Multistate Corporate Tax Guide

Volume I

Corporate Income Tax

JOHN C. HEALY

MICHAEL S. SCHADEWALD

CCH
a Wolters Kluwer business

ISBN: Set—978-0-8080-2606-8

4025 W. Peterson Ave.
Chicago, IL 60646-6085
1 800 248 3248
http://CCHGroup.com

Printed in the United States of America

Introduction

As a result of state legislation, administrative policy changes, and judicial decisions, significant changes have occurred across the country since publication of the 2011 edition of the *Multistate Corporate Tax Guide*. The *2012 Multistate Corporate Tax Guide* (*Guide*) is designed to provide quick access to each state's statement of its position on a sizable number of key issues in corporate and sales and use taxation. The easy-to-use chart format enables the reader to locate and compare how the states approach numerous aspects of corporate taxation. Information contained in each of the charts is based on the responses of state tax officials to a questionnaire that was prepared and administered by the University of Wisconsin—Milwaukee (UWM) Sheldon B. Lubar School of Business. The charts reflect state tax laws in effect on July 1, 2011, unless otherwise noted.

The charts or articles cover such significant areas as the following:

- Activities creating nexus for income, franchise, and sales/use tax purposes
- Conformity to the federal check-the-box regulations
- Information on non-income corporate taxes—Michigan, Ohio, Texas, and Washington
- First-year bonus depreciation
- NOL carryforwards and carrybacks in merger situations
- Components of the property, payroll, and sales factors
- Sales factor throwback and throwout rules
- Apportionment factors for specialized industries
- Apportionment of sales of services
- Cancellation of debt income
- Effects of a Section 338(h)(10) election
- Related party expense addback provisions
- Section 199 domestic production activities deduction
- Allocation of non-business income
- Taxation of corporate partners
- Whether the state requires a separate QSSS election
- Unitary business concept and reporting
- Time limits for reporting federal RARs
- Short year filing and NOL provisions applicable to an acquisition of a subsidiary
- The order in which a partial payment is applied to assessed tax, interest, and penalties
- Estimated tax payment rules
- Notification procedures to represent corporate taxpayers
- Required attachments to state returns
- Gulf Opportunity Zone Act
- Electronic filing of income tax returns
- Taxation of nonresident employees
- ASC 740 and uncertain income tax positions
- Sec. 179 asset expensing
- Activities creating nexus for an out-of-state seller
- Nexus and the cessation of filing requirements
- Sales/use taxation of computer consulting and services
- Sales/use tax filing requirements for LLCs and QSSSs
- Online filing of sales and use tax returns
- Statistical sampling in auditing sales/use tax

- Sales tax holidays
- Sales/use tax implications of distributing promotional items and catalogs
- Sales/use tax treatment of maintenance contracts
- Use tax on self-constructed machinery
- Sales/use tax treatment of shipping containers and packaging materials
- The Streamlined Sales Tax
- Sales/use tax treatment of software licenses
- Sales/use taxation of prepaid phone cards
- Sales/use tax treatment of cell phone-related transactions
- Sales/use tax treatment of architectural services
- Sales/use tax treatment of items consumed or destroyed in the manufacturing process
- Sales/use tax treatment of short-term rentals of tangible personal property
- Sales/use tax treatment of advertising agencies
- Sales/use tax treatment of airplanes, automobiles, and watercraft
- Sales/use tax treatment of drop shipments
- Sales/use tax compliance agreements
- Sales/use tax treatment of common and contract carriers
- Sales/use tax treatment of construction contractors
- Sales/use tax treatment of scaffolding and related charges
- Sales/use tax treatment of printers
- Sales/use tax treatment of temporary help
- Sales/use tax treatment of manufacturers
- Sales/use tax treatment of freight and shipping charges
- Sales/use tax treatment of fuel surcharges, hazardous material disposal charges, and special compliance charges
- Pollution control exemption
- Temporary storage exemption
- The Integrated Plant Doctrine and the manufacturing exemption for utilities consumed in manufacturing
- Taxation of landscaping services
- Sales/use tax treatment of purchases subsequently transferred to another state
- Motion picture production exemptions
- Sales/use tax treatment of certain energy-saving items
- Sales/use tax treatment of web design and hosting charges
- The Sales/use tax treatment of digital products
- The Sales/use tax treatment of cloud computing services
- Excise tax imposition
- The Sales/use tax treatment of travel-related expenses, including travel booked through online third-parties
- Personal responsibility statutes

The *2012 Multistate Corporate Tax Guide*, the recognized leader in its field, is a joint project of CCH, publisher of the Journal of State Taxation, and the University of Wisconsin—Milwaukee, Sheldon B. Lubar School of Business. In addition to serving as an excellent desk reference for practitioners, the *Multistate Corporate Tax Guide* is used as a text in the online graduate certificate program in state and local taxation, offered by the Sheldon B. Lubar School of Business at the University of Wisconsin—Milwaukee. Contact Matt Jensen at jensenmg@uwm.edu for information on this program, including special tuition assistance available to state department of revenue employees, or visit our Website, http://www.uwm.edu/dept/business/programs/certificates/certtax.html.

Organization of the book. The *2012 Multistate Corporate Tax Guide* is divided into two volumes. Volume I contains more than 160 charts with accompanying text and state-by-state summary analyses that focus on corporate income taxation. Volume II contains more than 135 charts accompanied by discussion and analysis of corporate sales and use tax issues; a state Internet address directory; the questionnaire that was sent to the state revenue officials and used to compile this guide; and a comprehensive subject index that references both income and franchise taxation (Volume I) and sales and use taxes (Volume II).

Notations. All 50 states and the District of Columbia responded to the UWM questionnaire, however the responses for Alaska and Nevada are based upon their responses to the 2010 survey. In cases where responses were not obtained for a specific question, the notation "NR" has been applied to indicate "Not reported." The notation "NA" indicates "Not applicable."

A word of appreciation. This book would not have been possible without the cooperation of the tax officials of the responding states and the District of Columbia. We appreciate their prompt and thorough responses to the questionnaire and their courtesy in answering follow-up inquiries.

Please contact John C. Healy at his e-mail address, jhealy@uwm.edu or at (414) 229-2262 (phone) or (414) 229-2265 (fax), or Michael S. Schadewald at his e-mail address, schade@uwm.edu or at (414) 229-5005 (phone) or (414) 229-2265 (fax) with your comments and suggestions.

John C. Healy, MST, CPA

Michael S. Schadewald, PhD, CPA

December 2011

About the Authors

JOHN C. HEALY, MST, CPA, is a senior lecturer in the graduate tax program at the University of Wisconsin—Milwaukee and the managing director of the Deloitte Multistate Tax Center at the University of Wisconsin—Milwaukee. His tax experience of more than 35 years includes tax management positions with Miller Brewing Company and GE Medical Systems. He is a frequent author and speaker on state and local taxation and is a past recipient of the Institute for Professionals in Taxation's Literary Award. He is also co-author of CCH's *Sales and Use Tax Answer Book* and author of CCH's *Surviving a Sales and Use Tax Audit*.

MICHAEL S. SCHADEWALD, PhD, CPA, is on the faculty of the University of Wisconsin-Milwaukee, where he teaches graduate and undergraduate courses in business taxation. A graduate of the University of Minnesota, Professor Schadewald has published numerous articles in academic and professional journals, and has served on many editorial boards. He also co-authors CCH's *Practical Guide to U.S. Taxation of International Transactions*, and writes a column for CCH's Journal of State Taxation.

Acknowledgments. The authors wish to acknowledge the *Multistate Corporate Tax Guide* Advisory Board for their contributions to the publication and continued support, and, in particular, to its chairperson, James T. Collins, for his visionary efforts in creating this publication. The authors also thank Susan Frayman of CCH for her outstanding editorial support in producing this book.

The *2012 Multistate Corporate Tax Guide* is dedicated to the representatives of the states' departments of revenue/taxation whose responses to the comprehensive questionnaire made this edition possible.

Gratitude is expressed for the fine efforts of the following faculty and alumni of the UWM MST programs, whose past efforts have contributed to the success of this book.

Editors Emeriti	***Production Manager***
James T. Collins	Linda Abrahamson
Zoltan Eszes	Jennifer Carstens
Lynn D. Fournier	
Jeffry A. Neuenschwander	
Judith A. Shanley	
William A. Raabe	

Multistate Corporate Tax Guide Advisory Board

2012 Multistate Corporate Tax Guide
Table of Contents

2012 Multistate Corporate Tax Guide
Table of Contents

VOLUME I: CORPORATE INCOME TAX

Part 1. MULTISTATE CORPORATE INCOME TAXES

Primer on Multistate Corporate Income Taxation

Introduction

Forty-five states and the District of Columbia impose some type of income-based tax on corporations. Nevada, Ohio, South Dakota, Washington, and Wyoming do not levy a corporate income tax. However, Ohio does impose a gross receipts tax called the *commercial activity tax*, Washington imposes a gross receipts tax called the *business and occupation tax*, and Texas imposes a tax on gross margin, called the *margin tax*.

The corporate income taxes of California, Florida, New York, and a number of other states are formally franchise taxes imposed on, for example, the privilege of doing business in the state. Nevertheless, because the value of the franchise is measured by the income derived from that privilege, the tax is computed in essentially the same manner as a direct income tax. This primer on multistate corporate income taxation is organized into two sections, as follows:

Basic Principles

- Nexus
- Computation of State Taxable Income
- Distinction between Business and Nonbusiness Income
- Apportionment Formulas
- Sales Factor
- Property Factor
- Payroll Factor
- Consolidated Returns and Combined Unitary Reporting
- Concept of a Unitary Business Group
- Basic Multistate Tax Planning Strategies

Advanced Concepts

- Nexus
- Specialized Industry Apportionment Formulas
- Sourcing Sales of Services
- Non-Income Taxes—Ohio, Texas and Washington
- Mechanisms Used by States to Limit Income Shifting
- Pass-Through Entities

BASIC PRINCIPLES

Nexus

Constitutional Nexus. A threshold issue for any corporation operating in more than one state is determining the states in which it must file returns and pay income tax. A state has jurisdiction to tax a corporation organized in another state only if the out-of-state corporation's contacts with the state are sufficient to create nexus. Historically, states have asserted that virtually any type of in-state business activity creates nexus for an out-of-state corporation. This approach reflects the reality that it is politically more appealing to collect taxes from out-of-state corporations than to raise taxes on in-state business interests. The desire of state lawmakers and tax officials to, in effect, export the local tax burden is counterbalanced by the Due Process Clause and Commerce Clause of the U.S. Constitution, both of which limit a state's ability to impose a tax obligation on an out-of-state corporation.

The landmark case on constitutional nexus is *Quill Corp. v. North Dakota.* [504 U.S. 298 (1992)] Quill was a mail-order vendor of office supplies that solicited sales through catalogs mailed to potential customers in North Dakota and made deliveries through common carriers. Quill was incorporated in Delaware and had facilities in California, Georgia, and Illinois. Quill had no office, warehouse, retail outlet, or other facility in North Dakota nor were any Quill employees or representatives physically present in North Dakota. During the years in question, Quill made sales to roughly 3,000 North Dakota customers and was the sixth largest office supply vendor in the state.

Under North Dakota law, Quill was required to collect North Dakota use tax on its mail-order sales to North Dakota residents. Quill challenged the constitutionality of this tax obligation. The Supreme Court held that Quill's economic presence in North Dakota was sufficient to satisfy the Due Process Clause's "minimal connection" requirement. On the other hand, the Court ruled that an economic presence was not, by itself, sufficient to satisfy the Commerce Clause's "substantial nexus" requirement. Consistent with its ruling 25 years earlier in *National Bellas Hess, Inc. v. Department of Revenue* [386 U.S. 753 (1967)], the Court ruled that a substantial nexus exists only if a corporation has a nontrivial physical presence in a state. In other words, the Court ruled that a physical presence is an essential prerequisite to establishing constitutional nexus, at least for sales and use tax purposes.

The Court did not address the issue of whether the physical presence test also applied for income tax purposes, which has resulted in a significant amount of controversy and litigation (see discussion below under the heading of Economic Nexus).

Public Law 86-272. Congress enacted Public Law 86-272 in 1959 to provide multistate corporations with a limited safe harbor from the imposition of state income taxes. Specifically, Public Law 86-272 prohibits a state from imposing a "net income tax" on a corporation organized in another state if the corporation's only in-state activity is (1) solicitation of orders by company representatives, (2) for sales of tangible personal property, (3) which orders are sent outside the state for approval or rejection, and (4) if approved, are filled by shipment or delivery from a point outside the state.

Although Public Law 86-272 can provide significant protections for a multistate business, it has several important limitations. First, it applies only to taxes imposed on net income and provides no protection against the imposition of a sales and use tax collection obligation, property taxes, gross receipts taxes (e.g., Ohio commercial activity tax, or Washington business and occupation tax), or corporate franchise taxes on net worth or capital.

Second, Public Law 86-272 protects only sales of tangible personal property. It does not protect activities such as leasing tangible personal property, selling services, selling or leasing real estate, or selling or licensing intangibles.

Third, for businesses that send employees into other states to sell tangible personal property, Public Law 86-272 applies only if those employees limit their in-state activities to the solicitation of orders that are sent outside the state for approval, and if approved, are filled by a shipment or delivery from a point outside the state. For example, if a salesperson exercises an authority to approve orders within a state, the company does not qualify for protection under Public Law 86-272. Likewise, Public Law 86-272 does not protect the presence of a salesperson who performs non-solicitation activities, such as repairs, customer training or technical assistance, within a state.

Although Public Law 86-272 does not define the phrase *solicitation of orders*, the meaning of the phrase was addressed by the Supreme Court in *Wisconsin Department of Revenue v. William Wrigley, Jr., Co.* [505 U.S. 214 (1992)]. In this case, the Court defined solicitation of orders as encompassing "requests for purchases" as well as "those activities that are entirely ancillary to requests for purchases—those that serve no independent business function apart from their connection to the soliciting of orders." Examples of activities that might serve an independent business function, apart from the solicitation of orders, include installation and start-up, customer training, engineering and design assistance, technical assistance, maintenance and repair, and credit and collection activities.

Computation of State Taxable Income

Most states that impose a corporate income tax use either the corporation's federal taxable income before the net operating loss and special deductions (federal Form 1120, Line 28) or the corporation's net federal taxable income (federal Form 1120, Line 30) as the starting place for computing state taxable income. The states that do not tie the computation of state taxable income directly to a corporation's federal tax return typically adopt the majority of the federal provisions governing items of gross income and deduction in defining the state tax base.

A corporation's state income tax liability generally is computed using the following steps:

Step 1. Begin with the amount of federal taxable income, which is the amount on Line 28 or Line 30 of the federal corporate income tax return, Form 1120. Add to (or subtract from) that amount the state addition and subtraction modifications. The resulting amount is the state tax base.

Step 2. If applicable, subtract from (or add to) the state tax base the total net allocable nonbusiness income (loss). The resulting amount is the total apportionable business income (loss).

Step 3. Multiply the total apportionable business income (loss) by the state's apportionment percentage. The resulting amount is the business income (loss) apportioned to the state.

Step 4. Add to (or subtract from) the business income apportioned to the state the total net allocable nonbusiness income (loss), if applicable, that is allocated to the state. The resulting amount is the state taxable income (loss).

Step 5. Multiply the state taxable income by the state tax rate to determine the state tax liability before credits.

Step 6. Subtract the state's tax credits from the state tax liability to arrive at the net income tax liability for the state.

The use of the federal tax base as the starting point for computing state taxable income is referred to as "piggybacking." Conformity with federal provisions simplifies tax compliance for multistate corporations, but complete conformity with the federal tax laws would effectively cede control over state tax policy to the federal government. States also must be wary of the effects of federal tax law changes on state tax revenues. Therefore, although federal taxable income generally is used as the starting point in computing state taxable income, numerous state modifications are required to reflect differences in federal and state policy objectives, as well as to eliminate income that a state is constitutionally prohibited from taxing.

The modifications to federal taxable income vary significantly among the states. Common addition modifications include the following:

- Interest income received on state and municipal debt obligations
- State income taxes
- Federal net operating loss carryover deductions
- Federal dividends-received deductions
- Royalties and interest expense paid to related parties
- Expenses related to state tax credits
- Federal domestic production activities deduction under Code Section 199
- Expenses related to income that is exempt for state tax purposes
- Federal bonus depreciation under Code Section 168(k)
- Federal Code Section 179 asset expensing

Common subtraction modifications include the following:

- Interest income received on federal debt obligations
- State net operating loss carryover deductions
- State dividends-received deductions
- Expenses related to federal tax credits
- Federal Subpart F income with respect to foreign subsidiaries
- Federal Code Section 78 gross-up income

Distinction Between Business and Nonbusiness Income

In 1957, a group of state tax officials promulgated the Uniform Division of Income for Tax Purposes Act (UDITPA) to provide uniformity among the states with respect to the taxation of multistate corporations. UDITPA has been adopted, at least in part, by many states. In an attempt to distinguish income derived from a corporation's regular trade or business from income derived from any activities that are unrelated to that trade or business, UDITPA makes a distinction between business income and nonbusiness income. Under the UDITPA approach, a taxpayer apportions a percentage of its business income to each state in which it has nexus, but specifically allocates the entire amount of any nonbusiness income to a single state. [UDITPA § § 4 and 9] Therefore, the principal consequence of classifying an item as nonbusiness income is that the income is excluded from the tax base of every nexus state except the state in which the nonbusiness income is taxable in full (e.g., the state of commercial domicile). Because the classification of an item as nonbusiness income can effectively remove the income from the tax base of one or more nexus states, the business versus nonbusiness income distinction has historically been an area of significant controversy between taxpayers and state tax authorities.

The distinction between business and nonbusiness income is related to the constitutional restrictions on the ability of a state to tax an out-of-state corporation. Based on these constitutional protections, taxpayers have challenged the ability of nexus states to tax an item of income that the taxpayer believes has no relationship to the business activity conducted in the state. As the Supreme Court stated in *Allied-Signal, Inc. v. Division of Taxation* [504 U.S. 768 (1992)], "the principle that a State may not tax value earned outside its borders rests on the fundamental requirement of both the Due Process and Commerce Clauses that there be 'some definite link, some minimum connection, between a state and the person, property or transaction it seeks to tax.' *Miller Bros. Co. v. Maryland*, 347 U.S. 340, 344-345 (1954)."

For example, the taxpayer in *Mobil Oil Corp. v. Commissioner of Taxes* [445 U.S. 425 (1980)] was an integrated petroleum company that was incorporated and commercially domiciled in New York. Mobil challenged Vermont's ability to tax the dividends that it received from its foreign subsidiaries. The essence of Mobil's argument that Vermont could not constitutionally tax the foreign dividends was that the activities of the foreign subsidiaries were unrelated to Mobil's business activities in Vermont, which were limited to distributing petroleum products. Stating that "the linchpin of apportionability in the field of state income taxation is the unitary business principle," the Supreme Court ruled that Vermont could tax an apportioned percentage of the dividends Mobil received from its foreign subsidiaries, because those subsidiaries were part of the same integrated petroleum enterprise as its distribution activities in Vermont. In other words, because they were received from unitary subsidiaries, the dividends were includible in Mobil's apportionable business income. The Court also indicated that if the business activities of the foreign subsidiaries had "nothing to do with the activities of the recipient in the taxing state, due process considerations might well preclude apportionability, because there would be no underlying unitary business."

Each state is free to adopt its own definitions of business and nonbusiness income, subject to the constitutional constraints discussed above. Most states have adopted a definition of nonbusiness income that more or less conforms to the UDITPA definition of nonbusiness income, which is "all income other than business income." [UDITPA § 1(e)] Thus, the key is the definition of business income. According to UDITPA Section 1(a), "business income is income arising from transactions and activity in the regular course of the taxpayer's trade or business and includes income from tangible and intangible property if the acquisition, management, and disposition of the property constitute integral parts of the taxpayer's regular trade or business operations."

Therefore, under UDITPA, an item of income is classified as business income if it either arises from a transaction in the regular course of the taxpayer's business (transactional test), or from property that is an integral part of the taxpayer's business (functional test) [MTC Reg. IV.1.(a)]. The transactional test looks at the frequency and regularity of the income-producing transaction in relation to the taxpayer's regular trade or business. The critical issue is whether the transaction is frequent in nature, as opposed to a rare or extraordinary event. In contrast, the functional test looks at the relationship between the underlying income-producing asset and the taxpayer's regular trade or business. The critical issue is whether the asset is integral, as opposed to incidental, to the taxpayer's business operations.

When an item of income is determined to be nonbusiness income, most states allocate the income to a specific state under guidelines similar to Sections 4 through 8 of UDITPA and the related Multistate Tax Commission (MTC) regulations. The basic thrust of these rules is that nonbusiness income derived from real and tangible personal property is allocable to the state in which the property is physically located, whereas nonbusiness income derived from intangible property is allocable to the state of commercial domicile (except for royalties, which are allocable to the state where the intangible asset is used). The MTC is an agency of state governments that was established in 1967 to promote fairness and uniformity in state tax laws.

Apportionment Formulas

A taxpayer's right to apportion its income is not automatic or elective; rather, it is a privilege that must be warranted by the corporation's activities. The requirements for establishing the right to apportion income vary from state to state, but generally entail carrying on business in another state, maintaining a regular place of business in another state, or being taxable in another state. Some states take the restrictive position that permits apportionment only if the corporation is actually filing returns and paying tax in another state.

Once a corporation has established its right to apportion income, the next step is to compute the applicable state apportionment percentages using the formulas provided by each taxing state. These formulas are usually based on the relative amounts of property, payroll, and/or sales that the corporation has in each taxing state. These formulas reflect the notion that a corporation's business activity in a state is properly measured by the amount of property, payroll, and sales in the state. These three components of an apportionment formula are referred to as "factors." For any given state, each factor equals the ratio of the corporation's property, payroll or sales in the state to its property, payroll or sales everywhere.

Factor weights vary from state to state. At present, about ten states use a three-factor apportionment formula that equally weights sales, property, and payroll. Most states use a modified three-factor formula, under which the sales factor is assigned more weight than the property or payroll factors. Many states double weight the sales factor (i.e., 50 percent sales, 25 percent property, and 25 percent payroll). About 15 states use a single-factor sales-only formula, including California (elective, starting in 2011), Colorado, Georgia, Illinois, Indiana (effective in 2011), Iowa, Maine, Michigan, Nebraska, New York, Oregon, South Carolina (effective in 2011), Texas, and Wisconsin. Other states that super weight the sales factor include Arizona (80 percent), Minnesota (93 percent in 2012), New Jersey (70 percent in 2012), and Pennsylvania (90 percent).

Assigning more weight to the sales factor than to the property or payroll factor tends to increase the percentage of an out-of-state corporation's income that is subject to tax, because the out-of-state corporation's principal activity in the state—sales of its product—is weighted more heavily than its payroll and property activities. At the same time, assigning more weight to the sales factor tends to reduce the tax on in-state corporations that have significant amounts of property and payroll in the state (factors that are given relatively less weight in the apportionment formula), but sales nationwide.

The standard three-factor formula was designed to apportion the income of multistate manufacturing and mercantile businesses and may not fairly apportion the income of businesses in other industries. To address this issue, many states provide special rules for computing apportionment percentages for businesses in certain industries. Typically, these special rules involve the modification or exclusion of the conventional factors or the use of unique, industry-specific factors. Examples of industries for which states provide special apportionment factor rules include airlines, railroads, trucking companies, financial institutions, television and radio broadcasters, publishers, telecommunication services companies, mutual funds, pipelines, ship transportation companies, and professional sports franchises.

In theory, apportionment prevents double taxation of a corporation's income. The practical reality, however, is that because each state is free to choose its own apportionment formula and make its own rules for computing the factors, apportionment does not provide a uniform division of a taxpayer's income among the taxing states. There are significant differences among the states in terms of factor weights, as well as variations in the computation of the factors themselves. This diversity can result in more than 100 percent of a corporation's income being subject to state taxation. Another potentially adverse consequence of apportionment occurs when a taxpayer's operations in one state result in a loss, but the corporation's overall operations are profitable. In such cases, the apportionment process will assign a percentage of the corporation's overall profit to the state in which the loss was incurred, even though no profit was generated by the taxpayer's operations in that state.

To address these issues, UDITPA Section 18 and the tax laws of most states allow a corporate taxpayer to petition for relief when the application of the state's apportionment formula does not fairly represent the taxpayer's business activity in the state. In such situations, UDITPA Section 18 lists several possible alternatives to the standard formula, including the use of separate accounting, the exclusion of one or more factors, the inclusion of one or more additional factors, or some other method that provides a more equitable apportionment of the taxpayer's income. Case law indicates, however, that there is a presumption that a state's apportionment method is equitable. In other words, to receive relief from distortions caused by the state's standard formula, a corporation must prove by clear and convincing evidence that the apportionment method in question grossly distorts the amount of income actually earned in the state.

Sales Factor

Under UDITPA Section 15, the sales factor is a fraction whose numerator is the total sales of the taxpayer in the state during the tax period and whose denominator is the total sales of the taxpayer everywhere during the tax period. Because the sales factor is used to apportion a corporation's business income, only sales that generate apportionable business income are includible in the fraction. Nonbusiness sales are excluded from the sales factor. Under UDITPA Section 1(g), the term *sales* means all gross receipts of the taxpayer other than receipts related to nonbusiness income. Consistent with this expansive view of the sales factor, MTC Regulation IV.15(b) provides that the sales factor generally includes all gross receipts derived by the taxpayer from transactions and activities in the regular course of its trade or business. Examples include gross receipts from sales of inventory, fees from services, interest, dividends, rentals, royalties, and other gains derived from other business assets and activities.

Under UDITPA Section 16(a), sales of tangible personal property are assigned to the sales factor numerator of the state into which the goods are delivered or shipped. This so-called destination test reflects the original purpose of including a sales factor in the apportionment formula, which was to provide tax revenue to the states in which customers are located. UDITPA Section 16(b) contains two exceptions to the destination test. The first exception applies to sales to the U.S. government, which are assigned to the state from which the goods are shipped rather than to the state in which the purchaser is located. The second exception is commonly known as "throwback," and requires that if the seller is not taxable in the destination state (in which case there is no sales factor numerator to which to assign the sale under the destination test), the sale is thrown back into the sales factor numerator of the state from which the goods are shipped. The rationale for throwback is to make sure that all of a company's sales are assigned to the numerator of some state's sales factor. Despite the logical basis for adopting a throwback rule, many states do not require throwback, primarily because that makes the state a more desirable place to locate a manufacturing or distribution facility from which to ship goods. The lack of a throwback rule results in "nowhere sales," which are sales that are not included in the numerator of any sales factor.

Under UDITPA Section 17, any sales other than sales of tangible personal property are considered in-state sales if the income-producing activity is performed in the state. This income-producing activity rule applies to fees for services, rental income, and income from intangibles (interest, dividends, royalties, and capital gains).

Under MTC Reg. IV.17(2), the term *income-producing activity* applies to each separate item of income and means the transactions and activity engaged in by the taxpayer in the regular course of its trade or business. Examples of income-producing activity include: (1) the rendering of personal services by employees or the use of tangible or intangible property by the taxpayer in performing a service; (2) the sale, rental, leasing, licensing or other use of real property; (3) the rental, leasing, licensing or other use of tangible personal property; and (4) the sale, licensing or other use of intangible personal property.

If the income-producing activity is performed in two or more states, the sale is assigned to the state in which the greater proportion of the income-producing activity is performed, based on cost of performance. [UDITPA § 17] Under MTC Reg. IV.17(3), the term *costs of performance* means direct costs determined in a manner consistent with generally accepted accounting principles and in accordance with accepted conditions or practices in the trade or business of the taxpayer. Direct costs include material and labor costs that have a causal relationship with the sale in question. Indirect costs, which include general and administrative expenses that are not associated with any specific sale, are not taken in account in determining the costs of performance.

Property Factor

Under UDITPA Section 10, the property factor is a fraction whose numerator is the average value of the taxpayer's real and tangible personal property owned or rented and used in the state during the tax year and whose denominator is the average value of all the taxpayer's real and tangible personal property owned or rented and used everywhere during the tax year. Under MTC Regulation IV.10(a), the definition of real and tangible personal property includes land, buildings, machinery, stocks of goods, equipment, and other real and tangible personal property. Intangible property, such as accounts receivable and marketable securities, generally is excluded from the property factor.

Property owned by the corporation is typically valued at its average original cost plus the cost of additions and improvements, but without any adjustments for depreciation. A few states require property to be included at its net book value or federal adjusted tax basis. Rented property is included in the property factor at a value equal to eight times the annual rental.

Only property that is used in producing apportionable business income is included in the property factor. Therefore, construction-in-progress, property that has been permanently withdrawn from service, and property that is used for producing nonbusiness income generally is excluded. Property that is temporarily idled, however, generally remains in the property factor.

Although the average value of the property is usually determined by averaging the beginning and ending property values, many states allow the average value to be calculated on a monthly or quarterly basis if the use of the annual computations substantially distorts the actual value of the property. This may occur if a significant amount of property is acquired or disposed of near the beginning or the end of the year.

Payroll Factor

Under UDITPA Section 13, the payroll factor is a fraction whose numerator is the total amount paid in the state during the tax year by the taxpayer for compensation and whose denominator is the total compensation paid everywhere during the tax year. For this purpose, compensation generally includes wages, salaries, commissions, and any other form of remuneration paid or accrued to an employee that is taxable to the employee for federal income tax purposes. Payments made to an independent contractor or to any other person who is not properly classifiable as an employee generally are excluded from the payroll factor. Compensation related to the production of nonbusiness income is also excluded from the payroll factor. In addition, in an attempt to make the state a more desirable place to locate a headquarters office, a few states exclude executive compensation from the payroll factor.

The rules for computing an employee's compensation and for assigning that compensation to a particular state parallel those used to compute the employer's federal and state unemployment taxes. Federal Form 940, *Employer's Annual Federal Unemployment Tax Return*, summarizes taxable compensation amounts on a state-by-state basis and is often used to compute state payroll factors. In computing the numerator of the payroll factor for a particular state, if an employee performs services exclusively within that state, that employee's compensation is included in the numerator for that state. If an employee performs services both within and without a state, the entire amount of the employee's compensation is still generally assigned to a single state, based on a hierarchy of factors, including (in the order in which they are applied) the employee's base of operations, where the employee is directed from, and the employee's state of residence. [UDITPA § 14]

Consolidated Returns and Combined Unitary Reporting

For financial reporting purposes, a parent corporation must issue consolidated financial statements that include all of its majority-owned subsidiaries. For federal income tax purposes, an affiliated group of corporations may elect to file a federal consolidated income tax return. [IRC § 1501] Thus, a federal consolidated return is not mandatory, and the members of an affiliated group have the option to file federal returns on a separate company basis. Filing a federal consolidated return is a popular election, primarily because it allows the group to offset the losses of one affiliate against the profits of other affiliates.

A federal *affiliated group* is defined as one or more chains of includible corporations connected through stock ownership with a common parent that is an includible corporation, provided that the common parent directly owns 80 percent or more of at least one of the other includible corporations, and stock meeting the 80 percent test in each includible corporation other than the common parent must be owned directly by one or more of the other includible corporations. [IRC § 1504(a)] An "includable corporation" is any corporation other than an exempt corporation, life insurance company, foreign corporation, Section 936 corporation, RIC, REIT, DISC or S corporation. [IRC § 1504(b)]

The states that impose corporate income taxes employ a wide variety of filing options for groups of commonly controlled corporations. This makes it difficult to generalize about state filing options. Roughly speaking, the different filing options fall into one of the following categories:

- Separate company returns
- Consolidated returns
- Combined unitary reporting

The lack of uniformity in state filing options means that tax practitioners must carefully analyze the filing options available in any given nexus state.

Separate Company Returns. Three states—Delaware, Maryland, and Pennsylvania—require each member of a commonly controlled group of corporations to compute its income and file a return as if it were a separate economic entity. Under this mandatory separate company return approach, consolidated returns and combined unitary reporting are not permitted or required under any circumstances.

The filing of separate company returns provides taxpayers with the opportunity to create legal structures and intercompany transactions that shift income from affiliates based in high-tax states to affiliates based in low-tax states. For example, if a multistate corporation's only activities in a high-tax state are sales and distribution, which are often relatively low-margin activities, and if the high-tax state allows separate company returns, the corporation may be able to insulate its higher-margin assets and activities from taxation in the high-tax state by forming a sales subsidiary that is responsible for marketing products in that state. Disadvantages of the separate company return approach include the inability to offset the losses of one affiliate against the profits of other affiliates and the need to develop defensible arm's-length transfer prices for intercompany transactions.

Consolidated Returns. Roughly 20 states (including Alabama, Florida, Georgia, Iowa, and South Carolina) generally allow affiliated corporations to file separate company returns but also permit or require such corporations to file a state consolidated return if certain conditions are met. The qualification requirements for including an affiliated corporation in a state consolidated return vary from state to state. In terms of stock ownership requirements, most states piggyback on the federal rule requiring 80 percent or more ownership. A number of states also require that an affiliated group file a federal consolidated return as a prerequisite to filing a state consolidated return. Examples of additional restrictions that a state may impose for including a specific affiliate in a state consolidated return include having nexus in the state, deriving income from sources in the state, and not being subject to a special apportionment formula such as those that often apply to financial institutions.

The advantages of filing a consolidated return include the ability to offset the losses of one affiliate against the profits of other affiliates, elimination of intercorporate dividends, deferral of gains on intercompany transactions, and the use of credits that would otherwise be limited by a lack of income. A disadvantage of filing a consolidated return is that it can prevent a taxpayer from creating legal structures and intercompany transactions to shift income from affiliates based in high-tax states to affiliates based in low-tax states.

Combined Unitary Reporting. Twenty-three states and the District of Columbia require members of a unitary business group to compute their taxable income on a combined basis. These states include Alaska, Arizona, California, Colorado, Hawaii, Idaho, Illinois, Kansas, Maine, Massachusetts, Michigan, Minnesota, Montana, Nebraska, New Hampshire, New York (for related corporations that have substantial intercorporate transactions), North Dakota, Oregon, Texas, Utah, Vermont, West Virginia, and Wisconsin.

Combined reporting is a methodology for apportioning the business income of a corporation that is a member of a commonly controlled group of corporations engaged in a unitary business. Generally speaking, a taxpayer member apportions its business income by multiplying the combined business income of all the members of the unitary business group by an apportionment percentage that is based on factors, the denominators of which include the factors everywhere of all group members, and the numerators of which include the in-state factors of only the taxpayer member.

Despite its surface-level resemblance to a consolidated return, combined unitary reporting differs from a federal consolidated return in several respects. First, whereas inclusion in a federal consolidated return requires 80 percent or more common ownership, inclusion in a combined unitary report generally requires more than 50 percent common ownership. Second, to be included in a combined report, an affiliate must be engaged in the same trade or business as the other group members, as exhibited by such factors as functional integration, centralized management and economies of scale. There is no unitary business requirement for inclusion in a federal consolidated return. Third, some states permit the inclusion of foreign corporations in a combined report. Finally, in many states, each group member that has nexus in the state is treated as a separate taxpayer, whereas the federal consolidated regulations treat a consolidated group as a single taxable entity.

The advantages and disadvantages of consolidated returns and combined reporting are similar. A primary disadvantage of both filing options is that they can limit a taxpayer's ability to use intercompany transactions to shift income from affiliates based in high-tax states to affiliates based in low-tax states. A major advantage of both filing options is that losses of one affiliate can be offset against the profits of other affiliates.

Numerous states, including New Jersey, North Carolina, and Virginia, generally allow commonly controlled corporations to file separate company returns but also require or permit a combined unitary report if certain conditions are satisfied. A common reason for requiring a combined report is the state tax authority's determination that a combined report is necessary to clearly reflect the group's income earned in the state or to prevent the evasion of taxes. For example, New Jersey does not permit an affiliated group to elect to file a consolidated return, nor does it require a unitary group to compute its income on a combined basis. Thus, every corporation with nexus in New Jersey is generally considered a separate entity and must file its own return. The Director of the Division of Taxation may, however, require members of an affiliated group or a controlled group to file a consolidated return "if the taxpayer cannot demonstrate by clear and convincing evidence that a report by a taxpayer discloses the true earnings of the taxpayer on its business carried on in this State." [N.J. Rev. Stat. 54:10A-10.c.]

Concept of a Unitary Business

Combined unitary reporting requires a determination of whether two or more corporations are engaged in a *unitary business*. Unfortunately, there is no simple, objective definition of what constitutes a unitary business. In fact, over the years the courts have developed a number of different tests for determining the existence of a unitary business. As one Supreme Court Justice observed, "the unitary business concept . . . is not, so to speak, unitary." Because of the many judicial interpretations of a unitary business, it is not always clear which of the available tests should be applied. In addition, even if a taxpayer knows which test will be used, the subjective nature of the tests makes them difficult to apply with any certainty.

Generally speaking, a vertically integrated business, in which each separate affiliate or division performs an interdependent step that leads to a finished product only when the steps are combined, will be treated as unitary. A horizontally integrated business, in which there are parallel operations in different geographic locations (e.g., a chain of retail stores), will also generally be considered unitary. A conglomerate may or may not be considered unitary, depending on whether there is strong centralized management, as exhibited by a centralized executive force and shared staff functions, as well as economies of scale in the form of common employee pension and benefit plans, common insurance policies, and so on.

As mentioned above, the courts have developed a number of different tests for determining the existence of a unitary business, including the three-unities test, the contribution or dependency test, the flow of value test, and the factors of profitability test. The three-unities test [*Butler Bros. v. McColgan*, 315 U.S. 501 (1942)] requires the presence of unity of ownership, unity of operation, and unity of use. Unity of ownership generally is satisfied when 50 percent or more of the corporation's stock is owned directly or indirectly by another corporation in the group. Unity of operation is evidenced by the performance of certain staff functions by one of the corporations on behalf of the entire group, such as centralized purchasing, advertising, accounting and legal services, and human resource functions. Unity of use is associated with common executive forces and general systems of operations and is evidenced by major policy decisions that are made by centralized management, intercompany product flow, and services that are provided by one affiliate to other group members.

The contribution or dependency test [*Edison Cal. Stores, Inc. v. McColgan*, 176 P.2d 697 (Cal. 1947)] focuses on whether the enterprise's in-state business operations depend on, or contribute to, the enterprise's out-of-state business operations. Examples of factors that suggest contributions by or dependency among commonly controlled corporations include intercompany loans, intercompany sales of goods or services, exchanges of products or expertise, and shared executive force and staff functions.

Under the flow of value test, "some sharing or exchange of value . . . beyond the mere flow of funds arising out of a passive investment" is needed to establish the existence of a unitary business. [*Container Corp. of Am. v. Franchise Tax Bd.*, 463 U.S. 159 (1983)] Finally, the factors of profitability test [*Allied-Signal, Inc. v. Division of Taxation*, 504 U.S. 768 (1992)] looks to functional integration, centralization of management, and economies of scale to determine the existence of a unitary business. Functional integration includes product flow among affiliates and centralized functions such as advertising, accounting, purchasing, manufacturing, and financing. Indicators of centralized management include interlocking boards of directors, interchange of personnel at upper management levels, and required parent company approval on major policy decisions.

In addition to judicial interpretations, state-specific statutes and regulations are important sources of authority regarding what constitutes a unitary business group. Like their judicial counterparts, however, they generally leave much to be desired in terms of providing detailed and objective guidance.

The MTC regulations portray the concept of a unitary business as follows:

> A unitary business is a single economic enterprise that is made up either of separate parts of a single business entity or of a commonly controlled group of business entities that are sufficiently interdependent, integrated and interrelated through their activities so as to provide a synergy and mutual benefit that produces a sharing or exchange of value among them and a significant flow of value to the separate parts. [MTC Reg. IV.1.(b)]

The regulations also provide that a unitary business is characterized by significant flows of value evidenced by the following factors:

- **Functional integration**—Examples include common marketing programs, transfers or pooling of technical information or intellectual property, common distribution systems, common purchasing, and common or intercompany financing.
- **Centralization of management**—Joint participation of corporate directors and officers in the management decisions that affect the different business units.
- **Economies of scale**—Centralized purchasing, centralized administrative functions, etc.

Finally, the MTC regulations identify same type of business, steps in a vertical process, and strong centralized management as indicators of a unitary business.

Basic Multistate Tax Planning Strategies

Multistate corporate income tax planning techniques generally involve an attempt either to reduce the total amount of the organization's taxable income subject to apportionment or to minimize the apportionment percentage in a given state. In determining which activities or entities to alter, the tax planner must carefully analyze the effects that each change has on the corporation's total state tax liability to ensure that the taxes saved in one state are not offset by tax increases in other states. Therefore, effective state tax planning requires a review of a corporation's activities in all states and an understanding of the apportionment formulas and other tax laws of the states in which the corporation does business. Moreover, any tax planning strategy must be reviewed in light of practical business considerations and the additional administrative or operational costs that might be incurred in implementing the strategy. The remainder of this section briefly discusses the following selected planning opportunities:

- Selecting the states in which to be taxed
- Establishing the right to apportion income
- Structure planning techniques
- Using the most beneficial group filing method

Selecting the States in Which to Be Taxed. When a corporation has only a limited connection with a state, it may be possible to discontinue that activity by using an alternative means of accomplishing the same result. For example, if maintaining a corporate office in a state creates an undesired nexus, the corporation might avoid nexus by providing the sales representatives with an office allowance rather than a formal company office.

When nexus is created by sales representatives performing repair and maintenance services in the state, one strategy would be to separately incorporate the sales division that operates in the state. Assuming the state does not require combined reporting, this would prevent the state from taxing the profits attributable to the parent corporation's out-of-state assets and activities. Such a technique will be successful only if the incorporated division is a bona fide business operation and the state does not successfully assert that the corporation continues to have nexus under the concepts of affiliate or agency nexus (discussed below). In addition, the pricing of any sales or services between the new subsidiary and the parent corporation must be at arm's length.

Although most planning techniques are designed to avoid nexus, there are situations in which a corporation can benefit from establishing nexus in a state. Creating nexus in a particular state can be beneficial if the corporation (1) currently does not have the right to apportion its income, (2) wants to avoid the application of a sales throwback rule by creating nexus in a destination state, or (3) wants to have a loss affiliate create nexus in a state that allows only nexus affiliates to join in filing a state consolidated return. Establishing nexus may not be difficult to accomplish because of the relatively low threshold for creating constitutional nexus and the limited nature of the protection afforded by Public Law 86-272.

Establishing the Right to Apportion Income. A corporation that has nexus in only one state cannot apportion its income and therefore is subject to tax on 100 percent of its income in that state. By establishing the right to apportion its income, the taxpayer may be able to reduce its state income tax costs substantially, particularly if the corporation is domiciled in a high-tax state. The income that is removed from the tax base of the state of domicile may escape state taxation altogether if the state in which the corporation establishes nexus does not impose a corporate income tax or imposes a corporate income tax but has more liberal nexus rules than the state of domicile.

Another major factor in determining the tax benefit of apportioning income is whether the state from which the taxpayer is shipping goods has a sales throwback rule. Many states do not require throwback, in which case sales in states where the taxpayer does not have nexus are not assigned to the numerator of any state's sales factor (so-called nowhere sales).

To acquire the right to apportion its income, the corporation generally must have nexus in at least one state other than its state of domicile. Whether a corporation's activities or contacts in another state are considered adequate to justify apportionment is generally determined by reference to the tax laws of the domicile state. Typically, a corporation must carry on business in another state, maintain an office or other regular place of business in another state, or be taxable in another state in order to apportion its income. Some states take the restrictive position that apportionment is permitted only if the corporation is actually filing returns and paying tax in another state. A corporation should analyze its current activities in and contacts with other states to determine which, if any, activities or contacts could be redirected so that the corporation will be granted the right to apportion its income.

Structure Planning Techniques. Numerous states allow a group of commonly controlled corporations to file returns on a separate company basis. This can provide a taxpayer with the opportunity to create legal structures and intercompany transactions that shift income from affiliates based in certain high-tax states to affiliates based in low-or no-tax states. For example, if a high-tax state allows separate company reporting and a multistate corporation's only activity in that state is sales and distribution (which are often relatively low-margin activities), the corporation may be able to insulate its out-of-state assets and activities from taxation in the high-tax state by forming a sales subsidiary that is responsible for marketing its products in the state.

Another example of structure planning is a financial institution that holds a significant portfolio of marketable securities. The taxpayer may be able to realize significant tax savings by transferring the securities to an intangible property holding company domiciled in Delaware, which does not tax the income of a corporation whose only activities in the state are the maintenance and management of intangible property or the collection and distribution of income from such property.

Historically, large corporations (in particular, retailers) used Delaware trademark holding companies to avoid state income taxes. By transferring valuable trademarks and trade names to an intangible property holding company domiciled in Delaware and then licensing the use of the intangibles back to the operating companies, a corporation could potentially avoid state taxation of the income attributable to the intangible assets. States have significantly curtailed the use of trademark holding companies by enacting combined reporting requirements, related-party expense add-back provisions, and economic nexus statutes.

Structure planning can also be used to take advantage of net operating losses in states that do not allow any form of consolidated or combined reporting. One way to use such losses is to merge an unprofitable affiliate into a profitable affiliate. Another potential strategy for better utilizing an affiliate's net operating losses is to convert the unprofitable affiliate into a single member limited liability company (LLC). A single-member LLC is generally treated as a disregarded entity for both federal and state income tax purposes, and therefore the use of a single-member LLC effectively produces the same result as a consolidated return. Care must be taken, however, when dealing with single-member LLCs because some states impose entity-level taxes on such entities.

Using the Most Beneficial Group Filing Method. In states that permit an affiliated group to elect to file a consolidated return, such an election can be beneficial when one affiliate has losses that can be offset against the income generated by other affiliates. Other potential benefits of filing a consolidated return include the elimination of intercorporate dividends, deferral of gains on intercompany transactions, and the use of credits that would otherwise be limited by the lack of income.

In choosing whether to file a consolidated return, the corporation should determine whether the advantages of a consolidated return can be realized without adverse consequences. For example, a corporation that is eligible to file a consolidated return in a given state may choose not to do so if it has significant losses on intercompany transactions and would lose the deduction as a result of the election. On the other hand, another member of the same affiliated group may elect to file a consolidated state return in another state to defer recognition of intercompany gains.

A major disadvantage of filing a consolidated return is that it can limit a taxpayer's ability to use intercompany transactions that shift income from affiliates based in high-tax states to affiliates based in low-tax states. Finally, most states that permit affiliated corporations to file a consolidated return have adopted a reporting-consistency requirement similar to that imposed for federal consolidated return purposes. Thus, once affiliated group begins filing a consolidated return, the group generally must continue to file on a consolidated basis, unless the group receives permission from state tax authorities to file separate company returns.

ADVANCED CONCEPTS

Nexus

Economic Nexus. In *Quill*, the Supreme Court ruled that a corporation satisfies the Commerce Clause's "substantial nexus" requirement only if the taxpayer has a physical presence in the state. Yet, in *Geoffrey, Inc. v. South Carolina Tax Commission* [437 S.E.2d 13 (S.C. 1993), *cert. denied* 510 U.S. 992, 1993], the South Carolina Supreme Court held that a trademark holding company that licensed its intangibles for use in South Carolina had nexus for income tax purposes despite the lack of any tangible property or employees in South Carolina. Geoffrey was the trademark holding company of the toy retailer, Toys "R" Us. Geoffrey was incorporated and domiciled in Delaware and had a license agreement with South Carolina retailers allowing them to use its trademarks and trade names, including the Toys "R" Us trademark. The court held that licensing intangibles for use in the state was sufficient to satisfy the minimum connection and substantial nexus requirements of the Due Process Clause and the Commerce Clause. The *Geoffrey* court did not follow the precedent established by *Quill*, because it believed that ruling applied only to the issue of nexus for sales and use tax purposes.

Since 1993, many states have adopted "economic nexus" standards that are based on the amount of income or sales derived from sources within a state. For example, the Connecticut corporate income tax applies to "[a]ny company that derives income from sources within this state, and that has a substantial economic presence within this state, evidenced by a purposeful direction of business toward this state, examined in light of the frequency, quantity and systematic nature of a company's economic contacts with this state, without regard to physical presence, and to the extent permitted by the Constitution of the United States." [Conn. Gen. Stat. § 12-216a]

Another approach to implementing the economic nexus concept is a factor presence standard, under which income tax nexus exists if in-state sales exceed a specified threshold. For example, for tax years beginning on or after January 1, 2011, an out-of-state corporation has income tax nexus in California if more than $500,000 of sales or 25 percent of its total sales are in California. [S.B. 15, Feb. 20. 2009]

In addition, there has been a significant amount of litigation related to the *Geoffrey* court's interpretation of the Commerce Clause's substantial nexus requirement.

In *Lanco, Inc. v. Division of Taxation* [908 A.2d 176 (N.J. 2006); *cert. denied*, U.S. Sup. Ct., 06-1236, June 18, 2007], the New Jersey Supreme Court ruled that the Delaware trademark holding company of the clothing retailer Lane Bryant had income tax nexus in New Jersey, even though it had no physical presence in the state. The court concluded that "the better interpretation of *Quill* is the one adopted by those states that limit the Supreme Court's holding to sales and use taxes." The court also stated that "we do not believe that the Supreme Court intended to create a universal physical-presence requirement for state taxation under the Commerce Clause."

In *Tax Commissioner v. MBNA America Bank, N.A.* [640 S.E.2d 226 (W. Va. 2006); *cert. denied*, U.S. Sup. Ct., 06-1228, June 18, 2007], the taxpayer was a Delaware bank that issued credit cards, extended unsecured credit, and serviced the credit card accounts of customers nationwide. Although MBNA did not have a physical presence in West Virginia, during one of the tax years in question, it derived over $10 million of gross receipts from West Virginia customers. The West Virginia Supreme Court of Appeals ruled that the physical presence test "applies only to state sales and use taxes and not to state business franchise and corporation net income taxes," and that MBNA had "a significant economic presence sufficient to meet the substantial nexus" test under the Commerce Clause.

In *Capital One Bank and Capital One F.S.B. v. Commissioner of Revenue* [No. SJC-10105 (Mass. Sup. Jud. Ct., Jan. 8, 2009); *cert. denied*, U.S. Sup. Ct., No. 08-1169, June 22, 2009], the Massachusetts Supreme

Judicial Court ruled that, despite the lack of any physical presence in the state, the two out-of-state credit card banks had substantial nexus in Massachusetts, because of their "purposeful, targeted marketing of their credit card business to Massachusetts customers . . . and their receipt of hundreds of millions of dollars in income from millions of transactions involving Massachusetts residents and merchants." Likewise, in *Geoffrey, Inc. v. Commissioner of Revenue* [No. SJC-10106, Mass. Sup. Jud. Ct., Jan. 8, 2009; *cert. denied*, U.S. Sup. Ct., No. 08-1207, June 22, 2009)], the Massachusetts Supreme Judicial Court ruled that, despite the lack of a physical presence in the state, a Delaware trademark holding company that received royalty income from licensing trademarks to affiliated entities that used the trademarks for retail business activities in Massachusetts had income tax nexus in Massachusetts.

In *KFC Corporation v. Iowa Department of Revenue* [No. 09-1032 (Ia. Sup. Ct., Dec. 30, 2010)], the Iowa Supreme Court ruled that the Commerce Clause does not require a physical presence in order to tax the income that a Delaware corporation (KFC) earned from the use of its intangibles in Iowa. The court concluded that the trademarks and other intangibles owned by KFC and licensed for use by independent franchisees doing business in Iowa "would be regarded as having a sufficient connection to Iowa to amount to the functional equivalent of 'physical presence' under *Quill*." The court also concluded that even if the use of the intangibles within the state does not amount to physical presence under *Quill*, the physical presence requirement should not be extended to prevent a state from imposing an income tax on revenue generated from the use of intangibles within the state.

Agency Nexus. Under the *Quill* decision, a corporation generally has constitutional nexus in any state in which it has property or employees located on a regular basis. What if, rather than conducting business in a state through employees (dependent agents), a corporation conducts business through independent contractors (independent agents)? Do the in-state activities of independent agents, acting on an out-of-state corporation's behalf, create constitutional nexus?

In *Scripto, Inc. v. Carson* [362 U.S. 207 (1960)], the Supreme Court addressed the issue whether the Florida marketing activities of ten independent sales representatives created Florida sales tax nexus for Scripto, a Georgia corporation that manufactured writing instruments. The Court held that for nexus purposes, the distinction between employees and independent contractors was "without constitutional significance," and that "to permit such formal 'contractual shifts' to make a constitutional difference would open the gates to a stampede of tax avoidance." The Court concluded that the critical fact was that the activities of the independent agents in Florida helped to create and maintain a commercial market for Scripto's goods. Thus, the presence of independent agents engaged in continuous local solicitation created Florida sales and use tax nexus for Scripto.

The Supreme Court reaffirmed these principles 25 years later in *Tyler Pipe Industries, Inc. v. Department of Revenue* [483 U.S. 232 (1987)], holding that the activities of an independent contractor residing in Washington were sufficient to create constitutional nexus for the out-of-state principal for purposes of the Washington business and occupation tax (a type of gross receipts tax). As in *Scripto*, the Court held that the critical test was "whether the activities performed in this state on behalf of the taxpayer are significantly associated with the taxpayer's ability to establish and maintain a market in this state for the sales."

In addition to protecting solicitation activities of employee-salespersons, Public Law 86-272 protects certain in-state activities conducted by independent contractors. Specifically, Public Law 86-272 provides that independent contractors can engage in the following in-state activities on behalf of an out-of-state corporation without creating income tax nexus for the principal: (1) soliciting sales, (2) making sales, and (3) maintaining an office. Thus, unlike employees, independent agents are permitted to maintain an in-state office without creating nexus for the principal.

The Supreme Court's decisions in *Scripto* and *Tyler Pipe* establish the principle that the use of independent agents to perform continuous local solicitation creates constitutional nexus for an out-of-state principal. Relying on these decisions, in Nexus Bulletin 95-1 [1995], the MTC took the position that the mail-order computer industry's practice of providing warranty services through third-party service providers creates constitutional nexus for sales and use tax purposes. See, for example, *Dell Catalog Sales L.P. v. New Mexico Taxation and Revenue Department* [No. 26,843 (N.M. Ct. of App., June 3, 2008); *cert.*

denied, U.S. No. 08-770, Mar. 23, 2009]; and *Louisiana v. Dell International, Inc.* [No. 2006-C-0996 (La. Ct. of App., Feb. 15, 2006)].

Affiliate Nexus. A number of states have taken the position that the existence of common ownership between a corporation that has a physical presence in a state (e.g., an in-state brick-and-mortar retailer) and an out-of-state corporation that has no physical presence in the state but makes substantial sales in the state (e.g., an affiliated out-of-state mail-order vendor) is sufficient to create constitutional nexus for the out-of-state mail-order affiliate. As with agency nexus, most of the litigation concerns the issue of nexus for sales and use tax purposes. For example, in *SFA Folio Collections, Inc. v. Tracy* [73 Ohio St. 3d 119, 652 N.E. 2d 693 (1995)], SFA Folio (Folio), a New York corporation, sold clothing and other merchandise by direct mail to customers in Ohio and delivered the merchandise using common carriers. Folio had no property or employees in Ohio, but Folio's parent corporation, Saks & Company, owned another subsidiary, Saks Fifth Avenue of Ohio (Saks-Ohio), which operated a retail store in Ohio.

Ohio tax authorities argued that Folio had "substantial nexus" in Ohio, because it was a member of an affiliated group that included a corporation that operated a store in Ohio and therefore was required to collect Ohio sales tax on its mail-order sales to Ohio customers. The state's position was based on a nexus-by-affiliate statute that the Ohio legislature had enacted, as well as the argument that Saks-Ohio was an "agent" of Folio. The agency argument was based on the fact that Saks-Ohio accepted some returns of Folio sales and distributed some Folio catalogs. The Ohio Supreme Court rejected the affiliate nexus argument, reasoning that to impute nexus to Folio merely because a sister corporation had a physical presence in Ohio ran counter to federal constitutional law and Ohio corporation law. The court also rejected the agency nexus argument because Saks-Ohio accepted Folio's returns according to its own policy (not Folio's) and charged the returns to its own inventory (not Folio's).

Consistent with the Ohio Supreme Court's ruling in *SFA Folio*, other states have generally been unsuccessful in their attempts to argue that common ownership, by itself, creates nexus for an out-of-state affiliate. [See, e.g., *Current, Inc. v. State Bd. of Equalization*, 24 Cal. App. 4th 382, 29 Cal. Rptr. 2d 407 (Ct. App. 1994); *SFA Folio Collections, Inc. v. Bannon*, 217 Conn. 220, 585 A.2d 666 (1991); *Bloomingdale's By Mail, Ltd. v. Commonwealth*, 130 Pa. Commw. 190, 567 A.2d 773 (Commw. Ct. 1989).] On the other hand, if an in-state affiliate functions as an agent for the out-of-state affiliate, the Supreme Court's decisions in *Scripto* and *Tyler Pipe* provide a basis for arguing that the activities of the in-state affiliate creates nexus for an out-of-state affiliate.

In *Borders Online, Inc.* [No. A105488 (Cal. Ct. of App., May 31, 2005)], the California Court of Appeals ruled that an out-of-state online retailer had a substantial nexus in California for sales and use tax purposes, because an affiliated corporation that sold similar products in brick-and-mortar stores in California performed return and exchange activities for the online retailer. The brick-and-mortar affiliate was considered to be an authorized representative of the online retailer because the online retailer posted a notice on its Web site that returns could be made to the brick-and-mortar retailer and the brick-and-mortar retailer's acceptance of returns was an integral part of the online retailer's sales operations. Therefore, under the relevant state statute, the online retailer was considered to be engaged in business in California and subject to the obligation to collect use tax on sales to California residents.

In *Barnesandnoble.com LLC v. State Bd. of Equalization* [No. CGC-06-456465 (Cal. Super. Ct., Oct. 11, 2007)], the California Superior Court ruled that an in-state brick-and-mortar affiliate's distribution of coupons that provided a discount on an online purchase did not create sales and use tax nexus for the related Internet retailer. The retail stores did not act as the Internet vendor's agent or representative. The court concluded that "[a]n essential element is that the agent (or representative) must have the authority to bind the principal." In the present case, the in-state retailer had no such authority and could do nothing but pass out the coupons created and distributed by Internet vendor.

Likewise, in *Barnesandnoble.com LLC* [N.M. Taxn. and Rev. Dept., No. 11-10, April 11, 2011], the New Mexico Taxation and Revenue Department ruled that the online bookseller did not have sufficient contacts with New Mexico to establish substantial nexus for gross receipts and compensating use tax purposes. The activities engaged in between the online bookseller, its parent corporation, and an affiliate that operated retail bookstores in New Mexico did not result in the affiliate establishing and maintaining a market in New Mexico for the online bookseller.

A number of states have enacted affiliate nexus statutes for sales and use taxes. For example, in H.B. 360 [Mar. 3, 2008], Idaho amended its definition of a "retailer engaged in business in this state"' for sales and use tax collection purposes to include a retailer with substantial nexus in the state. A retailer has "substantial nexus" with Idaho if both of the following apply: (1) the retailer and an in-state business maintaining one or more locations within Idaho are related parties; and (2) the retailer and the in-state business use an identical or substantially similar name, trade name, trademark, or goodwill to develop, promote, or maintain sales, or the in-state business provides services to, or that inure to the benefit of, the out-of-state business related to developing, promoting, or maintaining the in-state market. The above provisions do not apply to a retailer that had less than $100,000 in sales in Idaho in the previous year.

In recent years, a number of states have enacted click-through nexus requirements for sales and use tax purposes. For example, in 2011 California expanded the definition of "retailer engaged in business in this state" for use tax purposes to include any retailer who enters into an agreement under which a person in California, for a commission or other consideration, refers potential purchasers of tangible personal property to the retailer, whether by an Internet-based link, an Internet website, or otherwise, provided both of the following conditions are met: (1) the retailer's total sales of tangible personal property to California consumers that are referred pursuant to all of those agreements with a person(s) in California in the preceding 12 months are in excess of $10,000; and (2) the retailer's total sales of tangible personal property to California consumers in the preceding 12 months are in excess of $500,000. [A.B. 28, June 28, 2011]

Deliveries in Company-Owned Trucks. A corporation generally has constitutional nexus in any state in which it has property or employees located on a regular basis. Thus, a number of state courts have held that the regular and systematic presence of company-owned delivery trucks driven by company employees is sufficient to create sales and use tax nexus. [E.g., *Brown's Furniture, Inc. v. Wagner*, No. 78195 (Ill. 1996); *Town Crier, Inc. v. Zehnder*, No. 1-98-4251 (Ill. App. Ct. 2000); *John Swenson Granite Co. v. State Tax Assessor*, 685 A.2d 425 (Me. Super. Ct. 1996).]

For income tax purposes, Public Law 86-272 shields an out-of-state corporation from taxation if its only in-state activity is (1) solicitation of orders by company representatives (2) for sales of tangible personal property, (3) which orders are sent outside the state for approval or rejection, and (4) if approved, are filled by shipment or delivery from a point outside the state. Over the years, taxpayers have taken the position that the phrase *shipment or delivery* implies that a seller is protected by Public Law 86-272 regardless of whether it ships the goods into the state using a common carrier or its own delivery trucks. Some states, however, have taken the position that the seller's use of its own trucks to make deliveries is not protected by Public Law 86-272.

State supreme courts in Massachusetts and Virginia have ruled that deliveries in company-owned trucks is a protected activity under Public Law 86-272 [*National Private Truck Council v. Virginia Department of Taxation*, 253 Va. 74, 480 S.E.2d 500 (1997); and *National Private Truck Council v. Commissioner of Revenue*, 688 N.E.2d 936 (Mass. 1997), *cert. denied*]. In 2001, the MTC revised its Statement of Information Concerning Practices of Multistate Tax Commission and Signatory States Under Public Law 86-272 by removing from the list of unprotected activities the following item: "Shipping or delivering goods into this state by means of private vehicle, rail, water, air or other carrier, irrespective of whether shipment or delivery fee or other charge is imposed, directly or indirectly, upon the purchaser." Several state revenue departments have also indicated that deliveries using company-owned trucks is protected by Public Law 86-272. [Rev. Rul. 24-01-01, Neb. Dept. of Rev. (Feb. 22, 2001); Decision No. 2005-05-10-22, Okla. Tax Comn. (May 10, 2005); and Ala. Reg. 810-27-1-4-.19 (Feb. 28, 2006)]

De Minimis Rule. The existence of a *de minimis* rule in the nexus arena is supported by numerous authorities. With respect to constitutional nexus, the Supreme Court has ruled that the Commerce Clause requires a "substantial nexus" in a state. [*Complete Auto Transit, Inc. v. Brady*, 430 U.S. 274 (1977)] In addition, in *Quill*, the taxpayer held title to a few floppy diskettes that were located in North Dakota. The Supreme Court indicated that, although title to a few floppy diskettes located in a state "might constitute some minimal nexus, in *National Geographic Society v. California Bd. of Equalization*, 430 U.S. 551, 556 (1977), we expressly rejected a 'slightest presence' standard of constitutional nexus." [*Quill Corp. v. North Dakota*, 504 U.S. 298 n.8 (1992)] Thus, the presence of a few floppy diskettes did not satisfy the substantial nexus requirement of the Commerce Clause. With respect to Public Law 86-272, in *Wrigley* the Supreme Court indicated that a *de minimis* level of in-state non-solicitation activities does not cause a company to lose the protection afforded by Public Law 86-272.

State courts in Illinois and Michigan have adopted the "more than a slightest presence" test articulated in *Orvis Co., Inc. v. Tax Appeals Tribunal* and *Vermont Information Processing Inc. v. Tax Appeals Tribunal*, Nos. 138, 139 (N.Y. 1995)], in which the New York Court of Appeals concluded that although a physical presence is required to satisfy the *Quill* "substantial nexus" requirement, the in-state physical presence need not be substantial; instead, it must be "demonstrably more than a slightest presence." In *Brown's Furniture v. Wagner* [No. 78195 (Ill. 1996)], the Illinois Supreme Court concluded that "the Orvis court stated—correctly, we believe—the rule regarding substantial nexus." Likewise, in *MagneTek Controls, Inc. v. Michigan Department of Treasury* [No. 181612 (Mich. Ct. App. 1997)], the Michigan Court of Appeals stated that "we conclude that the court in *Orvis* correctly understood *Quill* and enunciated an appropriate test for applying *Quill*."

Specialized Industry Apportionment Formulas

The UDITPA equally weighted three-factor property, payroll and sales apportionment formula was designed to apportion the income of multistate manufacturing and mercantile businesses and may not fairly apportion the income of businesses in other industries. For example, the conventional UDITPA property and payroll factors are difficult to compute for property and payroll that is regularly in motion, such as that of interstate trucking companies, airlines, and railroads. In addition, since its adoption in 1957, the UDITPA Section 17 income producing activity rule for sourcing sales of services has been controversial. Many commentators have argued that its effect is often to merely mimic the property and payroll factor, rather than measure the customer base within a state. The drafters of UDITPA foresaw the limitations of the standard UDITPA apportionment formula, and, under Section 2, specifically excluded from UDITPA certain service businesses, including financial organizations (bank, trust company, savings bank, private banker, savings and loan association, credit union, investment company or insurance company), and public utilities (defined as any business entity that owns or operates for public use any plant, equipment, property, franchise or license for the transmission of communications, transportation of goods or persons or the production, storage, transmission, sale, delivery or furnishing of electricity, water, steam, oil, oil products or gas).

To address these issues, many states provide special rules for computing apportionment percentages for businesses in certain industries. Typically, these special rules involve the modification or exclusion of the conventional factors or the use of unique, industry-specific factors. Examples of industries for which states provide special apportionment rules include airlines, railroads, trucking companies, financial institutions, television and radio broadcasters, publishers, telecommunication services companies, mutual funds, pipeline companies, ship transportation companies, and professional sports franchises.

In many cases, the equitable relief provisions of UDITPA Section 18, which numerous states have incorporated into their statutes, serve as the basis for state revenue departments to adopt specialized formulas. UDITPA Section 18 provides that if the standard apportionment formula does not fairly reflect a taxpayer's in-state business activity, tax authorities may require the exclusion of one or more of the factors or the inclusion of additional factors that will fairly represent the taxpayer's business activity in the state. Under Section 18, the MTC has promulgated special apportionment regulations covering construction contractors [MTC Reg. IV.18(d)], airlines [MTC Reg. IV.18(e)], railroads [MTC Reg. IV.18(f)], trucking companies [MTC Reg. IV.18(g)], television and radio broadcasters [MTC Reg. IV.18(h)], and publishers [MTC Reg. IV.18(j)]. The MTC has also promulgated a model statute for apportioning the income of financial institutions (Nov. 17, 1994). In July 2008, the MTC approved a proposed model regulation for the apportionment of income from telecommunications services.

Sourcing Sales of Services

UDITPA Section 17. UDITPA provides two different rules for determining the numerator of the sales factor. UDITPA Section 16 applies to sales of tangible personal property, and UDITPA Section 17 applies to all sales other than sales of tangible personal property. UDIPTA Section 17 is a catch-all provision, which applies to fees from services, rental income, as well as interest, dividends, royalties, and gains derived from the sale of intangible property.

Most states employ some variation of the UDITPA Section 17 income producing activity rule to source sales of services. Under UDITPA Section 17(a), sales of services are attributed to the state in which "the income producing activity is performed." For example, assume a consulting firm receives a $100,000 fee for services performed by the taxpayer's employees at its offices in State P. Regardless of where the client is located, the $100,000 sale is attributed to State P, because that is where the underlying income producing activity (i.e., employee services) is performed.

Under UDIPTA Section 17(b), if the income producing activity is performed in two or more states, the sale is attributed to the state in which a greater proportion of the income producing activity is performed than in any other state, based on the "costs of performance." Thus, in order to source sales of services under the UDITPA income producing activity rule, the taxpayer must first determine what activity produced the income. Once the taxpayer has identified the applicable income producing activity, a cost of performance analysis is conducted. This involves determining the costs associated with the activity, as well as the states in which those costs were incurred.

The cost of performance rule is an all-or-nothing approach, whereby the entire sale is attributed to the single state in which the greater proportion of the costs of performance is incurred. For example, assume a consulting firm receives a $100,000 fee for services performed by its employees, and that 70 percent of the costs of performance are incurred in State P, and 30 percent of the costs of performance are incurred in State Q. Under UDIPTA Section 17(b), the entire $100,000 sale is attributed to State P, because that is where the greater proportion of the income producing activity is performed, based on costs of performance. In addition, and none of the $100,000 sale is attributed to State Q, despite the significant amount of costs of performance incurred in State Q.

UDITPA does not define the terms "income producing activity" or "costs of performance," but additional guidance is provided by the MTC regulations. Under MTC Reg. IV.17(2), the term *income producing activity* applies to each separate item of income and means the transactions and activity engaged in by the taxpayer in the regular course of its trade or business. Examples of income producing activity include: (1) the rendering of personal services by employees or the use of tangible or intangible property by the taxpayer in performing a service; (2) the sale, rental, leasing, licensing or other use of real property; (3) the rental, leasing, licensing or other use of tangible personal property; and (4) the sale, licensing or other use of intangible personal property. The mere holding of intangible personal property is not, by itself, an income producing activity.

Under MTC Reg. IV.17(3), the term *costs of performance* means direct costs determined in a manner consistent with generally accepted accounting principles and in accordance with accepted conditions or practices in the trade or business of the taxpayer. Direct costs include material and labor costs that have a causal relationship with the sale in question. In other words, a direct cost is a cost that was incurred for a specific purpose and is traceable to that purpose. For example, the direct costs associated with a service contract for maintaining business equipment would include both the cost of repair parts and the compensation costs of the service technicians. Indirect costs, which include general and administrative expenses that are not associated with any specific sale, are not taken in account in determining the costs of performance.

In 2007, the MTC amended this regulation to provide that a taxpayer's income-producing activity includes "transactions and activities performed on behalf of a taxpayer, such as those conducted on its behalf by an independent contractor," and that a taxpayer's cost of performance includes "payments to an agent or independent contractor for the performance of personal services and utilization of tangible and intangible property which give rise to the particular item of income."

MTC Reg. IV.17(4)(B)(c) provides a special rule for applying the UDITPA income producing activity rule to gross receipts for the performance of "personal services," under which a lump-sum payment for personal services performed in two or more states is prorated among the states in proportion to the time spent in each state, based on the premise that the services performed in each state constitute a separate income producing activity. The regulation does not define what constitutes "personal services."

Market-Based Source Rules. The original purpose of the sales factor was to include in the apportionment formula a measure of the taxpayer's customer base within a given state. Unlike the UDITPA Section 16 destination test for inventory sales, however, the UDITPA Section 17 income producing activity rule for sales of services does not accurately measure a service company's customer base when the seller (service provider) performs services in one state and the purchaser (service recipient) is located in another state. When UDITPA was drafted in 1957, it was rare for a service provider and service recipient to be located in different states. Today, however, it is more common for customers to do business with out-of-state service providers. In such cases, the income producing activity rule no longer measures the customer base within a state, but instead tends to mimic the property and payroll factors.

Due in part to this weakness of the income producing activity rule, some states have adopted a market-based approach for sales of services, whereby receipts from services are attributed to a state based on where the service recipient is located. In addition to providing a more accurate measure of the taxpayer's customer base, this approach has the political appeal of reducing the tax burden on service providers that have in-state facilities but provide services primarily to out-of-state customers. A market-based rule for services also creates an incentive for regional and national service providers to locate their facilities within the state's borders. Because most states use the income producing activity rule, a market-based source rule can result in no-where income for service providers that locate their facilities within the state. Finally, the tax revenue on in-state service providers that is lost from switching from the income producing activity rule to a market-based rule may be partially offset by increased taxes on out-of-state service providers that make sales to in-state customers.

The states that have adopted a market-based approach for sales of services include Alabama (effective in 2011), California (effective in 2011 for certain taxpayers), Georgia, Illinois, Iowa, Maine, Maryland, Michigan, Minnesota, Utah, and Wisconsin.

Alabama. For tax years beginning on or after December 31, 2010, sales of services are included in the numerator of the Alabama sales factor if the taxpayer's market for the sales is in Alabama. The determination of whether the market for a sale of services is in Alabama is based on whether the service is delivered to a location in the state. Under prior law, Alabama sourced sales of services using the cost of performance rule. [H.B. 434, June 9, 2011]

California. For tax years prior to 2011, California required the use of the UDITPA costs of performance rule for sourcing sales of services. Effective for tax years beginning on or after January 1, 2011, taxpayers who elect to use a single-factor sales apportionment formula must use a market-based sourcing rule for sales of services. Under the new law, sales of services are attributed to California "to the extent the purchaser of the service received the benefit of the service" in the state. Taxpayers who do not elect to use the single-factor sales apportionment formula, but instead continue to use a double-weighted sales formula, are required to use the costs of performance rule for sourcing sales of services. [S.B. 858, Oct. 19, 2010; and S.B. 15. Feb. 20, 2009]

Georgia. Sales of services are attributed to Georgia "if the receipts are derived from customers within this state or if the receipts are otherwise attributable to this state's marketplace." This gross receipts factor is designed to measure the marketplace for the taxpayer's goods and services. [Ga. Reg. § 560-7-7-.03(5)(c)(1)] A customer within Georgia means (1) a customer that is engaged in a trade or business and maintains a regular place of business within Georgia, or (2) a customer that is not engaged in a trade or business whose billing address is in Georgia.

Illinois. Effective for tax years ending on or after December 31, 2008, sales of services are attributed to Illinois if "the services are received" in Illinois. [S.B. 783, Jan. 11, 2008] Gross receipts from the performance of services provided to a corporation, partnership, or trust may only be attributed to a state where the service recipient has a fixed place of business. If the state where the services are received is not readily determinable or is a state where the service recipient does not have a fixed place of business, the services are deemed to be received at the location of the office of the customer from which the services were ordered in the regular course of the customer's trade or business. If the ordering office cannot be determined, the services are deemed to be received at the office of the customer to which the services are billed. If the taxpayer is not taxable in the state in which the services are received, the sale is excluded from both the numerator and the denominator of the sales factor.

Iowa. Sales of services are attributed to Iowa "if the recipient of the service receives all of the benefit of the service in Iowa." If the recipient of the service receives only some of the benefit of the service in Iowa, the sale is attributed to Iowa "in proportion to the extent the recipient receives benefit of the service in Iowa." [Iowa Admin. Code r. 701-54.6(422)]

Maine. Receipts from the performance of services are attributed to Maine if the services are received in Maine. If the state where the services are received is not readily determinable, the services are deemed to be received at the home of the customer or, in the case of a business, the office of the customer from which the services were ordered in the regular course of the customer's trade or business. If the ordering location cannot be determined, the services are deemed to be received at the home or office of the customer to which the services are billed. If the purchaser of the service is the federal government or the receipts are otherwise attributable to a state in which the taxpayer is not taxable, the receipts are attributed to Maine if a greater proportion of the income producing activity is performed in Maine than in any other state, based on costs of performance. [Me. Rev. Stat. Ann. tit. 36 § 5211(14)]

Maryland. Gross receipts from contracting or service-related activities are attributed to Maryland if the receipts are "derived from customers within" Maryland. [Md. Code Regs. 03.04.03.08.C(3)(c)] Customers within Maryland include individuals and business enterprises that are domiciled in Maryland. A business enterprise (e.g., a corporation, partnership or limited liability company) is domiciled in Maryland if a Maryland office or place of business provides the "principal impetus for the sale." If the principal impetus for the sale cannot be identified, then the business enterprise's domicile is the state in which the headquarters or principal place of business management is located. A special rule applies to construction services, under which the source of the sale is determined by the situs of the property. [Md. Code Regs. 03.04.03.08.D]

Michigan. Receipts from the performance of services are attributed to Michigan if the recipient of the services receives all of the benefit of the services in Michigan. If the recipient receives only some of the benefit of the services in Michigan, then the receipts are attributed to Michigan to the extent that the recipient receives the benefit of the services in Michigan. [Mich. Comp. Laws § 208.1305(2)]

Minnesota. Sales of services are attributed to Minnesota if the "services are received" in Minnesota. However, services provided to a corporation, partnership or trust may only be attributed to a state in which the customer has a fixed place of doing business. If the state where the services are received is not readily determinable or is a state where the corporation, partnership or trust receiving the service does not have a fixed place of doing business, the services are deemed to be received at the location of the office of the customer from which the services were ordered in the regular course of the customer's trade or business. If the ordering office cannot be determined, the services are deemed to be received at the office of the customer to which the services are billed. [Minn. Stat.§ 290.191(j)]

Utah. For tax years beginning on or after January 1, 2009, "a receipt from the performance of a service is considered to be in this state if the purchaser of the service receives a greater benefit of the service in this state than in any other state." [S.B. 136, Mar. 14, 2008]

Wisconsin. Sales of services are attributed to Wisconsin if the "purchaser of the service received the benefit of the service" in Wisconsin. [Wis. Stat. § 71.25(9)(dh)] The benefit of a service is received in Wisconsin if any of the following applies: (1) the service relates to real property that is located in Wisconsin; (2) the service relates to tangible personal property that is located in Wisconsin at the time that the service is received or tangible personal property that is delivered directly or indirectly to customers in Wisconsin; (3) the service is provided to an individual who is physically present in Wisconsin at the time that the service is received; or (4) the service is provided to a person engaged in a trade or business in Wisconsin and relates to that person's business in Wisconsin.

Non-Income Taxes—Ohio, Texas and Washington

Most states link their corporate tax structures to the federal net income tax model, primarily for ease of administration. Some states, however, base their corporate tax systems on different models, or impose specialized corporate taxes in addition to a regular corporate income tax.

Ohio Commercial Activity Tax. Ohio imposes a *commercial activity tax* (CAT) on a business entity's gross receipts. A flat tax of $150 is imposed on the first $1 million in taxable gross receipts. For amounts greater than $1 million, the tax rate is 0.26 percent.

The CAT applies to C corporations, S corporations, partnerships, and limited liability companies. Two or more commonly controlled corporations compute the CAT as either a consolidated elected taxpayer or as a combined taxpayer. Certain types of entities that are subject to other types of Ohio taxes are exempt from the CAT, including financial institutions, insurance companies, securities dealers and public utilities.

Generally, items that are treated as gross receipts for federal income tax purposes are treated as gross receipts for CAT purposes. Examples include the amounts realized from the sale of goods, the performance of services, or the use of property. There are a number of exemptions. Specifically, the following gross receipts are not subject to the CAT: interest (except on credit sales), dividends and capital gains, principal payments on a loan, proceeds from issuing stock, insurance proceeds (except business interruption insurance), damages from litigation, sales and use taxes collected from consumers, sales returns, allowances and discounts, and bad debts.

A taxable gross receipt is a gross receipt sitused to Ohio. Sales of inventory are attributed to Ohio if the property is received in Ohio by the purchaser, rents and royalties are attributed to Ohio if the property is located or used in Ohio, and fees for services are attributed to Ohio in the proportion that the purchaser's benefit in Ohio bears to the purchaser's benefit everywhere. Thus, examples of taxable gross receipts include sales of property delivered to locations within Ohio, rents from property used in Ohio, and fees for services where the purchaser receives the benefit in Ohio.

Texas Margin Tax. Texas imposes a business *margin tax*. Taxable entities include C corporations, S corporations, limited liability companies, partnerships, and other legal entities. Certain entities are not subject to the margin tax, including sole proprietorships (does not include single member limited liability companies), general partnerships with direct ownership entirely composed of natural persons, and certain passive entities. Taxable entities that are part of an affiliated group engaged in a unitary business must file a combined group report and compute their margin tax as if they were a single taxable entity. An affiliated group means a group of one or more taxable entities in which a controlling interest is owned by a common owner, either corporate or noncorporate, or by one or more of the member entities.

A taxable entity's margin is the lowest of three amounts: (1) total revenue minus cost of goods sold, (2) total revenue minus compensation, or (3) 70 percent of total revenue. The tax rate is 0.5 percent for taxpayers primarily engaged in retail or wholesale trade, and 1 percent for all other businesses. A taxable entity with total revenue of $10 million or less may elect to calculate its margin tax due by multiplying total revenue times the apportionment factor times 0.575 percent.

A taxable entity's total revenues are defined by reference to the amounts reported on its federal income tax return and include gross receipts or sales (less returns and allowances), dividends, interest, gross rents, gross royalties, capital gain net income, net gain or loss from the sale of trade or business assets (federal Form 4797), and other income. The following items may be excluded from gross revenue: bad debt expense, foreign dividends and royalties, net distributive income from a taxable entity treated as a partnership or S corporation for federal tax purposes, federal dividends received deduction, income from a disregarded entity for federal but not Texas margin tax purposes, dividends and interest from federal obligations, and certain other specified items.

A taxable entity may subtract cost of goods sold in computing its margin only if the entity owns the goods. Thus, service companies are generally not eligible to subtract cost of goods sold. In addition, numerous special rules apply in computing cost of goods sold for margin tax purposes; thus, the deduction will generally not be the same as the amount used in computing federal taxable income. For example, a taxable entity may elect to currently expense allowable costs associated with the goods purchased or produced, in which case the entity will have no beginning or ending inventory.

If a taxable entity subtracts compensation in computing its margin, the compensation deduction will include both the compensation amounts reported on the employees' Form W-2s (maximum of $320,000 per person 2010 tax reports), as well as deductible employee benefits, including workers' compensation, health care and retirement benefits.

Washington Business and Occupation Tax. The State of Washington imposes a gross receipts tax called the *business and occupation tax* (B&O tax). The B&O tax applies to C corporations, S corporations, partnerships, and sole proprietorships.

The B&O tax is imposed on a seller's gross receipts derived from business activities conducted in Washington. Taxable gross receipts generally include: (1) gross proceeds from sales of goods delivered to customers located in Washington, (2) gross receipts from sales of services rendered in Washington, and (3) the value of products manufactured in Washington. Gross proceeds from sales of goods that an in-state retailer or wholesaler delivers to customers located outside of Washington are generally not taxable. Generally, no deductions are allowed for cost of goods sold, salaries, supplies, taxes, or any other costs of doing business. There are a handful of exemptions, deductions and credits, however. For example, there is an exemption for the sale or rental of real estate (other than lodging), and deductions for bad debts as well as sales returns, allowances and discounts.

The B&O tax rate varies with the type of business activity. Moreover, it is possible for a single taxpayer to have gross receipts in two or more categories. The four primary business activity classifications are retailing, wholesaling, manufacturing, and service and other activities. The applicable tax rates are 0.471% for retailing, 0.484% for wholesaling, 0.484% for manufacturing, and 1.500% for service and other activities. In addition to the primary categories, there are numerous specialized categories, each with an associated tax rate. Examples include travel agents and tour operators (0.275 percent), manufacturing commercial aircraft (0.2904 percent), highway contractors (0.484 percent), royalties (0.484 percent), and public or nonprofit hospitals (1.5 percent).

Note. From 2008 through 2011, Michigan subjected corporations to the Michigan Business Tax, which included both a 4.95 percent business income tax and a 0.80 percent modified gross receipts tax. The modified gross receipts tax base equaled a taxpayer's gross receipts reduced by purchases of inventory, depreciable assets, materials, and supplies. Taxpayers paid the sum of the two taxes. These taxes applied to business entities generally, including C corporations, S corporations, partnerships, limited liability companies, and sole proprietorships. Effective January 1, 2012, Michigan replaced its business income and modified gross receipt taxes with a conventional 6 percent corporate income tax. [H.B. 4361 and 4362, May 25, 2011].

Mechanisms Used by States to Limit Tax Base Erosion

A principal planning objective is to create legal structures that minimize the state income taxes of the business enterprise as a whole. Through the use of separately incorporated affiliates and intercompany transactions (loans, licenses, inventory sales, etc.), income can be shifted from operations in high-tax states to operations in low-tax states. Such strategies are made possible by the large number of states that require or permit the filing of separate company returns, whereby each member of an affiliated group that has nexus in a state computes its income and files a return as if it were a separate and distinct economic entity.

States employ a number of mechanisms to limit the ability of multistate businesses to use related party structures and transactions to shift income. As discussed below, these include the theory of economic nexus, the judicial doctrines of economic substance and business purpose, combined reporting, IRC § 482-type reallocation provisions, and related party expense addback provisions.

Economic Nexus. The highest courts in several states have ruled that an economic presence, such as the licensing of trademarks for use within the state by affiliated companies, is sufficient to create constitutional nexus for income tax purposes [*Geoffrey, Inc. v. South Carolina Tax Commission*, 437 S.E.2d 13 (S.C. 1993), *cert. denied* 510 U.S. 992 (1993); *Lanco, Inc. v. Division of Taxation*, No. A-89-05 (N.J. Sup. Ct., Oct. 12, 2006); *cert. denied*, U.S. Sup. Ct., 06-1236 (2007); *Commissioner v. MBNA America Bank, N.A.*, No. 33049 (W.V. Sup. Ct. of App., Nov. 21, 2006); *cert. denied*, U.S. Sup. Ct., 06-1228 (2007); *Capital One Bank and Capital One F.S.B. v. Commissioner of Revenue*, No. SJC-10105 (Mass. Sup. Jud. Ct., Jan. 8, 2009); *cert. denied*, U.S. Sup. Ct., No. 08-1169 (2009); and *KFC Corporation v. Iowa Department of Revenue*, No. 09-1032 (Ia. Sup. Ct., Dec. 30, 2010)]

Economic Substance and Business Purpose. In *Gregory v. Helvering* [293 U.S. 465, 1935], the U.S. Supreme Court has ruled that a transaction is respected only if it has economic substance and serves a business purpose other than tax avoidance. The states have invoked the judicial doctrines of economic substance and business purpose as an argument to, for example, disallow deductions for royalty payments made by an operating company to a trademark holding company.

For example, in *Syms Corp. v. Commissioner of Revenue* [No. SJC-08513 (Mass. Sup. Jud. Ct., Apr. 10, 2002)], the Massachusetts Supreme Judicial Court ruled that the transfer and licensing back of trademarks between a retailer and its trademark holding company was a sham transaction, and therefore no deduction was allowed for the royalty payments. The Massachusetts courts reached similar conclusions in *Talbots, Inc. v. Commissioner of Revenue* [No. 09-P-1931 (Mass. App. Ct., Mar. 29, 2011)], *IDC Research v. Commissioner of Revenue* [No. 09-P-1533 (Mass. App. Ct., Nov. 30, 2010)], and *TJX Companies, Inc. vs. Commissioner of Revenue* [No. 09-P-1841 (Mass. App. Ct., July 23, 2010)]. On the other hand, in *The Sherwin-Williams., Co. v. Commissioner of Revenue* [No. SJC-08516 (Mass. Sup. Jud. Ct., Oct. 31, 2002)], the Massachusetts Supreme Judicial Court ruled that two trademark holding companies had economic substance and served valid business purposes.

In *HMN Financial, Inc. v. Commissioner of Revenue* [No. A09-1164 (Minn. Sup. Ct., May 20, 2010)], the Minnesota Supreme Court ruled that the commissioner did not have the authority to disregard the taxpayer's captive REIT structure, which was motivated solely by tax avoidance, because the taxpayer complied with the relevant corporate franchise tax statutes in structuring its business and reporting its income.

Combined Reporting. Requiring an out-of-state trademark holding company or financing company to file a combined report with an in-state operating company eliminates the tax benefits of intercompany royalty and interest payments. When computing the unitary group's combined income, the in-state operating company's royalty and interest expense deductions are offset by the royalty and interest income of the out-of-state holding and financing companies.

For example, New Jersey does not permit an affiliated group to elect to file a consolidated return nor does it require all unitary groups to compute their tax on a combined basis. Thus, every corporation with nexus in New Jersey generally is considered a separate entity and must file its own return. The Director of the Division of Taxation may, however, require members of an affiliated group or a controlled group to file a consolidated return "if the taxpayer cannot demonstrate by clear and convincing evidence that a report by a taxpayer discloses the true earnings of the taxpayer on its business carried on in this State." [N.J. Rev. Stat. 54:10A-10.c.]

Section 482-Type Reallocation. IRC Section 482 authorizes the IRS to reallocate income among commonly controlled corporations whenever necessary to prevent the evasion of taxes or to clearly reflect the income of the related entities. Congress enacted Section 482 to ensure that commonly controlled corporations report and pay tax on their actual share of income arising from intercompany transactions. Many states have enacted Section 482-type statutes, although the details of these statutes vary significantly from state to state. For example, Florida tax authorities may make adjustments to clearly reflect a taxpayer's income if an arrangement exists between related entities that causes a taxpayer's income to be "reflected improperly or inaccurately." [Fla. Stat. § 220.44]

Related Party Expense Add-Back Provisions. Another technique that many states use to limit income shifting is to require corporations to add back any royalty or interest payments made to related parties when computing state taxable income (hereinafter, referred to as "addback provisions").

Although the different state addback provisions share many common themes, there are significant differences, particularly with respect to the circumstances under which an exception applies and the related party expense need not be added back. Therefore, it is essential to thoroughly analyze each state's specific provisions to ensure compliance.

State related party expenses addback provisions are generally targeted at interest expenses and intangible expense. Most states define "interest expense" by reference to federal Internal Revenue Code Section 163. States generally define "intangible expenses" to include not only royalties, but also a broad range of other costs, expenses, and losses related to intangible property.

State addback provisions are designed to prevent taxpayers from using intercompany licensing and financing arrangements to avoid corporate income taxes. Under the general rules, however, state addback provisions apply automatically to all related party intangible and interest expenses, including those related party payments that are motivated by legitimate business purposes rather than tax avoidance. As a consequence, each state provides some relief in the form of exceptions from the automatic addback requirement. These exceptions are complex and vary from state to state. There are some common themes, however, including exceptions that apply when: (1) the related payee's corresponding income is subject to tax in another U.S. state or a foreign country, (2) the related payee pays the amount to an unrelated person, (3) the addback adjustment produces an unreasonable result, or (4) the taxpayer and the state tax authorities agree to an alternative adjustment.

Pass-Through Entities

States generally conform to the federal tax treatment of S corporations and partnerships as pass-through entities, as well as the federal "check-the-box" classification of an LLC as a partnership or a disregarded entity. Despite this broad conformity, numerous states impose entity-level taxes on S corporations, partnerships, and LLCs. Examples of states that impose entity-level taxes include, but are not limited to, the following:

Alabama. Alabama imposes a business privilege tax on limited partnerships, limited liability partnerships, and LLCs. The tax is based on Alabama net worth, with a $100 minimum and $15,000 maximum.

California. An S corporation doing business in California must pay the greater of an $800 minimum tax, or a 1.5 percent corporate franchise tax on the S corporation's income. The tax rate is 3.5 percent for S corporations that are financial corporations.

California imposes an annual tax of $800 on limited partnerships and limited liability partnerships doing business in California.

California also imposes an annual tax of $800 on any LLC doing business in California. An LLC must also pay a fee based on its total gross receipts attributable to California. The maximum fee is $11,790, and applies if the LLC's total gross receipts are $5 million or more. The fee applies even if the LLC is classified as a disregarded entity or partnership for federal income tax purposes.

District of Columbia. The District of Columbia does not conform to the federal pass-through entity treatment of an S corporation. As a consequence, S corporations are subject to the District's 9.975 percent corporate income tax.

The District of Columbia imposes a 9.975 percent income tax on unincorporated businesses, including partnerships and LLCs. The tax does not apply to a professional firm in which more than 80 percent of the gross income is derived from personal services and capital is not a material income-producing factor.

Illinois. Illinois imposes a 1.5 percent income tax (referred to as the personal property replacement tax) on S corporations, partnerships, and LLCs classified as partnerships.

Kansas. Prior to 2011, Kansas imposed a franchise tax on S corporations, partnerships, and LLCs classified as partnerships. The tax base is net worth (stockholders' equity or capital accounts), and the tax rate is $0.03125 per $1,000 of net worth in 2010, with a maximum tax of $20,000. The tax is repealed for tax years beginning after December 31, 2010.

Kentucky. S corporations, limited partnerships, limited liability partnerships, and LLCs are subject to a limited liability entity tax equal to the lesser of 0.095 percent of Kentucky gross receipts or 0.75 percent of Kentucky gross profits. The tax does not apply to entities with gross receipts or gross profits of $3 million or less and is reduced for entities with gross receipts or gross profits over $3 million but less than $6 million.

Massachusetts. An S corporation that has total annual receipts of $6 million or more is subject to a 2.3 percent (2010) corporate income tax. The rate increases to 3.45 percent (2010) for S corporations with total annual receipts of $9 million or more.

Michigan. From 2008 through 2011, Michigan subjected S corporations, partnerships, and LLCs to a 4.95 percent business income tax and 0.80 percent modified gross receipts tax. Taxpayers paid the sum of the two taxes.

New Hampshire. New Hampshire subjects S corporations, partnerships, and LLCs classified as partnerships to an 8.5 percent business profits tax and a 0.75 percent business enterprise tax. A credit against the business profits tax is allowed for any business enterprise tax paid.

Ohio. Ohio imposes a commercial activity tax (CAT) on the annual gross receipts of all business entities generally, including S corporations, partnerships, and LLCs. The tax rate is 0.26 percent. Examples of taxable gross receipts include sales of property delivered to locations within Ohio, fees for services where the purchaser receives the benefit in Ohio, and rents from property used in Ohio.

Pennsylvania. S corporations and LLCs are subject to a capital stock tax based on the entity's capital stock value, as determined by a statutory formula. The capital stock tax rate is 0.289 percent in 2011. The tax is scheduled to be repealed in 2014.

Tennessee. Tennessee imposes a 6.5 percent income tax and a 0.25 percent net worth tax on S corporations, LLCs, limited partnerships, and limited liability partnerships.

Texas. Texas subjects S corporations, partnerships, LLCs, and other pass-through entities to its margin tax. The tax base equals the lowest of three amounts: (1) total revenue minus cost of goods sold, (2) total revenue minus compensation, or (3) 70 percent of total revenue. The tax rate is 0.5 percent for taxable entities primarily engaged in retail or wholesale trade and 1 percent for all other entities. General partnerships with direct ownership entirely composed of natural persons and certain passive entities are exempt from the margin tax.

Washington. Washington subjects S corporations, partnerships, and LLCs, to its business and occupation (B&O) tax, which is a type of gross receipts tax. The B&O tax rate varies with the type of business activity, and generally is between 0.471 percent and 1.5 percent.

West Virginia. West Virginia imposes a business franchise tax on S corporations, partnerships, and LLCs classified as partnerships. For tax years beginning in 2011, the tax is 0.34 percent of the S corporation's capital or the partners' capital accounts. The tax is scheduled to be repealed in 2015.

Part 2. NEXUS

Activities Creating Franchise or Income Tax Nexus

Overview

A threshold issue for any corporation operating in more than one state is determining in which states it must file returns and pay income tax. A corporation generally is subject to income tax in the state in which it is incorporated, and also may be subject to income tax in any other states in which its property, employees, or other agents are physically present on a regular and systematic basis. *Nexus* is the term used to describe the types of contacts necessary to establish a state's right to impose an income tax obligation. Determining the nexus states for a large corporation that has customers nationwide can be a difficult task. Such corporations clearly have nexus in each state in which the company has offices and other facilities, accompanied by resident employees. A more difficult issue is determining in which, if any, market states the company has nexus.

Corporations with customers in multiple states generally want to minimize the number of states in which they must file returns and pay income tax. Fortunately, the U.S. Constitution and Public Law 86-272 provide important protections against state taxation. These federal protections also provide a degree of uniformity in state tax laws because they govern nexus determinations in all 50 states.

This section describes the principal considerations in determining whether a corporation has income tax nexus in a particular state, and is organized as follows:

- Constitutional Nexus
- Public Law 86-272
- *De Minimis* Rule
- Agency Nexus
- Affiliate Nexus
- Deliveries in Company-Owned Trucks
- Economic Nexus
- Factor Presence Nexus
- Other Nexus Issues
  - — State-Specific Statutory and Administrative Exemptions
  - — Ownership of Partnership Interest
  - — Ownership of Leased Property
  - — Ownership of Natural Gas or Electricity Flowing Through State
  - — Qualification to Do Business
  - — Gross Receipts Taxes
  - — Telecommuters
  - — Electronic Commerce

This section includes a multipart chart that summarizes the positions of the states on a wide range of potentially nexus-creating activities.

Constitutional Nexus

Due Process and Commerce Clause Restrictions. Historically, states have asserted that virtually any type of in-state business activity creates nexus for an out-of-state corporation. Such behavior reflects the reality that it is politically more appealing to tax out-of-state corporations than to raise taxes on in-state business interests. The desire of state lawmakers and tax officials to, in effect, export the local tax burden has been counterbalanced by the Due Process Clause and Commerce Clause of the U.S. Constitution.

The Due Process Clause states that no state shall "deprive any person of life, liberty or property, without due process of law." The U.S. Supreme Court has interpreted this clause as prohibiting a state from taxing an out-of-state corporation unless there is a "minimal connection" between the company's interstate activities and the taxing state. [E.g., *Mobil Oil Corporation v. Commissioner of Taxes*, 445 U.S. 425 (1980)] The Commerce Clause expressly authorizes Congress to "regulate Commerce with foreign Nations, and among the several States." The Supreme Court has interpreted the Commerce Clause as prohibiting states from enacting laws that might unduly burden or otherwise inhibit the free flow of trade among the states. More specifically, with respect to the nexus issue, the Supreme Court has interpreted the Commerce Clause as prohibiting a state from taxing an out-of-state corporation unless that company has a "substantial nexus" with the state. [*Complete Auto Transit, Inc. v. Brady*, 430 U.S. 274 (1977)]

In summary, a state cannot impose a tax obligation on an out-of-state corporation unless the Due Process Clause minimal connection and Commerce Clause substantial nexus requirements are satisfied. Therefore, a critical question in the nexus arena is, what do minimal connection and substantial nexus mean? The landmark case in this regard is *Quill Corporation v. North Dakota.* [504 U.S. 298 (1992)]

Quill (1992) Physical Presence Test. In *Quill*, the Supreme Court upheld the bright-line physical presence test that it established in *National Bellas Hess, Inc. v. Illinois* [386 U.S. 753 (1967)], an earlier mail-order/use tax collection case. Quill Corporation was a mail-order vendor of office supplies that solicited sales through catalogs mailed to potential customers in North Dakota and made deliveries using common carriers. Quill was a Delaware corporation with offices and warehouses in Illinois, California, and Georgia. Quill had no office, warehouse, retail outlet, or other facility in North Dakota, and no Quill employees or sales representatives were physically present in North Dakota. During the tax years in question, Quill made sales to roughly 3,000 North Dakota customers and was the sixth largest office supply vendor in the state.

North Dakota attempted to impose on Quill an obligation to collect North Dakota use tax on sales to North Dakota customers. The North Dakota Supreme Court ruled that Quill had constitutional nexus in North Dakota, reasoning that Quill's "economic presence" in North Dakota depended on services and benefits provided by the state, and therefore generated "a constitutionally sufficient nexus to justify imposition of the purely administrative duty of collecting and remitting the use tax."

The U.S. Supreme Court reversed the lower court's ruling, and held that, although an economic presence was sufficient to satisfy the Due Process Clause requirement of a minimal connection, it was not sufficient to satisfy the Commerce Clause requirement of substantial nexus. Consistent with its ruling 25 years earlier in *National Bellas Hess*, the Court further ruled that substantial nexus exists only if a corporation has a nontrivial physical presence in a state. Therefore, a physical presence is an essential prerequisite to establishing constitutional nexus, at least for sales and use tax purposes.

It is important to highlight the fact that *Quill* is a use tax case, and that the Supreme Court did not address the issue of whether the physical presence test also applied to income taxes. This has resulted in a significant amount of controversy and litigation (see discussion below under the heading of Economic Nexus).

Public Law 86-272

Limited Federal Safe Harbor. In *Northwestern States Portland Cement Co. v. Minnesota* [358 U.S. 450 (1959)], the Supreme Court held, for the first time, that the Commerce Clause did not prohibit a state from imposing a fairly apportioned, direct corporate income tax on an out-of-state corporation carrying on an exclusively interstate business within the taxing state. This ruling created a furor among the business community, which lobbied Congress to exercise its Commerce Clause powers to limit the ability of the states to tax out-of-state corporations.

Congress responded in 1959 by enacting Public Law 86-272, which provides multistate corporations with a limited safe harbor from the imposition of state taxes imposed on "net income." Specifically, Public Law 86-272 prohibits a state from taxing the income of a out-of-state corporation (i.e., a corporation that is not incorporated in the taxing state) if the company's only in-state activity is solicitation of orders by company representatives for sales of tangible personal property, which orders are sent outside the state for approval or rejection, and if approved, are filled by shipment or delivery from a point outside the state.

Although Public Law 86-272 can provide significant protections for a multistate business, it has several important limitations. First, it applies only to taxes imposed on net income, and therefore provides no protection against the imposition of a sales and use tax collection obligation, gross receipts taxes (e.g., Ohio commercial activity tax, or Washington business and occupation tax), or corporate franchise taxes on net worth or capital. Likewise, in *Home Impressions, Inc. v. Division of Taxation* [No. 000099-2003 (N.J. Tax Ct., June 7, 2004)], the New Jersey Tax Court ruled that Public Law 86-272 does not protect a taxpayer from the imposition of a flat dollar minimum tax that is part of the state's corporate business tax regime.

Second, the protection of Public Law 86-272 is available only to businesses that sell tangible personal property. It provides no protection to businesses that lease tangible personal property, sell services, sell or lease real estate, or sell or license intangibles. For example, *In re Personal Selling Power, Inc.* [No 380557 (Cal. State Bd. of Equal., Mar. 16, 2009)], the California State Board of Equalization ruled that Public Law 86-272 did not protect a Virginia media company from income tax nexus, because the employee solicitation of sales of advertisements in a magazine involved sales of a service rather than sales of tangible personal property.

Third, for businesses that do sell tangible personal property, their employees must limit their in-state activities to the solicitation of orders that are sent outside the state for approval, and if approved, are filled by shipment or delivery from a point outside the state. For example, Public Law 86-272 provides no protection if salespersons are given the authority to approve merchandise orders. Likewise, Public Law 86-272 does not protect the presence of salespersons who perform nonsolicitation activities, such as repairs, customer training, or technical assistance, within a state.

In *Schering-Plough Healthcare Products Sales Corp. v. Commonwealth* [161 MAP 2002 (Pa. Sup. Ct., Oct. 20, 2004), *aff'g* 805 A.2d 1284 (Pa. Commw. Ct. 2002)], the Pennsylvania Supreme Court ruled that Public Law 86-272 protected an out-of-state corporation that was a manufacturer's representative that limited its in-state activities to the solicitation of orders on behalf of its parent company, even though the taxpayer did not own the products it sold.

Meaning of Solicitation—Wrigley (1992). To qualify for the safe harbor provided by Public Law 86-272, a corporation must limit its employees' in-state activities to the solicitation of orders. Despite its importance as a qualification requirement, Public Law 86-272 does not define the phrase *solicitation of orders*; however, the proper interpretation of the phrase was addressed by the Supreme Court in *Wisconsin Department of Revenue v. William Wrigley, Jr., Co.* [505 U.S. 214 (1992)]Wrigley was a chewing gum manufacturer headquartered in Illinois. Wrigley marketed its goods in Wisconsin through employee sales representatives who were residents of Wisconsin. All Wisconsin orders were sent to Chicago for acceptance and were filled by shipment through common carrier from outside the state. Wrigley did not own or lease any offices or other facilities in Wisconsin.

In determining whether Wrigley's activities in Wisconsin exceeded the protection of Public Law 86-272, the Supreme Court was faced with two fundamental questions: 1) What is the scope of the phrase *solicitation of orders*? and 2) Does a *de minimis* exception exist for activities other than solicitation of orders? With respect to the first issue, Wisconsin argued that *solicitation of orders* should be narrowly construed to mean "any activity other than requesting the customer to purchase the product." Wrigley, on the other hand, argued for a much broader definition—specifically, "any activities that are ordinary and necessary business activities accompanying the solicitation process or are routinely associated with deploying a sales force to conduct the solicitation, so long as there is no office, plant, warehouse or inventory in the State." The Supreme Court rejected both definitions as too extreme, and instead crafted its own interpretation, defining *solicitation of orders* as encompassing "requests for purchases" and "those activities that are entirely ancillary to requests for purchases—those that serve no independent business function apart from their connection to the soliciting of orders."

The Court then applied this definition to the activities of Wrigley employees within Wisconsin. It found that providing a company-owned car or stock of free samples to salespeople; in-state recruitment, training, and evaluation of sales representatives; and use of hotels and homes for sales-related meetings were entirely ancillary to solicitation because they served no purpose apart from their role in facilitating requests for purchases. In contrast, the Court found that the replacement of stale gum, the supplying of gum through agency stock checks, and the storage of gum within the state were not ancillary to Wrigley's solicitation activities.

With respect to the issue of *de minimis* nonsolicitation activities, the Supreme Court held that a *de minimis* level of nonsolicitation activities does not cause a company to lose the protections afforded by Public Law 86-272, and that whether nonsolicitation activities are sufficiently *de minimis* to avoid the loss of tax immunity depends on whether that activity establishes a "nontrivial additional connection with the taxing state." The Court then held that, in the aggregate, Wrigley's unprotected activities (i.e., the replacement of stale gum, the supplying of gum through agency stock checks, and the storage of gum) did not meet its *de minimis* standard even though the relative magnitude of those activities was not large in comparison to Wrigley's total Wisconsin activities.

In summary, although taxpayers and the states can be expected to interpret the phrases *entirely ancillary* and *nontrivial additional connection* differently, the Supreme Court's ruling in *Wrigley* nevertheless provides a uniform standard applicable to all 50 states. Moreover, the *Wrigley* decision clearly establishes that there is a *de minimis* exception to the activities that are not protected by Public Law 86-272.

It does appear that some states will narrowly interpret the *Wrigley* definition of solicitation of orders. For example, in *Kennametal Inc. v. Massachusetts Commissioner of Revenue* [No. SJC-07448 (Mass. 1997)] the Massachusetts Supreme Judicial Court ruled that Kennametal's frequent in-plant presentations, inventory analyses for tool standardization programs, and sample testing using Kennametal's products exceeded solicitation. According to the court, those activities not only invited orders but also ingratiated customers to the company and assisted customers with making buying decisions.

Likewise, in *Amgen, Inc. v. Commissioner of Revenue* [No. SJC-07563 (Mass. 1998)], the Massachusetts Supreme Judicial Court held that the in-state activities of Amgen employees exceeded the mere solicitation of Amgen's pharmaceutical products. In particular, the employees monitored the research and clinical studies performed in Massachusetts, provided educational seminars, maintained ownership and control of the supplies used in such studies, and retained employees to review specific patient charts and answer patient-specific questions. The court ruled that these activities were not entirely ancillary to the solicitation of orders, but instead served an independent business purpose.

In *Alcoa Building Products, Inc. v. Commissioner of Revenue* [No. SJC-08939 (Mass. Sup. Jud. Ct., Oct. 21, 2003)], the Massachusetts Supreme Judicial Court held that various warranty claims activities performed by in-state sales personnel, such as initiating warranty claims, analyzing the merits of claims, and assisting customers in filing claims, exceeded mere solicitation and created income tax nexus for an out-of-state manufacturer.

Although taxpayers generally prefer to avoid nexus, a narrow interpretation of the meaning of "solicitation" can be helpful in avoiding the application of a state's sales factor throwback rule, as was illustrated in *Colgate-Palmolive Company v. Commissioner of Revenue* [No. C255116 (Mass. App. Tax Bd. April 3, 2003)]. On the other hand, the Texas Comptroller of Public Accounts rejected a taxpayer's argument that throwback did not apply to the company's sales to Alabama customers because while visiting family in Alabama, an employee checked the company's voice mail system and responded to work-related telephone calls. [Tex. Comp. of Pub. Accts., Hearing No. 42,586, Jan. 6, 2004]

MTC Statement of Practices: Protected vs. Unprotected Activities. Created in 1967, the Multistate Tax Commission (MTC) is an agency of state governments whose mission is to promote fairness and uniformity in state tax laws. The MTC adopted a policy statement in 1986 regarding the proper application of Public Law 86-272, modified the statement in 1993 and 1994 in light of the *Wrigley* decision, and modified it again in 2001 to remove deliveries in company-owned vehicles from the list of unprotected activities. In the MTC's Statement of Information Concerning Practices of Multistate Tax Commission and Signatory States Under Public Law 86-272, the states indicate that "it is the policy of the state signatories hereto to impose their net income tax, subject to State and Federal legislative limitations, to the fullest extent constitutionally permissible." The statement goes on to list activities that are considered to be entirely ancillary to the solicitation of orders (protected activities) and activities that are considered to serve an independent business function (unprotected activities).

Unprotected Activities. The following in-state activities (if they are not of a *de minimis* level) are not considered either the solicitation of orders or ancillary to the solicitation of orders or otherwise protected under Public Law 86-272 and will cause otherwise protected sales to lose their protection under Public Law 86-272:

- Making repairs or providing maintenance or service to the property sold or to be sold
- Collecting current or delinquent accounts, whether directly or by third parties, through assignment or otherwise
- Investigating creditworthiness
- Installation or supervision of installation at or after shipment or delivery
- Conducting training courses, seminars, or lectures for personnel other than personnel involved only in solicitation
- Providing any kind of technical assistance or service (including, but not limited to, engineering assistance or design service) when one of the purposes thereof is other than the facilitation of the solicitation of orders
- Investigating, handling, or otherwise assisting in resolving customer complaints, other than mediating direct customer complaints when the sole purpose of the mediation for sales personnel is to ingratiate themselves with customers
- Approving or accepting orders
- Repossessing property
- Securing deposits on sales
- Picking up or replacing damaged or returned property
- Hiring, training, or supervising personnel, other than personnel involved only in solicitation
- Using agency stock checks or any other instrument or process by which sales are made within the state by sales personnel
- Maintaining a sample or display room in excess of two weeks (14 days) at any one location within the state during the tax year
- Carrying samples for sale, exchange, or distribution in any manner for consideration or other value
- Owning, leasing, using, or maintaining any of the following facilities or property in the state:
  - — Repair shop
  - — Parts department
  - — Any kind of office other than an in-home office
  - — Warehouse
  - — Meeting place for directors, officers, or employees
  - — Stock of goods other than samples for sales personnel or samples whose use is entirely ancillary to solicitation
  - — Telephone answering service that is publicly attributed to the company or to employees or agents of the company in their representative status
  - — Mobile stores (i.e., vehicles with drivers who are sales personnel making sales from the vehicles)
  - — Real property or fixtures to real property of any kind
- Consigning stock of goods or other tangible personal property to any person, including an independent contractor, for sale
- Maintenance, by any employee or other representative, of an office or place of business of any kind (other than an in-home office located within the residence of the employee or representative 1) that is not publicly attributed to the company or to the employee or representative of the company in an employee or representative capacity, and 2) as long as the use of such office is

limited to soliciting and receiving orders from customers; to transmitting such orders outside the state for acceptance or rejection by the company; or to such other activities that are protected under Public Law 86-272)

- Entering into franchising or licensing agreements; selling or otherwise disposing of franchises and licenses; or selling or otherwise transferring tangible personal property pursuant to such franchise or license by the franchisor or licensor to its franchisee or licensee within the state
- Conducting any activity not listed as a protected activity (see below) that is not entirely ancillary to requests for orders, even if the activity helps to increase purchases

Protected Activities. The following in-state activities will not cause the loss of protection for otherwise protected sales:

- Solicitation of orders by any type of advertising
- Solicitation of orders by an in-state resident employee or representative of the company, as long as such person does not maintain or use any office or other place of business in the state other than an in-home office
- Carrying samples and promotional materials only for display or distribution without charge or other consideration
- Furnishing and setting up display racks and advising customers on the display of the company's products without charge or other consideration
- Providing automobiles to sales personnel for their use in conducting protected activities
- Passing orders, inquiries, and complaints on to the home office
- Missionary sales activities (i.e., the solicitation of indirect customers for the company's goods, which would include, for example, a manufacturer's solicitation of retailers to buy the manufacturer's goods from the manufacturer's wholesale customers if such solicitation activities were otherwise immune)
- Coordinating shipment or delivery without payment or other consideration and providing information relating thereto either prior or subsequent to the placement of an order
- Checking customers' inventories without charge (for reorder but not for other purposes such as quality control)
- Maintaining a sample or display room for two weeks (14 days) or less at any one location within the state during the tax year
- Recruiting, training, or evaluating sales personnel, including occasionally using homes, hotels, or similar places for meetings with sales personnel
- Mediating direct customer complaints when the purpose of the mediation is solely for sales personnel to ingratiate themselves with customers and to facilitate requests for orders
- Owning, leasing, or maintaining personal property for use in the employee's or representative's in-home office or automobile that is solely limited to conducting protected activities

It follows from the last item that use of personal property such as a cellular telephone, facsimile machine, duplicating equipment, personal computer, and computer software that is limited to carrying on protected solicitation and activity entirely ancillary to protected solicitation or permitted by the MTC's statement will not, by itself, remove the protection under the MTC's statement.

De Minimis Rule

The existence of a *de minimis* rule in the nexus arena is supported by numerous authorities. With respect to constitutional nexus and the *Quill* physical presence test, the Commerce Clause requires not just nexus, but a "substantial nexus" in a state. [*Complete Auto Transit, Inc. v. Brady*, 430 U.S. 274 (1977)] In addition, in *Quill*, the taxpayer did have property (specifically, a few floppy discs) in North Dakota. The Supreme Court indicated that, although title to a few floppy discs present in a state "might constitute some minimal nexus, in *National Geographic Society v. California Board of Equalization*, 430 U.S. 551, 556 (1977), we expressly rejected a 'slightest presence' standard of constitutional nexus." [*Quill Corporation v. North Dakota*, 504 U.S. 298 n.8 (1992)] Thus, the presence of a few floppy discs did not meet the substantial nexus requirement of the Commerce Clause. In addition, with respect to Public Law 86-272, in *Wrigley* the Supreme Court clearly indicated that a *de minimis* level of nonsolicitation activities does not cause a company to lose the protections afforded by Public Law 86-272.

State courts in Illinois and Michigan have adopted the "more than a slightest presence" test articulated in *Orvis Company, Inc. v. Tax Appeals Tribunal* and *Vermont Information Processing Inc. v. Tax Appeals Tribunal* [Nos. 138, 139 (N.Y. 1995)], in which the New York Court of Appeals concluded that although a physical presence is required to satisfy the *Quill* "substantial nexus" requirement, the in-state physical presence need not be substantial; instead, it must be "demonstrably more than a slightest presence." In *Brown's Furniture v. Wagner* [No. 78195 (Ill. 1996)], the Illinois Supreme Court concluded that "the Orvis court stated—correctly, we believe—the rule regarding substantial nexus." Likewise, in *Magne-Tek Controls, Inc. v. Michigan Department of Treasury* [No. 181612 (Mich. Ct. App. 1997)], the Michigan Court of Appeals stated that "we conclude that the court in *Orvis* correctly understood *Quill* and enunciated an appropriate test for applying *Quill*."

A common issue with respect to the *de minimis* rule is how many days of presence on the part of company employees is required to exceed a *de minimis* level of in-state business activity. There are a number of authorities in this regard, most of which deal with the issue of nexus for sales and use tax purposes. Under *Quill*, the decisive issue for sales and use tax nexus is whether the corporation has a nontrivial physical presence in the state. Public Law 86-272 does not apply, and thus the nature of the in-state activities (i.e., solicitation versus nonsolicitation activities) generally is a moot issue; however, under Public Law 86-272 and the Supreme Court's ruling in *Wrigley*, employees attending in-state business meetings that are entirely ancillary to the solicitation of sales of tangible personal property will not create income tax nexus, regardless of the frequency of the meetings, as long as the other requirements of Public Law 86-272 are satisfied.

In Determination No. 08-0117 [Wash. Dept. of Rev., App. Div., Apr. 29, 2008], the Washington Department of Revenue ruled that an out-of-state manufacturer who sent a salesman into Washington to meet with its Washington customers for only one day during the year had sufficient contact to establish nexus for purposes of the Washington business and occupation tax (a type of gross receipts tax). While the visit lasted only a day, the salesman intended to sell the taxpayer's products to the distributors, and the activity was clearly designed to help the taxpayer market its products in Washington.

In Private Letter Ruling No. P-2009-001 [Kan. Dept. of Rev., Feb. 4, 2009], the Kansas Department of Revenue ruled that out-of-state vendors that operate in Kansas at transient events such as trade shows, antique shows, and county fairs are required to collect Kansas sales tax. The ruling emphasizes that Kansas sales tax is imposed on the privilege of engaging in the business of selling tangible personal property at retail within the state. The imposition of sales tax does not depend on an out-of-state retailer making a certain number or dollar amount of sales in the state, nor does it depend on the duration of the retailer's operation within the state.

In *Share International, Inc. v. Florida Department of Revenue* [676 So. 2d 1362 (Fla. 1996)] a Texas mail-order vendor that had no offices or resident employees in Florida conducted a seminar in Florida for three days each year. Share's products were displayed and sold at the seminar. The Florida Supreme Court held that the company did not have substantial nexus with the state for purposes of collecting use tax on the company's mail-order sales.

In Technical Assistance Advisement No. 05A-045 [Fla. Dept. of Rev. (Nov. 2, 2005)], the Florida Department of Revenue advised that an out-of-state distributor of electrical wire and cable does not have sales and use tax nexus with Florida if the taxpayer's only physical contact with Florida is a once a year visit to one customer, where no sales orders are taken.

In Minnesota Revenue Notice 2000-10, the Minnesota Department of Revenue states, "[i]t is the department's position that an out-of-state business is maintaining a place of business in this state and has sufficient nexus to be required to collect Minnesota sales or use tax when it conducts business activity in Minnesota on at least four days during a 12-month period."

In *Appeal of Intercard, Inc.* [No. 83,802 (Kan. Sup. Ct., Dec. 8, 2000)], the Kansas Supreme Court ruled that 11 days of presence during a four-year audit period constituted an isolated and sporadic presence that was insufficient to establish nexus with Kansas for sales and use tax purposes. See also, e.g., *Care Computer Sys., Inc. v. Arizona Department of Revenue* [197 Ariz. 414, 4 P.3d 469 (Ct. App. 2000)].

With respect to Public Law 86-272, in *Wrigley* the Supreme Court indicated that nonsolicitation activities are not *de minimis* if they establish a "nontrivial additional connection with the taxing state." The Court then held that, in the aggregate, Wrigley's non-immune activities (i.e., the replacement of stale gum, the supplying of gum through agency stock checks, and the storage of gum) did not meet its *de minimis* standard even though the relative magnitude of those activities was not large in comparison to Wrigley's total Wisconsin activities. For example, Wrigley's gum sales through agency stock checks accounted for only 0.00007 percent of Wrigley's total annual Wisconsin sales, and in absolute terms amounted to only several hundred dollars a year. Expanding on the *Wrigley* decision, the MTC's Statement of Information Concerning Practices of Multistate Tax Commission and Signatory States Under Public Law 86-272 defines *de minimis* activities as follows:

> *De minimis* activities are those that, when taken together, establish only a trivial connection with the taxing State. An activity conducted within a taxing State on a regular or systematic basis or pursuant to a company policy (whether such policy is in writing or not) shall normally not be considered trivial. Whether or not an activity consists of a trivial or non-trivial connection with the State is to be measured on both a qualitative and quantitative basis. If such activity either qualitatively or quantitatively creates a non trivial connection with the taxing State, then such activity exceeds the protection of P.L. 86-272. Establishing that the disqualifying activities only account for a relatively small part of the business conducted within the taxing State is not determinative of whether a *de minimis* level of activity exists. The relative economic importance of the disqualifying in-state activities, as compared to the protected activities, does not determine whether the conduct of the disqualifying activities within the taxing State is inconsistent with the limited protection afforded by P.L. 86-272.

Agency Nexus

Agency Nexus Principle. Under the *Quill* decision, a corporation generally has constitutional nexus in any state in which the corporation's property or employees are physically present on a regular and systematic basis. What if, rather than conducting business in a state through employees (dependent agents), a corporation conducts business through independent contractors (independent agents)? Do the in-state activities of independent agents, acting on an out-of-state corporation's behalf, create constitutional nexus?

In *Scripto, Inc. v. Carson* [362 U.S. 207 (1960)], the Supreme Court addressed whether the Florida marketing activities of ten independent sales representatives created sales and use tax nexus for an out-of-state manufacturer of writing instruments. The Court held that for nexus purposes, the distinction between employees and independent contractors was "without constitutional significance" and that "to permit such formal 'contractual shifts' to make a constitutional difference would open the gates to a stampede of tax avoidance." The Court concluded that the critical fact was that the agents' activity in Florida helped create and maintain a commercial market for Scripto's goods. Thus, the presence of independent agents engaged in continuous local solicitation created Florida sales and use tax nexus for Scripto.

The U.S. Supreme Court reaffirmed these principles 25 years later in *Tyler Pipe Industries, Inc. v. Washington Department of Revenue* [483 U.S. 232 (1987)], holding that the activities of an independent contractor residing in Washington was sufficient to create constitutional nexus for the out-of-state principal (Tyler Pipe). As in *Scripto*, the Court held that the critical test was "whether the activities performed in this state on behalf of the taxpayer are significantly associated with the taxpayer's ability to establish and maintain a market in this state for the sales." [See also *Lamtec Corp. v. Department of Revenue*, No. 83579-9 (Wash. Sup. Ct., Jan. 20, 2011).]

In *Jafra Cosmetics, Inc. v. Massachusetts* [No. SJC-08265 (Mass. Jan. 25, 2001)], the Massachusetts Supreme Judicial Court ruled that independent contractors (called "consultants") who sold the products of an out-of-state cosmetics company (Jafra) in Massachusetts created sales tax nexus for Jafra. Although the consultants were not agents of Jafra, the nature of the relationship between the consultants and Jafra was such that the consultants did constitute representatives of Jafra, and, as such, created sales tax nexus for Jafra.

In *Appeal of Family of Eagles, Ltd.* [No. 88,118 (Kan. Sup. Ct. Apr. 18, 2003)], the Kansas Supreme Court ruled that a Texas corporation whose only physical presence in Kansas was through its independent sales representatives had nexus for sales tax purposes. The court found no constitutionally significant differences between the taxpayer's independent sales representatives and the independent contractors in *Scripto*.

In *Arco Building Systems, Inc. v. Chumley* [No. M2004-01872-COA-R3-CV (Tenn. Ct. of App., June 12, 2006)], the Tennessee Court of Appeals ruled that an out-of-state seller of pre-engineered metal buildings with no property or employees in the state had sales and use tax nexus in Tennessee, because the seller contracted with a unrelated Tennessee manufacturer to construct the buildings and relied on the in-state manufacturer to perform various services that were integral to the success of the seller's overall business in Tennessee. The in-state manufacturer was involved in the seller's Tennessee operations from beginning to end, including the preparation of price quotes, drawing up blueprints, fabricating the product, arranging for shipment, and accepting final payment. The in-state manufacturer also provided post-delivery consulting services and shipped replacement parts by in-state mail or common carrier.

On the other hand, in *Scholastic Book Clubs, Inc. v. Commissioner of Revenue Services* [Nos. CV 07 4013027 S and CV 07 4013028 S (Conn. Super. Ct., Apr. 9, 2009)] the Connecticut Superior Court ruled that an out-of-state book publisher that relied on in-state teachers to distribute catalogs and collect orders from students did not have sales tax nexus in Connecticut, because the activities of the school teachers did not rise to the level of representatives of the book publisher. Although the teachers performed an important administrative role for the publisher, they were not in-state order-takers seeking to produce revenue for themselves or the publisher.

In *Vestax Securities Corp. v. Department of Treasury* [No. 142535 (Mich. Sup. Ct., June 1, 2011)], the Michigan Supreme Court ruled that an out-of-state securities broker-dealer did not have substantial nexus with Michigan, because the evidentiary record did not support the conclusion that the independent registered representatives who were doing business in Michigan were agents of the taxpayer.

Public Law 86-272. In addition to protecting solicitation activities of employee-salespersons, Public Law 86-272 protects certain in-state activities conducted by an independent contractor. Specifically, Public Law 86-272 provides that independent contractors may engage in the following in-state activities on behalf of an out-of-state corporation without creating income tax nexus for the out-of-state principal: 1) soliciting sales, 2) making sales, and 3) maintaining an office. Thus, unlike employees, independent agents can maintain in-state offices without creating nexus for the principal. [See, e.g., *Universal Instruments Corp. v. Massachusetts Commissioner of Revenue*, No. 196059 (Mass. App. Tax Bd. 1998).]

For this purpose, the term *independent contractors* means a commission agent, broker, or other independent contractor who is engaged in selling, or soliciting orders for the sale of, tangible personal property for more than one principal and who holds him- or herself out as such in the regular course of his or her business activities.

In *Dart Industries, Inc.* [No. 04-03, N.M. Dept. of Rev., Feb. 26, 2004], the New Mexico Department of Revenue ruled that Public Law 86-272 did not protect an out-of-state manufacturer from income tax nexus. The taxpayer sold its goods in New Mexico through an in-state distributor that maintained an office in the state, but did not qualify as an independent contractor because the distributor was contractually bound to represent only the taxpayer. The distributor also handled customer complaints, which was another activity that is not protected by Public Law 86-272.

Likewise, in *Reader's Digest Association v. Franchise Tax Board* [No. C036307 (Cal. Ct. App. Dec. 31, 2001), *cert. denied*, Cal. Mar. 13, 2002], the California Court of Appeals held that Public Law 86-272 did not protect an out-of-state parent corporation from nexus in California because its California sales subsidiary had offices in the state, but did not qualify as an independent contractor because it represented only its parent company.

Under the MTC's Statement of Information Concerning Practices of Multistate Tax Commission and Signatory States Under Public Law 86-272, the maintenance of a stock of goods within a state by the independent contractor under consignment or any other type of arrangement with the out-of-state principal, except for purposes of display and solicitation, is not protected by Public Law 86-272.

MTC Nexus Bulletin 95-1. Nonancillary services, such as installation and repair services, performed by an employee-salesperson are not protected by Public Law 86-272 and will create income tax nexus for the employer if the unprotected activities are not *de minimis*. A number of states take the position that such in-state services create nexus even if they are performed by unrelated third-party repairpersons (i.e., independent agents). Unlike the use of independent agents to perform continuous local solicitation, the use of independent agents to perform services that are not ancillary to the solicitation has yet to be addressed by the Supreme Court. Thus, this remains an unsettled area of the law.

In Nexus Bulletin 95-1 (1995), the MTC and roughly two dozen signatory states took the position that with respect to mail-order computer vendors, the industry practice of providing in-state warranty repair services through third-party repair service providers creates constitutional nexus. As a consequence, the out-of-state mail-order vendors have nexus for sales and use tax purposes. This position is based on the Supreme Court's decision in *Scripto* and *Tyler Pipe*, both of which dealt with the use of independent sales representatives, as opposed to independent service providers. The computer mail-order industry and many practitioners believe that there is insufficient support in these two Supreme Court decisions for the position asserted by the MTC in Nexus Bulletin 95-1. Nevertheless, since its issuance, a number of states have taken a position similar to that espoused in Nexus Bulletin 95-1.

In *Dell Catalog Sales v. Commissioner of Revenue Services* [No. CV 00 0503146S (Conn. Super. Ct. July 10, 2003); a Texas-based Internet and mail-order computer vendor (Dell) had no property or employees in Connecticut. Nevertheless, Dell offered on-site computer repair services to customers that elected to purchase a service contract when purchasing a computer. The services were performed by a third-party repair company (BancTec). The Connecticut Superior Court ruled that Dell did not have sales tax nexus because no evidence was produced to indicate that the in-state service calls were frequent or substantial in nature.

In another case involving Dell and BancTec [*Louisiana v. Dell International, Inc.*, No. 2006-C-0996 (La. Ct. of App., Feb. 15, 2006)], the Louisiana Court of Appeal concluded that BancTec's on-site repair services were crucial to Dell's ability to establish and maintain a market for its goods in Louisiana, and that Dell retained control over many aspects of the services provided by BancTec, such as requiring customers to contact Dell directly to determine whether a BancTec technician was dispatched, setting the price for the on-site services, compensating BancTec based on the number of service calls made, and training the BancTec technicians on how to perform the services. As a consequence, the appellate court ruled that there was a genuine issue of fact as to whether Dell, through its contractual agreements with BancTec, had established constitutional nexus in Louisiana, and that the trial court had erred in granting summary judgment for Dell. Therefore, the case was remanded to the trial court for further proceedings.

In *Dell Catalog Sales L.P. v. New Mexico Taxation and Revenue Department* [No. 26,843 (N.M. Ct. of App., June 3, 2008); *cert. denied*, U.S. No. 08-770, Mar. 23, 2009], the New Mexico Court of Appeals ruled that, despite the lack of a direct physical presence in New Mexico, the use of an in-state third-party repair and installation service provider created "substantial nexus" for the Texas-based Internet and mail-order computer vendor (Dell). The third-party service provider's activities performed in the state on behalf of Dell were significantly associated with Dell's ability to establish and maintain a market in New Mexico for the sale of its products. The fact that the third-party service provider was not itself engaged in sales-related activities was a distinction without relevance.

Affiliate Nexus

Some states have taken the position that the existence of common ownership between a corporation that has a physical presence in a taxing state (e.g., an in-state brick-and-mortar retailer) and an out-of-state corporation that has no physical presence in the state but makes substantial sales into the state (e.g., an out-of-state mail-order or Internet vendor) is sufficient to create nexus for the out-of-state affiliate. As with agency nexus, many of these cases concern the existence of nexus for sales and use tax purposes.

For example, in *SFA Folio Collections, Inc. v. Tracy* [73 Ohio St. 3d 119, 652 N.E.2d 693 (1995)], the taxpayer (Folio) was a mail-order retailer of clothing and other merchandise. Folio had no property or employees in Ohio. Folio's parent corporation, Saks & Company, also owned another subsidiary, Saks Fifth Avenue of Ohio (Saks-Ohio), which operated a retail store in Ohio. The state tax authorities argued that Folio had "substantial nexus" in Ohio because it was a member of an affiliated group that included Saks-Ohio and therefore was required to collect Ohio sales tax on its mail-order sales to Ohio customers. The state's position was based on a nexus-by-affiliate statute that the Ohio legislature had enacted, as well as the argument that Saks-Ohio was an "agent" of Folio. The agency argument was based on the fact that Saks-Ohio accepted some returns of Folio sales and distributed some Folio catalogs. The Ohio Supreme Court rejected the affiliate nexus argument, reasoning that to impute nexus to Folio merely because a sister corporation had a physical presence in Ohio ran counter to federal constitutional law and Ohio corporation law. The court also rejected the agency nexus argument because Saks-Ohio accepted Folio's returns according to its own policy (not Folio's) and charged the returns to its inventory (not Folio's).

Consistent with the Ohio Supreme Court ruling in *SFA Folio*, other states have generally been unsuccessful in their attempts to argue that common ownership, by itself, creates nexus for an out-of-state affiliate. [See, e.g., *Current, Inc. v. State Board of Equalization*, 24 Cal. App. 4th 382, 29 Cal. Rptr. 2d 407 (Ct. App. 1994); *SFA Folio Collections, Inc. v. Bannon*, 217 Conn. 220, 585 A.2d 666 (1991); *Bloomingdale's By Mail, Ltd. v. Commonwealth*, 130 Pa. Commw. 190, 567 A.2d 773 (Pa. 1989).]

On the other hand, if an in-state affiliate functions as an agent for an out-of-state affiliate, the Supreme Court's decisions in *Scripto* and *Tyler Pipe* provide a basis for concluding that the activities of the in-state affiliate creates nexus for an out-of-state affiliate.

In *Borders Online, Inc.* [No. A105488 (Cal. Ct. of App., May 31, 2005)], the California Court of Appeals ruled that an out-of-state online retailer had a substantial nexus in California for sales tax purposes because an affiliated corporation, which sold similar products in brick-and-mortar stores in California, performed return and exchange activities for the online retailer. The brick-and-mortar affiliate was considered to be an authorized representative of the online retailer because the online retailer posted a notice on its Web site that returns could be made to the brick-and-mortar retailer, and the brick-and-mortar retailer's acceptance of returns was an integral part of the online retailer's sales operations. Therefore, under the relevant state statute, the online retailer was considered to be engaged in business in California and subject to the obligation to collect sales tax on sales to California residents.

In *Barnesandnoble.com LLC v. State Bd. of Equalization* [No. CGC-06-456465 (Cal. Super. Ct., Oct. 11, 2007)], the California Superior Court ruled that an in-state brick-and-mortar affiliate's distribution of coupons that provided a discount on an online purchase did not create sales and use tax nexus for the related Internet retailer. The retail stores did not act as the Internet vendor's agent or representative. The court concluded that "[a]n essential element is that the agent (or representative) must have the authority to bind the principal." In the present case, the in-state retailer had no such authority and could do nothing but pass out the coupons created and distributed by Internet vendor.

Likewise, in *Barnesandnoble.com LLC* [N.M. Taxn. and Rev. Dept., No. 11-10, Apr. 11, 2011], the New Mexico Taxation and Revenue Department ruled that the online bookseller did not have sufficient contacts with New Mexico to establish substantial nexus for gross receipts and compensating use tax purposes. The activities engaged in between the online bookseller, its parent corporation, and an affiliate that operated retail bookstores in New Mexico did not result in the affiliate establishing and maintaining a market in New Mexico for the online bookseller.

In *Reader's Digest Association v. Franchise Tax Board* [No. C036307 (Cal. Ct. App. Dec. 31, 2001), *cert. denied*, Cal. Mar. 13, 2002], the California Court of Appeals held that an out-of-state parent corporation (Reader's Digest) had nexus for California corporate income tax purposes as a result of solicitation activities performed by its wholly owned in-state subsidiary (Reader's Digest Sales & Services, Inc.). Public Law 86-272 did not protect the in-state affiliate's California activities because the subsidiary had offices in the state and did not qualify as an "independent contractor" with respect to its out-of-state parent.

In *J.C. Penney National Bank v. Johnson* [No. M1998-00497-COA-R3-CV (Tenn. Ct. App. Dec. 17, 1999)], the state argued that J.C. Penney National Bank (JCPNB) had "substantial nexus" in Tennessee, because JCPNB had a physical presence in Tennessee by virtue of the fact the J.C. Penney Company, JCPNB's parent, owned and operated J.C. Penney retail stores in Tennessee. The court rejected the argument and ruled that JCPNB did not have substantial nexus in Tennessee, because the retail stores conducted no activities that assisted JCPNB in maintaining its credit card business in Tennessee. Customers could not apply for JCPNB credit cards at the J.C. Penney stores, nor could customers make a payment on their accounts at the stores. The solicitation of potential new credit card customers, which was the most important function in allowing JCPNB to maintain its business, took place through the U.S. mail, and that, under the holding in *Quill*, does not allow a finding of substantial nexus.

In *Dillard National Bank, N.A. v. Johnson* [No. 96-545-III (Tenn. Ch. Ct., June 22, 2004)], the Tennessee Chancery Court ruled that an out-of-state subsidiary corporation that issued proprietary credit cards for use in a chain of in-state department stores that were operated by the parent corporation had income tax nexus in Tennessee because of the activities conducted on its behalf by the department stores and the store employees. These activities included placing advertisements in the stores, soliciting and taking credit card applications from store customers, answering questions for store customers regarding their credit card accounts, and accepting credit card payments in the stores. The Tennessee Chancery Court's ruling in *Dillard National Bank* is consistent with the nexus principles articulated by the Tennessee Court of Appeals in *America Online, Inc. v. Johnson* [No. M2001-00927-COA-R3-CV (Tenn. Ct. App. July 30, 2002)], in which the court stated that "substantial nexus may be established by activities carried on within the state by affiliates and independent contractors." In addition, the facts in *Dillard National Bank* are distinguishable from those in *J.C. Penney National Bank v. Johnson* [No. M1998-00497-COA-R3-CV (Tenn. Ct. App. Dec. 17, 1999)], in which the Tennessee Court of Appeals rejected the affiliate nexus argument because the in-state retail stores conducted no activities that assisted the affiliated out-of-state bank in maintaining its credit card business in Tennessee.

On the other hand, in *St. Tammany Parish Tax Collector v. Barnesandnoble.com* [No. 05-5695, (E.D. La., Mar. 22, 2007)], the U.S. District Court ruled that an Internet retailer of books, movies, and music with no physical presence in Louisiana did not have sales and use tax nexus merely because of its close business relationship with an affiliated bricks-and-mortar retailer. The court stated that the "existence of a close corporate relationship between companies and a common corporate name does not mean that the physical presence of one is imputed to the other," and that "attributional nexus does not apply merely by virtue of the affiliation between the companies."

Likewise, in Determination No. 08-0128 [Wash. Dept. of Rev., App. Div., May 14, 2008], the Washington Department of Revenue ruled that wholesale sales of the identical brand name products by an in-state affiliate did not establish business and occupation tax nexus for a remote seller that used television infomercials to promote telephone and online sales, because the in-state affiliate's wholesale-level sales activities were not significantly related to establishing a market for the remote seller.

In *Drugstore.com, Inc. v. Division of Taxation* [No. 000637-2003 (N.J. Tax Ct., Feb. 11, 2008)], the New Jersey Tax Court held that the operator of a drug store Web site had sales and use tax nexus, because it had a physical presence in New Jersey. Drugstore.com contended that its only roles in the sales to New Jersey customers were the operation of the Web site and the performance of certain administrative functions for its subsidiaries. One of those subsidiaries, DS Non-Pharmaceutical Sales, Inc. (DSNP Sales) was the nominal retail vendor of the merchandise and had no physical presence in New Jersey. The other subsidiary involved in the transactions was DS Distribution, Inc., which distributed the merchandise to New Jersey customers from a New Jersey warehouse. The taxpayer contended that DSNP Sales was the actual retail vendor of the merchandise and made the sales to New Jersey customers through a drop shipment transaction. The Tax Court rejected this contention and held that Drugstore.com was the actual seller of merchandise and liable for collecting tax.

Affiliate Nexus Statutes. A number of states have enacted affiliate nexus statutes for sales and use taxes. For example, effective January 1, 2012, the following retailers will be considered to be engaged in business in Texas for sales and use tax collection purposes: (1) a retailer that holds a substantial ownership interest in, or is owned in whole or in substantial part by, a person who maintains a business location in Texas, provided certain conditions are met; and (2) a retailer that holds a substantial ownership interest in, or is owned in whole or in substantial part by, a person who maintains a distribution center, warehouse, or similar location in Texas and who delivers property sold by the retailer to consumers. In addition, the definition of a "seller" or "retailer" is expanded to include a person who has been entrusted with the possession of property and has the power to sell, lease, or rent the property without further action by the owner. [S.B. 1, July 19, 2011]

In 2009, Wisconsin amended its definition of a retailer engaged in business in the state for sales and use tax collection purposes to include "any person who has an affiliate in this state, if the person is related to the affiliate and if the affiliate uses facilities or employees in this state to advertise, promote, or facilitate the establishment of or market for sales of items by the related person to purchasers in this state or for providing services to the related person's purchasers in this state, including accepting returns of purchases or resolving customer complaints." [A.B. 75, June 29, 2009]

Another example is Idaho, which in 2008 amended its definition of a "retailer engaged in business in this state" for sales and use tax collection purposes to include a retailer with substantial nexus in the state. A retailer has "substantial nexus" with Idaho if both of the following apply: (1) the retailer and an in-state business maintaining one or more locations within Idaho are related parties; and (2) the retailer and the in-state business use an identical or substantially similar name, trade name, trademark, or goodwill to develop, promote, or maintain sales, or the in-state business provides services to, or that inure to the benefit of, the out-of-state business related to developing, promoting, or maintaining the in-state market. These provisions do not apply to a retailer that had less than $100,000 in sales in Idaho in the previous year. [H.B. 360, Mar. 3, 2008]

Click-Through Nexus Requirements. In recent years, a number of states have enacted click-through nexus requirements for sales and use tax purposes. For example, in 2011, California expanded the definition of "retailer engaged in business in this state" for use tax purposes to include any retailer who enters into an agreement under which a person in California, for a commission or other consideration, refers potential purchasers of tangible personal property to the retailer, whether by an Internet-based link, an Internet website, or otherwise, provided both of the following conditions are met: (1) the retailer's total sales of tangible personal property to California consumers that are referred pursuant to all of those agreements with a person(s) in California in the preceding 12 months are in excess of $10,000; and (2) the retailer's total sales of tangible personal property to California consumers in the preceding 12 months are in excess of $500,000. [A.B. 28, June 28, 2011]

Likewise, in 2011, Illinois modified its definition of a "retailer maintaining a place of business" in the state for use tax purposes to include any retailer who has a contract with a person located in Illinois under which the person, for a commission or other consideration based upon the sale of tangible personal property by the retailer, directly or indirectly refers potential customers to the retailer by a link on the person's Internet website, but only if the cumulative gross receipts from sales of tangible personal property under the contract exceed $10,000 during the preceding four quarterly periods ending on the last day of March, June, September, and December. [H.B. 3659, Mar. 10, 2011]

Deliveries in Company-Owned Trucks

A corporation generally has constitutional nexus in any state in which it has property or employees located on a continuous basis. Thus, a number of state courts have held that the regular and systematic presence of company-owned delivery trucks driven by company employees is sufficient to create sales and use tax nexus. [E.g., *Brown's Furniture, Inc. v. Wagner*, No. 78195 (Ill. Apr. 18, 1996); *Town Crier, Inc. v. Zehnder*, No. 1-98-4251 (Ill. App. Ct. June 30, 2000); *John Swenson Granite Co. v. State Tax Assessor*, 685 A.2d 425 (Me. Super. Ct. 1996). But see *Miller Bros. Co. v. Maryland*, 347 U.S. 340 (1954) (ruling that "occasional delivery" of goods with no solicitation other than the "incidental effects of general advertising" was not sufficient to create nexus under the Due Process Clause).]

For income tax purposes, Public Law 86-272 shields an out-of-state corporation from taxation if its only in-state activity is solicitation of orders by company representatives for sales of tangible personal property, which orders are sent outside the state for approval or rejection, and if approved, are filled by shipment or delivery from a point outside the state. Over the years, taxpayers have taken the position that the phrase *shipment or delivery* implies that a seller is protected by Public Law 86-272 regardless of whether it ships the goods into the state using a common carrier or its own delivery trucks. Some states, however, have taken the position that the in-state delivery of goods in the seller's own delivery trucks exceeds solicitation and therefore is an activity that is not protected by Public Law 86-272.

State supreme courts in Massachusetts and Virginia have ruled that deliveries in company-owned trucks is a protected activity under Public Law 86-272 [*National Private Truck Council v. Virginia Department of Taxation*, 253 Va. 74, 480 S.E.2d 500 (1997); and *National Private Truck Council v. Commissioner of Revenue*, 688 N.E.2d 936 (Mass. 1997), *cert. denied*]. In 2001, the MTC revised its Statement of Information Concerning Practices of Multistate Tax Commission and Signatory States Under Public Law 86-272 by removing from the list of unprotected activities the following item: "Shipping or delivering goods into this state by means of private vehicle, rail, water, air or other carrier, irrespective of whether shipment or delivery fee or other charge is imposed, directly or indirectly, upon the purchaser." Several state revenue departments have also indicated that deliveries using company-owned trucks is protected by Public Law 86-272 [Rev. Rul. 24-01-01, Neb. Dept. of Rev. (Feb. 22, 2001); Decision No. 2005-05-10-22, Okla. Tax Comm'n. (May 10, 2005); and Ala. Reg. 810-27-1-4-.19 (Feb. 28, 2006)].

Although deliveries may be a protected activity, other activities of a delivery truck driver, such as collecting payments or accepting returns (back-hauling), are likely not protected by Public Law 86-272. For example, in *Asher, Inc. v. Division of Taxation* [No. 004061-2003 (N.J. Tax Ct., Jan. 5, 2006)], the New Jersey Tax Court ruled that Public Law 86-272 did not protect the New Jersey activities of a Pennsylvania company's delivery drivers, which included picking up damaged or returned goods and the collection of delinquent accounts. These activities were not ancillary to the solicitation of sales and were not sufficiently de minimis to avoid the loss of immunity under the standard established by the Supreme Court in *Wrigley*.

Likewise, In P.D. 08-168 [Va. Dept. of Taxn., Sept. 11, 2008], the Virginia Department of Taxation ruled that an out-of-state mail-order and Internet vendor that uses unrelated third party contract carriers to make deliveries would establish income tax nexus if the activities of the contract carriers, which include unpacking a purchased item at the customer's home, providing minor setup services, and inspecting the product for quality and damage, go beyond the making of sales and are not protected by Public Law 86-272.

Economic Nexus

In *Quill*, the Supreme Court ruled that a corporation satisfies the Commerce Clause's "substantial nexus" requirement only if the taxpayer has a physical presence in the state. Yet, in *Geoffrey, Inc. v. South Carolina Tax Commissioner* [437 S.E.2d 13 (S.C.), *cert. denied*, 510 U.S. 992 (1993)], the South Carolina Supreme Court held that a trademark holding company that licensed its intangibles for use in South Carolina had nexus for income tax purposes despite the lack of any tangible property or employees in South Carolina. Geoffrey was the trademark holding company of the toy retailer, Toys "R" Us. Geoffrey was incorporated and domiciled in Delaware and had a license agreement with South Carolina retailers allowing them to use its trademarks and trade names, including the Toys "R" Us trademark, in exchange for a percentage of net sales. The court rejected Geoffrey's claim that it had not purposefully directed its activities toward South Carolina and held that, by licensing intangibles for use in the state and receiving income in exchange for their use, Geoffrey had the minimum connection and substantial nexus with South Carolina required by the Due Process Clause and the Commerce Clause. The *Geoffrey* court did not follow the precedent established by *Quill* because it believed that ruling applied only to the issue of nexus for sales and use tax purposes.

Since 1993, many states have adopted "economic nexus" standards that are based on the amount of income or sales derived from sources within a state. For example, the Connecticut corporate income tax applies to "[a]ny company that derives income from sources within this state and that has a substantial economic presence within this state, evidenced by a purposeful direction of business toward this state, examined in light of the frequency, quantity and systematic nature of a company's economic contacts with this state, without regard to physical presence, and to the extent permitted by the Constitution of the United States." [Conn.Gen. Stat. § 12-216a] An exemption applies to a company that is treated as a foreign corporation for federal tax purposes and has no income effectively connected with a U.S. trade or business. The "bright-line test" for determining economic nexus is whether the company had $500,000 or more in business receipts attributable to Connecticut sources during the tax year. The in-state ownership and use of intangible property by a company in Connecticut would subject it to tax on its income when: (1) the intangible property generates, or is otherwise a source of, gross receipts within the state for the corporation, including through a license or franchise; (2) the activity through which the corporation obtains such gross receipts from its intangible property is purposeful (e.g., a contract with an in-state company); and (3) the corporation's presence within the state, as indicated by its intangible property and its activities with respect to that property, satisfies the bright-line test. [Informational Publication 2010(29.1), Conn. Dept. of Rev. Services, Dec. 28, 2010]

In addition, there has been a significant amount of litigation related to the *Geoffrey* court's interpretation of the Commerce Clause's substantial nexus requirement.

For example, in *Cerro Copper Products Inc. v. Department of Revenue* [No. 94-444 (Ala. Admin. L. Div. 1995)] and *Dial Bank v. Department of Revenue* [No. 95-289 (Ala. Admin. L. Div. 1998)], an administrative law judge could find no reason why the *Quill* physical presence test should not also apply to nexus for corporate income taxes.

Likewise, in *Bandag Licensing Corporation v. Rylander* [No. 03-99-00427-CV (Tex. App. May 11, 2000)], the Texas appeals court saw no principled distinction between sales taxes and income taxes when the underlying issue was whether the Commerce Clause permits a state to impose a tax obligation on an out-of-state corporation. The court concluded that, consistent with the ruling in *Quill*, a state cannot constitutionally impose its corporate franchise tax on an out-of-state corporation that lacks a physical presence in the state.

In *A&F Trademark, Inc. v. Tolson* [No. COA03-1203 (N.C. Ct. of App., Dec. 7, 2004); *appeal denied*, No. 23P05, N.C. Sup. Ct., Mar. 3, 2005; *cert. denied*, U.S. No. 04-1625, Oct. 3, 2005], the North Carolina Court of Appeals held that licensing intangibles for use in North Carolina was sufficient to establish income tax nexus for an out-of-state trademark holding company, even though the holding company had no physical presence in North Carolina.

In *Geoffrey, Inc. v. Tax Commission* [No. 99,938 (Okla. Ct. of Civ. App., Dec. 23, 2005)], the Oklahoma Court of Civil Appeals ruled that licensing intangibles for use in Oklahoma was sufficient to establish income tax nexus for a Delaware trademark holding company, even though the holding company had no physical presence in Oklahoma. The court concluded that the *Quill* physical presence test did not apply to taxes other than sales and use taxes.

In *Kmart Properties, Inc. v. Taxation and Revenue Department* [No. 21,140 (N.M. Ct. App. Nov. 27, 2001)], the taxpayer (Kmart Properties, Inc., or KPI) was a Michigan corporation that had no employees or property in New Mexico but did license trademarks to its parent corporation, which operated Kmart stores in New Mexico. The New Mexico Court of Appeal ruled that the use of the trademarks in New Mexico was sufficient to create income tax nexus for KPI, despite the lack of any direct physical presence in New Mexico. The court also concluded that the *Quill* physical presence requirement did not apply to income taxes, and that the presence in New Mexico of a licensee that was working on KPI's behalf to maintain and enhance the market for its intangibles created nexus for KPI under the agency nexus principles of *Scripto.* See also *Kmart Corp. v. Taxation and Revenue Department* [No. 27,269 (N.M. Sup. Ct., Dec. 29, 2005)].

In *ACME Royalty Co. and Brick Investment Co.* (Mo. S.Ct., No. SC84225 and SC84226, Nov. 26, 2002), the Missouri Supreme Court ruled that two trademark holding companies were not subject to the Missouri corporate income tax, because they did not have any activity in Missouri in the form of payroll, property, or sales.

In *SYL, Inc. v. Comptroller; Crown Cork & Seal Co. (Del.), Inc. v. Comptroller* [Nos. 76 and 80 (Md. Ct. of App., June 9, 2003)], the Maryland Court of Appeals held that the trademark holding companies in question had nexus in Maryland because they were unitary with their parent companies that were doing business in Maryland, and had no economic substance as separate entities from their parent corporations. The Maryland courts reached similar conclusions in *The Classics Chicago, Inc., et al. v. Comptroller of the Treasury* [No. 2047 (Md. Ct. of Spec. App., Jan. 4, 2010)] (Classics was a wholly-owned subsidiary of the retailer, Talbots); and *Nordstrom, Inc. v. Comptroller of the Treasury* [Nos. 07-IN-OO-0226, 06-IN-OO-00317, 07-IN-OO-0226, 06-IN-OO-00318, 07-IN-OO-0226; 06-IN-OO-00319 (Md. Tax Ct., Oct. 24, 2008); and No. 07-IN-00-0317 and No. 07-IN-00-0318 (Md. Tax Ct., Feb. 25, 2010)]; and *W. L. Gore v. Comptroller of Treasury* [No. 07-IN-OO-0084, No. 07-IN-OO-0085, No. 07-IN-OO-0086 (Md. Tax Ct., Nov. 9, 2010)].

In *Department of Revenue v. Gap (Apparel) Inc.* [No. 2004 CW 0263 (La. Ct. App., June 25, 2004)], the Louisiana Court of Appeal held that a California trademark holding company had income tax nexus in Louisiana, despite the lack of any type of physical presence in the state. The trademark holding company licensed its intangibles for use by affiliates which operated 2,600 retail stores nationwide, including about 40 stores in Louisiana. The court concluded that the trademark holding company's intangibles had "acquired a business situs in Louisiana" because the intangibles were an integral part of a business carried on within the state. See also *Bridges v. Geoffrey, Inc.* [No. 2007 CA 1063 (La. Ct. App., Feb.8, 2008)].

In *Bridges vs. Autozone Properties, Inc.* [No. 2004-C-814 (La. Sup. Ct., Mar. 24, 2005)], the Louisiana Supreme Court ruled that, based on the "minimum contacts" nexus standard of the Due Process Clause, the State of Louisiana could tax an out-of-state corporation on the dividends that it received as a shareholder of a real estate investment trust (REIT) that owned rental producing retail stores in Louisiana that were operated by another subsidiary of the taxpayer, because the state provided the "benefits, opportunities and protections that come from doing business in Louisiana."

In *Lanco, Inc. v. Division of Taxation* [No. A-89-05 (N.J. Sup. Ct., Oct. 12, 2006); *cert. denied*, U.S. Sup. Ct., 06-1236, June 18, 2007], the New Jersey Supreme Court ruled that the Delaware trademark holding corporation of the clothing retailer Lane Bryant (Lanco) had income tax nexus with New Jersey, even though the corporation had no physical presence in the state. The court stated that "we do not believe that the Supreme Court intended to create a universal physical-presence requirement for state taxation under the Commerce Clause," and concluded that "the better interpretation of Quill is the one adopted by those states that limit the Supreme Court's holding to sales and use taxes." See also *Praxair Technology, Inc. v. Division of Taxation* [No. A-91/92-08 (N.J. Sup. Ct., Dec. 15, 2009)].

In *Tax Commissioner v. MBNA America Bank, N.A.* [No. 33049 (W.V. Sup. Ct. of App., Nov. 21, 2006); *cert. denied*, U.S. Sup. Ct., 06-1228, June 18, 2007], the West Virginia Supreme Court of Appeals ruled that a Delaware bank that provided credit card services to customers in West Virginia had income tax nexus in West Virginia, even though it had no physical presence in the state. During the tax years in question, the bank regularly issued credit cards and extended unsecured credit to West Virginia customers, and derived significant gross receipts from these activities. The court concluded that the *Quill* physical presence test "applies only to state sales and use taxes and not to state business franchise and corporation net income taxes," and that MBNA had "a significant economic presence sufficient to meet the substantial nexus" test under the Commerce Clause.

In *MBNA America Bank v. Indiana Department of State Revenue* [No. 49T10-0506-TA-53 (Ind. Tax Ct., Oct. 20, 2008)], the Indiana Tax Court concluded that "the Supreme Court has not extended the physical presence requirement beyond the realm of sales and use taxes" and that a national bank's economic presence in Indiana was sufficient to create a substantial nexus.

In *Capital One Bank and Capital One F.S.B. v. Commissioner of Revenue* [No. SJC-10105 (Mass. Sup. Jud. Ct., Jan. 8, 2009); *cert. denied*, U.S. Sup. Ct., No. 08-1169, June 22, 2009], the Massachusetts Supreme Judicial Court held that imposition of the Massachusetts financial institution excise (income) tax "is determined not by *Quill's* physical presence test, but by the 'substantial nexus' test articulated in *Complete Auto.*" As a result, despite the lack of any physical presence in the state, the two out-of-state credit card banks had substantial nexus in Massachusetts, because of their "purposeful, targeted marketing of their credit card business to Massachusetts customers . . . and their receipt of hundreds of millions of dollars in income from millions of transactions involving Massachusetts residents and merchants." See also *Geoffrey, Inc. v. Commissioner of Revenue* [No. SJC-10106, Mass. Sup. Jud. Ct., Jan. 8, 2009; *cert. denied*, U.S. Sup. Ct., No. 08-1207, June 22, 2009)].

In *KFC Corporation v. Iowa Department of Revenue* [No. 09-1032 (Ia. Sup. Ct., Dec. 30, 2010)], the Iowa Supreme Court ruled that the Commerce Clause does not require a physical presence in order to tax the income that a Delaware corporation (KFC) earned from the use of its intangibles in Iowa. The court concluded that the trademarks and other intangibles owned by KFC and licensed for use by independent franchisees doing business in Iowa "would be regarded as having a sufficient connection to Iowa to amount to the functional equivalent of 'physical presence' under *Quill*." The court also concluded that even if the use of the intangibles within the state does not amount to physical presence under *Quill*, the physical presence requirement should not be extended to prevent a state from imposing an income tax on revenue generated from the use of intangibles within the state.

Factor Presence Nexus

Another approach to the economic nexus concept is a factor presence nexus standard, under which income tax nexus exists if in-state sales exceed a specified threshold. In 2002, the Multistate Tax Commission adopted a model statute, Factor Presence Nexus Standard for Business Activity Taxes (Oct. 17, 2002), which provides that a corporation organized outside the state has income tax nexus if its in-state activities exceed both the minimum standards of Public Law 86-272 and one of the following thresholds: $50,000 of property in the state, $50,000 of payroll in the state, $500,000 of sales in the state, or 25 percent of total property, payroll or sales in the state. The notion that $500,000 of in-state sales can, by itself, create income tax nexus is essentially an economic nexus standard.

A number of states have adopted nexus standards similar to the MTC's model law.

California. For tax years beginning on or after January 1, 2011, an out-of-state corporation has income tax nexus in California if it has more than $50,000 of property, $50,000 of payroll, $500,000 of sales, or 25 percent of its total property, payroll or sales in California. [S.B. 15, Feb. 20. 2009]

Colorado. Effective April 30, 2010, an out-of-state corporation has income tax nexus in Colorado if it has more than $50,000 of property, $50,000 of payroll, $500,000 of sales, or 25 percent of its total property, payroll or sales in Colorado. [Colo. Dept. of Rev., Reg. 39-22-301.1, Apr. 10, 2010]

Ohio. For purposes of the Ohio commercial activity tax (a gross receipts tax), an out-of-state corporation has nexus if it has at least $50,000 of property, $50,000 of payroll, $500,000 of taxable gross receipts, or 25 percent of its total property, payroll or gross receipts in Ohio. [Commercial Activity Tax Information Release CT 2005-02 (Ohio Dept. of Taxn., Sept. 2005)] In 2010, the Ohio Department of Taxation determined that L.L. Bean, an out-of-state mail order and Internet vendor, met the statutory bright-line presence test and was subject to the CAT, because it had annual taxable gross receipts of at least $500,000 in Ohio. [*In re L.L. Bean, Inc.*, Ohio Dept. of Taxn., Aug. 10, 2010]

Washington. Effective June 1, 2010, for purposes of imposing the Washington business and occupation tax (a gross receipts tax) on service activities and royalty income, an out-of-state corporation has nexus if it has more than $50,000 of property, $50,000 of payroll, $250,000 of receipts, or at least 25 percent of its total property, payroll, or receipts in Washington. [S.B. 6143, Feb. 20. 2009]

Other Nexus Issues

State-Specific Statutory and Administrative Exemptions. States generally attempt to impose their income taxes to the fullest extent permissible under the U.S. Constitution and Public Law 86-272. In the name of supporting in-state business interests, however, many states provide targeted exemptions for selected activities that would otherwise create nexus. For example, although the ownership of property in a state typically creates nexus, a number of states provide statutory or administrative exemptions for the ownership of raw materials or finished goods at an unrelated in-state printer, or the ownership of equipment or tooling in the state for use by an unrelated in-state manufacturer. For example, starting in 2009, Minnesota provides an exception for ownership of property on the premises of a printer when there is a contract for printing and the printer is not a member of a Minnesota unitary business. [S.F. 832, Apr. 6, 2009]

In addition, a number of states provide exemptions for employees attending in-state trade shows or conventions. For example, an out-of-state corporation does not have nexus in California if its only contact with the state is employees who (1) enter the state to attend conventions and trade shows for a total of no more than 15 days in a given year and (2) earn no more than $100,000 from those activities. [Cal. Rev. & Tax. Code § 6203(e)]

Ownership of Partnership Interest. States generally take the position that an ownership interest in a partnership doing business in the state is sufficient to create constitutional nexus for an out-of-state corporation. In asserting nexus, the states rely primarily on the aggregate theory of partnership, which holds that a partnership is the aggregation of its owners rather than an entity that is separate from its owners (unlike a corporation). Under this theory, the partners are viewed as direct owners of the partnership's assets. Based on the aggregate theory, most states take the position that the mere ownership of a partnership interest is sufficient to create constitutional nexus for an out-of-state corporation, regardless of whether the corporation is a general or limited partner.

Some states apply a different rule for limited partners. The basis for this distinction is that a limited partnership interest is a passive investment akin to shares of corporate stock. (See the section entitled Partnerships in Part 6 for more details.)

Ownership of Leased Property. In general, the ownership of business property in a state is sufficient to create nexus. In the case of leased property, the lessee is subject to the state's jurisdiction because the property is being used in the state and sufficient nexus may also be established for the lessor because of the in-state presence of owned business property. In addition to the presence of property, factors that help to support nexus include the negotiation or execution of the lease agreement in the state or the receipt of the rental payments in the state.

In the case of leased property that is immobile (e.g., machinery and equipment affixed within a manufacturing facility), the creation of nexus generally is easier to identify because, in negotiating the agreement or in addressing the shipment or delivery of the property to the lessee, the lessor is informed of the state in which the property is expected to be located during the rental period. In contrast, when mobile property (e.g., airplanes and other transportation vehicles) is at issue, the lessor typically has no control over where the property will be used. Moreover, unless otherwise specified in the lease agreement, the lessee may be under no contractual obligation to provide the lessor with any information about where the property has been used at any time during the lease.

The lessor typically is considered to have established nexus with each state where the leased immobile property is located. For leased mobile property, many states provide that an isolated landing or trip through the state will not create nexus. The presence of leased property in the state on a regular or systematic basis, however, is typically sufficient nexus with the state to subject the lessor to the state's corporate income tax. Therefore, in negotiating lease agreements, the lessor should annually require the lessee to supply the appropriate information about the states in which the property is used during the tax period. Without that information, the lessor cannot determine the states with which nexus has been established or compute its apportionment factors in the various states.

In *TTX Co. v. Idaho State Tax Commission* [128 Idaho 483 (1996)], the Idaho Supreme Court held that an out-of-state corporation that leased railcars to railroads operating within Idaho did not have nexus in Idaho. Likewise, in *Airoldi Bros., Inc. v. Illinois Department of Revenue* [Admin. Hearing Decision No. 98-IT-0330 (Ill. Dep't of Revenue Sept. 29, 2000)], the Illinois Department of Revenue ruled that a Wisconsin truck leasing company whose customers used its trucks in Illinois did not have income tax nexus in Illinois. In both *Comdisco, Inc. v. Indiana Department of Revenue* [No. 49T10-9903-TA-19, Ind. Tax Ct. Dec. 8, 2002)]and *Enterprise Leasing Company of Chicago v. Indiana Department of Revenue* [No. 49T10-9807-TA-74, Ind. Tax Ct. Dec. 8, 2002)], the Indiana Tax Court ruled that two out-of-state leasing companies were not subject to Indiana tax on income from equipment and autos leased to Indiana customers, because their ownership of the leased property was the companies' only contact with the state.

The out-of-state leasing companies did not exercise control over the leased equipment, and were not active participants in the leasing activities within the state.

On the other hand, in *Truck Renting & Leasing Association, Inc. v. Commissioner of Revenue* [No. SJC-08308 (Mass. Apr. 17, 2001)], the Massachusetts Supreme Judicial Court ruled that the imposition of the Massachusetts corporate income tax on an out-of-state corporation whose leased trucks operated in Massachusetts violated neither the Due Process Clause nor the Commerce Clause of the U.S. Constitution, even though the lessor had no physical presence in Massachusetts beyond the presence of the leased trucks. By providing registration and licensing services that allowed the lessees to operate the trucks in Massachusetts, the out-of-state lessee was purposefully availing itself of the privilege of doing business in the state, as required by the Due Process Clause. In addition, the physical presence of the taxpayer's trucks within the state on a regular and systematic basis created a substantial nexus, as required by the Commerce Clause.

In *Alabama Department of Revenue vs. Union Tank Car Co.* [No. 2050652 (Ala. Ct. of Civ. App., April 13, 2007)], the taxpayer (Union Tank) was a Delaware corporation that was headquartered in Illinois. Union Tank manufactured specialty railroad cars in Illinois and Texas and leased them to customers nationwide. Some of Union Tank's leased railcars were used to transport materials through Alabama and to destinations within Alabama. None of the railcars were used strictly within Alabama. The Department contended that Union Tank was subject to Alabama income tax, because the operative statute imposes an income tax on "[e]very corporation doing business in Alabama or deriving income from sources within Alabama, including income from property located in Alabama." The Alabama Court of Civil Appeals concluded, however, that Union Tank "derived income from the lease transactions in Illinois, not from sources in Alabama." Union Tank executed its lease contracts in Illinois, the railcars were picked up in Illinois or Texas, and the lessees made lease payments to Union Tank in Illinois. The amount of the lease payments were fixed, and UTCC had no control over where the railcars were used after they had been leased.

Ownership of Natural Gas or Electricity Flowing Through State. Many utility companies produce and distribute electricity and natural gas on a regional or nationwide basis. These companies need to determine whether the products they market, produce, or distribute qualify as tangible personal property, the solicitation of which will be protected under Public Law 86-272, or whether such products are sales of intangible assets or services, which are not afforded the protections of Public Law 86-272.

The states generally have not taken a uniform position on whether electricity and natural gas are properly classified as tangible personal property, services, or intangible property for corporate income or franchise tax purposes. The view that electricity is tangible personal property is explained by the fact that it can be touched, seen, and measured; however, the sale of electricity may also be viewed as the sale of intangible property or as the sale of a service. The view that providing electricity is the sale of a service arises from the fact that a transmission company is allowing its lines to be used to transmit electricity or that, although a generating company is creating a product, what the consumer is paying for is the distribution of the product to the consumer in a usable form. The latter view is comparable to the argument that an Internet service provider is providing information access instead of selling electrical impulses.

In *Appeal of PacifiCorp* [2002-SBE-005 (Cal. St. Bd. of Equalization Sept. 12, 2002)], the California State Board of Equalization ruled that electricity is an intangible asset. In addition, for purposes of apportioning the income of the Oregon utility company, sales of the generation and transmission of electricity are properly classified as sales of services that consisted of the taxpayer setting and keeping in motion electrically charged particles. Therefore, under the income-producing activity rule for sourcing sales of services, the sales were excluded from the numerator of the taxpayer's California sales factor because the generation and transmission services were performed mainly outside of California.

Qualification to Do Business. A number of states have statutes or regulations that require a corporation to file an income or franchise tax return and pay tax if the corporation has the authority to do business in the state. For example, under Texas Tax Code Annotated Section 171.001(a)(1), the state's corporate franchise tax applies to "each corporation that does business in this state or that is chartered or authorized to do business in this state." See also, e.g., Cal. Code Regs. tit. 18, § 23038(a); Mass. Regs. Code tit. 830, § 63.39.1.

The constitutionality of the Texas statute was tested in *Bandag Licensing Corp. v. Rylander*. [No. 03-99-00427-CV (Tex. App. May 11, 2000)] Bandag was incorporated in Iowa, did not own or use any property in Texas, and did not have any employees or other agents present in Texas. Nevertheless, the Texas Comptroller of Public Accounts imposed the Texas corporate franchise tax on Bandag solely on the basis that Bandag had obtained a certificate of authority to do business in Texas. The Texas appeals court saw no principled distinction between sales and income taxes when the underlying issue was whether the Commerce Clause permits a state to impose a tax obligation on an out-of-state corporation. The court went on to conclude that, consistent with the ruling in *Quill*, a state cannot constitutionally impose its corporate franchise tax on an out-of-state corporation that lacks a physical presence in the state. In response to the *Bandag* decision, the Comptroller issued a letter ruling indicating that an out-of-state corporation's possession of a certificate of authority to do business in Texas is not, by itself, sufficient to create nexus. [Comptroller's Letter No. 200106294L (Tex. Comptroller of Public Accounts, June 15, 2001)]

A related issue is whether the authority to do business in a state constitutes a separate business activity that is not protected by Public Law 86-272. For example, in *Commissioner of Revenue v. Kelly-Springfield Tire Co.* [419 Mass. 262 (1994)], the taxpayer had employees who were physically present in Massachusetts on a continuous basis. The parties agreed, however, that the activities of the in-state employees were protected by Public Law 86-272. At issue was whether the taxpayer's authority to do business in Massachusetts constituted a separate business activity that was sufficient to establish income tax nexus. The Massachusetts Supreme Judicial Court ruled that the authority to do business does not deny a corporation the protections afforded by Public Law 86-272. See also *Kelly-Springfield Tire Co. v. Bajorski* [228 Conn. 137 (1993)].

In *LSDHC Corp. v. Tracy* [No. 98-J-896 (Ohio Bd. of Tax App. Nov. 19, 2001)], the Ohio Board of Tax Appeals ruled that registration to do business was not, by itself, sufficient to create nexus for purposes of Ohio's corporate franchise tax on net income.

On the other hand, in *Buehner Block Company, Inc. v. Wyoming Department of Revenue* [No. 05-175 (Wyo. Sup. Ct., July 27, 2006)], the Wyoming Supreme Court ruled that, despite the lack of a physical presence in the state, the taxpayer had "substantial nexus" in the state because of its "historical connection with the Wyoming taxing system, including its voluntary possession and use of a Wyoming vendor's license, in combination with common-carrier delivery of its goods into this state."

Gross Receipts Taxes. Public Law 86-272 applies only to a "net income tax." It does not protect taxpayers against the imposition of a gross receipts tax.

Ohio imposes a gross receipts tax called the "commercial activity tax" (CAT). A person is subject to Ohio's CAT if the person: (1) owns or uses a part or all of its capital or property in this state; (2) holds a certificate of compliance with the laws of Ohio authorizing the person to do business in this state; (3) has bright-line presence in Ohio; or (4) has nexus with Ohio to an extent that the person can be required to remit the CAT under the U.S. Constitution. The Department of Taxation takes the position that the *Quill* physical presence test does not apply to the CAT. Even if a person has nexus under the U.S. Constitution, the Department of Taxation will only enforce nexus against persons who possess bright-line presence, which is a method of determining whether nexus exists that relies entirely upon quantitative criteria. A person has "bright-line presence" in Ohio if the person is domiciled in Ohio or during the calendar year, the person has $50,000 of property in Ohio, $50,000 of payroll in Ohio, $500,000 of taxable gross receipts in Ohio, or 25 percent of the person's total property, total payroll or total gross receipts in Ohio. [Commercial Activity Tax Information Release CT 2005-02 (Ohio Dept. of Taxn., Sept. 2005)] In 2010, the Ohio Department of Taxation determined that L.L. Bean, an out-of-state mail order and Internet vendor, met the statutory bright-line presence test and was subject to the CAT, because it had annual taxable gross receipts of at least $500,000 in Ohio. [*In re L.L. Bean, Inc.*, Ohio Dept. of Taxn., Aug. 10, 2010]

The State of Washington imposes a gross receipts tax called the "business and occupation" (B&O) tax. The B&O tax is imposed on the act or privilege of engaging in business activities in Washington, and is measured by the "value of products, gross proceeds of sales, or gross income of the business." [Wash.

Rev. Code § 82.04.220] Therefore, Public Law 86-272 does not prohibit the imposition of the B&O tax on sales solicited by in-state employees of an out-of-state manufacturer. Effective June 1, 2010, for purposes of imposing the Washington business and occupation tax (a gross receipts tax) on service activities and royalty income, an out-of-state corporation has nexus if it has more than $50,000 of property, $50,000 of payroll, $250,000 of receipts, or at least 25 percent of its total property, payroll, or receipts in Washington. [S.B. 6143, Feb. 20. 2009]

From 2008 through 2011, Michigan subjected corporations to the Michigan Business Tax (MBT), which includes both a 4.95 percent business income tax and a 0.80 percent modified gross receipts tax. Taxpayers pay the sum of the two taxes. The 'modified gross receipts tax' base equals a taxpayer's gross receipts reduced by purchases of inventory, depreciable assets, materials, and supplies. A taxpayer is subject to the MBT if it "has a physical presence in this state for a period of more than one day during the tax year or if the taxpayer actively solicits sales in this state and has gross receipts of $350,000 or more sourced to this state." [Mich. Comp. Laws § 208.1200(1)] According to Revenue Administrative Bulletin 2008-64 [Mich. Dept. of Treas., Oct. 21, 2008], physical presence for a portion of a day establishes physical presence for the entire day. Examples of active solicitation include sending mail order catalogs; sending credit applications; maintaining an Internet site offering online shopping, services, or subscriptions; and soliciting through media advertising, including Internet advertisements. Public Law 86-272 protects taxpayers from the imposition of the business income tax portion of the MBT, but not the modified gross receipts tax portion. Effective January 1, 2012, Michigan replaced its business income and modified gross receipt taxes with a 6 percent corporate income tax. [H.B. 4361 and 4362, May 25, 2011]

Texas imposes a tax on a business entity's "margin," which equals the lesser of total revenue minus cost of goods sold, total revenue minus compensation, or 70 percent of total revenue. Texas has taken the position that the margin tax does not qualify as a net income tax for purposes of applying Public Law 86-272. [34 Texas Admin. Code § 3.586(e)]

Telecommuters. In GIL-2009-010 [Colo. Dept. of Rev., Feb. 25, 2009], the Colorado Department of Revenue ruled that an out-of-state corporation will generally have nexus for corporate income tax purposes if it hires an employee who is a Colorado resident and works out of his home office that is located in Colorado. Most of the corporation's employees were based overseas providing analytical support to the U.S. military. The company had three administrative support employees who worked in direct support of the headquarters and were involved in recruitment, accounting, and business development activities for the company and not directly supporting a paying customer. The company was interested in hiring another administrative support employee to support the company's headquarters and he would like to perform his duties out of a home he has in Colorado. He would not be working in support of a customer or directly generating revenue for the company but would be strictly supporting the company in an overhead capacity. Nevertheless, the Department concluded that a company which has an employee residing in Colorado will generally have nexus for income tax purposes, and that the company's service income would be apportioned to Colorado in proportion to the cost of the one Colorado employee to the total cost of all its employees.

Electronic Commerce. As goods that have historically been sold by "brick-and-mortar" retailers (books, compact discs, and clothing) are increasingly sold over the Internet, states are likely to experience an erosion of their sales and use tax base. The states' predicament is largely due to the physical presence test for nexus, as mandated by the Supreme Court in *Quill.* Because electronic commerce allows companies to exploit a commercial market without establishing a physical presence in a state, the physical presence test significantly inhibits a state's ability to impose a tax obligation on an out-of-state Internet vendor.

On the other hand, the business community has legitimate concerns about the compliance burden of collecting sales and use taxes on a nationwide basis. There are currently thousands of sales tax jurisdictions (state, county, and city), which have different tax rates, different definitions of the tax base, and different administrative procedures. In recognition of the potential negative effect that state and local taxation could have on the growth of electronic commerce, in October 1998 Congress enacted the Internet Tax Freedom Act, which imposed a three-year moratorium on any "new" state or local taxes on Internet access. Subsequent legislation in 2001, 2004 and 2007 has extended the moratorium through November 1, 2014 (H.R. 3678, Oct. 31, 2007).

From the states' perspective, one potential solution is federal legislation that allows the states to impose tax obligations on out-of-state companies that have an economic presence, but no physical presence, within a state. Another potential solution is more uniform and simplified state and local tax systems. In fact, the states have initiated a major effort to simplify and modernize sales and use tax collection and administration through the Streamlined Sales Tax Project [see www.streamlinedsalestax.org]. The project was initiated in 2000, and includes representatives from state and local governments, as well as the private sector. The goals of the project are to create common definitions for key items in the sales tax base, restrict the number of tax rates that a state may impose, provide for state-level administration of local sales taxes, create uniform sourcing rules for interstate sales, simplify the administration of exempt transactions, develop uniform audit procedures, and provide partial state funding of the system for collecting tax. About 20 states conform their sales and use tax laws to the provisions of the agreement.

State-by-State Summary

The following chart summarizes the positions of the states with respect to a wide-range of potentially nexus-creating activities. For ease of presentation, the chart has been divided into 11 parts, as follows:

- Part 1: Licensing Intangibles
- Part 2: Ownership of Real or Tangible Property
- Part 3: Leasing
- Part 4: Sales Activities of Employees
- Part 5: Activities Other than Sales
- Part 6: Activities of Third Parties
- Part 7: *De Minimis* Physical Presence
- Part 8: Ownership Interest in Pass-Through Entity
- Part 9: Holding Title to Electricity or Natural Gas
- Part 10: Qualification to Do Business/Filing Requirements
- Part 11: Other

Activities Creating Franchise or Income Tax Nexus (Part 1)

Licensing Intangibles

Legend:

X	These activities create franchise or income tax nexus
NA	Not applicable
NR	Not reported

	Licensing Trademark/Trade Name	*Licensing Software*	*Licensing Other Intangible (e.g., Patents)*	*Licensing of Franchises*
Alabama	Alabama interprets nexus on case-by-case basis and as broadly as allowed under the Due Process and Commerce Clauses of the United States Constitution			
Alaska	X	X	X	X
Arizona	X	X	X	X
Arkansas	X	X	X	X
California	X	X	X	X
Colorado	X	X, if lease not sale		X
Connecticut				X
Delaware			X	
District of Columbia	X	X	X	X
Florida	X	X	X	X
Georgia	Georgia determines and interprets nexus on a case by case basis and as broadly as allowed, but within the Due Process and Commerce Clause of the United States Constitution.			Georgia determines and interprets nexus on a case-by-case basis and as broadly as allowed but within the Due Process and Commerce Clauses of the United States Constitution.
Hawaii	X	X	X	X
Idaho	X, unless *de minimis*	X, unless *de minimis*	X, unless *de minimis*	Depends on facts
Illinois	X	X	X	X

Activities Creating Franchise or Income Tax Nexus (Part 1)

Licensing Intangibles

Legend:

X	These activities create franchise or income tax nexus
NA	Not applicable
NR	Not reported

	Licensing Trademark/Trade Name	*Licensing Software*	*Licensing Other Intangible (e.g., Patents)*	*Licensing of Franchises*
	Nexus determinations can be made only in the context of an audit wherein the auditor would have full access to all pertinent information. Illinois determines "doing business" utilizing the prevailing principles of jurisprudence under the Commerce and Due Process Clauses of the United States Constitution as applied to the facts in each case. For further information see 86 Ill. Admin. Code § 100.9720.			
Indiana				
Iowa	X	X	X	X
Kansas	X	X	X	X
Kentucky	X	X	X	X
Louisiana	X			X
Maine	X	X	X	X
Maryland	X	X		X
Massachusetts	X		Depends on facts	Depends on facts, see DD 96-2.
Michigan (Michigan Business Tax—MBT)				X
Note. The CIT takes effect 01/01/12, and replaces the Michigan Business Tax (MBT) for most taxpayers. However, businesses that have been approved to receive, have received, or have been assigned certain certified credits may elect to file a return and pay the tax imposed by the MBT in lieu of the CIT until the certified credits are exhausted or extinguished.				
Minnesota	X	X	X	X
Mississippi	X	X	X	X
Missouri	X	X	X	X

Activities Creating Franchise or Income Tax Nexus (Part 1)

Licensing Intangibles

Legend:

X	These activities create franchise or income tax nexus
NA	Not applicable
NR	Not reported

	Licensing Trademark/Trade Name	*Licensing Software*	*Licensing Other Intangible (e.g., Patents)*	*Licensing of Franchises*
Montana	X	X	X	X
Nebraska	X	X	X	X
Nevada	Nevada does not impose a corporate income tax			
New Hampshire			X	X
New Jersey	X	X	X	X
New Mexico	X	X	X	X
New York	Responses apply only to Article 9-A franchise tax on business corporations			
North Carolina	X	X	X	X
North Dakota	X	X	X	X
Ohio	Ohio does not impose a corporate income tax			
Note. Effective 1/1/2010, the Ohio Franchise Tax was fully phased out and business will be taxed on gross receipts through the Commercial Activity Tax. Details about that tax can be found at: http//tax.ohio.gov/divisions/commercial_activities/index.stm				
Oklahoma	X, currently litigating	X	X	
Oregon	X		X	X
Pennsylvania				X
Rhode Island	X	X	X	X
South Carolina	X	X	X	X
South Dakota	South Dakota does not impose a corporate income tax			

Activities Creating Franchise or Income Tax Nexus (Part 1)

Licensing Intangibles

Legend:

X	These activities create franchise or income tax nexus
NA	Not applicable
NR	Not reported

	Licensing Trademark/Trade Name	*Licensing Software*	*Licensing Other Intangible (e.g., Patents)*	*Licensing of Franchises*
Tennessee				
Texas				X
Utah	X	X	X	X
Vermont	X	X	X	X
Virginia	X	X	X	X
Washington	Washington does not impose a corporate income tax			
West Virginia		X	X	X
Wisconsin	X	X	X	X
Wyoming	Wyoming does not impose a corporate income tax			

Activities Creating Franchise or Income Tax Nexus (Part 2)

Ownership of Real or Tangible Property (Section 1)

Legend:

X	These activities create franchise or income tax nexus
NA	Not applicable
NR	Not reported

	Owning Real Estate	*Owning Stock or Goods in Public Warehouse*	*Owning Stock or Goods on Consignment*	*Owning Display Racks*	*Operating Mobile Stores*
Alabama	Alabama interprets nexus on case-by-case basis and as broadly as allowed under the Due Process and Commerce Clauses of the United States Constitution				
Alaska	X	X	X	X	X
Arizona	X	X	X	X	X
Arkansas	X	X	X	X	X
California	X	X	X	X, See P.L. 86-272	X
Colorado	X, except in cases of foreclosure see Colo. Rev. Stat. § 39-22-303(7)	X	X	X	X
Connecticut	X	X	X		X
Delaware	X	X	X	X	X
District of Columbia	X	X	X	X	X
Florida	X	X	X	X	X
Georgia	X	X	X	X	X
Hawaii	X	X	X	X	X
Idaho	X	X	X	X	X
Illinois	X	X	X		X
	Nexus determinations can be made only in the context of an audit wherein the auditor would have full access to all pertinent information. Illinois determines "doing business" utilizing the prevailing principles of jurisprudence under the Commerce and Due Process Clauses of the United States Constitution as applied to the facts in each case. For further information see 86 Ill. Admin. Code § 100.9720.				

Activities Creating Franchise or Income Tax Nexus (Part 2)

Ownership of Real or Tangible Property (Section 1)

Legend:

X	These activities create franchise or income tax nexus
NA	Not applicable
NR	Not reported

	Owning Real Estate	*Owning Stock or Goods in Public Warehouse*	*Owning Stock or Goods on Consignment*	*Owning Display Racks*	*Operating Mobile Stores*
Indiana	X	X	X	X	X
Iowa	X	X, effective 1/1/06, this would not create nexus if retail sales are not made from the distribution facility for more than 12 days a year and no more than 10% of the dollar amount of goods from the distribution facility are shipped to Iowa customers.	X		X
Kansas	X	X	X	X	X
Kentucky	X	X	X		X
Louisiana	X	X	X		
Maine	X	X	X		X
Maryland	X	X	X	X	X
Massachusetts	X		X		X
Michigan (Business Tax)	X	X	X	X	X
Note. The CIT takes effect 01/01/12, and replaces the Michigan Business Tax (MBT) for most taxpayers. However, businesses that have been approved to receive, have received, or have been assigned certain certified credits may elect to file a return and pay the tax imposed by the MBT in lieu of the CIT until the certified credits are exhausted or extinguished.					
Minnesota	X		X		X

Activities Creating Franchise or Income Tax Nexus (Part 2)

Ownership of Real or Tangible Property (Section 1)

Legend:

X	These activities create franchise or income tax nexus
NA	Not applicable
NR	Not reported

	Owning Real Estate	*Owning Stock or Goods in Public Warehouse*	*Owning Stock or Goods on Consignment*	*Owning Display Racks*	*Operating Mobile Stores*
Mississippi	X	X	X		X
Missouri	X	X	X	X	X
Montana	X	X	X		X
Nebraska	X	X	X	X	X
Nevada	Nevada does not impose a corporate income tax				
New Hampshire	X	X	X	X	X
New Jersey	X	X	X	X	X
New Mexico	X	X	X	X	X
New York	X	X, unless fulfillment house	X		X
	Responses apply to New York Franchise Tax				
North Carolina	X	X	X	X	X
North Dakota	X	X	X		X
Ohio	Ohio does not impose a corporate income tax				
Note. Effective 1/1/2010, the Ohio Franchise Tax was fully phased out and business will be taxed on gross receipts through the Commercial Activity Tax. Details about that tax can be found at: http//tax.ohio.gov/divisions/commercial_activities/index.stm					
Oklahoma	X	X	X	X	X
Oregon	X	X	X		X
Pennsylvania	X	X	X	X, no if there is no change	X

Activities Creating Franchise or Income Tax Nexus (Part 2)
Ownership of Real or Tangible Property (Section 1)

Legend:

X	These activities create franchise or income tax nexus
NA	Not applicable
NR	Not reported

	Owning Real Estate	*Owning Stock or Goods in Public Warehouse*	*Owning Stock or Goods on Consignment*	*Owning Display Racks*	*Operating Mobile Stores*
Rhode Island	X	X	X	X	X
South Carolina	X	X	X	X	X
South Dakota	South Dakota does not impose a corporate income tax				
Tennessee	X	X	X		X
Texas	X	X	X	X	X
Utah	X	X	X	X	X
Vermont	X	X	X	X	X
Virginia	X		X		X
Washington	Washington does not impose a corporate income tax				
West Virginia	X			X	X
Wisconsin	X	X	X		X
Wyoming	Wyoming does not impose a corporate income tax				

Activities Creating Franchise or Income Tax Nexus (Part 2)

Ownership of Real or Tangible Property (Section 2)

Legend:

X	These activities create franchise or income tax nexus
NA	Not applicable
NR	Not reported

"Occasional" 1 to 3 times per year

	Occasional In-State Delivery via Company-Owned Truck	*Regular In-State Delivery via Company-Owned Truck*	*Raw Materials or Finished Goods at In-State Printer and Occasional Quality Control Visits by Employees*	*Tooling, Molds, Dies, etc., at In-State Manufacturer*	*Temporary Presence of Inventory for Sole Purpose of Processing by Unrelated Third Party*
Alabama	Alabama interprets nexus on case-by-case basis and as broadly as allowed under the Due Process and Commerce Clauses of the United States Constitution				
Alaska	X	X	X	X	X
Arizona			X	X	X
Arkansas	X	X		X	X
California	X, See P.L. 86-272 and FTB Form 1050	X, See P.L. 86-272 and FTB Form 1050	X	X	X
Colorado	X	X		X	X
Connecticut	No written guidance	X		X	No written guidance
Delaware		X	X	X	X
District of Columbia	X	X	X	X	X
Florida	X	X	X	X	X
Georgia	X	X		X	X
Hawaii	X	X	X	X	X
Idaho	X, unless *de minimis*	X, unless protected under P.L. 86-272	X	X	X
Illinois	X	X		X	

Activities Creating Franchise or Income Tax Nexus (Part 2)

Ownership of Real or Tangible Property (Section 2)

Legend:

X	These activities create franchise or income tax nexus
NA	Not applicable
NR	Not reported

"Occasional" 1 to 3 times per year

	Occasional In-State Delivery via Company-Owned Truck	*Regular In-State Delivery via Company-Owned Truck*	*Raw Materials or Finished Goods at In-State Printer and Occasional Quality Control Visits by Employees*	*Tooling, Molds, Dies, etc., at In-State Manufacturer*	*Temporary Presence of Inventory for Sole Purpose of Processing by Unrelated Third Party*
	Nexus determinations can be made only in the context of an audit wherein the auditor would have full access to all pertinent information. Illinois determines "doing business" utilizing the prevailing principles of jurisprudence under the Commerce and Due Process Clauses of the United States Constitution as applied to the facts in each case. For further information see 86 Ill. Admin. Code § 100.9720.				
Indiana		X		X	X
Iowa			X	X	X
Kansas	X	X	X	X	X
Kentucky	X	X		X	X
Louisiana	X	X	X	X	X
Maine			X	X	X
Maryland	If nontrivial	X	Maryland applies nexus law to full extent permitted.	Maryland applies nexus law to full extent permitted.	Maryland applies nexus law to full extent permitted.
Massachusetts	Depends on facts	Depends on facts			Depends on facts
Michigan (Business Tax)	X	X	X	X	X
Note. The CIT takes effect 01/01/12, and replaces the Michigan Business Tax (MBT) for most taxpayers. However, businesses that have been approved to receive, have received, or have been assigned certain certified credits may elect to file a return and pay the tax imposed by the MBT in lieu of the CIT until the certified credits are exhausted or extinguished.					
Minnesota				X	

Activities Creating Franchise or Income Tax Nexus (Part 2)

Ownership of Real or Tangible Property (Section 2)

Legend:

X	These activities create franchise or income tax nexus
NA	Not applicable
NR	Not reported

"Occasional" 1 to 3 times per year

	Occasional In-State Delivery via Company-Owned Truck	*Regular In-State Delivery via Company-Owned Truck*	*Raw Materials or Finished Goods at In-State Printer and Occasional Quality Control Visits by Employees*	*Tooling, Molds, Dies, etc., at In-State Manufacturer*	*Temporary Presence of Inventory for Sole Purpose of Processing by Unrelated Third Party*
Mississippi			X	X	X
Missouri	X	X	X	X	X
Montana			X	X	X
Nebraska			No position	No position	No position
Nevada	Nevada does not impose a corporate income tax				
New Hampshire	X	X	X	X	X
New Jersey	X	X	X	X	X
New Mexico	X	X	X	X	X
New York		X			
	Responses apply to New York Franchise Tax				
North Carolina			X	X	X
North Dakota			X	X	X
Ohio	Ohio does not impose a corporate income tax				
Note. Effective 1/1/2010, the Ohio Franchise Tax was fully phased out and business will be taxed on gross receipts through the Commercial Activity Tax. Details about that tax can be found at: http//tax.ohio.gov/divisions/commercial_activities/index.stm					
Oklahoma		X		X	
Oregon			X	X	X

Activities Creating Franchise or Income Tax Nexus (Part 2)

Ownership of Real or Tangible Property (Section 2)

Legend:

X	These activities create franchise or income tax nexus
NA	Not applicable
NR	Not reported

"Occasional" 1 to 3 times per year

	Occasional In-State Delivery via Company-Owned Truck	*Regular In-State Delivery via Company-Owned Truck*	*Raw Materials or Finished Goods at In-State Printer and Occasional Quality Control Visits by Employees*	*Tooling, Molds, Dies, etc., at In-State Manufacturer*	*Temporary Presence of Inventory for Sole Purpose of Processing by Unrelated Third Party*
Pennsylvania					
Rhode Island			X	X	
South Carolina				X	X
South Dakota	South Dakota does not impose a corporate income tax				
Tennessee					
Texas	X	X	X	X	X
Utah				X	X
Vermont				X	
Virginia	X, unless ancillary to P.L. 86-272 sales	X	See Va. Code § 58.1-401	X	
Washington	Washington does not impose a corporate income tax				
West Virginia	X	X			
Wisconsin		X, depending on facts	X, depending on facts		
Wyoming	Wyoming does not impose a corporate income tax				

Activities Creating Franchise or Income Tax Nexus (Part 3)

Leasing

Legend:

X	These activities create franchise or income tax nexus
NA	Not applicable
NR	Not reported
"Occasionally" 1 to 3 days per year	

	Leasing of Tangible Personal Property		
	Regularly Used by Lessee	*Occasionally Used by Lessee*	*Leasing of Mobile Assets (e.g., Trucks) Used Occasionally by Lessee*
Alabama	Alabama interprets nexus on case-by-case basis and as broadly as allowed under the Due Process and Commerce Clauses of the United States Constitution		
Alaska	X	X	X
Arizona	X	X	X
Arkansas	X	X	X
California	X	X	X, see *Appeal of John H. Grace Co.*, Oct. 28, 1980
Colorado	X		X
Connecticut	X	No written guidance	No written guidance
Delaware	X	X	
District of Columbia	X	X	X
Florida	X	X	X
Georgia	X		
Hawaii	X	X	X
Idaho	X	X	X
Illinois	X	X	X

Activities Creating Franchise or Income Tax Nexus (Part 3)

Leasing

Legend:

X	These activities create franchise or income tax nexus
NA	Not applicable
NR	Not reported

"Occasionally" 1 to 3 days per year

	Leasing of Tangible Personal Property		
	Regularly Used by Lessee	*Occasionally Used by Lessee*	*Leasing of Mobile Assets (e.g., Trucks) Used Occasionally by Lessee*
	Nexus determinations can be made only in the context of an audit wherein the auditor would have full access to all pertinent information. Illinois determines "doing business" utilizing the prevailing principles of jurisprudence under the Commerce and Due Process Clauses of the United States Constitution as applied to the facts in each case. For further information see 86 Ill. Admin. Code § 100.9720.		
Indiana	X	X	X
Iowa	X	X	X
Kansas	X	X	X
Kentucky	X	X	X
Louisiana	X	X	X
Maine	X	X	X
Maryland	X	X	X
Massachusetts	Depends on facts	Depends on facts	
Michigan (Business Tax)	X	X	X
Note. The CIT takes effect 01/01/12, and replaces the Michigan Business Tax (MBT) for most taxpayers. However, businesses that have been approved to receive, have received, or have been assigned certain certified credits may elect to file a return and pay the tax imposed by the MBT in lieu of the CIT until the certified credits are exhausted or extinguished.			
Minnesota	X	X	X
Mississippi	X		

Activities Creating Franchise or Income Tax Nexus (Part 3)

Leasing

Legend:

X	These activities create franchise or income tax nexus
NA	Not applicable
NR	Not reported

"Occasionally" 1 to 3 days per year

	Leasing of Tangible Personal Property		
	Regularly Used by Lessee	*Occasionally Used by Lessee*	*Leasing of Mobile Assets (e.g., Trucks) Used Occasionally by Lessee*
Missouri	X	X	X
Montana	X	X	X
Nebraska	X		
Nevada	Nevada does not impose a corporate income tax		
New Hampshire	X	X	X
New Jersey	X	X	X
New Mexico	X	X	X
New York	X		
	Responses apply to New York Franchise Tax		
North Carolina	X	X	X
North Dakota	X	X	X
Ohio	Ohio does not impose a corporate income tax		
Note. Effective 1/1/2010, the Ohio Franchise Tax was fully phased out and business will be taxed on gross receipts through the Commercial Activity Tax. Details about that tax can be found at: http//tax.ohio.gov/divisions/commercial_activities/index.stm			
Oklahoma	X		
Oregon	X	X	X
Pennsylvania	X	X	X

Activities Creating Franchise or Income Tax Nexus (Part 3)

Leasing

Legend:

X	These activities create franchise or income tax nexus
NA	Not applicable
NR	Not reported

"Occasionally" 1 to 3 days per year

	Leasing of Tangible Personal Property		
	Regularly Used by Lessee	*Occasionally Used by Lessee*	*Leasing of Mobile Assets (e.g., Trucks) Used Occasionally by Lessee*
Rhode Island	X		X
South Carolina	X	X	X
South Dakota	South Dakota does not impose a corporate income tax		
Tennessee	X	X	X
Texas	X	X	X
Utah	X		
Vermont	X		
Virginia	X	X	X
Washington	Washington does not impose a corporate income tax		
West Virginia	X		
Wisconsin	X	Depends on facts	Depends on facts
Wyoming	Wyoming does not impose a corporate income tax		

Activities Creating Franchise or Income Tax Nexus (Part 4)

Sales Activities of Employees

Legend:

X	These activities create franchise or income tax nexus
NA	Not applicable
NR	Not reported

	Soliciting Sales of: *Tangible Personal Property*	*Real Estate*	*Intangibles (e.g., Securities)*	*Services*	*Company Car for Salesperson*	*Setup of Promotional Items by Salesperson*	*Inventory Inspection by Salesperson*	*Attendance at Trade Shows 14 Days or Less per Year (Products Are Tangible Personal Property)*	*Attendance at Trade Shows 14 Days or Less per Year (Products Are Not Tangible Personal Property)*
Alabama	Alabama interprets nexus on case-by-case basis and as broadly as allowed under the Due Process and Commerce Clauses of the United States Constitution								
Alaska		X		X				X	X
Arizona	Depends, See Corp Tax Ruling CTR 99-5	X	X	Depends		Depends	X	See Corp Tax Ruling CTR 99-5	See Corp Tax Ruling CTR 99-5
Arkansas		X	X	X			X		
California	X, but see P.L. 86-272 and FTB Form 1050	X	X	X, depends on facts and circumstances	X, See P.L. 86-272 and FTB Form 1050	X, See P.L. 86-272, FTB Form 1050 and R&TC § 23104.	X	X, see R&TC § 23104	X, see R&TC § 23104
Colorado		X, see ownership	X	X					
Connecticut	X, unless protected by P.L. 86-272	X	X	X	X				
Delaware		X	X		X				

Activities Creating Franchise or Income Tax Nexus (Part 4)
Sales Activities of Employees

Legend:
X These activities create franchise or income tax nexus
NA Not applicable
NR Not reported

	Soliciting Sales of: Tangible Personal Property	Real Estate	Intangibles (e.g., Securities)	Services	Company Car for Salesperson	Setup of Promotional Items by Salesperson	Inventory Inspection by Salesperson	Attendance at Trade Shows 14 Days or Less per Year (Products Are Tangible Personal Property)	Attendance at Trade Shows 14 Days or Less per Year (Products Are Not Tangible Personal Property)
District of Columbia	X	X	X	X	X	X	X	X	X
Florida		X	X	X			X	X	X
Georgia		X	X	X		X	X	If activities do not exceed P.L. 86-272	X
Hawaii	X, with authority to accept orders	X	X, with authority to accept orders	X	No, if used for protected activity		X		
Idaho	X, unless protected by P.L. 86-242	X	X	X	No, if used for protected activity		X, unless for reorder		
Illinois	X	X	X	X			X		X

Nexus determinations can be made only in the context of an audit wherein the auditor would have full access to all pertinent information. Illinois determines "doing business" utilizing the prevailing principles of jurisprudence under the Commerce and Due Process Clauses of the United States Constitution as applied to the facts in each case. For further information see 86 Ill. Admin. Code § 100.9720.

	Tangible Personal Property	Real Estate	Intangibles (e.g., Securities)	Services	Company Car for Salesperson	Setup of Promotional Items by Salesperson	Inventory Inspection by Salesperson	Attendance at Trade Shows 14 Days or Less per Year (Products Are Tangible Personal Property)	Attendance at Trade Shows 14 Days or Less per Year (Products Are Not Tangible Personal Property)
Indiana	X	X	X	X				X	X
Iowa		X	X	X			X	X	X
Kansas		X	X			X	X		

Activities Creating Franchise or Income Tax Nexus (Part 4)

Sales Activities of Employees

Legend:

X	These activities create franchise or income tax nexus
NA	Not applicable
NR	Not reported

	Soliciting Sales of:								
	Tangible Personal Property	*Real Estate*	*Intangibles (e.g., Securities)*	*Services*	*Company Car for Salesperson*	*Setup of Promotional Items by Salesperson*	*Inventory Inspection by Salesperson*	*Attendance at Trade Shows 14 Days or Less per Year (Products Are Tangible Personal Property)*	*Attendance at Trade Shows 14 Days or Less per Year (Products Are Not Tangible Personal Property)*
Kentucky		X	X	X		X			
Louisiana				X					
Maine			X	X				X	X
Maryland		X	X	X		X, depends on where orders are approved			
Massachusetts	X		X	X	Depends on facts				
Michigan (Single Business Tax—VAT)	X	X	X	X	X	X	X	X, see I.(7)(g); nexus is created if orders for goods are taken and sales are made	X

Note. The CIT takes effect 01/01/12, and replaces the Michigan Business Tax (MBT) for most taxpayers. However, businesses that have been approved to receive, have received, or have been assigned certain certified credits may elect to file a return and pay the tax imposed by the MBT in lieu of the CIT until the certified credits are exhausted or extinguished.

Minnesota		X	X	X					X

Activities Creating Franchise or Income Tax Nexus (Part 4)

Sales Activities of Employees

Legend:

X	These activities create franchise or income tax nexus
NA	Not applicable
NR	Not reported

	Soliciting Sales of:								
	Tangible Personal Property	*Real Estate*	*Intangibles (e.g., Securities)*	*Services*	*Company Car for Salesperson*	*Setup of Promotional Items by Salesperson*	*Inventory Inspection by Salesperson*	*Attendance at Trade Shows 14 Days or Less per Year (Products Are Tangible Personal Property)*	*Attendance at Trade Shows 14 Days or Less per Year (Products Are Not Tangible Personal Property)*
Mississippi		X	X	X			X		
Missouri		X	X	X		X	X		
Montana		X	X	X			X	X	X
Nebraska	X	X	X	X		X	X		
Nevada	Nevada does not impose a corporate income tax								
New Hampshire		X	X	X			X		X
New Jersey		X	X	X		X	X		
New Mexico		X	X	X			X		
New York		X	X	X					
	Responses apply to New York Franchise Tax								
North Carolina		X	X	X					
North Dakota		X	X	X					
Ohio	Ohio does not impose a corporate income tax								

Activities Creating Franchise or Income Tax Nexus (Part 4)

Sales Activities of Employees

Legend:

X	These activities create franchise or income tax nexus
NA	Not applicable
NR	Not reported

	Soliciting Sales of:								
	Tangible Personal Property	*Real Estate*	*Intangibles (e.g., Securities)*	*Services*	*Company Car for Salesperson*	*Setup of Promotional Items by Salesperson*	*Inventory Inspection by Salesperson*	*Attendance at Trade Shows 14 Days or Less per Year (Products Are Tangible Personal Property)*	*Attendance at Trade Shows 14 Days or Less per Year (Products Are Not Tangible Personal Property)*
Note. Effective 1/1/2010, the Ohio Franchise Tax was fully phased out, and businesses will be taxed on gross receipts through the Commercial Activity Tax. Details about that tax can be found at: http//tax.ohio.gov/divisions/commercial_activities/index.stm									
Oklahoma		X	X				X		
Oregon		X	X	X			X		X
Pennsylvania	X	X	X	X		X, no if there is no charge	X, no if there is no charge and it is for purposes of reorder only	X, if more than 7 days, no if 7 days or less and annual Pennsylvania sales from all sources are $10,000 or less	X, if more than 7 days, no if 7 days or less and annual Pennsylvania sales from all sources are $10,000 or less
Rhode Island		X	X				X		
South Carolina		X	X	X			For reorder purposes only		X
South Dakota	South Dakota does not impose a corporate income tax								
Tennessee			X						
Texas	X	X	X	X	X	X	X		X

Activities Creating Franchise or Income Tax Nexus (Part 4)

Sales Activities of Employees

Legend:

X	These activities create franchise or income tax nexus
NA	Not applicable
NR	Not reported

	Soliciting Sales of: Tangible Personal Property	Real Estate	Intangibles (e.g., Securities)	Services	Company Car for Salesperson	Setup of Promotional Items by Salesperson	Inventory Inspection by Salesperson	Attendance at Trade Shows 14 Days or Less per Year (Products Are Tangible Personal Property)	Attendance at Trade Shows 14 Days or Less per Year (Products Are Not Tangible Personal Property)
Utah		X	X	X			X, unless for reorder		
Vermont		X	X	X					
Virginia		X	X		X, unless salesperson solicits only and is protected by P.L. 86-272	X	X, unless part of P.L. 86-272 solicitation		
Washington	Washington does not impose a corporate income tax								
West Virginia	X	X	X	X		X	X	X	
Wisconsin		X	X	X	Depends on facts		Depends on Facts		
Wyoming	Wyoming does not impose a corporate income tax								

Activities Creating Franchise or Income Tax Nexus (Part 5)
Activities Other than Sales (Section 1)

Legend:

X	These activities create franchise or income tax nexus
NA	Not applicable
NR	Not reported

	Listing Company in Phone Book	*Employees Repairing and Maintaining Products*	*Employee Working from Home Office, Performing Nonsolicitation Activities*	*Employees Providing In-State Consulting Services*	*Lease Employees to Another Company*	*Employees Inspecting Customer Installations of Products*	*Maintaining Telephone Answering Service*
Alabama	Alabama interprets nexus on case-by-case basis and as broadly as allowed under the Due Process and Commerce Clauses of the United States Constitution						
Alaska		X	X	X	X	X	X
Arizona	Depends	X	X	X	X	X	X
Arkansas	X	X	X	X	X	X	X
California	See FTB Form 1050	X	X			X	X
Colorado		X	X	X	X	X	X
Connecticut	No written guidance	X	X	X	No written guidance	X	X
Delaware		X	X	X	X		
District of Columbia	X	X	X	X	X	X	X
Florida		X	X	X	X	X	
Georgia	X	X	X	X	X	X	X
Hawaii		X	X	X	X	X	X
Idaho		X	Depends on facts	Depends on facts	Depends on facts	X	X
Illinois	X	X	X	X	X	X	X

Activities Creating Franchise or Income Tax Nexus (Part 5)

Activities Other than Sales (Section 1)

Legend:

X	These activities create franchise or income tax nexus
NA	Not applicable
NR	Not reported

	Listing Company in Phone Book	*Employees Repairing and Maintaining Products*	*Employee Working from Home Office, Performing Nonsolicitation Activities*	*Employees Providing In-State Consulting Services*	*Lease Employees to Another Company*	*Employees Inspecting Customer Installations of Products*	*Maintaining Telephone Answering Service*
Nexus determinations can be made only in the context of an audit wherein the auditor would have full access to all pertinent information. Illinois determines "doing business" utilizing the prevailing principles of jurisprudence under the Commerce and Due Process Clauses of the United States Constitution as applied to the facts in each case. For further information see 86 Ill. Admin. Code § 100.9720.							
Indiana		X	X	X	X	X	
Iowa		X	X	X	X	X	X
Kansas	X	X	X	X	X	X	X
Kentucky	X	X	X	X	X	X	X
Louisiana	X	X	X	X		X	X
Maine		X	X	X		X	X
Maryland		X	Perhaps	X	NR	X	
Massachusetts		X	X	X	X		
Michigan (Business Tax)		X	X		X		
Note. The CIT takes effect 01/01/12, and replaces the Michigan Business Tax (MBT) for most taxpayers. However, businesses that have been approved to receive, have received, or have been assigned certain certified credits may elect to file a return and pay the tax imposed by the MBT in lieu of the CIT until the certified credits are exhausted or extinguished.							
Minnesota	X	X	X	X	X	X	X
Mississippi		X	X	X	X	X	
Missouri	X	X	X	X	X	X	

Activities Creating Franchise or Income Tax Nexus (Part 5)

Activities Other than Sales (Section 1)

Legend:

X	These activities create franchise or income tax nexus
NA	Not applicable
NR	Not reported

	Listing Company in Phone Book	*Employees Repairing and Maintaining Products*	*Employee Working from Home Office, Performing Nonsolicitation Activities*	*Employees Providing In-State Consulting Services*	*Lease Employees to Another Company*	*Employees Inspecting Customer Installations of Products*	*Maintaining Telephone Answering Service*
Montana	X	X	X	X	X	X	
Nebraska		X	X	X	X	X	
Nevada	Nevada does not impose a corporate income tax						
New Hampshire	X	X	X	X	X	X	X
New Jersey	X	X	X	X	X		
New Mexico	X	X	X	X	X	X	X
New York		X	Fact driven	X	X	Insufficient facts to make a determination. Nexus is determined on an individual basis; each determination considers the facts and circumstances unique to that specific corporation.	Insufficient facts to make a determination. Nexus is determined on an individual basis; each determination considers the facts and circumstances unique to that specific corporation.
	Responses apply to New York Franchise Tax						
North Carolina		X	X	X	X	X	

Activities Creating Franchise or Income Tax Nexus (Part 5)
Activities Other than Sales (Section 1)

Legend:

X	These activities create franchise or income tax nexus
NA	Not applicable
NR	Not reported

	Listing Company in Phone Book	*Employees Repairing and Maintaining Products*	*Employee Working from Home Office, Performing Nonsolicitation Activities*	*Employees Providing In-State Consulting Services*	*Lease Employees to Another Company*	*Employees Inspecting Customer Installations of Products*	*Maintaining Telephone Answering Service*
North Dakota		X	X	X	X	X	
Ohio	Ohio does not impose a corporate income tax						
Note. Effective 1/1/2010, the Ohio Franchise Tax was fully phased out and business will be taxed on gross receipts through the Commercial Activity Tax. Details about that tax can be found at: http//tax.ohio.gov/divisions/commercial_activities/index.stm							
Oklahoma		X	X		X		
Oregon	X	X	X	X	X	X	X
Pennsylvania		X	X	X	X	X, no if 7 days or less and annual charges are $10,000 or less.	X
Rhode Island	X	X	X	X	X	X	X
South Carolina	X	X	X	X	X	X	X
South Dakota	South Dakota does not impose a corporate income tax						
Tennessee	X, if in state	X	No, only if non-income-producing activity	X	X		
Texas		X	X	X	X	X	X
Utah	X	X	X	X	X	X	X
Vermont	X	X	X	X	X	X	

Activities Creating Franchise or Income Tax Nexus (Part 5)
Activities Other than Sales (Section 1)

Legend:

X	These activities create franchise or income tax nexus
NA	Not applicable
NR	Not reported

	Listing Company in Phone Book	*Employees Repairing and Maintaining Products*	*Employee Working from Home Office, Performing Nonsolicitation Activities*	*Employees Providing In-State Consulting Services*	*Lease Employees to Another Company*	*Employees Inspecting Customer Installations of Products*	*Maintaining Telephone Answering Service*
Virginia		X	X	X	X	X	
Washington	Washington does not impose a corporate income tax						
West Virginia	X	X		X	X	X	X
Wisconsin	Depends on Facts	X	X	X	X	X	Depends on Facts
Wyoming	Wyoming does not impose a corporate income tax						

Activities Creating Franchise or Income Tax Nexus (Part 5)

Activities Other than Sales (Section 2)

Legend:

X	These activities create franchise or income tax nexus
NA	Not applicable
NR	Not reported

	Employees Providing Engineering or Design Functions Related to Sales of Customized Products	*Nonsalesperson Employee Working from Home Office (No Contact with In-State Customers, and the Home Is Not Used as a Place of Business for the Employer)*	*Presence of Employees for 20 or Fewer Days Solely to Purchase Goods from In-State Vendors*	*Having a Web Site Accessible in but Not Located on a Server in the State*	*Having a Web Site Accessible in and Located on a Server in the State*
Alabama	Alabama interprets nexus on case-by-case basis and as broadly as allowed under the Due Process and Commerce Clauses of the United States Constitution				
Alaska	X	Yes			X
Arizona	X	Yes	X		Depends
Arkansas	X	Yes			X
California	X	Yes	X		X
Colorado	X	Yes	X		X
Connecticut	X	No written guidance	No written guidance	No written guidance	No written guidance
Delaware		Yes	X		X
District of Columbia	X, if performed in state	No	X		X
Florida	X	Yes		X	X
Georgia	X	Yes	X		X
Hawaii	X	Yes			
Idaho	X	NR		Depends on facts	
Illinois	X	Yes	X		

Activities Creating Franchise or Income Tax Nexus (Part 5)

Activities Other than Sales (Section 2)

Legend:

X	These activities create franchise or income tax nexus
NA	Not applicable
NR	Not reported

	Employees Providing Engineering or Design Functions Related to Sales of Customized Products	*Nonsalesperson Employee Working from Home Office (No Contact with In-State Customers, and the Home Is Not Used as a Place of Business for the Employer)*	*Presence of Employees for 20 or Fewer Days Solely to Purchase Goods from In-State Vendors*	*Having a Web Site Accessible in but Not Located on a Server in the State*	*Having a Web Site Accessible in and Located on a Server in the State*
	Nexus determinations can be made only in the context of an audit wherein the auditor would have full access to all pertinent information. Illinois determines "doing business" utilizing the prevailing principles of jurisprudence under the Commerce and Due Process Clauses of the United States Constitution as applied to the facts in each case. For further information see 86 Ill. Admin. Code § 100.9720.				
Indiana	X	Yes			
Iowa	X	Yes	X		X
Kansas	X	Yes			X
Kentucky	X	Yes			X
Louisiana	X	Yes		X	
Maine	X	Yes			X
Maryland	No, see ARD No. 2, IV. G.	No	Apply nexus to full extent permitted under law	Apply nexus to full extent permitted under law	Apply nexus to full extent permitted under law
Massachusetts	Depends on facts				
Michigan (Business Tax)	X	Yes	X	X, if website constitutes "active solicitation" and taxpayer has $350,000 or more in Michigan gross receipts	X, if website constitutes "active solicitation" and taxpayer has $350,000 or more in Michigan gross receipts

Activities Creating Franchise or Income Tax Nexus (Part 5)

Activities Other than Sales (Section 2)

Legend:

X	These activities create franchise or income tax nexus
NA	Not applicable
NR	Not reported

	Employees Providing Engineering or Design Functions Related to Sales of Customized Products	*Nonsalesperson Employee Working from Home Office (No Contact with In-State Customers, and the Home Is Not Used as a Place of Business for the Employer)*	*Presence of Employees for 20 or Fewer Days Solely to Purchase Goods from In-State Vendors*	*Having a Web Site Accessible in but Not Located on a Server in the State*	*Having a Web Site Accessible in and Located on a Server in the State*
Note. The CIT takes effect 01/01/12, and replaces the Michigan Business Tax (MBT) for most taxpayers. However, businesses that have been approved to receive, have received, or have been assigned certain certified credits may elect to file a return and pay the tax imposed by the MBT in lieu of the CIT until the certified credits are exhausted or extinguished.					
Minnesota	X	Yes		X	X
Mississippi	X	No	X		
Missouri	X	No	X		X
Montana	X	Yes	X		X
Nebraska	X	Yes	X		X
Nevada	Nevada does not impose a corporate income tax				
New Hampshire	X	Yes	X		X
New Jersey		Yes		Possibly	
New Mexico	X	No	X		X
New York	X	Yes	X	No, assuming taxpayer does not own or lease the server	No, assuming taxpayer does not own or lease the server
	Responses apply to New York Franchise Tax				
North Carolina	X	Yes			X
North Dakota	X	Yes			X

Activities Creating Franchise or Income Tax Nexus (Part 5)

Activities Other than Sales (Section 2)

Legend:

X	These activities create franchise or income tax nexus
NA	Not applicable
NR	Not reported

	Employees Providing Engineering or Design Functions Related to Sales of Customized Products	*Nonsalesperson Employee Working from Home Office (No Contact with In-State Customers, and the Home Is Not Used as a Place of Business for the Employer)*	*Presence of Employees for 20 or Fewer Days Solely to Purchase Goods from In-State Vendors*	*Having a Web Site Accessible in but Not Located on a Server in the State*	*Having a Web Site Accessible in and Located on a Server in the State*
Ohio	Ohio does not impose a corporate income tax				
Note. Effective 1/1/2010, the Ohio Franchise Tax was fully phased out and business will be taxed on gross receipts through the Commercial Activity Tax. Details about that tax can be found at: http//tax.ohio.gov/divisions/commercial_activities/index.stm					
Oklahoma		Yes	X		
Oregon	X	Yes			X
Pennsylvania	X, no if 7 days or less and annual charges are $10,000 or less.	Yes			
Rhode Island	X	Yes		X	X
South Carolina	X	Yes	X		
South Dakota	South Dakota does not impose a corporate income tax				
Tennessee		No			
Texas	X	Yes			
Utah	X	Yes			X
Vermont	X	NR			
Virginia	X	Yes			Assumes taxpayer does not own server
Washington	Washington does not impose a corporate income tax				

Activities Creating Franchise or Income Tax Nexus (Part 5)

Activities Other than Sales (Section 2)

Legend:

X	These activities create franchise or income tax nexus
NA	Not applicable
NR	Not reported

	Employees Providing Engineering or Design Functions Related to Sales of Customized Products	*Nonsalesperson Employee Working from Home Office (No Contact with In-State Customers, and the Home Is Not Used as a Place of Business for the Employer)*	*Presence of Employees for 20 or Fewer Days Solely to Purchase Goods from In-State Vendors*	*Having a Web Site Accessible in but Not Located on a Server in the State*	*Having a Web Site Accessible in and Located on a Server in the State*
West Virginia	X	No			X
Wisconsin	X	Depends on facts	X	Depends on facts	Depends on Facts
Wyoming	Wyoming does not impose a corporate income tax				

Activities Creating Franchise or Income Tax Nexus (Part 6)
Activities of Third Parties

Legend:

X	These activities create franchise or income tax nexus
NA	Not applicable
NR	Not reported

	Hire Unrelated Third Party to Install Products	*In-State Warranty Repair Performed by Unrelated Third Parties for No Charge*	*In-State Warranty Repair Performed by Unrelated Third Parties for a Charge*	*In-State Fulfillment Company Fills Orders from Company-Owned Inventory Located at Fulfillment Company*	*Hire Unrelated Third Party to Repossess Property*	*Hire Unrelated Third Party to Collect Accounts*
Alabama	Alabama interprets nexus on case-by-case basis and as broadly as allowed under the Due Process and Commerce Clauses of the United States Constitution					
Alaska	X		X	X	X	
Arizona	X	X	X	X, if required by contract	X	X
Arkansas		X	X	X	X	
California	X	X	X	X	X	X
Colorado	X	X	X	X		X
Connecticut		No written guidance	No written guidance		No written guidance	
Delaware	X			X		
District of Columbia	X	X	X	X	X	X
Florida	X	X	X	X	X	X
Georgia	X	X	X	X	X	X
Hawaii	X	X	X	X	X	
Idaho	Depends on facts	Depends on facts	Depends on facts	X		
Illinois		Need more information	Need more information	X		

Activities Creating Franchise or Income Tax Nexus (Part 6)
Activities of Third Parties

Legend:

X	These activities create franchise or income tax nexus
NA	Not applicable
NR	Not reported

	Hire Unrelated Third Party to Install Products	*In-State Warranty Repair Performed by Unrelated Third Parties for No Charge*	*In-State Warranty Repair Performed by Unrelated Third Parties for a Charge*	*In-State Fulfillment Company Fills Orders from Company-Owned Inventory Located at Fulfillment Company*	*Hire Unrelated Third Party to Repossess Property*	*Hire Unrelated Third Party to Collect Accounts*
	Nexus determinations can be made only in the context of an audit wherein the auditor would have full access to all pertinent information. Illinois determines "doing business" utilizing the prevailing principles of jurisprudence under the Commerce and Due Process Clauses of the United States Constitution as applied to the facts in each case. For further information see 86 Ill. Admin. Code § 100.9720.					
Indiana	X	X		X		X
Iowa	X	X	X	X, taxpayer owned fulfillment company	X	X
Kansas	X	X	X	X	X	
Kentucky	X	X	X	X	X	X
Louisiana		X	X	X		
Maine	X	X	X		X	X
Maryland	X			X		No, see ADR No. 2, IV.F.
Massachusetts	X				X	Depends on facts
Michigan (Business Tax)	X	X	X	X	X	X
Note. The CIT takes effect 01/01/12, and replaces the Michigan Business Tax (MBT) for most taxpayers. However, businesses that have been approved to receive, have received, or have been assigned certain certified credits may elect to file a return and pay the tax imposed by the MBT in lieu of the CIT until the certified credits are exhausted or extinguished.						
Minnesota	X	X	X	X	X	X

Activities Creating Franchise or Income Tax Nexus (Part 6)

Activities of Third Parties

Legend:

X	These activities create franchise or income tax nexus
NA	Not applicable
NR	Not reported

	Hire Unrelated Third Party to Install Products	*In-State Warranty Repair Performed by Unrelated Third Parties for No Charge*	*In-State Warranty Repair Performed by Unrelated Third Parties for a Charge*	*In-State Fulfillment Company Fills Orders from Company-Owned Inventory Located at Fulfillment Company*	*Hire Unrelated Third Party to Repossess Property*	*Hire Unrelated Third Party to Collect Accounts*
Mississippi	X	X	X	X		
Missouri	X	X	X	X	X	X
Montana	X	X	X	X	X	X
Nebraska	X	X	X	X		
Nevada	Nevada does not impose a corporate income tax					
New Hampshire	X	X	X	X	X	X
New Jersey		X	X	X		
New Mexico	X	X	X		X	X
New York					Insufficient facts to make a determination. Nexus is determined on an individual basis; each determination considers the facts and circumstances unique to that specific corporation	
	Responses apply to New York Franchise Tax					
North Carolina	X	X	X	X	X	X

Activities Creating Franchise or Income Tax Nexus (Part 6)

Activities of Third Parties

Legend:

X	These activities create franchise or income tax nexus
NA	Not applicable
NR	Not reported

	Hire Unrelated Third Party to Install Products	*In-State Warranty Repair Performed by Unrelated Third Parties for No Charge*	*In-State Warranty Repair Performed by Unrelated Third Parties for a Charge*	*In-State Fulfillment Company Fills Orders from Company-Owned Inventory Located at Fulfillment Company*	*Hire Unrelated Third Party to Repossess Property*	*Hire Unrelated Third Party to Collect Accounts*
North Dakota	X	X	X	X	X	
Ohio	Ohio does not impose a corporate income tax					
Note: Effective 1/1/2010, the Ohio Franchise Tax was fully phased out and business will be taxed on gross receipts through the Commercial Activity Tax. Details about that tax can be found at: http//tax.ohio.gov/divisions/commercial_activities/index.stm						
Oklahoma				X		
Oregon	X	X	X	X	X	X
Pennsylvania	X	X, no if 7 days or less	X, no if 7 days or less and annual charges are $10,000 or less	X	X	X
Rhode Island		X	X	X	X	X
South Carolina	X	X	X	X	X	X
South Dakota	South Dakota does not impose a corporate income tax					
Tennessee				X		
Texas	X	X	X	X	X	X
Utah	X	X	X	X	X	X
Vermont			X			
Virginia				X, see P.D. 92-125	X	
Washington	Washington does not impose a corporate income tax					

Activities Creating Franchise or Income Tax Nexus (Part 6)

Activities of Third Parties

Legend:

X	These activities create franchise or income tax nexus
NA	Not applicable
NR	Not reported

	Hire Unrelated Third Party to Install Products	*In-State Warranty Repair Performed by Unrelated Third Parties for No Charge*	*In-State Warranty Repair Performed by Unrelated Third Parties for a Charge*	*In-State Fulfillment Company Fills Orders from Company-Owned Inventory Located at Fulfillment Company*	*Hire Unrelated Third Party to Repossess Property*	*Hire Unrelated Third Party to Collect Accounts*
West Virginia	X	X	X	X	X	
Wisconsin	Depends on Facts	Depends on Facts	Depends on Facts	X	Depends on Facts	Depends on Facts
Wyoming	Wyoming does not impose a corporate income tax					

Activities Creating Franchise or Income Tax Nexus (Part 7)
De Minimis *Physical Presence*

Legend:
X — These activities create franchise or income tax nexus
NA — Not applicable
NR — Not reported

	Occasional Business Meetings at Customer's Location	*Occasional Training Seminars for Customers*	*Occasional Board of Directors' Meetings*	*Occasional Attendance at Technical/Training Seminars Sponsored by Unrelated Parties*	*Has the State Defined "Occasional" or "De Minimis" Activity That Will Not Establish Nexus?*	*If Yes, What Is the Definition?*
Alabama	Alabama interprets nexus on case-by-case basis and as broadly as allowed under the Due Process and Commerce Clauses of the United States Constitution					
Alaska	X	X			No	
Arizona	X	X	X	X	Yes	See Arizona Corporate Income Tax Ruling CTR-995.
Arkansas		X			Yes	Activities that, when taken together, establish only a trivial or minor connection, Reg. 6.26-51-702.
California	X	X	X	X	No	See FTB Form 1050
Colorado					Yes	MTC's Factor Presence Nexus regulations 39-22-301.1
Connecticut	No written guidance	No written guidance		No written guidance	No	NA
Delaware	X	X		X	No	NA
District of Columbia	X				No	NA
Florida	X	X			No	NA

Activities Creating Franchise or Income Tax Nexus (Part 7)
De Minimis *Physical Presence*

Legend:

X	These activities create franchise or income tax nexus
NA	Not applicable
NR	Not reported

	Occasional Business Meetings at Customer's Location	*Occasional Training Seminars for Customers*	*Occasional Board of Directors' Meetings*	*Occasional Attendance at Technical/Training Seminars Sponsored by Unrelated Parties*	*Has the State Defined "Occasional" or "De Minimis" Activity That Will Not Establish Nexus?*	*If Yes, What Is the Definition?*
Georgia	X	X			No	NA
Hawaii	X	X			No	NA
Idaho	X, unless *de minimis*	X			Yes	MTC trucking regulation, which contains a *de minimis* nexus standard
Illinois	X	X			No	This is a factual determination.
	Nexus determinations can be made only in the context of an audit wherein the auditor would have full access to all pertinent information. Illinois determines "doing business" utilizing the prevailing principles of jurisprudence under the Commerce and Due Process Clauses of the United States Constitution as applied to the facts in each case. For further information see 86 III. Admin. Code § 100.9720.					
Indiana	X	X			No	NA
Iowa	X	X			No	NA
Kansas	X	X			No	NA
Kentucky		X			Yes	Follow Wisconsin Dept. of Revenue V. William J. Wrigley, Jr.
Louisiana		X			No	

Activities Creating Franchise or Income Tax Nexus (Part 7)
De Minimis *Physical Presence*

Legend:

X	These activities create franchise or income tax nexus
NA	Not applicable
NR	Not reported

	Occasional Business Meetings at Customer's Location	*Occasional Training Seminars for Customers*	*Occasional Board of Directors' Meetings*	*Occasional Attendance at Technical/Training Seminars Sponsored by Unrelated Parties*	*Has the State Defined "Occasional" or "De Minimis" Activity That Will Not Establish Nexus?*	*If Yes, What Is the Definition?*
Maine			X		Yes	Defined pursuant to 18-125 CMR 808, "Corporate Income Tax Nexus"
Maryland	X	X			NR	NR
Massachusetts				Yes	Yes	
Michigan (Business Tax)	X, see note.	X	To be determined, under review		Yes	Less than 2 days per year and active solicitation of sales in Michigan with gross receipts under $350,000 to Michigan. Policy regarding additional examples of *de minimis* activities under review.

Note. The CIT takes effect 01/01/12, and replaces the Michigan Business Tax (MBT) for most taxpayers. However, businesses that have been approved to receive, have received, or have been assigned certain certified credits may elect to file a return and pay the tax imposed by the MBT in lieu of the CIT until the certified credits are exhausted or extinguished.

Note. See RAB 1998-1; 1 visit does not create nexus; 2 or more visits create a rebuttable presumption of nexus.

Minnesota		X	X		No	NA
Mississippi	X	X			No	NA

Activities Creating Franchise or Income Tax Nexus (Part 7)
De Minimis *Physical Presence*

Legend:

X	These activities create franchise or income tax nexus
NA	Not applicable
NR	Not reported

	Occasional Business Meetings at Customer's Location	*Occasional Training Seminars for Customers*	*Occasional Board of Directors' Meetings*	*Occasional Attendance at Technical/Training Seminars Sponsored by Unrelated Parties*	*Has the State Defined "Occasional" or "De Minimis" Activity That Will Not Establish Nexus?*	*If Yes, What Is the Definition?*
Missouri		X			No	NR
Montana	X	X	X		Yes	ARM 42.26.274
Nebraska					No	NA
Nevada	Nevada does not impose a corporate income tax					
New Hampshire	X	X	X	X	No	NA
New Jersey	X	X			Yes	A trivial presence is exceeded when the presence arises from a regular and systematic business practice, the pursuit of an established company policy, an affirmative decision of management or ownership, or any steps taken to establish and maintain a market within New Jersey.

Activities Creating Franchise or Income Tax Nexus (Part 7)
De Minimis *Physical Presence*

Legend:

X	These activities create franchise or income tax nexus
NA	Not applicable
NR	Not reported

	Occasional Business Meetings at Customer's Location	*Occasional Training Seminars for Customers*	*Occasional Board of Directors' Meetings*	*Occasional Attendance at Technical/Training Seminars Sponsored by Unrelated Parties*	*Has the State Defined "Occasional" or "De Minimis" Activity That Will Not Establish Nexus?*	*If Yes, What Is the Definition?*
New Mexico					Yes	Definition of *de minimis* for trucking. Trucking company will not establish nexus if it does not (1) own or rent real or personal property in the state, except mobile property; (2) make any pick-ups or deliveries within the state; (3) travel more than 25,000 miles within the state provided that the total miles traveled in New Mexico does not exceed 3% of the total miles traveled in all states: nor (4) make more than 12 trips into New Mexico.
New York	X	X			No	NA
	Responses apply to New York Franchise Tax					
North Carolina		X			No	

Activities Creating Franchise or Income Tax Nexus (Part 7)
De Minimis *Physical Presence*

Legend:

X	These activities create franchise or income tax nexus
NA	Not applicable
NR	Not reported

	Occasional Business Meetings at Customer's Location	*Occasional Training Seminars for Customers*	*Occasional Board of Directors' Meetings*	*Occasional Attendance at Technical/Training Seminars Sponsored by Unrelated Parties*	*Has the State Defined "Occasional" or "De Minimis" Activity That Will Not Establish Nexus?*	*If Yes, What Is the Definition?*
North Dakota		X				No
Ohio	Ohio does not impose a corporate income tax					
Note: Effective 1/1/2010, the Ohio Franchise Tax was fully phased out and business will be taxed on gross receipts through the Commercial Activity Tax. Details about that tax can be found at: http//tax.ohio.gov/divisions/commercial_activities/index.stm						
Oklahoma					No	NA

Activities Creating Franchise or Income Tax Nexus (Part 7)
De Minimis *Physical Presence*

Legend:

X	These activities create franchise or income tax nexus
NA	Not applicable
NR	Not reported

	Occasional Business Meetings at Customer's Location	*Occasional Training Seminars for Customers*	*Occasional Board of Directors' Meetings*	*Occasional Attendance at Technical/Training Seminars Sponsored by Unrelated Parties*	*Has the State Defined "Occasional" or "De Minimis" Activity That Will Not Establish Nexus?*	*If Yes, What Is the Definition?*
Oregon	X	X			Yes	Definition of de minimis for trucking only. Trucking company will not establish nexus if it does not (1) own or rent real or personal property in the state, except mobile property; (2) make any pickups or deliveries within the state; (3) travel more than 25,000 miles within the state provided that the total miles traveled in Oregon does not exceed 3% of the total miles traveled in all states; not (4) make more than 12 trips into Oregon.

Activities Creating Franchise or Income Tax Nexus (Part 7)
De Minimis *Physical Presence*

Legend:

X	These activities create franchise or income tax nexus
NA	Not applicable
NR	Not reported

	Occasional Business Meetings at Customer's Location	*Occasional Training Seminars for Customers*	*Occasional Board of Directors' Meetings*	*Occasional Attendance at Technical/Training Seminars Sponsored by Unrelated Parties*	*Has the State Defined "Occasional" or "De Minimis" Activity That Will Not Establish Nexus?*	*If Yes, What Is the Definition?*
Pennsylvania	X, no if incidental to use or personal property sold and if free or for a nominal charge and a trivial part of the overall sale.	X, no if limited to no more than seven days and less than $10,000 in charges.			Yes	See Corporation Tax Bulletin 2004-01, Application of P.L. 86-272 and *de minimis* standards. May 13, 2004.
Rhode Island	X	X	X	Yes	Regulation CT-95-2	
South Carolina	X	X		Yes	Yes, *de minimis* activities are those that, when taken together, establish only a trivial connection with the taxing state. South Carolina Revenue Ruling #97-15	
South Dakota	South Dakota does not impose a corporate income tax					
Tennessee				No	NA	
Texas	X	X	X		No	

Activities Creating Franchise or Income Tax Nexus (Part 7)
De Minimis *Physical Presence*

Legend:

X	These activities create franchise or income tax nexus
NA	Not applicable
NR	Not reported

	Occasional Business Meetings at Customer's Location	*Occasional Training Seminars for Customers*	*Occasional Board of Directors' Meetings*	*Occasional Attendance at Technical/Training Seminars Sponsored by Unrelated Parties*	*Has the State Defined "Occasional" or "De Minimis" Activity That Will Not Establish Nexus?*	*If Yes, What Is the Definition?*
Utah	X	X			Yes	Activities that when taken together establish only a trivial connection with the taxing state. An activity conducted within Utah on a regular or systematic basis or pursuant to a company policy. Whether or not in writing, is not normally considered trivial.
Vermont			No	NA		
Virginia	X	X		Yes	See 23 VAC 10-120-90G	
Washington	Washington does not impose a corporate income tax					
West Virginia				No	NA	
Wisconsin	Depends on Facts	Depends on Facts		Depends on Facts	No	
Wyoming	Wyoming does not impose a corporate Income tax					

Activities Creating Franchise or Income Tax Nexus (Part 8)

Ownership Interest in Pass-Through Entity

Legend:

X	These activities create franchise or income tax nexus
NA	Not applicable
NR	Not reported

	Ownership of Interest in LLC Doing Business in State			
	Limited Interest	*General Interest*	*Ownership of Interest in LLC Doing Business in State*	*Ownership of Interest in Board-Managed LLC (Member Is Not on Board) Doing Business in State*
Alabama	Alabama interprets nexus on case-by-case basis and as broadly as allowed under the Due Process and Commerce Clauses of the United States Constitution			
Alaska	X	X	X	X
Arizona	X	X	X	X
Arkansas	X	X	X	X
California	X	X	X	X
Colorado	X	X	X	X
Connecticut	X	X	X	
Delaware	X	X	X	X
District of Columbia	X	X	X	X
Florida	X	X	X	X
Georgia	X	X	X	X
Hawaii	X	X	X	X
Idaho	X	X	X	X
Illinois	X	X		
	Nexus determinations can be made only in the context of an audit wherein the auditor would have full access to all pertinent information. Illinois determines "doing business" utilizing the prevailing principles of jurisprudence under the Commerce and Due Process Clauses of the United States Constitution as applied to the facts in each case. For further information see 86 Ill. Admin. Code § 100.9720.			

Activities Creating Franchise or Income Tax Nexus (Part 8)

Ownership Interest in Pass-Through Entity

Legend:

X	These activities create franchise or income tax nexus
NA	Not applicable
NR	Not reported

	Ownership of Interest in LLC Doing Business in State			
	Limited Interest	*General Interest*	*Ownership of Interest in LLC Doing Business in State*	*Ownership of Interest in Board-Managed LLC (Member Is Not on Board) Doing Business in State*
Indiana	X	X	X	X
Iowa	X	X	X	X
Kansas	X	X	X	X
Kentucky	X	X	X	X
Louisiana	X	X	X	X
Maine	X	X	X	
Maryland	X	X	X	X
Massachusetts	Depends on facts	X	X	Depends on facts
Michigan (Business Tax)				
Note. The CIT takes effect 01/01/12, and replaces the Michigan Business Tax (MBT) for most taxpayers. However, businesses that have been approved to receive, have received, or have been assigned certain certified credits may elect to file a return and pay the tax imposed by the MBT in lieu of the CIT until the certified credits are exhausted or extinguished.				
Minnesota	X	X	X	X
Mississippi	X	X	X	X
Missouri	X	X	X	X
Montana	X	X	X	X
Nebraska	X	X	X	X
Nevada	Nevada does not impose a corporate income tax			

Activities Creating Franchise or Income Tax Nexus (Part 8)

Ownership Interest in Pass-Through Entity

Legend:

X	These activities create franchise or income tax nexus
NA	Not applicable
NR	Not reported

	Ownership of Interest in LLC Doing Business in State			
	Limited Interest	*General Interest*	*Ownership of Interest in LLC Doing Business in State*	*Ownership of Interest in Board-Managed LLC (Member Is Not on Board) Doing Business in State*
New Hampshire				
New Jersey	Possibly	X	X	
New Mexico	X	X	X	X
New York	New York has special nexus rules for a foreign corporation that is a limited partner in a partnership-See NY Regs. § 1-3.2(a)(6).	X	New York has special nexus rules for a foreign corporation that is a limited partner in a partnership-See NY Regs. § 1-3.2(a)(6).	New York has special nexus rules for a foreign corporation that is a limited partner in a partnership-See NY Regs. § 1-3.2(a)(6).
	Responses apply to New York Franchise Tax			
North Carolina	X	X	X	X
North Dakota	X	X	X	X
Ohio	Ohio does not impose a corporate income tax			
Note: Effective 1/1/2010, the Ohio Franchise Tax was fully phased out and business will be taxed on gross receipts through the Commercial Activity Tax. Details about that tax can be found at: http//tax.ohio.gov/divisions/commercial_activities/index.stm				
Oklahoma	X	X	X	X
Oregon	X	X	X	X

Activities Creating Franchise or Income Tax Nexus (Part 8)

Ownership Interest in Pass-Through Entity

Legend:

X	These activities create franchise or income tax nexus
NA	Not applicable
NR	Not reported

	Ownership of Interest in LLC Doing Business in State			
	Limited Interest	*General Interest*	*Ownership of Interest in LLC Doing Business in State*	*Ownership of Interest in Board-Managed LLC (Member Is Not on Board) Doing Business in State*
Pennsylvania	X, unless the partnership is classified as a corporation for federal income tax purposes	X, unless the partnership is classified as a corporation for federal income tax purposes	X, unless the partnership is classified as a corporation for federal income tax purposes	X, unless the partnership is classified as a corporation for federal income tax purposes
Rhode Island		X	X	X
South Carolina	X	X	X	X
South Dakota	South Dakota does not impose a corporate income tax			
Tennessee	LPs subject to tax	X	LLCs subject to tax	LLCs subject to tax
Texas		X		
Utah	X	X	X	X
Vermont	X	X	X	X
Virginia	X	X	X	X
Washington	Washington does not impose a corporate income tax			
West Virginia	X	X	X	X
Wisconsin	X	X	X	X
Wyoming	Wyoming does not impose a corporate income tax			

Activities Creating Franchise or Income Tax Nexus (Part 9)

Holding Title to Electricity or Natural Gas

Legend:

X	These activities create franchise or income tax nexus
NA	Not applicable
NR	Not reported
SAF	Same as applicable federal rules

	Holding Title to Electricity Flowing Through Transmission Wire Within State (No Origination or Termination in State)	*Holding Title to Natural Gas Flowing Through Pipeline in State (No Origination or Termination in State)*	*For Purposes of Applying P.L. 86-272, Are the Following Energy Commodities Considered Tangible Personal Property?* — *Electricity*	*Natural Gas*
Alabama	Alabama interprets nexus on case-by-case basis and as broadly as allowed under the Due Process and Commerce Clauses of the United States Constitution			
Alaska	X	X	Yes	Yes
Arizona	Depending on utility deregulation	Depending on utility deregulation	Yes	Yes
Arkansas			No	No
California	Electricity is intangible.		No	Yes
Colorado	X	X	Yes, electricity as tangible personal property at issue in sales tax litigation	Yes
Connecticut	X	X	Yes	Yes
Delaware			No	No
District of Columbia	X	X	Yes	Yes
Florida	X	X	NR	NR
Georgia			Yes	Yes
Hawaii			No	No
Idaho	X	X	Yes	Yes

Activities Creating Franchise or Income Tax Nexus (Part 9)

Holding Title to Electricity or Natural Gas

Legend:

X	These activities create franchise or income tax nexus
NA	Not applicable
NR	Not reported
SAF	Same as applicable federal rules

	Holding Title to Electricity Flowing Through Transmission Wire Within State (No Origination or Termination in State)	*Holding Title to Natural Gas Flowing Through Pipeline in State (No Origination or Termination in State)*	*For Purposes of Applying P.L. 86-272, Are the Following Energy Commodities Considered Tangible Personal Property?*	
			Electricity	*Natural Gas*
Illinois			No	Yes
	Nexus determinations can be made only in the context of an audit wherein the auditor would have full access to all pertinent information. Illinois determines "doing business" utilizing the prevailing principles of jurisprudence under the Commerce and Due Process Clauses of the United States Constitution as applied to the facts in each case. For further information see 86 Ill. Admin. Code § 100.9720.			
Indiana			Yes	Yes
Iowa	X	X	Yes	Yes
Kansas	X	X	No	Yes
Kentucky			Yes	Yes
Louisiana	X	X	Yes	Yes
Maine	X	X	Yes	Yes
Maryland	NR	NR	Yes	Yes
Massachusetts				
Michigan (Business Tax)			Yes	Yes

Note. The CIT takes effect 01/01/12, and replaces the Michigan Business Tax (MBT) for most taxpayers. However, businesses that have been approved to receive, have received, or have been assigned certain certified credits may elect to file a return and pay the tax imposed by the MBT in lieu of the CIT until the certified credits are exhausted or extinguished.

Activities Creating Franchise or Income Tax Nexus (Part 9)

Holding Title to Electricity or Natural Gas

Legend:

X	These activities create franchise or income tax nexus
NA	Not applicable
NR	Not reported
SAF	Same as applicable federal rules

	Holding Title to Electricity Flowing Through Transmission Wire Within State (No Origination or Termination in State)	*Holding Title to Natural Gas Flowing Through Pipeline in State (No Origination or Termination in State)*	*For Purposes of Applying P.L. 86-272, Are the Following Energy Commodities Considered Tangible Personal Property?*	
			Electricity	*Natural Gas*
Minnesota	X	X	No	No
Mississippi			Yes	Yes
Missouri	X	X	Yes	Yes
Montana	X	X	NR	Yes
Nebraska			No	Yes
Nevada	Nevada does not impose a corporate income tax			
New Hampshire			Yes	Yes
New Jersey			Yes	Yes
New Mexico	X	X	Yes	Yes
New York			Yes	Yes
	Responses apply to New York Franchise Tax			
North Carolina			Yes	Yes
North Dakota			Yes	Yes
Ohio	Ohio does not impose a corporate income tax			

Note: Effective 1/1/2010, the Ohio Franchise Tax was fully phased out and business will be taxed on gross receipts through the Commercial Activity Tax. Details about that tax can be found at: http//tax.ohio.gov/divisions/commercial_activities/index.stm

Activities Creating Franchise or Income Tax Nexus (Part 9)

Holding Title to Electricity or Natural Gas

Legend:

X	These activities create franchise or income tax nexus
NA	Not applicable
NR	Not reported
SAF	Same as applicable federal rules

	Holding Title to Electricity Flowing Through Transmission Wire Within State (No Origination or Termination in State)	*Holding Title to Natural Gas Flowing Through Pipeline in State (No Origination or Termination in State)*	*For Purposes of Applying P.L. 86-272, Are the Following Energy Commodities Considered Tangible Personal Property?*	
			Electricity	*Natural Gas*
Oklahoma			NR	Yes
Oregon	X	X	Yes	Yes
Pennsylvania	NR	NR	NR	NR
Rhode Island	Public Service Corporation	Public Service Corporation	Public Service Corporation	Public Service Corporation
South Carolina	X	X	Yes	Yes
South Dakota	South Dakota does not impose a corporate income tax			
Tennessee			Yes	Yes
Texas	P.L. 86-272 does not apply	P.L. 86-272 does not apply	Yes	
Utah	X	X	Yes	Yes
Vermont			No	Yes
Virginia	X	X	Yes	Yes
Washington	Washington does not impose a corporate income tax			
West Virginia			No	No
Wisconsin			Yes	Yes
Wyoming	Wyoming does not impose a corporate income tax			

Activities Creating Franchise or Income Tax Nexus (Part 10)

Qualification to Do Business/Filing Requirements

Legend:

X	These activities create franchise or income tax nexus
NA	Not applicable
NR	Not reported

In the Case of a Corporation That is Qualified to do Business in State:

	Does the Mere Holding of a Certificate of Authority Subject the Corporation to an Income-Based Tax?	*Does the Mere Holding of a Certificate of Authority Subject the Corporation to a Flat Dollar Amount Minimum Tax?*	*Is a Tax Return Required to Be Filed Even if the Corporation Has Not Yet Begun to Do Business in the State?*	*Is a Tax Return Required to Be Filed Even if the Corporation's Activities Are Protected by P.L. 86-272 (i.e., Must File Return Noting That Corporation Is Protected Under the Public Law)?*
Alabama	Alabama interprets nexus on case-by-case basis and as broadly as allowed under the Due Process and Commerce Clauses of the United States Constitution			
Alaska	No	No	Yes	Yes
Arizona	No	No	No	No
Arkansas	No	No	No	No
California	No	Yes	Yes	Yes
Colorado	No	No	No	No
Connecticut	No	Yes	Yes	No written guidance
Delaware	No	No	No	No
District of Columbia	No	No	No	No
Florida	No	No	No	No
Georgia	No	NA	Yes, a resident domestic or foreign corporation doing business or owning property in Georgia, must file an initial net worth tax return on or before the 15th day of the 3rd calendar month after incorporation or qualification.	Yes

Activities Creating Franchise or Income Tax Nexus (Part 10)

Qualification to Do Business/Filing Requirements

Legend:

X	These activities create franchise or income tax nexus
NA	Not applicable
NR	Not reported

In the Case of a Corporation That is Qualified to do Business in State:

	Does the Mere Holding of a Certificate of Authority Subject the Corporation to an Income-Based Tax?	*Does the Mere Holding of a Certificate of Authority Subject the Corporation to a Flat Dollar Amount Minimum Tax?*	*Is a Tax Return Required to Be Filed Even if the Corporation Has Not Yet Begun to Do Business in the State?*	*Is a Tax Return Required to Be Filed Even if the Corporation's Activities Are Protected by P.L. 86-272 (i.e., Must File Return Noting That Corporation Is Protected Under the Public Law)?*
Hawaii	No	NA	No	No
Idaho	No	Yes	Yes	Yes
Illinois	No	Secretary of state administers franchise tax	Yes	Yes
	Nexus determinations can be made only in the context of an audit wherein the auditor would have full access to all pertinent information. Illinois determines "doing business" utilizing the prevailing principles of jurisprudence under the Commerce and Due Process Clauses of the United States Constitution as applied to the facts in each case. For further information see 86 Ill. Admin. Code § 100.9720.			
Indiana	No	No	No	No
Iowa	No	No	No	No
Kansas	No	No	No	Yes
Kentucky	No	Yes	Yes	Yes
Louisiana	No	No	Yes	No
Maine	No	No	No	No
Maryland	NR	NR	NR	NR
Massachusetts	Depends on facts	Yes	Yes	Depends on facts

Activities Creating Franchise or Income Tax Nexus (Part 10)

Qualification to Do Business/Filing Requirements

Legend:

X	These activities create franchise or income tax nexus
NA	Not applicable
NR	Not reported

	In the Case of a Corporation That is Qualified to do Business in State:			
	Does the Mere Holding of a Certificate of Authority Subject the Corporation to an Income-Based Tax?	*Does the Mere Holding of a Certificate of Authority Subject the Corporation to a Flat Dollar Amount Minimum Tax?*	*Is a Tax Return Required to Be Filed Even if the Corporation Has Not Yet Begun to Do Business in the State?*	*Is a Tax Return Required to Be Filed Even if the Corporation's Activities Are Protected by P.L. 86-272 (i.e., Must File Return Noting That Corporation Is Protected Under the Public Law)?*
Michigan (Business Tax)	No	No	No	A person whose activities are limited to that protected by P.L. 86-272 is not subject to the business income tax portion of the MBT. However, such a person otherwise having sufficient nexus with Michigan will be subject to the modified gross receipts tax portion of the MBT.

Note. The CIT takes effect 01/01/12, and replaces the Michigan Business Tax (MBT) for most taxpayers. However, businesses that have been approved to receive, have received, or have been assigned certain certified credits may elect to file a return and pay the tax imposed by the MBT in lieu of the CIT until the certified credits are exhausted or extinguished.

Minnesota	No	No	No	Yes
Mississippi	No	Yes	Yes	Yes
Missouri	Yes	No	No	Yes
Montana	No	No	Yes	Yes
Nebraska	No	No	No	No
Nevada	Nevada does not impose a corporate income tax			
New Hampshire	No	No	No	No

Activities Creating Franchise or Income Tax Nexus (Part 10)

Qualification to Do Business/Filing Requirements

Legend:

X	These activities create franchise or income tax nexus
NA	Not applicable
NR	Not reported

In the Case of a Corporation That is Qualified to do Business in State:

	Does the Mere Holding of a Certificate of Authority Subject the Corporation to an Income-Based Tax?	*Does the Mere Holding of a Certificate of Authority Subject the Corporation to a Flat Dollar Amount Minimum Tax?*	*Is a Tax Return Required to Be Filed Even if the Corporation Has Not Yet Begun to Do Business in the State?*	*Is a Tax Return Required to Be Filed Even if the Corporation's Activities Are Protected by P.L. 86-272 (i.e., Must File Return Noting That Corporation Is Protected Under the Public Law)?*
New Jersey	No	Yes	Yes	Yes
New Mexico	No	Yes, $50 franchise tax	Yes	Yes
New York	No	Yes, Form CT 245 or CT 240	Yes	Yes, if authorized to do business in the state
Note. Insufficient facts to make a determination. Nexus is determined on an individual basis; each determination considers the facts and circumstances unique to that specific corporation.				
	Responses apply to New York Franchise Tax			
North Carolina	No	No	Yes	Yes
North Dakota	No	No	No	Yes
Ohio	Ohio does not impose a corporate income tax			
Note: Effective 1/1/2010, the Ohio Franchise Tax was fully phased out and business will be taxed on gross receipts through the Commercial Activity Tax. Details about that tax can be found at: http//tax.ohio.gov/divisions/commercial_activities/index.stm				
Oklahoma	No	No, Oklahoma does not have a minimum income tax. Potential franchise tax may be due.	No	No
Oregon	No	No	No	No
Pennsylvania	No	No	Yes	Yes

Activities Creating Franchise or Income Tax Nexus (Part 10)

Qualification to Do Business/Filing Requirements

Legend:

X	These activities create franchise or income tax nexus
NA	Not applicable
NR	Not reported

In the Case of a Corporation That is Qualified to do Business in State:

	Does the Mere Holding of a Certificate of Authority Subject the Corporation to an Income-Based Tax?	*Does the Mere Holding of a Certificate of Authority Subject the Corporation to a Flat Dollar Amount Minimum Tax?*	*Is a Tax Return Required to Be Filed Even if the Corporation Has Not Yet Begun to Do Business in the State?*	*Is a Tax Return Required to Be Filed Even if the Corporation's Activities Are Protected by P.L. 86-272 (i.e., Must File Return Noting That Corporation Is Protected Under the Public Law)?*
Rhode Island	No	Yes	Yes	NR
South Carolina	No	No	Yes	No
South Dakota	South Dakota does not impose a corporate income tax			
Tennessee	No	Yes	Yes	Yes
Texas	No, per *Rylander v. Bandag Licensing Corp.*, 18 S.W.3d 296, policy is being updated.	No	No	P.L. 86-272 does not apply
Utah	Yes	NA	Yes	Yes
Vermont	No	No	Yes	Yes
Virginia	No	No	Yes	Yes
Washington	Washington does not impose a corporate income tax			
West Virginia	No	No	Yes	Yes
Wisconsin	No	No	Yes	Yes
Wyoming	Wyoming does not impose a corporate income tax			

Activities Creating Franchise or Income Tax Nexus (Part 11)

Other

Legend:

SAF	Same as applicable federal rules
NA	Not applicable
NR	Not reported

	If a Taxpayer Establishes Nexus During the Year, Is It Taxable for the Entire Year (i.e., Must File a Full-Year Return and Include in the Sales Factor Sales That Occurred Prior to Establishing Nexus)?	*Has the State Developed an Income Tax Nexus Questionnaire That Is Sent to Taxpayers That the State Believes May Be Doing Business in the State?*
Alabama	Alabama interprets nexus on case-by-case basis and as broadly as allowed under the Due Process and Commerce Clauses of the United States Constitution	
Alaska	Yes	No
Arizona	Yes	Yes. To obtain a questionnaire, call (602) 716-6453; or visit the ADOR website at http://www.azdor.gov/disclosure/Questionnaire.pdf for a fillable questionnaire. Also, visit the Department's Voluntary Disclosure link at http://www.azdor.gov/Audit/Disclosure.osp
Arkansas	Yes	Yes
California	Yes	Yes. Form FTB 1063A
Colorado	No	No
Connecticut	No written guidance	Yes
Delaware	Yes	Yes
District of Columbia	Yes	Yes
Florida	Yes	Yes
Georgia	Yes	Yes
Hawaii	No	Yes
Idaho	Yes	Yes

Activities Creating Franchise or Income Tax Nexus (Part 11)

Other

Legend:

SAF	Same as applicable federal rules
NA	Not applicable
NR	Not reported

	If a Taxpayer Establishes Nexus During the Year, Is It Taxable for the Entire Year (i.e., Must File a Full-Year Return and Include in the Sales Factor Sales That Occurred Prior to Establishing Nexus)?	*Has the State Developed an Income Tax Nexus Questionnaire That Is Sent to Taxpayers That the State Believes May Be Doing Business in the State?*
Illinois	Yes, DOR Letter Ruling IT96-0056 (3/3/96), p. 3: If a corporation exceeds the standard of "mere solicitation" in Illinois, it loses its immunity and will be liable for income tax and the additional personal property tax replacement income tax for the year.	No
	Nexus determinations can be made only in the context of an audit wherein the auditor would have full access to all pertinent information. Illinois determines "doing business" utilizing the prevailing principles of jurisprudence under the Commerce and Due Process Clauses of the United States Constitution as applied to the facts in each case. For further information see 86 Ill. Admin. Code § 100.9720.	
Indiana	Yes	No
Iowa	Yes	Yes
Kansas	Yes	Yes
Kentucky	Yes	Yes
Louisiana	Yes	Yes
Maine	Yes	Yes
Maryland	Yes	Yes
Massachusetts	NR	Yes, DD96-6. 830 CMR 63.39.1
Michigan (Business Tax)	Yes	Yes, Form 1353, Michigan Department of Treasury Nexus Questionnaire, can be found on Internet at http://www.michigan.gov/documents/1353_2719_7.pdf

Activities Creating Franchise or Income Tax Nexus (Part 11)

Other

Legend:

SAF	Same as applicable federal rules
NA	Not applicable
NR	Not reported

	If a Taxpayer Establishes Nexus During the Year, Is It Taxable for the Entire Year (i.e., Must File a Full-Year Return and Include in the Sales Factor Sales That Occurred Prior to Establishing Nexus)?	*Has the State Developed an Income Tax Nexus Questionnaire That Is Sent to Taxpayers That the State Believes May Be Doing Business in the State?*
Note. The CIT takes effect 01/01/12, and replaces the Michigan Business Tax (MBT) for most taxpayers. However, businesses that have been approved to receive, have received, or have been assigned certain certified credits may elect to file a return and pay the tax imposed by the MBT in lieu of the CIT until the certified credits are exhausted or extinguished.		
Minnesota	Yes	Yes
Mississippi	Yes	No
Missouri	Yes	Yes
Montana	Yes	Yes
Nebraska	Yes	Yes
Nevada	Nevada does not impose a corporate income tax	
New Hampshire	Yes	Yes
New Jersey	No	Yes
New Mexico	Yes	Yes
New York	No	No
	Responses apply to New York Franchise Tax	
North Carolina	Yes	Yes
North Dakota	Yes	Yes, can be found on Internet at www.state.nd.us/taxdtp/genpubs/28819.pdf
Ohio	Ohio does not impose a corporate income tax	

Note: Effective 1/1/2010, the Ohio Franchise Tax was fully phased out and business will be taxed on gross receipts through the Commercial Activity Tax. Details about that tax can be found at: http//tax.ohio.gov/divisions/commercial_activities/index.stm

Activities Creating Franchise or Income Tax Nexus (Part 11)

Other

Legend:

SAF	Same as applicable federal rules
NA	Not applicable
NR	Not reported

	If a Taxpayer Establishes Nexus During the Year, Is It Taxable for the Entire Year (i.e., Must File a Full-Year Return and Include in the Sales Factor Sales That Occurred Prior to Establishing Nexus)?	*Has the State Developed an Income Tax Nexus Questionnaire That Is Sent to Taxpayers That the State Believes May Be Doing Business in the State?*
Oklahoma	Yes	Yes
Oregon	No. If a foreign corporation had no prior activity in Oregon when the tax year started and during the year engaged in activities giving Oregon jurisdiction to tax, the numerator of the sales factor must include sales from the date when Oregon's jurisdiction to tax began. (not protected from state taxation by P.L. 86-272), the numerator of the sales factor must include sales from the date due process nexus arose. If a foreign corporation had no prior activity in Oregon when the tax year started and during the year engaged in activities giving Oregon jurisdiction to tax, the numerator of the sales factor must include sales from the date when Oregon's jurisdiction to tax began.	Yes
Pennsylvania	Yes	Yes
Rhode Island	NR	Yes
South Carolina	Yes	Yes
South Dakota	South Dakota does not impose a corporate income tax	. . . .
Tennessee	Yes	Yes
Texas	No	Yes
Utah	Yes	Yes
Vermont	NR	NR
Virginia	Yes	No

Activities Creating Franchise or Income Tax Nexus (Part 11)

Other

Legend:

SAF Same as applicable federal rules
NA Not applicable
NR Not reported

	If a Taxpayer Establishes Nexus During the Year, Is It Taxable for the Entire Year (i.e., Must File a Full-Year Return and Include in the Sales Factor Sales That Occurred Prior to Establishing Nexus)?	*Has the State Developed an Income Tax Nexus Questionnaire That Is Sent to Taxpayers That the State Believes May Be Doing Business in the State?*
Washington	Washington does not impose a corporate income tax	
West Virginia	Yes	Yes
Wisconsin	Yes	Yes
Wyoming	Wyoming does not impose a corporate income tax	

Activities Creating Nexus for Franchisers

A corporation must have sufficient contact with a state for the state to impose a tax on the corporation. When the activity of the corporation is sufficient to permit the state to impose a tax, the corporation has nexus with the state. Typically, the ownership or rental of property within the state or the presence of employees in the state is sufficient to establish nexus with the state; however, Public Law 86-272 restricts the states' right to impose an income tax on out-of-state corporations in limited situations relating to the solicitation of sales of tangible personal property. Since the business of a franchiser typically does not entail, or is not limited to, the sale of tangible personal property to the franchisee, Public Law 86-272 generally provides no protection for the franchiser.

Because service activities are not protected under Public Law 86-272, most states view any service activity greater than an undefined *de minimis* amount as sufficient to establish nexus with the state. A franchiser typically receives payments from the franchisee for supplies and merchandise and for the right to use a trade name or trademark (or both), as well as for management and accounting services. If any of those services are provided in the state, the corporation will not be protected from taxation under Public Law 86-272. Nexus, however, is not a clearly defined issue. The actual number of visits to the state and the other activities of the corporation within the state, if any, are important determinants of nexus. (See the charts entitled Activities Creating Franchise or Income Tax Nexus in this part for a detailed listing of general activities that create income tax nexus.)

Providing Services to Franchisees

To ensure that the franchisee is providing quality services or goods (or both) and otherwise maintaining the standards associated with the franchiser's trade names and trademarks, most franchisers employ "secret shoppers" (i.e., persons posing as regular shoppers who rate the services and products provided by the franchisee). Although such persons frequently are employees of the franchisers, many franchisers employ unrelated third-party companies to provide secret shopper services. Another service typically provided by franchisers is making equipment and supplies available for special events. For example, a fast-food restaurant franchiser may provide large posters and signs as well as a 50-foot trademarked hot-air balloon for the opening of a franchisee's restaurant.

In P.D. 92-64 [May 4, 1992], the Virginia Tax Commissioner ruled that an out-of-state corporation had nexus in Virginia as a result of the services it provided to its Virginia franchisees. The franchiser had no property in Virginia and received no fees for the franchises it granted in Virginia. The franchiser made only wholesale-level sales to its franchised retailers, and all sales orders were accepted and filled from outside the state. The franchiser did, however, provide technical services in the nature of support, training, and a liaison function to the franchisees. The Tax Commissioner held that because the technical services did not constitute solicitation, the franchiser's activities exceeded the protection of Public Law 86-272.

In an analogous situation involving an out-of-state manufacturer of tangible personal property that sold its products in Virginia through independent distributors, the Virginia Tax Commissioner has ruled that activities which exceed the mere solicitation of sales, and therefore are not protected by Public Law 86-272 (assuming they are not de minimis), include: "serving in a consultant's role for dealers for their product support operations; providing input for dealer business plan development; providing sales coverage analysis; providing dealer operations studies; assessing dealer management capabilities and addressing deficiencies including replacing dealers; assisting dealers in assessing sales personnel; providing technical training to the dealer's customers; and, resolving user, customer and dealer disputes and problems." [Va. P.D. 01-70, May 25, 2001]

In *Subway Real Estate Corp. v. Director of Taxation* [No. 26488 (Hawaii Sup. Ct., Feb. 28, 2006)], the taxpayer was a Delaware corporation responsible for signing and maintaining the leases and subleases for each Subway Sandwich shop in the United States, including Hawaii. Even though the sandwich shop franchisees made the lease payments directly to the owners of the sandwich shop properties, the Hawaii

Supreme Court ruled that the taxpayer was subject to Hawaii's general excise tax on its subleasing activities in Hawaii because it realized substantial economic benefits from the sublease agreements.

In *Norell Services, Inc. v. Indiana Dept. of Revenue* [No. 49T10-9904-TA-23 (Ind. Tax Ct., Sept. 21, 2004)], the Indiana Tax Court ruled that the franchise fees and royalties received by an out-of-state temporary services provider were not subject to Indiana tax because, based on an earlier Department of Revenue letter of finding, the franchiser's in-state activity was not sufficient to create income tax nexus.

Economic Nexus: Licensing of Trademarks and Trade Names

In *Quill Corporation v. North Dakota* [504 U.S. 298 (1992)], the Supreme Court ruled that a corporation satisfies the Commerce Clause's "substantial nexus" requirement only if the taxpayer has a physical presence in the state. Yet, in *Geoffrey, Inc. v. South Carolina Tax Commissioner* [437 S.E.2d 13 (S.C.), *cert. denied*, 114 S. Ct. 550 (1993)], the South Carolina Supreme Court held that a trademark holding company that licensed its intangibles for use in South Carolina had nexus for income tax purposes despite the lack of any tangible property or employees in South Carolina. Geoffrey was the trademark holding company of the toy retailer, Toys "R" Us. Geoffrey was incorporated and domiciled in Delaware and had a license agreement with South Carolina retailers allowing them to use its trademarks and trade names, including the Toys "R" Us trademark, in exchange for a percentage of net sales. The court rejected Geoffrey's claim that it had not purposefully directed its activities toward South Carolina and held that, by licensing intangibles for use in the state and receiving income in exchange for their use, Geoffrey had the minimum connection and substantial nexus with South Carolina required by the Due Process Clause and the Commerce Clause. The *Geoffrey* court did not follow the precedent established by *Quill*, because it believed that ruling applied only to the issue of nexus for sales and use tax purposes.

Since 1993, many states have enacted "economic nexus" standards that are based on the amount of income or sales derived from sources within a state. For example, the Connecticut corporate income tax applies to "[a]ny company that derives income from sources within this state and that has a substantial economic presence within this state, evidenced by a purposeful direction of business toward this state, examined in light of the frequency, quantity and systematic nature of a company's economic contacts with this state, without regard to physical presence, and to the extent permitted by the Constitution of the United States." [Conn. Gen. Stat. § 12-216a] The in-state ownership and use of intangible property by a company in Connecticut would subject it to tax on its income when: (1) the intangible property generates, or is otherwise a source of, gross receipts within the state for the corporation, including through a license or franchise; (2) the activity through which the corporation obtains such gross receipts from its intangible property is purposeful (e.g., a contract with an in-state company); and (3) the corporation's presence within the state, as indicated by its intangible property and its activities with respect to that property, satisfies the bright-line test. The "bright-line test" for determining economic nexus is whether the company had $500,000 or more in business receipts attributable to Connecticut sources during the tax year. [Informational Publication 2010(29.1), Conn. Dept. of Rev. Services, Dec. 28, 2010]

Another approach to the economic nexus concept is a factor presence nexus standard, under which income tax nexus exists if in-state sales exceed a specified threshold. For example, for tax years beginning on or after January 1, 2011, an out-of-state corporation has income tax nexus in California if it has more than $500,000 of sales or 25 percent of its total sales in California. [S.B. 15, Feb. 20. 2009] Effective April 30, 2010, an out-of-state corporation has income tax nexus in Colorado if it has more than $500,000 of sales or 25 percent of its total sales in Colorado. [Colo. Dept. of Rev., Reg. 39-22-301.1, Apr. 10, 2010] Effective June 1, 2010, for purposes of taxing service activities and royalty income, an out-of-state corporation has nexus in Washington if it has more than $250,000 of receipts or at least 25 percent of its total receipts in Washington. [S.B. 6143, Feb. 20. 2009]

In addition, there has been a significant amount of litigation related to the *Geoffrey* court's interpretation of the Commerce Clause's substantial nexus requirement.

In *Lanco, Inc. v. Division of Taxation* [No. A-89-05 (N.J. Sup. Ct., Oct. 12, 2006); *cert. denied*, U.S. Sup. Ct., 06-1236, June 18, 2007], the New Jersey Supreme Court ruled that the Delaware trademark holding corporation of the clothing retailer Lane Bryant (Lanco) had income tax nexus with New Jersey, even though the corporation had no physical presence in the state. The court concluded that the *Quill* physical presence test for sales and use tax nexus did not apply to income taxes.

In *Commissioner v. MBNA America Bank, N.A.* [No. 33049 (W.V. Sup. Ct. of App., Nov. 21, 2006); *cert. denied*, U.S. Sup. Ct., 06-1228, June 18, 2007], the West Virginia Supreme Court of Appeals ruled that a Delaware bank that provided credit card services to customers in West Virginia had income tax nexus in West Virginia, even though it had no physical presence in the state. During the tax years in question, the bank regularly engaged in direct mail, telephone solicitation, and promotion in the state that produced significant gross receipts from its West Virginia customers. The court concluded that the *Quill* physical presence test did not apply to taxes other than sales and use taxes and that MBNA had "a significant economic presence sufficient to meet the substantial nexus" test under the Commerce Clause.

In *Capital One Bank and Capital One F.S.B. v. Commissioner of Revenue* [No. SJC-10105 (Mass. Sup. Jud. Ct., Jan. 8, 2009); *cert. denied*, U.S. Sup. Ct., No. 08-1169, June 22, 2009], the Massachusetts Supreme Judicial Court held that imposition of the Massachusetts financial institution excise (income) tax "is determined not by *Quill's* physical presence test, but by the 'substantial nexus' test articulated in *Complete Auto*." As a result, despite the lack of any physical presence in the state, the two out-of-state credit card banks had substantial nexus in Massachusetts because of their "purposeful, targeted marketing of their credit card business to Massachusetts customers . . . and their receipt of hundreds of millions of dollars in income from millions of transactions involving Massachusetts residents and merchants." See also *Geoffrey, Inc. v. Commissioner of Revenue* [No. SJC-10106, Mass. Sup. Jud. Ct., Jan. 8, 2009; *cert. denied*, U.S. Sup. Ct., No. 08-1207, June 22, 2009)].

In *KFC Corporation v. Iowa Department of Revenue* [No. 09-1032 (Ia. Sup. Ct., Dec. 30, 2010)], the Iowa Supreme Court ruled that the Commerce Clause does not require a physical presence in order to tax the income that a Delaware corporation (KFC) earned from the use of its intangibles in Iowa. The court concluded that the trademarks and other intangibles owned by KFC and licensed for use by independent franchisees doing business in Iowa "would be regarded as having a sufficient connection to Iowa to amount to the functional equivalent of 'physical presence' under *Quill*." The court also concluded that even if the use of the intangibles within the state does not amount to physical presence under *Quill*, the physical presence requirement should not be extended to prevent a state from imposing an income tax on revenue generated from the use of intangibles within the state.

For a more detailed discussion of economic nexus, see the section in this part entitled Activities Creating Franchise or Income Tax Nexus.

In *Sonic Industries v. New Mexico* [No. 26,447 (N.M. Sup. Ct., Aug. 3, 2006)], the New Mexico Supreme Court held that an out-of-state franchiser's receipt of royalty fees paid by in-state franchisees for the right to operate fast food restaurants in New Mexico was not subject to the New Mexico gross receipts tax because the taxpayer's franchising activities constituted out-of-state sales. The state supreme court relied on its earlier decision in *Kmart Corp. v. Taxation & Revenue Department* [No. 27,269 (N.M. Sup. Ct., Dec. 29, 2005)], in which it ruled that the New Mexico gross receipts tax did not apply to the royalties received by an out-of-state intangible holding company for the use of its trademarks in New Mexico. The court reasoned that the franchising agreements between Sonic and its franchisees were comparable to the trademark license agreements in the *Kmart* case. Like the licensed property in *Kmart*, the subject matter of Sonic's franchise agreements was not sold in New Mexico, because the franchise agreements were purchased and signed in Oklahoma and the rights governed by those agreements were then employed in, not moved into, New Mexico.

In Decision of Hearing Officer case No. 200700083-C [Ariz. Dept. of Rev., Mar. 27, 2008], an out-of-state franchiser that received license and royalty fees from Arizona franchisees had sufficient nexus with Arizona to subject it to Arizona corporate income tax, despite the lack of a physical presence in the state. The hearing officer concluded that the *Quill* physical presence test applies only to sales and use taxes.

State-by-State Summary

The following chart summarizes the positions of the states with respect to a number of potential nexus-creating activities. For ease of presentation, the chart has been divided into three parts, as follows:

- Part 1: In-State Training/Bookkeeping Services/Visiting Franchisees
- Part 2: Licensing Intangibles/Promotional Equipment/Secret Shopper Visits
- Part 3: Central Purchasing/Field Training or Evaluations/Meetings/Deliveries

Activities Creating Nexus for Franchisers (Part 1)

In-State Training/Bookkeeping Services/Visiting Franchisees

Legend:

X	These activities create income tax nexus for out-of-state franchisers
NA	Not applicable
NR	Not reported

	Conduct In-State Management Training Courses	*Send Bookkeeping Out of State for Processing*	*Visit Franchisees to Advise on Business Matters*	
			Occasionally	*Frequently*
Alabama	Alabama interprets nexus on case-by-case basis and as broadly as allowed under the Due Process and Commerce Clauses of the United States Constitution			
Alaska	X		X	X
Arizona	X	X	X	X
Arkansas	X			X
California	X		X	X
Colorado	X		X	X
Connecticut				
Delaware	X		X	X
District of Columbia	X	X	X	X
Florida	X	X	X	X
Georgia	X		X	X
Hawaii	X		X	X
Idaho	X			X
Illinois	X		X	X
	See 86 Ill. Admin. Code § 100.9270			
Indiana	X			X
Iowa	X	X	X	X

Activities Creating Nexus for Franchisers (Part 1)

In-State Training/Bookkeeping Services/Visiting Franchisees

Legend:

X	These activities create income tax nexus for out-of-state franchisers
NA	Not applicable
NR	Not reported

			Visit Franchisees to Advise on Business Matters	
	Conduct In-State Management Training Courses	*Send Bookkeeping Out of State for Processing*	*Occasionally*	*Frequently*
Kansas	X		X	X
Kentucky	X	X	X	X
Louisiana	X	X	X	X
Maine	X		X	X
Maryland	X		X	X
Massachusetts	X			X
Michigan (Business Tax)	X	X	X	X

Note. The CIT takes effect 01/01/12, and replaces the Michigan Business Tax (MBT) for most taxpayers. However, businesses that have been approved to receive, have received, or have been assigned certain certified credits may elect to file a return and pay the tax imposed by the MBT in lieu of the CIT until the certified credits are exhausted or extinguished.

Minnesota	X	X	X	X
Mississippi	X			X
Missouri	X			X
Montana	X		X	X
Nebraska	X	X	X	X
Nevada	Nevada does not impose a corporate income tax			
New Hampshire	X		X	X
New Jersey	X		X	X

Activities Creating Nexus for Franchisers (Part 1)

In-State Training/Bookkeeping Services/Visiting Franchisees

Legend:

X	These activities create income tax nexus for out-of-state franchisers
NA	Not applicable
NR	Not reported

	Conduct In-State Management Training Courses	*Send Bookkeeping Out of State for Processing*	*Visit Franchisees to Advise on Business Matters*	
			Occasionally	*Frequently*
New Mexico	X		X	X
New York	X		X	X
North Carolina	X		X	X
North Dakota	X		X	X
Ohio	Ohio does not impose a corporate income tax			
Note: Effective 1/1/2010, the Ohio Franchise Tax was fully phased out and business will be taxed on gross receipts through the Commercial Activity Tax. Details about that tax can be found at: http//tax.ohio.gov/divisions/commercial_activities/index.stm				
Oklahoma	X			
Oregon	X		X	X
Pennsylvania	X		X	X
Rhode Island	X		X	X
South Carolina	X		X	X
South Dakota	South Dakota does not impose a corporate income tax			
Tennessee	X		X	X
Texas	X		X	X
Utah	X		X	X
Vermont	X			X
Virginia	X		X	X

Activities Creating Nexus for Franchisers (Part 1)

In-State Training/Bookkeeping Services/Visiting Franchisees

Legend:

X — These activities create income tax nexus for out-of-state franchisers

NA — Not applicable

NR — Not reported

	Conduct In-State Management Training Courses	*Send Bookkeeping Out of State for Processing*	*Visit Franchisees to Advise on Business Matters*	
			Occasionally	*Frequently*
Washington	Washington does not impose a corporate income tax			
West Virginia	X	X	X	X
Wisconsin	X		X	X
Wyoming	Wyoming does not impose a corporate income tax			

Activities Creating Nexus for Franchisers (Part 2)

Licensing Intangibles/Promotional Equipment/Secret Shopper Visits

Legend:

X	These items create income tax nexus
NA	Not applicable
NR	Not reported

	Licensing Trademark/Trade Name	*Providing Free-of-Charge Supplies or Equipment for Special Events*	*Occasional "Secret Shopper" Visits by Employees for Quality Control*	*Occasional "Secret Shopper" Visits by Unrelated Third Parties for Quality Control*
Alabama	Alabama interprets nexus on case-by-case basis and as broadly as allowed under the Due Process and Commerce Clauses of the United States Constitution			
Alaska	X	X	X	
Arizona	X	X	X	X
Arkansas	X			
California	X	X	X	X
Colorado	X	X	X	X
Connecticut	No written guidance	No written guidance	No written guidance	No written guidance
Delaware				
District of Columbia	X	X	X	X
Florida	X	X	X	X
Georgia		X	X	X
Hawaii	X	X	X	X
Idaho	X, unless *de minimis*	X, unless *de minimis*		
Illinois	X	X	X	X
	See 86 Ill. Admin. Code § 100.9720			
Indiana		X		
Iowa	X		X	X

Activities Creating Nexus for Franchisers (Part 2)

Licensing Intangibles/Promotional Equipment/Secret Shopper Visits

Legend:

X	These items create income tax nexus
NA	Not applicable
NR	Not reported

	Licensing Trademark/Trade Name	*Providing Free-of-Charge Supplies or Equipment for Special Events*	*Occasional "Secret Shopper" Visits by Employees for Quality Control*	*Occasional "Secret Shopper" Visits by Unrelated Third Parties for Quality Control*
Kansas	X	X	X	X
Kentucky	X	X	X	X
Louisiana	X		X	X
Maine			X	X
Maryland		If ongoing and continuous	If ongoing and continuous	If ongoing and continuous
Massachusetts	X, see DD 96-2			
Michigan (Business Tax)		X	X	X
Note. The CIT takes effect 01/01/12, and replaces the Michigan Business Tax (MBT) for most taxpayers. However, businesses that have been approved to receive, have received, or have been assigned certain certified credits may elect to file a return and pay the tax imposed by the MBT in lieu of the CIT until the certified credits are exhausted or extinguished.				
Minnesota	X	X	X	X
Mississippi	X	X		
Missouri	X			
Montana	X	X	X	X
Nebraska		X	X	
Nevada	Nevada does not impose a corporate income tax			
New Hampshire	X		X	X
New Jersey	X	X	X	X
New Mexico	X	X	X	X

Activities Creating Nexus for Franchisers (Part 2)
Licensing Intangibles/Promotional Equipment/Secret Shopper Visits

Legend:

X	These items create income tax nexus
NA	Not applicable
NR	Not reported

	Licensing Trademark/Trade Name	*Providing Free-of-Charge Supplies or Equipment for Special Events*	*Occasional "Secret Shopper" Visits by Employees for Quality Control*	*Occasional "Secret Shopper" Visits by Unrelated Third Parties for Quality Control*
New York			X	
North Carolina	X		X	X
North Dakota	X	X	X	
Ohio	Ohio does not impose a corporate income tax			
Note: Effective 1/1/2010, the Ohio Franchise Tax was fully phased out and business will be taxed on gross receipts through the Commercial Activity Tax. Details about that tax can be found at: http//tax.ohio.gov/divisions/commercial_activities/index.stm				
Oklahoma	X			X
Oregon	X. The franchise agreement itself is an intangible asset located in Oregon from which the franchiser usually derives income, making the franchisee subject to Oregon corporation income tax.	X, if franchiser retains ownership of equipment or supplies not consumed at special event	X	
Pennsylvania		X	X	X
Rhode Island	X		X	X
South Carolina	X	X	X	X
South Dakota	South Dakota does not impose a corporate income tax			
Tennessee				
Texas		X	X	X

Activities Creating Nexus for Franchisers (Part 2)

Licensing Intangibles/Promotional Equipment/Secret Shopper Visits

Legend:

X	These items create income tax nexus
NA	Not applicable
NR	Not reported

	Licensing Trademark/Trade Name	*Providing Free-of-Charge Supplies or Equipment for Special Events*	*Occasional "Secret Shopper" Visits by Employees for Quality Control*	*Occasional "Secret Shopper" Visits by Unrelated Third Parties for Quality Control*
Utah	X	X	X	X
Vermont	X			
Virginia	X	X	X	X
Washington	Washington does not impose a corporate income tax			
West Virginia				
Wisconsin	X	X	X	X
Wyoming	Wyoming does not impose a corporate income tax			

Activities Creating Nexus for Franchisers (Part 3)

Central Purchasing/Field Training or Evaluations/Meetings/Deliveries

Legend:

X	These activities create franchise or income tax nexus for out-of-state franchisers.
NA	Not applicable
NR	Not reported

	Central Purchasing	*Field Training*	*Field Operations Evaluations*	*In-State Regional Meetings*	*Delivery of Products via Company-Owned Vehicles*
Alabama	Alabama interprets nexus on case-by-case basis and as broadly as allowed under the Due Process and Commerce Clauses of the United States Constitution				
Alaska		X	X	X	X
Arizona	X	X	X		
Arkansas		X	X		X
California	X, depends on facts and circumstances	X	X	X	X
Colorado		X	X	X	X
Connecticut	No written guidance	No written guidance	No written guidance	No written guidance	No written guidance
Delaware			X	X	X
District of Columbia	X	X	X	X	X
Florida	X	X	X	X	X
Georgia		X	X	X	X
Hawaii		X	X	X	X
Idaho	X	X, in-state training if not occasional or *de minimis* will create nexus.	X, unless *de minimis*	X, if not occasional or *de minimis*	X
Illinois	X	X	X	X	X
	See 86 Ill. Admin. Code § 100.9720				
Indiana		X	X	X	

Activities Creating Nexus for Franchisers (Part 3)

Central Purchasing/Field Training or Evaluations/Meetings/Deliveries

Legend:

X	These activities create franchise or income tax nexus for out-of-state franchisers.
NA	Not applicable
NR	Not reported

	Central Purchasing	*Field Training*	*Field Operations Evaluations*	*In-State Regional Meetings*	*Delivery of Products via Company-Owned Vehicles*
Iowa		X	X	X	
Kansas	X	X	X	X	X
Kentucky	X	X	X	X	X
Louisiana				X	X
Maine	X		X	X	
Maryland					No, see ADR No. 2 III B.3(c).
Massachusetts	X			Depends on facts	
Michigan (Business Tax)	X	X	X	X	X
Note. The CIT takes effect 01/01/12, and replaces the Michigan Business Tax (MBT) for most taxpayers. However, businesses that have been approved to receive, have received, or have been assigned certain certified credits may elect to file a return and pay the tax imposed by the MBT in lieu of the CIT until the certified credits are exhausted or extinguished.					
Minnesota	X	X	X	X	
Mississippi		X			
Missouri		X	X	X	X
Montana	X	X	X	X	
Nebraska	X	X	X	X	
Nevada	Nevada does not impose a corporate income tax.				
New Hampshire		X	X	X	X
New Jersey	X	X	X	X	X

Activities Creating Nexus for Franchisers (Part 3)

Central Purchasing/Field Training or Evaluations/Meetings/Deliveries

Legend:

X	These activities create franchise or income tax nexus for out-of-state franchisers.
NA	Not applicable
NR	Not reported

	Central Purchasing	*Field Training*	*Field Operations Evaluations*	*In-State Regional Meetings*	*Delivery of Products via Company-Owned Vehicles*
New Mexico		X	X	X	X
New York	No, however, the franchiser may have nexus by being required or permitted to file a combined report with the franchisee if the substantial intercompany transactions test is met due to the purchase made by the franchisee from the franchiser and the other requirements of combined reporting are met.	X	X	X	X, unless activity is *de minimis*.
	Responses apply to New York Franchise Tax				
North Carolina		X	X	X	
North Dakota		X			
Ohio	Ohio does not impose a corporate income tax				
Note: Effective 1/1/2010, the Ohio Franchise Tax was fully phased out and business will be taxed on gross receipts through the Commercial Activity Tax. Details about that tax can be found at: http//tax.ohio.gov/divisions/commercial_activities/index.stm					
Oklahoma				X	
Oregon		X	X	X	X
Pennsylvania	X	X	X	X	X

Activities Creating Nexus for Franchisers (Part 3)

Central Purchasing/Field Training or Evaluations/Meetings/Deliveries

Legend:

X	These activities create franchise or income tax nexus for out-of-state franchisers.
NA	Not applicable
NR	Not reported

	Central Purchasing	*Field Training*	*Field Operations Evaluations*	*In-State Regional Meetings*	*Delivery of Products via Company-Owned Vehicles*
Rhode Island				X	
South Carolina	X	X	X	X	
South Dakota	South Dakota does not impose a corporate income tax				
Tennessee					
Texas	X	X	X	X	X
Utah		X	X	X	
Vermont			X		
Virginia		X	X	X	X
Washington	Washington does not impose a corporate income tax				
West Virginia	X	X			
Wisconsin		X	X	X	
Wyoming	Wyoming does not impose a corporate income tax				

Trucking Activities That Create Nexus

The state in which a business is incorporated has the jurisdiction to tax the corporation, regardless of the volume of business activity that the corporation conducts within that state. Whether a state can tax the income of a business that is incorporated in another state depends on whether the relationship between the state and the corporation is sufficient to establish nexus. Nexus describes the degree of business activity that must be present before a taxing jurisdiction has the right to impose a tax on a corporation. The measure of the relationship that is necessary to create nexus is defined by state statute, case law, and the Due Process Clause and the Commerce Clause of the U.S. Constitution. Typically, nexus for income tax purposes is established when a corporation uses owned or leased property in a state or employs personnel in a state.

Delivery in Company-Owned Vehicles

A corporation generally has constitutional nexus in any state in which it has property or employees located on a continuous basis. Thus, a number of state courts have held that the regular and systematic presence of company-owned delivery trucks driven by company employees is sufficient to create sales and use tax nexus. [E.g., *Brown's Furniture, Inc. v. Wagner*, No. 78195 (Ill. Apr. 18, 1996); *Town Crier, Inc. v. Zehnder*, No. 1-98-4251 (Ill. App. Ct. June 30, 2000); *John Swenson Granite Co. v. State Tax Assessor*, 685 A.2d 425 (Me. Super. Ct. 1996). But see *Miller Bros. Co. v. Maryland*, 347 U.S. 340 (1954) (ruling that "occasional delivery" of goods with no solicitation other than the "incidental effects of general advertising" was not sufficient to create nexus under the Due Process Clause).]

For income tax purposes, Public Law 86-272 shields an out-of-state corporation from taxation if its only in-state activity is solicitation of orders by company representatives for sales of tangible personal property, which orders are sent outside the state for approval or rejection, and if approved, are filled by shipment or delivery from a point outside the state. Over the years, taxpayers have taken the position that the phrase *shipment or delivery* implies that a seller is protected by Public Law 86-272 regardless of whether it ships the goods into the state using a common carrier or its own delivery trucks. Some states, however, have taken the position that the in-state delivery of goods in the seller's own delivery trucks exceeds solicitation and therefore is an activity that is not protected by Public Law 86-272.

State supreme courts in Massachusetts and Virginia have ruled that deliveries in company-owned trucks is a protected activity under Public Law 86-272 [*National Private Truck Council v. Virginia Department of Taxation*, 253 Va. 74, 480 S.E.2d 500 (1997); and *National Private Truck Council v. Commissioner of Revenue*, 688 N.E.2d 936 (Mass. 1997), *cert. denied*]. In 2001, the MTC revised its Statement of Information Concerning Practices of Multistate Tax Commission and Signatory States Under Public Law 86-272 by removing from the list of unprotected activities the following item: "Shipping or delivering goods into this state by means of private vehicle, rail, water, air or other carrier, irrespective of whether shipment or delivery fee or other charge is imposed, directly or indirectly, upon the purchaser." Several state revenue departments have also indicated that deliveries using company-owned trucks is protected by Public Law 86-272 [Rev. Rul. 24-01-01, Neb. Dept. of Rev. (Feb. 22, 2001); Decision No. 2005-05-10-22, Okla. Tax Comm'n. (May 10, 2005); and Ala. Reg. 810-27-1-4-.19 (Feb. 28, 2006)].

Although deliveries may be a protected activity, other activities of a delivery truck driver, such as collecting payments or accepting returns (back-hauling), are likely not protected by Public Law 86-272. For example, in *Asher Inc. v. Division of Taxation* [No. 004061-2003 (N.J. Tax Ct., Jan. 5, 2006)], the New Jersey Tax Court ruled that Public Law 86-272 did not protect the New Jersey activities of a Pennsylvania company's delivery drivers, which included picking up damaged or returned goods and the collection of delinquent accounts. These activities were not ancillary to the solicitation of sales and were not sufficiently *de minimis* to avoid the loss of immunity under the standard established by the Supreme Court in *Wrigley*.

Likewise, In P.D. 08-168 [Va. Dept. of Taxn., Sept. 11, 2008], the Virginia Department of Taxation ruled that an out-of-state mail-order and Internet vendor that uses unrelated third party contract carriers to make deliveries would establish income tax nexus if the activities of the contract carriers, which include unpacking a purchased item at the customer's home, providing minor setup services, and inspecting the product for quality and damage, go beyond the making of sales and are not protected by Public Law 86-272.

Trucking Companies and Common Carriers

The business activity of a trucking company or common carrier is unusual in that it is conducted across a number of states and the in-state activity can vary significantly from state to state. For example, a customer could hire a trucking company to pick up goods in State *A* and deliver the goods to State Z. In providing that transportation service, the company's truck may drive through several other states. The activities in those other states may be limited to driving on the highways, or they may extend to stopping for a meal, purchasing fuel, resting, and, on the return trip, picking up goods for back-hauling. Alternatively, the company may contract with independent truckers that use their trucks and drivers to provide the transportation services to its customers. As a result, the trucking company may be providing a service in the state, but it does not directly own or rent the vehicles that travel through the state, nor does it have any employees providing services within the state.

In *Spector Motor Service, Inc. v. O'Connor* [340 U.S. 602 (1950)], the taxpayer, a Missouri corporation engaged exclusively in interstate trucking, transported freight by motor truck. The tax at issue was the Connecticut franchise tax imposed on the corporation's franchise for the privilege of carrying on exclusively interstate transportation in the state. The U.S. Supreme Court concluded, as it had done in the past, that taxes on the privilege of carrying on a business that was exclusively interstate in character must be struck down.

In 1977, the Supreme Court overruled the *Spector* decision in *Complete Auto Transit, Inc. v. Brady.* [430 U.S. 274 (1977)] In its decision, the Court stated, "Not only has the philosophy underlying the [*Spector*] rule been rejected, but the rule itself has been stripped of any practical significance." The Court acknowledged that "net income from the interstate operations of a foreign corporation may be subjected to state taxation provided the levy is not discriminatory and is properly apportioned to local activities." [430 U.S. at 285 (citing *Northwestern Cement Co. v. Minnesota,* 358 U.S. 450 (1959))] Moreover, the Court concluded that, in applying the rule of *Northwestern Cement* to the facts of *Spector,* it was clear that Connecticut could have taxed Spector's apportioned net income. In other words, the Court concluded that a foreign interstate trucking company's income attributable to its business activities within a state could be subject to tax.

In *Commonwealth v. B.J. McAdams, Inc.* [317 S.E.2d 788 (Va. 1984)], the Virginia Supreme Court held that Virginia's income tax laws are constitutional as applied to common carriers whose business is purely interstate in nature and takes them through the state. The court found that the laws provide fair and reasonable compensation to Virginia for services and benefits provided to interstate carriers that use the state's highways.

If a state provides that the mere use of its highways creates nexus, it generally provides that a minimum highway use threshold must be satisfied before nexus is established. In other words, irregular and infrequent use of the highways typically would not create nexus.

Under the rules adopted by a number of other states, a trucking company or common carrier does not establish nexus unless its operations within the state include pickups and deliveries that begin or end in the state. For example, in *Erieview Cartage, Inc. v. Department of Revenue* [No. 1-93-2565 (Ill. App. Ct. Apr. 24, 1996)], an Illinois appellate court held that a transportation company was subject to Illinois corporate income tax on deliveries and pickups in Illinois because it derived income from furnishing transportation services in the state; however, the company was not subject to tax on income from shipments that merely passed through the state (i.e., shipments that did not originate or terminate in Illinois).

Similarly, in *Aloha Freightways Inc. v. Commissioner of Revenue* [701 N.E.2d 961 (Mass. 1998)], the Massachusetts Supreme Judicial Court affirmed the decision of the Massachusetts Appellate Tax Board holding that an Illinois-based shipping company had sufficient nexus with Massachusetts, because its in-state delivery and pickup services were regular, ongoing, and substantial during the tax year. During 1996, the taxpayer made 54 trips to Massachusetts, serviced customers in 32 separate Massachusetts cities and towns, and logged 10,926 miles on Massachusetts roads.

In *Cruise International Corp. v. Pennsylvania* [No. 667 F.R. 2004 (Pa. Commw. Ct, Jan. 18, 2007)], the taxpayer (Cruise) was a broker incorporated outside Pennsylvania and headquartered in New Jersey. Cruise contracted with independent truck drivers to make deliveries in Pennsylvania and other states for third party vendors. For example, in 1995, the independent truck drivers hired by Cruise made 242 trips back and forth and through Pennsylvania, totaling 15,000 miles. The truck drivers were independent contractors who owned the trucks used to make the deliveries. Cruise did not have any offices, employees, customers, or real or personal property in Pennsylvania. The Pennsylvania Commonwealth Court concluded that Cruise was engaged in the transportation of property in and through Pennsylvania and, through its lease agreements, it was using and employing property in Pennsylvania to accomplish its corporate purposes. As a consequence, Cruise had sufficient nexus with the state to be subject to the Pennsylvania franchise tax.

In Revenue Ruling 24-08-1 [Apr. 9, 2008], the Nebraska Department of Revenue ruled that trucking companies transporting goods over Nebraska roads are subject to the Nebraska corporate income tax, because their services are physically performed in Nebraska, and such services are not protected by Public Law 86-272. Under a *de minimis* rule, however, a trucking company is not required to apportion income to Nebraska if, during the course of the income year, the company neither (1) owns nor rents any real or personal property in this state, except mobile property; nor (2) makes any pick-ups or deliveries within this state; nor (3) travels more than 25,000 mobile property miles within this state; provided that the total mobile property miles traveled within this state during the income year does not exceed 3 percent of the total mobile property miles traveled in all states by the trucking company during that period; nor (4) makes more than 12 trips into this state.

Leased Trucks

In general, the ownership of business property in a state is sufficient to create nexus. In the case of leased property, the lessee is subject to the state's jurisdiction because the property is being used in the state. Sufficient nexus may also be established for the lessor because of the in-state presence of owned business property. In the case of mobile property, such as trucks, the lessor typically has no control over where the property will be used. Moreover, unless otherwise specified in the lease agreement, the lessee may be under no contractual obligation to provide the lessor with any information about where the property has been used at any time during the lease. As a consequence, many states provide that an isolated landing or trip through the state will not create nexus. The presence of leased property in the state on a regular or systematic basis, however, is typically sufficient nexus with the state to subject the lessor to the state's corporate income tax. Therefore, in negotiating lease agreements, the lessor should annually require the lessee to supply the appropriate information about the states in which the property is used during the tax period. Without that information, the lessor cannot determine the states with which nexus has been established or compute its apportionment factors in the various states.

In *Airoldi Bros., Inc. v. Illinois Department of Revenue* [Admin. Hearing Decision No. 98-IT-0330 (Ill. Dep't of Revenue Sept. 29, 2000)], the Illinois Department of Revenue ruled that a Wisconsin truck leasing company whose customers used its trucks in Illinois did not have income tax nexus in Illinois.

On the other hand, in *Truck Renting & Leasing Association, Inc. v. Commissioner of Revenue* [No. SJC-08308 (Mass. Apr. 17, 2001)], the Massachusetts Supreme Judicial Court ruled that the imposition of the Massachusetts corporate income tax on an out-of-state corporation whose leased trucks operated in Massachusetts violated neither the Due Process Clause nor the Commerce Clause of the U.S. Constitution, even though the lessor had no physical presence in Massachusetts beyond the presence of the leased trucks. By providing registration and licensing services that allowed the lessees to operate the trucks in Massachusetts, the out-of-state lessee was purposefully availing itself of the privilege of doing business in the state, as required by the Due Process Clause. In addition, the physical presence of the taxpayer's trucks within the state on a regular and systematic basis created a substantial nexus, as required by the Commerce Clause.

In a case involving mobile property other than trucks, the Idaho Supreme Court held that an out-of-state corporation that leased railcars to railroads operating within Idaho did not have nexus in Idaho [*TTX Co. v. Idaho State Tax Commission* [128 Idaho 483 (1996)]. Likewise, in both *Comdisco, Inc. v. Indiana Department of Revenue* [No. 49T10-9903-TA-19, Ind. Tax Ct. Dec. 8, 2002)] and *Enterprise Leasing Company of Chicago v. Indiana Department of Revenue* [No. 49T10-9807-TA-74, Ind. Tax Ct. Dec. 8, 2002)], the Indiana Tax Court ruled that two out-of-state leasing companies were not subject to Indiana tax on income from equipment and autos leased to Indiana customers, because their ownership of the leased property was the companies' only contact with the state. The out-of-state leasing companies did not exercise control over the leased equipment, and were not active participants in the leasing activities within the state.

Finally, in *Alabama Dept. of Revenue vs. Union Tank Car Co.* [No. 2050652 (Ala. Ct. of Civ. App., April 13, 2007)], the taxpayer (Union Tank) was a Delaware corporation that was headquartered in Illinois. Union Tank manufactured specialty railroad cars in Illinois and Texas and leased them to customers nationwide. Some of Union Tank's leased railcars were used to transport materials through Alabama and to destinations within Alabama. None of the railcars were used strictly within Alabama. The Department contended that Union Tank was subject to Alabama income tax, because the operative statute imposes an income tax on "[e]very corporation doing business in Alabama or deriving income from sources within Alabama, including income from property located in Alabama." The Alabama Court of Civil Appeals concluded, however, that Union Tank "derived income from the lease transactions in Illinois, not from sources in Alabama." Union Tank executed its lease contracts in Illinois, the railcars were picked up in Illinois or Texas, and the lessees made lease payments to Union Tank in Illinois. The amount of the lease payments were fixed, and UTCC had no control over where the railcars were used after they had been leased.

State-by-State Summary

The following chart indicates whether a number of activities, such as trucks passing through the state on a regular or irregular basis, the driver's residence, and in-state pickup or delivery of goods, create nexus with the state. The states use a variety of criteria in determining whether a multistate trucking company's activities are sufficient to create nexus. Most of the responding states indicated that nexus is created by trucks passing through the state on a regular basis.

Trucking Activities That Create Nexus

Legend:

X	These activities create income tax nexus
NA	Not applicable
NR	Not reported

	Company-Owned Trucks Pass Through State Without Delivering or Picking up Goods			*Company-Owned Trucks Are Used to:*	
	More Than 6 Times per Year	*More Than 12 Times per Year*	*Hire Unrelated Trucking Company to Deliver or Pick-up Goods*	*Back-Haul Goods Originating in State*	*Deliver or Pick-up Goods in State*
Alabama	Alabama interprets nexus on case-by-case basis and as broadly as allowed under the Due Process and Commerce Clauses of the United States Constitution				
Alaska			X	X	X
Arizona			Depends	X	X
Arkansas				X	X
California	See Cal. Code Regs., title 18, § 25137-11			X	X
Colorado		X	X	X	X
Connecticut	No written guidance	No written guidance	No written guidance	No written guidance	No written guidance
Delaware					X
District of Columbia			X	X	X
Florida	X	X		X	X
Georgia				X	X
Hawaii	NA	NA			X
Idaho		X, or travel more than 25,000 miles in state or total miles in state exceed 3% of total miles traveled in all states during the tax period			

Trucking Activities That Create Nexus

Legend:

X	These activities create income tax nexus
NA	Not applicable
NR	Not reported

	Company-Owned Trucks Pass Through State Without Delivering or Picking up Goods			*Company-Owned Trucks Are Used to:*	
	More Than 6 Times per Year	*More Than 12 Times per Year*	*Hire Unrelated Trucking Company to Deliver or Pick-up Goods*	*Back-Haul Goods Originating in State*	*Deliver or Pick-up Goods in State*
Illinois	X	X			
	Nexus determinations can only be made in the context of an audit wherein the auditor would have full access to all pertinent information. Please note that Illinois determines "doing business" utilizing the prevailing principles of jurisprudence under the Commerce and Due Process Clauses of the United States Constitution as applied to the facts in each case. For further information, see 86 Ill. Admin. Code § 100.9720.				
Indiana	X	X, no threshold			
Iowa	X	X			
Kansas			X, no nexus if Taxpayer hires driver who owns truck that makes deliveries	X	
Kentucky				X	X
Louisiana		X		X	X
Maine				X	
Maryland	X	X	X		X
Massachusetts		X		Depends on facts	Depends on facts

Trucking Activities That Create Nexus

Legend:

X	These activities create income tax nexus
NA	Not applicable
NR	Not reported

	Company-Owned Trucks Pass Through State Without Delivering or Picking up Goods			*Company-Owned Trucks Are Used to:*	
	More Than 6 Times per Year	*More Than 12 Times per Year*	*Hire Unrelated Trucking Company to Deliver or Pick-up Goods*	*Back-Haul Goods Originating in State*	*Deliver or Pick-up Goods in State*
Michigan (Business Tax)	X	X	No nexus as long as activity is not significantly associated with taxpayer's ability to establish and maintain a market in the state.	X	X
Note. The CIT takes effect 01/0112, and replaces the Michigan Business Tax (MBT) for most taxpayers. However, businesses that have been approved to receive, have received, or have been assigned certain certified credits may elect to file a return and pay the tax imposed by the MBT in lieu of the CIT until the certified credits are exhausted or extinguished.					
Minnesota			X	X	X
Mississippi					X
Missouri		X	X	X	X
Montana		X, or 25,000 miles within the state annually		X	
Nebraska	This activity may create nexus for trucking companies. See Revenue Ruling 24-08-01	This activity may create nexus for trucking companies. See Revenue Ruling 24-08-01		X	X
Nevada	Nevada does not impose a corporate income tax.				
New Hampshire				X	X
New Jersey			X	X	X

Trucking Activities That Create Nexus

Legend:
X These activities create income tax nexus
NA Not applicable
NR Not reported

	Company-Owned Trucks Pass Through State Without Delivering or Picking up Goods			*Company-Owned Trucks Are Used to:*	
	More Than 6 Times per Year	*More Than 12 Times per Year*	*Hire Unrelated Trucking Company to Deliver or Pick-up Goods*	*Back-Haul Goods Originating in State*	*Deliver or Pick-up Goods in State*
New Mexico		X, unless own no property in state other than mobile, make no pickups or delivery in state, travel no more than 25,000 miles in state, miles traveled do not exceed 3% of all miles, and make no more than 12 trips/year into state.			
New York				X, 3 or more	X, 3 or more
North Carolina			X	X	X
North Dakota		More than 12 trips into state, 3% of total miles, or 25,000 miles within the state annually		X	X
Ohio	Ohio does not impose a corporate income tax				
Note: Effective 1/1/2010, the Ohio Franchise Tax was fully phased out and business will be taxed on gross receipts through the Commercial Activity Tax. Details about that tax can be found at: http//tax.ohio.gov/divisions/commercial_activities/index.stm					
Oklahoma	X	X		X	X
Oregon		X			

Trucking Activities That Create Nexus

Legend:

X	These activities create income tax nexus
NA	Not applicable
NR	Not reported

	Company-Owned Trucks Pass Through State Without Delivering or Picking up Goods			*Company-Owned Trucks Are Used to:*	
	More Than 6 Times per Year	*More Than 12 Times per Year*	*Hire Unrelated Trucking Company to Deliver or Pick-up Goods*	*Back-Haul Goods Originating in State*	*Deliver or Pick-up Goods in State*
Pennsylvania		There is no limit on trips if there are no pickups or deliveries. If there are pickups or deliveries, then the trucking company is subject to tax reporting if it either: (1) makes at least one trip with a pickup or delivery and also has 50,000 loaded annual Pennsylvania miles or (2) makes more than 12 trips with pickups or deliveries and has a Pennsylvania mileage apportionment factor of more than 5%.		There is no limit on trips if there are no pickups or deliveries. If there are pickups or deliveries, then the trucking company is subject to tax reporting if it either: (1) makes at least one trip with a pickup or delivery and also has 50,000 loaded annual Pennsylvania miles or (2) makes more than 12 trips with pickups or deliveries and has a Pennsylvania mileage apportionment factor of more than 5%.	
Rhode Island					X
South Carolina		X, South CarolinaCode Sec. § 12-6-4920			
South Dakota	South Dakota does not impose a corporate income tax				
Tennessee		Must have intra-state receipts (both pick-up and delivery in state)			

Trucking Activities That Create Nexus

Legend:
X — These activities create income tax nexus
NA — Not applicable
NR — Not reported

	Company-Owned Trucks Pass Through State Without Delivering or Picking up Goods			*Company-Owned Trucks Are Used to:*	
	More Than 6 Times per Year	*More Than 12 Times per Year*	*Hire Unrelated Trucking Company to Deliver or Pick-up Goods*	*Back-Haul Goods Originating in State*	*Deliver or Pick-up Goods in State*
Texas			X, unless common carrier	X, related to sales only	X, related to sales only
Utah		X, travel > 25,000 mobile property miles and in-state mileage traveled > 3% of total revenue miles traveled (MTC rule)			
Vermont					
Virginia		X, or 50,000 miles or 5% of miles, see Va. Code § 58.1-417			
Washington	Washington does not impose a corporate income tax				
West Virginia				X	X
Wisconsin	Depends on facts	Depends on facts	Depends on facts	X	Depends on facts
Wyoming	Wyoming does not impose a corporate income tax				

Activities Creating Nexus for Financial Institutions

The state in which a business is incorporated has the jurisdiction to tax the corporation, regardless of the amount of business activity that is conducted within the state. Whether a state has the right to tax the income of a business that is incorporated in another state depends on the relationship between that state and the corporation. When a corporation's income is derived partly from property that is owned, or business that is conducted, in other states, the corporation will be subject to income tax if sufficient nexus is established with the state.

Constitutional Nexus

Nexus describes the degree of business activity that must be present before a taxing jurisdiction has the right to impose a tax on a corporation. The measure of the relationship that is necessary to create nexus is defined by state statute, case law, and the Due Process Clause and the Commerce Clause of the U.S. Constitution. Typically, sufficient nexus for income tax purposes is present when a corporation uses owned or leased property in the state or employs personnel in the state (if the extent of such in-state activities is not considered to be *de minimis*).

Two nexus requirements must be met for a state tax to be constitutionally valid. First, connection must be established between the transaction being taxed and the taxing state. Second, there must be a connection between the taxpayer and the taxing state. Under the Due Process Clause, the connection requirements are met based on a minimal connection standard. The minimal connection standard is met if the entity purposefully directs its activity into a jurisdiction. A more stringent connection standard exists under the Commerce Clause, which requires the taxpayer to have a "substantial nexus" in the state before the requisite connection is established.

Public Law 86-272

Public Law 86-272 prohibits a state from taxing the income of a corporation if the corporation's only business activities within the state consist of the solicitation of orders for sales of tangible personal property that are sent outside the state for approval and are filled and shipped from outside the state.

Immunity from an interstate income tax is limited under Public Law 86-272 to sales of tangible personal property. Because property ownership is not a protected activity, a corporation will not be protected under Public Law 86-272 if it owns tangible property that is not ancillary to soliciting orders or real property in the state. More important, leases, rentals, and other dispositions of tangible personal property are not protected. In addition, sales, leases, rentals, or other dispositions of real property and intangible property, as well as sales of services, are not provided immunity under Public Law 86-272.

Because financial institutions provide services, the protection under Public Law 86-272 is not available to them. As a result, solicitation of financial services by salespersons within a state (if such activities are not *de minimis*) creates nexus for a financial institution.

Economic Nexus

In *Quill*, the Supreme Court ruled that a corporation satisfies the Commerce Clause's "substantial nexus" requirement only if the taxpayer has a physical presence in the state. Yet, in *Geoffrey, Inc. v. South Carolina Tax Commissioner* [437 S.E.2d 13 (S.C.), *cert. denied*, 114 S. Ct. 550 (1993)], the South Carolina Supreme Court held that a trademark holding company that licensed its intangibles for use in South Carolina had nexus for income tax purposes despite the lack of any tangible property or employees in South Carolina. Geoffrey was the trademark holding company of the toy retailer, Toys "R" Us. Geoffrey was incorporated and domiciled in Delaware and had a license agreement with South Carolina retailers allowing them to use its trademarks and trade names, including the Toys "R" Us trademark, in exchange for a percentage of net sales. The court rejected Geoffrey's claim that it had not purposefully directed its activities toward South Carolina and held that, by licensing intangibles for use in the state and receiving income in exchange for their use, Geoffrey had the minimum connection and substantial nexus with South Carolina required by the Due Process Clause and the Commerce Clause. The *Geoffrey* court did not follow the precedent established by *Quill* because it believed that ruling applied only to the issue of nexus for sales and use tax purposes.

Since 1993, many states have enacted "economic nexus" standards that are based on the amount of income or sales derived from sources within a state. For example, the Connecticut corporate income tax applies to "[a]ny company that derives income from sources within this state and that has a substantial economic presence within this state, evidenced by a purposeful direction of business toward this state, examined in light of the frequency, quantity and systematic nature of a company's economic contacts with this state, without regard to physical presence, and to the extent permitted by the Constitution of the United States." [Conn. Gen. Stat. § 12-216a] The "bright-line test" for determining economic nexus is whether the company had $500,000 or more in business receipts attributable to Connecticut sources during the tax year. [Informational Publication 2010(29.1), Conn. Dept. of Rev. Services, Dec. 28, 2010]

Another approach to the economic nexus concept is a factor presence nexus standard, under which income tax nexus exists if in-state sales exceed a specified threshold. For example, for tax years beginning on or after January 1, 2011, an out-of-state corporation has income tax nexus in California if it has more than $500,000 of sales or 25 percent of its total sales in California. [S.B. 15, Feb. 20. 2009] Effective April 30, 2010, an out-of-state corporation has income tax nexus in Colorado if it has more than $500,000 of sales or 25 percent of its total sales in Colorado. [Colo. Dept. of Rev., Reg. 39-22-301.1, Apr. 10, 2010] Effective June 1, 2010, for purposes of taxing service activities and royalty income, an out-of-state corporation has nexus in Washington if it has more than $250,000 of receipts or at least 25 percent of its total receipts in Washington. [S.B. 6143, Feb. 20. 2009]

There has also been a significant amount of litigation related to the *Geoffrey* court's interpretation of the Commerce Clause's substantial nexus requirement.

In *Lanco, Inc. v. Division of Taxation* [908 A.2d 176 (N.J. 2006); *cert. denied*, U.S. Sup. Ct., 06-1236, June 18, 2007], the New Jersey Supreme Court ruled that the Delaware trademark holding company of the clothing retailer Lane Bryant had income tax nexus in New Jersey, even though it had no physical presence in the state. The court concluded that "the better interpretation of *Quill* is the one adopted by those states that limit the Supreme Court's holding to sales and use taxes. The court also stated that "we do not believe that the Supreme Court intended to create a universal physical-presence requirement for state taxation under the Commerce Clause.

In *Tax Commissioner v. MBNA America Bank, N.A.* [No. 33049 (W.V. Sup. Ct. of App., Nov. 21, 2006); *cert. denied*, U.S. Sup. Ct., 06-1228, June 18, 2007], the West Virginia Supreme Court of Appeals ruled that a Delaware bank that provided credit card services to customers in West Virginia had income tax nexus in West Virginia, even though it had no physical presence in the state. During the tax years in question, the bank regularly issued credit cards and extended unsecured credit to West Virginia customers, and derived significant gross receipts from these activities. The court concluded that the *Quill* physical presence test "applies only to state sales and use taxes and not to state business franchise and corporation net income taxes," and that MBNA had "a significant economic presence sufficient to meet the substantial nexus" test under the Commerce Clause.

In *MBNA America Bank v. Indiana Department of State Revenue* [No. 49T10-0506-TA-53 (Ind. Tax Ct., Oct. 20, 2008)], the Indiana Tax Court concluded that "the Supreme Court has not extended the physical presence requirement beyond the realm of sales and use taxes" and that a national bank's economic presence in Indiana was sufficient to create a substantial nexus.

In *Capital One Bank and Capital One F.S.B. v. Commissioner of Revenue* [No. SJC-10105 (Mass. Sup. Jud. Ct., Jan. 8, 2009); *cert. denied*, U.S. Sup. Ct., No. 08-1169, June 22, 2009], the Massachusetts Supreme Judicial Court held that imposition of the Massachusetts financial institution excise (income) tax "is determined not by *Quill's* physical presence test, but by the 'substantial nexus' test articulated in *Complete Auto*." As a result, despite the lack of any physical presence in the state, the two out-of-state credit card banks had substantial nexus in Massachusetts because of their "purposeful, targeted marketing of their credit card business to Massachusetts customers . . . and their receipt of hundreds of millions of dollars in income from millions of transactions involving Massachusetts residents and merchants." See also *Geoffrey, Inc. v. Commissioner of Revenue* [No. SJC-10106, Mass. Sup. Jud. Ct., Jan. 8, 2009; *cert. denied*, U.S. Sup. Ct., No. 08-1207, June 22, 2009)].

In *KFC Corporation v. Iowa Department of Revenue* [No. 09-1032 (Ia. Sup. Ct., Dec. 30, 2010)], the Iowa Supreme Court ruled that the Commerce Clause does not require a physical presence in order to tax the income that a Delaware corporation (KFC) earned from the use of its intangibles in Iowa. The court concluded that the trademarks and other intangibles owned by KFC and licensed for use by independent franchisees doing business in Iowa "would be regarded as having a sufficient connection to Iowa to amount to the functional equivalent of 'physical presence' under *Quill*." The court also concluded that even if the use of the intangibles within the state does not amount to physical presence under *Quill*, the physical presence requirement should not be extended to prevent a state from imposing an income tax on revenue generated from the use of intangibles within the state.

Affiliate Nexus

In *J.C. Penney National Bank v. Johnson* [No. M1998-00497-COA-R3-CV (Tenn. Ct. App. Dec. 17, 1999)], the state argued that J.C. Penney National Bank (JCPNB) had "substantial nexus" in Tennessee because JCPNB had a physical presence in Tennessee by virtue of the fact the J.C. Penney Company, JCPNB's parent, owned and operated J.C. Penney retail stores in Tennessee. The court rejected the argument, and ruled that JCPNB did not have substantial nexus in Tennessee, because the retail stores conducted no activities that assisted JCPNB in maintaining its credit card business in Tennessee. Customers could not apply for JCPNB credit cards at the J.C. Penney stores, nor could customers make a payment on their accounts at the stores. The solicitation of potential new credit card customers, which was the most important function in allowing JCPNB to maintain its business, took place through the U.S. mail, and that, under the holding in *Quill*, does not allow a finding of substantial nexus.

In *Dillard National Bank, N.A. v. Johnson* [No. 96-545-III (Tenn. Ch. Ct., June 22, 2004)], the Tennessee Chancery Court ruled that an out-of-state subsidiary corporation that issued proprietary credit cards for use in a chain of in-state department stores that were operated by the parent corporation had income tax nexus in Tennessee because of the activities conducted on its behalf by the department stores and the store employees. These activities included placing advertisements in the stores, soliciting and taking credit card applications from store customers, answering questions for store customers regarding their credit card accounts, and accepting credit card payments in the stores. The Tennessee Chancery Court's ruling in *Dillard National Bank* is consistent with the nexus principles articulated by the Tennessee Court of Appeals in *America Online, Inc. v. Johnson* [No. M2001-00927-COA-R3-CV (Tenn. Ct. App. July 30, 2002)], in which the court stated that "substantial nexus may be established by activities carried on within the state by affiliates and independent contractors." In addition, the facts in *Dillard National Bank* are distinguishable from those in *J.C. Penney National Bank v. Johnson* [No. M1998-00497-COA-R3-CV (Tenn. Ct. App. Dec. 17, 1999)], in which the Tennessee Court of Appeals rejected the affiliate nexus argument because the in-state retail stores conducted no activities that assisted the affiliated out-of-state bank in maintaining its credit card business in Tennessee.

State-by-State Summary

The following chart summarizes the positions of the states with respect to a number of potential nexus-creating activities. For ease of presentation, the chart has been divided into three parts, as follows:

- Part 1: Credit Cards/Loans/Closing Mortgages/Solicitation via Mail
- Part 2: Solicitation via Web Sites/Debt Obligations Secured by In-State Property
- Part 3: Servicing Loans/Telemarketing Firm/Foreclosures

Activities Creating Nexus for Financial Institutions (Part 1)

Credit Cards/Loans/Closing Mortgages/Solicitation via Mail

Legend:

X	These activities create income tax nexus
NA	Not applicable
NR	Not reported

	Residents of State Hold the Institution's Credit Cards	*Unsecured Consumer Loans Made to State Residents*	*Commercial Loans Made to State Residents*	*Mortgage Loans Made to State Residents Secured by In-State Realty*	*Hires In-State Unrelated Third Party to Close Mortgages*	*Solicits Loans or Credit Cards Through the Mail in State*
Alabama	Not subject to income tax levy					
Alaska	X	X	X	X	X	X
Arizona	X	X	X	X	X	
Arkansas	X	X	X	X	X	
California	Depends on facts	Depends on facts	Depends on facts	Depends on facts	X, See Corp Code Sec 2104	
Colorado	X	X	X	X		
Connecticut	X	X	X	X	NR	X
Note. See Informational Publication 2010 (29.1), Q&A on Economic Nexus						
Delaware	File with Delaware Bank Commissioners Office					
District of Columbia	X	X	X	X	X	X
Florida	X	X	X	X	X	
Georgia				X	X	
Hawaii					X	
	Subject to tax on financial corporations					
Idaho	X, effective 1-1-08	X, effective 1-1-08	X, effective 1-1-08	X, effective 1-1-08	X, effective 1-1-08	X, effective 1-1-08
Illinois	Nexus determinations can only be made in the context of an audit wherein the auditor would have full access to all pertinent information. Please note that Illinois determines "doing business" utilizing the prevailing principles of jurisprudence under the Commerce and Due Process Clauses of the United States Constitution as applied to the facts in each case. For further information, see 86 Ill. Admin. Code § 100.9720.					

Activities Creating Nexus for Financial Institutions (Part 1)

Credit Cards/Loans/Closing Mortgages/Solicitation via Mail

Legend:

X	These activities create income tax nexus
NA	Not applicable
NR	Not reported

	Residents of State Hold the Institution's Credit Cards	*Unsecured Consumer Loans Made to State Residents*	*Commercial Loans Made to State Residents*	*Mortgage Loans Made to State Residents Secured by In-State Realty*	*Hires In-State Unrelated Third Party to Close Mortgages*	*Solicits Loans or Credit Cards Through the Mail in State*
Indiana	X	X	X	X		X
Iowa	X	X	X	X	X	X
Kansas	X		X	X		
Kentucky						
Louisiana						
Maine	X		X	X		
Maryland						
Massachusetts	X	Depends on facts	Depends on facts	X	X	
Michigan (Business Tax)					X	X
Note. The CIT takes effect 01/0112, and replaces the Michigan Business Tax (MBT) for most taxpayers. However, businesses that have been approved to receive, have received, or have been assigned certain certified credits may elect to file a return and pay the tax imposed by the MBT in lieu of the CIT until the certified credits are exhausted or extinguished.						
Minnesota	X	X	X	X	X	
Mississippi						
Missouri	X	X	X	X	X	
Montana	X	X	X	X	X	
Nebraska						
Nevada	Nevada does not impose a corporate income tax					

Activities Creating Nexus for Financial Institutions (Part 1)
Credit Cards/Loans/Closing Mortgages/Solicitation via Mail

Legend:

X	These activities create income tax nexus
NA	Not applicable
NR	Not reported

	Residents of State Hold the Institution's Credit Cards	*Unsecured Consumer Loans Made to State Residents*	*Commercial Loans Made to State Residents*	*Mortgage Loans Made to State Residents Secured by In-State Realty*	*Hires In-State Unrelated Third Party to Close Mortgages*	*Solicits Loans or Credit Cards Through the Mail in State*
New Hampshire	X	X	X	X	X	
New Jersey	X, possibly	X, possibly	X, possibly	X		
New Mexico	X			X	X	
New York	Yes, if threshold number of in-state customers is exceeded	"Nexus requires physical presence in the state".	"Nexus requires physical presence in the state".	"Nexus requires physical presence in the state".	"Nexus requires physical presence in the state".	"Nexus requires physical presence in the state".
North Carolina	X			X	X	X
North Dakota	X		X	X	X	X
Ohio	Ohio does not impose a corporate income tax					
Note: Effective 1/1/2010, the Ohio Franchise Tax was fully phased out and business will be taxed on gross receipts through the Commercial Activity Tax. Details about that tax can be found at: http//tax.ohio.gov/divisions/commercial_activities/index.stm						
Oklahoma						
Oregon	X	X	X	X	X	X
Pennsylvania				X	X	
Rhode Island						
South Carolina	X	Depends on additional facts	Depends on additional facts	Depends on additional facts	X	X
South Dakota	South Dakota does not impose a corporate income tax					
Tennessee						

Activities Creating Nexus for Financial Institutions (Part 1)

Credit Cards/Loans/Closing Mortgages/Solicitation via Mail

Legend:

X	These activities create income tax nexus
NA	Not applicable
NR	Not reported

	Residents of State Hold the Institution's Credit Cards	*Unsecured Consumer Loans Made to State Residents*	*Commercial Loans Made to State Residents*	*Mortgage Loans Made to State Residents Secured by In-State Realty*	*Hires In-State Unrelated Third Party to Close Mortgages*	*Solicits Loans or Credit Cards Through the Mail in State*
Texas (for earned surplus)					X	
Utah	X	X	X	X	X	
Vermont						
Virginia						
Washington	Washington does not impose a corporate income tax					
West Virginia	X	X	X	X	X	
Wisconsin	X	Depends on facts	X	X		Depends on facts
Wyoming	Wyoming does not impose a corporate income tax					

Activities Creating Nexus for Financial Institutions (Part 2)

Solicitation via Web Sites/Debt Obligations Secured by In-State Property

Legend:

X	These activities create income tax nexus
NA	Not applicable
NR	Not reported

	Solicits Loans or Credit Cards Via Internet Web Site	*Purchased Mortgages in Secondary Market on In-State Property*	*Purchased Consumer Loans to State Residents in Secondary Market, Secured by Tangible Personal Property*	*Purchased Credit Card Receivables of State Residents in Secondary Markets*	*Made Consumer Loans Secured by In-State Tangible Personal Property to State Residents*
Alabama	Not subject to income tax levy				
Alaska	X	X	X	X	X
Arizona		X	X		X
Arkansas		X	X	X	X
California		See Corporation Code § 2104	X	See Corporation Code § 2104	See Corporation Code § 2104
Colorado		X	X	X	X
Connecticut	X	NR	X	NR	No written guidance
Delaware	File with Delaware Bank Commissioner's Office				
District of Columbia		X	X	X	X
Florida		X	X	X	X
Georgia					X
Hawaii	Subject to tax on financial corporations				
Idaho		X, effective 1-1-08	X, effective 1-1-08		X, effective 1-1-08
Illinois	Nexus determinations can only be made in the context of an audit wherein the auditor would have full access to all pertinent information. Please note that Illinois determines "doing business" utilizing the prevailing principles of jurisprudence under the Commerce and Due Process Clauses of the United States Constitution as applied to the facts in each case. For further information, see 86 Ill. Admin. Code § 100.9720.				
Indiana	X	X	X	X	X

Activities Creating Nexus for Financial Institutions (Part 2)

Solicitation via Web Sites/Debt Obligations Secured by In-State Property

Legend:

X	These activities create income tax nexus
NA	Not applicable
NR	Not reported

	Solicits Loans or Credit Cards Via Internet Web Site	*Purchased Mortgages in Secondary Market on In-State Property*	*Purchased Consumer Loans to State Residents in Secondary Market, Secured by Tangible Personal Property*	*Purchased Credit Card Receivables of State Residents in Secondary Markets*	*Made Consumer Loans Secured by In-State Tangible Personal Property to State Residents*
Iowa					X
Kansas					X
Kentucky					
Louisiana					
Maine		X	X	X	X
Maryland			X	X	X
Massachusetts		Depends on facts	Depends on facts	Depends on facts	Depends on facts
Michigan (Business Tax)	X				
Note. The CIT takes effect 01/0112, and replaces the Michigan Business Tax (MBT) for most taxpayers. However, businesses that have been approved to receive, have received, or have been assigned certain certified credits may elect to file a return and pay the tax imposed by the MBT in lieu of the CIT until the certified credits are exhausted or extinguished.					
Minnesota					X
Mississippi					
Missouri		X	X	X	X
Montana			X		
Nebraska					
Nevada	Nevada does not impose a corporate income tax.				
New Hampshire		X	X	X	X

Activities Creating Nexus for Financial Institutions (Part 2)

Solicitation via Web Sites/Debt Obligations Secured by In-State Property

Legend:

X	These activities create income tax nexus
NA	Not applicable
NR	Not reported

	Solicits Loans or Credit Cards Via Internet Web Site	*Purchased Mortgages in Secondary Market on In-State Property*	*Purchased Consumer Loans to State Residents in Secondary Market, Secured by Tangible Personal Property*	*Purchased Credit Card Receivables of State Residents in Secondary Markets*	*Made Consumer Loans Secured by In-State Tangible Personal Property to State Residents*
New Jersey					
New Mexico		X			X
New York	Nexus requires physical presence in the state				
North Carolina	X	X			X
North Dakota	X				X
Ohio	Ohio does not impose a corporate income tax				
Note: Effective 1/1/2010, the Ohio Franchise Tax was fully phased out and business will be taxed on gross receipts through the Commercial Activity Tax. Details about that tax can be found at: http//tax.ohio.gov/divisions/commercial_activities/index.stm					
Oklahoma					
Oregon	X	X	X	X	X
Pennsylvania		X	X		X
Rhode Island					
South Carolina	X	Depends on additional facts	Depends on additional facts	Depends on additional facts	
South Dakota	South Dakota does not impose a corporate income tax				
Tennessee					X
Texas					
Utah					X

Activities Creating Nexus for Financial Institutions (Part 2)
Solicitation via Web Sites/Debt Obligations Secured by In-State Property

Legend:

X	These activities create income tax nexus
NA	Not applicable
NR	Not reported

	Solicits Loans or Credit Cards Via Internet Web Site	*Purchased Mortgages in Secondary Market on In-State Property*	*Purchased Consumer Loans to State Residents in Secondary Market, Secured by Tangible Personal Property*	*Purchased Credit Card Receivables of State Residents in Secondary Markets*	*Made Consumer Loans Secured by In-State Tangible Personal Property to State Residents*
Vermont					
Virginia					
Washington	Washington does not impose a corporate income tax				
West Virginia		X	X		X
Wisconsin	Depends on facts	X	X	Depends on facts	X
Wyoming	Wyoming does not impose a corporate income tax				

Activities Creating Nexus for Financial Institutions (Part 3)

Servicing Loans/Telemarketing Firm/Foreclosures

Legend:

X	These activities create income tax nexus
NA	Not applicable
NR	Not reported

	Hires Unrelated Party In-State to Service Loans	*Hires Related Party In-State to Service Loans*	*Hires Telemarketing Firm In-State to Market Credit Cards or Loans*	*Forecloses on In-State Properties*
Alabama	Not subject to income tax levy			
Alaska	X	X	X	X
Arizona	X	X	X	X
Arkansas	X	X	X	X
California	X	X, See Corp Code Sec 2104	X	X, See Corp Code Sec 2104
Colorado				
Connecticut	NR	NR	X	X
Note. See Informational Publication 2010 (29.1), Q&A on Economic Nexus				
Delaware	File with Delaware Bank Commissioners Office			
District of Columbia	X	X		X
Florida	X	X	X	X
Georgia	X	X	X	X
Hawaii	X	X	X	Depends on facts and circumstances
	Subject to tax on financial corporations			
Idaho	X, effective 1/1/08	X, effective 1/1/08	X, effective 1/1/08	X, effective 1/1/08
Illinois	Nexus determinations can only be made in the context of an audit wherein the auditor would have full access to all pertinent information. Please note that Illinois determines "doing business" utilizing the prevailing principles of jurisprudence under the Commerce and Due Process Clauses of the United States Constitution as applied to the facts in each case. For further information, see 86 Ill. Admin. Code § 100.9720.			

Activities Creating Nexus for Financial Institutions (Part 3)

Servicing Loans/Telemarketing Firm/Foreclosures

Legend:

X	These activities create income tax nexus
NA	Not applicable
NR	Not reported

	Hires Unrelated Party In-State to Service Loans	*Hires Related Party In-State to Service Loans*	*Hires Telemarketing Firm In-State to Market Credit Cards or Loans*	*Forecloses on In-State Properties*
Indiana		X	X	
Iowa	X	X	X	X
Kansas		X		X
Kentucky				
Louisiana				X, unless taxpayer is an organization described in LSA R.S. § 42:302(K) and (L)
Maine	X	X		X
Maryland	Not if unrelated	X	X	
Massachusetts	X	X		X
Michigan (Business Tax)	X	X	X	X
Note. The CIT takes effect 01/0112, and replaces the Michigan Business Tax (MBT) for most taxpayers. However, businesses that have been approved to receive, have received, or have been assigned certain certified credits may elect to file a return and pay the tax imposed by the MBT in lieu of the CIT until the certified credits are exhausted or extinguished.				
Minnesota	X	X	X	
Mississippi				
Missouri	X	X		X
Montana	X		X	X
Nebraska		X		X, if a financial institution takes title to the property

Activities Creating Nexus for Financial Institutions (Part 3)

Servicing Loans/Telemarketing Firm/Foreclosures

Legend:

X	These activities create income tax nexus
NA	Not applicable
NR	Not reported

	Hires Unrelated Party In-State to Service Loans	*Hires Related Party In-State to Service Loans*	*Hires Telemarketing Firm In-State to Market Credit Cards or Loans*	*Forecloses on In-State Properties*
Nevada	Nevada does not impose a corporate income tax			
New Hampshire	X	X	X	X
New Jersey			X	X
New Mexico	X	X		X
New York	Nexus requires physical presence in the state			
North Carolina	X	X	X	X
North Dakota	X	X		X
Ohio	Ohio does not impose a corporate income tax			
Note. Effective 1/1/2010, the Ohio Franchise Tax was fully phased out and business will be taxed on gross receipts through the Commercial Activity Tax. Details about that tax can be found at: http//tax.ohio.gov/divisions/commercial_activities/index.stm				
Oklahoma				
Oregon	X	X	X	X
Pennsylvania	X	X		X
Rhode Island				X
South Carolina	X	X	X	X
South Dakota	South Dakota does not impose a corporate income tax			
Tennessee				X
Texas	X	X	X	X
Utah	X	X		X

Activities Creating Nexus for Financial Institutions (Part 3)
Servicing Loans/Telemarketing Firm/Foreclosures

Legend:
X — These activities create income tax nexus
NA — Not applicable
NR — Not reported

	Hires Unrelated Party In-State to Service Loans	*Hires Related Party In-State to Service Loans*	*Hires Telemarketing Firm In-State to Market Credit Cards or Loans*	*Forecloses on In-State Properties*
Vermont				
Virginia				X
Washington	Washington does not impose a corporate income tax			
West Virginia	X	X	X	X
Wisconsin		X	X	X
Wyoming	Wyoming does not impose a corporate income tax			

Nexus Standards for Foreign (Non-US) Corporations

Federal Nexus Standards

U.S. trade or business. The United States uses a two-pronged system to tax the income of a "foreign corporation," that is, a corporation which is created or organized under the laws of a foreign country or U.S. possession. [IRC § 7701(a)] If the foreign corporation is engaged in a trade or business within the United States, the net amount of income effectively connected with that U.S. trade or business is taxed at the regular graduated rates. [IRC § 882] In addition, the gross amount of a foreign corporation's U.S.-source dividend, interest, royalty and other investment-type income is subject to a flat-rate withholding tax of 30 percent. [IRC §§ 881(a) and 1442] Income tax treaties generally reduce the withholding tax rate to 15 percent or less, [IRS Pub. 515, Table 1], and a statutory exemption is provided for portfolio interest income. [IRC § 881(c)]

Under IRC Section 882(a), a foreign corporation's business profits are subject to U.S. taxation if the foreign corporation is "engaged in trade or business within the United States." However, neither the Code nor the Regulations provide a comprehensive definition of the term *trade or business*. Section 864(b) provides that a U.S. trade or business includes "the performance of personal services within the United States," but does not include the trading of stocks, securities or commodities, if such trades are either made through an independent agent or are made for the taxpayer's own account (unless the taxpayer is a dealer). These exceptions do not apply if the foreign corporation has an office in the United States through which the trades are made.

Case law suggests that a foreign corporation is engaged in a U.S. trade or business if its employees are engaged in considerable, continuous, and regular business activity within the United States [e.g., *Spermacet Whaling & Shipping Co. S/A v. Commissioner*, 30 T.C. 618 (1958); and *Inverworld, Inc. v. Commissioner*, 71 TCM 3231 (1996)]. The conduct of a U.S. trade or business by a domestic subsidiary corporation is not imputed to a foreign parent corporation [e.g., *Eugene Higgins v. Commissioner*, 312 U.S. 212 (1941)]. However, if a partnership, estate, or trust is engaged in a U.S. trade or business, then each partner or beneficiary is considered to be engaged in a U.S. trade or business. [IRC § 875]

Permanent establishment. The United States has entered into bilateral income tax treaties with approximately 60 foreign countries (see listing in table below).

Australia	Austria	Bangladesh	Barbados	Belgium
Bulgaria	Canada	China	Commonwealth of Independent States*	Cyprus
Czech Republic	Denmark	Egypt	Estonia	Finland
France	Germany	Greece	Hungary	Iceland
India	Indonesia	Ireland	Israel	Italy
Jamaica	Japan	Kazakhstan	Korea	Latvia
Lithuania	Luxembourg	Malta	Mexico	Morocco
Netherlands	New Zealand	Norway	Pakistan	Philippines
Poland	Portugal	Romania	Russia	Slovak Republic
Slovenia	South Africa	Spain	Sri Lanka	Sweden
Switzerland	Thailand	Trinidad and Tobago	Tunisia	Turkey
Ukraine	United Kingdom	Venezuela		

* The U.S.-U.S.S.R. income tax treaty applies to the countries of Armenia, Azerbaijan, Belarus, Georgia,Kyrgyzstan, Moldova, Tajikistan, Turkmenistan, and Uzbekistan. Source: IRS Pub. No. 515, Table 3 (Mar. 18, 2011)

The United States Model Income Tax Convention of November 15, 2006 (hereinafter the "U.S. Model Treaty") reflects the baseline negotiating position of the United States in establishing income tax treaties with other countries. Many treaties are patterned after, or have provisions similar to, the U.S. Model Treaty. Therefore, it is used as a reference point in the following discussion of treaty provisions. It is important to remember, however, that each tax treaty is separately negotiated and therefore is unique. As a consequence, to determine the impact of treaty provisions in any specific situation, one must consult the applicable treaty.

A primary goal of income tax treaties is to mitigate international double taxation through tax reductions or exemptions on certain types of income derived by residents of one treaty country from sources within the other treaty country. Prime examples are permanent establishment protections for business profits, and reduced withholding tax rates on dividend, interest, royalty and other investment-type income. These tax benefits are available only to a treaty country "resident," which is generally defined as any person who, under the country's internal laws, is subject to taxation by reason of domicile, residence, citizenship, place of management, place of incorporation, or other criterion of a similar nature. A resident does not include a person who is subject to tax in the country only with respect to income derived from sources in that country or on profits attributable to a permanent establishment in that country. [Article 4 of U.S. Model Treaty]

Under a permanent establishment provision, the business profits of a foreign corporation that is a resident of the treaty country are exempt from U.S. taxation unless the foreign corporation carries on business in the United States through a permanent establishment situated therein. If a foreign corporation has a permanent establishment in the United States, the United States may tax the foreign corporation business profits, but only to the extent those business profits are attributable to the permanent establishment. [Article 7 of U.S. Model Treaty]

A *permanent establishment* generally includes a fixed place of business, such as a place of management, a branch, an office, a factory, a workshop, or a mine, well, quarry, or other place of natural resource extraction. There are numerous exceptions, however. In particular, a permanent establishment does not include the following:

1. the use of facilities solely for the purpose of storage, display or delivery of goods or merchandise belonging to the foreign corporation;
2. the maintenance of a stock of goods or merchandise belonging to the foreign corporation solely for the purpose of storage, display or delivery;
3. the maintenance of a stock of goods or merchandise belonging to the foreign corporation solely for the purpose of processing by another enterprise;
4. the maintenance of a fixed place of business solely for the purpose of purchasing goods or merchandise, or of collecting information, for the foreign corporation;
5. the maintenance of a fixed place of business solely for the purpose of carrying on, for the foreign corporation, any other activity of a preparatory or auxiliary character;
6. the maintenance of a fixed place of business solely for any combination of the activities mentioned above, provided that the overall activity of the fixed place of business resulting from this combination is of a preparatory or auxiliary character.

A permanent establishment also exists if employees or other dependent agents of the foreign corporation habitually exercise in the United States an authority to conclude sales contracts in the taxpayer's name. Employees who limit their activities to auxiliary or preparatory functions, such as collecting information about potential customers, with sales concluded in the home country, will not create a permanent establishment. Marketing products in the United States solely through independent brokers or distributors also does not create a permanent establishment. Finally, the mere presence of a U.S. subsidiary does not create a permanent establishment for a parent company incorporated in another country. [Article 5 of U.S. Model Treaty]

Treaty permanent establishment provisions are not binding for state nexus purposes, however, because income tax treaties generally apply only to selected types of federal taxes. [Article 2 of U.S. Model

Treaty] As a consequence, it is possible for a foreign corporation to have nexus for state tax purposes but not federal income tax purposes.

State Nexus Standards

In contrast to the federal nexus standards of engaging in trade or business within the United States or carrying on business in the United States through a permanent establishment situated therein, state income tax nexus standards generally require only a physical presence within the state of a type that is not protected by Public Law 86-272. In addition, some states have adopted the theory of economic nexus, under which an in-state physical presence is not an absolute prerequisite for income tax nexus. Instead, a significant economic presence, such as licensing intangibles or making substantial sales in the state, is sufficient to create state income tax nexus.

As a consequence, it is possible for a foreign (non-U.S.) corporation to have nexus for state but not federal income tax purposes. For example, if a foreign corporation leases warehouse space in a state solely for the purpose of storing and delivering its merchandise to U.S. customers, the physical presence of company-owned inventory would generally create state income tax nexus, but not necessarily federal income tax nexus, because the mere storage of inventory does not constitute a permanent establishment.

Physical presence test. States generally attempt to impose their taxes on out-of-state corporations to the fullest extent permissible under federal law. The U.S Constitution prohibits a state from taxing an out-of-state corporation unless the requirements of both the Due Process Clause and the Commerce Clause are satisfied. The Due Process Clause provides that no state shall "deprive any person of life, liberty or property, without due process of law," and the Commerce Clause gives Congress the exclusive authority to regulate interstate commerce.

In *National Bellas Hess, Inc. v. Department of Revenue* [386 U.S. 753 (1967)], the Supreme Court established the principle that constitutional nexus requires an in-state physical presence, at least with respect to sales and use tax. In this case, the Court ruled that Illinois could not require a Missouri-based mail-order vendor to collect use tax on sales to Illinois residents, because the Missouri corporation had no offices, property, employees or any other type of physical presence in Illinois. In 1992, the Supreme Court reaffirmed the physical presence requirement in *Quill Corp. v. North Dakota* [504 U.S. 298 (1992)], which was another case involving the collection of use tax by an out-of-state mail-order company. However, the Court did not specifically address the issue of whether the physical presence test also applied to income tax nexus.

Economic nexus. An unsettled legal issue is whether the physical presence test for constitutional nexus applies to income taxes. In *Geoffrey, Inc. v. South Carolina Tax Commission* [437 S.E.2d 13 (S.C. 1993), *cert. denied* 510 U.S. 992 (1993)], the South Carolina Supreme Court ruled that an out-of-state corporation "need not have a tangible, physical presence in a state for income to be taxable there." Geoffrey, Inc. was the Delaware trademark holding company of the toy retailer, Toys "R" Us. Geoffrey licensed the use of its intangibles to affiliates operating stores in South Carolina, but did not have a physical presence in the state. The court concluded that "by licensing intangibles for use in this State and deriving income from their use here, Geoffrey has a 'substantial nexus' with South Carolina," as required by the Commerce Clause.

Since 1993, many states have enacted ''economic nexus'' standards that are based on the amount of income or sales derived from sources within a state. For example, the Connecticut corporate income tax applies to "[a]ny company that derives income from sources within this state and that has a substantial economic presence within this state, evidenced by a purposeful direction of business toward this state, examined in light of the frequency, quantity and systematic nature of a company's economic contacts with this state, without regard to physical presence, and to the extent permitted by the Constitution of the United States." [Conn. Gen. Stat. § 12-216a] An exemption applies to a company that is treated as a foreign corporation for federal tax purposes and has no income effectively connected with a U.S. trade or business. The "bright-line test" for determining economic nexus is whether the company had $500,000 or more in business receipts attributable to Connecticut sources during the tax year. [Informational Publication 2010(29.1), Conn. Dept. of Rev. Services, Dec. 28, 2010]

Another approach to the economic nexus concept is a factor presence nexus standard, under which income tax nexus exists if in-state sales exceed a specified threshold. For example, for tax years beginning on or after January 1, 2011, an out-of-state corporation has income tax nexus in California if it has more than $500,000 of sales or 25 percent of its total sales in California. [S.B. 15, Feb. 20. 2009] Effective April 30, 2010, an out-of-state corporation has income tax nexus in Colorado if it has more than $500,000 of sales or 25 percent of its total sales in Colorado. [Colo. Dept. of Rev., Reg. 39-22-301.1, Apr. 10, 2010] Effective June 1, 2010, for purposes of taxing service activities and royalty income, an out-of-state corporation has nexus in Washington if it has more than $250,000 of receipts or at least 25 percent of its total receipts in Washington. [S.B. 6143, Feb. 20. 2009]

There has also been a significant amount of litigation related to the *Geoffrey* court's interpretation of the Commerce Clause's substantial nexus requirement.

In *Lanco, Inc. v. Division of Taxation* [908 A.2d 176 (N.J. 2006); *cert. denied*, U.S. Sup. Ct., 06-1236, June 18, 2007], the New Jersey Supreme Court ruled that the Delaware trademark holding company of the clothing retailer Lane Bryant had income tax nexus in New Jersey, even though it had no physical presence in the state. The court concluded that "the better interpretation of *Quill* is the one adopted by those states that limit the Supreme Court's holding to sales and use taxes." The court also stated that "we do not believe that the Supreme Court intended to create a universal physical-presence requirement for state taxation under the Commerce Clause."

In *Tax Commissioner v. MBNA America Bank, N.A.* [640 S.E.2d 226 (W. Va. 2006); *cert. denied*, U.S. Sup. Ct., 06-1228, June 18, 2007], the taxpayer was a Delaware bank that issued credit cards, extended unsecured credit, and serviced the credit card accounts of customers nationwide. Although MBNA did not have a physical presence in West Virginia, during one of the tax years in question, it derived over $10 million of gross receipts from West Virginia customers. The West Virginia Supreme Court of Appeals ruled that the physical presence test "applies only to state sales and use taxes and not to state business franchise and corporation net income taxes," and that MBNA had "a significant economic presence sufficient to meet the substantial nexus" test under the Commerce Clause.

In *Capital One Bank and Capital One F.S.B. v. Commissioner of Revenue* [No. SJC-10105 (Mass. Sup. Jud. Ct., Jan. 8, 2009); *cert. denied*, U.S. Sup. Ct., No. 08-1169, June 22, 2009], the Massachusetts Supreme Judicial Court ruled that, despite the lack of any physical presence in the state, the two out-of-state credit card banks had substantial nexus in Massachusetts, because of their "purposeful, targeted marketing of their credit card business to Massachusetts customers . . . and their receipt of hundreds of millions of dollars in income from millions of transactions involving Massachusetts residents and merchants." See also *Geoffrey, Inc. v. Commissioner of Revenue* [No. SJC-10106, Mass. Sup. Jud. Ct., Jan. 8, 2009; *cert. denied*, U.S. Sup. Ct., No. 08-1207, June 22, 2009)].

In *KFC Corporation v. Iowa Department of Revenue* [No. 09-1032 (Ia. Sup. Ct., Dec. 30, 2010)], the Iowa Supreme Court ruled that the Commerce Clause does not require a physical presence in order to tax the income that a Delaware corporation (KFC) earned from the use of its intangibles in Iowa. The court concluded that the trademarks and other intangibles owned by KFC and licensed for use by independent franchisees doing business in Iowa "would be regarded as having a sufficient connection to Iowa to amount to the functional equivalent of 'physical presence' under *Quill*." The court also concluded that even if the use of the intangibles within the state does not amount to physical presence under *Quill*, the physical presence requirement should not be extended to prevent a state from imposing an income tax on revenue generated from the use of intangibles within the state.

Public Law 86-272. Another major federal restriction on state tax jurisdiction is Public Law 86-272 [15 U.S.C. 381], which Congress enacted in 1959 to provide out-of-state corporations with a limited safe harbor from the imposition of state taxes on "net income." Specifically, Public Law 86-272 prohibits a state from imposing a tax on the net income of an out-of-state corporation if the company's only in-state activity is the solicitation of orders by company representatives for sales of tangible personal property, which orders are sent outside the state for approval or rejection, and if approved, are filled by shipment or delivery from a point outside the state.

By its terms, Public Law 86-272 applies only to "interstate commerce." Individual states are free, however, to extend the protections of Public Law 86-272 to foreign commerce to ensure that foreign and interstate commerce are treated the same.

State-by-State Summary

The following chart summarizes whether a foreign corporation that has state income tax nexus, but is exempt from federal tax pursuant to an income tax treaty, is required to file a state income tax return, and if so, whether the starting point for computing state taxable income is federal taxable income computed as if the corporation were subject to federal income tax. The chart also summarizes the states' positions as to whether Public Law 86-272 protects a foreign (non-U.S.) corporation from income tax nexus if employees of the foreign corporation enter the state to solicit sales of tangible personal property.

Nexus Standards for Foreign (Non-U.S.) Corporations

Legend:

NA	Not applicable
NR	Not reported

	If a Foreign Corporation has Income Tax Nexus in Your State But is Exempt from Federal Income Tax Pursuant to a Tax Treaty, is the Foreign Corporation		*If Yes, What is The Starting Point for Computing State Taxable Income?*		
	Required to File an Income Tax Return in Your State?	*Subject to Income Tax in Your State?*	*Federal Taxable Income Computed as if the Corporation was Subject to Federal Income Tax?*	*Other, Explain:*	*If Employees of a Foreign Corporation Enter Your State to Solicit Sales of Tangible Personal Property Which are Approved and Shipped from Outside Your State, Does P.L. 86-272 Protect the Foreign Corporation from Income Tax Nexus in Your State?*
Alabama	Yes	Yes	X		Yes
Alaska	Yes	Yes		Can choose to use either FTI on an "as if" basis or financial statement income	Yes
Arizona	Yes	Yes	X, federal taxable income		Depends, see Arizona Corporate Tax Ruling, CTR 99-5
Arkansas	Yes	Yes		Computed based on income and deductions authorized in Arkansas income tax code	Yes
California	Yes	Yes	X		No
Colorado	Yes	Yes	X		Yes
Connecticut	Yes	Yes			No published position.
Delaware					
District of Columbia	Follows IRS Rules				

Nexus Standards for Foreign (Non-U.S.) Corporations

Legend:
NA Not applicable
NR Not reported

	If a Foreign Corporation has Income Tax Nexus in Your State But is Exempt from Federal Income Tax Pursuant to a Tax Treaty, is the Foreign Corporation		*If Yes, What is The Starting Point for Computing State Taxable Income?*		
	Required to File an Income Tax Return in Your State?	*Subject to Income Tax in Your State?*	*Federal Taxable Income Computed as if the Corporation was Subject to Federal Income Tax?*	*Other, Explain:*	*If Employees of a Foreign Corporation Enter Your State to Solicit Sales of Tangible Personal Property Which are Approved and Shipped from Outside Your State, Does P.L. 86-272 Protect the Foreign Corporation from Income Tax Nexus in Your State?*
Florida	No	No			Yes
Georgia				This issue is addressed on a case by case basis. Taxpayer is required to request a letter ruling.	No
Hawaii	NR	NR			

Nexus Standards for Foreign (Non-U.S.) Corporations

Legend:
NA — Not applicable
NR — Not reported

	If a Foreign Corporation has Income Tax Nexus in Your State But is Exempt from Federal Income Tax Pursuant to a Tax Treaty, is the Foreign Corporation		*If Yes, What is The Starting Point for Computing State Taxable Income?*		
	Required to File an Income Tax Return in Your State?	*Subject to Income Tax in Your State?*	*Federal Taxable Income Computed as if the Corporation was Subject to Federal Income Tax?*	*Other, Explain:*	*If Employees of a Foreign Corporation Enter Your State to Solicit Sales of Tangible Personal Property Which are Approved and Shipped from Outside Your State, Does P.L. 86-272 Protect the Foreign Corporation from Income Tax Nexus in Your State?*
Idaho	Yes	Yes		Idaho's starting point for determining Idaho taxable income is federal taxable income, which under this scenario would be zero. However, under Idaho Code § 63-3030(a)(3), a foreign corporation transacting business within Idaho would be required to file an Idaho income tax return and pay the Idaho Code § 63-3025 or 63-3025A minimum tax and the Idaho Code § 63-3082 Permanent Building Fund Tax.	Yes
Illinois	No, See IITA § 502(a)	No, See IITA § 203(e)(1)			Yes, See 86 Ill. Admin. Code 100.9720(c)(8)
Indiana	Yes	No			

Nexus Standards for Foreign (Non-U.S.) Corporations

Legend:
NA Not applicable
NR Not reported

	If a Foreign Corporation has Income Tax Nexus in Your State But is Exempt from Federal Income Tax Pursuant to a Tax Treaty, is the Foreign Corporation		*If Yes, What is The Starting Point for Computing State Taxable Income?*		
	Required to File an Income Tax Return in Your State?	*Subject to Income Tax in Your State?*	*Federal Taxable Income Computed as if the Corporation was Subject to Federal Income Tax?*	*Other, Explain:*	*If Employees of a Foreign Corporation Enter Your State to Solicit Sales of Tangible Personal Property Which are Approved and Shipped from Outside Your State, Does P.L. 86-272 Protect the Foreign Corporation from Income Tax Nexus in Your State?*
Iowa	No	No			Yes
Kansas	Yes	Yes		Unrelated business income taxable under the federal Internal Revenue Code.	Yes
Kentucky	No	No			Yes
Louisiana	No	No			Yes
Maine	No	No			Yes
Maryland	No	No			Yes
Massachusetts	No				Yes

Nexus Standards for Foreign (Non-U.S.) Corporations

Legend:
NA Not applicable
NR Not reported

	If a Foreign Corporation has Income Tax Nexus in Your State But is Exempt from Federal Income Tax Pursuant to a Tax Treaty, is the Foreign Corporation		*If Yes, What is The Starting Point for Computing State Taxable Income?*		
	Required to File an Income Tax Return in Your State?	*Subject to Income Tax in Your State?*	*Federal Taxable Income Computed as if the Corporation was Subject to Federal Income Tax?*	*Other, Explain:*	*If Employees of a Foreign Corporation Enter Your State to Solicit Sales of Tangible Personal Property Which are Approved and Shipped from Outside Your State, Does P.L. 86-272 Protect the Foreign Corporation from Income Tax Nexus in Your State?*
Michigan	Yes, unless exempt under § 208.1207(1)	Yes, unless exempt under § 208.1207(1)		The business income tax base of a foreign person includes the sum of business income and adjustments that are related to U.S. business activity and shall not include proceeds from cases where title passes outside the U.S.	Yes
Note. The CIT takes effect 01/0112, and replaces the Michigan Business Tax (MBT) for most taxpayers. However, businesses that have been approved to receive, have received, or have been assigned certain certified credits may elect to file a return and pay the tax imposed by the MBT in lieu of the CIT until the certified credits are exhausted or extinguished.					
Minnesota	Yes	Yes	X		Yes
Mississippi	Yes	Yes	X		
Missouri	Yes	Yes		Federal taxable income	Yes
Montana	Yes	Yes	X		NR
Nebraska	No	No			Yes

Nexus Standards for Foreign (Non-U.S.) Corporations

Legend:
NA Not applicable
NR Not reported

	If a Foreign Corporation has Income Tax Nexus in Your State But is Exempt from Federal Income Tax Pursuant to a Tax Treaty, is the Foreign Corporation		*If Yes, What is The Starting Point for Computing State Taxable Income?*		
	Required to File an Income Tax Return in Your State?	*Subject to Income Tax in Your State?*	*Federal Taxable Income Computed as if the Corporation was Subject to Federal Income Tax?*	*Other, Explain:*	*If Employees of a Foreign Corporation Enter Your State to Solicit Sales of Tangible Personal Property Which are Approved and Shipped from Outside Your State, Does P.L. 86-272 Protect the Foreign Corporation from Income Tax Nexus in Your State?*
Nevada	Nevada does not impose a corporate income tax				
New Hampshire	X	X			X
New Jersey	Yes	Yes	X		Yes
New Mexico	Yes	No			Yes
New York	Yes	Yes	X		Yes

Nexus Standards for Foreign (Non-U.S.) Corporations

Legend:
NA — Not applicable
NR — Not reported

	If a Foreign Corporation has Income Tax Nexus in Your State But is Exempt from Federal Income Tax Pursuant to a Tax Treaty, is the Foreign Corporation		*If Yes, What is The Starting Point for Computing State Taxable Income?*		
	Required to File an Income Tax Return in Your State?	*Subject to Income Tax in Your State?*	*Federal Taxable Income Computed as if the Corporation was Subject to Federal Income Tax?*	*Other, Explain:*	*If Employees of a Foreign Corporation Enter Your State to Solicit Sales of Tangible Personal Property Which are Approved and Shipped from Outside Your State, Does P.L. 86-272 Protect the Foreign Corporation from Income Tax Nexus in Your State?*
North Carolina	Yes	Yes		Federal taxable income is the NC starting point. However, a foreign corporation may still be subject to North Carolina income tax even though it is not subject to federal taxation as a result of a tax treaty. If the foreign corporation has any adjustments to federal taxable income in determining North Carolina net income pursuant to N.C. Gen. Stat. § 105-130.5, it may be subject to North Carolina corporate income tax.	Yes
North Dakota	Yes	Yes	X		Yes
Ohio	Ohio does not impose a corporate income tax				

Legend:
NA — Not applicable
NR — Not reported

Nexus Standards for Foreign (Non-U.S.) Corporations

	If a Foreign Corporation has Income Tax Nexus in Your State But is Exempt from Federal Income Tax Pursuant to a Tax Treaty, is the Foreign Corporation		*If Yes, What is The Starting Point for Computing State Taxable Income?*		
	Required to File an Income Tax Return in Your State?	*Subject to Income Tax in Your State?*	*Federal Taxable Income Computed as if the Corporation was Subject to Federal Income Tax?*	*Other, Explain:*	*If Employees of a Foreign Corporation Enter Your State to Solicit Sales of Tangible Personal Property Which are Approved and Shipped from Outside Your State, Does P.L. 86-272 Protect the Foreign Corporation from Income Tax Nexus in Your State?*
Note. Effective 1/1/2010, the Ohio Franchise Tax was fully phased out, and businesses will be taxed on gross receipts through the Commercial Activity Tax. Details about that tax can be found at: http//tax.ohio.gov/divisions/commercial_activities/index.stm					
Oklahoma	Yes	Yes			Yes
Oregon	Yes	Yes	X		Yes
Pennsylvania	Yes	Yes	X		Yes
Rhode Island	Yes	Yes	X		Yes
South Carolina	No	No	NA		No
South Dakota	South Dakota does not impose a corporate income tax				
Tennessee	No	No			Yes
Texas	Yes	Yes		Total revenue is tied to specific lines from the federal return. If no revenue is reported on the federal return, the entity owes no franchise tax but must file a no tax due report.	No

Nexus Standards for Foreign (Non-U.S.) Corporations

Legend:
NA Not applicable
NR Not reported

	If a Foreign Corporation has Income Tax Nexus in Your State But is Exempt from Federal Income Tax Pursuant to a Tax Treaty, is the Foreign Corporation		*If Yes, What is The Starting Point for Computing State Taxable Income?*		
	Required to File an Income Tax Return in Your State?	*Subject to Income Tax in Your State?*	*Federal Taxable Income Computed as if the Corporation was Subject to Federal Income Tax?*	*Other, Explain:*	*If Employees of a Foreign Corporation Enter Your State to Solicit Sales of Tangible Personal Property Which are Approved and Shipped from Outside Your State, Does P.L. 86-272 Protect the Foreign Corporation from Income Tax Nexus in Your State?*
Utah	Yes	Yes	X		Yes
Vermont	No	No			No
Virginia	No	No			Yes
Washington	Washington does not impose a corporate income tax				
West Virginia	No	No			Yes
Wisconsin	Yes	Yes		Starting point is gross income as determined under "Internal Revenue Code" and as modified by Wis. Stat. § 71.26(3), with due regard to any treaty obligation to which the United States is a party.	No
Wyoming	Wyoming does not impose a corporate income tax				

Part 3. CORPORATE TAXES AND TAX BASE

Income Tax Rates and Conformity to Federal Rules for Determining Taxable Income

The starting point for computing a corporation's state taxable income is usually either federal taxable income before the dividends-received and net operating loss deductions (Line 28 of federal Form 1120) or federal taxable income (Line 30 of federal Form 1120). Thus, the computation of state taxable income is directly affected by the Internal Revenue Code (Code). The adoption of the Code may be to either the current Code or the Code as of a specific reference date. A state that adopts the current Code automatically incorporates any changes in the federal statutes into the state statutes. In contrast, a state that adopts the Code as of a specific reference date must periodically update its statutes to ensure conformity to the current Code. For most states that adopt the federal provisions as of a specific reference date, annual legislation to ensure the update of state statutes becomes almost automatic. If adoption of federal statutory provisions is delayed, corporate taxpayers must consider the differences that may arise in the computation of state corporate taxable income.

Complete conformity to the federal statutory provisions would reduce both state administrative costs and taxpayer compliance costs. Numerous factors, however, make such conformity untenable. State judiciaries may consider a complete tie-in to be an unconstitutional delegation of legislative power to Congress, and state legislatures are concerned about the loss of control over state tax policy as well as the effects of federal tax law changes on state income tax revenues. Major revisions in the federal statutes can have negative effects on state income tax revenues. Generally, the states find it difficult to evaluate the effect of federal tax legislation on state revenues. Some states respond quickly with legislation affecting state tax laws; others defer their response until the impact of the federal tax changes is more fully known.

For example, a major component of the federal Job Creation and Worker Assistance Act of 2002 was bonus depreciation equal to 30 percent of the adjusted basis of qualified property placed in service between September 11, 2001, and September 10, 2004. The Congressional Research Service estimated that, if adopted, bonus depreciation could cost the states as much as $14 billion in lost tax revenues over the three-year period. As a consequence, many states, already under serious budgetary pressures due to the sagging economy, decided to "decouple" from the Code with respect to the bonus depreciation provisions.

States also may have difficulties with conformity to federal tax laws for other reasons. For example, in *Kraft General Foods, Inc. v. Iowa Department of Revenue & Finance* [505 U.S. 71 (1992)], the U.S. Supreme Court held that administrative convenience does not justify discrimination. Having found that Iowa's disparate treatment of domestic and foreign dividends discriminated against foreign commerce, the Supreme Court turned to the state's administrative convenience argument. Iowa argued that adopting the federal dividend treatment was administratively advantageous. The Court, however, found that the state could have retained its tie-in to federal taxable income with only minor adjustments. The Court held that Iowa's treatment of foreign dividends violated the Commerce Clause.

Recent Developments

Arizona. The Arizona corporate income tax rate is reduced from 6.968 percent to 6.5 percent for tax years beginning in 2014, 6 percent for tax years beginning in 2015, 5.5 percent for tax years beginning in 2016, and 4.9 percent for tax years beginning on or after January 1, 2017. [H.B. 2001, Feb. 17, 2011]

Connecticut. Effective for tax years beginning in 2009 to 2011, Connecticut imposes a 10 percent surcharge on the income tax liability (before credits) of corporations that have $100 million or more in annual gross revenues and a tax liability of $250 or more. [S.B. 2052, Oct. 5, 2009]

Illinois. The Illinois corporate tax rate increases from 7.3 percent to 9.5 percent for tax years 2011 through 2014. The corporate tax rate decreases to 7.75 percent for tax years 2015-2024, and to 7.3 percent on January 1, 2025. [S.B. 2505, Jan. 13, 2011]

Indiana. The Indiana corporate income tax rate is reduced from 8.5 percent to 8 percent for tax years beginning after June 30, 2012, 7.5 percent for tax years beginning after June 30, 2013, 7 percent for tax years beginning after June 30, 2014, and 6.5 percent for tax years beginning after June 30, 2015. [H.B. 1004, May 10, 2011]

Kansas. The state's top corporate income tax rate is reduced from 7.35 percent to 7.10 percent for tax year 2008, and is further reduced to 7.05 percent for tax years 2009 and 2010, and 7.00 percent for tax years after 2010. [H.B. 2434, Mar. 22, 2008]

In 2007, Kansas enacted legislation to phase out the Kansas corporation franchise tax on net worth (stockholders' equity) over a five-year period. The tax base is net worth (stockholders' equity), and the tax rate is $0.03125 per $1,000 of net worth in 2010, with a maximum tax of $20,000. The tax is repealed for tax years beginning after December 31, 2010.

Massachusetts. The corporate income tax rate of 9.5 percent is reduced to 8.75 percent in 2010, 8.25 percent in 2011, and 8.0 percent in tax years after 2011. The financial institution tax rate of 10.5 percent is reduced to 10 percent in 2010, 9.5 percent in 2011, and 9 percent in tax years after 2011. [H.B. 4904, July 3, 2008]

Maryland. The corporate income tax rate is increased from 7.0 percent to 8.25 percent for tax years beginning on or after January 1, 2008. [S.B. 2, Nov. 19, 2007]

Michigan. Effective in 2008, Michigan repealed its single business tax and replaced it with a 4.95 percent business income tax and a 0.80 percent modified gross receipts tax. [S.B. 94, July 12, 2007]

Effective January 1, 2012, Michigan replaced its business income and modified gross receipt taxes with a 6 percent corporate income tax. [H.B. 4361 and 4362, May 25, 2011]

Missouri. The Missouri corporate franchise tax rate is reduced from 1/30 of 1 percent to 1/37 of 1 percent in 2012, 1/50 of 1 percent in 2013, 1/75 of 1 percent in 2014, 1/150 of 1 percent in 2015, and is repealed in 2016. [S.B. 19 Apr. 26, 2011]

New Jersey. Effective for tax years ending on or after July 1, 2006, and before July 1, 2009, New Jersey imposes a 4 percent surcharge on a corporation's income tax liability before credits. [A.B. 4706, July 8, 2006] The surcharge was extended to apply to tax years ending before July 1, 2010. [A.B. 4105, June 29, 2009]

North Carolina. For tax years beginning in 2009 and 2010, North Carolina imposes a 3 percent surcharge on a corporation's income tax liability. [S.B. 202, Aug. 7, 2009]

North Dakota. For tax years beginning on or after January 1, 2009, the top North Dakota corporate income tax rate is reduced from 6.5 percent to 6.4 percent. [S.B. 2199, Apr. 30, 2009] For tax years beginning on or after January 1, 2011, the top North Dakota corporate income tax rate is reduced from 6.4 percent to 5.15 percent. [H.B. 1047, Apr. 27, 2011]

Ohio. In 2005, Ohio enacted a new "commercial activity tax" (CAT) which is imposed on a business entity's gross receipts [H.B. 66, June 30, 2005]. The tax is effective for gross receipts received on or after July 1, 2005, and the tax rate is phased in over a five-year period from 2005 through 2009. The initial top tax rate is 0.06 percent and will rise to 0.26 percent when the tax is fully phased in for gross receipts received after March 31, 2009.

Oregon. For tax years beginning in 2009 and 2010, the Oregon corporate income tax is 6.6 percent of the first $250,000 of taxable income, and 7.9 percent of taxable income in excess of $250,000. For tax years beginning in 2011 and 2012, the tax rate on income in excess of $250,000 decreases to 7.6 percent. For tax years beginning after 2012, the $250,000 threshold is increased to $10 million. [H.B. 3405, June 12, 2009] Prior to 2009, Oregon imposed a 6.6 percent corporate income tax.

Texas. For franchise tax reports due on or after January 1, 2008, Texas significantly modified its corporate franchise tax, replacing the prior tax based on capital and earned surplus with a new "margin tax." A taxable entity's margin is the lowest of three amounts: (1) total revenue minus cost of goods sold, (2) total revenue minus compensation, or (3) 70 percent of total revenue. The tax rate is 0.5 percent for taxpayers primarily engaged in retail or wholesale trade, and 1 percent for all other businesses. [H.B. 3, May 18, 2006]

West Virginia. The West Virginia corporate income tax rate is reduced from 8.75 percent in 2008 to 8.5 percent in 2009 to 2011, 7.75 percent in 2012, 7.0 percent in 2013, and 6.5 percent in 2014. The rate reductions for tax years beginning after 2011 are suspended if revenue in the state's shortfall reserve fund does not equal or exceed 10 percent of the general revenue fund budgeted for the fiscal year. [S.B. 680 and H.B. 4587, Mar. 31, 2008]

The West Virginia business franchise tax on taxable capital is repealed for tax years beginning after 2014. Prior to repeal, the tax rate is reduced each year, from 0.55 percent in 2008 to 0.48 percent in 2009, 0.41 percent in 2010, 0.34 percent in 2011, 0.27 percent in 2012, 0.21 percent in 2013, and 0.10 percent in 2014. [S.B. 680 and H.B. 4587, Mar. 31, 2008]

State-by-State Summary

The following chart indicates whether the state computation of taxable net income starts with a figure from federal Form 1120. Some states use final federal taxable income (Line 30 of federal Form 1120) as the starting point; others use federal taxable income before the dividends-received and net operating loss deductions (Line 28 of federal Form 1120). In addition, the chart indicates the date of adoption of federal tax statutes and includes tax rate information.

Income Tax Rates and Conformity to Federal Rules for Determining Taxable Income

Legend:
NA — Not applicable
NR — Not reported
SAF — Same as applicable federal rules

	Does State Computation of Taxable Net Income Start with a Figure from Federal Form 1120?	*Date of Adoption of Federal Income Tax Rules*	*Tax Rates*
Alabama	Yes, starts with taxable income after special deductions	1/1/2001	$6^{1}/_{2}$% for tax years after 12/31/00
Alaska	Yes, starts with taxable income before special deductions	Immediately, SAF	1% to 9.4% maximum
Arizona	Yes, starts with taxable income after special deductions	1/1/2006	6.968%, A.R.S. § 43-1111
Arkansas	No, income and deductions based on Arkansas Code	NA	First $3,000 @ 1%, next $3,000 @ 2%, next $5,000 @ 3%, next $14,000 @ 5%, next $75,000 @ 6%, over $100,000 @ 6.5%.
California	Yes, it starts with taxable income before special deductions.	Effective 01/01/2011, California adopts the 01/01/2009 IRC for taxable years beginning on or after 01/01/2010 (R&TC § 17024.5).	8.84%
Colorado	Yes, starts with taxable income after special deductions	1965	4.63%
Connecticut	Yes, starts with taxable income before special deductions	SAF	7.5%, for income years commencing on or after 1/01/2009 and prior to 1/1/2011 there is a 10% surtax. For income years commencing on or after 01/01/12 and prior to 01/01/14, there is a 20% surtax. See Conn. Gen. Stat. § 12-214(b), as amended by 2011 Conn. Pub. Acts. 6, § 76, and Conn. Gen. Stat. § 12-219, as amended by 2011 Conn. Pub. Acts. 6, § 79.
Delaware	Yes, starts with taxable income after special deductions	1/1/1958	8.70%

Income Tax Rates and Conformity to Federal Rules for Determining Taxable Income

Legend:

NA Not applicable
NR Not reported
SAF Same as applicable federal rules

	Does State Computation of Taxable Net Income Start with a Figure from Federal Form 1120?	*Date of Adoption of Federal Income Tax Rules*	*Tax Rates*
District of Columbia	No. starts with line 1 as Federal	Current	9.975% Surcharge rate of 2.3% built into tax rate to arrive at 9.975%
Florida	Yes, starts with taxable income after special deductions	1/1/2010	5.50%
Georgia	Yes, starts with taxable income after special deductions	1/1/2011; However, several IRC Sections are excluded pursuant to OCGA 48-1-2(14). Certain provisions of federal Acts passed during 2010 were retroactively accepted for tax year 2010.	6%
Hawaii	Yes, starts with taxable income before special deductions and NOL deductions	12/31/2001	$ 0-25,000: 4.4% 25,001-100,000: 5.4% 100,001 or more: 6.4%
Idaho	Yes, starts with taxable income after special deductions	1/1/2002	7.60%
Illinois	Yes, starts with taxable income after special deductions	Current	7.3%; 1.5% for S corporations
Indiana	Yes, starts with taxable income after dividends-received deduction but before NOL deduction	1/1/1998	See IC 6-3-2-1(b) Before 7/1/12: 8.5% 7/1/12-6/30/13: 8% 7/1/13-6/30/14: 7.5% 7/1/14-6/30/15: 7% After 6/30/15: 6.5%

Income Tax Rates and Conformity to Federal Rules for Determining Taxable Income

Legend:
NA Not applicable
NR Not reported
SAF Same as applicable federal rules

	Does State Computation of Taxable Net Income Start with a Figure from Federal Form 1120?	*Date of Adoption of Federal Income Tax Rules*	*Tax Rates*
Iowa	Yes, the federal net operating loss deduction on line 29(a) is not deductible on the Iowa return.	1/1/2011	$ 0-25,000: 6% 25,001-100,000: 8% 100,001-250,000: 10% 250,001 or more: 12%
Kansas	Yes, starts with taxable income after special deductions	Provisions of the IRC of 1986, and amendments thereto, and other provisions as may become effective at any time for the taxable year	Normal tax at 4% ,3 % surcharge on income > $50,000
Kentucky	Yes, starts with taxable income before special deductions	12/31/2006, except for depreciation and § 179 deductions which is 12/31/2001.	$ 0-50,000; 4%; 5% on $50,001-$100,000; and 6% on amount over $100,000 50,001-100,000: 5% 100,001 or more: 7%
Louisiana	Yes, starts with taxable income before special deductions	1/1/1987	$ 0-25,000: 4% 25,001-50,000: 25% 50,001-100,000: 6% 100,001-200,000: 7% 200,001 or more: 8%
Maine	Yes, starts with taxable income after special deductions	Maine conforms to the Code as of 12/31/2010.	$ 0-25,000: 3.5% 25,001-75,000: $875 + 7.93% over 25,000 75,001-250,000: $4,840 + 8.33% over 75,000 250,001 or more: $19,418 + 8.93% over 250,000 (See 36 MRSA § 5200)

Income Tax Rates and Conformity to Federal Rules for Determining Taxable Income

Legend:

NA	Not applicable
NR	Not reported
SAF	Same as applicable federal rules

	Does State Computation of Taxable Net Income Start with a Figure from Federal Form 1120?	*Date of Adoption of Federal Income Tax Rules*	*Tax Rates*
Maryland	Yes, starts with taxable income before special deductions	Current	7%
Massachusetts	Yes	Current	.095 corporate income, tangible, or net worth tax
Michigan (Business Tax)	Yes, starts with taxable income after special deductions	1/1/2008	4.9% on taxable income
Note. The CIT takes effect 01/01/12, and replaces the Michigan Business Tax (MBT) for most taxpayers. However, businesses that have been approved to receive, have received, or have been assigned certain certified credits may elect to file a return and pay the tax imposed by the MBT in lieu of the CIT until the certified credits are exhausted or extinguished.			
Minnesota	Yes, starts with taxable income before special deductions	As amended through 4/14/11	9.80%
Mississippi	Yes, starts with taxable income before special deductions	NA	$ 0-5,000: 3% 5,001-10,000: 4% 10,001 or more: 5%
Missouri	Yes, starts with taxable income after special deductions	No adoption. Section 143,431, RSMo refers to "federal taxable income for the taxable year."	6.25%
Montana	Yes, starts with taxable income before special deductions	NR	6.75%; 7% for water's edge filers
Nebraska	Yes, starts with taxable income after deductions	Current	$ 0-100,000: 5.58% 100,001 or more: 7.81%
Nevada	Nevada does not impose a corporate income tax		
New Hampshire	Yes, starts with taxable income before special deductions	12/31/2000	8.50%

Income Tax Rates and Conformity to Federal Rules for Determining Taxable Income

Legend:

NA	Not applicable
NR	Not reported
SAF	Same as applicable federal rules

	Does State Computation of Taxable Net Income Start with a Figure from Federal Form 1120?	*Date of Adoption of Federal Income Tax Rules*	*Tax Rates*
New Jersey	Yes, starts with taxable income before special deductions	Adopted by reference N.J.S.A. 54:10A-4(k).	7.5% for income of $100,000 or less; 9% for income > $100,000; 6.5% for income ≤ $50,000 for periods on and after 1/1/02
New Mexico	Yes, starts with taxable income before special deductions	IRS Code of 1986	< $500,000: 4.8% of net income; $500,000-$1,000,000: 6.4%; > $1,000,000: 7.6%
New York	Yes, starts with taxable income before special deductions	New York does not incorporate the IRC by reference in its definition of taxable income. For taxpayers, New York Entire Net Income is the same as taxable income reported for federal purposes under the current federal law, unless a specific modification to federal taxable income under the New York law is required to be made.	*Tax Base* / *Rate* Entire Net Income (ENI) Base for general business taxpayer: 7.1% generally, 6.5% for qualified New York manufacturers and emerging technology companies. ENI Base for small business taxpayers: ENI Base of $290,000 or less: 6.5%; ENI Base of more than $290,000 but not more than $390,000: Sum of $18,850, 7.1% of excess ENI over $290,000 4.35% of excess ENI over $350,000 Capital Base: 0.15%, with a $10,000,000 cap for non-manufacturers and a $350,000 cap for manufacturers. Alternative Minimum Tax: 1.5% Fixed Dollar Minimum Tax: $25-$5,000 depending on New York receipts Subsidiary Capital Tax: 0.09%
North Carolina	Yes, starts with taxable income after special deductions, but before NOL deduction	5/1/2010	6.90%

Legend:

NA Not applicable
NR Not reported
SAF Same as applicable federal rules

Income Tax Rates and Conformity to Federal Rules for Determining Taxable Income

	Does State Computation of Taxable Net Income Start with a Figure from Federal Form 1120?	*Date of Adoption of Federal Income Tax Rules*	*Tax Rates*
North Dakota	Yes, starts with taxable income after special deductions	Perpetual	$25,000 or less: 2.1% >$25,000 but not >$50,000: $525 plus 5.25% of the amount over $25,000 >$50,000: $1,837 plus 6.4% of the amount over $50,000 Water's Edge filers are subject to an additional 3.5% surtax on taxable income
Ohio	Ohio does not impose a corporate income tax		
Note. Effective 1/1/2010, the Ohio Franchise Tax was fully phased out and business will be taxed on gross receipts through the Commercial Activity Tax. Details about that tax can be found at: http//tax.ohio.gov/divisions/commercial_activities/index.stm			
Oklahoma	Yes, starts with taxable income before special deductions	Current	6%
Oregon	Yes, starts with taxable income before special deductions	Rolling tie to IRC with exceptions noted. All years: §§ 139A and 199. Tax years 2009 and 2010; IRC § 108(i), § 168(k) and § 179.	2011-2012; 6.6% of Oregon taxable income up to $250,000 plus 7.6% of taxable income over $250,000: 2013: 6.6% of Oregon taxable income up to $10 million plus 7.6% of taxable income over $10 million.
Pennsylvania	Yes, starts with taxable income before special deductions	Current	5%
Rhode Island	Yes, starts with taxable income before special deductions	Years ago	
South Carolina	Yes, starts with taxable income after special deductions	12/31/2010	5%
South Dakota	South Dakota does not impose a corporate income tax		.5% for qualifying entities in retail or wholesale trade and 1% for all others.
Tennessee	Yes, starts with taxable income before special deductions; LPs and LLCs use Form 1065	7/1/1976	5%

Income Tax Rates and Conformity to Federal Rules for Determining Taxable Income

Legend:
NA Not applicable
NR Not reported
SAF Same as applicable federal rules

	Does State Computation of Taxable Net Income Start with a Figure from Federal Form 1120?	*Date of Adoption of Federal Income Tax Rules*	*Tax Rates*
Texas	Other, for a taxable entity filing as a corporation for federal tax purposes, total revenue is the sum of the amounts reportable as income on Form 1120, lines 4-10. For a taxable entity other than a taxable entity treated as a corporation for federal income tax purposes, the total revenue is an amount determined in a manner substantially equivalent to the amount calculated for a corporation. See Comptroller's Rule 3.588.	The IRC of 1986 in effect for federal tax year beginning on 1/1/2007, not including any changes made by federal law after that date.	$ 0-$10,000: 7% $10,001-$25,000: 8.1% $25,001-$250,000: 9.2% $250,001 or more: 9.75%
Utah	Yes, starts with taxable income before special deductions	1/1/1994	6% flat rate
Vermont	Yes, starts with taxable income after special deductions	Current	
Virginia	Yes, starts with taxable income after special deductions. NOL deduction limited to reducing federal taxable income to $0.	12/31/2010	6% flat rate
Washington	Washington does not impose a corporate income tax		
West Virginia	Yes, starts with taxable income after special deductions	Current; updated yearly	8.5%

Income Tax Rates and Conformity to Federal Rules for Determining Taxable Income

Legend:
NA Not applicable
NR Not reported
SAF Same as applicable federal rules

	Does State Computation of Taxable Net Income Start with a Figure from Federal Form 1120?	*Date of Adoption of Federal Income Tax Rules*	*Tax Rates*
Wisconsin	Yes, starts with taxable income before special deductions. For certain types of corporations the applicable line of the federal return may be different. RICs use Form 1120-RIC, line 26. REMICs use Form 1066, Schedule J, line 4 plus line 9. REITs use Form 1120-REIT, line 22. Cooperative associations use Form 1120-C, line 25 minus line 26a. Corporations that are treated as S corporations federally, but are not treated as WI tax-option corporations, use Form 1120-S, line 21.	IRC as amended to 12/31/2008	7.9%, Permanent Economic Development Surcharge between $25 and $9,800
Wyoming	Wyoming does not impose a corporate income tax		

Alternative Minimum Taxes

Federal Tax Treatment

The Internal Revenue Code Section 55 corporate alternative minimum tax (AMT) is a separate income tax that is applied to a broader income base than the regular corporate income tax. The corporate AMT is 20 percent of the alternative minimum taxable income (AMTI) that exceeds the allowable exemption amount. The only credit allowable against the AMT is the foreign tax credit. For tax years beginning before 2005, the foreign tax credit is limited to 90 percent of the precredit AMT liability.

AMTI is the corporation's taxable income as modified by certain adjustments and increased by tax preference items. In determining AMTI, a corporation is allowed to deduct alternative tax net operating losses to the extent that such losses do not exceed 90 percent of the AMTI as computed before the AMT net operating loss deduction. A corporation also may be entitled to claim an AMT exemption. The corporate AMT exemption amount, $40,000, is reduced by 25 percent of the amount by which AMTI exceeds $150,000. Thus, the exemption is zero when a corporation's AMTI exceeds $310,000.

A "small corporation" is exempt from the AMT. A corporation qualifies as an exempt small corporation if its average gross receipts do not exceed $7.5 million for all three-year periods ending prior to the year for which an exemption is sought.

Code Sections 56 and 57 define the AMT adjustments and tax preference items for corporate taxpayers. Examples include:

- Accelerated depreciation on property placed in service after 1986
- Excess of accelerated depreciation over straight-line depreciation on pre-1987 real property
- Gains and losses on dispositions of depreciable property (adjusted basis may be different for AMT purposes)
- Seventy-five percent of the excess of the corporation's adjusted current earnings (ACE) over its pre-ACE alternative minimum taxable income (The ACE amount includes many income items that are taken into account in determining the taxpayer's current earnings and profits but are not included in the taxpayer's pre-adjustment AMTI.)
- Long-term contracts (must be accounted for using the percentage-of-completion method)
- Amortization of pollution control facilities
- Use of the installment method of accounting for dealer sales
- Tax-exempt interest on certain private activity bonds
- Reserves for losses on bad debts of financial institutions
- Percentage depletion deductions in excess of basis
- Excess mining exploration and development costs
- Intangible drilling costs
- Capital construction funds of shipping companies

Congress also enacted an AMT credit against the regular tax to alleviate the double taxation of adjustments and tax preference items that results from timing differences. These "deferral" preferences and adjustments are generally subject to the AMT before they are subject to the regular tax; consequently, without the allowance of a credit against the regular tax, they would be taxed under the AMT when the deferral originates and then taxed again under the regular tax when the deferral item reverses.

Recent Developments

District of Columbia. As of December 31, 2010, the minimum District of Columbia corporate franchise tax is increased from $100 to $250. If District gross receipts exceed $1 million, the minimum tax is $1,000. [D.C.B 19-203, July 22, 2011]

New Jersey. For tax years beginning after 2001 and on or before June 30, 2007, a corporation doing business in New Jersey must pay the higher of a 9 percent corporate business tax (CBT) on net income or an alternative minimum assessment (AMA). A taxpayer may elect to compute the AMA based on either gross receipts or gross profits. The applicable AMA tax rates vary with the tax base, gross receipts or gross profits. For example, the top AMA rates are 0.8 percent for gross profits of more than $37.5 million and 0.4 percent for gross receipts of more than $75 million. The maximum annual AMA is $5 million (or $20 million in the case of five or more affiliated corporations), and no AMA is due if the taxpayer's gross profits are $1 million or less or its gross receipts are $2 million or less. For corporations that file CBT returns, the AMA does not apply to tax years beginning on or after July 1, 2006. The AMA will continue to apply, however, to corporations that are exempt from the CBT because their New Jersey activities are protected by Public Law 86-272.

Oregon. For tax years beginning after 2008, all corporations subject to the Oregon corporate income tax must pay an annual minimum tax based on their Oregon sales. The minimum tax ranges from a $150 tax if Oregon sales are less than $500,000, to a $100,000 tax if Oregon sales are $100 million or more. [H.B. 3405, June 12, 2009]

State-by-State Summary

The chart that follows identifies the states that impose a corporate minimum tax, whether the minimum tax is similar to the federal AMT, the rate of tax imposed, and the adjustments and preference items that are included in the computation of the minimum tax.

For ease of presentation, the following chart has been divided into three parts, as follows:

- Part 1: Imposition of Minimum Tax/Conformity to Federal AMT/State AMT Rate
- Part 2: Tax Preference and Adjustment Items
- Part 3: Tax Preference and Adjustment Items (continued)

Alternative Minimum Taxes (Part 1)

Imposition of Minimum Tax/Conformity to Federal AMT/State AMT Rate

Legend:

NA Not applicable

NR Not reported

	Does State Impose Flat-Dollar Minimum Tax or Filing Fee? If Yes, Amount?	*Does State Impose Minimum Tax Similar to Federal AMT (IRC Section 55)? If Yes, What is State's AMT Rate?*	*Does State Impose Other Minimum Tax on Income? If Yes, Rate Schedule?*
Alabama	No	NA	NA
Alaska	No	Yes	
Arizona	Yes	No	Flat $50
Arkansas	No	No	No
California	Yes, $800 minimum franchise tax is imposed on C corporations organized, registered or doing business in California, if greater than graduated franchise tax. The minimum tax is not applicable to the first taxable year of a C corporation that is organized or registers in California on or after 01/01/00.	Yes, 6.65%	No
Colorado	No	NA	NA
Connecticut	Yes, $250	No	
Delaware	No	NA	NA
District of Columbia	No	No	$100
Florida	No	Yes, 3.3%	No
Georgia	No	No	Only a minimum new worth tax of $10
Hawaii	No	NA	NA
Idaho	Yes	No	Flat $20
Illinois	No	NA	NA

Alternative Minimum Taxes (Part 1)

Imposition of Minimum Tax/Conformity to Federal AMT/State AMT Rate

Legend:

NA **Not applicable**

NR **Not reported**

	Does State Impose Flat-Dollar Minimum Tax or Filing Fee? If Yes, Amount?	*Does State Impose Minimum Tax Similar to Federal AMT (IRC Section 55)? If Yes, What is State's AMT Rate?*	*Does State Impose Other Minimum Tax on Income? If Yes, Rate Schedule?*
Indiana	No	NA	NA
Iowa	Yes	Yes	NR
Kansas	No	NA	NA
Kentucky	No	No	LLE Tax which is the lesser of $.95 per $100 of KY gross receipts or $.75 per $100 of KY gross profits; or a minimum of $175. A credit equal to the LLE Tax less $175 is allowed against corporation income tax.
Louisiana	No	No	No
Maine	No	Yes. 5.4% (See 36 MRSA § 5203-C(A)(3))	No
Maryland	No	NA	NA
Massachusetts	Yes, flat rate $456	No	
Michigan (Business Tax)	No	No	No

Note. The CIT takes effect 01/01/12, and replaces the Michigan Business Tax (MBT) for most taxpayers. However, businesses that have been approved to receive, have received, or have been assigned certain certified credits may elect to file a return and pay the tax imposed by the MBT in lieu of the CIT until the certified credits are exhausted or extinguished.

Alternative Minimum Taxes (Part 1)

Imposition of Minimum Tax/Conformity to Federal AMT/State AMT Rate

Legend:

NA **Not applicable**

NR **Not reported**

	Does State Impose Flat-Dollar Minimum Tax or Filing Fee? If Yes, Amount?	*Does State Impose Minimum Tax Similar to Federal AMT (IRC Section 55)? If Yes, What is State's AMT Rate?*	*Does State Impose Other Minimum Tax on Income? If Yes, Rate Schedule?*
Minnesota	No	Yes, 6.4%	Yes, minimum fee based on Minnesota property, payroll and sales factors. <$500,000 will have a minimum tax of zero; $500,000 to $999,999 will have a minimum tax of $100; $1,000,000 to $4,999,999 will have a minimum tax of $500; $5,000,000 to $9,999,999 a minimum tax of $1,000, $10,000,000 to $19,999,9990 a minimum fee of $2,000; and over $5,000
Mississippi	No	No	No
Missouri	No	No	No
Montana	Yes	No	$50 minimum tax
Nebraska	No	NA	NA
Nevada	No	No	NR
New Hampshire	No	NA	NA
New Jersey	Yes, Alternative Minimum Assessment (AMA), not based on income.	No, it is based on gross profits or gross receipts	Graduated rates, see P.L. 2002, Chapter 40; 14; 7.b. Based upon NJ gross receipts or gross profits.
New Mexico	No	NA	NA
New York	Yes	Yes	1.5% of minimum taxable income base
North Carolina	No	NA	NA
North Dakota	No	NA	NA

Alternative Minimum Taxes (Part 1)

Imposition of Minimum Tax/Conformity to Federal AMT/State AMT Rate

Legend:

NA	**Not applicable**
NR	**Not reported**

	Does State Impose Flat-Dollar Minimum Tax or Filing Fee? If Yes, Amount?	*Does State Impose Minimum Tax Similar to Federal AMT (IRC Section 55)? If Yes, What is State's AMT Rate?*	*Does State Impose Other Minimum Tax on Income? If Yes, Rate Schedule?*
Ohio	Ohio does not impose a corporate income tax		
Note. Effective 1/1/2010, the Ohio Franchise Tax was fully phased out and business will be taxed on gross receipts through the Commercial Activity Tax. Details about that tax can be found at: http//tax.ohio.gov/divisions/commercial_activities/index.stm			
Oklahoma	No	NA	NA
Oregon	No	No	Yes, C-corporations subject to Oregon's excise tax must pay the greater of tax computed or minimum tax based on Oregon sales: Corporations with Oregon Sales of less than $500,000 will have a minimum tax of $150; $500,000 to $999,999 will have a minimum tax of $500; $1,000,000 to $1,999,999 will have a minimum tax of $1,000; $2,000,000 to $2,999,999 will have a minimum tax of $1,500; $3,000,000 to $4,999,999 will have a minimum tax of $2,000; $5,000,000 to $6,999,999 will have a minimum fee of $4,000; $7,000,000 to $9,999,999 will have a minimum fee of $7,500; $10,000,000 to $24,999,999 will have a minimum fee of $15,000; $25,000,000 to $49,999,999 will have a minimum fee of $30,000; $50,000,000 to $74,999,999 will have a minimum fee of $50,000; $75,000,000 to $99,999,999 will have a minimum fee of $75,000; and $100,000,000 or more will have a minimum fee of $100,000.

Alternative Minimum Taxes (Part 1)

Imposition of Minimum Tax/Conformity to Federal AMT/State AMT Rate

Legend:

NA — **Not applicable**

NR — **Not reported**

	Does State Impose Flat-Dollar Minimum Tax or Filing Fee? If Yes, Amount?	*Does State Impose Minimum Tax Similar to Federal AMT (IRC Section 55)? If Yes, What is State's AMT Rate?*	*Does State Impose Other Minimum Tax on Income? If Yes, Rate Schedule?*
Oregon	No	No	Yes, C-corporations subject to Oregon's excise tax must pay the greater of tax computed or minimum tax based on Oregon sales: Corporations with Oregon Sales of less than $500,000 will have a minimum tax of $150; $500,000 to $999,999 will have a minimum tax of $500; $1,000,000 to $1,999,999 will have a minimum tax of $1,000; $2,000,000 to $2,999,999 will have a minimum tax of $1,500; $3,000,000 to $4,999,999 will have a minimum tax of $2,000; $5,000,000 to $6,999,999 will have a minimum fee of $4,000; $7,000,000 to $9,999,999 will have a minimum fee of $7,500; $10,000,000 to $24,999,999 will have a minimum fee of $15,000; $25,000,000 to $49,999,999 will have a minimum fee of $30,000; $50,000,000 to $74,999,999 will have a minimum fee of $50,000; $75,000,000 to $99,999,999 will have a minimum fee of $75,000; and $100,000,000 or more will have a minimum fee of $100,000.
Pennsylvania	No	NA	NA
Rhode Island	Yes	No	Flat $500
South Carolina	Yes, $25 minimum license fee	NA	NA
South Dakota	South Dakota does not impose a corporate income tax		
Tennessee	No	NA	NA

Alternative Minimum Taxes (Part 1)

Imposition of Minimum Tax/Conformity to Federal AMT/State AMT Rate

Legend:
NA **Not applicable**
NR **Not reported**

	Does State Impose Flat-Dollar Minimum Tax or Filing Fee? If Yes, Amount?	*Does State Impose Minimum Tax Similar to Federal AMT (IRC Section 55)? If Yes, What is State's AMT Rate?*	*Does State Impose Other Minimum Tax on Income? If Yes, Rate Schedule?*
Texas	No	NA	NA
Utah	Yes	No	$100 per corporation
Vermont	Yes	No	Flat $250
Virginia	Only on telecommunications companies and electric suppliers.	NR	NR
Washington	Washington does not impose a corporate income tax		
West Virginia	No	NA	NA
Wisconsin	Various amounts, but these are imposed by the Wisconsin Department of Financial Institutions.	No	No
Wyoming	Wyoming does not impose a corporate income tax		

Alternative Minimum Taxes (Part 2)

Tax Preference and Adjustment Items

Legend:

X	These items are treated as state tax preference or adjustment items
AMT	Alternative minimum tax
SAF	Same as applicable federal rules
NA	Not applicable
NR	Not reported

	Depletion	*Bad-Debt Reserves of Financial Institutions*	*Depreciation*	*Mining Exploration and Development Costs*	*Pollution Control Facilities*	*Intangible Drilling Costs*
Alabama	Alabama does not impose an alternative minimum tax					
Alaska	X	X	X	X	X	X
Arizona	NA	NA	NA	NA	NA	NA
Arkansas	Arkansas does not impose an alternative minimum tax					
California	X		X	X	X	X
Colorado	Colorado does not impose an alternative minimum tax					
Connecticut	NA	NA	NA	NA	NA	NA
Delaware	Delaware does not impose an alternative minimum tax					
District of Columbia	No	NA	NA	NA	NA	NA
Florida	NR	NR	NR	NR	NR	NR
Georgia	Georgia does not impose an alternative minimum tax					
Hawaii	Hawaii does not impose an alternative minimum tax					
Idaho	NA	NA	NA	NA	NA	NA
Illinois	Illinois does not impose an alternative minimum tax					
Indiana	Indiana does not impose an alternative minimum tax					
Iowa		X	X	X	X	X
Kansas	Kansas does not impose an alternative minimum tax					

Alternative Minimum Taxes (Part 2)

Tax Preference and Adjustment Items

Legend:

X	These items are treated as state tax preference or adjustment items
AMT	Alternative minimum tax
SAF	Same as applicable federal rules
NA	Not applicable
NR	Not reported

	Depletion	*Bad-Debt Reserves of Financial Institutions*	*Depreciation*	*Mining Exploration and Development Costs*	*Pollution Control Facilities*	*Intangible Drilling Costs*
Kentucky	Kentucky does not impose an alternative minimum tax					
Louisiana	Louisiana does not impose an alternative minimum tax					
Maine	X	X	X	X	X	X
Maryland	Maryland does not impose an alternative minimum tax					
Massachusetts	NA	NA	NA	NA	NA	NA
Michigan (Business Tax)	Michigan does not impose an alternative minimum tax					
Note. The CIT takes effect 01/01/12, and replaces the Michigan Business Tax (MBT) for most taxpayers. However, businesses that have been approved to receive, have received, or have been assigned certain certified credits may elect to file a return and pay the tax imposed by the MBT in lieu of the CIT until the certified credits are exhausted or extinguished.						
Minnesota	X		X	X	X	X
Mississippi	Mississippi does not impose an alternative minimum tax					
Missouri	Missouri does not impose an alternative minimum tax					
Montana	NA	NA	NA	NA	NA	NA
Nebraska	Nebraska does not impose an alternative minimum tax					
Nevada	Nevada does not impose a corporate income tax					
New Hampshire	New Hampshire does not impose an alternative minimum tax					
New Jersey	NA	NA	NA	NA	NA	NA

Alternative Minimum Taxes (Part 2)

Tax Preference and Adjustment Items

Legend:

X	These items are treated as state tax preference or adjustment items
AMT	Alternative minimum tax
SAF	Same as applicable federal rules
NA	Not applicable
NR	Not reported

	Depletion	*Bad-Debt Reserves of Financial Institutions*	*Depreciation*	*Mining Exploration and Development Costs*	*Pollution Control Facilities*	*Intangible Drilling Costs*
New Mexico	New Mexico does not impose an alternative minimum tax					
New York	X		X	X		X
North Carolina	North Carolina does not impose an alternative minimum tax					
North Dakota	North Dakota does not impose an alternative minimum tax					
Ohio	Ohio does not impose an alternative minimum tax					
Note. Effective 1/1/2010, the Ohio Franchise Tax was fully phased out and business will be taxed on gross receipts through the Commercial Activity Tax. Details about that tax can be found at: http//tax.ohio.gov/divisions/commercial_activities/index.stm						
Oklahoma	Oklahoma does not impose an alternative minimum tax					
Oregon	NA	NA	NA	NA	NA	NA
Pennsylvania	Pennsylvania does not impose an alternative minimum tax					
Rhode Island	NA	NA	NA	NA	NA	NA
South Carolina	South Carolina does not impose an alternative minimum tax					
South Dakota	South Dakota does not impose a corporate income tax					
Tennessee	Tennessee does not impose an alternative minimum tax					
Texas	Texas does not impose an alternative minimum tax					
Utah	NA	NA	NA	NA	NA	NA
Vermont	NA	NA	NA	NA	NA	NA

Alternative Minimum Taxes (Part 2)

Tax Preference and Adjustment Items

Legend:

X	These items are treated as state tax preference or adjustment items
AMT	Alternative minimum tax
SAF	Same as applicable federal rules
NA	Not applicable
NR	Not reported

	Depletion	*Bad-Debt Reserves of Financial Institutions*	*Depreciation*	*Mining Exploration and Development Costs*	*Pollution Control Facilities*	*Intangible Drilling Costs*
Virginia	Virginia imposes an alternative minimum tax only on telecommunications companies and electric suppliers					
Washington	Washington does not impose a corporate income tax					
West Virginia	West Virginia does not impose an alternative minimum tax					
Wisconsin	Wisconsin does not impose an alternative minimum tax					
Wyoming	Wyoming does not impose a corporate income tax					

Alternative Minimum Taxes (Part 3)

Tax Preference and Adjustment Items (continued)

Legend:

X	These items are treated as state tax preference or adjustment items
AMT	Alternative minimum tax
SAF	Same as applicable federal rules
NA	Not applicable
NR	Not reported

	Completed Contract Method	*Installment Sales Method*	*Tax-Exempt Private Activity Bond Interest*	*Gain/Loss on Disposition of Property*	*Adjusted Current Earnings*
Alabama	Alabama does not impose an alternative minimum tax				
Alaska	X	X	X	X	X
Arizona	NA	NA	NA	NA	NA
Arkansas	Arkansas does not impose an alternative minimum tax				
California	X	X		X	X
Colorado	Colorado does not impose an alternative minimum tax				
Connecticut	NA	NA	NA	NA	NA
Delaware	Delaware does not impose an alternative minimum tax				
District of Columbia	NA	NA	NA	NA	NA
Florida	AMTI, as defined in IRC § 55(b)(2), less the exemption amount computed under § 55(d)				
Georgia	Georgia does not impose an alternative minimum tax				
Hawaii	Hawaii does not impose an alternative minimum tax				
Idaho	NA	NA	NA	NA	NA
Illinois	Illinois does not impose an alternative minimum tax				
Indiana	Indiana does not impose an alternative minimum tax				
Iowa	X	X		X	X
Kansas	Kansas does not impose an alternative minimum tax				

Alternative Minimum Taxes (Part 3)

Tax Preference and Adjustment Items (continued)

Legend:

X	These items are treated as state tax preference or adjustment items
AMT	Alternative minimum tax
SAF	Same as applicable federal rules
NA	Not applicable
NR	Not reported

	Completed Contract Method	*Installment Sales Method*	*Tax-Exempt Private Activity Bond Interest*	*Gain/Loss on Disposition of Property*	*Adjusted Current Earnings*
Kentucky	Kentucky does not impose an alternative minimum tax				
Louisiana	Louisiana does not impose an alternative minimum tax				
Maine	X	X	X, non Maine only		X
Maryland	Maryland does not impose an alternative minimum tax				
Massachusetts	NA	NA	NA	NA	NA
Michigan (Business Tax)	Michigan does not impose an alternative minimum tax				
Note. The CIT takes effect 01/01/12, and replaces the Michigan Business Tax (MBT) for most taxpayers. However, businesses that have been approved to receive, have received, or have been assigned certain certified credits may elect to file a return and pay the tax imposed by the MBT in lieu of the CIT until the certified credits are exhausted or extinguished.					
Minnesota					
Mississippi	Mississippi does not impose an alternative minimum tax				
Missouri	Missouri does not impose an alternative minimum tax				
Montana	NA	NA	NA	NA	NA
Nebraska	Nebraska does not impose an alternative minimum tax				
Nevada	Nevada does not impose a corporate income tax				
New Hampshire	New Hampshire does not impose an alternative minimum tax				
New Jersey	NA	NA	NA	NA	NA
New Mexico	New Mexico does not impose an alternative minimum tax				

Alternative Minimum Taxes (Part 3)
Tax Preference and Adjustment Items (continued)

Legend:

X	These items are treated as state tax preference or adjustment items
AMT	Alternative minimum tax
SAF	Same as applicable federal rules
NA	Not applicable
NR	Not reported

	Completed Contract Method	*Installment Sales Method*	*Tax-Exempt Private Activity Bond Interest*	*Gain/Loss on Disposition of Property*	*Adjusted Current Earnings*
New York	X	X		X	
North Carolina	North Carolina does not impose an alternative minimum tax				
North Dakota	North Dakota does not impose an alternative minimum tax				
Ohio	Ohio does not impose an alternative minimum tax				
Note. Effective 1/1/2010, the Ohio Franchise Tax was fully phased out and business will be taxed on gross receipts through the Commercial Activity Tax. Details about that tax can be found at: http//tax.ohio.gov/divisions/commercial_activities/index.stm					
Oklahoma	Oklahoma does not impose an alternative minimum tax				
Oregon	NA	NA	NA	NA	NA
Pennsylvania	Pennsylvania does not impose an alternative minimum tax				
Rhode Island	NA	NA	NA	NA	NA
South Carolina	South Carolina does not impose an alternative minimum tax				
South Dakota	South Dakota does not impose a corporate income tax				
Tennessee	Tennessee does not impose an alternative minimum tax				
Texas	Texas does not impose an alternative minimum tax				
Utah	NA	NA	NA	NA	NA
Vermont	NA	NA	NA	NA	NA
Virginia	Virginia imposes an alternative minimum tax only on telecommunications companies and electric suppliers				
Washington	Washington does not impose a corporate income tax				

Alternative Minimum Taxes (Part 3)
Tax Preference and Adjustment Items (continued)

Legend:

X	These items are treated as state tax preference or adjustment items
AMT	Alternative minimum tax
SAF	Same as applicable federal rules
NA	Not applicable
NR	Not reported

	Completed Contract Method	*Installment Sales Method*	*Tax-Exempt Private Activity Bond Interest*	*Gain/Loss on Disposition of Property*	*Adjusted Current Earnings*
West Virginia	West Virginia does not impose an alternative minimum tax				
Wisconsin	Wisconsin does not impose an alternative minimum tax				
Wyoming	Wyoming does not impose a corporate income tax				

Non-Income Corporate Taxes—Michigan, Ohio, Texas and Washington

Most states link their corporate tax structures to the federal net income tax model, primarily for ease of administration. Some states, however, base their corporate tax systems on different models, or impose specialized corporate taxes in addition to a regular corporate income tax. This section provides a brief overview of the following non-income corporate taxes:

- Michigan business tax (2008 to 2011)
- Ohio commercial activity tax
- Texas margin tax
- Washington business and occupation tax

Michigan Business Tax (2008 to 2011)

From 2007 to 2012, Michigan experienced two major business tax reforms. Prior to 2008, Michigan imposed a value-added tax called the *single business tax*. From 2008 to 2011, Michigan imposed both a business income tax and a modified gross receipts tax called the *Michigan business tax*. Starting in 2012, Michigan imposes a conventional corporate income tax.

Post-2011 corporate income tax. Effective January 1, 2012, Michigan replaced its business income and modified gross receipt taxes with a 6 percent corporate income tax. [H.B. 4361 and 4362, May 25, 2011]

2008-2011 Michigan Business Tax. Michigan repealed its single business tax effective December 31, 2007, and replaced it with a 4.95 percent business income tax and a 0.80 percent modified gross receipts tax that apply to business activity occurring on or after January 1, 2008. Both taxes apply to business entities generally, including C corporations, S corporations, partnerships, limited liability companies, and sole proprietorships. Taxpayers pay the sum of the two taxes. There is currently an annual surcharge equal to 21.99 percent of a taxpayer's Michigan business tax. The surcharge is capped at $6 million per year.

In lieu of the business income tax and modified gross receipts tax, insurance companies are subject to a premiums tax on gross direct premiums, and financial institutions are subject to a franchise tax on the value of their net capital.

The business income tax base is a taxpayer's federal taxable income, adjusted for numerous addition and subtraction modifications. The business income tax is imposed on every person with business activity in the state, unless prohibited by Public Law 86-272. The modified gross receipts tax base is a taxpayer's gross receipts reduced by purchases from other firms, which includes acquisitions of inventory, depreciable assets, and materials and supplies (including repair parts and fuel). The modified gross receipts tax is imposed on every person that has a physical presence in Michigan for more than one day or actively solicits sales in Michigan and has gross receipts of $350,000 or more sourced to Michigan. Examples of active solicitation include print, TV, radio or internet advertising, mail-order catalogs, or a website offering online shopping.

To provide relief for smaller businesses, taxpayers with less than $350,000 of Michigan gross receipts are exempt, and taxpayers with between $350,000 and $700,000 of Michigan gross receipts may claim a credit that provides a phase-in of the tax. In addition, taxpayers with gross receipts of $20 million or less, adjusted business income of $1.3 million or less, and officer compensation of $180,000 or less, may claim a small business credit.

A "unitary business group" must compute both the business income tax and the modified gross receipts tax on a combined basis. The term "unitary business group" is defined as (1) a group of U.S. persons, other than a foreign operating entity, one of which owns or controls more than 50 percent of the ownership interests with voting rights of the other U.S. persons, and (2) that has business activities or operations that result in a flow of value between or among persons included in the unitary business group or has business activities or operations that are integrated with, are dependent upon, or contribute to each other. The flow of value is determined by reviewing the totality of the facts and circumstances. A "foreign operating entity" is a U.S. person (e.g., a domestic corporation) that would otherwise be a part of a unitary business group, but has substantial operations outside the United States and at least 80 percent of its income is active foreign business income. Financial institutions and insurance companies are also excluded from the combined return.

All transactions between members of a unitary business group are eliminated from the business income tax base, the modified gross receipts tax base, and the apportionment formula. Thus, the business income of a unitary business group is the sum of the business income of each group member, less any items of income and related deductions arising from transactions (including dividends) between the group members. Likewise, the modified gross receipts of a unitary business group is the sum of the modified gross receipts of each group member, less any modified gross receipts arising from transactions between the group members.

The business income tax base and modified gross receipts tax base are both apportioned using a sales-only apportionment formula. In the case of a unitary business group filing a combined return, the Michigan sales include the Michigan sales of every group member, regardless of whether a member has nexus with Michigan (the so-called *Finnigan* rule), and any sales between group members are eliminated. There is no throwback rule for sales shipped from Michigan to a purchaser located in a state in which the taxpayer is not taxable. Royalties and other income received for the use of intangible property are attributed to Michigan to the extent the property is used by the purchaser in Michigan. Receipts from the performance of services are attributed to Michigan to the extent that the recipient receives the benefit of the services in Michigan.

Pre-2008 Single Business Tax. Prior to 2008, Michigan levied a 1.9 percent single business tax (SBT) that applied to all business entities, including C corporations, S corporations, partnerships, limited liability companies, and sole proprietorships. The SBT was a value-added tax, which was enacted in 1976 to replace seven other types of business taxes—hence the name "single" business tax. The value added by a corporation's operations consisted of three components: capital (measured by depreciation expense, plus net interest expense), labor (measured by compensation expense), and profit (measured by federal taxable income). Accordingly, the basic formula for computing the SBT tax base was federal taxable income, with addition modifications for depreciation expense, net interest expense, and compensation expense. The SBT tax basis was apportioned to Michigan using a three-factor apportionment formula that weights the sales factor 92.5 percent. Each member of an affiliated group of corporations with nexus in Michigan generally filed a Michigan single business tax return on a separate company basis, unless the commissioner exercised its discretionary authority to require or permit the filing of a consolidated return.

Ohio Commercial Activity Tax

Ohio imposes a *commercial activity tax* (CAT) on a business entity's gross receipts. A flat tax of $150 is imposed on the first $1 million in taxable gross receipts. For amounts greater than $1 million, the tax rate is 0.26 percent. The CAT applies to any business entities that have annual taxable gross receipts in excess of $150,000, including C corporations, S corporations, partnerships, and limited liability companies. Certain types of entities that are subject to other types of Ohio taxes are exempt from the CAT, including (1) financial institutions, which are subject to a corporate franchise tax; (2) insurance companies, which are subject to a premiums tax; (3) securities dealers, which are subject to a dealer in intangibles tax; and (4) public utilities, which are subject to a public utility excise tax.

Generally, items that are treated as gross receipts for federal income tax purposes are treated as gross receipts for CAT purposes. Examples include the amounts realized from the sale of goods, the performance of services, or the use of property. There are a number of exemptions. Specifically, the following gross receipts are not subject to the CAT: interest (except on credit sales), dividends and capital gains, principal payments on a loan, proceeds from issuing stock, insurance proceeds (except business interruption insurance), damages from litigation, sales and use taxes collected from consumers, sales returns, allowances and discounts, and bad debts.

A taxable gross receipt is a gross receipt sitused to Ohio. Sales of inventory are attributed to Ohio if the property is received in Ohio by the purchaser, rents and royalties are attributed to Ohio if the property is located or used in Ohio, and fees for services are attributed to Ohio in the proportion that the purchaser's benefit in Ohio bears to the purchaser's benefit everywhere. Thus, examples of taxable gross receipts include sales of property delivered to locations within Ohio, rents from property used in Ohio, and fees for services where the purchaser receives the benefit in Ohio.

Two or more commonly controlled corporations that have either 50 percent (or 80 percent) or more common ownership may elect to compute the CAT as a "consolidated elected taxpayer." If this election is made, receipts received between members of the group are not subject to the CAT. However, all commonly owned entities that are part of the group are included in the group, including entities that do not have nexus in Ohio on a separate company basis. The election is binding for two years, and the taxpayer may choose not to include non-U.S. entities. If the election is not made, any taxpayers with common ownership of more than 50 percent must file as a "combined taxpayer." A combined taxpayer may not exclude receipts between members of the group. However, combined taxpayers only need to include in the group those members who have nexus with Ohio. [General Information on the Commercial Activities Tax, Ohio Dept. of Taxation, July 2005].

In its Commercial Activity Tax Information Release CT 2005-02 [Sept. 2005], the Ohio Department of Taxation described the nexus standards that it will apply to determine whether a person is subject to the CAT. A person is subject to Ohio's CAT if the person: (1) owns or uses a part or all of its capital or property in this state; (2) holds a certificate of compliance with the laws of Ohio authorizing the person to do business in this state; (3) has bright-line presence in Ohio; or (4) has nexus with Ohio to an extent that the person can be required to remit the CAT under the U.S. Constitution. Even if a person has nexus under the U.S. Constitution, the Department of Taxation will only enforce nexus against persons who possess bright-line presence, which is a method of determining whether nexus exists that relies entirely upon quantitative criteria. A person has "bright-line presence" in Ohio if the person is domiciled in Ohio, or during the calendar year, the person has $50,000 of property in Ohio, $50,000 of payroll in Ohio, $500,000 of taxable gross receipts in Ohio, or 25 percent of the person's total property, total payroll or total gross receipts in Ohio. The Department of Taxation takes the position that the physical presence test for "substantial nexus" under the Commerce Clause, which the U.S. Supreme Court articulated in a case involving sales and use taxes [i.e., *Quill Corporation v. North Dakota*, 504 U.S. 298 (1992)], does not apply to the CAT. Public Law 86-272, which applies only to taxes imposed on net income, offers no protection from the CAT.

In 2010, the Ohio Department of Taxation determined that L.L. Bean, an out-of-state mail order and Internet vendor, met the statutory bright-line presence test and was subject to the CAT, because it had annual taxable gross receipts of at least $500,000 in Ohio. [*In re L.L. Bean, Inc.*, Ohio Dept. of Taxn., Aug. 10, 2010]

Corporate Franchise Tax. Prior to 2005, Ohio imposed a corporate franchise tax equal to the greater of 8.5 percent of net income or 0.4 percent of net worth (maximum of $150,000). Financial institutions were subject only to a 1.3 percent tax on net worth. Beginning in 2005, the corporate franchise tax is phased out over five years at a rate of 20 percent per year. Specifically, for tax years ending in 2005, 2006, 2007, 2008, and 2009, taxpayers pay 80 percent, 60 percent, 40 percent, 20 percent and 0 percent, respectively, of the franchise tax that would otherwise be due. For example, the tax rate is 1.7 percent in 2008. Financial institutions will continue to pay the full amount of the net worth tax, however. Roughly speaking, a corporation's "net worth" equals the net book value of its assets reduced by the net carrying value of its liabilities, as reflected in its GAAP financial statements.

Texas Margin Tax

In 2006, Texas significantly modified its corporate franchise tax, adopting a new business "margin tax." The margin tax is effective for franchise tax reports which are due on or after January 1, 2008, and which reflect taxpayer activity for calendar year 2007 or for fiscal years ending in 2007. Under prior law, the corporate franchise tax equaled the greater of 4.5 percent of net taxable earned surplus or 0.25 percent of net taxable capital.

A taxable entity's margin is the lowest of three amounts: (1) total revenue minus cost of goods sold, (2) total revenue minus compensation, or (3) 70 percent of total revenue. The tax rate is 0.5 percent for taxpayers primarily engaged in retail or wholesale trade and 1 percent for all other businesses. A taxable entity with total revenue of $10 million or less may elect to calculate its margin tax due by multiplying total revenue times the apportionment factor times 0.575 percent.

A taxable entity is primarily engaged in retail or wholesale trade if: (1) the total revenue from its activities in retail and wholesale trade is greater than the total revenue from its activities in trades other than the retail and wholesale trades; (2) except for eating and drinking places, less than 50 percent of the total revenue from activities in retail and wholesale trade comes from the sale of products the entity produces or products produced by an entity that is part of an affiliated group to which the taxable entity also belongs; and (3) the taxable entity does not provide retail or wholesale utilities, including telecommunications services, electricity or gas.

A taxable entity's total revenues are defined by reference to the amounts reported on its federal income tax return and include gross receipts or sales (less returns and allowances), dividends, interest, gross rents, gross royalties, capital gain net income, net gain or loss from the sale of trade or business assets (federal Form 4797), and other income. The following items may be excluded from gross revenue: bad debt expense, foreign dividends and royalties, net distributive income from a taxable entity treated as a partnership or S corporation for federal tax purposes, federal dividends received deduction, income from a disregarded entity for federal but not Texas margin tax purposes, dividends and interest from federal obligations, and certain other specified items.

A taxable entity may subtract cost of goods sold in computing its margin only if the entity owns the goods. Thus, service companies are generally not eligible to subtract cost of goods sold. In addition, numerous special rules apply in computing cost of goods sold for margin tax purposes; thus, the deduction will generally not be the same as the amount used in computing book income or federal taxable income. For example, a taxable entity may elect to currently expense allowable costs associated with the goods purchased or produced, in which case the entity will have no beginning or ending inventory.

If a taxable entity subtracts compensation in computing its margin, the compensation deduction will include both the compensation amounts reported on the employees' Form W-2s (maximum of $320,000 per person 2010 tax reports), as well as deductible employee benefits, including workers' compensation, health care and retirement benefits.

Texas has taken the position that the margin tax does not qualify as a net income tax for purposes of applying Public Law 86-272.

Taxable entities include C corporations, S corporations, limited liability companies, partnerships and other legal entities. Certain entities are not subject to the margin tax, including sole proprietorships (does not include single member limited liability companies), general partnerships with direct ownership entirely composed of natural persons, and passive entities. A partnership or a trust (other than a business trust) is a "passive entity" if at least 90 percent of its gross income consists of investment-type income and it does not derive more than 10 percent of its gross income from an active trade or business. A limited liability company cannot qualify as a passive entity.

Taxable entities that are part of an affiliated group engaged in a unitary business must file a combined report in lieu of individual reports. In addition to regular corporations, a combined report can include partnerships, limited liability companies and S corporations. Insurance companies that are subject to the Texas gross premium tax are not included, because they are not subject to the margin tax. The combined group is treated as a single taxable entity for purposes of calculating the margin tax and completing the required tax reports. The combined group's reporting entity files a combined report on the group's behalf and pays the margin tax imposed on the group. In addition, adjustments are made to eliminate the effect of intercompany transactions on the group's total revenue and its gross receipts factor.

Only those taxable entities that are part of an "affiliated group" engaged in a unitary business may file a Texas combined report. An affiliated group is a group of one or more entities in which a "controlling interest" is owned by a common owner, either corporate or non-corporate, or by one or more of the member entities." For a corporation, "controlling interest" means more than 50 percent direct or indirect ownership of the total combined voting power of all classes of stock of the corporation, or a more than 50 percent direct or indirect beneficial ownership interest in the voting stock of the corporation. A more than 50 percent ownership test also applies to limited liability companies and partnerships.

A taxable entity that conducts business outside the United States is excluded from a Texas combined report if 80 percent or more of its property and payroll are assigned to locations outside the United States. If either the property factor or the payroll factor is zero, the denominator is one. If a taxable entity that conducts business outside the United States has no property or payroll, the entity is excluded from the combined report if 80 percent or more of its gross receipts are assigned to locations outside the United States.

A unitary business means "a single economic enterprise that is made up of separate parts of a single entity or of a commonly controlled group of entities that are sufficiently interdependent, integrated, and interrelated through their activities so as to provide a synergy and mutual benefit that produces a sharing or exchange of value among them and a significant flow of value to the separate parts." Relevant factors in determining whether a unitary business exists include whether the activities of the group members are (1) in the same general line, such as manufacturing, wholesaling, retailing of tangible personal property, insurance, transportation, or finance; or (2) steps in a vertically structured enterprise or process, such as the steps involved in the production of natural resources, including exploration, mining, refining, and marketing. Another relevant factor is whether the members are functionally integrated through the exercise of strong centralized management, such as authority over purchasing, financing, product line, personnel, and marketing.

A taxable entity's margin is apportioned to Texas using an apportionment formula, the numerator of which is the taxable entity's gross receipts from business done in Texas and the denominator of which is the taxable entity's gross receipts from its entire business. There is no throwback rule for sales shipped from Texas to a purchaser located in a state in which the taxpayer is not taxable. Receipts from a service are apportioned to the location where the service is performed. In the case of a unitary group filing a combined report, Texas sales include only the sales of group members that have nexus with Texas on a separate company basis (the so-called *Joyce* rule).

Washington Business and Occupation Tax

The State of Washington does not impose either a corporate income tax or a personal income tax, but does impose a gross receipts tax called the *business and occupation ta x* (B&O tax). The B&O tax applies to C corporations, S corporations, partnerships, and sole proprietorships. Because it is not a net income tax, Public Law 86-272 provides no protection against the imposition of the B&O tax.

Effective June 1, 2010, for purposes of imposing the B&O tax on service activities and royalty income, an out-of-state corporation has nexus if it has more than $50,000 of property, $50,000 of payroll, $250,000 of receipts, or at least 25 percent of its total property, payroll, or receipts in Washington. [S.B. 6143, Feb. 20. 2009]

The B&O tax is imposed on a seller's gross receipts derived from business activities conducted in Washington. Taxable gross receipts generally include: (1) gross proceeds from sales of goods delivered to customers located in Washington, except for sales of goods that an in-state retailer or wholesaler delivers to customers located outside of Washington; (2) gross receipts from sales of services rendered in Washington; and (3) the value of products manufactured in Washington. Gross proceeds from sales of goods that an in-state retailer or wholesaler delivers to customers located outside of Washington are generally not taxable. Generally, no deductions are allowed for cost of goods sold, salaries, supplies, taxes, or any other costs of doing business. There are a handful of exemptions, deductions and credits, however. For example, there is an exemption for the sale or rental of real estate (other than lodging), and deductions for bad debts as well as sales returns, allowances and discounts.

One unusual aspect of the B&O tax is that the tax rate varies with the type of business activity. Moreover, it is possible for a single taxpayer to have gross receipts in two or more categories. The four primary business activity classifications are retailing, wholesaling, manufacturing, and service and other activities. The applicable rates are as follows:

Business Activity Classification	*Tax Rate*
Retailing	0.471%
Wholesaling	0.484%
Manufacturing	0.484%
Service and other activities	1.500%

In addition to the primary categories, there are numerous specialized categories, each with an associated tax rate. Examples include travel agents and tour operators (0.275 percent), manufacturing commercial aircraft (0.2904 percent), highway contractors (0.484 percent), royalties (0.484 percent), and public or nonprofit hospitals (1.5 percent).

If the same taxpayer engages in more than one type of taxable activity, that taxpayer is subject to more than one rate. For example, the same taxpayer may engage in manufacturing activities (taxed at 0.484 percent) and retailing activities (taxed at 0.471 percent). It also is possible for the same receipts to be taxed under two business activity classifications, in which case the taxpayer may claim a multiple activities credit to prevent double taxation.

Example: Acme Corporation both manufactures and sells at retail within Washington $1 million of goods. The B&O tax on the value of the goods manufactured is $4,840 ($1,000,000 × 0.484%), and the B&O tax on the gross proceeds from the sale of the goods is $4,710 ($1,000,000 × 0.471%). Acme is eligible to claim a multiple activities credit equal to the lesser of the two taxes (i.e., $4,710), which means that Acme's net B&O tax is only $4,840 ([$4,840 manufacturing tax + $4,710 retailing tax] – $4,710 multiple activities credit).

Addition Modifications to Federal Income

Most states piggyback on the federal system by adopting federal taxable income as the starting point for computing state taxable income. Some states use Line 28 of federal Form 1120 (federal taxable income before the federal dividends-received and net operating loss deductions) as the starting point for computing state taxable income, whereas other states use Line 30 of federal Form 1120 (federal taxable income, net of all deductions) as the starting point.

Conformity to the federal tax base is important, because it eases the administrative burden of computing state taxable income and creates some uniformity in state income tax systems. Despite the broad conformity to the federal tax base, each state has its own unique list of addition and subtraction modifications to federal taxable income. This section summarizes the most common types of addition modifications.

Bonus Depreciation

A major feature of the Job Creation and Worker Assistance Act of 2002 is Code Section 168(k) first year bonus depreciation equal to 30 percent of the adjusted basis of qualifying property acquired between September 11, 2001, and September 10, 2004. The Jobs and Growth Tax Relief Reconciliation Act of 2003 increased the bonus depreciation allowance from 30 percent to 50 percent for property acquired after May 5, 2003, and placed in service before 2005 (before 2006 in the case of property with a long production period and certain noncommercial aircraft).

Subsequent legislation reinstated the 50 percent bonus depreciation allowance for qualifying property acquired in 2008 (Economic Stimulus Act of 2008), 2009 (American Recovery and Reinvestment Act of 2009), and 2010 (Small Business Jobs Act of 2010). The 2010 Tax Relief Act boosted 50 percent bonus depreciation to 100 percent for property acquired after September 8, 2010 and placed in service before 2012 (before 2013 in the case of property with a long production period and certain noncommercial aircraft), and extended the 50 percent bonus depreciation allowance to qualified property placed in service during 2012 (2013 in the case of property with a long production period and certain noncommercial aircraft). (For a more detailed discussion, see the next section in this part entitled First-Year Bonus Depreciation.)

To the extent a depreciable asset's adjusted basis is different for federal and state tax purposes, an addition or subtraction modification for the difference between the federal and state gain or loss will be necessary on the disposition of an asset.

Interest Income

Another common addback to federal taxable income is interest income received on debt obligations issued by state and local governments. Such interest is excluded from federal taxable income under Code Section 103. Many states exempt interest paid on the state's own bonds, while taxing interest paid on bonds issued by other states. In such cases, an addition modification is required for interest income on bonds issued by other states. (See the section entitled Interest from Municipal Bonds in this part for a listing of each state's treatment of state and municipal interest income.)

Taxes

Most states require an addback of state and local income taxes paid to the taxpayer's own state and/ or other states. In addition, some states also require addition modifications for state and local capital stock and excise taxes. (Further details on this addition modification can be found in the section entitled Deductions for Tax Payments in this part.)

Some states allow a corporation to deduct federal income tax paid during the taxable year. If any of that tax is refunded in a later year, the taxpayer would be required to add back to state income the amount of the refund to the extent that the taxpayer received a tax benefit.

Net Operating Loss Deduction

In some states, the starting point for computing state taxable income is federal taxable income after the federal net operating loss (NOL) and dividends-received deductions (i.e., Line 30 of federal Form 1120). Unless the state requires an addition modification for an NOL deduction reported on the federal return, the corporation automatically is accorded the same NOL treatment for state and federal tax purposes. Many states do not conform to the federal NOL carryover rules, however. For example, many states do not permit an NOL carryback, whereas a two year carryback is permitted for federal tax purposes. (For further details regarding the states' treatment of NOL deductions, see the section entitled Net Operating Loss Carryovers in this part.)

Dividends-Received Deduction

As with the federal net operating loss deduction, if the starting point for computing state taxable income is Line 30 of federal Form 1120, the corporation automatically is accorded the same dividends-received deduction (DRD) treatment for state and federal tax purposes, unless the state requires an additional modification for the DRD reported on the federal return. Many states do not conform to the federal DRD rules, however. For example, state DRD provisions generally apply equally to dividends received from U.S. and foreign country corporations, whereas the federal DRD generally applies only to dividends received from a U.S. corporation. (For further details regarding the state DRD provisions, see the section entitled Treatment of Dividends in this part.)

Expenses Related to Exempt Income

Another typical addition modification relates to income that is taxable for federal purposes but either is exempt or is otherwise not subject to state tax. Several states provide that where certain types of gross income are not included in the tax base, direct (and, for some states, indirect) expenses related to generating that income also must be excluded or added back in computing the state tax base. For example, interest on obligations of the U.S. government is exempt from a pure state income tax. Accordingly, a number of states require that expenses related to generating such income must be added back to federal taxable income or offset against the exempt interest income before they are subtracted from federal taxable income. The states have different definitions for the expenses that may be considered to relate directly or indirectly to nontaxable income. Such expenses may include taxes, interest, payroll, associated office expenses (supplies, rent, and depreciation), transaction costs, and administrative fees related to the production of such income.

Expenses Related to State Credits

If a corporation is allowed a state tax credit for expenditures that were deducted on the corporation's federal income tax return, the taxpayer generally must add back those deductions in computing its state taxable income. The purpose of this addition modification is to prevent a double tax benefit for the same expenditures.

Related Party Royalty and Interest Expenses

To limit the ability of corporations to erode a state's income tax base through the use of intangible property companies and intercompany royalty and interest payments, many states require corporations to add-back deductions for royalty and interest payments made to related parties. These state add-back provisions contain numerous special rules and exceptions, and although the various state statutes share common themes, there are significant differences among the states. (For further details regarding addition modifications for related party royalty and interest expenses, see the section in this part entitled Related Party Expense Addback Provisions.)

Domestic Production Activities Deduction

Code Section 199 permits a corporation to claim a deduction equal to 9 percent of the lesser of its qualified production activities income (QPAI) or its taxable income (before the Section 199 deduction). The amount of the deduction is limited to 50 percent of the W-2 wages of the taxpayer that are allocable to domestic production gross receipts. (For further details regarding state conformity to Section 199, see the section in this part entitled Section 199 Domestic Production Activities Deduction.)

State-by-State Summary

For ease of presentation, the following chart has been divided into four parts, as follows:

- Part 1: State and local taxes
- Part 2: Depreciation
- Part 3: Amortization, depletion, and IRC Section 179 deductions
- Part 4: Municipal Interest/Carryovers
- Part 5: DRD/Refunds/Expenses Related to Credit or Excluded Income/Other

The states were not asked to list every possible addition to federal taxable income; thus, the chart does not exhaust all the possible addition modifications that may be required by each state.

Addition Modifications to Federal Income (Part 1)

State and Local Taxes

Legend:

X	**These items are added to federal taxable income in computing state income**
NA	**Not applicable**
NR	**Not reported**

	Local Income Taxes	*Franchise Taxes Based on Income (State & Local)*	*Foreign Income Taxes Deducted for Federal*	*Franchise Tax Based on Capital or Net Worth (State and Local)*	*State Income Taxes*
Alabama	X	X			X
Alaska	X	X	X		X
Arizona	X	X	X		X, added if Deducted in Computing Federal Income
Arkansas			X		X
California	X	X	X		X
Colorado					X, Colorado income tax only to the extent deducted in determining federal taxable income
Connecticut	Connecticut does not allow a deduction for any taxes imposed on or measured by the income or profits by any state, political subdivision or the District of Columbia.				
Delaware	X				X
District of Columbia	X	X	X		X
Florida		X	X		X, state income tax
Georgia	X	X	X		X, non-Georgia only
Hawaii					
Idaho	X	X			X
Illinois					

Addition Modifications to Federal Income (Part 1)

State and Local Taxes

Legend:

X — **These items are added to federal taxable income in computing state income**
NA — **Not applicable**
NR — **Not reported**

	Local Income Taxes	*Franchise Taxes Based on Income (State & Local)*	*Foreign Income Taxes Deducted for Federal*	*Franchise Tax Based on Capital or Net Worth (State and Local)*	*State Income Taxes*
Indiana		State only			X
Iowa	X				X
Kansas	X	X	X		X
Kentucky		X	X		X
Louisiana					
Maine		X	X		X
Maryland	X				X
Massachusetts					X
Michigan (Business Tax)	X	X	X		X
Note. The CIT takes effect 01/01/12, and replaces the Michigan Business Tax (MBT) for most taxpayers. However, businesses that have been approved to receive, have received, or have been assigned certain certified credits may elect to file a return and pay the tax imposed by the MBT in lieu of the CIT until the certified credits are exhausted or extinguished.					
Minnesota	X	X			X
Mississippi	X	X			X
Missouri	X	X			X
Montana	X	X	X		X
Nebraska					
Nevada	Nevada does not impose a corporate income tax				

Addition Modifications to Federal Income (Part 1)

State and Local Taxes

Legend:

X	These items are added to federal taxable income in computing state income
NA	Not applicable
NR	Not reported

	Local Income Taxes	*Franchise Taxes Based on Income (State & Local)*	*Foreign Income Taxes Deducted for Federal*	*Franchise Tax Based on Capital or Net Worth (State and Local)*	*State Income Taxes*
New Hampshire	X	X	X	X	X
New Jersey	X	X	X	X	X
New Mexico					
New York		X		X	X
North Carolina	X	X	X		X
North Dakota	X	X	X		X
Ohio	Ohio does not impose a corporate income tax				
	Note. Effective 1/1/2010, the Ohio Franchise Tax was fully phased out and business will be taxed on gross receipts through the Commercial Activity Tax. Details about that tax can be found at: http//tax.ohio.gov/divisions/commercial_activities/index.stm				
Oklahoma	X	X			X
Oregon	X	X	X		X
Pennsylvania	X	X	X		X
Rhode Island		X		X	X
South Carolina	X	X			X
South Dakota	South Dakota does not impose a corporate income tax				
Tennessee					
Texas					
Utah		X	X	X	X

Addition Modifications to Federal Income (Part 1)

State and Local Taxes

Legend:

X	**These items are added to federal taxable income in computing state income**
NA	**Not applicable**
NR	**Not reported**

	Local Income Taxes	*Franchise Taxes Based on Income (State & Local)*	*Foreign Income Taxes Deducted for Federal*	*Franchise Tax Based on Capital or Net Worth (State and Local)*	*State Income Taxes*
Vermont	X	X		X	X
Virginia	X	X	X		X
Washington	Washington does not impose a corporate income tax				
West Virginia	X	X	X		X
Wisconsin		X	X, unless taxed by Wisconsin law. See § 71.26(3)(f)(g)(h) and (hd), Wis. Stats.	X	
Wyoming	Wyoming does not impose a corporate income tax				

Addition Modifications to Federal Income (Part 2)

Depreciation

Legend:

X	These items are added to federal taxable income in computing state income
NA	Not applicable
NR	Not reported

	MACRS over State-Allowed Depreciation	*IRC Section 199 Domestic Production Activities Deduction*	*Related Party Royalty Expense*	*Related Party Interest Expenses*	*Federal First Year Bonus Depreciation*
Alabama		X	X	X	
Alaska	X	X			X
Arizona		Not Added	Depends	Depends	X
Arkansas		X	X	X	X
California	X	X	X	X	X
Colorado					
Connecticut			X	X	X
Delaware				X	
District of Columbia	X		X	Yes and no	X
Florida					X
Georgia		X	X	X	X
Note. All federal depreciation must be added back, then Georgia depreciation is computed as if §§ 168(k) and 1400L did not exist.					
Hawaii	X, but not 30% bonus	X			X

Addition Modifications to Federal Income (Part 2)

Depreciation

Legend:

X	These items are added to federal taxable income in computing state income
NA	Not applicable
NR	Not reported

	MACRS over State-Allowed Depreciation	*IRC Section 199 Domestic Production Activities Deduction*	*Related Party Royalty Expense*	*Related Party Interest Expenses*	*Federal First Year Bonus Depreciation*
Idaho					The modification is the difference between federal depreciation and depreciation computed without regard to the 30% bonus depreciation. The modification may be either an addition or a subtraction in arriving at Idaho taxable income.
Illinois			X	X	
Indiana		X	X	X	X
Iowa					X
Kansas					
Kentucky	X	X	X	X	X
Louisiana					
Maine		X			X
Maryland		X	X	X	X, only if the corporation included the 30% additional depreciation allowance in federal taxable income.

Addition Modifications to Federal Income (Part 2)

Depreciation

Legend:

X These items are added to federal taxable income in computing state income
NA Not applicable
NR Not reported

	MACRS over State-Allowed Depreciation	*IRC Section 199 Domestic Production Activities Deduction*	*Related Party Royalty Expense*	*Related Party Interest Expenses*	*Federal First Year Bonus Depreciation*
Massachusetts		X	X	X	
Michigan (Business Tax)	X		X	X	X

Note. The CIT takes effect 01/01/12, and replaces the Michigan Business Tax (MBT) for most taxpayers. However, businesses that have been approved to receive, have received, or have been assigned certain certified credits may elect to file a return and pay the tax imposed by the MBT in lieu of the CIT until the certified credits are exhausted or extinguished.

	MACRS over State-Allowed Depreciation	*IRC Section 199 Domestic Production Activities Deduction*	*Related Party Royalty Expense*	*Related Party Interest Expenses*	*Federal First Year Bonus Depreciation*
Minnesota		X			X
Mississippi		X	X	X	X
Missouri					X
Montana					
Nebraska			X	X	
Nevada	Nevada does not impose a corporate income tax				
New Hampshire		X			X
New Jersey		X	X	X	X
New Mexico					
New York	X, pre-1994	X			X, other than for Resurgence Zone or Liberty Zone Property
North Carolina	X	X			X
North Dakota					

Addition Modifications to Federal Income (Part 2)

Depreciation

Legend:

X	These items are added to federal taxable income in computing state income
NA	Not applicable
NR	Not reported

	MACRS over State-Allowed Depreciation	*IRC Section 199 Domestic Production Activities Deduction*	*Related Party Royalty Expense*	*Related Party Interest Expenses*	*Federal First Year Bonus Depreciation*
Ohio	Ohio does not impose a corporate income tax				
Note. Effective 1/1/2010, the Ohio Franchise Tax was fully phased out and business will be taxed on gross receipts through the Commercial Activity Tax. Details about that tax can be found at: http//tax.ohio.gov/divisions/commercial_activities/index.stm					
Oklahoma					
Oregon		X			2003 HB 2747 would disconnect from 30% bonus depreciation for specified four-wheeled motor vehicles not used for farm, wood production, or timber activities. It would be effective for property placed in service in tax years beginning on or after 1/1/04.
Pennsylvania			X	X	X
Rhode Island			X	X	X
South Carolina		X		X	X
South Dakota	South Dakota does not impose a corporate income tax				
Tennessee			X	X	
Texas					

Addition Modifications to Federal Income (Part 2)

Depreciation

Legend:

X	These items are added to federal taxable income in computing state income
NA	Not applicable
NR	Not reported

	MACRS over State-Allowed Depreciation	*IRC Section 199 Domestic Production Activities Deduction*	*Related Party Royalty Expense*	*Related Party Interest Expenses*	*Federal First Year Bonus Depreciation*
Utah					
Vermont					X
Virginia		X, for taxable years beginning on or after 1/1/10, there will be a partial add back of this deduction. Virginia will allow a deduction equal to two thirds of the federal deduction. Thus, taxpayers will be required to add back one third of the federal deduction.	X	X	X
Washington	Washington does not impose a corporate income tax				
West Virginia		X			

Addition Modifications to Federal Income (Part 2)

Depreciation

Legend:

X	These items are added to federal taxable income in computing state income
NA	Not applicable
NR	Not reported

	MACRS over State-Allowed Depreciation	*IRC Section 199 Domestic Production Activities Deduction*	*Related Party Royalty Expense*	*Related Party Interest Expenses*	*Federal First Year Bonus Depreciation*
Wisconsin	X	X, For taxable years beginning after 12/31/10, the Wisconsin definition of "Internal Revenue Code" for corporations, nonprofit organizations, regulated entities, tax - option(S) corporations, and insurance companies, decouples from the domestic production activities deduction provisions under section 199 of the federal IRC.	X	X	X
Wyoming	Wyoming does not impose a corporate income tax				

Addition Modifications to Federal Income (Part 3)
Amortization, Depletion, and Section 179 Deductions

Legend:

X	These items are added to federal income in computing state income
NA	Not applicable
NR	Not reported

	Federal Depletion in Excess of State Method	*Federal Amortization in Excess of State Method*	*IRC Section 179 Asset Expensing*	*Lower State Basis on Asset Disposition*
Alabama				X
Alaska	For oil/gas producers, pipelines only	For oil/gas producers, pipelines only		X
Arizona			X	X
Arkansas			X,, 2003-06 $25,000, 2007 $112,000, 2008 $115,000, 2009 $133,000, 2010 $134,000, 2011 $25,000	X
California	X	X	X, $10,000	X
Colorado				
Connecticut				
Delaware	X			
District of Columbia	X	X	X	X
Florida			X	
Georgia			X, to the extent of increases enacted federally during 2011. Georgia does not currently follow any federal Acts passed during 2011.	X

Addition Modifications to Federal Income (Part 3)

Amortization, Depletion, and Section 179 Deductions

Legend:

X	These items are added to federal income in computing state income
NA	Not applicable
NR	Not reported

	Federal Depletion in Excess of State Method	*Federal Amortization in Excess of State Method*	*IRC Section 179 Asset Expensing*	*Lower State Basis on Asset Disposition*
Hawaii				X, Hawaii has not conformed to the provisions of the Job Creation and Worker Assistance Act of 2002. See Department of Taxation Announcement 2002-5.
Idaho				
Illinois				
Indiana				
Iowa	X		X, 2009 only, has not yet coupled with the American Recovery and Reinvestment Act of 2009	X
Kansas				
Kentucky	X	X	X	X
Louisiana			X, SAF	
Maine			X, in excess of $25,000 for tax years prior to 2011	
Maryland	Oil percentage depletion deducted on federal return			
Massachusetts				

Addition Modifications to Federal Income (Part 3)

Amortization, Depletion, and Section 179 Deductions

Legend:

X	These items are added to federal income in computing state income
NA	Not applicable
NR	Not reported

	Federal Depletion in Excess of State Method	*Federal Amortization in Excess of State Method*	*IRC Section 179 Asset Expensing*	*Lower State Basis on Asset Disposition*
Michigan (Business Tax)				
Note. The CIT takes effect 01/01/12, and replaces the Michigan Business Tax (MBT) for most taxpayers. However, businesses that have been approved to receive, have received, or have been assigned certain certified credits may elect to file a return and pay the tax imposed by the MBT in lieu of the CIT until the certified credits are exhausted or extinguished.				
Minnesota	X		X	
Mississippi	X			X
Missouri				X
Montana				
Nebraska				
Nevada	Nevada does not impose a corporate income tax			
New Hampshire		X, limited to the IRC in effect at 12/31/00	X, limited to IRC of 1986 in effect on 12/31/00	X
New Jersey		Adjustment may be required	X, $25,000	
New Mexico				
New York			X, only for certain sport utility vehicles	
North Carolina				
North Dakota				
Ohio	Ohio does not impose a corporate income tax			

Addition Modifications to Federal Income (Part 3)

Amortization, Depletion, and Section 179 Deductions

Legend:

X	These items are added to federal income in computing state income
NA	Not applicable
NR	Not reported

	Federal Depletion in Excess of State Method	*Federal Amortization in Excess of State Method*	*IRC Section 179 Asset Expensing*	*Lower State Basis on Asset Disposition*
Note. Effective 1/1/2010, the Ohio Franchise Tax was fully phased out and business will be taxed on gross receipts through the Commercial Activity Tax. Details about that tax can be found at: http//tax.ohio.gov/divisions/commercial_activities/index.stm				
Oklahoma				
Oregon				
Pennsylvania				
Rhode Island		X, in excess of $25,000		
South Carolina			X	
South Dakota	South Dakota does not impose a corporate income tax			
Tennessee	X		X, as a result of 30% bonus depreciation add back	
Texas				
Utah				
Washington	Washington does not impose a corporate income tax			
West Virginia				
Wisconsin	X	X	X, $25,000 with a phase-out threshold of $200,000	X
Wyoming	Wyoming does not impose a corporate income tax			

Addition Modifications to Federal Income (Part 4)

Municipal Interest/Carryovers

Legend:

X	These items are added to federal income in computing state income
NA	Not applicable
NR	Not reported

	Municipal Bond Interest		*Federal Carryover Deductions*		
	Home State	*Other States*	*Net Capital Loss*	*Contributions*	*Federal NOL Carryover*
Alabama		X			
Alaska			X, Alaska specific items	X, Alaska specific items	X, Alaska specific items
Arizona		X			X
Arkansas		X	X	X	X
California		X	X	X	X
Colorado					X
Connecticut	X, all interest income exempt from federal taxation	X, all interest income exempt from federal taxation	X		
Delaware		X	X		X
District of Columbia			X	X	
Florida			X	X	X
Georgia		X			X

Addition Modifications to Federal Income (Part 4)
Municipal Interest/Carryovers

Legend:

X	These items are added to federal income in computing state income
NA	Not applicable
NR	Not reported

	Municipal Bond Interest		*Federal Carryover Deductions*		
	Home State	*Other States*	*Net Capital Loss*	*Contributions*	*Federal NOL Carryover*
Hawaii		X	X, see § 235-2.45(f), HRS. No capital loss carryback allowed. Capital loss carry-forward allowed by IRC § 1212(a) is limited to 5 years, except for qualified high technology business as defined in § 235-7.3, HRS, which is limited to 15 years.		
Idaho		X	X, for year with no Idaho nexus	X	
Illinois	X	X			For losses after 1986
Indiana					
Iowa	X	X			X
Kansas		X			X
Kentucky		X	X	X	X
Louisiana		Repealed by Acts 2005, No. 401 § 2 effective for all taxable periods after 12/31/05.			X
Maine		X			X, tax years 2009, 2010, and 2011

Addition Modifications to Federal Income (Part 4)

Municipal Interest/Carryovers

Legend:

X	These items are added to federal income in computing state income
NA	Not applicable
NR	Not reported

	Municipal Bond Interest		*Federal Carryover Deductions*		
	Home State	*Other States*	*Net Capital Loss*	*Contributions*	*Federal NOL Carryover*
Maryland		X	Carrybacks only		For the taxable year in which an NOL occurs, the loss is used to offset Maryland modifications; if the total of addition modifications exceeds the total of subtraction modifications, a modification to recapture the excess is required when claiming the corresponding NOL deduction.
Massachusetts	X	X	X		
Michigan (Business Tax)		X			X
Note. The CIT takes effect 01/01/12, and replaces the Michigan Business Tax (MBT) for most taxpayers. However, businesses that have been approved to receive, have received, or have been assigned certain certified credits may elect to file a return and pay the tax imposed by the MBT in lieu of the CIT until the certified credits are exhausted or extinguished.					
Minnesota	X	X	X		X
Mississippi		X	X	X	X
Missouri		X			
Montana	X	X	X	X	NA, Montana starts with federal line 28
Nebraska		X	X		X

Addition Modifications to Federal Income (Part 4)
Municipal Interest/Carryovers

Legend:

X	These items are added to federal income in computing state income
NA	Not applicable
NR	Not reported

	Municipal Bond Interest		*Federal Carryover Deductions*		
	Home State	*Other States*	*Net Capital Loss*	*Contributions*	*Federal NOL Carryover*
Nevada	Nevada does not impose a corporate income tax.				
New Hampshire					
New Jersey	X	X	X	X, federal limit on separate entity	
New Mexico		X			
New York					X
North Carolina		X	X	X	X
North Dakota		X			X
Ohio	Ohio does not impose a corporate income tax				
Note. Effective 1/1/2010, the Ohio Franchise Tax was fully phased out and business will be taxed on gross receipts through the Commercial Activity Tax. Details about that tax can be found at: http//tax.ohio.gov/divisions/commercial_activities/index.stm					
Oklahoma			X		X
Oregon		X			
Pennsylvania		X			
Rhode Island					X
South Carolina		X			X
South Dakota	South Dakota does not impose a corporate income tax				
Tennessee	X	X	X	X	
Texas					

Addition Modifications to Federal Income (Part 4)

Municipal Interest/Carryovers

Legend:

X These items are added to federal income in computing state income

NA Not applicable

NR Not reported

	Municipal Bond Interest		*Federal Carryover Deductions*		
	Home State	*Other States*	*Net Capital Loss*	*Contributions*	*Federal NOL Carryover*
Utah	X	X	X	X	X, required if taxpayer elected to deduct the capital loss in the year it was incurred.
Vermont		X			
Virginia		X			
Washington	Washington does not impose a corporate income tax				
West Virginia		X			X
Wisconsin	X	X			X, if previously deducted for Wisconsin.
Wyoming	Wyoming does not impose a corporate income tax				

Addition Modifications to Federal Income (Part 5)

DRD/Refunds/Expenses Related to Credit or Excluded Income/Other

Legend:

X	These items are added to federal income in computing state income
NA	Not applicable
NR	Not reported

	Federal Dividends-Received Deduction	*Federal Tax Refunds Included in State Income*	*Expenses Related to State Tax Credits*	*Expenditures Attributable to Items Included in Federal Taxable Income, but Excluded from State Taxable Income*	*Other Additions*
Alabama	X	X		X	
Alaska		X		X	X
Arizona	X	X	Most Credits	X	For oil and gas producers only
Arkansas	X		X	X	
California	X			X	
Colorado				X	On or after 1/1/08, an amount equal to business expense for labor services paid to an unauthorized alien that is deducted pursuant to § 162(a)(1) of the IRC but that is prohibited from being claimed as a deductible business expense for state income tax purposes pursuant to CRS 39-22-529
Connecticut	X	X		X	
Delaware					Loss on sale of U.S. or Delaware securities

Addition Modifications to Federal Income (Part 5)

DRD/Refunds/Expenses Related to Credit or Excluded Income/Other

Legend:

X	These items are added to federal income in computing state income
NA	Not applicable
NR	Not reported

	Federal Dividends-Received Deduction	*Federal Tax Refunds Included in State Income*	*Expenses Related to State Tax Credits*	*Expenditures Attributable to Items Included in Federal Taxable Income, but Excluded from State Taxable Income*	*Other Additions*
District of Columbia	Yes and no			X	
Florida			X		Tax exempt interest
Georgia				X	X, payments to Captive REITS. See O.C.G.A. §48-7-28.4
Hawaii			X		Credit for employment of vocational rehabilitation referrals determined under § 235-55.91, HRS; state and municipal bond interest not specifically exempt, see TIR 84-1; qualified research expense equal to amount of credit for research activities determined under § 235-110.91, HRS.
Idaho	X			X, includes expenses related to tax-exempt interest income and nonbusiness income	Non-Idaho state and local government interest and dividend income

Addition Modifications to Federal Income (Part 5)

DRD/Refunds/Expenses Related to Credit or Excluded Income/Other

Legend:

X	These items are added to federal income in computing state income
NA	Not applicable
NR	Not reported

	Federal Dividends-Received Deduction	*Federal Tax Refunds Included in State Income*	*Expenses Related to State Tax Credits*	*Expenditures Attributable to Items Included in Federal Taxable Income, but Excluded from State Taxable Income*	*Other Additions*
Illinois					P.A. 95-707 amended IITA §§ 203(b)(2)(E-12) effective for taxable years ending on and after 12/31/08. Extended related party expense disallowance for interest and intangible expenses to corporations that are not unitary under IITA § 1501(a)(27. P.A. added an addition modification at IITA § 293(b)(2)(E-14), effective 12/31/2008, for insurance premiums paid to certain related insurance companies and the amount of the federal dividends paid deduction allowed to REITs that is classified as a captive REIT under IITA § 1501(a)(1.5).
Indiana	X				

Addition Modifications to Federal Income (Part 5)

DRD/Refunds/Expenses Related to Credit or Excluded Income/Other

Legend:

X	These items are added to federal income in computing state income
NA	Not applicable
NR	Not reported

	Federal Dividends-Received Deduction	*Federal Tax Refunds Included in State Income*	*Expenses Related to State Tax Credits*	*Expenditures Attributable to Items Included in Federal Taxable Income, but Excluded from State Taxable Income*	*Other Additions*
Iowa		X	X, disallows charitable contributions for which a school tuition organization credit was claimed		Safe harbor lease expenses
Kansas			X, Specific credits require the addition of federal expenses and offers accelerated depreciation or amortization for state purposes. See KSA 79-32,138		State and municipal interest and amount of contributions for which the Community Services Contribution Credit is taken
Kentucky	X			X	
Louisiana	X			X	
Maine			X	X	

Addition Modifications to Federal Income (Part 5)

DRD/Refunds/Expenses Related to Credit or Excluded Income/Other

Legend:

X	These items are added to federal income in computing state income
NA	Not applicable
NR	Not reported

	Federal Dividends-Received Deduction	*Federal Tax Refunds Included in State Income*	*Expenses Related to State Tax Credits*	*Expenditures Attributable to Items Included in Federal Taxable Income, but Excluded from State Taxable Income*	*Other Additions*
Maryland					The amount of credit claimed for qualifying employees of an enterprise zone, the previous year's subtraction of certain reforestation and timber stand improvement expenses if the commercial land was decertified.
Massachusetts	X				
Michigan (Business Tax)					Losses from other taxable entities

Note. The CIT takes effect 01/01/12, and replaces the Michigan Business Tax (MBT) for most taxpayers. However, businesses that have been approved to receive, have received, or have been assigned certain certified credits may elect to file a return and pay the tax imposed by the MBT in lieu of the CIT until the certified credits are exhausted or extinguished.

Addition Modifications to Federal Income (Part 5)
DRD/Refunds/Expenses Related to Credit or Excluded Income/Other

Legend:
X These items are added to federal income in computing state income
NA Not applicable
NR Not reported

	Federal Dividends-Received Deduction	*Federal Tax Refunds Included in State Income*	*Expenses Related to State Tax Credits*	*Expenditures Attributable to Items Included in Federal Taxable Income, but Excluded from State Taxable Income*	*Other Additions*
Minnesota	X			X	Interest income exempt from federal income tax, exempt interest dividends under IRC § 852[b](5), deemed dividends from foreign operating corporations, foreign sale corporation adjustment, losses from mining operations subject to Minnesota occupation tax, partner's pro rata share of net income on which the partnership elects to pay tax, net income excluded under IRC § 114 (extra-territorial income deduction), Subpart F income (IRC § 952(a)), 80% of federal bonus depreciation
Mississippi	X		X	X	
Missouri		X		X	

Addition Modifications to Federal Income (Part 5)

DRD/Refunds/Expenses Related to Credit or Excluded Income/Other

Legend:

X	These items are added to federal income in computing state income
NA	Not applicable
NR	Not reported

	Federal Dividends-Received Deduction	*Federal Tax Refunds Included in State Income*	*Expenses Related to State Tax Credits*	*Expenditures Attributable to Items Included in Federal Taxable Income, but Excluded from State Taxable Income*	*Other Additions*
Montana	NA, Montana starts with federal line 28.	X	X	X	Tax exempt federal interest, extraterritorial income exclusion, income of unitary subsidiaries (foreign and unconsolidated domestic)
Nebraska					
Nevada	Nevada does not impose a corporate income tax				
New Hampshire				X	New Hampshire calculates federal taxable income using the IRC that was in effect on 12/31/00
New Jersey			X	X	
New Mexico					Non-New Mexico municipal bond interest

Addition Modifications to Federal Income (Part 5)

DRD/Refunds/Expenses Related to Credit or Excluded Income/Other

Legend:

X	These items are added to federal income in computing state income
NA	Not applicable
NR	Not reported

	Federal Dividends-Received Deduction	*Federal Tax Refunds Included in State Income*	*Expenses Related to State Tax Credits*	*Expenditures Attributable to Items Included in Federal Taxable Income, but Excluded from State Taxable Income*	*Other Additions*
New York			X	X	Income from worldwide activities of taxpayer not already included in federal taxable income; expenses attributable to subsidiary capital
North Carolina		X			Royalty payments required to be added back by GS 105-130.7A to the extent deducted in calculating federal taxable income
North Dakota	X			X	For tax years 2005-2006, the amount of extraterritorial income excluded under the 2004 A.J.C.A., §§ 101(d), (e), and (f). For tax years beginning after 12/31/05, the amount of the U.S. production tax activities deducted under IRC § 199 in calculating federal taxable income

Addition Modifications to Federal Income (Part 5)

DRD/Refunds/Expenses Related to Credit or Excluded Income/Other

Legend:

X	These items are added to federal income in computing state income
NA	Not applicable
NR	Not reported

	Federal Dividends-Received Deduction	*Federal Tax Refunds Included in State Income*	*Expenses Related to State Tax Credits*	*Expenditures Attributable to Items Included in Federal Taxable Income, but Excluded from State Taxable Income*	*Other Additions*
Ohio	Ohio does not impose a corporate income tax				
Note. Effective 1/1/2010, the Ohio Franchise Tax was fully phased out and business will be taxed on gross receipts through the Commercial Activity Tax. Details about that tax can be found at: http//tax.ohio.gov/divisions/commercial_activities/index.stm					
Oklahoma			X		
Oregon	X, in law but not on form, which starts with federal taxable income before dividends-received deduction	X		X	2003 HB 2914 would create an addition of the amount of contribution to a qualified forestry resource organization if such contribution was used to compute a credit, effective for tax years beginning on or after 1/1/04. 2003 HB 2182 requires add-back of extraterritorial income exclusion from federal return for tax years beginning on or after 1/1/03
Pennsylvania			X	X	Employer Incentive Payment Credit; tax preference; IRC § 168 K bonus depreciation

Addition Modifications to Federal Income (Part 5)

DRD/Refunds/Expenses Related to Credit or Excluded Income/Other

Legend:

X	These items are added to federal income in computing state income
NA	Not applicable
NR	Not reported

	Federal Dividends-Received Deduction	*Federal Tax Refunds Included in State Income*	*Expenses Related to State Tax Credits*	*Expenditures Attributable to Items Included in Federal Taxable Income, but Excluded from State Taxable Income*	*Other Additions*
Rhode Island					Tax exempt interest other than RI obligations
South Carolina				X	
South Dakota	South Dakota does not impose a corporate income tax				
Tennessee			X		Tax-exempt interest and depreciation computed under the federal Job Creation and Worker Assistance Act of 2002 (effective tax years ending on or after 7/15/02)

Addition Modifications to Federal Income (Part 5)

DRD/Refunds/Expenses Related to Credit or Excluded Income/Other

Legend:

X	These items are added to federal income in computing state income
NA	Not applicable
NR	Not reported

	Federal Dividends-Received Deduction	*Federal Tax Refunds Included in State Income*	*Expenses Related to State Tax Credits*	*Expenditures Attributable to Items Included in Federal Taxable Income, but Excluded from State Taxable Income*	*Other Additions*
Texas					Total revenue is determined based on revenue amounts reported for federal income tax minus statutory exclusions. Exclusions include: Bad debt expensed for federal income tax, Dividends and interest from federal obligations; Sch C dividends deduction; Foreign royalties and dividend from affiliated taxable entity that does not transact a substantial portion of its business or regularly maintain a substantial portion of its assets in the US including amounts determined under IRC § 78 or § § 951-964; Net distributive income from a taxable entity that is disregarded for

Addition Modifications to Federal Income (Part 5)

DRD/Refunds/Expenses Related to Credit or Excluded Income/Other

Legend:

X	These items are added to federal income in computing state income
NA	Not applicable
NR	Not reported

	Federal Dividends-Received Deduction	*Federal Tax Refunds Included in State Income*	*Expenses Related to State Tax Credits*	*Expenditures Attributable to Items Included in Federal Taxable Income, but Excluded from State Taxable Income*	*Other Additions*
					federal income tax; certain flow thru funds. For health care providers, revenues from Medicaid, Medicare, Children's Health Ins Prg, Worker's Comp claims, TRICARE and actual costs for uncompensated care. For health institutions, 50% of revenues for Medicaid, Medicare, Children's Health Ins Prg, Worker's Comp claims, TRICARE, and actual costs for uncompensated care; payments made to persons providing services, labor, or materials in connection with the provision of destination management services as defined in TX Tax Code § 151.0565 and effective

Addition Modifications to Federal Income (Part 5)

DRD/Refunds/Expenses Related to Credit or Excluded Income/Other

Legend:

X	These items are added to federal income in computing state income
NA	Not applicable
NR	Not reported

	Federal Dividends-Received Deduction	*Federal Tax Refunds Included in State Income*	*Expenses Related to State Tax Credits*	*Expenditures Attributable to Items Included in Federal Taxable Income, but Excluded from State Taxable Income*	*Other Additions*
					for reports originally due on or after 1/1/2010
Utah			X	X, (1) amounts withdrawn from a Utah Educational Savings Plan (2) Dividends paid deduction in connection with the statutorily required combination of a captive Real Estate Investment Trust.	
Vermont				X	
Virginia				X	Captive REITs must add back 50% of their deduction for dividends paid in 2009 and 2010, and 100% of their deduction for dividends paid thereafter.
Washington	Washington does not impose a corporate income tax				

Addition Modifications to Federal Income (Part 5)
DRD/Refunds/Expenses Related to Credit or Excluded Income/Other

Legend:

X	These items are added to federal income in computing state income
NA	Not applicable
NR	Not reported

	Federal Dividends-Received Deduction	*Federal Tax Refunds Included in State Income*	*Expenses Related to State Tax Credits*	*Expenditures Attributable to Items Included in Federal Taxable Income, but Excluded from State Taxable Income*	*Other Additions*
West Virginia					IRC § 572 unrelated business taxable income, tax-exempt interest, net foreign-source income
Wisconsin	X		X, the credit amounts themselves are addition modifications, except for the supplement to the Federal Historic Rehabilitation Credit and the Early State Seed Investment Credit, for which the basis of the assets must be reduced by the amount of the credits.	X	See Wis. Stat. § 71.26(3)
Wyoming	Wyoming does not impose a corporate income tax				

Subtraction Modifications to Federal Income

Most states "piggyback" on the federal system by adopting federal taxable income as the starting point for computing state taxable income. Some states use Line 28 of federal Form 1120 (federal taxable income before the federal dividends-received and net operating loss deductions) as the starting point for computing state taxable income, whereas other states use Line 30 of federal Form 1120 (federal taxable income, net of all deductions) as the starting point.

Conformity to the federal tax base is important because it eases the administrative burden of computing state taxable income and creates some uniformity in state income tax systems. Despite the broad conformity to the federal tax base, each state has its own unique list of addition and subtraction modifications to federal taxable income. This section summarizes the most common types of subtraction modifications.

State Net Operating Loss Deduction

For federal tax purposes, corporate taxpayers can carry net operating loss deductions back 2 years and forward 20 years. [IRC § 172]Most states also allow net operating loss deductions, but the specific rules vary significantly from state to state. As a consequence, there is often a difference between the amount of the federal and state net operating loss deductions.

These federal-state differences arise for a number of reasons, including (1) state carryover qualification requirements such as the requirement that the taxpayer have nexus in the year the net operating loss arises, (2) states' disallowance of carrybacks or having carryforward periods that differ from the 20-year federal carryforward, (3) state statutory limitations on the dollar amount of the carryover allowed, (4) different corporate group filing options for federal and state tax purposes, and (5) computation of the state net operating loss carryover on a pre- versus post-apportionment basis. Depending in part on whether the state uses Line 28 or Line 30 of federal Form 1120 as the starting point for computing state taxable income, the requisite adjustment may take the form of an addition and/or subtraction modification. (For a more detailed discussion, see the section entitled Net Operating Loss Carryovers in this part.)

State Dividends-Received Deduction

For federal tax purposes, a corporation generally is allowed to deduct 70 percent of the dividends received from a less-than-20 percent owned domestic corporation, 80 percent of the dividends received from a 20 percent or more owned nonaffiliated domestic corporation, and 100 percent of the dividends received from corporations that are members of an affiliated group with the recipient corporation. [IRC § 243]

Most states allow some form of dividends-received deduction, but the specific ownership requirements and deduction percentages vary significantly from one state to another. In addition, whereas the federal government does not allow a dividends-received deduction for dividends received from foreign subsidiaries, many states allow such a deduction. This federal-state difference is due in large part to the U.S. Supreme Court's decision in *Kraft General Foods, Inc. v. Iowa Department of Revenue & Finance* [505 U.S. 71 (1992)], in which the Court held that Iowa's disparate treatment of dividends from domestic versus foreign subsidiaries discriminated against foreign commerce in violation of the U.S. Constitution. If the state definition of corporate taxable income begins with Line 28 of federal Form 1120 (federal taxable income before the federal dividends-received and net operating loss deductions), the state dividends-received deduction may take the form of a subtraction modification. (For a more detailed discussion, see the section entitled Treatment of Dividends in this part.)

Section 78 Gross-up Income

For federal income tax purposes, a U.S. parent corporation can claim a deemed paid foreign tax credit for the foreign income taxes paid by a 10 percent or more owned foreign corporation. [IRC § 902] To prevent a double tax benefit, the U.S. parent must gross up its dividend income by the amount of the deemed paid credit. [IRC § 78] This federal income inclusion is referred to as the "Section 78 gross-up."

Because states do not allow a credit for foreign income taxes paid by a foreign subsidiary, a subtraction modification is typically provided for Section 78 gross-up income.

Subpart F Income

Under Subpart F [IRC §§ 951–964], a U.S. shareholder of a controlled foreign corporation must include in federal taxable income a deemed dividend equal to the U.S. shareholder's pro rata share of the controlled foreign corporation's insurance and foreign base company income, as well as any increase in earnings invested in U.S. property. States generally allow a subtraction modification for deemed dividends under Subpart F. (For a more detailed discussion, see the section entitled Income from Foreign Subsidiaries in Part 7.)

Interest Earned on Federal Obligations

Federal taxable income includes interest income derived from obligations of the federal government, such as U.S. Treasury notes. [Treas. Reg. § 1.61-7(b)(3)] However, federal law prohibits states from taxing federal interest, unless the tax imposed is a nondiscriminatory corporate franchise tax. [31 USC § 3124] Thus, most states provide a subtraction modification for federal interest income. Nevertheless, some states impose corporate franchise taxes, which are measured by income, on federal interest.

Expenses Related to Federal Credits

The federal government allows corporate taxpayers to claim a number of credits, such as the federal credit for research and experimentation expenditures. To the extent the taxpayer claims a credit for federal tax purposes, generally it must add back the related deductions in computing federal taxable income [IRC § 280C]. If a state does not provide a credit comparable to that claimed for federal purposes, the state will often provide a subtraction modification for the deductions disallowed at the federal level.

State-by-State Summary

The following chart, presented in three parts, provides information regarding common subtractions from federal income in computing state income, as follows:

Part 1

- State dividends-received deduction
- IRC Section 78 foreign dividend gross-up income
- Subpart F income
- Other foreign source income
- Foreign income taxes disallowed for federal purposes because a credit was claimed
- State NOL deduction

Part 2

- Federal interest income
- Expenses related to federal tax credits
- State income tax refunds included on the federal return
- Higher state basis on asset dispositions
- Federal income taxes

Part 3

- Subtraction for prior year addback of federal
  - First-year bonus depreciation
  - IRC Section 179 asset expensing
- Capital gain exclusion or deduction allowed by state
- Other subtractions

Subtraction Modifications to Federal Income (Part 1)

Legend:

X	These items are subtracted from federal income in computing state income
NA	Not applicable
NR	Not reported
SAF	Same as applicable federal rules

	State Dividends-Received Deduction	*IRC Section 78 Foreign Dividend Gross-Up Income*	*Subpart F Income*	*Other Foreign Source Income*	*Foreign Income Taxes Disallowed for Federal Purposes Because a Credit Was Claimed*	*State NOL Deduction*
Alabama	X	X	X		X	X
Alaska	X	X	X	X, 80% Royalties, see AC 43.20.073(b)(3)		X
Arizona	X	X	X			X
Arkansas	X	X	X		X	X
California	X	X	X			X
Colorado		X		X, see Colo. Rev. Stat. § 39-22-303(10)		X
Connecticut						
Delaware		X	X	Interest, royalties		
District of Columbia	X	X	X			X
Florida		X	X	X, eligible net income, international banking facility		X
Georgia		X	X			X

Subtraction Modifications to Federal Income (Part 1)

Legend:

X	These items are subtracted from federal income in computing state income
NA	Not applicable
NR	Not reported
SAF	Same as applicable federal rules

	State Dividends-Received Deduction	*IRC Section 78 Foreign Dividend Gross-Up Income*	*Subpart F Income*	*Other Foreign Source Income*	*Foreign Income Taxes Disallowed for Federal Purposes Because a Credit Was Claimed*	*State NOL Deduction*
Hawaii	X, see § 235-7(c), HRS	X, Hawaii does not conform to IRC § 902 under § 235-55(b)(1), HRS; therefore, the gross-up dividend requirement is not applicable.	X, Hawaii does not conform to IRC § 951 under § 235-2-3, HRS; thus, the inclusion of CFC's subpart F income by its U.S. shareholders is not required.		X, depends on facts and circumstances, see §§ 235-55 and 235-4(d), HRS.	X
Idaho		X	X, water's-edge taxpayers allowed a dividends received deduction; worldwide filers allowed a deduction in full if included in the unitary combined group			
Illinois		X	For tax years ending on or after 12/31/88	Foreign corporation dividends		X
Indiana	X	X	X	X		X
Iowa		X	X	X, other foreign dividend income		X
Kansas		X, 100% deduction	X, 80% deduction	X, all other foreign dividends 80% deduction		

Subtraction Modifications to Federal Income (Part 1)

Legend:

X	These items are subtracted from federal income in computing state income
NA	Not applicable
NR	Not reported
SAF	Same as applicable federal rules

	State Dividends-Received Deduction	*IRC Section 78 Foreign Dividend Gross-Up Income*	*Subpart F Income*	*Other Foreign Source Income*	*Foreign Income Taxes Disallowed for Federal Purposes Because a Credit Was Claimed*	*State NOL Deduction*
Kentucky	X	X	X			X
Louisiana		X	X			
Maine	X	X				
Maryland		X	Subpart F income, to the extent required to be included in federal taxable income, is treated as a subtraction; however, the corporation that has the allowable Subpart F income must own, directly or indirectly, 50% or more outstanding shares of capital stock of the controlled foreign corporation.			
Massachusetts	X					X
	State has its own NOL and dividend deduction provisions					

Subtraction Modifications to Federal Income (Part 1)

Legend:

X	These items are subtracted from federal income in computing state income
NA	Not applicable
NR	Not reported
SAF	Same as applicable federal rules

	State Dividends-Received Deduction	*IRC Section 78 Foreign Dividend Gross-Up Income*	*Subpart F Income*	*Other Foreign Source Income*	*Foreign Income Taxes Disallowed for Federal Purposes Because a Credit Was Claimed*	*State NOL Deduction*
Michigan (Business Tax)		X	X	Dividends and royalties from persons other than U.S. persons and foreign operating entities		
Note. The CIT takes effect 01/01/12, and replaces the Michigan Business Tax (MBT) for most taxpayers. However, businesses that have been approved to receive, have received, or have been assigned certain certified credits may elect to file a return and pay the tax imposed by the MBT in lieu of the CIT until the certified credits are exhausted or extinguished.						
Minnesota	X	X				X
Mississippi	X	X	X	X, interest		
Missouri	X	X	X			
Montana	X	X	X, If foreign corporation is included in combined unitary group			X
Nebraska	X	X	X			X
Nevada	Nevada does not impose a corporate income tax					
New Hampshire		X				X
New Jersey	X	X	X		X, but no after 1/1/02	X

Subtraction Modifications to Federal Income (Part 1)

Legend:	
X	These items are subtracted from federal income in computing state income
NA	Not applicable
NR	Not reported
SAF	Same as applicable federal rules

	State Dividends-Received Deduction	*IRC Section 78 Foreign Dividend Gross-Up Income*	*Subpart F Income*	*Other Foreign Source Income*	*Foreign Income Taxes Disallowed for Federal Purposes Because a Credit Was Claimed*	*State NOL Deduction*
New Mexico	X	X				X
New York	X	X	X	X, banks only		X
North Carolina		X	X			X
North Dakota		X, if unitary	X, if unitary			X
Ohio	Ohio does not impose a corporate income tax					
	Note. Effective 1/1/2010, the Ohio Franchise Tax was fully phased out and business will be taxed on gross receipts through the Commercial Activity Tax. Details about that tax can be found at: http//tax.ohio.gov/divisions/commercial_activities/index.stm					
Oklahoma		X	X			
Oregon	X	X				X
Pennsylvania	X	X				X
Rhode Island	X	X	X			X
South Carolina		X				X
South Dakota	South Dakota does not impose a corporate income tax					
Tennessee	X	X				
Texas						
Utah	X	X				
Vermont		X	X			

Subtraction Modifications to Federal Income (Part 1)

Legend:

X	These items are subtracted from federal income in computing state income
NA	Not applicable
NR	Not reported
SAF	Same as applicable federal rules

	State Dividends-Received Deduction	*IRC Section 78 Foreign Dividend Gross-Up Income*	*Subpart F Income*	*Other Foreign Source Income*	*Foreign Income Taxes Disallowed for Federal Purposes Because a Credit Was Claimed*	*State NOL Deduction*
Virginia	X	X	X	X, as defined in Va. Code Ann. § 58.1-302		
Washington	Washington does not impose a corporate income tax					
West Virginia		X	X	X, net foreign income		
Wisconsin	X	X	X		X	X
Wyoming	Wyoming does not impose a corporate income tax					

Legend:

X	These items are subtracted from federal income in computing state income
NA	Not applicable
NR	Not reported

Subtraction Modifications to Federal Income (Part 2)

	Federal Interest Income	*Expenses Related to Federal Tax Credits*	*State Income Tax Refunds Included on Federal Return*	*Higher State Basis on Asset Dispositions*	*Federal Income Taxes*
Alabama	X	X	X		X
Alaska			X		
Arizona	Subtracted if Included in Federal Taxable Income, See Corp Ruling CTR 06-1	X	X	Depends	
Arkansas	X	X		X	
California	X	X	X	X	
Colorado			X		
Connecticut	X				
Delaware	X	X	X		
District of Columbia	X	X	X	X	
Florida					
Georgia	X		X, Non-Georgia only	X	
Hawaii	X	X		X	
Idaho	X		X	X	

Subtraction Modifications to Federal Income (Part 2)

Legend:

X	These items are subtracted from federal income in computing state income
NA	Not applicable
NR	Not reported

	Federal Interest Income	*Expenses Related to Federal Tax Credits*	*State Income Tax Refunds Included on Federal Return*	*Higher State Basis on Asset Dispositions*	*Federal Income Taxes*
Illinois	X	X, certain Disallowed expenses may be subtracted, See ILCS 5/203(B)(2)(l).	X	X, upon disposition of bonus depreciation property, all prior addition and subtraction modifications are reversed. Thus, a subtraction modification is allowed for bonus depreciation previously added back, and an addition modification is required equal to the total IL subtraction modifications previously allowed for the property. See IL-4562.	
Indiana	X				
Iowa	X	X	X	X	X
Kansas	X	X, federal jobs or specific employee classes	X		
Kentucky	X	X	X	X	
Louisiana	X		X		

Subtraction Modifications to Federal Income (Part 2)

Legend:
X These items are subtracted from federal income in computing state income
NA Not applicable
NR Not reported

	Federal Interest Income	*Expenses Related to Federal Tax Credits*	*State Income Tax Refunds Included on Federal Return*	*Higher State Basis on Asset Dispositions*	*Federal Income Taxes*
Maine	X		X	X, for tax years beginning after 2008 with respect to bonus depreciation adjustments only for tax years beginning after 2007	
Maryland	X	X, Maryland has own Research Credit	X		
Massachusetts				X	
Michigan (Business Tax)	X		X		
Note. The CIT takes effect 01/01/12, and replaces the Michigan Business Tax (MBT) for most taxpayers. However, businesses that have been approved to receive, have received, or have been assigned certain certified credits may elect to file a return and pay the tax imposed by the MBT in lieu of the CIT until the certified credits are exhausted or extinguished.					
Minnesota		X	X		
Mississippi	X	X	X	X	
Missouri	X		X	X	X
Montana		X	X		
Nebraska	X				
Nevada					
New Hampshire	X, deduct U.S. government obligations only		X	X	

Subtraction Modifications to Federal Income (Part 2)

Legend:
X — These items are subtracted from federal income in computing state income
NA — Not applicable
NR — Not reported

	Federal Interest Income	*Expenses Related to Federal Tax Credits*	*State Income Tax Refunds Included on Federal Return*	*Higher State Basis on Asset Dispositions*	*Federal Income Taxes*
New Jersey			X		
New Mexico	X				
New York		X	X		
North Carolina	X	X	X	X	
North Dakota	X		X, if previously included on state tax return		X, for tax years beginning before 1/1/04
Ohio	Ohio does not impose a corporate income tax				
Note. Effective 1/1/2010, the Ohio Franchise Tax was fully phased out and business will be taxed on gross receipts through the Commercial Activity Tax. Details about that tax can be found at: http//tax.ohio.gov/divisions/commercial_activities/index.stm					
Oklahoma			X		
Oregon	X		X	X	
Pennsylvania	X	X	X, if previously included in taxable income base		
Rhode Island	X		X	X	
South Carolina	X	X	X	X	
South Dakota					
Tennessee		X		X	
Texas					
Utah		X			

Legend:
X These items are subtracted from federal income in computing state income
NA Not applicable
NR Not reported

Subtraction Modifications to Federal Income (Part 2)

	Federal Interest Income	*Expenses Related to Federal Tax Credits*	*State Income Tax Refunds Included on Federal Return*	*Higher State Basis on Asset Dispositions*	*Federal Income Taxes*
Vermont	X				
Virginia	X	X	X		
Washington					
West Virginia		X	X		
Wisconsin	X, if the corporation was subject to Wisconsin Income Tax rather than the Franchise Tax.	X	X	X	
Wyoming					

Subtraction Modifications to Federal Income (Part 3)

Legend:

X	**These items are subtracted from federal income in computing state income**
NA	**Not applicable**
NR	**Not reported**

	Subtraction for Prior Year Addback of Federal			
	First-Year Bonus Depreciation	*IRC Section 179 Asset Expensing*	*Capital Gain Exclusion or Deduction Allowed by State*	*Other Subtractions*
Alabama	X	X		SIDA assistance; oil and gas depletion and Small Business Health Insurance Premiums
Alaska				
Arizona	See ARS §§ 43-1121 and 43-1122	See ARS §§ 43-1121 and 43-1122		
Arkansas	X	X		
California				
Colorado			X, if qualified under 39-22-518 as a Colorado gain	
Connecticut			X, this only applies to state capital gain on preserved open space land transferred to the state.	Federal bonus depreciation recovery; exceptions to interest and intangible add-back; capital loss carryover if not deducted in computing federal capital gain
Delaware				
District of Columbia			X	
Florida				Florida net capital loss carryforward deduction
Georgia	NR	NR		Exceptions to intangible and interest expense addback. See OCGA 48-7-28.3 Exceptions to Captive REITS addback. OCGA 48-7-28.4

Legend:

X These items are subtracted from federal income in computing state income

NA Not applicable

NR Not reported

Subtraction Modifications to Federal Income (Part 3)

	Subtraction for Prior Year Addback of Federal			
	First-Year Bonus Depreciation	*IRC Section 179 Asset Expensing*	*Capital Gain Exclusion or Deduction Allowed by State*	*Other Subtractions*
Hawaii	X	X	X, see § 235-9.5, HRS.	Interest on federal obligations (see TIR 84-1); basis differences on asset dispositions; certain tax incentives available to qualified high technology businesses, see §§ 235-7.3, 235-9.5, and 235-111.5, HRS.
Idaho	X			U.S. interest less offset; donated technological equipment to qualifying institutions; federal bonus depreciation; effective 1/1/04, in certain circumstances, mutual insurance holding companies may exclude dividends or distributions issued by a stock insurance subsidiary to the mutual insurance holding company or intermediate holding company.
Illinois	X			P.A. 95-707 amended IITA § 203(b)(2)(W) & (X) to take into account §§ 203(b)(2)(E-12) & (E-13) and amended IITA § 203(b)(2)(O) to allow dividends-received deduction for dividends received from a captive REIT and added IITA § 203(b)(2)(E-14) to allow a subtraction for insurance premium income that is subject to the addition modification effective 12/31/08.
Indiana	X			Safe harbor lease income; federal TIP credit; alcohol fuel credit
Iowa	X			Income received by IA-based businesses related to qualified expenditures relating to film production approved by the IA Film Office effective for tax years beginning on or after 1-1-07.
Kansas				Interest on U.S. obligations
Kentucky	X	X	X	
Louisiana				
Maine	X	X		

Subtraction Modifications to Federal Income (Part 3)

Legend:

X	**These items are subtracted from federal income in computing state income**
NA	**Not applicable**
NR	**Not reported**

	Subtraction for Prior Year Addback of Federal			
	First-Year Bonus Depreciation	*IRC Section 179 Asset Expensing*	*Capital Gain Exclusion or Deduction Allowed by State*	*Other Subtractions*
Maryland				Gross receipts (less expenses) subject to public service company franchise tax; expenses incurred for the purchase and installation of certain farm conservation tillage and liquid manure soil injection equipment; income derived from any security, share of capital stock, or evidence of indebtedness of the development credit corporation of Maryland; relocation assistance payments; certain reforestation and timber land improvement expenses; expenses to convert an old furnace or purchase a new furnace to utilize used oil; expenses to purchase and install equipment to recycle used freon; job creation tax credit
Massachusetts	X			
Michigan (Business Tax)				• SE income of sole proprietorships and partnerships, income from other taxable entities

Note. The CIT takes effect 01/01/12, and replaces the Michigan Business Tax (MBT) for most taxpayers. However, businesses that have been approved to receive, have received, or have been assigned certain certified credits may elect to file a return and pay the tax imposed by the MBT in lieu of the CIT until the certified credits are exhausted or extinguished.

Legend:

X These items are subtracted from federal income in computing state income

NA Not applicable

NR Not reported

Subtraction Modifications to Federal Income (Part 3)

	Subtraction for Prior Year Addback of Federal			
	First-Year Bonus Depreciation	*IRC Section 179 Asset Expensing*	*Capital Gain Exclusion or Deduction Allowed by State*	*Other Subtractions*
Minnesota	X	X		• Dividend (not including any distribution in liquidation) paid within the taxable year by a national or state bank to the United States, or to any instrumentality of the United States exempt from income taxes, on the preferred stock of the bank owned by the United States or the instrumentality. • Amounts disallowed for intangible drilling costs due to differences between this chapter and the IRC in taxable years beginning before 1/1/87. • Amount for interest and expenses relating to income not taxable for federal income tax purposes if (1) the income is taxable under this chapter (Chapter 1, H.F. 8) and (2) the interest and expenses were disallowed as deductions under the provisions of IRC § 171(a)(2), § 265, or § 291 in computing federal taxable income. • In the case of mines, oil and gas wells, other natural deposits, and timber for which percentage depletion was disallowed pursuant to Minn. Stat. § 290.01, subd. 19c, clause (11), a reasonable allowance for depletion based on actual cost. • For certified pollution control facilities placed in service in a taxable year beginning before 12/31/86, and for which amortization deductions were elected under § 169 of the Internal Revenue Code of 1954, as amended through 12/31/85, an amount equal to the allowance for depreciation under Minnesota Statutes 1986 § 290.09, subd. 7. • 80% of royalties, fees, or other like income accrued

Legend:

Subtraction Modifications to Federal Income (Part 3)

X — **These items are subtracted from federal income in computing state income**
NA — **Not applicable**
NR — **Not reported**

Subtraction for Prior Year Addback of Federal: First-Year Bonus Depreciation	*Subtraction for Prior Year Addback of Federal: IRC Section 179 Asset Expensing*	*Capital Gain Exclusion or Deduction Allowed by State*	*Other Subtractions*
			or received from a foreign operating corporation or a foreign corporation which is part of the same unitary business as the receiving corporation. • Income or gains from the business of mining. • Disability access expenditures in the taxable year which are not allowed to be deducted or capitalized under IRC § 44(d)(7). • The amount of qualified research expenses not allowed for federal income tax purposes under IRC § 280C, but only to the extent that the amount exceeds the amount of credit allowed under Minn. Stat. § 290.068. • The amount of any refund of environmental taxes paid under IRC § 59A. • For taxable years beginning before January 1, 2008, the amount of the federal small ethanol producer credit allowed under IRC § 40(a)(3) which is included in gross income under IRC § 87. • For a corporation whose foreign sales corporation, as defined in IRC § 922, constituted a foreign operating corporation during any taxable year ending before 1/1/95, and a return was filed by 8/15/96, claiming the deduction under Minn. Stat. § 290.21, subd. 4, for income received from the foreign operating corporation, an amount equal to 1.23 multiplied by the amount excluded under IRC § 114, provided the income is not income of a foreign operating company. • Any decrease in Subpart F income, as defined in

Subtraction Modifications to Federal Income (Part 3)

Legend:

X — **These items are subtracted from federal income in computing state income**
NA — **Not applicable**
NR — **Not reported**

	Subtraction for Prior Year Addback of Federal			
	First-Year Bonus Depreciation	*IRC Section 179 Asset Expensing*	*Capital Gain Exclusion or Deduction Allowed by State*	*Other Subtractions*
equal to one-fifth of the amount of the addition.				
Mississippi		X	X	
Missouri	X			Expenses related to municipal interest
Montana				Current year capital losses
Nebraska				
Nevada				
New Hampshire				New Hampshire calculates federal taxable income using the IRC of 1986 in effect on 12/31/2000
New Jersey				
New Mexico				
New York			X, certain gains only	Income from subsidiary capital
North Carolina	X	X		
North Dakota				
Ohio	Ohio does not impose a corporate income tax			

Note. Effective 1/1/2010, the Ohio Franchise Tax was fully phased out and business will be taxed on gross receipts through the Commercial Activity Tax. Details about that tax can be found at: http//tax.ohio.gov/divisions/commercial_activities/index.stm

Subtraction Modifications to Federal Income (Part 3)

Legend:

X **These items are subtracted from federal income in computing state income**
NA **Not applicable**
NR **Not reported**

	Subtraction for Prior Year Addback of Federal			
	First-Year Bonus Depreciation	*IRC Section 179 Asset Expensing*	*Capital Gain Exclusion or Deduction Allowed by State*	*Other Subtractions*
Oklahoma				
Oregon	X	X		2003 HB 2991 allows election to not have capital gain on qualified sale of farmland or water right taxed if reinvestment or application to long-term farm debt made within one year, effective for tax years beginning on or after 1/1/04.
Pennsylvania	X	X		Deduction equal to reduction in employer's deduction for wages and salaries related to employer taking a FICA credit on its employer's tips or targeted jobs pursuant to IRC 45B or IRC 51. 72 PS § 7401(3)(c).
Rhode island	X	X		
South Carolina	X			
South Dakota				
Tennessee	X			Excess federal capital losses; cash donations to "qualified public school support organizations."

Subtraction Modifications to Federal Income (Part 3)

Legend:
X — **These items are subtracted from federal income in computing state income**
NA — **Not applicable**
NR — **Not reported**

	Subtraction for Prior Year Addback of Federal			
	First-Year Bonus Depreciation	*IRC Section 179 Asset Expensing*	*Capital Gain Exclusion or Deduction Allowed by State*	*Other Subtractions*
Texas				Total revenue is determined based on revenue amounts reported for federal income tax minus statutory exclusions. Exclusions include: Bad debt expensed for federal income tax, Dividends and interest from federal obligations; Sch C dividends deduction; Foreign royalties and dividend from affiliated taxable entity that does not transact a substantial portion of its business or regularly maintain a substantial portion of its assets in the US including amounts determined under IRC § 78 or § § 951-964; Net distributive income from a taxable entity that is disregarded for federal income tax; certain flow thru funds. For health care providers, revenues from Medicaid, Medicare, Children's Health Ins Prg, Worker's Comp claims, TRICARE and actual costs for uncompensated care. For health institutions, 50% of revenues for Medicaid, Medicare, Children's Health Ins Prg, Worker's Comp claims, TRICARE, and actual costs for uncompensated care; payments made to persons providing services, labor, or materials in connection with the provison of destination management services as defined in Texas Tax Code § 151.0565. The provision is effective for reports originally due on or after 1/1/2010
Utah				(1). Income previously taxed by Utah; (2) Utah charitable contributions deduction; (3) fifty percent of Foreign Operating Company income in the context of a Water's Edge Combined Report: (4) dividends received from insurance company subsidiaries that are exempt from corporation income/franchise taxation under the Utah Code based on their status as Utah Admitted Insurers; (5) amount of qualified investment in a Utah Educational Savings Plan that is not deducted on the federal corporation income tax return.
Vermont	X			

Subtraction Modifications to Federal Income (Part 3)

Legend:
X — **These items are subtracted from federal income in computing state income**
NA — **Not applicable**
NR — **Not reported**

	Subtraction for Prior Year Addback of Federal			
	First-Year Bonus Depreciation	*IRC Section 179 Asset Expensing*	*Capital Gain Exclusion or Deduction Allowed by State*	*Other Subtractions*
Virginia	X		X, limited to certain gains: effective for taxable years beginning on or after 01/01/11, any income taxable as a long-term capital gain for federal income tax purposes, or any income taxed as investment services partnership income for federal income tax purposes may be subtracted on the Virginia return if (1) the income is attributable to an investment that is made between 04/1/10 and 06/30/13, (2) the investment is made in a ''qualified business'' as defined in Va. Code § 58.1-339.4 or in another technology business approved by the Secretary of Technology, (3) the business has its	Gains on the sale of launch services to spaceflight participants or launch services that provide individuals training or experience of a launch, gain recognized for resupply services contracts for delivering payload entered into with NASA. (Effective for taxable years beginning on or after January 1, 2009.)

Subtraction Modifications to Federal Income (Part 3)

Legend:
- **X** — **These items are subtracted from federal income in computing state income**
- **NA** — **Not applicable**
- **NR** — **Not reported**

	Subtraction for Prior Year Addback of Federal			
	First-Year Bonus Depreciation	*IRC Section 179 Asset Expensing*	*Capital Gain Exclusion or Deduction Allowed by State*	*Other Subtractions*
			principal office or facility in Virginia, and (4) the business has less than $3 million in annual revenues for the fiscal year preceding the investment.	
Washington				
West Virginia			X	Interest expense disallowed in determining federal income; contributions to West Virginia medical savings accounts
Wisconsin	X	X, This takes the form of depreciation deductions		Listed in statute § 71.26(3)
Wyoming				

Depreciation

Federal MACRS Provisions

The Economic Recovery Tax Act of 1981 introduced the accelerated cost recovery system (ACRS), which applies to real and tangible personal property used in the trade or business or held for the production of income, and placed into service after 1980. The Tax Reform Act of 1986 made significant revisions to the ACRS provisions, creating more asset classes and slower depreciation deductions for real property. The modified accelerated cost recovery system (MACRS) provisions assign each item of depreciable real or tangible personal property to a MACRS recovery class, based on the property's asset depreciation range (ADR) midpoint life, as specified in Rev. Procs. 87-56 and 88-22. The MACRS recovery classes are as follows:

- *3-year property*—property with an ADR midpoint life of 4 years or less (e.g., special tools and truck tractors)
- *5-year property*—property with an ADR class life of more than 4 years and less than 10 years (e.g., cars, light trucks, and computers)
- *7-year property*—property with an ADR class life of 10 years or more but less than 16 years, including property that does not have a class life and is not included in another class (e.g., office furniture and fixtures, and most types of machinery)
- *10-year property*—property with an ADR class life of 16 years or more and less than 20 years (e.g., petroleum and food processing equipment)
- *15-year property*—property with an ADR class life of 20 years or more and less than 25 years (e.g., billboards and land improvements)
- *20-year property*—property with an ADR class life of 25 years or more, but not Section 1250 real property with an ADR midpoint life of 27.5 years or more (e.g., utilities and sewers)
- *27.5-year residential rental property*—buildings or structures that generate 80 percent or more of their gross rental income from dwelling units, which are defined as houses or apartments used to provide living accommodations in buildings or structures, but do not include units in a hotel, motel, inn, or other establishment where more than half of the units are used on a transient basis [For pre-1987 property, the ACRS recovery period ranged from 15 to 19 years.]
- *39-year nonresidential real property*—Section 1250 property that is neither residential rental property nor property with a class life of less than 27.5 years. [The MACRS recovery period was 31.5 years for property placed into service before May 13, 1993, and the ACRS recovery period for pre-1987 property ranged from 15 to 19 years.]

Assets that come under the MACRS provisions are depreciated under the following methods:

- The 200 percent declining-balance method with a switch to the straight-line method in the year that maximizes the deduction, which applies to 3-, 5-, 7-, and 10-year property
- The 150 percent declining-balance method with a switch to the straight-line method in the year that maximizes the deduction, which applies to 15- and 20-year property
- The straight-line method of depreciation, which applies to all nonresidential real property and residential rental property

In addition, the taxpayer may elect to depreciate assets using the straight-line method over the asset's regular recovery period. Such an election applies to all property within the same recovery class that is placed in service in the year of the election.

Assets that are subject to the MACRS rules are depreciated by using the following averaging conventions:

- The *half-year convention* applies to all recovery property other than residential rental property and nonresidential real property. This convention treats all property placed in service or disposed of in any taxable year as placed in service or disposed of in the middle of the year. Thus, a half year's depreciation is allowed in both the year the asset is placed in service and the year in which the asset is disposed of.

- Residential rental property and nonresidential real property are subject to a *mid-month convention* that treats all property placed in service during any month or disposed of during any month as placed in service or disposed of on the midpoint of the month. Thus, one-half month of depreciation is claimed for the month the property is placed in service or the month in which it is disposed of.
- A special *mid-quarter convention* applies to property, other than residential rental property and nonresidential real property, if more than 40 percent of the aggregate bases of such property is placed in service within the last three months of the taxable year. When the midquarter convention applies, all property placed in service or disposed of during any quarter of a taxable year is treated as if it had been placed in service or disposed of on the midpoint of such quarter.

Section 179 Deduction

Code Section 179 allows taxpayers to immediately expense a portion of the cost of property purchased for use in the active conduct of a trade or business. The maximum deduction is $250,000 for tax years beginning in 2008 to 2010, and $500,000 for tax years beginning in 2010 and 2011. The deduction is phased out dollar-for-dollar, based on the amount by which all qualifying property placed in service during the tax year exceeds the investment limitation. The investment limitation is $800,000 for tax years beginning in 2008 to 2010, and $2,000,000 for tax years beginning in 2010 and 2011. As a consequence, up to $2,500,000 ($500,000 plus $2,000,000) of qualifying property may be placed in service during 2010 or 2011 before the deduction is fully phased-out. (For a more detailed discussion, see the section in this part entitled Section 179 Asset Expensing.)

Federal Bonus Depreciation

A major feature of the Job Creation and Worker Assistance Act of 2002 is Code Section 168(k) first year bonus depreciation equal to 30 percent of the adjusted basis of qualifying property acquired between September 11, 2001, and September 10, 2004. The Jobs and Growth Tax Relief Reconciliation Act of 2003 increased the bonus depreciation allowance from 30 percent to 50 percent for property acquired after May 5, 2003, and placed in service before 2005 (before 2006 in the case of property with a long production period and certain noncommercial aircraft).

Subsequent legislation reinstated the 50 percent bonus depreciation allowance for qualifying property acquired in 2008 (Economic Stimulus Act of 2008), 2009 (American Recovery and Reinvestment Act of 2009), and 2010 (Small Business Jobs Act of 2010). The 2010 Tax Relief Act boosted 50 percent bonus depreciation to 100 percent for property acquired after September 8, 2010 and placed in service before 2012 (before 2013 in the case of property with a long production period and certain noncommercial aircraft), and extended the 50 percent bonus depreciation allowance to qualified property placed in service during 2012 (2013 in the case of property with a long production period and certain noncommercial aircraft). (For a more detailed discussion, see the next section in this part entitled First-Year Bonus Depreciation.)

State-by-State Summary

The following chart indicates which states conform to the federal MACRS and ADS depreciation systems.

Depreciation

Legend:
SAF **Same as applicable federal rules**
NA **Not applicable**
NR **Not reported**

	Modified Accelerated Cost Recovery System (MACRS)		*Alternative Depreciation System (ADS)*		
	Has State Adopted MACRS?	*Effective Date*	*Is ADS Adopted?*	*Effective Date*	*If ACRS, MACRS, or ADS Are Not Available, What Methods Are?*
Alabama	Yes	SAF	Yes	SAF	NA
Alaska	Yes	SAF	Yes	SAF	NA
Arizona	Yes	SAF	Yes	SAF	NA
Arkansas	Yes	In effect 1/1/09	Yes	In effect 1/1/09	NA
California	No	NA	Yes		150% declining balance; straight-line; sum of the year's digits
Colorado	Yes	SAF	Yes	SAF	NA
Connecticut	Yes	SAF	Yes	SAF	NA
Delaware	Yes	SAF	Yes	SAF	
District of Columbia	Yes	SAF	Yes	SAF	
Florida	Yes	SAF	Yes	SAF	
Georgia	Yes	3/11/1987	Yes	3/11/1987	
Hawaii	Yes	SAF	Yes	SAF	
	Hawaii has not conformed to the provisions of the Job Creation and Worker Assistance Act of 2002. See Department of Taxation Announcement 2002-5				
Idaho	Yes	SAF, as of 1/1/02	Yes	SAF, as of 1/1/02	
Illinois	No separate Illinois depreciation subtraction				

Depreciation

Legend:

SAF **Same as applicable federal rules**
NA **Not applicable**
NR **Not reported**

	Modified Accelerated Cost Recovery System (MACRS)		*Alternative Depreciation System (ADS)*		
	Has State Adopted MACRS?	*Effective Date*	*Is ADS Adopted?*	*Effective Date*	*If ACRS, MACRS, or ADS Are Not Available, What Methods Are?*
Indiana	Yes	SAF	Yes	SAF	
Iowa	Yes	SAF	Yes	SAF	
Kansas	Yes	SAF	Yes	SAF	
Kentucky	Yes	SAF	Yes	SAF	
Louisiana	Yes	1/1/1987	Yes	1/1/1987	
Maine	Yes	SAF	Yes	SAF	
Maryland	Yes	SAF	Yes	SAF	
Massachusetts	NR	NR	NR	NR	
Michigan (Business Tax)	Yes	SAF	Yes	SAF	
Note. The CIT takes effect 01/01/12, and replaces the Michigan Business Tax (MBT) for most taxpayers. However, businesses that have been approved to receive, have received, or have been assigned certain certified credits may elect to file a return and pay the tax imposed by the MBT in lieu of the CIT until the certified credits are exhausted or extinguished.					
Minnesota	Yes	Add Back with subsequent deduction	Yes	SAF	
Mississippi	Yes	SAF	Yes	SAF	
Missouri	Yes	SAF	Yes	SAF	
Montana	Yes	SAF	Yes	SAF	

Depreciation

Legend:

SAF Same as applicable federal rules
NA Not applicable
NR Not reported

	Modified Accelerated Cost Recovery System (MACRS)		*Alternative Depreciation System (ADS)*		
	Has State Adopted MACRS?	*Effective Date*	*Is ADS Adopted?*	*Effective Date*	*If ACRS, MACRS, or ADS Are Not Available, What Methods Are?*
Nebraska	Yes	SAF	Yes	SAF	
Nevada	Nevada does not impose a corporate income tax				
New Hampshire	Yes	SAF	Yes	SAF	
New Jersey	Yes	NR	Yes	NR	
	For years on and after 1/1/02, N.J. decouples from 30% and 50% bonus depreciation of the Federal Job Creation and Worker Assistance Act of 2002 and the Federal Jobs and Growth Tax Relief Reconciliation Act of 2003, P.L. 108-27.				
New Mexico	Yes	SAF	Yes	SAF	
New York	Yes	SAF	Yes	SAF	
North Carolina	Yes	SAF	Yes	SAF	
North Dakota	Yes	SAF	Yes	SAF	
Ohio	Ohio does not impose a corporate income tax				
Note. Effective 1/1/2010, the Ohio Franchise Tax was fully phased out and business will be taxed on gross receipts through the Commercial Activity Tax. Details about that tax can be found at: http//tax.ohio.gov/divisions/commercial_activities/index.stm					
Oklahoma	Yes	SAF	Yes	SAF	
Oregon	Yes	SAF	Yes	SAF	
Pennsylvania	Yes	SAF	Yes	SAF	
Rhode Island	NR	NR	NR	NR	

Depreciation

Legend:
SAF **Same as applicable federal rules**
NA **Not applicable**
NR **Not reported**

	Modified Accelerated Cost Recovery System (MACRS)		*Alternative Depreciation System (ADS)*		
	Has State Adopted MACRS?	*Effective Date*	*Is ADS Adopted?*	*Effective Date*	*If ACRS, MACRS, or ADS Are Not Available, What Methods Are?*
South Carolina	Yes	12/31/09	Yes	12/31/09	
South Dakota	South Dakota does not impose a corporate income tax				
Tennessee	Yes	SAF	Yes	SAF	
Texas	Yes	SAF	Yes	SAF	
Utah	Yes	SAF	Yes	SAF	
Vermont	Conform to federal depreciation with the exception of bonus depreciation				
Virginia	Yes	SAF	Yes	SAF	
Washington	Washington does not impose a corporate income tax				
West Virginia	Yes	SAF	Yes	SAF	
Wisconsin	Yes	SAF except Wisconsin does not allow bonus depreciation and limits § 179 expenses to $25,000.	Yes	SAF	
Wyoming	Wyoming does not impose a corporate income tax				

First-Year Bonus Depreciation

Federal Treatment

A major feature of the Job Creation and Worker Assistance Act of 2002 is Code Section 168(k) first year bonus depreciation equal to 30 percent of the adjusted basis of qualifying property acquired between September 11, 2001, and September 10, 2004. The Jobs and Growth Tax Relief Reconciliation Act of 2003 increased the bonus depreciation allowance from 30 percent to 50 percent for property acquired after May 5, 2003, and placed in service before 2005 (before 2006 in the case of property with a long production period and certain noncommercial aircraft).

Subsequent legislation reinstated the 50 percent bonus depreciation allowance for qualifying property acquired in 2008 (Economic Stimulus Act of 2008), 2009 (American Recovery and Reinvestment Act of 2009), and 2010 (Small Business Jobs Act of 2010). The 2010 Tax Relief Act boosted 50 percent bonus depreciation to 100 percent for property acquired after September 8, 2010 and placed in service before 2012 (before 2013 in the case of property with a long production period and certain noncommercial aircraft), and extended the 50 percent bonus depreciation allowance to qualified property placed in service during 2012 (2013 in the case of property with a long production period and certain noncommercial aircraft).

Property eligible for Section 168(k) bonus depreciation generally includes:

1. new MACRS property with a recovery period of 20 years or less, which this includes most tangible personal property other than buildings;
2. new computer software as defined in Section 167(f)(1) (i.e., off-the-shelf software with a three-year depreciation period);
3. new water utility property depreciated under MACRS; and
4. qualified leasehold improvement property depreciated under MACRS.

Acquisition-related intangibles that are amortized over 15 years under Section 197 do not qualify for the bonus depreciation.

Bonus depreciation is mandatory unless the taxpayer affirmatively elects out. A taxpayer reduces the adjusted basis of the property by the amount of bonus depreciation and then computes regular MACRS deductions based on the remaining basis. There is no limit on the total amount of a taxpayer's bonus deprecation deduction. In addition, bonus depreciation is deductible for both regular and alternative minimum tax purposes. Any Section 179 asset expensing allowance is claimed prior to the bonus depreciation deduction. If bonus depreciation is claimed on an automobile acquired from 2008 through 2012, the Section 280F luxury automobile limitation amount for the first year is increased by $8,000.

State Treatment

Due primarily to budgetary constraints, many states have decoupled their tax laws from the federal bonus depreciation provisions and require that the federal deduction be added back in computing state taxable income. For example, Florida requires an addition modification for 100 percent of the federal bonus depreciation deduction and permits a subtraction modification equal to one-seventh of the addback in the current tax year and the subsequent six tax years. Some states disallow most, but not all, of the bonus depreciation. For example, Minnesota requires an addition modification for 80 percent of the federal bonus depreciation deduction and permits a subtraction modification equal to one-fifth of the addback in each of the subsequent five tax years. Likewise, North Carolina requires an addition modification for 85 percent of the federal bonus depreciation deduction and permits a subtraction modification equal to one-fifth of the addback in each of the subsequent five tax years.

For tax years beginning in 2011 and 2012, Maine provides a nonrefundable tax credit equal to 10 percent of the federal bonus depreciation claimed with respect to property that is placed in service in Maine. An addition modification is required for the full amount of the federal deduction. No credit may be claimed for property placed in service outside Maine, but an addition modification is required only for the net increase in the federal depreciation deduction attributable to bonus depreciation. [L.D. 1043, June 20, 2011]

State-by-State Summary

The following chart, presented in two parts, indicates which states conform to the federal bonus depreciation provisions.

First-Year Bonus Depreciation (Part 1)

Legend:

NA	Not applicable
NR	Not reported
SAF	Same as applicable federal rules

	Does State Conform to Federal 30% Bonus Depreciation Provisions (2001 to 2004)?	*Does State Conform to Federal 50% Bonus Depreciation Provisions (2003 to 2004)?*	*Does State Conform to Federal 50% Bonus Depreciation Provisions (2008)?*	*If State Does Not Conform, Are Taxpayers Allowed to Claim a Portion of the Bonus Depreciation?*	*Is There a Form to Compute the Deduction?*
Alabama	Yes	Yes		No	No
Alaska	Yes	Yes	Yes		No
Arizona	No	No	No	Yes, Only Allowed if Bonus Deprec Taken under Gulf Opp Zone Act of 2005	No
Arkansas	No	No	No	No	No
California	No	No	No	No	No
Colorado	Yes	Yes	Yes	NA	NA
Connecticut	No	No		NA	Yes, Form CT-1120ATT
Delaware	Yes	Yes	Yes	NA	NA
District of Columbia	No	No		NR	NR
Florida	Yes	Yes		No	NR
Georgia	No	No	No	No	Yes, GA 4562
Hawaii	No	No		NA	No

First-Year Bonus Depreciation (Part 1)

Legend:

NA	Not applicable
NR	Not reported
SAF	Same as applicable federal rules

	Does State Conform to Federal 30% Bonus Depreciation Provisions (2001 to 2004)?	*Does State Conform to Federal 50% Bonus Depreciation Provisions (2003 to 2004)?*	*Does State Conform to Federal 50% Bonus Depreciation Provisions (2008)?*	*If State Does Not Conform, Are Taxpayers Allowed to Claim a Portion of the Bonus Depreciation?*	*Is There a Form to Compute the Deduction?*
Idaho	No	No	Yes	No, the taxpayer must recompute depreciation without the 30% or 50% bonus depreciation and provide an addition or subtraction modification to arrive at Idaho taxable income.	No
Illinois	No, see Note.	No		Yes	Yes, Form II-4562, Special Depreciation.
	Note. Taxpayers are required to add back the 30% federal bonus depreciation and are allowed to deduct the amount that would have been allowed on their federal return if the bonus depreciation law had not been enacted. The deduction is allowed for each year that depreciation is claimed for an asset, not just for the year in which the bonus depreciation on the asset is added back. If the federal gain on the asset is taxed by Illinois when the asset is sold, taxpayers will not receive a deduction for the entire cost of the asset. P.A. 92-603 requires all of the Illinois changes to bonus and regular depreciation for an asset to be reversed in the year the asset is sold. After the changes are reversed, total Illinois depreciation will equal total federal depreciation, and taxpayers will have received a deduction for the entire cost of the asset. See IDOR Information Bulletin 2002-03.				
Indiana	No	No		No	Yes, Commissioner's Directive #19
Iowa	No	Yes		No, MACRS depreciation allowed for the entire cost of the asset.	Yes, Form IA 4562A
Kansas	Yes	Yes	Yes	NA	NA

First-Year Bonus Depreciation (Part 1)

Legend:

NA	Not applicable
NR	Not reported
SAF	Same as applicable federal rules

	Does State Conform to Federal 30% Bonus Depreciation Provisions (2001 to 2004)?	*Does State Conform to Federal 50% Bonus Depreciation Provisions (2003 to 2004)?*	*Does State Conform to Federal 50% Bonus Depreciation Provisions (2008)?*	*If State Does Not Conform, Are Taxpayers Allowed to Claim a Portion of the Bonus Depreciation?*	*Is There a Form to Compute the Deduction?*
Kentucky	No	No		No	No
Louisiana	Yes	Yes	Yes	NA	NA
Maine	Yes for 2001 only	No		Yes, amounts denied in year 1 are recaptured over remaining life of asset.	Taxpayers must complete a ProForma Federal Form 4562
Maryland	No	No		No	Yes, Form 500 DM
Massachusetts	No	No		No	NA
Michigan (Business Tax)	No	No	Yes	No	No
Minnesota	No	No	No	80% addback and subtraction over 5 years.	No

Note. The CIT takes effect 01/01/12, and replaces the Michigan Business Tax (MBT) for most taxpayers. However, businesses that have been approved to receive, have received, or have been assigned certain certified credits may elect to file a return and pay the tax imposed by the MBT in lieu of the CIT until the certified credits are exhausted or extinguished.

First-Year Bonus Depreciation (Part 1)

Legend:

NA	Not applicable
NR	Not reported
SAF	Same as applicable federal rules

	Does State Conform to Federal 30% Bonus Depreciation Provisions (2001 to 2004)?	*Does State Conform to Federal 50% Bonus Depreciation Provisions (2003 to 2004)?*	*Does State Conform to Federal 50% Bonus Depreciation Provisions (2008)?*	*If State Does Not Conform, Are Taxpayers Allowed to Claim a Portion of the Bonus Depreciation?*	*Is There a Form to Compute the Deduction?*
Mississippi	No	No		Yes, since the Mississippi basis is not reduced by the bonus depreciation, it will be deducted as regular depreciation over the life of the asset. The addition is a separate add back on Form 83-122.	No
Missouri	No	Yes	Yes	No	NR
Montana	Yes	Yes	Yes	NA	NA

Legend:
NA Not applicable
NR Not reported
SAF Same as applicable federal rules

First-Year Bonus Depreciation (Part 1)

	Does State Conform to Federal 30% Bonus Depreciation Provisions (2001 to 2004)?	*Does State Conform to Federal 50% Bonus Depreciation Provisions (2003 to 2004)?*	*Does State Conform to Federal 50% Bonus Depreciation Provisions (2008)?*	*If State Does Not Conform, Are Taxpayers Allowed to Claim a Portion of the Bonus Depreciation?*	*Is There a Form to Compute the Deduction?*
Nebraska	Yes, allowed the full 30% additional depreciation deduction for the depreciation deduction, basis of the item, and gain and loss determinations. However, there is addition to income that is required to be added back to income that is equal to 85% of the bonus depreciation taken. The amount added back will be deductible in the future.	Yes	Yes	NA	NA
Nevada	Nevada does not impose a corporate income tax				
New Hampshire	No	No	No	No, depreciation is based on the Internal Revenue Code in effect on 12/31/2000.	Yes, Schedule R

First-Year Bonus Depreciation (Part 1)

Legend:
NA Not applicable
NR Not reported
SAF Same as applicable federal rules

	Does State Conform to Federal 30% Bonus Depreciation Provisions (2001 to 2004)?	*Does State Conform to Federal 50% Bonus Depreciation Provisions (2003 to 2004)?*	*Does State Conform to Federal 50% Bonus Depreciation Provisions (2008)?*	*If State Does Not Conform, Are Taxpayers Allowed to Claim a Portion of the Bonus Depreciation?*	*Is There a Form to Compute the Deduction?*
New Jersey	No, decoupled from federal for tax years beginning on and after 1/1/02 for corporate tax purposes; not decoupled for personal income tax.	No		No	Yes, Form CBT-100, Schedule S-Part II(B)
New Mexico	Yes	Yes	X, SAF	NA	NA
New York	New York fully conformed for tax years beginning in 2001 and 2002. For tax years beginning after 2002, depreciation is allowed, only for Qualified Resurgence Zone and Qualified Liberty Zone property.	No, Except for Qualified Resurgence Zone and Qualified Liberty Zone Property.	No, except for Qualified Resurgence Zone and Qualified Liberty Zone Property.	NA	Yes, Form CT-399, Depreciation Adjustment Schedule
North Carolina	No for 2001 through 2003, Yes for 2004	No		See Note	No

First-Year Bonus Depreciation (Part 1)

Legend:

NA	Not applicable
NR	Not reported
SAF	Same as applicable federal rules

	Does State Conform to Federal 30% Bonus Depreciation Provisions (2001 to 2004)?	*Does State Conform to Federal 50% Bonus Depreciation Provisions (2003 to 2004)?*	*Does State Conform to Federal 50% Bonus Depreciation Provisions (2008)?*	*If State Does Not Conform, Are Taxpayers Allowed to Claim a Portion of the Bonus Depreciation?*	*Is There a Form to Compute the Deduction?*
	Note. G.S. 105-130.5(a)(15) was added to require a taxpayer to add to federal taxable income a percentage of the 30% additional first-year depreciation deduction allowed for federal income tax purposes. The applicable percentage is 100% of the bonus depreciation for the tax year 2002, 70% for the tax year 2003, and 0% for the tax year 2004 and thereafter. Any taxpayer who claimed the bonus depreciation for federal purposes for the tax year 2001 and whose North Carolina return also reflected that deduction must also add back 100% of the deduction claimed for the tax year 2001 on the 2002 tax return. This adjustment does not result in a difference is basic of the affected assets for State and federal income tax purposes.				
North Dakota	Yes	Yes	Yes	NA	NA
Ohio	Ohio does not impose a corporate income tax				
	Note. Effective 1/1/2010, the Ohio Franchise Tax was fully phased out and business will be taxed on gross receipts through the Commercial Activity Tax. Details about that tax can be found at: http//tax.ohio.gov/divisions/commercial_activities/index.stm				
Oklahoma	No	NR		Yes. 80% disallowed, then 25% of disallowed amount allowed in years 2 through 5, applies to C corporations only.	No
Oregon	Yes	2001 through 2004	Yes	No	

First-Year Bonus Depreciation (Part 1)

Legend:

NA Not applicable
NR Not reported
SAF Same as applicable federal rules

	Does State Conform to Federal 30% Bonus Depreciation Provisions (2001 to 2004)?	*Does State Conform to Federal 50% Bonus Depreciation Provisions (2003 to 2004)?*	*Does State Conform to Federal 50% Bonus Depreciation Provisions (2008)?*	*If State Does Not Conform, Are Taxpayers Allowed to Claim a Portion of the Bonus Depreciation?*	*Is There a Form to Compute the Deduction?*
Pennsylvania	No	No		Yes, 3/7 of the MACRS depreciation under § 168(k) property until the disallowed bonus depreciation is recovered. If the disallowed bonus depreciation is not recovered at the time the asset is disposed of, the remaining disallowed depreciation may be recovered at that time.	Yes. Form REV-784 CT (Schedules C-3 and C-4)
Rhode Island	NR	No		Yes, Maximum of $25,000	No
South Carolina	No	NR		No	NR
South Dakota	South Dakota does not impose a corporate income tax				
Tennessee	No	No		Yes, the asset is depreciated at full value based on MACRS	No
Texas	No	No		No	No
Utah	Yes	Yes		NA	NA

First-Year Bonus Depreciation (Part 1)

Legend:
NA Not applicable
NR Not reported
SAF Same as applicable federal rules

	Does State Conform to Federal 30% Bonus Depreciation Provisions (2001 to 2004)?	*Does State Conform to Federal 50% Bonus Depreciation Provisions (2003 to 2004)?*	*Does State Conform to Federal 50% Bonus Depreciation Provisions (2008)?*	*If State Does Not Conform, Are Taxpayers Allowed to Claim a Portion of the Bonus Depreciation?*	*Is There a Form to Compute the Deduction?*
Vermont	No	Yes		No	No
Virginia	No	No	No	No	
Washington	Washington does not impose a corporate income tax				
West Virginia	Yes	Yes	Yes	NA	NA
Wisconsin	No	No	No	No	No
Wyoming	Wyoming does not impose a corporate income tax				

First-Year Bonus Depreciation (Part 2)

Legend:

NA	Not applicable
NR	Not reported
SAF	Same as Federal

	Does State Conform to Federal 50% Bonus Depreciation Provisions for 2009?	*If State Does Not Conform, are Taxpayers Allowed to Claim a Portion of the Bonus Depreciation?*	*If Yes, Explain Computation.*
Alabama	Yes	No	
Alaska	Yes		
Arizona	No, Currently Arizona has not conformed to federal changes made after 1/1/09, but anticipated conforming in early 2010 and so Arizona has answered the questions based on past history.		
Arkansas	No	No	
California		No	
Colorado	Yes		
Connecticut	No, Connecticut does not allow IRC § 168 deduction	No	
Delaware			
District of Columbia		No	
Florida		No	
Georgia			
Hawaii	NR		
Idaho	Yes	No	
Illinois		Yes	See IITA § 203(b)(2)(T)

First-Year Bonus Depreciation (Part 2)

Legend:

NA	Not applicable
NR	Not reported
SAF	Same as Federal

	Does State Conform to Federal 50% Bonus Depreciation Provisions for 2009?	*If State Does Not Conform, are Taxpayers Allowed to Claim a Portion of the Bonus Depreciation?*	*If Yes, Explain Computation.*
Indiana	Yes		
Iowa		Yes	Use MACRS depreciation method for entire asset life.
Kansas	Yes		
Kentucky		No	
Louisiana	Yes		
Maine		Yes	Amounts denied in year 1 may be recaptured over the remaining life of the asset.
Maryland	NR		
Massachusetts			
Michigan			
Note. The CIT takes effect 01/01/12, and replaces the Michigan Business Tax (MBT) for most taxpayers. However, businesses that have been approved to receive, have received, or have been assigned certain certified credits may elect to file a return and pay the tax imposed by the MBT in lieu of the CIT until the certified credits are exhausted or extinguished.			
Minnesota	Yes		80% add back, subtraction allowed in five subsequent years
Mississippi		No	
Missouri	Yes		
Montana	Yes		

First-Year Bonus Depreciation (Part 2)

Legend:
NA Not applicable
NR Not reported
SAF Same as Federal

	Does State Conform to Federal 50% Bonus Depreciation Provisions for 2009?	*If State Does Not Conform, are Taxpayers Allowed to Claim a Portion of the Bonus Depreciation?*	*If Yes, Explain Computation.*
Nebraska	Yes		
Nevada	Nevada does not impose a corporate income tax		
New Hampshire	No	No	
New Jersey		No	
New Mexico	Yes		
New York	*		*No, except for Qualified Resurgence Zone and Qualified Liberty Zone Property
North Carolina	No	Yes	Taxpayers would be required to make an addition adjustment equal to 85% of the deduction claimed on the federal return but could subsequently deduct the amount added back over a five year period.
North Dakota	Yes		
Ohio	Ohio does not impose a corporate income tax		
Oklahoma	Yes		80% add back, then 25% of add back deducted annually over next four years
Oregon		No	
Pennsylvania	No		

First-Year Bonus Depreciation (Part 2)

Legend:
NA Not applicable
NR Not reported
SAF Same as Federal

	Does State Conform to Federal 50% Bonus Depreciation Provisions for 2009?	*If State Does Not Conform, are Taxpayers Allowed to Claim a Portion of the Bonus Depreciation?*	*If Yes, Explain Computation.*
Rhode Island		Yes	Limited to $25,000 Total
South Carolina	No		
South Dakota	South Dakota does not impose a corporate income tax		
Tennessee		NR	
Texas			
Utah	Yes, (SAF)		
Vermont	No	No	
Virginia			Depreciation must be recomputed for Virginia purposes as if the assets did not receive the special depreciation deduction for federal purposes. If the total Virginia depreciation is less than federal depreciation for the taxable year, then the difference must be recognized as an addition on the Virginia return. If the total depreciation is more than the federal depreciation for the taxable year, then the difference must be recognized as a subtraction on the Virginia return.
Washington	Washington does not impose a corporate income tax		
West Virginia	No		

First-Year Bonus Depreciation (Part 2)

Legend:
NA Not applicable
NR Not reported
SAF Same as Federal

	Does State Conform to Federal 50% Bonus Depreciation Provisions for 2009?	*If State Does Not Conform, are Taxpayers Allowed to Claim a Portion of the Bonus Depreciation?*	*If Yes, Explain Computation.*
Wisconsin	No	No	
Wyoming	Wyoming does not impose a corporate income tax		

Section 179 Asset Expensing

Federal Treatment

Under Code Section 179, taxpayers may elect to immediately expense a portion of the cost of depreciable tangible personal property, rather than depreciating the cost over the applicable MACRS recovery period. The adjusted basis of the property is reduced by the amount of the expense allowance. The Section 179 asset expensing deduction operates independently of, and is claimed prior to, any Section 168(k) first year bonus depreciation deduction. Thus, the ordering of deductions is as follows: Section 179 asset expensing, bonus depreciation, and then MACRS depreciation is computed on the asset's remaining basis.

Eligible property. Property that is eligible for Section 179 expensing includes new or used tangible Section 1245 property that is depreciable under MACRS and is acquired by purchase for use in the active conduct of a trade or business. Land and buildings generally do not qualify for asset expensing, nor does property held for the production of income.

An exception applies for tax years beginning in 2010 or 2011, under which a taxpayer may elect to treat qualified real property that is depreciable and acquired by purchase as Section 179 property. Qualified real property generally consists of qualified leasehold improvements, qualified retail improvement property, and qualified restaurant improvement property. [IRC § 179(f)]

Maximum expense deduction. The amount of qualifying Section 179 property that a taxpayer may elect to expense is limited, and Congress has increased the maximum Section 179 deduction numerous times during the past decade. The Jobs and Growth Tax Relief Reconciliation Act of 2003 increased the maximum federal deduction from $25,000 to $100,000 for tax years beginning after 2002. The Small Business and Work Opportunity Tax Act of 2007 increased the dollar limitation to $125,000 for tax years beginning in 2007 through 2010. The Economic Stimulus Act of 2008 increased the dollar limitation to $250,000 for tax years that begin in 2008. The American Recovery and Reinvestment Act of 2009 extended the $250,000 limitation to 2009, and the 2010 Hiring Incentives to Restore Employment Act extended the $250,000 limitation to 2010. The Small Business Jobs Act of 2010 increased the limitation to $500,000 for tax years beginning in 2010 and 2011.

Maximum investment limitation. The maximum annual Section 179 deduction is phased out, dollar-for-dollar, based on the amount by which all qualifying property placed in service during the tax year exceeds the investment limitation. As with the maximum deduction, Congress has increased the investment limitation numerous times during the past decade. Most recently, the Economic Stimulus Act of 2008, American Recovery and Reinvestment Act of 2009, and The 2010 Hiring Incentives to Restore Employment Act increased the investment limitation to $800,000 for tax years that begin in 2008 through 2010, and the Small Business Jobs Act of 2010 increased the limitation to $2,000,000 for tax years beginning in 2010 and 2011. As a consequence, up to $2,500,000 ($500,000 plus $2,000,000) of qualifying property may be placed in service during 2010 or 2011 before the deduction is fully phased-out.

The maximum annual Section 179 deduction amounts and the investment limitation amounts are summarized in the following table:

Tax years beginning in:	*Maximum expense deduction*	*Maximum investment limitation*
2001 or 2002	$24,000	$200,000
2003	$100,000	$400,000
2004	$102,000	$410,000
2005	$105,000	$420,000
2006	$108,000	$430,000
2007	$125,000	$500,000
2008 or 2009	$250,000	$800,000
2010 or 2011	$500,000	$2,000,000

Taxable income limitation. In addition to the investment limitation, there is also a taxable income limitation, under which the total cost of the property that may be expensed in a tax year cannot exceed the total amount of the taxable income that the taxpayer derives from the active conduct of a trade or business during that tax year.

State Treatment

Due to budgetary constraints, a number of states have decoupled their tax laws from the numerous increases in the maximum Section 179 deduction during the past decade. Such states require addition modifications for the excess of the federal Section 179 expensing amount over the state maximum.

State-by-State Summary

The following chart, presented in two parts, indicates which states conform to the federal Section 179 asset expensing provisions.

Section 179 Asset Expensing (Part 1)

Legend:

NA	Not applicable
NR	Not reported
SAF	Same as Federal

		Does Your State's Dollar Limitation on the Amount of Expensing Conform to Recent Federal Changes			
	What is the allocable IRC Section 179 Deduction	*$250,000 for 2008 (Economic Stimulus Act of 2008)*	*$250,000 for 2009 (American Recovery and Reinvestment Act of 2009)*	*If No, What is the Limitation Amount for 2008?*	*If No, What is the Limitation Amount for 2009?*
Alabama	SAF	No	Yes	$128,000	
Alaska	SAF	Yes	Yes		
Arizona	Limited to $25,000; Arizona requires an adjustment to add back the federal § 179 expense taken at the federal level in excess of $25,000 and provides for a subtraction of the excess $25,000 § 179 deduction to be subtracted ratably over a 5-year period.	No	No, Currently Arizona has not conformed to federal changes made after 1/1/09, but anticipated conforming in early 2010, and so have answered the questions based on past history. Arizona required that all Section 179 amounts in excess of $25,000, be added back and then allowed as a subtraction over 5 years.	$25,000	$25,000
Arkansas	2006 $25,000 2007 $112,000 2008 $115,000 2009 $133,000	No	No	$115,000	$133,000

Section 179 Asset Expensing (Part 1)

Legend:

NA	Not applicable
NR	Not reported
SAF	Same as Federal

		Does Your State's Dollar Limitation on the Amount of Expensing Conform to Recent Federal Changes			
	What is the allocable IRC Section 179 Deduction	*$250,000 for 2008 (Economic Stimulus Act of 2008)*	*$250,000 for 2009 (American Recovery and Reinvestment Act of 2009)*	*If No, What is the Limitation Amount for 2008?*	*If No, What is the Limitation Amount for 2009?*
California	Corporations may not claim a deduction under IRC § 179; however, they are allowed a first year depreciation deduction of 20% on the first $10,000 of "qualified property" in the year acquired.	No	No	$200,000	$200,000
Colorado	SAF	Yes	Yes		
Connecticut	SAF	Yes	Yes		
Delaware	NR				
District of Columbia	SAF	No	No	$25,000	$25,000
Florida		No	No	$128,000	$128,000
Georgia	Yes, state's dollar limitations on the amount of expensing conform to changes in 2009 with limitations.	Yes	Yes		
Hawaii	$25,000	NR	NR		
Idaho	SAF	Yes	Yes		

Legend:

NA	Not applicable
NR	Not reported
SAF	Same as Federal

Section 179 Asset Expensing (Part 1)

		Does Your State's Dollar Limitation on the Amount of Expensing Conform to Recent Federal Changes			
	What is the allocable IRC Section 179 Deduction	*$250,000 for 2008 (Economic Stimulus Act of 2008)*	*$250,000 for 2009 (American Recovery and Reinvestment Act of 2009)*	*If No, What is the Limitation Amount for 2008?*	*If No, What is the Limitation Amount for 2009?*
Illinois	No separate Illinois depreciation subtraction	Yes	Yes		
Indiana	Yes	No	No	$25,000	$25,000
Iowa	Yes	Yes	No		$133,000
Kansas	Yes	Yes	Yes		
Kentucky	Yes	No	No	$25,000	$25,000
Louisiana	Yes	Yes	Yes		
Maine	Yes, SAF	No	No	$25,000	$25,000
Maryland	Yes	NR	NR		
Massachusetts	Yes	Yes	Yes		
Michigan	Yes	Yes	Yes		
Note. The CIT takes effect 01/01/12, and replaces the Michigan Business Tax (MBT) for most taxpayers. However, businesses that have been approved to receive, have received, or have been assigned certain certified credits may elect to file a return and pay the tax imposed by the MBT in lieu of the CIT until the certified credits are exhausted or extinguished.					
Minnesota	Yes	No	No	$25,000	$25,000
Mississippi	Yes	Yes	Yes		
Missouri	Yes	Yes	Yes		

Section 179 Asset Expensing (Part 1)

Legend:

NA	Not applicable
NR	Not reported
SAF	Same as Federal

	What is the allocable IRC Section 179 Deduction	*Does Your State's Dollar Limitation on the Amount of Expensing Conform to Recent Federal Changes* — *$250,000 for 2008 (Economic Stimulus Act of 2008)*	*$250,000 for 2009 (American Recovery and Reinvestment Act of 2009)*	*If No, What is the Limitation Amount for 2008?*	*If No, What is the Limitation Amount for 2009?*
Montana	Yes	Yes	Yes		
Nebraska	Yes	Yes	Yes		
Nevada	Nevada does not impose a corporate income tax				
New Hampshire	Yes, $25,000 set by IRC of 1986 in effect on 12/31/2010	No	No	$25,000	$25,000
New Jersey	Yes	No	No	$25,000	$25,000
New Mexico	Yes	Yes	Yes		
New York	Yes	Yes	Yes		
North Carolina	Yes	Yes	Yes		
North Dakota	Yes	Yes	Yes		
Ohio	Ohio does not impose a corporate income tax				
Note Effective 1/1/2010, the Ohio Franchise Tax was fully phased out and business will be taxed on gross receipts through the Commercial Activity Tax. Details about that tax can be found at: http//tax.ohio.gov/divisions/commercial_activities/index.stm					
Oklahoma	Yes	No	No		$175,000
Oregon	Yes, for property placed in service after 1984	Yes	No	$250,000	$133,000

Section 179 Asset Expensing (Part 1)

Legend:

NA	Not applicable
NR	Not reported
SAF	Same as Federal

		Does Your State's Dollar Limitation on the Amount of Expensing Conform to Recent Federal Changes			
	What is the allocable IRC Section 179 Deduction	*$250,000 for 2008 (Economic Stimulus Act of 2008)*	*$250,000 for 2009 (American Recovery and Reinvestment Act of 2009)*	*If No, What is the Limitation Amount for 2008?*	*If No, What is the Limitation Amount for 2009?*
Pennsylvania **Note. The Pennsylvania Section 179 expense is limited to $25,000, under the Personal Income Tax law. Therefore, a sole proprietor, partnership, or S-Corporation can only claim up to $25,000 of Section 179 expense in calculating personal taxable income. https://revenue-pa.custhelp.com/app/answers/detail/a_id/1539/kw/1539**	Yes	Yes	Yes		
Rhode Island	NR	No	No	$25,000	$25,000
South Carolina	Yes	Yes	Yes		$133,000
South Dakota	South Dakota does not impose a corporate income tax				
Tennessee	Yes	Yes	Yes		
Texas	Yes	No	No	$112,000	$115,000
Utah	Yes	Yes	Yes		

Section 179 Asset Expensing (Part 1)

Legend:

NA	Not applicable
NR	Not reported
SAF	Same as Federal

		Does Your State's Dollar Limitation on the Amount of Expensing Conform to Recent Federal Changes			
	What is the allocable IRC Section 179 Deduction	*$250,000 for 2008 (Economic Stimulus Act of 2008)*	*$250,000 for 2009 (American Recovery and Reinvestment Act of 2009)*	*If No, What is the Limitation Amount for 2008?*	*If No, What is the Limitation Amount for 2009?*
Vermont	Conform to federal depreciation with the exception of bonus depreciation	Yes	Yes		
Virginia	Yes	Yes	Yes		
Washington	Washington does not impose a corporate income tax				
West Virginia	Yes	Yes	Yes		
Wisconsin	Yes	No	No	$25,000	$25,000 ($120,000 if actively engaged in farming)
Wyoming	Wyoming does not impose a corporate income tax				

Legend:
NA Not applicable
NR Not reported

Section 179 Asset Expensing (Part 2)

	Does Your State's Dollar Limitation on the Amount of Expensing Conform to Recent Federal Changes?			
	$250,000 for 2010 (Hiring Incentives to Restore Employment Act of 2010)	*If No, What Are the Limitation Amounts for 2010?*	*If No, What Are the Limitation Amounts for 2009?*	*If No, What Are the Limitation Amounts for 2008?*
Alabama	Yes			$128,000
Alaska	Yes			
Arizona	Statutory adjustments are required.			
Arkansas	No	$125,000	$133,000	$115,000
California	No	$200,000	$200,000	$200,000
Colorado	Yes			
Connecticut	Yes			
Delaware	Yes			
District of Columbia	No	$25,000	$25,000	$25,000
Florida	Yes			
Georgia	Yes			$134,000
Hawaii	No	$25,000	$25,000	$25,000
Idaho	No	$125,000	$250,000	$250,000
Illinois	Yes	NR	NR	NR
Indiana	No	$25,000	$25,000	$25,000
Iowa	No	$500,000	$133,000	$250,000
Kansas	Yes			
Kentucky	No	$25,000	$25,000	$25,000

Section 179 Asset Expensing (Part 2)

Legend:

NA Not applicable

NR Not reported

	Does Your State's Dollar Limitation on the Amount of Expensing Conform to Recent Federal Changes?			
	$250,000 for 2010 (Hiring Incentives to Restore Employment Act of 2010)	*If No, What Are the Limitation Amounts for 2010?*	*If No, What Are the Limitation Amounts for 2009?*	*If No, What Are the Limitation Amounts for 2008?*
Louisiana	Yes			
Maine	No	$25,000	$25,000	$25,000
Maryland	No	$25,000	$25,000	$25,000
Massachusetts	Yes			
Michigan	Yes			

Note. The CIT takes effect 01/01/12, and replaces the Michigan Business Tax (MBT) for most taxpayers. However, businesses that have been approved to receive, have received, or have been assigned certain certified credits may elect to file a return and pay the tax imposed by the MBT in lieu of the CIT until the certified credits are exhausted or extinguished.

Minnesota	No	NR	NR	NR
Mississippi	Yes			
Missouri	Yes			
Montana	Yes			
Nebraska	Yes			
Nevada	Nevada does not impose a corporate income tax			
New Hampshire	No	$25,000	$25,000	$25,000
New Jersey	No	$25,000	$25,000	$25,000
New Mexico	Yes			
New York	Yes			
North Carolina	Yes			

Section 179 Asset Expensing (Part 2)

Legend:
NA Not applicable
NR Not reported

	Does Your State's Dollar Limitation on the Amount of Expensing Conform to Recent Federal Changes?			
	$250,000 for 2010 (Hiring Incentives to Restore Employment Act of 2010)	*If No, What Are the Limitation Amounts for 2010?*	*If No, What Are the Limitation Amounts for 2009?*	*If No, What Are the Limitation Amounts for 2008?*
North Dakota	Yes			
Ohio	Ohio does not impose a corporate income tax			
Oklahoma	Yes		$175,000	
Oregon	No	Due to conformity with ARRA 2009 & subsequent changes, the Oregon limitation for taxable years beginning 2009 through 2011 is $125,000 plus inflation adjustments as set in Internal Revenue Code.	$133,000	$250,000
Pennsylvania	Yes			
Rhode Island	No	$25,000	$25,000	$25,000
South Carolina	Yes			
South Dakota	South Dakota does not impose a corporate income tax			
Tennessee	Yes			

Section 179 Asset Expensing (Part 2)

Legend:
NA Not applicable
NR Not reported

	Does Your State's Dollar Limitation on the Amount of Expensing Conform to Recent Federal Changes?			
	$250,000 for 2010 (Hiring Incentives to Restore Employment Act of 2010)	*If No, What Are the Limitation Amounts for 2010?*	*If No, What Are the Limitation Amounts for 2009?*	*If No, What Are the Limitation Amounts for 2008?*
Texas	No	A taxable entity that elects to subtract cost of goods sold in computing margin may include in cost of goods sold § 179 asset expense reported on the federal income tax return, to the extent associated with and necessary for the production of goods and subject to the following limitations. The section 179 expense is limited to $112,000 for franchise tax reports due in 2008; $115,000 for reports due in 2009; and $120,000 for reports due in 2010.		
Utah	Yes			
Vermont	Yes			
Virginia	Yes			
Washington	Washington does not impose a corporate income tax			
West Virginia	Yes			
Wisconsin	No	$25,000	$25,000 ($120,000 for actively engaged in farming)	$25,000
Wyoming	Wyoming does not impose a corporate income tax			

Net Operating Loss Carryovers

If a corporation has cyclical earnings, the effective tax rate on the corporation's net earnings over time could significantly exceed the statutory tax rate if the corporation's taxable income is determined on a strict annual basis, in which case losses from one year could not offset profits from another year. To prevent such inequities, Congress enacted Code Section 172, which permits taxpayers to claim a net operating loss (NOL) deduction against current year taxable income in a carryover year. Generally, for federal tax purposes, NOLs can be carried back 2 years and forward 20 years. Section 172(b)(3) gives taxpayers the option to forgo the two-year carryback in favor of a carryforward.

Differences Between Federal and State NOLs

Most states allow NOL deductions, but the specific rules vary significantly from state to state. As a consequence, there is often a difference between the amount of the federal and state NOL deductions. These federal-state differences arise for a number of reasons, including:

1. States requiring that the taxpayer have nexus in the year the NOL arises in order to carryover the loss;
2. No state provision for NOL carrybacks, and state carryforward periods that are shorter than the 20 year federal carryforward;
3. State statutory limitations on the dollar amount of the carryover allowed;
4. Different group filing methods for federal and state tax purposes; and
5. The application of the state NOL deduction on a pre- versus post-apportionment basis.

Depending in part on whether the state uses Line 28 or Line 30 of federal Form 1120 as the starting point for computing state taxable income, the requisite adjustments to convert a federal NOL deduction to the state deduction may take the form of an addition and/or subtraction modification.

Carryover Periods. Code Section 172 generally permits taxpayers to carry an NOL back 2 years and forward 20 years and claim as a deduction in the carryover year. Most states allow NOL deductions, but the specific rules vary from state to state. Many states do not permit a carryback, and a number of states have carryforward periods that are shorter than 20 years. These differences are due in large part to state budgetary constraints; in particular, the negative tax revenue consequences of refund claims associated with NOL carrybacks. In addition, as a revenue raising measure, some states have temporarily suspended the NOL deduction.

During periods of economic recession, Congress has enacted enhanced carryback periods to infuse cash in the form of tax refunds into the economy. For example, the Job Creation and Worker Assistance Act of 2002 (Pub. L. No. 107-147) extended the carryback period to five years for NOLs arising in taxable years ending in 2001 and 2002.

The American Recovery and Reinvestment Act of 2009 (Pub. L. No. 111-5, Feb. 17, 2009) allows an eligible small business to elect up to a five-year carryback for an NOL sustained in a tax year beginning or ending in 2008. To be eligible, the business must satisfy a $15 million gross receipts test. An eligible business can carry back its 2008 NOL either three, four or five years.

The Worker, Homeownership, and Business Assistance Act of 2009 (Pub. L. No. 111-92, Nov. 06, 2009) significantly broadened the availability of the enhanced carryback. Under Public Law 111-92, any taxpayer may elect to carryback an NOL arising in either 2008 or 2009, but not both, for either three, four or five years. If a taxpayer elects a five-year carryback, however, the amount that can be carried back to the fifth preceding tax year is limited to 50 percent of the taxpayer's taxable income in the carryback year.

For most taxpayers, the extended carryback period applies for only one tax year, 2008 or 2009. However, an eligible small business that elected an extended carryback for a 2008 NOL under prior law may also elect an extended carryback for a 2009 NOL. In addition, the 50 percent of taxable income limitation does not apply to eligible small businesses which, under prior law, elected a five-year carryback for a 2008 NOL.

For alternative minimum tax purposes, the usual rule that an NOL deduction is limited to 90 percent of alternative minimum taxable income does not apply to 2008 or 2009 NOLs that are carried back either three, four or five years.

Federal law allows a taxpayer to forgo the automatic carryback period in favor of an NOL carryforward. [IRC § 172(b)(3)] Most states that allow a carryback also permit the election to forgo the state carryback, provided that the taxpayer has made the same election for federal purposes. If a loss corporation is a member of a consolidated return group, different rules may apply. For example, if the current year's loss is absorbed in the federal consolidated return, in certain separate company return states a state-only election to carry back or carry forward a state NOL may be available. Because most states follow the federal rules on paying interest on carrybacks (i.e., no interest is paid if the refund is made within 45 days after the claim for refund is filed), amended state returns using a federal carryback should be filed as soon as possible after the federal or state return generating the loss is filed.

Impact of Apportionment Percentage. Some states require that the total NOL generated in a loss year be adjusted by the loss year's apportionment percentage before it is applied in a carryover year, and then the apportioned NOL is offset against the amount of apportioned income in the carryover year. This is known as a *post-apportionment* NOL deduction. Other states require that the full amount of the loss year's NOL be offset against the carryover year's total apportionable income before applying the apportionment percentage for the carryover year to the net amount of apportionable income. This is known as a *pre-apportionment* NOL deduction. If there is a major change in the corporation's state apportionment percentage between the loss year and the carryover year, the amount of the NOL deduction can vary significantly with the method (pre-versus post-apportionment) employed by the state.

For example, assume that in 20X1 Acme Corporation sustains a $100 NOL and has a State X apportionment percentage of 50 percent. In 20X2, Acme has taxable income before the NOL deduction of $300 and a State X apportionment percentage of 70 percent. If State X applies an NOL on a pre-apportionment basis, Acme's 20X2 taxable income is $140 ([$300 – $100] x 70%). On the other hand, if State X applies an NOL on a post–apportionment basis, Acme's 20X2 taxable income is $160 ([$300 x 70%] – $50]).

Impact of Addition and Subtraction Modifications. Regardless of whether Line 28 or Line 30 of the federal income tax return is used as the starting point in computing state taxable income, each state requires a number of addition and subtraction modifications. Generally, states require that the same modifications used in determining state taxable income be reflected in the computation of a state NOL. In addition, a corporation must generally be subject to tax and file a state tax return in the loss year in order to establish a state NOL, although there are some exceptions.

Several states have statutory or regulatory provisions mandating that the starting point (i.e., federal taxable income) before state modifications may not be smaller than zero unless an NOL is generated in that year. Therefore, in those states, if the state-specified addition modifications exceed the subtraction modifications in a year in which a federal NOL deduction is being used, the taxpayer may have state taxable income even though it has no federal taxable income for that year.

Statutory Limitations. A number of states impose flat dollar limitations on the amount of an NOL carryback deduction. For example, Utah limits carrybacks to $1 million, and Idaho limits carrybacks to $100,000. Some states impose flat dollar or percentage limitations on NOL carryforward deductions. For example, in 2010, Pennsylvania limits NOL carryforward deductions to the greater of $3 million or 20 percent of taxable income. Some states impose temporary limitations on NOL carryforward deductions in response to fiscal constraints. For example, Illinois suspended its NOL for tax years ending in 2011 to 2014. The carryforward period for the suspended NOLs is extended by the number of years that the deduction is suspended. [S.B. 2505, Jan. 13, 2011]

Some states permit an NOL deduction only to the extent that such a deduction is allowed in computing federal taxable income. If such a state also requires a member of a federal consolidated group to file a separate company return for state purposes, the current year's NOLs that are absorbed by an affiliate on a federal consolidated return may never be available to the loss-generating corporation for state tax purposes because the loss will never be reflected as an NOL deduction on the loss corporation's federal return. The limitation is illustrated by the Oklahoma Supreme Court's decision in *Utica Bankshares Corp. v. Oklahoma Tax Commission.* [892 P.2d 979 (Okla. 1994)] The court held that the federal NOL can be used only to offset federal taxable income for the carryback year and not for positive modifications for years in which Oklahoma taxable income was greater than federal taxable income. In other words, the taxpayer may not claim on the state tax return an NOL deduction based on the federal NOL that is in excess of the federal NOL deduction actually allowed by the IRS for the corresponding tax years.

In *Sovran Bank/D.C. National v. District of Columbia* [731 A.2d 387 (D.C. Ct. of App. 1999)], the taxpayer successfully argued that because it was required to file a District of Columbia return on a separate company basis, the appropriate construction of the District's NOL provision was to determine NOL carrybacks as if the taxpayer had filed a separate federal return. [See also *School Street Associates Limited Partnership et al. and Sovran Bank/D.C. National v. District of Columbia*, 764 A.2d 798 (D.C. Ct. of App. Jan. 4, 2001)]. The District codified this decision by allowing NOLs to be computed on a separate company basis, regardless of how the NOL is used on a federal consolidated return. [D.C. Code Ann. § 47-1803.3(a)(14)(E)(ii)]

Different Federal and State Consolidation Rules. In the case of an affiliated group of corporations filing a federal consolidated return, the computation of a state NOL deduction may be complicated by the use of different group filing methods for state tax purposes, such as separate company returns, nexus consolidations, or combined unitary reporting. In such cases, the state NOL deduction may be determined on a federal pro forma basis, that is, what the allowable federal NOL carryover or deduction would be if only the separate company or the companies included in the state consolidated or combined return were included in the federal return. However, states that permit the filing of a consolidated or combined return may impose separate return limitation year (or SRLY) restrictions on the use of a specific affiliate's NOLs to reduce consolidated taxable income. For example, see *Weyerhaeuser USA Subsidiaries v. Alabama Dept. of Revenue* [No. CORP. 04-511 (Ala. Dept. of Revenue, Admin. Law Div., Mar. 11, 2005)].

In *Golden West Financial Corp. v. Florida Department of Revenue* [No. 1D07-0135, 975 (Fla. Dist. Ct., Feb. 19, 2008)], a Florida District Court of Appeal ruled that that a Florida regulation, which prohibited corporations that incurred losses when filing Florida returns on a separate company basis to share those losses with members of their affiliated group when electing to file on a consolidated basis, was invalid because it impermissibly contravened the specific provisions of the enabling statutes. The Florida Department of Revenue subsequently deleted the invalid provision [Fla. Dept. of Rev., Regs. 12C-1.013, Apr. 14, 2009], and such corporations are now permitted to share Florida NOL carryovers on a consolidated return.

North Carolina's Net Economic Loss Approach. For North Carolina tax purposes, an operating loss is deductible only if it is a "net economic loss," rather than a net operating loss. A net economic loss is the amount by which allowable deductions, other than prior years' losses, exceed income from all sources in the year, including nontaxable income. [N.C. Gen Stat. § 105-130.8].

Mergers and Acquisitions—Federal Tax Treatment

When the assets of a corporation that has NOL carryovers (a "loss corporation") are acquired by another corporation, an important issue for the acquiring corporation is whether it can use the loss corporation's pre-acquisition NOLs to offset the earnings from its other business activities. Over the years, Congress has enacted numerous restrictions to prevent the "trafficking in NOLs," that is, profitable corporations acquiring corporations with NOL carryovers merely as a device to avoid taxes. The principal provisions governing the transfer of NOLs in such situations are Code Sections 381 and 382.

Section 381. Section 381 provides that an acquiring corporation succeeds to the NOL carryovers of a loss corporation when it acquires the assets of the loss corporation (or target) in one of the following transactions:

- Subsidiary liquidation under Section 332;

- Type A reorganization (statutory merger or consolidation);
- Type C reorganization (acquisition of substantially all of the target's assets in exchange for the stock of the acquiring corporation);
- Nondivisive Type D reorganization (acquisition of substantially all of the target's assets in exchange for stock, where the acquiring corporation distributes the stock it receives);
- Type F reorganization (change of identity, form, or place of organization); or
- Type G reorganization (acquisition of substantially all of the target's assets in a bankruptcy proceeding).

Section 381 does not apply to:

- Partial liquidations (where the target remains intact and retains its tax attributes);
- Type B reorganizations (a stock-for-stock exchange in which the target becomes a subsidiary of the acquirer and retains its tax attributes);
- Divisive Type D reorganizations (where the tax attributes remain with the target in a spin-off or split-off, or expire upon the liquidation of the transferor in a split-up);
- Type E reorganizations (recapitalizations, which involve a single corporation);
- Taxable asset acquisitions (where the tax attributes remain with the target); or
- Taxable stock acquisitions where the new subsidiary is not liquidated (and the tax attributes remain with the target).

Section 382. For transactions in which the acquiring corporation succeeds to the NOL carryovers of the loss corporation (e.g., a statutory merger), Section 382 may limit the acquiring corporation's use of the target's pre-acquisition NOLs. Section 382 does not disallow an NOL deduction, but rather limits the amount of the deduction to the hypothetical future income that would be generated by the loss corporation's business capital. Limiting the use of the NOLs to the amount that would have been deductible by the loss corporation reflects the policy of Section 382, which is that a change in ownership of the loss corporation's assets should not make that corporation's NOL carryovers more or less valuable.

The restrictions of Section 382 apply when there has been a substantial change in the stock ownership of the loss corporation. More specifically, Section 382 applies when two requirements are met. First, there has either been a tax-free reorganization (other than a Type F, Type G, or divisive Type D), or a change in the stock ownership of persons owning 5 percent of more of the loss corporation's stock. Second, the percentage of stock owned by one or more 5-percent shareholders increases by more than 50 percentage points (by value) during a three-year testing period.

When the requisite change in stock ownership of the loss corporation has occurred, Section 382 limits the annual amount of NOL deductions available to the acquiring corporation to an amount equal to the fair market value of the loss corporation's stock before the ownership change multiplied by the federal long-term tax-exempt rate. Thus, Section 382 limits the use of the loss corporation's pre-acquisition NOLs to the hypothetical future income of the loss corporation, determined as if its stock were sold and the proceeds were reinvested in long-term tax-exempt securities. This federal long-term tax-exempt rate is published monthly by the Internal Revenue Service (IRS), and is computed specifically for the purpose of applying Section 382.

Section 382 also imposes a continuity of business enterprise requirement. Specifically, if the acquiring corporation does not continue the business enterprise of the loss corporation at all times during the two-year period following the stock ownership change, no amount of the loss corporation's pre-acquisition NOLs are deductible.

Other Statutory Restrictions. In addition to Section 382, Congress has enacted various other restrictions on the carryover of tax attributes in mergers and acquisitions, including Section 269, Section 383, and Section 384. The regulations issued under Section 1502 also restrict the use of separate return limitation year NOLs in consolidated tax returns.

Under Section 269, the IRS may disallow an NOL carryforward deduction if one corporation acquires another corporation and the principal purpose of the acquisition is to evade or avoid income tax by claiming the benefit of a deduction that would not otherwise be available. Section 269 is the Service's broadest and oldest weapon (first enacted in 1943) against trafficking in NOLs. The primary defense against the Service's use of Section 269 is to document a good business purpose for the acquisition.

Section 383 extends restrictions similar to those found in Section 382 to other types of carryovers, including carryovers of capital losses, general business credits, minimum tax credits, and foreign tax credits.

Section 384 prevents a corporation with unrealized built-in gains from acquiring a loss corporation in order to use the target's pre-acquisition NOLs to offset its built-in gains. Section 384 provides that during a five-year post-acquisition period, the loss corporation's pre-acquisition NOLs may not offset the recognized built-in gains of the acquiring corporation. Section 384 also prevents an acquiring corporation from offsetting its pre-acquisition NOLs against the built-in gains of the target corporation.

Finally, in the case of an affiliated group of corporations filing a consolidated tax return, if a member of the affiliated group acquires the stock of another corporation and the new affiliate joins in the filing of the consolidated return, the consolidated group's use of the acquired corporation's pre-acquisition NOLs to offset income generated by other members of the group is limited by the separate return limitation year rules of Treasury Regulation Section 1.1502-21. A separate return limitation year, or SRLY, generally is a tax year of a subsidiary during which the subsidiary was not a member of the group. Under the SRLY rules, the SRLY losses of one group member may be used to offset income of other group members only to the extent of the SRLY member's aggregate contribution to the group's consolidated taxable income.

Mergers and Acquisitions—State Tax Treatment

General Rules. Most states permit NOL deductions, but the specific rules vary significantly from state to state. A number of states incorporate the federal NOL provisions into their tax laws by directly referencing the applicable federal provisions. Those states generally follow the limitations imposed by Code Sections 381 and 382. Accordingly, if the acquiring corporation is not permitted to carry over the target corporation's pre-acquisition NOLs for federal purposes, then those pre-acquisition NOLs may not be carried over for state tax purposes.

States that use federal Form 1120, line 30 (i.e., federal taxable income net of all deductions, including the federal NOL deduction) as the starting point in computing state taxable income automatically accord a corporation the same NOL treatment for state and federal tax purposes, unless the state requires an addition modification for the federal NOL deduction. Some of the states that use Line 30 of the federal return as the starting point in computing state taxable income have no statutory provisions governing NOL deductions. In those states, an NOL deduction is allowable for state purposes to the extent that the NOL deduction is allowed in computing federal taxable income. By default, these states adopt the provisions of Sections 381 and 382.

Even if a state NOL deduction is determined based on the federal provisions or an amount reported on a federal return, the computation of the allowable state NOL deduction may be more complicated if state returns are filed on a separate company basis or the consolidated or combined group for state tax purposes differs from the federal consolidated group. In either case, the state NOL deduction generally is determined on a pro forma federal basis, that is, the allowable federal NOL deduction determined as if only the corporation filing on a separate company basis or the group of corporations included in the state consolidated or combined group were included in the federal return.

Some states have created their own NOL provisions in lieu of adopting the federal provisions. These states generally permit an NOL to be carried forward in transactions involving tax-free reorganizations. Some of these states, however, have not adopted provisions similar to Sections 381 and 382. In such states, it is possible that NOLs, which do not carry over for federal purposes, do carry over for state tax purposes.

Continuity of Business Enterprise Requirement. Even if a state does not impose Section 382-type limitations, it may impose a continuity of business enterprise restriction on the use of pre-acquisition NOLs, in which case NOLs carry over only if the acquiring corporation continues the business enterprise of the loss corporation. In *BellSouth Telecommunications, Inc. v. Department of Revenue* (No. COA96-558 [N.C. Ct. App., June 3, 1997]), the North Carolina Court of Appeals ruled that a corporation could not deduct a pre-merger net economic loss of a former subsidiary, because the continuity of business enterprise requirement was not satisfied.

Taxpayer in Year of NOL Requirement. Another common state restriction is that a corporation may claim an NOL deduction only if the corporation was doing business in the state in the year the NOL was incurred. For example, if a corporation incurs an NOL in year 1 while doing business in State *A*, and during year 2 expands its business to State *B*, State *B* may not permit the corporation to deduct the NOL carryover from year 1. The proper application of this restriction to a merger may be uncertain. For example, if a loss corporation is merged into a profitable corporation in a tax-free statutory merger, for federal tax purposes, the surviving corporation inherits the loss corporation's pre-merger NOLs. For state tax purposes, does the fact that the surviving corporation was doing business in the state before the merger influence the determination, or is whether the loss corporation was doing business in the state before the merger the only relevant factor?

In *American Home Products Corp. v. Tracy* (No. 02AP-759 [Ohio Ct. of App., Mar. 27, 2003]), the Ohio Court of Appeals ruled that a surviving corporation could not deduct an NOL carryforward generated by a predecessor, because neither corporation was an Ohio taxpayer in the year the loss was generated.

Restricting NOL Deduction to Corporation That Incurred the Loss. Some states restrict the carryover of a pre-acquisition NOL to the specific corporation that actually generated the loss. In such cases, if a loss corporation is merged into a profitable corporation, the loss corporation's NOLs may disappear for state tax purposes.

In *Richard's Auto City, Inc. v. Division of Taxation* (No. A-54 [N.J. Sup. Ct. June 21, 1995]), the New Jersey Supreme Court held that the Division of Taxation regulation limiting post-merger NOL carryovers to the same corporation that originally incurred the loss was valid. Thus, a corporate survivor of a merger may not deduct NOLs incurred by the merged corporation. See also *A.H. Robins Company, Inc. v. Division of Taxation* (No. A-96-2003 [N.J. Sup. Ct., Dec. 7, 2004]).

Likewise, in *Little Six Corp. v. Johnson* (No. 01-A-01-9806-CH-00285 [Tenn. Ct. App., May 28, 1999]), the Tennessee Court of Appeals held that the corporation surviving a statutory merger may not deduct NOLs incurred by the merged corporation. See also *AT&T Corp. v. Johnson* (No. M2003-00148-COA-R3-CV [Tenn. Ct. App., Apr. 8, 2004]).

In *Macy's East, Inc. v. Commissioner of Revenue* (No. SJC-09194 [Mass. Sup. Jud. Ct. May 27, 2004]), the Massachusetts Supreme Judicial Court ruled that the survivor of a merger may not deduct NOLs incurred by the merged corporation. Although the pre-merger NOLs carried over and were deductible by the surviving corporation for federal tax purposes, the state regulation that prohibited such carryovers was not unconstitutional.

Net Operating Losses—Recent Developments

California. For tax years beginning in 2010 and 2011, California does not allow an NOL deduction for taxpayers whose pre-apportionment income exceeds $300,000 (determined on an aggregate basis for members of a combined reporting group). For tax years beginning in 2008 and 2009, California does not allow an NOL deduction for taxpayers with taxable income of $500,000 or more. The carryforward period for the suspended NOLs is extended one year for an NOL incurred in 2010, two years for an NOL incurred in 2009, three years for an NOL incurred in 2008, and four years for an NOL incurred prior to 2008. On the other hand, beginning with NOLs incurred after 2012, California will allow a two year NOL carryback. During the phase-in period, the carryback will be limited to 50 percent of an NOL incurred in 2013, and 75 percent of an NOL incurred in 2014. After 2014, the full amount of an NOL can be carried back two years. [S.B. 858, Oct. 19, 2010; and A.B. 1452, Sept. 30, 2008]

Colorado. For tax years beginning in 2011 to 2013, the NOL deduction is limited to $250,000 per year. If the limitation prevents the use of any part of an NOL carryforward in a tax year, then all NOLs carried forward to such tax year may be carried forward one additional year for each tax year the restriction applies. Additionally, any portion of an NOL carryforward that cannot be used solely due to the limitation is increased by 3.25 percent per year until the loss is used. [H.B. 1199, Feb 24, 2010]

Idaho. Effective January 1, 2010, Idaho codified the Tax Commission's practice of applying federal law to determine whether NOLs survive after a merged corporation ceases to exist. Under the new statute, Idaho NOLs will, pursuant IRC Sections 381 and 382, survive a merger if (1) the transaction meets all federal laws, criteria, and procedures; (2) the liquidated or merged entity had an Idaho business activity and incurred an Idaho NOL; and (3) the continuity of business requirements are satisfied. [H.B. 381, Feb. 23, 2010]

Illinois. Illinois does not allow an NOL deduction for tax years ending in 2011 to 2014. The carryforward period for the suspended NOLs is extended by the number of years that the deduction is suspended. [S.B. 2505, Jan. 13, 2011]

Indiana. Effective January 1, 2012, Indiana eliminated its two-year NOL carryback. [H.B. 1004, May 10, 2011]

Iowa. In 2009, Iowa eliminated the two-year carryback, effective for NOLs incurred in tax years beginning on or after January 1, 2009. Corporations are still permitted a 20 year carryforward period. [S.B. 483, May 22, 2009]

Maine. Maine does not allow any NOL deductions for tax years beginning in 2009, 2010, and 2011. The NOL not deducted due to this restriction may be deducted in tax years beginning after 2011, subject to certain restrictions. [L.D. 353, May 28, 2009]

Massachusetts. Effective for tax years beginning on or after January 1, 2010, Massachusetts extends the NOL carryforward period from 5 years to 20 years. [S.B. 2582, Aug. 5, 2010]

New Jersey. Effective for NOLs incurred in tax years ending after June 30, 2009, New Jersey extends the NOL carryforward period from 7 years to 20 years. [S.B. 2130, Nov. 24, 2008]

Pennsylvania. Prior to 2007, Pennsylvania limited NOL carryforward deductions to $2 million. The cap increased to the greater of $3 million or 12.5 percent of taxable income for tax years beginning in 2007 and 2008 [H.B. 859, July 12, 2006], the greater of $3 million or 15 percent of taxable income for tax years beginning in 2009, and the greater of $3 million or 20 percent of taxable income for tax years beginning after 2009. [H.B. 1531, Oct. 9, 2009]

State-by-State Summary

For ease of presentation, the following chart has been divided into six parts, as follows:

- Part 1: Carryover periods, and election to forgo carryback
- Part 2: Pre- versus post-apportionment NOLs, doing business in year of NOL, conformity to Sections 381 and 382
- Part 3: Surviving entity's use the Merged entity's NOLs (Part 1)
- Part 4: Surviving entity's use the Merged entity's NOLs (Part 2)
- Part 5: Conformity to federal 5-year carryback of 2008 NOLs for small businesses
- Part 6: Conformity to federal 5-year carryback of 2008-2009 NOLs

Net Operating Loss Carryovers (Part 1)

Legend:
SAF Same as applicable federal rules
NA Not applicable
NR Not reported

	Does State Allow NOL				*Number of Years NOLs May Be Carried*	
	Carrybacks?	*Carryforwards?*	*May Taxpayer Elect to Forgo a Carryback?*	*Is a Separate State Election Required to Do So?*	*Back*	*Forward*
Alabama	No	Yes	NA	NA	NA	15
Alaska	Yes	Yes	Yes	No	SAF, extension from 2 to 5 years under the Job Creation and Worker Assistance Act of 2002	SAF
Arizona	No	Yes	NA	NA	NA	5
Arkansas	No	Yes	NA	NA	NA	5
California	No, note that 2-year carrybacks will be allowed for taxable years beginning on or after 1/1/2013.	Yes, 10 years for NOLs incurred in taxable years beginning on or after 1/1/01, and 20 years for NOLs incurred in taxable years beginning on or after 1/1/08	NA	NA	NA	10, 5 for tax years beginning before 2000
Colorado	No	Yes	NA	NA	NA	20, SAF
Connecticut	No	Yes, for income years commencing on or after 1/4/2000-20 years	NA	NA	NA	20, 5 years prior to 1/1/2000

Net Operating Loss Carryovers (Part 1)

Legend:

SAF	Same as applicable federal rules
NA	Not applicable
NR	Not reported

	Does State Allow NOL				*Number of Years NOLs May Be Carried*	
	Carrybacks?	*Carryforwards?*	*May Taxpayer Elect to Forgo a Carryback?*	*Is a Separate State Election Required to Do So?*	*Back*	*Forward*
Delaware	Yes	Yes	Yes	NR	SAF, extension from 2 to 5 years under the Job Creation and Worker Assistance Act of 2002	SAF
District of Columbia	No	Yes	Yes	NR	2	SAF
Florida	No	Yes	NA	NA	NA	20, SAF
Georgia	Yes	Yes	Yes	Yes	SAF	20, 15 years for tax years beginning before 8/7/97
Hawaii	Yes	Yes	Yes	Yes	2	20
	Hawaii has not conformed to the provisions of the Job Creation and Worker Assistance Act of 2002. See Department of Taxation Announcement 2002-5.					
Idaho	Yes	Yes	Yes	Must attach copy of federal or separate state election	2, 3 years for tax years beginning on or before 1/1/2000	20, 15 years for tax years beginning on or before 1/1/2000
Illinois	Yes	Yes	Yes	Yes	See Note	See Note

Net Operating Loss Carryovers (Part 1)

Legend:

SAF	Same as applicable federal rules
NA	Not applicable
NR	Not reported

	Does State Allow NOL				*Number of Years NOLs May Be Carried*	
	Carrybacks?	*Carryforwards?*	*May Taxpayer Elect to Forgo a Carryback?*	*Is a Separate State Election Required to Do So?*	*Back*	*Forward*
Note. SB 1634 was passed by both houses and is expected to be signed into law by the Governor at any time. For taxpayers other than individuals, it provides as follows: For taxable years ending on/after 12/31/99 and prior to 12/31/03, Illinois-apportioned net losses (Illinois Net Losses) are allowed as a carryback to each of the 2 taxable years preceding the taxable years of such loss and may be carried forward to each of the 20 years following the taxable year of the loss. For taxable years ending on/after 12/31/03, such Illinois Net Losses shall be allowed as a carryover to each of the 12 taxable years following the taxable years following the taxable year of the loss. Illinois net losses incurred in such years may not be carried back. For Illinois Net Losses incurred in taxable years ending prior to 12/31/03, the taxpayer may elect to relinquish the entire carry-back period with respect to such loss.						
Indiana	No, carryback eliminated 12/31/11	Yes	Yes	No	2, extension from 2 to 5 years under the Job Creation and Worker Assistance Act of 2002	NR
Iowa	No, for losses beginning on or after 1/1/09	Yes	Yes	Yes	2, Iowa did not adopt the 5-year carryback for losses incurred in 2001 and 2002.	20
Kansas	No	Yes	NA	NA	NA	SAF
Kentucky	No, for losses incurred for beginning on or after 1/1/05.	Yes	NA	NA	NA	20, SAF
Louisiana	Yes	Yes	Yes, prior to 1/1/87	No	3	15
Maine	No	Yes	NA	NA	NA	20
Maryland	Yes	Yes	NR	NR	SAF	SAF

Net Operating Loss Carryovers (Part 1)

Legend:

SAF	Same as applicable federal rules
NA	Not applicable
NR	Not reported

	Does State Allow NOL				*Number of Years NOLs May Be Carried*	
	Carrybacks?	*Carryforwards?*	*May Taxpayer Elect to Forgo a Carryback?*	*Is a Separate State Election Required to Do So?*	*Back*	*Forward*
Massachusetts	No	Yes	NA	NA	NA	5 years
Michigan (Business Tax)	No	Yes	NA	NA	NA	10
Note. The CIT takes effect 01/01/12, and replaces the Michigan Business Tax (MBT) for most taxpayers. However, businesses that have been approved to receive, have received, or have been assigned certain certified credits may elect to file a return and pay the tax imposed by the MBT in lieu of the CIT until the certified credits are exhausted or extinguished.						
Minnesota	No	Yes	NA	NA	NA	15
Mississippi	Yes	Yes	Yes	Yes	2	20
Missouri	Yes	Yes			SAF	NR
Montana	Yes	Yes	Yes	Yes	3	7
Nebraska	No	Yes	NA	NA	NA	5
Nevada	Nevada does not impose a corporate income tax					
New Hampshire	No	Yes	NA	NA	NA	10

Net Operating Loss Carryovers (Part 1)

Legend:

SAF	Same as applicable federal rules
NA	Not applicable
NR	Not reported

	Does State Allow NOL				*Number of Years NOLs May Be Carried*	
	Carrybacks?	*Carryforwards?*	*May Taxpayer Elect to Forgo a Carryback?*	*Is a Separate State Election Required to Do So?*	*Back*	*Forward*
New Jersey	No	An NOL for any privilege period ending after 6/30/09 shall be a NOL carryover to each of the 20 privilege periods following the period of the loss. NOLs accruing for privilege periods ending before 6/30/09 continue to have a NOL carryover to each of the 7 privilege periods following the period of the loss. N.J.S.A. 54:10A-4(k)(6)(E); N.J.A.C. 18:7-5.12; 18:7-5.13(a); 18:7-5.14.	NA	NA	NA	7, 2002 and 2003 suspended by statute, 2004 and 2005, 50% suspended
New Mexico	No	Yes	NR	NA	NA	5

Net Operating Loss Carryovers (Part 1)

Legend:

SAF	Same as applicable federal rules
NA	Not applicable
NR	Not reported

	Does State Allow NOL				*Number of Years NOLs May Be Carried*	
	Carrybacks?	*Carryforwards?*	*May Taxpayer Elect to Forgo a Carryback?*	*Is a Separate State Election Required to Do So?*	*Back*	*Forward*
New York	Yes, but pre-New York State taxability losses not allowed, capped at $10,000.	Yes, but pre-New York State taxability losses not allowed	SAF	No	2, except New York does conform to the 5-year carryback under the Job Creation and Worker Assistance Act of 2002.	20
North Carolina	No	Yes	NA	NA	NA	15
North Dakota	Yes, only for NOLs incurred in taxable years beginning before 7/1/03	Yes	Yes	Yes	NR	SAF
Ohio	Ohio does not impose a corporate income tax					
	Note Effective 1/1/2010, the Ohio Franchise Tax was fully phased out and business will be taxed on gross receipts through the Commercial Activity Tax. Details about that tax can be found at: http//tax.ohio.gov/divisions/commercial_activities/index.stm					
Oklahoma	Yes	Yes	Yes	Yes	2001 NOLs eligible for carryback, extension from 2 to 5 years under the Job Creation and Worker Assistance Act of 2002	1997-2000 losses

Net Operating Loss Carryovers (Part 1)

Legend:
SAF Same as applicable federal rules
NA Not applicable
NR Not reported

	Does State Allow NOL				*Number of Years NOLs May Be Carried*	
	Carrybacks?	*Carryforwards?*	*May Taxpayer Elect to Forgo a Carryback?*	*Is a Separate State Election Required to Do So?*	*Back*	*Forward*
Oregon	No	Yes	No	NA	NA	15
Pennsylvania	No	Yes	NA	NA	NA	20 years for losses in taxable years 1998 and after; 10 years for losses in taxable years 1995-1997.
Rhode Island	No	Yes	No	NA	NA	5
South Carolina	No	SAF	NR	NR	NA	20
South Dakota	South Dakota does not impose a corporate income tax					
Tennessee	No	Yes	NA	NA	NA	15
Texas	No	No			NA	NA
Utah	Yes	Yes	Yes	No	3	15 years with the exception of pre-1994 losses

Net Operating Loss Carryovers (Part 1)

Legend:

SAF	Same as applicable federal rules
NA	Not applicable
NR	Not reported

	Does State Allow NOL				*Number of Years NOLs May Be Carried*	
	Carrybacks?	*Carryforwards?*	*May Taxpayer Elect to Forgo a Carryback?*	*Is a Separate State Election Required to Do So?*	*Back*	*Forward*
Vermont	No refund is allowed, federal carryback is recognized	Yes	Federal election applies	NA	SAF, extension from 2 to 5 years under the Job Creation and Worker Assistance Act of 2002. However note that no refund is available from the carryback.	SAF
Virginia	Yes	Yes	Yes	No	2	SA
Washington	Washington does not impose a corporate income tax					
West Virginia	Yes	Yes	Yes	Yes	2 years; if tax year end begins before 8/5/97, 3 years; extension from 2 to 5 years under the Job Creation and Worker Assistance Act of 2002.	
Wisconsin	No	Yes	NA	NA	NA	15
Wyoming	Wyoming does not impose a corporate income tax					

Net Operating Loss Carryovers (Part 2)

Legend:
NA Not applicable
NR Not reported

	Is Carryforward Deduction Based on Loss-Year Apportionment Percentage?	*Is Deduction Allowed for an NOL Generated When Not Doing Business in the State?*	*Does State Follow Section 381 in Computing NOL Carryovers?*	*Does State Follow Section 382 in Computing NOL Carryovers?*	*If so, Does the State Limitation Amount Match the IRC Section 382 Limitation Amount?*
Alabama	Yes	No	Yes	Yes	Yes
Alaska	Yes	No	Yes	Yes	No
Arizona	Yes	No	No	No	NA
Arkansas	Yes	No	No	No	NR
California	Yes	No	Yes	Yes	California generally conforms to the federal IRC § 382, but California has its own limitations.
Colorado	Yes	No, apportions to zero	Yes	Yes	Yes
Connecticut	Yes	No	Yes	No	No
Delaware	No, based on carryover year apportionment percentage	Yes	Yes	Yes	Yes
District of Columbia	Yes	No	Yes	Yes	Yes
Florida	Yes	No	Yes	Depends	NA
Georgia	Yes	No	Yes	Yes	See GA Reg 560-7-3.13 and 560-7-3.06
Hawaii	Yes	No	Yes	Yes	Yes

Net Operating Loss Carryovers (Part 2)

Legend:

NA Not applicable

NR Not reported

	Is Carryforward Deduction Based on Loss-Year Apportionment Percentage?	*Is Deduction Allowed for an NOL Generated When Not Doing Business in the State?*	*Does State Follow Section 381 in Computing NOL Carryovers?*	*Does State Follow Section 382 in Computing NOL Carryovers?*	*If so, Does the State Limitation Amount Match the IRC Section 382 Limitation Amount?*
Idaho	Yes	No	Yes	Yes	Yes, IRC § 382 limitation is further limited by pre-merger ID apportionment factor.
Illinois	Yes	No, the Illinois NOL is the amount of loss allocated or apportioned to Illinois, so there would be no loss to carryover.	Yes	No	NA
Indiana	Yes	No	Yes	Yes	Yes
Iowa	Yes	No	Yes	Yes	Yes
Kansas	Yes	No	No	Yes	Yes
Kentucky	Yes	No	Yes	Yes	Yes
Louisiana	Yes	No	Yes	Yes	Yes
Maine	NR	Yes, if claimed at federal level	Yes	Yes	Yes
Maryland	NR	NR	NR	NR	NR
Massachusetts	NR	NR	No	Yes	See 830 CMR 63.30.2(R)
Michigan (Business Tax)	Yes, loss year apportionment percentage	No	Yes	Yes	Yes

Net Operating Loss Carryovers (Part 2)

Legend:
NA **Not applicable**
NR **Not reported**

	Is Carryforward Deduction Based on Loss-Year Apportionment Percentage?	*Is Deduction Allowed for an NOL Generated When Not Doing Business in the State?*	*Does State Follow Section 381 in Computing NOL Carryovers?*	*Does State Follow Section 382 in Computing NOL Carryovers?*	*If so, Does the State Limitation Amount Match the IRC Section 382 Limitation Amount?*
Note. The CIT takes effect 01/01/12, and replaces the Michigan Business Tax (MBT) for most taxpayers. However, businesses that have been approved to receive, have received, or have been assigned certain certified credits may elect to file a return and pay the tax imposed by the MBT in lieu of the CIT until the certified credits are exhausted or extinguished.					
Minnesota	Yes	No	Yes	Yes	No
Mississippi	Yes	No	No	No	NA
Missouri	No, carryover year apportionment percentage	Yes	Yes	Yes	Yes
Montana	Yes	No	No	NR	NA
Nebraska	Yes	No	Yes	Yes	Yes
Nevada	Nevada does not impose a corporate income tax				
New Hampshire	Yes	No	Yes	Yes	No
New Jersey	No	No, return must be filed	No	No, statutory computation	NA
New Mexico	No	Yes	Yes	Yes	Yes
New York	No	No	Yes	Yes	Yes
North Carolina	Yes	No	No	No	NA
North Dakota	Yes	No	No	No	NA
Ohio	Ohio does not impose a corporate income tax				

Net Operating Loss Carryovers (Part 2)

Legend:
NA **Not applicable**
NR **Not reported**

	Is Carryforward Deduction Based on Loss-Year Apportionment Percentage?	*Is Deduction Allowed for an NOL Generated When Not Doing Business in the State?*	*Does State Follow Section 381 in Computing NOL Carryovers?*	*Does State Follow Section 382 in Computing NOL Carryovers?*	*If so, Does the State Limitation Amount Match the IRC Section 382 Limitation Amount?*
	Note. Effective 1/1/2010, the Ohio Franchise Tax was fully phased out and business will be taxed on gross receipts through the Commercial Activity Tax. Details about that tax can be found at: http//tax.ohio.gov/divisions/commercial_activities/index.stm				
Oklahoma	Yes	No	Yes	Yes	Yes
Oregon	Yes	No	Yes	Yes	Yes
Pennsylvania	Yes	No	Yes	Yes	Yes
Rhode Island	Yes	No	Yes	Yes	Yes
South Carolina	Yes	No	Yes	Yes	Yes
South Dakota	South Dakota does not impose a corporate income tax				
Tennessee	Yes	No	No	NR	NA
Texas	NA	No	No	No	NA
Utah	Yes	No	No	No	NA
Vermont	No	Yes	Yes	Yes	Yes
Virginia	No	Yes	Yes	Yes	Yes
Washington	Washington does not impose a corporate income tax				
West Virginia	Yes	No	Yes	Yes	Yes
Wisconsin	Yes	No	Yes	Yes	Yes
Wyoming	Wyoming does not impose a corporate income tax				

Net Operating Loss Carryovers (Part 3)

Legend:

SAF	Same as applicable federal rules
NA	Not applicable
NR	Not reported

Assumptions:

Q	Corporation with federal NOL carryforwards
R	A profitable corporation, merged into Q and files in state

	Can the Surviving Entity (R) Use the Merged Entity's (Q's) NOLs?		*Limitations That Apply*	
	Q Was Doing Business in State Prior to the Merger	*Q Was Not Doing Business in State Prior to the Merger*	*Q Was Doing Business in State Prior to the Merger*	*Q Was Not Doing Business in State Prior to the Merger*
Alabama	No	No	To extent NOL was earned in Alabama by Q	NA
Alaska	Yes, Q's Alaska NOL available	No	NA	NA
Arizona	Yes	No	Limited to post-merger income from Q's operations	NA
Arkansas	Yes	No	Income of assets of Q after merger.	NA
California	Yes	No	NA	NA
Colorado	Yes	No		NA
Connecticut	No	No	NA	NA
Delaware	Yes	Yes	SAF, but carryback is limited to $30,000/yr	SAF, but carryback is limited to $30,000/yr
District of Columbia	Yes	No	Yes	Yes
Florida	Yes	No	SAF	NA
Georgia	Yes	No	SAF	NA
Hawaii	Yes	No	SRLY rules and IRC §§ 381, 382; further limited to NOL apportioned to Hawaii	NA

Net Operating Loss Carryovers (Part 3)

Legend:

SAF	Same as applicable federal rules
NA	Not applicable
NR	Not reported

Assumptions:

Q	Corporation with federal NOL carryforwards
R	A profitable corporation, merged into Q and files in state

	Can the Surviving Entity (R) Use the Merged Entity's (Q's) NOLs?		*Limitations That Apply*	
	Q Was Doing Business in State Prior to the Merger	*Q Was Not Doing Business in State Prior to the Merger*	*Q Was Doing Business in State Prior to the Merger*	*Q Was Not Doing Business in State Prior to the Merger*
Idaho	Yes	No	IRC § 382 further limited by Idaho apportionment factor	NA
Illinois	Illinois does not allow federal NOLs, but does allow the carryforward of net losses apportioned to Illinois. Therefore, company Q must have been previously operating in Illinois to have existing Illinois NOLs. However, if company Q had federal NOLs that would survive a merger with company R, it could also claim Illinois NOLs that would similarly survive the merger.			
Indiana	Yes	No	NR	NA
Iowa	Yes	No	SAF	NA
Kansas	Yes	No	Not to exceed R's Kansas taxable income	NA
	Federal NOLs are not allowed but NOLs apportioned to Kansas are. (Answer based on each entity establishing a Kansas NOL.)			
Kentucky	Yes	No	SAF	NA
Louisiana	Yes	No	NR	NA
Maine	Yes	Yes	SAF	SAF
Maryland	Yes	Yes	SAF	SAF
Massachusetts	No	No	NA	NA
Michigan (Business Tax)	Policy under review	No	Policy under review	NA

Net Operating Loss Carryovers (Part 3)

Legend:

SAF	Same as applicable federal rules
NA	Not applicable
NR	Not reported

Assumptions:

Q	Corporation with federal NOL carryforwards
R	A profitable corporation, merged into Q and files in state

	Can the Surviving Entity (R) Use the Merged Entity's (Q's) NOLs?		*Limitations That Apply*	
	Q Was Doing Business in State Prior to the Merger	*Q Was Not Doing Business in State Prior to the Merger*	*Q Was Doing Business in State Prior to the Merger*	*Q Was Not Doing Business in State Prior to the Merger*
Note. The CIT takes effect 01/01/12, and replaces the Michigan Business Tax (MBT) for most taxpayers. However, businesses that have been approved to receive, have received, or have been assigned certain certified credits may elect to file a return and pay the tax imposed by the MBT in lieu of the CIT until the certified credits are exhausted or extinguished.				
Minnesota	Yes	No	SAF	NA
Mississippi	Yes	No	Both entities must have been members of the same affiliated group when the loss was incurred.	NA
Missouri	Yes	Yes	SAF	SAF
Montana	No	No	NA	NA
			NOLs are lost in mergers, MCA § 15-31-119(8)	
Nebraska	Yes	No	SAF	NA
Nevada	Nevada does not impose a corporate income tax			
New Hampshire	Yes, see RSA 77-A: 4, xiii	No	NR	NA
New Jersey	No	No	NA	NA
New Mexico	No, if reporting as separate entity.	SAF	SAF	SAF
New York	Yes	No	SAF	NOL must be "earned" in NY

Net Operating Loss Carryovers (Part 3)

Legend:

SAF	Same as applicable federal rules
NA	Not applicable
NR	Not reported

Assumptions:

Q	Corporation with federal NOL carryforwards
R	A profitable corporation, merged into Q and files in state

	Can the Surviving Entity (R) Use the Merged Entity's (Q's) NOLs?		*Limitations That Apply*	
	Q Was Doing Business in State Prior to the Merger	*Q Was Not Doing Business in State Prior to the Merger*	*Q Was Doing Business in State Prior to the Merger*	*Q Was Not Doing Business in State Prior to the Merger*
			Different rules apply to highly leveraged transactions	
North Carolina	Yes	No	Only to the extent the assets of Q generated a profit	NA
North Dakota	No	No	NA	NA
Ohio	Ohio does not impose a corporate income tax			
Note. Effective 1/1/2010, the Ohio Franchise Tax was fully phased out and business will be taxed on gross receipts through the Commercial Activity Tax. Details about that tax can be found at: http//tax.ohio.gov/divisions/commercial_activities/index.stm				
Oklahoma	Yes	No	SAF	NA
Oregon	Yes	No	Only to extent Q had loss apportioned to Oregon and R has income apportioned to Oregon after the merger	NA
Pennsylvania	Yes	No	NR	NA
Rhode Island	Yes	No	SAF	NA
South Carolina	Yes	No, there would be no South Carolina NOL.	SAF	SAF
South Dakota	South Dakota does not impose a corporate income tax			
Tennessee	No	No	NA	NA

Net Operating Loss Carryovers (Part 3)

Legend:
SAF Same as applicable federal rules
NA Not applicable
NR Not reported

Assumptions:
Q Corporation with federal NOL carryforwards
R A profitable corporation, merged into Q and files in state

	Can the Surviving Entity (R) Use the Merged Entity's (Q's) NOLs?		*Limitations That Apply*	
	Q Was Doing Business in State Prior to the Merger	*Q Was Not Doing Business in State Prior to the Merger*	*Q Was Doing Business in State Prior to the Merger*	*Q Was Not Doing Business in State Prior to the Merger*
Texas	No	No	NA	NA
Utah	No, unless both in a unitary group when losses are incurred	No, unless both in a unitary group when losses are incurred	NA	NA
Vermont	Yes	Yes	SAF	SAF
Virginia	Yes	Yes	SAF	SAF
Washington	Washington does not impose a corporate income tax			
West Virginia	Yes	No	SRLY rules and IRC §§ 381 and 382 limitations	NA
Wisconsin	Yes, limited to Wisconsin NOL	No	Limited to Wisconsin NOLs and credits	Since 0% to Wisconsin, no NOL
Wyoming	Wyoming does not impose a corporate income tax			

Net Operating Loss Carryovers (Part 4)

Legend:

SAF	Same as applicable federal rules
NA	Not applicable
NR	Not reported

Assumptions:

Q	Corporation with federal NOL carryforwards is merged into R
R	Surviving entity, profitable corporation filing in state

	Can Surviving Entity (R) Use the Merged Entity's (Q's) NOLs?		*Limitations That Apply*	
	R Was Doing Business in State Prior to Merger	*R Was Not Doing Business in State Prior to Merger*	*R Was Doing Business in State Prior to Merger*	*R Was Not Doing Business in State Prior to Merger*
Alabama	Yes	Yes	To extent NOL was earned in state by Q	To extent NOL was earned in state by Q
Alaska	No	No	NA	NA
Arizona	Yes	Yes	Limited to post-merger income from Q's operations	Limited to post-merger income from Q's operations
Arkansas	Yes	Yes	Income of assets of Q after merger.	Income of assets of Q after merger.
California	Yes	Yes	NR	NR
Colorado	Yes	Yes		SAF
Connecticut	Yes	No	Continuity of business test	
Delaware	Yes	Yes	SAF, NOL limited to $30,000	SAF, NOL limited to $30,000
District of Columbia	Yes	Yes	SAF	SAF
Florida	Unknown	No		
Georgia	Yes, if Q had Georgia NOL carryforward, but subject to IRC § 381	Yes, if Q had Georgia NOL carryforward, but subject to IRC § 381	NA	NA

Net Operating Loss Carryovers (Part 4)

Legend:

SAF — Same as applicable federal rules
NA — Not applicable
NR — Not reported

Assumptions:

Q — Corporation with federal NOL carryforwards is merged into R
R — Surviving entity, profitable corporation filing in state

	Can Surviving Entity (R) Use the Merged Entity's (Q's) NOLs?		*Limitations That Apply*	
	R Was Doing Business in State Prior to Merger	*R Was Not Doing Business in State Prior to Merger*	*R Was Doing Business in State Prior to Merger*	*R Was Not Doing Business in State Prior to Merger*
Hawaii	No	No	SRLY rules and IRC §§ 381, 382, further limited to NOL apportioned to Hawaii	Assumption: Q was doing business in Hawaii and had Hawaii NOL. SRLY rules and IRC §§ 381, 382, further limited to NOL apportioned to Hawaii
Idaho	Yes, if Q had Idaho NOL	Yes, if Q had Idaho NOL	IRC § 382 and Idaho apportionment factor	IRC § 382 and Idaho apportionment factor
Illinois	Illinois does not allow federal NOLs, but does allow the carryforward of net losses apportioned to Illinois. Therefore, company Q must have been previously operating in Illinois to have existing Illinois NOLs. However, if company Q had federal NOLs that would survive a merger with company R, it could also claim Illinois NOLs that would similarly survive the merger.			
Indiana	Yes	No	NR	NA
Iowa	Yes, if Q has an Iowa NOL	Yes, if Q has an Iowa NOL	SAF	SAF
Kansas	No	Yes	Yes, not to exceed R's Kansas taxable income	Not to exceed R's Kansas taxable income
	Federal NOLs are not allowed but NOLs apportioned to Kansas are. (Answer based on each entity establishing a Kansas NOL.)			
Kentucky	Yes	Yes	SAF	SAF
Louisiana	Yes, Q was doing business in Louisiana.	No	NA	NA

Net Operating Loss Carryovers (Part 4)

Legend:

SAF	Same as applicable federal rules
NA	Not applicable
NR	Not reported

Assumptions:

Q	Corporation with federal NOL carryforwards is merged into R
R	Surviving entity, profitable corporation filing in state

	Can Surviving Entity (R) Use the Merged Entity's (Q's) NOLs?		*Limitations That Apply*	
	R Was Doing Business in State Prior to Merger	*R Was Not Doing Business in State Prior to Merger*	*R Was Doing Business in State Prior to Merger*	*R Was Not Doing Business in State Prior to Merger*
Maine	Yes	Yes	SAF	SAF
Maryland	NR	NR	NR	NR
Massachusetts	NR	NR	NR	NR
Michigan (Business Tax)	TBD, policy under review	TBD, policy under review	TBD, policy under review	TBD, policy under review
Note. The CIT takes effect 01/01/12, and replaces the Michigan Business Tax (MBT) for most taxpayers. However, businesses that have been approved to receive, have received, or have been assigned certain certified credits may elect to file a return and pay the tax imposed by the MBT in lieu of the CIT until the certified credits are exhausted or extinguished.				
Minnesota	Yes	Yes	SAF	SAF
Mississippi	Yes	Yes	Both entities must have been members of the same affiliated group when loss was incurred.	Both entities must have been members of the same affiliated group when loss was incurred.
Missouri	Yes	Yes	SAF	SAF
Montana	No	No	NA	NA
			NOLs are lost in mergers, MCA § 15-31-119(8)	
Nebraska	No	No	NA	NA
Nevada	Nevada does not impose a corporate income tax			
New Hampshire	Yes, see RSA 77-A:4, xiii	Yes, see RSA 77-A:4, xiii No	NA	NA

Net Operating Loss Carryovers (Part 4)

Legend:

SAF	Same as applicable federal rules
NA	Not applicable
NR	Not reported

Assumptions:

Q	Corporation with federal NOL carryforwards is merged into R
R	Surviving entity, profitable corporation filing in state

	Can Surviving Entity (R) Use the Merged Entity's (Q's) NOLs?		*Limitations That Apply*	
	R Was Doing Business in State Prior to Merger	*R Was Not Doing Business in State Prior to Merger*	*R Was Doing Business in State Prior to Merger*	*R Was Not Doing Business in State Prior to Merger*
New Jersey	No	No	NA	NA
New Mexico	SAF	SAF	NR	NR
New York	Yes, if Q was also doing business in NY	Yes, if Q was also doing business in NY	NOL must be earned in NY.	SAF
North Carolina	No	No	NA	NA
North Dakota	No	No	NA	NA
Ohio	Ohio does not impose a corporate income tax			
Note. Effective 1/1/2010, the Ohio Franchise Tax was fully phased out and business will be taxed on gross receipts through the Commercial Activity Tax. Details about that tax can be found at: http//tax.ohio.gov/divisions/commercial_activities/index.stm				
Oklahoma	Yes	No	SAF	NA
Oregon	Yes	Yes	Allowed on consolidated basis if Q did business in Oregon in loss year and R has income apportioned to Oregon after the merger	Allowed on consolidated basis if Q did business in Oregon in loss year and R has income apportioned to Oregon after the merger
Pennsylvania	Yes	Yes	NR	NR
Rhode Island	As long as Q was doing business	Yes	NR	NR

Net Operating Loss Carryovers (Part 4)

Legend:

SAF	Same as applicable federal rules
NA	Not applicable
NR	Not reported

Assumptions:

Q	Corporation with federal NOL carryforwards is merged into R
R	Surviving entity, profitable corporation filing in state

	Can Surviving Entity (R) Use the Merged Entity's (Q's) NOLs?		*Limitations That Apply*	
	R Was Doing Business in State Prior to Merger	*R Was Not Doing Business in State Prior to Merger*	*R Was Doing Business in State Prior to Merger*	*R Was Not Doing Business in State Prior to Merger*
South Carolina	Yes	Yes	SAF	SAF
South Dakota	South Dakota does not impose a corporate income tax			
Tennessee	No	No	NA	NA
Texas	No	No	NA	NA
Utah	No, unless both in a unitary group when losses are incurred	No, unless both in a unitary group when losses are incurred	NA	NA
Vermont	Yes	Yes	SAF	SAF
Virginia	Yes	Yes	SAF	SAF
Washington	Washington does not impose a corporate income tax			
West Virginia	Yes	No	SRLY rules and IRC §§ 381 and 382	NA
Wisconsin	Yes	Yes	Wisconsin NOLs and credits	Wisconsin NOLs and credits
Wyoming	Wyoming does not impose a corporate income tax			

Net Operating Loss Carryovers (Part 5)

Legend:
NA — Not applicable
NR — Not reported

	Does State Conform to Federal 5-Year Carryback of 2008 NOLs for Small Businesses (American Recovery and Reinvestment Act of 2009)?		
	Yes	*No*	*If Yes explain.*
Alabama		X	
Alaska	X		
Arizona	No, Currently Arizona hasn't conformed to federal changes made after 1/1/09. However, for corporate income tax purposes, Arizona adds back all federal net operating loss deductions taken and then allows an Arizona basis net operating loss which is carried forward 5 years with no carryback provision.		
Arkansas		X	
California		X	
Colorado		X	
Connecticut		X	
Delaware			
District of Columbia		X	
Florida		X	
Georgia		X	
Hawaii	NR		
Idaho		X	
Illinois	X		

Net Operating Loss Carryovers (Part 5)

Legend:
NA — Not applicable
NR — Not reported

	Does State Conform to Federal 5-Year Carryback of 2008 NOLs for Small Businesses (American Recovery and Reinvestment Act of 2009)?		
	Yes	*No*	*If Yes explain.*
Indiana		X	
Iowa		X	
Kansas		X	
Kentucky		X	
Louisiana		X	
Maine		X	
Maryland		X	
Massachusetts			

Net Operating Loss Carryovers (Part 5)

Legend:
NA — Not applicable
NR — Not reported

	Does State Conform to Federal 5-Year Carryback of 2008 NOLs for Small Businesses (American Recovery and Reinvestment Act of 2009)?		
	Yes	*No*	*If Yes explain.*
Michigan		No, Michigan does not calculate a net operating loss separate from the federal NOL. For Michigan Business Tax purposes, the starting point for the business income tax base is business income, which is defined as the part of federal taxable income attributable to business activity. This implies conformity with the IRC in the calculation and usage of federal NOLs. However, the calculation of the business tax base also requires an add-back of any federal NOL carryover or carryback used to arrive at federal taxable income. In contrast, an MBT loss, determined on a post-apportionment basis, may be carried forward to apply against a future MBT business income tax base for up to 10 years. See Mich. Comp. Laws § 208.1201.	

Note. The CIT takes effect 01/01/12, and replaces the Michigan Business Tax (MBT) for most taxpayers. However, businesses that have been approved to receive, have received, or have been assigned certain certified credits may elect to file a return and pay the tax imposed by the MBT in lieu of the CIT until the certified credits are exhausted or extinguished.

Minnesota		X	
Mississippi		X	
Missouri		X	
Montana		X	

Net Operating Loss Carryovers (Part 5)

Legend:
NA Not applicable
NR Not reported

	Does State Conform to Federal 5-Year Carryback of 2008 NOLs for Small Businesses (American Recovery and Reinvestment Act of 2009)?		
	Yes	*No*	*If Yes explain.*
Nebraska		X	
Nevada	Nevada does not impose a corporate income tax		
New Hampshire	X		
New Jersey		X	
New Mexico		X	
New York	X		In general, New York limits an NOL carryback to $10,000
North Carolina		X	
North Dakota		X	
Ohio	Ohio does not impose a corporate income tax		
Note. Effective 1/1/2010, the Ohio Franchise Tax was fully phased out, and businesses will be taxed on gross receipts through the Commercial Activity Tax. Details about that tax can be found at: http//tax.ohio.gov/divisions/commercial_activities/index.stm			
Oklahoma		X	
Oregon		X	
Pennsylvania		X	
Rhode Island		X	
South Carolina		X	
South Dakota	South Dakota does not impose a corporate income tax		
Tennessee		X	
Texas		X	

Net Operating Loss Carryovers (Part 5)

Legend:

NA Not applicable

NR Not reported

	Does State Conform to Federal 5-Year Carryback of 2008 NOLs for Small Businesses (American Recovery and Reinvestment Act of 2009)?		
	Yes	*No*	*If Yes explain.*
Utah		X	
Vermont		X	
Virginia		X	
Washington	Washington does not impose a corporate income tax		
West Virginia	X		
Wisconsin		X	
Wyoming	Wyoming does not impose a corporate income tax		

Net Operating Loss Carryovers (Part 6)

Legend:

SAF	Same as applicable federal rules
NA	Not applicable
NR	Not reported

	Does State Conform to the Federal 5-year Carryback of a 2008 or 2009 NOL for Corporation in General (Worker, Homeownership, and Business Assistance Act of 2009)		*If Yes, Are There Special Restrictions for Certain Tax Years?*	*May Taxpayer Elect to Forego a Carryback?*	*Is Separate State Election Required to Do So?*
	Yes	No			
Alabama		X			
Alaska	X		No	Yes, only if a federal election was made.	No
Arizona		X			
Arkansas		X			
California		X, note that 2 year carrybacks will be allowed for taxable years beginning on or after 01/01/2011 for NOLs attributable to taxable years beginning on or after 01/01/2011.			
Colorado		X			
Connecticut		X			
Delaware	X				
District of Columbia		X			
Florida		X			
Georgia		X, Georgia never allowed the 5 year carryback			
Hawaii		X			

Net Operating Loss Carryovers (Part 6)

Legend:

SAF	Same as applicable federal rules
NA	Not applicable
NR	Not reported

	Does State Conform to the Federal 5-year Carryback of a 2008 or 2009 NOL for Corporation in General (Worker, Homeownership, and Business Assistance Act of 2009)	*If Yes, Are There Special Restrictions for Certain Tax Years?*	*May Taxpayer Elect to Forego a Carryback?*	*Is Separate State Election Required to Do So?*
Idaho	X			
Illinois	X			
Indiana	X			
Iowa	X			
Kansas	X			
Kentucky	X			
Louisiana	X			
Maine	X			
Maryland	X			
Massachusetts	X			
Michigan	X			
Note. The CIT takes effect 01/01/12, and replaces the Michigan Business Tax (MBT) for most taxpayers. However, businesses that have been approved to receive, have received, or have been assigned certain certified credits may elect to file a return and pay the tax imposed by the MBT in lieu of the CIT until the certified credits are exhausted or extinguished.				
Minnesota	X	No		
Mississippi	X			
Missouri	X			
Montana	X			

Net Operating Loss Carryovers (Part 6)

Legend:
SAF Same as applicable federal rules
NA Not applicable
NR Not reported

	Does State Conform to the Federal 5-year Carryback of a 2008 or 2009 NOL for Corporation in General (Worker, Homeownership, and Business Assistance Act of 2009)	*If Yes, Are There Special Restrictions for Certain Tax Years?*	*May Taxpayer Elect to Forego a Carryback?*	*Is Separate State Election Required to Do So?*
Nebraska	X			
Nevada	Nevada does not impose a corporate income tax			
New Hampshire	X			
New Jersey	X			
New Mexico	X			
New York	X, in general, New York limits an NOL carryback to $10,000.			
North Carolina	X			
North Dakota	X			
Ohio	Ohio does not impose a corporate income tax			
Oklahoma	X			
Oregon	X			
Pennsylvania	X			
Rhode Island	X			
South Carolina	X			
South Dakota	South Dakota does not impose a corporate income tax			
Tennessee	X			
Texas	X			

Net Operating Loss Carryovers (Part 6)

Legend:

SAF	Same as applicable federal rules
NA	Not applicable
NR	Not reported

	Does State Conform to the Federal 5-year Carryback of a 2008 or 2009 NOL for Corporation in General (Worker, Homeownership, and Business Assistance Act of 2009)	*If Yes, Are There Special Restrictions for Certain Tax Years?*	*May Taxpayer Elect to Forego a Carryback?*	*Is Separate State Election Required to Do So?*
Utah	X			
Vermont	X			
Virginia	X			
Washington	Washington does not impose a corporate income tax			
West Virginia	X	No	Yes	No
Wisconsin	No			
Wyoming	Wyoming does not impose a corporate income tax			

Treatment of Dividends

Federal Tax Treatment

A corporation generally is allowed to deduct 70 percent of a dividend received from a less-than-20 percent owned domestic corporation, 80 percent of a dividend received from a 20 percent or more owned nonaffiliated domestic corporation, and 100 percent of a dividend received from a corporation that is a member of an affiliated group with the recipient corporation. [IRC § 243] The purpose of the dividends received deduction (DRD) is to prevent multiple layers of U.S. corporate-level income taxes being imposed on the same underlying earnings. For example, earnings of a domestic subsidiary are taxed when earned, and, if not for the DRD, would be taxed a second time when distributed to the parent corporation as a dividend.

A U.S. parent corporation generally may not claim a DRD with respect to dividends received from foreign (non-U.S.) corporations, because the receipt of the dividend generally is the U.S. Treasury's first opportunity to tax the underlying foreign earnings. A federal DRD is also generally not available with respect to any Subpart F income or Section 78 gross-up income attributable to investments in foreign corporations. A deduction may be available, however, with respect to the U.S. source portion of any dividends received from a foreign corporation. [IRC § 245]

The DRD permitted for dividends received from nonaffiliated domestic corporations is limited to the DRD percentage (i.e., 70 percent or 80 percent) of the recipient corporation's taxable income, computed without regard to any net operating loss deduction, DRD, or capital loss carryback. This limitation does not apply if, after reducing taxable income by the DRD (as determined without regard to the taxable income limitation), the recipient corporation has a net operating loss for the current taxable year.

Section 78 Gross-up. A U.S. parent corporation generally must include any dividends received from foreign subsidiaries in its federal taxable income. [IRC § 61] Because the amount of dividend income recognized is net of any foreign income taxes paid by the foreign subsidiary, the U.S. parent is implicitly allowed a deduction for those foreign taxes. The U.S. parent can also claim a deemed paid foreign tax credit for the foreign income taxes paid by a 10 percent or more owned foreign corporation. [IRC § 902] To prevent a double tax benefit, the U.S. parent must gross up its dividend income by the amount of the deemed paid credit, thereby eliminating the implicit deduction. [IRC § 78] This amount is generally referred to as the *Section 78 gross-up*.

Subpart F Inclusions. As a general rule, the U.S. federal government does not tax the undistributed foreign-source income of a foreign corporation, even if that foreign corporation is a wholly owned subsidiary of a U.S. parent corporation. Instead, U.S. taxation is deferred until those foreign earnings are repatriated by the U.S. parent corporation as a dividend. This policy, which is known as *deferral*, is designed to allow U.S. companies to compete in foreign markets on a tax parity with foreign competitors.

A policy of unrestricted deferral would also allow U.S. companies to avoid U.S. taxes by shifting passive investment income and inventory trading profits to base companies organized in low-tax foreign jurisdictions. As a consequence, in 1962, Congress enacted the Subpart F provisions [IRC §§ 951–964] to combat foreign base company tax avoidance schemes. Under Subpart F, certain types of undistributed foreign earnings of a controlled foreign corporation are subject to immediate U.S. taxation at the U.S. shareholder level. A foreign corporation is a controlled foreign corporation if U.S. shareholders own more than 50 percent of the stock, by vote or value, of the foreign corporation. U.S. shareholders of a controlled foreign corporation must include in gross income a deemed dividend equal to the U.S. shareholder's pro rata share of the controlled foreign corporation's insurance and foreign base company income, as well as any earnings invested in U.S. property. Foreign base company income includes portable income, such as investment income and inventory trading profits, which is easily shifted to a foreign corporation located in a low-tax foreign jurisdiction.

Section 965 Temporary Dividends-Received Deduction. As part of the American Jobs Creation Act of 2004 [Public Law 108-357], Congress enacted Code Section 965 in an attempt to stimulate the U.S. economy by triggering the repatriation of foreign earnings that otherwise would have remained reinvested abroad. Under this provision, a domestic corporation may elect to claim a deduction equal to 85 percent of the cash dividends received from controlled foreign corporations in excess of the average dividends received from controlled foreign corporations over a five-year base period, but only if the repatriated earnings are reinvested in the United States pursuant to a formal domestic reinvestment plan. The election is available only for either the taxpayer's last tax year that began before October 22, 2004 (2004, for calendar year taxpayers) or the taxpayer's first tax year that begins on or after October 22, 2004 (2005, for calendar year taxpayers).

State Tax Treatment

About half of the states conform to the federal DRD in terms of how they treat dividends from domestic corporations. The states that do not conform to the federal DRD also generally provide a deduction for domestic dividends, but the specific rules vary from state-to-state. In sharp contrast with federal law, which generally limits its DRD to dividends received from domestic corporations, most states provide a DRD or subtraction modification for dividends received from both domestic and foreign corporations. For example, consistent with how they treat domestic dividends, many states provide a 100 percent deduction for dividends received from an 80-percent-or-more-owned foreign corporation.

Some states use federal taxable income *after* the net operating loss deduction and DRD (i.e., Line 30 of the corporation's federal Form 1120) as the starting point for computing state taxable income. Unless the state requires an additional modification for all or a portion of the DRD reported on the federal return, the corporation automatically is accorded the same DRD treatment for state and federal tax purposes. For example, Georgia uses federal taxable income after the DRD (Form 1120, Line 30) as the starting point for computing taxable income and does not require an addition modification for the federal DRD. [Ga. § 48-7-21] Some of the "line 30" states require an add-back of the federal DRD, but also allow a subtraction modification for the state DRD.

States that use federal taxable income *before* the net operating loss deduction and DRD (i.e., Line 28 of the federal return) as the starting point for computing state taxable income generally provide a DRD in the form of a subtraction modification. For example, Pennsylvania uses federal taxable income before the DRD (Form 1120, Line 28) as the starting point for computing taxable income, but provides a subtraction modification for the federal DRD as well as foreign dividends included in federal taxable income (Form 1120, Line 29b). [See Form RCT-101, PA Corporate Tax Report, Schedule C-2, PA Dividend Deduction Schedule.]

State Treatment of Foreign (non-U.S.) Dividends

The Kraft Decision. In *Kraft General Foods, Inc. v. Department of Revenue* [505 U.S. 71 (1992)], the Supreme Court ruled that an Iowa law that allowed taxpayers to claim a dividends-received deduction for dividends from domestic, but not foreign, subsidiary corporations was unconstitutional. During the years in question, Iowa conformed to the federal dividends-received deduction. As a consequence, Iowa did not tax dividends received from domestic corporations, but did tax dividends received from foreign corporations unless the dividends represented distributions of U.S. earnings. The Court ruled that the Iowa provision, which taxed only dividends paid by foreign corporations out of their foreign earnings, facially discriminated against foreign commerce, in violation of the Commerce Clause.

Fallout from Kraft Decision. Since the *Kraft* decision, a number of state courts have also struck down dividends-received deduction provisions that favored dividends received from U.S. corporations over dividends received from foreign (non-U.S. corporations).

In *Dart Industries, Inc. v. Clark* [657 A.2d 1062 (R.I. Sup. Ct., 1995)], the Rhode Island Supreme Court ruled the Rhode Island provision that allowed a deduction for dividends from domestic but not foreign subsidiaries was discriminatory in violation of the Commerce Clause. Likewise, in *D.D.I Inc. v. North Dakota* [657 N.W.2d 228 (N.D. Sup. Ct., 2003)], the North Dakota Supreme Court declared unconstitutional a North Dakota statute that permitted a dividends-received deduction, but only to the extent the dividend payer's income was subject to North Dakota corporate income tax. In *Hutchinson Technology, Inc. v. Commissioner of Revenue* [698 N.W.2d 1 (Minn. Sup. Ct., 2005)], the Minnesota Supreme Court ruled that a state statute that excluded dividends paid by certain foreign sales corporations from the state's dividends-received deduction was discriminatory in violation of the Commerce Clause. In *Emerson Electric Co. v. Tracy* [735 N.E.2d 445 (Ohio Sup. Ct., 2000)], the Ohio Supreme Court declared unconstitutional an Ohio statute that permitted a 100 percent deduction for dividends from domestic subsidiaries, but only an 85 percent deduction for dividends from foreign subsidiaries. In *Conoco Inc. v. Taxation and Revenue Department* [122 N.M. 736 (N.M. Sup. Ct., 1996)], the New Mexico Supreme Court ruled that the New Mexico scheme under which foreign but not domestic dividends were included in the tax base facially discriminated against foreign commerce, even though the state allowed a taxpayer to include a portion of the dividend-paying foreign subsidiaries' property, payroll, and sales in the denominators of its apportionment factors, thereby reducing the state apportionment percentage.

In addition, the supreme courts in several water's-edge combined reporting states have focused on footnote 23 of the *Kraft* decision and ruled that it is constitutionally acceptable to include dividends from foreign subsidiaries in the tax base, while excluding dividends from domestic subsidiaries that are included in the water's-edge combined report. In footnote 23 of its decision in *Kraft*, the Supreme Court stated:

> If one were to compare the aggregate tax imposed by Iowa on a unitary business which included a subsidiary doing business throughout the United States (including Iowa) with the aggregate tax imposed by Iowa on a unitary business which included a foreign subsidiary doing business abroad, it would be difficult to say that Iowa discriminates against the business with the foreign subsidiary. Iowa would tax an apportioned share of the domestic subsidiary's entire earnings, but would tax only the amount of the foreign subsidiary's earnings paid as a dividend to the parent.

In *Appeal of Morton Thiokol, Inc.* [864 P.2d 1175 (Kan. Sup. Ct., 1993)], the Kansas Supreme Court noted that *Kraft* did not address the taxation of foreign dividends by water's-edge combined reporting states (because Iowa is an elective consolidation state) and that "the aggregate tax imposed by Kansas on a unitary business with a domestic subsidiary would not be less burdensome than that imposed by Kansas on a unitary business with a foreign subsidiary because the income of the domestic subsidiary would be combined, apportioned, and taxed while only the dividend of the foreign subsidiary would be taxed." Likewise, in *E.I. Du Pont de Nemours & Co. v. State Tax Assessor* [675 A.2d 82 (Me. Sup Ct., 1996)], the Maine Supreme Judicial Court held that Maine's water's-edge combined reporting method was distinguishable from Iowa's single-entity reporting method, because the income of a domestic subsidiary is included in the Maine combined report. Therefore, taxing dividends paid by foreign but not domestic subsidiaries did not constitute the kind of facial discrimination found in the Iowa system.

Finally, in *General Electric Company, Inc. v. Department of Revenue Administration* [No. 2005-668 (N.H. Sup. Ct., Dec. 5, 2006)], GE challenged the constitutionality of a New Hampshire statute that permits a U.S. parent corporation to claim a dividends-received deduction for dividends received from foreign subsidiaries only to the extent the foreign subsidiary has business activity and is subject to tax in New Hampshire. None of GE's unitary foreign subsidiaries had business activities in New Hampshire. Thus, GE could not claim a dividends-received deduction for the dividends received from those foreign subsidiaries. The New Hampshire Supreme Court ruled that the New Hampshire tax scheme did not discriminate against foreign commerce, because both a unitary business with foreign subsidiaries operating in New Hampshire and a unitary business with foreign subsidiaries not operating in New Hampshire are each taxed only one time. Thus, there is no differential treatment that benefits the former and burdens the latter.

Apportionment Factor Relief. The inclusion of dividends received from a foreign subsidiary in the apportionable income of a domestic parent corporation raises the issue of whether the parent's apportionment factors should reflect the foreign subsidiary's property, payroll, and sales. In his dissent in *Mobil Oil Corp.*, Justice Stevens raised the issue of factor representation, noting that "[u]nless the sales, payroll, and property values connected with the production of income by the payor corporations are added to the denominator of the apportionment formula, the inclusion of earnings attributable to those corporations in the apportionable tax base will inevitably cause Mobil's Vermont income to be overstated."

In *NCR Corp. v. Taxation and Revenue Department* [856 P.2d 982 (N.M. Ct. App. 1993), *cert. denied*, 512 U.S. 1245 (1994)], the New Mexico Court of Appeals rejected the taxpayer's argument that the taxation of dividends received by a domestic parent corporation from its foreign subsidiaries without factor representation resulted in constitutionally impermissible double taxation. Similar arguments made by NCR were also rejected by state supreme courts in Minnesota and South Carolina [*NCR Corp. v. Commissioner of Revenue*, 438 N.W.2d 86 (Minn. Sup. Ct., 1989), *cert. denied*, 493 U.S. 848 (1989); *NCR Corp. v. Tax Commission*, 439 S.E.2d 254 (S.C. Sup Ct., 1993), *cert. denied*, 512 U.S. 1245 (1994)]. Caterpillar, Inc. also litigated the issue of factor representation with respect to dividends received from foreign subsidiaries and met with limited success. See, for example, *Caterpillar, Inc. v. Commissioner of Revenue* [568 N.W.2d 695 (Minn. Sup Ct., 1997), *cert. denied*, 522 U.S. 1112 (1998)], and *Caterpillar, Inc. v. Department of Revenue Administration* [741 A.2d 56 (N.H. Sup Ct., 1999), cert. denied, 120 S. Ct. 1424 (2000)]. Finally, in *Unisys Corp. v. Commonwealth of Pennsylvania* [812 A.2d 448 (Pa. Sup. Ct., 2002)], the Pennsylvania Supreme Court ruled that factor representation was not constitutionally required, because the taxpayer failed to prove that the state was unfairly taxing income earned outside its jurisdiction.

Section 78 Gross-up and Subpart F Inclusions. The rationale for including the Code Section 78 gross-up amount in federal taxable income does not apply for state tax purposes because no state allows a domestic corporation to claim a credit for the foreign income taxes paid by a foreign subsidiary. Consequently, nearly all states provide a subtraction modification or dividends-received deduction for Section 78 gross-up income, in effect, excluding the federal gross-up amount from state taxation. In *Amerada Hess Corp. v. North Dakota* [704 N.W.2d 8 (N.D. Sup. Ct., 2005)], the North Dakota Supreme Court ruled that Section 78 gross-up amounts did not qualify as "foreign dividends" under the applicable North Dakota tax statute and therefore did not qualify for the partial exclusion from income under North Dakota water's-edge combined unitary reporting method of determining the state corporate income tax.

Consistent with the notion that a Subpart F inclusion is a deemed dividend from a controlled foreign corporation, most states provide a DRD or subtraction modification for income under Subpart F. A few states, including California, require that the income and apportionment factors of a controlled foreign corporation be included in a water's-edge combined report to the extent of the controlled foreign corporation's Subpart F income. [Cal. Rev. & Tax. Code § 25110] California does not provide a DRD for Subpart F income. In addition, some states provide only limited deductions for income under Subpart F. For example, an Idaho water's-edge group may claim only an 85 percent deduction [Idaho § 63-3027C], and a Utah water's-edge group may claim only a 50 percent deduction [Utah § 59-7-106].

California Dividends Received Deduction

In General. In *Farmer Bros. Co. v. Franchise Tax Board* [No. B160061 (Cal. Ct. of App., May 31, 2003); *cert. denied*, 124 S.Ct. 1411, Feb. 23, 2004], the California Court of Appeals ruled that California DRD statute (i.e., Cal. Rev. & Tax. Code § 24402) was unconstitutional, because it facially discriminated against interstate commerce in violation of the Commerce Clause. Under Section 24402, a taxpayer could claim a DRD with respect to dividends paid out of income that was included in the measure of the California income tax, but was denied a deduction for dividends received from a corporation that was not subject to California tax.

In response to *Farmer Bros.*, the state's policy has been to disallow all deductions under Section 24402 for tax years ending after November 30, 1999. The instructions for Form 100, *California Corporation Franchise or Income Tax Return*, state that "[a] statute that is held to be unconstitutional is invalid and unenforceable. Therefore, the deduction is not available." In *Abbott Laboratories et al. v. Franchise Tax Board* [No. B204210 (Calif. Ct. of App., July 21, 2009), and *River Garden Retirement Home v. Franchise Tax Board* [No. A123316 (Calif. Ct. of App., July 15, 2010)], the California Court of Appeals has affirmed the policy of not permitting a DRD under Section 24402, because the statute was declared unconstitutional.

Insurance Company Subsidiaries. In *Ceridian Corp. v. Franchise Tax Board* [No. A084298 (Cal. Ct. App. Jan. 26, 2001)], the California Court of Appeals ruled that a California statute that permitted a DRD for dividends received from an insurance company subsidiary only if the subsidiary is subject to the California insurance company tax at the time the dividend is paid and only to the extent the dividend is paid from California sources (as measured by the percentage of the payer's gross income from California sources) was unconstitutional, because it imposed a higher burden on out-of-state corporations than on similarly situated in-state corporations.

In response to *Ceridian*, in 2004, the California legislature enacted California Revenue and Taxation Code Section 24410, which provides a deduction for (post-2007) 85 percent of the qualified dividends received from an 80 percent or more owned insurance company subsidiary, regardless of whether the insurance company is doing business in California. [A.B. 263, Sept. 29, 2004]

Intercompany Dividends. California provides a 100 percent DRD for dividends received from unitary subsidiaries, but only to the extent paid from unitary earnings and profits accumulated while both the payee and payer were members of a combined report. [Cal. Rev. & Tax. Code § 25106] In addition, a 75 percent DRD is allowed for dividends received by a water's-edge combined reporting group from a 50-percent-or-more-owned corporation, but only if the average of the payer's property, payroll, and sales factors within the United States is less than 20 percent. The deduction percentage increases to 100 percent for dividends derived from certain foreign construction projects [Cal. Rev. & Tax. Code § 24411].

State-by-State Summary

The following chart, presented in two parts, provides information regarding whether each state requires addition or subtraction modifications with respect to federal and state DRDs, state DRD schedules, and the availability of a DRD for dividends, Subpart F income, and Section 78 gross-up income derived from foreign (non-U.S.) corporations.

Treatment of Dividends (Part 1)

Legend:

NA	Not applicable
NR	Not reported
SAF	Same as applicable federal rules

	Does State Computation of Taxable Net Income Start with a Figure from Federal Form 1120?	*Does State Require Addition Modification for the Federal Dividends-Received Deduction?*	*Does State Provide a Subtraction Modification for Dividends Received from Other Corporations?*	*What Is State's Schedule for the Dividends-Received Deduction?*
Alabama	Yes, starts with taxable income after special deductions	Yes	Yes	NR
Alaska	Yes, generally with taxable income before special deductions	Yes	Yes	SAF
Arizona	Yes, starts with taxable income after special deductions	Yes	Yes	100% deduction for ownership between 50% and 100%
Arkansas	No, income and deductions based on Arkansas Code	Yes	Yes	100% deduction for ownership between 80% and 100%

Treatment of Dividends (Part 1)

Legend:

NA	Not applicable
NR	Not reported
SAF	Same as applicable federal rules

	Does State Computation of Taxable Net Income Start with a Figure from Federal Form 1120?	*Does State Require Addition Modification for the Federal Dividends-Received Deduction?*	*Does State Provide a Subtraction Modification for Dividends Received from Other Corporations?*	*What Is State's Schedule for the Dividends-Received Deduction?*
California	Yes, starts with taxable income before special deductions. Allow California computation method if no federal tax liability	Yes	Yes	With respect to deductions under R&TC § 24404, for taxable years ending before 12/1/99, deductions will be allowed for certain dividends in certain circumstances subject to ownership requirements. For income years ending on or after 12/1/99, deductions will not be allowed under R&TC § 24402 because the statute has been declared unconstitutional and is void. See *Farmer Bros., Co. v. Franchise Tax Board* (2003) 108 Cal. App. 4th 976. With respect to deductions under R&TC § 24410, for taxable years ending before 12/1/97, all dividends received from an 80% owned insurance subsidiary are deductible. For taxable years ending on or after 12/1/1997, all R&TC § 24410 deductions are disallowed. See *Ceridian Corp. v. Franchise Tax Board* (2001) 85 Cal. App. 4th 875 (as modified

Treatment of Dividends (Part 1)

Legend:
NA Not applicable
NR Not reported
SAF Same as applicable federal rules

	Does State Computation of Taxable Net Income Start with a Figure from Federal Form 1120?	*Does State Require Addition Modification for the Federal Dividends-Received Deduction?*	*Does State Provide a Subtraction Modification for Dividends Received from Other Corporations?*	*What Is State's Schedule for the Dividends-Received Deduction?*
				86 Cal. App.4th 383). Generally, dividends received by any member of the water's-edge group which are paid by a corporation that, (a) has an average property, payroll and sales factor within the United States that is less than 20% and (b) has more than 50% its total voting stock owned directly or indirectly by the receiving water's edge group at the time the dividend is received may be entitled to a dividend received deduction under § 24411.
Colorado	Yes, starts with taxable income after special deductions	No	Yes	SAF
Connecticut	Yes, starts with taxable income before special deductions	No	Yes	70% deduction for ownership between 0% and 20%; 100% deduction for ownership between 20% and 100%
Delaware	Yes, starts with taxable income after special deductions	No	No	SAF
District of Columbia	No	No	Yes	Other

Treatment of Dividends (Part 1)

Legend:

NA — Not applicable
NR — Not reported
SAF — Same as applicable federal rules

	Does State Computation of Taxable Net Income Start with a Figure from Federal Form 1120?	*Does State Require Addition Modification for the Federal Dividends-Received Deduction?*	*Does State Provide a Subtraction Modification for Dividends Received from Other Corporations?*	*What Is State's Schedule for the Dividends-Received Deduction?*
Florida	Yes, starts with taxable income after special deductions	No	No	SAF
Georgia	Yes, starts with taxable income after special deductions	No	No	SAF
Hawaii	Yes, starts with taxable income before special deductions and NOL deductions	NA	Yes, see HRS § 235-7(c)	See HRS § 235-7(c)
Idaho	Yes, starts with taxable income after special deductions	Yes, see Idaho Code § 63-3022(d).	Yes, effective 1/1/04, in certain circumstances, mutual insurance holding companies may exclude from taxable income dividends or distributions issued by a stock insurance subsidiary to the mutual insurance holding company or intermediate holding company	NA

Treatment of Dividends (Part 1)

Legend:

NA Not applicable
NR Not reported
SAF Same as applicable federal rules

	Does State Computation of Taxable Net Income Start with a Figure from Federal Form 1120?	*Does State Require Addition Modification for the Federal Dividends-Received Deduction?*	*Does State Provide a Subtraction Modification for Dividends Received from Other Corporations?*	*What Is State's Schedule for the Dividends-Received Deduction?*
Illinois	Yes, starts with taxable income after special deductions	No	Yes	Illinois statute contains several different dividends-received deductions. IITA § 203(b)(2)(0) allows a dividends-received deduction for dividends received from a foreign corporation that corresponds to the percentage deduction allowed under federal law for dividends received from a domestic corporation. IITA §§ 203(b)(2)(K) and 202(b)(2)(L) provide deductions for dividends received from corporations that conduct a certain amount of business in an Illinois enterprise zone and foreign trade zone or sub-zone, respectively
Indiana	Yes, starts with taxable income after dividends-received deduction but before NOL deduction	No	Yes	SAF

Treatment of Dividends (Part 1)

Legend:

NA Not applicable
NR Not reported
SAF Same as applicable federal rules

	Does State Computation of Taxable Net Income Start with a Figure from Federal Form 1120?	*Does State Require Addition Modification for the Federal Dividends-Received Deduction?*	*Does State Provide a Subtraction Modification for Dividends Received from Other Corporations?*	*What Is State's Schedule for the Dividends-Received Deduction?*
Iowa	Yes, the federal NOL on Line 29(a) is not deductible on the Iowa return	No, related to domestic dividends only	Yes, foreign dividends only	70% deduction for ownership between 0% and 20%; 80% deduction for ownership between 20% and 80%; 100% deduction for ownership between 80% and 100%
Kansas	Yes, starts with taxable income after special deductions	No	Yes	100% deduction, IRC § 78 Gross Up; 80% deduction, Subpart F and other foreign dividends.
Kentucky	Yes, starts with taxable income before special deductions	Yes	Yes	100% for ownership between 0% and 100%
Louisiana	Yes, starts with taxable income before special deductions	Yes	Yes	Acts 2005, No 401 provides for an exemption for interest and dividends.
Maine	Yes, starts with taxable income after special deductions	No	Yes	SAF, 50% deduction for ownership between 50% and 100%.
Maryland	Yes, starts with taxable income before special deductions	No	Yes, if received from other related corporations	100% deduction for ownership between 50% and 100%, dividends from related foreign corporations
Massachusetts	Yes, starts with taxable income before special deductions	Yes	Yes	

Treatment of Dividends (Part 1)

Legend:

NA	Not applicable
NR	Not reported
SAF	Same as applicable federal rules

	Does State Computation of Taxable Net Income Start with a Figure from Federal Form 1120?	*Does State Require Addition Modification for the Federal Dividends-Received Deduction?*	*Does State Provide a Subtraction Modification for Dividends Received from Other Corporations?*	*What Is State's Schedule for the Dividends-Received Deduction?*
Michigan (Business Tax)	Yes, starts with taxable income after special deductions	Yes	Yes	SAF
Note. The CIT takes effect 01/01/12, and replaces the Michigan Business Tax (MBT) for most taxpayers. However, businesses that have been approved to receive, have received, or have been assigned certain certified credits may elect to file a return and pay the tax imposed by the MBT in lieu of the CIT until the certified credits are exhausted or extinguished.				
Minnesota	Yes, starts with taxable income after special deductions	Yes	Yes	70% deduction for ownership between 0%, 20%; 80% deduction for ownership between 20% and 100% for non unitary and 100% deduction for ownership between 50% and 100% for unitary combined.
Mississippi	No, but law closely follows federal; starts with taxable income before special deductions	NR	Yes	SAF
Missouri	Yes, starts with taxable income after special deductions	No	Yes	SAF
Montana	Yes, starts with taxable income before special deductions	NA, Montana starts with federal line 28	Yes	SAF
Nebraska	Yes, starts with taxable income after special deductions	No	Yes	SAF

Treatment of Dividends (Part 1)

Legend:
NA — Not applicable
NR — Not reported
SAF — Same as applicable federal rules

	Does State Computation of Taxable Net Income Start with a Figure from Federal Form 1120?	*Does State Require Addition Modification for the Federal Dividends-Received Deduction?*	*Does State Provide a Subtraction Modification for Dividends Received from Other Corporations?*	*What Is State's Schedule for the Dividends-Received Deduction?*
Nevada	Nevada does not impose a corporate income tax			
New Hampshire	Yes, starts with taxable income before special deductions	No	No	NR
New Jersey	Yes, starts with taxable income before special deductions	No	Yes	100% deduction for ownership between 80% and 100%; 50% deduction for ownership between 0% and less than 80%.
New Mexico	Yes, starts with taxable income before special deductions	No	No	70% deduction for ownership between 0% and less than 20%; 80% deduction for ownership between 20% and less than or equal to 50%; factor representation for ownership greater than 50%

Treatment of Dividends (Part 1)

Legend:
NA Not applicable
NR Not reported
SAF Same as applicable federal rules

	Does State Computation of Taxable Net Income Start with a Figure from Federal Form 1120?	*Does State Require Addition Modification for the Federal Dividends-Received Deduction?*	*Does State Provide a Subtraction Modification for Dividends Received from Other Corporations?*	*What Is State's Schedule for the Dividends-Received Deduction?*
New York	Yes, starts with taxable income before special deductions	No	Yes, dividends from subsidiaries, 50% of dividends from nonsubsidiaries, and any amount treated as dividends pursuant to IRC § 78 are not subject to tax; 50% of nonsubsidiary dividends may be included in investment income. The proportion of investment income that is taxed depends on the particular composition of the taxpayer's investment portfolio. Investment income is allocated using an investment allocation percentage. The amount of investment capital for each stock, bond, or other security is allocated to New York using an allocation percentage given by the issuer of the security. The investment allocation percentage is the proportion of all such allocated amounts to the taxpayer's total amount of investment capital.	100% deduction for ownership between greater than 50% and 100%; 50% deduction for ownership between 0% and 50%

Treatment of Dividends (Part 1)

Legend:

NA	Not applicable
NR	Not reported
SAF	Same as applicable federal rules

	Does State Computation of Taxable Net Income Start with a Figure from Federal Form 1120?	*Does State Require Addition Modification for the Federal Dividends-Received Deduction?*	*Does State Provide a Subtraction Modification for Dividends Received from Other Corporations?*	*What Is State's Schedule for the Dividends-Received Deduction?*
North Carolina	Yes, starts with taxable income after special deductions, but before NOL deduction	No	No	SAF
North Dakota	Yes, starts with taxable income after special deductions	Yes	Yes, provided corporations are unitary	100% deduction if received from a unitary affiliate
Ohio	Ohio does not impose a corporate income tax			
Note. Effective 1/1/2010, the Ohio Franchise Tax was fully phased out and business will be taxed on gross receipts through the Commercial Activity Tax. Details about that tax can be found at: http//tax.ohio.gov/divisions/commercial_activities/index.stm				
Oklahoma	Yes, starts with taxable income after special deductions	No	No	SAF
Oregon	Yes, starts with taxable income after special deductions	Yes. Statute starts with federal taxable income and adds back federal deductions. Form starts with federal taxable income before special deductions.	Yes	70% deduction for ownership less than 20%; 80% deduction for ownership between 20% and 100%
Pennsylvania	Yes, starts with taxable income before special deductions	Yes	Yes	SAF
Rhode Island	Yes, starts with taxable income before special deductions	Yes	Yes	SAF
South Carolina	Yes, starts with taxable income before special deductions	No	No	SAF

Treatment of Dividends (Part 1)

Legend:
NA — Not applicable
NR — Not reported
SAF — Same as applicable federal rules

	Does State Computation of Taxable Net Income Start with a Figure from Federal Form 1120?	*Does State Require Addition Modification for the Federal Dividends-Received Deduction?*	*Does State Provide a Subtraction Modification for Dividends Received from Other Corporations?*	*What Is State's Schedule for the Dividends-Received Deduction?*
South Dakota	South Dakota does not impose a corporate income tax			
Tennessee	Yes, starts with taxable income before special deductions; LPs and LLCs use Form 1065	No	Yes	100% deduction for ownership between 80% and 100%
Texas	Yes, starts with taxable income before special deductions	No	Yes	SAF
Utah	Yes, starts with taxable income before special deductions	No	Yes, in a water's edge combined report	50% exclusion for dividends received from unitary foreign subsidiaries that are >50% owned
Vermont	Yes, starts with taxable income after special deductions	No	No	SAF
Virginia	Yes, starts with taxable income after special deductions. NOL deduction is limited to reducing federal taxable income to $0.	No	Yes	100% deduction for ownership between 50% and 100%
Washington	Washington does not impose a corporate income tax			
West Virginia	Yes, starts with taxable income after special deductions	No	No	NR

Treatment of Dividends (Part 1)

Legend:

NA	Not applicable
NR	Not reported
SAF	Same as applicable federal rules

	Does State Computation of Taxable Net Income Start with a Figure from Federal Form 1120?	*Does State Require Addition Modification for the Federal Dividends-Received Deduction?*	*Does State Provide a Subtraction Modification for Dividends Received from Other Corporations?*	*What Is State's Schedule for the Dividends-Received Deduction?*
Wisconsin	Yes, starts with taxable income before special deductions	No, starting point is federal income before the federal dividends-received deduction	Yes	100% deduction for ownership between 70% and 100%, Wisconsin Schedule Y
Wyoming	Wyoming does not impose a corporate income tax			

Treatment of Dividends (Part 2)

Legend:
NA Not applicable
NR Not reported
SAF Same as applicable federal rules

	For Purposes of State's Dividends-Received Deduction, Are Dividends from Foreign (Non-U.S.) Corporations Treated DIFFERENTLY than Dividends from U.S. Corporations?	*Does the State Dividends-Received Deduction Apply to Federal Subpart F Income?*	*Does the State Dividends-Received Deduction Apply to Federal IRC Section 78 Gross-up Income?*
Alabama	No	Yes	Yes
Alaska	No	No	No
Arizona	Yes, all foreign dividends not taxable	Yes	Yes
Arkansas	No	Yes	Yes
California	Yes	No	No
Colorado	Yes, specific calculation under 39-22-303(11)	NR	No
Connecticut	No	Yes	Yes
Delaware	No	NR	NR
District of Columbia	No	No	No
Florida	SAF	NR	NR
Georgia	Yes, taxpayer can deduct dividends from sources outside the U.S. and from affiliated corporations within the U.S.	No	No
Hawaii	No	NA. Hawaii does not conform to IRC § 951.	NA. Hawaii does not conform to IRC § 902.
Idaho	NA	NR	NA

Treatment of Dividends (Part 2)

Legend:

NA	Not applicable
NR	Not reported
SAF	Same as applicable federal rules

	For Purposes of State's Dividends-Received Deduction, Are Dividends from Foreign (Non-U.S.) Corporations Treated DIFFERENTLY than Dividends from U.S. Corporations?	*Does the State Dividends-Received Deduction Apply to Federal Subpart F Income?*	*Does the State Dividends-Received Deduction Apply to Federal IRC Section 78 Gross-up Income?*
Illinois	No, generally dividends from neither are included in the base income of a corporation.	Yes	Yes; however, a separate subtraction modification is provided for § 78 gross-up income.
Indiana	Yes	No	No
Iowa	No	Yes	No, 100% of § 78 is always deducted
Kansas	Yes, SAF for domestic dividends; subtraction for foreign dividends; gross-up (100%); other foreign dividends including subpart F (80%)	Yes	Yes
Kentucky	No	Yes	Yes
Louisiana	NR	NR	NR
Maine	No	Yes	No
Maryland	Yes. Foreign dividends are allowable subtraction modifications, but domestic dividends are not (except when calculating NOL carryforwards).	Yes	Yes
Massachusetts	No	Yes	Yes
Michigan (Business Tax)	No	Yes	Yes

Note. The CIT takes effect 01/01/12, and replaces the Michigan Business Tax (MBT) for most taxpayers. However, businesses that have been approved to receive, have received, or have been assigned certain certified credits may elect to file a return and pay the tax imposed by the MBT in lieu of the CIT until the certified credits are exhausted or extinguished.

Treatment of Dividends (Part 2)

Legend:
NA Not applicable
NR Not reported
SAF Same as applicable federal rules

	For Purposes of State's Dividends-Received Deduction, Are Dividends from Foreign (Non-U.S.) Corporations Treated DIFFERENTLY than Dividends from U.S. Corporations?	*Does the State Dividends-Received Deduction Apply to Federal Subpart F Income?*	*Does the State Dividends-Received Deduction Apply to Federal IRC Section 78 Gross-up Income?*
Minnesota	No	Yes	No
Mississippi	Yes, per Reg. § 806, all non-U.S. dividends are excluded	Yes	Yes
Missouri	No	Yes	Yes
Montana	Yes, intercompany foreign dividend deduction allowed only if both payee and payor are members of a unitary group	Yes, if both payee and payor are members of a unitary group	Yes
Nebraska	Yes, foreign dividends may be subtracted from taxable income	Yes	Yes
Nevada	Nevada does not impose a corporate income tax		
New Hampshire			
New Jersey	No, foreign dividends received deduction for taxpayers electing to file as separate corporate entity; same as federal, foreign dividends received deduction for taxpayers electing to file combined unitary or consolidated.	Yes	Yes

Treatment of Dividends (Part 2)

Legend:

NA	Not applicable
NR	Not reported
SAF	Same as applicable federal rules

	For Purposes of State's Dividends-Received Deduction, Are Dividends from Foreign (Non-U.S.) Corporations Treated DIFFERENTLY than Dividends from U.S. Corporations?	*Does the State Dividends-Received Deduction Apply to Federal Subpart F Income?*	*Does the State Dividends-Received Deduction Apply to Federal IRC Section 78 Gross-up Income?*
New Mexico	Yes, 70% deduction for ownership between 0% and less than 20%; 80% deduction for ownership between 20% and less than or equal to 50%; factor representation for ownership greater than 50%	Yes	Yes
New York	No	Yes	Yes, dividends from subsidiaries are not subject to tax.
North Carolina	No	Yes	Yes
North Dakota	No	Yes	Yes
Ohio	Ohio does not impose a corporate income tax		
Note. Effective 1/1/2010, the Ohio Franchise Tax was fully phased out and business will be taxed on gross receipts through the Commercial Activity Tax. Details about that tax can be found at: http//tax.ohio.gov/divisions/commercial_activities/index.stm			
Oklahoma	No	No	No
Oregon	No	Yes	No, separate 100% deduction for § 78 gross up income.
Pennsylvania	No	No	Yes
Rhode Island	No	Yes	Yes
South Carolina	No	Yes	No
South Dakota	South Dakota does not impose a corporate income tax		

Treatment of Dividends (Part 2)

Legend:
NA Not applicable
NR Not reported
SAF Same as applicable federal rules

	For Purposes of State's Dividends-Received Deduction, Are Dividends from Foreign (Non-U.S.) Corporations Treated DIFFERENTLY than Dividends from U.S. Corporations?	*Does the State Dividends-Received Deduction Apply to Federal Subpart F Income?*	*Does the State Dividends-Received Deduction Apply to Federal IRC Section 78 Gross-up Income?*
Tennessee	Yes	Same as dividends from U.S. corporations	
Texas	Yes, Schedule C dividend deduction and foreign dividends from an affiliated taxable entity that does not transact a substantial part of its business or regularly maintain a substantial portion of its assets in the U.S., including amounts determined under IRC § 78 or §§ 951-964, are deducted from total revenue to compute margin.	Yes	Yes

Treatment of Dividends (Part 2)

Legend:
NA — Not applicable
NR — Not reported
SAF — Same as applicable federal rules

	For Purposes of State's Dividends-Received Deduction, Are Dividends from Foreign (Non-U.S.) Corporations Treated DIFFERENTLY than Dividends from U.S. Corporations?	*Does the State Dividends-Received Deduction Apply to Federal Subpart F Income?*	*Does the State Dividends-Received Deduction Apply to Federal IRC Section 78 Gross-up Income?*
Utah	Yes, as to dividends from greater than 50% owned companies, in the context of a water's-edge combined report, dividends from unitary U.S. subsidiaries are eliminated because the income of the subsidiary is included in the combined report, while dividends from unitary foreign subsidiaries are allowed a 50% exclusion. Note that a corporation may elect to file a worldwide combined report, in which case dividends from both U.S. and foreign subsidiaries are excluded as an intercompany elimination while the income of all subsidiaries is included in the income base.	Yes	No, already fully excluded
Vermont	NR	Yes	Yes
Virginia	Yes, dividends from foreign corporation subtracted as foreign source income net of related expenses	No, separate exemption applies	No, separate exemption applies
Washington	Washington does not impose a corporate income tax		
West Virginia	NR	No	No
Wisconsin	No	Yes, when paid as a dividend	Yes, when paid as a dividend
Wyoming	Wyoming does not impose a corporate income tax		

Deductions for Tax Payments

Federal Tax Treatment

For federal income tax purposes, Section 164 of Internal Revenue Code (Code) provides taxpayers with a deduction for the following taxes paid or accrued during the taxable year:

- State, local, and foreign real property taxes
- State and local personal property taxes
- State, local, and foreign income taxes
- Federal generation-skipping transfer (GST) tax imposed on income distributions

Except for the GST and Section 59A environmental tax, all of these taxes are imposed by a government other than the U.S. federal government.

Federal customs, excise, and payroll taxes (i.e., FICA and FUTA taxes) incurred in the course of conducting a trade or business or an income-producing activity are also deductible. [IRC §§ 162, 212] Under no circumstances are federal income taxes deductible in computing federal taxable income.

A taxpayer can claim a credit for foreign income taxes paid in lieu of claiming a deduction. [IRC § 901] Because a credit is generally more valuable than a deduction, taxpayers generally elect to claim a credit for foreign income taxes.

State Tax Treatment

Federal Income Taxes. Federal income taxes are not deductible in computing federal taxable income. Nevertheless, in computing state taxable income, a handful of states allow a subtraction modification for federal income taxes (see the section entitled Subtraction Modifications to Federal Income in this part).

Foreign Income Taxes. For federal tax purposes, taxpayers generally claim a credit for foreign income taxes. [IRC § 901] No state allows a credit for foreign income taxes, but some states allow a deduction for foreign income tax payments. Generally, a deduction is allowed only if the foreign income taxes are deducted for federal tax purposes. Because a credit is generally more valuable, taxpayers generally elect to claim a credit for foreign income taxes (see the section entitled Treatment of Foreign Income Tax Payments in Part 7).

State Income Taxes. State income taxes are deducted in computing federal taxable income. [IRC § 164] In computing state taxable income, however, most states require that state income taxes be added back (see the section entitled Addition Modifications to Federal Income in this part).

Whether or not a state tax qualifies as an income tax can be uncertain. For example, the tax base for the Texas margin tax is the lowest of three amounts: (1) total revenue minus cost of goods sold, (2) total revenue minus compensation, or (3) 70 percent of total revenue. The Virginia Department of Taxation ruled that, because it excludes the vast majority of business expenses normally permitted in determining net income, the Texas margin tax is not based on net income and is not added back when computing Virginia taxable income. [P.D. 08-169, Va. Dept. of Tax., Sept. 11, 2008] In contrast, South Carolina classifies the Texas margin tax as a nondeductible income tax. [Rev. Rul. No. 09-10, S.C. Dept. of Rev., July 17, 2009] The Kansas Department of Revenue ruled that if it is determined by deducting cost of goods sold or compensation from gross receipts, the Texas margin tax is a nondeductible income tax. [Opinion Letter No. O-2009-05, Kan. Dept. of Rev., Mar. 24, 2009] Finally, the California Franchise Tax Board states that it cannot provide a definitive characterization of the Texas margin tax that applies to each and every taxpayer. [Notice 2009-06, Calif. Franch. Tax Bd., July 20, 2009]

State Franchise Taxes Based on Capital Stock or Net Worth. Most states require that state income taxes be added back in computing state taxable income. The state statutes governing such addition modifications generally refer to a "net income" tax or a tax "measured by net income." In addition to corporate income taxes, a number of states impose corporate franchise taxes measured by capital stock or net worth. Capital stock and net worth taxes are excise taxes imposed on the privilege of doing business in the state or the privilege of existing as a corporation. Such taxes are measured by the book value of the corporation's net worth or its capital stock value. Corporations paying such taxes need to review the tax laws in every nexus state to determine if such franchise taxes are deductible in computing state taxable income.

Gross Receipts Taxes. Several states impose gross receipts taxes. Ohio imposes a commercial activity tax on a business entity's gross receipts. The State of Washington imposes a gross receipts tax called the business and occupation tax. Michigan imposes a tax on a business entity's modified gross receipts, which equals a taxpayer's gross receipts reduced by purchases of inventory, depreciable assets, materials, and supplies. Corporations paying such taxes need to review the tax laws in every nexus state to determine whether such taxes are deductible in computing state taxable income.

Local Income Taxes. Most states indicated that deductions for income taxes paid to local governments (e.g., New York City) are handled in the same manner as deductions for state income taxes.

State-by-State Summary

The following chart, presented in two parts, provides a state-by-state summary of the deductions available for different types of state taxes.

Deductions for Tax Payments (Part 1)

Legend:

X — Indicates allowable deductions for state income tax payments
NA — Not applicable
NR — Not reported
SAF — Same as applicable federal rules

	Income Taxes Paid to:					*Income Taxes Paid to Local Governments*			
	Home State	*Other States'*	*Michigan Single Business Tax (Pre-2008)*	*Michigan Business Tax, Based on Gross Receipts*	*Washington Business and Occupation Tax*	*In Home State*	*In Other States*	*Ohio Franchise Tax Based on Income (Pre-2010)*	*Texas Franchise Tax Based on Income (Pre-2007)*
Alabama				X	X			X	X
Alaska			X		X			X	X
Arizona	Not if tax is an income tax	Not if tax is an income tax	X	X	X	Not if tax is an income tax	Not if tax is an income tax		Not if tax is an income tax
Arkansas		X	X	X	X		X	X	X
California			X					X	X
Colorado	X	X	X	X	X	X	X	X	X
Connecticut			No written guidance	No written guidance	X				
Delaware			X		X				
District of Columbia	X		X	X	X				
Florida			X		X	X	X		
Georgia	X		X	NR	X				
Hawaii	X	X	X	X	X	X	X	X	X
Idaho			X	X	X				

Deductions for Tax Payments (Part 1)

Legend:

X	Indicates allowable deductions for state income tax payments
NA	Not applicable
NR	Not reported
SAF	Same as applicable federal rules

	Income Taxes Paid to:					*Income Taxes Paid to Local Governments*			
	Home State	*Other States'*	*Michigan Single Business Tax (Pre-2008)*	*Michigan Business Tax, Based on Gross Receipts*	*Washington Business and Occupation Tax*	*In Home State*	*In Other States*	*Ohio Franchise Tax Based on Income (Pre-2010)*	*Texas Franchise Tax Based on Income (Pre-2007)*
Illinois	The tax base in Illinois starts with federal taxable income, and so taxes deductible for federal income tax purposes are also deducted in computing Illinois net income. However, Illinois law requires an addition modification for taxes imposed under the Illinois Income Tax Act to the extent deducted in computing federal taxable income. Thus, no deduction is allowed for Illinois income taxes.								
Indiana			X						
Iowa		X	X	X	X	X	X	X	X
Kansas			X	X	X				
Kentucky			X			X	X		
Louisiana	X	X	X	X	X	X	X	X	X
Maine			X	X	X	X	X		
Maryland	X	X				X	X	X	X
Massachusetts	See DD 99-9								
Michigan (Business Tax)				X	X				
Note. The CIT takes effect 01/01/12, and replaces the Michigan Business Tax (MBT) for most taxpayers. However, businesses that have been approved to receive, have received, or have been assigned certain certified credits may elect to file a return and pay the tax imposed by the MBT in lieu of the CIT until the certified credits are exhausted or extinguished.									
Minnesota			X						

Legend:

X	Indicates allowable deductions for state income tax payments
NA	Not applicable
NR	Not reported
SAF	Same as applicable federal rules

Deductions for Tax Payments (Part 1)

	Income Taxes Paid to:					*Income Taxes Paid to Local Governments*			
	Home State	*Other States'*	*Michigan Single Business Tax (Pre-2008)*	*Michigan Business Tax, Based on Gross Receipts*	*Washington Business and Occupation Tax*	*In Home State*	*In Other States*	*Ohio Franchise Tax Based on Income (Pre-2010)*	*Texas Franchise Tax Based on Income (Pre-2007)*
Mississippi									
Missouri			X		X			X	X
Montana			X	X					
Nebraska	SAF	SAF	SAF		SAF	SAF	SAF	SAF	SAF
Nevada	Nevada does not impose a corporate income tax								
New Hampshire									
New Jersey	NJ. Admin. Code 18:7-5.2(a)1.v provides that the following must be added to federal taxable income when computing entire net income: All New Jersey franchise taxes paid or accrued under the Corporation Business Tax Act, whether measured by net worth, net income or otherwise, to the extent such taxes were deducted in computing Federal taxable income; and, with respect to accounting years beginning after July 7,1993, taxes paid or accrued to a possession or territory of the United States, a state, a political subdivision thereof, or the District of Columbia on or measured by profits or income, or business presence or business activity including, without limitation, the Michigan Single Business Tax and taxes measured in whole or in part by "net taxable capital" to the extent such taxes were deducted in computing Federal taxable income.								
New Mexico									
New York	X, local income based taxes, but not state income based taxes		X			X			

Deductions for Tax Payments (Part 1)

Legend:

X	Indicates allowable deductions for state income tax payments
NA	Not applicable
NR	Not reported
SAF	Same as applicable federal rules

	Income Taxes Paid to:					*Income Taxes Paid to Local Governments*			
	Home State	*Other States'*	*Michigan Single Business Tax (Pre-2008)*	*Michigan Business Tax, Based on Gross Receipts*	*Washington Business and Occupation Tax*	*In Home State*	*In Other States*	*Ohio Franchise Tax Based on Income (Pre-2010)*	*Texas Franchise Tax Based on Income (Pre-2007)*
North Carolina			X	X	X				
North Dakota		X	X	X	X				
Ohio	Ohio does not impose a corporate income tax								
Note. Effective 1/1/2010, the Ohio Franchise Tax was fully phased out and business will be taxed on gross receipts through the Commercial Activity Tax. Details about that tax can be found at: http//tax.ohio.gov/divisions/commercial_activities/index.stm									
Oklahoma									
Oregon			X	X	X	X	X		
Pennsylvania	Pennsylvania uses federal taxable income as its starting point and adds back state and local taxes imposed on or measured by net income that were deducted for federal income tax purposes.								
Rhode Island		X	X		X	X	X	X	X
South Carolina	See Rev. Rul. #09-10		X, See Rev. Rul. 03-06.	X, See Rev. Rul 09-10	X, See Rev. Rul. 09-10.	See Rev. Rul. 09-10.	See Rev. Rul. 09-10.	See Rev. Rul. 03-06.	
South Dakota	South Dakota does not impose a corporate income tax								
Tennessee		X	X	X	X	X	X	X	X
Texas									
Utah						X	X		

Deductions for Tax Payments (Part 1)

Legend:

X	Indicates allowable deductions for state income tax payments
NA	Not applicable
NR	Not reported
SAF	Same as applicable federal rules

	Income Taxes Paid to:					*Income Taxes Paid to Local Governments*			
	Home State	*Other States'*	*Michigan Single Business Tax (Pre-2008)*	*Michigan Business Tax, Based on Gross Receipts*	*Washington Business and Occupation Tax*	*In Home State*	*In Other States*	*Ohio Franchise Tax Based on Income (Pre-2010)*	*Texas Franchise Tax Based on Income (Pre-2007)*
Vermont			X		X				
Virginia			X	X	X				
Washington	Washington does not impose a corporate income tax								
West Virginia	X	X	X	X		X	X		
Wisconsin					X	X	X		
Wyoming	Wyoming does not impose a corporate income tax								

Deductions for Tax Payments (Part 2)

Legend:

X	**These items are deductible**
NA	**Not applicable**
NR	**Not reported**
SAF	**Same as applicable federal rules**

								Franchise Tax on Net Worth or Capital Paid to	
	Ohio Commercial Activity Tax	*Ohio Franchise Tax Based on Net Worth (Pre-2010)*	*Kentucky Limited Liability Entity Tax*	*New Hampshire Business Profits Tax*	*Texas Margin Tax*	*Texas Franchise Tax Based on Net Worth (Pre-2007)*	*Pennsylvania Capital Stock Tax*	*Other States*	*Home State*
Alabama	X	X		X		X	X	X	X
Alaska	X	X	X	X	X	X	X	X	
Arizona	X	X		X		X	X	X	
Arkansas	X	X	X	X	X	X	X	X	X
California		X				X			
Colorado	X	X	X	X	X	X	X	X	X
	All taxes are deductible to the extent allowed in determining federal taxable income except income taxes imposed by this state (However, "income taxes imposed by this state" does not include severance taxes (Article 29)								
Connecticut	No written guidance	X	No written guidance	No written guidance	No written guidance	X	No written guidance	X	X
Delaware	X	X	X	X	X	X	X	X	X
District of Columbia		X				X		X	DC allows deduction for franchise but not for DC franchise taxes.
Florida	X	X	X	X	X	X	X	X	

Legend:

X — **These items are deductible**
NA — **Not applicable**
NR — **Not reported**
SAF — **Same as applicable federal rules**

Deductions for Tax Payments (Part 2)

								Franchise Tax on Net Worth or Capital Paid to	
	Ohio Commercial Activity Tax	*Ohio Franchise Tax Based on Net Worth (Pre-2010)*	*Kentucky Limited Liability Entity Tax*	*New Hampshire Business Profits Tax*	*Texas Margin Tax*	*Texas Franchise Tax Based on Net Worth (Pre-2007)*	*Pennsylvania Capital Stock Tax*	*Other States*	*Home State*
Georgia	NR	X	X		X	X	X	X	X
Hawaii	X	X	X	X	X	X	X	X	X
Idaho	X	X	X		X	X	X	X	
Illinois	The tax base in Illinois starts with federal taxable income and so taxes deductible for federal income tax purposes are also deducted in computing Illinois net income. However, Illinois law requires an addition modification for taxes imposed under the Illinois Income Tax Act to the extent deducted in computing federal taxable income. Taxes, no deduction is allowed for Illinois income taxes.								
Indiana		X		X		X	X	X	
Iowa	X	X	X	X	X	X	X	X	IA only disallows IA state income tax expense deducted on federal return.
Kansas	X	X	X	X	X	X	X	X	X
Kentucky		X	X			X	X	X	
Louisiana			X	X	X	X	X	X	
Maine		X			X	X		X	
Maryland									

Deductions for Tax Payments (Part 2)

Legend:

X	**These items are deductible**
NA	**Not applicable**
NR	**Not reported**
SAF	**Same as applicable federal rules**

								Franchise Tax on Net Worth or Capital Paid to	
	Ohio Commercial Activity Tax	*Ohio Franchise Tax Based on Net Worth (Pre-2010)*	*Kentucky Limited Liability Entity Tax*	*New Hampshire Business Profits Tax*	*Texas Margin Tax*	*Texas Franchise Tax Based on Net Worth (Pre-2007)*	*Pennsylvania Capital Stock Tax*	*Other States*	*Home State*
Massachusetts	See DD 99-9								
Michigan (Business Tax)	X	X	X	X	X	X	X	X	
Note. The CIT takes effect 01/01/12, and replaces the Michigan Business Tax (MBT) for most taxpayers. However, businesses that have been approved to receive, have received, or have been assigned certain certified credits may elect to file a return and pay the tax imposed by the MBT in lieu of the CIT until the certified credits are exhausted or extinguished.									
Minnesota					X				
Mississippi		X				X	X	X	X
Missouri	X	X	X	X		X	X	X	X
Montana	X	X	X		X	X	X	X	X
Nebraska	SAF	SAF	SAF	SAF	SAF	SAF	SAF	X	X
Nevada	Nevada does not impose a corporate income tax								
New Hampshire									

Deductions for Tax Payments (Part 2)

Legend:

X	**These items are deductible**
NA	**Not applicable**
NR	**Not reported**
SAF	**Same as applicable federal rules**

								Franchise Tax on Net Worth or Capital Paid to	
	Ohio Commercial Activity Tax	*Ohio Franchise Tax Based on Net Worth (Pre-2010)*	*Kentucky Limited Liability Entity Tax*	*New Hampshire Business Profits Tax*	*Texas Margin Tax*	*Texas Franchise Tax Based on Net Worth (Pre-2007)*	*Pennsylvania Capital Stock Tax*	*Other States*	*Home State*
New Jersey	N.J. Admin. Code 18:7-5.2(a)1.v provides that the following must be added to federal taxable income when computing entire net income: All New Jersey franchise taxes paid or accrued under the Corporation Business Tax Act, whether measured by net worth, net income or otherwise, to the extent such taxes were deducted in computing Federal taxable income; and, with respect to accounting years beginning after July 7, 1993, taxes paid or accrued to a possession or territory of the United States, a state, a political subdivision thereof, or the District of Columbia on or measured by profits or income, or business presence or business activity including, without limitation, the Michigan Single Business Tax and taxes measured in whole or in part by "net taxable capital" to the extent such taxes were deducted in computing Federal taxable income.								
New Mexico									
New York									
North Carolina	X	X	X	X	X	X	X	X	
North Dakota	X	X	X	X	X	X	X	X	
Ohio	Ohio does not impose a corporate income tax								
Note. Effective 1/1/2010, the Ohio Franchise Tax was fully phased out and business will be taxed on gross receipts through the Commercial Activity Tax. Details about that tax can be found at: http//tax.ohio.gov/divisions/commercial_activities/index.stm									
Oklahoma									
Oregon	X	X	X	X	X	X	X	X	
Pennsylvania	Pennsylvania uses federal taxable income as its starting point and adds back state or local taxes imposed on or measured by net income that were deducted for federal income tax purposes.								
Rhode Island	X	X	X	X	X	X	X	X	

Deductions for Tax Payments (Part 2)

Legend:

X	**These items are deductible**
NA	**Not applicable**
NR	**Not reported**
SAF	**Same as applicable federal rules**

	Ohio Commercial Activity Tax	*Ohio Franchise Tax Based on Net Worth (Pre-2010)*	*Kentucky Limited Liability Entity Tax*	*New Hampshire Business Profits Tax*	*Texas Margin Tax*	*Texas Franchise Tax Based on Net Worth (Pre-2007)*	*Pennsylvania Capital Stock Tax*	*Franchise Tax on Net Worth or Capital Paid to Other States*	*Franchise Tax on Net Worth or Capital Paid to Home State*
South Carolina	See Rev. Rul. 09-10.	X, See Rev. Rul. 03-06.	X		See Rev. Rul. 03-06.	X, See Rev. Rul. 09-10.		X, See Rev. Rul. 03-06.	X, See Rev. Rul 09-10.
South Dakota	South Dakota does not impose a corporate income tax								
Tennessee	X	X	X	X	X	X	X	X	X
Texas									
Utah			X	X					
Vermont				X					
Virginia	X	X	X	X	X	X	X	X	X
Washington	Washington does not impose a corporate income tax								
West Virginia									
Wisconsin	X								
Wyoming	Wyoming does not impose a corporate income tax								

Related Party Expense Addback Provisions

Background

Many states do not require a group of commonly controlled corporations to file a combined or consolidated income tax return. Instead, states generally permit each affiliated corporation that has nexus in the state to compute its state taxable income on a separate company basis. The ability to file state company returns has historically allowed affiliated corporations to avoid state income taxes through the use of intangible property holding companies and similar planning techniques. For example, an affiliated group could establish a trademark holding company or financing subsidiary in Delaware or Nevada, neither of which impose income taxes on intangible property companies, and then use intercompany licensing and financing transactions to reduce the income reported by the operating affiliates.

To close this perceived loophole, many states have enacted laws that require a corporation to add back to federal taxable income any royalties or interest expense paid to related parties when computing its state taxable income (hereinafter, referred to as "addback provisions"). The Multistate Tax Commission has adopted a model statute that requires taxpayers to add back certain intangible and interest expenses in computing state taxable income [Model Statute Requiring the Add-back of Certain Intangible and Interest Expenses, Aug. 17, 2006].

Although the different state addback provisions share many common themes, there are significant differences, particularly with respect to the circumstances under which an exception applies and the related party expense need not be added back. Therefore, it is essential to thoroughly analyze each state's specific provisions to ensure compliance.

Expenses Targeted

State related party expense addback provisions are generally targeted at two broad categories of expenses: "intangible expenses" and "interest expense." Some state addback provisions apply to a more limited range of expenses.

Most states define "interest expense" by reference to federal Internal Revenue Code (Code) Section 163. For example, for purposes of the Maryland addback provision, interest expense means "an amount directly or indirectly allowed as a deduction under section 163 of the Internal Revenue Code for purposes of determining taxable income under the Internal Revenue Code" [Md. Code Ann. § 10-306.1(a)(7)].

For this purpose, "intangible expenses" generally include: (1) royalty, patent, technical, copyright, and licensing fees; (2) losses related to factoring or discounting transactions; and (3) other expenses related to the acquisition, ownership, use, or disposition of intangible property. Intangible property generally means patents, trade names, trademarks, service marks, copyrights, trade secrets, and similar types of intangible assets.

In some states, the interest expense addback provisions apply only to interest expense that is related to intangible property. For example, the Georgia addback provision applies to interest expense deductions "to the extent such expenses and costs are directly or indirectly for, related to, or in connection with the direct or indirect acquisition, use, maintenance, management, ownership, sale, exchange, or disposition of intangible property" [Ga. Code § 48-7-28.3(a)(6)]. Interest expense that is not related to intangible property need not be added back. For this purpose, intangible property includes "patents, patent applications, trade names, trademarks, service marks, copyrights, mask words, trade secrets, and similar types of intangible assets" [Ga. Code § 48-7-28.3(a)(5)]. Such provisions are aimed at tax planning structures where an operating company pays a royalty or other intangible expense to a related party, which then lends the funds back to the operating company. The interest paid by the operating company on the loan of funds generated by the intangible expenses is an example of intangible-related interest expense.

Addback provisions are also found in some mandatory combination states. For example, Illinois requires members of a unitary business group to compute their state taxable income on a combined unitary basis. A water's-edge combination, which excludes 80/20 companies, is required in the case of a multinational business group. An 80/20 company is a related corporation whose business activity outside the U.S. is 80 percent or more of its total business activity. In computing its Illinois taxable income, a unitary business group generally must add back otherwise deductible intangible expenses and interest expenses paid to an 80/20 company [Ill. Comp. Stat. Ch. 35, § 203]. Examples include interest or royalty payments made by a U.S. affiliate to an offshore financing subsidiary or intangible property company located in a foreign country. Without the addback requirement, such intangible and interest expenses would reduce the unitary business group's Illinois taxable income.

Definition of "Related Member"

State addback provisions apply to expenses that are directly or indirectly paid or accrued to a related person, which most statutes refer to as a "related member." The definition of a related member varies somewhat from state to state, but generally includes: (1) a component member of a controlled group of corporations under Code Section 1563, (2) a person to or from whom there is attribution of stock ownership under Code Section 1563(e), or (3) some other type of related entity, such as an individual or other stockholder who directly, indirectly or constructively owns 50 percent or more of the stock in the taxpayer.

For example, for purposes of the New Jersey addback provision, a "related member" means a person that, with respect to the taxpayer during all or part of the tax year, is: "(1) a related entity, (2) a component member as defined in subsection (b) of [Code] section 1563 . . . , (3) a person to or from whom there is attribution of stock ownership in accordance with subsection (e) of [Code] section 1563, or (4) a person that, notwithstanding its form of organization, bears the same relationship to the taxpayer as a person described in (1) through (3) of this definition." (N.J. Stat. Ann. § 54:10A-4.4(a)). A "related entity" means: "(1) a stockholder who is an individual, or a member of the stockholder's family enumerated in [Code] section 318, if the stockholder and the members of the stockholder's family own, directly, indirectly, beneficially or constructively, in the aggregate, at least 50 percent of the value of the taxpayer's outstanding stock; (2) a stockholder, or a stockholder's partnership, limited liability company, estate, trust or corporation, if the stockholder and the stockholder's partnerships, limited liability companies, estates, trusts and corporations own directly, indirectly, beneficially or constructively, in the aggregate, at least 50 percent of the value of the taxpayer's outstanding stock; or (3) a corporation, or a party related to the corporation in a manner that would require an attribution of stock from the corporation to the party or from the party to the corporation under the attribution rules of [IRC § 318], if the taxpayer owns, directly, indirectly, beneficially or constructively, at least 50 percent of the value of the corporation's outstanding stock" [N.J. Stat. Ann. § 54:10A-4.4(a)].

Exceptions

State addback provisions are designed to prevent taxpayers from using intercompany licensing and financing arrangements to avoid corporate income taxes. Under the general rules, however, state addback provisions apply automatically to all related party intangible and interest expenses, including those related party payments that are motivated by legitimate business purposes rather than tax avoidance. As a consequence, each state provides some relief in the form of exceptions from the automatic addback requirement. These exceptions are complex and vary from state to state. There are some common themes, however, including exceptions that apply when: (1) the related payee's corresponding income is subject to tax in another U.S. state or a foreign country, (2) the related payee pays the amount to an unrelated person, (3) the addback adjustment produces an unreasonable result, or (4) the taxpayer and the state tax authorities agree to an alternative adjustment.

Subject to tax exception. Many states permit a deduction for related party intangible and interest expenses if the related payee's corresponding income is subject to tax in a U.S. state or a foreign country. In many states, the subject to tax exception requires that the related payee's corresponding income be subject to a certain rate of taxation. For example, the New Jersey exception applies only if the related payee's interest income is subject to state tax at an effective rate that is within 3 percentage points of the "rate of tax applied to taxable interest" by New Jersey [N.J. Stat. Ann. § 54:10A-4(l)].

Conduit payment exception. Another common exception is the conduit payment exception, under which a state permits a deduction for related party intangibles and interest expenses if in the same tax year the related payee pays the amount to an unrelated person and tax avoidance was not a principal purpose of the related party payment. In such situations, the related payee serves as a conduit for the taxpayer's payment of intangible or interest expenses to an unrelated third party. An example of a conduit payment arrangement is centralized cash management, where the excess cash generated by some operating affiliates is used to pay the expenses of other affiliates.

For example, the Maryland addback provision provides an exception when "(1) The transaction giving rise to the payment of the interest expense or intangible expense between the corporation and the related member did not have as a principal purpose the avoidance of any portion of the tax due under this title; (2) The interest expense or intangible expense was paid pursuant to arm's-length contracts at an arm's-length rate of interest or price; and (3)(i). During the same taxable year, the related member directly or indirectly paid, accrued, or incurred the interest expense or intangible expense to a person who is not a related member" [Md. Code Ann. § 10-306.1].

Unreasonable result and alternative adjustment exceptions. Many states provide an exception if the taxpayer can establish that the addback of the related party intangible or interest expense produces an unreasonable result (for example, results in double taxation), or if the taxpayer and state tax authorities agree to an alternative adjustment. For example, the Connecticut addback provision provides that an addback is not required if "the corporation establishes by clear and convincing evidence that the adjustments are unreasonable, or the corporation and the Commissioner of Revenue Services agree in writing to the application or use of an alternative method of apportionment" [Conn. Gen. Stat. § 12-218c].

Other exceptions. Various other types of exceptions can be found in the state addback provisions. For example, Arkansas provides an exception when the related party recipient of the interest or intangible income operates an active trade or business in a "non-tax location," has a minimum of 50 full-time-equivalent employees and owns more than $1 million of real or tangible personal property in the non-tax location, and has revenues generated from sources within the non-tax location in excess of $1 million [Ark. Code Ann. § 26-51-423].

Recent Developments

Alabama. In *Surtees v. VFJ Ventures, Inc.* [No. 1070718 (Ala. Sup. Ct., Sept. 19, 2008); cert. denied, U.S. No. 08-916, Apr. 27, 2009], the taxpayer (VFJ) manufactures and markets jeanswear, primarily with the "Lee" and "Wrangler" brand names. VFJ had facilities in Alabama that employed approximately 600 employees. In 2001, VFJ paid over $100 million in royalties to two related Delaware trademark management corporations for the use of their trademarks. The court applied the "unreasonableness exception" found in the state's addback statute, and ruled that it was unreasonable to require VFJ to add back the royalties, because the payments had economic substance and a business purpose. The Alabama Court of Civil Appeals reversed the trial court's ruling and held that VFJ must add back the related party royalty payments. The appeals court concluded that the unreasonableness exception applies only if the resulting tax is out of proportion to the corporation's activities in Alabama and there is no evidence of distortion in the record. The appeals court also ruled that the statutory "subject-to-tax" exception applied to VFJ's royalty payments only to the extent the royalties were actually taxed by another state. The Alabama Supreme Court affirmed the decision by the Court of Civil Appeals. In response to the *VFJ Ventures* decision, the Alabama legislature amended the statute to clarify that the subject-to-tax exception applies only to that "portion of an item of income which is attributed to a taxing jurisdiction." [H.B. 62, June 9, 2008]

District of Columbia. Effective for tax years beginning on or after January 1, 2009, no deduction is allowed for interest or intangible expenses paid to a related member, unless (1) the principal purpose of the payments is not the avoidance of tax, (2) the payments are made at arm's length, and (3) the related payee pays tax on the interest or intangible payments in another jurisdiction at an effective tax rate of 4.5 percent or more. [D.C.B. 18-255, Dec. 18, 2009]

Illinois. For tax years ending on or after December 31, 2008, in computing Illinois taxable income, a corporation must add back any otherwise deductible interest expenses, intangible expenses, and insurance expenses paid to a financial organization, insurance company, or transportation company that would be a member of the same unitary group but for the fact that it is required to use a different apportionment formula. [S.B. 1544, Aug. 16, 2007]

Effective January 11, 2008, the add-back requirements do not apply to interest and intangible expenses paid to a person who is subject to an income tax in a foreign country or state with respect to the interest or expense, or if the taxpayer can establish that (1) the interest or intangible expense is paid to a person who is not a related member, (2) the transaction giving rise to the expense did not have as a principal purpose the avoidance of Illinois income tax, or (3) the adjustment with respect to the interest or intangible expense is unreasonable. [S.B. 783, Jan. 11, 2008]

Massachusetts. In *Kimberly-Clark Corporation v. Commissioner of Revenue* [Nos. C282754, C295077, C299008 (Mass. App. Tax Bd., Jan. 31, 2011)], the Massachusetts Appellate Tax Board ruled that interest, royalty and rebate expenses paid to related parties must be added back, because the taxpayer failed to show by clear and convincing evidence that tax avoidance was not a principal purpose of the transactions. The excess cash advances made within the taxpayer's cash-management system did not constitute bona-fide debt, because they were not intended to be repaid, there was an absence of security, default or collateral provisions attendant to the purported debt, and the taxpayer failed to establish that the promissory notes represented arm's-length transactions. The royalty expenses related to transfer and license back transactions were subject to add-back, because the taxpayer failed to demonstrate that the reduction of tax was not the principal purpose behind the transactions. Finally, purported rebate payments to related parties were also subject to the state's add-back provision, because they constituted embedded royalties.

The Massachusetts related party add-back requirement applies to deductions for the amortization of intangible property, based on IRC Section 197, if the deduction derives from the acquisition of intangible property from a related member. The amortization expense need not be added back, however, if the deduction is eligible for one of the statutory exceptions and the taxpayer can demonstrate by clear and convincing evidence that the transaction that gives rise to the purported expense was primarily entered into for a valid business purpose and is supported by economic substance. [Mass. Dept. of Rev., Directive 07-9, Oct. 10, 2007]

Minnesota. For tax years beginning on or after January 1, 2008, Minnesota requires that in computing its taxable income, a combined reporting group must add-back interest and intangible expenses paid to, as well as certain other types of income received by, a member of the unitary group that qualifies as a foreign operating corporation. [H.F. 3149, May 29, 2008]

New Jersey. In *Beneficial New Jersey, Inc. v. Director, Division of Taxation* [No. 009886-2007 (N.J. Tax Ct., Aug. 31, 2010)], a finance company was allowed to deduct interest it paid on a loan from its parent corporation. The finance company was in the business of making loans to consumers and it borrowed money from its parent corporation which, in turn, borrowed the money from third-party lenders. The finance company deducted the interest it paid to its parent, but the parent did not file a New Jersey tax return. The New Jersey Tax Court ruled that the taxpayer satisfied the unreasonable add-back exception, because the transactions between the taxpayer and its parent had economic substance, the parent received more favorable interest rates on loans than the taxpayer could receive, and the parent paid taxes in 17 jurisdictions on the interest income it received from the taxpayer. The court rejected the division's argument that the exception applied only in the case of double taxation or where the corporations had a centralized cash management system. [See *Technical Advisory Memorandum TAM-13* (N.J. Div. of Taxn., Feb. 24, 2011) for guidance regarding the impact of this decision.]

In a notice issued June 10, 2010, the New Jersey Division of Taxation identifies three circumstances in which a taxpayer would qualify for the "unreasonable" exception to the related member interest expense add back requirement: (1) the related party pays tax in New Jersey on the income stream and disallowance of the deduction to the payer would result in double taxation, (2) the taxpayer has both a receivable and a payable from the exact same entity that results in offsetting interest income and interest expense, or

(3) the taxpayer and its related members have entered into a qualifying cash sweep management agreement.

Oregon. For tax years beginning on or after January 1, 2010, intangible expenses paid by a corporation to a related member that is not included in the same state tax return as the taxpayer must be added back to federal taxable income. However, the taxpayer may claim a credit for any tax that the related member pays on the same income that has been added back. An addback is not required for intangible expenses that the related member pays to a unrelated person and the transaction was undertaken for a valid business purpose. [S.B. 181, June 18, 2009]

Wisconsin. For tax years beginning on or after January 1, 2008, Wisconsin requires taxpayers to add back interest and rent expenses paid to a related entity. [A.B. 1, May 16, 2008] A "related entity" is any person related to the taxpayer under IRC Section 267 or IRC Section 1563. However, the taxpayer may take an offsetting subtraction modification if the taxpayer discloses the transaction on Wisconsin Schedule RT and meets one of the statutory exceptions for reimbursement of expenses paid to unrelated entity, related entity subject to tax on the income, and transactions not primarily for tax avoidance.

Effective for tax years beginning on or after January 1, 2009, management fees and intangible expenses are included under existing provisions governing the treatment of certain rent and interest payments to related parties. [S.B. 62, Feb. 19, 2009]

State-by-State Summary

The following chart, presented in two parts, summarizes which states require corporate taxpayers to add back royalties or interest expenses paid to related parties, as well as the circumstances under which an addback is not required. Part 1 summarizes the treatment of royalty expenses, and Part 2 summarizes the treatment of interest expenses.

Related Party Expense Addback Provisions (Part 1)
Royalty Expense

Legend:

X	Condition applies
SAF	Same as federal
NA	Not applicable
NR	Not reported

	Is an Addition Modification Required for Royalty Payments Made to a Related Out-of-State Corporation?	*If "Yes," Under Which of the Following Circumstances, if any, Is an Addback Not Required?*				
		Related Royalty Recipient Pays the Amount to an Unrelated Party, and Tax Avoidance Is Not a Principal Purpose of the Related Party Royalty Payment	*Related Royalty Recipient's Income Is Subject to Tax in a U.S. State or a Foreign Country*	*Taxpayer Establishes that Addback Is Unreasonable*	*Taxpayer and Commissioner Agree to Alternative Adjustment*	*Other Circumstances in Which an Addback Is Not Required*
Alabama	Yes	X	X	X	X	NR
Alaska						Intercompany royalties are eliminated in combination.
Arizona	Yes, may require combined filing					
Arkansas	Yes					X, related royalty recipient files Arkansas Return and apportions income according to Ark. Reg. 1996-3.

Related Party Expense Addback Provisions (Part 1)
Royalty Expense

Legend:

X	Condition applies
SAF	Same as federal
NA	Not applicable
NR	Not reported

		If "Yes," Under Which of the Following Circumstances, if any, Is an Addback Not Required?				
	Is an Addition Modification Required for Royalty Payments Made to a Related Out-of-State Corporation?	*Related Royalty Recipient Pays the Amount to an Unrelated Party, and Tax Avoidance Is Not a Principal Purpose of the Related Party Royalty Payment*	*Related Royalty Recipient's Income Is Subject to Tax in a U.S. State or a Foreign Country*	*Taxpayer Establishes that Addback Is Unreasonable*	*Taxpayer and Commissioner Agree to Alternative Adjustment*	*Other Circumstances in Which an Addback Is Not Required*
California	No (if the entities in question are considered unitary, this would generally be considered an intercompany transaction, and would be eliminated.)					
Colorado	No					
Connecticut	Yes			X	X	
Delaware	No					
District of Columbia	Yes	X			X	
Florida	No, see F.S. § 220.44					

Related Party Expense Addback Provisions (Part 1)
Royalty Expense

Legend:

X	Condition applies
SAF	Same as federal
NA	Not applicable
NR	Not reported

		If "Yes," Under Which of the Following Circumstances, if any, Is an Addback Not Required?				
	Is an Addition Modification Required for Royalty Payments Made to a Related Out-of-State Corporation?	*Related Royalty Recipient Pays the Amount to an Unrelated Party, and Tax Avoidance Is Not a Principal Purpose of the Related Party Royalty Payment*	*Related Royalty Recipient's Income Is Subject to Tax in a U.S. State or a Foreign Country*	*Taxpayer Establishes that Addback Is Unreasonable*	*Taxpayer and Commissioner Agree to Alternative Adjustment*	*Other Circumstances in Which an Addback Is Not Required*
Georgia	Yes, certain interest expense only. See O.C.G.A. § 48-7-28.3		X		X	X, paid to an unrelated party and the transaction has a valid business purpose. Royalty expense must still be added back before exception subtraction deduction is allowed. See O.C.G.A. § 48-7-28.3
Hawaii	No					
Idaho	No					

Related Party Expense Addback Provisions (Part 1)
Royalty Expense

Legend:

X	Condition applies
SAF	Same as federal
NA	Not applicable
NR	Not reported

		If "Yes," Under Which of the Following Circumstances, if any, Is an Addback Not Required?				
	Is an Addition Modification Required for Royalty Payments Made to a Related Out-of-State Corporation?	*Related Royalty Recipient Pays the Amount to an Unrelated Party, and Tax Avoidance Is Not a Principal Purpose of the Related Party Royalty Payment*	*Related Royalty Recipient's Income Is Subject to Tax in a U.S. State or a Foreign Country*	*Taxpayer Establishes that Addback Is Unreasonable*	*Taxpayer and Commissioner Agree to Alternative Adjustment*	*Other Circumstances in Which an Addback Is Not Required*
Illinois	Yes, in certain cases if related party is a "foreign person," see chart on "Addition Modifications."	X	X	X	X	X, if Taxpayer establishes by clear and convincing evidence that the interest paid, accrued, or incurred relates to an agreement entered into at arm's length rates and terms and the principal purpose of the payment is not federal or Illinois tax avoidance.
Indiana	No					
Iowa	No					

Related Party Expense Addback Provisions (Part 1)
Royalty Expense

Legend:

X	Condition applies
SAF	Same as federal
NA	Not applicable
NR	Not reported

	Is an Addition Modification Required for Royalty Payments Made to a Related Out-of-State Corporation?	*If "Yes," Under Which of the Following Circumstances, if any, Is an Addback Not Required?*				
		Related Royalty Recipient Pays the Amount to an Unrelated Party, and Tax Avoidance Is Not a Principal Purpose of the Related Party Royalty Payment	*Related Royalty Recipient's Income Is Subject to Tax in a U.S. State or a Foreign Country*	*Taxpayer Establishes that Addback Is Unreasonable*	*Taxpayer and Commissioner Agree to Alternative Adjustment*	*Other Circumstances in Which an Addback Is Not Required*
Kansas	No					Kansas is a unitary domestic combination state. Income and expense would offset.
Kentucky	Yes	X	X		X, both parties must agree to an alternative apportionment method.	The entity makes a disclosure and establishes by evidence that the recipient engages in transactions with one or more unrelated parties on terms identical to that of the subject transaction.

Related Party Expense Addback Provisions (Part 1)
Royalty Expense

Legend:

X	Condition applies
SAF	Same as federal
NA	Not applicable
NR	Not reported

		If "Yes," Under Which of the Following Circumstances, if any, Is an Addback Not Required?				
	Is an Addition Modification Required for Royalty Payments Made to a Related Out-of-State Corporation?	*Related Royalty Recipient Pays the Amount to an Unrelated Party, and Tax Avoidance Is Not a Principal Purpose of the Related Party Royalty Payment*	*Related Royalty Recipient's Income Is Subject to Tax in a U.S. State or a Foreign Country*	*Taxpayer Establishes that Addback Is Unreasonable*	*Taxpayer and Commissioner Agree to Alternative Adjustment*	*Other Circumstances in Which an Addback Is Not Required*
Louisiana	No, but if certain conditions are met the Secretary may redistribute deductions between related parties to fairly reflect income.					
Maine	No					
Maryland	Yes	X				X subject to aggregate effective tax rate equal to or greater than 4%.
Massachusetts	Yes	X	X	X	X	
Michigan (Business Tax)	Yes	X	X	X	X	X, see MCL 208.9(4)(g)

Note. The CIT takes effect 01/01/12, and replaces the Michigan Business Tax (MBT) for most taxpayers. However, businesses that have been approved to receive, have received, or have been assigned certain certified credits may elect to file a return and pay the tax imposed by the MBT in lieu of the CIT until the certified credits are exhausted or extinguished.

Related Party Expense Addback Provisions (Part 1)
Royalty Expense

Legend:

X	Condition applies
SAF	Same as federal
NA	Not applicable
NR	Not reported

		If "Yes," Under Which of the Following Circumstances, if any, Is an Addback Not Required?				
	Is an Addition Modification Required for Royalty Payments Made to a Related Out-of-State Corporation?	*Related Royalty Recipient Pays the Amount to an Unrelated Party, and Tax Avoidance Is Not a Principal Purpose of the Related Party Royalty Payment*	*Related Royalty Recipient's Income Is Subject to Tax in a U.S. State or a Foreign Country*	*Taxpayer Establishes that Addback Is Unreasonable*	*Taxpayer and Commissioner Agree to Alternative Adjustment*	*Other Circumstances in Which an Addback Is Not Required*
Minnesota	Yes					X, intercompany transactions are eliminated in reporting the income of a unitary group.
Mississippi	Yes	X				
Missouri	No					
Montana	No					
Nebraska	No					
Nevada	Nevada does not impose a corporate income tax					
New Hampshire	No					
New Jersey	Yes	X	X	X	X	The addback is cited as N.J.S.A. 54:10A-4.4(c)
New Mexico	No					

Related Party Expense Addback Provisions (Part 1)
Royalty Expense

Legend:

X	Condition applies
SAF	Same as federal
NA	Not applicable
NR	Not reported

		If "Yes," Under Which of the Following Circumstances, if any, Is an Addback Not Required?				
	Is an Addition Modification Required for Royalty Payments Made to a Related Out-of-State Corporation?	*Related Royalty Recipient Pays the Amount to an Unrelated Party, and Tax Avoidance Is Not a Principal Purpose of the Related Party Royalty Payment*	*Related Royalty Recipient's Income Is Subject to Tax in a U.S. State or a Foreign Country*	*Taxpayer Establishes that Addback Is Unreasonable*	*Taxpayer and Commissioner Agree to Alternative Adjustment*	*Other Circumstances in Which an Addback Is Not Required*
New York	Yes	X				The royalty payments are paid or incurred to a related member organized under the laws of a foreign country, are subject to a comprehensive income tax treaty between such country and the U.S., and are taxed in such country at a tax rate at least equal to that imposed by New York.
North Carolina	Yes					Related royalty recipient includes the royalty income on its North Carolina return.

Related Party Expense Addback Provisions (Part 1)
Royalty Expense

Legend:

X	Condition applies
SAF	Same as federal
NA	Not applicable
NR	Not reported

	Is an Addition Modification Required for Royalty Payments Made to a Related Out-of-State Corporation?	*If "Yes," Under Which of the Following Circumstances, if any, Is an Addback Not Required?*				
		Related Royalty Recipient Pays the Amount to an Unrelated Party, and Tax Avoidance Is Not a Principal Purpose of the Related Party Royalty Payment	*Related Royalty Recipient's Income Is Subject to Tax in a U.S. State or a Foreign Country*	*Taxpayer Establishes that Addback Is Unreasonable*	*Taxpayer and Commissioner Agree to Alternative Adjustment*	*Other Circumstances in Which an Addback Is Not Required*
North Dakota	No	X				North Dakota is a combined unitary state so the royalty expense would be offset by royalty income to the affiliated entity.
Ohio	Ohio does not impose a corporate income tax					
Note. Effective 1/1/2010, the Ohio Franchise Tax was fully phased out and business will be taxed on gross receipts through the Commercial Activity Tax. Details about that tax can be found at: http//tax.ohio.gov/divisions/commercial_activities/index.stm						
Oklahoma	NR	NR	NR	NR	NR	NR
Oregon	No, unless a consolidated federal return is not filed and the transaction is structured to evade taxes or does not clearly reflect Oregon business activity.					

Related Party Expense Addback Provisions (Part 1)
Royalty Expense

Legend:

X	Condition applies
SAF	Same as federal
NA	Not applicable
NR	Not reported

		If "Yes," Under Which of the Following Circumstances, if any, Is an Addback Not Required?				
	Is an Addition Modification Required for Royalty Payments Made to a Related Out-of-State Corporation?	*Related Royalty Recipient Pays the Amount to an Unrelated Party, and Tax Avoidance Is Not a Principal Purpose of the Related Party Royalty Payment*	*Related Royalty Recipient's Income Is Subject to Tax in a U.S. State or a Foreign Country*	*Taxpayer Establishes that Addback Is Unreasonable*	*Taxpayer and Commissioner Agree to Alternative Adjustment*	*Other Circumstances in Which an Addback Is Not Required*
Pennsylvania	Yes	X				
Rhode Island	No					
South Carolina	No					
South Dakota	South Dakota does not impose a corporate income tax					
Tennessee	Yes	X				Taxpayer must file a disclosure form to support the intangible expense that has a legitimate business purpose.
Texas	No					
Utah	No, however, combined reporting state and the recipient of the royalty payment would likely be included in the unitary group.					

Related Party Expense Addback Provisions (Part 1)
Royalty Expense

Legend:

X	Condition applies
SAF	Same as federal
NA	Not applicable
NR	Not reported

	Is an Addition Modification Required for Royalty Payments Made to a Related Out-of-State Corporation?	*If "Yes," Under Which of the Following Circumstances, if any, Is an Addback Not Required?*				
		Related Royalty Recipient Pays the Amount to an Unrelated Party, and Tax Avoidance Is Not a Principal Purpose of the Related Party Royalty Payment	*Related Royalty Recipient's Income Is Subject to Tax in a U.S. State or a Foreign Country*	*Taxpayer Establishes that Addback Is Unreasonable*	*Taxpayer and Commissioner Agree to Alternative Adjustment*	*Other Circumstances in Which an Addback Is Not Required*
Vermont	No					
Virginia	Yes 01/01/04	X		X, See Note 1		
Note. Related member derives at least 1/3 of gross revenue from licensing intangible property to unrelated members, and the transaction was made at arm's length rates; taxpayer can demonstrate to Tax Commissioner's sole satisfaction that transaction had a valid business purpose other than the avoidance or reduction of tax.						
Washington	Washington does not impose a corporate income tax					
West Virginia	No					
Wisconsin	Yes, See § 71.80(23)					
Wyoming	Wyoming does not impose a corporate income tax					

Related Party Expense Addback Provisions (Part 2)
Interest Expense

Legend:

X	Condition applies
SAF	Same as federal
NA	Not applicable
NR	Not reported

		If "Yes," Under Which of the Following Circumstances, if any, Is an Addback Not Required?				
	Is an Addition Modification Required for Interest Payments Made to a Related Out-of-State Corporation?	*Related Interest Recipient Pays the Amount to an Unrelated Party, and Tax Avoidance Is Not a Principal Purpose of the Related Party Interest Payment*	*Related Interest Recipient's Income Is Subject to Tax in a U.S. State or a Foreign Country*	*Taxpayer Establishes that Addback Is Unreasonable*	*Taxpayer and Commissioner Agree to Alternative Adjustment*	*Other Circumstances in Which an Addback Is Not Required*
Alabama	Yes	X	X	X	X	
Alaska						Intercompany interest is eliminated in combination.
Arizona						Depends on circumstances.
Arkansas	Yes	X	X	X	X	X, $1,000,000 property, $1,000,000 sales and 50 employees in a non-tax location.
California	No (if the entities in question are considered unitary, this would generally be considered an intercompany transaction, and would be eliminated.)					

Related Party Expense Addback Provisions (Part 2)
Interest Expense

Legend:

X	Condition applies
SAF	Same as federal
NA	Not applicable
NR	Not reported

		If "Yes," Under Which of the Following Circumstances, if any, Is an Addback Not Required?				
	Is an Addition Modification Required for Interest Payments Made to a Related Out-of-State Corporation?	*Related Interest Recipient Pays the Amount to an Unrelated Party, and Tax Avoidance Is Not a Principal Purpose of the Related Party Interest Payment*	*Related Interest Recipient's Income Is Subject to Tax in a U.S. State or a Foreign Country*	*Taxpayer Establishes that Addback Is Unreasonable*	*Taxpayer and Commissioner Agree to Alternative Adjustment*	*Other Circumstances in Which an Addback Is Not Required*
Colorado	No					
Connecticut	Yes		X	X	X	X, related party is an insurance company or taxpayer elects to file a unitary return
Delaware	Yes					Interest paid to an affiliate is added back only if the affiliate receiving the interest subtracts an equal amount.
District of Columbia	Yes	X			X	
Florida	No, see F.S. § 220.44					

Related Party Expense Addback Provisions (Part 2)
Interest Expense

Legend:

X	Condition applies
SAF	Same as federal
NA	Not applicable
NR	Not reported

		If "Yes," Under Which of the Following Circumstances, if any, Is an Addback Not Required?				
	Is an Addition Modification Required for Interest Payments Made to a Related Out-of-State Corporation?	*Related Interest Recipient Pays the Amount to an Unrelated Party, and Tax Avoidance Is Not a Principal Purpose of the Related Party Interest Payment*	*Related Interest Recipient's Income Is Subject to Tax in a U.S. State or a Foreign Country*	*Taxpayer Establishes that Addback Is Unreasonable*	*Taxpayer and Commissioner Agree to Alternative Adjustment*	*Other Circumstances in Which an Addback Is Not Required*
Georgia	Certain interest expense only See OCGA § 48-7-28.3		X		X	X, related member paid to unrelated person and has valid business purpose. Interest expense must still be added back before exception deduction is allowed. See OCGA § 48-7-28.3.
Hawaii	No					
Idaho	No					

Related Party Expense Addback Provisions (Part 2)
Interest Expense

Legend:

X	Condition applies
SAF	Same as federal
NA	Not applicable
NR	Not reported

		If "Yes," Under Which of the Following Circumstances, if any, Is an Addback Not Required?				
	Is an Addition Modification Required for Interest Payments Made to a Related Out-of-State Corporation?	*Related Interest Recipient Pays the Amount to an Unrelated Party, and Tax Avoidance Is Not a Principal Purpose of the Related Party Interest Payment*	*Related Interest Recipient's Income Is Subject to Tax in a U.S. State or a Foreign Country*	*Taxpayer Establishes that Addback Is Unreasonable*	*Taxpayer and Commissioner Agree to Alternative Adjustment*	*Other Circumstances in Which an Addback Is Not Required*
Illinois	Yes, in certain cases if related party is a "foreign person," see chart on "Addition Modifications."	X	X	X	X	X, if Taxpayer establishes by clear and convincing evidence that the interest paid, accrued, or incurred relates to an agreement entered into at arm's length rates and terms and the principal purpose of the payment is not federal or Illinois tax avoidance.
Indiana	No					
Iowa	No					

Related Party Expense Addback Provisions (Part 2)
Interest Expense

Legend:

X	Condition applies
SAF	Same as federal
NA	Not applicable
NR	Not reported

		If "Yes," Under Which of the Following Circumstances, if any, Is an Addback Not Required?				
	Is an Addition Modification Required for Interest Payments Made to a Related Out-of-State Corporation?	*Related Interest Recipient Pays the Amount to an Unrelated Party, and Tax Avoidance Is Not a Principal Purpose of the Related Party Interest Payment*	*Related Interest Recipient's Income Is Subject to Tax in a U.S. State or a Foreign Country*	*Taxpayer Establishes that Addback Is Unreasonable*	*Taxpayer and Commissioner Agree to Alternative Adjustment*	*Other Circumstances in Which an Addback Is Not Required*
Kansas	No					Kansas is a unitary domestic combination state. Income and expense would offset.
Kentucky	Yes	X	X		X, both parties must agree to an alternative apportionment method.	The entity makes a disclosure and establishes by evidence that the recipient engages in transactions with one or more unrelated parties on terms identical to that of the subject transaction.

Related Party Expense Addback Provisions (Part 2)
Interest Expense

Legend:

X	Condition applies
SAF	Same as federal
NA	Not applicable
NR	Not reported

		If "Yes," Under Which of the Following Circumstances, if any, Is an Addback Not Required?				
	Is an Addition Modification Required for Interest Payments Made to a Related Out-of-State Corporation?	*Related Interest Recipient Pays the Amount to an Unrelated Party, and Tax Avoidance Is Not a Principal Purpose of the Related Party Interest Payment*	*Related Interest Recipient's Income Is Subject to Tax in a U.S. State or a Foreign Country*	*Taxpayer Establishes that Addback Is Unreasonable*	*Taxpayer and Commissioner Agree to Alternative Adjustment*	*Other Circumstances in Which an Addback Is Not Required*
Louisiana	No, but if certain conditions are met the Secretary may redistribute deductions between related parties to fairly reflect income.					
Maine	No					
Maryland	Yes					X, if the corporation and the related member are banks
Massachusetts	Depends on facts	X	X	X	X	
Michigan (Business Tax)	Yes	X	X	X	X	X, see MCL 208.9(4)(f)

Note. The CIT takes effect 01/01/12, and replaces the Michigan Business Tax (MBT) for most taxpayers. However, businesses that have been approved to receive, have received, or have been assigned certain certified credits may elect to file a return and pay the tax imposed by the MBT in lieu of the CIT until the certified credits are exhausted or extinguished.

Related Party Expense Addback Provisions (Part 2)
Interest Expense

Legend:

X	Condition applies
SAF	Same as federal
NA	Not applicable
NR	Not reported

		If "Yes," Under Which of the Following Circumstances, if any, Is an Addback Not Required?				
	Is an Addition Modification Required for Interest Payments Made to a Related Out-of-State Corporation?	*Related Interest Recipient Pays the Amount to an Unrelated Party, and Tax Avoidance Is Not a Principal Purpose of the Related Party Interest Payment*	*Related Interest Recipient's Income Is Subject to Tax in a U.S. State or a Foreign Country*	*Taxpayer Establishes that Addback Is Unreasonable*	*Taxpayer and Commissioner Agree to Alternative Adjustment*	*Other Circumstances in Which an Addback Is Not Required*
Minnesota	Yes					X, intercompany transactions are eliminated in reporting the income of a unitary group.
Mississippi	Yes	X				
Missouri	No					
Montana	No					
Nebraska	No					
Nevada	Nevada does not impose a corporate income tax					
New Hampshire	No	NR	NR	NR	NR	NR

Related Party Expense Addback Provisions (Part 2)
Interest Expense

Legend:

X	Condition applies
SAF	Same as federal
NA	Not applicable
NR	Not reported

		If "Yes," Under Which of the Following Circumstances, if any, Is an Addback Not Required?				
	Is an Addition Modification Required for Interest Payments Made to a Related Out-of-State Corporation?	*Related Interest Recipient Pays the Amount to an Unrelated Party, and Tax Avoidance Is Not a Principal Purpose of the Related Party Interest Payment*	*Related Interest Recipient's Income Is Subject to Tax in a U.S. State or a Foreign Country*	*Taxpayer Establishes that Addback Is Unreasonable*	*Taxpayer and Commissioner Agree to Alternative Adjustment*	*Other Circumstances in Which an Addback Is Not Required*
New Jersey	Yes	X	X, for foreign country; foreign states fall under the 3% rule discussed under other circumstances.	X	X	Paid to independent lender and taxpayer guarantees debt. Related member subject to tax in other state or foreign country; a measure of the tax includes interest received from related member, rate of tax paid is not less than 3% less than the New Jersey tax rate applied to Taxpayer. N.J.S.A. 4(k)(2)(l).
New Mexico	No					

Related Party Expense Addback Provisions (Part 2)
Interest Expense

Legend:

X	Condition applies
SAF	Same as federal
NA	Not applicable
NR	Not reported

		If "Yes," Under Which of the Following Circumstances, if any, Is an Addback Not Required?				
	Is an Addition Modification Required for Interest Payments Made to a Related Out-of-State Corporation?	*Related Interest Recipient Pays the Amount to an Unrelated Party, and Tax Avoidance Is Not a Principal Purpose of the Related Party Interest Payment*	*Related Interest Recipient's Income Is Subject to Tax in a U.S. State or a Foreign Country*	*Taxpayer Establishes that Addback Is Unreasonable*	*Taxpayer and Commissioner Agree to Alternative Adjustment*	*Other Circumstances in Which an Addback Is Not Required*
New York	Yes	X				The interest payments are paid or incurred to a related member organized under the laws of a foreign country, are subject to a comprehensive income tax treaty between such country and the U.S., and are taxed in such country at a tax rate at least equal to that imposed by New York.
North Carolina	No, except as required by G.S. 105-130.7A(b)(6)b.					

Related Party Expense Addback Provisions (Part 2)
Interest Expense

Legend:

X	Condition applies
SAF	Same as federal
NA	Not applicable
NR	Not reported

		If "Yes," Under Which of the Following Circumstances, if any, Is an Addback Not Required?				
	Is an Addition Modification Required for Interest Payments Made to a Related Out-of-State Corporation?	*Related Interest Recipient Pays the Amount to an Unrelated Party, and Tax Avoidance Is Not a Principal Purpose of the Related Party Interest Payment*	*Related Interest Recipient's Income Is Subject to Tax in a U.S. State or a Foreign Country*	*Taxpayer Establishes that Addback Is Unreasonable*	*Taxpayer and Commissioner Agree to Alternative Adjustment*	*Other Circumstances in Which an Addback Is Not Required*
North Dakota	No					North Dakota is a combined unitary state so the expense would be offset by income to the affiliated entity.
Ohio	Ohio does not impose a corporate income tax					
Note. Effective 1/1/2010, the Ohio Franchise Tax was fully phased out and business will be taxed on gross receipts through the Commercial Activity Tax. Details about that tax can be found at: http//tax.ohio.gov/divisions/commercial_activities/index.stm						
Oklahoma	NR	NR	NR	NR	NR	NR
Oregon	No, unless a consolidated federal return is not filed and the transaction is structured to evade taxes or does not clearly reflect Oregon business activity.					
Pennsylvania	Yes	X				

Related Party Expense Addback Provisions (Part 2)
Interest Expense

Legend:

X	Condition applies
SAF	Same as federal
NA	Not applicable
NR	Not reported

	Is an Addition Modification Required for Interest Payments Made to a Related Out-of-State Corporation?	*If "Yes," Under Which of the Following Circumstances, if any, Is an Addback Not Required?*				
		Related Interest Recipient Pays the Amount to an Unrelated Party, and Tax Avoidance Is Not a Principal Purpose of the Related Party Interest Payment	*Related Interest Recipient's Income Is Subject to Tax in a U.S. State or a Foreign Country*	*Taxpayer Establishes that Addback Is Unreasonable*	*Taxpayer and Commissioner Agree to Alternative Adjustment*	*Other Circumstances in Which an Addback Is Not Required*
Rhode Island	No					
South Carolina	Yes					§12-6-1130(14)
South Dakota	South Dakota does not impose a corporate income tax					
Tennessee	Yes	X				Taxpayer must file a disclosure form to support the intangible expense is a legitimate business purpose.
Texas	No	NR or Blank	NR or Blank	NR or Blank		
Utah	No, however, combined reporting state and the recipient of the interest payment would likely be included in the unitary group.					
Vermont	No					

Related Party Expense Addback Provisions (Part 2)
Interest Expense

Legend:

X	Condition applies
SAF	Same as federal
NA	Not applicable
NR	Not reported

		If "Yes," Under Which of the Following Circumstances, if any, Is an Addback Not Required?				
	Is an Addition Modification Required for Interest Payments Made to a Related Out-of-State Corporation?	*Related Interest Recipient Pays the Amount to an Unrelated Party, and Tax Avoidance Is Not a Principal Purpose of the Related Party Interest Payment*	*Related Interest Recipient's Income Is Subject to Tax in a U.S. State or a Foreign Country*	*Taxpayer Establishes that Addback Is Unreasonable*	*Taxpayer and Commissioner Agree to Alternative Adjustment*	*Other Circumstances in Which an Addback Is Not Required*
Virginia	Yes, for interest expenses related to intangibles	X	X			X, See Note
Note: Related member derives at least 1/3 of gross revenue from licensing intangible property to unrelated members, and the transaction was made at arm's length rates; taxpayer can demonstrate to Tax Commissioner's sole satisfaction that transaction had a valid business purpose other than the avoidance or reduction of tax.						
Washington	Washington does not impose a corporate income tax					
West Virginia	No					
Wisconsin	Yes					See § 71.80(23), Wis. Stats.
Wyoming	Wyoming does not impose a corporate income tax					

Section 199 Domestic Production Activities Deduction

IRC Section 199

Overview. Internal Revenue Code Section 199 was enacted as part of the American Jobs Creation Act of 2004 [Pub. L. No. 108-357]. Under Section 199, a corporation may claim a deduction equal to 9 percent of the lesser of its qualified production activities income (QPAI), or its taxable income (before the Section 199 deduction). The amount of the deduction is limited to 50 percent of the W-2 wages of the taxpayer which are allocable to domestic production gross receipts. The Section 199 deduction effectively reduces the federal corporate income tax rate on a taxpayer's QPAI from 35 percent to 31.85 percent (91% × 35%).

Both corporate and individual taxpayers are eligible to claim a Section 199 deduction. In the case of a partnership or S corporation, the Section 199 deduction is determined at the partner or S corporation shareholder level, with each owner taking into account its proportionate share of the pass-through entity's items of income, deduction, and other tax attributes that impact the computation of the Section 199 deduction. (IRC § 199(d)(1)).

Taxpayers may claim a Section 199 deduction for both regular income tax and alternative minimum tax purposes, but the amount of the Section 199 deduction for alternative minimum tax purposes is limited to 9 percent of the taxpayer's alternative minimum taxable income before the Section 199 deduction. (IRC § 199(d)(6)).

Domestic production gross receipts. A taxpayer's QPAI equals its *domestic production gross receipts* (DPGR), reduced by the cost of goods sold and other allocable direct and indirect expenses. Under Section 199(c), DPGR includes gross receipts of the taxpayer which are derived from the following qualifying production activities:

- Lease, rental, license, sale, exchange or other disposition of:
  - — Tangible personal property, computer software, or music recordings manufactured, produced, grown, or extracted by a taxpayer in whole or significant part within the U.S.;
  - — Certain films produced by the taxpayer where at least 50 percent of the total production compensation is for services performed in the U.S.;
- Sale, exchange or other disposition of electricity, natural gas, or potable water produced by the taxpayer in the U.S.;
- Construction performed in the U.S.; and
- Engineering and architectural services performed in the U.S. in connection with U.S. construction projects.

DPGR does not include gross receipts derived from the transmission or distribution of electricity, natural gas, or potable water. DPGR also does not include gross receipts from the sale of food and beverages prepared by the taxpayer at a retail establishment. On the other hand, gross receipts derived from the sale of food or beverages at the wholesale level may qualify. The term *construction* means the erection or substantial renovation of real property by a taxpayer that is engaged in a trade or business that is considered construction.

DPGR also does not include gross receipts that a taxpayer derives from "property leased, licensed, or rented" for use by a related person. (IRC § 199(c)(7)). On the other hand, a sale to a related party apparently can give rise to DPGR.

Qualified production activities income. QPAI equals the excess, if any, of the taxpayer's DPGR for the tax year over the sum of the cost of goods sold that are allocable to such receipts, and other expenses, losses, or deductions that are properly allocable to such receipts. (IRC § 199(c)(1)).

There are three methods for allocating and apportioning deductions to DPGR, including: (1) the Section 861 method, (2) the simplified deduction method for taxpayers with average annual gross receipts of $25 million or less, and (3) the small business simplified overall method for taxpayers with average annual gross receipts of $5 million or less, or a taxpayer that is eligible to use the cash method under Rev. Proc. 2002-28.

Expanded affiliated group. For purposes of computing the Section 199 deduction, all members of an expanded affiliated group are treated as a single corporation. (IRC § 199(d)(4)). In other words, a single Section 199 deduction is computed for all the group members by aggregating each member's QPAI, taxable income or loss, and W-2 wages.

The term *expanded affiliated group* (EAG) means an affiliated group, as defined in Section 1504, except that the requisite ownership threshold is more than 50 percent rather than 80 percent or more. Under Section 1504, the term *affiliated group* means one or more chains of includible corporations connected through stock ownership with a common parent corporation. A partnership is not includible in an affiliated group, nor is a corporation organized in a foreign country. Under a special rule, insurance companies and Section 936 companies are includible in an EAG, even though they are not includible in an affiliated group, as defined in Section 1504. (IRC § 199(d)(4)(B)(ii)).

For purposes of computing a group member's DPGR, each member of an EAG is generally treated as conducting the activities that are actually conducted by other group members. For example, the activities of a manufacturing affiliate may be attributed to a distribution affiliate for purposes of determining whether the distribution affiliate's gross receipts qualify as DPGR.

The single Section 199 deduction computed at the group level is allocated to each member of the EAG in proportion to each member's QPAI, regardless of whether a member has any taxable income or W-2 wages for the tax year. If a member's QPAI is negative, its QPAI is deemed to be zero for purposes of this allocation.

Affiliated corporations that join in filing a federal consolidated income tax return (i.e., a "consolidated group") are treated as a single member of an EAG. Thus, if the EAG consists exclusively of members of a consolidated group, the consolidated group's Section 199 deduction is determined based on the group's consolidated taxable income or loss and not the separate taxable income or loss amounts of the group members.

State-by-State Summary

The following chart summarizes which states have conformed to the Code Section 199 deduction.

Section 199 Domestic Production Activities Deduction

Legend:
SAF Same as applicable federal rules
NA Not applicable
NR Not reported

	Does State Conform to IRC Section 199 Domestic Production Activities Deduction?	*If "No," Does State Allow Taxpayers to Claim a Portion of the Federal Deduction?*	*If Taxpayers Are Allowed to Claim a Portion, What Is the Computation?*	*Is There a Form that Helps Taxpayers Compute the Deduction?*
Alabama	Yes	NR	NR	NR
Alaska	Yes	NA	NA	SAF
Arizona	Yes	NA	NA	NA
Arkansas	No	No	NA	No
California	No	No	If a taxpayer claims this deduction for federal purposes, the deduction should be added back to California taxable income as a state tax adjustment.	No
Colorado	Yes	NA	NA	Yes
Connecticut	Yes	NA		
Delaware	Yes	NA	NA	NA
District of Columbia	No	No	NR	NA
Florida	Yes	NA	NA	No
Georgia	No	No	NA	No
Hawaii	No	No	NA	No
Idaho	Yes	NA	NA	NA
Illinois	Yes	NA	NA	NA
Indiana	Yes	NA	NA	NA

Section 199 Domestic Production Activities Deduction

Legend:
SAF — Same as applicable federal rules
NA — Not applicable
NR — Not reported

	Does State Conform to IRC Section 199 Domestic Production Activities Deduction?	*If "No," Does State Allow Taxpayers to Claim a Portion of the Federal Deduction?*	*If Taxpayers Are Allowed to Claim a Portion, What Is the Computation?*	*Is There a Form that Helps Taxpayers Compute the Deduction?*
Iowa	Yes	NA	NA	NA
Kansas	Yes	NA	NA	No
Kentucky	Yes	NA	NA	8903-K
Louisiana	Yes	NA	NA	NA
Maine	No	No	NA	
Maryland	No	No	NA	No
Massachusetts	No	No	NA	No
Michigan (Business Tax)	No	No	NA	No
Note. The CIT takes effect 01/01/12, and replaces the Michigan Business Tax (MBT) for most taxpayers. However, businesses that have been approved to receive, have received, or have been assigned certain certified credits may elect to file a return and pay the tax imposed by the MBT in lieu of the CIT until the certified credits are exhausted or extinguished.				
Minnesota	No	No	NA	No
Mississippi	No	No	NA	No
Missouri	Yes	NA	NA	No
Montana	Yes	NR	NR	No
Nebraska	Yes	NA	NA	NA
Nevada	Nevada does not impose a corporate income tax			
New Hampshire	No	No	New Hampshire conforms to the IRC of 1986 in effect on 12/31/00	No

Section 199 Domestic Production Activities Deduction

Legend:

SAF	Same as applicable federal rules
NA	Not applicable
NR	Not reported

	Does State Conform to IRC Section 199 Domestic Production Activities Deduction?	*If "No," Does State Allow Taxpayers to Claim a Portion of the Federal Deduction?*	*If Taxpayers Are Allowed to Claim a Portion, What Is the Computation?*	*Is There a Form that Helps Taxpayers Compute the Deduction?*
New Jersey	No	Yes	See Note	Yes, Form 501
Note: Under P.L. 2005, c. 127, a deduction is allowed for the gross receipts from qualifying property manufactured or produced by taxpayer. The uncoupling will apply (the deduction will not be allowed) for gross receipts from the qualifying production property that was grown or extracted by the taxpayer and to the gross receipts from the other activities set forth in the American Jobs Creation Act of 2004.				
New Mexico	Yes	NA	NA	NA
New York	No, after 2007	No	NA	NA
North Carolina	Yes	NA	NA	NA
North Dakota	No	No	NA	NR
Ohio	Ohio does not impose a corporate income tax			
Note. Effective 1/1/2010, the Ohio Franchise Tax was fully phased out and business will be taxed on gross receipts through the Commercial Activity Tax. Details about that tax can be found at: http//tax.ohio.gov/divisions/commercial_activities/index.stm				
Oklahoma	NR	NR	NR	NR
Oregon	Yes	NR	NA	NR
If HB 2542 passes in its current form, then Oregon would not conform to the deduction, but would have an add-back provision for the amount deducted on the federal return. This is a specific exception to the general acceptance of the changes made by the *American Jobs Creation Act*.				
Pennsylvania	Yes	NA	NA	NA
Rhode Island	No	No	NA	NA
South Carolina	No	No	No	No
South Dakota	South Dakota does not impose a corporate income tax			
Tennessee	No	No	NA	No

Section 199 Domestic Production Activities Deduction

Legend:
SAF Same as applicable federal rules
NA Not applicable
NR Not reported

	Does State Conform to IRC Section 199 Domestic Production Activities Deduction?	*If "No," Does State Allow Taxpayers to Claim a Portion of the Federal Deduction?*	*If Taxpayers Are Allowed to Claim a Portion, What Is the Computation?*	*Is There a Form that Helps Taxpayers Compute the Deduction?*
Texas	No	No	NA	No
Utah	Yes	NA	NA	NA
Vermont	Yes	NA	NA	NA
Virginia	No, for taxable years beginning on and after 01/01/10, Virginia will allow two-thirds of the federal deduction. This is equivalent to allowing a deduction of 6% of the qualifying income as has been the practice in the last three taxable years (2007 through 2009).	No, for taxable years beginning on and after 01/01/10, Virginia will allow two-thirds of the federal deduction. This is equivalent to allowing a deduction of 6% of the qualifying income as has been the practice in the last three taxable years (2007 through 2009).	NA	No
Washington	Washington does not impose a corporate income tax			
West Virginia	No	No	For taxable years beginning on and after 1/1/10, Virginia will allow two-thirds of the federal deduction. This is equivalent to allowing a deduction of 6% of the qualifying income as has been the practice in the last three taxable years (2007 through 2009).	NR
Wisconsin	No	No		No
Wyoming	Wyoming does not impose a corporate income tax			

Interest from Federal Obligations

The federal government generally does not tax interest income derived from obligations of states or their political subdivisions. [IRC § 103] In contrast, the federal government generally taxes interest income derived from federal obligations, such as U.S. Treasury notes. [Treas. Reg. § 1.61-7(b)(3)] State taxation of interest income derived from federal obligations is governed by the intergovernmental immunity doctrine. Observing that "the power to tax involves the power to destroy" [*McCulloch v. Maryland* (1819)], Chief Justice John Marshall established the doctrine of federal immunity from state taxation. From *McCulloch* evolved the doctrine of intergovernmental immunity, which holds that the U.S. system of sovereign federal-state governments implicitly prohibits the federal government from taxing state governments, and state governments from taxing the federal government.

In 31 U.S.C. Section 3124, Congress codified this principle with respect to interest earned on federal obligations, as follows:

> (a) Stocks and obligations of the United States Government are exempt from taxation by a State or political subdivision of a State. The exemption applies to each form of taxation that would require the obligation, the interest on the obligation, or both, to be considered in computing a tax, except—
>
> (1) A nondiscriminatory franchise tax or another nonproperty tax instead of a franchise tax imposed on a corporation; and
>
> (2) An estate or inheritance tax.
>
> (b) The tax status of interest on obligations and dividends, earnings, or other income from evidences of ownership issued by the Government or an agency and the tax treatment of gain and loss from the disposition of those obligations and evidences of ownership is decided under the Internal Revenue Code. . . .

Under 31 U.S.C. § 3124, states that impose a direct corporate income tax must exempt interest earned on federal obligations from taxation. In contrast, states that impose a nondiscriminatory corporate franchise tax are not prohibited from taxing federal interest, even if the value of the franchise is measured by net income. A *franchise tax* is an excise tax on doing business or owning property within a state, whereas a direct income tax is a tax on the income derived from sources within a state's borders.

As required by 31 U.S.C. Section 3124, a franchise tax must be "nondiscriminatory" before the state can tax federal interest. A franchise tax is nondiscriminatory if the state taxes both federal interest and interest derived from the state's own obligations. In *Memphis Bank & Trust Co. v. Garner* [459 U.S. 392 (1983)], the U.S. Supreme Court held that a Tennessee tax that statutorily included interest on federal obligations but excluded interest on Tennessee obligations did not qualify as a nondiscriminatory franchise tax. In essence, the Court ruled that a state cannot exempt interest from in-state obligations while taxing interest from U.S. obligations. Instead, the state must either tax or exempt both types of interest.

States that exempt federal interest generally extend that exemption to dividends received from a registered investment company (i.e., mutual fund) to the extent the distribution is attributable to federal interest. In other words, interest earned by a mutual fund retains its tax-exempt character in the hands of the mutual fund shareholders.

A state that does not tax interest derived from debt obligations issued directly by the federal government (e.g., U.S. Treasury bills and notes) may nevertheless tax interest derived from debt obligations issued by quasi-public agencies, such as Ginnie Mae or Sallie Mae, even though the U.S. government guarantees the obligation. In *Rockford Life Insurance v. Illinois Department of Revenue* [482 U.S. 182 (1987)], the Supreme Court ruled that 31 U.S.C. Section 3124 did not prohibit states from taxing interest derived from Ginnie Mae bonds because the private institution in question (i.e., the Government National Mortgage Association, or Ginnie Mae) issued the debt and bore the primary obligation to repay the debt. In contrast, the federal government's role as guarantor makes the federal government's obligation secondary and contingent. As a consequence, the state tax treatment of "federal" interest also depends on the specific type of obligation involved. Examples include the following:

- U.S. Treasury bills and notes

- Federal Home Loan Bank System (FHLBS)
- Federal Farm Credit Bank System
- Federal National Mortgage Association (Fannie Mae)
- Government National Mortgage Association (Ginnie Mae)
- Student Loan Marketing Association (Sallie Mae)
- Federal Home Loan Mortgage Corporation (Freddie Mac)
- Federal Agricultural Mortgage Corporation (Farmer Mac)
- Dividends from mutual funds that invest solely in U.S. Treasury obligations
- Dividends from mutual funds to extent of income related to U.S. Treasury obligations

State-by-State Summary

The following chart, presented in two parts, provides a state-by-state summary of the taxation of the different types of federal interest.

Interest from Federal Obligations (Part 1)

Legend:

X	Interest and dividends from these federal obligations are included in income
FHLB	Federal Home Loan Board
Farmer Mac	Federal Agricultural Mortgage Corporation
SAF	Same as applicable federal rules
NA	Not applicable
NR	Not reported

	U.S. Treasury	*FHLB*	*Farmer Mac*	*Federal Farm Credit Bank*
Alabama			X	
Alaska			X	
Arizona				Not Allowed
Arkansas			X	
California	X	X	X	X
Colorado		X		
Connecticut	X	X	X	X
Delaware		X		X
District of Columbia		X	X	
Florida	X	X	X	X
Georgia			NR	
Hawaii	See TIR 84-1			X
Idaho				X
Illinois				X
Indiana				
Iowa			X	
Kansas				X
Kentucky				

Interest from Federal Obligations (Part 1)

Legend:

X	Interest and dividends from these federal obligations are included in income
FHLB	Federal Home Loan Board
Farmer Mac	Federal Agricultural Mortgage Corporation
SAF	Same as applicable federal rules
NA	Not applicable
NR	Not reported

	U.S. Treasury	*FHLB*	*Farmer Mac*	*Federal Farm Credit Bank*
Louisiana				
Maine				
Maryland				
Massachusetts	X	X	X	X
Michigan (Business Tax)				
Note. The CIT takes effect 01/01/12, and replaces the Michigan Business Tax (MBT) for most taxpayers. However, businesses that have been approved to receive, have received, or have been assigned certain certified credits may elect to file a return and pay the tax imposed by the MBT in lieu of the CIT until the certified credits are exhausted or extinguished.				
Minnesota	X	X	X	X
Mississippi				X
Missouri			X	
Montana	X	X		X
Nebraska				
Nevada	Nevada does not impose a corporate income tax			
New Hampshire				
New Jersey	X	X		X, NJAC 18:7-5.2(a)iv
New Mexico				X
New York	X	X		

Interest from Federal Obligations (Part 1)

Legend:

X	Interest and dividends from these federal obligations are included in income
FHLB	Federal Home Loan Board
Farmer Mac	Federal Agricultural Mortgage Corporation
SAF	Same as applicable federal rules
NA	Not applicable
NR	Not reported

	U.S. Treasury	*FHLB*	*Farmer Mac*	*Federal Farm Credit Bank*
North Carolina				X
North Dakota	X	X		
Ohio	Ohio does not impose a corporate income tax			
Note. Effective 1/1/2010, the Ohio Franchise Tax was fully phased out and business will be taxed on gross receipts through the Commercial Activity Tax. Details about that tax can be found at: http//tax.ohio.gov/divisions/commercial_activities/index.stm				
Oklahoma				
Oregon			X	
	Interest on federal obligations taxed under excise tax program, but not under income tax program			
Pennsylvania				X
Rhode Island				
South Carolina			X	
South Dakota	South Dakota does not impose a corporate income tax			
Tennessee	X	X		X
Texas				
Utah	X	X		X
Vermont				
Virginia			X	
Washington	Washington does not impose a corporate income tax			

Interest from Federal Obligations (Part 1)

Legend:

X	Interest and dividends from these federal obligations are included in income
FHLB	Federal Home Loan Board
Farmer Mac	Federal Agricultural Mortgage Corporation
SAF	Same as applicable federal rules
NA	Not applicable
NR	Not reported

	U.S. Treasury	*FHLB*	*Farmer Mac*	*Federal Farm Credit Bank*
West Virginia				
Wisconsin	X	X	X	X
	Included in the measure for franchise tax			
Wyoming	Wyoming does not impose a corporate income tax			

Interest from Federal Obligations (Part 2)

Legend:

X	Interest and dividends from these federal obligations are included in income
Freddie Mac	Federal Home Loan Mortgage Corporation
Fannie Mae	Federal National Mortgage Association
Ginnie Mae	Government National Mortgage Association
Sallie Mae	Student Loan Marketing Association
SAF	Same as applicable federal rules
NA	Not applicable
NR	Not reported

	Freddie Mac	*Fannie Mae*	*Ginnie Mae*	*Sallie Mae*	*Dividends from Mutual Funds That Invest Solely in U.S. Treasury Obligations*	*Dividends from Mutual Funds to Extent of Income Related to U.S. Treasury Obligations*
Alabama	X	X	X			
Alaska	X	X	X	X		
Arizona	X	X	X			
Arkansas	X	X	X			
California	X	X	X	X	X	X
Colorado		X	X		X	X
Connecticut	X	X	X	X	X	X
Delaware	NR	X	X	X		
District of Columbia	X	X	X	X	X	
Florida	X	X	X	X	X	X
Georgia	NR	X	X	NR		
Hawaii	See TIR 84-1					
Idaho	X	X	X			
Illinois	X	X	X	X		

Interest from Federal Obligations (Part 2)

Legend:

X	Interest and dividends from these federal obligations are included in income
Freddie Mac	Federal Home Loan Mortgage Corporation
Fannie Mae	Federal National Mortgage Association
Ginnie Mae	Government National Mortgage Association
Sallie Mae	Student Loan Marketing Association
SAF	Same as applicable federal rules
NA	Not applicable
NR	Not reported

	Freddie Mac	*Fannie Mae*	*Ginnie Mae*	*Sallie Mae*	*Dividends from Mutual Funds That Invest Solely in U.S. Treasury Obligations*	*Dividends from Mutual Funds to Extent of Income Related to U.S. Treasury Obligations*
Indiana	X	X	X		X	X
Iowa						
Kansas	X	X	X	X		
Kentucky	X	X	X	X		
Louisiana						
Maine		X	X	X	X	X
Maryland	X	X	X			Percentage of fund attributed to U.S. obligations is not taxed.
Massachusetts	X	X	X	X	X	
Michigan (Business Tax)	X	X	X			

Note. The CIT takes effect 01/01/12, and replaces the Michigan Business Tax (MBT) for most taxpayers. However, businesses that have been approved to receive, have received, or have been assigned certain certified credits may elect to file a return and pay the tax imposed by the MBT in lieu of the CIT until the certified credits are exhausted or extinguished.

Interest from Federal Obligations (Part 2)

Legend:

X	Interest and dividends from these federal obligations are included in income
Freddie Mac	Federal Home Loan Mortgage Corporation
Fannie Mae	Federal National Mortgage Association
Ginnie Mae	Government National Mortgage Association
Sallie Mae	Student Loan Marketing Association
SAF	Same as applicable federal rules
NA	Not applicable
NR	Not reported

	Freddie Mac	*Fannie Mae*	*Ginnie Mae*	*Sallie Mae*	*Dividends from Mutual Funds That Invest Solely in U.S. Treasury Obligations*	*Dividends from Mutual Funds to Extent of Income Related to U.S. Treasury Obligations*
Minnesota	X	X	X	X	X	X
Mississippi		X	X	X		
Missouri	X	X	X	X		
Montana	X	X	X	X	X	X
Nebraska		X	X			
Nevada	Nevada does not impose a corporate income tax					
New Hampshire	X	X	X		X	X
New Jersey	X	X	X	X	X	X
New Mexico		X	X	X		
New York	X	X	X	X	X	X
North Carolina	X	X	X		Yes, if supported by statement/ prospectus	Yes, if supported by statement/ prospectus
North Dakota	X				X	X
Ohio	Ohio does not impose a corporate income tax					

Interest from Federal Obligations (Part 2)

Legend:

X	Interest and dividends from these federal obligations are included in income
Freddie Mac	Federal Home Loan Mortgage Corporation
Fannie Mae	Federal National Mortgage Association
Ginnie Mae	Government National Mortgage Association
Sallie Mae	Student Loan Marketing Association
SAF	Same as applicable federal rules
NA	Not applicable
NR	Not reported

	Freddie Mac	*Fannie Mae*	*Ginnie Mae*	*Sallie Mae*	*Dividends from Mutual Funds That Invest Solely in U.S. Treasury Obligations*	*Dividends from Mutual Funds to Extent of Income Related to U.S. Treasury Obligations*
Note. Effective 1/1/2010, the Ohio Franchise Tax was fully phased out and business will be taxed on gross receipts through the Commercial Activity Tax. Details about that tax can be found at: http//tax.ohio.gov/divisions/commercial_activities/index.stm						
Oklahoma	X	X	X	X		X
Oregon	X	X	X			
	Interest on federal obligations taxed under excise tax program, but not under income tax program					
Pennsylvania		X	X	NR		
Rhode Island		X	X	X		
South Carolina	X	X	X			
South Dakota	South Dakota does not impose a corporate income tax					
Tennessee	X	X	X	X	X	X
Texas					X	X
Utah	X	X	X	X	X	X
Vermont			X	NR		

Interest from Federal Obligations (Part 2)

Legend:

X	Interest and dividends from these federal obligations are included in income
Freddie Mac	Federal Home Loan Mortgage Corporation
Fannie Mae	Federal National Mortgage Association
Ginnie Mae	Government National Mortgage Association
Sallie Mae	Student Loan Marketing Association
SAF	Same as applicable federal rules
NA	Not applicable
NR	Not reported

	Freddie Mac	*Fannie Mae*	*Ginnie Mae*	*Sallie Mae*	*Dividends from Mutual Funds That Invest Solely in U.S. Treasury Obligations*	*Dividends from Mutual Funds to Extent of Income Related to U.S. Treasury Obligations*
Virginia		X	X	X		No, unless the shareholder can substantiate the portion attributable to interest on extempt exempt obligations. See Tax Bulletin 82-3, published as PD No. 82-38
Washington	Washington does not impose a corporate income tax					
West Virginia						
Wisconsin	X	X	X	X	X	X
	Included in the measure for franchise tax					
Wyoming	Wyoming does not impose a corporate income tax					

Interest from Municipal Bonds

Federal Tax Treatment

Code Section 103 excludes interest income received from bonds issued by state and local governments (e.g., state agencies, counties, school districts, port authorities, etc.) from federal taxable income. The federal exemption for municipal interest does not apply, however, to interest paid on state and municipal bonds issued to finance certain private activities, as described in Sections 141 to 150. [IRC § 103(b)] No deduction is allowed for any expenses allocable to tax-exempt interest. [IRC § 265]

State Tax Treatment

Many states exempt interest paid on the state's own bonds, while taxing interest paid on bonds issued by other states. In such cases, an addition modification is required for interest income on bonds issued by other states. Because expenses related to such interest are not deductible in computing federal taxable income, some states permit taxpayers to reduce the amount of the addition modification by the amount of related expenses.

In *Kentucky Department of Revenue v. Davis* [553 US 328, 2008], the U.S. Supreme Court upheld the traditional state tax treatment of municipal bond interest under which a state exempts from its corporate and personal income taxes the interest on bonds issued by the state and its own localities, but not the interest on bonds issued by other states and their localities. The Court held that limiting the exemption to the interest on in-state bonds does not violate the Commerce Clause, because the exemption permissibly favors a traditional government function (issuing debt securities to pay for public projects), rather than favoring in-state private interests while disfavoring out-of-state private interests. Thus, this conduct does not represent the sort of "private protectionism" the Commerce Clause was designed to prevent. The Court also observed that the current tax treatment is critical to the operation of the municipal bond market.

The state tax treatment of gains realized on the disposition of municipal bonds may differ from the treatment of the interest income earned on those bonds [see the section in this part entitled Municipal Bonds: Treatment of Gain (Loss) and Premiums (Discounts)].

Recent Developments

Indiana. Effective for bonds acquired after December 31, 2011, Indiana no longer provides an exclusion for interest received from debt obligations issued by other states and their localities. However, bonds issued by Indiana or its localities will remain exempt. [H.B. 1004, May 10, 2011]

State-by-State Summary

The following chart provides a state-by-state summary of the taxation of the different types of municipal bond interest.

Interest from Municipal Bonds

Legend:

X	Interest and dividends from these federal obligations are included in income
FHLB	Federal Home Loan Board
Farmer Mac	Federal Agricultural Mortgage Corporation
SAF	Same as applicable federal rules
NA	Not applicable
NR	Not reported

	For Corporate Taxpayer: *Is Interest from Municipal and State Bonds Issued by the Home State Taxable?*	*For Corporate Taxpayer:* *Is Interest from Municipal and State Bonds Issued by Other States Taxable?*	*Must Municipal Bonds Be Registered to Be Tax Exempt?*
Alabama	No	Yes	Yes
Alaska	No	No	No
Arizona	No	Yes	No
Arkansas	No	Yes	Yes
California	Yes, franchise taxpayers (Chapter 2) only	Yes, franchise taxpayers (Chapter 2) only	No
Colorado	No	Yes	
Connecticut	Yes	Yes	
Delaware	No	Yes	NR
District of Columbia		Yes	NR
Florida	Yes	Yes	NA
Georgia	No	Yes	No
Hawaii	See TIR 84-1.	See TIR 84-1.	See TIR 84-1.
Idaho	No	Yes	Yes
Illinois	Yes, except for some specific exemptions in the statute	Yes	No
Indiana	No	Yes	Yes

Legend:

X	Interest and dividends from these federal obligations are included in income
FHLB	Federal Home Loan Board
Farmer Mac	Federal Agricultural Mortgage Corporation
SAF	Same as applicable federal rules
NA	Not applicable
NR	Not reported

Interest from Municipal Bonds

	For Corporate Taxpayer:		
	Is Interest from Municipal and State Bonds Issued by the Home State Taxable?	*Is Interest from Municipal and State Bonds Issued by Other States Taxable?*	*Must Municipal Bonds Be Registered to Be Tax Exempt?*
Iowa	Yes	Yes	NA
Kansas	No	Yes	Yes
Kentucky	No	Yes	Yes
Louisiana	No	Yes	No
Maine	No	Yes	Yes
Maryland	No	Yes	Yes
Massachusetts	Yes	No	Yes
Michigan (Business Tax)	No	Yes	NR

Note. The CIT takes effect 01/01/12, and replaces the Michigan Business Tax (MBT) for most taxpayers. However, businesses that have been approved to receive, have received, or have been assigned certain certified credits may elect to file a return and pay the tax imposed by the MBT in lieu of the CIT until the certified credits are exhausted or extinguished.

Minnesota	Yes	Yes	NR
Mississippi	No	Yes	No
Missouri	No	Yes	Yes
Montana	Yes	Yes	NR
Nebraska	No	Yes	NR

Interest from Municipal Bonds

Legend:

X	Interest and dividends from these federal obligations are included in income
FHLB	Federal Home Loan Board
Farmer Mac	Federal Agricultural Mortgage Corporation
SAF	Same as applicable federal rules
NA	Not applicable
NR	Not reported

	For Corporate Taxpayer:		
	Is Interest from Municipal and State Bonds Issued by the Home State Taxable?	*Is Interest from Municipal and State Bonds Issued by Other States Taxable?*	*Must Municipal Bonds Be Registered to Be Tax Exempt?*
Nevada	Nevada does not impose a corporate income tax		
New Hampshire	No	No	NR
New Jersey	Yes	Yes	NA, not exempt
New Mexico	No	Yes	Yes
New York	Yes	Yes	NA, not exempt
North Carolina	No	Yes	No
North Dakota	No	Yes	No
Ohio	Ohio does not impose a corporate income tax		
Note. Effective 1/1/2010, the Ohio Franchise Tax was fully phased out and business will be taxed on gross receipts through the Commercial Activity Tax. Details about that tax can be found at: http//tax.ohio.gov/divisions/commercial_activities/index.stm			
Oklahoma	Yes	Yes	Yes
Oregon	No	Yes	Yes
Pennsylvania	No	No	No
Rhode Island	No	Yes	NA
South Carolina		Yes	No
South Dakota	South Dakota does not impose a corporate income tax		

Interest from Municipal Bonds

Legend:

X	Interest and dividends from these federal obligations are included in income
FHLB	Federal Home Loan Board
Farmer Mac	Federal Agricultural Mortgage Corporation
SAF	Same as applicable federal rules
NA	Not applicable
NR	Not reported

	For Corporate Taxpayer:		
	Is Interest from Municipal and State Bonds Issued by the Home State Taxable?	*Is Interest from Municipal and State Bonds Issued by Other States Taxable?*	*Must Municipal Bonds Be Registered to Be Tax Exempt?*
Tennessee	Yes	Yes	NA
Texas	Interest exempt for federal income tax purposes is not included in total revenue in calculating margin.		
Utah	Yes	Yes	NA
Vermont	No	Yes	NR
Virginia	No	Yes	No
Washington	Washington does not impose a corporate income tax		
West Virginia	No	Yes	NR
Wisconsin	Yes	Yes	No
Wyoming	Wyoming does not impose a corporate income tax		

Municipal Bonds: Treatment of Gain (Loss) and Premiums (Discounts)

Generally, the taxation of bonds varies depending on whether the bond is tax exempt, issued at a discount, or issued at a premium. Discount on bonds is classified into two categories: 1) original issue discount and 2) market discount. Federal law requires that original issue discount be recognized currently using the effective yield method. Market discount may be recognized currently, or deferred and recognized upon disposition if elected; however, federal law allows holders of tax-exempt bonds purchased with market discount to amortize the discount currently, thereby increasing the basis of the bond. For federal tax purposes, the amortization of discount is treated as interest from a municipal bond and is therefore excluded from federal taxation. Premium on municipal bonds must be amortized with a corresponding decrease in the basis of the municipal bond.

Unlike interest income received from municipal bonds that is exempt from federal tax, upon disposition of the bond the difference between the proceeds and the adjusted basis of the bond is taxable. Although gain may be recognized, the federal requirement that tax-exempt bond premium must be amortized precludes any taxable loss for federal tax purposes on the maturity of a tax-exempt bond previously purchased at a premium.

The majority of states tax some or all state and municipal bond interest income that is exempt from federal taxation. In addition to the coupon portion of municipal bond interest, the interest income or expense generated from amortization of premium, original issue discount, and market discount by state tax authorities may or may not be taxable or deductible.

In *NACCO Industries, Inc. v. Tracy* [681 N.E.2d 900 (Ohio 1997), *cert. denied,* 118 S. Ct. 882 (1998)], the taxpayer challenged the constitutionality of Ohio corporate franchise tax provisions that taxed gains from dispositions of federal debt obligations, while exempting gains from dispositions of obligations issued by the State of Ohio. The Ohio Supreme Court found that, although 31 U.S.C. Section 3124(a) exempts interest on federal obligations from tax, it does not exempt gains from the sale of such obligations arising from the exchange of the obligations between two private parties. Similarly, the constitutional doctrine of intergovernmental immunity does not extend to the state taxation of gains with respect to a contract between two private parties.

Effective January 11, 2008, in computing Illinois taxable income, the add-back for exempt income derived from bonds is amended to provide that the amount exempted is the interest, net of bond premium amortization. [S.B. 783, Jan. 11, 2008]

State-by-State Summary

The following chart highlights each state's treatment of gain or loss from the disposition of a home state's or other state's municipal bond and indicates whether premium or discount on municipal bonds can (or must) be amortized.

Municipal Bonds: Treatment of Gain (Loss) and Premiums (Discounts)

Legend:

SAF	Same as applicable federal rules
NA	Not applicable
NR	Not reported

	For Corporate Taxpayers:		
	Is Gain (Loss) on Sale of Home State Municipal Bonds Taxed?	*Is Gain (Loss) on Sale of Other States' Municipal Bonds Taxed?*	*How is Premium (Discount) on Municipal Bonds Amortized?*
Alabama	SAF	SAF	SAF
Alaska	Yes	Yes	SAF
Arizona	Yes	Yes	SAF
Arkansas		Yes	SAF
California	Yes	Yes	Franchise taxpayers (Chapter 2) only.
Colorado	Yes	Yes	Yes
Connecticut	Yes	Yes	SAF
Delaware	No	No	NR
District of Columbia		Yes	Yes
Florida	Yes	Yes	SAF
Georgia	Yes	Yes	SAF
Hawaii	Yes	NR	NR
Idaho	Yes	Yes	Yes
Illinois	Yes	Yes	Yes
Indiana	No	No	No
Iowa	No	Yes	NR
Kansas	Yes	Yes	SAF
Kentucky	Yes	Yes	SAF

Municipal Bonds: Treatment of Gain (Loss) and Premiums (Discounts)

Legend:

SAF	Same as applicable federal rules
NA	Not applicable
NR	Not reported

	For Corporate Taxpayers:		
	Is Gain (Loss) on Sale of Home State Municipal Bonds Taxed?	*Is Gain (Loss) on Sale of Other States' Municipal Bonds Taxed?*	*How is Premium (Discount) on Municipal Bonds Amortized?*
Louisiana	Yes	Yes	No, Amortization not required
Maine	No	Yes	SAF
Maryland	No	Yes	SAF
Massachusetts	Yes		NR
Michigan (Business Tax)	Yes	Yes	SAF
Note. The CIT takes effect 01/01/12, and replaces the Michigan Business Tax (MBT) for most taxpayers. However, businesses that have been approved to receive, have received, or have been assigned certain certified credits may elect to file a return and pay the tax imposed by the MBT in lieu of the CIT until the certified credits are exhausted or extinguished.			
Minnesota	Yes	Yes	Yes, SAF
Mississippi	Yes	Yes	Yes
Missouri	Yes	Yes	SAF
Montana	Yes	Yes	No
Nebraska	Yes	Yes	SAF
Nevada	Nevada does not impose a corporate income tax		
New Hampshire	No	No	No
New Jersey	Yes	Yes	No
New Mexico	Yes	Yes	SAF
New York	Yes	Yes	SAF
North Carolina	Yes	Yes	Yes

Municipal Bonds: Treatment of Gain (Loss) and Premiums (Discounts)

Legend:

SAF	Same as applicable federal rules
NA	Not applicable
NR	Not reported

	For Corporate Taxpayers:		
	Is Gain (Loss) on Sale of Home State Municipal Bonds Taxed?	*Is Gain (Loss) on Sale of Other States' Municipal Bonds Taxed?*	*How is Premium (Discount) on Municipal Bonds Amortized?*
North Dakota	No	Yes	No
Ohio	Ohio does not impose a corporate income tax		
Note. Effective 1/1/2010, the Ohio Franchise Tax was fully phased out and business will be taxed on gross receipts through the Commercial Activity Tax. Details about that tax can be found at: http//tax.ohio.gov/divisions/commercial_activities/index.stm			
Oklahoma	Yes	Yes	No
Oregon	Yes	Yes	SAF
Pennsylvania	NR	Yes	SAF
Rhode Island	Yes	Yes	No
South Carolina	Yes	Yes	SAF
South Dakota	South Dakota does not impose a corporate income tax		
Tennessee	Yes	Yes	No
Texas			
Utah	Yes	Yes	SAF
Vermont	Yes	Yes	NR
Virginia	No	Yes	SAF
Washington	Washington does not impose a corporate income tax		
West Virginia	No	Yes	Yes
Wisconsin	Yes	Yes	SAF

Municipal Bonds: Treatment of Gain (Loss) and Premiums (Discounts)

Legend:
SAF Same as applicable federal rules
NA Not applicable
NR Not reported

	For Corporate Taxpayers:		
	Is Gain (Loss) on Sale of Home State Municipal Bonds Taxed?	*Is Gain (Loss) on Sale of Other States' Municipal Bonds Taxed?*	*How is Premium (Discount) on Municipal Bonds Amortized?*
Wyoming	Wyoming does not impose a corporate income tax		

Capital Gains and Losses

Internal Revenue Code (Code) Section 1221 defines a "capital asset" as property held by the taxpayer other than those assets which are specifically excluded. The principal exclusions are inventory; real or depreciable property used in a trade or business; a copyright, or a literary, musical, or artistic composition held by a taxpayer whose personal efforts created such property; accounts or notes receivable acquired in the ordinary course of a trade or business for services rendered or from the sale of property; and supplies of the type regularly consumed by the taxpayer in its trade or business.

A gain or loss from the disposition of a capital asset is classified as long-term if the taxpayer held the asset for more than one year, and short-term if the asset is held for one year or less. Code Section 1222 provides netting rules, and the taxpayer has a "net capital gain" for the year if the taxpayer's net long-term capital gains exceeds its net short-term capital losses.

Under Code Section 1(h), the maximum tax rate on an individual's net capital gain is 15 percent, except for net gains from collectibles and unrecaptured Section 1250 gains, for which the maximum tax rates are 28 percent and 25 percent, respectively. There is no preferential capital gain rate for corporate taxpayers.

Under Code Section 1211, a corporation may offset its capital losses only against its capital gains. In other words, a net capital loss is not deductible against ordinary income. Individuals are allowed a deduction against ordinary income equal to the lesser of the net capital loss for the year or $3,000. Code Section 1212 permits a corporation to carry a net capital loss back 3 years and forward 5 years, and offset it against capital gains in the carryover year. Individuals may not carry back a net capital loss, but may carry it forward indefinitely.

Code Sections 1231, 1245, and 1250 provide complex depreciation recapture provisions and netting rules, which apply to real or depreciable property used in a trade or business and held for more than one year. Under these rules, a gain on the disposition of such property may be treated as a long-term capital gain if the amount of the gain exceeds the recapture of the depreciation deductions taken with respect to the property, provided various other requirements are met.

The treatment of capital gains and losses for state tax purposes generally follows the federal approach. One difference is that many states restrict the use of capital loss carryforwards that arose in a tax year during which the taxpayer was not doing business in the state.

State-by-State Summary

The following chart, presented in two parts, summarizes how the states treat a corporation's capital gains and losses, as follows:

Part 1

- Preferential tax rate for capital gains
- Capital gains deduction or exclusion
- Holding period for long-term capital gains

Part 2

- Deductibility of a net capital loss
- Dollar limitation on a net capital loss deduction
- Carryover period for a nondeductible net capital loss

Capital Gains and Losses (Part 1)

Legend:

X	Indicates that there is a carryback and/or carryforward period
SAF	Same as applicable federal rules
NA	Not applicable
NR	Not reported

	For Corporations, Does State Allow		
	Preferential Tax Rate for Capital Gains?	*Capital Gains Deduction or Exclusion?*	*Holding Period for Long-Term Capital Gains*
Alabama	No	No	NR
Alaska	Yes, 4.5%	No	SAF
Arizona	No	No	SAF
Arkansas	No	No	NA
California	No	No	
Colorado	No	Yes	SAF, depends on TABOR excess status
Connecticut	No	Yes	5 years
Delaware	No	Yes	SAF
District of Columbia	No	No	SAF
Florida	No	No	NA
Georgia	No	No	SAF
Hawaii	Yes, 4%	No	SAF
Idaho	No	No	SAF
Illinois	No	No	NA
Indiana	No	No	NA
Iowa	No	No	SAF
Kansas	No	No	SAF

Capital Gains and Losses (Part 1)

Legend:

X	Indicates that there is a carryback and/or carryforward period
SAF	Same as applicable federal rules
NA	Not applicable
NR	Not reported

	For Corporations, Does State Allow		
	Preferential Tax Rate for Capital Gains?	*Capital Gains Deduction or Exclusion?*	*Holding Period for Long-Term Capital Gains*
Kentucky	No	NR	SAF
Louisiana	No	No	NA
Maine	No	No	NA
Maryland	No	No	SAF
Massachusetts	No	No	NR
Michigan (Business Tax)	No	SAF	SAF
Note. The CIT takes effect 01/01/12, and replaces the Michigan Business Tax (MBT) for most taxpayers. However, businesses that have been approved to receive, have received, or have been assigned certain certified credits may elect to file a return and pay the tax imposed by the MBT in lieu of the CIT until the certified credits are exhausted or extinguished.			
Minnesota	No	No	NA
Mississippi	No	No	SAF
Missouri	No	No	
Montana	No	No	SAF
Nebraska	No	No	SAF
Nevada	Nevada does not impose a corporate income tax		
New Hampshire	No	No	
New Jersey	No	No	SAF
New Mexico	No	No	NR

Capital Gains and Losses (Part 1)

Legend:

X	Indicates that there is a carryback and/or carryforward period
SAF	Same as applicable federal rules
NA	Not applicable
NR	Not reported

	For Corporations, Does State Allow		
	Preferential Tax Rate for Capital Gains?	*Capital Gains Deduction or Exclusion?*	*Holding Period for Long-Term Capital Gains*
New York	No	100% from subsidiaries only	SAF
North Carolina	No	No	SAF
North Dakota	No	No	SAF
Ohio	Ohio does not impose a corporate income tax		
Note. Effective 1/1/2010, the Ohio Franchise Tax was fully phased out and business will be taxed on gross receipts through the Commercial Activity Tax. Details about that tax can be found at: http//tax.ohio.gov/divisions/commercial_activities/index.stm			
Oklahoma	No	No	SAF
Oregon	No	No	NA
Pennsylvania	No	No	SAF
Rhode Island	No	No	SAF
South Carolina	No	No	SAF
South Dakota	South Dakota does not impose a corporate income tax		
Tennessee	No	No	NA
Texas	No	No	NA
Utah	No	No	NA, gains are not distinguished between short and long term or ordinary and capital
Vermont	No	NR	NR

Capital Gains and Losses (Part 1)

Legend:

X	Indicates that there is a carryback and/or carryforward period
SAF	Same as applicable federal rules
NA	Not applicable
NR	Not reported

	For Corporations, Does State Allow		
	Preferential Tax Rate for Capital Gains?	*Capital Gains Deduction or Exclusion?*	*Holding Period for Long-Term Capital Gains*
Virginia	No	Yes, limited to certain gains: effective for taxable years beginning on or after 01/01/11, any income taxable as a long-term capital gain for federal income tax purposes, or any income taxed as investment services partnership income for federal income tax purposes may be subtracted on the Virginia return if (1) the income is attributable to an investment that is made between 04/1/10 and 06/30/13, (2) the investment is made in a "qualified business" as defined in Va. Code § 58.1-339.4 or in another technology business approved by the Secretary of Technology, (3) the business has its principal office or facility in Virginia, and (4) the business has less than $3 million in annual revenues for the fiscal year preceding the investment.	SAF
Washington	Washington does not impose a corporate income tax		

Capital Gains and Losses (Part 1)

Legend:

X	Indicates that there is a carryback and/or carryforward period
SAF	Same as applicable federal rules
NA	Not applicable
NR	Not reported

	For Corporations, Does State Allow		
	Preferential Tax Rate for Capital Gains?	*Capital Gains Deduction or Exclusion?*	*Holding Period for Long-Term Capital Gains*
West Virginia	No	No	SAF
Wisconsin	No	No	SAF
Wyoming	Wyoming does not impose a corporate income tax		

Capital Gains and Losses (Part 2)

Legend:

X	Indicates that there is a carryback and/or carryforward period
SAF	Same as applicable federal rules
NA	Not applicable
NR	Not reported

	Are Net Capital Losses Currently Deductible?	*If Yes, Is There a Dollar Limitation on Capital Loss Deductions?*	*Carryover Period for Net Capital Losses*		*Is Carryforward Allowed for Net Loss from Year Taxpayer Did Not Have Nexus*
			Carrybacks	*Carryforwards*	
Alabama	No	SAF	SAF	SAF	SAF
Alaska	No	NA	SAF	SAF	No
Arizona	No	NA	SAF	SAF	
Arkansas	Yes, basis	No	None	None	No
California	No	NA	None	SAF	No
Colorado	SAF	SAF	SAF	SAF	No
Connecticut	No	NA	None	5 years	NR
Delaware	SAF	NR	SAF	SAF	
District of Columbia	Yes	SAF	SAF	SAF	No
Florida	No	NA	None	SAF	No
Georgia	No	Yes, SAF	SAF	SAF	No
Hawaii	No	NA	No	Yes	
Idaho	Yes	SAF	SAF	SAF	
Illinois	No, SAF	SAF	SAF	SAF	
Indiana	Yes	SAF, for Indiana losses	SAF	SAF	
Iowa	No	NR	3 years	5 years	

Capital Gains and Losses (Part 2)

Legend:

X	Indicates that there is a carryback and/or carryforward period
SAF	Same as applicable federal rules
NA	Not applicable
NR	Not reported

	Are Net Capital Losses Currently Deductible?	*If Yes, Is There a Dollar Limitation on Capital Loss Deductions?*	*Carryover Period for Net Capital Losses*		*Is Carryforward Allowed for Net Loss from Year Taxpayer Did Not Have Nexus*
			Carrybacks	*Carryforwards*	
Kansas	Yes	NR	SAF	SAF	X
Kentucky	No	NR	SAF	SAF	No
Louisiana	Yes	No	SAF	SAF	No
Maine	No	NA	NA	NA	Yes
Maryland	No	NA	None	SAF	
Massachusetts	Yes	NR	None	None	
Michigan (Business Tax)	Yes	SAF	SAF	SAF	
Note. The CIT takes effect 01/01/12, and replaces the Michigan Business Tax (MBT) for most taxpayers. However, businesses that have been approved to receive, have received, or have been assigned certain certified credits may elect to file a return and pay the tax imposed by the MBT in lieu of the CIT until the certified credits are exhausted or extinguished.					
Minnesota	NR	NR	15 years	SAF	No
Mississippi	No	SAF	3 years	5 years	
Missouri	Yes	NR	SAF	SAF	Yes
Montana	Yes	No	None	None	
Nebraska	No	NA	None	Yes, 5 years	No
Nevada	Nevada does not impose a corporate income tax				
New Hampshire	No	NA	SAF	SAF	

Capital Gains and Losses (Part 2)

Legend:

X	Indicates that there is a carryback and/or carryforward period
SAF	Same as applicable federal rules
NA	Not applicable
NR	Not reported

	Are Net Capital Losses Currently Deductible?	*If Yes, Is There a Dollar Limitation on Capital Loss Deductions?*	*Carryover Period for Net Capital Losses*		*Is Carryforward Allowed for Net Loss from Year Taxpayer Did Not Have Nexus*
			Carrybacks	*Carryforwards*	
New Jersey	No	NA	Yes	Yes	
New Mexico	Yes	NR	Yes, SAF	Yes, SAF	Yes
New York	SAF	NA	SAF	SAF	
North Carolina	Yes	NA	None	None	
North Dakota	No	NA	No	No	
Ohio	Ohio does not impose a corporate income tax				
Note. Effective 1/1/2010, the Ohio Franchise Tax was fully phased out and business will be taxed on gross receipts through the Commercial Activity Tax. Details about that tax can be found at: http//tax.ohio.gov/divisions/commercial_activities/index.stm					
Oklahoma	Yes	SAF	NR	NR	
Oregon	Yes	Yes, SAF	SAF	SAF	SAF
Pennsylvania	No	NA	NR	NR	
Rhode Island	Yes	NR	NR	NR	
South Carolina	Yes	SAF	None	SAF	
South Dakota	South Dakota does not impose a corporate income tax				
Tennessee	Yes	None	No	No	
Texas	No	NA	SAF	SAF	Yes
Utah	Yes	None	No	SAF	

Capital Gains and Losses (Part 2)

Legend:

X	Indicates that there is a carryback and/or carryforward period
SAF	Same as applicable federal rules
NA	Not applicable
NR	Not reported

			Carryover Period for Net Capital Losses		
	Are Net Capital Losses Currently Deductible?	*If Yes, Is There a Dollar Limitation on Capital Loss Deductions?*	*Carrybacks*	*Carryforwards*	*Is Carryforward Allowed for Net Loss from Year Taxpayer Did Not Have Nexus*
Vermont	SAF	SAF	Federal NOL is allowed	Federal NOL is allowed	
Virginia	No	NA	SAF	SAF	
Washington	Washington does not impose a corporate income tax				
West Virginia	Yes	NR	SAF, 3 years	SAF	
Wisconsin	No	SAF	SAF, 5 years	SAF	Yes
Wyoming	Wyoming does not impose a corporate income tax				

Nontaxable Exchanges

For federal tax purposes, the law recognizes that certain exchanges of property result in a change in the form but not the substance of the taxpayer's economic position. The new property received in the exchange may be viewed as substantially a continuation of the old investment. Therefore, the gain or loss is not permanently excluded but instead is deferred. The common threads providing for deferral in the applicable provisions are that the transaction does not change the taxpayer's economic position and that the taxpayer does not have the wherewithal to pay a tax.

Like-Kind Exchanges

Section 1031(a) of the Internal Revenue Code (Code) provides that no gain or loss is recognized on the exchange of property held for productive use in a trade or business or for investment if such property is exchanged solely for "property of a like kind" that is to be held either for productive use in a trade or business or for investment. Properties are of a like kind if they are of the same character or nature; however, the grade or quality of the properties need not be the same for them to qualify as like kind. Qualifying properties can be either trade or business properties or investment properties, and the taxpayer may switch from one category to the other. Nonqualifying properties include stock in trade (inventory) or other property held primarily for sale (subdivision of real estate); stocks, bonds, or notes; other securities or evidence of indebtedness or interest; and partnership interests.

The nonrecognition provisions still apply if a taxpayer gives cash in a transaction; however, if cash or other property is received, gain or loss may be recognized. For such purpose, consideration received in the form of an assumption of liabilities is generally treated as though the party assuming the liabilities gave cash to the other party to the transaction. The tax basis of the replacement like-kind property is generally the same as that of the property exchanged, decreased by the amount of any money received and increased by the amount of any gain recognized.

Property to be received in a like-kind exchange transaction must be identified within 45 days of the initial property transfer, and the exchange must be completed within 180 days of the initial property transfer—but not later than the due date (including extensions) of the taxpayer's return. Replacement property may be identified in one of three ways: 1) actual receipt of the replacement property within the 45-day identification period; 2) designation of the replacement property in an unambiguous fashion in a written document signed by the seller and sent to the other party; or 3) designation of the replacement property in an unambiguous fashion in a written exchange agreement signed by all parties.

Exchanges of property between related persons under Code Section 1031 will lose the benefit of the nonrecognition provisions if either the property received or the property transferred is disposed of within two years of the last transfer in the exchange. For purposes of Code Section 1031 related parties are the same as those defined in Code Section 267(b) or 707(b)(1). The two-year time period will not be applied to certain dispositions lacking in tax avoidance motive, arising from involuntary conversions, or arising after a taxpayer's death.

The majority of the states follow the federal like-kind exchange rules. Some states impose an additional limitation—the replacement property must be located in the state in order to qualify for nonrecognition.

Involuntary Conversions

A taxpayer suffering an involuntary conversion of property may postpone recognition of realized gains from the conversion under Code Section 1033. Involuntary conversion is defined as including destruction, theft, seizure, condemnation, or the threat or imminence of condemnation. Gain is recognized only to the extent that the amount realized exceeds the amount reinvested in replacement property.

If the taxpayer directly converts property into qualifying replacement property, nonrecognition of gain is mandatory. When a taxpayer receives money or other dissimilar property as payment in an involuntary conversion, nonrecognition of gain is elective. Code Section 1033 does not apply to losses. Any losses on involuntary conversions may be deductible under other provisions of the Code.

Qualifying replacement property must be "similar or related in service or use" to the original property. The replacement property must be purchased; property acquired through gift or nontaxable exchange does not qualify. The Section 1033 rules do not apply to the receipt of severance damages or special assessments, and such amounts may be recognized as taxable income unless they are used to restore the damaged property or to purchase qualifying replacement property. Involuntary conversion benefits are available only to the taxpayer that held the property that was involuntarily converted. The taxpayer has two years (three years for condemnations of real property) after the close of the taxable year in which any gain is realized from the involuntary conversion to replace the property.

The majority of the states follow the federal involuntary conversion rules. Some states impose an additional limitation—the replacement property must be located in the state in order to qualify for nonrecognition.

Recent Developments

Effective July 1, 2009, Minnesota enacted legislation requiring a qualified intermediary to file a return relating to transactions for which the intermediary acted to facilitate an exchange under Code Section 1031. The return must include the name, address, and state or federal tax identification number or Social Security number of each of the parties to the exchange, information relating to the property subject to the exchange, and any other information required by the commissioner. [H.B. 1298, May 16, 2009]

State-by-State Summary

The following chart indicates which states conform to the federal rules for like-kind exchanges and involuntary conversions, including the replacement periods. The chart also indicates whether both properties must be located within the state for the deferral to apply.

Nontaxable Exchanges

Legend:

X — Federal rules are followed for involuntary conversions
SAF — Same as applicable federal rules
NA — Not applicable

	Like-Kind Exchanges (IRC Section 1031)		*Involuntary Conversions (IRC Section 1033)*	
	Does State Follow Federal Rules?	*Both Properties Must Be Located in State for Deferral to Apply*	*Does State Follow Federal Rules?*	*Both Properties Must Be Located in State for Deferral to Apply*
Alabama	Yes	No	Yes	No
Alaska	Yes	No	Yes	No
Arizona	Yes	No	Yes	No
Arkansas	No	No	Yes	No
California	Yes	No	Yes	No
Colorado	Yes	Under review	Yes	Under review
Connecticut	No written guidance	No written guidance	No written guidance	No written guidance
Delaware	Yes	Yes	Yes	SAF
District of Columbia	Yes	No	Yes	No
Florida	Yes	SAF	Yes	SAF
Georgia	Yes	No	Yes	No
Hawaii	Yes	No	Yes	No
Idaho	Yes	No	Yes	No
Illinois	Yes	No	Yes	No
Indiana	Yes	No	Yes	No
Iowa	Yes	No	Yes	No
Kansas	Yes	No	Yes	No
Kentucky	Yes	No	Yes	No

Nontaxable Exchanges

Legend:

X — Federal rules are followed for involuntary conversions
SAF — Same as applicable federal rules
NA — Not applicable

	Like-Kind Exchanges (IRC Section 1031)		*Involuntary Conversions (IRC Section 1033)*	
	Does State Follow Federal Rules?	*Both Properties Must Be Located in State for Deferral to Apply*	*Does State Follow Federal Rules?*	*Both Properties Must Be Located in State for Deferral to Apply*
Louisiana	Yes	Yes	Yes	Yes
Maine	Yes	No	Yes	No
Maryland	Yes	NR	Yes	NR
Massachusetts	Yes	No	Yes	No
Michigan (Business Tax)	Yes	No	Yes	No
Note. The CIT takes effect 01/01/12, and replaces the Michigan Business Tax (MBT) for most taxpayers. However, businesses that have been approved to receive, have received, or have been assigned certain certified credits may elect to file a return and pay the tax imposed by the MBT in lieu of the CIT until the certified credits are exhausted or extinguished.				
Minnesota	Yes	No	Yes	No
Mississippi	Yes	Yes	Yes	Yes
Missouri	Yes	No	Yes	No
Montana	Yes	No	Yes	No
Nebraska	Yes	No	Yes	No
Nevada	Nevada does not impose a corporate income tax.			
New Hampshire	Yes	No	Yes	No
New Jersey	Yes	No	Yes	No
New Mexico	Yes	No	Yes	No
New York	Yes	No	Yes	No

Nontaxable Exchanges

Legend:
X — Federal rules are followed for involuntary conversions
SAF — Same as applicable federal rules
NA — Not applicable

	Like-Kind Exchanges (IRC Section 1031)		*Involuntary Conversions (IRC Section 1033)*	
	Does State Follow Federal Rules?	*Both Properties Must Be Located in State for Deferral to Apply*	*Does State Follow Federal Rules?*	*Both Properties Must Be Located in State for Deferral to Apply*
North Carolina	Yes	No	Yes	No
North Dakota	Yes	No	Yes	No
Ohio	Ohio does not impose a corporate income tax.			
Note. Effective 1/1/2010, the Ohio Franchise Tax was fully phased out and business will be taxed on gross receipts through the Commercial Activity Tax. Details about that tax can be found at: http//tax.ohio.gov/divisions/commercial_activities/index.stm				
Oklahoma	Yes	No	Yes	No
Oregon	Yes	No	Yes	No
Pennsylvania	Yes	No	Yes	No
Rhode Island	Yes	No	Yes	Yes
South Carolina	Yes	No	Yes	No
South Dakota	South Dakota does not impose a corporate income tax			
Tennessee	Yes	No	Yes	No
Texas	Yes	No	Yes	No
Utah	Yes	No	Yes	No
Vermont	Yes	No	Yes	No
Virginia	Yes	No	Yes	No
Washington	Washington does not impose a corporate income tax			
West Virginia	Yes	No	Yes	No

Nontaxable Exchanges

Legend:

X	Federal rules are followed for involuntary conversions
SAF	Same as applicable federal rules
NA	Not applicable

	Like-Kind Exchanges (IRC Section 1031)		*Involuntary Conversions (IRC Section 1033)*	
	Does State Follow Federal Rules?	*Both Properties Must Be Located in State for Deferral to Apply*	*Does State Follow Federal Rules?*	*Both Properties Must Be Located in State for Deferral to Apply*
Wisconsin	Yes	No	Yes	Property must not produce nonbusiness income and taxpayer must have nexus when property is replaced.
Wyoming	Wyoming does not impose a corporate income tax			

Passive Losses and Credits

Internal Revenue Code Section 469 was enacted as part of the Tax Reform Act of 1986. Under Section 469, certain types of taxpayers may not deduct a net loss from passive activities against either portfolio income or income from non-passive activities.

The passive activity limitations apply to individuals, estates, trusts, closely held C corporations, and personal service corporations. For purposes of the passive activity loss limitations and the at-risk rules, a closely held corporation is defined as a corporation in which more than 50 percent of the value of the outstanding stock was owned directly or indirectly by five or fewer individuals at any time during the last half of the taxable year and which is not a personal service corporation. A personal service corporation is any C corporation whose principal activity is the performance of personal services by the corporation's employee-owners. For such purpose, an employee-owner is defined as any employee who, on any day during the taxable year, owns any of the outstanding stock of the personal service corporation.

In general, there are two kinds of passive activities: trade or business activities in which the taxpayer does not materially participate and rental activities regardless of the taxpayer's participation. A taxpayer is considered to materially participate in an activity if the taxpayer is involved in the operations of the activity on a regular, continuous, and substantial basis. Various quantitative and qualitative tests have been developed by Treasury regulations to determine whether an activity is a passive activity. For a closely held C corporation that is a personal service corporation, material participation in an activity requires that at least one shareholder holding in excess of 50 percent of the value of the outstanding stock materially participate in such activity. In the case of a closely held C corporation other than a personal service corporation, the qualified-business requirements, as defined in Code Section 465(c)(7)(C), must be satisfied.

Investment interest expense of the taxpayer must be allocated between the taxpayer's passive and active investments. The portion allocated to passive activities is netted against the taxpayer's passive income to determine net passive income.

Taxpayers may deduct passive losses to the extent of net passive income. Passive losses in excess of the taxpayer's passive income are suspended. The suspended passive losses are carried forward indefinitely to offset future passive income. In addition, any suspended losses are available in the year a passive activity is sold or otherwise disposed of. In the year of disposition, the suspended loss is used first to reduce any net income or gain from passive activities for the tax year. Any remaining loss may be deducted against nonpassive income; however, such loss recognition may be limited under the capital loss limitation rules.

Tax credits from all passive activities for a taxable year that are in excess of the tax liability for passive activities are suspended and carried forward to offset the tax liability from passive activities in future years; however, unlike suspended losses, suspended credits are not allowed upon the disposition of a taxpayer's interest in a passive activity.

State-by-State Summary

The following chart summarizes the states' application of the passive activity limitations, including the corporate entities affected by the limitations, and any limitations on the carryforward period for the suspended losses and credits.

Passive Losses and Credits

Legend:

SAF	Same as applicable federal rules
NA	Not applicable
NR	Not reported

	For Corporations, Does State Conform to IRC Section 469 Limitations on:		*Corporations Subject to Limitations on Passive Losses and Credits*		
	Passive Losses?	*Passive Credits?*	*Closely Held C Corporations*	*Personal Service Corporations*	*Can Disallowed Losses and Credits Be Carried Forward?*
Alabama	Yes	Yes	SAF	SAF	No
Alaska	Yes	Yes	SAF	SAF	SAF
Arizona	SAF	SAF	NR	NR	SAF
Arkansas	Yes	Yes	NR	NR	SAF
California	Yes	Yes	NR	SAF	SAF
Colorado	Yes	Yes	SAF	SAF	Yes
Connecticut	No written guidance	No written guidance	No written guidance	No written guidance	No written guidance
Delaware	SAF	SAF	SAF	SAF	NR
District of Columbia	Yes	No	SAF	SAF	NR
Florida	Yes	Yes	SAF	SAF	SAF
Georgia	Yes	NR	NR	SAF	SAF
Hawaii	SAF	NR	NR	NR	NR
Idaho	SAF	No	SAF	SAF	SAF
Illinois	SAF	No	SAF	SAF	SAF
Indiana	SAF, but loss must be attributable to Indiana	SAF	SAF	SAF	SAF
Iowa	NR	SAF	SAF	SAF	SAF
Kansas	Yes	No	SAF	SAF	SAF

Passive Losses and Credits

Legend:

SAF	Same as applicable federal rules
NA	Not applicable
NR	Not reported

	For Corporations, Does State Conform to IRC Section 469 Limitations on:		*Corporations Subject to Limitations on Passive Losses and Credits*		
	Passive Losses?	*Passive Credits?*	*Closely Held C Corporations*	*Personal Service Corporations*	*Can Disallowed Losses and Credits Be Carried Forward?*
Kentucky	Yes	Yes	SAF	SAF	SAF
Louisiana	No	Yes	SAF	SAF	SAF
Maine	Yes	Yes	SAF	SAF	Yes
Maryland	SAF	Maryland does not recognize federal credits	SAF, passive losses only	SAF	SAF, losses only
Massachusetts	Yes	Yes	All corporations	All corporations	SAF
Michigan (Business Tax)	Yes	Yes	SAF	SAF	SAF
Note. The CIT takes effect 01/01/12, and replaces the Michigan Business Tax (MBT) for most taxpayers. However, businesses that have been approved to receive, have received, or have been assigned certain certified credits may elect to file a return and pay the tax imposed by the MBT in lieu of the CIT until the certified credits are exhausted or extinguished.					
Minnesota	Yes	No	SAF	SAF	Yes
Mississippi	SAF	Yes			SAF
Missouri	Yes	Yes	SAF	SAF	SAF
Montana	No	No			SAF
Nebraska	SAF	No	NR	NR	SAF
Nevada	Nevada does not impose a corporate income tax.				
New Hampshire	SAF	SAF	SAF	SAF	SAF
New Jersey	SAF	NR			NR
New Mexico	SAF	SAF			SAF

Passive Losses and Credits

Legend:
SAF Same as applicable federal rules
NA Not applicable
NR Not reported

	For Corporations, Does State Conform to IRC Section 469 Limitations on:		*Corporations Subject to Limitations on Passive Losses and Credits*		
	Passive Losses?	*Passive Credits?*	*Closely Held C Corporations*	*Personal Service Corporations*	*Can Disallowed Losses and Credits Be Carried Forward?*
New York	SAF	NA	SAF	SAF	SAF
North Carolina	SAF	NA	SAF	SAF	No
North Dakota	SAF	SAF			SAF
Ohio	Ohio does not impose a corporate income tax				
Note. Effective 1/1/2010, the Ohio Franchise Tax was fully phased out and business will be taxed on gross receipts through the Commercial Activity Tax. Details about that tax can be found at: http//tax.ohio.gov/divisions/commercial_activities/index.stm					
Oklahoma	SAF	SAF	SAF	SAF	No
Oregon	Yes	Yes	SAF	SAF	NA
Pennsylvania	SAF	No	SAF	SAF	SAF
Rhode Island	SAF	SAF	NR	NR	
South Carolina	Yes	Yes			Yes
South Dakota	South Dakota does not impose a corporate income tax				
Tennessee	SAF	NA	NR	NR	NR
Texas	SAF	No credit is allowed	SAF	SAF	SAF for losses, federal credits not allowed
Utah	SAF	SAF	SAF	SAF	SAF
Vermont	SAF	NR	NR	NR	NR
Virginia	SAF	SAF	SAF	SAF	SAF

Passive Losses and Credits

Legend:

SAF — Same as applicable federal rules
NA — Not applicable
NR — Not reported

	For Corporations, Does State Conform to IRC Section 469 Limitations on:		*Corporations Subject to Limitations on Passive Losses and Credits*		
	Passive Losses?	*Passive Credits?*	*Closely Held C Corporations*	*Personal Service Corporations*	*Can Disallowed Losses and Credits Be Carried Forward?*
Washington	Washington does not impose a corporate income tax				
West Virginia	SAF	SAF	SAF	SAF	SAF
Wisconsin	Yes	No	SAF	SAF	Yes
Wyoming	Wyoming does not impose a corporate income tax				

Depletion

Taxpayers are not permitted to deduct the full purchase price of a capital asset in the year of acquisition. Instead, the Internal Revenue Code (Code) typically allows a ratable deduction over a number of years to reflect use or consumption. That consumption or depreciation expense is a reasonable allowance for the physical exhaustion of, and wear and tear on, property used in the trade or business and includes a reasonable allowance for obsolescence.

Similarly, natural resources cannot be fully expensed in the year of acquisition; the cost of such assets is subject to a depletion deduction. Federal law provides two methods of calculating the depletion deduction: cost depletion and percentage depletion. The choice between the two is made annually; therefore, for each taxable year, the depletion deduction should be calculated using both methods, and the method that results in the largest deduction generally should be selected.

Cost Depletion. Cost depletion is the basic method of computing depletion. The first step in the calculation of cost depletion is to estimate the number of units (e.g., tons or barrels) of the natural resource acquired. Next, the adjusted basis of the asset is divided by the estimated number of units to arrive at a dollar value of depletion per unit. The dollar value of depletion per unit is then multiplied by the number of units extracted or used to arrive at the depletion allowed for a given year. If it is later discovered that the number of remaining recoverable units is materially greater or less than the number remaining from the prior estimate, a new dollar value of depletion per unit must be calculated; however, the amount of depletion taken cannot exceed the adjusted basis of the asset. Cost depletion is similar to unit-of-production depreciation in that it represents the amortization of the cost of a property over its productive life on the basis of units produced.

Percentage Depletion. Percentage depletion is the method of computing depletion for mines, wells, and other natural resource deposits listed in Code Section 613(b); it uses specified percentage factors provided in the Code. The percentage depletion factor varies according to the type of mineral interest (e.g., 5 percent for gravel, 15 percent for gold and silver). Percentage depletion is calculated by multiplying the gross income from the property by the depletion percentage appropriate for a specific mineral; however, in a given year the amount of percentage depletion may not be greater than 50 percent (100 percent in the case of oil and gas properties) of the taxable income from the property before the allowance for depletion.

Percentage depletion is based on gross income from the property, rather than on the cost of the asset. Accordingly, depletion under the percentage method may exceed the cost of the asset; however, if percentage depletion is used, the adjusted basis of the property must be reduced by the amount of depletion taken until the basis of the property reaches zero.

State-by-State Summary

The following chart indicates which states allow use of the cost depletion method, the percentage depletion method, or some other method of depletion, and whether the same methods are allowed for in-state and out-of-state property.

Depletion

Legend:
SAF Same as applicable federal rules
NA Not applicable
NR Not reported

	Does State Conform to IRC Sections 611-613 Rules for Computing Depletion on:					
	In-State Property?			*Out-of-State Property?*		
	Cost Depletion	*Percentage Depletion*	*Other Method*	*Cost Depletion*	*Percentage Depletion*	*Other Method*
Alabama	X	X		X	X	
Alaska	X, oil and gas companies restricted to cost depletion only	X, however not for oil and gas companies	X	X, oil and gas companies restricted to cost depletion only	X, however not for oil and gas companies	X
Arizona	SAF	SAF	SAF	SAF	SAF	SAF
Arkansas	X	X		X	X	
California	X	X		X	X	
Colorado	X	X	No	X	X	No
Connecticut	No written guidance	No written guidance		No written guidance	No written guidance	
Delaware	X			X		
District of Columbia	X	X		X	X	
Florida	X	X		X	X	
Georgia	X	X	X	X	X	SAF
Hawaii	X	X		X	X	
Idaho	SAF	SAF		SAF	SAF	
Illinois	SAF	SAF	SAF	SAF	SAF	SAF
Indiana	SAF	SAF		SAF	SAF	
Iowa	X			X		

Depletion

Legend:

SAF	Same as applicable federal rules
NA	Not applicable
NR	Not reported

	Does State Conform to IRC Sections 611-613 Rules for Computing Depletion on:					
	In-State Property?			*Out-of-State Property?*		
	Cost Depletion	*Percentage Depletion*	*Other Method*	*Cost Depletion*	*Percentage Depletion*	*Other Method*
Kansas	X	X	No	X	X	No
Kentucky	X	X		X	X	
Louisiana	X	X		X	X	
Maine	X	X	No	X	X	No
Maryland	SAF	X, oil percentage depletion is not an allowable deduction.		SAF	X, oil percentage depletion is not an allowable deduction.	
Massachusetts	X		All allowable federal methods			SAF
Michigan (Business Tax)	X	X		X	X	
Note. The CIT takes effect 01/01/12, and replaces the Michigan Business Tax (MBT) for most taxpayers. However, businesses that have been approved to receive, have received, or have been assigned certain certified credits may elect to file a return and pay the tax imposed by the MBT in lieu of the CIT until the certified credits are exhausted or extinguished.						
Minnesota			X, reasonable allowance based on cost			X, reasonable allowance based on cost
Mississippi	X	X, total taken cannot exceed cost basis.		X	X, total taken cannot exceed cost basis.	
Missouri	X	X		X	X	
Montana	X	X		X	X	

Depletion

Legend:

SAF Same as applicable federal rules
NA Not applicable
NR Not reported

	Does State Conform to IRC Sections 611-613 Rules for Computing Depletion on:					
	In-State Property?			*Out-of-State Property?*		
	Cost Depletion	*Percentage Depletion*	*Other Method*	*Cost Depletion*	*Percentage Depletion*	*Other Method*
Nebraska	X	X		X	X	
Nevada	Nevada does not impose a corporate income tax					
New Hampshire	X	X		X	X	
New Jersey	X	X		X	X	
New Mexico	X	X		X	X	
New York	X	X		X	X	
North Carolina	X	X		X		
North Dakota	X	X		X	X	
Ohio	Ohio does not impose a corporate income tax					
Note. Effective 1/1/2010, the Ohio Franchise Tax was fully phased out and business will be taxed on gross receipts through the Commercial Activity Tax. Details about that tax can be found at: http//tax.ohio.gov/divisions/commercial_activities/index.stm						
Oklahoma	X	X		NA	NA	NA
Oregon	X	X		X	X	
Pennsylvania	SAF	SAF	SAF	SAF	SAF	SAF
Rhode Island	NR	NR	NR	NR	NR	NR
South Carolina	X	X	No	X	X	No
South Dakota	South Dakota does not impose a corporate income tax					
Tennessee	X			X		

Depletion

Legend:

SAF	Same as applicable federal rules
NA	Not applicable
NR	Not reported

	Does State Conform to IRC Sections 611-613 Rules for Computing Depletion on:					
	In-State Property?			*Out-of-State Property?*		
	Cost Depletion	*Percentage Depletion*	*Other Method*	*Cost Depletion*	*Percentage Depletion*	*Other Method*
Texas	A taxable entity that elects to subtract cost of goods sold in computing margin may include in cost of goods sold depletion reported on the federal income tax return, to the extent associated with and necessary for the production of goods.					
Utah	X	X	No	X	X	No
Vermont	SAF	SAF		SAF	SAF	
Virginia	X	X		X	X	SAF
Washington	Washington does not impose a corporate income tax					
West Virginia	SAF	SAF		SAF	SAF	
Wisconsin	X			X		No
Wyoming	Wyoming does not impose a corporate income tax					

Section 338 Elections

Federal Tax Treatment

Background. The acquisition by one corporation (acquirer) of the business operations of another corporation (target) can be accomplished through the purchase of either the target corporation's assets or the target corporation's stock. If the acquisition is structured as an asset purchase, the target recognizes gain or loss on the sale of its assets, and the acquirer takes a basis in the assets equal to the purchase price (i.e., market value). In other words, the basis of the acquired assets gets stepped-up or stepped-down to market value. On the other hand, the acquirer does not inherit the net operating loss (NOL) carryforwards, earnings and profits, and other tax attributes of the target corporation. These tax attributes remain with the target, which may use any of its NOL carryforwards to offset the gains from the asset sale.

If the acquisition is structured as a stock purchase, once the acquirer obtains a controlling interest in the stock of the target corporation, the acquirer may either continue to operate the target as a separate subsidiary or liquidate the target to obtain direct control of the target's assets. In a stock purchase where the acquirer then continues to operate the target as a separate subsidiary, only the target shareholders recognize gain or loss. Neither the acquirer nor the target recognize any gain or loss on the acquisition, there is no change in the basis of the target's assets, and the target's NOL carryforwards and other tax attributes remain with the target. If the acquirer liquidates the target, the subsidiary liquidation is generally tax-free to both the acquirer and target under Internal Revenue Code (Code) Sections 332 and 337, the target's basis in its assets carries over to the acquirer (i.e., there is no step-up or step-down to market value), and the target's tax attributes carry over to the acquirer.

A corporation making a qualifying stock purchase also has the option to make an Section 338 election. If the acquirer makes a Section 338 election, the purchase of a controlling interest in the target's stock is treated as if it were an asset purchase, which means the target recognizes gain or loss on the fictional asset sale, and the acquirer takes a basis in the target's assets equal to the purchase price of the stock plus the liabilities assumed (i.e., market value). Section 338 reflects the judicial principle that the purchase of a target corporation's stock in order to obtain the target's assets should be treated as a single transaction involving the acquirer's acquisition of the target's assets (see, e.g., *Kimbell-Diamond Milling Co. v. Commissioner*, 187 F.2d 718 [CA-5, 1951]). In 1954, Congress codified this principle by enacting Section 334(b)(2), which in 1982 was replaced by Section 338.

Section 338(g) Election. Under Section 338(g), a corporation that makes a qualifying stock purchase may elect to have the target corporation treated as if both of the following has occurred: (1) on the stock acquisition date, the target sells all of its assets at fair market value in a single transaction, and (2) on the day after the stock acquisition date, the target is a new corporation that purchases all of the old target's assets. Note that the acquirer acts alone in making a Section 338(g) election and the election has no effect on the seller of the target corporation stock.

The acquirer is eligible to make a Section 338(g) election if, within a 12-month acquisition period, the acquirer obtains by purchase at least 80 percent of both the total voting power and total value of the stock of the target corporation. Stock acquired from a related party or stock acquired in a tax-free transaction (e.g., a Section 351 transaction) is not taken into account in applying the 80 percent ownership test. The acquirer must make a Section 338(g) election no later than the fifteenth day of the ninth month beginning after the month in which the acquisition date occurs. The acquisition date is the first day during the 12-month acquisition period on which the 80 percent stock ownership requirement is satisfied. The election is made on federal Form 8023, *Elections Under Section 338 for Corporations Making Qualified Stock Purchases.*

In effect, a Section 338(g) election results in a hypothetical asset sale by the target corporation ("old target") to a new corporation ("new target"). The old target must recognize gains and losses on the hypothetical asset sale, after which the old target no longer exists for federal income tax purposes and its tax attributes do not carry over to the new target, but instead expire. Thus, a Section 338 election triggers immediate gain recognition with respect to the target corporation's appreciated assets. The target's gains on the deemed asset sale are in addition to any gain recognized by the target's shareholders on the actual sale of the target's stock. For this reason, it is generally not beneficial to make a Section 338(g) election unless the target corporation has NOL carryforwards that can be used to offset the gains triggered by the deemed asset sale.

Any gain or loss resulting from the deemed asset sale is included in the final tax return of the old target. That final return covers old target's final tax year, which ends at the close of the stock acquisition date. When old target is a member of an affiliated group filing a consolidated return, absent a Section 338(h)(10) election (which is discussed in the next section), the old target is disaffiliated from that group immediately before its deemed sale of assets under Section 338(g) and must file a final return on a separate company basis that includes only the gain or loss from the deemed asset sale and certain carryforward items (Treas. Reg. § 1.338-10(a)(2)). The separate final return is referred to as a "one-day return."

The new target is considered to be a newly formed corporation for federal income tax purposes, and the basis of the assets acquired from old target gets stepped-up or stepped-down to market value. The acquirer may, but need not, liquidate the new target corporation. If the new target is liquidated, the new target's stepped-up or stepped-down basis in its assets carries over to the acquiring corporation.

The price at which the old target is deemed to have sold all of its assets to the new target is referred to as the "aggregate deemed sales price" (Treas. Reg. § 1.338-4), whereas the price at which the new target is deemed to have paid to purchase the old target's assets is referred to as the "adjusted grossed-up basis" (Treas. Reg. § 1.338-5). Both amounts are determined by reference to the acquiring corporation's basis in the target's stock and the liabilities of old target. To compute its gains and losses, old target allocates the deemed sales price among its assets under rules substantially similar to those applicable to purchase price allocations under Section 1060, which generally requires the use of the residual method to allocate the purchase price of applicable asset acquisitions among the individual assets purchased. The new target applies the same allocation principles to allocate the deemed sales price among the assets it acquired (Treas. Reg. § 1.338-6). Under these principles, the deemed sales price is allocated among seven asset classes in priority order, starting with Class I assets (cash and cash equivalents), then Class II assets, then Class III assets, and so on, with any residual amount allocated to Class VII assets (goodwill and going concern value). The amount allocated to a specific asset, other than the Class VII assets, cannot exceed the asset's fair market value. To report the basis allocation, both old target and new target must attach to their respective federal tax returns Form 8883 (Asset Allocation Statement Under Section 338).

Section 338(h)(10) Election. Section 338(h)(10) provides a special election that is available when one corporation is purchasing the stock of another corporation that is either a member of an affiliated group of corporations or an S corporation. As with a Section 338(g) election, a Section 338(h)(10) election triggers a deemed sale of the target corporation's assets that results in both gain or loss recognition and a step-up or step-down in the basis of the target's assets. In contrast to a Section 338(g) election, however, the gain or loss on the actual sale of target's stock is ignored. Therefore, a Section 338(h)(10) election results in a single level of taxation, rather than the two levels of taxation associated with a Section 338(g) election. For this reason, Section 338(h)(10) elections are more popular than Section 338(g) elections.

A Section 338(h)(10) election may be made if the target corporation is a member of an affiliated group of corporations, regardless of whether the group members are filing a consolidated return or separate returns. If a Section 338(h)(10) election is made, the stock sale is treated as an asset sale by the old target to the new target, followed by the complete liquidation of the new target. In addition, any gain or loss recognized on the stock sale is ignored.

The first part of the fiction created by a Section 338(h)(10) election is that the old target is deemed to have sold all of its assets to the new target in a single transaction. If old target was a member of an affiliated group filing a consolidated return (i.e., a "selling consolidated group"), the asset sale is deemed to occur before the close of the acquisition date while old target is still a member of the selling consolidated group, and therefore the gain or loss is included in the selling consolidated group's federal consolidated return (Treas. Reg. § 1.338(h)(10)-1(d)(3)). If the old target was a member of a affiliated group filing separate returns, the gain or loss is included in old target's separately filed final tax return.

The basis of the assets that new target is deemed to have purchased from old target gets stepped-up or stepped-down to market value.

The second part of the fiction created by a Section 338(h)(10) election is the deemed liquidation of the old target. After the deemed asset sale but before the close of the acquisition date, and while the old target is a member of the selling consolidated group (or owned by the selling affiliate), the old target is treated as having distributed the sales proceeds to the selling consolidated group or the selling affiliate as part of a complete liquidation to which Section 332 (tax-free liquidation of subsidiary) applies, and the tax attributes of the old target carry over to the selling consolidated group or selling affiliate under Section 381 (Treas. Reg. § 1.338(h)(10)-1(d)(4)).

A Section 338(h)(10) election also may be made by S corporation shareholders when the stock of the S corporation is purchased by another corporation. The gain or loss from the deemed asset sale is included in old target's separately filed final tax return. The target's S corporation status continues in effect through the close of the acquisition date. Therefore, the S corporation shareholders take their pro rata share of the deemed sale tax consequences into account under Section 1366, and increase or decrease their basis in the target corporation's stock under Section 1367 (Treas. Reg. § 1.338(h)(10)-1(d)(5)). After the deemed asset sale but before the close of the acquisition date, the old target is treated as having transferred all of its assets to the S corporation shareholders as part of a complete liquidation to which Section 331 (taxable exchange of S corporation stock) applies.

Note that unlike a Section 338(g) election, where any gains from the deemed asset sale are taxed to the stock purchaser, a Section 338(h)(10) election causes the stock seller to report and pay the tax on any gains from the deemed asset sale. As a consequence, a Section 338(h)(10) election must be made jointly on Form 8023 by both the seller and the purchaser (Treas. Reg. § 1.338(h)(10)-1(c)(3)).

State Tax Treatment

States generally conform to the federal income tax treatment of an election made under Section 338(g). See, for example, California Franchise Tax Board Legal Ruling 2006-03 [May 5, 2006]. Accordingly, for state income tax purposes, the selling corporation recognizes gain or loss on the stock sale, and the target's deemed asset sale results in both gain or loss recognition and a step-up or step-down in the basis of the target's assets.

Most states also conform to the federal treatment of a Section 338(h)(10) election. As a consequence, for state income tax purposes, a Section 338(h)(10) election causes a deemed sale of the target corporation's assets that results in both gain or loss recognition and a step-up or step-down in the basis of the target's assets, whereas the seller's gain or loss on the actual sale of the target's stock is ignored.

Inclusion of Gain from Deemed Asset Sale in Apportionable Income. States generally treat the gains and losses resulting from a deemed asset sale under Section 338 as apportionable business income. However, courts in some states have ruled that such gains are specifically allocable nonbusiness income.

In *Canteen Corp. v. Commonwealth of Pennsylvania* [854 A.2d 440 (Pa. Sup. Ct., 2004)], the Pennsylvania Supreme Court ruled that the gains triggered by a Section 338(h)(10) election were nonbusiness income, because the transaction met neither the transactional test nor the functional test for treatment as "business income." Referring to the standards established in *Laurel Pipe Line Comp. v. Board of Finance and Revenue* [642 A.2d 472 (Pa. Sup. Ct. 1994)], the court noted that the transactional test was not met, because the "fictional liquidation" of assets stemming from the parent corporation's Section 338 election is not a type of transaction in which the taxpayer regularly engages. The functional test also was not met because, as in *Laurel Pipe*, the taxpayer liquidated and distributed the proceeds to its shareholders. In 2001, the Pennsylvania legislature broadened the definition of business income to include "all income which is apportionable under the Constitution of the United States." In Corporate Tax Statement of Policy 2004-01 [Nov. 9, 2004], the Pennsylvania Department of Revenue announced that due to the statutory amendments to the definition of "business income" that were enacted in 2001, the ruling in *Canteen* does not apply to tax years beginning after 1998, and the taxable income generated as a result of a Section 338 election will be treated as business income.

In *ABB C-E Nuclear Power, Inc. v. Director of Revenue* [No. SC87811 (Mo. Sup. Ct., Jan. 30, 2007)], the Missouri Supreme Court ruled that a $227 million gain from the sale and liquidation of a subsidiary in a Section 338(h)(10) transaction was nonbusiness income that was not apportionable to Missouri. The court concluded that the sale and liquidation was not a type of business transaction in which the subsidiary regularly engaged, nor was it a disposition of the sort that constituted an integral part of the subsidiary's ordinary business. Therefore, the transaction was a one-time, extraordinary event that did not generate business income under either the transactional test or the functional test.

In *American States Insurance Co. v. Illinois Department of Revenue* [No. 1-03-1646 (Ill. App. Ct., Aug. 27, 2004)]; *appeal denied*, No. 99589 [Ill. Jan. 26, 2005]), the Illinois Appellate Court ruled that the gains arising from a Section 338(h)(10) election made in 1997 were nonbusiness income, because the gains were related to the complete liquidation and cessation of business operations, and therefore, the functional test was not met. In *Nicor v. Illinois Department of Revenue* [No. 1-07-1359 & 1-07-1591 (Ill. App. Ct., Dec. 5, 2008)], the Illinois appellate court ruled that a Section 338(h)(10) election made in 1993 gave rise to nonbusiness income. Relying on the earlier ruling in *American States Insurance*, the appellate court held that the taxpayer's sale must be treated as a complete liquidation and cessation of business resulting in nonbusiness income. The court also noted that in 2004, the Illinois Legislature broadened its definition of "business income" to include "all income that may be treated as apportionable business income under the Constitution of the United States." [S.B. 2207, 2004] As a result, the functional test no longer exists and the arguments raised in this appeal are no longer relevant.

In *McKesson Water Products Company v. Division of Taxation* [No. A-5423-06T3 (N.J. Super. Ct., July 16, 2009)], the New Jersey Superior Court ruled that a gain from the sale of a corporation's stock that was part of a Section 338(h)(10) transaction was neither operational income nor investment income serving an operational function. As a consequence, the gain was not subject to New Jersey corporation income tax, but instead was non-operational income allocable to the taxpayer's principal state of business, California.

On the other hand, in *General Mills, Inc. v. Commissioner of Revenue* [440 Mass. 154, 795 N.E.2d 552 (Mass. Sup. Jud. Ct., 2003)], the taxpayer argued that the gains arising from a Section 338(h)(10) election were a federal tax fiction, and the reality of the transaction (i.e., a sale of stock) should be respected, in which case the gains were nonbusiness income. The Massachusetts Supreme Judicial Court rejected the taxpayer's argument, and ruled that the gains from the deemed asset sale were properly included in the Massachusetts income tax base, consistent with the federal tax treatment of the transaction.

Likewise, in S.C. Revenue Ruling No. 09-4 [Mar. 31, 2009], the South Carolina Department of Revenue ruled that if the target subsidiary uses the assets in its trade or business, the gains triggered by a Section 338(h)(10) election are apportionable business income. An exception applies to gains from the deemed sale of real property, which are allocated to South Carolina if the real property is located in South Carolina or to the extent of depreciation previously deducted in computing South Carolina taxable income.

Also, in *Newell Window Furnishing, Inc. v. Johnson* [No. M2007-02176-COA-R3-CV (Tenn. Ct. of App., Dec. 9, 2008)], the Tennessee Court of Appeals ruled that where a corporation sold the stock of its subsidiary and the sale was treated as a sale of assets under Section 338(h)(10), the gain from the deemed asset sale had to be included in the subsidiary's Tennessee corporate income tax base as apportionable business income.

In *Centurytel, Inc. v. Department of Revenue* [No. TC 4826 (Ore. Tax Ct., Aug. 9, 2010)], the Oregon Tax Court ruled that the gain from the sale of stock by a telecommunications company in a Section 338(h)(10) transaction was business income, because the proceeds were used to acquire additional telecommunications assets and to pay debts previously occurred in the business.

Inclusion of Gross Receipts from Deemed Asset Sale in Sales Factor. Most states apply their standard apportionment rules to the target corporation's deemed asset sale. Thus, the gross receipts from the deemed asset sale are generally included in the target corporation's sales factor. For example, in Ruling No. 2003-3 [July 14, 2003], the Connecticut Department of Revenue ruled that gains arising from a Section 338(h)(10) election are reflected in the target corporation's sales factor. Likewise, in S.C. Revenue Ruling No. 09-4 [Mar. 31, 2009], the South Carolina Department of Revenue ruled that gains arising from a

Section 338(h)(10) election are included in the sales factor, except for gains from real property, which are treated as allocable income.

In *Combustion Engineering, Inc. v. Commissioner of Revenue* (No. F228740 [Mass. App. Tax Bd., Mar. 29, 2000]), the Massachusetts Appellate Tax Board ruled that a parent corporation's gross receipts from the sale of a subsidiary's stock were not includible in the parent's sales factor, even though a federal Section 338(h)(10) election resulted in the stock sale being treated as a deemed asset sale, the gains from which were included in apportionable income. Consistent with this decision, the Massachusetts Department of Revenue took the position that the receipts from a Section 338 deemed asset sale are excluded from the sales factor [see Technical Information Release 01-11, Aug. 28 2001]. In 2004, however, the Massachusetts legislature enacted an amendment that clarifies that effective for tax years beginning on or after January 1, 2005, if an acquiring corporation makes a Section 338 election, the target corporation will be treated as having sold its assets for Massachusetts apportionment purposes. [H.B. 4744, Aug. 9, 2004] This amendment effectively reversed the result in *Combustion Engineering*. In response to this legislation, in Technical Information Release 04-22 [Dec. 8, 2004], the Massachusetts Department of Revenue indicated that it will amend its regulations to reflect the legislative intent to harmonize the treatment of the gains and gross receipts arising from Section 338 transactions.

Special Apportionment Rule for Section 338(h)(10) Gains. New Jersey generally requires the receipts from a deemed asset sale under Section 338(h)(10) to be allocated and sourced to New Jersey by multiplying the gain by a three-year average of the allocation factors used by a target corporation for its three tax return periods immediately prior to the sale. [N.J. Admin. Code 18:7-8.12, New Jersey Division of Taxation]

State-by-State Summary

The following chart, presented in three parts, provides information regarding the state tax treatment of Section 338 elections.

Section 338 Elections (Part 1)

Legend:
SAF — **Same as applicable federal rules**
NA — **Not applicable**
NR — **Not reported**

	Does State Conform to Federal Treatment of a IRC Section 338 Election?	*How Are IRC Section 338 Gains Apportioned?*	*To Report Gains from Deemed Asset Sale, Is a One-Day Return Required?*
Alabama	Yes	By, using standard short-period apportionment formula	No
Alaska	Yes	By using standard short-period apportionment formula	No
Arizona	SAF	By using prior-year apportionment percentages	SAF
Arkansas	Yes	By using standard short-period apportionment formula	Yes
California	Yes	By using standard short-period apportionment formula	Yes
Colorado	Yes	By using prior-year apportionment percentages	No
Connecticut	Yes	By using prior-year apportionment percentages	SAF
Delaware	SAF	By using prior-year apportionment percentages	SAF
District of Columbia	Yes	By using standard short-period apportionment formula	Yes
Florida	Yes	By using standard short-period apportionment formula; other method if standard short period does not clearly reflect Florida income.	Yes

Section 338 Elections (Part 1)

Legend:

SAF Same as applicable federal rules

NA Not applicable

NR Not reported

	Does State Conform to Federal Treatment of a IRC Section 338 Election?	*How Are IRC Section 338 Gains Apportioned?*	*To Report Gains from Deemed Asset Sale, Is a One-Day Return Required?*
Georgia	Yes	By using prior-year apportionment percentages if a one day return is filed; by using standard short-period apportionment formula for non one day return situations	No
Hawaii	No	NA	Yes
Idaho	Yes	By using standard short-period apportionment formula	SAF
Illinois	Yes, to the extent included in federal taxable income	By using standard short-period apportionment formula	Yes, if required for federal income tax purposes
Indiana	SAF	By using standard short-period apportionment formula	SAF
Iowa	Yes	By using standard short-period apportionment formula	Yes
Kansas	Yes	By using standard short-period apportionment formula	Yes
Kentucky	Yes	By using standard short-period apportionment formula	Yes
Louisiana	Yes	Current year apportionment factor	No
Maine	Yes	By using standard short-period apportionment formula	No
Maryland	Yes	Single factor formula of property in effect on date of transaction	Yes

Section 338 Elections (Part 1)

Legend:
SAF **Same as applicable federal rules**
NA **Not applicable**
NR **Not reported**

	Does State Conform to Federal Treatment of a IRC Section 338 Election?	*How Are IRC Section 338 Gains Apportioned?*	*To Report Gains from Deemed Asset Sale, Is a One-Day Return Required?*
Massachusetts	Yes	See TIR 01-11.	Yes
Michigan (Business Tax)	Yes	By using standard short-period apportionment formula or prior-year apportionment percentages	NR
Note. The CIT takes effect 01/01/12, and replaces the Michigan Business Tax (MBT) for most taxpayers. However, businesses that have been approved to receive, have received, or have been assigned certain certified credits may elect to file a return and pay the tax imposed by the MBT in lieu of the CIT until the certified credits are exhausted or extinguished.			
Minnesota	Yes	By using prior-year apportionment percentages	No
Mississippi	Yes	It depends upon facts and circumstances	No
Missouri	Yes	By using standard short-period apportionment formula	Yes
Montana	Yes	By using standard short-period apportionment formula	SAF
Nebraska	Yes	By using standard short-period apportionment formula	Yes
Nevada	Nevada does not impose a corporate income tax		
New Hampshire	Yes	By using standard short-period apportionment formula	Yes
New Jersey	Yes	By using standard short-period apportionment formula	No

Section 338 Elections (Part 1)

Legend:
SAF — **Same as applicable federal rules**
NA — **Not applicable**
NR — **Not reported**

	Does State Conform to Federal Treatment of a IRC Section 338 Election?	*How Are IRC Section 338 Gains Apportioned?*	*To Report Gains from Deemed Asset Sale, Is a One-Day Return Required?*
New Mexico	Yes	Standard short-period apportionment formula	No
New York	Yes	By using standard short-period apportionment formula	No
North Carolina	Yes	Gain apportioned using prior-year apportionment percentages.	Yes
North Dakota	Yes	By using prior-year apportionment percentages	Yes
Ohio	Ohio does not impose a corporate income tax		
Note. Effective 1/1/2010, the Ohio Franchise Tax was fully phased out and business will be taxed on gross receipts through the Commercial Activity Tax. Details about that tax can be found at: http//tax.ohio.gov/divisions/commercial_activities/index.stm			
Oklahoma	Yes	By using direct allocation	Yes
Oregon	Yes	By using prior-year apportionment percentages	No
Pennsylvania	Yes	By using standard short-period apportionment formula	SAF
Rhode Island	NR	NR	NR
South Carolina	Yes	By using prior-year apportionment percentages	No
South Dakota	South Dakota does not impose a corporate income tax		
Tennessee	Yes	By using standard short-period apportionment formula	SAF

Section 338 Elections (Part 1)

Legend:
SAF — **Same as applicable federal rules**
NA — **Not applicable**
NR — **Not reported**

	Does State Conform to Federal Treatment of a IRC Section 338 Election?	*How Are IRC Section 338 Gains Apportioned?*	*To Report Gains from Deemed Asset Sale, Is a One-Day Return Required?*
Texas	Yes	The receipts from the deemed sale of assets is apportioned using the regular apportionment rules based on the nature of the deemed assets sold.	No
Utah	Yes	Must use most recent tax year consisting of at least 180 days.	Yes
Vermont	Yes	By using prior-year apportionment percentages	Yes
Virginia	Yes	By using standard short-period apportionment formula	No
Washington	Washington does not impose a corporate income tax		
West Virginia	Yes	By using prior-year apportionment percentages	Yes
Wisconsin	Yes	Standard short-period apportionment formula	No
Wyoming	Wyoming does not impose a corporate income tax		

Section 338 Elections (Part 2)

Election Under Section 338(h)(10)

Legend:
SAF Same as applicable federal rules
NA Not applicable
NR Not reported

	Describe the Effects of an Election Under IRC Section 338(h)(10)						
	Does State Conform to Federal Treatment of IRC Section 338(h)(10) Election?	*Is It Also Available for Shareholders of an S Corporation?*	*How Is the Target's Resulting Gain Treated?*	*What Amount from the Deemed Asset Sale Is Included in Target's Sales Factor?*	*How Is the Resulting Gain Apportioned?*	*Do Target's State Filing Periods Follow Those for Federal Purposes?*	*Can a Corporation Making a Federal Election Choose Not to Make a Corresponding State Election?*
Alabama	No	Yes	Apportionable income	Gross proceeds	Standard short-period apportionment formula	No	No
Alaska	Yes	Only if elected for federal	The tests for business income apply	No, net also no	Facts and circumstances	Yes	No
Arizona	Yes	Yes	Apportionable income	No, net also no	Prior year apportionment percentages	Yes	No
Arkansas	Yes	Yes	Apportionable income	Gross proceeds unless it distorts factor	Standard short-period apportionment formula	Yes	No

Section 338 Elections (Part 2)

Election Under Section 338(h)(10)

Legend:

SAF	Same as applicable federal rules
NA	Not applicable
NR	Not reported

Describe the Effects of an Election Under IRC Section 338(h)(10)

	Does State Conform to Federal Treatment of IRC Section 338(h)(10) Election?	*Is It Also Available for Shareholders of an S Corporation?*	*How Is the Target's Resulting Gain Treated?*	*What Amount from the Deemed Asset Sale Is Included in Target's Sales Factor?*	*How Is the Resulting Gain Apportioned?*	*Do Target's State Filing Periods Follow Those for Federal Purposes?*	*Can a Corporation Making a Federal Election Choose Not to Make a Corresponding State Election?*
California	Yes	Yes	Apportionable income	None	Standard short-period apportionment formula	Yes	Yes, election is filed on or before federal due date, irrespective of federal extension to file election; however S corporations are not permitted to make non-conforming elections (see R&TC § 23806).
Colorado	Yes	Yes	Apportionable income	Gross proceeds	Prior year apportionment percentages	Yes	No
Connecticut	Yes	No written guidance	Apportionable income	Gross proceeds	Standard short-period apportionment formula	Yes	No

Section 338 Elections (Part 2)

Election Under Section 338(h)(10)

Legend:

SAF	Same as applicable federal rules
NA	Not applicable
NR	Not reported

	Describe the Effects of an Election Under IRC Section 338(h)(10)						
	Does State Conform to Federal Treatment of IRC Section 338(h)(10) Election?	*Is It Also Available for Shareholders of an S Corporation?*	*How Is the Target's Resulting Gain Treated?*	*What Amount from the Deemed Asset Sale Is Included in Target's Sales Factor?*	*How Is the Resulting Gain Apportioned?*	*Do Target's State Filing Periods Follow Those for Federal Purposes?*	*Can a Corporation Making a Federal Election Choose Not to Make a Corresponding State Election?*
Delaware	SAF	NR	Apportionable income	Yes	Prior-year apportionment percentages	Yes	No
District of Columbia	Yes	No	Apportionable income	Gross proceeds	Standard short-period apportionment formula	Yes	No
Florida	Yes, unless distortive	Yes	Apportionable income generally; depends on nature of income	Gross proceeds	Generally standard short-period apportionment formula	Yes	No
Georgia	Yes	Yes	Normal rules on asset sales apply	None	Standard short-period apportionment formula	Yes	No
Hawaii	Yes	No	NA	NR	NR	Yes	NR
Idaho	Yes	Only if elected for federal	Apportionable income Yes, unless distortive	Standard short-period apportionment formula	Yes	No	

Section 338 Elections (Part 2)
Election Under Section 338(h)(10)

Legend:
SAF Same as applicable federal rules
NA Not applicable
NR Not reported

Describe the Effects of an Election Under IRC Section 338(h)(10)

	Does State Conform to Federal Treatment of IRC Section 338(h)(10) Election?	*Is It Also Available for Shareholders of an S Corporation?*	*How Is the Target's Resulting Gain Treated?*	*What Amount from the Deemed Asset Sale Is Included in Target's Sales Factor?*	*How Is the Resulting Gain Apportioned?*	*Do Target's State Filing Periods Follow Those for Federal Purposes?*	*Can a Corporation Making a Federal Election Choose Not to Make a Corresponding State Election?*
Illinois	Yes	Only if elected for federal	Asset-by-asset determination	No, net yes but may be excluded if distortive	Standard short-period apportionment formula	Yes	No
Indiana	SAF	Only if elected for federal	Apportionable income	Yes	Standard short-period apportionment formula	Yes	No
Iowa	Yes	Only if elected for federal	Apportionable income	No	Standard short-period apportionment formula	NR	No
Kansas	Yes	Only if elected for federal	Apportionable income	Yes	Current year's apportionment percentage	Yes	No
Kentucky	Yes	Yes	Apportionable income	Gross proceeds	Standard short-period apportionment formula	Yes	No

Section 338 Elections (Part 2)

Election Under Section 338(h)(10)

Legend:

SAF	Same as applicable federal rules
NA	Not applicable
NR	Not reported

	Describe the Effects of an Election Under IRC Section 338(h)(10)						
	Does State Conform to Federal Treatment of IRC Section 338(h)(10) Election?	*Is It Also Available for Shareholders of an S Corporation?*	*How Is the Target's Resulting Gain Treated?*	*What Amount from the Deemed Asset Sale Is Included in Target's Sales Factor?*	*How Is the Resulting Gain Apportioned?*	*Do Target's State Filing Periods Follow Those for Federal Purposes?*	*Can a Corporation Making a Federal Election Choose Not to Make a Corresponding State Election?*
Louisiana	Yes	Yes	Apportionable income	None	Current year's apportionment factor	Per LAC 61:1.1148D. Change in Ownership 1. Except as otherwise provided herein, when a change in ownership results in no change to the accounting period but results in the income of the taxpayer being reported on two separate federal returns, the taxpayer may either file one return for the entire accounting period or file two short period returns. 2. Except as otherwise provided herein, when a change in	No

Section 338 Elections (Part 2)
Election Under Section 338(h)(10)

Legend:

SAF	Same as applicable federal rules
NA	Not applicable
NR	Not reported

	Describe the Effects of an Election Under IRC Section 338(h)(10)						
	Does State Conform to Federal Treatment of IRC Section 338(h)(10) Election?	*Is It Also Available for Shareholders of an S Corporation?*	*How Is the Target's Resulting Gain Treated?*	*What Amount from the Deemed Asset Sale Is Included in Target's Sales Factor?*	*How Is the Resulting Gain Apportioned?*	*Do Target's State Filing Periods Follow Those for Federal Purposes?*	*Can a Corporation Making a Federal Election Choose Not to Make a Corresponding State Election?*
						ownership results in a change to the accounting period, the filing of two short period returns is required. 3. When a one-day return is required under federal law, that one-day is a separate accounting period for Louisiana reporting purposes. A separate return is required for that one day. This will usually result in the filing of three short period returns.	

Section 338 Elections (Part 2)

Election Under Section 338(h)(10)

Legend:

SAF	Same as applicable federal rules
NA	Not applicable
NR	Not reported

	Describe the Effects of an Election Under IRC Section 338(h)(10)						
	Does State Conform to Federal Treatment of IRC Section 338(h)(10) Election?	*Is It Also Available for Shareholders of an S Corporation?*	*How Is the Target's Resulting Gain Treated?*	*What Amount from the Deemed Asset Sale Is Included in Target's Sales Factor?*	*How Is the Resulting Gain Apportioned?*	*Do Target's State Filing Periods Follow Those for Federal Purposes?*	*Can a Corporation Making a Federal Election Choose Not to Make a Corresponding State Election?*
Maine	Yes	Yes	Apportionable income	Net gain	Standard short-period apportionment formula	Yes	No
Maryland	NR	NR	NR	NR	NR	NR	NR
Massachusetts	NR	Only if elected for federal	NR	NR	NR	Yes	No
Michigan (Business Tax)	Yes	Yes	Apportionable income	Only the portion related to inventory	Standard short-period apportionment formula	Yes	No

Note. The CIT takes effect 01/01/12, and replaces the Michigan Business Tax (MBT) for most taxpayers. However, businesses that have been approved to receive, have received, or have been assigned certain certified credits may elect to file a return and pay the tax imposed by the MBT in lieu of the CIT until the certified credits are exhausted or extinguished.

Minnesota	Yes	Yes	Apportionable income	None	Prior year apportionment percentages	Yes	No
Mississippi	Yes, but only if elected for federal	Only if elected for federal	Apportionable income	No, net yes	Apportionable income or business gain	No	No

Section 338 Elections (Part 2)

Election Under Section 338(h)(10)

Legend:

SAF Same as applicable federal rules
NA Not applicable
NR Not reported

	Describe the Effects of an Election Under IRC Section 338(h)(10)						
	Does State Conform to Federal Treatment of IRC Section 338(h)(10) Election?	*Is It Also Available for Shareholders of an S Corporation?*	*How Is the Target's Resulting Gain Treated?*	*What Amount from the Deemed Asset Sale Is Included in Target's Sales Factor?*	*How Is the Resulting Gain Apportioned?*	*Do Target's State Filing Periods Follow Those for Federal Purposes?*	*Can a Corporation Making a Federal Election Choose Not to Make a Corresponding State Election?*
Missouri	Yes	Yes	Allocable/non-business income	None	Not apportioned	Yes	No
Montana	No, not taxes	NR	Apportionable income, not attributes are carried forward	SAF	Standard short-period apportionment formula	Yes	No
Nebraska	Yes	Only if elected for federal	Apportionable income	Gross proceeds	NR	Yes	No
Nevada	Nevada does not impose a corporate income tax						
New Hampshire	Yes	Yes	Apportionable income	No, net yes	Standard short-period apportionment formula	Yes	No
New Jersey	Yes	Yes	Apportionable income	Gross proceeds	Standard short-period apportionment formula	Yes	No
New Mexico	SAF	SAF	UDITPA	UDITPA	UDITPA	Yes	No

Section 338 Elections (Part 2)

Election Under Section 338(h)(10)

Legend:
SAF — Same as applicable federal rules
NA — Not applicable
NR — Not reported

	Describe the Effects of an Election Under IRC Section 338(h)(10)						
	Does State Conform to Federal Treatment of IRC Section 338(h)(10) Election?	*Is It Also Available for Shareholders of an S Corporation?*	*How Is the Target's Resulting Gain Treated?*	*What Amount from the Deemed Asset Sale Is Included in Target's Sales Factor?*	*How Is the Resulting Gain Apportioned?*	*Do Target's State Filing Periods Follow Those for Federal Purposes?*	*Can a Corporation Making a Federal Election Choose Not to Make a Corresponding State Election?*
New York	Yes	Yes	Included in C corporation income and resident shareholder income	No, net also no	Standard short-period apportionment formula	Yes	No
North Carolina	Yes	Yes	Apportionable income, allocable/ non-business income	No, net also no	Prior-year apportionment percentages	Yes	No
North Dakota	No	Only if elected for federal	Apportionable income	No, net also no	Prior-year apportionment percentages	Yes	No
Ohio	Ohio does not impose a corporate income tax						
Note. Effective 1/1/2010, the Ohio Franchise Tax was fully phased out and business will be taxed on gross receipts through the Commercial Activity Tax. Details about that tax can be found at: http//tax.ohio.gov/divisions/commercial_activities/index.stm							
Oklahoma	Yes	Only if elected for federal	Apportionable income	Gross proceeds	Standard short-period apportionment formula	Yes	No

Section 338 Elections (Part 2)

Election Under Section 338(h)(10)

Legend:

SAF	Same as applicable federal rules
NA	Not applicable
NR	Not reported

Describe the Effects of an Election Under IRC Section 338(h)(10)

	Does State Conform to Federal Treatment of IRC Section 338(h)(10) Election?	*Is It Also Available for Shareholders of an S Corporation?*	*How Is the Target's Resulting Gain Treated?*	*What Amount from the Deemed Asset Sale Is Included in Target's Sales Factor?*	*How Is the Resulting Gain Apportioned?*	*Do Target's State Filing Periods Follow Those for Federal Purposes?*	*Can a Corporation Making a Federal Election Choose Not to Make a Corresponding State Election?*
Oregon	Yes	Only if elected federal	Depends on nature of asset, see ORS 314.610, OARs 150-314.610(1)(A)	No	Apportionment factor computed through date of the stock sale.	Yes	No
Pennsylvania	Not separate from federal	No	Apportionable income	No, net also no	Standard short-period apportionment formula	Yes	No
Rhode Island	Yes	Only if elected for federal	Apportionable income	No	Standard short-period apportionment formula	Yes	No
South Carolina	Yes	SAF	Apportionable income	Net gain	Prior-year apportionment percentages	Yes	No
South Dakota	South Dakota does not impose a corporate income tax						
Tennessee	Yes	No	Apportionable income	No, net yes	Standard short-period apportionment formula	Yes	No

Section 338 Elections (Part 2)
Election Under Section 338(h)(10)

Legend:

SAF	Same as applicable federal rules
NA	Not applicable
NR	Not reported

	Describe the Effects of an Election Under IRC Section 338(h)(10)						
	Does State Conform to Federal Treatment of IRC Section 338(h)(10) Election?	*Is It Also Available for Shareholders of an S Corporation?*	*How Is the Target's Resulting Gain Treated?*	*What Amount from the Deemed Asset Sale Is Included in Target's Sales Factor?*	*How Is the Resulting Gain Apportioned?*	*Do Target's State Filing Periods Follow Those for Federal Purposes?*	*Can a Corporation Making a Federal Election Choose Not to Make a Corresponding State Election?*
Texas	Yes	Only if elected for federal	For receipts from deemed sale of property under § 338 use regular apportionment based on nature of items sold.	Sales of items are included in the sales factor at gross unless the item is an investment or capital asset. Only the net gain on sales of investments and capital assets is included.	If the income is unitary, the gain on the deemed sale is apportioned as though the assets were actually sold. Sales of items are included in the sales factor at gross unless the item is an investment or capital asset. Only the net gain on sales of Investments and capital assets is included. See Rule 3.591	No	No

Section 338 Elections (Part 2)

Election Under Section 338(h)(10)

Legend:
SAF Same as applicable federal rules
NA Not applicable
NR Not reported

	Describe the Effects of an Election Under IRC Section 338(h)(10)						
	Does State Conform to Federal Treatment of IRC Section 338(h)(10) Election?	*Is It Also Available for Shareholders of an S Corporation?*	*How Is the Target's Resulting Gain Treated?*	*What Amount from the Deemed Asset Sale Is Included in Target's Sales Factor?*	*How Is the Resulting Gain Apportioned?*	*Do Target's State Filing Periods Follow Those for Federal Purposes?*	*Can a Corporation Making a Federal Election Choose Not to Make a Corresponding State Election?*
Utah	Yes	Only if elected for federal	Apportionable income	No, net also no	Standard short-period (or if apportionment formula target corporation is a member of a unitary group, gain would be included in the combined income of the unitary group).	Yes	No
Vermont	Yes	Only if elected for federal	Apportionable income	NR	Prior-year apportionment percentages	Yes	No
Virginia	Yes, SAF	Only if elected for federal	Apportionable income	Gross proceeds	Standard short-period apportionment formula	Yes	No
Washington	Washington does not impose a corporate income tax						

Section 338 Elections (Part 2)

Election Under Section 338(h)(10)

Legend:

SAF	Same as applicable federal rules
NA	Not applicable
NR	Not reported

	Describe the Effects of an Election Under IRC Section 338(h)(10)						
	Does State Conform to Federal Treatment of IRC Section 338(h)(10) Election?	*Is It Also Available for Shareholders of an S Corporation?*	*How Is the Target's Resulting Gain Treated?*	*What Amount from the Deemed Asset Sale Is Included in Target's Sales Factor?*	*How Is the Resulting Gain Apportioned?*	*Do Target's State Filing Periods Follow Those for Federal Purposes?*	*Can a Corporation Making a Federal Election Choose Not to Make a Corresponding State Election?*
West Virginia	Yes	Only if elected for federal	If capital, allocated as business, if other, ordinary, apportioned	No, net yes	Prior-year apportionment percentages	Yes	No
Wisconsin	Yes	Yes	Apportionable income	Yes, only to extent of deemed sales of inventory.	Standard short-period apportionment formula	Yes	Yes, both Corps include a statement with the WI return filed.
Wyoming	Wyoming does not impose a corporate income tax						

Section 338 Elections (Part 3)

Election Under Section 338(h)(10)

Legend:

X — **These activities indicate tax attribute carryover.**
SAF — **Same as federal**
NA — **Not applicable**
NR — **Not reported**

	Describe the Effects of an Election Under IRC Section 338(h)(10)			
	Is the Selling Parent Subject to Tax on Gain from Sale of the Target's Stock?	*Is the Target Subject to Tax on the Deemed Sale of Assets?*	*How Are Target's Tax Attributes Treated?*	*Is a Separate "State" Section 338(h)(10) Election Required?*
Alabama	SAF	SAF	SAF	NR
Alaska	SAF	SAF	SAF	No
Arizona	No	Yes	Depends on attributes	No
Arkansas	SAF	SAF	SAF except NOL must follow state rules	No
California	SAF	SAF	SAF	No
Colorado	SAF	SAF	SAF	No
Connecticut		Yes	No written guidance	No
Delaware	NR	NR	NR	No
District of Columbia	SAF	Yes	SAF	No
Florida	SAF	SAF	SAF	No
Georgia	SAF	SAF	SAF	No
Hawaii	NR	NR	NR	Yes
Idaho	Yes, if included in federal taxable income	Yes, if included in federal taxable income	X	No
Illinois	No, based upon the extent included in federal taxable income	Yes, based upon the extent included in federal taxable income	SAF	No

Section 338 Elections (Part 3)

Election Under Section 338(h)(10)

Legend:

X — **These activities indicate tax attribute carryover.**
SAF — **Same as federal**
NA — **Not applicable**
NR — **Not reported**

	Describe the Effects of an Election Under IRC Section 338(h)(10)			
	Is the Selling Parent Subject to Tax on Gain from Sale of the Target's Stock?	*Is the Target Subject to Tax on the Deemed Sale of Assets?*	*How Are Target's Tax Attributes Treated?*	*Is a Separate "State" Section 338(h)(10) Election Required?*
Indiana	No	Yes	SAF	No
Iowa	No	Yes	X	No
Kansas	SAF	SAF	SAF	No
Kentucky	SAF	SAF	SAF	No
Louisiana	The parent is not taxed on any gain from the sale of subsidiary stock.	Apportionable income	SAF	No
Maine	SAF	SAF	SAF	No
Maryland	NR	NR	NR	NR
Massachusetts	SAF	SAF	Other	No
Michigan (Business Tax)	SAF	SAF	SAF	No
Note. The CIT takes effect 01/01/12, and replaces the Michigan Business Tax (MBT) for most taxpayers. However, businesses that have been approved to receive, have received, or have been assigned certain certified credits may elect to file a return and pay the tax imposed by the MBT in lieu of the CIT until the certified credits are exhausted or extinguished.				
Minnesota	SAF	SAF	SAF	No
Mississippi	Yes	Yes		No
Missouri	SAF	SAF	SAF	No
Montana	SAF	SAF		No

Section 338 Elections (Part 3)

Election Under Section 338(h)(10)

Legend:

X	**These activities indicate tax attribute carryover.**
SAF	**Same as federal**
NA	**Not applicable**
NR	**Not reported**

	Describe the Effects of an Election Under IRC Section 338(h)(10)			
	Is the Selling Parent Subject to Tax on Gain from Sale of the Target's Stock?	*Is the Target Subject to Tax on the Deemed Sale of Assets?*	*How Are Target's Tax Attributes Treated?*	*Is a Separate "State" Section 338(h)(10) Election Required?*
Nebraska	No	Yes		No
Nevada	Nevada does not impose a corporate income tax			
New Hampshire	Treated as target asset sale	Treated as target asset sale	Treated as target asset sale	No
New Jersey	No	Yes	X	No
New Mexico	SAF	SAF	SAF	No
New York	No	No	X, SAF	No
North Carolina	No	Yes		No
North Dakota	Yes	No		No
Ohio	Ohio does not impose a corporate income tax			

Note. Effective 1/1/2010, the Ohio Franchise Tax was fully phased out and business will be taxed on gross receipts through the Commercial Activity Tax. Details about that tax can be found at: http//tax.ohio.gov/divisions/commercial_activities/index.stm

Oklahoma	Yes	Yes		No
Oregon	SAF	SAF	SAF	NR
Pennsylvania	No	Yes	X	NR
Rhode Island	No	Yes	X	NR
South Carolina	SAF	SAF	SAF	No
South Dakota	South Dakota does not impose a corporate income tax			

Section 338 Elections (Part 3)

Election Under Section 338(h)(10)

Legend:

X	**These activities indicate tax attribute carryover.**
SAF	**Same as federal**
NA	**Not applicable**
NR	**Not reported**

	Describe the Effects of an Election Under IRC Section 338(h)(10)			
	Is the Selling Parent Subject to Tax on Gain from Sale of the Target's Stock?	*Is the Target Subject to Tax on the Deemed Sale of Assets?*	*How Are Target's Tax Attributes Treated?*	*Is a Separate "State" Section 338(h)(10) Election Required?*
Tennessee	Yes	Yes	X	No
Texas	No	Yes	NA	No
Utah	No	See Note		No
Note. Yes, if the target corporation is not a member of a unitary group immediately preceding the acquisition date				
Vermont	NR	NR	NR	No
Virginia	Yes	Yes	X, see P.D. 99-91 (4/21/99), coal credits stay with target.	No
Washington	Washington does not impose a corporate income tax			
West Virginia	SAF	SAF	SAF	No
Wisconsin	SAF	SAF	SAF	No, unless a different election is made for WI than that made for federal purposes.
Wyoming	Wyoming does not impose a corporate income tax			

Cancellation of Debt Income

Generally, a taxpayer must recognize income from a creditor's non-gratuitous forgiveness of a portion or all of the taxpayer's debt. [IRC § 61(a)(12) and Treas. Reg. § 1.61-12] The amount of cancellation of debt (COD) income (also known as discharge of indebtedness income) equals the amount by which the taxpayer's debt is reduced. COD income can arise when the taxpayer's debt is forgiven, repurchased by the taxpayer at less than face value, exchanged for a new debt, or significantly modified. If the taxpayer repurchases its debt at a discount, the amount of COD income equals the excess of the adjusted issue price over the price paid for the debt [Treas. Reg. § 1.61-12(c)(2)(ii)] A significant modification of a debt agreement, such as a change in interest rates or a deferral of principal or interest payments, is treated as an exchange of the old debt for a new debt. Transactions that give rise to taxable COD income can create an ability-to-pay problem for taxpayers, because COD income often does not provide any cash to pay the tax.

Code Section 108(a) provides an exception, under which a debtor can exclude COD income if: (1) the discharge occurs in a title 11 bankruptcy case, (2) the discharge occurs when the taxpayer is insolvent, (3) the debt discharged is qualified farm indebtedness, (4) the debt discharged is qualified real property business indebtedness (does not apply if taxpayer is a C corporation), or (5) the debt is qualified principal residence indebtedness that is discharged before January 1, 2013.

Code Section 108(b) requires a taxpayer who excludes COD income to reduce certain tax attributes to the extent of the excluded COD income. Thus, the effect of Section 108 is to defer rather than exclude COD income. Generally, the following seven tax attributes are reduced in the following order: (1) net operating loss carryovers; (2) general business credits; (3) minimum tax credits; (4) capital loss carryovers; (5) basis of property; (6) passive activity loss and credit carryovers; and (7) foreign tax credit carryovers.

Under Section 108(b)(5), a taxpayer who excludes COD income may elect to first reduce the basis in its depreciable property before it reduces the specified tax attributes. The amount of the reduction is limited to the total adjusted basis of the taxpayer's depreciable property, and any remaining exclusion amount is then applied to reduce the seven tax attributes.

The American Recovery and Reinvestment Tax Act of 2009 [Pub. L. No. 111-5, Feb. 17, 2009] added a new subsection (i) to Code Section 108, which allows taxpayers to elect to defer recognition of COD income in connection with the reacquisition in 2009 or 2010 of a debt instrument. The income is deferred until 2014 and then included in gross income ratably over a five-year period (i.e., 20 percent per year in each of the tax years 2014 to 2018). This deferral is available, regardless of whether the taxpayer is insolvent or in bankruptcy. Congress enacted Section 108(i) to enable taxpayers to restructure their debt without triggering any current income recognition.

State-by-State Summary

The following chart summarizes which states conform to the Section 108(a) exclusion for COD income, the Section 108(b) requirements for reducing tax attributes, the election under Section 108(b)(5) to reduce the basis of property rather than tax attributes, and the Section 108(i) election to defer recognition of COD income.

Cancellation of Debt Income

Legend:
NA — Not applicable
NR — Not reported
SAF — Same as applicable federal rules

	Does State Conform to the IRC § 108(a) Exclusion for Cancellation of Debt (COD) Income When the Taxpayer Is Bankrupt or Insolvent? If No, Explain.	*Is the Exclusion Only Available if the Taxpayer Reduces its NOLs and Other Tax Attributes by the Excluded Amount as Required by IRC § 108(b)? If No, Explain.*	*Can the Taxpayer Elect to Reduce the Basis of its Depreciable Property, Rather than its Tax Attributes? If No, Explain.*	*Does State Conform to IRC § 108(i), as Added by the American Recovery and Reinvestment Tax Act of 2009*
Alabama	Yes	Yes	Yes	Yes
Alaska	Yes	Yes	Yes	Yes
Arizona	Yes	Yes, Arizona adopts the various provisions of the Internal Revenue Code. Unless otherwise provided, Arizona generally conforms to changes made to the Internal Revenue Code during the prior year.	Yes, Arizona adopts the various provisions of the Internal Revenue Code. Unless otherwise provided, Arizona generally conforms to changes made to the Internal Revenue Code during the prior year.	No
Arkansas	Yes	No		No
California	Yes	Yes	Yes	No
Colorado	Yes	Yes, must reduce state tax attributes.	No	Yes
Connecticut	Yes	Connecticut has no written guidance on this issue.	Connecticut has no written guidance on this issue.	No, 2009 Conn. Pub. Acts 2, § 4 (June Spec. Sess.)
Delaware	Yes			Yes
District of Columbia	No, decoupled with IRC.	No, decoupled in total.	No	No
Florida	Yes			Florida requires an addition to Florida income equal to the amount of income deferred and allows a subtraction when it is included in federal income.

Cancellation of Debt Income

Legend:

NA	Not applicable
NR	Not reported
SAF	Same as applicable federal rules

	Does State Conform to the IRC § 108(a) Exclusion for Cancellation of Debt (COD) Income When the Taxpayer Is Bankrupt or Insolvent? If No, Explain.	*Is the Exclusion Only Available if the Taxpayer Reduces its NOLs and Other Tax Attributes by the Excluded Amount as Required by IRC § 108(b)? If No, Explain.*	*Can the Taxpayer Elect to Reduce the Basis of its Depreciable Property, Rather than its Tax Attributes? If No, Explain.*	*Does State Conform to IRC § 108(i), as Added by the American Recovery and Reinvestment Tax Act of 2009*
Georgia	Yes, Generally follow but see Reg. 560-7-3-.06 for differences in federal treatment.	Yes	Yes	No
Hawaii	Yes	Yes	Yes	No
Idaho	Yes, Idaho Income Tax Administrative Rule 210 provides guidance on the reduction of Idaho attributes and basis when income from indebtedness discharged in bankruptcy is excluded from gross income.			Yes
Illinois	Yes	No, the exclusion applies to the same extent it applies federally.		Yes
Indiana	Yes	Yes	Yes	No
Iowa	Yes	Yes	Yes	No
Kansas	Yes	Yes	Yes	Yes
Kentucky	Yes	Yes	Yes	No
Louisiana	Yes	Yes	Yes	Yes
Maine	Yes	Yes	Yes	No
Maryland	Yes	Yes	Yes	No

Cancellation of Debt Income

Legend:
NA — Not applicable
NR — Not reported
SAF — Same as applicable federal rules

	Does State Conform to the IRC § 108(a) Exclusion for Cancellation of Debt (COD) Income When the Taxpayer Is Bankrupt or Insolvent? If No, Explain.	*Is the Exclusion Only Available if the Taxpayer Reduces its NOLs and Other Tax Attributes by the Excluded Amount as Required by IRC § 108(b)? If No, Explain.*	*Can the Taxpayer Elect to Reduce the Basis of its Depreciable Property, Rather than its Tax Attributes? If No, Explain.*	*Does State Conform to IRC § 108(i), as Added by the American Recovery and Reinvestment Tax Act of 2009*
Massachusetts	Yes, TIR 09-21	Yes	Yes	No, TIR 09-21
Michigan	NR	NR	NR	NR
Note. The CIT takes effect 01/01/12, and replaces the Michigan Business Tax (MBT) for most taxpayers. However, businesses that have been approved to receive, have received, or have been assigned certain certified credits may elect to file a return and pay the tax imposed by the MBT in lieu of the CIT until the certified credits are exhausted or extinguished.				
Minnesota	Yes	Yes	Yes	Yes
Mississippi	No, Mississippi does not have statutory authority to follow cancellation of debt; therefore, it must be recognized in the tax year it is cancelled without the benefit of deferral.			No
Missouri	Yes	Yes	Yes	Yes
Montana	Yes	Yes	Yes	Yes
Nebraska	Yes	Yes	Yes	Yes
Nevada	Nevada does not impose a corporate income tax			
New Hampshire	Yes	Yes	Yes	New Hampshire conforms to the IRC of 1986 in effect on 12/31/00.

Cancellation of Debt Income

Legend:

NA	Not applicable
NR	Not reported
SAF	Same as applicable federal rules

	Does State Conform to the IRC § 108(a) Exclusion for Cancellation of Debt (COD) Income When the Taxpayer Is Bankrupt or Insolvent? If No, Explain.	*Is the Exclusion Only Available if the Taxpayer Reduces its NOLs and Other Tax Attributes by the Excluded Amount as Required by IRC § 108(b)? If No, Explain.*	*Can the Taxpayer Elect to Reduce the Basis of its Depreciable Property, Rather than its Tax Attributes? If No, Explain.*	*Does State Conform to IRC § 108(i), as Added by the American Recovery and Reinvestment Tax Act of 2009*
New Jersey	Yes	No, the New Jersey net operating loss deduction is calculated independently of the federal tax attributes (N.J.S.A. 54:10A-4(k)(6)), and at the present time there is no provision to reduce tax attributes connected with discharge of indebtedness. Thus, New Jersey would not require the corporation to reduce New Jersey net operating loss with respect to discharge of indebtedness for corporation business tax purposes.		No, New Jersey corporation business tax is decoupled from IRC § 108, as added by the American Recovery and Reinvestment Act of 2009. New Jersey corporate taxpayers will not be able to defer this income and must report the income in the year it is earned. Nevertheless, corporate taxpayers may exclude the income from New Jersey taxable income in future years when it is required to be recognized as taxable income for federal income tax purposes. Accordingly, the income will not be taxed twice in New Jersey. N.J.A.C. 18:7-5.2(a)(2)(viii).
New Mexico	Yes	Yes	Yes	Yes
New York	Yes	Yes	Yes	
North Carolina	Yes		Yes	No
North Dakota	NR	NR	NR	NR
Ohio	Ohio does not impose a corporate income tax			

Cancellation of Debt Income

Legend:
NA Not applicable
NR Not reported
SAF Same as applicable federal rules

	Does State Conform to the IRC § 108(a) Exclusion for Cancellation of Debt (COD) Income When the Taxpayer Is Bankrupt or Insolvent? If No, Explain.	*Is the Exclusion Only Available if the Taxpayer Reduces its NOLs and Other Tax Attributes by the Excluded Amount as Required by IRC § 108(b)? If No, Explain.*	*Can the Taxpayer Elect to Reduce the Basis of its Depreciable Property, Rather than its Tax Attributes? If No, Explain.*	*Does State Conform to IRC § 108(i), as Added by the American Recovery and Reinvestment Tax Act of 2009*
Oklahoma	No, required to include this income in Oklahoma taxable income in the year the debt is forgiven and is not recognized in the year included in federal taxable income (the deferred years).			No
Oregon	Yes	Yes	Yes	No
Pennsylvania	Yes	No, Pennsylvania uses federal taxable income to determine Pennsylvania taxable income. If income is excluded on the federal return accepted by the IRS, Pennsylvania will allow the exclusion. There is no provision in Pennsylvania law to adjust Pennsylvania NOL's or credits.		Yes
Rhode Island	Yes	Yes	Yes	No
South Carolina	Yes	Yes	Yes	No
South Dakota	South Dakota does not impose a corporate income tax			

Cancellation of Debt Income

Legend:
NA — Not applicable
NR — Not reported
SAF — Same as applicable federal rules

	Does State Conform to the IRC §108(a) Exclusion for Cancellation of Debt (COD) Income When the Taxpayer Is Bankrupt or Insolvent? If No, Explain.	*Is the Exclusion Only Available if the Taxpayer Reduces its NOLs and Other Tax Attributes by the Excluded Amount as Required by IRC §108(b)? If No, Explain.*	*Can the Taxpayer Elect to Reduce the Basis of its Depreciable Property, Rather than its Tax Attributes? If No, Explain.*	*Does State Conform to IRC §108(i), as Added by the American Recovery and Reinvestment Tax Act of 2009*
Tennessee	Yes	No, COD income is only a part of the excise tax base if it is recognized in federal taxable income, regardless of any other federal treatment.		Yes
Texas	Yes	SAF	SAF	Yes
Utah	Yes	No, Utah Code piggybacks federal amounts used to determine the taxable income shown on Form 1120, line 28. Therefore, Utah follows the reduction in basis of assets (and capital loss carryovers in certain circumstances). The current Utah statute does not address reduction in Utah loss carryovers and credits.	Yes	Yes, Utah piggybacks federal deferred amount.
Vermont	Yes	Yes	Yes	Yes

Cancellation of Debt Income

Legend:
NA Not applicable
NR Not reported
SAF Same as applicable federal rules

	Does State Conform to the IRC § 108(a) Exclusion for Cancellation of Debt (COD) Income When the Taxpayer Is Bankrupt or Insolvent? If No, Explain.	*Is the Exclusion Only Available if the Taxpayer Reduces its NOLs and Other Tax Attributes by the Excluded Amount as Required by IRC § 108(b)? If No, Explain.*	*Can the Taxpayer Elect to Reduce the Basis of its Depreciable Property, Rather than its Tax Attributes? If No, Explain.*	*Does State Conform to IRC § 108(i), as Added by the American Recovery and Reinvestment Tax Act of 2009*
Virginia	Yes	Yes	Yes	No, taxpayers that defer cancellation of debt income from transactions occurring on or before 04/21/10, may elect to report the Virginia addition required by conformity in equal amounts over three taxable years. Taxpayers incurring this income in 2010 will be required to add back the entire amount resulting from transactions after 04/21/10.
Washington	Washington does not impose a corporate income tax			
West Virginia	Yes	Yes	Yes	Yes
Wisconsin	Yes	No	Yes	No
Wyoming	Wyoming does not impose a corporate income tax			

Part 4. GROUP FILING OPTIONS

Group Filing Options—Overview

Background: GAAP and Federal Income Tax

A large business enterprise is often structured as a parent corporation with multiple subsidiary corporations. For financial reporting purposes, a parent corporation generally must issue consolidated financial statements that include all of its majority-owned U.S. and foreign subsidiaries. [FASB ASC 810] Thus, consolidated financial statements are mandatory for generally accepted accounting principles (GAAP) purposes. The rationale for requiring consolidated financial statements is the presumption that consolidated statements are more meaningful than separate statements and that they are usually necessary for a fair presentation when one of the companies in the group directly or indirectly has a controlling financial interest in the other companies. Consolidated statements reflect the practical reality that a group of commonly controlled corporations often functions as a single economic entity. Consistent with the single entity view of a multicorporate group, any income or expense arising from intercompany transactions is eliminated so that the group's reported earnings reflect only the items of income and expense arising from transactions with unrelated third parties.

For federal income tax purposes, an affiliated group of corporations may elect to file a federal consolidated income tax return. [IRC § 1501] Thus, a federal consolidated return is not mandatory, and the members of an affiliated group have the option of filing federal returns on a separate company basis. Filing a federal consolidated return is a popular election, primarily because it allows the group to offset the losses of one affiliate against the profits of other affiliates.

A federal *affiliated group* is defined as one or more chains of includible corporations connected through stock ownership with a common parent that is an includible corporation, provided that the common parent directly owns 80 percent or more of at least one of the other includible corporations, and stock meeting the 80 percent test in each includible corporation other than the common parent must be owned directly by one or more of the other includible corporations. [IRC § 1504(a)] An "includible corporation" is any corporation other than an exempt corporation, life insurance company, foreign corporation, Section 936 corporation, RIC, REIT, DISC or S corporation. [IRC § 1504(b)]

Therefore, unlike GAAP, federal tax law does not generally allow foreign country subsidiaries to be included in the consolidation. On the other hand, the consolidated federal taxable income of an affiliated group is computed as if the group were a single economic entity. To achieve this objective, the group's taxable income reflects only the earnings derived from transactions with unrelated third parties. A major advantage of electing to file a federal consolidated return is that losses of one affiliate can be offset against the profits of other affiliates.

Overview of State Filing Options

The states that impose corporate income taxes employ a variety of filing options for groups of commonly controlled corporations. This makes it difficult to generalize about group filing options. To complicate matters further, some states use terms such as *consolidated return* and *combined reporting* to mean different things. For example, Connecticut uses the term *combined return* for what is generally referred to as a *consolidated return*. With these qualifications in mind, roughly speaking, state filing options fall into one of the following categories:

1. Separate company returns,
2. Consolidated returns, and
3. Combined unitary reporting.

The lack of uniformity in state filing options means that tax practitioners must carefully analyze the filing options available in any given nexus state.

The Multistate Tax Commission has approved a model combined reporting statute. [Proposed Model Statute for Combined Reporting, August 17, 2006]

Separate Company Returns. Three states—Delaware, Maryland and Pennsylvania—require each member of a commonly controlled group of corporations to compute its income and file a return as if it were a separate economic entity. Under this mandatory separate company return approach, consolidated returns and combined reporting are not permitted or required under any circumstances.

The filing of separate company returns provides taxpayers with the opportunity to create legal structures and intercompany transactions that shift income from affiliates based in high-tax states to affiliates based in low- or no-tax states. For example, if a multistate corporation's only activities in a high-tax state are sales and distribution, which are often relatively low-margin activities, and the high-tax state allows separate company returns, the corporation may be able to insulate its higher-margin assets and activities from taxation in the high-tax state by forming a sales subsidiary that is responsible for marketing products in that state. Disadvantages of the separate company return approach include the inability to offset the losses of one affiliate against the profits of other affiliates and the need to develop defensible arm's-length transfer prices for intercompany transactions.

Consolidated Returns. Roughly 20 states, including Alabama, Florida, Georgia, Iowa, and South Carolina, permit or require affiliated corporations to file a state consolidated return if certain conditions are met. The qualification requirements for including an affiliated corporation in a state consolidated return vary from state to state. In terms of stock ownership requirements, many states piggyback on the federal rule requiring 80 percent or more ownership. A number of states also require that an affiliated group file a federal consolidated return as a prerequisite to filing a state consolidated return. Examples of additional restrictions that a state may impose for including a specific affiliate in a state consolidated return include having nexus in the state, deriving income from sources in the state, and not being subject to a special apportionment formula such as those that often apply to financial institutions.

The advantages of filing a consolidated return include the ability to offset the losses of one affiliate against the profits of other affiliates, elimination of intercorporate dividends, deferral of gains on intercompany transactions, and the use of credits that would otherwise be limited by a lack of income. A disadvantage of filing a consolidated return is that it can prevent a taxpayer from creating legal structures and intercompany transactions to shift income from affiliates based in high-tax states to affiliates based in low-tax states.

State consolidated returns are discussed in more detail in the section entitled Consolidated Returns.

Combined Unitary Reporting. Twenty-three states and the District of Columbia require members of a unitary business group to compute their taxable income on a combined basis. These states include Alaska, Arizona, California, Colorado, Hawaii, Idaho, Illinois, Kansas, Maine, Massachusetts (effective in 2009), Michigan (effective in 2008), Minnesota, Montana, Nebraska, New Hampshire, New York (effective in 2007 for related corporations that have substantial intercorporate transactions), North Dakota, Oregon, Texas (effective in 2007), Utah, Vermont, West Virginia (effective in 2009) and Wisconsin (effective in 2009).

Despite its surface-level resemblance to a consolidated return, combined unitary reporting differs from a federal consolidated return in several respects. First, whereas inclusion in a federal consolidated return requires 80 percent or more common ownership, inclusion in a combined unitary report generally requires more than 50 percent common ownership. Second, to be included in a combined report, an affiliate must be engaged in the same trade or business as the other group members, as exhibited by such factors as functional integration, centralized management and economies of scale. There is no unitary business requirement for inclusion in a federal consolidated return. Third, some states permit the inclusion of foreign corporations in a combined report. Finally, in many states, each group member that has nexus in the state is treated as a separate taxpayer, whereas the federal consolidated regulations treat a consolidated group as a single taxable entity.

Numerous states, including New Jersey, North Carolina, and Virginia, generally allow commonly controlled corporations to file separate company returns, but also require or permit a combined unitary report if certain conditions are satisfied. A common reason for requiring a combined report is the state tax authority's determination that a combined report is necessary to clearly reflect the group's income earned in the state or to prevent the evasion of taxes.

Combined unitary reporting is discussed in more detail in the section entitled Combined Unitary Reporting.

Group Filing Options in the Most Populous States

To illustrate the use of the different group filing options, the requirements of the ten most populous states (other than New York) are summarized below.

California. For purposes of computing the California corporate franchise tax, if two or more commonly-controlled corporations are engaged in a unitary business, the taxpayer members must apportion their income on a combined basis. The control test is more than 50 percent common control. If a taxpayer member does not make a water's-edge election, the California combined report includes all members of the unitary group, including foreign (non-U.S.) corporations.

Florida. Each affiliate with nexus in Florida is generally considered a separate taxable entity and must file a return on a separate company basis. Florida does not require or permit combined unitary reporting. However, if the parent company of a federal affiliated group has nexus in Florida, it may elect to file a consolidated return, regardless of whether the other group members have nexus in Florida. To qualify, the same affiliated group must file a federal consolidated return and each member of the group must consent to filing a Florida consolidated return. In addition, the Florida Director of Revenue has the authority to require nexus affiliates to file a consolidated return if the filing of separate company returns would "improperly reflect" the taxable incomes of such corporations. [Fla. Stat. Ann. § 220.131(2)]

Georgia. Each affiliate with nexus in Georgia is generally considered a separate taxable entity and must file a return on a separate company basis. Georgia does not require combined unitary reporting. An affiliated group of corporations that files a federal consolidated return may request permission to file a Georgia consolidated return. A Georgia consolidated group consists of all the members of the federal consolidated group that are subject to Georgia income tax. The Georgia Department of Revenue must grant permission if a consolidated return will clearly and equitably reflect the Georgia income of the corporations. The Department also has the authority to require members of an affiliated group filing a federal consolidated return to file a Georgia consolidated return if the filing of separate returns would not clearly and equitably reflect the income attributable to activities in Georgia, but the filing of a consolidated return would clearly and equitably reflect such income.

Illinois. For purposes of computing the Illinois corporate income tax, if two or more commonly-controlled corporations are engaged in a unitary business, the taxpayer members must apportion their income on a combined basis. The control test is more than 50 percent common control. The unitary group does not include any members whose business activity outside the United States is 80 percent or more of the member's total business activity, as measured by its property and payroll factors.

Michigan. From 2008 to 2011, Michigan imposed a 4.95 percent business income tax and 0.80 percent modified gross receipts tax. A unitary business group must file a combined return for purposes of computing the business income tax and modified gross receipts tax.

Effective January 1, 2012, Michigan replaced its business income and modified gross receipt taxes with a 6 percent corporate income tax. In computing the corporate income tax, unitary business groups are required to file combined tax returns. [H.B. 4361 and 4362, May 25, 2011]

North Carolina. In 2011, North Carolina repealed the Department of Revenue's existing statutory authority to adjust a corporation's net income or require a combined return, effective for tax years beginning on or after January 1, 2012. [H.B. 619, June 30, 2011] Under the new law, the Department may redetermine the net income of a corporation if the Department finds that the company's transactions lack economic substance or are not at fair market value. The Department may redetermine net income by adding back, eliminating or otherwise adjusting intercompany transactions. The Secretary may also require a combined return, but only if other adjustments to intercompany transactions are not adequate to redetermine net income. [Important Notice Regarding the Secretary's Authority to Adjust the Net Income of a Corporation or to Require a Corporation to File a Combined Report (N.C. Dept. of Rev., July 13, 2011)]

In 2010, North Carolina authorized the Department of Revenue to adopt regulations that describe the circumstances under which the Department can require a corporation to file a consolidated or combined return. [S.B. 897, June 30, 2010] The adoption of these rules did not limit the Department's authority to require a consolidated or combined return if it determines that a report by a corporation does not disclose the true earnings of the corporation on its business carried on in North Carolina. In addition, a corporation filing a federal consolidated return may be permitted or required to file a consolidated or combined return if: (1) it is directed to file a combined report because the corporation's report does not disclose the true net earnings of the corporation, because payments have been made in excess of fair compensation between such a corporation and its parent, subsidiary, or affiliate; (2) it falls within the rules requiring the filing of a combined return; or (3) pursuant to a written request from the corporation, the Department has provided written advice to the corporation stating that a combined return is required under the facts and circumstances set out in the request and the corporation files a combined return in accordance with that written advice.

Ohio. Ohio does not impose a corporate income tax. However, corporations are subject to the Ohio commercial activity tax (CAT), which is a 0.26 percent tax on Ohio gross receipts. For purposes of computing the Ohio commercial activity tax (CAT), commonly controlled corporations may elect to compute the CAT as a "consolidated elected taxpayer." If this election is made, receipts received between members of the group are not subject to the CAT. However, all commonly owned entities that are part of the group are included in the group, including entities that do not have nexus in Ohio on a separate company basis. The election is binding for two years. If the election is not made, any taxpayers with common ownership of more than 50 percent must file as a "combined taxpayer." A combined taxpayer may not exclude receipts between members of the group. However, combined taxpayers only need to include in the group those members who have nexus with Ohio. [General Information on the Commercial Activities Tax, Ohio Dept. of Taxation, July 2005].

Pennsylvania. Pennsylvania does not permit or require combined unitary reports or consolidated returns. Therefore, each affiliate with nexus in Pennsylvania is considered a separate taxable entity and must file a return on a separate company basis.

Texas. Texas does not have a traditional corporate income tax, but instead imposes a 1.0 percent tax (0.5 percent for retailers or wholesalers) on a taxable entity's margin. Taxable entities that are part of an affiliated group engaged in a unitary business must file a combined report. Only members of an affiliated group, which requires more than 50 percent common control, are included in the combined report. A taxable entity that conducts business outside the United States is excluded from a Texas combined report if 80 percent or more of its property and payroll are assigned to locations outside the United States.

State-by-State Summary

Three states—Delaware, Maryland and Pennsylvania—generally do not permit or require consolidated returns or combined reporting under any circumstances. In these states, each member of a commonly controlled group of corporations must compute its income and file a return as if it were a separate economic entity.

The other states that impose corporate income taxes make use of some form of consolidated returns or combined reporting. The states that permit the filing of consolidated returns are discussed in the section entitled Consolidated Returns, and the states that require or permit combined unitary reporting are discussed in the section entitled Combined Unitary Reporting.

Consolidated Returns

Federal Consolidated Returns

For federal income tax purposes, an affiliated group of corporations may elect to file a federal consolidated income tax return. [IRC § 1501] Thus, a federal consolidated return is not mandatory, and the members of an affiliated group have the option of filing federal returns on a separate company basis. Filing a federal consolidated return is a popular election, primarily because it allows the group to offset the losses of one affiliate against the profits of other affiliates.

A federal *affiliated group* is defined as one or more chains of includible corporations connected through stock ownership with a common parent that is an includible corporation, provided that the common parent directly owns 80 percent or more of at least one of the other includible corporations, and stock meeting the 80 percent test in each includible corporation other than the common parent must be owned directly by one or more of the other includible corporations. [IRC § 1504(a)] An "includible corporation" is any corporation other than an exempt corporation, life insurance company, foreign corporation, Section 936 corporation, RIC, REIT, DISC or S corporation. [IRC § 1504(b)]

Under the statutory authority provided by Code Section 1502, the Treasury Department has issued voluminous regulations regarding how an affiliated group computes its consolidated federal income tax liability. These regulations generally adopt the single-entity approach to determining the tax of a consolidated group. Under this approach, the members of a consolidated group are treated as divisions of a single taxpayer.

State Consolidated Returns

Roughly 20 states, including Alabama, Florida, Georgia, Iowa, and South Carolina, permit or require affiliated corporations to file a state consolidated return if certain conditions are met. The advantages of filing a state consolidated return include the ability to offset the losses of one affiliate against the profits of other affiliates, elimination of intercorporate dividends, deferral of gains on intercompany transactions, and the use of credits that would otherwise be limited by a lack of income. A disadvantage of filing a consolidated return is that it may prevent the taxpayer from creating legal structures and intercompany transactions that shift income from affiliates based in high-tax states to affiliates based in low-tax states.

The qualification requirements for including an affiliated corporation in a state consolidated return vary from state to state. In terms of stock ownership requirements, many states piggyback on the federal rule requiring 80 percent or more ownership. A number of states also require that an affiliated group file a federal consolidated return as a prerequisite to filing a state consolidated return. Examples of additional restrictions that a state may impose for including a specific affiliate in a state consolidated return include having nexus in the state, deriving income from sources in the state, and not being subject to a special apportionment formula such as those that often apply to financial institutions.

Any restrictions that a state imposes on the filing of a consolidated return cannot violate U.S. Constitutional requirements. For example, prior to 1998, an affiliated group was allowed to file a Missouri consolidated return only if at least 50 percent of the group's income was derived from Missouri sources. In *General Motors Corp. v. Director of Revenue* [No. 80853 (Mo. 1998)], the Missouri Supreme Court ruled that the 50 percent requirement violated the Commerce Clause's anti-discrimination requirement, because it facially discriminated against affiliated groups based outside Missouri.

Florida. Florida permits members of a federal affiliated group to elect to file a consolidated return, but only if the group has filed a federal consolidated return and the parent corporation has nexus in Florida. Once the election is made, it remains in effect even if the parent corporation's nexus in Florida is terminated. All of the affiliates that file a federal consolidated return generally must be included in the Florida consolidated return. Thus, unlike some other states (e.g., Iowa and Virginia, see below), Florida does not limit its consolidated return to corporations that have nexus in the state. The Florida Director of Revenue has the authority to require nexus affiliates to file a consolidated return if the filing of separate company returns would "improperly reflect" the taxable incomes of such corporations. [Fla. Stat. Ann. § 220.131(2)]

Georgia. Under Georgia law, an affiliated group of corporations that files a federal consolidated return may request permission to file a Georgia consolidated return. A Georgia consolidated group consists of all the members of the federal consolidated group that are subject to Georgia income tax. The Georgia Department of Revenue must grant permission if a consolidated return will clearly and equitably reflect the Georgia income of the corporations. The Department also has the authority to require members of an affiliated group filing a federal consolidated return to file a Georgia consolidated return if the filing of separate returns would not clearly and equitably reflect the income attributable to activities in Georgia, but the filing of a consolidated return would clearly and equitably reflect such income.

Iowa. Iowa permits (and may require) members of a federal affiliated group that file a federal consolidated return and have nexus in Iowa to file a consolidated return. This approach is known as a "nexus consolidation."

Virginia. Virginia also employs a nexus consolidation approach, whereby members of a federal affiliated group may file a consolidated return, but the return may not include corporations that are exempt from Virginia income tax or which are not subject to Virginia income tax if separate returns are filed.

In P.D. 04-188 [Oct. 8, 2004], the Virginia Tax Commissioner ruled that a group of six out-of-state subsidiaries that reported net operating losses must be removed from the taxpayer's Virginia consolidated return because the subsidiaries tried "to create nexus artificially" by leasing warehouse space in Virginia. The Commissioner determined that, based on the facts of the case, the sole reason for placing property in Virginia was to allow the net operating losses of the out-of-state affiliates to be included in the taxpayer's consolidated return. On the other hand, the Commissioner required the income of two other out-of-state subsidiaries to be included in the consolidated return because they lacked economic substance and loans between these entities were not at arm's length.

Reporting Consistency

Most states that permit affiliated corporations to file a consolidated return have adopted a reporting-consistency provision similar to that imposed for federal consolidated return purposes. Thus, once an election to file a consolidated return is made, the affiliated group generally must continue to file on a consolidated basis unless the group receives permission from state tax authorities to file separate company returns. There are some exceptions. For example, Connecticut permits an affiliated group to revoke an election after five years, and Colorado permits an election to be revoked after four years.

In *Kidde America, Inc. v. Director of Revenue* [No. SC87192 (Mo. Sup. Ct., June 30, 2006)], the Missouri Supreme Court ruled that an affiliated group of corporations was entitled to file a consolidated Missouri corporate income tax return and receive the resulting refund, even though the group did not make a timely election to file a Missouri consolidated return. The group would have been eligible for the federal good faith exception for failing to make a timely election (i.e., Treas. Reg. § 301.9100-3), and a Missouri statute mandates that the Director of Revenue should follow "as nearly as practicable" the federal regulations.

Methodologies for Computing Taxable Income

In determining whether an affiliated group should elect to file a state consolidated return, the state's methodology for computing the group's consolidated taxable income should be analyzed. In particular, a number of states that permit affiliates to file a consolidated return require each affiliate to compute and apportion its income separately.

For example, Georgia determines an affiliated group's consolidated taxable income as follows: (1) the taxable net income of each affiliate is computed separately, and then apportioned separately to Georgia; and (2) the apportioned income of all of the affiliates is aggregated to determine the group's consolidated taxable income. This post-apportionment form of consolidation limits the ability of taxpayers to realize the full benefits of offsetting the losses of one affiliate against the profits of other affiliates. For example, if a loss affiliate's Georgia apportionment percentage, computed on a separate company basis, is only 5 percent, then only 5 percent of that affiliate's loss can be deducted against the Georgia income of the other affiliates.

Another example of how a post-apportionment consolidation differs from the single entity theory of a federal consolidation is the limitation on charitable contributions. For example, each member of an affiliated group filing an Alabama consolidated return that has nexus in Alabama must calculate its Alabama taxable income on a separate company basis. As a consequence, federal limitations calculated at the consolidated group level for federal tax purposes, such as the 10 percent limitation on the charitable contribution deduction under IRC Section 170(b)(2), must be recalculated on a separate-entity basis when computing Alabama taxable income. Federal limitations must also be adjusted to reflect the fact that the members with nexus in Alabama must calculate taxable income on a post-apportionment basis. [Amended Rule 810-3-1.1-.01, Ala. Dept. of Rev., Aug. 31, 2009]

On the other hand, some states (e.g., Florida) use a pre-apportionment form of consolidation that is more consistent with the federal method of computing consolidated taxable income. Under this approach, the taxable income or loss of each affiliate is first aggregated to arrive at the group's consolidated income, which is then apportioned using apportionment factors that reflect the aggregate property, payroll, and sales of all group members. This approach allows an affiliated group to realize more of the benefits of filing a consolidated return. In particular, the full amount of a loss affiliate's net operating loss is offset against the profits of the other affiliates before applying the state's apportionment percentage to the group's consolidated income or loss.

State-by-State Summary

The following chart, presented in three parts, indicates the conditions under which consolidated returns are required or permitted, the qualification requirements for inclusion of specific affiliated group members in a consolidated return, whether an election to file a consolidated return is binding for future years, and whether the income of individual group members is consolidated before or after applying the state's apportionment percentages.

Consolidated Returns (Part 1)

Legend:
X — **Indicates filing options available to a group of two or more commonly controlled corporations**
NA — **Not applicable**
NR — **Not reported**

	Consolidated Returns Are Mandatory	*Consolidated Returns Are Not Allowed Under Any Circumstances*	*State Has Authority to Require a Consolidated Return if Certain Conditions Are Met*	*State Has Authority to Grant Permission to File a Consolidated Return if Certain Conditions Are Met*	*Taxpayer May Elect to File a Consolidated Return if Certain Conditions Are Met*	*Other*
Alabama					X	
Alaska	X					
Arizona			X	X	X	
Arkansas					X	
California						California does not follow the federal consolidated return regulations provided under IRC Code § 1502. The only exception is for affiliated railroads pursuant to California Revenue & Taxation Code § 23362.
Colorado					X	
Connecticut					X, See Conn. Gen. Stat. § 12-223a	
Delaware		X				
District of Columbia			X	X	X	
Florida			X		X	
Georgia			X	X		
Hawaii		X	X			
Idaho		X				Group returns are allowed.

Consolidated Returns (Part 1)

Legend:
X **Indicates filing options available to a group of two or more commonly controlled corporations**
NA **Not applicable**
NR **Not reported**

	Consolidated Returns Are Mandatory	*Consolidated Returns Are Not Allowed Under Any Circumstances*	*State Has Authority to Require a Consolidated Return if Certain Conditions Are Met*	*State Has Authority to Grant Permission to File a Consolidated Return if Certain Conditions Are Met*	*Taxpayer May Elect to File a Consolidated Return if Certain Conditions Are Met*	*Other*
Illinois		X				
Indiana			X			
Iowa			X	X	X	
Kansas			X	X	X, must be 100% Kansas for all companies	
Kentucky						An election to file a consolidated return prior to 1/1/05 will be honored during the 8 year election period.
Louisiana			X			
Maine		X				
Maryland	NA	NA	NA	NA	NA	NA
Massachusetts				X		
Michigan (Business Tax)		X	X			If the group of commonly controlled corporations comprise a unitary business group, combined reporting is mandatory. Otherwise, each corporation must file separately.

Note. The CIT takes effect 01/01/12, and replaces the Michigan Business Tax (MBT) for most taxpayers. However, businesses that have been approved to receive, have received, or have been assigned certain certified credits may elect to file a return and pay the tax imposed by the MBT in lieu of the CIT until the certified credits are exhausted or extinguished.

Consolidated Returns (Part 1)

Legend:
X — **Indicates filing options available to a group of two or more commonly controlled corporations**
NA — **Not applicable**
NR — **Not reported**

	Consolidated Returns Are Mandatory	*Consolidated Returns Are Not Allowed Under Any Circumstances*	*State Has Authority to Require a Consolidated Return if Certain Conditions Are Met*	*State Has Authority to Grant Permission to File a Consolidated Return if Certain Conditions Are Met*	*Taxpayer May Elect to File a Consolidated Return if Certain Conditions Are Met*	*Other*
Minnesota		X				
Mississippi		X				
Missouri					X	
Montana				X	X	
Nebraska	X					
Nevada	Nevada does not impose a corporate income tax					
New Hampshire		X				
New Jersey			X, (there are special rules for casino companies, N.J. Stat. Ann. §§ 5:12-148b	X	X, if air carrier, N.J.S.A. 54: 10A-18.1	
New Mexico					X	
New York					Only corporate parent and tax-exempt domestic international sales corporation	

Consolidated Returns (Part 1)

Legend:
X **Indicates filing options available to a group of two or more commonly controlled corporations**
NA **Not applicable**
NR **Not reported**

	Consolidated Returns Are Mandatory	*Consolidated Returns Are Not Allowed Under Any Circumstances*	*State Has Authority to Require a Consolidated Return if Certain Conditions Are Met*	*State Has Authority to Grant Permission to File a Consolidated Return if Certain Conditions Are Met*	*Taxpayer May Elect to File a Consolidated Return if Certain Conditions Are Met*	*Other*
North Carolina			X, G.S. 105-130.6 is repealed 1/1/12 (See Session Law 2011-390)			
North Dakota	Consolidated returns are just a convenience allowing all companies with nexus to file one return rather than each filing their own; each nexus company must still report its own taxable income and income tax.					
Ohio	Ohio does not impose a corporate income tax					
Note. Effective 1/1/2010, the Ohio Franchise Tax was fully phased out and business will be taxed on gross receipts through the Commercial Activity Tax. Details about that tax can be found at: http//tax.ohio.gov/divisions/commercial_activities/index.stm						
Oklahoma				X	X	
Oregon	X, if certain conditions are met					
Pennsylvania		X				
Rhode Island					95% or more stock ownership	
South Carolina			Mandatory after first consolidated return, unless permission is granted.	X	X	
South Dakota	South Dakota does not impose a corporate income tax					
Tennessee			X	X		

Consolidated Returns (Part 1)

Legend:

X	**Indicates filing options available to a group of two or more commonly controlled corporations**
NA	**Not applicable**
NR	**Not reported**

	Consolidated Returns Are Mandatory	*Consolidated Returns Are Not Allowed Under Any Circumstances*	*State Has Authority to Require a Consolidated Return if Certain Conditions Are Met*	*State Has Authority to Grant Permission to File a Consolidated Return if Certain Conditions Are Met*	*Taxpayer May Elect to File a Consolidated Return if Certain Conditions Are Met*	*Other*
Texas		X				
Utah						Only unitary groups can file on a consolidated basis.
Vermont					X	
Virginia					X	
Washington	Washington does not impose a corporate income tax					
West Virginia					X	
Wisconsin		X				
Wyoming	Wyoming does not impose a corporate income tax					

Consolidated Returns (Part 2)

Legend:

NA **Not applicable**
NR **Not reported**
SAF **Same as federal**

	What Is the Ownership Percentage for Inclusion in the Consolidated Return?	*In Addition to Stock Ownership, What Other Conditions Must an Affiliate Satisfy to Be Included in a Consolidated Return?*	*Must an Affiliated Group File a Federal Consolidated Return to File a State Consolidated Return?*	*If an Affiliated Group Must File a Federal Consolidated Return, Must the State Consolidated Return Include All Members Included in the Federal Return?*
Alabama	80% or more stock ownership	Must be part of federal consolidation and have Alabama nexus	Yes	No
Alaska	50% or more stock ownership	Affiliate must have nexus in state	No	NA
Arizona	80% or more stock ownership	Affiliate must be included in federal consolidated return.	Yes	Yes
Arkansas	80% or more stock ownership	Affiliate must be included in federal consolidated return and must have nexus in state.	Yes	No
California	N/A	At the time specified by R&TC § 23361 (1) at least 80% of the stock of each of the corporation, except the common parent corporation, is owned directly by one or more of the other corporations, and (2) the common parent corporation owns directly at least 80%.	No	NA
Colorado	SAF except only entities with nexus	Affiliate must have nexus in state.	NR	NA
Connecticut	80% or more	Must have nexus in state	Yes	Yes

Note. Answers are for Connecticut combined return which is similar to a "consolidated return". See Conn. Gen. Stat. § 12-223a.

Consolidated Returns (Part 2)

Legend:

- NA — Not applicable
- NR — Not reported
- SAF — Same as federal

	What Is the Ownership Percentage for Inclusion in the Consolidated Return?	*In Addition to Stock Ownership, What Other Conditions Must an Affiliate Satisfy to Be Included in a Consolidated Return?*	*Must an Affiliated Group File a Federal Consolidated Return to File a State Consolidated Return?*	*If an Affiliated Group Must File a Federal Consolidated Return, Must the State Consolidated Return Include All Members Included in the Federal Return?*
Delaware	NA	NA	NA	NA
District of Columbia	SAF	Affiliate must be included in federal consolidated return; must have nexus in state and must have in state gross receipts.	Yes	No
Florida	80% or more stock ownership	Affiliate must be included in federal consolidated return.	Yes	Yes
Georgia	NR	Affiliate must be included in federal consolidated return and must have nexus in state.	Yes	No
Hawaii	80% or more stock ownership		No	NA
Idaho	NA	NA	NA	NA
Illinois	NA	NA	NA	NA
Indiana	80% or more stock ownership	Affiliate must have nexus in state.	No	NA
Iowa	80% or more stock ownership	Affiliate must be included in federal consolidated return and must have nexus in state.	Yes	No
Kansas	General rule is more than 50% stock ownership; however, actual control is the measurement	Affiliate must derive all of its income from sources in the state and must have nexus in state.	No	NA

Legend:

NA	**Not applicable**
NR	**Not reported**
SAF	**Same as federal**

	What Is the Ownership Percentage for Inclusion in the Consolidated Return?	*In Addition to Stock Ownership, What Other Conditions Must an Affiliate Satisfy to Be Included in a Consolidated Return?*	*Must an Affiliated Group File a Federal Consolidated Return to File a State Consolidated Return?*	*If an Affiliated Group Must File a Federal Consolidated Return, Must the State Consolidated Return Include All Members Included in the Federal Return?*
Kentucky	80% or more stock ownership	Affiliate and common parent must have nexus in state.	No	NA
Louisiana	See La. Rev. Stat. Ann. § 47:280.480(3)	Affiliate must have nexus in state.	No	NA
Maine	NA	NA	NA	NA
Maryland	NA	NA	NA	NA
Massachusetts	NR	NR	Yes	Yes
Michigan (Business Tax)	NA	NA	NA	NA
Note. The CIT takes effect 01/01/12, and replaces the Michigan Business Tax (MBT) for most taxpayers. However, businesses that have been approved to receive, have received, or have been assigned certain certified credits may elect to file a return and pay the tax imposed by the MBT in lieu of the CIT until the certified credits are exhausted or extinguished.				
Minnesota	NA	NA	NA	NA
Mississippi	80% or more stock ownership	Affiliate must derive all of its income from sources in state.	No	NA
Missouri	SAF	Affiliate must be included in federal consolidated return.	Yes	Yes
Montana	80% or more stock ownership	Affiliate must derive all of its income from sources in state.	No	Yes
Nebraska	50% or more stock ownership	Must be part of the unitary group.	No	NA

Consolidated Returns (Part 2)

Legend:

NA Not applicable
NR Not reported
SAF Same as federal

	What Is the Ownership Percentage for Inclusion in the Consolidated Return?	*In Addition to Stock Ownership, What Other Conditions Must an Affiliate Satisfy to Be Included in a Consolidated Return?*	*Must an Affiliated Group File a Federal Consolidated Return to File a State Consolidated Return?*	*If an Affiliated Group Must File a Federal Consolidated Return, Must the State Consolidated Return Include All Members Included in the Federal Return?*
Nevada	Nevada does not impose a corporate income tax			
New Hampshire	NA	NA	NA	NA
New Jersey	80% or more stock ownership	Affiliate must be included in federal consolidated return.	Yes, if required by the Director, except for air carriers	Yes
New Mexico	80% or more stock ownership	Affiliate must be included in federal consolidated return.	Yes	Yes
New York	80% or more stock ownership; only a domestic international sales corporation can file a consolidated return with its parent.	NA	NA	NA
North Carolina	NR	NR	NR	NR
North Dakota	NR	NR	NR	NR
Ohio	Ohio does not impose a corporate income tax			
Note. Effective 1/1/2010, the Ohio Franchise Tax was fully phased out and business will be taxed on gross receipts through the Commercial Activity Tax. Details about that tax can be found at: http//tax.ohio.gov/divisions/commercial_activities/index.stm				
Oklahoma	Requires federal consolidation	Requires federal consolidation	Yes	Yes, but only companies with nexus in Oklahoma

Consolidated Returns (Part 2)

Legend:

NA	**Not applicable**
NR	**Not reported**
SAF	**Same as federal**

	What Is the Ownership Percentage for Inclusion in the Consolidated Return?	*In Addition to Stock Ownership, What Other Conditions Must an Affiliate Satisfy to Be Included in a Consolidated Return?*	*Must an Affiliated Group File a Federal Consolidated Return to File a State Consolidated Return?*	*If an Affiliated Group Must File a Federal Consolidated Return, Must the State Consolidated Return Include All Members Included in the Federal Return?*
Oregon	80% or more stock ownership	Must be part of a unitary group with one or more corporations having nexus in Oregon and affiliate must be included in federal consolidated return	Yes	No
Pennsylvania	NA	NA	NA	NA
Rhode Island	NR	Affiliate must have nexus in state.	No	NA
South Carolina	80% or more stock ownership	Must have nexus in state and must be subject to South Carolina corporate income tax	No	NA
South Dakota	South Dakota does not impose a corporate income tax			
Tennessee	Based on details of variance	NR	NR	NR
Texas	NA	NA	NA	NA
Utah	More than 50% stock ownership			
Vermont	Members of federal affiliated group	Affiliate must have nexus in state and must be included in federal consolidated return.	No	All members with Vermont nexus
Virginia	80% or more stock ownership, SAF	Affiliate must have nexus in state.	No	NA

Consolidated Returns (Part 2)

Legend:
NA **Not applicable**
NR **Not reported**
SAF **Same as federal**

	What Is the Ownership Percentage for Inclusion in the Consolidated Return?	*In Addition to Stock Ownership, What Other Conditions Must an Affiliate Satisfy to Be Included in a Consolidated Return?*	*Must an Affiliated Group File a Federal Consolidated Return to File a State Consolidated Return?*	*If an Affiliated Group Must File a Federal Consolidated Return, Must the State Consolidated Return Include All Members Included in the Federal Return?*
Washington	Washington does not impose a corporate income tax			
West Virginia	NR	NR	NR	NR
Wisconsin	NA	NA	NA	NA
Wyoming	Wyoming does not impose a corporate income tax			

Consolidated Returns (Part 3)

Legend:

X	Indicates may be included in a state consolidated return
NA	Not applicable
NR	Not reported
SAF	Same as applicable federal rules

	Are the Following Types of Companies Included in a State Consolidated Return?					
	Transportation Companies	*Insurance Companies*	*Financial Services Companies*	*Must the Year-End for the State Consolidated Return Be the Same as That Used for the Federal Consolidated Return?*	*Must an Affiliated Group Continue to File a State Consolidated Return Once It Has Elected to Do So?*	*What Procedure Applies for Apportioning Income?*
Alabama	X			Yes	Yes	Income of members is consolidated *after* each member apportions its income individually.
Alaska	X	X	X	Yes	Yes	Income of members is consolidated *before* applying the state's apportionment percentage.
Arizona	X		X	Yes	Yes	Income of members is consolidated *before* applying the state's apportionment percentage.
Arkansas	X	X	X	Yes	Until federal parent changes or department approves.	Income of members is consolidated *after* each member apportions its income individually.
California	X, affiliated railroad companies only			Yes	Yes	Income of members is consolidated *before* applying the state's apportionment percentage.
Colorado	X	X	X	Yes	Yes	Income of members is consolidated *before* applying the state's apportionment percentage.

Consolidated Returns (Part 3)

Legend:

X	Indicates may be included in a state consolidated return
NA	Not applicable
NR	Not reported
SAF	Same as applicable federal rules

	Are the Following Types of Companies Included in a State Consolidated Return?					
	Transportation Companies	*Insurance Companies*	*Financial Services Companies*	*Must the Year-End for the State Consolidated Return Be the Same as That Used for the Federal Consolidated Return?*	*Must an Affiliated Group Continue to File a State Consolidated Return Once It Has Elected to Do So?*	*What Procedure Applies for Apportioning Income?*
Connecticut	X		X	Yes	Yes, for at least 5 years.	Income of members is consolidated *after* each member apportions its income individually.
Delaware	NA	NA	NA	NA	NA	NA
District of Columbia				Yes	Yes	Income of members is consolidated *before* applying the state's apportionment percentage.
Florida	X	X	X	Yes	Yes	Income of members is consolidated *before* applying the state's apportionment percentage.
Georgia	X	X, unless exempt	X	Yes	Yes, unless they stop filing a federal consolidated return, they request to stop filing, or the Department of Revenue revokes permission	Income of members is consolidated *after* each member individually apportions its income.

Consolidated Returns (Part 3)

Legend:

X	Indicates may be included in a state consolidated return
NA	Not applicable
NR	Not reported
SAF	Same as applicable federal rules

	Are the Following Types of Companies Included in a State Consolidated Return?					
	Transportation Companies	*Insurance Companies*	*Financial Services Companies*	*Must the Year-End for the State Consolidated Return Be the Same as That Used for the Federal Consolidated Return?*	*Must an Affiliated Group Continue to File a State Consolidated Return Once It Has Elected to Do So?*	*What Procedure Applies for Apportioning Income?*
Hawaii	X			Yes	Yes	Income of members is consolidated *before* applying the state's apportionment percentage.
Idaho	NA	NA	NA	NA	NA	NA
Illinois	NA	NA	NA	NA	NA	NA
Indiana	X	X	X	Yes	Yes	Income of members is consolidated *before* applying the state's apportionment percentage.
Iowa	X		X	Yes	Yes	Income of members is consolidated *before* applying the state's apportionment percentage.
Kansas	X		X, not banks, savings & loans, or credit unions	Yes	Yes	Income of members is consolidated *before* applying the state's apportionment percentage
Kentucky	X	X, includible only if not exempt from tax under Ky. Rev. Stat. Ann. 141.040(1)(f)	X, includible only if not exempt from tax under Ky. Rev. Stat. Ann. 141.040(1)(b), (c), (d), or (e)	Yes	An election to file a consolidated return made prior to 1/1/05, must continue during the eight-year election period.	Income of members is consolidated *before* applying the state's apportionment percentage.

Consolidated Returns (Part 3)

Legend:

X	Indicates may be included in a state consolidated return
NA	Not applicable
NR	Not reported
SAF	Same as applicable federal rules

	Are the Following Types of Companies Included in a State Consolidated Return?					
	Transportation Companies	*Insurance Companies*	*Financial Services Companies*	*Must the Year-End for the State Consolidated Return Be the Same as That Used for the Federal Consolidated Return?*	*Must an Affiliated Group Continue to File a State Consolidated Return Once It Has Elected to Do So?*	*What Procedure Applies for Apportioning Income?*
Louisiana				Yes	No, if mandated, continue until notified otherwise	Income of members is consolidated *before* applying the state's apportionment percentage.
Maine	NA	NA	NA	NA	NA	NA
Maryland	NA	NA	NA	NA	NA	NA
Massachusetts		X	Depends on facts	Yes	Yes	NR
Michigan (Business Tax)	NA	NA	NA	NA	NA	NA
Note. The CIT takes effect 01/01/12, and replaces the Michigan Business Tax (MBT) for most taxpayers. However, businesses that have been approved to receive, have received, or have been assigned certain certified credits may elect to file a return and pay the tax imposed by the MBT in lieu of the CIT until the certified credits are exhausted or extinguished.						
Minnesota						
Mississippi	X	X	X	Yes	Yes	Income of members is consolidated *after* each member apportions its income individually.
Missouri	X	X	X	Yes	Yes	Income of members is consolidated *before* applying the state's apportionment percentage.

Consolidated Returns (Part 3)

Legend:

X	Indicates may be included in a state consolidated return
NA	Not applicable
NR	Not reported
SAF	Same as applicable federal rules

	Are the Following Types of Companies Included in a State Consolidated Return?					
	Transportation Companies	*Insurance Companies*	*Financial Services Companies*	*Must the Year-End for the State Consolidated Return Be the Same as That Used for the Federal Consolidated Return?*	*Must an Affiliated Group Continue to File a State Consolidated Return Once It Has Elected to Do So?*	*What Procedure Applies for Apportioning Income?*
Montana	X	X	X	Yes	Yes	NA, all income derived from sources within the state, no multistate groups may file a consolidated return.
Nebraska	X			Yes	NR	Income of members is consolidated *before* applying the state's apportionment percentage.
Nevada	Nevada does not impose a corporate income tax					
New Hampshire	NA	NA	NA	NA	NA	NA
New Jersey	X	X	X	Yes	No	Income of members is consolidated *before* applying the state's apportionment percentage.
New Mexico	X	X	X	Yes	Yes	Income of members is consolidated *before* applying the state's apportionment percentage.
New York	NA	NA	NA	NA	NA	NA
North Carolina	NR	NR	NR	NR	NR	NR
North Dakota	NR	NR	NR	NR	NR	NR
Ohio	Ohio does not impose a corporate income tax					

Consolidated Returns (Part 3)

Legend:

X	Indicates may be included in a state consolidated return
NA	Not applicable
NR	Not reported
SAF	Same as applicable federal rules

	Are the Following Types of Companies Included in a State Consolidated Return?					
	Transportation Companies	*Insurance Companies*	*Financial Services Companies*	*Must the Year-End for the State Consolidated Return Be the Same as That Used for the Federal Consolidated Return?*	*Must an Affiliated Group Continue to File a State Consolidated Return Once It Has Elected to Do So?*	*What Procedure Applies for Apportioning Income?*
Note. Effective 1/1/2010, the Ohio Franchise Tax was fully phased out and business will be taxed on gross receipts through the Commercial Activity Tax. Details about that tax can be found at: http//tax.ohio.gov/divisions/commercial_activities/index.stm						
Oklahoma	SAF	SAF	SAF	Yes	Yes	Income of members is consolidated *after* each member apportions its income individually.

Consolidated Returns (Part 3)

Legend:

X	Indicates may be included in a state consolidated return
NA	Not applicable
NR	Not reported
SAF	Same as applicable federal rules

	Are the Following Types of Companies Included in a State Consolidated Return?					
	Transportation Companies	*Insurance Companies*	*Financial Services Companies*	*Must the Year-End for the State Consolidated Return Be the Same as That Used for the Federal Consolidated Return?*	*Must an Affiliated Group Continue to File a State Consolidated Return Once It Has Elected to Do So?*	*What Procedure Applies for Apportioning Income?*
Oregon	X	Domestic insurance companies may file consolidated returns with other domestic insurance companies only. Foreign insurance companies must file separate returns. Insurance companies subject to Oregon taxation may not be included in Oregon consolidated groups of non-insurance corporations.	Financial organizations without Oregon Nexus that are unitary with nonfinancial corporations may be part of the Oregon Consolidated group. Special provisions cover unitary consolidated groups including both financial organizations and nonfinancial corporations subject to Oregon tax.	Yes. Insurance companies must use a calendar year for state consolidated returns no matter what fiscal year-end can be used on the federal consolidated return.	The Oregon filing method is based on the federal filing method and the existence of a unitary relationship among the affiliates in a federal consolidated group.	Income of members is consolidated *before* applying the state's apportionment percentage.
Pennsylvania	NA	NA	NA	NA	NA	NA

Consolidated Returns (Part 3)

Legend:

X	Indicates may be included in a state consolidated return
NA	Not applicable
NR	Not reported
SAF	Same as applicable federal rules

	Are the Following Types of Companies Included in a State Consolidated Return?					
	Transportation Companies	*Insurance Companies*	*Financial Services Companies*	*Must the Year-End for the State Consolidated Return Be the Same as That Used for the Federal Consolidated Return?*	*Must an Affiliated Group Continue to File a State Consolidated Return Once It Has Elected to Do So?*	*What Procedure Applies for Apportioning Income?*
Rhode Island	X		X	Yes	No, must request approval each year	Income of members is consolidated *after* each member apportions its income individually.
South Carolina	X		X	Yes	Until permission is granted by the South Carolina Department of Revenue	Income of members is consolidated *after* each member apportions its income individually
South Dakota	South Dakota does not impose a corporate income tax					
Tennessee	NR	NR	NR	NR	NR	NR
Texas	NA	NA	NA	NA	NA	NA
Utah						Income of members is consolidated *before* applying the state's apportionment percentage.
Vermont	X		X	Yes	Yes	Income of members is consolidated *before* applying the state's apportionment percentage.

Consolidated Returns (Part 3)

Legend:

X	Indicates may be included in a state consolidated return
NA	Not applicable
NR	Not reported
SAF	Same as applicable federal rules

	Are the Following Types of Companies Included in a State Consolidated Return?					
	Transportation Companies	*Insurance Companies*	*Financial Services Companies*	*Must the Year-End for the State Consolidated Return Be the Same as That Used for the Federal Consolidated Return?*	*Must an Affiliated Group Continue to File a State Consolidated Return Once It Has Elected to Do So?*	*What Procedure Applies for Apportioning Income?*
Virginia	X		X	Yes	Yes	Income of members is consolidated *before* applying the state's apportionment percentage for Virginia consolidated returns. Income of members is consolidated *after* each member apportions its income individually for Virginia "Combined" returns.
Washington	Washington does not impose a corporate income tax					
West Virginia	X	X	X	Yes	Yes	Income of members is consolidated *before* applying the state's apportionment percentage.
Wisconsin	NA	NA	NA	NA	NA	NA
Wyoming	Wyoming does not impose a corporate income tax					

Combined Unitary Reporting

Background

As noted by Justice Blackmun in *Mobil Oil Corp. v. Commissioner of Taxes* [445 U.S. 425 (1980)], "the linchpin of apportionability in the field of state income taxation is the unitary business principle." The unitary business principle was first applied in the 1800s, as states sought to impose property taxes on railroad companies that operated across state lines. The essential idea of the unitary business principle is that to effectively tax a business enterprise whose operations span numerous states, all of the activities constituting that single trade or business must be viewed as a whole, rather than as separate activities conducted in a given taxing state.

In the corporate income tax arena, combined unitary reporting is a methodology for apportioning the business income of a corporation that is a member of a commonly controlled group of corporations engaged in a unitary business. Generally speaking, a taxpayer member apportions its business income by multiplying the combined business income of all the members of the unitary business group by an apportionment percentage that is based on factors, the denominators of which include the factors everywhere of all group members, and the numerators of which include the in-state factors of only the taxpayer member. From a state's perspective, a major benefit of combined reporting is that it limits the ability of large business enterprises to erode the state's income tax base by using related party transactions to shift income from in-state affiliates to out-of-state affiliates.

The unitary business principle ignores the separate legal existence of separately incorporated affiliates, and instead focuses on the practical reality that different affiliates often function as a single business enterprise. In *Container Corporation of America v. Franchise Tax Board* (463 U.S. 159, 1983), the Supreme Court noted that using "geographical or transactional accounting" to compute state taxable income "captures inadequately the many subtle and largely unquantifiable transfers of value that take place among the components of a single enterprise," whereas the unitary business method "apportion[s] the total income of th[e] 'unitary business' between the taxing jurisdiction and the rest of the world on the basis of a formula taking into account objective measures of the corporation's activities within and without the jurisdiction."

Based on the unitary business principle, a state can require a corporation that has divisions located both within and without the state to compute its income using formulary apportionment rather than geographic separate accounting if the out-of-state divisions conduct a unitary business with the in-state divisions. [*Butler Bros. v. McColgan*, 315 U.S. 501 (1942); *Exxon Corp. v. Wisconsin Dep't of Revenue*, 447 U.S. 207 (1980)] Likewise, the unitary business principle allows states to require a commonly controlled group of corporations to apportion their income on a combined basis if the out-of-state affiliates are engaged in a unitary business with the in-state affiliates. [*Edison Cal. Stores, Inc. v. McColgan*, 176 P.2d 697 (Cal. 1947)]

Combined Reporting Versus Consolidated Returns

Despite its surface-level resemblance to a federal consolidated return, combined unitary reporting differs from a consolidated return in a number of important respects:

1. *Apportionment methodology versus type of return.* A federal consolidated return involves the filing of a single return for a group of affiliated corporations and the computation of the group's federal income tax as if the group were a single economic entity. In contrast, combined unitary reporting is not so much a type of return as the name given to the calculations (akin to a spreadsheet) by which a unitary business group apportions its income. For example, in many combined reporting states, each group member that has nexus in the state is treated as a separate taxpayer, in contrast to the single entity theory of a federal consolidated return. Under California's combined unitary reporting scheme, the first step is to compute the aggregate business income of all group members. The group's combined business income is then apportioned, first to California (based on the group's apportionment percentage), and then to each of the individual group members that have nexus in California (based on the ratio of each member's factors to the group's factors). The second level of apportionment is necessary because each group member

that has nexus in California is treated as a separate taxpayer. This is true even if taxpayers that are members of the same combined reporting group satisfy their reporting obligation by filing a single group return on which they report the sum of their individual tax liabilities. The importance of this distinction was illustrated in *General Motors Corp. v. Franchise Tax Board* [No. S127086 (Cal. Sup. Ct., Aug. 18, 2006)], in which the California Supreme Court ruled that a research and development credit could reduce the tax of only the member that earned the credit and can not be used to reduce the tax of any other group members. However, not all combined reporting states require each member of a unitary group to compute its own tax separately. For example, Illinois requires a unitary business group to file a single Illinois combined report. In that report, the business income of each group member is aggregated, and then the combined income is apportioned to Illinois using the aggregated apportionment factors of the unitary group.

2. *Common ownership requirements.* Inclusion in a state consolidated return generally requires 80 percent or more common ownership (which piggybacks on the ownership threshold for inclusion in a federal consolidated return), whereas membership in a combined unitary report generally requires more than 50 percent common ownership.
3. *Unitary business requirement.* To be included in a combined report, an affiliate must be engaged in the same trade or business as the other group members, as exhibited by such factors as functional integration, centralized management and economies of scale. This "unitary business" test is not a requirement for inclusion in an elective consolidated return.
4. *Worldwide combinations.* Consistent with the federal approach to consolidation, affiliates organized in a foreign country generally are not includible in a state consolidated return. On the other hand, some states permit the inclusion of foreign corporations in a combined unitary report.

Despite these differences, the advantages and disadvantages of consolidated returns and combined reporting are similar. Major advantages of both filing options include the ability to offset the losses of one affiliate against the profits of other affiliates, elimination of intercorporate dividends, and deferral of gains on intercompany transactions. A primary disadvantage of both filing options is that they can prevent a taxpayer from creating legal structures and intercompany transactions that shift income from affiliates based in high-tax states to affiliates based in low-tax states.

Finally, it is worth noting that the comparison of consolidated returns and combined unitary reporting is complicated by the wide variety of filing options employed by the states, which makes it difficult to generalize.

Mandatory Combined Reporting

Twenty-three states and the District of Columbia require taxpayer members of a unitary business group to compute their taxable income on a combined basis. These states include Alaska, Arizona, California, Colorado, Hawaii, Idaho, Illinois, Kansas, Maine, Massachusetts (effective in 2008), Michigan (effective in 2008), Minnesota, Montana, Nebraska, New Hampshire, New York (effective in 2007 for related corporations that have substantial intercorporate transactions), North Dakota, Oregon, Texas (effective in 2007), Utah, Vermont, West Virginia (effective in 2009), and Wisconsin (effective in 2009).

California. If two or more corporations are engaged in a unitary business, the combined reporting group's "taxpayer members" (i.e., members that are required to file a California income tax return) must apportion the combined income of the entire unitary group in order to compute their tax. [Cal. Rev. & Tax. Code § 25102] Generally, every taxpayer member of the same combined reporting group is required to file its own tax return. As an administrative convenience, however, two or more taxpayer members may annually elect to file a group return. [Calif. Code of Regs. § 25106.5-11] Filing a group return does not change the tax liabilities of any members.

Illinois. If two or more corporations are engaged in a unitary business, a part of which is conducted in Illinois, the business income of the taxpayer members must be apportioned on a combined basis. [35 Ill. Comp. Stat. § 5/304(e)] Members of the same unitary business group are treated as one taxpayer for purposes of determining the group's tax liability and filing tax returns. [35 Ill. Comp. Stat. § 5/502(e)]

Group members must designate a common agent to represent all the members in tax matters, pay taxes, and file the combined return. [86 Ill. Adm. Code § 100.5220(a)]

Texas. Texas does not have a traditional corporate income tax, but instead imposes a 1.0 percent margin tax (0.5 percent for retailers or wholesalers). Taxable entities that are part of an affiliated group engaged in a unitary business must file a combined report. [Tex. Tax Code § 171.1014(a)] In addition to regular corporations, a combined report can include partnerships, limited liability companies and S corporations. [34 Tex. Admin. Code § 3.590(b)]

The combined group is treated as a single taxable entity for purposes of calculating the margin tax and completing the required tax reports. [Tex. Tax Code § 171.1014(b)] The combined group's reporting entity files a combined report on the group's behalf and pays the margin tax imposed on the group. [34 Tex. Admin. Code § 3.590(e)]

Discretionary Combined Reporting

In addition to the mandatory combined reporting states, numerous states (including New Jersey, North Carolina, and Virginia) generally allow commonly controlled corporations to file separate company returns, but also require or permit a combined unitary report if certain conditions are satisfied. A common reason for requiring a combined report is the state tax authority's determination that a combined report is necessary to clearly reflect the group's income earned in the state or to prevent the evasion of taxes.

Indiana. The Indiana Department of Revenue may require commonly controlled corporations to file a combined return, but only if the Department is unable to fairly reflect the taxpayer's income through other statutory means. [Ind. Code § 6-3-2-2(p)]. For instance, in Letter of Findings No. 05-0175 [Ind. Dept. of Rev., May 1, 2006], a manufacturing corporation that divided its operations among various subsidiaries was required to file a combined Indiana income tax return to fairly reflect its income from Indiana sources. On a separate company basis, the parent had a loss of $25 million during the four-year audit period, while the other companies in the group had a profit of $500 million. The parent and its subsidiaries engaged in numerous intercompany transactions and were part of a unitary business.

New Jersey. New Jersey does not permit an affiliated group to elect to file a consolidated return, nor does it require all unitary groups to compute their tax on a combined basis. Thus, every corporation with nexus in New Jersey generally is considered a separate entity and must file its own return. The Director of the Division of Taxation may, however, require members of an affiliated group or a controlled group to file a consolidated return "if the taxpayer cannot demonstrate by clear and convincing evidence that a report by a taxpayer discloses the true earnings of the taxpayer on its business carried on in this State." [N.J. Rev. Stat. 54:10A-10.c.]

North Carolina. In 2011, North Carolina repealed the Department of Revenue's existing statutory authority to adjust a corporation's net income or require a combined return, effective for tax years beginning on or after January 1, 2012. [H.B. 619, June 30, 2011] Under the new law, the Department may redetermine the net income of a corporation if the Department finds that the company's transactions lack economic substance or are not at fair market value. The Department may redetermine net income by adding back, eliminating or otherwise adjusting intercompany transactions. The Secretary may also require a combined return, but only if other adjustments to intercompany transactions are not adequate to redetermine net income. [Important Notice Regarding the Secretary's Authority to Adjust the Net Income of a Corporation or to Require a Corporation to File a Combined Report (N.C. Dept. of Rev., July 13, 2011)]

In 2010, North Carolina authorized the Department of Revenue to adopt regulations that describe the circumstances under which the Department can require a corporation to file a consolidated or combined return. [S.B. 897, June 30, 2010] The adoption of these rules did not limit the Department's authority to require a consolidated or combined return if it determines that a report by a corporation does not disclose the true earnings of the corporation on its business carried on in North Carolina. In addition, a corporation filing a federal consolidated return may be permitted or required to file a consolidated or combined return if: (1) it is directed to file a combined report, because the corporation's report does not disclose the true net earnings of the corporation because payments have been made in excess of fair compensation between such a corporation and its parent, subsidiary, or affiliate; (2) it falls within the rules requiring the filing of a combined return; or (3) pursuant to a written request from the corporation, the Department has provided written advice to the corporation stating that a combined return is required under the facts and circumstances set out in the request and the corporation files a combined return in accordance with that written advice.

In *Wal-Mart Stores East, Inc. v. Secretary of Revenue* [No. COA08-450 (N.C. Ct. of App., May 19, 2009)], the North Carolina Court of Appeals ruled that the Department of Revenue could require a large retailer to file on a combined basis in order to determine the retailer's "true earnings" from its business in North Carolina. The taxpayer's parent company had restructured its divisions to establish the taxpayer operating company, a real estate investment trust (REIT) subsidiary that owned the retail stores in North Carolina and another property company subsidiary. The reorganization was designed to avoid North Carolina tax by enabling the taxpayer to claim a rent deduction for rent paid by the operating company to the REIT and a dividends-received deduction for dividends paid to the taxpayer by the out-of-state subsidiary property company from the rental income distributed to it by the REIT. See also *Delhaize America, Inc. v. Lay* [No. 06 CVS 08416, N.C. Supr. Ct., Jan. 12, 2011].

Virginia. In P.D. 05-139 [Va. Dept. of Taxn., Aug. 23, 2005], the Virginia Department of Taxation ruled that the income of a taxpayer and its three out-of-state subsidiaries had to be consolidated, because the transactions between the taxpayer and the subsidiaries lacked economic substance and were not at arm's length. The taxpayer had created the subsidiaries to hold its trademarks, trade names, real estate mortgages, and to make loans to the taxpayer.

Common Ownership Requirements

California. Two or more corporations are required to file a California combined report only if they are members of a "commonly controlled group," which means any of the following:

1. A parent corporation and one or more corporations or chains of corporations where the parent owns more than 50 percent of the voting power of at least one corporation and (if applicable) more than 50 percent of the voting power of each of the corporations, except the parent, is cumulatively owned by the parent, a corporation controlled by the parent, or other group member;
2. Two or more corporations, if more than 50 percent of the voting power of the corporations is owned by the same person;
3. Two or more corporations that constitute stapled entities; or
4. Two or more corporations, if more than 50 percent of the voting power of the corporations is cumulatively owned (ignoring the constructive ownership rules) by members of the same family. [Cal. Rev. & Tax. Code § 25105(a)]

Constructive ownership rules apply in determining a person's stock ownership.

Illinois. To qualify as members of an Illinois unitary business group, two or more corporations must be related through "common ownership," which means direct or indirect control or ownership of more than 50 percent of the outstanding voting stock. [35 Ill. Comp. Stat. § 1501(a)(27)] In the case of an entity other than a corporation, common ownership means direct or indirect ownership of an interest sufficient to exercise control over the activities of the entity. In the case of individuals, indirect control is determined by applying the attribution rules found in IRC § 318(a). [86 Ill. Adm. Code § 100.9700]

Texas. Only those taxable entities that are part of an "affiliated group" may file a Texas combined report. [Tex. Tax Code § 171.1014(a)] An affiliated group is a group of one or more entities in which a "controlling interest" is owned by a common owner, either corporate or non-corporate, or by one or more of the member entities. For a corporation, a "controlling interest" means more than 50 percent direct or indirect ownership of the total combined voting power of all classes of stock of the corporation, or a more than 50 percent direct or indirect beneficial ownership interest in the voting stock of the corporation. A more than 50 percent ownership test also applies to limited liability companies and partnerships. [Tex. Tax Code § 171.0001]

Concept of a Unitary Business

The various statutory definitions and judicial interpretations of a "unitary business" are discussed in the section in this part entitled Concept of a Unitary Business.

Worldwide Versus Water's-Edge Combined Reporting

Background. When a unitary group is required to compute its tax on a combined basis, there are two general approaches to dealing with unitary group members that are incorporated in a foreign country and/or conduct most of their business abroad:

1. *Worldwide combination.* The combined report includes all members of the unitary business group, regardless of the country in which the member is incorporated or the country in which the member conducts business.
2. *Water's-edge combination.* The combined report includes all members of the unitary business group, except for certain unitary group members that are incorporated in a foreign country or conduct most of their business abroad. A common approach is to exclude so-called 80/20 corporations. An 80/20 corporation is a corporation whose business activity outside the United States, as measured by some combination of apportionment factors, is 80 percent or more of the corporation's total business activity.

Requiring the use of worldwide combined reporting is controversial for a number of reasons, including the following: 1) distortions in the property or payroll factors caused by significantly lower wage rates and/or property values in developing countries; 2) the difficulty of converting books and records maintained under foreign accounting principles and in a foreign currency into a form that is acceptable to the states; 3) the inability of states to readily access or audit records located in foreign countries; and 4) uncertainties about which affiliates are properly included in the unitary group.

Despite the practical difficulties of apportioning income on a worldwide basis, the constitutionality of requiring a corporation to compute its state taxable income on a worldwide combined basis has been firmly established. In *Container Corp. of America v. Franchise Tax Board* [463 U.S. 159 (1983)], the Supreme Court held that California's worldwide combined reporting method was constitutional with respect to a U.S.-based parent corporation and its foreign country subsidiaries. In *Barclays Bank plc v. Franchise Tax Board* [512 U.S. 298 (1994)], the Supreme Court held that California's worldwide combined reporting method was also constitutional with respect to a foreign-based parent corporation and its U.S. subsidiaries. California repealed mandatory worldwide combined reporting in 1988 and permits a unitary group to make a water's-edge election.

Although a water's-edge combination generally reduces the compliance burden, it may also increase the taxpayer member's state tax liability if the unitary group's U.S. operations are more profitable than its foreign operations. Although the inclusion of a foreign member's profits increases the combined income of the group, the inclusion of the foreign member's property, payroll, and/or sales in the denominators of the apportionment factors generally reduces the state's apportionment percentage. The net effect can be a reduction in state taxable income if the group's foreign operations are less profitable than its U.S. operations and an increase in state taxable income if the group's foreign operations are more profitable than its U.S. operations.

In *Irving Pulp & Paper, Ltd. v. Maine State Tax Assessor* [No. Ken-04-580 (Me. Sup. Jud. Ct., Aug. 9, 2005)], the Maine Supreme Judicial Court addressed the issue of whether the references to property, payroll and sales "everywhere" in the apportionment statutes of Maine, which requires water's-edge reporting, refer to the taxpayer's worldwide property, payroll, and sales, or only the taxpayer's property, payroll, and sales within the United States. The court ruled that the taxpayer, a Canadian corporation, could not include its worldwide property, payroll, and sales in the denominators of the Maine apportionment factors, because Maine's water's-edge method of reporting looks only to a taxpayer's U.S. activities in determining its taxable income and because Maine taxable income is based on federal taxable income. In the case of a foreign corporation, federal taxable income generally includes only the income effectively connected with the foreign corporation's U.S. trade or business activities.

Different state approaches. California, Idaho, Montana and North Dakota require a worldwide combination, but give taxpayers the option to elect a water's-edge combination. The District of Columbia, Massachusetts, Utah and West Virginia require a water's-edge combination, but give taxpayers the option to elect a worldwide combination. Alaska requires a water's-edge combination, except for oil and gas companies, which must use worldwide combined reporting. The other mandatory combined reporting states, such as Illinois, Michigan and Texas, require a water's-edge combination.

Regardless of whether a water's-edge combination is mandatory or elective, a key issue is determining which members of the unitary group are excluded. One approach is to exclude any member that is incorporated in a foreign country. For example, Oregon requires corporations that are engaged in a unitary business and file a federal consolidated return to file an Oregon consolidated return. Because foreign corporations are not includible in a federal consolidated return, they are also not included in an Oregon consolidated return. [Ore. § 317.710]Moreover, a domestic corporation is not excluded from the Oregon consolidated return even if it conducts its business operations abroad.

Another approach is to exclude any member of the unitary group, regardless of the country of incorporation, which qualifies as a so-called "80/20 company." For example, a Colorado combined report excludes a member if 80 percent or more of its property and payroll are assigned to locations outside the United States. [Colo. § 39-22-303] Under this approach, the water's-edge group excludes a domestic corporation if its average property and payroll within the United States is 20 percent or less, and includes a foreign corporation if its average property and payroll within the United States is more than 20 percent.

Some states, such as Massachusetts, take a hybrid approach that looks at both the country of incorporation and the location of business activities. A Massachusetts' water's-edge group includes all domestic corporations, as well as any foreign corporation if its average property, payroll, and sales factors within the United States is 20 percent or more. [Mass. Ch. 63, § 32B]

Other variations on the theme water's-edge reporting include: (1) Montana and West Virginia require the inclusion of tax haven corporations, (2) Montana and North Dakota require taxpayers that make a water's-edge election to pay tax at a higher rate, and (3) Maine and New Mexico require foreign corporations to be included if they are required to file a federal income tax return (i.e., are engaged in a U.S. trade or business).

To close a perceived loophole with water's-edge reporting, Illinois requires a water's-edge group to add back certain interest and royalty expenses paid to 80/20 companies in computing its Illinois taxable income. Likewise, Oregon requires a unitary group to add back certain royalties and other intangible expenses paid to a related party that is excluded from the Oregon combined report, such as a domestic retailer paying royalties to a trademark holding company incorporated in Bermuda. [Ore. Reg. OAR § 150-314.295] Starting in 2008, Minnesota also requires a combined reporting group to add back interest and intangible expenses paid to a member of the unitary group that qualifies as a foreign operating corporation. [H.F. 3149, May 29, 2008]

California. If a member of the combined reporting group that is required to file a California income tax return does not make a water's-edge election, the California combined report includes the income and apportionment factors of all the members of the unitary business, including corporations organized in foreign countries. For members that are incorporated in a foreign country, the amount included in combined income is generally determined by preparing an income statement in the corporation's functional currency, making adjustments to conform the income amount to U.S. GAAP and California tax accounting standards, and translating the income amount and the related apportionment factors into U.S. dollars. [Calif. Code of Regs. § 25106.5-10]

In lieu of a California combined report that includes all the members of the unitary business, taxpayer members have the option to make a water's-edge election, under which the income and apportionment factors of foreign (non-U.S.) corporations are generally, but not always, excluded from the combined report.

To be eligible to make a water's-edge election, a taxpayer member must consent to the taking of depositions from key employees or officers of the water's-edge group and to the acceptance of subpoenas for producing documents. In addition, the taxpayer must agree to treat as apportionable business income any dividends received from (1) a corporation that is more than 50 percent owned by the unitary group and engaged in the same general line of business as the unitary group, and (2) any corporation that is either a significant source of supply for or a significant purchaser of the output of the members of the water's-edge group, or that sells a significant part of its output or obtains a significant part of its raw materials or input from the unitary business. Significant means an amount equal to 15 percent or more of either input or output. [Cal. Rev. & Tax. Code § 25110]

A water's-edge combined report includes the income and apportionment factors of only those members of the unitary group that meet one of the following criteria:

1. Any corporation incorporated in the United States (other than an IRC Section 936 corporation) if more than 50 percent of its stock is controlled by the same interests;
2. Any corporation (other than a bank), regardless of its country of incorporation, if the average of its property, payroll, and sales factors within the United States is 20 percent or more;
3. Controlled foreign corporation, as defined in IRC Section 957, but only to the extent of its Subpart F income and the apportionment factors related thereto;
4. Domestic international sales corporation (DISC), foreign sales corporation (FSC), or export trade corporation, as defined in the IRC;
5. Any other corporation, but only to the extent of its U.S. located income and factors (e.g., a foreign corporation's income effectively connected a U.S. trade or business). [Cal. Rev. & Tax. Code § 25110]

A water's-edge election may be terminated without the consent of the Franchise Tax Board (FTB) only after the election has been in effect for at least 84 months. An election may be terminated before the expiration of the 84-month period only with the consent of the FTB. [Cal. Rev. & Tax. Code § 25113]

Illinois. For purposes of computing the Illinois corporate income tax, a unitary business group does not include any those members whose business activity outside the United States is 80 percent or more of the member's total business activity, as measured by its property and payroll factors. [35 Ill. Comp. Stat. § 1501(a)(27)] If a foreign (non-U.S.) corporation is not excluded from the unitary business group under the 80/20 rule, IRC Section 882 limits the foreign corporation's federal taxable income to the amount of its income effectively connected with a U.S. trade or business. As a consequence, using the foreign corporation's worldwide apportionment factors to determine how much of its U.S. business income is apportioned to Illinois would not fairly represent that taxpayer's business activities within Illinois. Accordingly, only the factors related to the foreign corporation's U.S. business income are included in the numerators and denominators of the Illinois apportionment factors. [86 Ill. Adm. Code § 100.3380(e)]

A water's-edge group must add-back certain interest and royalty payments made to 80/20 companies in computing Illinois taxable income. [Ill. Comp. Stat. Ch. 35, § 203] Examples include interest or royalty payments made by a U.S. affiliate to an offshore financing subsidiary or intangible property company located in a foreign country.

Massachusetts. Massachusetts permits the taxable members of a combined group (i.e., members that have income tax nexus in the state) to elect to determine their apportioned share of the taxable net income of the combined group on a worldwide reporting basis, which takes into account the income and apportionment factors of all the members includible in the combined group. The worldwide reporting election is binding for 10 years. If the taxable members do not elect worldwide reporting, they must determine their apportioned share of the taxable net income of the combined group on a water's-edge basis. A Massachusetts' water's-edge group includes all domestic corporations, as well as any foreign corporation if its average property, payroll, and sales factors within the United States is 20 percent or more. [Mass. Ch. 63, § 32B] However, an item of income of a foreign corporation is excluded from the income of a water's-edge group if it is exempt from federal taxation under an income tax treaty. Moreover, a foreign corporation's inclusion in a combined group is determined only with regard to any items of income that are not exempt, taking into account items of expense and apportionment factors associated with such items of nonexempt income to the extent provided by regulation. [S.B. 2582, Aug. 5, 2010]

Michigan. A Michigan combined report is limited to U.S. persons, as defined in IRC Section 7701(a)(30). [Mich. Comp. Laws § 208.1117] Foreign (non-U.S.) corporations are not includible in the unitary business group. [Mich. Comp. Laws § 208.1511]A U.S. person that qualifies as a "foreign operating entity" is also not included in a unitary business group. [Mich. Comp. Laws § 208.1117(6)]A "foreign operating entity" is a U.S. person (e.g., a corporation organized in the United States) that would otherwise be a part of a unitary business group but has substantial operations outside the United States, and at least 80 percent of its income is active foreign business income. [Mich. Comp. Laws § 208.1109(5)]

Texas. For purposes of computing the Texas margin tax, a taxable entity that conducts business outside the United States is excluded from a Texas combined report if 80 percent or more of its property and payroll are assigned to locations outside the United States. If either the property factor or the payroll factor is zero, the denominator is one. If a taxable entity that conducts business outside the United States has no property or payroll, the entity is excluded from the combined report if 80 percent or more of its gross receipts are assigned to locations outside the United States. [Tex. Tax Code § 171.1014(a)]

West Virginia. Water's-edge combined reporting is the default method in West Virginia. Taxpayers have the option, however, to elect to file on a worldwide combined reporting basis. The election is binding for 10 years, and may be withdrawn only upon a written request to the Tax Commissioner for reasonable cause based on extraordinary hardship. [W. Va. Code § 11.24]

Recent Developments

District of Columbia. Effective for tax years beginning on or after January 1, 2011, commonly controlled corporations engaged in a unitary business must allocate and apportion their District taxable income on a combined basis. [D.C.B. 18-255, Dec. 18, 2009] A water's-edge combination is required, unless the taxpayer makes a worldwide combined reporting election. A worldwide election is binding for the tax year it is made and all tax years thereafter for a period of 10 years. [D.C.B 19-203, July 22, 2011]

Maryland. A corporation that files a Maryland income tax return and is a member of a corporate group is required to file a pro-forma (information only) water's-edge combined report. This reporting requirement sunsets for tax years beginning on or after January 1, 2011. [H.B. 664, Apr. 24, 2008]

Massachusetts. Effective for tax years beginning on or after January 1, 2009, a corporation subject to Massachusetts corporate income tax and engaged in a unitary business with one or more other corporations must calculate its Massachusetts taxable income based on its share of the combined group's apportionable income that is attributable to Massachusetts. [H.B. 4904 July 3, 2008] Under prior law, Massachusetts permitted affiliated corporations filing a federal consolidated return to elect to file a Massachusetts consolidated return, but only those affiliates that had nexus in Massachusetts were included in the consolidated return.

Michigan. From 2008 to 2011, Michigan imposed a 4.95 percent business income tax and 0.80 percent modified gross receipts tax. A unitary business group must file a combined return for purposes of computing the business income tax and modified gross receipts tax.

Effective January 1, 2012, Michigan replaced its business income and modified gross receipt taxes with a 6 percent corporate income tax. In computing the corporate income tax, unitary business groups are required to file combined tax returns. [H.B. 4361 and 4362, May 25, 2011]

Minnesota. For tax years beginning on or after January 1, 2008, Minnesota requires that in computing its taxable income, a combined reporting group must add-back interest and intangible expenses paid to, as well as certain other types of income received by, a member of the unitary group that qualifies as a foreign operating corporation. [H.F. 3149, May 29, 2008]

Rhode Island. For tax years beginning in 2011 or 2012, each corporation that is part of a unitary business is required to provide pro-forma (information only) combined reporting disclosures. [H.B. 5894, June 30, 2011]

South Carolina. South Carolina generally requires separate company reporting and does not require or permit the use of combined reporting. However, in *Media General Communications, Inc. v. Department of Revenue* [No. 26828 (S.C. Sup. Ct., June 14, 2010)], the South Carolina Supreme Court ruled that a group of communication companies could determine their taxable income on a combined basis under an equitable relief provision similar to UDITPA Section 18.

Texas. Effective for franchise tax reports originally due on or after January 1, 2008, Texas significantly modified the corporate franchise tax, replacing the prior tax based on capital and earned surplus with a new "margin tax." For purposes of computing the margin tax, "taxable entities that are part of an affiliated group engaged in a unitary business" must file a combined report. [H.B. 3, May 18, 2006] In contrast, under prior law each corporation that had nexus in Texas filed a return on a separate company basis, and a combined report was not required or permitted under any circumstances.

West Virginia. Effective for tax years beginning on and after January 1, 2009, any corporation engaged in a unitary business with one or more other corporations must compute its tax on a combined basis. An affiliated group of corporations is no longer allowed to file a consolidated return for tax years beginning after 2008. Each taxpayer member is responsible for tax based on its taxable income to West Virginia, including the member's apportioned share of the business income of the combined group. [S.B. 749, April 4, 2007]

Wisconsin. Effective for tax years beginning on or after January 1, 2009, a corporation engaged in a unitary business with one or more other corporations must report its share of income from that unitary business as determined by a combined report. [S.B. 62, Feb. 19, 2009] Prior to 2009, Wisconsin required the use of separate company reporting.

State-by-State Summary

The chart that follows summarizes each state's combined reporting requirements. For ease of presentation, the chart is divided into six parts, as follows:

- Part 1: Group Filing Options
- Part 2: Combined Reporting Group
- Part 3: Worldwide or Water's-Edge Reporting
- Part 4: Apportioning Income and Intercompany Transactions
- Part 5: Tax Credits, NOLs, and Dividends

Combined Unitary Reporting (Part 1)
Group Filing Options

Legend:
NA Not applicable
NR Not reported

Which filing options are available to a group of two or more corporations engaged in a unitary business?

State	*Combined Unitary Reporting Is Mandatory*	*Combined Unitary Reporting Is NOT Allowed Under Any Circumstances*	*State May Require Combined Unitary Reporting if Certain Conditions Are Met*	*State May Grant Permission to File a Combined Unitary Report if Certain Conditions Are Met*	*Taxpayer May Elect Combined Unitary Report if Certain Conditions Are Met*	*Other—Please Specify*
Alabama		X				
Alaska	X					
Arizona	Required if unitary	Required if unitary, See ARS §§ 43-941 and 43-942				
Arkansas		X				
California	X, Exceptions: R&TC § 25101.15 allows corporations conducting a unitary business wholly within the state to elect to use a combined report, and, R&TC § 25110 allows a qualified business to exclude certain income and apportionment factors pursuant to a water's-edge election.			See RTC § 25102		

Combined Unitary Reporting (Part 1)
Group Filing Options

Legend:
NA Not applicable
NR Not reported

Which filing options are available to a group of two or more corporations engaged in a unitary business?

State	*Combined Unitary Reporting Is Mandatory*	*Combined Unitary Reporting Is NOT Allowed Under Any Circumstances*	*State May Require Combined Unitary Reporting if Certain Conditions Are Met*	*State May Grant Permission to File a Combined Unitary Report if Certain Conditions Are Met*	*Taxpayer May Elect Combined Unitary Report if Certain Conditions Are Met*	*Other—Please Specify*
Colorado	X					X, must have at least 3 of 6 factors to combine. 39-22-303, C.R.S.
Connecticut				X, see Conn. Gen. Stat. § 12-223(a)	X, if it has related party interest. See Conn. Gen. Stat § 12-218(c)	
Delaware		X				
District of Columbia	X		X	X	X	X, District Council passed legislation "Combined Reporting Act of 2011" to require combined reporting, "Section 47-1805.02a" effective after tax year end 12/31/10. General Council at present is working on details and regulations.
Florida		X				
Georgia						Combined returns are generally not required or allowed.

Combined Unitary Reporting (Part 1)
Group Filing Options

Legend:
NA Not applicable
NR Not reported

Which filing options are available to a group of two or more corporations engaged in a unitary business?

State	*Combined Unitary Reporting Is Mandatory*	*Combined Unitary Reporting Is NOT Allowed Under Any Circumstances*	*State May Require Combined Unitary Reporting if Certain Conditions Are Met*	*State May Grant Permission to File a Combined Unitary Report if Certain Conditions Are Met*	*Taxpayer May Elect Combined Unitary Report if Certain Conditions Are Met*	*Other—Please Specify*
Hawaii	X					
Idaho	X					
Illinois	X					
Indiana			X	X		
Iowa		X				Iowa allows a "nexus consolidated" return whereby only those companies in the federal affiliated group that have nexus can be included in the Iowa consolidated return.
Kansas			X	X	X	
Kentucky		X				
Louisiana			X			
Maine	X					
Maryland		X				Separate company filing only
Massachusetts	X					

Combined Unitary Reporting (Part 1)
Group Filing Options

Legend:
NA Not applicable
NR Not reported

Which filing options are available to a group of two or more corporations engaged in a unitary business?

State	*Combined Unitary Reporting Is Mandatory*	*Combined Unitary Reporting Is NOT Allowed Under Any Circumstances*	*State May Require Combined Unitary Reporting if Certain Conditions Are Met*	*State May Grant Permission to File a Combined Unitary Report if Certain Conditions Are Met*	*Taxpayer May Elect Combined Unitary Report if Certain Conditions Are Met*	*Other—Please Specify*
Michigan (Business Tax)	X					

Note. The CIT takes effect 01/01/12, and replaces the Michigan Business Tax (MBT) for most taxpayers. However, businesses that have been approved to receive, have received, or have been assigned certain certified credits may elect to file a return and pay the tax imposed by the MBT in lieu of the CIT until the certified credits are exhausted or extinguished.

State	*Combined Unitary Reporting Is Mandatory*	*Combined Unitary Reporting Is NOT Allowed Under Any Circumstances*	*State May Require Combined Unitary Reporting if Certain Conditions Are Met*	*State May Grant Permission to File a Combined Unitary Report if Certain Conditions Are Met*	*Taxpayer May Elect Combined Unitary Report if Certain Conditions Are Met*	*Other—Please Specify*
Minnesota	X					
Mississippi		X	X			
Missouri		X				
Montana	X					
Nebraska	X					
Nevada	Nevada does not impose a corporate income tax					
New Hampshire	X					
New Jersey		X				
New Mexico					X	
New York	X, but only if there is substantial intercompany transactions		X	X		Required if there is substantial intercompany transactions
North Carolina				X		

Combined Unitary Reporting (Part 1)
Group Filing Options

Legend:
NA Not applicable
NR Not reported

Which filing options are available to a group of two or more corporations engaged in a unitary business?

State	*Combined Unitary Reporting Is Mandatory*	*Combined Unitary Reporting Is NOT Allowed Under Any Circumstances*	*State May Require Combined Unitary Reporting if Certain Conditions Are Met*	*State May Grant Permission to File a Combined Unitary Report if Certain Conditions Are Met*	*Taxpayer May Elect Combined Unitary Report if Certain Conditions Are Met*	*Other—Please Specify*
North Dakota	X					
Ohio	Ohio does not impose a corporate income tax					
Note. Effective 1/1/2010, the Ohio Franchise Tax was fully phased out and business will be taxed on gross receipts through the Commercial Activity Tax. Details about that tax can be found at: http//tax.ohio.gov/divisions/commercial_activities/index.stm						
Oklahoma		X				OK uses combined reporting/separate company calculation
Oregon						
Pennsylvania	NR	NR	NR	NR	NR	
Rhode Island					X	
South Carolina			X, mandatory after first consolidated return, unless permission granted		X	
South Dakota	South Dakota does not impose a corporate income tax					
Tennessee	Only for entities defined as Financial Institutions, TCA § 67-4-2004(4) and (11)		X	X		
Texas	X					

Combined Unitary Reporting (Part 1)
Group Filing Options

Legend:
NA Not applicable
NR Not reported

Which filing options are available to a group of two or more corporations engaged in a unitary business?

State	*Combined Unitary Reporting Is Mandatory*	*Combined Unitary Reporting Is NOT Allowed Under Any Circumstances*	*State May Require Combined Unitary Reporting if Certain Conditions Are Met*	*State May Grant Permission to File a Combined Unitary Report if Certain Conditions Are Met*	*Taxpayer May Elect Combined Unitary Report if Certain Conditions Are Met*	*Other—Please Specify*
Utah	X					
Vermont	X					
Virginia		X				
Washington	Washington does not impose a corporate income tax					
West Virginia	X, effective 1/1/09					Written petition required and must be approved by Tax Commissioner.
Wisconsin	X					
Wyoming	Wyoming does not impose a corporate income tax					

Combined Unitary Reporting (Part 2)
Combined Reporting Group

Legend:
NA Not applicable
NR Not reported

			If Unitary, Are the Following Types of Business Entities Included in the Combined Reporting Group?		
State	*Does Your State Require Taxpayers to Complete a Questionnaire to Determine Whether a Unitary Relationship Exists?*	*If Combined Unitary Reporting Is Required or Permitted, What Is the Stock Ownership Percentage for Inclusion in the Combined Reporting Group?*	*Transportation Companies*	*Financial Services Companies*	*Insurance Companies*
Alabama	No				
Alaska	Yes	More than 50%	X	X	X
Arizona	See AAC R15-2D-401.	More than 50%	X	X	See ARS § 43-1201(14).
Arkansas	No	NA			
California	No	More than 50% voting stock, see R&TC § 25105.	X	X	
Colorado	Yes	More than 50%	X		
Connecticut	Yes	80% or more	No written guidance	No written guidance	No written guidance
Delaware					
District of Columbia	Work in progress	50% or more	X		X
Florida	NA				
Georgia					
Hawaii	No	More than 50%	X	X	X
Idaho	No	More than 50%	X	X	X
Illinois	No	Direct or indirect control or ownership of more than 50% of the outstanding voting stock	X	X	X

Combined Unitary Reporting (Part 2)
Combined Reporting Group

Legend:

NA Not applicable

NR Not reported

State	*Does Your State Require Taxpayers to Complete a Questionnaire to Determine Whether a Unitary Relationship Exists?*	*If Combined Unitary Reporting Is Required or Permitted, What Is the Stock Ownership Percentage for Inclusion in the Combined Reporting Group?*	*If Unitary, Are the Following Types of Business Entities Included in the Combined Reporting Group?*		
			Transportation Companies	*Financial Services Companies*	*Insurance Companies*
Indiana	Yes	80% or more	X	X	X
Iowa	No				
Kansas	No	General rule is more than 50%; however actual control demonstrated is the measurement.	X, using a bifurcated formula	X, not banks, trusts or credit unions.	X, captive insurance companies may be included in certain circumstances
Kentucky	NR				
Louisiana	No	Stock ownership by same interest-no minimum ownership required			
Maine	No	More than 50%	X	X	X
Maryland	No				
Massachusetts	No	More than 50%	X	X	X
Michigan (Business Tax)	No	More than 50%	X		

Note. The CIT takes effect 01/01/12, and replaces the Michigan Business Tax (MBT) for most taxpayers. However, businesses that have been approved to receive, have received, or have been assigned certain certified credits may elect to file a return and pay the tax imposed by the MBT in lieu of the CIT until the certified credits are exhausted or extinguished.

Minnesota	Yes	More than 50%	X	X	

Combined Unitary Reporting (Part 2)
Combined Reporting Group

Legend:
NA Not applicable
NR Not reported

State	*Does Your State Require Taxpayers to Complete a Questionnaire to Determine Whether a Unitary Relationship Exists?*	*If Combined Unitary Reporting Is Required or Permitted, What Is the Stock Ownership Percentage for Inclusion in the Combined Reporting Group?*	*If Unitary, Are the Following Types of Business Entities Included in the Combined Reporting Group?*		
			Transportation Companies	*Financial Services Companies*	*Insurance Companies*
Mississippi	No	80% or more			
Missouri					
Montana	No	More than 50%	X	X	X
Nebraska	Yes	50% or more	X		
Nevada	Nevada does not impose a corporate income tax				
New Hampshire	No	No per se requirement	X	X	X
New Jersey	No				
New Mexico	No	More than 50%	X	X	X
New York	No	80% or more	X	X	
North Carolina	No				
North Dakota	No	More than 50%	X	X	
Ohio	Ohio does not impose a corporate income tax				
Note. Effective 1/1/2010, the Ohio Franchise Tax was fully phased out and business will be taxed on gross receipts through the Commercial Activity Tax. Details about that tax can be found at: http//tax.ohio.gov/divisions/commercial_activities/index.stm					
Oklahoma					

Combined Unitary Reporting (Part 2)
Combined Reporting Group

Legend:

NA Not applicable

NR Not reported

State	*Does Your State Require Taxpayers to Complete a Questionnaire to Determine Whether a Unitary Relationship Exists?*	*If Combined Unitary Reporting Is Required or Permitted, What Is the Stock Ownership Percentage for Inclusion in the Combined Reporting Group?*	*If Unitary, Are the Following Types of Business Entities Included in the Combined Reporting Group?* — *Transportation Companies*	*Financial Services Companies*	*Insurance Companies*
Oregon					Yes, if no Oregon presence, no if Oregon presence—must file separate Form 20-INS
Pennsylvania	NR	NR	NR	NR	NR
Rhode Island	No	More than 50%	X		
South Carolina	No	More than 80%	X	X	
South Dakota	South Dakota does not impose a corporate income tax				
Tennessee	No	All factors on a case-by-case basis will be evaluated whether to require or grant permission to file a combined return TCA § 67-4-2014.		X	
Texas	No	More than 50%	X	X	X, unless exempt
Utah	Yes	More than 50%	X	X	Depends
Vermont	No	More than 50%	X	X	X
Virginia					
Washington	Washington does not impose a corporate income tax				

Combined Unitary Reporting (Part 2)
Combined Reporting Group

Legend:
NA Not applicable
NR Not reported

State	*Does Your State Require Taxpayers to Complete a Questionnaire to Determine Whether a Unitary Relationship Exists?*	*If Combined Unitary Reporting Is Required or Permitted, What Is the Stock Ownership Percentage for Inclusion in the Combined Reporting Group?*	*If Unitary, Are the Following Types of Business Entities Included in the Combined Reporting Group?*		
			Transportation Companies	*Financial Services Companies*	*Insurance Companies*
West Virginia	No	50% or more	X	X	
Wisconsin	No	50% or more	X	X	X
Wyoming	Wyoming does not impose a corporate income tax				

Combined Unitary Reporting (Part 3)
Worldwide or Water's-Edge Reporting

Legend:

NA Not applicable

NR Not reported

State	*What Is Your State's Policy Regarding Worldwide versus Water's-Edge Reporting?*	*If Water's-Edge Reporting Is Required or Elected, which Types of Corporations Are Excluded from the Combined Reporting Group?*	*If a Unitary Foreign Entity Is Treated as a Corporation for Foreign Country Purposes, but a Branch for U.S. Tax Purposes, Is this "Check-the-Box" Foreign Branch Included in the Combined Reporting Group?*	*If a Member of the Combined Reporting Group Is a Partner in a Partnership that Is Unitary with the Partner, Is a Distributive Share of the Partnership's Income Included in the Combined Report?*
Alabama	NR			
Alaska	Oil and gas producers and pipeline companies are required to prepare Worldwide combined reports that include all unitary corporations. Water's-Edge is mandatory for all other companies.	Corporations organized in a foreign country.	Yes	Yes
Arizona	Water's-edge is mandatory.	See ARS § 43-1101(5).	Yes	See AZ Corp Tax Ruling 94-1.
Arkansas	NA	NA	NA	NA

Combined Unitary Reporting (Part 3)
Worldwide or Water's-Edge Reporting

Legend:
NA Not applicable
NR Not reported

State	*What Is Your State's Policy Regarding Worldwide versus Water's-Edge Reporting?*	*If Water's-Edge Reporting Is Required or Elected, which Types of Corporations Are Excluded from the Combined Reporting Group?*	*If a Unitary Foreign Entity Is Treated as a Corporation for Foreign Country Purposes, but a Branch for U.S. Tax Purposes, Is this "Check-the-Box" Foreign Branch Included in the Combined Reporting Group?*	*If a Member of the Combined Reporting Group Is a Partner in a Partnership that Is Unitary with the Partner, Is a Distributive Share of the Partnership's Income Included in the Combined Report?*
California	Worldwide is required unless taxpayer makes water's-edge election.	Corporations organized in a foreign country, except the taxpayer must take into account the entire income and apportionment factors of: (1) a domestic international sales corporation and foreign sales corporations (2) any corporation (other than a bank), regardless of where incorporated if the average of its property, payroll and sales factors within the U.S. is 20% or more (3) corporations incorporated in the U.S., excluding those making an election pursuant to IRC §§ 931-936, and (4) export trade corporations. See R&TC § 25110(a)(1).	Yes	Yes, see CA Code Reg Title 18, § 25137-1.
Colorado	Water's-edge is mandatory.	80/20 Companies	X	No, partnership is treated as a member of the group (i.e., all of partnership's income and all of its factors are considered part of partner's income and factors).
Connecticut	No written guidance	No written guidance	No written guidance	No written guidance

Combined Unitary Reporting (Part 3)
Worldwide or Water's-Edge Reporting

Legend:
NA Not applicable
NR Not reported

State	*What Is Your State's Policy Regarding Worldwide versus Water's-Edge Reporting?*	*If Water's-Edge Reporting Is Required or Elected, which Types of Corporations Are Excluded from the Combined Reporting Group?*	*If a Unitary Foreign Entity Is Treated as a Corporation for Foreign Country Purposes, but a Branch for U.S. Tax Purposes, Is this "Check-the-Box" Foreign Branch Included in the Combined Reporting Group?*	*If a Member of the Combined Reporting Group Is a Partner in a Partnership that Is Unitary with the Partner, Is a Distributive Share of the Partnership's Income Included in the Combined Report?*
Delaware				
District of Columbia	Water's-edge is mandatory unless taxpayer makes waters-edge election.	The one not in unitary group	Yes, regulations are pending.	Yes
Florida				
Georgia				
Hawaii	Yes	Foreign affiliate as defined by § 18-235-38.5-02 HAR	No	Yes
Idaho	Worldwide is required unless taxpayer makes water's-edge election.	Corporations organized in a foreign country, IRC § 936 companies	Yes	Yes
Illinois	Water's-edge is mandatory.	80/20 Companies, at least 80% business activity outside the US	Yes, assumes foreign branch does not cause the entity to be an 80/20 company.	Yes
Indiana	Water's-edge is mandatory.	Corporations organized in a foreign country, 80/20 Companies	Yes	Yes
Iowa				
Kansas	Domestic combination		Yes	Yes
Kentucky				

Combined Unitary Reporting (Part 3)
Worldwide or Water's-Edge Reporting

Legend:
NA Not applicable
NR Not reported

State	*What Is Your State's Policy Regarding Worldwide versus Water's-Edge Reporting?*	*If Water's-Edge Reporting Is Required or Elected, which Types of Corporations Are Excluded from the Combined Reporting Group?*	*If a Unitary Foreign Entity Is Treated as a Corporation for Foreign Country Purposes, but a Branch for U.S. Tax Purposes, Is this "Check-the-Box" Foreign Branch Included in the Combined Reporting Group?*	*If a Member of the Combined Reporting Group Is a Partner in a Partnership that Is Unitary with the Partner, Is a Distributive Share of the Partnership's Income Included in the Combined Report?*
Louisiana			No	Yes
Maine	Water's-edge is mandatory, factor relief for foreign dividend payors is dependent on a worldwide equivalent calculations.	Corporations not required to file a US federal income tax return	Yes	Yes
Maryland				
Massachusetts	Water's-edge is mandatory. Worldwide election is permitted	830 CMR 63.32B.2(5)	Yes	Yes
Michigan (Business Tax)	Water's-edge is mandatory.	80/20 corporations defined as a U.S. person that (a) would otherwise be part of a unitary business group, (b) has substantial operations outside the US, DC, PR, any territory or possession of the US or is a political subdivision of any of the foregoing and (c) at least 80% of its income is active foreign business income as defined in IRC §. 861(c)(1)(B) also known under MBT as a "foreign operating entity."	No	No

Combined Unitary Reporting (Part 3)
Worldwide or Water's-Edge Reporting

Legend:

NA	Not applicable
NR	Not reported

State	*What Is Your State's Policy Regarding Worldwide versus Water's-Edge Reporting?*	*If Water's-Edge Reporting Is Required or Elected, which Types of Corporations Are Excluded from the Combined Reporting Group?*	*If a Unitary Foreign Entity Is Treated as a Corporation for Foreign Country Purposes, but a Branch for U.S. Tax Purposes, Is this "Check-the-Box" Foreign Branch Included in the Combined Reporting Group?*	*If a Member of the Combined Reporting Group Is a Partner in a Partnership that Is Unitary with the Partner, Is a Distributive Share of the Partnership's Income Included in the Combined Report?*
Note. The CIT takes effect 01/01/12, and replaces the Michigan Business Tax (MBT) for most taxpayers. However, businesses that have been approved to receive, have received, or have been assigned certain certified credits may elect to file a return and pay the tax imposed by the MBT in lieu of the CIT until the certified credits are exhausted or extinguished.				
Minnesota	Water's-edge is mandatory.	Corporations organized in a foreign country. Domestic corporations that qualify as foreign operating corporations.	No	Yes
Mississippi	Only companies that have nexus in MS can file in a combined return, then, all corporations that have nexus in MS must file on the combined return.		Yes	Yes
Missouri				
Montana	World wide is required unless taxpayer makes water's-edge election.	Corporations organized in a foreign country, 80/20 Companies- incorporated in US, in a unitary relationship with the taxpayer and has more than 80% of its payroll and property assignable to locations outside the US.	NR	Yes
Nebraska	All members subject to IRC		Yes	Yes

Combined Unitary Reporting (Part 3)
Worldwide or Water's-Edge Reporting

Legend:
NA Not applicable
NR Not reported

State	*What Is Your State's Policy Regarding Worldwide versus Water's-Edge Reporting?*	*If Water's-Edge Reporting Is Required or Elected, which Types of Corporations Are Excluded from the Combined Reporting Group?*	*If a Unitary Foreign Entity Is Treated as a Corporation for Foreign Country Purposes, but a Branch for U.S. Tax Purposes, Is this "Check-the-Box" Foreign Branch Included in the Combined Reporting Group?*	*If a Member of the Combined Reporting Group Is a Partner in a Partnership that Is Unitary with the Partner, Is a Distributive Share of the Partnership's Income Included in the Combined Report?*
Nevada	Nevada does not impose a corporate income tax			
New Hampshire	Water's-edge is mandatory.	Corporations organized in a foreign country, 80/20 Companies; see Rev. 301.12	No	No, but partnership would be brought into group
New Jersey	Water's-edge reporting not used since entire net income of affiliated group is reported and determined on separate entity basis.			Yes, NJAC 17.9
New Mexico	Neither is allowed.		Yes	Yes
New York	Corporations organized under the laws of a non-US country are never required or permitted to be included in a combined report.		Only if it is treated as a disregarded entity and its income is included with its US parent for federal purposes.	Yes
North Carolina				
North Dakota	Worldwide is required unless taxpayer makes water's-edge election.	Corporations organized in a foreign country, 80/20 companies.	No	Yes
Ohio	Ohio does not impose a corporate income tax			

Note. Effective 1/1/2010, the Ohio Franchise Tax was fully phased out and business will be taxed on gross receipts through the Commercial Activity Tax. Details about that tax can be found at: http//tax.ohio.gov/divisions/commercial_activities/index.stm

Combined Unitary Reporting (Part 3)
Worldwide or Water's-Edge Reporting

Legend:
NA — Not applicable
NR — Not reported

State	*What Is Your State's Policy Regarding Worldwide versus Water's-Edge Reporting?*	*If Water's-Edge Reporting Is Required or Elected, which Types of Corporations Are Excluded from the Combined Reporting Group?*	*If a Unitary Foreign Entity Is Treated as a Corporation for Foreign Country Purposes, but a Branch for U.S. Tax Purposes, Is this "Check-the-Box" Foreign Branch Included in the Combined Reporting Group?*	*If a Member of the Combined Reporting Group Is a Partner in a Partnership that Is Unitary with the Partner, Is a Distributive Share of the Partnership's Income Included in the Combined Report?*
Oklahoma				
Oregon				
Pennsylvania	NR	NR	NR	NR
Rhode Island	Worldwide is required unless taxpayer makes water's-edge election.	Corporations organized in a foreign country.	Yes	Yes
South Carolina	Worldwide is mandatory		No	X
South Dakota	South Dakota does not impose a corporate income tax			
Tennessee				

Combined Unitary Reporting (Part 3)
Worldwide or Water's-Edge Reporting

Legend:
NA Not applicable
NR Not reported

State	*What Is Your State's Policy Regarding Worldwide versus Water's-Edge Reporting?*	*If Water's-Edge Reporting Is Required or Elected, which Types of Corporations Are Excluded from the Combined Reporting Group?*	*If a Unitary Foreign Entity Is Treated as a Corporation for Foreign Country Purposes, but a Branch for U.S. Tax Purposes, Is this "Check-the-Box" Foreign Branch Included in the Combined Reporting Group?*	*If a Member of the Combined Reporting Group Is a Partner in a Partnership that Is Unitary with the Partner, Is a Distributive Share of the Partnership's Income Included in the Combined Report?*
Texas	Water's edge is mandatory	80/20 companies defined as: A combined group may not include a taxable entity that conducts business outside the U.S. if 80% or more of the taxable entity's property and payroll are assigned to locations outside the U.S. Additionally, the combined group may not include a taxable entity that conducts business outside the U.S. and has no property or payroll if 80% or more of the taxable entity's gross receipts are assigned to locations outside the U.S. Taxable entities that are part of an affiliated group engaged in a unitary business must file a combined group report. The net distributive income from a taxable entity treated as a partnership or as an S corporation for federal income tax is excluded from total revenue.	No	A combined group may not include a taxable entity that conducts business outside the U.S. if 80% or more of the taxable entity's property and payroll are assigned to locations outside the U.S. Additionally, the combined group may not include a taxable entity that conducts business outside the U.S. and has no property or payroll if 80% or more of the taxable entity's gross receipts are assigned to locations outside the U.S. Taxable entities that are part of an affiliated group engaged in a unitary business must file a combined group report. The net distributive income from a taxable entity treated as a partnership or as an S corporation for federal income tax is excluded from total revenue.

Combined Unitary Reporting (Part 3)
Worldwide or Water's-Edge Reporting

Legend:
NA Not applicable
NR Not reported

State	*What Is Your State's Policy Regarding Worldwide versus Water's-Edge Reporting?*	*If Water's-Edge Reporting Is Required or Elected, which Types of Corporations Are Excluded from the Combined Reporting Group?*	*If a Unitary Foreign Entity Is Treated as a Corporation for Foreign Country Purposes, but a Branch for U.S. Tax Purposes, Is this "Check-the-Box" Foreign Branch Included in the Combined Reporting Group?*	*If a Member of the Combined Reporting Group Is a Partner in a Partnership that Is Unitary with the Partner, Is a Distributive Share of the Partnership's Income Included in the Combined Report?*
Utah	Worldwide is required unless taxpayer makes water's-edge election.	Corporations organized in a foreign country.	Yes	Yes
Vermont	Water's-edge is mandatory	80/20 companies, defined as 80% of payroll and property ordinarily outside US.	NR	Yes
Virginia				
Washington	Washington does not impose a corporate income tax			
West Virginia	X	Corporations organized in a foreign country	No	Yes

Combined Unitary Reporting (Part 3)
Worldwide or Water's-Edge Reporting

Legend:
NA Not applicable
NR Not reported

State	*What Is Your State's Policy Regarding Worldwide versus Water's-Edge Reporting?*	*If Water's-Edge Reporting Is Required or Elected, which Types of Corporations Are Excluded from the Combined Reporting Group?*	*If a Unitary Foreign Entity Is Treated as a Corporation for Foreign Country Purposes, but a Branch for U.S. Tax Purposes, Is this "Check-the-Box" Foreign Branch Included in the Combined Reporting Group?*	*If a Member of the Combined Reporting Group Is a Partner in a Partnership that Is Unitary with the Partner, Is a Distributive Share of the Partnership's Income Included in the Combined Report?*
Wisconsin	Water's edge is mandatory	80% or more of corporation's worldwide gross income is "active foreign business income" as defined in IRC § 861(c)(1)(B). See Rule Tax § 2.61(4). A "domestic 80/20" may be partially excluded. See Rule Tax § 2.61(4)(d). A "foreign 80/20" is generally excluded. See Rule Tax § 2.61(4)(e). Emergency rules for combined reporting are available at http://www.revenue.wi.gov/combrept/rules.html.	Yes	Yes
Wyoming	Wyoming does not impose a corporate income tax			

Combined Unitary Reporting (Part 4)
Apportioning Income and Intercompany Transactions

Legend:
NA Not applicable
NR Not reported

	What Procedure Applies for Apportioning the Income of the Combined Reporting Group?		*What Adjustments Are Made for Income Derived from Transactions between Members of the Combined Reporting Group?*			
State	*Income of Members Is Combined BEFORE Applying the State's Apportionment Percentage*	*Income of Members Is Combined AFTER Each Member Individually Apportions Its Income*	*No Adjustment Is Made for Intercompany Transactions*	*Same as Those Required by Treasury Reg. § 1.1502-13 for Federal Consolidated Return Purposes*	*Same as Treasury Reg. § 1.1502-13, with Exceptions*	*Other—Please Specify*
Alabama	NR	NR	NR	NR	NR	
Alaska	X			X		
Arizona	X					See AAC R15-2D-405
Arkansas	NA	NA	NA	NA	NA	
California	X			As modified by R&TC § 25106.5, also see CA Code Regs Title 18, § 25106.5-1.		
Colorado	X			X		
Connecticut	No written guidance	No written guidance	No written guidance	No written guidance	No written guidance	No written guidance
Delaware						
District of Columbia		X		X		
Florida						
Georgia						
Hawaii	X				X	

Combined Unitary Reporting (Part 4)
Apportioning Income and Intercompany Transactions

Legend:
NA Not applicable
NR Not reported

	What Procedure Applies for Apportioning the Income of the Combined Reporting Group?		*What Adjustments Are Made for Income Derived from Transactions between Members of the Combined Reporting Group?*			
State	*Income of Members Is Combined BEFORE Applying the State's Apportionment Percentage*	*Income of Members Is Combined AFTER Each Member Individually Apportions Its Income*	*No Adjustment Is Made for Intercompany Transactions*	*Same as Those Required by Treasury Reg. § 1.1502-13 for Federal Consolidated Return Purposes*	*Same as Treasury Reg. § 1.1502-13, with Exceptions*	*Other—Please Specify*
Idaho	X					Eliminate intercompany transactions to the extent necessary to properly reflect combined income and to properly compute the apportionment factor.
Illinois	X			X		
Indiana	X			X		
Iowa						
Kansas	X			X		
Kentucky						
Louisiana	X			X		
Maine	X					Pursuant to MRS Reg. 810 (Similar to federal consolidated return)
Maryland						
Massachusetts	X					

Combined Unitary Reporting (Part 4)
Apportioning Income and Intercompany Transactions

Legend:

NA Not applicable

NR Not reported

State	*What Procedure Applies for Apportioning the Income of the Combined Reporting Group?* — *Income of Members Is Combined BEFORE Applying the State's Apportionment Percentage*	*Income of Members Is Combined AFTER Each Member Individually Apportions Its Income*	*What Adjustments Are Made for Income Derived from Transactions between Members of the Combined Reporting Group?* — *No Adjustment Is Made for Intercompany Transactions*	*Same as Those Required by Treasury Reg. § 1.1502-13 for Federal Consolidated Return Purposes*	*Same as Treasury Reg. § 1.1502-13, with Exceptions*	*Other—Please Specify*
Michigan (Business Tax)	X					Each member included in a unitary business group shall be treated as a single person and all transactions between those persons shall be eliminated from the business income tax base and the apportionment formula.
Note. The CIT takes effect 01/01/12, and replaces the Michigan Business Tax (MBT) for most taxpayers. However, businesses that have been approved to receive, have received, or have been assigned certain certified credits may elect to file a return and pay the tax imposed by the MBT in lieu of the CIT until the certified credits are exhausted or extinguished.						
Minnesota	X					Intercompany transactions are eliminated
Mississippi		X	X			
Missouri						
Montana	X			X		
Nebraska	X			X		
Nevada	Nevada does not impose a corporate income tax					

Combined Unitary Reporting (Part 4)
Apportioning Income and Intercompany Transactions

Legend:
NA Not applicable
NR Not reported

	What Procedure Applies for Apportioning the Income of the Combined Reporting Group?		*What Adjustments Are Made for Income Derived from Transactions between Members of the Combined Reporting Group?*			
State	*Income of Members Is Combined BEFORE Applying the State's Apportionment Percentage*	*Income of Members Is Combined AFTER Each Member Individually Apportions Its Income*	*No Adjustment Is Made for Intercompany Transactions*	*Same as Those Required by Treasury Reg. § 1.1502-13 for Federal Consolidated Return Purposes*	*Same as Treasury Reg. § 1.1502-13, with Exceptions*	*Other—Please Specify*
New Hampshire	X					All intercompany transactions are eliminated.
New Jersey		X				A blended allocation factor is used. NJAC 18:7-17.9.
New Mexico	X			X		
New York	X					All corporations in the combined group should make all the adjustments required for the federal consolidated return on a separate basis. See § 3-2.10 of the Business Corporation Franchise Tax Regulations.
North Carolina						
North Dakota	X					These intercompany transactions are eliminated.
Ohio	Ohio does not impose a corporate income tax.					

Combined Unitary Reporting (Part 4)
Apportioning Income and Intercompany Transactions

Legend:

NA	Not applicable
NR	Not reported

	What Procedure Applies for Apportioning the Income of the Combined Reporting Group?		*What Adjustments Are Made for Income Derived from Transactions between Members of the Combined Reporting Group?*			
State	*Income of Members Is Combined BEFORE Applying the State's Apportionment Percentage*	*Income of Members Is Combined AFTER Each Member Individually Apportions Its Income*	*No Adjustment Is Made for Intercompany Transactions*	*Same as Those Required by Treasury Reg. § 1.1502-13 for Federal Consolidated Return Purposes*	*Same as Treasury Reg. § 1.1502-13, with Exceptions*	*Other—Please Specify*
Note. Effective 1/1/2010, the Ohio Franchise Tax was fully phased out and business will be taxed on gross receipts through the Commercial Activity Tax. Details about that tax can be found at: http//tax.ohio.gov/divisions/commercial_activities/index.stm						
Oklahoma						
Oregon						
Pennsylvania	NR	NR	NR	NR	NR	
Rhode Island		X	X			
South Carolina		X	X			
South Dakota	South Dakota does not impose a corporate income tax					
Tennessee						
Texas	X					Items of total revenue received from a member of the combined group are eliminated.
Utah	X			X		
Vermont		X				
Virginia						
Washington	Washington does not impose a corporate income tax					
West Virginia	X			X		

Combined Unitary Reporting (Part 4)
Apportioning Income and Intercompany Transactions

Legend:
NA Not applicable
NR Not reported

	What Procedure Applies for Apportioning the Income of the Combined Reporting Group?		*What Adjustments Are Made for Income Derived from Transactions between Members of the Combined Reporting Group?*			
State	*Income of Members Is Combined BEFORE Applying the State's Apportionment Percentage*	*Income of Members Is Combined AFTER Each Member Individually Apportions Its Income*	*No Adjustment Is Made for Intercompany Transactions*	*Same as Those Required by Treasury Reg. § 1.1502-13 for Federal Consolidated Return Purposes*	*Same as Treasury Reg. § 1.1502-13, with Exceptions*	*Other—Please Specify*
Wisconsin	X				X, except as provided by rule	
Wyoming	Wyoming does not impose a corporate income tax					

Combined Unitary Reporting (Part 5)
Tax Credits, NOLs, and Dividends

Legend:

NA Not applicable

NR Not reported

State	*Can a Tax Credit Earned by One Member of the Combined Reporting Group Be Used to Reduce the Tax Liability of Another Group Member?*	*Can an NOL Carryforward Attributable to One Member of the Combined Reporting Group Be Deducted by Another Group Member?*	*Are Dividends Paid by One Member of the Combined Reporting Group to Another Group Member Eliminated from the Income of the Recipient?*	*Is Each Group Member with Nexus in the State Separately Responsible for the Tax on Its Income Apportioned to the State?*
Alabama	NR	NR	NR	NR
Alaska	Yes	Yes	Yes	Yes
Arizona	Yes, of the entire unitary group	Yes, of the entire unitary group	Depends, see ARS § 43-1122(4).	No
Arkansas	NA	NA	NA	NA
California	No, see R&TC, § 23663, which permits credit assignments between wholly-owned unitary affiliates.	No	Yes, see R&TC, § 25106; only if paid out of E&P of the unitary business that was included in a combined report.	Yes
Colorado	Yes	Yes	Only if paid from E&P of unitary business included in combined report	No
Connecticut	Yes	Yes	No	No
Delaware				
District of Columbia	No	No, final regulations pending decision at present.	Yes, only if paid from E & P of the unitary business that was included in a combined report.	Yes
Florida				
Georgia				
Hawaii	No	No	Yes, 18-235-22-03(b)(1)	No

Combined Unitary Reporting (Part 5)
Tax Credits, NOLs, and Dividends

Legend:
NA Not applicable
NR Not reported

State	*Can a Tax Credit Earned by One Member of the Combined Reporting Group Be Used to Reduce the Tax Liability of Another Group Member?*	*Can an NOL Carryforward Attributable to One Member of the Combined Reporting Group Be Deducted by Another Group Member?*	*Are Dividends Paid by One Member of the Combined Reporting Group to Another Group Member Eliminated from the Income of the Recipient?*	*Is Each Group Member with Nexus in the State Separately Responsible for the Tax on Its Income Apportioned to the State?*
Idaho	Yes	No	Only if paid out of E&P of the unitary business that was included in a combined report.	Yes
Illinois	Yes	Yes	Yes	No, joint and severable liability for the group's tax liability
Indiana	Yes	Yes	Yes	Yes
Iowa				
Kansas	No	No	Yes	Yes
Kentucky				
Louisiana	No	No	Yes	Yes
Maine	Yes	Yes	Yes	Yes
Maryland				
Massachusetts	Yes, depending on the credit and the facts.		NR	Yes

Combined Unitary Reporting (Part 5)
Tax Credits, NOLs, and Dividends

Legend:

NA	Not applicable
NR	Not reported

State	*Can a Tax Credit Earned by One Member of the Combined Reporting Group Be Used to Reduce the Tax Liability of Another Group Member?*	*Can an NOL Carryforward Attributable to One Member of the Combined Reporting Group Be Deducted by Another Group Member?*	*Are Dividends Paid by One Member of the Combined Reporting Group to Another Group Member Eliminated from the Income of the Recipient?*	*Is Each Group Member with Nexus in the State Separately Responsible for the Tax on Its Income Apportioned to the State?*
Michigan (Business Tax)	Yes, under the MBT, the unitary business group is the taxpayer. In most cases, a credit earned by a member of a unitary business group can be applied to the tax liability of the unitary business group	No	Yes	No, the Department will look to the designated member of a unitary business group to file returns and remit payments. However, all members of a unitary business group that have nexus with MI shall be jointly and severally liable for the MBT
Note. The CIT takes effect 01/01/12, and replaces the Michigan Business Tax (MBT) for most taxpayers. However, businesses that have been approved to receive, have received, or have been assigned certain certified credits may elect to file a return and pay the tax imposed by the MBT in lieu of the CIT until the certified credits are exhausted or extinguished.				
Minnesota	No	No	Yes	Yes
Mississippi	No	Yes	Yes	No
Missouri				
Montana	No	No	Yes	Yes
Nebraska	Yes, a single return is required for the combined unitary group	No	Yes	No
Nevada	Nevada does not impose a corporate income tax			
New Hampshire	See Rev 306	No	Yes	No
New Jersey				Yes

Combined Unitary Reporting (Part 5)
Tax Credits, NOLs, and Dividends

Legend:
NA — Not applicable
NR — Not reported

State	*Can a Tax Credit Earned by One Member of the Combined Reporting Group Be Used to Reduce the Tax Liability of Another Group Member?*	*Can an NOL Carryforward Attributable to One Member of the Combined Reporting Group Be Deducted by Another Group Member?*	*Are Dividends Paid by One Member of the Combined Reporting Group to Another Group Member Eliminated from the Income of the Recipient?*	*Is Each Group Member with Nexus in the State Separately Responsible for the Tax on Its Income Apportioned to the State?*
New Mexico	Yes	No	Yes	No
New York	The credit is applied to the tax liability of the combined group.	See § 3-8.7 of the Business Franchise Tax Regulations.	Yes	See § 8-1.3 of the Business Corporation Franchise Tax Regulations.
North Carolina				
North Dakota	Only for installation of an energy device and the research expenditure credit	No	Yes	Yes
Ohio	Ohio does not impose a corporate income tax			
Note. Effective 1/1/2010, the Ohio Franchise Tax was fully phased out and business will be taxed on gross receipts through the Commercial Activity Tax. Details about that tax can be found at: http//tax.ohio.gov/divisions/commercial_activities/index.stm				
Oklahoma				
Oregon				
Pennsylvania	NR	NR	NR	NR
Rhode Island	No	No	No	No
South Carolina	Yes		No	Yes
South Dakota	South Dakota does not impose a corporate income tax			
Tennessee				
Texas	Yes		Yes	No, all members are jointly and severally liable

Combined Unitary Reporting (Part 5)
Tax Credits, NOLs, and Dividends

Legend:
NA — Not applicable
NR — Not reported

State	*Can a Tax Credit Earned by One Member of the Combined Reporting Group Be Used to Reduce the Tax Liability of Another Group Member?*	*Can an NOL Carryforward Attributable to One Member of the Combined Reporting Group Be Deducted by Another Group Member?*	*Are Dividends Paid by One Member of the Combined Reporting Group to Another Group Member Eliminated from the Income of the Recipient?*	*Is Each Group Member with Nexus in the State Separately Responsible for the Tax on Its Income Apportioned to the State?*
Utah	Yes	No	Yes	No
Vermont	No	No	Yes	Yes
Virginia				
Washington	Washington does not impose a corporate income tax			
West Virginia	No	No	Yes	No
Wisconsin	Yes, limited to research credits, except the super research and development credits.		Only if paid from E&P of unitary business included in combined report.	Yes, joint and several liability applies
Wyoming	Wyoming does not impose a corporate income tax			

Concept of a Unitary Business

Combined unitary reporting requires a determination of whether two or more corporations are engaged in a "unitary business." Unfortunately, there is no simple, objective definition of what constitutes a unitary business. In fact, over the years the courts have developed a number of different tests for determining the existence of a unitary business. As one Supreme Court Justice observed, "the unitary business concept . . . is not, so to speak, unitary." Because of the many judicial interpretations of a unitary business, it is not always clear which of the available tests should be applied. In addition, even if a taxpayer knows which test will be used, the subjective nature of the tests makes them difficult to apply with any certainty.

Generally speaking, a vertically integrated business, in which each of the separate affiliates or divisions performs an interdependent step that leads to a finished product only when the steps are combined, will be treated as unitary. A horizontally integrated business, in which there are parallel operations in different geographic locations (e.g., a chain of retail stores), will generally be considered unitary if there is centralized management. A conglomerate may or may not be considered unitary, depending on whether there is strong centralized management, as exhibited by a centralized executive force and shared staff functions, as well as economies of scale in the form of common employee pension and benefit plans, common insurance policies, and so on.

Judicial Interpretations of a Unitary Business

Over the years the courts have developed a number of different tests for determining the existence of a unitary business, including (1) the three-unities test, (2) the contribution or dependency test, (3) the flow of value test, and (4) the factors of profitability test.

Three-Unities Test. The Supreme Court articulated the three-unities test in *Butler Bros. v. McColgan.* [315 U.S. 501 (1942)] Under this test, a unitary business exists if each of three factors is present:

1. *Unity of ownership.* Generally, other than the common parent, more than 50 percent of each corporation's voting stock must be owned, directly or indirectly, by another corporation in the group to establish unity of ownership. It is notable that the unitary theory does not recognize minority interests. Thus, if "control" is established through a 51 percent ownership interest, all of the income of that corporation and all of its property, payroll, and sales factors are included in the combined report, even though there is a substantial minority interest.
2. *Unity of operation.* Unity of operation is exhibited by centralized staff functions performed by one of the corporations on behalf of the entire group. Examples include centralized purchasing, advertising, accounting and legal services, and human resources functions, as well as common personnel policies, pension and employee benefit plans, and insurance.
3. *Unity of use.* Unity of use is similar to unity of operation, except that unity of use is associated with line functions (executive force and general systems of operation), whereas unity of operation relates to staff functions. Unity of use is exhibited by a centralized executive force (e.g., shared officers and directors) that makes major decisions regarding strategy and operations, as well as by intercompany transfers of products, know-how, and expertise.

Contribution or Dependency Test. A second judicial test for the existence of a unitary business is whether "the operation of the portion of the business done within the state is dependent upon or contributes to the operation of the business without the state." [*Edison Cal. Stores, Inc. v. McColgan*, 176 P.2d 697 (Cal. 1947)] Examples of factors that suggest contributions by or dependency among commonly controlled corporations include intercompany loans, intercompany sales of goods or services, exchanges of products or expertise, and a shared executive force and staff functions. Some courts have made a distinction between essential contributing activities and other contributing activities. Examples of activities that may be considered essential are substantial borrowing from out-of-state operations to finance in-state operations, transfers of top-level executives from out-of-state operations, and transfers of manufacturing equipment and raw materials from out-of-state operations.

Factors of Profitability Test. The U.S. Supreme Court has referred to the factors of profitability test in several cases, including *Mobil Oil Corp. v. Commissioner of Taxes* [445 U.S. 425 (1980)], *F.W. Woolworth Co. v. Taxation & Revenue Department* [458 U.S. 354 (1982)], and *Allied-Signal, Inc. v. Division of Taxation* [504 U.S. 768 (1992)]. The indicia of a unitary business, or so-called factors of profitability, include functional integration, centralization of management, and economies of scale. Functional integration is exhibited by intercompany flows of goods, services, personnel, and expertise. Centralization of management is indicated by shared directors and officers, exchanges of upper-level management, and required parent corporation approval of major policy decisions. Economies of scale are demonstrated by the collective negotiation and purchase of goods and services, shared staff functions, and common insurance policies and employee pension and benefit plans.

Flow of Value Test. In *Container Corp. of America v. Franchise Tax Board* [463 U.S. 159 (1983)], the Supreme Court arguably established a fourth test for the existence of a unitary business. Under the flow of value test, a parent corporation and its subsidiary are unitary if "there [is] some sharing or exchange of value not capable of precise identification or measurement—beyond the mere flow of funds arising out of a passive investment or a distinct business operation." The Court also indicated that "the prerequisite to a constitutionally acceptable finding of unitary business is a flow of value, not a flow of goods."

MTC Model Regulations

Created in 1967, the Multistate Tax Commission (MTC) is an agency of state governments whose mission is to promote fairness and uniformity in state tax laws. To help states determine the existence of a unitary business, in 2004 the Multistate Tax Commission adopted MTC Reg. IV.1.(b), Principles for Determining the Existence of a Unitary Business. This model regulation describes the concept of a unitary business as follows:

> A unitary business is a single economic enterprise that is made up either of separate parts of a single business entity or of a commonly controlled group of business entities that are sufficiently interdependent, integrated and interrelated through their activities so as to provide a synergy and mutual benefit that produces a sharing or exchange of value among them and a significant flow of value to the separate parts.

More specifically, a unitary business is characterized by significant flows of value evidenced by factors such as those described in the U.S. Supreme Court's decision in *Mobil Oil Corporation v. Vermont* [445 U.S. 425 (1980)], which include:

- *Functional integration*—Includes, but is not limited to, transfers or pooling with respect to the unitary business's products or services, technical information, marketing information, distribution systems, purchasing, and intangibles such as patents, trademarks, service marks, copyrights, trade secrets, know-how, formulas, and processes.
- *Centralization of management*—Exists when directors, officers, and/or other management employees jointly participate in the management decisions that affect the respective business activities and that may also operate to the benefit of the entire economic enterprise.
- *Economies of scale*—Refers to a relation among and between business activities resulting in a significant decrease in the average per unit cost of operational or administrative functions due to the increase in operational size.

The MTC regulation also identifies same type of business, steps in a vertical process, and strong centralized management as indicators of a unitary business. [MTC Reg. IV(b)(3)]

These factors provide evidence of whether the business activities operate as an integrated whole or exhibit substantial mutual interdependence. [MTC Reg. IV(b)(2)]

State Definitions of Unitary Business

Other important sources of authority regarding the meaning of the term unitary business are state statutes, regulations, and administrative rulings. Like their judicial counterparts, however, they generally do not provide any bright-line tests.

California. California has not adopted a statutory definition of a unitary business, but the California courts have applied the three unities test (*Butler Brothers v. McColgan,* 315 U.S. 501, 1942) and the contribution or dependency test (*Edison California Stores v. McColgan,* 30 Calif. 2d 472, 1947). Both tests are discussed above. Businesses are unitary if either test is satisfied. [*A.M. Castle & Company v. Franchise Tax Board,* 36 Cal. App. 4th 1794 (1995)]

The U.S. Supreme Court has also stated that "[t]he prerequisite to a constitutionally acceptable finding of a unitary business is a flow of value" [*Container Corporation of America v. Franchise Tax Board,* 463 U.S. 159, 178 (1983)], and that a unitary business exhibits "contributions to income resulting from functional integration, centralization of management, and economies of scale" [e.g., *Allied Signal v. Director, Taxation Division* 504 U.S. 768 (1992)].

The California regulations state that there is a "strong presumption" that the taxpayer's activities are unitary if any one of the following three factors is present: (1) same type of business, such as a corporation that operates a chain of retail grocery stores; (2) steps in a vertical process, such as a corporation that explores for and mines copper ores, concentrates smelts and refines the copper ores, and fabricates the refined copper into consumer products; and (3) strong centralized management. Thus, a conglomerate may be considered a unitary business if the central executive officers are normally involved in the operations of the various divisions and there are centralized offices that perform for the divisions the normal matters that a truly independent business would perform for itself, such as accounting, personnel, insurance, legal, purchasing, advertising, or financing. [Calif. Code of Regs. § 25120(b)]

Colorado. The Colorado statutory definition of a unitary business is noteworthy, because it represents a rather unique attempt to provide a bright-line test for the existence of a unitary business. Specifically, Colorado Revised Statutes Section 39-22-303 provides that a unitary business exists if there is common ownership and three of the following six factors are present for the current tax year and the two preceding tax years:

1. Intercompany sales or leases constitute 50 percent or more of the gross operating receipts of the affiliate making the sales or leases (or 50 percent or more of the cost of goods sold or leases of the affiliate making the purchases or leases).
2. Five or more of the following services are provided by one or more affiliates for the benefit of other affiliates: (a) advertising and public relations services; (b) accounting and bookkeeping services; (c) legal services; (d) personnel services; (e) sales services; (f) purchasing services; (g) research and development services; (h) insurance procurement and servicing exclusive of employee benefit programs; and (i) employee benefit programs, including pension, profit-sharing, and stock purchase plans.
3. Twenty percent or more of the long-term debt (defined as debt due more than one year after it is incurred) of one affiliate is owed to or guaranteed by another affiliate.
4. One affiliate substantially uses the patents, trademarks, service marks, logo-types, trade secrets, copyrights, or other proprietary materials owned by another affiliate.
5. Fifty percent or more of the members of the board of directors of one affiliate are members of the board of directors or are corporate officers of another affiliate.
6. Twenty-five percent or more of the 20 highest ranking officers of one affiliate are members of the board of directors or are corporate officers of another affiliate.

Illinois. For Illinois tax purposes, the term unitary business group means "a group of persons related through common ownership whose business activities are integrated with, dependent upon and contribute to each other." A unitary business ordinarily exists if the following two conditions are met:

1. The activities of the members are in the same general line (such as manufacturing, wholesaling, retailing of tangible personal property, insurance, transportation or finance); or are steps in a vertically structured enterprise or process (such as the steps involved in the production of natural resources, which might include exploration, mining, refining, and marketing); and
2. In either instance, the members are functionally integrated through the exercise of strong centralized management (where, for example, authority over such matters as purchasing, financ-

ing, tax compliance, product line, personnel, marketing and capital investment is not left to each member). [35 Ill. Comp. Stat. § 1501(a)(27)]

Thus, members of a unitary business group will ordinarily be in the same general line of business, or steps in a vertically structured enterprise or process. On the other hand, two or more corporations can not be unitary unless they are functionally integrated through the exercise of strong centralized management, because "[i]t is this exercise of strong centralized management that is the primary indicator of mutual dependency, mutual contribution and mutual integration between persons that is necessary to constitute them members of the same unitary business group." [86 Ill. Adm. Code § 100.9700]

A unitary business group does not include any member that is required to apportion its business income using specialized apportionment formulas [35 Ill. Comp. Stat. § 1501(a)(27)], including insurance companies, financial organizations and transportation services [35 Ill. Comp. Stat. § 304(b), (c) and (d)]. However, two or more insurance companies may constitute their own separate unitary business group, as may two or more financial organizations or two or more transportation companies. [35 Ill. Comp. Stat. § 1501(a)(27)] Thus, a taxpayer first identifies all the entities that are engaged in a unitary business and then creates subgroups consisting of the separate unitary business groups required to use either the standard apportionment formula or the specialized formulas for insurance companies, financial organizations, or transportation services companies. [86 Ill. Adm. Code § 100.9700(d)]

In *Borden, Inc. v. Department of Revenue* [No. 1-96-2408 (Ill. App. Ct. 1998)], Borden was a manufacturer and distributor of food, consumer, and chemical products that owned 100 percent of the Pepsi-Subs, which were independent bottlers that operated under an exclusive agreement with PepsiCo. Despite the general lack of functional integration in key areas such as manufacturing and marketing, the court held that the two companies constituted a unitary business group because of the restrictive nature of the bottling agreements between the Pepsi-Subs and PepsiCo. There was strong centralized management, as evidenced by shared staff functions, such as accounting, internal audit, tax compliance, cash management, employee relations, legal, insurance, and employee benefit programs. In addition, Borden had control over the Pepsi-Subs' operating budgets, capital expenditures, appointment of officers, and determination of officer salaries.

On the other hand, in *The Dow Chemical Company v. Department of Revenue* [No. 1-03-1657 (Ill. App. Ct., June 27, 2005)], the Illinois Appellate Court ruled that a subsidiary was not a member of its parent corporation's unitary business, because there was no integration, centralized management, or economies of scale.

In *Envirodyne Industries, Inc.* [No. 02-1632 (U.S. Ct. of App., 7th Cir., Jan. 6, 2004)], which involved a bankruptcy matter, the U.S. Court of Appeals ruled that despite the existence of common management, several steel manufacturing subsidiaries were not unitary with several food packaging subsidiaries, because there was no functional integration of the activities of the two subsets of subsidiaries. As a consequence, the losses of the steel subsidiaries could not offset the income of the food-packaging subsidiaries for Illinois tax purposes. In making this determination, the federal court relied on a "wheel and spoke" theory of unity, under which unity between the common parent and the steel subsidiaries was not sufficient to establish unity between the steel subsidiaries and the food packaging subsidiaries.

Massachusetts. The term unitary business means the activities of a group of two or more corporations under common ownership that are "sufficiently interdependent, integrated or interrelated through their activities so as to provide mutual benefit and produce a significant sharing or exchange of value among them or a significant flow of value between the separate parts." The term is construed to the broadest extent permitted under the U.S. constitution. [Mass. Gen. Laws, Ch. 63, Code § 32B(b)(1)]

Michigan. A unitary business group is defined as a group of commonly controlled U.S. persons, other than a foreign operating entity, that have "business activities or operations that result in a flow of value between or among persons included in the unitary business group or has business activities or operations that are integrated with, are dependent upon, or contribute to each other." The flow of value is determined by reviewing the totality of the facts and circumstances. [Mich. Comp. Laws § 208.1117(6)]

Minnesota. A unitary business is defined as business activities that result in a flow of value, as determined by all of the facts and circumstances. Business activities conducted by two or more commonly controlled corporations are presumed to be unitary when:

1. The business activities or operations are of mutual benefit, dependent on, or contributory to one another individually or as a group;
2. There is unity of operation evidenced by staff functions, such as centralized advertising, accounting, financing, management, or centralized, group, or committee purchasing; or
3. There is unity of use evidenced by line functions, centralized executive force, and general system of operation.

Two or more commonly controlled corporations are also presumed to be unitary when contributions to income result from functional integration, centralized management, and economies of scale. [Minn. Dept. of Rev. Reg. § § 8019.0100 and 8019.0405]

Based on the state's statutory definition of a unitary business for the tax years in question (1986 to 1990), in *Amoco Corporation v. Commissioner of Revenue* [658 N.W.2d 859 (Minn. Sup. Ct. Apr. 3, 2003)], the Minnesota Supreme Court ruled that an oil company's exploration and production subsidiary was not unitary with its refining, marketing, and transportation subsidiary, because the two companies did not depend on or contribute to one another in order to earn a profit. The two subsidiaries were independently managed, and their operations were driven by market conditions rather than each other's needs. In addition, all sales of crude oil by the exploration and production business were at market prices, including sales to its sister company.

Oregon. A unitary business means a business enterprise in which there exists directly or indirectly between the members or parts of the enterprise a sharing or exchange of value as demonstrated by:

1. centralized management or a common executive force;
2. centralized administrative services or functions resulting in economies of scale; or
3. flow of goods, capital resources or services demonstrating functional integration. [Ore. Sec. 317.705]

Oregon corporate income taxpayers may be considered a unitary group if only one or two of the above factors are present. [OAR 150-317.705(3)(a)(2)]

Texas. A unitary business means "a single economic enterprise that is made up of separate parts of a single entity or of a commonly controlled group of entities that are sufficiently interdependent, integrated, and interrelated through their activities so as to provide a synergy and mutual benefit that produces a sharing or exchange of value among them and a significant flow of value to the separate parts." Relevant factors in determining whether a unitary business exists include whether the activities of the group members are (1) in the same general line, such as manufacturing, wholesaling, retailing of tangible personal property, insurance, transportation, or finance; or (2) steps in a vertically structured enterprise or process, such as the steps involved in the production of natural resources, including exploration, mining, refining, and marketing. Another relevant factor is whether the members are functionally integrated through the exercise of strong centralized management, such as authority over purchasing, financing, product line, personnel, and marketing. [Tex. Tax Code § 171.0001(17)]

Utah. In 2008, the Utah Tax Commission modified its definition of a "unitary business" to conform to changes in the MTC regulations, as follows: "A unitary business is a single economic enterprise that is made up either of separate parts of a single business entity or of a commonly controlled group of business entities that are sufficiently interdependent, integrated and interrelated through their activities so as to provide a synergy and mutual benefit that produces a sharing or exchange of value among them and a significant flow of value to the separate parts." [Rule R865-6F-8, Utah Admin. Code, Sept. 9, 2008]

Wisconsin. Effective for tax years beginning on or after January 1, 2009, Wisconsin requires combined reporting. [S.B. 62, Feb. 19, 2009] Wisconsin Statute Section 71.255 defines a "unitary business" as a commonly controlled group of business entities that are "sufficiently interdependent, integrated, and interrelated through their activities so as to provide a synergy and mutual benefit that produces a sharing or exchange of value among them and a significant flow of value to the separate parts." Two or more business entities are presumed to be unitary if the businesses have "unity of ownership, operation, and use as indicated by a centralized management or a centralized executive force; centralized purchasing, advertising, or accounting; intercorporate sales or leases; intercorporate services, including administrative, employee benefits, human resources, legal, financial, and cash management services; intercorporate debts; intercorporate use of proprietary materials; interlocking directorates; or interlocking corporate officers."

On March 16, 2010, the Wisconsin Department of Revenue issued final regulations interpreting the state's new combined reporting statutes.

Recent Developments

Arizona. In *R.R. Donnelley & Sons Co. v. Arizona Department of Revenue* [No. 1 CA-TX 08-0007 (Ariz. Ct. of App. Apr. 29, 2010)], the Arizona Court of Appeals ruled that a printing business and a subsidiary that owned trademarks used by the printing business were engaged in a unitary business. The trademarks appeared on shipping labels, invoices, business cards, locations, signage, letterhead, the company website, as well as miscellaneous promotional items or other items that would be used to identify taxpayer. Thus, the trademarks were a core part of the taxpayer's operations, because they were operationally integrated with the delivery and distribution of the commercial printing materials the taxpayer produced. On the other hand, two other subsidiaries that provided accounts receivables and investment services were not part of the unitary business. The accounts receivables and investment services did not create a unitary relationship, because they were "accessory services" rather than basic operational components of the taxpayer's core business.

State-by-State Summary

The chart that follows summarizes which factors each state considers in determining whether business entities are engaged in a unitary business.

Concept of a Unitary Business

Legend:
NA Not applicable
NR Not reported

State	*Which Factors Are Considered When Determining Whether Business Entities Are Engaged in a Unitary Business?*							
	Functional Integration	*Economies of Scale*	*Centralized Executive Force*	*Centralized Administrative Services*	*Same Type or Line of Business*	*Steps in a Vertical Enterprise or Process*	*Operations Dependent Upon or Contribute to One Another*	*Other—Please Specify*
Alabama	X	X	X	X	X		X	
Alaska	X	X	X	X	X	X	X	
Arizona	X	X	X	X	X	X	X	See AAC R15-2D-101; AAC R15-2D-401
Arkansas	X	X	X	X	X	X	X	X, used to determine business or non-business income only.
California	X	X	X	X	X	X	X	Three unities test-ownership, operations and use.
Colorado	X	X	X	X	X		X	X, CRS 39-22-303
Connecticut	X	X	X	X	X	X	X	
Delaware								

Legend:
NA Not applicable
NR Not reported

Concept of a Unitary Business

	Which Factors Are Considered When Determining Whether Business Entities Are Engaged in a Unitary Business?							
State	*Functional Integration*	*Economies of Scale*	*Centralized Executive Force*	*Centralized Administrative Services*	*Same Type or Line of Business*	*Steps in a Vertical Enterprise or Process*	*Operations Dependent Upon or Contribute to One Another*	*Other—Please Specify*
District of Columbia	X	X	X	X	X	X	X	X, commonly controlled group of business entities that are sufficiently interdependent, integrated, and interrelated through their activities as to provide a synergy and mutual benefit that produces a sharing or exchange of value among them and a significant flow of value to the parts.
Florida								
Georgia								
Hawaii	X	X	X		X	X	X	
Idaho	X	X	X	X	X	X	X	
Illinois	X	X	X	X	X	X		

Legend:
NA Not applicable
NR Not reported

Concept of a Unitary Business

State	*Which Factors Are Considered When Determining Whether Business Entities Are Engaged in a Unitary Business?*							
	Functional Integration	*Economies of Scale*	*Centralized Executive Force*	*Centralized Administrative Services*	*Same Type or Line of Business*	*Steps in a Vertical Enterprise or Process*	*Operations Dependent Upon or Contribute to One Another*	*Other—Please Specify*
Indiana	X	X	X	X	X	X	X	
Iowa	X	X	X	X	X	X	X	
Kansas	X	X	X	X	X	X	X	
Kentucky								
Louisiana								
Maine	X	X	X	X	X	X	X	
Maryland								
Massachusetts								U.S. Constitutional Standards
Michigan (Business Tax)	X	X	X	X	X	X	X	
Note. The CIT takes effect 01/01/12, and replaces the Michigan Business Tax (MBT) for most taxpayers. However, businesses that have been approved to receive, have received, or have been assigned certain certified credits may elect to file a return and pay the tax imposed by the MBT in lieu of the CIT until the certified credits are exhausted or extinguished.								
Minnesota	X	X	X	X	X	X	X	Flow of value
Mississippi	X	X	X	X	X	X	X	
Missouri								
Montana	X	X	X	X	X	X	X	
Nebraska	X	X	X	X	X	X	X	

Concept of a Unitary Business

Legend:
NA Not applicable
NR Not reported

Which Factors Are Considered When Determining Whether Business Entities Are Engaged in a Unitary Business?

State	*Functional Integration*	*Economies of Scale*	*Centralized Executive Force*	*Centralized Administrative Services*	*Same Type or Line of Business*	*Steps in a Vertical Enterprise or Process*	*Operations Dependent Upon or Contribute to One Another*	*Other—Please Specify*
Nevada	Nevada does not impose a corporate income tax							
New Hampshire	X	X	X	X	X	X	X	See RSAS 77-A:1, XIV
New Jersey	X	X						Centralized Management
New Mexico	X	X	X	X	X	X	X	Flow of value
New York								See § 6-2.2(b) of the Business Corp Tax Regulations.
North Carolina								
North Dakota	X	X	X	X	X	X	X	Common ownership
Ohio	Ohio does not impose a corporate income tax							
Note. Effective 1/1/2010, the Ohio Franchise Tax was fully phased out and business will be taxed on gross receipts through the Commercial Activity Tax. Details about that tax can be found at: http//tax.ohio.gov/divisions/commercial_activities/index.stm								
Oklahoma								
Oregon								
Pennsylvania	NR	NR	NR	NR	NR	NR	NR	NR
Rhode Island								All businesses must have activities in RI.

Legend:
NA Not applicable
NR Not reported

Concept of a Unitary Business

	Which Factors Are Considered When Determining Whether Business Entities Are Engaged in a Unitary Business?							
State	*Functional Integration*	*Economies of Scale*	*Centralized Executive Force*	*Centralized Administrative Services*	*Same Type or Line of Business*	*Steps in a Vertical Enterprise or Process*	*Operations Dependent Upon or Contribute to One Another*	*Other—Please Specify*
South Carolina	X	X	X		X	X	X	
South Dakota	South Dakota does not impose a corporate income tax							
Tennessee								All factors on a case by case basis will be evaluated whether to require or grant permission to file a combined return TCA § 67-4-2014.
Texas	X	X	X	X	X	X	X	
Utah	X	X	X					
Vermont	X	X	X	X	X	X	X	
Virginia								
Washington	Washington does not impose a corporate income tax							
West Virginia	X				X			
Wisconsin	X	X	X	X	X	X	X	To the extent permitted by the U.S. Constitution
Wyoming	Wyoming does not impose a corporate income tax							

Net Operating Loss Carryovers: Combined Reporting and Consolidated Returns

NOLs in a Federal Consolidated Return

Under IRC Section 1501, an affiliated group of corporations may elect to file a federal consolidated income tax return. Thus, a federal consolidated return is not mandatory, and the members of an affiliated group have the option of filing federal returns on a separate company basis. A federal *affiliated group* is defined as one or more chains of includible corporations connected through stock ownership with a common parent that is an includible corporation, provided that the common parent directly owns 80 percent or more of at least one of the other includible corporations, and stock meeting the 80 percent test in each includible corporation other than the common parent must be owned directly by one or more of the other includible corporations. [IRC § 1504(a)] An "includible corporation" is any corporation other than an exempt corporation, life insurance company, foreign corporation, Section 936 corporation, RIC, REIT, DISC or S corporation. [IRC § 1504(b)]

Offsetting losses of one affiliate against the profits of another. Under the statutory authority provided by Section 1502, the Treasury Department has issued voluminous regulations regarding how an affiliated group computes its consolidated federal income tax liability. These regulations generally adopt the single-entity approach to determining the tax of a consolidated group. Under this approach, the members of a consolidated group are treated as divisions of a single taxpayer. Thus, a major advantage of filing a federal consolidated return is that a net operating loss (NOL) sustained by one group member can offset income earned by other group members in computing consolidated taxable income. [Treas. Reg. § 1.1502-11]

Carryover of CNOL to consolidated return year. In computing its consolidated taxable income, a consolidated group may claim a deduction for the consolidated NOL (CNOL), which is the aggregate of the NOL carryovers to the consolidated return year, as determined under the principles of Section 172, and includes both any CNOLs of the consolidated group, as well as any NOLs of the members arising in separate return years. [Treas. Reg. § 1.1502-21(a)]

Carryover of CNOL to separate return year. The rules governing the carryover of a CNOL to a separate return year are found in Treasury Regulation Section 1.1502-21(b). A CNOL that is attributable to a member may be carried back to a separate return year of that member. However, that same loss may not be carried back to an equivalent, or earlier, consolidated return year of the group. The portion of a CNOL that is attributable to a member is determined by a fraction, the numerator of which is the separate NOL of the member for the year of the loss and the denominator of which is the sum of the separate NOLs for that year of all members having such losses.

If a corporation ceases to be a member during a consolidated return year, any portion of a CNOL carryforward attributable to the departing member which is not absorbed by the consolidated group in that year may be carried forward to the departing member's first separate return year. However, that same loss may not be carried forward to an equivalent, or subsequent, consolidated return year of the group.

Limitations on NOLs from separate return limitation years. If an acquired corporation joins the acquiring corporation in the filing of a consolidated return, the use of the acquired corporation's pre-acquisition NOLs to offset income generated by other members of the consolidated group is limited by both the separate return limitation year (SRLY) rules of Treasury Regulation Section 1.1502-21(c), and the Section 382 limitation. A SRLY is a tax year of a subsidiary during which the subsidiary was not a member of the consolidated group.

Under Section 382, if a more than 50 percentage point change in stock ownership occurs with respect to a loss corporation, the use of the loss corporation's NOL carryforwards is limited. The Section 382 limitation for a tax year of a loss corporation after an ownership change generally equals the fair market value of the corporation's stock immediately before the ownership change multiplied by the long-term tax-exempt rate.

To simplify the calculation of the loss limitations, Treasury Regulation Section 1.1502-21(g) contains an "overlap rule," under which the Section 382 limitations, rather than the SRLY limitations, apply if certain requirements are met. If, after applying the overlap rule, the SRLY limitations apply, an acquired subsidiary's SRLY losses may be deducted by the consolidated group only to the extent of that member's cumulative contribution to the group's consolidated taxable income.

NOLs in State Combined Reporting and Consolidated Returns

States employ a variety of filing options for groups of commonly controlled corporations, including separate company reporting, consolidated returns, and combined unitary reporting. Under separate company reporting, each member of a commonly controlled group of corporations computes its income and files a return as if it were a separate economic entity. Some states permit or require affiliated corporations to file a state consolidated return if certain requirements are met. Combined unitary reporting is a methodology for apportioning the business income of a taxpayer member of a commonly controlled group of corporations that is engaged in a unitary business.

In contrast to the federal single-entity approach to determining the tax of a consolidated group, some states treat each member of a combined reporting group (or each affiliate in a state consolidated return) that has nexus in the state as a separate taxpayer that must pay its own tax and file its own return. For example, under California's combined reporting regime, each "taxpayer member" of the unitary business group (i.e., a member that has income tax nexus in California) generally must separately compute its own tax. Consistent with this separate-entity approach to combined reporting, a California source NOL incurred by one member of the combined reporting group cannot be used to offset the income of other group members in a subsequent tax year. [Calif. Code Regs. tit. 18 § 25106.5-(e)]

Consistent with the federal tax regulations, some states have SRLY-type rules that restrict the use of an acquired subsidiary's pre-acquisition NOLs. For example, Oregon requires that if a consolidated Oregon return is filed, the SRLY rules found in Treasury Regulation Section 1.1502-1 must be followed. [Ore. Reg. OAR 150-317.476(4)]

State-by-State Summary

The following chart, presented in two parts, summarizes whether an NOL of a state combined or consolidated group is attributed to specific members, and if so, whether an NOL attributable to one group member can offset the income of other members in a subsequent tax year. The chart also summarizes whether a combined or consolidated group that acquires a new member that has an NOL carryforward can offset that carryforward against the income of other group members, and if so, whether SRLY-type rules restrict the group's use of that new member's pre-acquisition NOL carryforwards.

Part 1 summarizes the rules for combined reporting groups, and Part 2 summarizes the rules for consolidated groups.

Net Operating Loss Carryovers: Combined Reporting and Consolidated Returns (Part 1)

Combined Reporting Group

Legend:

NA — **Not applicable**
NR — **Not reported**

	If a Combined Reporting Group has a Taxable Loss, is the Resulting NOL Carried Forward at the Group Level or Member Level?					
	NOL Carryforward of Group	*NOL Carryforward Attributed to Specific Members*	*If NOL Carryforwards are Attributed to Specific Members, can an NOL Carryforward Attributable to One Group Member Offset the Income of Other Group Members?*	*When a Combined Reporting Group Acquires a New Member that has NOL Carryforwards in your State, can those Carryforwards offset the Income of Other Group Members?*	*If Yes, are there SRLY-Type Restrictions on the Use of the New Member's NOL Carryforwards?*	*If Yes, Explain.*
Alabama						
Alaska		X	Yes	No		
Arizona	See Ariz. Admin Code R15-2D-302; See Arizona Corporate Tax Ruling CTR 91-2	See Ariz. Admin Code R15-2D-302; See Arizona Corporate Tax Ruling CTR 91-2	See Ariz. Admin Code R15-2D-302; See Arizona Corporate Tax Ruling CTR 91-2			
Arkansas		X				SRLY limits are explained in Reg. 2.26-51-805(f)
California		X	No	No		
Colorado	NR	NR	Yes	Yes	Yes	
Connecticut	No written guidance	No written guidance	No written guidance	No written guidance	No written guidance	No written guidance
Delaware						

Net Operating Loss Carryovers: Combined Reporting and Consolidated Returns (Part 1)

Combined Reporting Group

Legend:

NA Not applicable
NR Not reported

	If a Combined Reporting Group has a Taxable Loss, is the Resulting NOL Carried Forward at the Group Level or Member Level?					
	NOL Carryforward of Group	*NOL Carryforward Attributed to Specific Members*	*If NOL Carryforwards are Attributed to Specific Members, can an NOL Carryforward Attributable to One Group Member Offset the Income of Other Group Members?*	*When a Combined Reporting Group Acquires a New Member that has NOL Carryforwards in your State, can those Carryforwards offset the Income of Other Group Members?*	*If Yes, are there SRLY-Type Restrictions on the Use of the New Member's NOL Carryforwards?*	*If Yes, Explain.*
District of Columbia		X	No, final regulation pending decision at present.	No		
Florida	NA	NA	NA	NA	NA	NA
Georgia						
Hawaii	NR	NR	NR	NR		
Idaho		X	No	No		
Illinois		X	Yes	Yes	No	
Indiana	X	N/A	Yes	Yes	Yes	SRLY-type limitations applied by looking at new member's previous Indiana losses line effect
Iowa			NA	NA	NA	NA

Net Operating Loss Carryovers: Combined Reporting and Consolidated Returns (Part 1)

Combined Reporting Group

Legend:

NA — **Not applicable**
NR — **Not reported**

	If a Combined Reporting Group has a Taxable Loss, is the Resulting NOL Carried Forward at the Group Level or Member Level?					
	NOL Carryforward of Group	*NOL Carryforward Attributed to Specific Members*	*If NOL Carryforwards are Attributed to Specific Members, can an NOL Carryforward Attributable to One Group Member Offset the Income of Other Group Members?*	*When a Combined Reporting Group Acquires a New Member that has NOL Carryforwards in your State, can those Carryforwards offset the Income of Other Group Members?*	*If Yes, are there SRLY-Type Restrictions on the Use of the New Member's NOL Carryforwards?*	*If Yes, Explain.*
Kansas		X	No	No		
Kentucky						
Louisiana		X	No	No		
Maine	NR	NR	NR	NR	NR	
Maryland	NR	NR	NR	NR	NR	
Massachusetts		X	Depends on facts	No		
Michigan	X			Yes	No	
Note. The CIT takes effect 01/01/12, and replaces the Michigan Business Tax (MBT) for most taxpayers. However, businesses that have been approved to receive, have received, or have been assigned certain certified credits may elect to file a return and pay the tax imposed by the MBT in lieu of the CIT until the certified credits are exhausted or extinguished.						
Minnesota		X	No	No		
Mississippi		X	Yes	No		
Missouri						
Montana		X	No	No		

Net Operating Loss Carryovers: Combined Reporting and Consolidated Returns (Part 1)

Combined Reporting Group

Legend:

NA	**Not applicable**
NR	**Not reported**

	If a Combined Reporting Group has a Taxable Loss, is the Resulting NOL Carried Forward at the Group Level or Member Level?					
	NOL Carryforward of Group	*NOL Carryforward Attributed to Specific Members*	*If NOL Carryforwards are Attributed to Specific Members, can an NOL Carryforward Attributable to One Group Member Offset the Income of Other Group Members?*	*When a Combined Reporting Group Acquires a New Member that has NOL Carryforwards in your State, can those Carryforwards offset the Income of Other Group Members?*	*If Yes, are there SRLY-Type Restrictions on the Use of the New Member's NOL Carryforwards?*	*If Yes, Explain.*
Nebraska	X		Yes	No		
Nevada	Nevada does not impose a corporate income tax					
New Hampshire		X	Yes	Yes	Yes	Follow IRC 382 and RSA 77-A:5, XIII
New Jersey		X	No	No	No	
New Mexico	X		NA	Yes, if target not filing as SCE.	Yes	SAF
New York	X			Yes	Yes	See 20 NYCRR § 3-8.7
North Carolina						
North Dakota		X	No	No		
Ohio	Ohio does not impose a corporate income tax					

Note. Effective 1/1/2010, the Ohio Franchise Tax was fully phased out, and businesses will be taxed on gross receipts through the Commercial Activity Tax. Details about that tax can be found at: *http//tax.ohio.gov/divisions/commercial_activities/index.stm*

Net Operating Loss Carryovers: Combined Reporting and Consolidated Returns (Part 1)

Combined Reporting Group

Legend:

NA **Not applicable**
NR **Not reported**

	If a Combined Reporting Group has a Taxable Loss, is the Resulting NOL Carried Forward at the Group Level or Member Level?					
	NOL Carryforward of Group	*NOL Carryforward Attributed to Specific Members*	*If NOL Carryforwards are Attributed to Specific Members, can an NOL Carryforward Attributable to One Group Member Offset the Income of Other Group Members?*	*When a Combined Reporting Group Acquires a New Member that has NOL Carryforwards in your State, can those Carryforwards offset the Income of Other Group Members?*	*If Yes, are there SRLY-Type Restrictions on the Use of the New Member's NOL Carryforwards?*	*If Yes, Explain.*
Oklahoma		X	Yes	No		
Oregon						
Pennsylvania		X	No	No		
Rhode Island		X	No	No		
South Carolina	X			SAF	SAF	
South Dakota	South Dakota does not impose a corporate income tax					
Tennessee	X			Yes	No	
Texas	NA	NA	No, NOLs not recognized	No, NOLs not recognized		
Utah	X	NA	No	NA	NA	
Vermont		X	No	No		
Virginia	Virginia does not allow combined unitary reporting					
Washington	Washington does not impose a corporate income tax					
West Virginia		X	No	No		

Net Operating Loss Carryovers: Combined Reporting and Consolidated Returns (Part 1)

Combined Reporting Group

Legend:

NA — **Not applicable**
NR — **Not reported**

	If a Combined Reporting Group has a Taxable Loss, is the Resulting NOL Carried Forward at the Group Level or Member Level?					
	NOL Carryforward of Group	*NOL Carryforward Attributed to Specific Members*	*If NOL Carryforwards are Attributed to Specific Members, can an NOL Carryforward Attributable to One Group Member Offset the Income of Other Group Members?*	*When a Combined Reporting Group Acquires a New Member that has NOL Carryforwards in your State, can those Carryforwards offset the Income of Other Group Members?*	*If Yes, are there SRLY-Type Restrictions on the Use of the New Member's NOL Carryforwards?*	*If Yes, Explain.*
Wisconsin		X	Yes	Depends on facts		Wisconsin's combined reporting law includes SRLY-type limitations. IRC § 381 controls whether the acquiring corporation succeeds to the corporations net business loss carryforward. Wisconsin treatment of Section 381 is modified by Wis. Stat. § 71.26(3)(n), so that it applies to WI net business loss carryforwards

Legend:

NA **Not applicable**
NR **Not reported**

Net Operating Loss Carryovers: Combined Reporting and Consolidated Returns (Part 1)

	Combined Reporting Group					
	If a Combined Reporting Group has a Taxable Loss, is the Resulting NOL Carried Forward at the Group Level or Member Level?					
	NOL Carryforward of Group	*NOL Carryforward Attributed to Specific Members*	*If NOL Carryforwards are Attributed to Specific Members, can an NOL Carryforward Attributable to One Group Member Offset the Income of Other Group Members?*	*When a Combined Reporting Group Acquires a New Member that has NOL Carryforwards in your State, can those Carryforwards offset the Income of Other Group Members?*	*If Yes, are there SRLY-Type Restrictions on the Use of the New Member's NOL Carryforwards?*	*If Yes, Explain.*
						instead of federal net operating loss carryovers.
Wyoming	Wyoming does not impose a corporate income tax					

Net Operating Loss Carryovers: Combined Reporting and Consolidated Returns (Part 2)

Consolidated Group

Legend:
NA Not applicable
NR Not reported

	If a Consolidated Group has a Taxable Loss, is the Resulting NOL Carried Forward at the Group Level or Member Level?					
	NOL Carryforward of Group	*NOL Carryforward Attributed to Specific Members*	*If NOL Carryforwards are Attributed to Specific Members, can an NOL Carryforward Attributable to One Group Member Offset the Income of Other Group Members?*	*When a Consolidated Group Acquires a New Member that has NOL Carryforwards in your State, can those Carryforwards offset the Income of Other Group Members?*	*If Yes, are there SRLY-Type Restrictions on the Use of the New Member's NOL Carryforwards?*	*If Yes, Explain.*
Alabama	Yes		No	No		
Alaska		X	Yes	No		
Arizona	See Ariz. Admin. Code R15-2D-302; See Arizona Corporate Tax Ruling CTR 91-2.	See Ariz. Admin. Code R15-2D-302; See Arizona Corporate Tax Ruling CTR 91-2.				
Arkansas		X	Yes	No	Yes	SRLY limits are explained in Reg. 2.26-51-805(f)
California	X		Yes	No		
Colorado			Yes	Yes	Yes	
Connecticut		X	Yes	No		
Delaware						
District of Columbia	X		No	No		
Florida	X		Yes, federal limitations apply	Yes	Yes, SAF	

Net Operating Loss Carryovers: Combined Reporting and Consolidated Returns (Part 2)

Consolidated Group

Legend:

NA Not applicable

NR Not reported

	If a Consolidated Group has a Taxable Loss, is the Resulting NOL Carried Forward at the Group Level or Member Level?					
	NOL Carryforward of Group	*NOL Carryforward Attributed to Specific Members*	*If NOL Carryforwards are Attributed to Specific Members, can an NOL Carryforward Attributable to One Group Member Offset the Income of Other Group Members?*	*When a Consolidated Group Acquires a New Member that has NOL Carryforwards in your State, can those Carryforwards offset the Income of Other Group Members?*	*If Yes, are there SRLY-Type Restrictions on the Use of the New Member's NOL Carryforwards?*	*If Yes, Explain.*
Georgia	X		Yes, but only if the NOL carryforward occurred after filing the first consolidated return. Prior, separate NOLs are subject to GSRLY and can only be used by the specific company that had generated the original, separate NOL.	No	Yes	Only NOLs generated while filing as a consolidated group can offset the income of other group members.
Hawaii	NR	NR	NR	NR		
Idaho	NA	NA	NA	NA	NA	NA
Illinois						
Indiana	X		NA	Yes	Yes	NR

Net Operating Loss Carryovers: Combined Reporting and Consolidated Returns (Part 2)

Consolidated Group

Legend:

NA Not applicable

NR Not reported

	If a Consolidated Group has a Taxable Loss, is the Resulting NOL Carried Forward at the Group Level or Member Level?					
	NOL Carryforward of Group	*NOL Carryforward Attributed to Specific Members*	*If NOL Carryforwards are Attributed to Specific Members, can an NOL Carryforward Attributable to One Group Member Offset the Income of Other Group Members?*	*When a Consolidated Group Acquires a New Member that has NOL Carryforwards in your State, can those Carryforwards offset the Income of Other Group Members?*	*If Yes, are there SRLY-Type Restrictions on the Use of the New Member's NOL Carryforwards?*	*If Yes, Explain.*
Iowa	X		N/A	Yes	Yes	Based on the ratio of Iowa Sales of the New Member to Total Iowa Sales of the Consolidated Group in Accordance with Iowa Admin. Code r. 701-53.15(7)
Kansas		X	No	No		
Kentucky	X		NR	Yes	No	
Louisiana		X	No	No		
Maine	NA	NA	NA	NA	NA	
Maryland	NR	NR	NR	NR	NR	
Massachusetts						
Michigan						

Net Operating Loss Carryovers: Combined Reporting and Consolidated Returns (Part 2)

Consolidated Group

Legend:

NA	Not applicable
NR	Not reported

	If a Consolidated Group has a Taxable Loss, is the Resulting NOL Carried Forward at the Group Level or Member Level?					
	NOL Carryforward of Group	*NOL Carryforward Attributed to Specific Members*	*If NOL Carryforwards are Attributed to Specific Members, can an NOL Carryforward Attributable to One Group Member Offset the Income of Other Group Members?*	*When a Consolidated Group Acquires a New Member that has NOL Carryforwards in your State, can those Carryforwards offset the Income of Other Group Members?*	*If Yes, are there SRLY-Type Restrictions on the Use of the New Member's NOL Carryforwards?*	*If Yes, Explain.*

Note. The CIT takes effect 01/01/12, and replaces the Michigan Business Tax (MBT) for most taxpayers. However, businesses that have been approved to receive, have received, or have been assigned certain certified credits may elect to file a return and pay the tax imposed by the MBT in lieu of the CIT until the certified credits are exhausted or extinguished.

Minnesota	NA	NA	NA	NA	NA	
Mississippi		X	Yes	No		
Missouri	X			No		
Montana						
Nebraska		X	Yes	No		
Nevada	Nevada does not impose a corporate income tax					
New Hampshire						
New Jersey		X	No	No	No	
New Mexico	X	NA	NA	Yes, if target not filing as separate corporate entity	Yes	
New York	NA	NA	NA	NA	NA	
North Carolina						

Net Operating Loss Carryovers: Combined Reporting and Consolidated Returns (Part 2)

Consolidated Group

Legend:
NA Not applicable
NR Not reported

	If a Consolidated Group has a Taxable Loss, is the Resulting NOL Carried Forward at the Group Level or Member Level?					
	NOL Carryforward of Group	*NOL Carryforward Attributed to Specific Members*	*If NOL Carryforwards are Attributed to Specific Members, can an NOL Carryforward Attributable to One Group Member Offset the Income of Other Group Members?*	*When a Consolidated Group Acquires a New Member that has NOL Carryforwards in your State, can those Carryforwards offset the Income of Other Group Members?*	*If Yes, are there SRLY-Type Restrictions on the Use of the New Member's NOL Carryforwards?*	*If Yes, Explain.*
North Dakota		X	No	No		
Ohio	Ohio does not impose a corporate income tax					
Note. Effective 1/1/2010, the Ohio Franchise Tax was fully phased out, and businesses will be taxed on gross receipts through the Commercial Activity Tax. Details about that tax can be found at: *http//tax.ohio.gov/divisions/commercial_activities/index.stm*						
Oklahoma		X	Yes	No		
Oregon		X	Yes	Yes	Yes	Federal SRLY rules apply, limitations multiplied by applicable year's Oregon apportionment percentage.
Pennsylvania		X	No	No		
Rhode Island		X	No	No		
South Carolina	X			SAF	SAF	
South Dakota	South Dakota does not impose a corporate income tax					

Net Operating Loss Carryovers: Combined Reporting and Consolidated Returns (Part 2)

Consolidated Group

Legend:

NA Not applicable

NR Not reported

	If a Consolidated Group has a Taxable Loss, is the Resulting NOL Carried Forward at the Group Level or Member Level?					
	NOL Carryforward of Group	*NOL Carryforward Attributed to Specific Members*	*If NOL Carryforwards are Attributed to Specific Members, can an NOL Carryforward Attributable to One Group Member Offset the Income of Other Group Members?*	*When a Consolidated Group Acquires a New Member that has NOL Carryforwards in your State, can those Carryforwards offset the Income of Other Group Members?*	*If Yes, are there SRLY-Type Restrictions on the Use of the New Member's NOL Carryforwards?*	*If Yes, Explain.*
Tennessee		X	No	No		
Texas	NA	NA	NA	NA		
Utah	NA	NA	NA	NA	NA	
Vermont		X	Yes	Yes	Yes	Follow I.R.C § 382
Virginia		X	Yes	Yes	Yes	Virginia conforms to federal rules for NOL carryforwards related to SRLY years.
Washington	Washington does not impose a corporate income tax					
West Virginia	X			X		
Wisconsin	NA	NA	NA	NA	NA	NA
Wyoming	Wyoming does not impose a corporate income tax					

Provisions That Limit Related Party Planning

Income Shifting Strategies

A principal planning objective is to create legal structures that minimize the state income taxes of the business enterprise as a whole. Through the use of separately incorporated affiliates and intercompany transactions (loans, licenses, inventory sales, etc.), income can be shifted from operations in high tax states to operations in low tax states. Such strategies are made possible by the large number of states that require or permit the filing of separate company returns, whereby each member of an affiliated group that has nexus in a state computes its income and files a return as if it were a separate and distinct economic entity.

Historically, one common planning strategy has been the use of trademark holding companies. This strategy involves transferring an operating company's trademarks, trade names and service marks to a separately incorporated subsidiary, which then licenses the marks back for use by the operating affiliates. The subsidiary is often incorporated in Delaware, which does not tax the income of a corporation whose only activity in Delaware is the ownership and management of intangible assets. Therefore, as long as the trademark holding company has nexus only in the tax haven state, this structure provides the operating company with a royalty expense deduction, while the corresponding royalty income is not subject to tax in any state. Other examples of corporate tax avoidance strategies based on the creation of special-purpose subsidiaries include the use of Delaware or Nevada passive investment companies (which hold stocks or bonds), captive insurance companies, and captive real estate investment trusts.

Mechanisms Used by States to Limit Income Shifting

States employ a number of mechanisms to limit the ability of multistate businesses to use related party structures and transactions to shift income. As discussed below, these include the theory of economic nexus, the judicial doctrines of economic substance and business purpose, combined reporting, IRC Section 482-type reallocation provisions, and deduction disallowance provisions.

Economic Nexus. Based on the theory of economic nexus, an out-of-state trademark holding company has nexus by virtue of the royalty income it derives from the state, in which case the in-state operating company's royalty expense deduction is, in effect, offset by the holding company's royalty income. In *Geoffrey, Inc.* (S.C. Sup. Ct., No. 23886, July 6, 1993), the South Carolina Supreme Court ruled that a Delaware trademark holding company had constitutional nexus in South Carolina for income tax purposes because it licensed its intangibles for use in South Carolina. The court stated that it did not apply the *Quill* physical presence test because, in its view, the *Quill* nexus standard applies only for sales and use tax purposes.

Since 1993, many states have adopted *Geoffrey* rules or regulations, and there has been a significant amount of litigation related to the *Geoffrey* court's interpretation of the Commerce Clause substantial nexus requirement. For example, the Connecticut corporate income tax applies to "[a]ny company that derives income from sources within this state and that has a substantial economic presence within this state, evidenced by a purposeful direction of business toward this state, examined in light of the frequency, quantity and systematic nature of a company's economic contacts with this state, without regard to physical presence, and to the extent permitted by the Constitution of the United States." [Conn. Gen. Stat.§ 12-216a]

One approach to implementing the economic nexus concept is a factor presence standard under which income tax nexus exists if in-state sales exceed a specified threshold. For example, for tax years beginning on or after January 1, 2011, an out-of-state corporation has income tax nexus in California if more than $500,000 of sales or 25 percent of its total sales are in California. [S.B. 15, Feb. 20. 2009] Effective April 30, 2010, an out-of-state corporation has income tax nexus in Colorado if more than $500,000 of sales or 25 percent of its total sales in Colorado. [Colo. Dept. of Rev., Reg. 39-22-301.1, Apr. 10, 2010] Effective June 1, 2010, for purposes of imposing the Washington business and occupation tax (a gross receipts tax) on service activities and royalty income, an out-of-state corporation has nexus if it has more than $250,000 of receipts or at least 25 percent of its total receipts in Washington. [S.B. 6143, Feb. 20. 2009]

In *Lanco, Inc. v. Division of Taxation* [No. A-89-05 (N.J. Sup. Ct., Oct. 12, 2006); *cert. denied*, U.S. Sup. Ct., 06-1236, June 18, 2007], the New Jersey Supreme Court ruled that the Delaware trademark holding corporation of the clothing retailer Lane Bryant (Lanco) had income tax nexus with New Jersey, even though the corporation had no physical presence in the state. The court concluded that the Quill physical presence test for sales and use tax nexus did not apply to income taxes.

In *Commissioner v. MBNA America Bank, N.A.* [No. 33049 (W.V. Sup. Ct. of App., Nov. 21, 2006); *cert. denied*, U.S. Sup. Ct., 06-1228, June 18, 2007], the West Virginia Supreme Court of Appeals ruled that a Delaware bank that provided credit card services to customers in West Virginia had income tax nexus in West Virginia, even though it had no physical presence in the state. During the tax years in question, the bank regularly engaged in direct mail, telephone solicitation, and promotion in the state that produced significant gross receipts from its West Virginia customers. The court concluded that the Quill physical presence test did not apply to taxes other than sales and use taxes and that MBNA had "a significant economic presence sufficient to meet the substantial nexus" test under the Commerce Clause.

In *Capital One Bank and Capital One F.S.B. v. Commissioner of Revenue* [No. SJC-10105 (Mass. Sup. Jud. Ct., Jan. 8, 2009); *cert. denied*, U.S. Sup. Ct., No. 08-1169, June 22, 2009], the Massachusetts Supreme Judicial Court held that imposition of the Massachusetts financial institution excise (income) tax "is determined not by *Quill's* physical presence test, but by the 'substantial nexus' test articulated in *Complete Auto.*" As a result, despite the lack of any physical presence in the state, the two out-of-state credit card banks had substantial nexus in Massachusetts, because of their "purposeful, targeted marketing of their credit card business to Massachusetts customers . . . and their receipt of hundreds of millions of dollars in income from millions of transactions involving Massachusetts residents and merchants." See also *Geoffrey, Inc. v. Commissioner of Revenue* [No. SJC-10106, Mass. Sup. Jud. Ct., Jan. 8, 2009; *cert. denied*, U.S. Sup. Ct., No. 08-1207, June 22, 2009)].

In *KFC Corporation v. Iowa Department of Revenue* [No. 09-1032 (Ia. Sup. Ct., Dec. 30, 2010)], the Iowa Supreme Court ruled that the Commerce Clause does not require a physical presence in order to tax the income that a Delaware corporation (KFC) earned from the use of its intangibles in Iowa. The court concluded that the trademarks and other intangibles owned by KFC and licensed for use by independent franchisees doing business in Iowa, "would be regarded as having a sufficient connection to Iowa to amount to the functional equivalent of 'physical presence' under *Quill.*" The court also concluded that even if the use of the intangibles within the state does not amount to physical presence under *Quill*, the physical presence requirement should not be extended to prevent a state from imposing an income tax on revenue generated from the use of intangibles within the state.

For a detailed discussion of economic nexus, see the section in Part 2 entitled Activities Creating Franchise or Income Tax Nexus.

Economic Substance and Business Purpose. In *Gregory v. Helvering* [293 U.S. 465, 1935], the U.S. Supreme Court has ruled that a transaction is respected only if it has economic substance and serves a business purpose other than tax avoidance. The states have invoked the judicial doctrines of economic substance and business purpose as an argument for disallowing deductions for royalty payments made by an operating company to a trademark holding company.

In *Syms Corp. v. Commissioner of Revenue* [No. SJC-08513 (Mass. Sup. Jud. Ct., Apr. 10, 2002)], the Massachusetts Supreme Judicial Court ruled that the transfer and licensing back of trademarks between a retailer and its trademark holding company was a sham transaction, and therefore no deduction was allowed for the royalty payments. The Massachusetts courts reached similar conclusions in *Talbots, Inc. v. Commissioner of Revenue* [No. 09-P-1931 (Mass. App. Ct., Mar. 29, 2011)], *IDC Research v. Commissioner of Revenue* [No. 09-P-1533 (Mass. App. Ct., Nov. 30, 2010)], and *TJX Companies, Inc. vs. Commissioner of Revenue* [No. 09-P-1841 (Mass. App. Ct., July 23, 2010)]. On the other hand, in *The Sherwin-Williams., Co. v. Commissioner of Revenue* [No. SJC-08516 (Mass. Sup. Jud. Ct., Oct. 31, 2002)], the Massachusetts Supreme Judicial Court ruled that two trademark holding companies had economic substance and served valid business purposes.

In *SYL, Inc. v. Comptroller; Crown Cork & Seal Co. (Del.), Inc. v. Comptroller* [Nos. 76 and 80 (Md. Ct. of App. June 9, 2003)], the Maryland Court of Appeals held that the trademark holding companies in question had nexus in Maryland, because they were unitary with their parent companies, which were doing business in Maryland, and had no economic substance as separate entities from their parent corporations. The Maryland courts reached similar conclusions in *W. L. Gore v. Comptroller of Treasury* [No. 07-IN-OO-0084, No. 07-IN-OO-0085, No. 07-IN-OO-0086 (Md. Tax Ct., Nov. 9, 2010)]; *The Classics Chicago, Inc., et al. v. Comptroller of the Treasury* [No. 2047 (Md. Ct. of Spec. App., Jan. 4, 2010)] (Classics was a wholly-owned subsidiary of the retailer, Talbots) and *Nordstrom, Inc. v. Comptroller of the Treasury* [Nos. 07-IN-OO-0226, 06-IN-OO-00317, 07-IN-OO-0226, 06-IN-OO-00318, 07-IN-OO-0226, and 06-IN-OO-00319 (Md. Tax Ct., Oct. 24, 2008); and No. 07-IN-00-0317 and No. 07-IN-00-0318 (Md. Tax Ct., Feb. 25, 2010)].

In *TD Banknorth, N.A. v. Department of Taxes* [No. 2007-127 (Vt. Sup. Ct., Sept. 19, 2008)], the Vermont Supreme Court applied the economic substance doctrine to disregard the existence of a taxpayers' holding companies for Vermont bank franchise tax purposes, because the holding companies were merely shell corporations established for the sole purpose of tax avoidance, with no independent economic substance.

In *Wal-Mart Stores East, Inc. v. Secretary of Revenue* [No. COA08-450 (N.C. Ct. of App., May 19, 2009)], the North Carolina Court of Appeals ruled that the Department of Revenue could require a large retailer to file on a combined basis in order to determine the retailer's "true earnings" from its business in North Carolina. The taxpayer's parent company had restructured its divisions to establish the taxpayer operating company, a real estate investment trust (REIT) subsidiary that owned the retail stores in North Carolina, and another property company subsidiary. The reorganization was designed to avoid North Carolina tax by enabling the taxpayer to claim a rent deduction for rent paid by the operating company to the REIT and a dividends-received deduction for dividends paid to the taxpayer by the out-of-state subsidiary property company from the rental income distributed to it by the REIT.

In *HMN Financial, Inc. v. Commissioner of Revenue* [No. A09-1164 (Minn. Sup. Ct., May 20, 2010)], the Minnesota Supreme Court ruled that the commissioner did not have the authority to disregard the taxpayer's captive REIT structure, which was motivated solely by tax avoidance, because the taxpayer complied with the relevant corporate franchise tax statutes in structuring its business and reporting its income.

Combined Reporting. Requiring an out-of-state trademark holding company to file a combined report with an in-state operating company eliminates the tax benefits of intercompany royalty payments because the operating company's royalty deduction is, in effect, offset by the holding company's royalty income.

For a detailed discussion of combined reporting, see the section in this Part entitled Combined Unitary Reporting.

Section 482-Type Reallocation. IRC Section 482 authorizes the IRS to reallocate income among commonly controlled corporations whenever necessary to prevent the evasion of taxes or to clearly reflect the income of the related entities. Congress enacted Section 482 to ensure that commonly controlled corporations report and pay tax on their actual share of income arising from intercompany transactions. Many states have enacted Section 482-type statutes, although the details of these statutes vary significantly from state to state. For example, Florida tax authorities may make adjustments to clearly reflect a taxpayer's income if an arrangement exists between related entities which causes a taxpayer's income to be "reflected improperly or in accurately" [Fla. Stat. ch. § 220.44].

Related Party Royalty and Interest Expense Add-Back Provisions. Another method of combating the use of trademark holding company planning structures is to enact laws that disallow deductions for royalty and interest payments made to related parties. By enacting a statute that requires an in-state operating company to add-back deductions for royalty and interest payments made to related parties, states deny the tax benefit of establishing an out-of-state trademark holding company.

For a more detailed discussion of these provisions, see the section in Part 3 entitled Related Party Expense Addback Provisions.

State-by-State Summary

The following chart, presented in two parts, summarizes which states limit the use of related party planning structures through the use of the different mechanisms outlined above.

Provisions That Limit Related Party Planning (Part 1)

Legend:

X	Condition applies
NA	Not applicable
NR	Not reported

	Which of the Following Methods Does State Use in Dealing with Related Party Transactions?			
	Forced Combination of the Related Entities	*Reallocation of Income Among Related Entities*	*Denial of Deductions for Intercompany Payments*	*Assert Out-of-State Entity Has Nexus for Corporate Income Tax Purposes*
Alabama		Reallocation of income when related party transactions are not at arm's length. Effective 2007, denial of dividends paid deduction for captive REITS.	X, interest expenses and intangible expenses made to related parties must be added back.	
Alaska				X
Arizona	X	X	X	
Arkansas		X, royalties subject to Reg 1996-3. Other intangible inter-company transactions subject to ACA 26-51-423(g).	X, royalties subject to Reg 1996-3. Other intangible inter-company transactions subject to ACA 26-51-423(g).	X, royalties subject to Reg 1996-3. Other intangible inter-company transactions subject to ACA 26-51-423(g).
California	X, related entities are part of unitary business, unless the taxpayer has made a water's-edge election and the related entity is outside the water's edge.	X, in California, IRC § 482-type adjustments are only necessary if the taxpayer has made a water's-edge election and the related party transaction is with an affiliate that is outside the water's edge.	X, for related transactions which are not considered intercompany transactions. See Cal. Code Regs., tit. 18 § 25106.5-1(b)(1)(B).	X, for taxable years beginning on or after 1/1/2011, R&TC § 23101 is amended to provide a bright-line test for economic nexus.
Colorado	X, 3 of 6 tests. See C.R.S. 39-22-303	X, § 39-22-303(b) C.R.S.	X, § 39-22-303(b) C.R.S.	X
Connecticut		Where taxpayer's income is not properly reflected under Conn. Gen. Stat. § 12-226a.	Required addback of interest payments and royalty payments; Conn. Gen. Stat. §§ 12-218c and 12-218d.	

Provisions That Limit Related Party Planning (Part 1)

Legend:

X	Condition applies
NA	Not applicable
NR	Not reported

	Which of the Following Methods Does State Use in Dealing with Related Party Transactions?			
	Forced Combination of the Related Entities	*Reallocation of Income Among Related Entities*	*Denial of Deductions for Intercompany Payments*	*Assert Out-of-State Entity Has Nexus for Corporate Income Tax Purposes*
Delaware	NR	NR	NR	NR
District of Columbia		X, DC Code § 47-1810.3	X	X
Florida				X, earning income as described in FL statutes and rules.
Georgia			X, for tax years beginning on or after 1/1/10, see O.C.G.A. § 48-7-28.3 and O.C.G.A. § 48-7-28.4	
Hawaii				X, assert either economic nexus or attributional nexus
Idaho				

Legend:

X — Condition applies
NA — Not applicable
NR — Not reported

Provisions That Limit Related Party Planning (Part 1)

	Which of the Following Methods Does State Use in Dealing with Related Party Transactions?			
	Forced Combination of the Related Entities	*Reallocation of Income Among Related Entities*	*Denial of Deductions for Intercompany Payments*	*Assert Out-of-State Entity Has Nexus for Corporate Income Tax Purposes*
Illinois	X, under IITA § 304, members of a Unitary Business Group are required to apportion business income using the combined apportionment method. IITA § 1501(a)(27) defines "unitary business group," which does not include members with 80% or more of total business activity outside the U.S., nor does it include members required to apportion business income under a different subsection of IITA § 304.	X, see IITA § 404.	See IITA § 404. Modifications related to interest and intangible expenses to a related party are required when paid to a foreign entity who would be a member of the unitary business group, but 80% or more of its business activity is outside the United States. Modifications for dividends received required, see IITA § 203(b)(2)(E-12), (E-13).	X, the Department will seek enforcement against any entity liable for Illinois income tax under the IITA unless federal law precludes the exercise of tax jurisdiction.
Indiana				
Iowa		X, if the net income reported to Iowa results in a distortion, see Iowa Code § 422.36(3).		X, if the out-of-state entity has income from intangible property located or having situs in Iowa.
Kansas	X, if it is determined the two parties conduct a unitary business			

Provisions That Limit Related Party Planning (Part 1)

Legend:

X Condition applies
NA Not applicable
NR Not reported

	Which of the Following Methods Does State Use in Dealing with Related Party Transactions?			
	Forced Combination of the Related Entities	*Reallocation of Income Among Related Entities*	*Denial of Deductions for Intercompany Payments*	*Assert Out-of-State Entity Has Nexus for Corporate Income Tax Purposes*
Kentucky			X, KRS 141.205 provides for disallowance of the deduction for intangible expenses, intangible interest expense and management fees if: 1) not taxed in its state or country of commercial domicile, 2) the recipient is not engaged in a business for the maintenance and protection of the intangible property, and 3) the intangible transaction was not made at a commercially reasonable rate and at terms comparable to an arm's length transaction.	
Louisiana	X, if deemed necessary by the Secretary to prevent evasion of taxes or to clearly reflect the evasion of taxes or to clearly reflect the income of such organizations LSA R.S. 47:287, 480(2).	X, if deemed necessary by the Secretary to prevent evasion of taxes or to clearly reflect the evasion of taxes or to clearly reflect the income of such organizations LSA R.S. 47:287, 480(2).		X, either economic or attributional
Maine	Intercompany transactions are eliminated, see MRS Reg 810.			
Maryland				X, the Maryland Court of Appeals is currently deciding.

Provisions That Limit Related Party Planning (Part 1)

Legend:

X	Condition applies
NA	Not applicable
NR	Not reported

	Which of the Following Methods Does State Use in Dealing with Related Party Transactions?			
	Forced Combination of the Related Entities	*Reallocation of Income Among Related Entities*	*Denial of Deductions for Intercompany Payments*	*Assert Out-of-State Entity Has Nexus for Corporate Income Tax Purposes*
Massachusetts	Depends			
Michigan (Business Tax)	The entities will be required to file a combined return if they constitute a unitary business group.			
Note. The CIT takes effect 01/01/12, and replaces the Michigan Business Tax (MBT) for most taxpayers. However, businesses that have been approved to receive, have received, or have been assigned certain certified credits may elect to file a return and pay the tax imposed by the MBT in lieu of the CIT until the certified credits are exhausted or extinguished.				
Minnesota	X, combined unitary reporting is mandatory with elimination of intercompany transactions.	X, SAF	X, elimination of intercompany transactions of unitary group	X, nexus questionnaire required
Mississippi	X, can be used by the Commissioner		X	
Missouri				X
Montana	X, if unitary relationship exists			
Nebraska	X, all members of any unitary group are required to be included in a single return, unless some members have a special apportionment formula.			
Nevada	Nevada does not impose a corporate income tax			

Provisions That Limit Related Party Planning (Part 1)

Legend:

X	Condition applies
NA	Not applicable
NR	Not reported

	Which of the Following Methods Does State Use in Dealing with Related Party Transactions?			
	Forced Combination of the Related Entities	*Reallocation of Income Among Related Entities*	*Denial of Deductions for Intercompany Payments*	*Assert Out-of-State Entity Has Nexus for Corporate Income Tax Purposes*
New Hampshire	Combined reporting	Combined reporting	Combined reporting	See RSA 77-A"1, XII, business activity
New Jersey	X, if taxpayer cannot demonstrate its report reflects true earnings, Director may require consolidated returns. N.J.S.A. 54:10A-10, 18:7-5.10	X, if distortion occurs in Director's opinion, N.J.A.C. 18.7-5.10, N.J.S.A. 54:10A-10	X, if distortion occurs in Director's opinion, N.J.A.C. 18.7-5.10, N.J.S.A. 54:10A-10	X, *Lanco, Inc. v. Director* (*Geoffrey*-type case), Tax Court of New Jersey, Docket ##005329-1997.
New Mexico				X, economic
New York				

Provisions That Limit Related Party Planning (Part 1)

Legend:
X — Condition applies
NA — Not applicable
NR — Not reported

	Which of the Following Methods Does State Use in Dealing with Related Party Transactions?			
	Forced Combination of the Related Entities	*Reallocation of Income Among Related Entities*	*Denial of Deductions for Intercompany Payments*	*Assert Out-of-State Entity Has Nexus for Corporate Income Tax Purposes*
North Carolina	X, when taxpayer's income with its affiliated company is more accurately reflective of the true earnings of taxpayer from its business activities conducted in state. G.S. 105-130.6 is repealed 1/1/12 (See Session Law 2011-390)		X, G.S. 105-130.7A sets out reporting options for royalty payments and income. Under the options, royalty income from the use of a trademark in North Carolina may be reported in either of two ways if the payer and the recipient are related entities. First, the recipient of the payments can include the payments in its North Carolina income and the company making the payments can deduct the payments from the company's North Carolina income. Second, the recipient of the payments can exclude the payments from its North Carolina income and the company making the payments can add the payments to the company's North Carolina income. The options in G.S. 105-130.7A are reporting options and not filing options.	X, a corporation that receives royalty payments for the use of trademarks in this State is doing business in this State and must file an income tax return and a franchise tax return. [NCAC T17:5C.0102(a)(5)(C)]
North Dakota				

Provisions That Limit Related Party Planning (Part 1)

Legend:
X — Condition applies
NA — Not applicable
NR — Not reported

	Which of the Following Methods Does State Use in Dealing with Related Party Transactions?			
	Forced Combination of the Related Entities	*Reallocation of Income Among Related Entities*	*Denial of Deductions for Intercompany Payments*	*Assert Out-of-State Entity Has Nexus for Corporate Income Tax Purposes*
Ohio	Ohio does not impose a corporate income tax			
Note. Effective 1/1/2010, the Ohio Franchise Tax was fully phased out and business will be taxed on gross receipts through the Commercial Activity Tax. Details about that tax can be found at: http//tax.ohio.gov/divisions/commercial_activities/index.stm				
Oklahoma	Currently litigating issue, have asserted nexus for the out-of-state holding company			
Oregon	X, an Oregon consolidated return is required when a federal consolidated return is filed and the related parties are unitary with two or more affiliates subject to Oregon tax.		X, intercompany transactions between the unitary members of an Oregon consolidated group are eliminated, when the company making the payment is unitary with but may not be included in the consolidated return of the company to which payments are made.	X, nexus for income tax purposes is acquired when an out-of-state corporation has income from tangible or intangible property located within Oregon. If intangible property is used in Oregon by the operating company, the statutory provision is met. Nexus for excise tax purposes is acquired when an out-of-state corporation has a representative in the state that does not qualify as "independent" and the representative's activities are not protected by P.L. 86-272.
Pennsylvania				
Rhode Island				

Provisions That Limit Related Party Planning (Part 1)

Legend:

X	Condition applies
NA	Not applicable
NR	Not reported

	Which of the Following Methods Does State Use in Dealing with Related Party Transactions?			
	Forced Combination of the Related Entities	*Reallocation of Income Among Related Entities*	*Denial of Deductions for Intercompany Payments*	*Assert Out-of-State Entity Has Nexus for Corporate Income Tax Purposes*
South Carolina			Sec. 12-6.1130(14) disallows a deduction for accrual of an expense or interest if the payee is a related person and the payment is not made in the tax year of accrual or before the payor's income tax is due, without regard to extensions, for the tax year of accrual.	
South Dakota	South Dakota does not impose a corporate income tax			
Tennessee			X, if the intangible expense deduction is not disclosed on the return; the law provides for a disclosure on the face of the return and a schedule within the return.	
Texas	X, taxable entities that are part of an affiliated group engaged in a unitary business must file a combined group report.		X, a payment made by one member of an affiliated group to another member of that affiliated group not included in the combined group may be subtracted as cost of goods sold only if the transaction is at arm's length.	

Provisions That Limit Related Party Planning (Part 1)

Legend:
X Condition applies
NA Not applicable
NR Not reported

Which of the Following Methods Does State Use in Dealing with Related Party Transactions?

	Forced Combination of the Related Entities	*Reallocation of Income Among Related Entities*	*Denial of Deductions for Intercompany Payments*	*Assert Out-of-State Entity Has Nexus for Corporate Income Tax Purposes*
Utah	X, a licensing arrangement is highly likely to result in the finding of a unitary business and the income of the entities would end up being required to be combined. If not, Utah also has similar authority to IRC § 482, UDITPA § 18 authority.			
Vermont				
Virginia	X, determination is based on facts and circumstances of each case that improperly reflects business done in Virginia, see Va. Code § 58.1-446.	X, determination is based on facts and circumstances of each case that improperly reflects business done in Virginia, see Va. Code § 58.1-446.	X, determination is based on facts and circumstances of each case that improperly reflects business done in Virginia, see Va. Code § 58.1-446. For 2004 and after, corporations must add back expenses for royalties and certain interest paid to intangible holding companies.	X, determination is based on facts and circumstances of each case that improperly reflects business done in Virginia, see Va. Code § 58.1-446. Nexus based on existence of arrangement allowing consolidation, authority not used to assert *Geoffrey* nexus directly on the out-of-state corporation.
Washington	Washington does not impose a corporate income tax			
West Virginia				

Legend:

X	Condition applies
NA	Not applicable
NR	Not reported

Provisions That Limit Related Party Planning (Part 1)

	Which of the Following Methods Does State Use in Dealing with Related Party Transactions?			
	Forced Combination of the Related Entities	*Reallocation of Income Among Related Entities*	*Denial of Deductions for Intercompany Payments*	*Assert Out-of-State Entity Has Nexus for Corporate Income Tax Purposes*
Wisconsin	Where facts are appropriate	X, IRC § 482 type provision or § 71.30(2) Wis. Stats. (2001-2002) provisions	For rent and interest expense deductions, an addback statute applies effective for taxable years beginning on or after 1/1/08. See § § 71.26(2)(a)7 - 9 and 71.80(23), as enacted by 2007 Wis. Act 226. The addback statute is in addition to and not a limitation of or dependent on the Department's authority under § 71.30(2), Wis. Stat.	Where facts are appropriate.
Wyoming	Wyoming does not impose a corporate income tax			

Provisions That Limit Related Party Planning (Part 2)

Legend:

X	Condition applies
NA	Not applicable
NR	Not reported

	Which of the Following Methods Does State Use in Dealing with Related Party Transactions?		
	Disregard the Existence of the Related Party Transactions	*Require Alternative Apportionment Method*	*Other*
Alabama	NR	NR	NR
Alaska			
Arizona		X	
Arkansas	X, royalties subject to Reg 1996-3. Other intangible inter-company transactions subject to ACA 26-51-423(g).	X, royalties subject to Reg 1996-3. Other intangible inter-company transactions subject to ACA 26-51-423(g).	
California	X, only necessary if the taxpayer has made a water's edge election and the related party transaction is with an affiliate that is outside the water's edge.		
Colorado	X, sham transactions or sham entities	X, § 39-22-303(5)(b) and (6) C.R.S.	
Connecticut	See Conn. Gen. Stat. § 12-226a and Conn. Agencies Regs. § 12-226a-1.		
Delaware	NR	NR	NR
District of Columbia	X	X	NR
Florida			X, may require any of the preceding remedies depending on the specific facts and circumstances.
Georgia	NR	NR	NR
Hawaii			

Provisions That Limit Related Party Planning (Part 2)

Legend:

X	Condition applies
NA	Not applicable
NR	Not reported

	Which of the Following Methods Does State Use in Dealing with Related Party Transactions?		
	Disregard the Existence of the Related Party Transactions	*Require Alternative Apportionment Method*	*Other*
Idaho			X, state does not have any special related party transaction provisions. If they meet the requirements to be combined, state would combine them. Would follow federal reallocations or denial of deductions. The nexus rules applicable to all corporations would apply.
Illinois	X, See IITA § 404. Under appropriate circumstances, the Department may seek to invoke the economic substance, business purpose, sham transaction, or similar doctrine.	X, 86 Ill. Admin. Code 100.3380 allows the Department to require an alternative apportionment method in the instances described in that section.	
Indiana			X, Department has statutory authority to adjust income so that Indiana-source income is fairly represented.
Iowa			
Kansas			
Kentucky			
Louisiana			
Maine		No	
Maryland			
Massachusetts	X	X	

Provisions That Limit Related Party Planning (Part 2)

Legend:

X	Condition applies
NA	Not applicable
NR	Not reported

	Which of the Following Methods Does State Use in Dealing with Related Party Transactions?		
	Disregard the Existence of the Related Party Transactions	*Require Alternative Apportionment Method*	*Other*
Michigan (Business Tax)			
Note. The CIT takes effect 01/01/12, and replaces the Michigan Business Tax (MBT) for most taxpayers. However, businesses that have been approved to receive, have received, or have been assigned certain certified credits may elect to file a return and pay the tax imposed by the MBT in lieu of the CIT until the certified credits are exhausted or extinguished.			
Minnesota	Elimination of intercompany transactions of unitary group	When the prescribed apportionment method does not fairly reflect the income attributable to the state, another method may be used	
Mississippi			
Missouri			
Montana			
Nebraska			
Nevada	Nevada does not impose a corporate income tax		
New Hampshire	See RSA 21-J:38-a, sham transactions	See RSA 77-A:3, II(a). apportionment	
New Jersey	X, disallow deduction of royalty payments and interest, N.J.S.A. 54:10A-4.4.	X, to correct distortions	
New Mexico			
New York			New York may use one or more of these methods depending on the facts and circumstances.
North Carolina			

Provisions That Limit Related Party Planning (Part 2)

Legend:

X	Condition applies
NA	Not applicable
NR	Not reported

	Which of the Following Methods Does State Use in Dealing with Related Party Transactions?		
	Disregard the Existence of the Related Party Transactions	*Require Alternative Apportionment Method*	*Other*
North Dakota			Mandatory combination if unitary
Ohio	Ohio does not impose a corporate income tax		
Note. Effective 1/1/2010, the Ohio Franchise Tax was fully phased out and business will be taxed on gross receipts through the Commercial Activity Tax. Details about that tax can be found at: http//tax.ohio.gov/divisions/commercial_activities/index.stm			
Oklahoma	Currently litigating issue, have asserted nexus for the out-of-state holding company.		
Oregon	X, when the related parties are a principal subject to Oregon tax and its related FSC or Interest Charge DISC.	X, if the application of the allocation and apportionment provisions of ORS 314.605 to 314.675 do not fairly represent the extent of the taxpayer's business activity in state. (UDITPA § 18 type equitable relief provision)	
Pennsylvania	X, income is calculated as it would have been reported to the IRC on a separate company basis.		
Rhode Island			Must separately apportion based upon activities or physical presence in state.
South Carolina		The Department may require if allocation and apportionment provisions do not fairly represent the extent of the taxpayer's business activity in this state.	Special methods allowed under § 12-6-2320(A)
South Dakota	South Dakota does not impose a corporate income tax		

Provisions That Limit Related Party Planning (Part 2)

Legend:

X — Condition applies
NA — Not applicable
NR — Not reported

	Which of the Following Methods Does State Use in Dealing with Related Party Transactions?		
	Disregard the Existence of the Related Party Transactions	*Require Alternative Apportionment Method*	*Other*
Tennessee			
Texas		X, corporations report on a separate entity basis. The mere licensing of intangible into Texas does not subject a corporation to nexus in Texas.	
Utah			
Vermont			Depends upon circumstances
Virginia	X, determination is based on facts and circumstances of each case that improperly reflects business done in Virginia, see Va. Code § 58.1-446.		X, determination is based on facts and circumstances of each case.
Washington	Washington does not impose a corporate income tax		
West Virginia			
Wisconsin	X, where facts are appropriate	X, if income properly assignable to the State of Wisconsin cannot be ascertained with reasonable certainty by the standard apportionment methods.	
Wyoming	Wyoming does not impose a corporate income tax		

Part 5. APPORTIONMENT

Apportionment Formulas

When a corporation does business in more than one state, such that the corporation is or could be taxed by more than one state, the question arises as to how to determine the portion of the corporation's income attributable to each state. When, as is often the case, a corporation consists of separate but interdependent departments and divisions that are integrated vertically or horizontally, it is generally not possible to assign the corporation's income precisely among the several states in which it does business. Because the results obtained by using a separate accounting method for each business unit are often arbitrary, states use allocation and apportionment procedures to determine the portion of a corporation's income that is attributable to a particular state.

Allocation

Allocation generally refers to the assignment of nonbusiness income to a particular state. Generally, "nonbusiness income" means all income other than business income, and "business income" means income that arises from the regular course of the taxpayer's trade or business or is derived from property that is an integral part of the taxpayer's regular trade or business operations. For example, rental income received by a manufacturing corporation for a piece of real property that is located outside the state in which the corporation carries on its manufacturing activities and that is not related to those manufacturing activities. Nonbusiness income is usually allocated to the state in which the property giving rise to the income is located, or in the case of income from intangible property, to the state in which the corporation has its commercial domicile. (See the section entitled Allocation of Nonbusiness Income in this part for further details regarding the allocation of nonbusiness income.)

Apportionment

A corporation that is taxable in more than one state has the constitutional right to have its income fairly apportioned among the taxing states. [*Complete Auto Transit v. Brady*, 430 U.S. 274 (1977)] A taxpayer apportions its income by computing the percentage of its business income that is taxable in each nexus state using the formulas provided by those states. To determine a state's apportionment percentage, a ratio is established for each of the factors included in the state's formula. Each ratio is calculated by comparing the level of a specific business activity within a state to the total corporate activity of that type. The ratios are then appropriately weighted and summed to determine the corporation's apportionment percentage for each state.

Apportionment does not necessarily provide a uniform division of a corporation's income among the nexus states (i.e., a corporation's apportionment percentages may not sum to 100 percent) because each state is free to choose the type and number of factors it will use as indicative of the amount of business activity conducted within its borders. Moreover, each state makes its own rules for computing the factors included in its apportionment formula. The lack of uniformity can result in either double taxation or "nowhere income."

In 1957, state tax officials promulgated the Uniform Division of Income for Tax Purposes Act (UDITPA), which is a model law for apportioning the income of a corporation that is taxable in two or more states. UDITPA provides for the use of an equally-weighted three-factor formula that includes a sales factor, property factor, and payroll factor. In *Moorman Manufacturing Co. v. Bair* [437 U.S. 267 (1978)], the Supreme Court ruled that a three-factor formula is not constitutionally required, and that Iowa could use a sales-only apportionment formula. Consistent with its prior rulings, the Court stated that a state's choice of apportionment formulas generally will be upheld unless a taxpayer can prove by clear and cogent evidence that the formula attributes income to the state that is out of all appropriate proportion to the business transacted by the taxpayer in that state.

At present, about ten states use a three-factor apportionment formula that equally weights sales, property, and payroll. Most states use a modified three-factor formula, under which the sales factor is assigned more weight than the property or payroll factors. Many states double weight the sales factor (i.e., 50 percent sales, 25 percent property, and 25 percent payroll). About 15 states use a single-factor sales-only formula, including Colorado, Georgia, Illinois, Indiana (effective in 2011), Iowa, Maine, Michigan, Nebraska, New York, Oregon, South Carolina (effective in 2011), Texas, and Wisconsin. Other states that super weight the sales factor include Arizona (80 percent), Minnesota (93 percent in 2012), New Jersey (70 percent in 2012), and Pennsylvania (90 percent).

For tax years beginning on or after January 1, 2011, California taxpayers may make an annual election to use a single factor sales-only formula. However, the election is not available to a taxpayer that derives more than 50 percent of its gross business receipts from conducting an agricultural, extractive, banking or financial business activity. [S.B. 15. Feb. 20, 2009] On July 7, 2011, the California Franchise Tax Board approved regulations that provide procedures for making the election. [Reg. 25128.5]

The political appeal of an apportionment formula that weights the sales factor more heavily than the property and payroll factors is that it tends to reduce the tax liabilities of corporations that are based in the state, while potentially increasing the tax liabilities of out-of-state corporations. Specifically, placing more weight on the sales factor tends to pull a larger percentage of an out-of-state corporation's income within the taxing jurisdiction of the state because the corporation's major activity within the state—sales of its product—is weighted more heavily than its payroll and property activities. For corporations that are based in the state, however, placing more weight on the sales factor provides tax relief because those corporations generally own significantly more property and incur more payroll costs (factors that are given relatively less weight in the apportionment formula) within the state than do out-of-state corporations.

If a state uses a three-factor apportionment formula and one of the factors is not present (e.g., a corporation has no payroll), generally the computation of the apportionment percentage is adjusted accordingly. For example, if a state uses an equally weighted three-factor formula and the taxpayer has no payroll, the apportionment percentage is determined by dividing the sum of the property and sales factors by two. [e.g., Colo. Dept. of Rev. Reg. IV.18(a), effective Apr. 30, 2010; and *Rentco Trailer Corp. v. Director of Revenue*, No. 97-001373 RI (Mo. Admin. Hearing Comm., July 31, 1998)]

Right to Apportion

Not all corporations are entitled to apportion their income. The requirements for establishing the right to apportion income vary from state to state, but generally entail carrying on business in another state, maintaining a regular place of business in another state, or being taxable in another state. Some states take the restrictive position that permits apportionment only if the corporation is actually filing returns and paying tax in another state. UDITPA provides that any taxpayer having income from business activity that is taxable both within and without this state shall allocate and apportion its net income. [UDITPA Section 2] For this purpose, a corporation is "taxable in another state if (1) in that state the corporation is subject to a net income tax, a franchise tax measured by net income, a franchise tax for the privilege of doing business, or a corporate stock tax, or (2) that state has jurisdiction to subject the corporation to a net income tax regardless of whether, in fact, the state does or does not." [UDITPA Section 3]

Kentucky. In *Publishers Printing Company and Subsidiaries v. Finance and Administration Cabinet* [No. K08-R-10 (Ky. Bd. of Tax App., Jan. 20, 2010)], six affiliated companies filed a unitary return in Kentucky. Only one of the affiliates conducted business outside Kentucky, doing business in Colorado where the group also filed a unitary return. The Kentucky Board of Tax Appeals ruled that apportionment did not fairly represent the extent of the taxpayer's business activity in Kentucky, and that because all of the taxpayer's property and payroll was in Kentucky, all its net income was taxable by Kentucky.

New Jersey. In *River Systems, Inc. v. Division of Taxation* [No. A-2741-01T3 (N.J. Super. Ct., Mar. 14, 2003)], the New Jersey Superior Court ruled that the income of a New Jersey corporation is 100 percent taxable in New Jersey, because the taxpayer's use of telemarketers in New York did not satisfy New Jersey's statutory requirement that, in order to apportion its income, a taxpayer must "maintain a regular place of business" outside New Jersey. [N.J.S.A. § 54:10A-6]

In *New Jersey Natural Gas Co. v. Division of Taxation* [Nos. 000240-2005 and 007284-2005 (N.J. Tax Ct., Apr. 17, 2008)], the New Jersey Tax Court ruled that the taxpayer must allocate all of its income to New Jersey, because an employee's home office in Connecticut did not constitute a regular place of business outside New Jersey. In order for an out-of-state location to be considered the taxpayer's regular place of business, the taxpayer must either own or rent the facility in its own name and must be directly responsible for the expenses incurred in maintaining the place of business. In this case, the taxpayer did not own or rent the employee's home and the employee was contractually responsible for all expenses related to the home office.

In December 2008, New Jersey enacted legislation to eliminate the requirement that a corporation have a "regular place of business" in another state in order to apportion its income, effective for privilege periods beginning on or after July 1, 2010. [A.B. 2722, Dec. 19, 2008]

Missouri. In *Jay Wolfe Imports Missouri, Inc. v. Director of Revenue* [No. SC89568 (Mo. Sup. Ct., May 5, 2009)], the Missouri Supreme Court ruled that a Missouri car dealership located two blocks from the Missouri-Kansas state line was not entitled to apportion its income, because it derived income from sources entirely in Missouri. The fact that some out-of-state customers purchased cars and then drove them back to their out-of-state addresses did not mean that the sales themselves were conducted partly within and partly outside the state. Missouri law provides that sales partly within and partly without the state occur only if the seller's shipping point and the purchaser's destination point are in different states. In this case, the dealership did not ship cars purchased at its Missouri facility to out-of-state customers. Instead, the out-of-state customers completed their sales transactions and took possession of their purchased car in Missouri and then drove them to their out-of-state addresses.

In *Moberly Regional Center v. Director of Revenue* [No. 07-0283 RI (Mo. Admin. Hearing Comm., Oct. 6, 2008)], the Missouri Administrative Hearing Commission ruled that a hospital located in and transacting business in Missouri that contracted with an affiliated out-of-state company to perform management functions was not entitled to apportion its income, because it did not employ any labor or capital outside Missouri. Paying an affiliated out-of-state company to perform management services did not constitute the employment of labor outside the state of Missouri. All of the hospital's employees and property were located in Missouri, and all of its patients were treated in Missouri. The hospital did not earn any income in any other state and thus had no income to apportion between Missouri and any other state.

In *TSI Holding Co. v. Director of Revenue* [No. SC85179, SC85180, and SC85181 (Mo. Sup. Ct., Nov. 4, 2003)], a case dealing with the Missouri franchise tax, the Missouri Supreme Court ruled that three related Missouri investment holding companies were not entitled to apportion their income because they did business solely in Missouri. The corporations did not do business in any other state, did not have offices in any other state, and did not file franchise tax returns in any other state.

Massachusetts. In *Tech-Etch, Inc. v. Commissioner of Revenue* [No. 05-P-1012 (Mass. App. Ct., Nov. 3, 2006)], the Massachusetts Appeals Court ruled that a Massachusetts manufacturer was not entitled to apportion its income in connection with sales of goods shipped to customers located in foreign countries, because the taxpayer failed to establish that it was taxable in another state or foreign country.

Equitable Relief Provisions

The divergent apportionment formulas used by the states, along with different rules for computing the factors in each state's formula, can result in a corporation's being subject to tax on more than 100 percent of its income. An equally adverse consequence of apportionment may result when the operations in a state result in a loss, as determined by a separate geographic accounting. When a corporation as a whole generates a profit, the use of an apportionment formula results in the corporation's incurring an income tax liability in the state in which the loss operation is located, even though no profit is generated in that state.

To provide relief in inequitable situations, UDITPA Section 18 provides that if the standard allocation and apportionment provisions do not fairly represent the extent of the taxpayer's business activity in a state, the taxpayer may petition for, or the tax administrator may require, with respect to all or any part of the taxpayer's business activity, if reasonable, use of separate accounting, exclusion of any one or more of the factors, inclusion of one or more additional factors, or employment of any other method that will result in "an equitable allocation and apportionment of the taxpayer's income." For example, California's equivalent of UDITPA Section 18, California Revenue and Taxation Code Section 25137 (Equitable Adjustment of Standard Allocation or Apportionment), states:

> If the allocation and apportionment provisions of this act do not fairly represent the extent of the taxpayer's business activity in this state, the taxpayer may petition for or the Franchise Tax Board may require, in respect to all or any part of the taxpayer's business activity, if reasonable:
>
> (a) Separate accounting;
>
> (b) The exclusion of any one or more of the factors;
>
> (c) The inclusion of one or more additional factors which will fairly represent the taxpayer's business activity in this state; or
>
> (d) The employment of any other method to effectuate an equitable allocation and apportionment of the taxpayer's income.

California Code of Regulations Title 18, Section 25137, states that "Section 25137 may be invoked only in specific cases where unusual fact situations (which ordinarily will be unique and nonrecurring) produce incongruous results under the apportionment and allocation provisions contained in these regulations."

There is a presumption developed by judicial precedent that a state's apportionment provisions are equitable. Thus, the taxpayer must do more than merely demonstrate that there is an inequity in its tax liability under the state's apportionment formula. To receive relief from the state's standard formula, the corporation generally must prove by clear and convincing evidence that the apportionment formula grossly distorts the amount of income actually earned in the state. Taxpayers generally find it difficult to prove that a state's standard apportionment provisions are inequitable. [E.g., *Hans Rees' Sons, Inc. v. North Carolina*, 283 U.S. 123 (1931); *Moorman Mfg. Co. v. Bair*, 437 U.S. 267 (1978); *Container Corp. of Am. v. Franchise Tax Bd.*, 463 U.S. 159 (1983); *Unisys Corp. v. Pa. Bd. of Fin. and Rev.*, 812 A2d 448 (Pa. Sup. Ct. 2002); and *Colgate-Palmolive Company, Inc. v. Bower* (No. 01 L 50195, Ill. Cir. Ct., Cook Cty., Oct. 15, 2002).]

In *Home Interiors & Gifts, Inc. v. Strayhorn* [No. 03-04-00660-CV (Tex. Ct. of App., Sept. 22, 2005)], the Texas Court of Appeals ruled that the interplay between Public Law 86-272 and the Texas throwback provision caused the franchise tax to be internally inconsistent; therefore, it failed *Complete Auto*'s fair apportionment requirement.

In *Media General Communications, Inc. v. Department of Revenue* [No. 26828 (S.C. Sup. Ct., June 14, 2010)], the South Carolina Supreme Court ruled that a group of communication companies could determine their taxable income on a combined basis under an equitable relief provision similar to UDITPA Section 18.

Specialized Industry Formulas

A three-factor formula typically is used to apportion the income of manufacturers and mercantile businesses. The accompanying chart reflects the apportionment factors used in apportioning the income of such businesses. Most apportionment statutes, however, also contain special provisions for apportioning the income of multistate businesses in certain industries, such as transportation companies, financial institutions, utilities, insurance companies, and construction companies. Special-apportionment provisions typically use factors that are appropriate to the particular industry. For example, mileage methods are frequently used in apportioning the income of a trucking company. (See the section in this part entitled Specialized Industry Formulas for a state-by-state listing of the apportionment formulas that have been adopted for certain industries.)

Recent Developments

Alabama. For tax years beginning on or after December 31, 2010, Alabama adopts a double-weighted sales formula. [H.B. 434, June 9, 2011] For tax years beginning before December 31, 2010, Alabama employed an equally weighted three-factor formula.

Arizona. Prior to 2007, Arizona used a double-weighted sales formula. In 2005, Arizona enacted legislation that will give taxpayers the option to use an alternative apportionment formula, under which the sales factor would be weighted 60 percent for tax years beginning in 2007, 70 percent for tax years beginning in 2008, and 80 percent for tax years beginning after 2008. [H.B. 2139, May 20, 2005]

In 2011, Arizona increased the weight on the sales factor in the optional enhanced sales factor apportionment formula to 85 percent for tax years beginning in 2014, 90 percent for tax years beginning in 2015, 95 percent for tax years beginning in 2016, and 100 percent for tax years beginning after 2016. [H.B. 2001, Feb. 17, 2011]

California. California uses a double-weighted sales apportionment formula. However, for tax years beginning on or after January 1, 2011, a taxpayer may make an annual election to use a single factor sales-only formula. The election is not available to a taxpayer that derives more than 50 percent of its gross business receipts from conducting an agricultural, extractive, banking or financial business activity. [S.B. 15. Feb. 20, 2009] On July 7, 2011, the California Franchise Tax Board approved regulations that provide procedures for making the election. [Reg. 25128.5]

Colorado. For tax years beginning on or after January 1, 2009, Colorado adopts a single-factor sales formula. [H.B. 1380, May 20, 2008] For tax years beginning before 2009, Colorado permitted corporations to choose between an equally-weighted three-factor formula, and a two-factor (property and sales) formula.

District of Columbia. For tax years beginning on or after January 1, 2011, the District of Columbia adopts a double-weighted sales formula. [D.C.B 19-203, July 22, 2011] For tax years beginning before 2011, the District employed an equally weighted three-factor formula.

Florida. Florida uses a double-weighted sales apportionment formula. However, a corporation that makes qualified capital expenditures exceeding $250 million within a two-year period beginning after June 30, 2011, may elect to use a single-factor sales apportionment formula (but not before the tax year that begins after 2012). Certain financial organizations are not eligible.

Georgia. For tax years beginning before 2006, Georgia used a double-weighted sales formula. In 2005, Georgia enacted legislation to phase in a sales-only formula over a three-year period. The sales factor will be weighted 80 percent for tax years beginning in 2006, 90 percent for tax years beginning in 2007, and 100 percent for tax years beginning on or after January 1, 2008. [H.B. 191, Apr. 6, 2005]

Indiana. For tax years beginning before 2007, Indiana used a double-weighted sales formula. In 2006, Indiana enacted legislation to phase in a sales-only formula from 2007 through 2011. The sales factor will be weighted 60 percent in 2007, 70 percent in 2008, 80 percent in 2009, 90 percent in 2010, and 100 percent for tax years beginning on or after January 1, 2011. [H.B. 1001, Mar. 24, 2006]

Kansas. A manufacturer that builds a new facility in Kansas costing at least $100 million, employs at least 100 new employees at the facility after July 1, 2007 and prior to December 31, 2009, and pays the employees higher than average wages may use a sales-only apportionment formula. [S.B. 240, Mar. 20, 2007] If certain requirements are met, the Kansas Secretary of Revenue may extend the deadline until June 30, 2010. [H.B. 2270, Mar. 27, 2009]

Minnesota. For tax years beginning before 2007, Minnesota used a 75-12.5-12.5 apportionment formula weighted in favor of sales. In 2005, Minnesota enacted legislation to phase in a sales-only formula over an eight-year period beginning in 2007. The sales-only formula will be fully phased in by 2014. [H.F. 138, July 14, 2005]

New Mexico. In 2009, New Mexico extended the time period for a manufacturer's optional use of a double-weighted sales apportionment formula from 2010 through 2019. [H.B. 75, Apr. 7, 2009]

New York City. Prior to 2009, New York City used an equally-weighted three-factor property, payroll and sales factor formula. Beginning in 2009, a sales-only apportionment formula is being phased in over 10 years. A 53-23.5-23.5 formula applies for 2011, and a 60-20-20 formula applies for 2012. [A.B. 8867, July 11, 2009]

New Jersey. For tax years beginning before 2012, New Jersey used a double-weighted sales formula. In 2011, New Jersey enacted legislation to phase in a sales-only formula. The sales factor will be weighted 70 percent for tax years beginning in 2012, 90 percent for tax years beginning in 2013, and 100 percent for tax years beginning on or after January 1, 2014. [S.B. 2753, Apr. 28, 2011]

Pennsylvania. For tax years beginning after 2008, the formula places an 83 percent weight on sales and an 8.5 percent weight on both property and payroll. For tax years beginning after 2009, the formula places a 90 percent weight on sales, and a 5 percent weight on both property and payroll. [H.B. 1531, Oct. 13, 2009]

South Carolina. For tax years beginning after 2006, taxpayers whose principal business is manufacturing or dealing in tangible personal property in South Carolina, apportion their income using a sales-only formula. Prior to 2007, such taxpayers used a double-weighted sales formula. For tax years beginning in 2007 through 2010, these taxpayers must apportion their income using both a double-weighted sales formula and a sales-only formula. If the calculation using the sales-only formula reduces the amount of income apportioned to South Carolina, 20 percent of the reduction is allowed for tax years beginning in 2007, 40 percent for tax years beginning in 2008, 60 percent for tax years beginning in 2009, and 80 percent for tax years beginning in 2010. For tax years beginning on or after January 1, 2011, manufacturers and dealers in tangible personal property will use a sales-only apportionment formula. [H.B. 4874, June 14, 2006] For additional guidance, see Revenue Ruling No. 09-15. [S.C. Dept. of Rev., Nov. 17 2009]

Virginia. Effective for tax years beginning on or after July 1, 2011, but before July 1, 2013, manufacturing companies may elect to use a triple-weighted sales apportionment formula. For tax years beginning on or after July 1, 2013, but before July 1, 2014, manufacturers may elect to use a quadruple-weighted sales formula. For tax years beginning on or after July 1, 2014, manufacturers may elect to use a sales-only formula. A manufacturer that makes this election is required to maintain a base year level of employment in Virginia and must certify that the average weekly wages of its full-time employees are greater than the lower of the state or local average weekly wages for the taxpayer's industry. [H.B. 2437, Apr. 14, 2009]

Wisconsin. For tax years beginning before 2006, Wisconsin uses a double-weighted sales formula. In 2003, Wisconsin enacted legislation to phase in a sales-only formula. The sales factor will be weighted 60 percent for tax years beginning in 2006, 80 percent for tax years beginning in 2007, and 100 percent for tax years beginning on or after January 1, 2008. [S.B. 197, July 31, 2003]

State-by-State Summary

The following chart is divided into two parts for ease of presentation. The first indicates whether the state follows UDITPA and identifies the factors and their weighting in the states' standard apportionment formulas. The second part indicates whether the states allow separate accounting and allow (or require) allocation of specific items when the standard apportionment formula does not fairly represent the extent of the taxpayer's business activity in the state. The second part also identifies whether a factor is eliminated in computing the states' apportionment percentages if either the numerator or the denominator of the factor is zero.

Apportionment Formulas (Part 1)

Legend:

X	These factors are used in apportioning business income
NA	Not applicable
NR	Not reported

	Does State Conform to UDITPA?	*Generally Used Factors*			*How Are the Factors Weighted?*
		Sales	*Property*	*Payroll*	
Alabama	Yes, with minor variations	X	X	X	50% sales, 25% property and 25% payroll
Alaska	Yes, modified apportionment formula for oil and gas producers and pipeline companies	X	X	X	Equally weighted
Arizona	Yes	X	X	X	Effective from and after 12/31/07 for taxable years beginning from and after 12/31/06, the weighting of the apportionment factors changes. See A.R.S. § 43-1139 and Laws 2005, 47th Legislature First Regular Session, ch.289, H.B. 2139.
Arkansas	Yes, double-weighted sales factor	X	X	X	50% Sales, 25% Property and 25% Payroll

Apportionment Formulas (Part 1)

Legend:
X These factors are used in apportioning business income
NA Not applicable
NR Not reported

	Does State Conform to UDITPA?	*Generally Used Factors* Sales	Property	Payroll	*How Are the Factors Weighted?*
California	Yes, however, unlike UDIPTA itself. California applies the apportionment and allocation rules of UDIPTA to financial corporations and utilities. In addition, unlike UDIPTA, California double weighs the sales factor for most taxpayers. California also has special statutory variations from UDIPTA dealing with 1) apportionment of sea and air transportation 2) gain on the sale of a nonbusiness partnership interest, and 3) professional athletic teams. Operating under authority of UDIPTA's § 18, California also has regulatory variations from the standard provision of UDIPTA. (Cal. Code Regs., tit. 18, § § 25137 through 25137-14.	X	X	X	Sales double-weighted. However, there is an exception to the double-weighted sales factor formula for some extractive and agricultural business activity, saving and loan activity, and banking or financial business activity. For these, all factors are 1/3. In addition, for taxable years beginning on or after 1/1/11, elective single sales factor apportionment is allowed.
Colorado	Partly, generally for sales factor but see specific types of sales	X			100%
Connecticut	No	X			100% for manufacturer, financial services, broadcasters and other services. 3-factor double weighted for all others
Delaware	No	X	X	X	Equally weighted
District of Columbia	Yes	X	X	X	Equally weighted

Apportionment Formulas (Part 1)

Legend:

X	These factors are used in apportioning business income
NA	Not applicable
NR	Not reported

		Generally Used Factors			
	Does State Conform to UDITPA?	*Sales*	*Property*	*Payroll*	*How Are the Factors Weighted?*
Florida	Partly	X	X	X	Property 25%; payroll 25%; sales 50%.
Georgia	No	X			As of 1-1-08, 100% Sales
Hawaii	Yes	X	X	X	Equally weighted
Idaho	Yes, Idaho version also applies to utilities and financial institutions; in addition, state's version contains a stronger presumption that all income is business income unless proven otherwise.	X	X	X	Property 25%; payroll 25%; sales 50%
Illinois	Yes, alternative apportionment provisions are provided for insurance companies, financial organizations, and transportation companies.	X			After 2000, 100% sales. The payroll and property factors remain relevant, however, for purposes of the 80/20 test that is used for determining membership in a unitary business group under IITA 1501(a)(27).
Indiana	Generally consistent with UDITPA	X			Sales 100%
Iowa	No	X			Sales 100%
Kansas	Yes	X	X	X	Equally weighted
Kentucky	Double weighted sales factor.	X	X	X	Property 25%; payroll 25%; sales 50%
Louisiana	No	X			100% Sales

Apportionment Formulas (Part 1)

Legend:

X	These factors are used in apportioning business income
NA	Not applicable
NR	Not reported

	Does State Conform to UDITPA?	*Generally Used Factors*			*How Are the Factors Weighted?*
		Sales	*Property*	*Payroll*	
Maine	Partly, Maine does not distinguish between business & non-business income. Single sales factor enacted for 2007 and forward, COP repealed. *Finnigan* approach adopted for 2010 forward.	X			Single sales factor enacted 2007 and forward
Maryland	No	X	X	X	Sales double-weighted
Massachusetts	No	X	X	X	Sales double-weighted, only sales factor for defense manufacturers and mutual fund companies.
Michigan (Business Tax)	No	X			100% sales factor
Note. The CIT takes effect 01/01/12, and replaces the Michigan Business Tax (MBT) for most taxpayers. However, businesses that have been approved to receive, have received, or have been assigned certain certified credits may elect to file a return and pay the tax imposed by the MBT in lieu of the CIT until the certified credits are exhausted or extinguished.					
Minnesota	No	X	X	X	Property 5%; payroll 5%; sales 90%, moving to 100% sales in 2014
Mississippi	No	X	X	X	Equally weighted
Missouri	Yes, completely	X	X	X	Equally weighted
Montana	Yes, completely	X	X	X	Equally weighted
Nebraska	No	X			No, 100% sales factor
Nevada	Nevada does not impose a corporate income tax				
New Hampshire	No	X	X	X	Property 25%; payroll 25%; sales 50%
New Jersey	No	X	X	X	Sales double-weighted

Apportionment Formulas (Part 1)

Legend:

X	These factors are used in apportioning business income
NA	Not applicable
NR	Not reported

	Does State Conform to UDITPA?	*Generally Used Factors*			*How Are the Factors Weighted?*
		Sales	*Property*	*Payroll*	
Note. Single Sales Factor Phase-in: P.L. 2011, c. 59, signed on 4/28/11, applicable to privilege periods beginning on or after 1/1/12 replaces the three factor allocation formula with a single sales factor formula. The change is phased in over three years, beginning with privilege periods beginning on or after 1/1/12. For privilege period beginning on or after 1/1/12 but before 1/1/13, the sales fraction will account for 70% of the allocation, and the property and payroll fractions will each account for 15% of the allocation. For privilege periods beginning on or after 1/1/13 but before 1/1/14, the sales factor will account for 90% of the allocation, and the property and payroll fractions will each account for 5% of the allocation. For privilege periods beginning on or after 1/1/14, the sales fraction will account for 100% of the allocation.					
New Mexico	Yes	X	X	X	Property 25%; payroll 25%; sales 50%
New York	No	X			For tax years beginning on or after 1/1/07, 100% sales
North Carolina	Yes, officers' salaries excluded from the payroll factor; sales factor excludes casual sales	X	X	X	Property 25%; payroll 25%; sales 50%
North Dakota	Yes	X	X	X	Equally weighted
Ohio	Ohio does not impose a corporate income tax.				
Note A. Effective 1/1/2010, the Ohio Franchise Tax was fully phased out and business will be taxed on gross receipts through the Commercial Activity Tax. Details about that tax can be found at: http//tax.ohio.gov/divisions/commercial_activities/index.stm					
Oklahoma	No	X	X	X	Sales factor double-weighted under some circumstances

Apportionment Formulas (Part 1)

Legend:

X	These factors are used in apportioning business income
NA	Not applicable
NR	Not reported

	Does State Conform to UDITPA?	*Generally Used Factors* Sales	Property	Payroll	*How Are the Factors Weighted?*
Oregon	Yes, but double-weighted sales factor. XXX No. For tax years beginning on or after 5/1/05, For tax years beginning on or after 5/1/05, sales 90%, property 5%, payroll 5%. For tax years sales 90%, property 5%, payroll 5%. For tax beginning on or after 5/1/07, sales 100% years beginning on or after 5/1/07, sales 100%	X			For tax years beginning on or after 5/1/05, sales 90%, property 5%, payroll 5%. For tax years beginning on or after 5/1/07, sales 100%
Pennsylvania	Not officially adopted or enacted; however, many statutory provisions are similar to UDITPA.	X	X	X	Property 20%; payroll 20%; sales 60%
Rhode Island	No	X	X	X	Equally weighted, however, for years beginning 1/1/04 or later, manufacturers can phase in double weighted sales over 2004 and 2005.
South Carolina	Yes	X			Sales 100%
South Dakota	South Dakota does not impose a corporate income tax				
Tennessee	Yes, except no throwback	X	X	X	Sales factor double-weighted
Texas	No	X			Sales 100%
Utah	Yes	X	X	X	Equally weighted
Vermont	No	X	X	X	Equally weighted
Virginia	Yes, UDITPA not adopted, but Virginia law is similar	X	X	X	Sales factor double-weighted

Apportionment Formulas (Part 1)

Legend:

X	These factors are used in apportioning business income
NA	Not applicable
NR	Not reported

		Generally Used Factors			
	Does State Conform to UDITPA?	*Sales*	*Property*	*Payroll*	*How Are the Factors Weighted?*
Washington	Washington does not impose a corporate income tax				
West Virginia	Yes	X	X	X	Property 25%; payroll 25%; sales 50%
Wisconsin	Partly, see Wis. Stat. § 71.25.	X			After 12/31/05 and before 1/1/07; 60% sales, 20% property, and 20% payroll; after 12/31/06 and before 1/1/08; 80% sales, 10% property, 10% payroll; and after 12/31/07; 100% sales
Wyoming	Wyoming does not impose a corporate income tax				

Apportionment Formulas (Part 2)

Legend:
NA **Not applicable**
NR **Not reported**

	If Normal Rules Do Not Fairly Apportion Income, Does State Allow Separate Accounting?	*If Normal Rules Do Not Fairly Apportion Income, Does State Allow Allocation of Specific Items?*	*Does State Eliminate Factor if*	
			Denominator Is Zero?	*Numerator Is Zero?*
Alabama	Yes, written permission required.	Yes, written permission required	Yes	No
Alaska	Yes, when apportionment provisions do not fairly represent the extent of business activity in Alaska	Yes, when apportionment provisions do not fairly represent the extent of business activity in Alaska	Yes	No
Arizona	Yes	Yes	Yes	No
Arkansas	Yes, approved by Department	Yes, partnership income and nonbusiness income.	Yes	No
California	Yes, the taxpayer may petition or the FTB may require separate accounting when the allocations and apportionment provisions of the California Rev. & Tax. Code do not fairly represent the extent of the taxpayer's business activity in this state. Cal. Rev. & Tax Code 25137.	Yes, the taxpayer may petition or the FTB may require separate accounting when the allocation and apportionment provisions of the California Rev. & Tax. Code do not fairly represent the extent of the taxpayer's business activity in this state. Cal. Rev. & Tax Code 25137.	Yes	No, except the FTB will disregard a factor if there is no amount in the denominator. The FTB may disregard a factor if there are significant values. See R&TC § 25137; Cal Code Regs., tit. 18, § 25137; Appeal of Oscar Enterprises Ltd., 87-SBE-069, October 6, 1987.

Legend:

NA **Not applicable**

NR **Not reported**

Apportionment Formulas (Part 2)

	If Normal Rules Do Not Fairly Apportion Income, Does State Allow Separate Accounting?	*If Normal Rules Do Not Fairly Apportion Income, Does State Allow Allocation of Specific Items?*	*Does State Eliminate Factor if*	
			Denominator Is Zero?	*Numerator Is Zero?*
Colorado	Yes, determined on a case by case basis, written permission required.	Yes, determined on a case by case basis, written permission required—very rare.	Yes, generally required pursuant to Colo. Rev. Stat. § 39-22-303(6).	No
Connecticut	Yes, non-unitary partnerships, Conn. Gen. Stat. § 12-218(h); unique and non recurring circumstances Conn. Gen. Stat § 12-22a		Yes	No
Delaware	No	Yes, statute requires allocation of rents, royalties, interest, and gains or losses on real and tangible property.	Yes	No
District of Columbia	Yes, see § 47-1810.02(h)	Yes, See § 47-1810.02(h)	Yes	No
Florida	Yes, with permission (varies depending on the taxpayer's situation).	Yes, in specific cases, with permission only (varies depending on the taxpayer's situation).	Yes	No
Georgia	Yes, with permission from revenue department	Yes, requires approval from revenue department	Yes	No, neither applicable after 1/1/08
Hawaii	Yes	Yes	Yes	No

Apportionment Formulas (Part 2)

Legend:
NA **Not applicable**
NR **Not reported**

	If Normal Rules Do Not Fairly Apportion Income, Does State Allow Separate Accounting?	If Normal Rules Do Not Fairly Apportion Income, Does State Allow Allocation of Specific Items?	Does State Eliminate Factor if Denominator Is Zero?	Does State Eliminate Factor if Numerator Is Zero?
Idaho	Yes, when separate accounting is a more accurate reflection; taxpayer holds burden of proof.	Yes, nonbusiness income and all deductions relating to its production must be allocated.	Yes	No
Illinois	Yes, separate accounting (to determine where income was earned) is used only with Revenue Director's approval and only if statutory apportionment formula does not fairly represent extent of business activity in state, see 86 Ill. Admin. Code § 100.3390.	Yes, only with Director's approval	Yes	No
Indiana	Yes, may petition for use if standard apportionment does not fairly reflect income derived in state.	Yes, may petition for use if standard apportionment does not fairly reflect income derived in state.	Yes	No
Iowa	Yes, if activities in state are not unitary with activities outside of Iowa.	Yes, for any item of income that qualifies for nonbusiness income.	NA	NA

Legend:
NA — **Not applicable**
NR — **Not reported**

Apportionment Formulas (Part 2)

	If Normal Rules Do Not Fairly Apportion Income, Does State Allow Separate Accounting?	*If Normal Rules Do Not Fairly Apportion Income, Does State Allow Allocation of Specific Items?*	*Does State Eliminate Factor if Denominator Is Zero?*	*Does State Eliminate Factor if Numerator Is Zero?*
Kansas	Yes, with prior approval from Secretary of Revenue and taxpayer demonstrates the statutory method of apportionment does not fairly reflect activity in Kansas.	Yes, if income is not earned in the regular course of business.	Yes	No
Kentucky	Yes, a corporation must demonstrate that the statutory apportionment factor does not fairly represent the corporation's business activity in Kentucky and receive approval from the Kentucky Department of Revenue to use an alternative method.	No	Yes	No
Louisiana	Yes, LA Rev. Stat. 47:207394(C) provides that the Secretary may grant permission to use the separate accounting method if the taxpayer shows that the apportionment method produces manifestly unfair result.	Yes, Rev. Stat. 47:243	Yes	No
Maine	Yes, if gross distortion exists and the taxpayer petition is approved by the State Tax Assessor.	Yes, if gross distortion exists and the taxpayer petition is approved by the State Tax Assessor.	NA	No
Maryland	No	Yes, but only with prior written approval from the Comptroller's Office.	No	No

Apportionment Formulas (Part 2)

Legend:
NA **Not applicable**
NR **Not reported**

	If Normal Rules Do Not Fairly Apportion Income, Does State Allow Separate Accounting?	*If Normal Rules Do Not Fairly Apportion Income, Does State Allow Allocation of Specific Items?*	*Does State Eliminate Factor if*	
			Denominator Is Zero?	*Numerator Is Zero?*
Massachusetts	Yes	Yes	Yes	Yes
Michigan (Business Tax)	Yes, requires approval by State Treasurer	Yes, requires approval by State Treasurer	No	No
Note. The CIT takes effect 01/01/12, and replaces the Michigan Business Tax (MBT) for most taxpayers. However, businesses that have been approved to receive, have received, or have been assigned certain certified credits may elect to file a return and pay the tax imposed by the MBT in lieu of the CIT until the certified credits are exhausted or extinguished.				
Minnesota	Yes, approval by the Commissioner	Yes, approval by the Commissioner	Yes	No
Mississippi	Yes, at Commissioner's discretion	Yes, at Commissioner's discretion	Yes	No
Missouri	No	No	Yes	No
Montana	Yes, depends on facts	Yes, depends on facts	Yes	No
Nebraska	In unique and nonrecurring situations	In unique and non-recurring situations	NA	NA
Nevada	Nevada does not impose a corporate income tax			
New Hampshire	No	No	Yes	No
New Jersey	No	No	Yes	No
New Mexico	Yes	Yes, nonbusiness items	Yes	No
New York	Yes, fact driven	Yes, discretionary as to facts and circumstances	Yes	No

Legend:

NA **Not applicable**

NR **Not reported**

Apportionment Formulas (Part 2)

			Does State Eliminate Factor if	
	If Normal Rules Do Not Fairly Apportion Income, Does State Allow Separate Accounting?	*If Normal Rules Do Not Fairly Apportion Income, Does State Allow Allocation of Specific Items?*	*Denominator Is Zero?*	*Numerator Is Zero?*
North Carolina	No	No	Yes	No
North Dakota	No	Yes	Yes	No
Ohio	Ohio does not impose a corporate income tax			
Note A. Effective 1/1/2010, the Ohio Franchise Tax was fully phased out and business will be taxed on gross receipts through the Commercial Activity Tax. Details about that tax can be found at: http//tax.ohio.gov/divisions/commercial_activities/index.stm				
Oklahoma	Yes, generally oil and gas companies	Yes	Yes	No
Oregon	Yes, when application of standard apportionment and allocation provisions do not fairly represent the extent of the taxpayer's business activities in Oregon. (ORS 317.670)	Yes, nonbusiness income from net rents, royalties, capital gains and losses, interest, dividends, lottery prizes, patent and copyright royalties is allocated.	Yes	No
Pennsylvania	Yes	Yes	Yes	No
Rhode Island	No	No	Yes	No
South Carolina	Yes, Department approval, § 12-6.2320	Yes, Department approval § 12-6.2320	Yes	No
South Dakota	South Dakota does not impose a corporate income tax			
Tennessee	Yes, requires approval of variance	Yes, requires approval of variance	Yes	No

Apportionment Formulas (Part 2)

Legend:
NA — **Not applicable**
NR — **Not reported**

			Does State Eliminate Factor if	
	If Normal Rules Do Not Fairly Apportion Income, Does State Allow Separate Accounting?	*If Normal Rules Do Not Fairly Apportion Income, Does State Allow Allocation of Specific Items?*	*Denominator Is Zero?*	*Numerator Is Zero?*
Texas	No	No	If either numerator or denominator of gross receipts factor is zero, the apportionment percentage is zero.	If either numerator or denominator of gross receipts factor is zero, the apportionment percentage is zero.
Utah	Rarely allowable; burden of proof on party seeking to deviate from the UDITPA formula	Yes, follow LJPITPA and only allow allocation when income constitutes nonbusiness income.	Yes	No
Vermont	No	No	Yes	No
Virginia	No alternative methods may be requested, but rarely granted.	Yes, if it would be unconstitutional under Allied-Signal to include an item in the apportionable income of a corporation that is neither commercially domiciled in VA nor organized under VA law.	Yes	No
Washington	Washington does not impose a corporate income tax			
West Virginia	Yes	Yes, nonbusiness income	Yes	No

Apportionment Formulas (Part 2)

Legend:
NA **Not applicable**
NR **Not reported**

			Does State Eliminate Factor if	
	If Normal Rules Do Not Fairly Apportion Income, Does State Allow Separate Accounting?	*If Normal Rules Do Not Fairly Apportion Income, Does State Allow Allocation of Specific Items?*	*Denominator Is Zero?*	*Numerator Is Zero?*
Wisconsin	Yes, when business is not unitary.	Yes, nonbusiness income and winnings from lottery tickets purchased in Wisconsin are allocated to Wisconsin.	Yes	No
Wyoming	Wyoming does not impose a corporate income tax			

Specialized Industry Formulas

Overview

The Uniform Division of Income for Tax Purposes Act (UDITPA) equally weighted three-factor property, payroll and sales apportionment formula was designed to apportion the income of multistate manufacturing and mercantile businesses, and may not fairly apportion the income of businesses in other industries. For example, the conventional UDITPA property factor is difficult to compute for property that is regularly in motion, such as that of interstate trucking companies, airlines and railroads. Likewise, since its adoption in 1957, the UDITPA Section 17 income producing activity rule for sourcing sales of services has been controversial. Many commentators have argued that its effect is often to merely mimic the property and payroll factor, rather than measure the customer base within a state (See discussion in the section entitled Sales Factor: Receipts from Services). The drafters of UDITPA foresaw the limitations of the standard UDITPA apportionment formula, and, under Section 2, specifically excluded from UDITPA certain service businesses, including financial organizations (bank, trust company, savings bank, private banker, savings and loan association, credit union, investment company, or insurance company), and public utilities (defined as any business entity which owns or operates for public use any plant, equipment, property, franchise, or license for the transmission of communications, transportation of goods or persons, or the production, storage, transmission, sale, delivery, or furnishing of electricity, water, steam, oil, oil products or gas).

To address these issues, many states provide special rules for computing apportionment percentages for businesses in certain industries. Typically, these special rules involve the modification or exclusion of the conventional factors, or the use of unique, industry-specific factors. In some instances, a primary motive for adopting specialized industry apportionment rules is to provide an economic incentive for certain businesses to maintain or locate operations within the state. Examples of industries for which states provide special apportionment rules include airlines, railroads, trucking companies, financial institutions, television and radio broadcasters, publishers, telecommunication services companies, mutual funds, pipeline companies, ship transportation companies, and professional sports franchises.

In many cases, the equitable relief provisions of UDITPA Section 18, which numerous states have incorporated into their statutes, serves as the basis for state revenue departments to adopt specialized formulas. UDITPA Section 18 provides that if the standard apportionment formula does not fairly reflect a taxpayer's in-state business activity, tax authorities may require the exclusion of one or more of the factors, or the inclusion of additional factors which will fairly represent the taxpayer's business activity in the state. Under Section 18, the Multistate Tax Commission (MTC) has promulgated special apportionment regulations covering construction contractors (MTC Reg. IV.18(d)), airlines (MTC Reg. IV.18(e)), railroads (MTC Reg. IV.18(f)), trucking companies (MTC Reg. IV.18(g)), television and radio broadcasters (MTC Reg. IV.18(h)), and publishers (MTC Reg. IV.18(j)). The MTC has also promulgated a model statute for apportioning the income of financial institutions (Nov. 17, 1994). In July 2008, the MTC approved a proposed model regulation for the apportionment of income from telecommunications services.

As a general rule, only those taxpayers engaged in the type of business activity for which the special apportionment rules were developed are permitted to apply the special rules (e.g., *Cooper Tire & Rubber Co. v. Limbach*, 70 Ohio St. 3d 347 [1994]; *TTX Co. v. Whitley*, No. 1-98-3604 [Ill. App. Ct., Mar. 31, 2000]). In most instances, when a corporation is required to use a specialized apportionment formula, all its income is apportioned using that formula. For example, in *Texaco-Cities Service Pipeline Company v. McGaw* (182 Ill. 2d 269 [1998]), the Illinois Supreme Court ruled that the taxpayer's gain from the sale of its 90 percent interest in a pipeline was apportionable under Illinois's sales-only apportionment formula for transportation services businesses. On the other hand, in *Buckeye Pipeline Co. v. Commonwealth* [689 A.2d 366 (Pa. Commw. Ct. 1997)], a one percent general partner of four limited partnerships engaged in the interstate transportation of petroleum products through pipelines was permitted to use the single-factor revenue barrel mile apportionment formula for pipeline companies to apportion the portion of its gross receipts attributable to its distributive share of partnership receipts, but also was required to use the standard three-factor formula to apportion gross receipts attributable to management fees received from the partnerships.

Airlines

Many states provide special apportionment formulas for airlines. MTC Regulation IV.18(e), which the MTC adopted in 1983, addresses the apportionment of a multistate airline's business income. As discussed below, this regulation modifies the standard three-factor property, payroll, and sales formula, primarily by basing the computation of the factor numerators on the ratio of in-state aircraft departures, weighted by the cost and value of aircraft, to the total departures everywhere, similarly weighted. Some states have adopted the MTC approach, in whole or in part. Other states have adopted their own special formulas, such as formulas based on revenue miles.

Property Factor. In general, the property factor denominator includes the average value of all owned and rented real and tangible personal property used by the airline in its trade or business. The numerator includes all owned and rented property used in the state. MTC Regulation IV.18(e) provides a special rule for sourcing aircraft ready for flight. Such aircraft are includible in a particular state's numerator based on the ratio of in-state departures, weighted by the cost and value of aircraft, to the total departures everywhere, similarly weighted. Aircraft ready for flight are defined as aircraft owned or acquired through rental or lease that are in the possession of the taxpayer and are available for service on the taxpayer's routes.

Payroll Factor. The denominator of the payroll factor includes all compensation paid everywhere by the airline, and the numerator is the total compensation paid in the state. MTC Regulation IV.18(e) provides a special rule for sourcing compensation paid to flight personnel. The payroll of such employees is includible in the state's payroll factor numerator based on the ratio of in-state departures, weighted by the cost and value of aircraft, to the total departures everywhere, similarly weighted.

Sales Factor. Under MTC Regulation IV.18(e), the sales factor denominator includes all revenues that the airline derives from transactions and activities in the regular course of its trade or business, except for passive income and net gains or losses from the sale of aircraft. The sales factor numerator is the taxpayer's total in-state revenue, which includes the sum of: (1) the total transportation revenue multiplied by the ratio of in-state departures, weighted by the cost and value of aircraft, to the total departures everywhere, similarly weighted; plus (2) any nonflight revenues directly attributable to the state.

Railroads

Many states provide special apportionment formulas for railroads. MTC Regulation IV.18(f), which the MTC adopted in 1981, addresses the apportionment of a multistate railroad's business income. The manner in which the regulation modifies the standard equally-weighted three-factor property, payroll, and sales formula, is summarized below.

Property Factor. In general, the property factor denominator includes the average value of all owned and rented real and tangible personal property used by the railroad in its trade or business. Railroad cars owned by other railroads and temporarily used by the taxpayer for a per diem charge are not included in the property factor as rented property, whereas railroad cars owned by the taxpayer and temporarily used by other railroads for a per diem charge are included in the property factor. The numerator includes all owned and rented property used in the state. A special rule applies to sourcing mobile property, such as passenger cars, freight cars, locomotives and freight containers, which are located within and without this state during the year. Such property is included in the property factor numerator based on the ratio of locomotive-miles or car-miles in the state to locomotive-miles or car-miles everywhere.

Payroll Factor. The denominator of the payroll factor includes all compensation paid everywhere by the railroad, and the numerator is the total compensation paid in the state. A special rule applies to sourcing compensation paid to enginemen and trainmen performing services on interstate trains. The payroll of such employees is included in the state's payroll factor numerator based on the compensation required to be reported by such employees for purposes of determining their state personal income tax liabilities.

Sales Factor. Under MTC Regulation IV.18(f), the sales factor denominator includes all revenues derived by the railroad from transactions and activities in the regular course of its trade or business, except per diem and mileage charges. The sales factor numerator is the railroad's total revenues in the state. The taxpayer in-state revenues from hauling freight, mail and express include the entire amount of the receipts from intrastate shipments (i.e., the shipment both originates and terminates within the state); and a pro-rata portion of the receipts from interstate shipments (i.e., shipments passing through, into, or out of the state), determined by the ratio of the miles traveled by the shipment in the state to the total miles traveled by the shipment from its point of origin to its destination. Likewise, the taxpayer's in-state revenues from hauling passengers includes the entire amount of the receipts from the intrastate transportation of passengers, and a pro-rata portion of the receipts from the interstate transportation of passengers, determined by the ratio of the revenue passenger miles in the state to the revenue passenger miles everywhere. The in-state portion of any revenues, other than revenue from hauling freight, passengers, mail and express, is determined under the standard UDITPA rules for sourcing sales.

Trucking Companies

Many states provide special apportionment formulas for trucking companies. MTC Regulation IV.18(g), which the MTC adopted in 1986 and amended in 1989, addresses the apportionment of a multistate trucking company's business income. As discussed below, this regulation modifies the standard equally three-factor property, payroll, and sales formula, primarily by basing the computation of the factor numerators on the ratio of the mobile property miles in the state to the mobile property miles everywhere. Some states have adopted the MTC approach, in whole or in part. Other states have adopted their own special formulas, such as formulas based on revenue miles.

MTC Regulation IV.18(g) defines a "trucking company" as a motor common carrier, a motor contract carrier, or an express carrier which primarily transports tangible personal property of others by motor vehicle for compensation.

Property Factor. In general, the property factor denominator includes the average value of all owned and rented real and tangible personal property used by the trucking company in its trade or business. The numerator includes all owned and rented property used in the state. A special sourcing rule applies to motor vehicles and trailers ("mobile property"), which is included in the state's numerator based on the ratio of mobile property miles in the state to total mobile property miles. A mobile property mile is defined as the movement of a unit of mobile property a distance of one mile, whether loaded or unloaded.

Payroll Factor. The denominator of the payroll factor includes all compensation paid everywhere by a trucking company, and the numerator is the total compensation paid in a particular state. A special rule applies to sourcing compensation paid to employees performing services within and without the state. The payroll of such employees is includible in the state's payroll factor numerator based on the ratio of mobile property miles in the state to total mobile property miles.

Sales Factor. Under MTC Regulation IV.18(g), the sales factor denominator includes all revenue derived from transactions and activities in the regular course of the trucking company's trade or business. The sales factor numerator is the trucking company's total revenues in the state. The taxpayer in-state revenues from hauling freight, mail and express include the entire amount of the receipts from intrastate shipments (i.e., the shipment both originates and terminates within the state); and a pro-rata portion of the receipts from interstate shipments (i.e., shipments passing through, into, or out of the state), determined by the ratio of the mobile property miles traveled by the shipment in the state to the total mobile property miles traveled by the shipment from its point of origin to its destination. The in-state portion of any revenues, other than revenue from hauling freight, mail and express, is determined under the standard UDITPA rules for sourcing sales.

Television and Radio Broadcasters

Some states provide special apportionment formulas for television and radio broadcasters. MTC Regulation IV.18(h), which the MTC adopted in 1990 and amended in 1996, addresses the apportionment of a multistate television or radio broadcaster's business income. The regulation covers taxpayers engaged in broadcasting over the public airwaves, by cable, satellite transmission, or by any other means of communication. The manner in which the regulation modifies the standard equally-weighted three-factor property, payroll, and sales formula, is summarized below.

Property Factor. In general, the property factor denominator includes the average value of all owned and rented real and tangible personal property used by the broadcaster in its trade or business. However, outer-jurisdictional film and radio programming property are excluded from the property factor. Outer-jurisdictional property includes orbiting satellites, undersea transmission cables, and like property that is owned or rented by the taxpayer and used in its broadcasting business, but is not physically located in any particular state. Discs and similar medium containing film or radio programming and intended for sale or rental by the taxpayer for home viewing or listening are included in the property factor. The numerator includes owned and rented property used in the state, as determined under the standard UDITPA rules for sourcing property.

Payroll Factor. The denominator of the payroll factor includes all compensation, including residual and profit participation payments, paid to employees, including that paid to directors, actors, newscasters and other talent in their status as employees. The numerator includes the total compensation paid in the state, as determined under the standard UDITPA rules for sourcing payroll.

Sales Factor. Under MTC Regulation IV.18(h), the sales factor denominator includes all gross receipts that the broadcaster derives from transactions and activities in the regular course of its trade or business. The sales factor numerator is the broadcaster's gross receipts in the state. Gross receipts, including advertising revenue, from television film or radio programming in release to or by television and radio stations is pro-rated to a state based on an audience factor, which equals the ratio of the broadcaster's in-state viewing (listening) audience to its total viewing (listening) audience. A cable television system's audience factor is the ratio of the system's in-state subscribers to its total subscribers. Receipts from the sale, rental, or licensing of discs and similar media intended for home viewing or listening are sourced under the standard UDITPA rules for sourcing sales of tangible personal property.

Publishing

Some states provide special apportionment formulas for taxpayers engaged in the publishing, sale, licensing or other distribution of books, newspapers, magazines, periodicals, trade journals or other printed material. MTC Regulation IV.18(j), which the MTC adopted in 1993, modifies the standard equally-weighted three-factor property, payroll, and sales formula, as summarized below.

Property Factor. In general, the property factor denominator includes the average value of all owned and rented real and tangible personal property, including outer-jurisdictional (e.g., orbiting satellites and undersea transmission cables) used by the publisher in its trade or business. The numerator includes owned and rented property used in the state. Outer-jurisdictional property is pro-rated to a state based on the ratio of number of uplink and downlink transmissions in the state to the total number of uplink and downlink transmissions everywhere. If uplink and downlink information is not available, outer-jurisdictional property is pro-rata to the state based on the ratio of the amount of time the property was used to make transmissions in the state to the total amount of time the property was used for transmissions everywhere.

Payroll Factor. The denominator of the payroll factor includes all compensation paid everywhere by the taxpayer, and the numerator is the total compensation paid in the state, as determined under the standard UDITPA rules for sourcing payroll.

Sales Factor. Under MTC Regulation IV.18(j), the sales factor denominator includes all gross receipts derived by the taxpayer from transactions and activities in the regular course of its trade or business, and the sales factor numerator is the taxpayer's gross receipts in the state. Gross receipts derived from the sale of printed materials are sourced to the state in which the material is delivered or shipped to the purchaser or subscriber. A throwback rule applies if the purchaser or subscriber is the U.S. government or the taxpayer is not taxable in a state in which the printed materials are shipped or delivered. Gross receipts derived from advertising and the sale or rental of the taxpayer's customer lists are pro-rated to the state based on the taxpayer's circulation factor. A separate circulation factor is computed for each publication of printed material, and equals the ratio of the in-state purchasers and subscribers to the purchasers and subscribers everywhere, as determined by reference to rating statistics.

Telecommunications Services

Some states provide special apportionment formulas for telecommunications service companies, and in 2008 the MTC has promulgated a Proposed Model Regulation for Apportionment of Income from the Sale of Telecommunications and Ancillary Services.

For this purpose, the term *telecommunications service* means the electronic transmission of voice, data, audio, video, or any other information or signals, and includes a transmission, conveyance, or routing in which computer processing applications are used to act on the content for purposes of transmission, conveyance or routing without regard to whether such service is referred to as voice over Internet protocol services or is classified by the Federal Communications Commission as enhanced or value-added. The term *telecommunications service* includes but is not limited to, the following services: wireline, fixed wireless, mobile wireless, paging, prepaid calling, prepaid wireless calling, private communication, value-added non-voice data, coin-operated telephone and pay telephone services.

Property Factor. In general, the property factor denominator includes the average value of all owned and rented real and tangible personal property used by the telecommunications service company in its trade or business. An exception applies to outer-jurisdictional property, which is excluded from the property factor. Outer-jurisdictional property includes orbiting satellites, undersea transmission cables, and like property that is owned or rented by the taxpayer and used in its telecommunications service business, but is not physically located in any particular state. The numerator includes owned and rented property used in the state, as determined under the standard UDITPA rules for sourcing property.

Payroll Factor. The denominator of the payroll factor includes all compensation paid everywhere by the taxpayer, and the numerator is the total compensation paid in the state, as determined under the standard UDITPA rules for sourcing payroll.

Sales Factor. The sales factor denominator includes all gross receipts that the taxpayer derives from transactions and activities in the regular course of its telecommunications service business. The sales factor numerator includes all gross receipts of the taxpayer from sources within the state. The regulation provides numerous specialized sourcing rules for sales of telecommunications services. For example, gross receipts from the sale of mobile telecommunications services, other than air-to-ground radiotelephone service and prepaid calling service, are attributed to the state when the customer's place of primary use is pursuant to the Mobile Telecommunications Sourcing Act.

Financial Institutions

Some state impose special franchise taxes on banks and other financial institutions, while other states subject financial institutions to the state's standard corporate income tax. In addition, many states provide special apportionment formulas for financial institutions. In 1994, the MTC adopted a model statute for apportioning the income of a financial institution, which adopts the standard UDITPA equally-weighted three-factor apportionment formula. The manner in which model statute modifies the computation of the property, payroll, and sales factors is summarized below.

Property Factor. In general, the property factor denominator includes the average value of all owned and rented real and tangible personal property used by the financial institution in its trade or business. The property factor also includes two intangible assets, loans and credit card receivables, which are valued at their average outstanding principal balance, without regard to any reserve for bad debts, but reduced by any amount written-off for Federal income tax purposes.

The property factor numerator includes owned and rented real and tangible personal property that is physically located or used in the state. A loan is attributed to the state if it is properly assigned to a regular place of business of the taxpayer within the state. A loan is properly assigned to the place of business with which it has a preponderance of substantive contacts, as determined by such activities as the solicitation, investigation, negotiation, approval and administration of the loan. The location of credit card receivables is determined in the same manner as loans.

Payroll Factor. The denominator of the payroll factor includes all compensation paid everywhere by the taxpayer, and the numerator is the total compensation paid in the state, as determined under the standard UDITPA rules for sourcing payroll.

Sales Factor. The sales factor denominator includes all gross receipts that the financial institution derives from transactions and activities in the regular course of its trade or business. The sales factor numerator is the financial institution's gross receipts in the state. Interest from loans secured by real property is attributed to the state in which the real property is located, whereas interest from loans not secured by real property is attributed to the state in which the borrower is located. Interest from credit card receivables and fees charged to card holders is attributed to the state in which the billing address of the card holder is located. Net gains from the sale of loans and loan servicing fees are sourced in the same manner as the loan interest. Likewise, net gains from the sale of credit card receivables are sourced in the same manner as the interest on the credit card receivables. Interest, dividends and net gains from investment and trading assets and activities are attributed to the state if such receipts are properly assigned to a regular place of business of the taxpayer within the state, based on where the day-to-day decisions regarding the assets or activities occur. Finally, under a throwback rule, all receipts which would be assigned to a state in which the taxpayer is not taxable are attributed to the state in which the financial institution has its commercial domicile.

Insurance Companies

Many states do not subject insurance companies to the state's standard corporate income tax. Those states that do impose a corporate income tax on insurance companies generally require insurance companies to apportion their income using a single-factor premiums formula. The MTC has not promulgated a special apportionment formula for insurance companies.

Recent Developments

Alaska. In determining their Alaska property, payroll, and sales factors, water transport companies (i.e., companies engaged in the transportation of goods or passengers by ship or barge) must use a days-spent-in-port ratio that represents the number of 24-hour days spent in Alaska ports during the tax year divided by the total number of days spent in all ports during the tax year. [Alaska Dept. of Rev., Reg. § 15 ACC 19.1490, effective Aug. 8, 2007]

California. Effective April 18, 2010, the California regulations governing the computation of the property, payroll and sales factors for air transportation companies (e.g., in-state arrivals and departures) are amended to require that aircraft be grouped by model (e.g., Boeing 737 versus Boeing 767). Under the prior regulations, aircraft were grouped by type (e.g., two-engine versus four-engine). [Cal. Code Regs. tit. 18, § § 25101.3 and 25137-7]

Colorado. For tax years beginning on or after January 1, 2009, Colorado adopts a sales-only apportionment formula. [H.B. 1380, May 20, 2008] The Colorado Department of Revenue has adopted new special regulations to implement sales-only apportionment for taxpayer in the following industries: airlines, contractors, publishing, railroads, television and radio broadcasting, trucking, financial institutions, and telecommunications. [Colo. Dep't of Rev., Special Regs. 1A to 8A and Regs. 39-22–303.5.7(A), 39-22-303.7.1, and 39-22-303.7.2, June 10, 2010]

For tax years beginning on or after January 1, 2009, a mutual fund service corporation that provides management, distribution, and administrative services for a regulated investment company must source mutual fund sales to Colorado based on the percentage of shareholders in the regulated investment company that are domiciled in the state. [H.B. 1311, May 18, 2009]

Delaware. For tax years beginning on or after January 1, 2009, an asset management corporation may apportion income using a single-factor gross receipts formula. An asset management corporation is a corporation that derives 90 percent or more of its gross receipts from investment services. [S.B. 213, June 3, 2008]

Illinois. Effective for tax years ending on or after December 31, 2008, receipts from the sale of broadcasting services are sourced to Illinois if the broadcasting services are received in Illinois. Numerous rules are provided for determining the location of the recipient of different types of revenues received by broadcasting. For advertising revenue from broadcasting, the customer is the advertiser and the service is received in Illinois if the commercial domicile of the advertiser is in Illinois. [S.B. 1739, Aug. 25, 2009]

As detailed below, Illinois made numerous changes to its apportionment rules in 2007 [S.B. 1544, Aug. 16, 2007] and 2008 [S.B. 783, Jan. 11, 2008]. These changes generally are effective for tax years ending on or after December 31, 2008.

Income derived by a financial organization is apportioned to Illinois based on the ratio of the receipts from sources within Illinois or otherwise attributable to the state's marketplace, to the receipts everywhere. Receipts from investment or trading assets and activities are attributed to Illinois if they are properly assigned, based on the preponderance of substantive contacts, to a fixed place of business of the taxpayer within Illinois. If the fixed place of business that has a preponderance of substantive contacts can not be determined, the asset or activity is assigned to the state in which the taxpayer's commercial domicile is located. [35 Ill. Comp. Stat. § 5/304(c)]

Receipts from the sale of telecommunications services or mobile telecommunications service are attributed to Illinois, with certain exceptions, if the customer's service address is in the state. [35 Ill. Comp. Stat. § 5/304(a)(3)(B-5)]

Income from providing airline transportation services is apportioned to Illinois based on the ratio of revenue miles in the state to revenue miles everywhere. A revenue mile is the transportation of one passenger or one net ton of freight the distance of one mile for consideration. [35 Ill. Comp. Stat. § 5/304(d)]

Income from providing transportation services other than airline services is apportioned using a formula, the numerator of which includes (1) all receipts from any movement or shipment of people or goods that both originates and terminates in Illinois, plus (2) that portion of the receipts from movements or shipments of people or goods passing through, into, or out of Illinois, that is determined by the ratio that the miles traveled in Illinois bears to total miles from point of origin to point of destination. The denominator is all receipts derived from the movement or shipment of people or goods. [35 Ill. Comp. Stat. § 5/304(d)]

Kansas. Effective June 20, 2008, if a unitary group includes one or more members engaged in railroad or interstate motor carrier operations and one or more members not engaged in railroad or interstate motor carrier operations, a three-factor formula is used to apportion the income of the entire unitary group to those members engaged in railroad or interstate motor carrier operations, and then a single-factor mileage formula is used to apportion the income of each member engaged in railroad or interstate motor carrier operations to Kansas. [Kan. Dept. of Rev., Regs. § 92-12-114]

Kentucky. For tax years beginning on or after January 1, 2008, a passenger airline determines its property, payroll, and sales factors by multiplying the total average value of its aircraft, total flight personnel compensation, and total transportation revenues, by the ratio of Kentucky revenue passenger miles to total revenue passenger miles. [H.B. 258, Apr. 9, 2008]

Massachusetts. In November 2007, the Massachusetts Department of Revenue issued new regulations for apportioning income derived from sales of electricity, unforced capacity, electricity brokerage services, ancillary services related to electricity, electricity transmission and distribution services, and from buying and selling financial instruments related to electricity. [830 Mass. Code Regs. 63.38.10, effective for tax years beginning on or after Nov. 30, 2007]

Michigan. Effective in 2007, media receipts from sales by taxpayers whose business activities include television programming or live radio are attributable to Michigan if the commercial domicile of the customer is in Michigan, and if the customer has a direct connection with the taxpayer pursuant to a contract under which the media receipts are derived. Media receipts from the sale of advertising to a customer who is commercially domiciled in Michigan and who receives some of the benefit of the advertising sale in Michigan are attributable to Michigan in proportion to the extent that the customer receives benefit from the advertising in Michigan. Media receipts from the sale of advertising to a customer who is a broadcaster and who receives some of the benefit of the advertising in Michigan are proportioned based on the ratio that the broadcaster's listening or viewing audience in Michigan bears to its total listening or viewing audience everywhere. [H.B. 5460, Dec. 27, 2007]

Minnesota. For tax years beginning on or after January 1, 2010, receipts from management, distribution, or administrative services performed by a corporation or trust for a mutual fund are attributed to the state in which the shareholders of the fund reside for purposes of computing the Minnesota sales factor. [H.B. 3149, May 29, 2008]

Montana. In 2011, the Montana Department of Revenue adopted new rules for apportioning the income for telecommunications service providers, which generally conform to the MTC model apportionment regulations for the telecommunications industry. These rules are effective for tax years beginning on or after January 1, 2012. [ARM 42.26.1201 to 42.26.1205, Mont. Dept. of Rev., Apr. 14, 2011]

New Jersey. Effective for tax years beginning on or after January 1, 2012, a sales factor for airlines based on departures (weighted by cost or value) will be replaced by a sales factor based on revenue miles.

Oregon. Effective for tax years beginning on or after January 1, 2007, insurance companies must use a sales-only apportionment formula. [S.B. 179, June 28, 2007] Under prior law, insurance companies used an equally-weighted three-factor formula.

Pennsylvania. In *FedEx Ground Package System, Inc. v. Pennsylvania* [Nos. 302 F.R. 2003 and 303 F.R. 2003 (Penn. Commw. Ct., Apr. 27, 2007)], the Pennsylvania Commonwealth Court ruled that the numerator of a trucking company's revenue miles apportionment formula should be computed by multiplying the total number of miles that the company transported packages in Pennsylvania by the company's average receipts per mile for transporting packages "in Pennsylvania" (rather than the average receipts per mile "everywhere," which was the Department of Revenue's standard practice). For this purpose, revenue mile means the average receipts derived from the transportation by the taxpayer of persons or property for one mile. During the tax year in question, FedEx's average receipts per mile everywhere were $3.93 per mile, and its average receipts per mile in Pennsylvania were $2.94. The court determined that its interpretation follows the plain language of the statute and is consistent with the principle that an apportionment factor numerator should only reflect activity in Pennsylvania. The Pennsylvania Supreme Court affirmed the lower court's decision [Nos. 55-56 MAP 2007 (Pa. Sup. Ct., Dec. 27, 2007)]

Utah. Starting in 2011, a sales-only apportionment formula is phased in for taxpayers in selected industries. [S.B. 165, Mar. 25, 2010] For tax years beginning in 2011, the Utah apportionment fraction is computed by adding the property factor, the payroll factor, and four times the sales factor and dividing by six. For tax years beginning in 2012, the fraction is computed by adding the property factor, the payroll factor, and 10 times the sales factor and dividing by 12. For tax years beginning on or after January 1, 2013, the property and payroll factors are eliminated. The enhanced sales factor formulas are not available for taxpayers in the following industries: mining, manufacturing, transportation and warehousing, information (except other information services), and finance and insurance.

For tax years beginning on or after January 1, 2008, an airline determines its property, payroll, and sales factors by multiplying the total average value of its mobile flight equipment, total flight personnel compensation, and total transportation revenues, by the ratio of Utah revenue ton miles to total revenue ton miles. Separate computations are made for each aircraft type. [S.B. 237, Mar. 17, 2008]

Multistate Tax Commission. At its annual meeting on July 31, 2008, the MTC approved the "Model Uniform Regulation for the Apportionment of Income from Telecommunications and Similar Services."

State-by-State Summary

The chart that follows is divided into three parts for ease of presentation. Part 1 summarizes the apportionment formulas for airlines, trucking companies, telecommunications companies, and sports and entertainment companies. Part 2 covers financial institutions, insurance companies, and mutual funds. Part 3 summarizes the apportionment formulas for service companies, retailers, and broadcasters.

Specialized Industry Formulas (Part 1)

Legend:
NA — Not applicable
NR — Not reported

	Interstate Air	*Weighted Equally?*	*Interstate Motor Vehicles*	*Weighted Equally?*	*Telecommunications*	*Weighted Equally?*	*Sports/ Entertainment Activities*	*Weighted Equally?*
Alabama	Gross receipts or sales; payroll; tangible property; mileage	Yes	Gross receipts or sales; payroll; tangible property; mileage	Yes	Tangible property; gross receipts or sales; payroll	Yes	Tangible property; gross receipts or sales; payroll;	Yes
Alaska	Tangible property; gross receipts or sales; payroll	Yes	Tangible property; gross receipts or sales; payroll	Yes	Tangible property; gross receipts or sales; payroll	Yes	Tangible property; gross receipts or sales; payroll	Yes
Arizona	Revenue miles	NA. See A.R.S. § 43-1139(B)	Tangible property; gross receipts or sales; payroll	NA. See A.R.S. § 43-1139(A)	Tangible property; gross receipts or sales; payroll	NA. See A.R.S. § 43-1139(A)	Tangible property; gross receipts or sales; payroll	NA. See A.R.S. § 43-1139(A)
Arkansas	Gross receipts or sales	NA	Mileage	NA	Tangible property; gross receipts or sales; payroll	No, sales double-weighted	Tangible property; gross receipts or sales; payroll	No, sales double-weighted
California	Tangible property; gross receipts or sales; payroll	No, sales double-weighted	Tangible property; gross receipts or sales; payroll	No, sales double-weighted	Tangible property; gross receipts or sales; payroll	No, sales double-weighted	Tangible property; gross receipts or sales; payroll	No, sales double-weighted
Colorado	MTC special regs	NR		NR	MTC special regs	NR		NR
Connecticut	Revenue miles		Revenue miles					

Specialized Industry Formulas (Part 1)

Legend:
NA **Not applicable**
NR **Not reported**

	Interstate Air	*Weighted Equally?*	*Interstate Motor Vehicles*	*Weighted Equally?*	*Telecommunications*	*Weighted Equally?*	*Sports/ Entertainment Activities*	*Weighted Equally?*
Delaware	Tangible property; gross receipts or sales; payroll	Yes	Tangible property; gross receipts or sales; payroll	Yes	Tangible property; gross receipts or sales; payroll	Yes	Tangible property; gross receipts or sales; payroll	Yes
District of Columbia	Tangible property; gross receipts or sales; payroll; exempt from tax		Tangible property; gross receipts or sales; payroll; exempt from tax		Tangible property; gross receipts or sales; payroll	Yes	Tangible property; gross receipts or sales; payroll	Yes
Florida	Revenue miles, 100%	NA	Revenue miles, 100%	NA	Tangible property; gross receipts or sales; payroll	No, sales double-weighted	Tangible property; gross receipts or sales; payroll	No, sales double-weighted
Georgia	See O.C.G.A § 48-7-31(d)(2.1)		Revenue miles 100%	NA	Gross receipts or sales	Sales 100%	Gross receipts or sales	Sales 100%
Hawaii	Revenue tons; flight originating revenue; flight operating hours	Yes	NA	NA	Tangible property; gross receipts or sales; payroll	Yes	Tangible property; gross receipts or sales; payroll	Yes
Idaho	Tangible property; gross receipts or sales; payroll	No, sales double-weighted	Tangible property; gross receipts or sales; payroll	No, sales double-weighted	Tangible property; gross receipts or sales; payroll	No, sales double-weighted; single weighted sales factor for telephone corporations	Tangible property; gross receipts or sales; payroll	No, sales double-weighted

Specialized Industry Formulas (Part 1)

Legend:
NA **Not applicable**
NR **Not reported**

	Interstate Air	*Weighted Equally?*	*Interstate Motor Vehicles*	*Weighted Equally?*	*Telecommunications*	*Weighted Equally?*	*Sports/ Entertainment Activities*	*Weighted Equally?*
Illinois	Revenue miles	IITA § 304(d)(4)	Revenue miles	IITA § 304(d)(3)	Gross receipts or sales	See Note. IITA § 304(a)(3)(B-5)	Gross receipts or sales	See Note 1.
Note. For taxable years ending on or after 12/31/00, the apportionment factor for taxpayers with business income is calculated using only the sales factor. See IITA § 304(a), (h). For taxable years ending after 12/31/99 and before 12/31/00, property 8 1/3, payroll 83 1/3.								
Indiana	100% Sales	NA	100% Sales	NA	100% Sales	NA	100% Sales	NA
Iowa	Mileage	NA	Mileage	NA	Gross receipts or sales	NA	Gross receipts or sales	NA
Kansas	Tangible property; gross receipts or sales; payroll	Yes	100% Mileage	NA	100% Fiberoptic mileage	NA	Tangible property; gross receipts or sales; payroll	Yes
Kentucky	Tangible property; payroll; revenue miles	No, sales double-weighted	Tangible property; payroll; revenue miles	No, sales double-weighted	Tangible property; gross receipts or sales; payroll	No, sales double-weighted	Tangible property; gross receipts or sales; payroll	No, sales double-weighted
Louisiana	Tangible property; gross receipts or sales	Yes	Tangible property; gross receipts or sales	Yes	Tangible property; gross receipts or sales; payroll	Yes	Tangible property; gross receipts or sales; payroll *or* payroll and sales	Yes
Maine								

Legend:

NA **Not applicable**

NR **Not reported**

Specialized Industry Formulas (Part 1)

	Interstate Air	*Weighted Equally?*	*Interstate Motor Vehicles*	*Weighted Equally?*	*Telecommunications*	*Weighted Equally?*	*Sports/ Entertainment Activities*	*Weighted Equally?*
Maryland	Tangible property; gross receipts or sales; payroll	Yes	One-factor formula of sales allocated on basis of revenue miles	NA	Gross receipts or sales; tangible property; payroll	No, sales double-weighted	Gross receipts or sales; tangible property; payroll	No, sales double-weighted.
Massachusetts	Tangible property; gross receipts or sales; payroll	No, sales double-weighted.	Tangible property; payroll; gross receipts or sales	No, sales double-weighted.	NR	NR	NR	NR
Michigan (Business Tax)	Revenue miles	NA	Revenue miles	NA				

Note. The CIT takes effect 01/01/12, and replaces the Michigan Business Tax (MBT) for most taxpayers. However, businesses that have been approved to receive, have received, or have been assigned certain certified credits may elect to file a return and pay the tax imposed by the MBT in lieu of the CIT until the certified credits are exhausted or extinguished.

Specialized Industry Formulas (Part 1)

Legend:
NA — Not applicable
NR — Not reported

	Interstate Air	*Weighted Equally?*	*Interstate Motor Vehicles*	*Weighted Equally?*	*Telecommunications*	*Weighted Equally?*	*Sports/ Entertainment Activities*	*Weighted Equally?*
Minnesota	Gross receipts; payroll; tangible property	No, 5%, 5%, 90%	Tangible property; payroll; gross receipts or sales	No, 5%, 5%, 90%	Property; payroll; gross receipts or sales	No, 5%, 5%, 90%	Property; payroll; gross receipts or sales. All income from the operation of an athletic team when the visiting team does not share in the gate receipts is assigned to the state in which the team's operation is based.	No, 5%, 5%, 90%
Mississippi	Revenue miles, or flight miles	NA	Revenue tons; or vehicle miles	NA	Gross receipts or sales	NA	Gross receipts or sales	NA
Missouri	Revenue miles	NA	Revenue miles	NA	Line mileage of public utilities	NA	Property; payroll gross receipts or sales	Yes
Montana	Other, see ARM 42.26.801-807	Yes	Tangible property; gross receipts or sales; payroll; revenue miles	Yes	Tangible property; gross receipts or sales; payroll	Yes	Tangible property; gross receipts or sales; payroll	Yes
Nebraska	Departures weighted to cost and value	NA	Mobile property miles	NA	Gross receipts or sales	NA	Gross receipts or sales	NA

Legend:

NA **Not applicable**
NR **Not reported**

Specialized Industry Formulas (Part 1)

	Interstate Air	*Weighted Equally?*	*Interstate Motor Vehicles*	*Weighted Equally?*	*Telecommunications*	*Weighted Equally?*	*Sports/ Entertainment Activities*	*Weighted Equally?*
Nevada	Nevada does not impose a corporate income tax							
New Hampshire	Rev. 304.07	NR	Rev 304.11	NR	NR	NR	NR	NR
New Jersey	Tangible property; gross receipts or sales; payroll (special rules on tangible personal property) **Note.** Beginning 1/1/12, the sales factor for air carriers shall be based on revenue miles.	No, sales double-weighted	Tangible property; gross receipts or sales; payroll (special rule for receipts)	No, sales double-weighted	Tangible property; gross receipts or sales; payroll	No, sales double-weighted	Tangible property; gross receipts or sales; payroll	No, sales double-weighted
New Mexico	Tangible property; gross receipts or sales; payroll	Yes	Revenue miles	NA	Tangible property; gross receipts or sales; payroll	Yes	Tangible property; gross receipts or sales; payroll	Yes
New York	Arrivals/ departures; originating revenue; revenue tons	Yes	Revenue miles	NA	NA	NA	Gross receipts	NA
	Does not reflect special sourcing for receipts of many of these industries							

Specialized Industry Formulas (Part 1)

Legend:
NA **Not applicable**
NR **Not reported**

	Interstate Air	*Weighted Equally?*	*Interstate Motor Vehicles*	*Weighted Equally?*	*Telecommunications*	*Weighted Equally?*	*Sports/ Entertainment Activities*	*Weighted Equally?*
North Carolina	Revenue miles	NA	Revenue miles	NA	Gross receipts or sales	NA	Tangible property; gross receipts or sales; payroll	No, sales double-weighted
North Dakota	Tangible property; gross receipts or sales; payroll	Yes	Tangible property; gross receipts or sales; payroll (revenue miles for interstate)	Yes	Tangible property; gross receipts or sales; payroll	Yes	Tangible property; gross receipts or sales; payroll	Yes
Ohio	Ohio does not impose a corporate income tax							
Note A. Effective 1/1/2010, the Ohio Franchise Tax was fully phased out and business will be taxed on gross receipts through the Commercial Activity Tax. Details about that tax can be found at: http//tax.ohio.gov/divisions/commercial_activities/index.stm								
Oklahoma	Tangible property; payroll; revenue miles	Yes	Tangible property; payroll; revenue tons	Yes	Tangible property; gross receipts or sales; payroll	Yes	Tangible property; gross receipts or sales; payroll	Yes
Oregon	Revenue miles	100%	Revenue miles	100%	Tangible property; gross receipts or sales; payroll	100% of gross receipts or sales or 25%, 50%, 25%	In-state appearance	100%
Pennsylvania	Revenue miles	NA	Revenue miles	NA	Tangible property; gross receipts or sales; payroll	No, 20%, 60%, 20%	Tangible property; gross receipts or sales; payroll	No, 20%, 60%, 20%

Legend:

NA	**Not applicable**
NR	**Not reported**

Specialized Industry Formulas (Part 1)

	Interstate Air	*Weighted Equally?*	*Interstate Motor Vehicles*	*Weighted Equally?*	*Telecommunications*	*Weighted Equally?*	*Sports/ Entertainment Activities*	*Weighted Equally?*
Rhode Island	Special regulation	NA	Special regulation	NA	Special regulation	NA	Tangible property; gross receipts or sales; payroll	Yes
South Carolina	Revenue tons	NA	Vehicle miles	NA	Gross receipts or sales	NA	Gross receipts or sales	NA
South Dakota	South Dakota does not impose a corporate income tax							
Tennessee	Gross receipts or sales; revenue miles	Yes	Gross receipts or sales; revenue miles	Yes	Tangible property; gross receipts or sales; payroll	No, sales double-weighted	Tangible property; gross receipts or sales; payroll	No, sales double-weighted
Texas	Gross receipts	NA	Gross receipts	NA	Gross receipts	NA	Gross receipts	NA
Utah	Tangible property; gross receipts or sales; payroll	Yes	Tangible property; gross receipts or sales; payroll	Yes	Tangible property; gross receipts or sales; payroll	Yes	Tangible property; gross receipts or sales; payroll	Yes
Vermont	Tangible property; gross receipts or sales; payroll	Yes	Tangible property; gross receipts or sales; payroll	Yes	Tangible property; gross receipts or sales; payroll	Yes	Tangible property; gross receipts or sales; payroll	Yes

Specialized Industry Formulas (Part 1)

Legend:
NA **Not applicable**
NR **Not reported**

	Interstate Air	*Weighted Equally?*	*Interstate Motor Vehicles*	*Weighted Equally?*	*Telecommunications*	*Weighted Equally?*	*Sports/ Entertainment Activities*	*Weighted Equally?*
Virginia	Tangible property; gross receipts or sales; payroll, property and sales factors are calculated using mileage, including over-flight miles, in the numerator and denominator with use of departures as an alternative.	No, sales double-weighted	Mileage	NA	Tangible property; gross receipts or sales; payroll	No, sales double-weighted	Tangible property; gross receipts or sales; payroll	No, sales double-weighted
Washington	Washington does not impose a corporate income tax							
West Virginia	Tangible property; gross receipts or sales; payroll	No, sales double-weighted	Revenue miles	NA	Tangible property; gross receipts or sales; payroll	No, sales double-weighted	Tangible property; gross receipts or sales; payroll	No, sales double-weighted
Wisconsin	Revenue tons handled; arrivals/ departures; originating revenue; Rule Tax 2.46	Yes	Originating revenue; revenue or ton miles; Rule Tax 2.47	Yes	Tangible property; gross receipts or sales; payroll	Yes	Gross receipts or sales; Rule Tax 2.505	No, 100% gross receipts or sales

Legend:

NA **Not applicable**

NR **Not reported**

Specialized Industry Formulas (Part 1)

	Interstate Air	*Weighted Equally?*	*Interstate Motor Vehicles*	*Weighted Equally?*	*Telecommunications*	*Weighted Equally?*	*Sports/ Entertainment Activities*	*Weighted Equally?*
Wyoming	Wyoming does not impose a corporate income tax							

Specialized Industry Formulas (Part 2)

Legend:
NA Not applicable
NR Not reported

	Financial Institutions	*Weighted Equally?*	*Insurance Companies*	*Weighted Equally?*	*Mutual Funds*	*Weighted Equally?*
Alabama	NA, financial institutions must file an excise tax return.	NA	NA, insurance companies pay premium tax (Dept. of Insurance).	NA	Tangible property; gross receipts or sales; payroll	Yes
Alaska	Tangible property; gross receipts or sales; payroll	Yes	Exempt	NA	Tangible property; gross receipts; payroll	Yes
Arizona	Tangible property; gross receipts or sales; payroll	NA. See A.R.S. § 43-1139(A).	Tangible property; gross receipts or sales; payroll	NA. See A.R.S. § 43-1139(A).	Tangible property; gross receipts or sales; payroll	NA. See A.R.S. § 43-1139(A).
Arkansas	Tangible property; gross receipts or sales; payroll	Yes	Exempt if pay Arkansas premium tax; if taxable, tangible property; gross receipts or sales; payroll	No, sales double-weighted	Tangible property; gross receipts or sales; payroll	Yes
California	Tangible property; gross receipts or sales; payroll	Yes	NA	NA	Gross receipts or sales; payroll	No, sales double-weighted
Colorado	MTC special regs	NR		NR	Special regs	NR
Connecticut	Gross receipts or sales	100%	Gross receipts or sales	100%	Gross receipts or sales	100%
Delaware	NA, exempt from corporate income tax	NA	NA, exempt from corporate income tax	NA	Tangible property; gross receipts or sales; payroll	Yes
District of Columbia	Gross receipts or sales; payroll	Yes	NA, exempt from corporate income tax	NA	Tangible property; gross receipts or sales; payroll	Yes
Florida	Intangibles and tangible property; gross receipts or sales; payroll	No, sales double-weighted	Premiums written	NA	Tangible property; gross receipts or sales; payroll	No, sales double-weighted
Georgia	Gross receipts or sales	Sales 100%	NA, exempt if subject to premiums tax	NA	Gross receipts or sales	Sales 100%

Legend:
NA Not applicable
NR Not reported

Specialized Industry Formulas (Part 2)

	Financial Institutions	*Weighted Equally?*	*Insurance Companies*	*Weighted Equally?*	*Mutual Funds*	*Weighted Equally?*
Hawaii	NA	NA	NA	NA	Tangible property; gross receipts or sales; payroll	Yes
Idaho	Tangible property; gross receipts or sales; payroll	No, sales double-weighted	Exempt if pay a premiums tax.	NA	Tangible property; gross receipts or sales; payroll	No, sales double-weighted
Illinois	Gross receipts or sales	IITA § 304(c)(3)	Premiums written	NA	Business income sourced in Illinois, see IITA § 304(c)	NA
Indiana	100% Sales	NA	100% Sales	NA	100% Sales	NA
Iowa	Subject to Iowa franchise tax	NA	Subject to Iowa premiums tax	NA	Exempt from tax	NA
Kansas	.33 tangible property/ receivables, .33 gross receipts or sales, .33 payroll (includes banks and trusts subject to Privilege Tax)	NA	100% premiums written	NA	See K.S.A. 79-3279(b)(5) for apportionment method for investment fund service corporations.	NA
Kentucky	Tangible property; gross receipts or sales; payroll;	No, sales double-weighted	Exempt from corporate income tax	NA	Tangible property; gross receipts or sales; payroll	No, sales double-weighted
Louisiana	Tangible property; payroll	Yes	Other. See La. Rev. Stat. 47:221 and 47:227	NA	NA, no specific apportionment formula exists	NA
Maine						

Specialized Industry Formulas (Part 2)

Legend:
NA Not applicable
NR Not reported

	Financial Institutions	*Weighted Equally?*	*Insurance Companies*	*Weighted Equally?*	*Mutual Funds*	*Weighted Equally?*
Maryland	Gross receipts or sales; tangible property; payroll	No, sales double-weighted	Gross receipts or sales; tax administered by the Department of Licensing and Regulation, Insurance Division	NA	Exempt from tax	NA
Massachusetts	See TIRs 95-6, 00-6 04-6	NA	NR	NA	NR	NA
Michigan (Business Tax)	Gross business	NA		NA		
Note. The CIT takes effect 01/01/12, and replaces the Michigan Business Tax (MBT) for most taxpayers. However, businesses that have been approved to receive, have received, or have been assigned certain certified credits may elect to file a return and pay the tax imposed by the MBT in lieu of the CIT until the certified credits are exhausted or extinguished.						
Minnesota	Tangible property (includes intangibles); payroll; gross receipts or sales	No, 5%, 5%, 90%	Exempt from tax	NA	Gross receipts or sales; tangible property; payroll	No, 90%, 5%, 5%
Mississippi	Tangible property; payroll; sales or gross receipts	Yes	Separate accounting	NA	Gross receipts or sales	NA
Missouri	Tangible property; gross receipts or sales; payroll	Yes	Premiums	100%	In-state appearances	100%
Montana	Tangible property; gross receipts or sales; payroll	Yes	Subject to premiums tax	NA	Tangible property; gross receipts or sales; payroll	Yes
Nebraska	Exempt from tax	NA	Premiums written	NA	Gross receipts or sales	NA
Nevada	Nevada does not impose a corporate income tax					
New Hampshire	Rev 304.10	NR	NR	NR	NR	NR

Specialized Industry Formulas (Part 2)

Legend:
NA Not applicable
NR Not reported

	Financial Institutions	*Weighted Equally?*	*Insurance Companies*	*Weighted Equally?*	*Mutual Funds*	*Weighted Equally?*
New Jersey	Tangible property; gross receipts or sales; payroll	Sales double-weighted; special rate for regulated investment companies	Taxed under insurance premium tax	NA	Tangible property; gross receipts; payroll (special rules for management companies and special rate for regulated investment companies)	Sales double-weighted
New Mexico	Tangible property; gross receipts or sales; payroll	Yes	Tangible property; gross receipts or sales; payroll	Yes	Tangible property; gross receipts or sales; payroll	Yes
New York	For banks only, receipts; payroll (except general executive officers); deposits	No, receipts and deposits both double-weighted	Premium written; salaries	No, 90%, 10% for life insurers, 100% premiums written for all others	Gross receipts or sales	NA
	Does not reflect special sourcing rules for receipts of many of these industries					
North Carolina	Gross receipts or sales	NA	Premiums written	NA	Gross receipts or sales	NA
North Dakota	Use NDCC Ch. 57-35.3	NA	Exempt if Premiums Tax paid	NA	Tangible property; gross receipts or sales; payroll	Yes
Ohio	Ohio does not impose a corporate income tax					
Note A. Effective 1/1/2010, the Ohio Franchise Tax was fully phased out and business will be taxed on gross receipts through the Commercial Activity Tax. Details about that tax can be found at: http//tax.ohio.gov/divisions/commercial_activities/index.stm						
Oklahoma	Separate accounting	NA	Exempt (premiums tax imposed)	NA	Tangible property; gross receipts or sales; payroll	Yes
Oregon	Gross receipts or sales	NA	Premiums written	NA	Gross receipts or sales	NA
Pennsylvania	Value of shares	NA	Premiums written	NA	NA	NA
Rhode Island	Tangible property; gross receipts or sales; payroll	Yes	Premiums written	NA	Tangible property; gross receipts or sales; payroll	Yes

Specialized Industry Formulas (Part 2)

Legend:
NA Not applicable
NR Not reported

	Financial Institutions	*Weighted Equally?*	*Insurance Companies*	*Weighted Equally?*	*Mutual Funds*	*Weighted Equally?*
South Carolina	Gross receipts or sales	NA	Taxed by Dept. of Insurance	NA	Allocated	NA
South Dakota	South Dakota does not impose a corporate income tax					
Tennessee	Receivables (all financing income)	NA	Premiums written	NA	Gross receipts or sales	NA
Texas	Gross receipts or sales	NA	Exempt from franchise tax if annual gross premiums insurance tax is paid	NA	Gross receipts or sales	NA
Utah	Tangible property; gross receipts or sales; payroll	Yes	Tangible property; gross receipts or sales; payroll	Yes	Tangible property; gross receipts or sales; payroll	Yes
Vermont	Tangible property; gross receipts or sales; payroll	Yes	Exempt	NA	Tangible property; gross receipts or sales; payroll	Yes
Virginia	Cost of performance	NA	Exempt (premium tax in lieu of income tax)	NA	Exempt (pass through entity)	NA
Washington	Washington does not impose a corporate income tax					
West Virginia	Gross receipts or sales	NA	Tangible property; gross receipts or sales; payroll	No, sales double weighted	Tangible property; gross receipts or sales; payroll	No, sales double-weighted
Wisconsin	Gross receipts or sales; Rule Tax 2.49	No, 100% gross receipts or sales	Premiums written: (s. 71.45, Wis Stats)	No, 100%, premiums written	Gross receipts or sales	No, 100% gross receipts or sales
Wyoming	Wyoming does not impose a corporate income tax					

Legend:

NA — **Not applicable**

NR — **Not reported**

Specialized Industry Formulas (Part 3)

	Service Business	*Weighted Equally?*	*Retailers*	*Weighted Equally?*	*Broadcasting*	*Weighted Equally?*
Alabama	Tangible property; gross receipts or sales; payroll	Yes	Tangible property; gross receipts or sales; payroll	Yes	Tangible property; gross receipts or sales; payroll	Yes
Alaska	Tangible property; gross receipts or sales; payroll	Yes	Tangible property; gross receipts or sales; payroll	Yes	Tangible property; gross receipts or sales; payroll	Yes
Arizona	Tangible property; gross receipts or sales; payroll	No, see A.R.S. § 43-1139	Tangible property; gross receipts or sales; payroll	No, see A.R.S. § 43-1139	Tangible property; gross receipts or sales; payroll	No, see A.R.S. § 43-1139
Arkansas	Tangible property; gross receipts or sales; payroll	No, sales double-weighted	Tangible property; gross receipts or sales; payroll	No, sales double-weighted	Tangible property; gross receipts or sales; payroll	No, sales double-weighted
California	Tangible property; gross receipts or sales; payroll	No, sales double-weighted	Tangible property; gross receipts or sales; payroll	No, sales double-weighted	Tangible property; gross receipts or sales; payroll	No, sales double-weighted
Colorado	NR	NR	NR	NR	MTC special regs	NR
Connecticut	Gross receipts or sales	100%	Tangible property; gross receipts or sales; payroll	No, sales double-weighted	Gross receipts or sales	100%
Delaware	Tangible property; gross receipts or sales; payroll	Yes	Tangible property; gross receipts or sales; payroll	Yes	Tangible property; gross receipts or sales; payroll	Yes
District of Columbia	Tangible property; gross receipts or sales; payroll	Yes	Tangible property; gross receipts or sales; payroll	Yes	Tangible property; gross receipts or sales; payroll	Yes
Florida	Tangible property; gross receipts or sales; payroll	No, sales double-weighted	Tangible property; gross receipts or sales; payroll	No, sales double-weighted	Tangible property; gross receipts or sales; payroll	No, sales double-weighted
Georgia	Gross receipts or sales	Sales 100%	Gross receipts or sales	Sales 100%	Audience factor	100%
Hawaii	Tangible property; gross receipts or sales; payroll	Yes	Tangible property; gross receipts or sales; payroll	Yes	Tangible property; gross receipts or sales; payroll	Yes

Legend:

NA **Not applicable**

NR **Not reported**

Specialized Industry Formulas (Part 3)

	Service Business	*Weighted Equally?*	*Retailers*	*Weighted Equally?*	*Broadcasting*	*Weighted Equally?*
Idaho	Tangible property; gross receipts or sales; payroll	No, sales double-weighted; single-weighted sales factor for electrical companies	Tangible property; gross receipts or sales; payroll	No, sales double-weighted; single-weighted sales factor for electrical companies	Tangible property; gross receipts or sales; payroll	No, sales factor doubled
Illinois	Gross receipts or sales	See Note.	Gross receipts or sales	See Note.	Gross receipts or sales	See Note.
Note. For taxable years ending on or after 12/31/00, the apportionment factor for taxpayers with business income is calculated using only the sales factor. See IITA § 304(a), (h). For taxable years ending after 12/31/99 and before 12/31/00, property 8$^{1}/_{3}$, payroll 8$^{1}/_{3}$, and sales 83$^{1}/_{3}$.						
Indiana	100% Sales	NA	100% Sales	NA	100% Sales	NA
Iowa	Gross receipts or sales	NA	Gross receipts or sales	NA	Population	NA
Kansas	Tangible property; gross receipts or sales; payroll	Yes	Tangible property; gross receipts or sales; payroll	Yes	Tangible property; gross receipts or sales; payroll	Yes
Kentucky	Tangible property; gross receipts or sales; payroll	No, sales double-weighted	Tangible property; gross receipts or sales; payroll	No, sales double-weighted	Tangible property; gross receipts or sales; payroll	No, sales double-weighted
Louisiana	Gross receipts or sales; payroll	Yes	Tangible property; gross receipts or sales; payroll	No, sales double-weighted	Television, radio, and other broadcasting, see R.S. § 47.287.95(k)	NA
Maine						
Maryland	Gross receipts or sales; tangible property; payroll	No, sales double weighted	Tangible property; gross receipts or sales; payroll	No, sales double-weighted	Gross receipts or sales; tangible property; payroll	No, sales double-weighted
Massachusetts	NR	NR	NR	NR	NR	NR
Michigan (Business Tax)						

Legend:

NA **Not applicable**
NR **Not reported**

Specialized Industry Formulas (Part 3)

	Service Business	*Weighted Equally?*	*Retailers*	*Weighted Equally?*	*Broadcasting*	*Weighted Equally?*
Note. The CIT takes effect 01/01/12, and replaces the Michigan Business Tax (MBT) for most taxpayers. However, businesses that have been approved to receive, have received, or have been assigned certain certified credits may elect to file a return and pay the tax imposed by the MBT in lieu of the CIT until the certified credits are exhausted or extinguished.						
Minnesota	Tangible property; payroll; gross receipts or sales	No, 5%, 5%, 90%	Tangible property; payroll; gross receipts or sales	No, 5%, 5% and 90%	Tangible property; payroll; gross receipts or sales	No, 5%, 5% and 90%
Mississippi	Gross receipts or sales	NA	Gross receipts or sales	NA	Gross receipts or sales	NA
Missouri	Tangible property; gross receipts or sales; payroll	Yes	Tangible property; gross receipts or sales; payroll	Yes	Tangible property; gross receipts or sales; payroll	Yes
Montana	Tangible property; gross receipts or sales; payroll	Yes	Tangible property; gross receipts or sales; payroll	Yes	Tangible property; gross receipts or sales; payroll	Yes
Nebraska	Gross receipts or sales	NA	Gross receipts or sales	NA	Gross receipts or sales	NA
Nevada	Nevada does not impose a corporate income tax					
New Hampshire	NR	NR	NR	NR	Rev 304.09	NR
New Jersey	Tangible property; gross receipts or sales; payroll (special rule for receipts)	No, sales double-weighted	Tangible property; gross receipts or sales; payroll	No, sales double-weighted	Tangible property; gross receipts or sales; payroll (special rule for receipts)	No, sales double-weighted
New Mexico	Tangible property; gross receipts or sales; payroll	Yes	Tangible property; gross receipts or sales; payroll	Yes	Tangible property; gross receipts or sales; payroll	Yes
New York	Gross receipts	NA	Gross receipts	NA	Gross receipts	NA
	Does not reflect special sourcing rules for receipts of many of these industries					
North Carolina	Tangible property; gross receipts or sales; payroll	No, sales double-weighted	Tangible property; gross receipts or sales; payroll	No, sales double-weighted	Gross receipts or sales	NA

Specialized Industry Formulas (Part 3)

Legend:
NA **Not applicable**
NR **Not reported**

	Service Business	*Weighted Equally?*	*Retailers*	*Weighted Equally?*	*Broadcasting*	*Weighted Equally?*
North Dakota	Tangible property; gross receipts or sales; payroll	Yes	Tangible property; gross receipts or sales; payroll	Yes	Tangible property; gross receipts or sales; payroll	Yes
Ohio	Ohio does not impose a corporate income tax					
Note A. Effective 1/1/2010, the Ohio Franchise Tax was fully phased out and business will be taxed on gross receipts through the Commercial Activity Tax. Details about that tax can be found at: http//tax.ohio.gov/divisions/commercial_activities/index.stm						
Oklahoma	Tangible property; gross receipts or sales; payroll	Yes	Tangible property; gross receipts or sales; payroll	Yes	Tangible property; gross receipts or sales; payroll	Yes
Oregon	Gross receipts or sales	100%	Gross receipts or sales	100%	Audience factor	100%
Pennsylvania	Tangible property; gross receipts or sales; payroll	No, 20%, 60%, 20%	Tangible property; gross receipts or sales; payroll	No, 20%, 60%, 20%	Tangible property; gross receipts or sales; payroll	Yes
Rhode Island	Tangible property; gross receipts or sales; payroll	Yes	Tangible property; gross receipts or sales; payroll	Yes	Specialty Regulation	NA
South Carolina	Gross receipts or sales	NA	B	No, sales double-weighted	Gross receipts or sales	NA
South Dakota	South Dakota does not impose a corporate income tax					
Tennessee	Tangible property; gross receipts or sales; payroll	No, sales double-weighted	Tangible property; gross receipts or sales; payroll	No, sales double-weighted	Tangible property; gross receipts or sales; payroll	No, sales double-weighted
Texas	Gross receipts	NA	Gross receipts	NA	Gross receipts	NA
Utah	Tangible property; gross receipts or sales; payroll	Yes	Tangible property; gross receipts or sales; payroll	Yes	Tangible property; gross receipts or sales; payroll	Yes
Vermont	Tangible property; gross receipts or sales; payroll	Yes	Tangible property; gross receipts or sales; payroll	Yes	Tangible property; gross receipts or sales; payroll	Yes
Virginia	Tangible property; gross receipts or sales; payroll	No, sales double-weighted	Tangible property; gross receipts or sales; payroll	No, sales double-weighted	Tangible property; gross receipts or sales; payroll	No, sales double-weighted

Legend:

NA **Not applicable**

NR **Not reported**

Specialized Industry Formulas (Part 3)

	Service Business	*Weighted Equally?*	*Retailers*	*Weighted Equally?*	*Broadcasting*	*Weighted Equally?*
Washington	Washington does not impose a corporate income tax					
West Virginia	Tangible property; gross receipts or sales; payroll	No, sales double-weighted	Tangible property; gross receipts or sales; payroll	No, sales double-weighted	Tangible property; gross receipts or sales; payroll	No, sales double-weighted
Wisconsin	Gross receipts or sales; Rule Tax 2.39	100% gross receipts or sales	100% gross receipts or sales; Rule Tax 2.39	100% gross receipts or sales	Gross receipts or sales; Rule Tax 2.39	100% gross receipts or sales
Wyoming	Wyoming does not impose a corporate income tax					

Allocation of Nonbusiness Income

Constitutional Restrictions on Inclusions in Apportionable Income

The U.S. Constitution prohibits a state from taxing an out-of-state corporation on income derived from an unrelated activity that has nothing to do with the business activity of the corporation in the taxing state. This principle reflects the fundamental requirement of the Due Process and Commerce Clauses that there be "some definite link, some minimum connection, between a state and the person, property or transaction it seeks to tax." [*Miller Bros. Co. v. Maryland*, 347 U.S. 340, 1954] Under the unitary business principle, if a corporation's interstate activities form a unitary business, a state need not isolate the corporation's in-state activities from the rest of the business in determining the corporation's taxable income. Instead, the state may tax an apportioned percentage of the income generated by the multistate unitary business. The unitary business principle was originally developed in the 19th century to address the issues that arose when states attempted to impose property taxes on interstate railroad and telegraph companies. For example, to fairly determine the value of an interstate railroad's track located within a state for property tax purposes, it was necessary to apportion a share of the value of the entire multistate business rather than attempt to isolate the value of the in-state property.

In *Mobil Oil Corp. v. Commissioner of Taxes* [445 U.S. 425 (1980)], the Supreme Court stated that "the linchpin of apportionability in the field of state income taxation is the unitary business principle." Mobil was an integrated petroleum company that was incorporated and commercially domiciled in New York. Mobil challenged Vermont's ability to tax dividends that the taxpayer received from its foreign subsidiaries. The essence of Mobil's argument that Vermont could not constitutionally tax the foreign dividends was that the activities of the foreign subsidiaries were "unrelated" to Mobil's activities in Vermont, which were limited to distributing petroleum products. The Supreme Court ruled that Vermont could tax an apportioned percentage of the dividends Mobil received from its foreign subsidiaries, because those subsidiaries were part of the same integrated petroleum enterprise as the business operations conducted in Vermont. In other words, the dividends were apportionable income, because they were received from unitary subsidiaries. The Court also indicated that if the business activities of the foreign subsidiaries had "nothing to do with the activities of the recipient in the taxing state, due process considerations might well preclude apportionability, because there would be no underlying unitary business."

The two most recent Supreme Court decisions regarding apportionable income are *Allied-Signal* and *MeadWestvaco*.

Allied-Signal. In *Allied-Signal, Inc. v. Director, Division of Taxation* [504 U.S. 768, 1992], the taxpayer was Bendix Corporation (Allied-Signal was the successor in interest to Bendix), a Delaware corporation that was commercially domiciled in Michigan and conducted business in all 50 states. In 1981, Bendix realized a $211.5 million gain from the sale of 20.6 percent of the stock of ASARCO, Inc. The Supreme Court ruled that the State of New Jersey was constitutionally prohibited from including the gain in the taxpayer's apportionable income, because none of the factors that would indicate that Bendix and ASARCO were engaged in a unitary business (e.g., functional integration, centralized management, or economies of scale) were present. As a result, the Court concluded that Bendix and ASARCO were "unrelated business enterprises each of whose activities had nothing to do with the other." In addition, the ownership of ASARCO stock did not serve an operational function in Bendix's business—"the mere fact that an intangible asset was acquired pursuant to a long-term corporate strategy of acquisitions and dispositions does not convert an otherwise passive investment into an integral operational one."

In arriving at its decision in *Allied-Signal*, the Supreme Court stated that "the payee and the payer need not be engaged in the same unitary business as a prerequisite to apportionment in all cases . . . What is required instead is that the capital transaction serve an operational rather than an investment function." As an example of an asset that serves an operational function, the Court mentions "interest earned on short-term deposits . . . if that income forms part of the working capital of the corporation's unitary business." The Court's reference to an operational function in this case was widely interpreted as creating a new test for apportionable income. Under the alleged operational function test, even if no unitary business exists between the payee (taxpayer) and payer (asset), a state may still tax an apportioned percentage of the income from an intangible asset if that asset serves an operational function rather than an investment function in the taxpayer's business.

MeadWestvaco. In *MeadWestvaco Corporation v. Illinois Department of Revenue* [553 U.S. 16, 2008], the issue was whether Illinois was constitutionally prohibited from taxing an apportioned share of the $1 billion gain realized by Mead Corporation in 1994 when it sold its investment in Lexis/Nexis. MeadWestvaco is the successor in interest to Mead, which was an Ohio corporation. Lexis/Nexis (Lexis) was one of Mead's business divisions. The Illinois trial court concluded that although Mead and Lexis were not engaged in a unitary business, the gain nevertheless qualified as apportionable income, because Mead's investment in Lexis served an operational purpose. The Illinois appeals court affirmed the trial court's decision that Lexis served an "operational function" in Mead's business, but did not address the issue of whether Mead and Lexis were engaged in a unitary business.

The U.S. Supreme Court vacated the Illinois appeals court decision on the grounds that it misinterpreted the Court's references to "operational function" in *Allied-Signal* as modifying the unitary business principle to add a new basis for apportionment. The Court explained that the operational function concept described in *Allied-Signal* merely recognizes the reality that an asset can be part of a taxpayer's unitary business even if there is no unitary relationship between the payee (taxpayer) and payer (asset). The Court explained that its reference to "operational function" in *Allied-Signal* was "not intended to modify the unitary business principle by adding a new ground for apportionment." Instead, "[t]he concept of operational function simply recognizes that an asset can be a part of a taxpayer's unitary business even if what we may term a 'unitary relationship' does not exist between the 'payor and payee.'" Thus, whether an asset serves an operational function in the taxpayer's business is "merely instrumental to the constitutionally relevant conclusion that the asset was a unitary part of the business being conducted in the taxing State."

The Court illustrated this point using examples drawn from its earlier decisions. In *Allied-Signal*, the Supreme Court stated that apportionable income includes "interest earned on short-term deposits in a bank located in another State if that income forms part of the working capital of the corporation's unitary business, notwithstanding the absence of a unitary relationship between the corporation and the bank." The taxpayer is not unitary with the payer of the income (the bank), but the taxpayer's deposits (working capital and thus operational assets) are clearly unitary with the taxpayer's business. Likewise, in *Container Corporation of America v. Franchise Tax Board* [463 U.S. 159, 1983], the Supreme Court stated that "capital transactions can serve either an investment function or an operational function," and noted that it had made this distinction in another context in *Corn Products Refining Co.* v. *Commissioner*. [350 U. S. 46, 1955] In *Corn Products*, a manufacturer purchased commodity futures to secure supplies of raw materials at an economical price. Thus, the taxpayer was not unitary with the payer of the income (the counterparty to the futures contracts), but the taxpayer's futures contracts (hedges against the risk of a price increase for raw materials) were clearly unitary with the taxpayer's business.

Finally, the Supreme Court indicated that because the Illinois appeals court did not rule on whether Mead and Lexis formed a unitary business, the Illinois appeals court may take up that issue on remand.

State Statutory Restrictions on Inclusions in Apportionable Income

The Uniform Division of Income for Tax Purposes Act (UDITPA) is a model law for apportioning the income of a corporation. The apportionment laws of most states conform, to vary degrees, to UDITPA. Under UDITPA, "business income" is apportioned among the states in which the taxpayer has nexus, whereas the entire amount of an item of "nonbusiness income" is specifically allocated to a single state. Therefore, the principal consequence of classifying an item as nonbusiness income is that the income is excluded from the tax base of every nexus state except the state in which the nonbusiness income is taxable in full (often, the state of commercial domicile). Because the classification of an item as nonbusiness income effectively removes the income from the tax base of one or more states, the business versus nonbusiness income distinction has historically been an area of significant controversy.

UDITPA Section 1(e) defines nonbusiness income as "all income other than business income." According to UDITPA Section 1(a), business income is:

> [I]ncome arising from transactions and activity in the regular course of the taxpayer's trade or business and includes income from tangible and intangible property if the acquisition, management, and disposition of the property constitute integral parts of the taxpayer's regular trade or business operations.

Therefore, under UDITPA, an item of income is classified as business income if it either arises from transactions and activity in the regular course of the taxpayer's trade or business (transactional test) or from tangible and intangible property, if the acquisition, management, and disposition of the property constitute integral parts of the taxpayer's regular trade or business operations (functional test). [MTC Reg. IV.1.(a)]

Each state is free to adopt its own definition of nonbusiness income, subject to U.S. Constitutional constraints. This can result in the same item of income being treated differently in different states. For example, when a grocery store chain sold its leasehold assets, the gain on the sale was held to be nonbusiness income in Kansas [*In re Kroger Co.*, No. 93-15316-DT (Kan. B.T.A. Feb. 13, 1997)], but business income in Illinois [*Kroger Co. v. Department of Revenue*, Nos. 1-95-1658, 1-95-2232 (Ill. App. Ct. Sept. 17, 1996)]. The Kansas court focused on the unusual nature of the sale transaction, whereas the Illinois court focused on the integral nature of the leasehold assets to the taxpayer's trade or business. Such inconsistent treatment can result in double taxation of the income in question.

Another example is a Delaware law that allocates the entire amount of a gain from the sale of property, including business property, to the state in which the asset is located. [30 Del. Code § 1903(b)] In *Director of Revenue v. CNA Holdings. Inc., f/k/a Hoechst Celanese Corp.* [No. 51, 2002 (Del. Sup. Ct. Mar. 21, 2003)], the Delaware Supreme Court ruled that a multistate corporation must comply with this statute and allocate to Delaware 100 percent of the gain from the sale of a Delaware plant, even though other states were also taxing an apportioned percentage of the gain. Although Delaware's approach resulted in double taxation, the court concluded that the statute was not unreasonable because, to the extent that Delaware may be taxing more than its share of in-state property sales, it is taxing less than its share of out-of-state property sales.

In *Oracle Corporation v. Department of Revenue* [No. TC-MD 070762C (Ore. Tax Ct., Feb. 11, 2010)], the taxpayer reported gains from the sale of stock as business income in California, its state of commercial domicile, but reported the same income as nonbusiness income on its Oregon return. The Oregon Department of Revenue argued that the taxpayer's treatment violated a duty of uniform reporting of income under UDITPA, as codified in Oregon statutes. The Tax Court rejected this argument and agreed with the taxpayer that, because of differences in state law, its method of reporting the sale of stock under California law was not controlling for Oregon tax purposes. Instead, whether the gains were business or nonbusiness income for Oregon income tax purposes was an issue to be decided on the basis of Oregon law.

Controversy Regarding Existence of Two-Part Test

In determining whether an item of income is business or nonbusiness in nature, state courts have been divided on whether the UDITPA definition of business income includes both a transactional test (i.e., "income arising from transactions and activity in the regular course of the taxpayer's trade or business") and a functional test (i.e., "income from tangible and intangible property if the acquisition, management, and disposition of the property constitute integral parts of the taxpayer's regular trade or business operations"), or just a transactional test. The transactional test looks to the frequency and regularity of the income-producing transaction in relation to the taxpayer's regular trade or business. The critical issue is whether the transaction is frequent in nature, as opposed to a rare and extraordinary event. In contrast, the functional test looks to the relationship between the underlying income-producing asset and the taxpayer's regular trade or business. The critical issue is whether the asset is integral, as opposed to incidental, to the taxpayer's business operations.

The majority view is that the UDITPA definition of business income includes both a transactional test and a functional test, and that an item of income is properly classified as business in nature if either test is met. Nevertheless, as discussed below, supreme courts in Alabama, Iowa, Kansas, Minnesota and Tennessee have held that the UDITPA definition contains only a transactional test. In each case, the decision has been followed by a legislative change to broaden the statute to include a functional test. In

2003, the Multistate Tax Commission amended MTC Regulation IV.1(a) to provide that business income means income that meets either the transactional test or the functional test.

Alabama. In *Uniroyal Tire Co. v. State Department of Revenue* [No. 1981928 (Ala. Aug. 4, 2000), the Alabama Supreme Court held that the Alabama statute (adopted verbatim from UDITPA) contained only a transactional test. In 1986, Uniroyal formed a 50-50 partnership with B.F. Goodrich, wherein Uniroyal transferred all of its business assets to the partnership and thereafter its only asset was the partnership interest. In 1990, Uniroyal sold its entire partnership interest at a gain. Despite the fact that the partnership interest produced business income prior to its sale, the Alabama Supreme Court held that the Alabama statute contained only a transactional test and that Uniroyal's complete liquidation and cessation of business did not give rise to business income under the transactional test. In 2001, the Alabama legislature broadened the statutory definition of business income to explicitly include a functional-type test. [Ala. H.B. 7 (Dec. 28, 2001)]

California. In *Hoechst Celanese Corp. v. Franchise Tax Board* [No. S085091 (Cal. May 14, 2001), *cert. denied*, No. 01-265 (U.S. Nov. 26, 2001)], the California Supreme Court analyzed the legislative history of the California definition of business income, as well as rulings in other states regarding the UDITPA definition, and concluded that the definition included both a transactional test and a functional test. The court then applied the two-part definition to the taxpayer's $389 million of pension plan reversion income and ruled that, although the transactional test was not satisfied because the pension plan reversion was an extraordinary event rather than a normal trade or business activity, the functional test was satisfied, because the pension plan assets "materially contributed" to the production of business income and therefore were integral to the taxpayer's trade or business.

In *Jim Beam Brands Co. v. Franchise Tax Board* [No. A107209 (Cal. Ct. of App., Oct. 17, 2005)], the California Court of Appeal ruled that there was no partial liquidation exception to the functional test and no independent requirement that the disposition of the property be an integral part of the corporation's trade or business operations.

Illinois. In another case involving the sale of a pipeline, *Texaco-Cities Service Pipeline Co. v. McGaw* [*182 Ill. 2d 269* (1998)], the Illinois Supreme Court interpreted the applicable state statute (which was similar to the UDITPA definition) as including both a transactional test and a functional test. Unlike the taxpayer in *Laurel Pipeline*, however, this taxpayer remained in the pipeline business after the sale, and the proceeds from the sale were immediately reinvested in the operations of the business rather than distributed as a dividend to the shareholders. Accordingly, the court ruled that the gain on the sale of pipeline assets was business in nature.

On the other hand, in *Blessing/White Inc. et al. v. Dept. of Revenue* [No. 1 01 0733 (Ill. App. Ct. 1st Dist., Mar. 29, 2002)], the Illinois Appellate Court for the First District ruled that the gain realized from a complete liquidation was nonbusiness income, because the proceeds were distributed to the shareholders and not reinvested in the business. Likewise, in *National Holdings, Inc. v. Zehnder* [No. 4-06-0148 (Ill. App. Ct. 4th Dist., Jan. 19, 2007], the Illinois Appellate Court for the Fourth District joined the First District in recognizing a business-liquidation exception to the functional test, and the court concluded that the exception applied in this case. Thus, the court ruled that the gain was nonbusiness income, because all of the liquidation proceeds were distributed to the parent company and were not reinvested in the ongoing business.

Iowa. In *Phillips Petroleum Co. v. Iowa Department of Revenue* [511 N.W.2d 608 (Iowa 1993)], the taxpayer purchased a substantial amount of its outstanding stock to stave off a hostile takeover attempt. To retire the debt incurred for this purchase, the corporation sold at a gain a significant portion of its gas and oil-producing assets, none of which were located in Iowa. Even though the assets in question had been used in the taxpayer's regular trade or business, the Iowa Supreme Court held that the gain was not business income. The court interpreted the applicable state statute (adopted verbatim from UDITPA) as "basically transactional" in nature, stating that the so-called functional test was "added to include transactions involving disposal of fixed assets by taxpayers who emphasize the trading of assets as an integral part of regular business." Noting that the enormity of the disposition was "unprecedented" and "clearly a once-in-a-corporate-lifetime occurrence," the court concluded that the gain failed the transactional test, and thus was nonbusiness income. In response to this decision, the Iowa legislature amended the Iowa statute to expressly include a functional test. [Iowa Code Ann. § 422.32]

Kansas. In 1994, the Kansas Supreme Court held that a gain on the sale of a subsidiary's stock was nonbusiness income because the Kansas statute contained only a transactional test. [*In re Chief Indus., Inc.*, No. 69972 (Kan. June 3, 1994)] In response to this decision, the Kansas legislature modified the state's statute governing the treatment of nonbusiness income. In addition, to ensure that corporations that have their headquarters office (commercial domicile) in Kansas would not be at a disadvantage with regard to treatment of nonbusiness income, Kansas passed legislation that allows corporations to elect to have all income arising from the acquisition, management, use, or disposition of tangible or intangible property treated as business income.

Minnesota. In *Firstar Corp. v. Commissioner of Revenue* [No. CX-97-600 (Minn. Mar. 12, 1998)], the Minnesota Supreme Court held that the gain realized by a Wisconsin-based bank on the sale of its headquarters office in Milwaukee was nonbusiness income. In making this determination, the court focused on two factors: 1) the frequency and regularity of similar transactions and the former business practices of the taxpayer, and 2) the subsequent use of the sale proceeds. With respect to the first factor, the sale of the headquarters office was an isolated transaction in the bank's history. In fact, prior to the sale of the headquarters office, Firstar had never sold a commercial office property. With respect to the second factor, the proceeds from the sale were not reinvested in the taxpayer's ongoing business operations, but were instead used to retire the bonds secured by the headquarters office, pay the taxes on the gain from the sale, pay a dividend to shareholders, and redeploy the capital of Firstar into acquisitions of new banks. In response to this decision, in 1999 the Minnesota legislature amended the statute to define nonbusiness income as "income of the trade or business that cannot be apportioned to this state because of the United States Constitution . . . [,] includ[ing] income that cannot constitutionally be apportioned to this state because it is derived from a capital transaction that solely serves an investment function."

Montana. In *Gannett Satellite Information Network, Inc. v. Montana Department of Revenue* [No. DA 08-0026 (Mt. Sup. Ct., Jan. 13, 2009)], the Montana Supreme Court ruled that the state's definition of "business income," which is based on UDITPA, contains both a transactional test and an independent functional test. As a result, the taxpayer's $2.54 billion gain from the sale of its cable subsidiary was apportionable business income, because the income arose from the sale of property that was regularly used in the combined reporting group's regular course of conducting its telecommunications business.

North Carolina. In *Polaroid Corp. v. Offerman* [No. 70PA98 (N.C. Oct. 12, 1998)], the North Carolina Supreme Court held that the North Carolina definition of business income includes both a transactional test and a functional test, and that "once a corporation's assets are found to constitute integral parts of the corporation's regular trade or business, income resulting from the acquisition, management, and/or disposition of those assets constitutes business income regardless of how that income is received." Under this approach, the court treated damages that the taxpayer received in a patent infringement lawsuit as business income.

In *Union Carbide Corp. v. Offerman* [No. 453A98-2 (N.C. Feb. 4, 2000)], the North Carolina Supreme Court ruled that income from a pension plan reversion did not meet the functional test because the taxpayer held only a contingent property right in the excess funds in the event of a plan termination and that contingent property right was not integral or essential to the taxpayer's regular trade or business. Moreover, the assets of the pension plan were not used to generate income in the regular business operations, were not working capital, were not used as collateral in borrowing, and were not relied on to purchase equipment or support research and development.

In *Lenox, Inc. v. Offerman* [No. 17A01 (N.C. July 20, 2001)], the North Carolina Supreme Court held that a consumer products company's gain on the complete cessation and sale of a separate and distinct operating division (a fine jewelry business) and the distribution of the sale proceeds to the corporation's parent company satisfied neither the transactional test nor the functional test, and therefore qualified as nonbusiness income. In effect, the court created an exception for dispositions of assets in a complete liquidation of a separate trade or business. Had the assets in question been disposed of under different circumstances, the sale would have given rise to business income because the assets were an integral part of the company's business.

Ohio. In *Kemppel v. Zaino* [No. 00-358, Oh. Sup. Ct. May 23, 2001)], the Ohio Supreme Court ruled that gains realized by an S corporation on the liquidating sale of its assets were nonbusiness income, because the gains were not from a sale in the regular course of a trade or business, but rather from a liquidation of assets followed by a dissolution of the corporation.

Oregon. In *Williamette Industries, Inc. v. Oregon Department of Revenue* [331 Or. 311, 15 P.3d 18 (2000)], the Oregon Supreme Court held that the Oregon definition of business income included both a transactional test and a functional test. The court also ruled that the royalty income received by an Oregon lumber company from oil and gas drilling performed on land it owned in Louisiana and Arkansas was not business income under either test. The royalty income did not satisfy the transactional test because the taxpayer's business was growing timber and making wood products, not producing oil and gas. In addition, the court refused to apply the functional test, stating that the test applies only to the sale or disposition of property, and the taxpayer had not disposed of the property in question.

In *Pennzoil Co. v. Department of Revenue* [No. S47561 (Or. Oct. 4, 2001)], Pennzoil received a $3 billion settlement from Texaco in a lawsuit involving Texaco's alleged interference with Pennzoil's negotiations to purchase Getty Oil stock. Despite the extraordinary nature of the settlement, the Oregon Supreme Court ruled that the settlement proceeds were business income under the transactional test because the settlement arose from Pennzoil's loss of a contract with Getty Oil and Pennzoil's attempt to gain access to Getty Oil's oil reserves was in the regular course of Pennzoil's petroleum business.

Pennsylvania. In *Laurel Pipeline Co. v. Commonwealth* [615 A.2d 841 (Pa. 1994)], the Pennsylvania Supreme Court interpreted the applicable state statute (adopted verbatim from UDITPA) as including both a transactional test and a functional test. In this case, the taxpayer realized a gain on the sale of a pipeline, the use of which was discontinued three years prior to the sale. The proceeds from the sale were distributed as a dividend to the corporation's shareholders immediately after the sale. Both parties agreed that the gain on the sale of the pipeline failed the transactional test. In addition, because the taxpayer was not in the business of buying and selling pipelines and the pipeline was not an integral part of the taxpayer's business at the time of its sale (its use had been discontinued three year earlier), the court held that the gain was nonbusiness income. [See also *Ross-Araco Corp. v. Commonwealth*, No. J-224-1995 (Pa. Apr. 18, 1996) (holding that the gain from the sale of undeveloped land from which the taxpayer never derived any rental or royalty income was nonbusiness income).]

Tennessee. In *Associated Partnership I, Inc. v. Huddleston* [No. 01S01-9203-CH-00045 (Tenn. Oct. 17, 1994)], the Tennessee Supreme Court ruled that a capital gain from the sale of a partnership interest that produced business income prior to its sale was nonbusiness income, because the sale was not a transaction in the regular course of the taxpayer's trade or business. The Tennessee legislature later amended the statute to incorporate a functional test. [Tenn. Code Ann. § 67-4-2004]

Nonbusiness Income Allocation Rules

When an item of income is determined to be nonbusiness income, the majority of states allocate the income to a specific state under the guidelines of Sections 4 through 8 of UDITPA and the related MTC regulations. The basic thrust of these rules is that nonbusiness income derived from real and tangible personal property is allocable to the state in which the property is physically located, whereas nonbusiness income derived from intangible property is allocable to the state of commercial domicile (except for royalties, which are allocable to the state where the intangible asset is used).

Rents, Royalties, and Gains from Realty. Nonbusiness rental, royalty, and capital gain income derived from real property is generally allocable to the state in which the underlying property is located.

Rents and Gains from Tangible Personal Property. Nonbusiness rental and capital gain income derived from tangible personal property is generally allocable to the state in which the underlying property is located if the income is taxable in that state. If the income is not taxable in the state in which the property is located, a throwback concept applies whereby the income is allocable to the state of commercial domicile. In addition, in the case of movable property, the income is allocated based on the proportionate days of use in each state.

Interest, Dividends, and Capital Gains from Intangibles. Nonbusiness capital gains from the sale of stocks, bonds, and other intangible assets are generally allocable to the state of commercial domicile. Likewise, nonbusiness interest and dividend income is generally allocable to the state of commercial domicile.

Royalties from Patents and Copyrights. Nonbusiness royalty income derived from patents or copyrights is usually allocable to the state in which the intangible asset is used if the royalties are taxable in that state. If the royalties are not taxable in the state in which the intangible is used, a throwback concept applies whereby the income is allocable to the state of commercial domicile.

For this purpose, a patent is considered used in a state to the extent that it is employed in production, fabrication, manufacturing, or other processing in the state, or to the extent a patented product is produced in the state. If the state in which the patent is used cannot be reasonably ascertained, the income is allocable to the state of commercial domicile.

Commercial Domicile. UDITPA defines commercial domicile as "the principal place from which the trade or business of the taxpayer is directed or managed." [UDITPA Section 1(b)] The commercial domicile of a corporation may or may not be the same as the state of incorporation. The MTC comments to UDITPA state that the phrase "'directed or managed' is not intended to permit both the state where the board of directors meets and the state where the company is managed to claim the commercial domicile. Instead, the phrase 'directed or managed' is intended as two words serving the same end, not as two separate concepts."

The phrase *commercial domicile* was first used by the Supreme Court in *Wheeling Steel Corp. v. Fox.* [298 U.S. 193 (1936)] Wheeling was a Delaware corporation that challenged the constitutionality of a West Virginia property tax imposed on its intangible assets. The tax was upheld on the basis that the taxpayer's "actual seat of corporate government" was located in West Virginia and that was where the "management functioned."

In the *Matter of the Appeal of Downey Toy Company* [No. 306793 (Cal. State Bd. of Equal., Jan. 31, 2008)], the California State Board of Equalization ruled that an investment holding company that was incorporated in Delaware and had no employees or operating assets was commercially domiciled in California, because that was the state from which the company "was managed and controlled and from which it received its greatest benefits and protections." As a consequence, the corporation's gain from the sale of a European company was subject to California corporate income tax. The taxpayer had argued that the company had a commercial domicile in Europe, because its only directors and shareholders (Chris Downey and his wife) traveled to Europe on the company's behalf and managed and controlled the company during those trips.

Expenses Attributable to Nonbusiness Income

Generally, if a taxpayer treats an item as nonbusiness income, any interest expense or other expenses attributable to that nonbusiness income cannot be deducted against apportionable business income. In other words, expenses attributable to nonbusiness income may be offset only against the related nonbusiness income. For example, California Code of Regulations Title 18, Section 25120(d), provides:

> In most cases an allowable deduction of a taxpayer will be applicable only to the business income arising from a particular trade or business or to a particular item of nonbusiness income. In some cases an allowable deduction may be applicable to the business incomes of more than one trade or business and/or to several items of nonbusiness income. In such cases the deduction shall be prorated among such trades or businesses and such items of nonbusiness income in a manner which fairly distributes the deduction among the classes of income to which it is applicable.

California historically required the use of the so-called interest-offset rule [Cal. Rev. & Tax. Code § 24344(b)] to compute the amount of a taxpayer's interest expense that was attributable to nonbusiness income. In *Hunt-Wesson, Inc. v. Franchise Tax Board* [120 S. Ct. 1022 (2000)], the Supreme Court ruled that

California's interest-offset rule was unconstitutional. Under California's interest-offset rule, the amount of interest expense that an out-of-state corporation could deduct against apportionable business income equaled the amount by which the taxpayer's total interest expense exceeded its nonbusiness interest and dividend income. The purpose of this rule was to prevent an out-of-state corporation from borrowing funds, making investments that generate nonbusiness income that is not subject to taxation in California, and then deducting the related interest expense against apportionable business income.

The California interest-offset rule effectively assumed that any borrowings were used first to make investments that produce nonbusiness income, even if there was no evidence to support this assumption. The Court concluded that it was not reasonable to expect that a rule that attributed all borrowings first to investments that produce nonbusiness income would accurately reflect the amount of interest expense related to nonbusiness income. Because California's offset provision was not a reasonable allocation of expense deductions to nonbusiness income, it effectively resulted in taxing the underlying nonbusiness income in violation of the Due Process Clause and Commerce Clause of the U.S. Constitution. California FTB Notice 2000-9 [Dec. 19, 2000] discusses the changes in California's interest expense allocation policy in light of the *Hunt-Wesson* decision.

In *Kroger Co.* [No. 69972 (Kan. Nov. 3, 2000)], the Kansas Supreme Court held that the interest expense incurred on a loan to defend against a hostile takeover was a nonbusiness expense and thus could not be deducted against apportionable business income. The taxpayer, an Ohio corporation operating grocery stores in Kansas, borrowed $4.1 billion to pay a special dividend to shareholders. The borrowing resulted in large amounts of interest expense, which the taxpayer deducted on its federal income tax return. Applying the transactional test (Kansas recognized only the transactional test during the years at issue, 1989–1992), the court determined that borrowing money to defend against a hostile takeover is not an expense in the regular course of business, but rather an extraordinary event. As a result, the interest expense was a nonbusiness expense allocable to Kroger's state of commercial domicile, and not apportionable to Kansas.

In *American General Realty Investment Corp., Inc.* [No. 156726 (Cal. St. Bd. of Equalization, June 25, 2003)], the California State Board of Equalization held that the taxpayer could not deduct interest expenses related to dividends that were not subject to the California corporation franchise tax.

Section 338 Elections

For a discussion of the proper treatment of gains and losses triggered by a federal Code Section 338 election as business or nonbusiness income, see the section in Part 3 entitled Section 338 Elections.

Trend in Statutory Definition of "Business Income"

Many states have broadened their definition of "business income." during the past decade.

In 1999, Minnesota amended its definition of nonbusiness income to mean "income of the trade or business that cannot be apportioned to this state because of the United States Constitution . . . [,] includ[ing] income that cannot constitutionally be apportioned to this state because it is derived from a capital transaction that solely serves an investment function" [Minn. § 290.17].

In 2001, Alabama broadened its definition of nonbusiness income to explicitly include a functional test [H.B. 7, 2001]; Mississippi amended its definition to include any income, other than income that fails both a transactional and a functional test [A.B. 1695, 2001]; and Pennsylvania broadened its definition to include "all income which is apportionable under the Constitution of the United States" [H.B. 334, 2001].

In 2002, New Jersey amended its apportionment statute to provide that "100% of the nonoperational income of a taxpayer that has its principal place from which the trade or business of the taxpayer is directed or managed in this State shall be specifically assigned to this State to the extent permitted under the Constitution and statutes of the United States" [A.B. 2501, 2002]; and North Carolina broadened its definition of business income to include "all income that is apportionable under the U.S. Constitution" [S.B. 1115, 2002].

In 2004, Illinois broadened its definition of business income to include "all income that may be treated as apportionable business income under the Constitution of the United States." [S.B. 2207, 2004] This legislation also requires the recapture of expenses related to an asset or activity if income previously classified as business income from that asset or activity is determined in a later year to be nonbusiness income. In addition, in 2004 the Oregon Department of Revenue adopted a regulation, which provides that business income includes income of any type or class, and from any activity, that meets either the transactional test or the functional test. [OAR 150-314.610(1)-(A)(2)]

In 2005, Georgia amended its apportionment statute to provide that the state's corporate income tax applies to a corporation's income "to the extent permitted by the United States Constitution." [H.B. 488, 2005]

In 2006, the Kentucky Department of Revenue adopted an emergency regulation, which provides that the department will apply both the transactional test and the functional test in determining whether income is business income [Ky. Reg. 103 KAR 16:060E, Feb. 1, 2006].

In 2008, Kansas broadened its definition of "business income" to include: (1) income arising from transactions and activity in the regular course of the taxpayer's trade or business; (2) income arising from transactions and activity involving tangible and intangible property or assets used in the operation of the taxpayer's trade or business; or (3) income of the taxpayer that may be apportioned to this state under the provisions of the Constitution of the United States and laws thereof, except that a taxpayer may elect that all income constitutes business income. [H.B. 2434, May 22, 2008]

In addition, the Utah Tax Commission changed its regulatory definition of "business income" to conform to the MTC regulations, which provide that "business income" means income that meets either the transactional test or the functional test. [Rule R865-6F-8, Utah Admin. Code, Sept. 9, 2008]

Recent Developments

Alabama. In *Kimberly-Clark Corporation v. Department of Revenue* [No. 1070925 (Ala. Sup. Ct., Feb. 26, 2010)], Kimberly-Clark (KC) was a manufacturer of paper-related consumer products. In 1962, KC purchased a pulp/paper mill and 375,000 acres of timberland located in Alabama ("Coosa properties"). Production from the Coosa properties constituted the majority of KC's pulp production. In the early 1990s, KC changed its corporate strategy from being primarily a manufacturer of consumer-paper products to becoming a global consumer-products company. Consistent with its new strategy, KC sought to reduce its dependence on internally produced pulp. To further this goal, in 1998, KC sold the Coosa properties for $600 million. Based on its ruling in *Uniroyal Tire Company v. State Department of Revenue* [779 So.2d 227, 2000] that the state's statutory definition of business income during the 1990s contained only a transactional test, the Supreme Court of Alabama ruled that KC's sale of the Coosa properties was an extraordinary transaction that did not generate business income under the transactional test. The Supreme Court of Alabama reasoned that "[i]t is difficult to conceive how the sale of properties that had been operated by the company as part of its business for 34 years and were sold because of a new corporate strategy could be said to be in the 'regular course of business' for KC."

Louisiana. In *BP Products North America, Inc. v. Bridges* [No. 2010 CA 1860 (La. Ct. of App., Aug. 10, 2011)], the taxpayer was engaged in oil and gas exploration, production, transportation, refining and distribution. In 2000, as part of a larger strategic plan of examining all refineries owned by the taxpayer, parent, and other subsidiaries, the taxpayer sold its Louisiana refinery at a $496 million gain and treated the gain as apportionable income. The Department of Revenue argued that the gain was allocable income that was taxable in full in Louisiana, because the taxpayer was not in the business of buying and selling refineries for profit, and the transaction was a one-time asset divesture rather than a sale in the regular course of business. The appellate court rejected the Department's argument, and held that the gain was apportionable income, because the sale was part of the company's strategic plan to streamline its refining operations, and because this type of sale was a regular practice of the company. BP had bought and sold many refineries over the years, and neither the taxpayer nor its parent went out of business after this sale or similar sales. The gain from the sale was invested in other segments of the company's business and was not distributed to shareholders.

Maine. In *Gannett Co., Inc. v. State Tax Assessor* [No. Ken-07-629 (Me. Sup. Jud. Ct., Nov. 18, 2008)], the Maine Supreme Judicial Court held that a corporation's cable, broadcast news, and newspaper affiliates constituted a single unitary business. As a result, it was constitutionally permissible for Maine to tax an apportioned share of the corporation's $2.54 billion gain from the sale of its cable affiliate. In concluding that a unitary business existed, the court noted that the corporation provided intercompany services to the affiliates at cost, the affiliates shared operational expertise and legal services, centralized health and benefit plans were in place, a system of interlocking directors and officers existed, and a common pool of cash was available for capital and operating expenses.

Massachusetts. In *W.R. Grace & Co.-Conn. v. Commissioner of Revenue* [No. C271787 (Mass. App. Tax Bd., Apr. 6, 2009)], the Massachusetts Appellate Tax Board ruled that interest and dividend income received by an out-of-state parent corporation as a result of internal financing transactions undertaken to raise capital for the parent was not apportionable business income, because the parent and the subsidiaries were not engaged in a unitary business. In concluding that a unitary business did not exist, the court noted that there was no functional integration, centralization of management, or economies of scales between the parties. Moreover, the transactions that gave rise to the income served an investment purpose, rather than an operational function. The board also ruled that the affiliates had no actual or expected use of the interest or dividend income for their operations within Massachusetts.

Michigan. In *Reynolds Metals Company LLC v. Department of Treasury* [No. 08-68-MT (Mich. Ct. of Cl., Aug. 16, 2010)], the Michigan Court of Claims held that a parent corporation's capital gain on the sale of stock of a subsidiary was not includible in the Michigan single business tax base, because there was little evidence of functional integration, centralization of management, and economies of scale.

Pennsylvania. In *Glatfelter Pulpwood Co. v. Commonwealth of Pennsylvania* [No. 362 F.R. 2007, Pa. Commw. Ct., May 4, 2011], the Pennsylvania Commonwealth Court ruled that the taxpayer's $55 million gain from the sale of timberland met the definition of business income. The taxpayer was in the business of procuring pulpwood from either company-owned timberland or from unrelated third parties. Based on a business decision, the taxpayer began selling off some of its company-owned timberland, reducing the percentage of pulpwood received from company timber from 25 percent to 5 percent. During the tax year in question, the taxpayer sold off some acres in Delaware and realized a net gain of $55 million. The taxpayer then distributed all of the proceeds from this sale to its parent who then used the funds to pay off debt and to pay dividends. The Delaware sale did not satisfy the transactional test, because it was a one-time event. The taxpayer argued that the sale also did not satisfy the functional test, because it constituted a partial liquidation of a unique aspect of its assets. The court concluded that the sale was not a partial liquidation but rather the disposition of property used in producing business income, in which case the functional test was satisfied.

Tennessee. In *Blue Bell Creameries v. Commissioner,* Department of Revenue [No. M2009-00255-SC-R11-CV, Jan. 24, 2011], the Tennessee Supreme Court ruled that a $120 million capital gain realized by a subsidiary from stock redemption qualified as business income. The stock redemption did not satisfy the transactional test, because it was a one-time, extraordinary transaction. However, it did satisfy the functional test, because the acquisition and sale of the stock contributed materially to the production of business earnings. The taxpayer was in the business of producing and distributing ice cream, and the stock redemption was part of a reorganization of the business entities that constituted the ice cream business. The reorganization reduced expenses and removed one level of federal taxation on the earnings arising from the ice cream business. Taxation of the gain was also constitutional under the unitary business principle, because the reorganization served an operational function and both subsidiary and the parent derived their income from a single underlying activity.

State-by-State Summary

The following chart, divided into two parts, indicates how each state distinguishes between business and nonbusiness income, and the states' allocation provisions for various types of nonbusiness income, such as gains and losses from sales of tangible and intangible property, patent or copyright royalties, dividends, interest, and rents from tangible personal property and from real property.

Allocation of Nonbusiness Income (Part 1)

Legend:
NA Not applicable
NR Not reported

	How Does State Define Business Income?	*How Does State Define Nonbusiness Income?*
Alabama	All income that arises from the conduct of trade or business operations of a taxpayer is business income.	Nonbusiness income means all income other than business income. Apply either a functional and transactional test.
Alaska	UDITPA definition.	UDITPA definition. Apply either a transactional or a functional test.
Arizona	UDITPA definition.	UDITPA definition.
Arkansas	UDITPA definition.	UDITPA definition. An item is business income if it meets transactional and functional test.
California	Income arising from transactions (see R&TC § 25120(a)) and activity in the regular course of the taxpayer's trade or business and includes income from tangible and intangible property if the acquisition, management, and disposition of the property constitute integral parts of the taxpayer's regular trade or business operations.	All income other than business income. See R&TC §§ 25120, 25120(d). Apply both a transactional or functional test. See *Hoechst Celanese Corp. v. FTB*, 25 Cal. 4th 508 (2001).
Colorado	UDITPA definitions	UDITPA; apply both a transactional and a functional test.
Connecticut	No written guidance	No written guidance
Delaware	All income apportioned, except allocated nonbusiness income.	Rents, royalties, interest, gain (loss) on sales of tangible and real property.
District of Columbia	Same as UDITPA	Same as UDITPA, either the transactional test or the functional test
Florida	Activities and transactions in the regular course of taxpayer's trade or business. Includes any amounts that could be included in apportionable income without violating the due process clause.	All income other than business income

Allocation of Nonbusiness Income (Part 1)

Legend:
NA — Not applicable
NR — Not reported

	How Does State Define Business Income?	*How Does State Define Nonbusiness Income?*
Georgia	All income except certain limited types of investment income. See O.C.G.A. § 48-7-31(a).	GA does not use the term, non-business income. GA allocates investment income as well as gains or losses from the sale of assets not held, owned, or used in connection with the trade or business of the corporation. Apply either a transactional or functional test.
Hawaii	Follow MTC guidelines.	Follow MTC guidelines; apply either a transactional or a functional test.
Idaho	Income from transactions and activities in the regular course of taxpayer's trade or business. Business income is also income from the acquisition, management, or disposition of tangible and intangible property when such acquisition, management, or disposition constitute integral or necessary parts of the taxpayer's trade or business operations.	All income other than business income; apply either a transactional or a functional test.
Illinois	35 ILCS 5/1501(a)(1), all income that may be treated as apportionable business income under the U.S. Constitution.	35 ILCS 5/1501(a)(1), all income other than business income and compensation.
Indiana	Income from transactions and activity in the regular course of the taxpayer's trade or business, including income from tangible and intangible property if the acquisition, management, and disposition of the property are integral parts of the taxpayer's regular trade or business.	All income other than business income; apply both a transactional and a functional test.
Iowa	Income earned as part of a unitary business.	Income not earned as part of a unitary business.
Kansas	Income from transactions and activities in the regular course of taxpayer's trade or business. Income arising from transactions and activities involving tangible and intangible property or assets used in the operation of the taxpayer's trade or business. Income of the taxpayer that may be apportioned to this state under the provisions of the Constitution of the U.S. and laws thereof, except that a taxpayer may elect that all income constitutes business income.	Any income other than business income, both the transactional test and functional test

Allocation of Nonbusiness Income (Part 1)

Legend:

NA Not applicable

NR Not reported

	How Does State Define Business Income?	How Does State Define Nonbusiness Income?
Kentucky	Same as UDITPA.	Both the transactional or functional test.
Louisiana	Louisiana does not apply the business/nonbusiness concepts outlined by the MTC. The two classes of income are apportionable and allocable.	Louisiana does not apply the business/nonbusiness concepts outlined by the MTC. The two classes of income are apportionable and allocable.
Maine	All unless non-apportionable	Those that are constitutionally excluded.
Maryland	All items are considered business income.	None, all items are considered business income.
Massachusetts	Full apportionment modified by *Allied-Signal.*	Investment income on nondomiciliary corporations is excluded from apportionable income base to the extent required by Allied-Signal. See TIR 92-5. Do not recognize nonbusiness income.
Michigan (Business Tax)	Business income means that part of federal taxable income derived from business activity. For MBT purposes, federal taxable income means taxable income as defined by IRC § 63, except that federal taxable income shall be calculated as if IRC § 168(k) [as applied to qualified property placed in service after 12/31/07] and IRC § 199 were not in effect. For a partnership or S corporation (or LLC federally taxed as such), business income includes payments and items of income and expense that are attributable to business activity of the partnership or S corporation and separately reported to the partners or shareholders.	Not defined under MBT
Note. The CIT takes effect 01/01/12, and replaces the Michigan Business Tax (MBT) for most taxpayers. However, businesses that have been approved to receive, have received, or have been assigned certain certified credits may elect to file a return and pay the tax imposed by the MBT in lieu of the CIT until the certified credits are exhausted or extinguished.		
Minnesota	All income other than that income that cannot constitutionally be apportioned to the state.	Income of a trade or business that cannot constitutionally be apportioned to the state; apply constitutional test.

Allocation of Nonbusiness Income (Part 1)

Legend:
NA Not applicable
NR Not reported

	How Does State Define Business Income?	*How Does State Define Nonbusiness Income?*
Mississippi	Business income means income arising from transactions and activities in the regular course of the taxpayer's trade or business and includes income from real, tangible, and intangible property if the acquisition, management, and disposition of the property constitute integral parts of the taxpayer's regular trade or business operations. In essence, all income that arises from the conduct of trade or business operations of a taxpayer is business income. The income of the taxpayer is business income unless clearly classifiable as nonbusiness income.	All nonbusiness income; non-US interest and dividends; U.S. government interest; apply either a transactional or a function test.
Missouri	See MTC and MO regulations.	See MTC regulations, apply both the transactional and functional test.
Montana	Same as UDITPA	Same as UDITPA, either the transactional test or the functional test
Nebraska	All income is presumed to be business income.	None
Nevada	Nevada does not impose a corporate income tax	
New Hampshire	All income is business income unless excluded pursuant to federal constitutional law	New Hampshire has no nonbusiness income provision
New Jersey	Operational income, analogous to the Allied Signal case.	No definitions for business and nonbusiness income. New Jersey has constitutional exclusion for "non-operational" income. See *Allied Signal v. Director*, 504 U.S. 768 (1992) and N.J. Stat. Ann 54:10A-6.1. See instructions on CBT-100, Schedule O. Apply a transactional, functional, and operational test (did property serve an operational rather than investment function).
New Mexico	UDITPA definition.	UDITPA definition.

Allocation of Nonbusiness Income (Part 1)

Legend:
NA Not applicable
NR Not reported

	How Does State Define Business Income?	*How Does State Define Nonbusiness Income?*
New York	All income is either business, investment, or subsidiary in nature. Stock ownership of more than 50% is subsidiary, less than 50% is investment.	All income is either business, investment, or subsidiary in nature. Stock ownership of more than 50% is subsidiary, less than 50% is investment.
North Carolina	Effective 8/14/2003, North Carolina replaced the term "business income" with "apportionable income'. The state uses the term "apportionable income", which is defined as "all income that is apportionable under the U.S. Constitution. G.S. 105-130.4(a)(1).	Income from unrelated business activities that make up a discrete business enterprise is "nonbusiness income." Effective 8/14/2003, North Carolina replaced the term "nonbusiness income" with "nonapportionable income". "Nonapportionable income" means all income other than apportionable income.
North Dakota	UDITPA definition.	UDITPA definition; apply both a transactional and a functional test.
Ohio	Ohio does not impose a corporate income tax	
Note. Effective 1/1/2010, the Ohio Franchise Tax was fully phased out and business will be taxed on gross receipts through the Commercial Activity Tax. Details about that tax can be found at: http//tax.ohio.gov/divisions/commercial_activities/index.stm		
Oklahoma	NA	NA
Oregon	Income arising from transactions and activities in the regular course of the taxpayer's trade or business and includes income from tangible and intangible property if the acquisition, management, use or rental and disposition of the property constitute integral parts of the taxpayer's regular trade or business operations. This includes sales of product or services, rents and royalties from real and tangible personal property, gains and losses from sales of assets, interest, dividends, patent and copyright royalties.	All income other than business income. This includes income from investments not related to or used in the operation of the taxpayer's business. Specific statutory provisions for allocation of nonbusiness rents, royalties, capital gains and losses, interest, dividends, lottery prizes, and patent and copyright royalties. Apply both a transactional and a functional test.
Pennsylvania	All income arising from normal and usual transactions; all income apportionable under the U.S. Constitution.	All other items of income; apply both a transactional and a functional test.
Rhode Island	All	None

Allocation of Nonbusiness Income (Part 1)

Legend:
NA Not applicable
NR Not reported

	How Does State Define Business Income?	*How Does State Define Nonbusiness Income?*
South Carolina	Any income that is part of the taxpayer's unitary business.	Income earned from sources other than the taxpayer's unitary business.
South Dakota	South Dakota does not impose a corporate income tax	
Tennessee	Earnings arising from transactions and activities in the regular course of the taxpayer's trade or business or earnings from tangible and intangible property if the acquisition, use management, or disposition of the property constitutes an integral part of the taxpayer's regular trade or business operations. See 67-4-2004(1) TCA.	All income other than "business" earnings. Apply both a transactional and a functional test.
Texas	All income except income that a state could not tax even if the corporation had nexus in that state.	Income a state could not tax even if the corporation had nexus in that state; constitutional standard.
Utah	Standard UDITPA definition, included if income satisfies an operational function; Utah employs both a transactional and functional test, either of which if met will require apportionment.	All income that is not business income. Meeting either transactional or function test generates business income.
Vermont	Receipts from regular business activities.	Receipts unrelated to regular business activities; apply either a transactional or a functional test.
Virginia	Virginia does not distinguish business and nonbusiness income. Statute allocates only dividends, and apportions all other income. Taxpayers may request allocation of specific items of income under VA code 58.1-421 for which apportionment would be unconstitutional under *Allied Signal*.	Virginia does not distinguish business and nonbusiness income; apply both a transactional and a functional test.
Washington	Washington does not impose a corporate income tax	

Allocation of Nonbusiness Income (Part 1)

Legend:
NA — Not applicable
NR — Not reported

	How Does State Define Business Income?	*How Does State Define Nonbusiness Income?*
West Virginia	Income from transactions and activities in the regular course of taxpayer's trade or business, including income from tangible and intangible property if the acquisition, management, and disposition of the property constitute integral parts of taxpayer's regular trade or business operations.	Rentals, royalties, capital gains (losses), interest, and dividends, if the taxpayer's commercial domicile is in West Virginia; patent, copyright royalties, and partnership income. Apply both a transactional and a functional test.
Wisconsin	All income except nonbusiness items.	Income other than business income. Apply both a transactional and a functional test.
Wyoming	Wyoming does not impose a corporate income tax	

Allocation of Nonbusiness Income (Part 2)

Legend:
NA Not applicable
NR Not reported

	Gains (Losses) from Sales of Tangible Personal Property	*Gains (Losses) from Sales of Intangible Property*	*Patent/Copyright Royalties*	*Dividends*	*Interest*	*Rents/Royalties from Tangible Personal Property*	*Rents/Royalties from Real Property*
Alabama	Situs of property	Commercial domicile	Commercial domicile or state where the income is generated	Commercial domicile or state where the income is generated	Commercial domicile or state where the income is generated	Commercial domicile or state where the income is generated	Situs of property
Alaska	Situs of property but commercial domicile if taxpayer is not taxable in state where property had a situs.	Commercial domicile	State where utilized but commercial domicile if taxpayer is not taxable in state where utilized.	Commercial domicile	Commercial domicile	State where income is generated but commercial domicile if taxpayer is not taxable in state where income was generated.	Situs of property
Arizona	Situs of property	Commercial domicile or state where the income is generated	Commercial domicile or state where income is generated	Commercial domicile or state where income is generated	Commercial domicile or state where income is generated	Situs of the income-producing property	Situs of property
Arkansas	Situs of property	Commercial domicile	Situs of property	Commercial domicile	Commercial domicile	Situs of property	Situs of property

Allocation of Nonbusiness Income (Part 2)

Legend:
NA — Not applicable
NR — Not reported

	Gains (Losses) from Sales of Tangible Personal Property	*Gains (Losses) from Sales of Intangible Property*	*Patent/Copyright Royalties*	*Dividends*	*Interest*	*Rents/Royalties from Tangible Personal Property*	*Rents/Royalties from Real Property*
California	Situs of property, but commercial domicile of taxpayer if the taxpayer is not taxable in the state where the property had a situs. See R&TC § 25125(b).	Commercial domicile, except for sale of partnership interest. See R&TC § 25125(c) and (d).	State in which income is generated, unless no nexus in state of use, then commercial domicile. See R&TC § 25127(b).	Commercial domicile	Commercial domicile	Situs of property, but commercial domicile of taxpayer if the taxpayer is not taxable in the state where the property had a situs	Situs of property
Colorado	Situs of property	Commercial domicile	Situs of property	Commercial domicile	Commercial domicile	Situs of property	Situs of property
	Under MTC 3-factor election						
Connecticut	Apportioned unless prohibited by US Constitution	Apportioned unless prohibited by US Constitution	Apportioned unless prohibited by US Constitution	Apportioned unless prohibited by US Constitution	Apportioned unless prohibited by US Constitution	Apportioned unless prohibited by US Constitution	Apportioned unless prohibited by US Constitution
Delaware	Situs of property	Apportioned	Situs of property	Apportioned	Situs of property	Situs of property	Situs of property

Allocation of Nonbusiness Income (Part 2)

Legend:
NA Not applicable
NR Not reported

	Gains (Losses) from Sales of Tangible Personal Property	*Gains (Losses) from Sales of Intangible Property*	*Patent/Copyright Royalties*	*Dividends*	*Interest*	*Rents/Royalties from Tangible Personal Property*	*Rents/Royalties from Real Property*
District of Columbia	Situs of property, state where income generated	Situs of property, state where income generated	State where the income is generated, commercial domicile, situs of property	State where income is generated, situs of property, commercial domicile	State where income is generated, situs of property, commercial domicile	Situs of property, state where income generated	Situs of property, state where income generated
Florida	Situs of property	Commercial domicile	State in which property generating income is located	Commercial domicile	Commercial domicile	Situs of property	Situs of property
Georgia	Situs of property	Actual situs or business situs	Actual situs or business situs	Actual situs or business situs	Actual situs or business situs	Situs of property	Situs of property
Hawaii	Situs of property, taxpayer's commercial domicile in Hawaii	Situs of property, taxpayer's commercial domicile in Hawaii	Situs of property, taxpayer's commercial domicile in Hawaii	Situs of property, taxpayer's commercial domicile in Hawaii	Situs of property, taxpayer's commercial domicile in Hawaii	Situs of property, taxpayer's commercial domicile in Hawaii	Situs of property

Allocation of Nonbusiness Income (Part 2)

Legend:
NA Not applicable
NR Not reported

	Gains (Losses) from Sales of Tangible Personal Property	*Gains (Losses) from Sales of Intangible Property*	*Patent/Copyright Royalties*	*Dividends*	*Interest*	*Rents/Royalties from Tangible Personal Property*	*Rents/Royalties from Real Property*
Idaho	Situs of property, but commercial domicile of taxpayer if taxpayer is not taxable in state where property had a situs	Commercial domicile	State in which income is generated unless not taxable in that state, then commercial domicile	Commercial domicile	Commercial domicile	To the extent used in state or entirely commercial domicile if in Idaho and the taxpayer is not taxable in the state where property used	Situs of property
Illinois	Situs of property. Commercial domicile if corporation is taxable in state where property had situs or usage	Commercial domicile	Situs of property. Commercial domicile if corporation is taxable in state where property had situs or usage	Commercial domicile	Commercial domicile	State where the income is generated, commercial domicile if corporation is taxable in state where property had situs or usage	Situs of property
Indiana	Situs of property	Commercial domicile	Commercial domicile	Commercial domicile	Commercial domicile	Situs of property	Situs of property
Iowa	Situs of property	Commercial domicile	Commercial domicile	Commercial domicile	Commercial domicile	Situs of property	Situs of property
Kansas	Situs of property	Commercial domicile	State where the income is generated	Commercial domicile	Commercial domicile	Situs of property	Situs of property

Allocation of Nonbusiness Income (Part 2)

Legend:
NA — Not applicable
NR — Not reported

	Gains (Losses) from Sales of Tangible Personal Property	*Gains (Losses) from Sales of Intangible Property*	*Patent/Copyright Royalties*	*Dividends*	*Interest*	*Rents/Royalties from Tangible Personal Property*	*Rents/Royalties from Real Property*
Kentucky	Situs of property	Commercial domicile	Situs of property	Not taxed	Commercial domicile	Situs of property	Situs of property
Louisiana	Apportioned	Apportioned	Situs of property	Not taxed	Not taxed	State where the income is generated	State where the income is generated
Maine	NA	NA	NA	NA	NA	NA	NA
Maryland	No distinction made between business and nonbusiness; apportioned in the usual manner						
Massachusetts	No distinction made between business and nonbusiness; apportioned in the usual manner						
Michigan (Business Tax)	No distinction made between business and nonbusiness; apportioned in the usual manner						
Note. The CIT takes effect 01/01/12, and replaces the Michigan Business Tax (MBT) for most taxpayers. However, businesses that have been approved to receive, have received, or have been assigned certain certified credits may elect to file a return and pay the tax imposed by the MBT in lieu of the CIT until the certified credits are exhausted or extinguished.							
Minnesota	Situs of property	Commercial domicile	Commercial domicile	Commercial domicile	Commercial domicile	Situs of property	Situs of property
Mississippi	Situs of property	Commercial domicile or situs of property	Situs of property	Commercial domicile	Situs of property	Situs of property	Situs of property
Missouri	Situs of property	Commercial domicile	Commercial domicile	Exempt	Commercial domicile	Situs of property	Situs of property
Montana	Situs of property	Situs of property or commercial domicile	Situs of property or commercial domicile	Commercial domicile	State where is income generated	Situs of property	Situs of property

Allocation of Nonbusiness Income (Part 2)

Legend:
NA Not applicable
NR Not reported

	Gains (Losses) from Sales of Tangible Personal Property	*Gains (Losses) from Sales of Intangible Property*	*Patent/Copyright Royalties*	*Dividends*	*Interest*	*Rents/Royalties from Tangible Personal Property*	*Rents/Royalties from Real Property*
Nebraska	NA	NA	NA	NA	NA	NA	NA
Nevada	Nevada does not impose a corporate income tax						
New Hampshire	NA	NA	NA	NA	NA	NA	NA
New Jersey	Nonbusiness income is not subject to apportionment but is "assigned." 100% of nonoperational income of a taxpayer whose principal place of management is in New Jersey is assigned to New Jersey.						
New Mexico	Situs of property	Commercial domicile	Situs of property	Commercial domicile	Situs of property	Situs of property	Situs of property
New York	Apportioned	Apportioned	Apportioned	Apportioned	Apportioned	Apportioned	Apportioned
North Carolina	Situs of property	Commercial domicile	State where the income is generated; situs of property	Commercial domicile	Commercial domicile	Situs of property	Situs of property
North Dakota	Situs of property	Domicile of property	Domicile of payee, where utilized	Domicile of payee	State where income is generated	Situs of property	Situs of property
Ohio	Ohio does not impose a corporate income tax						

Note A. Effective 1/1/2010, the Ohio Franchise Tax was fully phased out and business will be taxed on gross receipts through the Commercial Activity Tax. Details about that tax can be found at: http//tax.ohio.gov/divisions/commercial_activities/index.stm

Oklahoma	Apportioned	Situs of property	Apportioned	Commercial domicile	Commercial domicile	Situs of property	Situs of property

Allocation of Nonbusiness Income (Part 2)

Legend:
NA — Not applicable
NR — Not reported

	Gains (Losses) from Sales of Tangible Personal Property	*Gains (Losses) from Sales of Intangible Property*	*Patent/Copyright Royalties*	*Dividends*	*Interest*	*Rents/Royalties from Tangible Personal Property*	*Rents/Royalties from Real Property*
Oregon	Situs of property	Commercial domicile	State where income is generated	Commercial domicile of recipient	Commercial domicile of recipient	Situs of property	Situs of property
Pennsylvania	Situs of property	Commercial domicile	Commercial domicile	Excluded	Commercial domicile	Situs of property	Situs of property
Rhode Island	NA	NA	NA	NA	NA	NA	NA
South Carolina	Apportioned	Commercial domicile or individual's state of domicile	Commercial domicile, or individual's state of domicile	Commercial domicile or individual's state of domicile	Commercial domicile or individual's state of domicile	Situs of property	Situs of property
	South Carolina does not adopt the UDITPA definitions of business/nonbusiness income						
South Dakota	South Dakota does not impose a corporate income tax						
Tennessee	Situs of property	Commercial domicile	State where income is generated	Commercial domicile	Commercial domicile	Situs of property	Situs of property
Texas	Apportioned	Apportioned	Apportioned	Apportioned	Apportioned	Apportioned	Apportioned
Utah	Situs of property	Commercial domicile	Commercial domicile	Commercial domicile	Commercial domicile	Situs of property	Situs of property
Vermont	Situs of property	Commercial domicile	State in which income is generated	Commercial domicile	Commercial domicile	Situs of property	Situs of property
Virginia	Apportioned	Apportioned	Apportioned	Commercial domicile	Apportioned	Apportioned	Apportioned

Allocation of Nonbusiness Income (Part 2)

Legend:
NA Not applicable
NR Not reported

	Gains (Losses) from Sales of Tangible Personal Property	*Gains (Losses) from Sales of Intangible Property*	*Patent/Copyright Royalties*	*Dividends*	*Interest*	*Rents/Royalties from Tangible Personal Property*	*Rents/Royalties from Real Property*
Washington	Washington does not impose a corporate income tax						
West Virginia	Situs of property	Commercial domicile	State in which income is generated	Commercial domicile	Commercial domicile	Commercial domicile	Situs of property
Wisconsin	Situs of property	Apportioned	Apportioned	Apportioned	Apportioned	Situs of property	Situs of property
Wyoming	Wyoming does not impose a corporate income tax						

Property Factor

Despite the trend towards a single-factor sales-only apportionment formula, most states that impose a corporate income tax still employ a three-factor formula that includes a property factor. Thus, the computation of the property factor remains a regular chore for multistate taxpayers. The provisions governing the determination of the property factor generally conform to the guidance provided by the Uniform Division of Income for Tax Purposes Act (UDITPA) and the associated Multistate Tax Commission (MTC) regulations.

Meaning of "Property"

Under UDITPA, the property factor is a fraction, the numerator of which is the average value of the taxpayer's real and tangible personal property owned or rented and used in the state during the tax year and the denominator of which is the average value of all the taxpayer's real and tangible personal property owned or rented and used during the tax year. [UDITPA Section 10] Under the MTC regulations, real and tangible personal property includes "land, buildings, machinery, stocks of goods, equipment, and other real and tangible personal property but does not include coin or currency." [MTC Reg. IV.10.(a)] Leasehold improvements are generally treated as property owned by the taxpayer regardless of whether the taxpayer is entitled to remove the improvements or the improvements revert to the lessor at the end of the lease. [e.g., Cal. Code of Regs. § 25130(b)(5)] Business assets other than real and tangible personal property, such as accounts receivable, marketable securities, patents, trademarks and other intangibles, are excluded from the property factor.

Business Use Requirement

Real and tangible personal property owned or rented by the taxpayer is included in the property factor only if it is "used during the tax period in the regular course of the trade or business." [MTC Reg. IV.10.(a)] Property used to produce nonbusiness income is excluded from the property factor. Property used both in the regular course of the taxpayer's trade or business and in the production of nonbusiness income is included in the property factor only to the extent that the property is used in the regular course of the taxpayer's trade or business, based on the facts of each case. [MTC Reg. IV.10.(a)]

Idle property. The business use requirement is satisfied if the property is "actually used or is available for or capable of being used during the tax period in the regular course of the trade or business of the taxpayer." Thus, standby facilities, a plant that is temporarily idle, and raw material reserves not currently being processed are all includable in the factor. For example, if a taxpayer closes a manufacturing plant and puts the property up for sale, even if the property remains vacant until its sale one year later, the value of the plant is included in the property factor until the plant is sold. [MTC Reg. IV.10.(b), Example (i)]

Property is removed from the property factor, however, if its permanent withdrawal from service is established by an identifiable event, such as an extended period of time (normally, five years) during which the property is no longer held for use in the trade or business. [MTC Reg. IV.10.(b)] For example, if a chain of retail grocery stores closes one of its stores and remodels the space into three small retail stores (e.g., a dress shop, dry cleaner, and barber shop) that are leased to unrelated parties, the taxpayer removes the store from the property factor upon commencement of the remodeling. [MTC Reg. IV.10.(b), Example (iv)]

Construction-in-progress. With the exception of inventoriable goods, property or equipment that is under construction during the tax year is excluded from the property factor until the date on which the property is placed into service and actually used in the regular course of the taxpayer's trade or business. If the property is partially used in the regular course of the taxpayer's trade or business while under construction, the construction-in-progress ("CIP") costs are included in the property factor to the extent the property is used. [MTC Reg. IV.10.(b)]

In Technical Advice Memorandum 2011-1 [Cal. Fran. Tax Bd., Jan. 6, 2011], the California Franchise Tax Board ruled that a home builder's or developer's CIP is excluded from the California property factor, because it is not property owned or rented and used in California during the tax year. On the other hand, real property that has not yet become CIP or that is not CIP because it has been completed and is held for sale is includible in the property factor. Examples include undeveloped and partially developed land (regardless of whether development activities for that land are actual or planned), completed lots purchased prior to house construction, completed houses under sales contract, completed speculative houses, completed model houses (whether used as models or available for sale), and completed community improvements such as parks, libraries, clubhouses, community centers, and parkways.

For example, in *Lockheed Martin Corporation v. State Tax Commissio* n [142 Idaho 790 (Idaho Sup. Ct., 2006)], the Idaho Supreme Court ruled that the taxpayer was not required to include in its property factor the CIP costs associated with a building that the taxpayer was constructing to clean up nuclear and hazardous waste, because it was not being used in the regular course of the taxpayer's trade or business.

On the other hand, in *Commissioner of Revenue v. New England Power Company* [411 Mass. 418 (Mass. Sup. Jud. Ct., 1991)], the Massachusetts Supreme Judicial Court ruled that a public utility company properly included in the property factor the CIP costs associated with the construction of two nuclear power plants. The taxpayer's construction of the power plants was a necessary function of its business, and the inclusion of the CIP costs in the federally set rate base indirectly generated income for the taxpayer. Therefore, although the power plants would not be producing income or be available for use until they were completed, the taxpayer was using the plants to meet its responsibilities as a public utility and the CIP costs were properly included in its property factor.

Consistency in reporting requirement. Under the MTC regulations, if a taxpayer modifies the manner of excluding, including or valuing property in the property factor used in prior year returns, the taxpayer must disclose the nature of the modification in its current year return. In addition, if the state tax returns filed by the taxpayer are not uniform in the valuation of property and in the exclusion of property from or the inclusion of property in the property factor, the taxpayer must disclose the nature of the variance in its tax returns. [MTC Reg. IV.10.(c)]

Numerator of Property Factor

The numerator of the property factor is the value of the taxpayer's property owned or rented and used in the state during the tax year. [UDITPA Section 10] Given that only real or tangible personal property are included in the property factor, the physical location of the property's use is the controlling factor in determining the numerator of the property factor.

Mobile property. The value of mobile property, such as trucks, construction equipment, or leased electronic equipment, which is located both within and without this state during the tax year is included in the numerator of the property factor based on the total time within the state during the tax year. [MTC Reg. IV.10.(d)] Generally, different rules apply to taxpayers in specialized industries, such as airlines, trucking companies and construction contractors. For example, under the MTC regulations, an airline includes its aircraft in a state's numerator based on the ratio of in-state departures, weighted by the value of aircraft, to the total departures everywhere, similarly weighted. [MTC Reg. IV.18(e)] Another example is motor vehicles and trailers operated by a trucking company, which are included in a state's numerator based on the ratio of mobile property miles in the state to total mobile property miles. [MTC Reg. IV.18(g)]

An automobile assigned to a traveling employee is included in the numerator of the property factor of the state to which the employee's compensation is assigned for purposes of computing the payroll factor or in the numerator of the state in which the automobile is licensed. [MTC Reg. IV.10.(d)]

Property in transit. Property owned by the taxpayer and in transit between locations of the taxpayer is included in the numerator of the destination state. Likewise, property in transit between a buyer and seller which is included by a taxpayer in the denominator of its property factor in accordance with its regular accounting practices is included in the numerator of the destination state. [MTC Reg. IV.10.(d)]

In *Appeal of Craig Corporation* [87-SBE-013 (Cal. St. Bd. of Equalization, Mar. 3, 1987)], the California State Board of Equalization held that when inventory in transit is gathered, sorted, and inspected by the taxpayer at its facilities in California, following its importation from Asia but prior to its shipment to the taxpayer's facilities in other states, the inventory is no longer considered to be "in transit" if the temporary stoppage is not the result of a lack of immediate transportation but is for the taxpayer's own purposes. Accordingly, the inventory is included in the numerator of the California property factor even though the goods will be shipped to regional centers in other states after they are inspected and separated for shipment. Likewise, in *Comptroller of the Treasury v. Mercedes-Benz of North America, Inc.* [No. 8834940/CL88967 (Md. Cir. Ct. July 21, 1989)], a Maryland Circuit Court ruled that the taxpayer, which operated a vehicle preparation center in Maryland for vehicles imported from Europe, was required to include the value of vehicles in transit across the ocean in the numerator of the state's property factor.

Valuation of Owned Property

Property owned by the taxpayer is valued at its "original cost." [UDITPA Section 11] Generally, original cost is the basis of the property for federal income tax purposes at the time of acquisition, adjusted by any subsequent capital additions or improvements or partial dispositions, but not reduced by federal depreciation deductions. For example, if a taxpayer purchased a factory building at a cost of $500,000, spent $100,000 for major remodeling of the building, and claimed $22,000 of depreciation deductions, the value of the building included in the property factor is $600,000. A special rule applies to capitalized intangible drilling and development costs, which are included in the property factor even if they are expensed for either federal or state tax purposes. If the original cost of property is unascertainable, the property is included in the property factor at its fair market value as of the acquisition date. [MTC Reg. IV.11(a)(1)] A few states, such as Connecticut and New Jersey, require taxpayers to value property at its net book value (i.e., original cost less accumulated depreciation) rather than original cost.

Inventory. Inventory is included in the property factor "in accordance with the valuation method used for federal income tax purposes." [MTC Reg. IV.11(a)(2)] Consistent with the MTC regulations, most states permit the use of the last-in, first-out (LIFO) method if the taxpayer has adopted LIFO for federal tax purposes. Likewise, if a state requires strict conformity to the federal tax value, by default, the Code Section 263A uniform capitalization rules will apply to the extent the method is required for federal tax purposes.

Average value. Generally, the average value of property owned by the taxpayer is determined by averaging the values at the beginning and end of the tax year. [UDITPA Section 12] The tax administrator may require or allow averaging by monthly values if that method of averaging is required to properly reflect the average value of the taxpayer's property for the tax year. Averaging by monthly values is generally used if substantial fluctuations in the values of the property occur during the tax year or if property is acquired after the beginning of the tax year or disposed of before the end of the tax year. [MTC Reg. IV.12]

Valuation of Rented Property

Property rented by the taxpayer is valued at "eight times the net annual rental rate." [UDITPA Section 11] If property owned by others is used by the taxpayer at no charge or rented by the taxpayer for a nominal rate, the net annual rental rate for the property is based on a reasonable market rental rate for the property. [MTC Reg. IV.18.(b)(2)]

Whether a payment constitutes "rent" can be uncertain. For example, in *Nelson's Office Supply Stores, Inc. v. Commissioner of Revenue*[508 N.W.2d 776 (Minn. Sup. Ct., 1993)], the Minnesota Supreme Court ruled that, for purposes of computing the property factor for a retailer that rented space in several shopping centers, the capitalized rentals include the real property taxes, utilities, and common area expenses required to be paid under the lease.

In *Foodways National, Inc. v. Commissioner* [232 Conn. 325 (Conn. Sup Ct., 1995)], the Connecticut Supreme Court ruled that, for purposes of computing the property factor for a frozen food manufacturer, storage fees paid to public warehouses were properly treated as rentals, rather than a fee for services. The product storage contracts at issue provided that a warehouse would supply the taxpayer with a specified amount of cubic storage space for a given quantity of frozen food products but did not designate a specific section of a warehouse to be set aside for the taxpayer's use. Thus, the warehouse, rather than the taxpayer, determined the place within a warehouse where items would be stored.

Subrents. If a taxpayer subleases the property it is renting, the "net annual rental rate" is the annual rental rate paid by the taxpayer less the annual subrental rates received by the taxpayer from the subtenants. Subrents are not deducted, however, if they constitute business income because the property that produces the subrents is used by the taxpayer in the regular course of a trade or business in producing such income. [MTC Reg. IV.11(b)(1)] For example, if a grocery store receives subrents from an in-store bakery concession, the subrents are business income and are not deducted from the rent paid by the taxpayer for the store. [MTC Reg. IV.11(b)(1), Example (i)] In contrast, assume a taxpayer rents a 20-story office building, and uses the lower two stories for its corporate headquarters while subleasing the remaining 18 floors to others. The subrents are nonbusiness income that is deducted from the rent paid by the taxpayer because the rental of the 18 floors is separate from the operation of the taxpayer's trade or business. [MTC Reg. IV.11(b)(1), Example (iii)]

If nonbusiness subrents that are taken into account in determining the net annual rental rate produce a negative or clearly inaccurate value for an item of rented property, another method that properly reflects the value of the property may be required or allowed by the tax administrator. In no case, however, can the value be less than an amount that bears the same ratio to the annual rental rate paid by the taxpayer for the property as the fair market value of that portion of the property used by the taxpayer bears to the total fair market value of the rented property. [MTC Reg. IV.18.(b)(1)] For example, if a taxpayer, who rents a 10-story building at an annual rental rate of $1,000,000, occupies two stories and sublets eight stories for $1,000,000 a year, the net annual rental rate of the taxpayer must not be less than two-tenths of the taxpayer's annual rental rate for the entire year, or $200,000. [MTC Reg. IV.18.(b)(1), Example]

Payments for license agreements. In *Meredith Corp.* [No. 822396 (N.Y. Tax App. Trib., Mar. 10, 2011)], the Tax Appeals Tribunal ruled that the taxpayer could not treat amounts paid by the taxpayer's TV stations under license agreements to broadcast TV programs as payments for the rental of tangible personal property. The taxpayer argued that the payments were includible in the property factor, because the programming was delivered by satellite transmission and backup tapes, which constituted personal property. The Tribunal disagreed, concluding that the method of delivery was not dispositive of whether the payments for broadcast licenses could be included in the property factor. Under the license agreements, the stations acquired the exclusive rights to broadcast TV programs within a given market. The programming material was delivered to the stations for the sole purpose of enabling the stations to broadcast the material. The TV stations had no interest in or right to use the programming beyond the terms of the license agreements. The right to broadcast programs is equivalent to a copyright, which constitutes an intangible asset. Accordingly, the amounts paid for intangible broadcast rights could not be included in the property factor calculation, because they constituted intangible property.

State-by-State Summary

For ease of presentation, the following chart has been divided into five parts, as follows:

- Part 1: Valuation method, averaging, excluded property
- Part 2: CIP, idle property, leasehold improvements and in-transit property
- Part 3: Rented property
- Part 4: Inventory
- Part 5: Mobile property

Property Factor (Part 1)

Valuation Method, Averaging, Excluded Property

Legend:
NA — Not applicable
NR — Not reported

	Property Factor Valuation Methods			
	Property	*Depletable Assets*	*What Averaging Method is Used to Determine "Annual" Value?*	*Property Specifically Excluded from the Property Factor*
Alabama	Cost	Cost	Averaging of beginning and year-end balances.	Intangibles; property used to produce nonbusiness income; construction in progress
Alaska	Cost	Cost	Average of beginning and year-end balances.	Intangibles; property used to produce nonbusiness income; construction in progress
Arizona	Cost	Cost	Average of beginning and year-end balances	Intangibles; property used to produce nonbusiness income (see Corporate Income Tax Ruling CTR 01-2); construction in progress; custom software; supplies inventory
Arkansas	Cost	Cost	Averaging of beginning and year-end balances	Intangibles, except financial institutions; custom software; property used to produce nonbusiness income; construction in progress

Property Factor (Part 1)

Valuation Method, Averaging, Excluded Property

Legend:

NA	Not applicable
NR	Not reported

	Property Factor Valuation Methods			
	Property	*Depletable Assets*	*What Averaging Method is Used to Determine "Annual" Value?*	*Property Specifically Excluded from the Property Factor*
California	Cost, original cost adjusted by subsequent capital additions and improvements and partial dispositions thereof by sale, exchange, abandonment, etc.; if original cost of property is unascertainable, the property is included in the factor at its fair market value as of the date of acquisition by the taxpayer. Cal. Code Regs., tit. 18, § 25130	Cost, original cost adjusted by subsequent capital additions and improvements and partial dispositions thereof by sale, exchange, abandonment, etc.; if original cost of property is unascertainable, the property is included in the factor at its fair market value as of the date of acquisition by the taxpayer. Cal. Code Regs., tit. 18, § 25130	Averaging of beginning and year-end. See CA Code Regs., tit. 18 R&TC § 25131.	Intangibles (subject to R&TC § 25137); custom software; construction in progress (unless it is partially used in a trade or business while under construction. CA Code Regs., tit. 18 § 25129(b); property used to produce nonbusiness income; coin or currency
Colorado				
Connecticut	Net book value	Net book value	Monthly	Intangible assets
Delaware	Cost	Cost	Averaging of beginning and year-end balances	Construction in progress; intangibles; custom software
District of Columbia	Cost	Cost	Averaging of beginning and year-end balances	Intangibles and property used to produce nonbusiness income; construction in progress; custom and canned software
Florida	Cost	Cost	Averaging of beginning and year-end balances. Monthly average will be allowed or required when substantial fluctuations occurred.	Intangibles, custom software; property used to produce nonbusiness income.

Property Factor (Part 1)
Valuation Method, Averaging, Excluded Property

Legend:
NA Not applicable
NR Not reported

	Property Factor Valuation Methods			
	Property	*Depletable Assets*	*What Averaging Method is Used to Determine "Annual" Value?*	*Property Specifically Excluded from the Property Factor*
Georgia	Georgia uses only sales factor			
Hawaii	Cost	Cost	Averaging of beginning and year-end balances	Custom software, intangibles, property used to produce nonbusiness income, construction in progress
Idaho	Cost	Cost	Averaging of beginning and year-end balances	Intangibles; property used to produce nonbusiness income; construction in progress
Illinois	Illinois uses only sales factor			
Indiana	Indiana uses only sales factor			
Iowa	Iowa uses only sales factor			
Kansas	Cost	Cost	Averaging of beginning and year-end balances. When property is owned for less than the entire taxable year, a weighted average is used.	Construction in progress; property used to produce nonbusiness income; intangibles
Kentucky	Cost	Cost	Averaging of beginning and year-end balances	Intangibles, property used to produce nonbusiness income, construction in progress, pollution control facilities for which a tax exemption certificate is issued by the KY Dept of Rev.
Louisiana	Net book value	Net book value	Averaging of beginning and year-end balances	Custom software; intangible assets; construction in progress

Property Factor (Part 1)

Valuation Method, Averaging, Excluded Property

Legend:
NA Not applicable
NR Not reported

	Property Factor Valuation Methods			
	Property	*Depletable Assets*	*What Averaging Method is Used to Determine "Annual" Value?*	*Property Specifically Excluded from the Property Factor*
Maine	NA, effective 2007 forward, ME enacted single sales factor			
Maryland	Cost	Cost	Averaging of beginning and year-end balances	Construction-in-progress; intangible property; property idle 5 years or more
Massachusetts	Cost	Cost	Quarterly averaging	
Michigan (Business Tax)	Michigan uses only sales factor			
Note. The CIT takes effect 01/01/12, and replaces the Michigan Business Tax (MBT) for most taxpayers. However, businesses that have been approved to receive, have received, or have been assigned certain certified credits may elect to file a return and pay the tax imposed by the MBT in lieu of the CIT until the certified credits are exhausted or extinguished.				
Minnesota	Cost	Cost	Averaging of beginning and year-end balances	Intangible assets, property used to produce nonbusiness income, construction in progress; software (custom and canned)
Mississippi	Net book value	Net book value	Averaging of beginning and year-end balances	General and administrative property; custom software; intangible property; transportation equipment; property used to produce nonbusiness income; construction in progress
Missouri	Cost	Cost	Averaging of beginning and year-end balances	Intangible assets; property used to produce nonbusiness income; construction in progress

Property Factor (Part 1)

Valuation Method, Averaging, Excluded Property

Legend:

NA Not applicable

NR Not reported

	Property Factor Valuation Methods			
	Property	*Depletable Assets*	*What Averaging Method is Used to Determine "Annual" Value?*	*Property Specifically Excluded from the Property Factor*
Montana	Cost	Cost	Averaging of beginning and year-end balances	Intangibles; construction in progress; property used to produce nonbusiness income
Nebraska	Nebraska uses only sales factor			
Nevada	Nevada does not impose a corporate income tax			
New Hampshire	Cost	Cost	Averaging of beginning and year-end balances	Intangible assets; construction in progress; custom software
New Jersey	Net book value	Net book value	Quarterly average, unless distortion would result	Intangibles
New Mexico	Cost	Cost	Average of beginning and year-end balances	Property used to produce nonbusiness income; intangible assets; construction in progress
New York	Net book value; historical cost except real property at FMV	Net book value; historical cost	Quarterly or more frequent average	Property used to produce nonbusiness income; intangibles
Note. Property and payroll factors only relate to the MTA surcharge and prior year amended returns				
North Carolina	Cost	Cost	Averaging of beginning and year-end balances	Property used to produce nonbusiness income; construction in progress; custom software; supplies inventory

Property Factor (Part 1)

Valuation Method, Averaging, Excluded Property

Legend:

NA	Not applicable
NR	Not reported

	Property Factor Valuation Methods			
	Property	*Depletable Assets*	*What Averaging Method is Used to Determine "Annual" Value?*	*Property Specifically Excluded from the Property Factor*
North Dakota	Cost	Cost	Averaging of beginning and year-end balances	Property used to produce nonbusiness income; construction in progress; intangibles
Ohio	Ohio does not impose a corporate income tax			
Note Effective 1/1/2010, the Ohio Franchise Tax was fully phased out and business will be taxed on gross receipts through the Commercial Activity Tax. Details about that tax can be found at: http//tax.ohio.gov/divisions/commercial_activities/index.stm				
Oklahoma	Cost	Direct accounting	Averaging of beginning and year-end balances	Intangibles; property used to produce nonbusiness and directly allocable income; custom software
Oregon	Oregon uses only sales factor			
Pennsylvania	Cost	Cost	Averaging of beginning and year-end balances	Intangibles; custom software; construction in progress
Rhode Island	Net book value	Net book value	Averaging of beginning and year-end balances	Intangibles
South Carolina	South Carolina uses only sales factor			
South Dakota	South Dakota does not impose a corporate income tax			
Tennessee	Federal tax value	Cost	Averaging of beginning and year-end balances	Intangibles; property that produces nonbusiness income; construction in progress
Texas	Texas uses only sales factor			

Property Factor (Part 1)

Valuation Method, Averaging, Excluded Property

Legend:

NA Not applicable

NR Not reported

	Property Factor Valuation Methods			
	Property	*Depletable Assets*	*What Averaging Method is Used to Determine "Annual" Value?*	*Property Specifically Excluded from the Property Factor*
Utah	State tax value	Cost	Averaging of beginning and year-end balances	Intangibles; property used to produce nonbusiness income; custom software; construction in progress
Vermont	Cost	Cost	Averaging of beginning and year-end balances	Intangible assets; construction in progress; property used to produce nonbusiness income
Virginia	Cost	Cost	Averaging of beginning and year-end balances	Intangibles; construction in progress; software (custom and canned), property used to produce nonbusiness income
Washington	Washington does not impose a corporate income tax			
West Virginia	Cost	Cost	Averaging of beginning and year-end balances	Property used to produce nonbusiness income; construction in progress; intangibles; custom software
Wisconsin	Wisconsin uses only sales factor			
Wyoming	Wyoming does not impose a corporate income tax			

Property Factor (Part 2)

CIP, Idle Property, Leasehold Improvements and In-Transit Property

Legend:

X	These items are included in the property factor
NA	Not applicable
NR	Not required

		Treatment of Idle Property Previously Used by Taxpayers		*Property Factor Includes*		
	Is Construction in Progress Included in the Property Factor?	*Included if Retained for Later Use*	*Included if Retained for Disposition*	*Leasehold Improvements*	*In-Transit Property*	*Mobile Property*
Alabama	By the construction contractor	X	X	X, at average cost	X, if in transit between taxpayer and customer, or between two of taxpayers facilities.	X
Alaska	No	Depends on facts	Depends on facts	X, at average cost	X	X
Arizona	By the construction contractor	5 years		X, at average cost	X	X
Arkansas	By the construction contractor	5 years	5 years	X, at average cost	X	X
California	By the construction contractors and owner of constructed property if the property is partially used in the trade or business while under construction. Cal. Code Regs., tit. 18, § 25129(b).	X; property held for future business use remains in property factor until it is converted to a nonbusiness use. Cal Code Regs., tit 18, § 25129(b)	X; property held pending a sale remains in property factor until its sale or the lease of an extended period of time, normally 5 years. See 18 CCR § 25129(b).	X, at original cost	X, if in transit between taxpayer and customer, numerator is according to the state of destination or between two of taxpayer's facilities.	X, numerator is determined on the basis of total time within the state. R&TC § 25129(d)
Colorado						
Connecticut	By the owner of the constructed property	X, unless alternate method of apportionment	X, unless alternate method of apportionment	X, no written guidance for valuation	X	X

Property Factor (Part 2)

CIP, Idle Property, Leasehold Improvements and In-Transit Property

Legend:

X	These items are included in the property factor
NA	Not applicable
NR	Not required

		Treatment of Idle Property Previously Used by Taxpayers		*Property Factor Includes*		
	Is Construction in Progress Included in the Property Factor?	*Included if Retained for Later Use*	*Included if Retained for Disposition*	*Leasehold Improvements*	*In-Transit Property*	*Mobile Property*
Delaware	By the construction contractors	X		X, at average cost		
District of Columbia	No	X	Not included in the property factor	X, at average cost	X, property in transit between two of taxpayer's facilities	X
Florida	By the construction contractors and owner of constructed property	X, Included indefinitely	X, Included indefinitely	X, at average cost	X, between taxpayer and customer, or between two of taxpayers facilities.	X
Georgia	Georgia uses only sales factor					
Hawaii	By the construction contractor	X		X, at average cost	X	X
Idaho	By the construction contractors	Included until permanently withdrawn by an identifiable event, e.g., sale or abandonment	Included until permanently withdrawn by an identifiable event, e.g., sale or abandonment	X, at average cost	X	X
Illinois	Illinois uses only sales factor					
Indiana	Indiana uses only sales factor					
Iowa	Iowa uses only sales factor					

Property Factor (Part 2)

CIP, Idle Property, Leasehold Improvements and In-Transit Property

Legend:

X	These items are included in the property factor
NA	Not applicable
NR	Not required

		Treatment of Idle Property Previously Used by Taxpayers		*Property Factor Includes*		
	Is Construction in Progress Included in the Property Factor?	*Included if Retained for Later Use*	*Included if Retained for Disposition*	*Leasehold Improvements*	*In-Transit Property*	*Mobile Property*
Kansas	Excluded from property factor		5 years	X, at average cost	X, between two of taxpayer's facilities or property in transit between taxpayer and customer	X
Kentucky	By the construction contractor	X	X	X, at average cost	X	X
Louisiana	No	X		X, capitalization of amortization expense	X, between two of taxpayer's facilities	
Maine	Maine uses only sales factor					
Maryland	Construction-in-progress included to the extent it is used in the regular course of trade or business	5 years	5 years	X	X	X
Massachusetts	NR			X	X, if in transit between taxpayer and customer, or between two of taxpayers facilities	X
Michigan (Business Tax)	Michigan uses only sales factor					

Property Factor (Part 2)

CIP, Idle Property, Leasehold Improvements and In-Transit Property

Legend:

X	These items are included in the property factor
NA	Not applicable
NR	Not required

	Is Construction in Progress Included in the Property Factor?	*Treatment of Idle Property Previously Used by Taxpayers*: *Included if Retained for Later Use*	*Treatment of Idle Property Previously Used by Taxpayers*: *Included if Retained for Disposition*	*Property Factor Includes*: *Leasehold Improvements*	*Property Factor Includes*: *In-Transit Property*	*Property Factor Includes*: *Mobile Property*
Note. The CIT takes effect 01/01/12, and replaces the Michigan Business Tax (MBT) for most taxpayers. However, businesses that have been approved to receive, have received, or have been assigned certain certified credits may elect to file a return and pay the tax imposed by the MBT in lieu of the CIT until the certified credits are exhausted or extinguished.						
Minnesota	By the owner of the constructed property	Not included	Not included	X, at average cost	X, if in transit between taxpayer and customer, or between two of taxpayers facilities	X
Mississippi	No	Until permanent withdrawal		X, at net book value	X	
Missouri	No, excluded from property factor	X, SAF	X, SAF	X, at average cost	X	X
Montana	No	X, remains in property factor for 5 years	X, remains in property factor for 5 years	X, at average cost	X	X
Nebraska	Nebraska uses only sales factor					
Nevada	Nevada does not impose a corporate income tax					
New Hampshire	By construction contractors	Until sold	Until sold	X, at average cost	X, between two of taxpayer's facilities; between taxpayer and customer	X
New Jersey	By construction contractors	X		X, at average cost	X	X

Property Factor (Part 2)

CIP, Idle Property, Leasehold Improvements and In-Transit Property

Legend:

X	These items are included in the property factor
NA	Not applicable
NR	Not required

	Is Construction in Progress Included in the Property Factor?	*Treatment of Idle Property Previously Used by Taxpayers* — *Included if Retained for Later Use*	*Included if Retained for Disposition*	*Property Factor Includes* — *Leasehold Improvements*	*In-Transit Property*	*Mobile Property*
New Mexico	By construction contractors	5 years	5 years	X, at average cost	X, between two of taxpayer's facilities	X
New York	Construction contractors to the extent owned by the contractor and the corporation or by owner of constructed property if in use	Included in factor until disposed	Included in factor until disposed	X, at average cost	X	X
	Note. Property and payroll factors only relate to the MTA surcharge and prior year amended returns					
North Carolina	No	Not included	Not included	X, at average cost	X	X
North Dakota	By construction contractors	5 years	5 years	X, at average cost	X	X
Ohio	Ohio does not impose a corporate income tax					
	Note. Effective 1/1/2010, the Ohio Franchise Tax was fully phased out and business will be taxed on gross receipts through the Commercial Activity Tax. Details about that tax can be found at: http//tax.ohio.gov/divisions/commercial_activities/index.stm					
Oklahoma	By construction contractors, and owner of constructed property	X		X, at average cost	X	X
Oregon	Oregon uses only sales factor					

Property Factor (Part 2)

CIP, Idle Property, Leasehold Improvements and In-Transit Property

Legend:

X	These items are included in the property factor
NA	Not applicable
NR	Not required

		Treatment of Idle Property Previously Used by Taxpayers		*Property Factor Includes*		
	Is Construction in Progress Included in the Property Factor?	*Included if Retained for Later Use*	*Included if Retained for Disposition*	*Leasehold Improvements*	*In-Transit Property*	*Mobile Property*
Pennsylvania	By construction contractors	NR	NR		X, between taxpayer and customer	
Rhode Island	By construction contractors, the owner of the constructed property, and/or whenever on books	Whenever on books	Whenever on books	X		NR
South Carolina	South Carolina only uses sales factor					
South Dakota	South Dakota does not impose a corporate income tax					
Tennessee	If it is held for sale or lease by taxpayer	X	X	X, federal basis	X	X
Texas	Texas uses only sales factor					
Utah	By construction contractors	3 years		X, state tax basis	X	X
Vermont	NR	NR	NR	X, at average cost	X	X
Virginia	By the owner of constructed property	X, until identifiable event		X, at average cost	X	X
Washington	Washington does not impose a corporate income tax					

Property Factor (Part 2)

CIP, Idle Property, Leasehold Improvements and In-Transit Property

Legend:

X	These items are included in the property factor
NA	Not applicable
NR	Not required

		Treatment of Idle Property Previously Used by Taxpayers		*Property Factor Includes*		
	Is Construction in Progress Included in the Property Factor?	*Included if Retained for Later Use*	*Included if Retained for Disposition*	*Leasehold Improvements*	*In-Transit Property*	*Mobile Property*
West Virginia	By construction contractors	Stays in the factor until disposed of by sale, exchange, abandonment, or other disposition	Stays in the factor until disposed of by sale, exchange, abandonment, or other disposition	X, at average cost	X	X
Wisconsin	Wisconsin uses only sales factor					
Wyoming	Wyoming does not impose a corporate income tax					

Property Factor (Part 3)

Rented Property

Legend:

X	Indicates that gross rentals are used, rather than net rentals
NA	Not applicable
NR	Not required

	What is the Capitalization Rate if State Includes Rental Property in the Property Factor?	*If Rental Property is Subleased, What is Property Factor Based on, Assuming Subrents Are:* Business Income	Nonbusiness Income
Alabama	8 times annual rental	Gross rents	Net rents
Alaska	8 times annual rental	Gross rents	Net rents
Arizona	8 times annual rental	X	Net rents
Arkansas	8 times annual rental	Net rents	NR
California	8 times net annual rental rate, Cal. Code Regs. tit. 18, § 25130	X, gross rents See Cal. Code Regs. tit. 18, § 25130(b)	Net rents
Colorado			
Connecticut	8 times annual rental	Gross rents	Gross rents
Delaware	8 times annual rental	X	Excluded
District of Columbia	8 times annual rental	Net rents	Net rents
Florida	8 times annual rental	Net rents	Net rents
Georgia	Georgia uses only sales factor		
Hawaii	8 times annual rental	X	NR
Idaho	8 times annual rental	X	X, less nonbusiness subrents. Excluded if all rent is nonbusiness.
Illinois	Illinois uses only sales factor		
Indiana	Indiana uses only sales factor		
Iowa	Iowa uses only sales factor		

Property Factor (Part 3)
Rented Property

Legend:

X	Indicates that gross rentals are used, rather than net rentals
NA	Not applicable
NR	Not required

	What is the Capitalization Rate if State Includes Rental Property in the Property Factor?	*If Rental Property is Subleased, What is Property Factor Based on, Assuming Subrents Are:*	
		Business Income	*Nonbusiness Income*
Kansas	8 times annual rental	Gross rents	Net rents
Kentucky	8 times annual rental	Net Rents	
Louisiana	Rental assets are not included in the property factor.	NA	NA
Maine	Maine uses only sales factor		
Maryland	8 times annual rental	X	X
Massachusetts	8 times annual rental	Gross rents	Gross rents
Michigan (Business Tax)	Michigan uses only sales factor		

Note. The CIT takes effect 01/01/12, and replaces the Michigan Business Tax (MBT) for most taxpayers. However, businesses that have been approved to receive, have received, or have been assigned certain certified credits may elect to file a return and pay the tax imposed by the MBT in lieu of the CIT until the certified credits are exhausted or extinguished.

Minnesota	8 times annual rental	Net rents	Net rents
Mississippi	8 times annual rental	NR	NR
Missouri	8 times annual rental	Gross rents	Net rents
Montana	8 times annual rental	X	Net rents
Nebraska	Nebraska uses only sales factor		
Nevada	Nevada does not impose a corporate income tax		
New Hampshire	8 times annual rental	Net rents	NA

Property Factor (Part 3)

Rented Property

Legend:

X	Indicates that gross rentals are used, rather than net rentals
NA	Not applicable
NR	Not required

	What is the Capitalization Rate if State Includes Rental Property in the Property Factor?	*If Rental Property is Subleased, What is Property Factor Based on, Assuming Subrents Are:* *Business Income*	*Nonbusiness Income*
New Jersey	8 times annual rental	X	NR
New Mexico	8 times annual rental	Net rents	Net rents
New York	8 times annual rental	X	NA
	Note. Property and payroll factors only relate to the MTA surcharge and prior year amended returns		
North Carolina	8 times annual rental	X	Net rents
North Dakota	8 times annual rental	X	Net rents
Ohio	Ohio does not impose a corporate income tax		
	Note. Effective 1/1/2010, the Ohio Franchise Tax was fully phased out and business will be taxed on gross receipts through the Commercial Activity Tax. Details about that tax can be found at: http//tax.ohio.gov/divisions/commercial_activities/index.stm		
Oklahoma	8 times annual rental	Net rents	Net rents
Oregon	Oregon uses only sales factor		
Pennsylvania	8 times annual rental	Net rents	Net rents
Rhode Island	8 times annual rent	Net rents	NR
South Carolina	South Carolina uses only sales factor		
South Dakota	South Dakota does not impose a corporate income tax		
Tennessee	8 times annual rental	X	Net rents
Texas	Texas uses only sales factor.		
Utah	8 times annual rental	X	Net rents

Property Factor (Part 3)
Rented Property

Legend:
X — Indicates that gross rentals are used, rather than net rentals
NA — Not applicable
NR — Not required

	What is the Capitalization Rate if State Includes Rental Property in the Property Factor?	*If Rental Property is Subleased, What is Property Factor Based on, Assuming Subrents Are:* *Business Income*	*Nonbusiness Income*
Vermont	8 times annual rent	X	X
Virginia	8 times annual rental	X	X, unless *Allied Signal*, prevents inclusion in apportionable income
Washington	Washington does not impose a corporate income tax		
West Virginia	8 times annual rental	8 times annual rent	Not included if nonbusiness
Wisconsin	Wisconsin uses only sales factor		
Wyoming	Wyoming does not impose a corporate income tax		

Property Factor (Part 4)

Inventory

Legend:

NA	Not applicable
NR	Not reported
SAF	Same as applicable federal rules

	What Valuation Method is Used For Inventory?	*Is the LIFO Method Allowed in Deriving the Property Factor?*	*Is the Section 263A Uniform Capitalization Method Required in Determining Inventory Amount Included in Property Factor?*
Alabama	Tax value	NR	NR
Alaska	Generally tax value	Yes	Yes
Arizona		Yes	Yes
Arkansas	Tax value	Yes	Yes
California	Tax value (see R&TC § 25130(a)(2).)	Yes	Yes
Colorado			
Connecticut	Book value	Yes	No written guidance
Delaware	Book value	Yes	No
District of Columbia	SAF	No	Yes
Florida	SAF	Yes	Yes
Georgia	NA	NA	NA
Hawaii	Tax value	Yes	Yes
Idaho	Tax value	SAF	SAF
Illinois	Illinois uses only sales factor		
Indiana	Indiana uses only sales factor		
Iowa	Iowa uses only sales factor		
Kansas	Book value	Yes	No
Kentucky	Tax value	Yes	Yes

Property Factor (Part 4)
Inventory

Legend:

NA	Not applicable
NR	Not reported
SAF	Same as applicable federal rules

	What Valuation Method is Used For Inventory?	*Is the LIFO Method Allowed in Deriving the Property Factor?*	*Is the Section 263A Uniform Capitalization Method Required in Determining Inventory Amount Included in Property Factor?*
Louisiana	Book value	NR	No
Maine	NA, effective 2007 forward, ME enacted a single sales factor		
Maryland	Tax value	NR	Yes, if required for federal purposes
Massachusetts	NR	NR	Yes
Michigan (Business Tax)	Michigan uses only sales factor		
Note. The CIT takes effect 01/01/12, and replaces the Michigan Business Tax (MBT) for most taxpayers. However, businesses that have been approved to receive, have received, or have been assigned certain certified credits may elect to file a return and pay the tax imposed by the MBT in lieu of the CIT until the certified credits are exhausted or extinguished.			
Minnesota	Tax value	Yes	Yes
Mississippi	Book value	NR	Yes
Missouri	Tax value	Yes	No
Montana	Tax value	SAF	SAF
Nebraska	Nebraska uses only sales factor		
Nevada	Nevada does not impose a corporate income tax		
New Hampshire	Tax value	Yes	Yes
New Jersey	Book value	Yes	Yes
New Mexico	Tax value	Yes	Yes
New York	Book value	Yes	Yes
	Note. Property and payroll factors only relate to the MTA surcharge and prior year amended returns		

Property Factor (Part 4)
Inventory

Legend:

NA	Not applicable
NR	Not reported
SAF	Same as applicable federal rules

	What Valuation Method is Used For Inventory?	*Is the LIFO Method Allowed in Deriving the Property Factor?*	*Is the Section 263A Uniform Capitalization Method Required in Determining Inventory Amount Included in Property Factor?*
North Carolina	Book value	No	Yes
North Dakota	Book value	NR	No
Ohio	Ohio does not impose a corporate income tax		
	Note A. Effective 1/1/2010, the Ohio Franchise Tax was fully phased out and business will be taxed on gross receipts through the Commercial Activity Tax. Details about that tax can be found at: http//tax.ohio.gov/divisions/commercial_activities/index.stm		
Oklahoma	Book value	Yes	Yes
Oregon	Oregon uses only sales factor		
Pennsylvania	Tax value	Yes	Yes
Rhode Island	Book value	NR	NR
South Carolina	South Carolina uses only sales factor		
South Dakota	South Dakota does not impose a corporate income tax		
Tennessee	Tax value	Yes	Yes
Texas	Texas uses only sales factor		
Utah	Tax value	Yes	Yes
Vermont	Book value	NR	NR
Virginia	Tax value	Yes	Yes
Washington	Washington does not impose a corporate income tax		

Property Factor (Part 4)
Inventory

Legend:

NA Not applicable
NR Not reported
SAF Same as applicable federal rules

	What Valuation Method is Used For Inventory?	*Is the LIFO Method Allowed in Deriving the Property Factor?*	*Is the Section 263A Uniform Capitalization Method Required in Determining Inventory Amount Included in Property Factor?*
West Virginia	Book value	Yes	Yes
Wisconsin	Wisconsin uses only sales factor		
Wyoming	Wyoming does not impose a corporate income tax		

Property Factor (Part 5)
Mobile Property

Legend:

NA Not applicable

NR Not reported

	Airplanes	*Ships*	*Autos and Trucks*	*Autos Used by Sales Representatives*
Alabama	Cost	Cost	Cost	Cost
Alaska	Ground time	Port days	Terminal days	Average cost
Arizona	No property factor for airlines	NR	Mileage	Assigned to state where registered
Arkansas	Cost	Cost	Cost	Cost
California	Time in state and ratio of arrivals and departures from airports within the state compared with the total number of arrivals and departures from airports within and without the state see 18 CCR § 25137-7(b)(1); R&TC § § 25101.3, 25101.	Number of voyage days during which the ship was within the State over total number of days of voyages. Cal. Code Regs., tit. 18 § 25101(b).	Time in state, see 18 CCR § 25129(d). For trucking companies, see Cal. Code Regs., tit. 18 § 25137-11.	Where employee payroll is assigned or where vehicle licensed. See 18 CCR § 25129(d).
Colorado				
Connecticut	Net book value or 8 times rent	Net book value or 8 times rent	Net book value or 8 times rent	Net book value or 8 times rent
Delaware	NR	NR	NR	NR
District of Columbia	Miles	Miles	Miles	Time in state
Florida	Miles, see Rule 12c-1.0153, F.A.C.	Port days, see Rule 12c-1.0153, F.A.C.	Miles	Where employee compensation is included
Georgia	Georgia uses only sales factor			
Hawaii	Number of days in the state	Number of days in the state	Number of days in the state	Number of days in the state

Property Factor (Part 5)
Mobile Property

Legend:
NA Not applicable
NR Not reported

	Airplanes	*Ships*	*Autos and Trucks*	*Autos Used by Sales Representatives*
Idaho	Departures	NA	Miles	Where employee payroll is assigned or where vehicle is licensed.
Illinois	Illinois uses only sales factor			
Indiana	Indiana uses only sales factor			
Iowa	Iowa uses only sales factor			
Kansas	Cost and departures	NA	Mileage	Usage
Kentucky	Allocated based on revenue passenger miles	Excluded from sales factor	Autos included based on time in KY. Over the road trucks excluded from sales factor	Included in state of domicile
Louisiana	Excluded	State miles/total miles	State miles/total miles	State miles/total miles
Maine	Maine uses only sales factor			
Maryland	Time in state	Time in state	Time in state	Time in state
Massachusetts	Aircraft value of aircraft ready for flight, owned and used in Mass, times percentage of departures of that airline and aircraft in Mass.	Vessel value times days located and used in state	Total value of motor carrier's mobile property times percentage of miles traveled by carrier's mobile property in state, see 830 CMR 63.38.1(7).	NR
Michigan (Business Tax)	Michigan uses only sales factor			

Note. The CIT takes effect 01/01/12, and replaces the Michigan Business Tax (MBT) for most taxpayers. However, businesses that have been approved to receive, have received, or have been assigned certain certified credits may elect to file a return and pay the tax imposed by the MBT in lieu of the CIT until the certified credits are exhausted or extinguished.

Minnesota	Mileage	Mileage	Mileage	Mileage

Property Factor (Part 5)

Mobile Property

Legend:

NA — Not applicable

NR — Not reported

	Airplanes	*Ships*	*Autos and Trucks*	*Autos Used by Sales Representatives*
Mississippi	Excluded	Excluded	Excluded	Excluded
Missouri	Time	Time	Time	Time
Montana	Cost and departures	Cost	Cost and mileage	Cost and mileage
Nebraska	Nebraska uses only sales factor			
Nevada	Nevada does not impose a corporate income tax			
New Hampshire	Departures, Rev. 304.07	Miles, Rev. 304.11	Miles, Rev. 304.11	Cost
New Jersey	Takeoffs	Days of operation	Departures	Days of operation
New Mexico	Departures	NA	Mileage	NA
New York	Net book	Net book	Net book	Net book
	Note. Property and payroll factors only relate to the MTA surcharge and prior year amended returns			
North Carolina	NR	NR	NR	NR
North Dakota	Cost	Cost	Cost	Cost
Ohio	Ohio does not impose a corporate income tax			
	Note A. Effective 1/1/2010, the Ohio Franchise Tax was fully phased out and business will be taxed on gross receipts through the Commercial Activity Tax. Details about that tax can be found at: http//tax.ohio.gov/divisions/commercial_activities/index.stm			
Oklahoma	Air miles	NA	Mileage	Cost
Oregon	Oregon uses only sales factor			
Pennsylvania	Cost	Cost	Cost	Cost
Rhode Island	NR	NR	NR	NR
South Carolina	South Carolina uses only sales factor			

Property Factor (Part 5)
Mobile Property

Legend:
NA Not applicable
NR Not reported

	Airplanes	*Ships*	*Autos and Trucks*	*Autos Used by Sales Representatives*
South Dakota	South Dakota does not impose a corporate income tax			
Tennessee	Percentage of time	Percentage of time	Percentage of time	Domicile of employee
Texas	Texas uses only sales factor			
Utah	State tax basis	State tax basis	State tax basis	State tax basis
Vermont	Proportional use	Proportional use	Proportional use	Employee location
Virginia	Average value based on days used in state, mileage acceptable	Average value based on days used in state	Specific mileage formula	Average value (days in state or state where representatives payroll factor included)
Washington	Washington does not impose a corporate income tax			
West Virginia	Time utilized			
Wisconsin	Wisconsin uses only sales factor			
Wyoming	Wyoming does not impose a corporate income tax			

Payroll Factor

Despite the trend towards a single-factor sales-only apportionment formula, most states that impose a corporate income tax still employ a three-factor formula that includes a payroll factor. Thus, the computation of the payroll factor remains a regular chore for multistate taxpayers. The provisions governing the determination of the payroll factor generally conform to the guidance provided by the Uniform Division of Income for Tax Purposes Act (UDITPA) and the associated Multistate Tax Commission (MTC) regulations.

Under UDITPA Section 13, a state's payroll factor is a fraction, the numerator of which is the total amount paid in the state during the tax year by the taxpayer for compensation, and the denominator of which is the total compensation paid everywhere during the tax year.

Denominator of Payroll Factor

Definition of compensation. The denominator of the payroll factor is the total compensation paid everywhere. For this purpose, "compensation means wages, salaries, commissions and any other form of remuneration paid to employees for personal services." [UDITPA Section 1(c)] California provides the following guidance for determining a taxpayer's total compensation.

> The term "compensation" means wages, salaries, commissions and any other form of remuneration paid to employees for personal services. Payments made to an independent contractor or any other person not properly classifiable as an employee are excluded. Only amounts paid directly to employees are included in the payroll factor. Amounts considered paid directly include the value of board, rent, housing, lodging, and other benefits or services furnished to employees by the taxpayer in return for personal services provided that such amounts constitute income to the recipient under the federal Internal Revenue Code. In the case of employees not subject to the federal Internal Revenue Code, e.g., those employed in foreign countries, the determination of whether such benefits or services would constitute income to the employees shall be made as though such employees were subject to the federal Internal Revenue Code. [Cal. Code of Regs. § 25132(a)(3)]

Definition of employee. The proper classification of a worker as an employee or an independent contractor can be uncertain. For example, in P.D. 03-24 [Mar. 24, 2003], the Virginia Tax Commissioner ruled that the compensation of sales personnel was properly excluded from the payroll factor where the overall weight of the evidence suggested that the sales personnel should be classified as independent contractors.

California provides the following guidance for distinguishing employees from independent contractors.

> The term "employee" means (A) any officer of a corporation or (B) any individual who, under the usual common-law rules applicable in determining the employer-employee relationship, has the status of an employee. Generally, a person will be considered to be an employee if he is included by the taxpayer as an employee for purposes of the payroll taxes imposed by the Federal Insurance Contributions Act; except that, since certain individuals are included within the term "employees" in the Federal Insurance Contributions Act who would not be employees under the usual common-law rules, it may be established that a person who is included as an employee for purposes of the Federal Insurance Contributions Act is not an employee for purposes of this regulation. [Cal. Code of Regs. § 25132(a)(4)]

Exclusions. Only compensation paid by the taxpayer in the regular course of its trade or business is included in the payroll factor. [MTC Reg. 13.(a).(1)] Compensation that is related to the production of nonbusiness income is excluded from the payroll factor. [MTC Reg. 13.(a).(2)] For example, if an employee's only duty is managing a portfolio of securities that the employer holds as investments that are separate and apart from its trade or business, the employee's salary is excluded from the payroll factor. [MTC Reg. 13.(a).(2), Example (ii)]

Most states include officer compensation in the payroll factor. A few states provide exclusions, in an attempt to make the state a more attractive location for a corporation's headquarters office. For example, North Carolina excludes compensation paid to general executive officers, including the "chairman of the board, president, vice-presidents, secretary, treasurer, comptroller, and any other officer serving in similar capacities." [N.C. Gen. Stat. § 105-130.4(k)(1)]

Method of accounting. The total amount of compensation "paid" to employees is determined based upon the taxpayer's method of accounting. If the taxpayer uses the accrual method, all compensation that is properly accrued is deemed to have been paid. [MTC Reg. 13.(a).(2)] For example, if the taxpayer treats as a capital expenditure the wages paid to employees who constructed a building that the taxpayer uses in its trade or business, those wages are still included in the payroll factor. [MTC Reg. 13.(a).(2), Example (ii)]

Regardless of the taxpayer's method of accounting, if the taxpayer is required to use the cash method to report compensation for unemployment compensation purposes, the taxpayer may elect to use the cash method in determining the payroll factor. [MTC Reg. 13.(a).(2)]

Salaries are generally included in the payroll factor of the taxpayer for which the services were performed; in most cases, that would be the same corporation that is paying the employees. In *Philip Morris, Inc. v. Director of Revenue* [760 SW 2d 888 (Mo. Sup. Ct. Dec. 13, 1988)], however, the Missouri Supreme Court ruled that a Virginia parent corporation was required to include in the numerator of its Missouri payroll factor the salaries that the parent paid to the top executives of its wholly-owned Missouri subsidiary. The court reached this conclusion, even though the executives devoted all of their time to the subsidiary's business and the subsidiary reimbursed the parent for the payroll costs.

On the other hand, in Letter of Findings No. 01-0129 [July 1, 2002], the Indiana Department of Revenue ruled that an Indiana parent corporation that performed payroll functions for subsidiaries in Ohio and Michigan could not include the payroll expenses of the subsidiaries' out-of-state employees in the denominator of the taxpayer's Indiana payroll factor, because the taxpayer received a management fee from the subsidiaries for performing the payroll services.

Payroll in states in which the taxpayer is not taxable. The denominator of the payroll factor is the total compensation paid everywhere during the tax year. Accordingly, compensation paid to employees whose services are performed entirely in a state where the taxpayer is immune from taxation, for example, by Public Law 86-272, is included in the denominator of the payroll factor. [MTC Reg. 13.(b)] For example, if a corporation has employees in several states, including employees whose services are performed entirely in a state in which the corporation is immune from taxation under Public Law 86-272, the compensation of these employees is assigned to the state in which their services are performed even though the taxpayer is not taxable in that state. [MTC Reg. 13.(b), Example] As a result, this payroll is included in the denominator but not the numerator of any state's payroll factor.

Numerator of Payroll Factor

The numerator of a state's payroll factor is the total amount paid in this state during the tax year by the taxpayer for compensation. Under UDITPA Section 14 and MTC Regulation 14, compensation is "paid in this state" if any one of the following tests, applied consecutively, are met:

1. The employee's service is performed entirely within the state.
2. The employee's service is performed both within and without the state, but the service performed without the state is "incidental" (i.e., temporary or transitory in nature, or which is rendered in connection with an isolated transaction) to the employee's service within the state.
3. If the employee's services are performed both within and without this state, the employee's compensation is attributed to this state:
    a. If the employee's base of operations is in this state; or
    b. If there is no base of operations in any state in which some part of the service is performed, but the place from which the service is directed or controlled (i.e., the place from which the power to direct or control is exercised by the taxpayer) is in this state; or
    c. If the base of operations or the place from which the service is directed or controlled is not in any state in which some part of the service is performed, but the employee's residence is in this state.

The above tests for sourcing compensation are derived from the Model Unemployment Compensation Act. Accordingly, if compensation is included in the payroll factor based on the cash method of accounting or if the taxpayer is required to report compensation on a cash basis for unemployment compensation purposes, then it is presumed that the total wages reported by the taxpayer to this state for unemployment compensation purposes constitute compensation paid in this state for purposes of the payroll factor (except for compensation related to nonbusiness income). The presumption may be overcome by satisfactory evidence that an employee's compensation is not properly reportable to this state for unemployment compensation purposes. [MTC Reg. 13.(c)]

Definition of base of operations. The MTC regulations define an employee's base of operations as "the place of more or less permanent nature from which the employee starts his work and to which he customarily returns in order to receive instructions from the taxpayer or communications from his customers or other persons or to replenish stock or other materials, repair equipment, or perform any other functions necessary to the exercise of his trade or profession at some other point or points." [MTC Reg. 14]

In *O.H. Materials Co. v. Commissioner* [Ohio Ct. App., 3rd Dist., No. 5-89-2 (Nov. 26, 1990)], the Ohio Appeals Court ruled that wages paid by an Ohio company to employees working at two job sites in New Jersey were included in the numerator of the Ohio payroll factor, even though New Jersey also required inclusion of the wages in the numerator of its payroll factor. One project lasted 15 months and the other project lasted 10 months. New Jersey included the wages, because the services were performed in New Jersey, whereas Ohio included the wages because, the employee's "base of operations" was in Ohio. This case illustrates that companies with employees at various work sites throughout the country should be careful to establish and identify an employee's base of operations.

Leased Employees

Employee leasing generally refers to a situation where a third-party company "employs" the taxpayer's staff by taking over various legal responsibilities, including distributing paychecks, withholding and depositing personal income taxes, making FICA contributions, providing worker's compensation insurance, and administering other employee benefits. In return for this service, the taxpayer pays the third-party company a cost-plus fee. In many cases, the taxpayer maintains significant control over the activities of a leased employee. As a consequence, a leased employee may be considered an employee of the service recipient under the common-law rules.

The UDITPA and the MTC regulations are silent regarding how the compensation costs associated with leased employees are properly treated for purposes of computing the payroll factor. One approach is to include a leased employee's compensation in the payroll factor of the employee leasing company (the lessor), because that is the entity directly paying the individual in question. An alternative approach is to include a leased employee's compensation in the payroll factor of the common-law employer, which could be either the employee leasing company or the entity for which the employees are providing services (the lessee).

Some states provide specific guidance regarding the treatment of leased employees, but many states do not. For example, for purposes of computing the Massachusetts payroll factor, compensation paid for personal services rendered by leased employees is included in the payroll factor of the recipient of the services of the leased employee and is excluded from the payroll factor of the employee leasing company. [830 Mass. Code Regs. 63.38.1] For purposes of computing the New Mexico payroll factor, compensation paid for personal services rendered by leased employees is included in the payroll factor of the recipient of the services of the leased employee if the recipient is considered to be the employer or joint employer of the leased employee for payroll tax purposes. [N.M. Admin. Code tit. 3, § 5.14.8]

In *UPS Worldwide Forwarding, Inc. v. Commw. of Pennsylvania* [Nos. 62-65 F.R. 2001 (Pa. Commw. Ct., Dec. 8, 2004)], UPS Worldwide Forwarding, Inc. (Taxpayer) and UPS Aviation Services, Inc. (UPS-AS) were wholly-owned subsidiaries of UPS-America (UPS). Taxpayer had no employees. Instead, all of Taxpayer's services were performed by employees of affiliated companies and independent contractors. Taxpayer paid UPS-AS for the payroll costs it incurred for its employees who performed network planning and logistic functions for Taxpayer, and Taxpayer recorded these costs on its books as payroll expenses. The Pennsylvania Commonwealth Court ruled that the amounts Taxpayer paid UPS-AS did not constitute compensation expenses of the type includible in the Taxpayer's payroll factor, because the individuals in question were not Taxpayer's employees and there was no written agreement between Taxpayer and UPS-AS with respect to the individuals. The Pennsylvania Supreme Court affirmed the lower court's decision. [No.1-4 MAP 2005 (Pa. Sup. Ct., Dec. 30, 2005)]

In *Plantation Pipeline Co. v. Department of Revenue* [No. Corp. 05-948 (Ala. Admin. Law Div., May 23, 2006)], Plantation Pipeline Company (Taxpayer) was an interstate oil pipeline company that conducted business in Alabama and numerous other states. Taxpayer was owned by an affiliate of ExxonMobil Pipeline Company (Exxon), Kinder Morgan Operating L.P. "D" (KMLP-D), and Kinder Morgan Operating L.P. "A." In December 2000, Taxpayer entered into an agreement with Plantation Services, LLC (PS LLC), which required PS LLC to perform all of Taxpayer's operational and administrative functions. PS LLC then subcontracted for KMLP-D to perform those functions for Taxpayer beginning in January 2001. PS LLC was owned by Exxon and KMLP-D. Pursuant to the agreement, Taxpayer transferred all of its employees to KMLP-D, effective January 1, 2001. Those employees thereafter continued to perform the same services for Taxpayer as they had performed as direct employees of Taxpayer before 2001.

The Alabama Administrative Law Division previously addressed the issue of whether compensation paid for leased employees should be included in a taxpayer's payroll factor in *C&D Chemical Products, Inc. v. Department of Revenue.* [No. 2000-288 (Ala. Admin. Law Div. Feb. 9, 2001)] The taxpayer was a partner in a partnership that operated in Alabama using leased employees provided by a related corporation. The partnership compensated the related corporation for the cost of the employees, and the taxpayer included the compensation paid for the leased employees in its Alabama payroll factor. The judge ruled that even though the employees in question were not direct employees of the partnership, a pro-rata share of the amounts paid for the leased employees were properly included in the corporate partner's payroll factor, because the applicable statute did not require that the compensation be paid to an employee.

Consistent with the ruling in *C&D Chemical Products*, the judge in *Plantation Pipeline Co.* ruled that the compensation paid by Taxpayer to an affiliated corporation in 2001 for the services performed by the transferred employees was properly included in Taxpayer's Alabama payroll factor. The individuals who performed Taxpayer's operational and administrative functions as employees of the affiliated corporation were the same individuals who performed those duties as direct employees of Taxpayer in prior years and contributed to Taxpayer's production of business income to the same extent as they had in the prior years. Therefore, Taxpayer's income producing activities were more accurately identified and attributed to Alabama if the compensation paid by Taxpayer for the transferred employees was included in its Alabama payroll factor.

Recent Developments

In *Kentucky Revenue Cabinet v. Marquette Transportation Company, Inc.* [No. 2006-CA-002639-MR (Ky. Ct. of App., Apr. 3, 2009)], the Kentucky Court of Appeals ruled that the compensation of company employees who operated towboats along the Mississippi River and Illinois River was not included in the numerator of the Kentucky payroll factor, because there was no evidence that the company's towboat employees actually performed services in Kentucky. Although the company maintained its headquarters in Kentucky, it had no customers in Kentucky and its towboats never stopped in Kentucky. The company had about 35 employees who worked in the Kentucky headquarters office and 700 employees who worked on the towboats. Only the compensation paid to the towboat employees was in dispute. The fact that the company paid unemployment insurance tax for all of its employees to Kentucky was not relevant, because the Kentucky payroll factor statute does not mention unemployment taxes.

State-by-State Summary

The following chart is presented in three parts. Part 1 indicates whether throwback rules apply to payroll; whether any form of common paymaster procedure is recognized in computing the payroll factor; whether salary paid to an employee who is a state resident for services performed in another state is prorated in arriving at the numerator; whether the federal Form 940 basis and the state unemployment tax return basis are acceptable in computing the payroll factor; and whether the state requires the use of a specific form to compute the payroll factor.

Part 2 indicates whether the payroll factor includes officers' payroll, deferred employee compensation contributed to a 401(k) plan, payments to independent contractors, imputed income, sick pay, and fees paid to affiliated corporations for personal services.

Part 3 indicates whether compensation paid to a leased employee is included in the payroll factor of the common-law employer, the entity at which the employee provides services, or the entity that provides paychecks to the employee.

Payroll Factor (Part 1)

Legend:

X	These items are included in the payroll factor
NA	Not applicable
NR	Not reported

	Does State Apply a Throwback Rule to Payroll?	*Any Form of "Common Paymaster" Procedure Recognized in Computing Payroll Factor?*	*Numerator of Payroll Factor Is Prorated for Salary Paid to a State Resident for Services Rendered in Another State*	*Are Amounts From Federal Form 940 Acceptable?*	*Are Amounts From State Unemployment Tax Return Acceptable?*	*Does State Require a Specific Form Be Used to Compute the Payroll Factor?*
Alabama	Yes	No	No	Yes	Yes	NR
Alaska	No	No	No	Yes	Yes	No
Arizona	No	No	No	Yes	Yes	No
Arkansas	No	No	Yes	Yes	Yes	No
California	No, see example in 18 § CCR 25132(b).	No	No, but see 18 CCR §§ 25137-1-25137-14 for special rules for certain industries.	Yes	Yes	Yes, Schedule R
Colorado						
Connecticut	No	No written guidance	No written guidance	No written guidance	No written guidance	No
Delaware	No	No	NR	Yes	NR	NR
District of Columbia	Yes	No	Yes	Yes	Yes	No
Florida	No	No	No	No	Yes	No
Georgia	Georgia uses only sales factor					
Hawaii	No	No	No	No	Yes	No
Idaho	No	No	No	Yes	Yes	No
Illinois	Illinois uses only sales factor					
Indiana	Indiana uses only sales factor					

Payroll Factor (Part 1)

Legend:

X — These items are included in the payroll factor
NA — Not applicable
NR — Not reported

	Does State Apply a Throwback Rule to Payroll?	*Any Form of "Common Paymaster" Procedure Recognized in Computing Payroll Factor?*	*Numerator of Payroll Factor Is Prorated for Salary Paid to a State Resident for Services Rendered in Another State*	*Are Amounts From Federal Form 940 Acceptable?*	*Are Amounts From State Unemployment Tax Return Acceptable?*	*Does State Require a Specific Form Be Used to Compute the Payroll Factor?*
Iowa	Iowa uses only sales factor					
Kansas	No	No	No	Yes	Yes	No
Kentucky	No	No	Yes	Yes	No	Yes, Form 41A720A
Louisiana	No	Yes	Yes	No	No	Yes, Form ICFT 620A
Maine	Maine uses only sales factor					
Maryland	No	NR	No	No	Yes	NR
Massachusetts	No	NR	No	NR	NR	No
Michigan (Business Tax)	Michigan uses only sales factor					

Note. The CIT takes effect 01/01/12, and replaces the Michigan Business Tax (MBT) for most taxpayers. However, businesses that have been approved to receive, have received, or have been assigned certain certified credits may elect to file a return and pay the tax imposed by the MBT in lieu of the CIT until the certified credits are exhausted or extinguished.

Minnesota	No	No	No	Yes	Yes	No
Mississippi	No	No	No	NR	NR	NR
Missouri	Yes	Yes	No	Yes	Yes	No
Montana	No	No	No	Yes	Yes	No
Nebraska	Nebraska uses only sales factor					
Nevada	Nevada does not impose a corporate income tax					

Payroll Factor (Part 1)

Legend:

X	These items are included in the payroll factor
NA	Not applicable
NR	Not reported

	Does State Apply a Throwback Rule to Payroll?	*Any Form of "Common Paymaster" Procedure Recognized in Computing Payroll Factor?*	*Numerator of Payroll Factor Is Prorated for Salary Paid to a State Resident for Services Rendered in Another State*	*Are Amounts From Federal Form 940 Acceptable?*	*Are Amounts From State Unemployment Tax Return Acceptable?*	*Does State Require a Specific Form Be Used to Compute the Payroll Factor?*
New Hampshire	No	No	No	Yes	Yes	No
New Jersey	No	It depends on whether all entities of the group file in New Jersey	No, state where unemployment tax paid is where payroll located	Yes, as backup. Use Sch J of CBT-100	No	Yes, Schedule I, part III of CBT-100
New Mexico	No	No	No	Yes	Yes	No
New York	No	No	No	NA	NA	No
	Note. Property and payroll factors only relate to the MTA surcharge and prior year amended returns					
North Carolina	No	Yes	No	Yes	No	No
North Dakota	Yes	No	Yes	Yes	Yes	Yes, Form 40, Schedule B
Ohio	Ohio does not impose a corporate income tax					
Note. Effective 1/1/2010, the Ohio Franchise Tax was fully phased out and business will be taxed on gross receipts through the Commercial Activity Tax. Details about that tax can be found at: http//tax.ohio.gov/divisions/commercial_activities/index.stm						
Oklahoma	No	No	Yes	Yes	Yes	No
Oregon	Oregon uses only sales factor					
Pennsylvania	No	No	NR	Yes	Yes	Yes, Form RCT 106
Rhode Island	No	Yes	Yes	Yes	Yes	Yes, Form 941
South Carolina	South Carolina uses only sales factor					

Payroll Factor (Part 1)

Legend:

X	These items are included in the payroll factor
NA	Not applicable
NR	Not reported

	Does State Apply a Throwback Rule to Payroll?	*Any Form of "Common Paymaster" Procedure Recognized in Computing Payroll Factor?*	*Numerator of Payroll Factor Is Prorated for Salary Paid to a State Resident for Services Rendered in Another State*	*Are Amounts From Federal Form 940 Acceptable?*	*Are Amounts From State Unemployment Tax Return Acceptable?*	*Does State Require a Specific Form Be Used to Compute the Payroll Factor?*
South Dakota	South Dakota does not impose a corporate income tax					
Tennessee		No	No	Yes	Yes	No
Texas	Texas uses only sales factor.					NA
Utah	No	No	No	Yes	Yes	No
Vermont	No	No	No	Yes	Yes	NR
Virginia	No	No	No	Yes	Yes, required for numerator	Yes, Virginia Unemployment Tax return
Washington	Washington does not impose a corporate income tax					
West Virginia	No	NR	NR	No, use figures from Form 1120.	No	Yes, Form 1120
Wisconsin	Wisconsin uses only sales factor					
Wyoming	Wyoming does not impose a corporate income tax					

Payroll Factor (Part 2)

Legend:

X	These items are included in the payroll factor
NA	Not applicable
NR	Not reported

	Payroll Factor Includes					
	Officers' Payroll	*Tax-Deferred Compensation Contributed to a § 401(k) Plan*	*Payments to Independent Contractors*	*Imputed Fringe Benefits Income (§ 79)*	*Sick Pay*	*Fees Paid to Affiliated Corporation for Personal Services*
Alabama	X	X		X	X	
Alaska	X			X	X	
Arizona	X					
Arkansas	X				X	
California	X, see 18 CRR § 25132(a)(4).	X		X	X, see 18 CCR § 25132(a)(3).	
Colorado						
Connecticut	X	X		X	X	
Delaware		X		X	X	
District of Columbia	X	X		X	X	
Florida	X	X		X	X	
Georgia	Georgia uses only sales factor					
Hawaii	X		X	X	X	
Idaho	X	X		X	X	
Illinois	Illinois uses only sales factor					
Indiana	Indiana uses only sales factor					
Iowa	Iowa uses only sales factor					

Payroll Factor (Part 2)

Legend:

X	These items are included in the payroll factor
NA	Not applicable
NR	Not reported

	Payroll Factor Includes					
	Officers' Payroll	*Tax-Deferred Compensation Contributed to a § 401(k) Plan*	*Payments to Independent Contractors*	*Imputed Fringe Benefits Income (§ 79)*	*Sick Pay*	*Fees Paid to Affiliated Corporation for Personal Services*
Kansas	X	X		X	X	
Kentucky	X	X		X	X	
Louisiana	X	X				X
Maine	Maine uses only sales factor					
Maryland	X	X			X	
Massachusetts	X	X			X	
Michigan (Business Tax)	Michigan uses only sales factor					
Note. The CIT takes effect 01/01/12, and replaces the Michigan Business Tax (MBT) for most taxpayers. However, businesses that have been approved to receive, have received, or have been assigned certain certified credits may elect to file a return and pay the tax imposed by the MBT in lieu of the CIT until the certified credits are exhausted or extinguished.						
Minnesota	X	X			X	
Mississippi				X		
Missouri	X	X				
Montana	X	X		X	X	
Nebraska	Nebraska uses only sales factor					
Nevada	Nevada does not impose a corporate income tax					
New Hampshire	X	X		X	X	
New Jersey	X			X		

Payroll Factor (Part 2)

Legend:

X	These items are included in the payroll factor
NA	Not applicable
NR	Not reported

	Payroll Factor Includes					
	Officers' Payroll	*Tax-Deferred Compensation Contributed to a § 401(k) Plan*	*Payments to Independent Contractors*	*Imputed Fringe Benefits Income (§ 79)*	*Sick Pay*	*Fees Paid to Affiliated Corporation for Personal Services*
New Mexico	X			X	X	
New York		X		X	X	
	Note. Property and payroll factors only relate to the MTA surcharge and prior year amended returns					
North Carolina		X		X		
North Dakota	X	X		X	X	
Ohio	Ohio does not impose a corporate income tax					
Note. Effective 1/1/2010, the Ohio Franchise Tax was fully phased out and business will be taxed on gross receipts through the Commercial Activity Tax. Details about that tax can be found at: http//tax.ohio.gov/divisions/commercial_activities/index.stm						
Oklahoma		X			X	
Oregon	Oregon uses only sales factor					
Pennsylvania	X	X			X	
Rhode Island	X	X		X	X	X
South Carolina	South Carolina uses only sales factor					
South Dakota	South Dakota does not impose a corporate income tax					
Tennessee	X	X			X	
Texas	Texas uses only sales factor					
Utah	X	X			X	
Vermont	X	X		X	X	

Payroll Factor (Part 2)

Legend:

X	These items are included in the payroll factor
NA	Not applicable
NR	Not reported

	Payroll Factor Includes					
	Officers' Payroll	*Tax-Deferred Compensation Contributed to a § 401(k) Plan*	*Payments to Independent Contractors*	*Imputed Fringe Benefits Income (§ 79)*	*Sick Pay*	*Fees Paid to Affiliated Corporation for Personal Services*
Virginia	X					
Washington	Washington does not impose a corporate income tax					
West Virginia	X	X		X	X	
Wisconsin	Wisconsin uses only sales factor					
Wyoming	Wyoming does not impose a corporate income tax					

Payroll Factor (Part 3)
Leased Employees

Legend:
X — These items are included in the payroll factor
NA — Not applicable
NR — Not reported

	Compensation paid to a leased employee is included in the payroll factor of:			
	Common Law Employer	*Entity at Which Employee Provides Services*	*Entity Providing Paycheck to Employee*	*Other*
Alabama	X			
Alaska	X			
Arizona	Depends on facts	Depends on facts		
Arkansas			X	
California	X			
Colorado				
Connecticut				
Delaware			X	
District of Columbia	Depends on facts	X	Depends on facts	
Florida			X	
Georgia	Georgia uses only sales factor			
Hawaii	X			
Idaho				Based upon facts and circumstances; preference for entity reporting on federal Form 941
Illinois	Illinois uses only sales factor			
Indiana	Indiana uses only sales factor			
Iowa	Iowa uses only the sales factor			

Payroll Factor (Part 3)

Leased Employees

Legend:

X	These items are included in the payroll factor
NA	Not applicable
NR	Not reported

	Compensation paid to a leased employee is included in the payroll factor of:			
	Common Law Employer	*Entity at Which Employee Provides Services*	*Entity Providing Paycheck to Employee*	*Other*
Kansas		X	X	
Kentucky			X	
Louisiana			X	
Maine	Maine uses only sales factor			
Maryland	NR	NR	NR	NR
Massachusetts	X			
Michigan (Business Tax)	Michigan uses only sales factor			
Note. The CIT takes effect 01/01/12, and replaces the Michigan Business Tax (MBT) for most taxpayers. However, businesses that have been approved to receive, have received, or have been assigned certain certified credits may elect to file a return and pay the tax imposed by the MBT in lieu of the CIT until the certified credits are exhausted or extinguished.				
Minnesota			X	
Mississippi		X		
Missouri		X		
Montana	X		X	
Nebraska	Nebraska uses only the sales factor			
Nevada	Nevada does not impose a corporate income tax			
New Hampshire	X			
New Jersey			X	The entity that pays the payroll tax

Payroll Factor (Part 3)

Leased Employees

Legend:

X	These items are included in the payroll factor
NA	Not applicable
NR	Not reported

Compensation paid to a leased employee is included in the payroll factor of:

	Common Law Employer	*Entity at Which Employee Provides Services*	*Entity Providing Paycheck to Employee*	*Other*
New Mexico			X	
New York	X		X	
	Note. Property and payroll factors only relate to the MTA surcharge and prior year amended returns			
North Carolina	X			
North Dakota			X	
Ohio	Ohio does not impose a corporate income tax			
Note. Effective 1/1/2010, the Ohio Franchise Tax was fully phased out and business will be taxed on gross receipts through the Commercial Activity Tax. Details about that tax can be found at: http//tax.ohio.gov/divisions/commercial_activities/index.stm				
Oklahoma	X			
Oregon	Oregon uses only sales factor			
Pennsylvania	X			
Rhode Island		X		
South Carolina	South Carolina uses only sales factor			
South Dakota	South Dakota does not impose a corporate income tax			
Tennessee			X	
Texas	Texas uses only the sales factor			
Utah			X	
Vermont	X			

Payroll Factor (Part 3)
Leased Employees

Legend:

X	These items are included in the payroll factor
NA	Not applicable
NR	Not reported

	Compensation paid to a leased employee is included in the payroll factor of:			
	Common Law Employer	*Entity at Which Employee Provides Services*	*Entity Providing Paycheck to Employee*	*Other*
Virginia			X	
Washington	Washington does not impose a corporate income tax			
West Virginia			X	
Wisconsin	Wisconsin uses only sales factor			
Wyoming	Wyoming does not impose a corporate income tax			

Sales Factor

Under Section 15 of the Uniform Division of Income for Tax Purposes Act (UDITPA), "the sales factor is a fraction, the numerator of which is the total sales of the taxpayer in this state during the tax period, and the denominator of which is the total sales of the taxpayer everywhere during the tax period." Because the sales factor is used to apportion a corporation's business income, only sales that generate apportionable business income are includible in the fraction. Nonbusiness sales or receipts are excluded from the sales factor. Business income means "income arising from transactions and activity in the regular course of the taxpayer's trade or business and includes income from tangible and intangible property if the acquisition, management, and disposition of the property constitute integral parts of the taxpayer's regular trade or business operations" (UDITPA Section 1(a)).

Meaning of "Sales"

Under UDITPA Section 1(g), the term *sales* means all gross receipts of the taxpayer other than receipts related to nonbusiness income. Thus, the sales factor generally includes all gross receipts from transactions and activity in the regular course of the taxpayer's trade or business, including sales of goods and services, as well as rentals, royalties, and any other gains and profits derived from other business assets or activities. For example, in *Appeal of Polaroid Corp.* [No. 62415 (Cal. State Bd. of Equal., May 28, 2003)], the California State Board of Equalization held that a $837 million damages award received from a patent infringement lawsuit should be included in the sales factor. (For a discussion of the inclusion in the sales factor of gains triggered by a Code Section 338 election, see the section in Part 3 entitled Section 338 Elections.)

Consistent with this expansive view of the sales factor, Multistate Tax Commission (MTC) Regulation IV.15(b) provides that the sales factor generally includes the total gross receipts derived by the taxpayer from transactions and activity in the regular course of its trade or business. This includes interest income, service charges, carrying charges, and time-price differential charges incidental to such sales, as well as federal and state excise taxes and state sales taxes if such taxes are passed on to the buyer or are included in the selling price of the goods. For example, in *Amoco Oil Co. v. Commissioner of Revenue* [Nos. 7223–7231 (Minn. T.C., Nov. 9, 2001)], the Minnesota Tax Court ruled that federal and state gasoline excise taxes paid by a gasoline distributor were included in the sales factor. Receipts from transactions with related corporations are also generally included in the sales factor, unless a consolidated or combined return is filed with the payor, in which case intercompany receipts are generally excluded from the sales factor.

For purposes of computing the sales factor, MTC Regulation IV.2.(a).(5) defines "gross receipts" as follows:

> "Gross receipts" are the gross amounts realized (the sum of money and the fair market value of other property or services received) on the sale or exchange of property, the performance of services, or the use of property or capital (including rents, royalties, interest and dividends) in a transaction which produces business income, in which the income or loss is recognized (or would be recognized if the transaction were in the United States) under the Internal Revenue Code. Amounts realized on the sale or exchange of property are not reduced for the cost of goods sold or the basis of property sold. Gross receipts, even if business income, do not include such items as, for example:
>
> 1. repayment, maturity, or redemption of the principal of a loan, bond, or mutual fund or certificate of deposit or similar marketable instrument;
> 2. the principal amount received under a repurchase agreement or other transaction properly characterized as a loan;
> 3. proceeds from issuance of the taxpayer's own stock or from sale of treasury stock;
> 4. damages and other amounts received as the result of litigation;
> 5. property acquired by an agent on behalf of another;
> 6. tax refunds and other tax benefit recoveries;
> 7. pension reversions;
> 8. contributions to capital (except for sales of securities by securities dealers);
> 9. income from forgiveness of indebtedness; or

10. amounts realized from exchanges of inventory that are not recognized by the Internal Revenue Code.

Exclusion of an item from the definition of "gross receipts" is not determinative of its character as business or nonbusiness income. Nothing in this definition shall be construed to modify, impair or supersede any provision of Section IV.18.

MTC Regulation IV.18(c)(1) and (2) provides an exception for incidental or occasional sales, as follows:

(1) Where substantial amounts of gross receipts arise from an incidental or occasional sale of a fixed asset used in the regular course of the taxpayer's trade or business, those gross receipts shall be excluded from the sales factor. For example, gross receipts from the sale of a factory or plant will be excluded.

(2) Insubstantial amounts of gross receipts arising from incidental or occasional transactions or activities may be excluded from the sales factor unless their exclusion would materially affect the amount of income apportioned to this state. For example, the taxpayer ordinarily may include in or exclude from the sales factor gross receipts from transactions such as the sale of office furniture, business automobiles, etc.

Consistent with the MTC regulation, California Regulation Section 25137(c) provides that if substantial amounts of gross receipts arise from an occasional sale of a fixed business asset (e.g., the sale of a factory, patent, or affiliate's stock), such gross receipts are excluded from the sales factor. For this purpose, a sale is *substantial* if its exclusion from the sales factor "results in a five percent or greater decrease in the sales factor denominator of the taxpayer." Illinois requires that all gross receipts arising from an incidental or occasional sale of business assets be excluded from the sales factor, regardless of whether the amount is substantial or insubstantial [86 Ill. Adm. Code 100.3380].

MTC Regulation IV.18(c)(3) provides an exception for income from intangible property that cannot readily be attributed to any particular income producing activity of the taxpayer, as follows:

(3) Where the income producing activity in respect to business income from intangible personal property can be readily identified, the income is included in the denominator of the sales factor and, if the income producing activity occurs in this state, in the numerator of the sales factor as well. For example, usually the income producing activity can be readily identified in respect to interest income received on deferred payments on sales of tangible property . . . and income from the sale, licensing or other use of intangible personal property . . .

Where business income from intangible property cannot readily be attributed to any particular income producing activity of the taxpayer, the income cannot be assigned to the numerator of the sales factor for any state and shall be excluded from the denominator of the sales factor. For example, where business income in the form of dividends received on stock, royalties received on patents or copyrights, or interest received on bonds, debentures or government securities results from the mere holding of the intangible personal property by the taxpayer, the dividends and interest shall be excluded from the denominator of the sales factor.

Effective June 10, 2011, any gain on the sale of an asset designated as goodwill and treated as a Class VII asset for federal tax purposes is excluded from both the numerator and the denominator of the Tennessee sales factor. [H.B. 1994, June 10, 2011]

Treatment of Treasury Function Receipts

States have struggled with the issue of how to apply the UDITPA sales factor rules to the gross receipts arising from the cash management activities of corporate treasury departments; in particular, the receipts arising from short-term investments in marketable securities. Under UDITPA Section 1(g), the term "sales" means all gross receipts of the taxpayer other than nonbusiness income. Thus, under the general rules, the sales factor would include not only the net gain derived from sales of short-term marketable securities, but also the return of principal portion of such investments. MTC Regulation IV.18(c)(4), however, provides the following special sales factor rule regarding a taxpayer's treasury functions:

(A) . . . If a taxpayer holds liquid assets in connection with one or more treasury functions of the taxpayer, and the liquid assets produce business income when sold, exchanged or otherwise disposed, the overall net gain from those transactions for each treasury function for the tax period is included in the sales factor . . .

(B) For purposes of this subsection, a liquid asset is an asset (other than functional currency or funds held in bank accounts) held to provide a relatively immediate source of funds to satisfy the liquidity needs of the trade or business. Liquid assets include foreign currency (and trading positions therein) other than functional currency used in the regular course of the taxpayer's trade or business; marketable instruments (including stocks, bonds, debentures, options, warrants, futures contracts, etc.); and mutual funds which hold such liquid assets . . .

(C) For purposes of this subsection, a treasury function is the pooling and management of liquid assets for the purpose of satisfying the cash flow needs of the trade or business, such as providing liquidity for a taxpayer's business cycle, providing a reserve for business contingencies, business acquisitions, etc. A taxpayer principally engaged in the trade or business of purchasing and selling instruments or other items included in the definition of liquid assets set forth herein is not performing a treasury function with respect to income so produced.

(D) Overall net gain refers to the total net gain from all transactions incurred at each treasury function for the entire tax period, not the net gain from a specific transaction.

California. In *Microsoft Corp. v. Franchise Tax Board* [No. S133343 (Cal. Sup. Ct., Aug. 17, 2006)], the California Supreme Court ruled that, based on the statutory definition of "sales," both the net gain and the return of capital portion of the proceeds from redeeming marketable securities at maturity is includible in the sales factor. However, the court also ruled that the standard apportionment provisions did not fairly represent Microsoft's business activities in California and that an alternate formula that included only Microsoft's net gains from its redemptions in the California sales factor should be used. The court observed that the essential problem with including the full redemption price in the sales factor is that such short-term investments involve profit margins that are dramatically lower than those of Microsoft's main line of business. During the tax year in question, Microsoft's profit margin on its redemptions of marketable securities was 0.2 percent compared to a profit margin in its primary business of 31.4 percent. The UDITPA sales factor assumes that a taxpayer's profit margin on gross receipts does not vary significantly from state to state. Thus, applying Microsoft's average margin to its California gross receipts would severely underestimate the amount of income attributable to Microsoft's activities in California. As a consequence, mixing the gross receipts from Microsoft's short-term investments with the gross receipts from its main line of business seriously distorted the representation of Microsoft's business activity in California. See also *Microsoft Corporation v. Franchise Tax Board* [No. CGC08-471260 (Cal. Super. Ct., Feb. 17, 2011)], in which the court ruled that only the net receipts from the taxpayer's redemptions of its marketable securities were includible in the denominator of the California sales factor.

Other recent California cases dealing with the issue of the proper treatment of gross receipts from dispositions of short-term marketable securities include *Appeal of Home Depot U.S.A., Inc.* [No. 298683 (Cal. State Bd. of Equal., Dec. 18, 2008)], *The Limited Stores Inc. v. Franchise Tax Board* [No. A102915 (Cal. Ct. of App., June 8, 2007)], *General Motors Corp. v. Franchise Tax Board* [No. S127086 (Cal. Sup. Ct., Aug. 17, 2006)], and *Toys "R" Us, Inc. v. Franchise Tax Board.* [C045386 (Cal. Ct. of App., Apr. 5, 2006)] See also *General Mills, Inc. v. Franchise Tax Board* [No. CGC-05-439929 (Cal. Super. Ct., Nov. 1, 2010); and No. A120492 (Cal. Ct. of App., Apr. 15, 2009], which deals with sales of commodity futures.

For tax years beginning on or after January 1, 2007, treasury function receipts are excluded from both the numerator and the denominator of the California sales factor. [California Franchise Tax Board, Reg. § 25137(c)(1)(D), May 29, 2008] The exclusion applies to interest and dividends from intangible assets held in connection with the taxpayer's treasury function, as well as the gross receipts and overall net gains from the maturity, redemption, sale, exchange or other disposition of such intangible assets. "Treasury function" is defined as the pooling, management, and investment of intangible assets for the purpose of satisfying the cash flow needs of the taxpayer's trade or business, such as providing liquidity for a taxpayer's business cycle, providing a reserve for business contingencies, business acquisitions, etc. It includes the use of futures and options contracts to hedge foreign currency fluctuations, but not futures and option contracts to hedge the price risks of the products or commodities consumed, produced, or sold by the taxpayer. This regulation does not apply to a registered broker-dealer or other taxpayer that is principally engaged in the trade or business of purchasing and selling intangible assets of the type typically held in a treasury function. The exclusion also does not apply to banks and financial corporations that use the specialized apportionment formula found in Cal. Code of Regs. § 25137-4.2.

Beginning with the 2011 taxable year, California adopts a statutory definition of "gross receipts" that specifically excludes treasury function receipts. [S.B. 15, Feb 20, 2009] The legislation declares that the changes constitute clarifying, non-substantive changes.

Other states. In *Mead Corp. v. Illinois Department of Revenue* [No. 1-03-1160 (Ill. App. Ct., Jan. 12, 2007)], the Illinois Appellate Court ruled that the taxpayer could not include the gross receipts from sales of interest-bearing financial instruments in the sales factor, because doing so would not have resulted in a fair representation of the corporation's business activity in the state.

In *Walgreen Arizona Drug Co. v. Arizona Department of Revenue* [No. 1 CA-TX 03-0009 (Ariz. Ct. of App., Sept. 23, 2004)], the Arizona Court of Appeals ruled that the return of capital portion of short-term investments of surplus cash was not includible in the denominator of the Arizona sales factor, because it would distort the sales factor by double-counting the same receipt, first as a retail sale and a second time as a receipt from the disposition of an investment of excess cash. In an analogous case, the Arizona Court of Appeals ruled that a corporation could include in the denominator of its Arizona sales factor only the net gains, not the gross amounts, from its subsidiary's sales of mortgages and mortgage servicing rights. [See also *M.D.C. Holdings, Inc. v. Arizona Department of Revenue* (No. 1 CA-TX 07-0011, Ariz. Ct. of App., Oct. 6, 2009)]

In *Union Pacific Corp. v. Idaho State Tax Commission* [No. 29219 (Idaho Sup. Ct., Jan. 4, 2004)], the Idaho Supreme Court ruled that an alternative apportionment method that was proposed by the tax commission and excluded sales of accounts receivable from the sales factor denominator was reasonable, because it more accurately represented the taxpayer's Idaho business activity. The taxpayer had originally included both the proceeds from the original freight sale and the proceeds from the subsequent sale of the accounts receivable in the sales factor denominator, which resulted in double-counting that artificially inflated denominator of the sales factor.

In *Sherwin-Williams Co. v. Department of Revenue* [No. 4127 (Or. T.C. Oct. 1998), *aff'd*, No. S46023 (Or. Sup. Ct. Jan. 27, 2000)], the Oregon Supreme Court ruled that the Department of Revenue erred in not including gross receipts from the company's investment securities in the sales factor when apportioning income for corporate excise tax purposes. The Department had argued that including gross receipts in the sales factor would result in a misrepresentation or distortion of Sherwin-Williams's true business activities. The court explained that, although this might be true, if a statute results in distortion, the legislature, not the Department, must correct the problem. Effective in 2001, under Rule 150.314.665(6), a taxpayer's primary business activity determines whether the gross receipts or net gains from dispositions of intangible assets are included in the Oregon sales factor.

In *Sherwin-Williams Co. v. Commissioner* [No. 01-A-01-9711-CH-00651 (Tenn. Ct. App., Oct. 21, 1998)], the Tennessee Court of Appeals held that the plain language of the applicable statute requires that the return of principal be included in the sales factor denominator. The court also held, however, that the Commissioner's exclusion of returns of principal was justified under the Tennessee equitable relief statute, which provides that the Commissioner may require use of an alternative apportionment method when the standard apportionment method results "do not fairly represent the extent of the taxpayer's business in this state."

In *Sherwin-Williams Co. v. Indiana Department of State Revenue* [No. 49T10-9412-TA-00273 (Ind. T.C., Dec. 2, 1996)], the Indiana Tax Court held that the principal portion of the proceeds from sales of interest-bearing securities are not included in the sales factor, even though the interest income generated from the investments was included in apportionable business income.

For tax years beginning on or after January 1, 2008, the Kansas sales factor includes only the overall net gains from the sale in the ordinary course of business of intangible business assets. [H.B. 2434, May 22, 2008]

For tax years beginning on or after January 1, 2008, the Kentucky sales factor includes only the net gain from treasury function transactions. This rule does not apply to a corporation principally engaged in the sale of stock or securities. [H.B. 258, Apr. 9, 2008]

Reimbursed Expenses

When the parent corporation of an affiliated group of entities incurs costs that relate to the operations of its subsidiaries, those costs typically are allocated to the subsidiaries for which they were incurred. Similarly, some parent holding companies allocate to their subsidiaries all of the overhead costs that are incurred by the parent in managing and overseeing the subsidiaries. Such transactions may be recorded as receipts or as a reduction of the expenses incurred by the parent corporation. In either case, the issue arises as to whether the parent includes such reimbursements in its sales factor?

Neither UDITPA nor the MTC regulations directly address the issue of whether reimbursed costs or expenses are includible in the sales factor. The general assumption is that if a transaction is recorded as a reduction of an expense, the item would not be included in the sales factor. From the point of view of substance over form, however, the manner in which the transaction is recorded should not control its inclusion or exclusion from the sales or receipts factor. This issue was addressed in *Petrie Stores Corp. v. Comptroller of the Treasury* [No. 5629 (Md. T.C. Apr. 18, 1996)], in which the Maryland Tax Court held that a taxpayer may not include in the sales factor amounts received from its subsidiaries as reimbursements for expenses.

Reimbursed expenses associated with clients or customers occur in numerous industries. For example, an advertising agency may directly pay a photographer for photographs that a client has chosen for an advertising campaign. Under the contract between the advertising agency and its client, all photography costs are passed on to the client. Because those amounts represent reimbursement of expenses, rather than a receipt for services, should (or may) the amounts be included in the sales factor?

This issue was addressed in *Bechtel Power Corp.* [Nos. 91R-1084, 93R-1225, 96R-98822 (Cal. St. Bd. of Equalization Mar. 19, 1997)], in which the California State Board of Equalization (SBE) ruled that the costs of client-furnished materials under a cost-plus contract should be included in the California sales factor of a multistate contractor. Many of the taxpayer's contracts were cost-plus contracts under which the customer agreed to pay the actual costs of materials and payroll plus an additional fee for various services. Materials under the contracts were purchased by the taxpayer in a number of ways, including as the customer's agent. When the customer issued its own purchase order for the materials, the supplier invoices were paid directly by the customer after the taxpayer's approval, and the materials were considered to be client-furnished materials. The California regulations provide that for cost-plus contracts, sales include the entire reimbursed cost plus the fee. The SBE therefore found that the taxpayer's income-producing business activity and the taxable income produced by that activity were the same, whether procurement was from the taxpayer's account or from its client's account. The SBE held that the level of income-producing business activity to be represented by the sales factor was best represented by including the full amount of the cost-plus contract—including the client-furnished materials.

Sales Factor Numerator: Destination Test for Sales of Tangible Personal Property

Most states employ the UDITPA Section 16(a) destination test to assign a receipt from the sale of tangible personal property (e.g., inventory) to a particular state. The destination test reflects the underlying policy reason for including a sales factor in the apportionment formula, which is to provide tax revenue to market states, that is, the states in which customers are located. Under UDITPA Section 16(a), sales of tangible personal property are in this state if the "property is delivered or shipped to a purchaser . . . within this state, regardless of the f.o.b. point or other conditions of the sale." For example, if a taxpayer makes a sale to a purchaser located in State Y, under UDITPA Section 16, the sale is attributed to State Y, regardless of the state from which the goods are shipped. UDITPA Section 16(b) provides an exception to the destination test, however, under which a sale is assigned to the state from which the goods were shipped if the purchaser is the U.S. government or the seller is not taxable in the destination state.

Dock Sales. The proper application of the UDITPA Section 16 destination test is unclear in situations where an out-of-state purchaser uses its own trucks or hires a third-party common carrier to take delivery (i.e., possession) of the goods at the seller's loading dock, and then transports the goods back to its place of business in another state. These are known as *dock sales*. In such situations, UDITPA Section 16 can be interpreted as requiring the application of either a *place of delivery rule* or an *ultimate destination rule*. Under a place of delivery rule, the dock sale is attributed to the state in which the property is delivered to the purchaser at the seller's loading dock. Under an ultimate destination rule, the dock sale is attributed to the state in which the purchaser is located.

For example, assume that XYZ Corporation makes a sale to a purchaser located in State Y, and the purchaser uses its own trucks to pick up the goods at XYZ's factory in State X and transport them back to its place of business in State Y. Under the place of delivery rule, XYZ would attribute the sale to State X (seller's loading dock). In contrast, under the ultimate destination rule, XYZ would attribute the sale to State Y (purchaser's location).

State courts have consistently ruled that a dock sale should be assigned to the state in which the purchaser is located, reasoning that the phrase "within the state" in UDITPA Section 16(a) refers to the "purchaser," and that the intended purpose of the sales factor is to measure the customer base within a state [e.g., *Pennsylvania v. Gilmour Manufacturing Co.*, 822 A.2d 676 (Penn. Sup. Ct. 2003); *McDonnell Douglas Corp. v. Franchise Tax Bd.*, 33 Cal. Rptr. 2d 129 (Cal. Ct. of App. 1994); *Pabst Brewing Co. v. Dept. of Revenue*, 387 N.W.2d 121 (Wis. Ct. of App. 1986); *Olympia Brewing Co. v. Comr. of Revenue*, 326 N.W.2d 642 (Minn. Sup. Ct. 1982); and *Dept. of Revenue v. Parker Banana Co.*, 391 So. 2d 762 (Fla. Ct. of App. 1980)].

From an administrative perspective, one downside to this approach is that the seller (taxpayer) may not know the ultimate destination state, because the seller has no control over the shipment once the goods are picked up by the purchaser. The Pennsylvania Department of Revenue has issued guidance regarding the documentation necessary to establish that any dock sales made by in-state sellers are, in fact, destined to an out-of-state location. [Reg. § 170.11 (Pa. Dept. of Rev., July 15, 2006)]. Documentation sufficient to establish an out-of-state sale includes: (i) bills of lading of the carrier establishing that the goods were destined for or delivered to an out-of-state location, (ii) delivery instructions from the purchaser to the carrier establishing that the goods were to be transported out of Pennsylvania, (iii) warehouse receipts of the purchaser showing that the goods were delivered to an out-of-state location, and (iv) invoices issued by the seller to the purchaser showing an out-of-state delivery address. Documentation which is not sufficient to establish that the ultimate destination of goods is to an out-of-state location includes: (i) invoices issued by the taxpayer/seller to the purchaser showing an out-of-state mailing address, and (ii) affidavits or other declarations from the taxpayer/seller, its employees or agents that the ultimate destination of the goods is an out-of-state location. In the absence of sufficient evidence establishing that the ultimate destination of the sale is an out-of-state location, deliveries of goods in Pennsylvania are attributed to Pennsylvania.

In *Miller Brewing Co. v. Indiana Dept. of State Rev.* [831 N.E.2d 859 (Ind. Tax Ct. 2005)], the Indiana Tax Court ruled that dock sales made by an out-of-state corporation to purchasers located in Indiana were not included in the numerator of the seller's Indiana sales factor. Upon receiving a purchase order, Miller Brewing would produce the beer for pick up at one of its breweries outside of Indiana. The purchaser typically had three options for transporting the beer from the brewery to the ultimate destination: (1) the purchaser could use its own trucks to transport the beer; (2) the purchaser could hire a third-party common carrier to transport the beer; or (3) Miller could arrange for a common carrier to transport the beer, in which case the purchaser would reimburse Miller for the freight charges. In all cases, title to the beer transferred to the purchasers at the breweries. A Department of State Revenue regulation required that a sale not be attributed to Indiana "if the purchaser picks up the goods at an out-of-state location and brings them back into Indiana in his own conveyance." In the present fact pattern, the third-party common carriers hired by the Indiana purchasers were acting as agents of the purchasers, and possession, title, and risk of loss of the beer transferred from Miller to the purchasers when the common carriers picked up the beer outside of Indiana. Based on the regulation, the court ruled that the sales were not included in the numerator of Miller's Indiana sales factor. In the 2005 ruling, the tax years in question were 1994 to 1996. Based on the same regulation, the Indiana Tax Court came to the same conclusion for tax years 1997 to 1999. [*Miller Brewing Co. v. Indiana Dept. of State Rev.* [No. 49T10-0607-TA-69 (Ind. Tax Ct., Aug. 18, 2011)]

Finally, in *Paccar, Inc. v. Alabama Dept. of Rev.* (Ala. Admin. Law Div., No. Corp. 04-715, Jan. 11, 2006), an administrative law judge ruled that a sale of goods is attributed to Alabama if the goods are ultimately delivered to a purchaser in Alabama, regardless of where the seller initially delivers the goods or passes title. Paccar hired a third-party common carrier to pick up the trucks it manufactured at its facilities located outside of Alabama and deliver them to dealers in Alabama. The risk of loss, title, and control over the trucks passed from Paccar to the dealers at the out-of-state shipping dock. As a matter of statutory construction, the judge concluded that the issue could reasonably be decided either way. Therefore, the judge looked to the legislative intent of the sales factor, which is to recognize the contribution of the market states in the production of income, and ruled that the ultimate destination rule applies to Paccar's dock sales.

Sales Factor Numerator: Throwback

Under UDITPA Section 16(b), if the purchaser is the U.S. government or the seller is not taxable in the state of the purchaser, a sale of tangible personal property is not attributed to the state in which the purchaser is located, but instead is attributed to the state from which the property is shipped from an office, store, warehouse, factory, or other place of storage. Under this so-called "throwback rule," a sale is thrown back to the sales factor numerator of the state from which the goods were shipped if either the purchaser is the U.S. government or the seller is not taxable in the destination state. About half of the states have adopted a throwback rule.

See the section in this part entitled Sales Factor: Throwback Rules for a detailed summary of state throwback provisions.

Sales Factor Numerator: Receipts Other than Sales of Tangible Personal Property

Under UDITPA Section 17, any sales other than sales of tangible personal property are considered in-state sales if the income-producing activity is performed in the state. This income-producing activity rule applies to fees for services, rental income from real or tangible personal property, income from intangibles (interest, dividends, royalties, and capital gains), and gains from the sale of real property.

Under MTC Regulation IV.17(2), the term *income-producing activity* applies to each separate item of income and means the transactions and activity engaged in by the taxpayer in the regular course of its trade or business. Examples of income-producing activity include: (i) the rendering of personal services by employees or the use of tangible or intangible property by the taxpayer in performing a service; (ii) the sale, rental, leasing, licensing or other use of real property; (iii) the rental, leasing, licensing or other use of tangible personal property; and (iv) the sale, licensing or other use of intangible personal property. The mere holding of intangible personal property is not, by itself, an income-producing activity.

In terms of determining the state in which the income-producing activity is performed, gross receipts from the sale or lease of real property are assigned to the state in which the real property is located. [MTC Reg. IV.17(4)(B)(a)] Determining where the underlying income-producing activity is located can be more difficult in the case of income from intangible assets, such as royalties, interest, dividends, and capital gains. One approach is to assume that the income-producing activity is the management of the intangible assets (e.g., the corporation's treasury function), in which case the receipts are assigned to the state of commercial domicile. Under MTC Regulation IV.18(c)(3), if income from intangible property cannot be readily attributed to any particular income-producing activity of the taxpayer, the income is excluded from both the numerator and the denominator of the sales factor. Texas takes a somewhat unique approach with respect to interest and dividends. For purposes of computing the Texas sales factor, interest and dividends received from a corporation are attributed to the state of incorporation of the payer. [TAC 34, § 3.557(3)]

In *Appeal of Polaroid Corp.* [No. 62415 (Cal. St. Bd. of Equalization, May 28, 2003)], the California State Board of Equalization held that the income-producing activity with respect to a damages award received from a patent infringement lawsuit was not the litigation, which all occurred in Massachusetts, but rather the lost sales of cameras and film resulting from the patent infringment, and had these lost sales occurred, they would have been included in the California sales factor numerator to the extent the sales occurred in California. [see also *In re Polaroid Corp.*, No. 62415 (Cal. State Bd. of Equal., Jan. 27, 2004)]

In P.D. 03-78 [Va. Dept. of Taxn., Nov. 3, 2003], the Virginia Department of Taxation ruled that the proceeds from the sale of intangible assets in the form of manufacturing contracts were not included in the numerator of the Virginia sales factor because the income-producing activity with regard to the sale occurred outside Virginia. The sale of manufacturing contracts was part of a larger sale of an out-of-state manufacturing division to an out-of-state buyer. The taxpayer (seller) had its corporate headquarters in Virginia. Although the taxpayer's employees in Virginia provided certain approval and oversight for the sale, the greater proportion of the costs directly associated with the sale, that is, gathering of data, negotiations, and due diligence, were incurred outside Virginia.

Cost of Performance Rule. If the income-producing activity is performed in two or more states, the sale is assigned to the state where the greater proportion of the income-producing activity is performed, based on cost of performance. [UDITPA Section 17] For example, if 40 percent of the cost of performance is incurred in State *X*, 30 percent in State *Y*, and 30 percent in State *Z*, the entire sale is assigned to State X. Thus, the cost of performance rule is an all-or-nothing approach, whereby the entire sale is assigned to the single state in which the greater proportion of the cost is incurred.

Under MTC Regulation IV.17(3), the term *costs of performance* means direct costs determined in a manner consistent with generally accepted accounting principles and in accordance with accepted conditions or practices in the trade or business of the taxpayer. Direct costs include material and labor costs that have a causal relationship with the sale in question. In other words, a direct cost is a cost that was incurred for a specific purpose and is traceable to that purpose. For example, the direct costs associated with a service contract for maintaining business equipment would include both the cost of repair parts and the compensation costs of the service technicians. Indirect costs, which include general and administrative expenses that are not associated with any specific sale, are not taken in account in determining the costs of performance.

MTC Regulation IV.17(B) provides a special rule for rental income, whereby receipts from the rental of tangible personal property that is used in two or more states are prorated among the states in proportion to the time the property was physically present or used in each state. For example, if a taxpayer owns ten railroad cars that are present in State *Z* for 50 days, the rental income attributable to State *Z* equals the total rental income multiplied by 500 days/3,650 days. [MTC Reg. IV.17(B)(b), Example.]

In *General American Transportation Corp. v. Department of Revenue* [No. Corp. 02-384 (Ala. Dept. of Rev., Admin. L. Div., April 4, 2003], an administrative law judge ruled that in the absence of information regarding the time that leased railcars were physically presence within and without Alabama, miles traveled within and without Alabama more accurately measured the taxpayer's receipts from business done in Alabama than a measure based on customer billing addresses.

Royalties. A number of states take a market-based approach to sourcing royalties derived from patents, copyrights, trade names, and other intangibles, whereby the royalty receipts are assigned to the state in which the intangible is used by the licensee. For example, for purposes of computing the Massachusetts sales factor, the income producing activity is considered to be performed in Massachusetts to the extent the intangible property is used by the licensee in Massachusetts. [Mass. Gen. Laws, Ch. 63, § 38(f)] For purposes of determining the place of use of intangible property, the regulations distinguish between royalties and licensing fees derived from "marketing intangibles" as opposed to "non-marketing intangibles." [830 Mass. Code Regs. 63.38.1]

Royalties and licensing fees derived from marketing intangibles are attributed to Massachusetts to the extent the income is attributable to the sale of goods or services purchased by Massachusetts customers. In the absence of actual evidence of the licensee's receipts derived from Massachusetts customers, the income is attributed to Massachusetts based upon the percentage of the Massachusetts population in the geographic area in which the licensee is permitted to use the intangible property to market its goods or services. If the license is for the right to use the intangible property in connection with sales at wholesale rather than directly to retail customers, the income is attributed to Massachusetts based upon the percentage of the Massachusetts population in the U.S. geographic area in which the licensee's goods or services are ultimately marketed using the intangible property. [830 Mass. Code Regs. 63.38.1(9)(d)3.c.ii.(A)]

Royalties and licensing fees derived from non-marketing intangibles are attributed to Massachusetts to the extent that the use for which the fees are paid takes place in Massachusetts. It is presumed that the use takes place in the state of the licensee's commercial domicile, unless the taxpayer or the Commissioner can reasonably establish the location of the actual use. If the Commissioner can reasonably establish that some of the actual use of the intangible takes place in Massachusetts, it is presumed that the entire use is in Massachusetts, unless the taxpayer can demonstrate that some of the actual use takes place outside Massachusetts. [830 Mass. Code Regs. 63.38.1(9)(d)3.c.ii.(B)]

Gross Receipts from Sales of Services. For a discussion of how gross receipts from sales of services are accounted for in computing the sales factor, see the section in this part entitled Sales Factor: Receipts from Services.

Nature of Product Sold: Tangible Personal Property, Intangible Property, or Service

Identifying whether the product that the taxpayer sells constitutes tangible personal property, intangible property, or a service is critical to determining which sales factor attribution rule, destination test or income-producing activity rules, to use. Generally, the classification of an item sold is not an issue, but there are exceptions.

In *Microsoft Corporation v. Franchise Tax Board* [No. CGC08-471260 (Cal. Super. Ct., Feb. 17, 2011)], Microsoft received royalties from the licensing of its software products to original equipment manufacturers (OEMs) and other licensees. The licensing agreements gave the OEMs the right to install the taxpayer's software into its computers and then sell the computer with the pre-installed software. Microsoft shipped master disks to the OEMs, which then copied the software onto the hard drives of the computers that they were assembling. Microsoft argued that the royalties were attributable to the licensing of intangible personal property and were excluded from the numerator of the California sales factor, because the greater proportion of the costs of performance relating to the licensed products was incurred in another state. The California Franchise Tax Board argued that the royalties were attributable to the licensing of tangible personal property, in which case the royalties were properly assigned to California in accordance with the California location to which those licensed products were delivered. The court ruled the royalties were derived from the licensing of tangible personal property, because (1) state courts from a number of jurisdictions have determined that computer software constitutes tangible personal property; (2) California appellate courts have determined that, for sales and use tax purposes, a transfer of tangible personal property (such as a master tape or master recording) that is physically useful in the manufacturing process results in a taxable sale even where the true object of the transfer is an intangible property right like a copyright; (3) "canned" software is treated as tangible personal property for California sales and use tax purposes; and (4) the Nebraska Supreme Court held that computerized information goods licensed by the taxpayer to other businesses were tangible personal property for purposes of computing the sales factor. After concluding that the royalties were derived from the licensing of tangible personal property, the court then determined that the royalties received from OEMs with California billing addresses were properly assigned to the California sales factor numerator.

In *TGS-NOPEC Geophysical Co. v. Combs* [No. 08-1056 (Tex. Sup. Ct., May 27, 2011)], the Texas Supreme Court ruled that for purposes of computing the Texas sales factor, receipts from the licensing of geophysical and seismic data to customers in Texas are properly classified as receipts from a limited sale of an intangible asset rather than receipts derived from the use of a license. As a consequence, the receipts are allocated under the location-of-the-payer rule for sales of intangibles rather than allocating them according to the place-of-use rule for licenses.

In *American Business Information, Inc., et al. v. Department of Revenue* [650 N.W. 2d 251 (Neb. Sup. Ct. Aug. 16, 2002)], the Nebraska Supreme Court was faced with the issue of whether the sale of licenses to use marketing data, sold in the form of prospect lists, index cards, computer diskettes, magnetic tapes, and CD-ROMs, should be treated as sales of tangible personal property for purposes of the Nebraska corporate income tax. The court ruled that the sales of the data products were sales of tangible personal property because these data products had a tangible, physical manifestation or embodiment, and because the customers acquired no intangible intellectual property rights to the products. The court also treated online sales where the taxpayer delivered the data electronically over telephone lines as sales of tangible personal property.

In 2003, the Texas Comptroller of Public Accounts ruled that the gross receipts of an Internet advertising company, which earns revenues through banner and click advertising, transactions, and broadcasting services, are properly classified as receipts derived from the performance of a service, and should be apportioned to the place where the service is performed. [Tex. Comp. of Pub. Accts., Letter No. 200305904L, May 16, 2003]

Sales of Electricity and Natural Gas. The states generally have not yet adopted a uniform position on whether, for corporate franchise or income tax purposes, sales of electricity and natural gas are considered sales of tangible personal property, services, or intangible property. To the extent sales of electricity or natural gas are considered sales of tangible personal property, the sales are assigned to a state based on the destination test. In contrast, to the extent such sales are considered sales of services or sales of intangible property, either the traditional UDITPA cost of performance rule or a market-based source rule applies.

The idea that electricity or natural gas is tangible personal property is based on its perceptibility to the senses. For example, for purposes of computing the Oregon sales factor, "'tangible personal property' means personal property that can be seen, weighed, measured, felt, or touched, or that is in any other manner perceptible to the senses. 'Tangible personal property' includes electricity, water, gas, steam, and prewritten computer software." [OAR 150-314.665(2)-(A)(1)]

The idea that providing electricity is the sale of a service arises from the fact that a transmission company is allowing its lines to be used to transmit electricity or that, although a generating company is creating a product, what the consumer is paying for is the distribution of the product to the consumer in a usable form. The latter view is comparable to the argument that an Internet service provider is providing information access instead of selling electrical impulses.

In *Appeal of PacifiCorp* [2002-SBE-005 (Cal. St. Bd. of Equalization Sept. 12, 2002)], the California State Board of Equalization ruled that electricity is an intangible asset. In addition, for purposes of apportioning the income of the Oregon utility company, sales of the generation and transmission of electricity are properly classified as sales of services that consist of the taxpayer setting and keeping in motion electrically charged particles. Therefore, under the income-producing activity rule for sourcing sales of services, the sales were excluded from the numerator of the taxpayer's California sales factor, because the generation and transmission services were performed mainly outside of California.

In *EUA Ocean State Corporation, et al. v. Commissioner of Revenue* [Nos. C258405-406, C258424-425, C258882-883, C259158-159, C259653, and C262566-568 (Mass. App. Tax Bd., April 24, 2006)], the Massachusetts Appellate Tax Board ruled that sales of electricity were not sales of tangible personal property for Massachusetts corporate income tax purposes, and therefore are attributed to the state in which the taxpayer incurred the greater proportion of the cost of performing the income-producing activity. [See also Technical Information Release 06-9 (Mass. Dept. of Rev., June 12, 2006)]

State-by-State Summary

For ease of presentation, the following chart has been divided into six parts, as follows:

- Part 1: Receipts Included in Sales Factor
- Part 2: Attribution Rules for Sales of Goods
- Part 3: Reimbursed Costs and Dock Sales

- Part 4: Sales of Electricity
- Part 5: Dispositions of Fixed Assets, Investments and Intangibles
- Part 6: Occasional Sales and Foreign Sales

Sales Factor (Part 1)

Receipts Included in Sales Factor

Legend:

X	Receipts from these items are included in sales factor
NA	Not applicable
NR	Not reported

		Sales Factor Includes Receipts from						
	What Is the Basis for Determining the Sales Factor?	*Rents*	*Royalties*	*Dividend Income*	*Interest Income*	*Franchise Fees*	*Service Income*	*Does State Permit an Amended Return to Adjust Sales if Another State Successfully Asserts Nexus?*
Alabama	Gross receipts (Ala. Code § 40-27-1; AAC 810-27-1-4)	X	X	Gross income amount	Receivables; working capital, federal interest, taxable municipal bonds, tax free municipal bonds		X	Yes
Alaska	Gross receipts (Alaska Admin. Code tit. 15 §§19.251; 19.271)	X	X				X	Yes
Arizona	Gross receipts (Ariz. Rev. Stat. § 43-1145; Ariz. Admin. Code R 15-2D-801.A)	X	X	Amount included in taxable income after dividends-received deduction	Receivables; working capital	X	X	Yes

Sales Factor (Part 1)
Receipts Included in Sales Factor

Legend:

X	Receipts from these items are included in sales factor
NA	Not applicable
NR	Not reported

		Sales Factor Includes Receipts from						
	What Is the Basis for Determining the Sales Factor?	*Rents*	*Royalties*	*Dividend Income*	*Interest Income*	*Franchise Fees*	*Service Income*	*Does State Permit an Amended Return to Adjust Sales if Another State Successfully Asserts Nexus?*
Arkansas	Gross receipts (Ark. Code Ann. § 26-51-715)	X	X	Amount included in taxable income after dividends-received deduction	Receivables; working capital; taxable municipal bonds	X	X	Yes
California	Gross receipts, see tit.18 CCR § 25134(a)(1)	X, provided they are business income, see R&TC §§ 25123, 25134(a)(1)(C)	X, provided they are business income, see R&TC §§ 25123, 25134(a)(1)(D)	Amount included in taxable income after dividends-received deduction, unless dividends are non-business income	Receivables; working capital; federal interest; taxable municipal bonds	X	X, See R&TC Code, § 25123, 25134(a)(1)(C)	Yes, generally
Colorado	Gross receipts	X	X	Gross income amount	Receivables; working capital; federal interest; taxable municipal bonds; tax-free municipal bonds	X	X	Yes

Sales Factor (Part 1)
Receipts Included in Sales Factor

Legend:

X	Receipts from these items are included in sales factor
NA	Not applicable
NR	Not reported

		Sales Factor Includes Receipts from						
	What Is the Basis for Determining the Sales Factor?	*Rents*	*Royalties*	*Dividend Income*	*Interest Income*	*Franchise Fees*	*Service Income*	*Does State Permit an Amended Return to Adjust Sales if Another State Successfully Asserts Nexus?*
Connecticut	Gross receipts	X	X	Gross amount	Receivables; working capital; nontaxable municipal bonds, federal interest, taxable municipal bonds	X	X	Yes, assuming statute remains open
Delaware	Gross receipts (Del. Code § 9303(b)(6)(c))			Gross income amount		X	X	Yes
District of Columbia	Gross receipts (D.C. Code § 47-1810.02(g))	X	X	Gross income amount	Receivables; working capital; taxable municipal bonds; tax-free municipal bonds	X	X	Yes
Florida	Gross receipts (Fla. Stat. § 220.15(5))	X	X	Gross income amount		X	X	No

Sales Factor (Part 1)

Receipts Included in Sales Factor

Legend:

X Receipts from these items are included in sales factor
NA Not applicable
NR Not reported

	What Is the Basis for Determining the Sales Factor?	*Sales Factor Includes Receipts from*						*Does State Permit an Amended Return to Adjust Sales if Another State Successfully Asserts Nexus?*
		Rents	*Royalties*	*Dividend Income*	*Interest Income*	*Franchise Fees*	*Service Income*	
Georgia	Gross receipts	See O.C.G.A. § 48-7-31 and Ga. Comp. R. & Regs. r. 560-7-7-.03	See O.C.G.A. § 48-7-31 and Ga. Comp. R. & Regs. r. 560-7-7-.03	See O.C.G.A. § 48-7-31 and Ga. Comp. R. & Regs. r. 560-7-7-.03	See O.C.G.A. § 48-7-31 and Ga. Comp. R. & Regs. r. 560-7-7-.03	See O.C.G.A. § 48-7-31 and Ga. Comp. R. & Regs. r. 560-7-7-.03	See O.C.G.A. § 48-7-31 and Ga. Comp. R. & Regs. r. 560-7-7-.03	See O.C.G.A. § 48-7-31 and Ga. Comp. R. & Regs. r. 560-7-7-.03
Hawaii	Gross receipts (Haw. Rev. Stat. § 235-35)	X	X	Amount included in taxable income after dividends-received deduction	Receivables; working capital; taxable state and local obligations	X	X	Yes
Idaho	Gross receipts less returns and allowances (Idaho Code § 63-3027(a))	X	X	Amount included in taxable income after dividends-received deduction	Receivables; working capital; taxable state and local obligations	X	X	Yes, provided statute of limitations is still open

Sales Factor (Part 1)

Receipts Included in Sales Factor

Legend:

X	Receipts from these items are included in sales factor
NA	Not applicable
NR	Not reported

	What Is the Basis for Determining the Sales Factor?	*Sales Factor Includes Receipts from* Rents	Royalties	Dividend Income	Interest Income	Franchise Fees	Service Income	*Does State Permit an Amended Return to Adjust Sales if Another State Successfully Asserts Nexus?*
Illinois	Gross receipts (less returns and allowances), except for those allocated as non-business income.(Ill. Admin. Code tit. 86 § 100.3370(a)(1)(A))	X, only if royalties and other income from intangible assets total more than 50% of gross receipts	X, amount included in taxable income after dividends-received deduction.	Excluded from 1995-1997	Receivables; working capital; taxable and non-taxable state and municipal obligations	X	X	Yes, however this does not extend or re-open the statute of limitations.
Indiana	Gross receipts (45 Ind. Admin. Code §§ 3.1-1-51 and 3.1-1-52; Ind. Code § 6-3-2-2)	X	X, if business income	Amount included in taxable income after dividends-received deduction	Receivables; working capital	X, if business income	X	Yes
Iowa	Gross receipts (Iowa Code § 422.33(e))	X	X	Amount included in taxable income after dividends-received deduction	Receivables; working capital; taxable state and local obligations	X	X	Yes

Sales Factor (Part 1)
Receipts Included in Sales Factor

Legend:

X	Receipts from these items are included in sales factor
NA	Not applicable
NR	Not reported

	What Is the Basis for Determining the Sales Factor?	*Sales Factor Includes Receipts from* Rents	Royalties	Dividend Income	Interest Income	Franchise Fees	Service Income	*Does State Permit an Amended Return to Adjust Sales if Another State Successfully Asserts Nexus?*
Kansas	Gross receipts net returns and allowances	X	X	Net amount included in taxable income after dividends-received deduction (including state modifications allowed on foreign source dividends)	Receivables; working capital; nontaxable and taxable state and municipal obligations	X	X	Yes, provided within statute of limitations
Kentucky	Gross receipts (Ky. Rev. Stat. § 141.120)	X	X	NA	Receivables; working capital; taxable municipal bonds	X	X	Yes
Louisiana	Net sales (La. Reg. § 1134.D.3)						X	Yes
Maine	Gross receipts, (See 18-125 CMR 801.06.A)	X	X	Amount included in taxable income after dividends-received deduction	Receivables; working capital; taxable state and municipal obligations		X	Yes, provided within statute of limitations

Sales Factor (Part 1)
Receipts Included in Sales Factor

Legend:

X	Receipts from these items are included in sales factor
NA	Not applicable
NR	Not reported

	What Is the Basis for Determining the Sales Factor?	*Sales Factor Includes Receipts from* Rents	Royalties	Dividend Income	Interest Income	Franchise Fees	Service Income	*Does State Permit an Amended Return to Adjust Sales if Another State Successfully Asserts Nexus?*
Maryland	Gross receipts (less returns and allowances. See Md. Code Regs. 03.04.03.08(c)(3))	X	X	Amount included in taxable income after dividends received deduction	Receivables; working capital; taxable state and municipal obligations		X	Yes. (Only if the taxpayer's activity in the other state meets Maryland's nexus requirements)
Massachusetts	Gross sales (Mass. Gen. Laws ch. 63 § 38(f))	X	X	Not included, see TIR 04-10	Not included		X	Yes
Michigan (Business Tax)	Gross sales (Mich. Comp. Laws § 208.1303(1))	X	X	Only if investing and trading are only business	X	X	X	Yes

Note. The CIT takes effect 01/01/12, and replaces the Michigan Business Tax (MBT) for most taxpayers. However, businesses that have been approved to receive, have received, or have been assigned certain certified credits may elect to file a return and pay the tax imposed by the MBT in lieu of the CIT until the certified credits are exhausted or extinguished.

	What Is the Basis for Determining the Sales Factor?	Rents	Royalties	Dividend Income	Interest Income	Franchise Fees	Service Income	*Does State Permit an Amended Return to Adjust Sales if Another State Successfully Asserts Nexus?*
Minnesota	Gross receipts (Minn. Stat. § 290.191(5)(a))	X	X			X	X	No

Sales Factor (Part 1)

Receipts Included in Sales Factor

Legend:

X	Receipts from these items are included in sales factor
NA	Not applicable
NR	Not reported

	What Is the Basis for Determining the Sales Factor?	*Sales Factor Includes Receipts from* Rents	Royalties	Dividend Income	Interest Income	Franchise Fees	Service Income	*Does State Permit an Amended Return to Adjust Sales if Another State Successfully Asserts Nexus?*
Mississippi	Net sales (Reg. 35.111.8.06)	X	X		Receivables; working capital; taxable state and municipal obligations	X	X	Yes
Missouri	Gross receipts	X	X		Receivables; working capital	X	X	Yes
Montana	Gross receipts (Mont. Code Ann. § 15-31-302)	X	X	Amount included in taxable income after dividends-received deduction	Receivables; all government obligations; working capital	X	X	Yes, if within statute of limitations, return subject to audit
Nebraska	Gross receipts (less returns and allowances. See Reg. §§ 24-035.01A, 24-036, 24-037, Neb. Rev. Stat. 77-2734.04(7))	X	X	Amount included in taxable income after dividends received deduction	Receivables; working capital; taxable state and local obligations; federal obligations	X	X	Yes
Nevada	Nevada does not impose a corporate income tax							

Sales Factor (Part 1)

Receipts Included in Sales Factor

Legend:

X	Receipts from these items are included in sales factor
NA	Not applicable
NR	Not reported

		Sales Factor Includes Receipts from						
	What Is the Basis for Determining the Sales Factor?	*Rents*	*Royalties*	*Dividend Income*	*Interest Income*	*Franchise Fees*	*Service Income*	*Does State Permit an Amended Return to Adjust Sales if Another State Successfully Asserts Nexus?*
New Hampshire	Net sales (code NH Rule Rev. 304.04(b))	X	X	Gross amount	Receivables; working capital; taxable municipal bonds	X	X	Yes, if within statute of limitations
New Jersey	Gross receipts (used in computation of net income for federal income tax purposes. See N.J. Admin. Code 34:10A-6(B))	X	X	Amount included in taxable income after dividends-received deduction	Receivables; working capital; federal obligations; taxable and nontaxable state and municipal obligations	X	X	Depends on facts and circumstances
New Mexico	Gross receipts	X	X	Amount included in taxable income after dividends received deduction	Receivables; working capital; taxable state and municipal obligations	X	X	Yes

Sales Factor (Part 1)

Receipts Included in Sales Factor

Legend:

X	Receipts from these items are included in sales factor
NA	Not applicable
NR	Not reported

		Sales Factor Includes Receipts from						
	What Is the Basis for Determining the Sales Factor?	*Rents*	*Royalties*	*Dividend Income*	*Interest Income*	*Franchise Fees*	*Service Income*	*Does State Permit an Amended Return to Adjust Sales if Another State Successfully Asserts Nexus?*
New York	Gross sales (Business receipts, i.e. gross income used in computation of taxpayer's net income. See NYCRR § 4-4.1)	X	X		Receivables; working capital unless election made to treat that as investment capital	X	X	NA
North Carolina	Gross sales (Gross receipts less returns and allowances. See N.C. Admin. Code § 17.05C.1002; Reg. 05C.1001)	X	X	Amount included in taxable income after dividends-received deduction	Receivables; working capital; taxable state and local obligations	X	X	Yes
North Dakota	Federal line 1 (N.D. Cent. Code § 57-38.1-15)	X, if rental business					X	Yes
Ohio	Ohio does not impose a corporate income tax							

Sales Factor (Part 1)

Receipts Included in Sales Factor

Legend:

X	Receipts from these items are included in sales factor
NA	Not applicable
NR	Not reported

	What Is the Basis for Determining the Sales Factor?	*Sales Factor Includes Receipts from*						*Does State Permit an Amended Return to Adjust Sales if Another State Successfully Asserts Nexus?*
		Rents	*Royalties*	*Dividend Income*	*Interest Income*	*Franchise Fees*	*Service Income*	
Note. Effective 1/1/2010, the Ohio Franchise Tax was fully phased out and business will be taxed on gross receipts through the Commercial Activity Tax. Details about that tax can be found at: http//tax.ohio.gov/divisions/commercial_activities/index.stm								
Oklahoma	Gross sales (Rule. 710:50-17-71; Okla. Stat. § 2358)							Yes

Sales Factor (Part 1)
Receipts Included in Sales Factor

Legend:

X	Receipts from these items are included in sales factor
NA	Not applicable
NR	Not reported

	What Is the Basis for Determining the Sales Factor?	*Sales Factor Includes Receipts from* Rents	Royalties	Dividend Income	Interest Income	Franchise Fees	Service Income	*Does State Permit an Amended Return to Adjust Sales if Another State Successfully Asserts Nexus?*
Oregon	Gross receipts, for tax years beginning on or after 1/1/99, net gain from sale, exchange, redemption, or holding of intangible assets, if such income is business income but not derived from the taxpayer's primary business activity. (OR. Rev. Stat. § 314.665)	X	X, only if derived from taxpayer's primary business activity in years beginning on or after 1/1/95, per ORS 314.665(6)(a).	Amount included in taxable income after dividends-received deduction.	Receivables	X, only if derived from taxpayer's primary business activity in years beginning on or after 1/1/95, per ORS 314.665(6)(a).	X	Yes
Pennsylvania	Gross receipts (72 PA. Cons. Stat. § 7401(3)2.(a))	X	X		Receivables, working capital, taxable state and municipal obligations	X	X	Yes

Sales Factor (Part 1)

Receipts Included in Sales Factor

Legend:

X	Receipts from these items are included in sales factor
NA	Not applicable
NR	Not reported

	What Is the Basis for Determining the Sales Factor?	*Sales Factor Includes Receipts from* Rents	Royalties	Dividend Income	Interest Income	Franchise Fees	Service Income	*Does State Permit an Amended Return to Adjust Sales if Another State Successfully Asserts Nexus?*
Rhode Island	Gross receipts (R.I. Gen. Laws § 44-11-14(2))	X	X	Amount included in taxable income after dividends received deduction	Receivables, working capital, taxable state and municipal obligations	X	X	Yes
South Carolina	Gross receipts except net gain for property used in a trade or business	X	X	X Gross amount	Receivables; working capital; taxable municipal bonds	X	X	No
South Dakota	South Dakota does not impose a corporate income tax							
Tennessee	Gross receipts (less returns and allowances. See Reg. § 1320-6-1-.32; Tenn. code ANN. § 67-4-2012)	X	X	Gross income amount	Receivables; working capital; taxable and non-taxable state and municipal obligations; federal obligations		X	Yes, if within statute of limitations

Sales Factor (Part 1)

Receipts Included in Sales Factor

Legend:

X	Receipts from these items are included in sales factor
NA	Not applicable
NR	Not reported

	What Is the Basis for Determining the Sales Factor?	*Sales Factor Includes Receipts from* Rents	*Royalties*	*Dividend Income*	*Interest Income*	*Franchise Fees*	*Service Income*	*Does State Permit an Amended Return to Adjust Sales if Another State Successfully Asserts Nexus?*
Texas	Gross receipts (Tex. Tax Code tit.2 ch. 171 § 105)	X	X	Receivables; working capital; taxable municipal bonds; tax-free municipal bonds	X	X	X	No, Texas does not apply a throwback rule.
Utah	Gross sales (Gross receipts less returns and allowances. See Utah Admin. Code R865-6F-8(9)(a))	X	X		Receivables	X	X	Yes, if within statute of limitations
Vermont	Gross receipts (VT. Stat. Ann. tit. 32 § 5833)	X	X	Amount included in taxable income after dividends received deduction.	Receivables; working capital; taxable state and municipal obligations if business income	X	X	Yes, if original return was in error and Statute of Limitations has not expired

Sales Factor (Part 1)
Receipts Included in Sales Factor

Legend:

X	Receipts from these items are included in sales factor
NA	Not applicable
NR	Not reported

		Sales Factor Includes Receipts from						
	What Is the Basis for Determining the Sales Factor?	*Rents*	*Royalties*	*Dividend Income*	*Interest Income*	*Franchise Fees*	*Service Income*	*Does State Permit an Amended Return to Adjust Sales if Another State Successfully Asserts Nexus?*
Virginia	Gross receipts, net gain on sales of intangible property only (VA. Code § 58.1-414; 23 VAC 10-120-210.B)	X	X	None, all dividends are allocated. See Va. Code § 58.1-407.	Receivables, working capital, taxable state and municipal obligations	X	X	Yes
Washington	Washington does not impose a corporate income tax							
West Virginia	Gross receipts (less returns and allowances. See W.VA. Code 311-24-7(e)(10))	X	X	Gross income amount	Taxable state and municipal obligations		X	Yes
Wisconsin	Gross receipts (Wis. Stat. § 71.25(9)(e))	X	X		Receivables	X	X	Yes, does not apply if taxpayer merely files return(s) in that/those state(s).
Wyoming	Wyoming does not impose a corporate income tax							

Sales Factor (Part 2)

Attribution Rules for Sales of Goods

Legend:

X	**The methods are used for attributing sales of tangible personal property to the numerator of the sales factor**
NA	**Not applicable**
NR	**Not reported**

	Ignoring Application of Throwback Rule (if any), Method Used to Attribute Sales of Tangible Personal Property to Numerator of Sales Factor				
	Destination State	*Sales Office Negotiating Sale*	*If Purchaser is U.S. Government, State From Which Goods are Shipped*	*State of Sales Activity*	*State Where Shipment Terminates, Even Though Subsequently Transferred to Another State*
Alabama	X				
Alaska	X		X		X
Arizona	X		Not included, See AAC R15-2D-805		See AAC R15-2D-804
Arkansas	X		X		X
California	X		X		X
	See 18 CRR § 25135(a)				
Colorado	X				X
Connecticut	X				X
Delaware	X			X	
District of Columbia	X			X	X
Florida	X	X		X	X
Georgia	X				
Hawaii	X		X		X
Idaho	X		X		X
Illinois	X		X		

Sales Factor (Part 2)

Attribution Rules for Sales of Goods

Legend:

X	**The methods are used for attributing sales of tangible personal property to the numerator of the sales factor**
NA	**Not applicable**
NR	**Not reported**

	Ignoring Application of Throwback Rule (if any), Method Used to Attribute Sales of Tangible Personal Property to Numerator of Sales Factor				
	Destination State	*Sales Office Negotiating Sale*	*If Purchaser is U.S. Government, State From Which Goods are Shipped*	*State of Sales Activity*	*State Where Shipment Terminates, Even Though Subsequently Transferred to Another State*
Indiana	X	X	X	X	X
Iowa	X				
Kansas	X		X		X
Kentucky	X		X		X
Louisiana	X				
Maine	X				
Maryland	X			X	
Massachusetts	X	X			
Michigan (Business Tax)	X				
Note. The CIT takes effect 01/01/12, and replaces the Michigan Business Tax (MBT) for most taxpayers. However, businesses that have been approved to receive, have received, or have been assigned certain certified credits may elect to file a return and pay the tax imposed by the MBT in lieu of the CIT until the certified credits are exhausted or extinguished.					
Minnesota	X				X
Mississippi	X		X		X
Missouri	X				X
Montana	X		X		

Sales Factor (Part 2)

Attribution Rules for Sales of Goods

Legend:

X	**The methods are used for attributing sales of tangible personal property to the numerator of the sales factor**
NA	**Not applicable**
NR	**Not reported**

	Ignoring Application of Throwback Rule (if any), Method Used to Attribute Sales of Tangible Personal Property to Numerator of Sales Factor				
	Destination State	*Sales Office Negotiating Sale*	*If Purchaser is U.S. Government, State From Which Goods are Shipped*	*State of Sales Activity*	*State Where Shipment Terminates, Even Though Subsequently Transferred to Another State*
Nebraska	X		X		
Nevada	Nevada does not impose a corporate income tax				
New Hampshire	X		X		
New Jersey	X				X
New Mexico	X		X		
New York	X				
North Carolina	X				X
North Dakota	X, throwback rule applies				
Ohio	Ohio does not impose a corporate income tax				
Note. Effective 1/1/2010, the Ohio Franchise Tax was fully phased out and business will be taxed on gross receipts through the Commercial Activity Tax. Details about that tax can be found at: http//tax.ohio.gov/divisions/commercial_activities/index.stm					
Oklahoma	X				
Oregon	X		X		
Pennsylvania	X				X
Rhode Island	X				X
South Carolina	X				

Sales Factor (Part 2)

Attribution Rules for Sales of Goods

Legend:

X	**The methods are used for attributing sales of tangible personal property to the numerator of the sales factor**
NA	**Not applicable**
NR	**Not reported**

	Ignoring Application of Throwback Rule (if any), Method Used to Attribute Sales of Tangible Personal Property to Numerator of Sales Factor				
	Destination State	*Sales Office Negotiating Sale*	*If Purchaser is U.S. Government, State From Which Goods are Shipped*	*State of Sales Activity*	*State Where Shipment Terminates, Even Though Subsequently Transferred to Another State*
South Dakota	South Dakota does not impose a corporate income tax				
Tennessee	X		X		X
Texas	X				X
Utah	X		X		X
Vermont	X		X		X
Virginia	X				
Washington	Washington does not impose a corporate income tax				
West Virginia	X		X		X
Wisconsin	X	X			
Wyoming	Wyoming does not impose a corporate income tax				

Sales Factor (Part 3)

Reimbursed Costs and Dock Sales

Legend:

NA	Not applicable
NR	Not reported
X	These items are included in the sales factor computation

	Reimbursement for Costs Shared Among Affiliated Group Members	*Reimbursement for Expenses Paid on Behalf of Customers*	*Attribution Rule for Goods Picked up by Out-of- State Customer at Taxpayer's In-State Manufacturing Facility*
Alabama			State in which goods are picked up.
Alaska			Destination state
Arizona			Destination state
Arkansas			State in which goods are picked up.
California			Destination state; however, see *McDonell Douglas v. FTB*, 26 Cal. App. 4th 1789 (1994) for special rule when goods are immediately taken into another state.
Colorado	X	X	NR
Connecticut			Destination state
Delaware			State in which goods are picked up.
District of Columbia	X	X	State in which goods are picked up.
Florida			State in which goods are picked up.
Georgia			Destination state
Hawaii		X	Destination state
Idaho		In the case of cost-plus-fixed-fee contracts sales include the entire reimbursed amount.	Destination state
Illinois		X	State in which goods picked up. See DOR Letter Ruling 88-0223 (8/4/88). Under UDITPA, as construed by MTC and Ill. Admin. Code § 100.337(c)(1)(C), these types of sales are assigned to the state of pickup.

Sales Factor (Part 3)

Reimbursed Costs and Dock Sales

Legend:

NA	Not applicable
NR	Not reported
X	These items are included in the sales factor computation

	Reimbursement for Costs Shared Among Affiliated Group Members	*Reimbursement for Expenses Paid on Behalf of Customers*	*Attribution Rule for Goods Picked up by Out-of- State Customer at Taxpayer's In-State Manufacturing Facility*
Indiana			State in which goods are picked up.
Iowa			Destination state
Kansas			State in which goods are picked up.
Kentucky		X	Destination state
Louisiana			Destination state
Maine			
Maryland			
Massachusetts			NR
Michigan (Business Tax)			Destination state
Note. The CIT takes effect 01/01/12, and replaces the Michigan Business Tax (MBT) for most taxpayers. However, businesses that have been approved to receive, have received, or have been assigned certain certified credits may elect to file a return and pay the tax imposed by the MBT in lieu of the CIT until the certified credits are exhausted or extinguished.			
Minnesota	X		State in which goods are picked up.
Mississippi			State in which goods are picked up.
Missouri			State in which goods are picked up.
Montana			Destination state
Nebraska			Destination state
Nevada	Nevada does not impose a corporate income tax		
New Hampshire			Destination state

Sales Factor (Part 3)

Reimbursed Costs and Dock Sales

Legend:

NA	Not applicable
NR	Not reported
X	These items are included in the sales factor computation

	Reimbursement for Costs Shared Among Affiliated Group Members	*Reimbursement for Expenses Paid on Behalf of Customers*	*Attribution Rule for Goods Picked up by Out-of- State Customer at Taxpayer's In-State Manufacturing Facility*
New Jersey			Destination if customer is the end user.
New Mexico			State in which goods are picked up.
New York	X	X	State of destination
North Carolina			NR
North Dakota			State of destination
Ohio	Ohio does not impose a corporate income tax		
Note. Effective 1/1/2010, the Ohio Franchise Tax was fully phased out and business will be taxed on gross receipts through the Commercial Activity Tax. Details about that tax can be found at: http//tax.ohio.gov/divisions/commercial_activities/index.stm			
Oklahoma			NR
Oregon			Destination state; however, this is a policy change and not a legislative change.
Pennsylvania	X	X	NR
Rhode Island			State in which goods are picked up.
South Carolina			State in which goods are picked up
South Dakota	South Dakota does not impose a corporate income tax		
Tennessee	X		Destination state

Sales Factor (Part 3)

Reimbursed Costs and Dock Sales

Legend:

NA	Not applicable
NR	Not reported
X	These items are included in the sales factor computation

	Reimbursement for Costs Shared Among Affiliated Group Members	*Reimbursement for Expenses Paid on Behalf of Customers*	*Attribution Rule for Goods Picked up by Out-of- State Customer at Taxpayer's In-State Manufacturing Facility*
Texas	The treatment of reimbursements depends on the facts. Certain flow-through funds are allowed as a deduction from total revenue. If the reimbursement qualifies as a flow-through fund and is excluded from total revenue, the reimbursement is not included in the apportionment factor.		State in which goods are picked up.
Utah			State in which goods are picked up, unless the purchaser is not a Utah purchaser.
Vermont			Destination state if known; otherwise state in which goods are picked up.
Virginia	X		Destination state if known; otherwise state in which goods are picked up.
Washington	Washington does not impose a corporate income tax		
West Virginia			State in which goods are picked up.
Wisconsin			Destination state
Wyoming	Wyoming does not impose a corporate income tax		

Sales Factor (Part 4)
Sales of Electricity

Legend:

X	Condition applies
NA	Not applicable
NR	Not reported

	For Apportionment Purposes, Is the Sale of Electricity Considered the Sale of (a/an):			
	Service	*Intangible Property*	*Tangible Personal Property*	*Other*
Alabama			X	
Alaska			X	
Arizona			X	
Arkansas	X			
California		X		
Colorado	X			
Connecticut			X	
Delaware				Commodity, included in sales factor
District of Columbia	X		X	
Florida		X		
Georgia			X	
Hawaii		X		
Idaho			X	
Illinois			X	
Indiana			X	
Iowa			X	
Kansas	X		X	

Sales Factor (Part 4)
Sales of Electricity

Legend:

X	Condition applies
NA	Not applicable
NR	Not reported

	For Apportionment Purposes, Is the Sale of Electricity Considered the Sale of (a/an):			
	Service	*Intangible Property*	*Tangible Personal Property*	*Other*
Kentucky			X	
Louisiana			X	
Maine			X	
Maryland	NR	NR	NR	NR
Massachusetts			X	
Michigan (Business Tax)			X	

Note. The CIT takes effect 01/01/12, and replaces the Michigan Business Tax (MBT) for most taxpayers. However, businesses that have been approved to receive, have received, or have been assigned certain certified credits may elect to file a return and pay the tax imposed by the MBT in lieu of the CIT until the certified credits are exhausted or extinguished.

Minnesota			X	
Mississippi			X	
Missouri			X	
Montana			X	
Nebraska	X			
Nevada	Nevada does not impose a corporate income tax			
New Hampshire			X	
New Jersey			X	
New Mexico			X	
New York	NR	NR	NR	NR

Sales Factor (Part 4)

Sales of Electricity

Legend:

X	Condition applies
NA	Not applicable
NR	Not reported

	For Apportionment Purposes, Is the Sale of Electricity Considered the Sale of (a/an):			
	Service	*Intangible Property*	*Tangible Personal Property*	*Other*
North Carolina	X		X	
North Dakota			X	
Ohio	Ohio does not impose a corporate income tax			
Note. Effective 1/1/2010, the Ohio Franchise Tax was fully phased out and business will be taxed on gross receipts through the Commercial Activity Tax. Details about that tax can be found at: http//tax.ohio.gov/divisions/commercial_activities/index.stm				
Oklahoma	NR	NR	NR	NR
Oregon			X	
Pennsylvania			X	
Rhode Island				File Public Service Tax
South Carolina			X	
South Dakota	South Dakota does not impose a corporate income tax			
Tennessee			X	
Texas			X	
Utah		X		X
Vermont			X	X
Virginia			X	X
Washington	Washington does not impose a corporate income tax			
West Virginia	X			X

Sales Factor (Part 4)
Sales of Electricity

Legend:

X	Condition applies
NA	Not applicable
NR	Not reported

	For Apportionment Purposes, Is the Sale of Electricity Considered the Sale of (a/an):			
	Service	*Intangible Property*	*Tangible Personal Property*	*Other*
Wisconsin			X	X
Wyoming	Wyoming does not impose a corporate income tax			

Sales Factor (Part 5)

Dispositions of Fixed Assets, Investments and Intangibles

Legend:

X — Receipts from these items are included in sales factor
NA — Not applicable
NR — Not reported

	Assuming Sale Is Not Excluded Under Special Rule For Occasional Transactions, Sales Factor Includes Receipts from								
	Disposition of Fixed Assets (e.g., machinery and equipment) Used in Business			*Disposition of Short-Term Investments of Working Capital*			*Disposition of Other Intangible Business Property (e.g., patents)*		
	Gross Proceeds	*Net Gain*	*Other*	*Gross Proceeds*	*Net Gain*	*Other*	*Gross Proceeds*	*Net Gain*	*Other*
Alabama	X			X				X	
Alaska	X					Generally excluded			Generally excluded
Arizona			Depends on facts		X				X, depends on circumstances
Arkansas	X, but excluded if distorts factor				X (gains only, net losses)		X		
California	X			X, unless inclusion is distortive under Rev. & Tax. Code § 25137, see *Microsoft Corporation v. FTB* (2006) 39 Cal.4th 750.	X, applies to repurchase agreements; see *General Motors Corporation v. FTB* (2006) 29 Cal.4th 773.		X, provided the activity is not substantial and occasional, see CCR § 25137(c)(1)(A).		
Colorado	X			X	X			X	
Connecticut		X			X			X	
Delaware					X				

Sales Factor (Part 5)

Dispositions of Fixed Assets, Investments and Intangibles

Legend:

X	Receipts from these items are included in sales factor
NA	Not applicable
NR	Not reported

	Assuming Sale Is Not Excluded Under Special Rule For Occasional Transactions, Sales Factor Includes Receipts from								
	Disposition of Fixed Assets (e.g., machinery and equipment) Used in Business			*Disposition of Short-Term Investments of Working Capital*			*Disposition of Other Intangible Business Property (e.g., patents)*		
	Gross Proceeds	*Net Gain*	*Other*	*Gross Proceeds*	*Net Gain*	*Other*	*Gross Proceeds*	*Net Gain*	*Other*
District of Columbia		X			X			X	
Florida	X			X			X		
Georgia	NR	NR	NR	NR	NR	NR	NR	NR	NR
Hawaii	X				X			X	
Idaho	X			X, if a sale; may modify if distortive			X, if a sale; may modify if distortive		

Sales Factor (Part 5)

Dispositions of Fixed Assets, Investments and Intangibles

Legend:

X — Receipts from these items are included in sales factor
NA — Not applicable
NR — Not reported

	Assuming Sale Is Not Excluded Under Special Rule For Occasional Transactions, Sales Factor Includes Receipts from								
	Disposition of Fixed Assets (e.g., machinery and equipment) Used in Business			*Disposition of Short-Term Investments of Working Capital*			*Disposition of Other Intangible Business Property (e.g., patents)*		
	Gross Proceeds	*Net Gain*	*Other*	*Gross Proceeds*	*Net Gain*	*Other*	*Gross Proceeds*	*Net Gain*	*Other*
Illinois	X, but excluded if from an incidental/ occasional sale of a fixed asset used in the regular course of business, 86 Ill. Adm. Code § 100.3380(b).			X, 86 Ill. Adm. Code § 100.3370(a)(2) addresses gross receipts not included in the sales factor, e.g., interest on federal obligations subtracted under IITA §§ 203(a)(2)(N), 203(b)(2)(J), 203(c)(2)(K), or 203(d)(2)(G).			X, as defined in 86 Ill. Adm. Code § 100.3370(a)(3)		
Indiana	X			X			X		
Iowa		X			X			X	
Kansas	X				X			X	
Kentucky	X				X		X		
Louisiana									
Maine									

Sales Factor (Part 5)

Dispositions of Fixed Assets, Investments and Intangibles

Legend:

X	Receipts from these items are included in sales factor
NA	Not applicable
NR	Not reported

	Assuming Sale Is Not Excluded Under Special Rule For Occasional Transactions, Sales Factor Includes Receipts from								
	Disposition of Fixed Assets (e.g., machinery and equipment) Used in Business			*Disposition of Short-Term Investments of Working Capital*			*Disposition of Other Intangible Business Property (e.g., patents)*		
	Gross Proceeds	*Net Gain*	*Other*	*Gross Proceeds*	*Net Gain*	*Other*	*Gross Proceeds*	*Net Gain*	*Other*
Maryland	X			X			X		
Massachusetts									
Michigan (Business Tax)	X			X			X		
Note. The CIT takes effect 01/01/12, and replaces the Michigan Business Tax (MBT) for most taxpayers. However, businesses that have been approved to receive, have received, or have been assigned certain certified credits may elect to file a return and pay the tax imposed by the MBT in lieu of the CIT until the certified credits are exhausted or extinguished.									
Minnesota	X			X			X		
Mississippi		X			X			X	
Missouri		X			X			X	
Montana		X			X			X	
Nebraska	X				X			X	
Nevada									
New Hampshire		X			X			X	
New Jersey		X			X			X	
New Mexico	X				X			X	

Sales Factor (Part 5)

Dispositions of Fixed Assets, Investments and Intangibles

Legend:

X	Receipts from these items are included in sales factor
NA	Not applicable
NR	Not reported

	Assuming Sale Is Not Excluded Under Special Rule For Occasional Transactions, Sales Factor Includes Receipts from								
	Disposition of Fixed Assets (e.g., machinery and equipment) Used in Business			*Disposition of Short-Term Investments of Working Capital*			*Disposition of Other Intangible Business Property (e.g., patents)*		
	Gross Proceeds	*Net Gain*	*Other*	*Gross Proceeds*	*Net Gain*	*Other*	*Gross Proceeds*	*Net Gain*	*Other*
New York				X, only if considered business capital, not investment or subsidiary capital			X, only if considered business receipts		
North Carolina		X			X			X	
North Dakota									
Ohio	Ohio does not impose a corporate income tax								

Note. Effective 1/1/2010, the Ohio Franchise Tax was fully phased out and business will be taxed on gross receipts through the Commercial Activity Tax. Details about that tax can be found at: http//tax.ohio.gov/divisions/commercial_activities/index.stm

Oklahoma	NR	NR	NR	NR	NR	NR	NR	NR	NR
Oregon	X, but excluded if incidental or occasional				X		X		
Pennsylvania	X					Proceeds, but only if securities dealers	X		

Sales Factor (Part 5)

Dispositions of Fixed Assets, Investments and Intangibles

Legend:

X	Receipts from these items are included in sales factor
NA	Not applicable
NR	Not reported

	Assuming Sale Is Not Excluded Under Special Rule For Occasional Transactions, Sales Factor Includes Receipts from								
	Disposition of Fixed Assets (e.g., machinery and equipment) Used in Business			*Disposition of Short-Term Investments of Working Capital*			*Disposition of Other Intangible Business Property (e.g., patents)*		
	Gross Proceeds	*Net Gain*	*Other*	*Gross Proceeds*	*Net Gain*	*Other*	*Gross Proceeds*	*Net Gain*	*Other*
Rhode Island		X			X			X	
South Carolina		X			X		X		
South Dakota	South Dakota does not impose a corporate income tax								
Tennessee	X			X			X		
Texas	Gross receipts is the general rule. Only the net gain from the sale of investments and capital assets is included in gross receipts.								
Utah	NR	X	NR	NR	NR	NR	NR	Not typically included because it is not generally sourced or sourceable to any particular state-generally earned in all states where T/P operates. If it were sourceable, only the net gain would be included.	Not typically included because it is not generally sourced or sourceable to any particular state-generally earned in all states where T/P operates. If it were sourceable, only the net gain would be included.
Vermont		X			X			X	

Sales Factor (Part 5)

Dispositions of Fixed Assets, Investments and Intangibles

Legend:

X	Receipts from these items are included in sales factor
NA	Not applicable
NR	Not reported

	Assuming Sale Is Not Excluded Under Special Rule For Occasional Transactions, Sales Factor Includes Receipts from								
	Disposition of Fixed Assets (e.g., machinery and equipment) Used in Business			*Disposition of Short-Term Investments of Working Capital*			*Disposition of Other Intangible Business Property (e.g., patents)*		
	Gross Proceeds	*Net Gain*	*Other*	*Gross Proceeds*	*Net Gain*	*Other*	*Gross Proceeds*	*Net Gain*	*Other*
Virginia	X				X			X	
Washington	Washington does not impose a corporate income tax								
West Virginia	X				X		X	X	
Wisconsin		Not included				Not included			Generally not included
Wyoming	Wyoming does not impose a corporate income tax								

Sales Factor (Part 6)

Inclusion of Occasional Sales and Foreign Sales

Legend:

X	These items are included in the sales factor denominator
NA	Not applicable
NR	Not reported

	Substantial Amount of Receipts From Occasional Sales of Fixed Assets	*Insubstantial Amount of Receipts From Occasional Sales*	*Sales Shipped to Purchasers in a Foreign Country*
Alabama	X	X	X
Alaska	X		
Arizona	See AAC R15-2D-903.	See AAC R15-2D-903.	Excluded only if income is not subject to tax under Title 43.
Arkansas		X	X
California	Excluded, see 18 CCR § 25137(c)(1)(A).	X, See 18 CCR § 25317(c)(1)(B).	X, includes total gross receipts of taxpayer derived from transactions and activity in the regular course of its trade or business; see 18 CCR, § 25134.
Colorado			X
Connecticut	X	X	X
Delaware	X	X	X
District of Columbia	X	X	X
Florida	X		
Georgia			
Hawaii			X
Idaho	X	X	X
Illinois			X
Indiana	X	X	
Iowa	X	X	X, if sales included in federal return

Sales Factor (Part 6)

Inclusion of Occasional Sales and Foreign Sales

Legend:

X	These items are included in the sales factor denominator
NA	Not applicable
NR	Not reported

	Substantial Amount of Receipts From Occasional Sales of Fixed Assets	*Insubstantial Amount of Receipts From Occasional Sales*	*Sales Shipped to Purchasers in a Foreign Country*
Kansas		X, included if exclusion would materially affect amount of income to Kansas.	X
Kentucky	X	X	X
Louisiana			
Maine			X
Maryland	X		X
Massachusetts	X	X	Depends on facts, must have right to apportion
Michigan (Business Tax)			

Note. The CIT takes effect 01/01/12, and replaces the Michigan Business Tax (MBT) for most taxpayers. However, businesses that have been approved to receive, have received, or have been assigned certain certified credits may elect to file a return and pay the tax imposed by the MBT in lieu of the CIT until the certified credits are exhausted or extinguished.

Minnesota			X
Mississippi	X	X	X
Missouri	X	X	X
Montana	X	X	X, throwback
Nebraska	X	X	X
Nevada	Nevada does not impose a corporate income tax		
New Hampshire	X	X	X

Sales Factor (Part 6)

Inclusion of Occasional Sales and Foreign Sales

Legend:

X	These items are included in the sales factor denominator
NA	Not applicable
NR	Not reported

	Substantial Amount of Receipts From Occasional Sales of Fixed Assets	*Insubstantial Amount of Receipts From Occasional Sales*	*Sales Shipped to Purchasers in a Foreign Country*
New Jersey	X	X	X
New Mexico	X	X	X
New York			X
North Carolina		X	X
North Dakota	X, determination based on facts and circumstances		X
Ohio	Ohio does not impose a corporate income tax		
Note. Effective 1/1/2010, the Ohio Franchise Tax was fully phased out and business will be taxed on gross receipts through the Commercial Activity Tax. Details about that tax can be found at: http//tax.ohio.gov/divisions/commercial_activities/index.stm			
Oklahoma			
Oregon		X	X
Pennsylvania	X	X	X
Rhode Island	X	X	X
South Carolina	X	X	X
South Dakota	South Dakota does not impose a corporate income tax		
Tennessee		X	X
Texas	X	X	
Utah		X	X
Vermont	X	X	X

Sales Factor (Part 6)

Inclusion of Occasional Sales and Foreign Sales

Legend:

X	These items are included in the sales factor denominator
NA	Not applicable
NR	Not reported

	Substantial Amount of Receipts From Occasional Sales of Fixed Assets	*Insubstantial Amount of Receipts From Occasional Sales*	*Sales Shipped to Purchasers in a Foreign Country*
Virginia	X	X	X
Washington	Washington does not impose a corporate income tax		
West Virginia	X		
Wisconsin	Depends on facts	Depends on facts	Denominator only
Wyoming	Wyoming does not impose a corporate income tax		

Sales Factor: Throwback Rules

Under UDITPA Section 15, the sales factor is a fraction, the numerator of which is the total sales of the taxpayer in this state during the tax period, and the denominator of which is the total sales of the taxpayer everywhere during the tax period. Under UDITPA Section 16, sales of tangible personal property are in this state if the "property is delivered or shipped to a purchaser . . . within this state." This so-called *destination test* reflects the original rationale for including a sales factor in the apportionment formula, which is to recognize the contribution of the market states.

UDITPA Section 16(b) provides two exceptions to the destination test, both of which take the form of a *throwback rule*. The first exception applies if "the purchaser is the United States government," in which case the sale of tangible personal property is not attributed to the state in which the purchaser is located, but instead is attributed to the state in which "the property is shipped from an office, store, warehouse, factory, or other place of storage." This exception reflects the U.S. government's centralized purchasing practices and the difficulty this creates in ascertaining the ultimate destination for such sales.

The second exception found in UDITPA Section 16(b) applies if "the taxpayer is not taxable in the state of the purchaser," in which case the sale is also attributed to the state in which "the property is shipped from an office, store, warehouse, factory, or other place of storage." This exception is designed to ensure that all of a taxpayer's sales are attributed to a state in which the taxpayer is taxable. By doing so, it prevents no-where sales, that is, sales that are included in the denominators but not in any of the numerators of the taxpayer's sales factors. Nevertheless, many states do not require throwback, including Arizona, Connecticut, Delaware, Florida, Georgia, Iowa, Louisiana, Maryland, Michigan, Minnesota, Nebraska, New York, North Carolina, Pennsylvania, South Carolina, Texas and Virginia. The lack of a throwback rule makes a state a more attractive location for a manufacturing or distribution facility.

In 2009, Wisconsin modified its sales throwback rule, which previously required the throwback of 50 percent of sales shipped to states in which the taxpayer was not taxable. Effective for tax years beginning on or after January 1, 2009, 100 percent of such sales must be thrown back to Wisconsin. [A.B. 75, June 29, 2009]

Taxable in Another State

Under UDITPA Section 3, a corporation is "taxable in another state" if it meets either a subject-to-tax test or a jurisdiction-to-tax test. Under the subject-to-tax test, a corporation is taxable in another state if it "is subject to a net income tax, a franchise tax measured by net income, a franchise tax for the privilege of doing business, or a corporate stock tax." In other words, the corporation "carries on business activities in a state and the state imposes such a tax thereon." [MTC Reg. IV.3.(b)] If a taxpayer asserts that it satisfies the subject-to-tax test in one state, another state that has a throwback rule may request proof that the taxpayer has filed tax returns and paid the requisite tax in the other state. A taxpayer does not satisfy this test if it "voluntarily files and pays one or more of such taxes when not required to do so by the laws of that state." [MTC Reg. IV.3(b)]

Under the jurisdiction-to-tax test, a taxpayer is taxable in another state if "that state has jurisdiction to subject the taxpayer to a net income tax regardless of whether, in fact, the state does or does not." A taxpayer meets this test if "the taxpayer's business activity is sufficient to give the state jurisdiction to impose a net income tax by reason of such business activity under the Constitution and statutes of the United States." [MTC Reg. IV.3.(c)] In *National Bellas Hess, Inc. v. Department of Revenue* [386 U.S. 753 (1967)], the U.S. Supreme Court established the principle that constitutional nexus requires an in-state physical presence, at least with respect to sales and use tax. In this case, the Court ruled that Illinois could not require a Missouri-based mail-order vendor to collect use tax on sales to Illinois residents, because the Missouri corporation had no offices, property, employees or any other type of physical presence in Illinois. In 1992, the U.S. Supreme Court reaffirmed the physical presence requirement in *Quill Corp. v. North Dakota* [504 U.S. 298 (1992)], which was another case involving the collection of use tax by an out-of-state mail-order company. However, the Court did not specifically address the issue of whether the physical presence test also applied to income tax nexus.

The jurisdiction-to-tax test is also not met if "the state is prohibited from imposing the tax by reason of the provisions of Public Law 86-272." [MTC Reg. IV.3.(c)] Congress enacted Public Law 86-272 (15 U.S.C. 381) in 1959 to provide out-of-state corporations with a limited safe harbor from the imposition of state taxes on "net income." Specifically, Public Law 86-272 prohibits a state from imposing a tax on the net income of an out-of-state corporation if the company's only in-state activity is the solicitation of orders by company representatives for sales of tangible personal property, which orders are sent outside the state for approval or rejection, and if approved, are filled by shipment or delivery from a point outside the state.

Alabama. In *Knauf Fiber Glass GMBH, Inc. v. Alabama Dept. of Revenue* [No. CORP. 05-970 (Ala. Dept. of Rev., Admin. Law Div., Nov. 30, 2006)], an administrative law judge ruled that sales made in Michigan and Washington did not have to be thrown back to Alabama, because the taxes imposed by those states (Michigan single business tax and Washington business and occupation tax) both qualify as a "franchise tax" for throwback purposes. Sales made in Mississippi and Tennessee also did not have to be thrown back to Alabama, even through the taxpayer did not file returns or pay tax in either state, because the taxpayer was engaged in significant business activities in both states.

Illinois. In order to satisfy the "taxable in another state" requirement and avoid throwback for Illinois tax purposes, a taxpayer must not only be subject to tax in another state, but must also pay tax in that other state. [86 Ill. Adm. Code § 100.3200(a)(2)] The Illinois Appellate Court upheld this regulation in *Dover Corp. et al. v. Department of Revenue.* [No. 1-93-3340 (Ill. App. Ct., 1st Dist., 1995)]

Indiana. The Indiana Department of Revenue ruled that income earned by an Indiana corporation in another state was not subject to Indiana's throwback rule, because the company's activities in the destination state exceeded mere solicitation, and thus were not protected by Public Law 86-272. Accordingly, the company was subject to tax in the state where the income was earned. The Department said it was irrelevant whether the taxpayer actually filed income tax returns in the states in which it was subject to tax. [Ind. Dep't of Revenue, Letter of Findings No. 98-0568 (released Sept. 2001) and No. 98-0084 (released Dec. 2001)]

Massachusetts. The Massachusetts throwback rule applies if (1) the taxpayer is not taxable in the state in which the property is delivered to the purchaser; and (2) the property is not sold by an agent of the taxpayer who is chiefly situated at, connected with, or sent out from the taxpayer's owned or rented business premises located outside Massachusetts. [830 CMR 63.38.1(9)(c)2] In other words, Massachusetts requires throwback of sales into states in which the taxpayer is not taxable, unless the taxpayer can prove the property was sold by an agent who works out of an office located in a state other than Massachusetts.

In *Colgate-Palmolive Company v. Commissioner of Revenue* [No. C255116 (Mass. App. Tax Bd. Apr. 3, 2003)], the Massachusetts Appellate Tax Board ruled that a company's sales of medical supplies to customers in thirty-three other states should not be thrown back to Massachusetts, because some of the activities of the taxpayer's sales representatives in the other states were not entirely ancillary to the solicitation of sales (based on state court decisions in Massachusetts that narrowly interpreted the meaning of "solicitation"), and therefore created a taxable nexus in the destination states.

Sales to Purchasers in a Foreign Country

The application of the jurisdiction-to-tax test for determining whether a taxpayer is taxable in another state can be ambiguous when dealing with export sales made by a U.S. corporation to purchasers located in a foreign country. One possible jurisdictional standard is U.S. constitutional nexus standards. A second possible standard is U.S. constitutional nexus standards, as limited by Public Law 86-272. A third possible standard is the foreign country's nexus standard for taxing the business profits of a U.S. corporation. Generally, that standard is doing business in the foreign country through a *permanent establishment*. The U.S. has bilateral income tax treaties with over 60 countries. These treaties usually prohibit a foreign country from taxing the business profits of a U.S. corporation unless that corporation conducts business through a permanent establishment situated in the foreign country (e.g., Articles 5 and 7, U.S. Model Income Tax Treaty of 2006). A permanent establishment generally means a fixed place of business, such as a sales office.

For purposes of both the subject-to-tax test and the jurisdiction-to-tax test, the term "state" means any U.S. state, the District of Columbia, Puerto Rico, any U.S. territory or possession, or any foreign country or political subdivision thereof. [UDITPA Section 1(h)]

According to MTC Regulation IV.3.(c), the determination of whether a taxpayer's business activity in a foreign country satisfies the jurisdiction-to-tax test is made as if the jurisdictional standards applicable to a U.S. state applied in the foreign country, and the impact of any tax treaty provisions is ignored. As discussed above, the jurisdictional standards applicable to a U.S. state are U.S. constitutional nexus, as limited by Public Law 86-272. By its terms, Public Law 86-272 applies only to "interstate commerce." Thus, the states are not required to extend the protections of Public Law 86-272 to foreign commerce.

California. In *Appeal of Dresser Industries, Inc.* (82-SBE-307, June 29, 1982, rehearing 83-SBE-118, Oct. 26, 1983), the California State Board of Equalization (SBE) ruled that for purposes of applying the California throwback rule to foreign sales, Public Law 86-272 did not apply when determining whether a corporation was taxable in a foreign country. Instead, the determination of whether the corporation is taxable in a foreign country is made based solely upon U.S. constitutional nexus standards.

In *Appeal of Galvantech, Inc.* [No. 288289 (Cal. State Bd. of Equal., Feb. 1, 2006)], the California SBE ruled that the taxpayer's sales to purchasers in foreign countries must be thrown back to California because, among other things, the taxpayer could not provide sufficient documentation to establish constitutional nexus in the foreign countries to which its products were shipped.

Illinois. In *Morton International, Inc. v. Illinois Dept. of Revenue* [No. 01 L 50752 (Ill. Cir. Ct., Cook Cty., July 8, 2004)], the Illinois Circuit Court ruled that $13 million of sales of goods shipped from Illinois to purchasers in foreign countries did not have to be thrown back to Illinois, because the U.S. exporter was taxable in the foreign destination countries for purposes of the Illinois throwback rule. Morton received two types of income: (1) proceeds from sales of goods shipped from an Illinois facility to buyers in six foreign countries—Australia, Belgium, Brazil, Canada, France and Mexico; and (2) royalties from patent licenses in the same countries and dividends from foreign corporations in Belgium and Brazil. Morton's royalty and dividend income had no direct relationship to its sales of goods. Although Morton did not pay foreign income taxes on the $13 million of export sales, it did pay foreign withholding taxes on the royalty and dividend income that was unrelated to the sales. The department of revenue argued that for throwback purposes, the term "taxable" means that the tax must be paid on the particular sales at issue. The court rejected this argument and ruled that the plain meaning of the Illinois throwback statute did not require that the taxpayer be taxable on the sales in question to avoid throwback. Instead, the taxpayer need only be subject to some type of income tax in the destination jurisdiction to avoid throwback. Therefore, the $13 million of export sales did not have to be thrown back to Illinois, because Morton was clearly taxable in the six foreign countries, albeit on unrelated royalty and dividend income.

Massachusetts. Massachusetts has a throwback rule, but it does not apply to sales of tangible personal property delivered or shipped to a purchaser in a foreign country. A statutory exception known as the *foreign sales presumption* provides that "[a] taxpayer is taxable in the state of the purchaser if tangible personal property is delivered or shipped to a purchaser in a foreign country." [830 CMR 63.38.1(9)(c)2.b.ii.]

In *Tech-Etch, Inc. v. Commissioner of Revenue* [No. C260139 (Mass. App. Tax Bd., June 3, 2005)], the taxpayer did not have income tax nexus in any U.S. state other than Massachusetts or in any foreign country. Nevertheless, based on the foreign sales presumption, Tech-Etch argued that it should be deemed taxable in the foreign countries in which its products were shipped, in which case it could both apportion its income and exclude its foreign sales from the numerator of the Massachusetts sales factor. The Massachusetts Appellate Tax Board rejected this argument, based on the plain language of the foreign sales presumption, which stated that the special rule applied only for purposes of computing the sales factor. Therefore, Tech-Etch was not entitled to apportion its income, and all of its income was taxable in

Massachusetts. The Appeals Court of Massachusetts affirmed the Board's decision. [No. 05-P-1012, Nov. 3, 2006]

Drop Shipment Sales and Double-Throwback

Drop-shipment sales are sales that are made by an in-state vendor to an out-of-state customer, but are not directly filled by the in-state vendor. Instead, the vendor directs an out-of-state supplier to ship the goods directly to the customer. For example, a distributor located in State *A* sells to a customer located in State *B* goods that are manufactured by a company in State C. To save time and transportation costs, the State *A* distributor has the State *C* manufacturer ship the goods directly to the State *B* customer. Under the UDITPA destination test, if the distributor has nexus in the destination state (State *B*), the sale is assigned to State *B*. If the distributor does not have nexus in the destination state (State *B*) but does have nexus in the state from which the goods were shipped (State C), the sale is assigned to State C under the UDITPA throwback rule. But what happens if the distributor does not have nexus in either the destination state or the origination state? MTC Regulation IV.16(a)(7) resolves this issue by providing a double-throwback rule, whereby drop-shipment sales that are not assigned to either the destination state or the origination state are assigned to the state in which the taxpayer is located (in the example, State *A*).

In *Southern Indiana Gas and Electric Co. v. Department of Revenue* [No. 49T10-0201-TA-4 (Ind. Tax Ct., Mar. 3, 2004], the Indiana Tax Court held that Indiana's double throwback rule did not apply to sales of natural gas that was purchased by the taxpayer (a utility company) from out-of-state producers and then transported to out-of-state customers using interstate pipelines that operated as common carriers. The third-party gas producers did not ship the natural gas to the ultimate customer, because the taxpayer took possession of the gas from the producer prior to its transport to the customer. The interstate pipelines also did not ship the natural gas, but merely acted as carriers of the gas. Because no third party shipped the natural gas, the Indiana double throwback rule did not apply.

In *Stryker Corp. v. Division of Taxation* [No. A-27-00 (N.J. Sup. Ct., June 14, 2001)], the New Jersey Supreme Court held that a manufacturer's sales to its New Jersey marketing subsidiary of goods that the manufacturer drop-shipped to the subsidiary's customers located outside New Jersey were nevertheless assigned to the numerator of the manufacturer's New Jersey sales factor, because the shipments were considered to be sales to the New Jersey subsidiary, despite the fact that the goods were not physically delivered to points in New Jersey.

Combined Reporting States: *Joyce vs. Finnigan*

Twenty-three states, including California, Illinois, Massachusetts and Texas, require combined unitary reporting. Combined reporting is a method for apportioning the business income of a "taxpayer member," that is, a member of a unitary group that has nexus in the state. Generally, the taxpayer member apportions its income by multiplying the combined business income of all the group members by an apportionment percentage that is based on factors, the denominators of which include the factors everywhere of all group members, and the numerators of which include the in-state factors of only the taxpayer member. As with state generally, most combined reporting states use either a double-weighted sales apportionment formula or a single-factor sales apportionment formula.

Under UDITPA Section 15, the numerator of the sales factor is the "sales of the taxpayer" in the state, and the denominator is the "sales of the taxpayer" everywhere. Under UDITPA Section 16, in-state sales include sales of tangible personal property that are delivered or shipped to a purchaser in the state (*destination test*), as well as property that is shipped from the state and either the purchaser is the U.S. government or "the taxpayer is not taxable in the state of the purchaser" (*throwback rule*).

When applying the destination test in a combined reporting state, an issue arises as to whether the phrase "sales of the taxpayer" means only the specific members of the unitary group that have nexus in the state, or all group members including those that do not separately have nexus in the taxing state. Likewise, when applying the throwback rule in a combined reporting state, an issue arises as to whether the phrase "the taxpayer is not taxable" in the destination state means only the specific member of the unitary group that makes the sale, or all group members.

In *Appeal of Joyce, Inc.* [SBE-XIV-215, 66-SBE-070 (Cal. St. Bd. of Equal. Nov. 23, 1966)], the California SBE ruled that the in-state sales made by a member of a unitary group that does not separately have nexus in California are not included in the numerator of the California sales factor. This member-by-member approach to determining in-state sales is known as the *Joyce* rule. Another implication of the *Joyce* rule is that throwback is avoided only if the specific member that is making the sale has nexus in the destination state. Therefore, in terms of computing the numerator of the California sales factor, the *Joyce* rule is advantageous with respect to sales shipped into California, but disadvantageous with respect to sales shipped out of California.

In *Appeal of Finnigan Corp.* [88-SBE-022-A, 88SBE022-A (Cal. St. Bd. of Equal., Jan. 24, 1990)], the California SBE overturned its position in *Joyce*, ruling that for purposes of applying the California throwback rule, throwback is avoided if any group member has nexus in the destination state. Another implication of the so-called *Finnigan* rule is that an out-of-state member's sales into California are included in the numerator of the California sales factor even if the selling member does not separately have nexus in California. Thus, the *Finnigan* rule produces results opposite those of the *Joyce* rule, and therefore is advantageous with respect to sales shipped out of California but disadvantageous with respect to sales shipped into California.

In *Appeal of Huffy Corp.* [No. 99-SBE-005 (Cal. St. Bd. of Equal., Apr. 22, 1999)], the California SBE re-adopted the *Joyce* rule and held that the renewed implementation of the *Joyce* rule applies only to income years beginning on or after April 22, 1999. Effective for tax years beginning on or after January 1, 2011, California will apply the *Finnigan* rule. [S.B. 15, Feb. 20, 2009]

Most combined reporting states, including Colorado and Illinois, employ the *Joyce* rule. Examples of combined reporting states that employ the *Finnigan* rule include California (post-2010), Kansas, Maine, Massachusetts, Utah and Wisconsin.

Throwout Rule

Maine. Prior to 2009, Maine had a throwback rule. For tax years beginning on or after January 1, 2009, Maine replaced its throwback rule with a throwout rule. [L.D. 353, May 28, 2009] Under a throwout rule, sales of tangible personal property delivered or shipped to a purchaser in a state in which the taxpayer is not taxable are excluded from both the numerator and the denominator of the sales factor.

Maine is a combined reporting state. For tax years beginning on or after January 1, 2010, Maine applies the *Finnigan* rule, which means that throwout is avoided if any group member has nexus in the destination state. [H.P. 1183, Mar. 31, 2010]

New Jersey. For tax years beginning before July 1, 2010, New Jersey had a throwout rule. The throwout rule is repealed effective for tax years beginning on or after July 1, 2010 [A.B. 2722, Dec. 19, 2008].

In *Whirlpool Properties, Inc. v. Director, Division of Taxation* [No. 066595, N.J Sup. Ct., July 28, 2011)], the New Jersey Supreme Court ruled that the former throwout rule was facially constitutional and did not violate the Due Process or Commerce Clauses. The rule arguably is externally consistent when applied to untaxed receipts that are thrown out, because the taxpayer does not have nexus in the state, due to insufficient contacts or Public Law 86-272. On the other hand, throwing out receipts because a state chooses not to impose an income tax is externally inconsistent, and thus results in an unfair apportionment, because that decision is independent of a taxpayer's business activity and has no bearing on how much income is attributable to New Jersey. Construing the throwout rule narrowly so that it generally operates constitutionally, the court interpreted the rule as operating only to throw out receipts from states without taxing jurisdiction, which is consistent with the legislative intent to close a loophole and throw out no-where sales from the sales fraction.

West Virginia. West Virginia, which is a combined reporting state, has a throwout rule. West Virginia applies the *Joyce* rule, which means that throwout is avoided only if the selling member has nexus in the destination state.

State-by-State Summary

The chart that follows is presented in two parts to provide a detailed summary of the throwback provisions that have been adopted by the states.

Sales Factor: Throwback Rules (Part 1)

Legend:
NA Not applicable
NR Not reported

	Does State Apply Throwback Rule to Sales?	*Does State Apply "Double Throwback" Rule to Drop Shipments?*	*To Avoid Throwback of Domestic Sales, Does State Require Proof of Taxability in Other State?*	*Does Throwback Rule Extend to Foreign Sales?*	*What Jurisdictional Standards Apply to Determine Taxability in a Foreign Country?*	*To Avoid Throwback on Foreign Sales, Does State Require Proof of Taxability in Foreign Country?*
Alabama	Yes, state goods shipped from	No	Yes, filing of a tax return	Yes	Foreign country's nexus standards	Yes, filing of a tax return
Alaska	Yes	Yes	Yes, proof of taxable presence	Yes	P.L. 86-272	Yes
Arizona	No	NA	NA	NA	NA	NA
Arkansas	Yes, state goods shipped from	No	Yes, or proof of taxability in the foreign country or destination or origin, filing of a tax return or proof of tax payment	Yes	Filing of return and payment of tax	Yes, or proof of taxable presence, filing of a tax return or proof of tax payment
California	Yes, state goods shipped from	Yes	Yes, proof of taxable presence	Yes	U.S. constitutional standard. See *Appeal of Dresser Industries, Inc.*, Calif. St. Bd. of Equal., 10/26/83.	Yes, proof of taxable presence
Colorado	Yes		Yes, proof of taxable presence	Yes	P.L. 86-272	Yes, proof of a taxable presence
Connecticut	No	No	NA	No	No	NA
Delaware	No	No	NA	NA	NA	NA

Sales Factor: Throwback Rules (Part 1)

Legend:
NA Not applicable
NR Not reported

	Does State Apply Throwback Rule to Sales?	*Does State Apply "Double Throwback" Rule to Drop Shipments?*	*To Avoid Throwback of Domestic Sales, Does State Require Proof of Taxability in Other State?*	*Does Throwback Rule Extend to Foreign Sales?*	*What Jurisdictional Standards Apply to Determine Taxability in a Foreign Country?*	*To Avoid Throwback on Foreign Sales, Does State Require Proof of Taxability in Foreign Country?*
District of Columbia	Yes, state goods shipped from	No	No, the filing of a return; proof of taxable presence; proof of a tax payment	Yes	State nexus standards, considering P.L. 86-272	No, the filing of a return; proof of a taxable presence; proof of a tax payment
Florida	No	No	NA	NA	NA	NA
Georgia	No	No	NA	No	NA	NA
Hawaii	Yes, state goods shipped from	Yes	Yes	Yes	P.L. 86-272 standard	Yes
Idaho	Yes, state goods shipped from	Yes	Yes	Yes	U.S. jurisdictional standards	Yes
Illinois	Yes, state goods shipped from, see IITA § 304(a)(3)(B)	Yes, see Ill. Admin. Code § 100.3380(b)(1)	Yes, if there is actual proof of tax being paid or if the mere filing of a return substantiates taxability.	No	P.L. 86-272	No, actual tax paid or jurisdiction to tax exists. The filing of a return if the return substantiates taxability.
Indiana	Yes, state goods shipped from	Yes	Yes, filing of a return or proof of taxability in other state	Yes	P.L. 86-272 or foreign country's standards	Yes or filing the return
Iowa	No	No	NA	No	NA	NA
Kansas	Yes, state goods shipped from	Yes	Yes, proof of taxable presence	Yes	P.L. 86-272	Proof of taxable presence

Legend:
NA — Not applicable
NR — Not reported

Sales Factor: Throwback Rules (Part 1)

	Does State Apply Throwback Rule to Sales?	*Does State Apply "Double Throwback" Rule to Drop Shipments?*	*To Avoid Throwback of Domestic Sales, Does State Require Proof of Taxability in Other State?*	*Does Throwback Rule Extend to Foreign Sales?*	*What Jurisdictional Standards Apply to Determine Taxability in a Foreign Country?*	*To Avoid Throwback on Foreign Sales, Does State Require Proof of Taxability in Foreign Country?*
Kentucky	No	No	The corporation must file a tax return in at least one state other than Kentucky	No	No	The corporation must file a tax return in at least one state other than Kentucky
Louisiana	No	NR	NA	NA	NA	NA
Maine	No	No	N/A, no throwback rule	No		N/A, no throwback rule
Maryland	No	No	NA	NA	NA	NA
Massachusetts	Yes, state where order was processed	NR	Yes, proof of taxable presence	No	Shipment to foreign country	NR
Michigan (Business Tax)	No	No	NA	No	NA	NA
Note. The CIT takes effect 01/01/12, and replaces the Michigan Business Tax (MBT) for most taxpayers. However, businesses that have been approved to receive, have received, or have been assigned certain certified credits may elect to file a return and pay the tax imposed by the MBT in lieu of the CIT until the certified credits are exhausted or extinguished.						
Minnesota	No	No	NA	NA	NA	NA
Mississippi	Yes, state goods shipped from	Yes	Yes, also proof of a tax payment	Yes	Mississippi nexus standards	Yes, also proof of a tax payment
Missouri	Yes, state goods shipped from	Yes	Yes, also proof of taxable presence, a tax payment, and the filing of a return	Yes	P.L. 86-272	Yes, proof of taxable presence, a tax payment, and the filing of a return

Sales Factor: Throwback Rules (Part 1)

Legend:
NA Not applicable
NR Not reported

	Does State Apply Throwback Rule to Sales?	*Does State Apply "Double Throwback" Rule to Drop Shipments?*	*To Avoid Throwback of Domestic Sales, Does State Require Proof of Taxability in Other State?*	*Does Throwback Rule Extend to Foreign Sales?*	*What Jurisdictional Standards Apply to Determine Taxability in a Foreign Country?*	*To Avoid Throwback on Foreign Sales, Does State Require Proof of Taxability in Foreign Country?*
Montana	Yes, state goods shipped from	Yes	Yes, also, proof of a tax payment and the filing of a return	Yes	P.L. 86-272	Yes, and proof of a tax payment
Nebraska	No	No	NA	NA	NA	NA
Nevada	Nevada does not impose a corporate income tax					
New Hampshire	Yes, state goods shipped from	No	Yes, proof of taxable presence	Yes	Foreign country's standards	Yes, proof of a taxable presence
New Jersey	No	No	NA	NA	NA	NA
New Mexico	Yes, state goods shipped from	Yes	Yes, proof of taxable presence.	Yes	State nexus standards considering P.L. 86-272	Yes, proof of taxable presence.
New York	No	NA	NA	NA	NA	NA
North Carolina	No	No	NA	NA	NA	NA
North Dakota	Yes, state goods shipped from	Yes	Yes, also proof of a tax payment	Yes	P.L. 86-272	Yes, also proof of a tax payment
Ohio	Ohio does not impose a corporate income tax					
Note. Effective 1/1/2010, the Ohio Franchise Tax was fully phased out and business will be taxed on gross receipts through the Commercial Activity Tax. Details about that tax can be found at: http//tax.ohio.gov/divisions/commercial_activities/index.stm						
Oklahoma	Yes, state goods shipped from	No	Yes	Yes	P.L. 86-272	Yes

Legend:
NA Not applicable
NR Not reported

Sales Factor: Throwback Rules (Part 1)

	Does State Apply Throwback Rule to Sales?	*Does State Apply "Double Throwback" Rule to Drop Shipments?*	*To Avoid Throwback of Domestic Sales, Does State Require Proof of Taxability in Other State?*	*Does Throwback Rule Extend to Foreign Sales?*	*What Jurisdictional Standards Apply to Determine Taxability in a Foreign Country?*	*To Avoid Throwback on Foreign Sales, Does State Require Proof of Taxability in Foreign Country?*
Oregon	Yes, state goods shipped from	Yes	Yes, and documentation of taxable activities	Yes	P.L. 86-272; foreign country's standards; and standards that apply to U.S. states	Yes, and documentation of taxable activities
Pennsylvania	No	No	Yes	No	NA	NA
Rhode Island	No	No	NA, no throwback rule	NA	NA	NA, no throwback rule
South Carolina	No	No	NA	NA	NA	NA
	If no other state can tax (due to P.L. 86-272) all income is taxed by South Carolina					
South Dakota	South Dakota does not impose a corporate income tax					
Tennessee	No	No	NA	No	NA	NA
Texas	No	No	NA	No	NA	NA, no throwback rule
Utah	Yes, state goods shipped from	Yes	Yes, proof nexus created	Yes	P.L. 86-272	Yes
Vermont	Yes, state goods shipped from	No	Yes	Yes	Foreign country's standards	Yes
Virginia	No	No	NA	NA	NA	NA
Washington	Washington does not impose a corporate income tax					
West Virginia	No	No	NA	NA	NA	NA
Wisconsin	Yes, but not for foreign sales; state goods shipped from	Yes	Yes, proof of taxpayer's taxable presence	No	NA	

Sales Factor: Throwback Rules (Part 1)

Legend:
NA — Not applicable
NR — Not reported

	Does State Apply Throwback Rule to Sales?	*Does State Apply "Double Throwback" Rule to Drop Shipments?*	*To Avoid Throwback of Domestic Sales, Does State Require Proof of Taxability in Other State?*	*Does Throwback Rule Extend to Foreign Sales?*	*What Jurisdictional Standards Apply to Determine Taxability in a Foreign Country?*	*To Avoid Throwback on Foreign Sales, Does State Require Proof of Taxability in Foreign Country?*
Note. Throwback for tangible personal property was increased from 50% to 100%, per Wisconsin Act 28. Throwback sales other than tangible personal property were repealed, per Act 28.						
Wyoming	Wyoming does not impose a corporate income tax					

Sales Factor: Throwback Rules (Part 2)

Legend:

MTC Multistate Tax Compact
NA Not applicable
NR Not reported

	If No Throwback Rule Is Used, Is the Denominator of the Sales Factor Reduced for Sales to States in Which the Corporation Is Not Subject to Tax?	*Would the State Contest Another State's Right to Tax Sales If the Other State's Statutes Include Sales in the Sales Factor?*	*Does State Apply Throwback Rule to Sales to the U.S. Government?*	*If State Applies a Throwback Rule and Requires Combined Reporting, Which Rule Is Used?*
Alabama	NA	Yes	No	NA
Alaska	State has throwback rule	No	No	*Joyce*
Arizona	No	NA	No	NA
Arkansas	State has throwback rule	No	Yes	State does not have combined reporting.
California	State has throwback rule	No	No	*Finnigan*, for taxable years beginning prior to 4/22/99 and for taxable years beginning on or after 1/1/11. See Appeal of Huffy Corp. 99-SBE-005A, 9/1/99. *Joyce*, for taxable years beginning on or after 4/22/99. See Appeal of Huffy Corp., 99-SBE-005A, 9/1/99
Colorado	NA, state has a throwback rule	No	No	*Joyce*
Connecticut	No	NA, no throwback rule	NA	NA
Delaware	No	NR	No	NA
District of Columbia	NA	Yes	Yes	NA
Florida	No	NA, no throwback rule	NA	NA
Georgia	No	NA, no throwback rule	NR	NA
Hawaii	NR	No	Yes	*Joyce*

Sales Factor: Throwback Rules (Part 2)

Legend:
MTC Multistate Tax Compact
NA Not applicable
NR Not reported

	If No Throwback Rule Is Used, Is the Denominator of the Sales Factor Reduced for Sales to States in Which the Corporation Is Not Subject to Tax?	*Would the State Contest Another State's Right to Tax Sales If the Other State's Statutes Include Sales in the Sales Factor?*	*Does State Apply Throwback Rule to Sales to the U.S. Government?*	*If State Applies a Throwback Rule and Requires Combined Reporting, Which Rule Is Used?*
Idaho	NA	No	NR	*Joyce*
Illinois	No	Depends, Illinois would not contest a direct sale.	Yes	*Joyce*
Indiana	NA	No	NR	*Finnigan*
Iowa	No	No	No	NA
Kansas	NA	No	No	*Finnigan*
Kentucky	No	No	Yes	NA
Louisiana	No	NA, no throwback rule	No	NA
Maine	Yes	No	Yes	N/A, state does not have throwback rule or combined reporting
Maryland	No	NA	NA	
Massachusetts	NR	NR	Depends on facts	*Joyce*
Michigan (Business Tax)	No	NA	No	NA

Note. The CIT takes effect 01/01/12, and replaces the Michigan Business Tax (MBT) for most taxpayers. However, businesses that have been approved to receive, have received, or have been assigned certain certified credits may elect to file a return and pay the tax imposed by the MBT in lieu of the CIT until the certified credits are exhausted or extinguished.

Minnesota	NA, no throwback rule	NA, no throwback rule	No	NA
Mississippi	No	Yes	Yes	NA

Sales Factor: Throwback Rules (Part 2)

Legend:

MTC	Multistate Tax Compact
NA	Not applicable
NR	Not reported

	If No Throwback Rule Is Used, Is the Denominator of the Sales Factor Reduced for Sales to States in Which the Corporation Is Not Subject to Tax?	*Would the State Contest Another State's Right to Tax Sales If the Other State's Statutes Include Sales in the Sales Factor?*	*Does State Apply Throwback Rule to Sales to the U.S. Government?*	*If State Applies a Throwback Rule and Requires Combined Reporting, Which Rule Is Used?*
Missouri	NA, no throwback rule	No	No	NA, state does not have throwback rule or combined reporting
Montana	NR	No	No	*Joyce*
Nebraska	No	No	Yes	NA
Nevada	Nevada does not impose a corporate income tax			
New Hampshire	State has throwback rule	No	Yes	*Joyce*
New Jersey	Yes, See *Pfizer, Inc v. Director Div of Taxation*—Docket Nos 000055-2006, 008807-2006, 08806-2006 and 000066-2007.	It depends upon the facts and circumstances.	No	NA
New Mexico	No	Yes	Yes	NR
New York	NA	NA	No	NA
North Carolina	No	No	No	NA
North Dakota	NA	No	No	*Joyce*
Ohio	Ohio does not impose a corporate income tax			
Note. Effective 1/1/2010, the Ohio Franchise Tax was fully phased out and business will be taxed on gross receipts through the Commercial Activity Tax. Details about that tax can be found at: http//tax.ohio.gov/divisions/commercial_activities/index.stm				
Oklahoma	NA	No	No	NR
Oregon	NA	No	Yes	*Joyce*

Sales Factor: Throwback Rules (Part 2)

Legend:
MTC Multistate Tax Compact
NA Not applicable
NR Not reported

	If No Throwback Rule Is Used, Is the Denominator of the Sales Factor Reduced for Sales to States in Which the Corporation Is Not Subject to Tax?	*Would the State Contest Another State's Right to Tax Sales If the Other State's Statutes Include Sales in the Sales Factor?*	*Does State Apply Throwback Rule to Sales to the U.S. Government?*	*If State Applies a Throwback Rule and Requires Combined Reporting, Which Rule Is Used?*
Pennsylvania	No	No	No	NA
Rhode Island	No	No	No	NA
South Carolina	No	Yes	No, throwout	NA
	If no other state can tax due to P.L. 86-272, all income is taxed in South Carolina			
South Dakota	South Dakota does not impose a corporate income tax			
Tennessee	No	No	No	NA
Texas	No	No	No	NA
Utah	NA	No	Yes	*Finnigan*
Vermont	NA	No, not if properly included	Yes	NR
Virginia	No	No	No	NA
Washington	Washington does not impose a corporate income tax			
West Virginia	Yes	No	No	NA
Wisconsin	NA, no throwback rule	No	Yes	*Finnigan*
Wyoming	Wyoming does not impose a corporate income tax			

Sales Factor: Receipts from Services

UDITPA Framework

Under UDITPA Section 15, the sales factor is a fraction, the numerator of which is the total sales of the taxpayer attributed to the state, and the denominator of which is the total sales of the taxpayer everywhere. With respect to sales of tangible personal property, states generally employ the UDITPA Section 16 *destination test* to attribute the sale to the numerator of the sales factor. Under this test, sales of tangible personal property are attributed to the state if the "property is delivered or shipped to a purchaser . . . within this state." The destination test reflects the original policy of the sales factor, which is to provide tax revenue for the states in which the taxpayer's customers are located. With respect to sales, other than sales of tangible personal property, most states employ the UDITPA Section 17 *costs of performance rule* to attribute the sale to the numerator of the sales factor. UDIPTA Section 17 is a catch-all provision which applies to all sales other than sales of tangible personal property, including fees from services.

Under UDITPA Section 17(a), sales of services are attributed to the state in which "the income producing activity is performed." For example, assume a consulting firm receives a $100,000 fee for services performed by the taxpayer's employees at its offices in State P. Regardless of where the client is located, the $100,000 sale is attributed to State P, because that is where the underlying income producing activity (i.e., employee services) is performed.

Under UDIPTA Section 17(b), if the income producing activity is performed in two or more states, the sale is attributed to the state in which a greater proportion of the income producing activity is performed than in any other state, based on the "costs of performance." Thus, in order to source sales of services under the UDITPA costs of performance rule, the taxpayer must first determine what activity produced the income. Once the taxpayer has identified the applicable income producing activity, a cost of performance analysis is conducted. This involves determining the costs associated with the activity, as well as the states in which those costs were incurred.

The UDITPA cost of performance rule is generally an all-or-nothing approach, whereby the entire sale is attributed to the single state in which the greater proportion of the costs of performance is incurred. For example, assume a consulting firm receives a $100,000 fee for services performed by its employees, and that 70 percent of the costs of performance are incurred in State P, and 30 percent of the costs of performance are incurred in State Q. Under UDITPA Section 17(b), the entire $100,000 sale is attributed to State P, because that is where the greater proportion of the income producing is performed, based on costs of performance. In addition, none of the $100,000 sale is attributed to State Q, despite the significant amount of costs of performance incurred in State Q.

UDITPA does not define the terms income producing activity. Under MTC Regulation IV.17(2), the term *income producing activity* applies to each separate item of income and means the transactions and activity engaged in by the taxpayer in the regular course of its trade or business. Examples of income producing activity include: (1) the rendering of personal services by employees or the use of tangible or intangible property by the taxpayer in performing a service; (2) the sale, rental, leasing, licensing or other use of real property; (3) the rental, leasing, licensing or other use of tangible personal property; and (4) the sale, licensing or other use of intangible personal property. The mere holding of intangible personal property is not, by itself, an income producing activity.

UDITPA also does not define the term costs of performance. Under MTC Regulation IV.17(3), the term *costs of performance* means direct costs determined in a manner consistent with generally accepted accounting principles and in accordance with accepted conditions or practices in the trade or business of the taxpayer. Direct costs include material and labor costs that have a causal relationship with the sale in question. In other words, a direct cost is a cost that was incurred for a specific purpose and is traceable to that purpose. For example, the direct costs associated with a service contract for maintaining business equipment would include both the cost of repair parts and the compensation costs of the service technicians. Indirect costs, which include general and administrative expenses that are not associated with any specific sale, are not taken in account in determining the costs of performance.

Income Producing Activity: Transactional versus Operational Approach

As noted above, MTC Regulation IV.17(2) provides that the term income producing activity "applies to each separate item of income." For example, if a consulting firm does work on multiple projects for the single client, then a separate costs of performance analysis is performed for each separate item of income. In such cases, an issue may arise as to what constitutes a "separate item of income."

In *Boston Professional Hockey Association, Inc. v. Commissioner of Revenue* [No. SJC-09287, Mass. Sup. Jud. Ct. (Jan. 13, 2005)], the Massachusetts Supreme Judicial Court addressed the issue of what constitutes an income producing activity with respect to the gate receipts received by a professional sports franchise. Boston Professional Hockey Association, Inc. (BPHA) owned and operated the Boston Bruins professional hockey club and had its principal place of business in Boston. One issue in this case was whether each Bruins game constituted a separate income producing activity, the costs of which must be individually analyzed to determine whether the gate receipts are attributed to Massachusetts ("transactional approach"), or whether the income producing activity underlying gate receipts included not only the actual games themselves, but also various subsidiary activities (e.g., scheduling and contract negotiation) that were necessary in creating a viable sports franchise. BPHA's operations, including its public and press relations departments, finance department, sales and marketing department, legal department, general manager, and administrative staff, were all located at the team's offices in Boston ("operational approach"). The court ruled that with respect to gate receipts, the income producing activity was the "operation of an NHL franchise" that included, but was not limited to, the playing of individual games. Moreover, the greater proportion of the costs incurred in that income producing activity were incurred in Massachusetts, where the franchise was physically located, administered and managed, and where the team played almost one-half of its games.

The Massachusetts Appellate Tax Board addressed a similar issue in *The Interface Group v. Commissioner of Revenue* [Nos. C266670-76, C266680 (Mass. App. Tax Bd., Oct. 17, 2008)]. The taxpayer (Interface) was a Massachusetts-based public charter tour operator which assembled and marketed vacation travel packages by negotiating with airlines, hotels and ground transportation operators for bulk purchases of the necessary tickets and accommodations. The assembled vacation packages were then sold to the public through independent travel agents. The Massachusetts Commissioner of Revenue argued that the taxpayer's income producing activity was its overall operation of a charter tour business (operational approach), in which case a greater proportion of the taxpayer's income producing activity costs were incurred in Massachusetts, where the vast majority of the taxpayer's employees were located. The taxpayer argued that the income producing activity was each individual sale of a travel package to a particular customer (transactional approach), which would require analyzing the taxpayer's costs on a per-trip basis by comparing the Massachusetts cost of performance for producing a single travel package to the performance costs for that package in the destination state. In recognition of the taxpayer's business model, which was to assemble and then market vacation packages in bulk so as to obtain discounted prices, the Appellate Tax Board held that the taxpayer's income producing activity was its overall operation of bundling travel packages, rather than the individual sales of those travel packages.

In *AT&T Corp. v. Commissioner of Revenue* [No. C293831 (Mass. App. Tax Bd., June 8, 2011)], the Massachusetts Appellate Tax Board ("Board") ruled that AT&T's receipts from providing telecommunications services to Massachusetts customers were not attributable to Massachusetts under the state's costs of performance rule for sourcing sales of services. The Commissioner of Revenue argued that because AT&T used a transaction-based billing system, its income-producing activity was its provision of each telephone call or data transmission made by a customer in Massachusetts. Under this transactional approach, a greater proportion of AT&T's costs of performance was incurred in Massachusetts than in any other single state, in which case the sales were attributable to Massachusetts. On the other hand, AT&T argued that its income-producing activity was the operation of a global telecommunications network that had its operational hub and administrative headquarters located in New Jersey. Under this operational approach, a greater proportion of AT&T's costs of performance was incurred in New Jersey than in Massachusetts, in which case the sales were not attributable to Massachusetts. Consistent with its previous rulings in *Interface Group* and *Boston Professional Hockey Association*, the Board concluded that an operational approach was the proper method for determining AT&T's income-producing activity for purposes of calculating the Massachusetts sales factor.

On the other hand, in *Honigman Miller Schwartz and Cohn LLP v. Department of Treasury* [No. 282768 (Mich. Ct. of App., July 30, 2009)], the Michigan Court of Appeals addressed the issue of what constitutes an income producing activity with respect to a law firm. The taxpayer was a limited liability partnership that provided legal services to clients inside Michigan and to clients in other states. The taxpayer's offices were located in Michigan. The taxpayer's attorneys billed their clients in 15-minute intervals. The taxpayer did not enter into a formal contract for services with its clients. Rather, the taxpayer's attorneys performed services for clients as those services were requested or became necessary. During the tax years in question (1999 to 2001), sales of services were attributed to Michigan if "the business activity is performed in this state" or "the business activity is performed both in and outside this state and, based on costs of performance, a greater proportion of the business activity is performed in this state than is performed outside this state." [Mich. Comp. Laws § 208.53] The taxpayer contended that each 15-minute increment of work was a unique business activity, in which case all of the taxpayer's business activities were sourced to the state in which the service was performed. In contrast, the Michigan Department of Treasury contended that the taxpayer's business activity was the representation of a client, and that every 15-minute increment of service to a client had to be aggregated. Therefore, if in the course of representing a client, the taxpayer billed the client for a total of 60 hours of service for activities performed in Michigan and 15 hours of service for activities performed elsewhere, all 75 hours of service would be attributed to Michigan because the majority of the entire contract was executed in Michigan. The Michigan Court of Appeals ruled that each quantum of work performed by the taxpayer's attorneys was a distinct service, and that the Department's aggregation theory improperly inserted language into the statutory provision that was not authorized by the Legislature.

Other Income Producing Activity Cases

In *Westcott Communications, Inc. v. Strayhorn* [No. 03-02-00351-CV, Tex. Ct. of App. (Mar. 20, 2003)], the taxpayer produced educational, informational, and training programming and delivered the programming to subscribers throughout the nation via satellite broadcast and videotape. These educational and training services were provided to schools, law enforcement personnel, nurses, and other professionals. The taxpayer's headquarters, broadcast transmission equipment, and production facilities were located in Texas. Additionally, the taxpayer produced, filmed, edited, and broadcast its training services in and from Texas. The taxpayer provided its subscribers with satellite dishes and supporting equipment to receive the programming. For purposes of computing the Texas sales factor, sales of services are attributed to the state in which the service is performed. [34 TAC § 3.591(e)(26)] The taxpayer argued that the true nature of its services is analogous to providing live seminars and transmitting cable television services, both of which would be taxed based on the location of the service recipients. However, the Texas Court of Appeals ruled that the training programs produced, filmed, edited, and broadcast in and from Texas, but subsequently delivered via satellite to customers located outside Texas, constituted services performed within Texas. Construing where the "service is performed" to mean where the "act is done," the court ruled that the services in question were performed in Texas.

In *Ameritech Publishing, Inc. v. Wisconsin Department of Revenue* [No. 2009AP445 (Wis. Ct. App., June 24, 2010)], the Wisconsin Court of Appeals ruled that an out-of-state corporation's performance of advertising services for advertisements placed in Wisconsin telephone directories from 1994 to 1997 constituted the performance of income producing activities in Wisconsin, even though most of the employees producing the advertisements were located outside Wisconsin. Relying on an earlier decision regarding the sale of television advertising [*The Hearst Corp. v. Wisconsin Department of Revenue*, No. I-8511 (Wis. Tax App. Comm., May 15, 1990)], the Court of Appeals concluded that the taxpayer's income producing activity was providing access to a Wisconsin audience. Although the taxpayer's employees working outside Wisconsin performed tasks related to the sale and production of the ads, the taxpayer's customers did not pay primarily for the taxpayer to service their accounts, design their ads, or send their ad copy with the completed directory to the printer; instead, they paid for the broad access to a Wisconsin audience which the taxpayer could provide through the distribution of telephone directories.

Special Rule for Personal Services

Under UDITPA Section 17(a), sales of services are attributed to the state in which "the income producing activity is performed." Under UDIPTA Section 17(b), if the income producing activity is performed in two or more states, the sale is attributed to the state in which a greater proportion of the income producing activity is performed than in any other state, based on the "costs of performance." Thus, the UDITPA cost of performance rule is generally an all-or-nothing approach, whereby the entire sale is attributed to the single state in which the greater proportion of the costs of performance is incurred.

MTC Regulation IV.17(4)(B)(c) provides the following special rule for the performance of personal services:

> Gross receipts for the performance of personal services are attributable to this state to the extent that such services are performed in this state. If services relating to a single item of income are performed partly within and partly without this state, the gross receipts from the performance of such services shall be attributable to this state only if the greater proportion of the services was performed in the state, based on costs of performance. Usually, where services are performed partly within and partly without this state, the services performed in each state will constitute a separate income producing activity; in such cases, the gross receipts from the performance of services attributable to this state shall be measured by the ratio which the time spent in performing the services in this state bears to the total time spent in performing the services everywhere. Time spent in performing services includes the amount of time expended in the performance of a contract or other obligation which gives rise to such gross receipts. Personal service not directly connected with the performance of the contract or other obligation, as for example time expended in negotiating the contract, is excluded from the computations.
>
> The regulation provides the following two examples:
>
> **Example** *(i)*: Taxpayer, a road show, gave theatrical performances at various locations in State X and in this state during the tax period. All gross receipts from performances given in this state are attributed to this state.
>
> **Example** *(ii)*: The taxpayer, a public opinion survey corporation, conducted a poll by means of its employees in State X and in this state for the sum of $9,000. The project required 600 man hours to obtain the basic data and prepare the survey report. Two hundred of the 600 man hours were expended in this state. The receipts attributable to this state are $3,000. (200/600 $9,000 = $3,000)

In essence, the special rule found in MTC Regulation IV.17(4)(B)(c) provides that a lump-sum payment for personal services performed in two or more states is prorated among the states in proportion to the time spent in each state, based on the premise that the services performed in each state constitute a separate income producing activity. The regulation does not define what constitutes "personal services."

California Regulation Section 25136 adopts the MTC's special rule for sales of personal services, under which the time each employee spends in each state constitutes a separate income producing activity, and the sale is attributed to California based on the ratio of the time spent performing such services in California to the total time spent performing such services everywhere (so-called "time-spread method"). In Legal Ruling 2005-1 [Mar. 21, 2005], the California Franchise Tax Board (FTB) provides guidance regarding what constitutes a personal service for this purpose. The FTB rejected both a broad definition of personal services that includes virtually all services, as well as a narrow definition, such as limiting personal services to specialized services performed by one individual for the personal benefit of another (e.g., a doctor) or professional services. Instead, the FTB concluded that "personal services" is not limited to professional services or to specialized services performed by one individual for the personal benefit of another. Instead, "personal services" means any service performed where capital is not a material income producing factor. Note: Effective for tax years beginning on or after January 1, 2011, California taxpayers who elect to use a single-factor sales apportionment formula must use a market-based sourcing rule for sales of services.

Costs of Performance and Independent Contractors

UDITPA does not define the terms income producing activity. Under MTC Regulation IV.17(2), the term *income producing activity* applies to each separate item of income and means the transactions and activity engaged in by the taxpayer in the regular course of its trade or business. Prior to 2007, MTC

Regulation IV.17(2) provided that a taxpayer's income producing activity "does not include transactions and activities performed on behalf of a taxpayer, such as those conducted on its behalf by an independent contractor." Thus, if a taxpayer out sources some aspect of performing a service for a customer, the payments that the taxpayer makes to the independent contractor are excluded from the costs of performance analysis.

Consistent with the MTC's pre-2007 regulations, the Virginia Department of Taxation had promulgated regulations which provided that the costs of performance do not "include activities performed on behalf of a taxpayer, such as those performed on its behalf by an independent contractor." *In General Motors Corp. v. Virginia Dept. of Taxn.* [Va. Sup. Ct., No. 032533 (Sept. 17, 2004)], the Virginia Supreme Court ruled that a Virginia Department of Taxation regulation which excluded payments made to independent contractors from the costs of performance was not valid, because the regulation was inconsistent with the plain language of the statute, which did not expressly limit the costs of performance to the cost of activities directly performed by the taxpayer. As a result, General Motors Acceptance Corporation (GMAC), which was a subsidiary of General Motors doing business in Virginia, could take into account payments to independent contractors when computing its cost of performance ratio, which reduced its Virginia apportionment percentage. The Department argued the regulation was a practical interpretation of the statute, because it may be impossible to audit an independent contractor's cost of performance, given that the independent contractor could be located anywhere in the world and may not be obligated to cooperate with the Department. In ruling for the taxpayer, the court recognized the potential practical difficulties that the Department may face, but concluded that this was a matter to be addressed by the state legislature rather than the court.

In 2007, the MTC amended MTC Regulation IV.17 to provide that a taxpayer's income producing activity includes "transactions and activities performed on behalf of a taxpayer, such as those conducted on its behalf by an independent contractor," and that a taxpayer's cost of performance includes "payments to an agent or independent contractor for the performance of personal services and utilization of tangible and intangible property which give rise to the particular item of income."

In addition, MTC Reg. IV.17(4)(C) provides the following hierarchy of rules for determining whether an independent contractor performs its income producing activities in a state: (i) whether the taxpayer can reasonably determine where the income producing activity is actually performed, (ii) whether the contract between the taxpayer and the independent contractor indicates where the income producing activity is to be performed, (iii) whether the contract between the taxpayer and the taxpayer's customer indicates where the income producing activity is to be performed, and (iv) where the taxpayer's customer is domiciled. If the location of the income producing activity performed by the independent contractor cannot be determined or is in a state in which the taxpayer is not taxable, such income producing activity is disregarded.

Since 2007, numerous states have conformed to the new MTC regulations. For example, in 2008, the Oregon Department of Revenue amended its regulations to provide that costs incurred by a third party on behalf of a taxpayer are included in the calculation of direct costs when computing the costs of performance for purposes of determining the numerator of the Oregon sales factor. [OAR 150-314.665(4)] In 2009, the Idaho State Tax Commission amended its regulations for sourcing sales of services to include in the cost of performance any payments that the taxpayer makes to an independent contractor. [Rules 35.01.01.550] In 2010, the California corporation franchise and income tax regulation governing the sourcing of sales other than sales of tangible personal property [Reg. § 25136] was amended to treat activities performed on behalf of a taxpayer by an independent contractor in a similar manner as activities performed directly by a taxpayer. The change applies retroactively to taxable years beginning on or after January 1, 2008.

Special Apportionment Methods for Certain Industries

The UDITPA equally weighted three-factor property, payroll and sales apportionment formula was designed to apportion the income of multistate manufacturing and mercantile businesses, and may not fairly apportion the income of businesses in other industries. The drafters of UDITPA foresaw the limitations of the standard UDITPA apportionment formula, and, under Section 2, specifically excluded from UDITPA certain service businesses, including financial organizations (bank, trust company, savings bank, private banker, savings and loan association, credit union, investment company, insurance company, etc.), and public utilities (a business entity which owns or operates for public use any plant, equipment, property, franchise, or license for the transmission of communications, transportation of goods or persons, or the production, storage, transmission, sale, delivery, or furnishing of electricity, water, steam, oil, oil products or gas). Many states provide special apportionment methods for financial institutions and public utilities. The MTC has also promulgated a model statute for apportioning the income of financial institutions [Nov. 17, 1994].

In many cases, the equitable relief provisions of UDITPA Section 18, which numerous states have incorporated into their statutes, serves as the basis for state revenue departments to adopt specialized formulas. UDITPA Section 18 provides that if the standard apportionment formula does not fairly reflect a taxpayer's in-state business activity, tax authorities may require the exclusion of one or more of the factors, or the inclusion of additional factors which will fairly represent the taxpayer's business activity in the state. Under Section 18, the MTC has promulgated special apportionment regulations covering construction contractors (MTC Reg. IV.18(d)), airlines (MTC Reg. IV.18(e)), railroads (MTC Reg. IV.18(f)), trucking companies (MTC Reg. IV.18(g)), television and radio broadcasters (MTC Reg. IV.18(h)), and publishers (MTC Reg. IV.18(j)). In July 2008, the MTC approved a proposed model regulation for the apportionment of income from telecommunications services.

Market-Based Approach for Sourcing Sales of Services

The original purpose of the sales factor was to include in the apportionment formula a measure of the taxpayer's customer base within a given state. Unlike the UDITPA Section 16 destination test for inventory sales, however, the UDITPA Section 17 costs of performance rule for sales of services does not accurately measure a service company's customer base when the seller (service provider) performs services in one state and the purchaser (service recipient) is located in another state. When UDITPA was drafted in 1957, it was rare for a service provider and service recipient to be located in different states. Today, however, it is more common for customers to do business with out-of-state service providers. In such cases, the costs of performance rule no longer measures the customer base within a state, but instead tends to mimic the property and payroll factors.

For example, in *Bellsouth Advertising & Publishing Corp. v. Chumley* [No. M2008-0129-COA-R3-CV (Tenn. Ct. of App., Aug. 26, 2009)], the Tennessee Court of Appeals ruled that the Tennessee Department of Revenue exercised reasonable discretion by imposing a variance from the standard cost of performance rule in connection with the sale of advertising by a taxpayer engaged in the business of publishing telephone directories. The unusual fact situation in this case was that the costs of production occurred outside of Tennessee, but the revenue derived from the end product only occurred when the product was distributed in Tennessee, which only then obligated the customers to pay for the sale of the advertising.

Due in part to this weakness of the costs of performance rule, some states have adopted a market based approach for sales of services, whereby receipts from services are attributed to a state based on where the service recipient is located. In addition to providing a more accurate measure of the taxpayer's customer base, this approach has the political appeal of reducing the tax burden on service providers that have in-state facilities but provide services primarily to out-of-state customers. A market-based rule for services also creates an incentive for regional and national service providers to locate their facilities within the state's borders. Because most states apply the UDITPA costs of performance rule, a market based source rule can result in no-where income for service providers that locate their facilities within the state. Finally, the tax revenue on in-state service providers that is lost from switching from the costs of performance rule to a market-based rule may be partially offset by increased taxes on out-of-state service providers that make sales to in-state customers.

The states that have adopted a market-based approach for sales of services include Alabama (effective in 2011), California (effective in 2011), Georgia, Illinois, Iowa, Maine, Maryland, Michigan, Minnesota, Utah, and Wisconsin.

Alabama. For tax years beginning on or after December 31, 2010, sales of services are included in the numerator of the Alabama sales factor if the taxpayer's market for the sales is in Alabama. The determination of whether the market for a sale of services is in Alabama is based on whether the service is delivered to a location in the state. If the taxpayer is not taxable in a state to which a sale is assigned or if the state of assignment cannot be determined, the sale is excluded from the denominator of the sales factor (throwout rule). Under prior law, Alabama sourced sales of services using the cost of performance rule. [H.B. 434, June 9, 2011]

California. For tax years prior to 2011, California required the use of the UDITPA costs of performance rule for sourcing sales of services. Effective for tax years beginning on or after January 1, 2011, taxpayers who elect to use a single-factor sales apportionment formula must use a market-based sourcing rule for sales of services. Under the new law, sales of services are attributed to California "to the extent the purchaser of the service received the benefit of the service" in the state. Taxpayers who do not elect to use the single-factor sales apportionment formula, but instead continue to use a double-weighted sales formula, are required to use the costs of performance rule for sourcing sales of services [S.B. 858, Oct. 19, 2010; and S.B. 15. Feb. 20, 2009].

Georgia. Sales of services are attributed to Georgia "if the receipts are derived from customers within this state or if the receipts are otherwise attributable to this state's marketplace." This gross receipts factor is designed to measure the marketplace for the taxpayer's goods and services. [Ga. Reg. § 560-7-7-.03(5)(c)(1)]

A customer within Georgia means (1) a customer that is engaged in a trade or business and maintains a regular place of business within Georgia, or (2) a customer that is not engaged in a trade or business whose billing address is in Georgia. A regular place of business means an office, factory, warehouse, or other business location at which the customer conducts business in a regular and systematic manner and which is continuously maintained, occupied and used by employees, agents or representatives of the customer. A billing address means the location indicated in the books and records of the taxpayer as the address of record where any notice, statement and/or bill relating to a customer's account is mailed. [Ga. Reg. § 560-7-7-.03(5)(c)(3) to (5)]

Gross receipts for the performance of services are attributable to the state's marketplace if the recipient of the service receives all of the benefit of the service in Georgia. If the recipient of the service receives some of the benefit of the service in Georgia, the gross receipts are attributed to Georgia in proportion to the extent the recipient receives benefit of the service in Georgia. [Ga. Reg. § 560-7-7-.03(5)(c)(6)(ii)] The regulation provides numerous examples, including the following:

> A corporation headquartered in State A is building an office complex in Georgia. The corporation from State A contracts with an engineering firm from State B to oversee construction of the buildings on the site. The engineering firm performs some of their service in Georgia at the building site and additional service in State B. All of the gross receipts from the engineering service are attributable to Georgia and are included in the numerator of the apportionment factor because the recipient of the service received all of the benefit of the service in Georgia.

Illinois. Effective for tax years ending on or after December 31, 2008, sales of services are attributed to Illinois if "the services are received" in Illinois. [S.B. 783, Jan. 11, 2008] Gross receipts from the performance of services provided to a corporation, partnership, or trust may be attributed to Illinois only if the service recipient has a fixed place of business in Illinois. If the state where the services are received is not readily determinable or is a state where the service recipient does not have a fixed place of business, the services are deemed to be received at the location of the office of the customer from which the services were ordered in the regular course of the customer's trade or business. If the ordering office cannot be determined, the services are deemed to be received at the office of the customer to which the services are billed. If the taxpayer is not taxable in the state in which the services are received, the sale is excluded from both the numerator and the denominator of the sales factor (a throw-out rule). Prior to 2008, Illinois generally conformed to the UDITPA costs of performance rule to source sales of services.

Iowa. Sales of services are attributed to Iowa "if the recipient of the service receives all of the benefit of the service in Iowa." If the recipient of the service receives only some of the benefit of the service in Iowa, the sale is attributed to Iowa "in proportion to the extent the recipient receives benefit of the service in Iowa.'' [Iowa Admin. Code Rule 701-54.6(422)] The regulation provides the following example, which illustrates that sales of services are not always attributed to the state in which the customer is located, but instead are attributed to the state in which the customer receives the benefit of the service.

> A real estate development firm from State A is developing a tract of land in Iowa. The real estate development firm from State A engages a surveying company from State B to survey the tract of land in Iowa. The survey work is completed and the plats are drawn in Iowa. The gross receipts from this survey work are attributable to Iowa and included in the numerator of the apportionment factor because the recipient of the service received all of the benefits of the service in Iowa.

Maine. Receipts from the performance of services are attributed to Maine if the services are received in Maine. If the state where the services are received is not readily determinable, the services are deemed to be received at the home of the customer or, in the case of a business, the office of the customer from which the services were ordered in the regular course of the customer's trade or business. If the ordering location cannot be determined, the services are deemed to be received at the home or office of the customer to which the services are billed. If the purchaser of the service is the federal government or the receipts are otherwise attributable to a state in which the taxpayer is not taxable, the receipts are attributed to Maine if a greater proportion of the income producing activity is performed in Maine than in any other state, based on costs of performance. [36 Me. Rev. Stat. Ann. § 5211(14)]

Maryland. Gross receipts from contracting or service-related activities are attributed to Maryland if the receipts are ''derived from customers within'' Maryland. [Md. Code Regs. § 03.04.03.08.C(3)(c)] Customers within Maryland include individuals and business enterprises that are domiciled in Maryland. A business enterprise (e.g., a corporation, partnership or limited liability company) is domiciled in Maryland if a Maryland office or place of business provides the ''principal impetus for the sale.'' If the principal impetus for the sale cannot be identified, then the business enterprise's domicile is the state in which the headquarters or principal place of business management is located. A special rule applies to construction services, under which the source of the sale is determined by the situs of the property. [Md. Code Regs. § 03.04.03.08.D] The regulation provides the following examples, which illustrate the determination of whether the principal impetus for a sale is in Maryland.

> **Example 3:** Service provider C contracts with corporation D, a multistate enterprise, to redesign the operating software for D's customer billing operation. The principal impetus for this contract is to provide a benefit to the central billing computers. If those computers are located within Maryland, then the revenue earned from these services is included in the numerator of C's [Maryland]sales factor.
>
> **Example 4:** Service provider E contracts with corporation F, a multistate enterprise, to redesign all the operating software of F's multistate computer network. If no particular office or place of business can be identified as the principal impetus for this contract, then the revenue earned from this contract shall be included in the numerator of E's [Maryland]sales factor only if F's headquarters or principal place of business management is located within Maryland.

Michigan. For purposes of the Michigan business tax, which took effect on January 1, 2008, receipts from the performance of services are attributed to Michigan if the recipient of the services receives all of the benefit of the services in Michigan. If the recipient receives only some of the benefit of the services in Michigan, then the receipts are attributed to Michigan to the extent that the recipient receives the benefit of the services in Michigan. [Mich. Comp. Laws § 208.1305(2)] The statute also provides special sourcing rules for selected types of services. These include, but not limited to, securities brokerage services, transportation services, and telecommunications services. The general rule applies to receipts received from the performance of all other services.

In 2010, the Michigan Department of Treasury issued Revenue Administrative Bulletin (RAB) 2010-5, which provides the following guidance for determining whether the service recipient receives the benefit of the service in Michigan:

1. The service relates to real property that is located in Michigan.
2. The service relates to tangible personal property that (a) is owned or leased by the purchaser and located in Michigan at the time that the service is received, or (b) is delivered to the purchaser in Michigan.
3. The service is provided to a purchaser who is an individual physically present in Michigan at the time that the service is received.

4. The services are received in Michigan and are in the nature of personal services (e.g., consulting, counseling, training, speaking, or providing entertainment) that are typically conducted or performed first-hand, on a direct, one-to-one or one-to-many basis.
5. The service is provided to a purchaser that is engaged in a trade or business in Michigan and relates to the trade or business of that purchaser in Michigan.
6. The service relates to the use of intangible property (e.g., computer software, licenses, designs, processes, patents, or copyrights) which is used in Michigan.
7. The services provided are professional in nature (e.g., legal or accounting services), and are provided to a purchaser that is an individual domiciled in Michigan, or to a purchaser with business operations in Michigan.

If where the benefit of the services is received cannot be determined, the receipt is sourced to the customer's location.

Minnesota. Sales of services are attributed to Minnesota if the "services are received" in Minnesota. However, services provided to a corporation, partnership, or trust may only be attributed to a state in which the customer has a fixed place of doing business. If the state where the services are received is not readily determinable or is a state where the corporation, partnership, or trust receiving the service does not have a fixed place of doing business, the services are deemed to be received at the location of the office of the customer from which the services were ordered in the regular course of the customer's trade or business. If the ordering office cannot be determined, the services are deemed to be received at the office of the customer to which the services are billed. [Minn. Rev. Stat. § 290.191(j)]

Utah. For tax years beginning on or after January 1, 2009, "a receipt from the performance of a service is considered to be in this state if the purchaser of the service receives a greater benefit of the service in this state than in any other state." [S.B. 136, Mar. 14, 2008] Prior to 2009, Utah used the UDITPA costs of performance rule to source sales of services.

Wisconsin. Sales of services are attributed to Wisconsin if the "purchaser of the service received the benefit of the service" in Wisconsin. [Wis. § 71.25(9)(dh)] The benefit of a service is received in Wisconsin if any of the following applies:

1. The service relates to real property that is located in Wisconsin.
2. The service relates to tangible personal property that is located in Wisconsin at the time that the service is received or tangible personal property that is delivered directly or indirectly to customers in Wisconsin.
3. The service is provided to an individual who is physically present in Wisconsin at the time that the service is received.
4. The service is provided to a person engaged in a trade or business in Wisconsin and relates to that person's business in Wisconsin.

Under the original version of this law [A.B. 100, July 25, 2005, effective for tax years beginning after 2004], if the taxpayer is not subject to income tax in the state in which the benefit of the service is received, the benefit of the service is deemed to be received in Wisconsin to the extent that the taxpayer's employees or representatives performed services from a location in Wisconsin. Fifty percent of the taxpayer's sales that are considered to be received in Wisconsin under this throwback rule are included in the numerator of the sales factor [Wis. Sec. 71.25(9)(dh)]. In 2009, Wisconsin repealed its throwback rule for sales of services, effective for tax years beginning on or after January 1, 2009. [A.B. 75, June 29, 2009]

State-by-State Summary

For ease of presentation, the following chart has been divided into four parts, as follows:

- Part 1: Costs of Performance Rule
- Part 2: Computing the Costs of Performance
- Part 3: Market-Based Sourcing Rules
- Part 4: Other Sourcing Rules

Sales Factor: Receipts from Services (Part 1)

Costs of Performance Rule

Legend:
X — Indicates basis for inclusion in the sales factor numerator
NA — Not applicable
NR — Not reported

		If YES, How Is the Amount Attributed to Your State Determined When the Income-Producing Activity Is Performed in More Than One State?			
	Does the State Attribute Sales of Services to the Numerator of the Sales Factor Based on where the Income-Producing Activity Is Performed?	*UDITPA Greater "Costs of Performance" Standard*	*Percentage of Total "Costs of Performance" Incurred*	*Ratio of Time Spent Performing the Service to the Total Time Spent Performing the Service*	*Other*
Alabama	Yes	X			
Alaska	Yes	X			
Arizona	Yes	X, R15-2D-806			
Arkansas	No				
California	Yes	X, See R&TC 25136(b); Cal. Code Regs., tit. 18, § 25136(a).		X, for gross receipts from the performance of personal services. See R&TC 25136(d)(2)C.	
Colorado	Yes		X		
Connecticut	Yes				
Delaware	Yes		X	X	
District of Columbia	Yes	X			
Florida	Yes			X	
Georgia	No				
Hawaii	Yes				
Idaho	Yes	X			
Illinois	No				

Sales Factor: Receipts from Services (Part 1)

Costs of Performance Rule

Legend:

X	Indicates basis for inclusion in the sales factor numerator
NA	Not applicable
NR	Not reported

		If YES, How Is the Amount Attributed to Your State Determined When the Income-Producing Activity Is Performed in More Than One State?			
	Does the State Attribute Sales of Services to the Numerator of the Sales Factor Based on where the Income-Producing Activity Is Performed?	*UDITPA Greater "Costs of Performance" Standard*	*Percentage of Total "Costs of Performance" Incurred*	*Ratio of Time Spent Performing the Service to the Total Time Spent Performing the Service*	*Other*
Indiana	Yes		X		
Iowa	No				
Kansas	Yes	X			
Kentucky	Yes			X	
Louisiana	Yes			X	
Maine	No				
Maryland	No				
Massachusetts	Yes	X			
Michigan	No				
Note. The CIT takes effect 01/01/12, and replaces the Michigan Business Tax (MBT) for most taxpayers. However, businesses that have been approved to receive, have received, or have been assigned certain certified credits may elect to file a return and pay the tax imposed by the MBT in lieu of the CIT until the certified credits are exhausted or extinguished.					
Minnesota	No				
Mississippi	Yes				
Missouri	Yes	X			
Montana	NR	NR	NR	NR	NR

Sales Factor: Receipts from Services (Part 1)

Costs of Performance Rule

Legend:

X	Indicates basis for inclusion in the sales factor numerator
NA	Not applicable
NR	Not reported

		If YES, How Is the Amount Attributed to Your State Determined When the Income-Producing Activity Is Performed in More Than One State?			
	Does the State Attribute Sales of Services to the Numerator of the Sales Factor Based on where the Income-Producing Activity Is Performed?	*UDITPA Greater "Costs of Performance" Standard*	*Percentage of Total "Costs of Performance" Incurred*	*Ratio of Time Spent Performing the Service to the Total Time Spent Performing the Service*	*Other*
Nebraska	Yes	X			
Nevada	Nevada does not impose a corporate income tax				
New Hampshire	Yes	X			
New Jersey	Yes		X	X	
New Mexico	Yes	X			
New York	Yes			X	
North Carolina	Yes			X	
North Dakota	Yes	X			
Ohio	Ohio does not impose a corporate income tax				

Note A. Effective 1/1/2010, the Ohio Franchise Tax was fully phased out and business will be taxed on gross receipts through the Commercial Activity Tax. Details about that tax can be found at: http://tax.ohio.gov/divisions/commercial_activities/index.stm

Sales Factor: Receipts from Services (Part 1)

Costs of Performance Rule

Legend:

X	Indicates basis for inclusion in the sales factor numerator
NA	Not applicable
NR	Not reported

		If YES, How Is the Amount Attributed to Your State Determined When the Income-Producing Activity Is Performed in More Than One State?			
	Does the State Attribute Sales of Services to the Numerator of the Sales Factor Based on where the Income-Producing Activity Is Performed?	*UDITPA Greater "Costs of Performance" Standard*	*Percentage of Total "Costs of Performance" Incurred*	*Ratio of Time Spent Performing the Service to the Total Time Spent Performing the Service*	*Other*
Oklahoma	Receipts from the performance of services shall be included in the numerator of the fraction if the receipts are derived from customers within this state or if the receipts are otherwise attributable to this state's marketplace (see 68 O.S. § 2358(A)(5)). A customer within Oklahoma "means" 1) a customer that is engaged in a trade or business and maintains a regular place of business in Oklahoma, or 2) a customer that is not engaged in a trade or business whose billing address is in Oklahoma. A "billing address" means the location indicated in the books and records of the taxpayer as the address of record where the bill relating to the customer's account is mailed.				
Oregon	Yes	X		X	

Sales Factor: Receipts from Services (Part 1)

Costs of Performance Rule

Legend:

X	Indicates basis for inclusion in the sales factor numerator
NA	Not applicable
NR	Not reported

	Does the State Attribute Sales of Services to the Numerator of the Sales Factor Based on where the Income-Producing Activity Is Performed?	*If YES, How Is the Amount Attributed to Your State Determined When the Income-Producing Activity Is Performed in More Than One State?*			
		UDITPA Greater "Costs of Performance" Standard	*Percentage of Total "Costs of Performance" Incurred*	*Ratio of Time Spent Performing the Service to the Total Time Spent Performing the Service*	*Other*
Pennsylvania	Yes	X			
Rhode Island	Yes			X	
South Carolina	Yes			X	
South Dakota	South Dakota does not impose a corporate income tax				
Tennessee	Yes	X			
Texas	Yes				X, based on fair value of services performed.
Utah	No				Sourced to Utah if the purchaser of the service receives a greater benefit in Utah than in any other state.

Sales Factor: Receipts from Services (Part 1)

Costs of Performance Rule

Legend:

X	Indicates basis for inclusion in the sales factor numerator
NA	Not applicable
NR	Not reported

	Does the State Attribute Sales of Services to the Numerator of the Sales Factor Based on where the Income-Producing Activity Is Performed?	*If YES, How Is the Amount Attributed to Your State Determined When the Income-Producing Activity Is Performed in More Than One State?* UDITPA Greater "Costs of Performance" Standard	*Percentage of Total "Costs of Performance" Incurred*	*Ratio of Time Spent Performing the Service to the Total Time Spent Performing the Service*	*Other*
Vermont	Yes				Receipts for services are apportioned to Vermont if the services are performed in Vermont. When compensation for services are in payment of services performed both within and outside of Vermont, sales are apportioned to this state if a greater proportion of the income producing activity is performed in Vermont.
Virginia	Yes	X			
Washington	Washington does not impose a corporate income tax				
West Virginia	Yes		X		
Wisconsin	No				
Wyoming	Wyoming does not impose a corporate income tax				

Sales Factor: Receipts from Services (Part 2)

Computing the Costs of Performance

Legend:

X Condition applies
NA Not applicable
NR Not reported

If State Sources Sales of Services Based on Cost of Performance, the Taxpayer's Cost of Performance Includes:

	Direct Cost Based on GAAP	*Direct Cost Based on Industry Standards*	*Cost Associated with Obtaining and Retaining Clients, Including Contract Negotiations*	*Charges from Unrelated Subcontractors Performing Some or All of the Services*	*Charges from Related Entities Performing Some or All of the Services*	*Other*
Alabama	X					
Alaska	X					
Arizona	See R15-2D-806.	See R15-2D-806.				
Arkansas						
California						Direct costs determined in a manner consistent with GAAP and in accordance with accepted conditions or practices in the trade or business of the taxpayer. See Cal. Code Regs., tit. 18, § 25136(c).
Colorado	X	X	X		X	
Connecticut						
Delaware	X					
District of Columbia	X	X		X	X	
Florida						
Georgia						

Sales Factor: Receipts from Services (Part 2)

Computing the Costs of Performance

Legend:

X	Condition applies
NA	Not applicable
NR	Not reported

If State Sources Sales of Services Based on Cost of Performance, the Taxpayer's Cost of Performance Includes:

	Direct Cost Based on GAAP	*Direct Cost Based on Industry Standards*	*Cost Associated with Obtaining and Retaining Clients, Including Contract Negotiations*	*Charges from Unrelated Subcontractors Performing Some or All of the Services*	*Charges from Related Entities Performing Some or All of the Services*	*Other*
Hawaii	X	X				
Idaho	X	X				Idaho Income Tax Administrative Rule 35.01.01.550.03 states, in pertinent part, "Included in the taxpayer's cost of performance are taxpayer's payments to an agent or independent contractor for the performance of personal services and utilization of tangible and intangible property that give rise to the particular item of income."
Illinois						
Indiana	X	X		X	X	
Iowa						
Kansas	X	X				
Kentucky						

Sales Factor: Receipts from Services (Part 2)

Computing the Costs of Performance

Legend:

X	Condition applies
NA	Not applicable
NR	Not reported

If State Sources Sales of Services Based on Cost of Performance, the Taxpayer's Cost of Performance Includes:

	Direct Cost Based on GAAP	*Direct Cost Based on Industry Standards*	*Cost Associated with Obtaining and Retaining Clients, Including Contract Negotiations*	*Charges from Unrelated Subcontractors Performing Some or All of the Services*	*Charges from Related Entities Performing Some or All of the Services*	*Other*
Louisiana						
Maine						
Maryland						
Massachusetts	X	Depends on facts	Depends on facts	Depends on facts	Depends on facts	
Michigan						

Note. The CIT takes effect 01/01/12, and replaces the Michigan Business Tax (MBT) for most taxpayers. However, businesses that have been approved to receive, have received, or have been assigned certain certified credits may elect to file a return and pay the tax imposed by the MBT in lieu of the CIT until the certified credits are exhausted or extinguished.

	Direct Cost Based on GAAP	*Direct Cost Based on Industry Standards*	*Cost Associated with Obtaining and Retaining Clients, Including Contract Negotiations*	*Charges from Unrelated Subcontractors Performing Some or All of the Services*	*Charges from Related Entities Performing Some or All of the Services*	*Other*
Minnesota						
Mississippi						
Missouri	X					
Montana	NR	NR	NR	NR	NR	NR
Nebraska						
Nevada	Nevada does not impose a corporate income tax					
New Hampshire	X	X				
New Jersey		X				
New Mexico	X	X				
New York						

Sales Factor: Receipts from Services (Part 2)

Computing the Costs of Performance

Legend:

X	Condition applies
NA	Not applicable
NR	Not reported

If State Sources Sales of Services Based on Cost of Performance, the Taxpayer's Cost of Performance Includes:

	Direct Cost Based on GAAP	*Direct Cost Based on Industry Standards*	*Cost Associated with Obtaining and Retaining Clients, Including Contract Negotiations*	*Charges from Unrelated Subcontractors Performing Some or All of the Services*	*Charges from Related Entities Performing Some or All of the Services*	*Other*
North Carolina						
North Dakota	X					
Ohio	Ohio does not impose a corporate income tax					
Note A. Effective 1/1/2010, the Ohio Franchise Tax was fully phased out and business will be taxed on gross receipts through the Commercial Activity Tax. Details about that tax can be found at: http://tax.ohio.gov/divisions/commercial_activities/index.stm						
Oklahoma						
Oregon	X	X		X	X	
Pennsylvania						All options may be considered. It depends on the facts and circumstances and the available information.
Rhode Island						
South Carolina						
South Dakota	South Dakota does not impose a corporate income tax					
Tennessee	X	X				
Texas						
Utah						
Vermont						

Sales Factor: Receipts from Services (Part 2)

Computing the Costs of Performance

Legend:

X Condition applies
NA Not applicable
NR Not reported

If State Sources Sales of Services Based on Cost of Performance, the Taxpayer's Cost of Performance Includes:

	Direct Cost Based on GAAP	*Direct Cost Based on Industry Standards*	*Cost Associated with Obtaining and Retaining Clients, Including Contract Negotiations*	*Charges from Unrelated Subcontractors Performing Some or All of the Services*	*Charges from Related Entities Performing Some or All of the Services*	*Other*
Virginia						The cost of all activities performed by the taxpayer for the ultimate purpose of producing the sale to be apportioned. After a regulation limiting costs to direct costs and excluding costs paid for financial corporations to independent contractors was overturned by the court, the Virginia Department of Taxation issued Tax Bulletin 05-3 allowing taxpayers to elect to follow the regulation or the court holding.
Washington	Washington does not impose a corporate income tax					
West Virginia	X	X		X	X	
Wisconsin						
Wyoming	Wyoming does not impose a corporate income tax					

Sales Factor: Receipts from Services (Part 3)

Market-Based Sourcing Rule

Legend:

X	Condition applies
NA	Not applicable
NR	Not reported

		If YES, what factors are considered in determining where the benefit of the service is received (check all that apply)?						
	Does the State Attribute Sales of Services to the Numerator of the Sales Factor Based on where the Benefit of the Service is Received by the Purchaser?	*Service Relates to Real Property that is Located in the State*	*Service Relates to Tangible Personal Property that is Located in State at Time the Service is Received*	*Service Relates to Intangible Property Used at Time Service is Received*	*Service is Provided to Purchaser who is an Individual Physically Present at Time Service is Received*	*Service is Provided to Person Engaged in Trade or Business in State and Service Relates to that Person's Business in State*	*Service is Received in State and is a Personal Service that is Performed on a Direct, One-to-One Basis*	*Service is Professional in Nature, and is Provided to a Purchaser who is an Individual Domiciled in State, or to a Purchaser with Business Operations in State*
Alabama	No							
Alaska	No							
Arizona								
Arkansas	No							
California	No							
Colorado	No							
Connecticut								
Delaware	No							
District of Columbia	Yes	X	X	X	X	X	X	X
Florida	No							
Georgia	Yes, see GA. Code. § 48-7-31 and GA. Comp. R. & Regs. 560-7-7-.03.							

Sales Factor: Receipts from Services (Part 3)
Market-Based Sourcing Rule

Legend:

X	Condition applies
NA	Not applicable
NR	Not reported

		If YES, what factors are considered in determining where the benefit of the service is received (check all that apply)?						
	Does the State Attribute Sales of Services to the Numerator of the Sales Factor Based on where the Benefit of the Service is Received by the Purchaser?	*Service Relates to Real Property that is Located in the State*	*Service Relates to Tangible Personal Property that is Located in State at Time the Service is Received*	*Service Relates to Intangible Property Used at Time Service is Received*	*Service is Provided to Purchaser who is an Individual Physically Present at Time Service is Received*	*Service is Provided to Person Engaged in Trade or Business in State and Service Relates to that Person's Business in State*	*Service is Received in State and is a Personal Service that is Performed on a Direct, One-to-One Basis*	*Service is Professional in Nature, and is Provided to a Purchaser who is an Individual Domiciled in State, or to a Purchaser with Business Operations in State*
Hawaii	No							
Idaho	No							

Sales Factor: Receipts from Services (Part 3)

Market-Based Sourcing Rule

Legend:

X	Condition applies
NA	Not applicable
NR	Not reported

		If YES, what factors are considered in determining where the benefit of the service is received (check all that apply)?						
	Does the State Attribute Sales of Services to the Numerator of the Sales Factor Based on where the Benefit of the Service is Received by the Purchaser?	*Service Relates to Real Property that is Located in the State*	*Service Relates to Tangible Personal Property that is Located in State at Time the Service is Received*	*Service Relates to Intangible Property Used at Time Service is Received*	*Service is Provided to Purchaser who is an Individual Physically Present at Time Service is Received*	*Service is Provided to Person Engaged in Trade or Business in State and Service Relates to that Person's Business in State*	*Service is Received in State and is a Personal Service that is Performed on a Direct, One-to-One Basis*	*Service is Professional in Nature, and is Provided to a Purchaser who is an Individual Domiciled in State, or to a Purchaser with Business Operations in State*
Illinois	Yes, special apportionment formulas apply to insurance companies, financial organizations, and transportation companies, and special rules apply to gross receipts from telecommunication services and from broadcasting services. Otherwise, gross receipts from services are in Illinois if the	X	X	X	X	X	X	X

Sales Factor: Receipts from Services (Part 3)

Market-Based Sourcing Rule

Legend:
X Condition applies
NA Not applicable
NR Not reported

		If YES, what factors are considered in determining where the benefit of the service is received (check all that apply)?						
	Does the State Attribute Sales of Services to the Numerator of the Sales Factor Based on where the Benefit of the Service is Received by the Purchaser?	*Service Relates to Real Property that is Located in the State*	*Service Relates to Tangible Personal Property that is Located in State at Time the Service is Received*	*Service Relates to Intangible Property Used at Time Service is Received*	*Service is Provided to Purchaser who is an Individual Physically Present at Time Service is Received*	*Service is Provided to Person Engaged in Trade or Business in State and Service Relates to that Person's Business in State*	*Service is Received in State and is a Personal Service that is Performed on a Direct, One-to-One Basis*	*Service is Professional in Nature, and is Provided to a Purchaser who is an Individual Domiciled in State, or to a Purchaser with Business Operations in State*
	"services are received in Illinois" 35 ILCS 304(a)(3)(C-5)(iv).							
Indiana	Yes	X	X	X	X	X	X	
Iowa	Yes	X	X	X	X	X	X	X
Kansas	No							
Kentucky	No							
Louisiana	Yes	X	X	X	X	X	X	X
Maine	Yes, where service is received or customer is located.							
Maryland	Yes	X	X	X	X	X	X	X
Massachusetts	No							

Sales Factor: Receipts from Services (Part 3)

Market-Based Sourcing Rule

Legend:

X	Condition applies
NA	Not applicable
NR	Not reported

	Does the State Attribute Sales of Services to the Numerator of the Sales Factor Based on where the Benefit of the Service is Received by the Purchaser?	*If YES, what factors are considered in determining where the benefit of the service is received (check all that apply)?*						
		Service Relates to Real Property that is Located in the State	*Service Relates to Tangible Personal Property that is Located in State at Time the Service is Received*	*Service Relates to Intangible Property Used at Time Service is Received*	*Service is Provided to Purchaser who is an Individual Physically Present at Time Service is Received*	*Service is Provided to Person Engaged in Trade or Business in State and Service Relates to that Person's Business in State*	*Service is Received in State and is a Personal Service that is Performed on a Direct, One-to-One Basis*	*Service is Professional in Nature, and is Provided to a Purchaser who is an Individual Domiciled in State, or to a Purchaser with Business Operations in State*
Michigan	Yes	X	X	X	X	X	X	X
Note. The CIT takes effect 01/01/12, and replaces the Michigan Business Tax (MBT) for most taxpayers. However, businesses that have been approved to receive, have received, or have been assigned certain certified credits may elect to file a return and pay the tax imposed by the MBT in lieu of the CIT until the certified credits are exhausted or extinguished.								
Minnesota	Yes	X	X	X	X	X	X	X
Mississippi	Yes				X			
Missouri	No							
Montana	NR	NR	NR	NR	NR	NR	NR	NR
Nebraska	No							
Nevada	Nevada does not impose a corporate income tax							
New Hampshire	No							
New Jersey	No							
New Mexico	No							
New York	No							

Sales Factor: Receipts from Services (Part 3)

Market-Based Sourcing Rule

Legend:

X	Condition applies
NA	Not applicable
NR	Not reported

		If YES, what factors are considered in determining where the benefit of the service is received (check all that apply)?						
	Does the State Attribute Sales of Services to the Numerator of the Sales Factor Based on where the Benefit of the Service is Received by the Purchaser?	*Service Relates to Real Property that is Located in the State*	*Service Relates to Tangible Personal Property that is Located in State at Time the Service is Received*	*Service Relates to Intangible Property Used at Time Service is Received*	*Service is Provided to Purchaser who is an Individual Physically Present at Time Service is Received*	*Service is Provided to Person Engaged in Trade or Business in State and Service Relates to that Person's Business in State*	*Service is Received in State and is a Personal Service that is Performed on a Direct, One-to-One Basis*	*Service is Professional in Nature, and is Provided to a Purchaser who is an Individual Domiciled in State, or to a Purchaser with Business Operations in State*
North Carolina	No							
North Dakota	No							
Ohio	Ohio does not impose a corporate income tax							

Note A. Effective 1/1/2010, the Ohio Franchise Tax was fully phased out and business will be taxed on gross receipts through the Commercial Activity Tax. Details about that tax can be found at: http://tax.ohio.gov/divisions/commercial_activities/index.stm

Sales Factor: Receipts from Services (Part 3)
Market-Based Sourcing Rule

Legend:

X	Condition applies
NA	Not applicable
NR	Not reported

	Does the State Attribute Sales of Services to the Numerator of the Sales Factor Based on where the Benefit of the Service is Received by the Purchaser?	*If YES, what factors are considered in determining where the benefit of the service is received (check all that apply)?* Service Relates to Real Property that is Located in the State	Service Relates to Tangible Personal Property that is Located in State at Time the Service is Received	Service Relates to Intangible Property Used at Time Service is Received	Service is Provided to Purchaser who is an Individual Physically Present at Time Service is Received	Service is Provided to Person Engaged in Trade or Business in State and Service Relates to that Person's Business in State	Service is Received in State and is a Personal Service that is Performed on a Direct, One-to-One Basis	Service is Professional in Nature, and is Provided to a Purchaser who is an Individual Domiciled in State, or to a Purchaser with Business Operations in State
Oklahoma	Receipts from the performance of services shall be included in the numerator of the fraction if the receipts are derived from customers within this State or if the receipts are otherwise attributable to this State's marketplace (see 68 O.S. §2358(A)(5)). A customer within Oklahoma "means" (1) a customer that is engaged in a							

Sales Factor: Receipts from Services (Part 3)

Market-Based Sourcing Rule

Legend:

X Condition applies
NA Not applicable
NR Not reported

	Does the State Attribute Sales of Services to the Numerator of the Sales Factor Based on where the Benefit of the Service is Received by the Purchaser?	*If YES, what factors are considered in determining where the benefit of the service is received (check all that apply)?* Service Relates to Real Property that is Located in the State	*Service Relates to Tangible Personal Property that is Located in State at Time the Service is Received*	*Service Relates to Intangible Property Used at Time Service is Received*	*Service is Provided to Purchaser who is an Individual Physically Present at Time Service is Received*	*Service is Provided to Person Engaged in Trade or Business in State and Service Relates to that Person's Business in State*	*Service is Received in State and is a Personal Service that is Performed on a Direct, One-to-One Basis*	*Service is Professional in Nature, and is Provided to a Purchaser who is an Individual Domiciled in State, or to a Purchaser with Business Operations in State*
	trade or business and maintains a regular place of business in Oklahoma, or (2) a customer that is not engaged in a trade or business whose billing address is in Oklahoma. A "billing address" means the location indicated in the books and records of the taxpayer as the address of record where							

Sales Factor: Receipts from Services (Part 3)

Market-Based Sourcing Rule

Legend:

X	Condition applies
NA	Not applicable
NR	Not reported

	Does the State Attribute Sales of Services to the Numerator of the Sales Factor Based on where the Benefit of the Service is Received by the Purchaser?	*If YES, what factors are considered in determining where the benefit of the service is received (check all that apply)?* Service Relates to Real Property that is Located in the State	*Service Relates to Tangible Personal Property that is Located in State at Time the Service is Received*	*Service Relates to Intangible Property Used at Time Service is Received*	*Service is Provided to Purchaser who is an Individual Physically Present at Time Service is Received*	*Service is Provided to Person Engaged in Trade or Business in State and Service Relates to that Person's Business in State*	*Service is Received in State and is a Personal Service that is Performed on a Direct, One-to-One Basis*	*Service is Professional in Nature, and is Provided to a Purchaser who is an Individual Domiciled in State, or to a Purchaser with Business Operations in State*
	the bill relating to the customer's account is mailed.							
Oregon	No							
Pennsylvania	Where the benefit of the service is received may be considered in determining where the income-producing activity occurred.							
Rhode Island	Yes	X	X	X	X	X	X	
South Carolina	No							

Sales Factor: Receipts from Services (Part 3)

Market-Based Sourcing Rule

Legend:

X	Condition applies
NA	Not applicable
NR	Not reported

	Does the State Attribute Sales of Services to the Numerator of the Sales Factor Based on where the Benefit of the Service is Received by the Purchaser?	*If YES, what factors are considered in determining where the benefit of the service is received (check all that apply)?* Service Relates to Real Property that is Located in the State	Service Relates to Tangible Personal Property that is Located in State at Time the Service is Received	Service Relates to Intangible Property Used at Time Service is Received	Service is Provided to Purchaser who is an Individual Physically Present at Time Service is Received	Service is Provided to Person Engaged in Trade or Business in State and Service Relates to that Person's Business in State	Service is Received in State and is a Personal Service that is Performed on a Direct, One-to-One Basis	Service is Professional in Nature, and is Provided to a Purchaser who is an Individual Domiciled in State, or to a Purchaser with Business Operations in State
South Dakota	South Dakota does not impose a corporate income tax							
Tennessee	No							
Texas	No							
Utah	Yes	X	X	X	X	X		
Vermont	Yes	X	X	X	X	X	X	X
Virginia	No							
Washington	Washington does not impose a corporate income tax							
West Virginia	No							
Wisconsin	Yes	X	X		X	X		
Wyoming	Wyoming does not impose a corporate income tax							

Sales Factor: Receipts from Services (Part 4)

Other Sourcing Rules

Legend:

X	Condition applies
NA	Not applicable
NR	Not reported

	Does the State Attribute Sales of Services to the Numerator of the Sales Factor Based on a Criteria Other than Where the Income-Producing Activity is Performed or Where Benefit is Received by the Purchaser?	
	Yes, Explain	*No*
Alabama		X
Alaska		X
Arizona		
Arkansas	X, compute all three factors excluding sales of service and apply factor to sales of service.	
California		X
Colorado		X
Connecticut		
Delaware		X
District of Columbia	X, if taxpayer's commercial domicile is in the District of Columbia and taxpayer is not subject to tax in another state.	
Florida	No	
Georgia	See GA. Code. § 48-7-31 and GA. Comp. R. & Regs. 560-7-7-.03.	
Hawaii		X
Idaho		X
Illinois		X
Indiana		X
Iowa		X

Sales Factor: Receipts from Services (Part 4)

Other Sourcing Rules

Legend:

X	Condition applies
NA	Not applicable
NR	Not reported

Does the State Attribute Sales of Services to the Numerator of the Sales Factor Based on a Criteria Other than Where the Income-Producing Activity is Performed or Where Benefit is Received by the Purchaser?

	Yes, Explain	*No*
Kansas		X
Kentucky		X
Louisiana		X
Maine		X
Maryland		X
Massachusetts		X
Michigan	X, the sourcing of sales derived from certain specific types of services, such as securities brokerage services and telecommunications services, are addressed separately in the statute.	

Note. The CIT takes effect 01/01/12, and replaces the Michigan Business Tax (MBT) for most taxpayers. However, businesses that have been approved to receive, have received, or have been assigned certain certified credits may elect to file a return and pay the tax imposed by the MBT in lieu of the CIT until the certified credits are exhausted or extinguished.

	Yes, Explain	*No*
Minnesota		X
Mississippi		X
Missouri		X
Montana	NR	NR
Nebraska		X
Nevada	Nevada does not impose a corporate income tax	
New Hampshire		X

Sales Factor: Receipts from Services (Part 4)

Other Sourcing Rules

Legend:

X	Condition applies
NA	Not applicable
NR	Not reported

	Does the State Attribute Sales of Services to the Numerator of the Sales Factor Based on a Criteria Other than Where the Income-Producing Activity is Performed or Where Benefit is Received by the Purchaser?	
	Yes, Explain	*No*
New Jersey	X, allocation depends on the type of service. N.J.A.C. 18:7-8.10.	
New Mexico		X
New York	X, special rules exist for broadcasters, publishers, and securities broker/dealers. See Business Corporation Franchise Tax Regulations § 4-4.3 for details.	
North Carolina		X
North Dakota		X
Ohio	Ohio does not impose a corporate income tax	
Oklahoma	Receipts from the performance of services shall be included in the numerator of the fraction if the receipts are derived from customers within this State or if the receipts are otherwise attributable to this State's marketplace (see 68 O.S. § 2358(A)(5)). A customer within Oklahoma "means" (1) a customer that is engaged in a trade or business and maintains a regular place of business in Oklahoma, or (2) a customer that is not engaged in a trade or business whose billing address is in Oklahoma. A "billing address" means the location indicated in the books and records of the taxpayer as the address of record where the bill relating to the customer's account is mailed.	
Oregon		X
Pennsylvania		X

Sales Factor: Receipts from Services (Part 4)

Other Sourcing Rules

Legend:

X	Condition applies
NA	Not applicable
NR	Not reported

Does the State Attribute Sales of Services to the Numerator of the Sales Factor Based on a Criteria Other than Where the Income-Producing Activity is Performed or Where Benefit is Received by the Purchaser?

	Yes, Explain	*No*
Rhode Island		X
South Carolina		X
South Dakota	South Dakota does not impose a corporate income tax	
Tennessee		X
Texas		X
Utah		X, only in connection with Utah special industry statutes or rules applicable to trucking companies, railroads, publishing companies, financial institutions, telecommunications, registered securities or commodities brokers or dealer, airlines, and the sale of certain services to or on behalf of a regulated investment company. The foregoing rules generally employ a market approach in connection with the sales factor.
Vermont	NR	
Virginia		X
Washington	Washington does not impose a corporate income tax	
West Virginia		X
Wisconsin		X
Wyoming	Wyoming does not impose a corporate income tax	

Part 6. PASS-THROUGH ENTITIES

S Corporations

Federal Tax Treatment

The federal government taxes earnings of a regular corporation twice, imposing both a corporate-level tax when the income is earned and a shareholder-level tax when the corporation distributes its earnings as a dividend to individual shareholders. In 1958, Congress enacted the Subchapter S provisions [IRC §§ 1361–1379] to permit closely held corporations to enjoy the nontax advantages of the corporate form (e.g., limited liability and ownership interests that are readily transferable) without being subject to double taxation of corporate income. This is achieved by allowing the income of an S corporation to be taxed once at the shareholder level alone. The S corporation form also allows entity-level operating losses to pass through to shareholders, who can claim a deduction for those losses on their individual income tax returns.

To be eligible to make an S corporation election, a domestic corporation must have only one class of stock and no more than 100 shareholders. In addition, the shareholders must all be either individuals who are U.S. citizens or resident aliens, estates, or certain types of trusts. [IRC § 1361] The election is made by filing federal Form 2553.

Although an S corporation's year-to-year operating profits are taxed much like those of a partnership, Subchapter C provisions still generally apply to incorporation, reorganization and liquidation transactions. In addition, entity-level taxes may be imposed on an S corporation that was a C corporation in a prior taxable year. These include taxes on excess passive investment income [IRC § 1375], built-in gains [IRC § 1374], and the LIFO recapture amount. [IRC § 1363(d)]

A qualified Subchapter S subsidiary (QSSS) is a domestic corporation that qualifies as an S corporation, that is owned 100 percent by another S corporation, and whose parent S corporation elects to treat it as a QSSS. [IRC § 1361] For reporting purposes, the assets, liabilities, income, deductions, and other tax attributes of the QSSS are combined with those of its S corporation parent and reported on the parent's tax return.

State Conformity to Federal Pass-Through Treatment

States generally conform to the federal pass-through treatment of S corporations, but only if the corporation has filed a valid S corporation election for federal tax purposes. Although most states provide that the filing of a federal S corporation election automatically qualifies the corporation as an S corporation for state tax purposes, a handful of states require taxpayers to comply with additional special procedures in order to make a valid S corporation election. For example, a federal S corporation that wishes to be recognized as an S corporation for New Jersey income tax purposes must make a separate New Jersey S corporation election using New Jersey form CBT-2553.

States That Impose Entity-Level Taxes on S Corporations

Although most states treat S corporations as pass-through entities, a number of states impose special entity-level taxes on S corporations. In many cases, the entity-level tax is imposed in addition to a shareholder-level personal income tax. For example, California imposes a 1.5 percent income tax on S corporations doing business in California, and also imposes a personal income tax on a shareholder's pro rata share of an S corporation's income. Examples of states that impose entity-level taxes on S corporations include, but are not limited to, the following:

California. An S corporation doing business in California must pay the greater of an $800 minimum tax, or a 1.5 percent corporate franchise tax on the S corporation's income. The tax rate is 3.5 percent for S corporations that are financial corporations.

District of Columbia. The District of Columbia does not conform to the federal pass-through entity treatment of an S corporation. As a consequence, S corporations are subject to the District's 9.975 percent corporate income tax.

Illinois. Illinois imposes a 1.5 percent income tax (referred to as the personal property replacement tax) on S corporations.

Kansas. Prior to 2011, Kansas imposed a franchise tax on S corporations. The tax base is net worth (stockholders' equity), and the tax rate is $0.03125 per $1,000 of net worth in 2010, with a maximum tax of $20,000. The tax is repealed for tax years beginning after December 31, 2010.

Kentucky. S corporations are subject to a limited liability entity tax equal to the lesser of 0.095 percent of Kentucky gross receipts or 0.75 percent of Kentucky gross profits. The tax does not apply to S corporations with gross receipts or gross profits of $3 million or less and is reduced for S corporations with gross receipts or gross profits over $3 million but less than $6 million.

Massachusetts. Massachusetts subjects larger S corporations to an income tax. The tax rate for S corporations with total annual receipts of $9 million or more equals the excess of the corporate tax rate over the personal income tax rate (3.45 percent in 2010). The tax rate for S corporations with total annual receipts of at least $6 million but less than $9 million is 2/3 of the rate for larger S corporations (2.3 percent in 2010). S corporations with total annual receipts of less than $6 million are not subject to an entity-level income tax.

Michigan. From 2008 to 2011, Michigan subjected S corporations to a 4.95 percent business income tax and 0.80 percent modified gross receipts tax. Effective January 1, 2012, Michigan replaced its business income and modified gross receipt taxes with a 6 percent corporate income tax. S corporations are not subject to the corporate income tax. [H.B. 4361 and 4362, May 25, 2011]

New Hampshire. New Hampshire subjects S corporation to an 8.5 percent business profits tax and a 0.75 percent business enterprise tax. A credit against the business profits tax is allowed for any business enterprise tax paid.

New York City. New York City does not recognize a federal or New York State S corporation election. Therefore, S corporations are subject to New York City's 8.85 percent corporate income tax.

Ohio. Ohio imposes a 0.26 percent commercial activity tax (CAT) on the annual gross receipts of an S corporation. Examples of taxable gross receipts include sales of property delivered to locations within Ohio, fees for services where the purchaser receives the benefit in Ohio, and rents from property used in Ohio.

In addition, an S corporation with a qualifying investor (e.g., a nonresident individual for whom the S corporation does not file an Ohio composite nonresident shareholder return) is subject to a 5 percent pass-through entity tax. The tax is imposed on the qualifying investor's distributive share of the S corporation's taxable income apportioned to Ohio, and the qualifying investor can claim a credit for his or her share of the pass-through entity tax paid by the S corporation.

Pennsylvania. S corporations are not subject to the Pennsylvania corporate income tax; however, S corporations are subject to a capital stock tax based on the corporation's capital stock value, as determined by a statutory formula. The capital stock tax rate is 0.289 percent in 2011. The tax is scheduled to be repealed in 2014.

Tennessee. Tennessee taxes S corporations in the same manner as it taxes regular corporations. Thus, S corporations are subject to both the Tennessee corporate excise tax, which equals 6.5 percent of net earnings, and the Tennessee corporate franchise tax, which equals 0.25 percent of net worth.

Texas. Texas subjects S corporations to its margin tax. The tax base equals the lowest of three amounts: (1) total revenue minus cost of goods sold, (2) total revenue minus compensation, or (3) 70 percent of total revenue. The tax rate is 0.5 percent for S corporations primarily engaged in retail or wholesale trade and 1 percent for all other S corporations.

Washington. Washington subjects S corporations to its business and occupation (B&O) tax, which is a type of gross receipts tax. The B&O tax rate varies with the type of business activity, and generally is between 0.471 percent and 1.5 percent.

West Virginia. West Virginia imposes a business franchise tax on S corporations. For tax years beginning in 2011, the tax is 0.34 percent of the S corporation's capital. The tax is scheduled to be repealed in 2015.

State Taxation of Shareholders

Shareholders of an S corporation must be either individuals who are U.S. citizens or resident aliens, estates, or certain types of trusts. [IRC § 1361] Therefore, to the extent a state conforms to the federal pass-through treatment of an S corporation, the operative state income tax is usually the individual income tax; however, not all states have an individual income tax. Alaska, Florida, Nevada, South Dakota, Texas, Washington, and Wyoming do not impose individual income taxes. In addition, New Hampshire and Tennessee tax only selected types of income, not including salaries or wages.

The state in which an S corporation shareholder resides generally taxes the entire amount of the resident shareholder's pro rata share of S corporation income, regardless of where the income is earned. In contrast, states in which the shareholder does not reside tax a nonresident shareholder's distributive share of S corporation income only if the S corporation has nexus in the state, and then only to the extent the nonresident shareholder's pro rata share of income is attributable to sources within the state.

If a portion of a shareholder's pro rata share of income is subject to tax in two states (one by virtue of the shareholder's residence and the other by virtue of the source of the S corporation's income), the state of residence usually allows the individual to claim a credit for income taxes paid to the other state as a means of mitigating double taxation. Some states, such as California, also allow a shareholder to claim a credit for income taxes imposed directly on the S corporation.

Composite Returns and Withholding Requirements

The requirement that nonresident shareholders file returns and pay taxes in every state in which an S corporation has nexus can create a significant compliance burden for shareholders of an S corporation that has nexus in numerous states. One method of enhancing compliance is to require or permit an S corporation to file a composite return on behalf of the nonresident shareholders. A composite return is a single filing in which the participating shareholders report their pro rata shares of the S corporation's income and the S corporation pays the state tax on behalf of the nonresident shareholders.

Example. A State X Subchapter S corporation has five shareholders, all of whom are individuals who reside in State X. The S corporation also has nexus in State Z, and State Z allows an S corporation to file a composite return on behalf of shareholders who are nonresidents. The five shareholders do not have to file separate State Z tax returns. Instead, the S corporation can file a single composite State Z return on their behalf.

Most states allow shareholders to file a composite return. Examples of qualification requirements include (1) the participant must be a full-year nonresident, (2) the participant's income from the S corporation must be his or her only income derived from sources within the state, and (3) a minimum number of shareholders must participate in the composite filing. The composite tax generally equals the sum of the participating shareholders' pro rata shares of income apportioned to the state multiplied by the maximum tax rate applicable to individuals.

Another technique for promoting compliance on the part of nonresident shareholders is to require the S corporation to withhold and remit tax from distributions to nonresident shareholders or from the nonresident shareholders' pro rata shares of income. The amount withheld generally equals the highest marginal tax rate applicable to the nonresident shareholder multiplied by the shareholder's pro rata share of income apportioned to the state. Some states require withholding only if the S corporation fails to obtain a consent agreement from the shareholder or if the shareholder does not agree to be included in a composite return. A shareholder consent agreement is an agreement to submit to income tax jurisdiction in the state, file a return, and pay the tax due on the income sourced to the state.

The Multistate Tax Commission has adopted a model statute governing reporting options for nonresident owners of pass-through entities, including composite returns and withholding requirements.

[Proposed Statutory Language on Reporting Options for Non-resident Members of Pass-through Entities with Withholding Requirement, Dec. 18, 2003].

State-by-State Summary

For ease of presentation, the following chart has been divided into five parts, as follows:

- Part 1: Recognition of S Corporation Status/Conformity to Federal Rules
- Part 2: Entity-Level Taxes/Withholding Requirements
- Part 3: NOLs/Separate State Election/Composite Returns/Elect C Corporation Status
- Part 4: Qualified S Corporation Subsidiaries (QSSSs)

S Corporations (Part 1)

Recognition of S Corporation Status/Conformity to Federal Rules

Legend:

SAF	Same as applicable federal rules
NA	Not Applicable
NR	Not Reported

	Does State Recognize Federal S Corporation Status?	Does State Impose Special Eligibility Requirements?		Is Shareholder Basis in S Corp Stock Always the Same for State and Federal Purposes?
		State Resident	*Agree to Pay Tax*	
Alabama	Yes			No
Alaska	Yes	NR	NR	Yes
Arizona	Yes			Yes
Arkansas	Yes			Yes
California	Yes			No, a shareholder's basis is adjusted according to amounts using California law.
Colorado	Yes			Yes, generally
Connecticut	Yes	No	No	Yes
Delaware	Yes			Yes
District of Columbia	No	No	No	Yes
Florida	Yes			Yes
Georgia	Yes		X	No, various factors due to the difference in federal and state conformity can affect basis.
Hawaii	Yes			No, see § 235-124 Hawaii Revised Statutes.
Idaho	Yes			Yes
Illinois	Yes			Yes

S Corporations (Part 1)

Recognition of S Corporation Status/Conformity to Federal Rules

Legend:

SAF	Same as applicable federal rules
NA	Not Applicable
NR	Not Reported

	Does State Recognize Federal S Corporation Status?	*Does State Impose Special Eligibility Requirements?*		*Is Shareholder Basis in S Corp Stock Always the Same for State and Federal Purposes?*
		State Resident	*Agree to Pay Tax*	
Indiana	Yes			Yes
Iowa	Yes			Yes
Kansas	Yes	No	No	Yes
Kentucky	Yes			No, differences, such as depreciation, as provided by KRS 141.010 affect basis
Louisiana	Yes			Yes
Maine	Yes			Yes
Maryland	Yes			Yes
Massachusetts	Yes	NR	NR	NR
Michigan (Business Tax)	Yes			Yes
Note. The CIT takes effect 01/01/12, and replaces the Michigan Business Tax (MBT) for most taxpayers. However, businesses that have been approved to receive, have received, or have been assigned certain certified credits may elect to file a return and pay the tax imposed by the MBT in lieu of the CIT until the certified credits are exhausted or extinguished.				
Minnesota	Yes			Yes
Mississippi	Yes			No
Missouri	Yes	No	No	Yes
Montana	Yes			NR

S Corporations (Part 1)

Recognition of S Corporation Status/Conformity to Federal Rules

Legend:
SAF Same as applicable federal rules
NA Not Applicable
NR Not Reported

	Does State Recognize Federal S Corporation Status?	*Does State Impose Special Eligibility Requirements?*		*Is Shareholder Basis in S Corp Stock Always the Same for State and Federal Purposes?*
		State Resident	*Agree to Pay Tax*	
Nebraska	Yes			NR
Nevada	Nevada does not impose a corporate income tax			
New Hampshire	No, New Hampshire does not recognize S. Corp. status; treated as regular corporation			Yes
New Jersey	Yes		X	No, see N.J.S.A. 54:10A:5-11.
New Mexico	Yes			Yes
New York	Yes		X	Yes, generally
North Carolina	Yes		X	No
North Dakota	Yes			Yes
Ohio	Ohio does not impose a corporate income tax			
Note. Effective 1/1/2010, the Ohio Franchise Tax was fully phased out and business will be taxed on gross receipts through the Commercial Activity Tax. Details about that tax can be found at: http//tax.ohio.gov/divisions/commercial_activities/index.stm				
Oklahoma	Yes			Yes

S Corporations (Part 1)

Recognition of S Corporation Status/Conformity to Federal Rules

Legend:
SAF Same as applicable federal rules
NA Not Applicable
NR Not Reported

	Does State Recognize Federal S Corporation Status?	*Does State Impose Special Eligibility Requirements?*		*Is Shareholder Basis in S Corp Stock Always the Same for State and Federal Purposes?*
		State Resident	*Agree to Pay Tax*	
Oregon	Yes			No, assets contributed by a shareholder may have a different basis. Also different state and federal increase or decrease in basis due to different state and federal income and loss each year.
Pennsylvania	Yes			No, calculated on a Pennsylvania basis.
Rhode Island	Yes			Yes
South Carolina	Yes	No		Yes
South Dakota	South Dakota does not impose a corporate income tax			
Tennessee	No			Yes
Texas	No			Yes
Utah	Yes			Yes
Vermont	Yes	NR	NR	Yes
Virginia	Yes			NR
Washington	Washington does not impose a corporate income tax			
West Virginia	Yes			Yes

S Corporations (Part 1)

Recognition of S Corporation Status/Conformity to Federal Rules

Legend:

SAF	Same as applicable federal rules
NA	Not Applicable
NR	Not Reported

	Does State Recognize Federal S Corporation Status?	*Does State Impose Special Eligibility Requirements?*		*Is Shareholder Basis in S Corp Stock Always the Same for State and Federal Purposes?*
		State Resident	*Agree to Pay Tax*	
Wisconsin	Yes, under IRC as amended to 12/31/10. with exceptions: See Wis. Stat. §§ 71.34.			No, see Wisconsin Dept. of Revenue Publication 102 for difference.
Wyoming	Wyoming does not impose a corporate income tax			

S Corporations (Part 2)

Entity-Level Taxes/Withholding Requirements

Legend:
SAF — **Same as applicable federal rules**
NA — **Not Applicable**
NR — **Not Reported**

	Does State Impose Any of the Following Entity-Level Taxes on an S Corporation?						
	Flat-Dollar Amount Minimum Tax or Filing Fee	*Income-Based Tax*	*Franchise Tax Based on Net Worth or Capital*	*Withholding Taxes on Shareholders*	*Built-in Gains Tax*	*Excessive Net Passive Income Tax*	*LIFO Recapture Tax*
Alabama			X	X	X	X	X
Alaska					X	X	X
Arizona					X	X	X, payable on final C corporation return
Arkansas			X, 0.3% of Arkansas capital stock or specified dollar amount (minimum $150), whichever is applicable	X	X	X	X

S Corporations (Part 2)

Entity-Level Taxes/Withholding Requirements

Legend:

SAF	**Same as applicable federal rules**
NA	**Not Applicable**
NR	**Not Reported**

Does State Impose Any of the Following Entity-Level Taxes on an S Corporation?

	Flat-Dollar Amount Minimum Tax or Filing Fee	*Income-Based Tax*	*Franchise Tax Based on Net Worth or Capital*	*Withholding Taxes on Shareholders*	*Built-in Gains Tax*	*Excessive Net Passive Income Tax*	*LIFO Recapture Tax*
California	X, minimum corporate franchise tax of $800 is imposed on S corporations organized, registered, or doing business in California, if greater than graduated franchise tax (R&TC § 23802(c)). The minimum corporate franchise tax is not applicable to the first taxable year of an S corporation that is organized or registers in California on or after 1/1/00 (R&TC § 23153(f)(1)).	X, franchise or income tax is imposed at 1.5%, (R&TC § 23802)(b)(1))		X, S corporations must withhold tax on distributions out of California source taxable income to domestic (U.S.) shareholders (R&TC § 18662).	X, R&TC § 23809	X R&TC § 23811	X, R&TC § 23800, § 23802
Colorado				X, non-resident individuals only			
Connecticut	X, $250						
Delaware	X, for fee schedule contact the Delaware Secretary of State, Corporate Division	X, for fee schedule contact the Delaware Secretary of State					

S Corporations (Part 2)

Entity-Level Taxes/Withholding Requirements

Legend:
SAF Same as applicable federal rules
NA Not Applicable
NR Not Reported

Does State Impose Any of the Following Entity-Level Taxes on an S Corporation?

	Flat-Dollar Amount Minimum Tax or Filing Fee	*Income-Based Tax*	*Franchise Tax Based on Net Worth or Capital*	*Withholding Taxes on Shareholders*	*Built-in Gains Tax*	*Excessive Net Passive Income Tax*	*LIFO Recapture Tax*
District of Columbia		X		X			
Note. Gross Receipts							
Florida					X	X	X
Georgia		X, 6% (built-in gains and excessive passive income)	X, variable tax, from $10 to $5,000	X	X	X	X
Hawaii	See www.state.hi.us/dcca/breg-seu			X	X	X	X
Idaho		X, 7.6% corporate rate if paying the tax for shareholders who are individuals with a filing requirement plus $20 minimum tax			X	X	X
Illinois	There is an entity level Personal Property Replacement Income Tax.	X, 1.5%	There is an entity level Personal Property Replacement Income Tax.				

S Corporations (Part 2)

Entity-Level Taxes/Withholding Requirements

Legend:

SAF	**Same as applicable federal rules**
NA	**Not Applicable**
NR	**Not Reported**

	Does State Impose Any of the Following Entity-Level Taxes on an S Corporation?						
	Flat-Dollar Amount Minimum Tax or Filing Fee	*Income-Based Tax*	*Franchise Tax Based on Net Worth or Capital*	*Withholding Taxes on Shareholders*	*Built-in Gains Tax*	*Excessive Net Passive Income Tax*	*LIFO Recapture Tax*
Indiana				X	X	X	X
Iowa					X	X	
Kansas	X, $55 profits; $40 non-profits	X, 0.125% if Kansas apportioned net worth $1,000,000 or more, $20,000 maximum					
Kentucky		X, Lesser of $.095/$100 KY gross receipts or $.75/$100 KY gross profits or $175 minimum.		X	X	X	X
Louisiana		X, same rates as Corporation	X, $1.50 per $1,000 on 1st $300,000; $3 per $1,000 on excess				
Maine				X	X	X	
Maryland		X, only if S corporation has federal taxable income		X			

S Corporations (Part 2)

Entity-Level Taxes/Withholding Requirements

Legend:

SAF	**Same as applicable federal rules**
NA	**Not Applicable**
NR	**Not Reported**

Does State Impose Any of the Following Entity-Level Taxes on an S Corporation?

	Flat-Dollar Amount Minimum Tax or Filing Fee	*Income-Based Tax*	*Franchise Tax Based on Net Worth or Capital*	*Withholding Taxes on Shareholders*	*Built-in Gains Tax*	*Excessive Net Passive Income Tax*	*LIFO Recapture Tax*
Massachusetts		X			X		X
Michigan (Business Tax)	X, $15	X, 4.95% of taxable income	X, 0.235% on financial institutions only	X			
Note. The CIT takes effect 01/01/12, and replaces the Michigan Business Tax (MBT) for most taxpayers. However, businesses that have been approved to receive, have received, or have been assigned certain certified credits may elect to file a return and pay the tax imposed by the MBT in lieu of the CIT until the certified credits are exhausted or extinguished.							
Minnesota	Fee based on Minnesota factors						
Mississippi			X, $2.50 per $1,000, $25 minimum				X
Missouri			X	X	X	X	X
Montana				X	X, taxed at individual level		
Nebraska				X			
Nevada	Nevada does not impose a corporate income tax						
New Hampshire		X, 8.5%					

S Corporations (Part 2)

Entity-Level Taxes/Withholding Requirements

Legend:

SAF Same as applicable federal rules

NA Not Applicable

NR Not Reported

Does State Impose Any of the Following Entity-Level Taxes on an S Corporation?

	Flat-Dollar Amount Minimum Tax or Filing Fee	*Income-Based Tax*	*Franchise Tax Based on Net Worth or Capital*	*Withholding Taxes on Shareholders*	*Built-in Gains Tax*	*Excessive Net Passive Income Tax*	*LIFO Recapture Tax*
New Jersey	X, $50 (N.J.S.A. 14A:15-2(6))	For periods ending on or after 1/1/01 but before 6/30/06, 1.33%; for periods ending on or after 7/1/06 but before 6/30/07, 0.67%; for periods ending on or after 7/1/07, no tax. If entire net income is $100,000 or less, then no tax for periods ending on or after 6/30/01 (N.J.S.A. 54:10A5(c)).			X	X	
New Mexico			X	X	X	X	
New York	X	Fixed Dollar Minimum Tax of $100-$1,500, based on gross payroll.					

S Corporations (Part 2)

Entity-Level Taxes/Withholding Requirements

Legend:

SAF	**Same as applicable federal rules**
NA	**Not Applicable**
NR	**Not Reported**

	Does State Impose Any of the Following Entity-Level Taxes on an S Corporation?						
	Flat-Dollar Amount Minimum Tax or Filing Fee	*Income-Based Tax*	*Franchise Tax Based on Net Worth or Capital*	*Withholding Taxes on Shareholders*	*Built-in Gains Tax*	*Excessive Net Passive Income Tax*	*LIFO Recapture Tax*
North Carolina	X, Annual Report if registered with Secretary of State ($20 fee)		X, $1.50 per $1,000				
North Dakota				X, for nonresidents only	X	X	
Ohio	Ohio does not impose a corporate income tax						
Note. Effective 1/1/2010, the Ohio Franchise Tax was fully phased out and business will be taxed on gross receipts through the Commercial Activity Tax. Details about that tax can be found at: http//tax.ohio.gov/divisions/commercial_activities/index.stm							
Oklahoma			X				
Oregon	X, $150 if "doing business" in Oregon. See ORS 317.010(4) for definition.		X	X	X	X	X
Pennsylvania		X, 9.99% built-in gains	X, 6.99 mills	X	X		
Rhode Island			X, $500 minimum	X	X	X	X
South Carolina	Minimum $25 license fee	X, 5% of taxable income	X, §§12-20-50, 12-20-100	X	X	X, 5% on nonresident shareholder's taxable income	X
South Dakota	South Dakota does not impose a corporate income tax.						

S Corporations (Part 2)

Entity-Level Taxes/Withholding Requirements

Legend:

SAF — **Same as applicable federal rules**
NA — **Not Applicable**
NR — **Not Reported**

	Does State Impose Any of the Following Entity-Level Taxes on an S Corporation?						
	Flat-Dollar Amount Minimum Tax or Filing Fee	*Income-Based Tax*	*Franchise Tax Based on Net Worth or Capital*	*Withholding Taxes on Shareholders*	*Built-in Gains Tax*	*Excessive Net Passive Income Tax*	*LIFO Recapture Tax*
Tennessee		X, 6.5% excise tax	X, 0.25%				
Texas		X, .5% for qualifying entities in retail or wholesale trade and 1% for all others					
Utah		X, 5%			X	X	X
Vermont	X, $250			X	X		
Virginia			Banks only	X, Effective for taxable years beginning 1/1/08 and after.			
Washington	Washington does not impose a corporate income tax						
West Virginia			X, 0.7% or $50, whichever is greater				

S Corporations (Part 2)

Entity-Level Taxes/Withholding Requirements

Legend:

SAF Same as applicable federal rules
NA Not Applicable
NR Not Reported

Does State Impose Any of the Following Entity-Level Taxes on an S Corporation?

	Flat-Dollar Amount Minimum Tax or Filing Fee	*Income-Based Tax*	*Franchise Tax Based on Net Worth or Capital*	*Withholding Taxes on Shareholders*	*Built-in Gains Tax*	*Excessive Net Passive Income Tax*	*LIFO Recapture Tax*
Wisconsin	X, various amounts, but these are imposed by the Wisconsin Dept. of Financial Institutions.	X, Economic Development Surcharge between $25 and $9,800 may apply and 7.9% of Wisconsin income from certain state and federal gov't bonds.		X, nonresident shareholders	X		X
Wyoming	Wyoming does not impose a corporate income tax						

S Corporations (Part 3)

NOLs/Separate State Election/Composite Returns/Elect C Corporation Status

Legend:

NA	Not applicable
NR	Not reported
SAF	Same as applicable federal rules

	Can a Nonresident S Corporation Shareholder Carry Forward State (Non-Federal) NOLs?	*Does State Require Filing of a Separate S Corporation Election?*	*Does State Have Provisions for Composite Filings for S Corporation Shareholders Who Are Nonresidents?*	*Can an S Corporation Elect Not to Be Treated as an S Corporation for State Purposes?*
Alabama	Yes	No	Yes, Form PTE-C	No
Alaska	Yes	No	No	No
Arizona	No	No	Yes, Form 140 NR, for individuals only	No
Arkansas	Yes	Yes	Yes, Form AR1100CR	Yes, Form AR1000CT
California	Yes. To the extent attributable to CA Sources, R&TC § 17041(i)(3).	No	Yes, Form 540 NR, (R&TC § 18535)	No
Colorado	No	No	Yes, Form 106	No
Connecticut	Yes	No	Yes, CT-1065/CT-1120 SI	No
Delaware	NR	NR	Yes, Form 200C	No
District of Columbia	No	No	No	No
Florida	No	No	No	No
Georgia	Yes	No	Yes, Form IT-CR	Yes, only if they have 1 or more nonresident shareholders. The corporation files as a "C" corporation.
Hawaii	Yes	No	Yes, Form N-15	No
Idaho	Yes, to extent from Idaho activities	No	Yes, if individual shareholder elects to have S corporation pay tax on his or her share of the S corporation income tax paid on Idaho Form 41S.	No
Illinois	No	No	Yes, Form IL-1023-C	No

S Corporations (Part 3)

NOLs/Separate State Election/Composite Returns/Elect C Corporation Status

Legend:

NA	Not applicable
NR	Not reported
SAF	Same as applicable federal rules

	Can a Nonresident S Corporation Shareholder Carry Forward State (Non-Federal) NOLs?	*Does State Require Filing of a Separate S Corporation Election?*	*Does State Have Provisions for Composite Filings for S Corporation Shareholders Who Are Nonresidents?*	*Can an S Corporation Elect Not to Be Treated as an S Corporation for State Purposes?*
Indiana	No	No	Yes	No
Iowa	Yes	No	Yes, Form IA 1040C	No
Kansas	Yes	No	Yes, Form K-40C & K-40	No
Kentucky	Yes	No	Yes, Form 740-NP-WH	No
Louisiana	Yes	No	No	No
Maine	No	No	Yes, Form 1040 ME with Sch 1040C-ME and NRC.	No
Maryland	No, can only carry over the amount included in federal adjusted gross income	Yes	Yes, Form 50S	No
Massachusetts	NR	NR	Yes	No
Michigan (Business Tax)	Yes	No	Yes, Form 807	No
Note. The CIT takes effect 01/01/12, and replaces the Michigan Business Tax (MBT) for most taxpayers. However, businesses that have been approved to receive, have received, or have been assigned certain certified credits may elect to file a return and pay the tax imposed by the MBT in lieu of the CIT until the certified credits are exhausted or extinguished.				
Minnesota	No	No	Yes, Form M-8	No
Mississippi	Yes	No	Yes, Form 85-105	No
Missouri	No	No	Yes, MO 1040	No
Montana	No	No	Yes, schedule on CLT-4S	No

S Corporations (Part 3)

NOLs/Separate State Election/Composite Returns/Elect C Corporation Status

Legend:

NA — Not applicable
NR — Not reported
SAF — Same as applicable federal rules

	Can a Nonresident S Corporation Shareholder Carry Forward State (Non-Federal) NOLs?	*Does State Require Filing of a Separate S Corporation Election?*	*Does State Have Provisions for Composite Filings for S Corporation Shareholders Who Are Nonresidents?*	*Can an S Corporation Elect Not to Be Treated as an S Corporation for State Purposes?*
Nebraska	No	No	No	No
Nevada	Nevada does not impose a corporate income tax			
New Hampshire	No	No	No	No
New Jersey	No	Yes	Yes, Form NJ-1080C	Yes, the election is made by not filing NJ-CBT-2553 to become a New Jersey S corporation.
New Mexico	Yes	No	Yes, Form PTE	No
New York	NA	Yes, generally	No, combined filing may be required or permitted.	Yes, assumed C corporation unless S status elected; however, federal S Corporations may be deemed to be NY S-Corporations if their investment income is more than half of their federal gross income.
North Carolina	No	No	Yes, Form CD-401S	No
North Dakota	No	No	Yes, use Form ND-1	No
Ohio	Ohio does not impose a corporate income tax.			
Note. Effective 1/1/2010, the Ohio Franchise Tax was fully phased out and business will be taxed on gross receipts through the Commercial Activity Tax. Details about that tax can be found at: http//tax.ohio.gov/divisions/commercial_activities/index.stm				
Oklahoma	Yes	No	Yes, Oklahoma Form 512S	No
Oregon	Yes	No	Yes, Form 40 NR with Schedule	No
Pennsylvania	No	No	Yes, Form PA 40NRC	Yes, no action required

S Corporations (Part 3)

NOLs/Separate State Election/Composite Returns/Elect C Corporation Status

Legend:

NA	Not applicable
NR	Not reported
SAF	Same as applicable federal rules

	Can a Nonresident S Corporation Shareholder Carry Forward State (Non-Federal) NOLs?	*Does State Require Filing of a Separate S Corporation Election?*	*Does State Have Provisions for Composite Filings for S Corporation Shareholders Who Are Nonresidents?*	*Can an S Corporation Elect Not to Be Treated as an S Corporation for State Purposes?*
Rhode Island	Yes	No	Yes	No
South Carolina	Yes	No	Yes, Form SC1040, 1-348	No
South Dakota	South Dakota does not impose a corporate income tax.			
Tennessee	NA	No	NA	No
Texas	Franchise tax imposed on the corporation not the individual.	No	NA	NA
Utah	No	No	Yes, Form TC-20S, composite returns are required for nonresident shareholders.	No
Vermont	No	No	Yes	No
Virginia	No	No	Yes, Form 765	No
Washington	Washington does not impose a corporate income tax			
West Virginia	Yes	No	Yes, Form IT-140 NRC	No
Wisconsin	Yes	No	Yes, file Form 1CNS	Yes, make the election on or before the extended due date of the return by filing Wisconsin Form 5E with the Wisconsin Form 4 or 5.
Wyoming	Wyoming does not impose a corporate income tax			

S Corporations (Part 4)

Qualified S Corporation Subsidiaries (QSSS)

Legend:

X	Condition applies
NA	Not applicable
NR	Not reported
QSSS	Qualified Subchapter S Subsidiary

	Does State Conform to Federal Entity Classification of QSSS?	*Does State Require the Filing of a Separate QSSS Election?*	*If State Imposes a Franchise Tax Based on Net Worth or Capital, Are a QSSS and its Parent S Corporation Required to File?*		
			Two Separate Returns	*Single Combined Return*	*State Does Not Impose a Franchise Tax*
Alabama	Yes	No	X		
Alaska	Yes	Yes, same form for federal			X
Arizona	Yes	No			
Arkansas	Yes	Yes, Form AR 1103	X		
California	Yes, a QSSS is subject to an annual tax equal to minimum corporate franchise tax of $800 under § 23153 (R&TC § 23800.5). A QSSS does not file a separate return.	No			X
Colorado	Yes	No			X
Connecticut	Yes	No			X
Delaware	Yes	No	X		
District of Columbia	No	No			X
Florida	Yes	No			X
Georgia	Yes	No	X		

S Corporations (Part 4)

Qualified S Corporation Subsidiaries (QSSS)

Legend:

X	Condition applies
NA	Not applicable
NR	Not reported
QSSS	Qualified Subchapter S Subsidiary

	Does State Conform to Federal Entity Classification of QSSS?	*Does State Require the Filing of a Separate QSSS Election?*	*If State Imposes a Franchise Tax Based on Net Worth or Capital, Are a QSSS and its Parent S Corporation Required to File?*		
			Two Separate Returns	*Single Combined Return*	*State Does Not Impose a Franchise Tax*
Hawaii	Yes	Yes, attach a copy of the completed and filed federal Form 8869 to the first Hawaii S corporation income tax return filed following the federal QSSS election.			X
Idaho	Yes	No			
Illinois	Yes	No	See Secretary of State		
Indiana	Yes	No			X
Iowa	Yes	No	NR	NR	NR
Kansas	Yes	No			X
Kentucky	Yes	No			
Louisiana	Yes	No	X		
Maine	Yes	No			X
Maryland	Yes	No	NR	NR	NR
Massachusetts	Yes, TIR 08-11, 03-02	NR	NR	NR	NR

S Corporations (Part 4)

Qualified S Corporation Subsidiaries (QSSS)

Legend:

X	Condition applies
NA	Not applicable
NR	Not reported
QSSS	Qualified Subchapter S Subsidiary

	Does State Conform to Federal Entity Classification of QSSS?	*Does State Require the Filing of a Separate QSSS Election?*	*If State Imposes a Franchise Tax Based on Net Worth or Capital, Are a QSSS and its Parent S Corporation Required to File?*		
			Two Separate Returns	*Single Combined Return*	*State Does Not Impose a Franchise Tax*
Michigan	Policy under review	No		X	X, except on financial institutions
Note. The CIT takes effect 01/01/12, and replaces the Michigan Business Tax (MBT) for most taxpayers. However, businesses that have been approved to receive, have received, or have been assigned certain certified credits may elect to file a return and pay the tax imposed by the MBT in lieu of the CIT until the certified credits are exhausted or extinguished.					
Minnesota	Yes	No			X
Mississippi	Yes	No		X	
Missouri	Yes	No	X		
Montana	Yes	No			X
Nebraska	Yes	No	NR	NR	NR
Nevada	Nevada does not impose a corporate income tax				
New Hampshire	No	No			X
New Jersey	Not totally; QSSSs must register and pay the minimum tax.	Yes, Form NJ-2553			X
New Mexico	Yes	No			X
New York	Yes	No		X	
North Carolina	Yes	No	X		

S Corporations (Part 4)

Qualified S Corporation Subsidiaries (QSSS)

Legend:

X	Condition applies
NA	Not applicable
NR	Not reported
QSSS	Qualified Subchapter S Subsidiary

	Does State Conform to Federal Entity Classification of QSSS?	*Does State Require the Filing of a Separate QSSS Election?*	*If State Imposes a Franchise Tax Based on Net Worth or Capital, Are a QSSS and its Parent S Corporation Required to File?*		
			Two Separate Returns	*Single Combined Return*	*State Does Not Impose a Franchise Tax*
North Dakota	Yes	No	NR	NR	
Ohio	Ohio does not impose a corporate income tax.				
Note. Effective 1/1/2010, the Ohio Franchise Tax was fully phased out and business will be taxed on gross receipts through the Commercial Activity Tax. Details about that tax can be found at: http//tax.ohio.gov/divisions/commercial_activities/index.stm					
Oklahoma	Yes	No	NR	NR	
Oregon	Yes	No			X
Pennsylvania	Yes	Form Rev 1640 filed by parent for group	X		
Rhode Island	Yes	Yes, attachment to Rhode Island Form 1120S	X		
South Carolina	Yes	No		X	
South Dakota	South Dakota does not impose a corporate income tax				
Tennessee	No	No	X		
Texas	No	No			X
Utah	Yes	No			X
Vermont	Yes	No			X
Virginia	Yes	No			X

S Corporations (Part 4)

Qualified S Corporation Subsidiaries (QSSS)

Legend:

X	Condition applies
NA	Not applicable
NR	Not reported
QSSS	Qualified Subchapter S Subsidiary

			If State Imposes a Franchise Tax Based on Net Worth or Capital, Are a QSSS and its Parent S Corporation Required to File?		
	Does State Conform to Federal Entity Classification of QSSS?	*Does State Require the Filing of a Separate QSSS Election?*	*Two Separate Returns*	*Single Combined Return*	*State Does Not Impose a Franchise Tax*
Washington	Washington does not impose a corporate income tax				
West Virginia	Yes	No		X	
Wisconsin	Yes	No			X
Wyoming	Wyoming does not impose a corporate income tax				

Partnerships

In General

A partnership is an unincorporated trade or business owned and managed by two or more persons. For federal income tax purposes, a partnership is not a taxpaying entity. Instead, it is treated as a flow-through entity, whereby its gross income, deductions, and credits flow through to the partners, who report the items on their own tax returns. For federal tax purposes, each year a partnership must file a tax return (Form 1065) to report its results from operations, and must send each partner a statement (Schedule K-1 of Form 1065) that details the partner's distributive share of the partnership's gross income, deductions, and credits. Each partner then reports these items on its Form 1120 in the case of a corporate partner or Form 1040 in the case of a partner who is an individual.

A partnership generally takes one of two legal forms, that of a general partnership or a limited partnership. In a general partnership, each partner has unlimited liability for the partnership's debts and has the right to participate in the management of the partnership. In a limited partnership, there must be at least one general partner and one limited partner. A general partner has unlimited liability and is responsible for managing the partnership. In contrast, a limited partner cannot lose more than its investment in the partnership and generally may not participate in the management of the partnership. A third partnership form is the limited liability partnership, which allows partners of certain types of professional service firms (e.g., public accounting firms) to reduce their exposure to lawsuits relative to operating as a general partnership.

The principal state income tax issues with respect to partnerships include 1) conformity to the federal flow-through treatment of partnerships, 2) state entity-level taxes on partnerships, 3) nexus considerations for corporate general and limited partners, 4) apportionment of a corporate partner's distributive share of partnership income, 5) state taxation of partners who are individuals, 6) composite returns and withholding requirements, and 7) limited liability companies (LLCs).

State Conformity to Federal Flow-Through Treatment

The federal income tax treatment of a partnership is determined by an elective system for entity classification. [Treas. Reg. § 301.7701-3] The regime is known as "check-the-box" because an entity's owners can merely check a box on federal Form 8832 to determine an eligible entity's classification. If Form 8832 is not filed, default classification rules determine an eligible entity's classification for federal income tax purposes. Under these regulations, the owners of a partnership organized in the United States have the option of electing to have the entity classified as a regular corporation. If no election is made, the entity is classified as a partnership under the default rules.

The check-the-box regime also applies to a partnership organized under the laws of a foreign country, although the default classification rules are different. Under the default rules, a foreign partnership that does not affirmatively make an election is classified as a corporation if all the partners have limited liability, and as a partnership if at least one of the partners does not have limited liability. Like the owners of a domestic partnership, however, the owners of a foreign partnership have the option of electing a different classification than that provided by the default rules, as long as the entity is not on the Treasury Department's list of "per se" corporations. [Treas. Reg. § 301.7701-3]

Virtually all of the states conform to the federal classification rules for partnerships. Thus, in the vast majority of cases, an entity that is treated as a partnership for federal tax purposes is also treated as a partnership for state income tax purposes. State conformity to the federal flow-through treatment of a partnership generally extends to an LLC classified as a partnership for federal tax purposes. Under the federal check-the-box regulations, the default classification for a domestic LLC that has two or more members is a partnership.

States That Impose Entity-Level Taxes on Partnerships

Although most states treat partnerships as flow-through entities, a number of states impose special entity-level taxes on partnerships. Examples include, but are not limited to, the following:

Alabama. Alabama imposes a business privilege tax on limited partnerships and limited liability partnerships. The tax is based on Alabama net worth. The tax is a minimum of $100 and a maximum of $15,000.

California. California imposes an annual tax of $800 on limited partnerships and limited liability partnerships doing business in California.

District of Columbia. The District of Columbia imposes a 9.975 percent income tax on unincorporated businesses, including partnerships. The tax does not apply to a professional firm in which more than 80 percent of the gross income is derived from personal services and capital is not a material income-producing factor.

Illinois. Illinois imposes a 1.5 percent income tax (referred to as the personal property replacement tax) on partnerships. An exemption is provided for investment partnerships.

Kansas. Prior to 2011, Kansas imposed a franchise tax on limited partnerships and limited liability partnerships that have net capital accounts located or used in Kansas. The tax rate is $0.03125 per $1,000 of net worth in 2010, with a maximum tax of $20,000. The tax is repealed for tax years beginning after December 31, 2010.

Kentucky. Limited partnerships and limited liability partnerships are subject to a limited liability entity tax equal to the lesser of 0.095 percent of Kentucky gross receipts or 0.75 percent of Kentucky gross profits. The tax does not apply to partnerships with gross receipts or gross profits of $3 million or less and is reduced for partnerships with gross receipts or gross profits over $3 million but less than $6 million.

Michigan. From 2008 to 2011, Michigan subjected partnerships to a 4.95 percent business income tax and 0.80 percent modified gross receipts tax. Effective January 1, 2012, Michigan replaced its business income and modified gross receipt taxes with a 6 percent corporate income tax. Partnerships are not subject to the corporate income tax. [H.B. 4361 and 4362, May 25, 2011]

New Hampshire. New Hampshire subjects partnerships to an 8.5 percent business profits tax and a 0.75 percent business enterprise tax. A credit against the business profits tax is allowed for any business enterprise tax paid.

New Jersey. A limited partnership with a nonresident partner must pay 1) a 6.37 percent tax on a nonresident noncorporate partner's share of partnership income apportioned to New Jersey, and 2) a 9 percent tax on a nonresident corporate partner's share of partnership income apportioned to New Jersey. If the nonresident partner files a New Jersey return, it may claim a credit for its share of the tax paid by the partnership.

New York City. New York City imposes a 4 percent income tax on partnerships.

Ohio. Ohio imposes a 0.26 percent commercial activity tax (CAT) on the annual gross receipts of a partnership. Examples of taxable gross receipts include sales of property delivered to locations within Ohio, fees for services where the purchaser receives the benefit in Ohio, and rents from property used in Ohio.

In addition, a partnership with a qualifying individual investor (i.e., a nonresident individual for whom the partnership does not file an Ohio composite nonresident return) is subject to a 5 percent pass-through entity tax. The tax is imposed on the qualifying investor's distributive share of the partnership's taxable income apportioned to Ohio, and the investor can claim a credit for its share of the tax paid by the partnership.

Tennessee. Tennessee imposes a 6.5 percent income tax and a 0.25 percent net worth tax on limited partnerships and limited liability partnerships.

Texas. Texas subjects partnerships to its margin tax. General partnerships directly owned entirely by natural persons and passive investment partnerships are exempted, however. The tax base equals the lowest of three amounts: (1) total revenue minus cost of goods sold, (2) total revenue minus compensation, or (3) 70 percent of total revenue. The tax rate is 0.5 percent for partnerships primarily engaged in retail or wholesale trade and 1 percent for all other partnerships. General partnerships with direct ownership entirely composed of natural persons and certain passive entities are exempt from the margin tax.

Washington. Washington subjects partnerships to its business and occupation (B&O) tax, which is a type of gross receipts tax. The B&O tax rate varies with the type of business activity, and generally is between 0.471 percent and 1.5 percent.

West Virginia. West Virginia imposes a business franchise tax on partnerships. For tax years beginning in 2011, the tax is 0.34 percent of the partners' capital accounts. The tax is scheduled to be repealed in 2015.

In addition, a number of states single out LLPs for selected taxes. For example, Minnesota imposes an entity-level fee (maximum of $5,000), Wisconsin imposes an entity-level tax (maximum of $9,800), and other states impose either entity-level or partner-level flat rate annual taxes or filing fees.

Nexus Issue

A state has jurisdiction to tax a corporation organized in another state only if the out-of-state corporation's contacts with the taxing state are sufficient to create nexus. The types of contacts that create nexus are determined by U.S. constitutional law, Public Law 86-272, and the applicable state statutes. The principal issue with respect to corporate partners is whether a state has jurisdiction to tax the income of an out-of-state corporation that has no contacts with the state other than its ownership interest in a partnership doing business in the state.

Most states take the position that an ownership interest in a partnership doing business in the state is sufficient to create constitutional nexus for an out-of-state corporation. In asserting nexus, the states rely primarily on the aggregate theory of partnership, which holds that a partnership (unlike a corporation) is the aggregation of its owners rather than an entity that is separate and distinct from its owners. Under this theory, the partners are viewed as direct owners of the partnership's assets. Based on the aggregate theory, most states take the position that the mere ownership of a partnership interest is sufficient to create constitutional nexus for an out-of-state corporation, regardless of whether the corporation is a general or limited partner.

Some states provide exemptions for corporate limited partners, as well as interests in investment partnerships or publicly-traded limited partnerships. These exceptions reflect the view that some partnership interests are more comparable to corporate stock than a traditional general partnership interest.

The issue of whether a state has jurisdiction to tax an out-of-state corporation whose only contact with the state is through a limited partnership interest has been litigated in a number of cases, with the taxpayer prevailing in some cases [e.g., *BIS LP, Inc. v. Division of Taxation*, No. 007847-2007 (N.J. Tax Ct., July 30, 2009); *Appeals of Amman & Schmid Finanz AG*, No. 96-SBE-008 (Cal. St. Bd. of Equalization Apr. 11, 1996)], and state tax authorities prevailing in other cases [e.g., *In re Borden Chem. & Plastics, LP*, No. 96-L-51039 (Ill. Cir. Ct. Oct. 7, 1998); *In re CRIV Invs., Inc.*, No. 4046 (Or. T.C. Apr. 23, 1997); *In re Perkins Restaurants, Inc.*, N.C. Admin. Decision 351 (Jan. 28, 1999); and *Revenue Cabinet v. Asworth Corporation*, Nos. 2007-CA-002549-MR, 2008-CA-000023-MR (Ky. Ct. of App., Nov. 20, 2009)].

In *SAHI USA Inc. v. Commissioner of Revenue* [No. C262668 (Mass. App. Tax Bd., Oct. 27, 2006)], the taxpayer (SAHI) was a Delaware corporation and a limited partner in a New York partnership that invested in a Massachusetts joint venture, which owned and operated a hotel in Boston. The higher-tier New York partnership sold its interest in the lower-tier Massachusetts partnership, and the income from the sale was distributed to partners, including SAHI. The Massachusetts Appellate Tax Board ruled that because both the higher-tier and lowest-tier partnerships were doing business in Massachusetts, their income-producing activities were imputed to SAHI through the tiered-partnership arrangement. Because SAHI had income tax nexus with Massachusetts through a tiered-partnership arrangement, the income that SAHI realized from the sale of the lower-tier partnership interest was taxable by Massachusetts.

Apportionment of Partnership Income

There are two approaches to apportioning a corporate partner's distributive share of partnership income, partner-level apportionment and partnership-level apportionment.

Partner-level apportionment is analogous to the federal conduit theory, under which the partnership's items of income and deduction pass through and are reported on the tax returns of the partners. Under this approach, the partnership's activities are treated as part of the same trade or business as the corporate partner's other activities. Accordingly, when a state adopts this approach, the corporate partner's entire distributive share of partnership income is combined with the partner's other income to determine the total apportionable income of the single trade or business. Likewise, the partner computes its state apportionment percentage by combining its share of the partnership's property, payroll, and sales with its other apportionment factors. In other words, the corporate partner is allowed factor relief with respect to the inclusion of the entire distributive share of partnership income in the partner's apportionable income tax base. [E.g., *Homart Dev. Co. v. Norberg*, 529 A.2d 115 (R.I. 1987).] The numerator of the apportionment formula equals the corporate partner's property, payroll, and sales within the state, plus its share of the partnership's property, payroll, and sales within the state. The denominator equals the corporate partner's property, payroll, and sales everywhere, plus its share of the partnership's property, payroll, and sales everywhere. The corporate partner's state tax base is determined by multiplying the partner's apportionable income (which includes its distributive share of partnership income) by the partner's apportionment percentage (which reflects the partner's share of the partnership's factors).

Partnership-level apportionment treats the corporate investment in the partnership as a separate trade or business. Under this approach, the corporate partner's distributive share of partnership income is apportioned to the nexus state based solely on the property, payroll, and sales of the partnership. In effect, the partnership's activities are treated as a trade or business that is separate and distinct from the trade or business of the corporate partner. As a consequence, the corporate partner's distributive share of partnership income is not combined with the partner's other apportionable income, nor is the partner's share of the partnership's property, payroll, and sales combined with the partner's other apportionment factors. Instead, the corporate partner's distributive share of partnership income is independently apportioned to the state by multiplying the distributive share of partnership income by the partnership's apportionment percentage. The corporate partner's state tax base is then determined by combining the apportioned partnership income with any other income that the corporate partner allocates or apportions to the state by virtue of its other (non-partnership) activities.

Most states require partner-level apportionment if the corporate partner and the partnership are engaged in a unitary business, and require partnership-level apportionment if the corporate partner and partnership are engaged in separate trades or businesses. However, some states require partner-level apportionment, regardless of whether there is a unitary relationship between the partner and the partnership, and other states require partnership-level apportionment, irrespective of unity. For example, California Code of Regulations Title 18, Section 25137-1 (Apportionment and Allocation of Partnership Income), states:

> If the partnership's activities and the taxpayer's activities constitute a unitary business under established standards, disregarding ownership requirements, the taxpayer's share of the partnership's trade or business shall be combined with the taxpayer's trade or business as constituting a single trade or business. . . . When the activities of the partnership and the taxpayer do not constitute a unitary business under established standards, disregarding ownership requirements, the taxpayer's share of the partnership's trade or business shall be treated as a separate trade or business of the taxpayer.

New Jersey Administrative Code Title 18, Section 7-7.6 (Corporate Partners), adopts essentially the same principle, as follows:

> For purposes of apportionment (allocation) of corporate income, where the subject corporation and the partnership are not part of a single unitary business, including a business carried on directly by the foreign corporate partner, separate accounting apportionment should be used to arrive at corporate income. If the New Jersey business of the partnership is part of a single unitary business including a business carried on directly by the foreign corporate partner, flow through accounting apportionment should be used with respect to the income of the two entities.

See also *Chiron Corp. vs. Director, Division of Taxation*, No. 000120-1999 (N.J. Tax Ct., Nov. 19, 2004); *BP Oil Pipeline Co. v. Zehnder*, Nos. 1-01-2364 and 1-01-2365 (Ill. App. Ct., May 21, 2004); and *Exxon Corp. v. Bower*, No. 1-01-3302 (Ill. App. Ct., May 21, 2004).

In determining whether a corporate partner is unitary with a partnership, the conventional tests for the existence of a unitary business generally apply [e.g., *Luhr Bros., Inc. v. Director of Revenue*, 780 S.W.2d 55 (Mo. 1989)], with the exception of the more-than-50 percent ownership requirement [e.g., *Appeal of Willamette Indus., Inc.*, No. 87-SBE-053 (Cal. St. Bd. of Equalization, June 17, 1987)]. The control test that typically applies to subsidiary corporations is of less significance in the context of a partnership interest, because the corporate partner is taxed only on its distributive share of partnership income. Generally, states consider factors such as functional integration, centralization of management, and economies of scale to determine whether the activities of a partner and the partnership are sufficiently interdependent as to constitute a single economic enterprise. As a rule of thumb, a general partner is typically unitary with the partnership, whereas a limited partner may or may not be unitary, depending on the facts of the case [e.g., *Appeals of GasCo Gasoline, Inc.*, 88-SBE-017 (Cal. St. Bd. of Equalization, June 1, 1988].

In *Sasol North America v. Commissioner of Revenue* [No. C273084 (Mass. App. Tax Bd., Sept. 5, 2007)], the Massachusetts Appellate Tax Board ruled that an out-of-state corporation's distributive share of the income of a limited partnership was subject to apportionment, rather than being 100 percent allocable to the state, because the business activities of the limited partnership were closely related to that of the corporation and served an operational rather than a passive investment function. Treating the income as entirely allocable to Massachusetts would also be improper, because other states in which the corporate partner conducted business operations were entitled to tax an apportioned share of the limited partnership interest.

Partners Who Are Individuals

The operative state income tax for partners who are individuals is the state individual income tax; however, not all states have an individual income tax. Alaska, Florida, Nevada, South Dakota, Texas, Washington, and Wyoming do not impose individual income taxes. In addition, New Hampshire and Tennessee tax only selected types of income, not including salaries and wages.

The state in which a partner resides generally taxes the entire amount of a resident partner's distributive share of partnership income, regardless of where the income is earned. In contrast, states in which the partner does not reside tax a nonresident partner's distributive share of partnership income only if the partnership has nexus in the state, and then only to the extent the nonresident partner's distributive share of income is attributable to sources within the state. If a portion of a partner's distributive share of income is subject to tax in two states (one by virtue of the partner's residence and the other by virtue of the source of the partnership's income), the state of residence usually allows the partner to claim a credit for income taxes paid to the other state as a means of mitigating double taxation. Some states also allow an individual partner to claim a credit for income taxes imposed directly on the partnership.

Composite Returns and Withholding Requirements

The requirement that out-of-state partners file returns and pay taxes in every state in which a partnership has nexus can create a significant compliance burden for partners in a partnership that has nexus in numerous states. One method of enhancing compliance is to require or permit a partnership to file a composite return on behalf of the out-of-state partners. A composite return is a single filing in which the participating partners report their distributive shares of the partnership's income and the partnership pays the state tax on behalf of the partners.

Example. A State *X* partnership has five partners, all of whom are individuals who reside in State *X*. The partnership also has nexus in State *Z*, and State *Z* allows a partnership to file a composite return on behalf of partners who are nonresidents. The five partners do not have to file separate State *Z* tax returns. Instead, the partnership can file a single composite State *Z* return on their behalf.

Most states allow partners to file a composite return. Examples of qualification requirements include (1) the participant must be a full-year nonresident, (2) the participant's income from the partnership must be his or her only income derived from sources within the state, and (3) a minimum number of partners must participate in the composite filing. The composite tax generally equals the sum of the participating partners' distributive shares of income apportioned to the state multiplied by the maximum tax rate applicable to individuals.

Another technique for promoting compliance on the part of nonresident partners is to require the partnership to withhold and remit tax from distributions to nonresident partners or from the nonresident partners' distributive shares of income. The amount withheld generally equals the highest marginal tax rate applicable to the nonresident partner multiplied by the partner's distributive share of income apportioned to the state. Some states require withholding only if the partnership fails to obtain a consent agreement from the partner or if the partner does not agree to be included in a composite return. A partner consent agreement is an agreement to submit to income tax jurisdiction in the state, file a return, and pay the tax due on the income sourced to the state.

The Multistate Tax Commission has adopted a model statute governing reporting options for nonresident owners of pass-through entities, including composite returns and withholding requirements. [Proposed Statutory Language on Reporting Options for Non-resident Members of Pass-through Entities with Withholding Requirement, Dec. 18, 2003]

State-by-State Summary

For ease of presentation, the following chart has been divided into five parts, as follows:

- Part 1: General Partnerships—Entity-Level Taxes and Withholding Requirements
- Part 2: Limited Partnerships—Entity-Level Taxes and Withholding Requirements/ Composite Returns
- Part 3: Nexus Rules for Out-of-State Corporate Partners
- Part 4: How Corporate Partner Treats Distributive Share of Partnership Income
- Part 5: Impact of Partnership Interest on Corporate Partner's Apportionment Percentage

Partnerships (Part 1)

General Partnerships—Entity-Level Taxes and Withholding Requirements

Legend:

X	Indicates state imposes tax
NA	Not applicable
NR	Not reported

	Does State Impose Any of the Following Entity-Level Taxes on a General Partnership?			
	Flat-Dollar Amount Minimum Tax or Filing Fee	*Income-Based Tax*	*Franchise Tax Based on Net Worth or Capital*	*Withholding Taxes Partners*
Alabama				X
Alaska	Alaska does not impose any of the above taxes			
Arizona	Arizona does not impose any of the above taxes			
Arkansas			X	X
California				X, partnerships must withhold tax on distributions out of California source taxable income to a domestic (U.S.) partners (R&TC § 18662). Partnerships must withhold tax on allocations of California source income to foreign (non-U.S.) partners. (R&TC § 18666).
Colorado				X, nonresident individuals only
Connecticut				
Delaware				X
District of Columbia		X		X
Florida				
Georgia				X

Partnerships (Part 1)

General Partnerships—Entity-Level Taxes and Withholding Requirements

Legend:

X	Indicates state imposes tax
NA	Not applicable
NR	Not reported

	Does State Impose Any of the Following Entity-Level Taxes on a General Partnership?			
	Flat-Dollar Amount Minimum Tax or Filing Fee	*Income-Based Tax*	*Franchise Tax Based on Net Worth or Capital*	*Withholding Taxes Partners*
Hawaii	See www.state.hi.us/dcca/breg-seu.			
Idaho		X, 7.6% corporate rate if paying the tax for partners who are individuals with a filing requirement.		
Illinois	Administered by Secretary of State	X	Administered by Secretary of State	
Indiana				X
Iowa				
Kansas	X, $55 profits; $40 non-profits		Not subject to franchise tax	X
Kentucky				X
Louisiana	Louisiana does not impose any of the above taxes			
Maine				X
Maryland				X
Massachusetts				
Michigan (Business Tax)		4.95% on taxable income	0.235% on financial institutions only	X

Note. The CIT takes effect 01/01/12, and replaces the Michigan Business Tax (MBT) for most taxpayers. However, businesses that have been approved to receive, have received, or have been assigned certain certified credits may elect to file a return and pay the tax imposed by the MBT in lieu of the CIT until the certified credits are exhausted or extinguished.

Partnerships (Part 1)

General Partnerships—Entity-Level Taxes and Withholding Requirements

Legend:

X	Indicates state imposes tax
NA	Not applicable
NR	Not reported

	Does State Impose Any of the Following Entity-Level Taxes on a General Partnership?			
	Flat-Dollar Amount Minimum Tax or Filing Fee	*Income-Based Tax*	*Franchise Tax Based on Net Worth or Capital*	*Withholding Taxes Partners*
Minnesota	X, minimum fee is progressive based on Minnesota property, payroll and sales.			
Mississippi				
Missouri				X
Montana				X
Nebraska				X
Nevada	Nevada does not impose a corporate income tax			
New Hampshire		X, 8.5%		
New Jersey	X, for tax years starting on and after 1/1/02; $150 for each owner if entity has more than 2 owners, N.J.S.A. 54A:8-6	X, 6.37% on nonresident, noncorporate partner's allocated (apportioned) share of entire net income plus 9% on same of nonresident corporate partners, N.J.S.A. 54:10A-15.11		
New Mexico			X	

Note. Withholding tax on nonresident

Partnerships (Part 1)

General Partnerships—Entity-Level Taxes and Withholding Requirements

Legend:

X	Indicates state imposes tax
NA	Not applicable
NR	Not reported

	Does State Impose Any of the Following Entity-Level Taxes on a General Partnership?			
	Flat-Dollar Amount Minimum Tax or Filing Fee	*Income-Based Tax*	*Franchise Tax Based on Net Worth or Capital*	*Withholding Taxes Partners*
New York	X, $2,500-$4,500, depending on New York source gross income. General partnerships with income, less than lst 1 million are exempt			X, estimated tax for nonresidents only
North Carolina				
North Dakota				X, for non-residents only
Ohio	Ohio does not impose a corporate income tax.			
Note. Effective 1/1/2010, the Ohio Franchise Tax was fully phased out and business will be taxed on gross receipts through the Commercial Activity Tax. Details about that tax can be found at: http//tax.ohio.gov/divisions/commercial_activities/index.stm				
Oklahoma				
Oregon	Flat-dollar minimum fee; $150 if transacting business in Oregon and required to file a partnership return			
Pennsylvania				X
Rhode Island	Refer to R.I.G.L. 44-30			
South Carolina				X, 5% withholding required on taxable income of nonresident partners.
South Dakota	South Dakota does not impose a corporate income tax			
Tennessee				

Partnerships (Part 1)

General Partnerships—Entity-Level Taxes and Withholding Requirements

Legend:

X	Indicates state imposes tax
NA	Not applicable
NR	Not reported

	Does State Impose Any of the Following Entity-Level Taxes on a General Partnership?			
	Flat-Dollar Amount Minimum Tax or Filing Fee	*Income-Based Tax*	*Franchise Tax Based on Net Worth or Capital*	*Withholding Taxes Partners*
Texas	Tax is not imposed on a general partnership where direct ownership is composed entirely of natural persons.	.5% for qualifying entities in retail or wholesale trade and 1% for all others.		
Utah				X, withholding tax on nonresident pass-through entity taxpayers.
Vermont	X, $250			X
Virginia				X, effective for taxable years beginning 1/1/08 and after.
Washington	Washington does not impose a corporate income tax			
West Virginia			0.7% or $50, whichever is greater	
Wisconsin		X, Economic Development surcharge of $25 to $9500 may apply.		X, nonresident partners.
Wyoming	Wyoming does not impose a corporate income tax			

Partnerships (Part 2)

Limited Partnerships—Entity-Level Taxes and Withholding Requirements/Composite Returns

Legend:

X	Indicates state imposes tax
NA	Not applicable
NR	Not reported

	Does State Impose Any of the Following Entity-Level Taxes on a Limited Partnership?				*Composite Returns for:*	
	Flat-Dollar Amount Minimum Tax or Filing Fee	*Income-Based Tax*	*Franchise Tax Based on Net Worth or Capital*	*Withholding Taxes on Partners*	*Partners Who Are Individuals?*	*Corporate Partners?*
Alabama			X	X	No	No
Alaska					No	No
Arizona	Arizona does not impose any of the above taxes				Yes, Form 140NR	
Arkansas			X	X	Yes, AR1000CR	No

Partnerships (Part 2)

Limited Partnerships—Entity-Level Taxes and Withholding Requirements/Composite Returns

Legend:

X	Indicates state imposes tax
NA	Not applicable
NR	Not reported

	Does State Impose Any of the Following Entity-Level Taxes on a Limited Partnership?				*Composite Returns for:*	
	Flat-Dollar Amount Minimum Tax or Filing Fee	*Income-Based Tax*	*Franchise Tax Based on Net Worth or Capital*	*Withholding Taxes on Partners*	*Partners Who Are Individuals?*	*Corporate Partners?*
California	X, annual tax in amount equal to minimum corporate franchise tax of $800 is imposed on limited partnerships organized, registered, or doing business in California (R&TC § 17935). Annual tax in amount equal to minimum corporate franchise tax of $800 is imposed on limited liability partnerships organized, registered, or doing business in California (R&TC 17948).			X, same as for general partnerships	Yes, (group return) Form FTB 540NR, see R&TC § 18535	No
Colorado				X, non-resident individuals only	Yes	No
Connecticut		X, $250			Yes, Form CT1065-1120SI	No

Partnerships (Part 2)

Limited Partnerships—Entity-Level Taxes and Withholding Requirements/Composite Returns

Legend:

X	Indicates state imposes tax
NA	Not applicable
NR	Not reported

	Does State Impose Any of the Following Entity-Level Taxes on a Limited Partnership?				*Composite Returns for:*	
	Flat-Dollar Amount Minimum Tax or Filing Fee	*Income-Based Tax*	*Franchise Tax Based on Net Worth or Capital*	*Withholding Taxes on Partners*	*Partners Who Are Individuals?*	*Corporate Partners?*
Delaware				X	Yes, Form 200C	
District of Columbia		X			No	No
Note: Gross Receipts						
Florida					No	No
Georgia				X	Yes, Form IT-CR	Yes, Form IT-CR
Hawaii		See www.state.hi.us/dcca/breg-seu.				
Idaho		X, 7.6% corporate rate if paying the tax for partners who are individuals with a filing requirement.			Yes, Idaho Form 65	
Illinois	Administered by Secretary of State	X, 1.5% of net income	Administered by Secretary of State		Yes, Form 1023-C	
Indiana				X	Yes	
Iowa					Yes, Form IA1040C	
Kansas	X, $55, profits; $40, non-profits			X	Yes, Form K-40C & J-40	No

Partnerships (Part 2)

Limited Partnerships—Entity-Level Taxes and Withholding Requirements/Composite Returns

Legend:

X	Indicates state imposes tax
NA	Not applicable
NR	Not reported

	Does State Impose Any of the Following Entity-Level Taxes on a Limited Partnership?				*Composite Returns for:*	
	Flat-Dollar Amount Minimum Tax or Filing Fee	*Income-Based Tax*	*Franchise Tax Based on Net Worth or Capital*	*Withholding Taxes on Partners*	*Partners Who Are Individuals?*	*Corporate Partners?*
Kentucky		X, Lesser of $.095/ $100 KY gross receipts or $.75/$100 KY gross profits or $175 minimum.		X	Yes, Form 740-NPWH	No
Louisiana	Louisiana does not impose any of the above taxes				Yes, Form R6922	No
Maine				X	Yes, nonresident individuals Form 1040 ME	
Maryland				X	Yes, Form 505	
Massachusetts						
Michigan (Business Tax)		4.95% on taxable income	0.235% on financial institutions only		Yes, Form 807	No
Note. The CIT takes effect 01/01/12, and replaces the Michigan Business Tax (MBT) for most taxpayers. However, businesses that have been approved to receive, have received, or have been assigned certain certified credits may elect to file a return and pay the tax imposed by the MBT in lieu of the CIT until the certified credits are exhausted or extinguished.						
Minnesota					Yes,	No, M3
Mississippi					Yes, Form 86-106	
Missouri				X	Yes, MO-1040	No
Montana				X	Yes, schedule on PR-1	Yes, schedule on PR-1

Partnerships (Part 2)

Limited Partnerships—Entity-Level Taxes and Withholding Requirements/Composite Returns

Legend:

X	Indicates state imposes tax
NA	Not applicable
NR	Not reported

	Does State Impose Any of the Following Entity-Level Taxes on a Limited Partnership?				*Composite Returns for:*	
	Flat-Dollar Amount Minimum Tax or Filing Fee	*Income-Based Tax*	*Franchise Tax Based on Net Worth or Capital*	*Withholding Taxes on Partners*	*Partners Who Are Individuals?*	*Corporate Partners?*
Nebraska				X	No	No
Nevada	Nevada does not impose a corporate income tax					
New Hampshire		X, 8.5%			No	No
New Jersey	X, $50 N.J.S.A. 42:2A-68. For years starting on and after 1/1/02, $150 for each owner if entity has more than 2 owners, N.J.S.A. 54A:8-6.	X, 6.37% on nonresident, noncorporate partner's allocated (apportioned) share of entire net income plus 9% on same of nonresident corporate partners, N.J.S.A. 54:10A-15.11		Yes, Form NJ-1080C		
New Mexico				Yes	Yes, Form PTE	Yes, Form PTE
Note. Withholding tax on nonresidents						
New York	X, $25-$4,500 depending on NY source gross income.			X	X	
North Carolina						
North Dakota				Yes, Form ND-1 for nonresident members only		
Ohio	Ohio does not impose a corporate income tax.					

Partnerships (Part 2)

Limited Partnerships—Entity-Level Taxes and Withholding Requirements/Composite Returns

Legend:

X	Indicates state imposes tax
NA	Not applicable
NR	Not reported

	Does State Impose Any of the Following Entity-Level Taxes on a Limited Partnership?				*Composite Returns for:*	
	Flat-Dollar Amount Minimum Tax or Filing Fee	*Income-Based Tax*	*Franchise Tax Based on Net Worth or Capital*	*Withholding Taxes on Partners*	*Partners Who Are Individuals?*	*Corporate Partners?*
Note. Effective 1/1/2010, the Ohio Franchise Tax was fully phased out and business will be taxed on gross receipts through the Commercial Activity Tax. Details about that tax can be found at: http//tax.ohio.gov/divisions/commercial_activities/index.stm						
Oklahoma				Yes, Form 514	Yes	
Oregon	X, $150 if transacting business in Oregon and required to file a partnership return.			Yes, Form 40 MNR	Yes, Form OC	
Pennsylvania			X	Yes, Form PA 40 NRC		
Rhode Island	X				Yes	No
South Carolina				X, 5% withholding required on taxable income of nonresidents partners	Yes, 1-348, Form SC1040	No
South Dakota	South Dakota does not impose a corporate income tax					
Tennessee		X, excise tax .25%	X, excise tax .25%			
Texas		.5% for qualifying entities in retail or wholesale trade and 1% for all others.				

Partnerships (Part 2)

Limited Partnerships—Entity-Level Taxes and Withholding Requirements/Composite Returns

Legend:

X	Indicates state imposes tax
NA	Not applicable
NR	Not reported

	Does State Impose Any of the Following Entity-Level Taxes on a Limited Partnership?				*Composite Returns for:*	
	Flat-Dollar Amount Minimum Tax or Filing Fee	*Income-Based Tax*	*Franchise Tax Based on Net Worth or Capital*	*Withholding Taxes on Partners*	*Partners Who Are Individuals?*	*Corporate Partners?*
Utah				X, withholding tax on nonresident pass-through entity taxpayers.	Yes, Form TC-65, nonresident partners only	
Vermont	X, $250			X	Yes	Yes
Virginia				X, effective for taxable years beginning 1/1/08 and after.	Form 765	Form 765 with permission
Washington	Washington does not impose a corporate income tax					
West Virginia			0.7% or $50, whichever is greater.			
Wisconsin	X, various amounts, but these are imposed by the Wisconsin Dept. of Financial Institutions.	X, Economic Development Surcharge between $25 to $9800 may apply		X, nonresidents only	Yes, Form 1CNP	No
Wyoming	Wyoming does not impose a corporate income tax					

Partnerships (Part 3)

Nexus Rules for Out-of-State Corporate Partners

Legend:

X — Out-of-state corporation is subject to state income tax if only connection is ownership interest of this type of pass-through entity which is doing business in your state

NA — Not applicable

NR — Not reported

	Limited Interest, Operating Partnership	*Limited Interest, Investment Partnership*	*General Partnership Interest*	*Limited Liability Company*
Alabama	X	X	X	X
Alaska	X	X	X	X
Arizona	X	X	X	X
Arkansas	X	X	X	X
California	X, but mere receipt of dividends and interest does not create nexus, See CA Code Reg Title 18 § 23101(b)	X, but mere receipt of dividends and interest does not create nexus, See CA Code Reg Title 18 § 23101(b)	X, but mere receipt of dividends and interest does not create nexus, See CA Code Reg Title 18 § 23101(b)	X, but mere receipt of dividends and interest does not create nexus, See CA Code Reg Title 18 § 23101(b)
Colorado	X	X	X	X
Connecticut	X		X	X
Delaware	X	X	X	X
District of Columbia	X	X	X	X
Florida	X	X	X	X
Georgia	X	X, certain exemptions depending upon activity and ownership	X	X
Hawaii	X	X	X	X
Idaho	X	X	X	X
Illinois	Insufficient information			

Partnerships (Part 3)

Nexus Rules for Out-of-State Corporate Partners

Legend:

X	Out-of-state corporation is subject to state income tax if only connection is ownership interest of this type of pass-through entity which is doing business in your state
NA	Not applicable
NR	Not reported

	Limited Interest, Operating Partnership	*Limited Interest, Investment Partnership*	*General Partnership Interest*	*Limited Liability Company*
Indiana	X	X	X	X
Iowa	X	X	X	X
Kansas	X	X	X	X
Kentucky	X	X	X	
Louisiana	X	X	X	X
Maine	X	X	X	X
Maryland	X	X		
Massachusetts	X	Depends on facts	X	X
Michigan (Business Tax)				
Note. The CIT takes effect 01/01/12, and replaces the Michigan Business Tax (MBT) for most taxpayers. However, businesses that have been approved to receive, have received, or have been assigned certain certified credits may elect to file a return and pay the tax imposed by the MBT in lieu of the CIT until the certified credits are exhausted or extinguished.				
Minnesota	X	X	X	X
Mississippi	X	X	X	X
Missouri	X	X	X	X
Montana	X	X	X	X

Partnerships (Part 3)

Nexus Rules for Out-of-State Corporate Partners

Legend:

X	Out-of-state corporation is subject to state income tax if only connection is ownership interest of this type of pass-through entity which is doing business in your state
NA	Not applicable
NR	Not reported

	Limited Interest, Operating Partnership	*Limited Interest, Investment Partnership*	*General Partnership Interest*	*Limited Liability Company*
Nebraska	X	X	X	X
Nevada	Nevada does not impose a corporate income tax			
New Hampshire	NA	NA	NA	NA
New Jersey	See N.J.A.C., 18:7-7.b and P.L. 2001, c.136 approved 6/29/01 which creates consent and deemed payment provisions against such entities. For periods on or after 1/1/02, N.J.A.C. 54:10A-15.11 provides that the partnership pays tax for the foreign partner. No consent is needed.			X
New Mexico	X	X	X	X
New York	X	X, unless portfolio investment partnership	X	X
North Carolina	X	X	X	X
North Dakota	X	X	X	X
Ohio	Ohio does not impose a corporate income tax.			
Note. Effective 1/1/2010, the Ohio Franchise Tax was fully phased out and business will be taxed on gross receipts through the Commercial Activity Tax. Details about that tax can be found at: http//tax.ohio.gov/divisions/commercial_activities/index.stm				
Oklahoma	X	X	X	X
Oregon	X	X	X	X
Pennsylvania	X	X	X	X
Rhode Island			X	X

Partnerships (Part 3)

Nexus Rules for Out-of-State Corporate Partners

Legend:

X	Out-of-state corporation is subject to state income tax if only connection is ownership interest of this type of pass-through entity which is doing business in your state
NA	Not applicable
NR	Not reported

	Limited Interest, Operating Partnership	*Limited Interest, Investment Partnership*	*General Partnership Interest*	*Limited Liability Company*
South Carolina	X	X	X	X, unless taxed like C corporation
South Dakota	South Dakota does not impose a corporate income tax			
Tennessee			X, if the entity is a general partnership	
Texas	Taxable entities that are part of an affiliated group engaged in a unitary business must file a combined group report, regardless of whether an entity has nexus on a separate entity basis. All members of the combined group are included in the calculation of total revenue and in the denominator of the apportionment factor, regardless of whether the entity has nexus in Texas. The receipts for all members that have nexus in Texas are included in the numerator of the apportionment factor. The apportionment factor is calculated for the combined group and not on a separate entity basis.			
Utah	X	X	X	X
Vermont	X		X	X
Virginia	X	See Tax Bulletin 05-6 published as PD No. 05-69.	X	X
Washington	Washington does not impose a corporate income tax			
West Virginia	X	X	X	X
Wisconsin	X	X	X	X
Wyoming	Wyoming does not impose a corporate income tax			

Partnerships (Part 4)

How Corporate Partner Treats Distributive Share of Partnership Income

Legend:

A	Separate Accounting
B	Treat as Allocable Income
C	Combine with X's Income
D	Other method
NA	Not Applicable
NR	Not Reported

	Out-of-State Corporation "A" Is Subject to State Tax Because of Its Ownership Interest in "X," the Indicated Form. How Does "A" Treat its Distributive Share of X's Income?			
	Limited Interest, Operating Partnership	*Limited Interest, Investment Partnership*	*General Partnership Interest*	*Limited Liability Company*
Alabama	D, reported as apportionable income	D, reported as apportionable income unless the partnership is a qualified investment partnership, then income is exempt.	D, reported as apportionable income	D, reported as apportionable income
Alaska	C	C	C	C
Arizona	B, if nonbusiness income; C, if business income	B, if nonbusiness income; C, if business income	B, if nonbusiness income; C, if business income	B, if nonbusiness income; C, if business income
Arkansas	B	B	B	B

Partnerships (Part 4)

How Corporate Partner Treats Distributive Share of Partnership Income

Legend:

A	Separate Accounting
B	Treat as Allocable Income
C	Combine with X's Income
D	Other method
NA	Not Applicable
NR	Not Reported

Out-of-State Corporation "A" Is Subject to State Tax Because of Its Ownership Interest in "X," the Indicated Form. How Does "A" Treat its Distributive Share of X's Income?

	Limited Interest, Operating Partnership	*Limited Interest, Investment Partnership*	*General Partnership Interest*	*Limited Liability Company*
California	B, if A and X are not unitary, then (1) A's distributive share that is a nonbusiness income is allocated pursuant to R&TC § 25154-25127 and (2) A's distributive share of partnership business income is apportioned by the formula set forth in Cal. Code Regs., tit. 18 § 25137-1(f) and (g). C, if A and X are unitary, A's distributive share of X business income is combined with A's business income.	B, if A and X are not unitary, then (1) A's distributive share that is a nonbusiness income is allocated pursuant to R&TC § 25154-25127 and (2) A's distributive share of partnership business income is apportioned by the formula set forth in Cal. Code Regs., tit. 18 § 25137-1(f) and (g). C, if A and X are unitary, A's distributive share of X busienss income is combined with A's business income.	B, if A and X are not unitary, then (1) A's distributive share that is a nonbusiness income is allocated pursuant to R&TC § 25154-25127 and (2) A's distributive share of partnership business income is apportioned by the formula set forth in Cal. Code Regs., tit. 18 § 25137-1(f) and (g). C, if A and X are unitary, A's distributive share of X business income is combined with A's business income.	B, if A and X are not unitary, then (1) A's distributive share that is a nonbusiness income is allocated pursuant to R&TC § 25154-25127 and (2) A's distributive share of partnership business income is apportioned by the formula set forth in Cal. Code Regs., tit. 18 § 25137-1(f) and (g). C, if A and X are unitary, A's distributive share of X business income is combined with A's business income.
Colorado	B	B	B C, apportion if unitary	B C, apportion if unitary
Connecticut	See Conn. Gen. Stat. § 12-218(h)	See Conn. Gen. Stat. § 12-214(a)(3)(A)	C	D, treated same as a operating partnership—See Conn. Gen. Stat. § 12-218(h)
Delaware	All partnerships report their distributive share of income or loss with corporate partners' income, then allocate and apportion.			

Partnerships (Part 4)

How Corporate Partner Treats Distributive Share of Partnership Income

Legend:

A	Separate Accounting
B	Treat as Allocable Income
C	Combine with X's Income
D	Other method
NA	Not Applicable
NR	Not Reported

	Out-of-State Corporation "A" Is Subject to State Tax Because of Its Ownership Interest in "X," the Indicated Form. How Does "A" Treat its Distributive Share of X's Income?			
	Limited Interest, Operating Partnership	*Limited Interest, Investment Partnership*	*General Partnership Interest*	*Limited Liability Company*
District of Columbia	D, subject to tax less the portion that was taxed at "X" level	D, subject to tax if actively engaged	D, subject to tax if actively engaged	D, subject to tax if actively engaged
Florida	C, based on combined factors	C, based on combined factors	C, based on combined factors	C, based on combined factors
Georgia	C	C, unless exempt	C	C
Hawaii	A, B, C, D	A, B, C, D	A, B, C, D	A, B, C, D
Idaho	C, if business income to the partner; B, if nonbusiness income to the partner	C, if business income to the partner; B, if nonbusiness income to the partner	C, if business income to the partner; B, if nonbusiness income to the partner	C, if business income to the partner; B, if nonbusiness income to the partner
Illinois	C, in the case of a corporate business owner engaged in a unitary business with X; otherwise A	C, in the case of a corporate business owner engaged in a unitary business with X; otherwise A	C, in the case of a corporate business owner engaged in a unitary business with X; otherwise A	C, in the case of a corporate business owner engaged in a unitary business with X; otherwise A
Indiana	B	B	C	B
Iowa	Aggregate with A's income	Aggregate with A's income	Aggregate with A's income	Aggregate with A's income
Kansas	C, to the extent of ownership, combined apportionment factor	C, to the extent of ownership, combined apportionment factor	C, to the extent of ownership, combined apportionment factor	C, to the extent of ownership, combined apportionment factor
Kentucky	C	C	C	C

Partnerships (Part 4)

How Corporate Partner Treats Distributive Share of Partnership Income

Legend:

A	Separate Accounting
B	Treat as Allocable Income
C	Combine with X's Income
D	Other method
NA	Not Applicable
NR	Not Reported

Out-of-State Corporation "A" Is Subject to State Tax Because of Its Ownership Interest in "X," the Indicated Form. How Does "A" Treat its Distributive Share of X's Income?

	Limited Interest, Operating Partnership	*Limited Interest, Investment Partnership*	*General Partnership Interest*	*Limited Liability Company*
Louisiana	B	B	B	SAF based on the "check the box" election.
Maine	C	B	C	C
Maryland	NR	NR	A, B	A, B, if treated as partnership, B, if treated as corporation
Massachusetts	A,B	B	C	D, depends on facts
Michigan (Business Tax)	NA	NA	NA	NA

Note. The CIT takes effect 01/01/12, and replaces the Michigan Business Tax (MBT) for most taxpayers. However, businesses that have been approved to receive, have received, or have been assigned certain certified credits may elect to file a return and pay the tax imposed by the MBT in lieu of the CIT until the certified credits are exhausted or extinguished.

Minnesota	D, separate accounting or allocable based on whether there is unitary relationship between "A" and "X:	D, separate accounting or allocable based on whether there is unitary relationship between "A" and "X:	D, separate accounting or allocable based on whether there is unitary relationship between "A" and "X:	D, separate accounting or allocable based on whether there is unitary relationship between "A" and "X:
Mississippi	B	B	B	B
Missouri	Combine with A's income	Combine with A's income	Combine with A's income	Combine with A's income
Montana	C, if unitary with group; if not, A	C, if unitary with group; if not, A	C, if unitary with group; if not, A	C, if unitary with group; if not, A

Partnerships (Part 4)

How Corporate Partner Treats Distributive Share of Partnership Income

Legend:

A	Separate Accounting
B	Treat as Allocable Income
C	Combine with X's Income
D	Other method
NA	Not Applicable
NR	Not Reported

Out-of-State Corporation "A" Is Subject to State Tax Because of Its Ownership Interest in "X," the Indicated Form. How Does "A" Treat its Distributive Share of X's Income?

	Limited Interest, Operating Partnership	*Limited Interest, Investment Partnership*	*General Partnership Interest*	*Limited Liability Company*
Nebraska	C	C	C	C
Nevada	Nevada does not impose a corporate income tax			
New Hampshire	NR	NR	NR	NR
New Jersey	B, if A and X are not unitary, create an allocation factor for X and apply that to the distributive share.	Qualified investment partnership has no nexus	B, if A and X are not unitary, create an allocation factor for X and apply that to the distributive share.	B, if A and X are not unitary, create an allocation factor for X and apply that to the distributive share.
New Mexico	C	C	C	C
New York	A optional, C	Not taxable	C	C, unless treated as a C corporation for federal purposes
North Carolina	B, if nonbusiness; uses X apportionment factor if business	B, if nonbusiness; uses X apportionment factor if business	B, if nonbusiness; uses X apportionment factor if business	B, if nonbusiness; uses X apportionment factor if business
North Dakota	C	C	C	C
Ohio	Ohio does not impose a corporate income tax.			

Note. Effective 1/1/2010, the Ohio Franchise Tax was fully phased out and business will be taxed on gross receipts through the Commercial Activity Tax. Details about that tax can be found at: http//tax.ohio.gov/divisions/commercial_activities/index.stm

Partnerships (Part 4)

How Corporate Partner Treats Distributive Share of Partnership Income

Legend:

A	Separate Accounting
B	Treat as Allocable Income
C	Combine with X's Income
D	Other method
NA	Not Applicable
NR	Not Reported

Out-of-State Corporation "A" Is Subject to State Tax Because of Its Ownership Interest in "X," the Indicated Form. How Does "A" Treat its Distributive Share of X's Income?

	Limited Interest, Operating Partnership	*Limited Interest, Investment Partnership*	*General Partnership Interest*	*Limited Liability Company*
Oklahoma	A	A	A	A
Oregon	B, if not unitary, business income is allocable; C, if unitary, business income is combined with X's income.	B, if not unitary, business income is allocable; C, if unitary, business income is combined with X's income.	B, if not unitary, business income is allocable; C, if unitary, business income is combined with X's income.	B, if not unitary, business income is allocable; C, if unitary, business income is combined with X's income.
Pennsylvania	C	NR	NR	NR
Rhode Island	D, protected under CT 95-2 (Nexus)	D, protected under CT 95-2 (Nexus)	D, pro rate share based upon assets, payroll, and receipts	D, pro rate share based upon assets, payroll, and receipts
South Carolina	A	B	Allocable if non-unitary; apportionable if unitary	A single member LLC that has not elected to be taxed as a corporation is not regarded as an entity separate from its owner.
South Dakota	South Dakota does not impose a corporate income tax			
Tennessee	Entity X is subject to tax	Entity X is subject to tax	C	Entity X is subject to tax
Texas	Taxable entities that are part of an affiliated group engaged in a unitary business must file a combined group report, regardless of whether an entity has nexus on a separate entity basis. All members of the combined group are included in the calculation of total revenue and in the denominator of the apportionment factor, regardless of whether the entity has nexus in Texas. The receipts for all members that have nexus in Texas are included in the numerator of the apportionment factor. The apportionment factor is calculated for the combined group and not on a separate entity basis.			

Partnerships (Part 4)

How Corporate Partner Treats Distributive Share of Partnership Income

Legend:

A	Separate Accounting
B	Treat as Allocable Income
C	Combine with X's Income
D	Other method
NA	Not Applicable
NR	Not Reported

Out-of-State Corporation "A" Is Subject to State Tax Because of Its Ownership Interest in "X," the Indicated Form. How Does "A" Treat its Distributive Share of X's Income?

	Limited Interest, Operating Partnership	*Limited Interest, Investment Partnership*	*General Partnership Interest*	*Limited Liability Company*
Utah	C	C	C	C
Vermont	B, if nonbusiness income;	B	C	C
	C, if business income			
Virginia	C	NA	C	C
Washington	Washington does not impose a corporate income tax.			
West Virginia	B	B	B	B
Wisconsin	C	C	C	C
Wyoming	Wyoming does not impose a corporate income tax			

Partnerships (Part 5)

Impact of Partnership Interest on Corporate Partner's Apportionment Percentage

Legend:

A	Based only on A's apportionment factors
B	Combine A's apportionment factors with A's distributive share of partnership or LLC's (X's) apportionment factors
C	Based on A's apportionment factors, plus the inclusion in the receipts' factor of the K-1 income from the partnership or LLC (X)
NA	Not applicable
NR	Not reported
X	The partnership or LLC treated as a partnership

	If Separate Accounting Is Not Permissible and the Pass-Through Entity Income Is Not Treated as Allocable Income, How Is A's (the Out-of-State Corporate Owner's) Apportionment Percentage Determined?			
	Limited Interest, Operating Partnership	*Limited Interest, Investment Partnership*	*General Partnership Interest*	*Limited Liability Company Interest*
Alabama	B	B	B	B
Alaska	B	B	B	B
Arizona	B	B	B	B
Arkansas	NA	NA	NA	NA
California	If A and X are unitary, see Cal. Code. Regs, tit. 18 § 25137-1(f); if A and X are not unitary, A should apportion to CA its distributive share of X's business income apportioned to CA based on X's' factors. See Cal. Code Regs. tit. 18, § 25137-1(g).	If A and X are unitary, see Cal. Code. Regs, tit. 18 § 25137-1(f); if A and X are not unitary, A should apportion to CA its distributive share of X's business income apportioned to CA based on X's' factors. See Cal. Code Regs. tit. 18, § 25137-1(g).	If A and X are unitary, see Cal. Code. Regs, tit. 18 § 25137-1(f); if A and X are not unitary, A should apportion to CA its distributive share of X's business income apportioned to CA based on X's' factors. See Cal. Code Regs. tit. 18, § 25137-1(g).	If A and X are unitary, see Cal. Code. Regs, tit. 18 § 25137-1(f); if A and X are not unitary, A should apportion to CA its distributive share of X's business income apportioned to CA based on X's' factors. See Cal. Code Regs. tit. 18, § 25137-1(g).
Colorado			Partnership is treated as disregarded if unitary.	Partnership is treated as disregarded if unitary.
Connecticut	B		B	B
Delaware	NR	NR	NR	NR
District of Columbia	NR	NR	A	NR
Florida	B	B	B	B

Partnerships (Part 5)

Impact of Partnership Interest on Corporate Partner's Apportionment Percentage

Legend:

A	Based only on A's apportionment factors
B	Combine A's apportionment factors with A's distributive share of partnership or LLC's (X's) apportionment factors
C	Based on A's apportionment factors, plus the inclusion in the receipts' factor of the K-1 income from the partnership or LLC (X)
NA	Not applicable
NR	Not reported
X	The partnership or LLC treated as a partnership

	If Separate Accounting Is Not Permissible and the Pass-Through Entity Income Is Not Treated as Allocable Income, How Is A's (the Out-of-State Corporate Owner's) Apportionment Percentage Determined?			
	Limited Interest, Operating Partnership	*Limited Interest, Investment Partnership*	*General Partnership Interest*	*Limited Liability Company Interest*
Georgia	B	B, unless exempt	B	B
Hawaii	B	B	B	B
Idaho	B, limited to A's interest	B, limited to A's interest	B, limited to A's interest	B, limited to A's interest
Illinois	A; B, if corporate partners engaged in unitary business with partnership	A; B, if corporate partners engaged in unitary business with partnership	A; B, if corporate partners engaged in unitary business with partnership	A; B, if corporate partners engaged in unitary business with partnership
Indiana	Based on X's factor	Based on X's factor	B	Based on X's factor
Iowa	C	C	C	C
Kansas	B, to extent of ownership	B, to extent of ownership	B, to extent of ownership	B, to extent of ownership
Kentucky	B	B	Based on A's factors and its share of X's factors.	B
Louisiana	NA	NA	NA	NA
Maine	B	NR	B	B
Maryland	NR	NR	NR	NR
Massachusetts	NR	NR	NR	NR
Michigan (Business Tax)	NA	NA	NA	NA

Partnerships (Part 5)

Impact of Partnership Interest on Corporate Partner's Apportionment Percentage

Legend:

A	Based only on A's apportionment factors
B	Combine A's apportionment factors with A's distributive share of partnership or LLC's (X's) apportionment factors
C	Based on A's apportionment factors, plus the inclusion in the receipts' factor of the K-1 income from the partnership or LLC (X)
NA	Not applicable
NR	Not reported
X	The partnership or LLC treated as a partnership

If Separate Accounting Is Not Permissible and the Pass-Through Entity Income Is Not Treated as Allocable Income, How Is A's (the Out-of-State Corporate Owner's) Apportionment Percentage Determined?

	Limited Interest, Operating Partnership	*Limited Interest, Investment Partnership*	*General Partnership Interest*	*Limited Liability Company Interest*
Note. The CIT takes effect 01/01/12, and replaces the Michigan Business Tax (MBT) for most taxpayers. However, businesses that have been approved to receive, have received, or have been assigned certain certified credits may elect to file a return and pay the tax imposed by the MBT in lieu of the CIT until the certified credits are exhausted or extinguished.				
Minnesota	B	B	B	B
Mississippi	NA	NA	NA	NA
Missouri	B	B	B	B
Montana	B, if X is unitary with A; if not unitary, A	B, if X is unitary with A; if not unitary, A	B, if X is unitary with A; if not unitary, A	B, if X is unitary with A; if not unitary, A
Nebraska	C	C	C	C
Nevada	Nevada does not impose a corporate income tax.			
New Hampshire	NA	NA	NA	NA
New Jersey	Based on partnership allocation factor	Based on partnership allocation factor	Based on partnership allocation factor	Based on partnership allocation factor
New Mexico			B	B, if managing member; A's plus share of X's; other members: A's plus K-1.
New York	A, optional; B	NA	B	B, unless C corporation treatment is elected for federal purposes

Partnerships (Part 5)

Impact of Partnership Interest on Corporate Partner's Apportionment Percentage

Legend:

A	Based only on A's apportionment factors
B	Combine A's apportionment factors with A's distributive share of partnership or LLC's (X's) apportionment factors
C	Based on A's apportionment factors, plus the inclusion in the receipts' factor of the K-1 income from the partnership or LLC (X)
NA	Not applicable
NR	Not reported
X	The partnership or LLC treated as a partnership

	If Separate Accounting Is Not Permissible and the Pass-Through Entity Income Is Not Treated as Allocable Income, How Is A's (the Out-of-State Corporate Owner's) Apportionment Percentage Determined?			
	Limited Interest, Operating Partnership	*Limited Interest, Investment Partnership*	*General Partnership Interest*	*Limited Liability Company Interest*
North Carolina	B, if business income	B, if business income	B, if business income	B, if business income
North Dakota	B	B	B	B
Ohio	Ohio does not impose a corporate income tax.			
Note. Effective 1/1/2010, the Ohio Franchise Tax was fully phased out and business will be taxed on gross receipts through the Commercial Activity Tax. Details about that tax can be found at: http//tax.ohio.gov/divisions/commercial_activities/index.stms				
Oklahoma	NR	NR	NR	NR
Oregon	B, X's factors included based on A's ownership interest in the entity	B, X's factors included based on A's ownership interest in the entity	B, X's factors included based on A's ownership interest in the entity	B, X's factors included based on A's ownership interest in the entity
Pennsylvania	B	NR	NR	NR
Rhode Island	C, protected under CT 95-2 business nexus	C, protected under CT 95-2 business nexus	C, protected under CT 95-2 business nexus	C, protected under CT 95-2 business nexus
South Carolina	NR	NR	A	A
South Dakota	South Dakota does not impose a corporate income tax.			
Tennessee	Entity X is subject to tax	Entity X is subject to tax	B	Entity X is subject to tax

Partnerships (Part 5)

Impact of Partnership Interest on Corporate Partner's Apportionment Percentage

Legend:

A	Based only on A's apportionment factors
B	Combine A's apportionment factors with A's distributive share of partnership or LLC's (X's) apportionment factors
C	Based on A's apportionment factors, plus the inclusion in the receipts' factor of the K-1 income from the partnership or LLC (X)
NA	Not applicable
NR	Not reported
X	The partnership or LLC treated as a partnership

	If Separate Accounting Is Not Permissible and the Pass-Through Entity Income Is Not Treated as Allocable Income, How Is A's (the Out-of-State Corporate Owner's) Apportionment Percentage Determined?			
	Limited Interest, Operating Partnership	*Limited Interest, Investment Partnership*	*General Partnership Interest*	*Limited Liability Company Interest*
Texas	For earned surplus component, the partner's share of the partnership gross receipts are included in computing the partner's receipts. For the taxable capital component, the partner includes the partner's share of the partnership net income unless GAAP allows the partner to report the partner's share of the partnership gross receipts.			
Utah	Based on A's factors plus the portion of X's factors that reflect the amount of A's ownership in X	Based on A's factors plus the portion of X's factors that reflect the amount of A's ownership in X	Based on A's factors plus the portion of X's factors that reflect the amount of A's ownership in X	Based on A's factors plus the portion of X's factors that reflect the amount of A's ownership in X
Vermont	B	NR	B	B
Virginia	B	NA	B	B
Washington	Washington does not impose a corporate income tax			
West Virginia	B	B	B	B
Wisconsin	B	B	B	B
Wyoming	Wyoming does not impose a corporate income tax			

Limited Liability Companies

Federal Tax Treatment

The federal income tax treatment of a limited liability company (LLC) is determined by an elective system of entity classification. [Treas. Reg. § 301.7701-3] The regime is known as "check-the-box" because an entity's owners can merely check a box on federal Form 8832 to determine an entity's classification. If Form 8832 is not filed, default classification rules determine the entity's classification. For example, for an LLC that is organized in the United States and has two or more members, the default classification is partnership. The default classification for a single-member limited liability company (SMLLC) is branch if the single member is a corporation, and sole proprietorship if the single member is an individual. In other words, the separate legal existence of an SMLLC is disregarded for federal income tax purposes. In the case of both multi-member LLCs and SMLLCs, the members have the option of electing to have the LLC classified as a regular corporation for federal tax purposes.

Different default classification rules apply to an LLC organized in a foreign country. If the foreign LLC has two or more owners and at least one owner does not have limited liability, the foreign LLC is classified as a partnership. If the foreign LLC has only one owner and that member does not have limited liability, the entity is treated as a disregarded entity. If all the members have limited liability, the foreign LLC is classified as a corporation. Like the owners of a domestic LLC, however, the owners of a foreign LLC have the option of electing a different classification than that prescribed by the default rule, as long as the foreign entity is not on the Treasury Department's list of "per se" corporations. [Treas. Reg. § 301.7701-3]

State Conformity to Federal Flow-Through Treatment

Virtually all of the states conform to the federal approach of allowing an LLC to be treated as a partnership or a disregarded entity. As discussed below, however, a number of states that conform to the federal classification of an LLC as a flow-through entity nevertheless impose an entity-level tax on LLCs.

When structuring new operations, a major advantage of using the LLC form is that an SMLLC that is treated as a disregarded entity can provide results similar to those provided by a combined or consolidated return in a separate company return state. In other words, the disregarded entity's start-up losses can be used to offset the profits of the corporate parent. If the new operations are structured as a subsidiary corporation, the losses cannot be used by the corporate parent in separate company return states, but instead have to be carried forward and offset against the future profits, if any, of the subsidiary.

States That Impose Entity-Level Taxes on LLCs

Although virtually all states conform to the federal classification of an LLC as a flow-through entity, a number of states impose special entity-level taxes on LLCs. Examples include, but are not limited to, the following:

Alabama. Alabama imposes a business privilege tax on LLCs. The tax is based on Alabama net worth. The tax is a minimum of $100 and a maximum of $15,000.

California. California imposes an annual tax of $800 on any LLC doing business in California. An LLC must also pay a fee based on its total gross receipts attributable to California. The maximum fee is $11,790, and applies if the LLC's total gross receipts are $5 million or more. The fee applies even if the LLC is classified as a disregarded entity or partnership for federal income tax purposes.

Prior to 2007, the LLC fee was based on an LLC's gross receipts without apportionment. In both *Northwest Energetic Services, LLC v. Franchise Tax Board* [No. A114805 (Cal. Ct. of App., Jan. 31, 2008)], and *Ventas Finance I, LLC v. Franchise Tax Board* [No. A116277 (Cal. Ct. of App., Aug. 11, 2008); *cert. denied*, U.S. No. 08-1022, Apr. 6, 2009], state appellate courts ruled that basing the fee on an LLC's total gross receipts without apportionment is contrary to the Commerce Clause's fair apportionment requirement, and therefore the fee was an unconstitutional tax. California Franchise Tax Board Notice 2009-4 [May 22, 2009] provides guidance regarding the processing of refund claims.

District of Columbia. The District of Columbia imposes a 9.975 percent income tax on unincorporated businesses, including LLCs. The tax does not apply to a professional firm in which more than 80 percent of the gross income is derived from personal services and capital is not a material income-producing factor, or a single member LLC owned by an entity subject to tax in the District.

Illinois. Illinois imposes a 1.5 percent income tax (referred to as the personal property replacement tax) on LLCs classified as partnerships.

Kansas. Prior to 2011, Kansas imposed a franchise tax on LLCs. The tax base is net worth (stockholders' equity), and the tax rate is $0.03125 per $1,000 of net worth in 2010, with a maximum tax of $20,000. The tax is repealed for tax years beginning after December 31, 2010.

Kentucky. LLCs are subject to a limited liability entity tax equal to the lesser of 0.095 percent of Kentucky gross receipts or 0.75 percent of Kentucky gross profits. The tax does not apply to LLCs with gross receipts or gross profits of $3 million or less and is reduced for LLCs with gross receipts or gross profits over $3 million but less than $6 million.

Michigan. From 2008 to 2011, Michigan subjected LLCs to a 4.95 percent business income tax and 0.80 percent modified gross receipts tax. Effective January 1, 2012, Michigan replaced its business income and modified gross receipt taxes with a 6 percent corporate income tax. LLCs are not subject to the corporate income tax. [H.B. 4361 and 4362, May 25, 2011]

New Hampshire. New Hampshire subjects LLCs classified as partnerships to an 8.5 percent business profits tax and a 0.75 percent business enterprise tax. A credit against the business profits tax is allowed for any business enterprise tax paid.

New Jersey. An LLC that is treated as a partnership and has a nonresident member must pay a 6.37 percent tax on a nonresident noncorporate member's share of LLC income apportioned to New Jersey, and a 9 percent tax on a nonresident corporate member's share of LLC income apportioned to New Jersey. If the nonresident member files a New Jersey return, it may claim a credit for its share of the tax paid by the LLC.

Ohio. Ohio imposes a 0.26 percent commercial activity tax (CAT) on the annual gross receipts of an LLC. Examples of taxable gross receipts include sales of property delivered to locations within Ohio, fees for services where the purchaser receives the benefit in Ohio, and rents from property used in Ohio.

In addition, an LLC with a qualifying individual investor (i.e., a nonresident for whom the LLC does not file an Ohio composite nonresident return) is subject to a 5 percent pass-through entity tax. The tax is imposed on the qualifying investor's distributive share of the LLC's taxable income apportioned to Ohio, and the investor can claim a credit for its share of the tax paid by the LLC.

Pennsylvania. An LLC is subject to a capital stock tax based on the LLC's capital stock value, as determined by a statutory formula. The capital stock tax rate is 0.289 percent in 2011. The tax is scheduled to be repealed in 2014.

Tennessee. Tennessee imposes a 6.5 percent income tax and a 0.25 percent net worth tax on LLCs.

Texas. Texas subjects LLCs to its margin tax. The tax base equals the lowest of three amounts: (1) total revenue minus cost of goods sold, (2) total revenue minus compensation, or (3) 70 percent of total revenue. The tax rate is 0.5 percent for LLCs primarily engaged in retail or wholesale trade, and 1 percent for all other LLCs.

Washington. Washington subjects LLCs to its business and occupation (B&O) tax, which is a type of gross receipts tax. The B&O tax rate varies with the type of business activity, and generally is between 0.471 percent and 1.5 percent.

West Virginia. West Virginia imposes a business franchise tax on LLCs classified as partnerships. For tax years beginning in 2011, the tax is 0.34 percent of the partners' capital accounts. The tax is scheduled to be repealed in 2015.

In addition, Minnesota imposes an entity-level fee (maximum of $5,000), Wisconsin imposes an entity-level tax (maximum of $9,800), and other states impose either entity-level or member-level flat rate annual taxes or filing fees.

State Taxes Other Than Income Taxes

Treating an LLC as a disregarded entity for income tax purposes does not necessarily relieve the LLC from liability as a separate legal entity for other tax purposes, such as registration fees, sales and use taxes, employment taxes, and property taxes. Such taxes generally are imposed on each separate legal entity, and an LLC is a legal entity separate from its members, even if the LLC's existence is disregarded for income tax purposes. For example, a state may require an SMLLC and its corporate owner to file separate sales and use tax reports, even though for income tax purposes the SMLLC is viewed as a branch of the corporate parent. In a similar fashion, although intercompany transactions between a disregarded entity and its owner are ignored for income tax purposes, such transactions could create a sales and use tax or real estate transfer tax liability. The payroll tax consequences of operating a disregarded entity must also be analyzed on a state-by-state basis.

Nexus Issue

A state has jurisdiction to tax a corporation organized in another state only if the out-of-state corporation's contacts with the taxing state are sufficient to create nexus. The types of contacts that create nexus are determined by U.S. constitutional law, Public Law 86-272, and the applicable state statutes. As discussed in the previous section, states generally take the position that an ownership interest in a partnership doing business in the state is sufficient to create constitutional nexus for an out-of-state corporation. In asserting nexus, the states rely on nexus theories developed primarily for general partnerships. For example, under the aggregate theory of partnership, the partners are viewed as direct owners of fractional interests in the partnership's assets. Therefore, the physical presence of any partnership assets within a state is imputed to the partners. Based on these nexus theories, states generally take the position that they have jurisdiction to tax an out-of-state corporate member of an LLC that is doing business in the state, even if the member has no other contacts with the state.

For example, in Directive No. CD-02-1 [May 31, 2002], the North Carolina Department of Revenue ruled that a corporate member of an LLC doing business in North Carolina has nexus with the state if the LLC is treated as a partnership or a disregarded entity for federal income tax purposes.

Likewise, in FTB Legal Ruling 2011-01 [Cal. Franch. Tax Bd., Jan. 11, 2011], the California Franchise Tax Board ruled that a corporate owner of a disregarded entity that is doing business in California has nexus in the state even if that corporation has no activities in the state other than those of its disregarded entity. The activities of an LLC that is a disregarded entity are treated in the same manner as the activities of a branch or division of the corporate owner. Thus, if the LLC is doing business in California, those activities create nexus for the corporate owner.

Members Who Are Individuals

If an LLC is classified as a flow-through entity, the operative state income tax for members who are individuals is the state individual income tax; however, not all states have an individual income tax. Alaska, Florida, Nevada, South Dakota, Texas, Washington, and Wyoming do not impose an individual income tax. In addition, New Hampshire and Tennessee tax only selected types of income, not including salaries and wages. The state in which a member resides generally taxes the entire amount of a resident member's distributive share of LLC income, regardless of where the income was earned. In contrast, states in which the member does not reside tax a nonresident member's distributive share of LLC income only if the LLC has nexus in the state, and then only to the extent the nonresident member's distributive share of income is attributable to sources within the state. If a portion of a member's distributive share of income is subject to tax in two states (one by virtue of the member's residence and the other by virtue of the source of the LLC's income), the state of residence usually allows the member to claim a credit for income taxes paid to the other state as a means of mitigating double taxation. Some states also allow a credit for income taxes imposed directly on the LLC.

Composite Returns and Withholding Requirements

The requirement that nonresident members file returns and pay taxes in every state in which an LLC that is treated as a partnership has nexus can create a significant compliance burden for members of an LLC that has nexus in numerous states. One method of enhancing compliance is to require or permit an LLC to file a composite return on behalf of the nonresident members. Another technique for promoting compliance on the part of nonresident members is to require the LLC to withhold and remit tax from distributions to nonresident members or from the nonresident members' distributive shares of income. (For further details regarding composite returns and withholding requirements, see the section entitled Partnerships in this part.)

State-by-State Summary

For ease of presentation, the following chart has been divided into three parts, as follows:

- Part 1: Conformity to Federal Check-the-Box Regulations/Composite Returns
- Part 2: Entity-Level Taxes and Withholding: Multi-Member LLCs
- Part 3: Entity-Level Taxes and Withholding: Single-Member LLCs

Limited Liability Companies (Part 1)

Conformity to Federal Check-the-Box Regulations/Composite Returns

Legend:

SAF	Same as applicable federal rules
NA	Not applicable
NR	Not reported

	Does State Conform to the Federal Classification of:		In the Case of an LLC That Is Treated as a Partnership, Does State Permit Composite Returns for:	
	Single Member LLCs	*Two or More Member LLCs*	*Members Who Are Individuals?*	*Corporate Members?*
Alabama	Yes	Yes	No	No
Alaska	Yes	Yes	No	No
Arizona	Yes	Yes	Yes, Form 140NR	
Arkansas	Yes	Yes	Yes, Form AR-1000CR	No
California	Yes, exceptions: SMLLCs which are per se corporations for federal purposes under some provisions of Treas. Reg. § 301.7701-2(b) are not per se corporations for California purposes	Yes	Yes, (group return) Form FTB 540NR, see R&TC § 18535 and FTB Publication 1067	No
	California has regulations similar to federal regulations. See Cal. Code Reg. Title 18 §§ 23038-1 to -3.			
Colorado	Yes	Yes	Yes, Form 106, Part II	No
Connecticut	Yes	Yes	Yes, Forms CT-1065/CT-1120SI	No
Delaware	Yes	Yes	Yes, Form 200C	
District of Columbia	Yes	Yes	No	No
Florida	Yes	Yes	No	No
Georgia	Yes	Yes	Yes, Form IT-CR	Yes, Form IT-CR
Hawaii	Yes	Yes	Yes, Form N-15	

Limited Liability Companies (Part 1)

Conformity to Federal Check-the-Box Regulations/Composite Returns

Legend:

SAF	**Same as applicable federal rules**
NA	**Not applicable**
NR	**Not reported**

	Does State Conform to the Federal Classification of:		*In the Case of an LLC That Is Treated as a Partnership, Does State Permit Composite Returns for:*	
	Single Member LLCs	*Two or More Member LLCs*	*Members Who Are Individuals?*	*Corporate Members?*
Idaho	Yes	Yes	Yes, Idaho Form 65	
Illinois	Yes	Yes	Yes, Form 1023-C	
Indiana	Yes	Yes	Yes	
Iowa	Yes	Yes	Yes, Form IA 1040C	
Kansas	Yes	Yes	Yes, Form K-40C & D-40	No
Kentucky	Yes	Yes	Yes, 740NP-WH	No
Louisiana	Yes	Yes	Yes, Form IT-540B for nonresidents	No
Maine	Yes	Yes	Yes, nonresident individuals, Form 1040 ME	No
Maryland	Yes	Yes	Yes, Form 505	
Massachusetts	Yes	Yes	Yes	No
Michigan (Business Tax)	Policy under review	Yes	Yes, Form MI-807	No
Note. The CIT takes effect 01/01/12, and replaces the Michigan Business Tax (MBT) for most taxpayers. However, businesses that have been approved to receive, have received, or have been assigned certain certified credits may elect to file a return and pay the tax imposed by the MBT in lieu of the CIT until the certified credits are exhausted or extinguished.				
Minnesota	Yes	Yes	Yes, Form M3	No
Mississippi	Yes	Yes	Yes, Form 86-106	
Missouri	Yes	Yes	Yes, MO 1040	No

Limited Liability Companies (Part 1)

Conformity to Federal Check-the-Box Regulations/Composite Returns

Legend:

SAF	**Same as applicable federal rules**
NA	**Not applicable**
NR	**Not reported**

	Does State Conform to the Federal Classification of:		*In the Case of an LLC That Is Treated as a Partnership, Does State Permit Composite Returns for:*	
	Single Member LLCs	*Two or More Member LLCs*	*Members Who Are Individuals?*	*Corporate Members?*
Montana	Yes	Yes	Yes, Schedule on PR-1	Yes, Schedule on PR-1
Nebraska	Yes	Yes		
Nevada	Nevada does not impose a corporate income tax			
New Hampshire	No	No	No	No
New Jersey	Yes	Yes	Yes, Form NJ-1080C	
New Mexico	Yes	Yes	Yes, Form PTE	Yes, Form PTE
New York	Yes	Yes		
North Carolina	Yes	Yes		
North Dakota	Yes	Yes	Yes, Form ND-1 for nonresident members only	
Ohio	Ohio does not impose a corporate income tax			
Note. Effective 1/1/2010, the Ohio Franchise Tax was fully phased out and business will be taxed on gross receipts through the Commercial Activity Tax. Details about that tax can be found at: http//tax.ohio.gov/divisions/commercial_activities/index.stm				
Oklahoma	Yes	Yes	Yes, Form 514	Yes
	Oklahoma generally conforms to IRS accounting periods and methods. See 68 O.S. 2353 and 2360.			
Oregon	Yes	Yes	Yes, Form 40MNR	Yes, Form OC
Pennsylvania	Yes	Yes	Yes, Form PA 40NRC	
Rhode Island	Yes	Yes	Yes, Form 1040 C	No

Limited Liability Companies (Part 1)

Conformity to Federal Check-the-Box Regulations/Composite Returns

Legend:

SAF **Same as applicable federal rules**
NA **Not applicable**
NR **Not reported**

	Does State Conform to the Federal Classification of:		*In the Case of an LLC That Is Treated as a Partnership, Does State Permit Composite Returns for:*	
	Single Member LLCs	*Two or More Member LLCs*	*Members Who Are Individuals?*	*Corporate Members?*
South Carolina	Yes	Yes	Yes, 1-34 Form SC 1040C, 8,	No
South Dakota	South Dakota does not impose a corporate income tax			
Tennessee	Yes, but must be a corporate member	Yes		
Texas	No	No	NA	NA
Utah	Yes	Yes	Yes, Form TC-65, nonresident members only	
Vermont	Yes	Yes	Yes	Yes
Virginia	Yes	Yes	Form 764. Yes for non-resident members who are individuals-Form 765.	Form 764 with permission. Yes for nonresident members who are corporations-Form 765 with permission.
Washington	Washington does not impose a corporate income tax			
West Virginia	Yes	Yes		
Wisconsin	Yes	Yes	Yes, Form 1CNP	No
Wyoming	Wyoming does not impose a corporate income tax			

Limited Liability Companies (Part 2)

Entity-Level Taxes and Withholding: Multi-Member LLCs

Legend:

X	Indicates state imposes tax
NA	Not applicable
NR	Not reported

	Does State Impose Any of the Following Entity-Level Taxes on Multi-Member LLC That Is Classified as a Partnership for Tax Purposes?			
	Flat Dollar Amount Minimum Tax or Filing Fee	*Income-Based Tax*	*Franchise Tax Based on Net Worth or Capital*	*Withholding Taxes on Members*
Alabama			X	X
Alaska	Alaska does not impose any of the above taxes			
Arizona	Arizona does not impose any of the above taxes			
Arkansas			X, minimum $150	X

Limited Liability Companies (Part 2)

Entity-Level Taxes and Withholding: Multi-Member LLCs

Legend:

X	Indicates state imposes tax
NA	Not applicable
NR	Not reported

	Does State Impose Any of the Following Entity-Level Taxes on Multi-Member LLC That Is Classified as a Partnership for Tax Purposes?			
	Flat Dollar Amount Minimum Tax or Filing Fee	*Income-Based Tax*	*Franchise Tax Based on Net Worth or Capital*	*Withholding Taxes on Members*
California	X, annual tax in amount equal to minimum corporate franchise tax of $800 is imposed on LLC's organized, registered or doing business in California. (R&TC § 17941). Tax is due on the 15th day of the 4th month of the current taxable year.			X, LLC must pay tax for nonresident members that do not sign consent to file return, pay tax on distributive share of LLC income, and be subject to personal jurisdiction for collection of tax. (R&TC § 18633.5(e)(1)). The tax is imposed at the highest marginal rate on each non-consenting member's distributive share of LLC's California source income. An LLC may reduce the tax by amounts of tax withheld on members pursuant to withholding provisions applicable to partners. LLCs must withhold tax on distributions out of California source taxable income to domestic (U.S) partners. (R&TC § 18662). LLCs must withhold tax on California source distributive share of income of foreign (non-U.S.) partners. (R&TC § 18662)

Limited Liability Companies (Part 2)
Entity-Level Taxes and Withholding: Multi-Member LLCs

Legend:

X	Indicates state imposes tax
NA	Not applicable
NR	Not reported

	Does State Impose Any of the Following Entity-Level Taxes on Multi-Member LLC That Is Classified as a Partnership for Tax Purposes?			
	Flat Dollar Amount Minimum Tax or Filing Fee	*Income-Based Tax*	*Franchise Tax Based on Net Worth or Capital*	*Withholding Taxes on Members*
Note. Annual fee according to tiered fee schedule is imposed on LLCs organized, registered or doing business in California. (R&TC § 17942) If "total income", defined as gross income plus cost of goods sold that are paid or incurred in connection with a trade or business from all sources derived from or attributable to California is: less than $250,000, the fee is zero; at least $250,000, but less than $1,000,000, the fee is $2,500; at least $1,000,000, but less than $5,000,000, the fee is $6,000; $5,000,000 or more, the fee is $11,790. The fee must be estimated and paid by the 15th day of the 6th month of the LLCs current taxable year (R&TC § 17942(d)). A 10% penalty applies to the amount of underpayment of the estimated fee (R&TC § 17942(d).				
Colorado				X, nonresident individuals only
Connecticut	X, $250 Business Entity Tax			
Delaware	X, for fee schedule contact the Delaware Secretary of State, Corporate Division.			X
District of Columbia		X, 9.975%		X
Note. Personal Property Tax, Sales and Use Tax, Ball Park Fee.				
Florida				
Georgia				X
Hawaii	See www.state.hi.us/dcca			
Idaho		X, 8% corporate rate if paying the tax for members who are individuals with a filing requirement		
Illinois	Administered by the Secretary of State	X, 1.5%	Administered by the Secretary of State	

Limited Liability Companies (Part 2)

Entity-Level Taxes and Withholding: Multi-Member LLCs

Legend:

X	Indicates state imposes tax
NA	Not applicable
NR	Not reported

Does State Impose Any of the Following Entity-Level Taxes on Multi-Member LLC That Is Classified as a Partnership for Tax Purposes?

	Flat Dollar Amount Minimum Tax or Filing Fee	*Income-Based Tax*	*Franchise Tax Based on Net Worth or Capital*	*Withholding Taxes on Members*
Indiana				X
Iowa				
Kansas	X, $55, profits; $40, non-profits			X
Kentucky		X, Lesser of $.095/$100 KY gross receipts or $.75/$100 KY gross profits or $175 minimum.		X
Louisiana	Louisiana does not impose any of the above taxes.	Composite return required by entity for nonresident shareholders.		Composite return required by entity for nonresident shareholders.
Maine				X
Maryland				X
Massachusetts			X	
Michigan (Business Tax)		4.95% on taxable income	0.235% on financial institutions only	X
Note. The CIT takes effect 01/01/12, and replaces the Michigan Business Tax (MBT) for most taxpayers. However, businesses that have been approved to receive, have received, or have been assigned certain certified credits may elect to file a return and pay the tax imposed by the MBT in lieu of the CIT until the certified credits are exhausted or extinguished.				
Minnesota	X, minimum fee if elects partnership treatment			
Mississippi				
Missouri				X

Limited Liability Companies (Part 2)

Entity-Level Taxes and Withholding: Multi-Member LLCs

Legend:

X	Indicates state imposes tax
NA	Not applicable
NR	Not reported

Does State Impose Any of the Following Entity-Level Taxes on Multi-Member LLC That Is Classified as a Partnership for Tax Purposes?

	Flat Dollar Amount Minimum Tax or Filing Fee	*Income-Based Tax*	*Franchise Tax Based on Net Worth or Capital*	*Withholding Taxes on Members*
Montana				X
Nebraska				X
Nevada	Nevada does not impose a corporate income tax			
New Hampshire		X, 8.5%		
New Jersey	X, $50 annual filing fee (N.J.S.A. 42:2B-65a(b)). For years starting on or after 1/1/02, $150 for each owner if entity has more than 2 owners, N.J.S.A. 54A:8-6.	X, 6.37% on nonresident, noncorporate members' allocated (apportioned) share of entire net income plus 9% on same of nonresident corporate members, N.J.S.A. 54:10A-15.11		
New Mexico				
Note. Withholding tax on nonresidents				
New York	X, $25-$4,500 depending on New York source gross income			X, estimated tax for nonresidents only
North Carolina	X, $200 filing fee (N.C. Gen. Stat. § 57C-1-22(a)(25))			
North Dakota				X, non-residents only
Ohio	Ohio does not impose a corporate income tax			

Note. Effective 1/1/2010, the Ohio Franchise Tax was fully phased out and business will be taxed on gross receipts through the Commercial Activity Tax. Details about that tax can be found at: http//tax.ohio.gov/divisions/commercial_activities/index.stm

Limited Liability Companies (Part 2)

Entity-Level Taxes and Withholding: Multi-Member LLCs

Legend:

X	Indicates state imposes tax
NA	Not applicable
NR	Not reported

Does State Impose Any of the Following Entity-Level Taxes on Multi-Member LLC That Is Classified as a Partnership for Tax Purposes?

	Flat Dollar Amount Minimum Tax or Filing Fee	*Income-Based Tax*	*Franchise Tax Based on Net Worth or Capital*	*Withholding Taxes on Members*
Oklahoma				X, distributions to non-resident members after 8/29/03
Oregon	Yes, Flat-dollar minimum tax or filing fee; $150 if transacting business in Oregon and required to file a partnership return.			
Pennsylvania			X, 6.99 mills for 2004	X
Rhode Island	Yes, fee equal to Rhode Island minimum corporate fee.			
South Carolina				X, 5% withholding taxable income of nonresidents members
South Dakota	South Dakota does not impose a corporate income tax.			
Tennessee		X, excise tax 6.5%	X, .25%	
Texas		X, .5% for qualifying entities in retail or wholesale trade and 1% for all others.		
Utah		Any partnership may choose to file a composite return on behalf of nonresident individuals.		X
Vermont	X, $250			X
Virginia				X, effective for tax years beginning 01/1/08 and after
Washington	Washington does not impose a corporate income tax			

Limited Liability Companies (Part 2)
Entity-Level Taxes and Withholding: Multi-Member LLCs

Legend:

X	Indicates state imposes tax
NA	Not applicable
NR	Not reported

	Does State Impose Any of the Following Entity-Level Taxes on Multi-Member LLC That Is Classified as a Partnership for Tax Purposes?			
	Flat Dollar Amount Minimum Tax or Filing Fee	*Income-Based Tax*	*Franchise Tax Based on Net Worth or Capital*	*Withholding Taxes on Members*
West Virginia			0.7% or $50, whichever is greater	
Wisconsin	X, various amounts, but these are imposed by the Wisconsin Dept. of Financial Institutions.	X, Economic Development Surcharge of $25-$9800 may apply.		X, nonresident members.
Wyoming	Wyoming does not impose a corporate income tax			

Limited Liability Companies (Part 3)

Entity-Level Taxes and Withholding: Single-Member LLCs

Legend:

X	Indicates state imposes tax
NA	Not applicable
NR	Not reported

	Does State Impose Any of the Following Entity-Level Taxes on Single-Member LLC That Is Classified as a Disregarded Entity for Tax Purposes?			
	Flat Dollar Amount Minimum Tax or Filing Fee	*Income-Based Tax*	*Franchise Tax Based on Net Worth or Capital Stock*	*Withholding Taxes on Members*
Alabama			X, Business Privilege Tax	X
Alaska	Alaska does not impose any of the above taxes.			
Arizona	Arizona does not impose any of the above taxes.			
Arkansas			X, minimum $150	X
California	X, annual tax in amount equal to minimum corporate franchise tax of $800 is imposed on LLC's organized, registered or doing business in California. (R&TC § 17941)			X, LLC must pay tax of non-resident owner that does not sign consent to California tax jurisdiction. (R&TC § 18633.5(i)
Note. Annual fee according to tiered fee schedule is imposed on LLCs organized, registered or doing business in California. (R&TC § 17942) If "total income", defined as gross income plus cost of goods sold that are paid or incurred in connection with trade or business from all sources derived from or attributable to California is: less than $250,000, the fee is zero; at least $250,000, but less than $1,000,000, the fee is $2,500; at least $1,000,000, but less than $5,000,000, the fee is $6,000; $5,000,000 or more, the fee is $11,790. The fee must be estimated and paid by 15th day of the 6th month of the LLC's current taxable year (R&TC § 17942(d)). A 10% penalty applies to the amount of underpayment of the estimated fee (R&TC § 17942(d)).				
Colorado				X, nonresident individuals only
Connecticut	X, $250			
Delaware	X, for fee schedule contact the Delaware Secretary of State, Corporate Division.			

Limited Liability Companies (Part 3)

Entity-Level Taxes and Withholding: Single-Member LLCs

Legend:

X	Indicates state imposes tax
NA	Not applicable
NR	Not reported

	Does State Impose Any of the Following Entity-Level Taxes on Single-Member LLC That Is Classified as a Disregarded Entity for Tax Purposes?			
	Flat Dollar Amount Minimum Tax or Filing Fee	*Income-Based Tax*	*Franchise Tax Based on Net Worth or Capital Stock*	*Withholding Taxes on Members*
District of Columbia				X
Note. Single Member Limited Liability Companies must pay other taxes, Sales/Use and Personal Property Tax. Owner must pay income tax.				
Florida				
Georgia				
Hawaii	See www.state.hi.us/dcca/breg-seu.			
Idaho		X, 7.6% corporate rate if paying the tax for members who are individuals with a filing requirement		
Illinois	Administered by Secretary of State		Administered by Secretary of State	
Indiana		X		
Iowa				
Kansas	X, $55, profits; $40, non-profits	X, normal rate 4%, 3.35% surtax on amounts over $50,000		X
Kentucky		X, Lesser of $.095/$100 Kentucky gross receipts or $.75/$100 Kentucky gross profits or $175 minimum.		X

Limited Liability Companies (Part 3)

Entity-Level Taxes and Withholding: Single-Member LLCs

Legend:

X	Indicates state imposes tax
NA	Not applicable
NR	Not reported

	Does State Impose Any of the Following Entity-Level Taxes on Single-Member LLC That Is Classified as a Disregarded Entity for Tax Purposes?			
	Flat Dollar Amount Minimum Tax or Filing Fee	*Income-Based Tax*	*Franchise Tax Based on Net Worth or Capital Stock*	*Withholding Taxes on Members*
Louisiana	Louisiana does not impose any of the above taxes.	Composite return required by entity for nonresident shareholders		Composite return required by entity for nonresident shareholders
Maine				X
Maryland				
Massachusetts				
Michigan (Business Tax)		4.95% on taxable income	0.235% on financial institutions only	X
Note. The CIT takes effect 01/01/12, and replaces the Michigan Business Tax (MBT) for most taxpayers. However, businesses that have been approved to receive, have received, or have been assigned certain certified credits may elect to file a return and pay the tax imposed by the MBT in lieu of the CIT until the certified credits are exhausted or extinguished.				
Note. Policy under review				
Minnesota				
Mississippi				
Missouri				X
Montana				X
Nebraska				
Nevada	Nevada does not impose a corporate income tax.			

Limited Liability Companies (Part 3)

Entity-Level Taxes and Withholding: Single-Member LLCs

Legend:

X	Indicates state imposes tax
NA	Not applicable
NR	Not reported

Does State Impose Any of the Following Entity-Level Taxes on Single-Member LLC That Is Classified as a Disregarded Entity for Tax Purposes?

	Flat Dollar Amount Minimum Tax or Filing Fee	*Income-Based Tax*	*Franchise Tax Based on Net Worth or Capital Stock*	*Withholding Taxes on Members*
New Hampshire		X, 8.5%		
New Jersey	X, $50, N.J.S.A. 42:2B-65a.(b)			
New Mexico		X		X, if S corporation or partnership owner
New York	X, $25			
North Carolina	X, $200 filing fee (N.C. Gen. Stat. § 57C-1-22(a)(25))			
North Dakota				
Ohio	Ohio does not impose a corporate income tax			
Note. Effective 1/1/2010, the Ohio Franchise Tax was fully phased out and business will be taxed on gross receipts through the Commercial Activity Tax. Details about that tax can be found at: http//tax.ohio.gov/divisions/commercial_activities/index.stm				
Oklahoma				X, distributions to non-resident members after 8/29/03
Oregon	$20 paid to Corporate Division, not a tax			
Pennsylvania			X, 6.99 mills for 2004	
Rhode Island	X, fee equal to Rhode Island minimum corporate fee.	X, 9% if member is a corporation.		X
South Carolina				
South Dakota	South Dakota does not impose a corporate income tax			

Limited Liability Companies (Part 3)

Entity-Level Taxes and Withholding: Single-Member LLCs

Legend:

X	Indicates state imposes tax
NA	Not applicable
NR	Not reported

	Does State Impose Any of the Following Entity-Level Taxes on Single-Member LLC That Is Classified as a Disregarded Entity for Tax Purposes?			
	Flat Dollar Amount Minimum Tax or Filing Fee	*Income-Based Tax*	*Franchise Tax Based on Net Worth or Capital Stock*	*Withholding Taxes on Members*
Tennessee		X, excise tax 6.5%	X, .25%	
Texas		X, 4.5% of net taxable earned surplus	X, .25% of net taxable capital	
Utah				
Vermont				
Virginia				
Washington	Washington does not impose a corporate income tax			
West Virginia				
Wisconsin	X, $130, imposed by the WI Dept. of Financial Institutions.	X, Economic Development Surcharge between $25 to $9800 may apply,		X, nonresident members only
Wyoming	Wyoming does not impose a corporate income tax			

Fiscal-Year Elections: Partnerships, S Corporations, and Personal Service Corporations

Federal Tax Treatment

Personal Service Corporations. A regular corporation's taxable income is subject to tax at graduated rates; that is, the first $50,000 of income is taxed at 15 percent, the next $25,000 of income is taxed at 25 percent, and so on. A personal service corporation (PSC) is denied the benefit of these low tax brackets. Instead, a 35 percent flat tax is imposed on all of the PSC's taxable income. Code Section 448 defines a PSC is as a corporation that meets the following two tests:

1. Substantially all of its activities involve performing services in accounting, actuarial science, architecture, consulting, engineering, health, law, or the performing arts.
2. Substantially all of its stock (by value) is held directly or indirectly by employees performing the services, retired employees who performed the services in the past, their estates, or persons who hold stock by reason of the death of an employee or retired employee within the past two years.

From a tax planning perspective, this rule encourages shareholder-employees to withdraw all of the earnings of a PSC as deductible salary payments.

Fiscal-Year Restrictions on Pass-Through Entities. A partnership generally must adopt the same tax year as one or more partners that own more than 50 percent of the partnership. [IRC § 706] For example, if all of the partners of a partnership are calendar-year individuals, the partnership also must file its tax returns on a calendar-year basis. A similar rule applies to S corporations and PSCs. [IRC § 1378] The purpose of these restrictions is to prevent owners of a pass-through entity from deferring income by choosing a different tax year for the partnership, S corporation, or PSC. For example, calendar-year shareholders of an S corporation might choose a January 31 tax year for the S corporation, thereby deferring the taxation of the S corporation's income because that income is deemed to pass through to the shareholders on the last day of the S corporation's tax year. In a similar fashion, a PSC owned by calendar-year individuals might choose a January 31 year-end, and then wait each fiscal year until January to distribute a significant portion of the income earned from February to December of the prior year, thereby achieving a deferral of income at the shareholder level.

An exception applies if a partnership, S corporation, or PSC can establish to the satisfaction of the IRS that there is a substantial business purpose for adopting a different tax year. [Treas. Reg. § 1.441-1(c)(2)] The primary method for establishing a substantial business purpose is to satisfy a mechanical "natural business year" test. A natural business year is one in which at least 25 percent of the taxpayer's gross receipts are received in the last two months of the 12-month period. [Rev. Proc 2002-38]

Section 444 Elections. Many pass-through entities are unable to meet the IRS's strict business purpose test. This led Congress to create the Code Section 444 election, which allows partnerships, S corporations, and PSCs to elect a tax year that results in a tax deferral of three months or less. The deferral period signifies the number of months from the beginning of the entity's fiscal year to December 31. Therefore, an S corporation or PSC with calendar-year shareholders may elect a September 30, October 31, or November 30 year-end. A Section 444 election is made on federal Form 8716. A partnership or S corporation making a Section 444 election must reimburse the IRS for the benefit of the tax deferral obtained when a fiscal year is used. Under Code Section 7519, the required payment is the product of the maximum tax rate for individuals plus 1 percent times the previous year's taxable income times a deferral ratio. The deferral ratio equals the number of months in the deferral period divided by the number of months in the tax year.

PSCs that elect a fiscal year are not required to reimburse the IRS for the benefit of the tax deferral, but instead must make minimum distributions to shareholders during the deferral period. [IRC § 280H] These minimum distributions are designed to prevent a distribution pattern that achieves a deferral of income at the shareholder level. Roughly speaking, these rules require that deductible payments made to shareholder-employees during the deferral period be made at a rate that is no lower than the rate at which they were made during the previous fiscal year.

State-by-State Summary

The following chart indicates whether a state requires a partnership or S corporation making a Section 444 election to make special tax payments similar to those mandated by Section 7519 and whether a state's graduated rate schedule (if applicable) is denied to PSCs.

Fiscal-Year Elections: Partnerships, S Corporations, and Personal Service Corporations

Legend:

SAF	Same as applicable federal rules
FR	Flat income tax rate used; graduated rates are not applicable
NA	Not applicable
NR	No response

	If It Does Not Use Required Tax Year, Must Partnerships and S Corporations Make Special State-Required Payments (Similar to IRC § 7519)?	*Are Graduated Rates Denied to PSCs?*
Alabama	No	NA, state has flat rate corporate income tax
Alaska	NR	NR
Arizona	No	FR
Arkansas	No	No
California	No	NA, state has flat-rate corporate income tax
Colorado	No	NA
Connecticut	No	NA
Delaware	NR	Yes
District of Columbia	Yes	No, state has flat-rate corporate income tax
Florida	No	Yes
Georgia	No	NA, state has flat-rate corporate income tax
Hawaii	No	No
Idaho	No	FR
Illinois	No	FR
Indiana	No	FR
Iowa	No	No
Kansas	No	No
Kentucky	No	No

Fiscal-Year Elections: Partnerships, S Corporations, and Personal Service Corporations

Legend:

SAF	Same as applicable federal rules
FR	Flat income tax rate used; graduated rates are not applicable
NA	Not applicable
NR	No response

	If It Does Not Use Required Tax Year, Must Partnerships and S Corporations Make Special State-Required Payments (Similar to IRC § 7519)?	*Are Graduated Rates Denied to PSCs?*
Louisiana	Yes	No
Maine	No	No
Maryland	No	FR
Massachusetts	No	Yes
Michigan (Business Tax)	NA	NA, state has flat rate corporate income tax.
Note. The CIT takes effect 01/01/12, and replaces the Michigan Business Tax (MBT) for most taxpayers. However, businesses that have been approved to receive, have received, or have been assigned certain certified credits may elect to file a return and pay the tax imposed by the MBT in lieu of the CIT until the certified credits are exhausted or extinguished.		
Minnesota	No	FR
Mississippi	No	No
Missouri	No	FR
Montana	NR	NR
Nebraska	No	No
Nevada	Nevada does not impose a corporate income tax	
New Hampshire	NR	NA, state has flat-rate corporate income tax
New Jersey	No	No
New Mexico	No	No
New York	No	No
North Carolina	No	No

Fiscal-Year Elections: Partnerships, S Corporations, and Personal Service Corporations

Legend:

SAF	Same as applicable federal rules
FR	Flat income tax rate used; graduated rates are not applicable
NA	Not applicable
NR	No response

	If It Does Not Use Required Tax Year, Must Partnerships and S Corporations Make Special State-Required Payments (Similar to IRC § 7519)?	*Are Graduated Rates Denied to PSCs?*
North Dakota	No	No
Ohio	Ohio does not impose a corporate income tax	
Note. Effective 1/1/2010, the Ohio Franchise Tax was fully phased out and business will be taxed on gross receipts through the Commercial Activity Tax. Details about that tax can be found at: http//tax.ohio.gov/divisions/commercial_activities/index.stm		
Oklahoma	No	Yes
Oregon	No	NA, only 6.6% rate
Pennsylvania	No	NA
Rhode Island	NR	No
South Carolina	No	NA
South Dakota	South Dakota does not impose a corporate income tax	
Tennessee	No	NA
Texas	No	NA, state has flat-rate corporate income tax
Utah	No	NA
Vermont	No	No
Virginia	No	NA, FR for all corporations
Washington	Washington does not impose a corporate income tax	
West Virginia	NR	NR
Wisconsin	No	No, state has a flat-rate corporate income tax

Fiscal-Year Elections: Partnerships, S Corporations, and Personal Service Corporations

Legend:

SAF	Same as applicable federal rules
FR	Flat income tax rate used; graduated rates are not applicable
NA	Not applicable
NR	No response

	If It Does Not Use Required Tax Year, Must Partnerships and S Corporations Make Special State-Required Payments (Similar to IRC § 7519)?	*Are Graduated Rates Denied to PSCs?*
Wyoming	Wyoming does not impose a corporate income tax	

Part 7. FOREIGN OPERATIONS

Income From Foreign Subsidiaries

Federal Tax Treatment

Domestic Consolidation and Deferral. The globalization of business has made state taxation of a U.S. multinational corporation's foreign earnings an important issue. Federal tax law plays an important role in state taxation of a domestic corporation's foreign earnings because states generally use federal taxable income (federal Form 1120, line 28 or 30) as the starting point for computing state taxable income. The federal government taxes the worldwide income of a domestic corporation [IRC § 61], and allows a credit for the foreign income taxes imposed on foreign-source income. [IRC § 901] On the other hand, the federal government generally does not tax the undistributed foreign-source income of a foreign corporation, even if the foreign corporation is a wholly-owned subsidiary of a domestic corporation. [IRC §§ 881 and 882] Moreover, foreign corporations are not includible in a federal consolidated income tax return. [IRC § 1504] Consequently, if a domestic corporation operates abroad through foreign subsidiaries, the foreign earnings of those foreign corporations are generally not subject to U.S. taxation until the earnings are repatriated to the domestic parent through a dividend distribution. This policy, which is known as deferral, is designed to allow U.S. companies to compete in foreign markets on a tax parity with foreign competitors.

Dividends and Section 78 Gross-up Income. A domestic parent corporation's receipt of a dividend distribution from a foreign subsidiary corporation generally represents the U.S. federal government's first opportunity to tax the underlying foreign earnings. Therefore, the domestic corporation generally includes any foreign dividends in its federal taxable income [IRC § 61], and is not allowed an offsetting dividends-received deduction. [IRC § 243]A dividends-received deduction may be available, however, if a 10-percent-or-more-owned foreign corporation distributes a dividend out of earnings that are attributable to income derived from the conduct of a U.S. trade or business or dividends received from an 80-percent-or-more-owned domestic corporation. [IRC § 245]

To mitigate double taxation of a foreign subsidiary's earnings, upon receiving a dividend from a foreign subsidiary, a domestic parent corporation may claim a deemed paid foreign tax credit for the foreign income taxes that a 10 percent-or-more-owned foreign corporation pays on its earnings. [IRC § 902] Because the amount of dividend income recognized by a domestic parent corporation is net of any foreign income taxes paid by a foreign subsidiary, the domestic corporation is implicitly allowed a deduction for those foreign taxes. To prevent a double tax benefit, the domestic corporation must gross up its dividend income by the amount of the deemed paid foreign taxes, which offsets the implicit deduction. [IRC § 78] The domestic corporation reports its gross-up income as Dividends on Line 4 of Form 1120 (see Schedule C, Line 15).

Subpart F Inclusions. A policy of unrestricted deferral would create an opportunity to avoid U.S. taxes on portable income, such as passive investment income or inventory trading profits, that is easily shifted to a foreign corporation located in a tax haven country. In 1962, Congress attempted to close this loophole by enacting Subpart F (Code Secs. 951-965), which denies deferral to certain types of tainted income earned through a foreign corporation. Code Section 951 requires a U.S. shareholder of a controlled foreign corporation (CFC) to recognize a Subpart F inclusion equal to a pro rata share of the CFC's Subpart F income. Examples of Subpart F income include foreign personal holding company income and foreign base company sales income. Foreign personal holding company income includes dividends, interest, rents, and royalties, whereas foreign base company sales income includes income from the sale of goods that the CFC buys from or sells to a related person and are neither manufactured nor sold for use in the CFC's country of incorporation. [IRC § 954] A foreign corporation is a CFC if U.S. shareholders own more than 50 percent of the stock of the foreign corporation, by vote or value. [IRC § 957] A U.S. shareholder must also recognize a Subpart F inclusion for its share of a CFC's investment of earnings in U.S. property under Section 956. A Subpart F inclusion is reported as dividends on Line 4 of Form 1120 (see Schedule C, Line 14).

State Tax Treatment—Worldwide Combined Reporting

Twenty-three states and the District of Columbia require taxpayer members of a unitary business group to compute their taxable income on a combined basis. These states include Alaska, Arizona, California, Colorado, Hawaii, Idaho, Illinois, Kansas, Maine, Massachusetts, Michigan, Minnesota, Montana, Nebraska, New Hampshire, New York, North Dakota, Oregon, Texas, Utah, Vermont, West Virginia, and Wisconsin. These states take one of two general approaches to dealing with unitary group members that are incorporated in a foreign country or conduct most of their business abroad:

1. *Worldwide combination*. The combined report includes all members of the unitary business group, regardless of the country in which the member is incorporated or the country in which the member conducts business.
2. *Water's-edge combination*. The combined report includes all members of the unitary business group, except for certain unitary group members that are incorporated in a foreign country or conduct most of their business abroad. A common approach is to exclude so-called 80/20 corporations. An 80/20 corporation is a corporation whose business activity outside the United States, as measured by some combination of apportionment factors, is 80 percent or more of the corporation's total business activity.

California, Idaho, Montana and North Dakota require a worldwide combination, but give taxpayers the option to elect a water's-edge combination. Massachusetts, Utah and West Virginia require a water's-edge combination, but give taxpayers the option to elect a worldwide combination. Alaska requires a water's-edge combination, except for oil and gas companies, which must use worldwide combined reporting. The other mandatory combined reporting states, such as Illinois, Michigan and Texas, require a water's-edge combination.

See the section entitled "Combined Unitary Reporting" in Part 4 for a comprehensive discussion of worldwide and water's-edge combined reporting.

State Tax Treatment—Dividends from Foreign Subsidiaries

Most states do not permit worldwide combined reporting, in which case the foreign income of a foreign subsidiary is not included in the U.S. parent corporation's state taxable income until those earnings are distributed as a dividend. Thus, consistent with the federal policy of deferral, a state's first opportunity to tax the foreign income of a foreign subsidiary is generally when those earnings are repatriated by the U.S. parent corporation as a dividend.

Inclusion in Apportionable Income. Assuming either the activities of the foreign corporation or the stock of the foreign corporation is a unitary part of the business conducted by the U.S. parent in the states in which the parent has nexus, the dividend is included in the parent's apportionable business income. [See *MeadWestvaco Corporation v. Illinois Department of Revenue* (553 U.S. 16, 2008), and *Allied-Signal, Inc. v. Director, Division of Taxation* (504 U.S. 768, 1992)] On the other hand, if the activities and the stock of the foreign corporation have nothing to do with the activities of the U.S. parent in the taxing state, then the dividend may be nonbusiness income that is allocable only to the U.S. parent's state of commercial domicile.

In *Mobil Oil Corp. v. Commissioner of Taxes* [445 U.S. 425 (1980)], the Supreme Court addressed the issue of whether dividends from foreign corporations are business or nonbusiness income. Mobil was a vertically integrated petroleum company that was commercially domiciled in New York. Mobil argued that Vermont could not constitutionally tax the dividends that Mobil received from its foreign subsidiaries, because the activities of the foreign subsidiaries were unrelated to Mobil's activities in Vermont, which were limited to marketing petroleum products. Stating that "the linchpin of apportionability in the field of state income taxation is the unitary business principle," the Supreme Court ruled that Vermont could tax an apportioned percentage of the dividends, because the foreign subsidiaries were part of the same integrated petroleum enterprise as the business operations conducted in Vermont. In other words, dividends received from unitary subsidiaries are business income. The Court also noted that if the business activities of the foreign subsidiaries had "nothing to do with the activities of the recipient in the taxing state, due process considerations might well preclude apportionability, because there would be no underlying unitary business."

Dividends-Received Deductions. In sharp contrast with federal law, which generally limits its dividends-received deduction to dividends received from domestic corporations, most states provide a deduction for dividends received from both domestic and foreign corporations. For example, consistent with how they treat domestic dividends, many states provide a 100 percent deduction for dividends received from an 80-percent-or-more-owned foreign corporation.

In *Kraft General Foods, Inc. v. Department of Revenue* [505 U.S. 71 (1992)], the Supreme Court ruled that an Iowa law that allowed taxpayers to claim a dividends-received deduction for dividends from domestic, but not foreign, subsidiary corporations was unconstitutional. During the years in question, Iowa conformed to the federal dividends-received deduction. As a consequence, Iowa did not tax dividends received from domestic corporations, but did tax dividends received from foreign corporations unless the dividends represented distributions of U.S. earnings. The Court ruled that the Iowa provision which taxed only dividends paid by foreign corporations out of their foreign earnings facially discriminated against foreign commerce, in violation of the Commerce Clause.

Since the *Kraft* decision, a number of state courts have also struck down dividends-received deduction provisions that favored dividends received from domestic corporations over dividends received from foreign corporations.

In *Dart Industries, Inc. v. Clark* [657 A.2d 1062 (R.I. Sup. Ct., 1995)], the Rhode Island Supreme Court ruled the Rhode Island provision that allowed a deduction for dividends from domestic but not foreign subsidiaries was discriminatory in violation of the Commerce Clause. Likewise, in *D.D.I Inc. v. North Dakota* [657 N.W.2d 228 (N.D. Sup. Ct., 2003)], the North Dakota Supreme Court declared unconstitutional a North Dakota statute that permitted a dividends-received deduction, but only to the extent the dividend payer's income was subject to North Dakota corporate income tax. In *Hutchinson Technology, Inc. v. Commissioner of Revenue* [698 N.W.2d 1 (Minn. Sup. Ct., 2005)], the Minnesota Supreme Court ruled that a state statute that excluded dividends paid by certain foreign sales corporations from the state's dividends-received deduction was discriminatory in violation of the Commerce Clause. In *Emerson Electric Co. v. Tracy* [735 N.E.2d 445 (Ohio Sup. Ct., 2000)], the Ohio Supreme Court declared unconstitutional an Ohio statute that permitted a 100 percent deduction for dividends from domestic subsidiaries, but only an 85 percent deduction for dividends from foreign subsidiaries. In *Conoco Inc. v. Taxation and Revenue Department* [122 N.M. 736 (N.M. Sup. Ct., 1996)], the New Mexico Supreme Court ruled that the New Mexico scheme under which foreign but not domestic dividends were included in the tax base facially discriminated against foreign commerce, even through the state allowed a taxpayer to include a portion of the dividend-paying foreign subsidiaries' property, payroll, and sales in the denominators of its apportionment factors, thereby reducing the state apportionment percentage.

Dividends-Received Deductions in a Water's-Edge Combined Report. In footnote 23 of its decision in Kraft, the Supreme Court stated:

> If one were to compare the aggregate tax imposed by Iowa on a unitary business which included a subsidiary doing business throughout the United States (including Iowa) with the aggregate tax imposed by Iowa on a unitary business which included a foreign subsidiary doing business abroad, it would be difficult to say that Iowa discriminates against the business with the foreign subsidiary. Iowa would tax an apportioned share of the domestic subsidiary's entire earnings, but would tax only the amount of the foreign subsidiary's earnings paid as a dividend to the parent.

The state supreme courts in several water's-edge combined reporting states have focused on this footnote and ruled that it is constitutionally acceptable to include dividends from foreign subsidiaries in the tax base, while excluding dividends from domestic subsidiaries that are included in the water's-edge combined report.

In *Appeal of Morton Thiokol, Inc.* [864 P.2d 1175 (Kan. Sup. Ct., 1993)], the Kansas Supreme Court noted that *Kraft* did not address the taxation of foreign dividends by water's-edge combined reporting states (because Iowa is an elective consolidation state), and that "the aggregate tax imposed by Kansas on a unitary business with a domestic subsidiary would not be less burdensome than that imposed by

Kansas on a unitary business with a foreign subsidiary because the income of the domestic subsidiary would be combined, apportioned, and taxed while only the dividend of the foreign subsidiary would be taxed." Likewise, in *E.I. Du Pont de Nemours & Co. v. State Tax Assessor* [675 A.2d 82 (Maine Sup Ct., 1996)], the Maine Supreme Judicial Court held that Maine's water's-edge combined reporting method was distinguishable from the Iowa's single-entity reporting method because the income of a domestic subsidiary is included in the Maine combined report. Therefore, taxing dividends paid by foreign but not domestic subsidiaries did not constitute the kind of facial discrimination found in the Iowa system.

Finally, in *General Electric Company, Inc. v. Department of Revenue Administration* [No. 2005-668 (N.H. Sup. Ct., Dec. 5, 2006)], GE challenged the constitutionality of a New Hampshire statute that permits a U.S. parent corporation to claim a dividends-received deduction for dividends received from foreign subsidiaries only to the extent the foreign subsidiary has business activity and is subject to tax in New Hampshire. None of GE's unitary foreign subsidiaries had business activities in New Hampshire during the tax years in question. Thus, it could not claim a dividends-received deduction for the dividends received from those foreign subsidiaries. The New Hampshire Supreme Court ruled that the New Hampshire tax scheme did not discriminate against foreign commerce because both a unitary business with foreign subsidiaries operating in New Hampshire and a unitary business with foreign subsidiaries not operating in New Hampshire are each taxed only one time. Thus, there was no differential treatment that benefits the former and burdens the latter.

Apportionment Factor Relief. The inclusion of dividends received from a foreign subsidiary in the apportionable income of a domestic parent corporation raises the issue of whether the parent's apportionment factors should reflect the foreign subsidiary's property, payroll, and sales. In his dissent in *Mobil Oil Corp.,* Justice Stevens raised the issue of factor representation, noting that "[u]nless the sales, payroll, and property values connected with the production of income by the payor corporations are added to the denominator of the apportionment formula, the inclusion of earnings attributable to those corporations in the apportionable tax base will inevitably cause Mobil's Vermont income to be overstated."

In *NCR Corp. v. Taxation and Revenue Department* [856 P.2d 982 (N.M. Ct. App. 1993), *cert. denied,* 512 U.S. 1245 (1994)], the New Mexico Court of Appeals rejected the taxpayer's argument that the taxation of dividends received by a domestic parent corporation from its foreign subsidiaries without factor representation resulted in constitutionally impermissible double taxation. Similar arguments made by NCR were also rejected by state supreme courts in Minnesota and South Carolina [*NCR Corp. v. Commissioner of Revenue,* 438 N.W.2d 86 (Minn. Sup. Ct., 1989), cert. denied, 493 U.S. 848 (1989); *NCR Corp. v. Tax Commission,* 439 S.E.2d 254 (S.C. Sup Ct., 1993), cert. denied, 512 U.S. 1245 (1994)]. Caterpillar, Inc. also litigated the issue of factor representation with respect to dividends received from foreign subsidiaries, and met with limited success. See, for example, *Caterpillar, Inc. v. Commissioner of Revenue* [568 N.W.2d 695 (Minn. Sup Ct., 1997), cert. denied, 522 U.S. 1112 (1998)], and *Caterpillar, Inc. v. Department of Revenue Administration* [741 A.2d 56 (N.H. Sup Ct., 1999), cert. denied, 120 S. Ct. 1424 (2000)]. Finally, in *Unisys Corp. v. Commonwealth of Pennsylvania* [812 A.2d 448 (Pa. Sup. Ct., 2002)], the Pennsylvania Supreme Court ruled that factor representation was not constitutionally required because the taxpayer failed to prove that the state was unfairly taxing income earned outside its jurisdiction.

State Tax Treatment—Section 78 Gross-up and Subpart F Inclusions

The rationale for including the Code Section 78 gross-up amount in federal taxable income does not apply for state tax purposes because no state allows a domestic corporation to claim a credit for the foreign income taxes paid by a foreign subsidiary. As a consequence, nearly all states provide a subtraction modification or dividends-received deduction for Section 78 gross-up income, in effect, excluding the federal gross-up amount from state taxation. In *Amerada Hess Corp. v. North Dakota* [704 N.W.2d 8 (N.D. Sup. Ct., 2005)], the North Dakota Supreme Court ruled that Section 78 gross-up amounts did not qualify as "foreign dividends" under the applicable North Dakota tax statute, and therefore did not qualify for the partial exclusion from income under North Dakota water's-edge combined unitary reporting method of determining the state corporate income tax.

Consistent with the notion that a Subpart F inclusion is a deemed dividend from a controlled foreign corporation, most states provide a dividends-received deduction or subtraction modification for income under Subpart F. A few states, including California, require that the income and apportionment factors of a controlled foreign corporation be included in a water's-edge combined report to the extent of the controlled foreign corporation's Subpart F income. [Cal. Rev. & Tax. Code § 25110] California does not provide a dividends-received deduction for Subpart F income. In addition, some states provide only limited deductions for income under Subpart F. For example, an Idaho water's-edge group may claim only an 85 percent deduction [Idaho Code Ann. § 63-3027C], and a Utah water's-edge group may claim only a 50 percent deduction [Utah Code Ann. § 59-7-106].

IRC Section 965 Temporary Dividends-Received Deduction

As part of the American Jobs Creation Act of 2004 (Pub. L. No. 108-357), Congress enacted Code Section 965 in an attempt to stimulate the U.S. economy by triggering the repatriation of foreign earnings that otherwise would have remained reinvested abroad. Under Section 965, a domestic corporation may elect to claim a dividends received deduction equal to 85 percent of certain cash dividends received from CFCs. To qualify, the domestic corporation must reinvest the repatriated earnings in the United States pursuant to a formal domestic reinvestment plan. The amount of dividends that qualify for the 85 percent dividends-received deduction may not exceed the greater of $500 million or the amount of earnings reported in the taxpayer's financial statements as permanently reinvested abroad [IRC § 965(b)]. The election is available only for either the taxpayer's last tax year that began before October 22, 2004, or the taxpayer's first tax year that begins on or after October 22, 2004 [IRC § 965(f)]. Thus, a calendar year taxpayer must make the election for either its 2004 or 2005 tax year.

State-by-State Summary

For ease of presentation, the following chart has been divided into four parts, as follows:

- Part 1: Dividends
- Part 2: Interest, Royalties, Technical Fees, Section 965
- Part 3: Subpart F Income
- Part 4: Section 78 Gross-Up

Income From Foreign Subsidiaries (Part 1)

Dividends

Legend:

X	Condition applies
NA	Not applicable
NR	Not reported
SAF	Same as applicable federal rules

	With Respect to Dividends Received from Foreign (Non-U.S.) Corporations, State Provides			
	Dividends-Received Deduction	*Other Subtraction Modification*	*No Adjustment*	*Other*
Alabama	X			
Alaska	See Note.			

Note. For a water's-edge combination in which payor is not included in water's-edge group, 80% of dividend is excluded by statute. For a worldwide combination in which payor is not part of unitary group, dividends-received deduction follows federal percentages and is computed without regard to foreign or domestic status of payor. If payor is included in combined group, dividends are eliminated in combination and foreign corporation income (book earnings or E&P) is included in apportionable income.

	Dividends-Received Deduction	*Other Subtraction Modification*	*No Adjustment*	*Other*
Arizona	X			
Arkansas	X			
California	X			
Colorado		X		
Connecticut	NR	NR	NR	NR
Delaware		X		
District of Columbia			SAF	
Florida		X		
Georgia	X			
Hawaii	See HRS § 235-7(c)			

Income From Foreign Subsidiaries (Part 1)

Dividends

Legend:

X	Condition applies
NA	Not applicable
NR	Not reported
SAF	Same as applicable federal rules

	With Respect to Dividends Received from Foreign (Non-U.S.) Corporations, State Provides			
	Dividends-Received Deduction	*Other Subtraction Modification*	*No Adjustment*	*Other*
Idaho		X, unless filing water's edge. A unitary business may elect to forgo the filing of the domestic disclosure spreadsheet; however, the 85% exclusion of dividends from foreign corporations and from IRC § 936 corporations must be reduced to 80%.		
Illinois		X		
Indiana	X			
Iowa		X		
Kansas		X		
Kentucky	X			
Louisiana				See Note.

Note. Dividends on stock having a situs in Louisiana that are received by a corporation from another corporation that is controlled by the former, through ownership of 50% or more of the voting stock of the latter, must be allocated to the state or states in which is earned the income from which the dividends are paid, in proportion to the respective amounts of such income earned in each state.

Maine		X		
Maryland	X, as a subtraction modification			
Massachusetts	X, SAF	SAF	SAF	SAF

Income From Foreign Subsidiaries (Part 1)

Dividends

Legend:

X	Condition applies
NA	Not applicable
NR	Not reported
SAF	Same as applicable federal rules

	With Respect to Dividends Received from Foreign (Non-U.S.) Corporations, State Provides			
	Dividends-Received Deduction	*Other Subtraction Modification*	*No Adjustment*	*Other*
Michigan (Business Tax)		X		
Note. The CIT takes effect 01/01/12, and replaces the Michigan Business Tax (MBT) for most taxpayers. However, businesses that have been approved to receive, have received, or have been assigned certain certified credits may elect to file a return and pay the tax imposed by the MBT in lieu of the CIT until the certified credits are exhausted or extinguished.				
Minnesota	X			
Mississippi	X			
Missouri	X			
Montana				Intercompany dividend elimination
Nebraska	X			
Nevada	Nevada does not impose a corporate income tax			
New Hampshire				See RSA 77-A:3, II(b)
New Jersey	X			
New Mexico	X			70% deduction for ownership between 0% and less than 20%; 80% deduction for ownership between 20% and less than or equal to 50%; factor representation for ownership greater than 50%

Income From Foreign Subsidiaries (Part 1)

Dividends

Legend:

X	Condition applies
NA	Not applicable
NR	Not reported
SAF	Same as applicable federal rules

	With Respect to Dividends Received from Foreign (Non-U.S.) Corporations, State Provides			
	Dividends-Received Deduction	*Other Subtraction Modification*	*No Adjustment*	*Other*
New York	X			
North Carolina		X		
North Dakota				X, 100% elimination if received from unitary affiliate
Ohio	Ohio does not impose a corporate income tax			
Note. Effective 1/1/2010, the Ohio Franchise Tax was fully phased out and business will be taxed on gross receipts through the Commercial Activity Tax. Details about that tax can be found at: http//tax.ohio.gov/divisions/commercial_activities/ index.stm				
Oklahoma			X	
Oregon	X			
Pennsylvania	X			
Rhode Island	X			
South Carolina	X			
South Dakota	South Dakota does not impose a corporate income tax			
Tennessee	X, when greater than 80% owned			

Income From Foreign Subsidiaries (Part 1)
Dividends

Legend:

X	Condition applies
NA	Not applicable
NR	Not reported
SAF	Same as applicable federal rules

	With Respect to Dividends Received from Foreign (Non-U.S.) Corporations, State Provides			
	Dividends-Received Deduction	*Other Subtraction Modification*	*No Adjustment*	*Other*
Texas				Foreign royalties and foreign dividends from an affiliated taxable entity that does not transact a substantial portion of its business or regularly maintain a substantial portion of its assets in the U.S., including amounts determined under IRC § 78 or §§ 951-964, are deducted from total revenue to compute margin.
Utah		X		
Vermont			X	
Virginia	X, for 50-100% owned	X, for less than 50% owned		
Washington	Washington does not impose a corporate income tax			
West Virginia		X		
Wisconsin	X			
Wyoming	Wyoming does not impose a corporate income tax			

Income from Foreign Subsidiaries (Part 2)

Interest, Royalties, and Technical Fees, Section 965

Legend:

X	Condition applies
NA	Not applicable
NR	Not reported
SAF	Same as applicable federal rules

	State Provides a Subtraction Modification for the Following Types of Income Derived from a Foreign (Non-U.S.) Subsidiary Corporation					
	Interest Income	*Royalty Income*	*Technical Fees*	*None*	*Other*	*Does State Conform to the IRC § 965 Temporary Dividends Received Deduction?*
Alabama				X		Yes
Alaska		X, 80% in a water's-edge combination				Yes
Arizona				X		Yes
Arkansas				X		No
California				X		No
Colorado	X	X	X			Yes
Connecticut				X		Yes
Delaware	X	X				Yes
District of Columbia				X		No
Florida				X		No
Georgia				X		Yes
Hawaii					Depends on facts and circumstances	No
Idaho				X	Only if nonbusiness income	Yes, SAF
Illinois				X		Yes

Income from Foreign Subsidiaries (Part 2)

Interest, Royalties, and Technical Fees, Section 965

Legend:

X	Condition applies
NA	Not applicable
NR	Not reported
SAF	Same as applicable federal rules

	State Provides a Subtraction Modification for the Following Types of Income Derived from a Foreign (Non-U.S.) Subsidiary Corporation					
	Interest Income	*Royalty Income*	*Technical Fees*	*None*	*Other*	*Does State Conform to the IRC § 965 Temporary Dividends Received Deduction?*
Indiana				X		No
Iowa				X		Yes
Kansas				X		Yes
Kentucky	X			X		No
Louisiana	X					Yes
Maine				X		Yes
Maryland				X		No
Massachusetts				NR		NR
Michigan (Business Tax)		X			Dividends	Yes
Note. The CIT takes effect 01/01/12, and replaces the Michigan Business Tax (MBT) for most taxpayers. However, businesses that have been approved to receive, have received, or have been assigned certain certified credits may elect to file a return and pay the tax imposed by the MBT in lieu of the CIT until the certified credits are exhausted or extinguished.						
Minnesota					X, 80% for foreign royalties, fees and other like income	No
Mississippi	X					No
Missouri		X				Yes

Income from Foreign Subsidiaries (Part 2)

Interest, Royalties, and Technical Fees, Section 965

Legend:

X	Condition applies
NA	Not applicable
NR	Not reported
SAF	Same as applicable federal rules

	State Provides a Subtraction Modification for the Following Types of Income Derived from a Foreign (Non-U.S.) Subsidiary Corporation					
	Interest Income	*Royalty Income*	*Technical Fees*	*None*	*Other*	*Does State Conform to the IRC § 965 Temporary Dividends Received Deduction?*
Montana				X		No
Nebraska				X		Yes
Nevada	Nevada does not impose a corporate income tax					
New Hampshire						
New Jersey				X		Yes
New Mexico				X		Yes
New York					All income from subsidiary capital is deductible in the computation of taxable income.	Yes
North Carolina	NR	NR	NR	NR	NR	Yes
North Dakota				X		No
Ohio	Ohio does not impose a corporate income tax					
Note. Effective 1/1/2010, the Ohio Franchise Tax was fully phased out and business will be taxed on gross receipts through the Commercial Activity Tax. Details about that tax can be found at: http//tax.ohio.gov/divisions/commercial_activities/index.stm						
Oklahoma				X		NR

Income from Foreign Subsidiaries (Part 2)

Interest, Royalties, and Technical Fees, Section 965

Legend:

X	Condition applies
NA	Not applicable
NR	Not reported
SAF	Same as applicable federal rules

	State Provides a Subtraction Modification for the Following Types of Income Derived from a Foreign (Non-U.S.) Subsidiary Corporation					
	Interest Income	*Royalty Income*	*Technical Fees*	*None*	*Other*	*Does State Conform to the IRC § 965 Temporary Dividends Received Deduction?*
Oregon				X	Subtraction for taxes paid to a foreign country on the payment of interest or royalties arising from sources within such foreign country if not deductible for federal tax purposes and interest of royalties are included in Oregon taxable income.	Yes, only for tax years beginning before 1/1/07.
Pennsylvania				X		NA
Rhode Island	NR	NR	NR	NR	NR	Yes
South Carolina				X		No
South Dakota	South Dakota does not impose a corporate income tax					
Tennessee				X		The only deductions permitted are those used to determine Line 28 of federal Form 1120.

Income from Foreign Subsidiaries (Part 2)

Interest, Royalties, and Technical Fees, Section 965

Legend:

X	Condition applies
NA	Not applicable
NR	Not reported
SAF	Same as applicable federal rules

	State Provides a Subtraction Modification for the Following Types of Income Derived from a Foreign (Non-U.S.) Subsidiary Corporation					
	Interest Income	*Royalty Income*	*Technical Fees*	*None*	*Other*	*Does State Conform to the IRC § 965 Temporary Dividends Received Deduction?*
Texas		X				No
Utah				X		No
Vermont				X		Yes
Virginia	X	X	X		Dividends, rents, and gains on sales of intangible or real property	Yes
Washington	Washington does not impose a corporate income tax					
West Virginia	X	X	X			Yes
Wisconsin				X		No
Wyoming	Wyoming does not impose a corporate income tax					

Income from Foreign Subsidiaries (Part 3)

Subpart F Income

Legend:

X	Condition applies
NA	Not applicable
NR	Not reported
SAF	Same as applicable federal rules

	With Respect to Federal Subpart F Income, State Provides			
	Dividends-Received Deduction	*Other Subtraction Modification*	*No Adjustment*	*Other*
Alabama	X			
Alaska	See Note.			
Note. If a water's-edge combination in which payor is not included in the water's-edge group, 80% of dividend is excluded by statute. For a worldwide combination in which payor is not part of unitary group, dividends-received deduction follows federal percentages and is computed without regard to foreign or domestic status of payor. If payor is included in combined group, dividends eliminated in combination and foreign corporation income (book earnings or E&P) is included in apportionable income.				
Arizona	X			
Arkansas	X			
California				California does not conform to the Subpart F provisions under the IRC; therefore, a subtraction modification removing IRC §951 Subpart F income is required to convert federal taxable income into California state taxable income. No further adjustment to IRC §951 Subpart F income is necessary or allowed.
Colorado		X		
Connecticut	NR	NR	NR	NR
Delaware		X		
District of Columbia		X		

Income from Foreign Subsidiaries (Part 3)

Subpart F Income

Legend:

X	Condition applies
NA	Not applicable
NR	Not reported
SAF	Same as applicable federal rules

	With Respect to Federal Subpart F Income, State Provides			
	Dividends-Received Deduction	*Other Subtraction Modification*	*No Adjustment*	*Other*
Florida		X		
Georgia		X		Amount of Subpart F Income
Hawaii		X, Hawaii does not conform to IRC § 951.		
Idaho			X	
Illinois		X		
Indiana	X			
Iowa		X		
Kansas		X		
Kentucky	X			
Louisiana		X		
Maine		X		
Maryland	X, as a subtraction modification			
Massachusetts	X, SAF	SAF	SAF	SAF
Michigan (Business Tax)		X		

Note. The CIT takes effect 01/01/12, and replaces the Michigan Business Tax (MBT) for most taxpayers. However, businesses that have been approved to receive, have received, or have been assigned certain certified credits may elect to file a return and pay the tax imposed by the MBT in lieu of the CIT until the certified credits are exhausted or extinguished.

Income from Foreign Subsidiaries (Part 3)

Subpart F Income

Legend:

X	Condition applies
NA	Not applicable
NR	Not reported
SAF	Same as applicable federal rules

	With Respect to Federal Subpart F Income, State Provides			
	Dividends-Received Deduction	*Other Subtraction Modification*	*No Adjustment*	*Other*
Minnesota	X			
Mississippi	X			
Missouri	X			
Montana				Intercompany dividend elimination
Nebraska	X			
Nevada	Nevada does not impose a corporate income tax			
New Hampshire				See RSA 77-A:3, II(s)
New Jersey	X			
New Mexico	X			70% deduction for ownership between 0% and less than 20%; 80% deduction for ownership between 20% and less than or equal to 50%; factor representation for ownership greater than 50%
New York	X			
North Carolina		X		
North Dakota				X, 100% elimination if received from unitary affiliate

Income from Foreign Subsidiaries (Part 3)

Subpart F Income

Legend:

X	Condition applies
NA	Not applicable
NR	Not reported
SAF	Same as applicable federal rules

	With Respect to Federal Subpart F Income, State Provides			
	Dividends-Received Deduction	*Other Subtraction Modification*	*No Adjustment*	*Other*
Ohio	Ohio does not impose a corporate income tax			
Note. Effective 1/1/2010, the Ohio Franchise Tax was fully phased out and business will be taxed on gross receipts through the Commercial Activity Tax. Details about that tax can be found at: http//tax.ohio.gov/divisions/commercial_activities/index.stm				
Oklahoma			X	
Oregon	X			
Pennsylvania			X	
Rhode Island				
South Carolina	X			
South Dakota	South Dakota does not impose a corporate income tax			
Tennessee	X, when greater than 80% owned			
Texas				Foreign royalties and foreign dividends from an affiliated taxable entity that does not transact a substantial portion of its business or regularly maintain a substantial portion of its assets in the U.S., including amounts determined under IRC § 78 or §§ 951-964, are deducted from total revenue to compute margin.
Utah		X		Subpart F deemed dividends treated similar to paid dividends

Income from Foreign Subsidiaries (Part 3)

Subpart F Income

Legend:

X	Condition applies
NA	Not applicable
NR	Not reported
SAF	Same as applicable federal rules

	With Respect to Federal Subpart F Income, State Provides			
	Dividends-Received Deduction	*Other Subtraction Modification*	*No Adjustment*	*Other*
Vermont	X			
Virginia		X		
Washington	Washington does not impose a corporate income tax			
West Virginia		X		
Wisconsin		X		
Wyoming	Wyoming does not impose a corporate income tax			

Income from Foreign Subsidiaries (Part 4)

Section 78 Gross-Up

Legend:

X	Condition applies
NA	Not applicable
NR	Not reported
SAF	Same as applicable federal rules

	With Respect to Federal IRC § 78 Gross-Up Income, State Provides			
	Dividends-Received Deduction	*Other Subtraction Modification*	*No Adjustment*	*Other*
Alabama	X			
Alaska		X		
Arizona	X			
Arkansas	X			
California				California does not conform to IRC § 78 foreign dividends gross up provision; therefore, a subtraction modification removing such gross-up income is required to convert federal taxable income into California state taxable income. No further adjustments to IRC § 78 gross-up income is necessary or allowed.
Colorado		X		
Connecticut	NR	NR	NR	NR
Delaware		X		
District of Columbia		X		
Florida		X		
Georgia				X, amount of IRC § 78 Gross-up Income

Income from Foreign Subsidiaries (Part 4)
Section 78 Gross-Up

Legend:

X	Condition applies
NA	Not applicable
NR	Not reported
SAF	Same as applicable federal rules

	With Respect to Federal IRC § 78 Gross-Up Income, State Provides			
	Dividends-Received Deduction	*Other Subtraction Modification*	*No Adjustment*	*Other*
Hawaii		X, Hawaii does not conform to IRC § 902.		
Idaho		X, see Idaho Code § 63-3022(e).		
Illinois		X		
Indiana	X			
Iowa		X		
Kansas		X		
Kentucky	X			
Louisiana		X		
Maine		X		
Maryland	X, as a subtraction modification			
Massachusetts	SAF	SAF	SAF	SAF
Michigan (Business Tax)		X		

Note. The CIT takes effect 01/01/12, and replaces the Michigan Business Tax (MBT) for most taxpayers. However, businesses that have been approved to receive, have received, or have been assigned certain certified credits may elect to file a return and pay the tax imposed by the MBT in lieu of the CIT until the certified credits are exhausted or extinguished.

Minnesota		X		
Mississippi	X			

Income from Foreign Subsidiaries (Part 4)
Section 78 Gross-Up

Legend:

X	Condition applies
NA	Not applicable
NR	Not reported
SAF	Same as applicable federal rules

	With Respect to Federal IRC § 78 Gross-Up Income, State Provides			
	Dividends-Received Deduction	*Other Subtraction Modification*	*No Adjustment*	*Other*
Missouri	X			
Montana	X			
Nebraska	X			
Nevada	Nevada does not impose a corporate income tax			
New Hampshire				See RSA 77-A:4, XI
New Jersey	X			
New Mexico	X			
New York	X, dividends from subsidiaries are not subject to tax.			
North Carolina		X		
North Dakota				X, 100% elimination if received from unitary affiliate
Ohio	Ohio does not impose a corporate income tax			
Note. Effective 1/1/2010, the Ohio Franchise Tax was fully phased out and business will be taxed on gross receipts through the Commercial Activity Tax. Details about that tax can be found at: http//tax.ohio.gov/divisions/commercial_activities/index.stm				
Oklahoma			X	
Oregon	X			
Pennsylvania	X			
Rhode Island				

Income from Foreign Subsidiaries (Part 4)

Section 78 Gross-Up

Legend:

X	Condition applies
NA	Not applicable
NR	Not reported
SAF	Same as applicable federal rules

	With Respect to Federal IRC § 78 Gross-Up Income, State Provides			
	Dividends-Received Deduction	*Other Subtraction Modification*	*No Adjustment*	*Other*
South Carolina	X			
South Dakota	South Dakota does not impose a corporate income tax			
Tennessee	X, regardless of ownership percentage			
Texas				Foreign royalties and foreign dividends from an affiliated taxable entity that does not transact a substantial portion of its business or regularly maintain a substantial portion of its assets in the U.S., including amounts determined under IRC § 78 or §§ 951-964, are deducted from total revenue to compute margin.
Utah		X		
Vermont	X			
Virginia		X		
Washington	Washington does not impose a corporate income tax			
West Virginia		X		
Wisconsin		X		
Wyoming	Wyoming does not impose a corporate income tax			

Check-the-Box Foreign (Non-U.S.) Branches

Federal Tax Treatment

If a domestic corporation operates abroad through an unincorporated foreign branch rather than a separately incorporated subsidiary, the foreign-source income of the foreign branch represents income earned directly by the domestic corporation. Historically, U.S. companies generally have not operated abroad through an unincorporated branch for many reasons, including the desire for limited liability or to have a local corporate presence. Since the check-the-box regulations [Treas. Reg. § 301.7701] took effect in 1997, however, it has been possible to organize a foreign entity that is recognized as a separate corporation for foreign tax purposes but is treated as a disregarded entity or partnership for U.S. tax purposes.

State Tax Treatment

States generally conform to the federal check-the-box rules for state income tax purposes. Thus, a foreign entity that is a corporation for foreign tax purposes but is a branch or partnership for U.S. federal tax purposes is generally treated as a branch or partnership for state income tax purposes.

In *Manpower Inc. v. Commissioner of Revenue* [No. A06-468 (Minn. Sup. Ct., Dec. 7, 2006)], a domestic corporation owned 99 percent of Manpower France S.A.R.L (MPF), a French entity analogous to a U.S. limited liability company. In 1999, MPF made a federal check-the-box election, which caused the liquidation of a foreign corporation (MPF's previous federal tax status) and a contribution of the distributed assets to a new partnership. For Minnesota tax purposes, income of "foreign corporations and other foreign entities" is not included in apportionable income. The Commissioner argued that when the French subsidiary elected to be classified as a partnership for federal tax purposes, a newly formed partnership was created under U.S. law. The taxpayer argued that, despite the federal check-the-box election, MPF still qualified as a "foreign entity" for Minnesota tax purposes, because it was created in France under French law and operated in France. The Minnesota Supreme Court agreed, ruling that the check-the-box election changed the French entity's legal nature but not its nationality. The subsidiary was still a foreign entity, and the only effect of its check-the-box election was to convert it from a foreign corporation to a foreign partnership for federal income tax purposes.

State-by-State Summary

The following chart indicates which states provide some type of deduction or subtraction modification with respect to foreign source income that a domestic corporation earns through a foreign entity that is treated as a branch for U.S. tax purposes but a separately incorporated subsidiary for foreign tax purposes.

Check-the-Box Foreign (Non-U.S.) Branches

Legend:

X	Condition applies
NA	Not applicable
NR	Not reported
SAF	Same as applicable federal rules

	With Respect to the Foreign Source Taxable Income of a "Check-the-Box" Foreign Branch (i.e., A 100%-Owned Foreign Country Corporation That Is Treated as a Disregarded Entity for U.S. Tax Purposes) Included in Taxpayer's Federal Taxable Income, State Provides:			
	Dividends-Received Deduction	*Other Subtraction Modification*	*No Adjustment*	*Other*
Alabama			X	
Alaska			X	
Arizona			X	
Arkansas	X			
California			X	
Colorado		X		
Connecticut	NR	NR	NR	NR
Delaware	NR	NR	NR	NR
District of Columbia		X		
Florida			X	
Georgia			X	
Hawaii				Depends on facts and circumstances
Idaho			X	
Illinois			X	
Indiana			X	
Iowa			X	
Kansas			X	

Check-the-Box Foreign (Non-U.S.) Branches

Legend:

X	Condition applies
NA	Not applicable
NR	Not reported
SAF	Same as applicable federal rules

	With Respect to the Foreign Source Taxable Income of a "Check-the-Box" Foreign Branch (i.e., A 100%-Owned Foreign Country Corporation That Is Treated as a Disregarded Entity for U.S. Tax Purposes) Included in Taxpayer's Federal Taxable Income, State Provides:			
	Dividends-Received Deduction	*Other Subtraction Modification*	*No Adjustment*	*Other*
Kentucky	X			
Louisiana			X	
Maine			X	
Maryland			X	
Massachusetts	NR	NR	NR	NR
Michigan (Business Tax)		X		
Note. The CIT takes effect 01/01/12, and replaces the Michigan Business Tax (MBT) for most taxpayers. However, businesses that have been approved to receive, have received, or have been assigned certain certified credits may elect to file a return and pay the tax imposed by the MBT in lieu of the CIT until the certified credits are exhausted or extinguished.				
Minnesota				Foreign entity not included in Minnesota unitary family
Mississippi			X	
Missouri	X			
Montana			X	
Nebraska			X	
Nevada	Nevada does not impose a corporate income tax			
New Hampshire				See RSA 77_A:, XIX
New Jersey			X	
New Mexico			X	

Check-the-Box Foreign (Non-U.S.) Branches

Legend:

X	Condition applies
NA	Not applicable
NR	Not reported
SAF	Same as applicable federal rules

With Respect to the Foreign Source Taxable Income of a "Check-the-Box" Foreign Branch (i.e., A 100%-Owned Foreign Country Corporation That Is Treated as a Disregarded Entity for U.S. Tax Purposes) Included in Taxpayer's Federal Taxable Income, State Provides:

	Dividends-Received Deduction	*Other Subtraction Modification*	*No Adjustment*	*Other*
New York			X	
North Carolina	NR	NR	NR	NR
North Dakota			X	
Ohio	Ohio does not impose a corporate income tax			
Note. Effective 1/1/2010, the Ohio Franchise Tax was fully phased out and business will be taxed on gross receipts through the Commercial Activity Tax. Details about that tax can be found at: http//tax.ohio.gov/divisions/commercial_activities/index.stm				
Oklahoma			X	
Oregon			X	
Pennsylvania			X	
Rhode Island	NR	NR	NR	NR
South Carolina	X			
South Dakota	South Dakota does not impose a corporate income tax			
Tennessee			X	
Texas	X			
Utah	X			
Vermont	X			
Virginia	X			
Washington	Washington does not impose a corporate income tax			

Check-the-Box Foreign (Non-U.S.) Branches

Legend:

X	Condition applies
NA	Not applicable
NR	Not reported
SAF	Same as applicable federal rules

	With Respect to the Foreign Source Taxable Income of a "Check-the-Box" Foreign Branch (i.e., A 100%-Owned Foreign Country Corporation That Is Treated as a Disregarded Entity for U.S. Tax Purposes) Included in Taxpayer's Federal Taxable Income, State Provides:			
	Dividends-Received Deduction	*Other Subtraction Modification*	*No Adjustment*	*Other*
West Virginia	X			
Wisconsin			X	
Wyoming	Wyoming does not impose a corporate income tax			

Treatment of Foreign Income Tax Payments

Federal Tax Treatment

For federal tax purposes, a domestic corporation may claim either a deduction or a credit for foreign income tax payments, but not both [Code Secs. 164, 275 and 901]. If the taxpayer elects to claim a foreign tax credit, the credit is limited to the portion of the domestic corporation's pre-credit U.S. tax attributable to its foreign source taxable income [IRC § 904]. A domestic corporation that receives a dividend from a foreign corporation in which it owns at least 10 percent of the voting stock may also claim a deemed paid credit for the foreign income taxes paid by the foreign corporation on the earnings from which the dividends were paid [IRC § 902]. When a domestic corporation claims a deemed paid foreign tax credit, it must gross up its dividend income by the amount of the deemed paid foreign income taxes [IRC § 78].

State Tax Treatment

In contrast to federal law, no state allows a credit for foreign income taxes. However, some states allow a deduction for foreign income taxes, but generally only if a deduction is claimed for federal tax purposes. Because a credit is usually more valuable than a deduction, for federal tax purposes, taxpayers generally elect to claim a foreign tax credit under IRC Section 901 rather than a deduction under IRC Section 164. A handful of states allow a deduction even if the taxpayer claims the credit for federal tax purposes. Many states, such as California, do not permit a deduction for foreign income taxes, regardless of whether a deduction or a credit is claimed for federal tax purposes [Cal. Rev. & Tax. Code § 24345].

State-by-State Summary

The following chart indicates whether a state allows a credit for foreign income tax payments; whether a deduction for foreign income taxes is allowed for state purposes when a federal deduction is claimed; and whether a deduction is allowed for state purposes when a credit for foreign income taxes if taken for federal purposes.

Treatment of Foreign Income Tax Payments

Legend:
NA Not applicable
NR Not reported

	May Corporations Claim a Credit for Foreign Income Tax	*If Deduction for Foreign Income Tax Is Taken for Federal Purposes, Does State Allow a Deduction for State Purposes?*	*If Credit for Foreign Income Tax Is Taken for Federal Purposes, Does State Allow a Deduction for State Purposes?*
Alabama	No	Yes	Yes
Alaska	No	No	No
Arizona	No	No	No
Arkansas	No	Yes	Yes
California	No	No	No
Colorado	No	Yes	Yes
Connecticut	No	Yes	No
Delaware	No	No	No
District of Columbia	No	Yes	No
Florida	No	No	No
Georgia	No	No, if the tax was on income.	No
Hawaii	NR	NR	NR
Idaho	No	Yes	No
Illinois	No	Yes	No
Indiana	No	Yes	No
Iowa	No	Yes	No
Kansas	No	No	No
Kentucky	No	No	No

Treatment of Foreign Income Tax Payments

Legend:
NA — Not applicable
NR — Not reported

	May Corporations Claim a Credit for Foreign Income Tax	*If Deduction for Foreign Income Tax Is Taken for Federal Purposes, Does State Allow a Deduction for State Purposes?*	*If Credit for Foreign Income Tax Is Taken for Federal Purposes, Does State Allow a Deduction for State Purposes?*
Louisiana	No	Yes	No
Maine	No	No	No
Maryland	No	Yes	No
Massachusetts	No	No	No
Michigan (Business Tax)	No	Yes	No
Note. The CIT takes effect 01/01/12, and replaces the Michigan Business Tax (MBT) for most taxpayers. However, businesses that have been approved to receive, have received, or have been assigned certain certified credits may elect to file a return and pay the tax imposed by the MBT in lieu of the CIT until the certified credits are exhausted or extinguished.			
Minnesota	No	Yes	No
Mississippi	No	No	No
Missouri	No	Yes	No
Montana	No	No	No
Nebraska	No	Yes	No
Nevada	Nevada does not impose a corporate income tax		
New Hampshire	No	No	No
New Jersey	No	No	No
New Mexico	No	Yes	No
New York	No	No, unless foreign tax is not an income tax	No
North Carolina	No	No	No

Legend:
NA Not applicable
NR Not reported

Treatment of Foreign Income Tax Payments

	May Corporations Claim a Credit for Foreign Income Tax	*If Deduction for Foreign Income Tax Is Taken for Federal Purposes, Does State Allow a Deduction for State Purposes?*	*If Credit for Foreign Income Tax Is Taken for Federal Purposes, Does State Allow a Deduction for State Purposes?*
North Dakota	No	Yes, to the extent the deduction is included in line 30.	The foreign tax credit is considered in the calculation of the federal tax deduction allowable.
Ohio	Ohio does not impose a corporate income tax		
Note. Effective 1/1/2010, the Ohio Franchise Tax was fully phased out and business will be taxed on gross receipts through the Commercial Activity Tax. Details about that tax can be found at: http//tax.ohio.gov/divisions/commercial_activities/index.stm			
Oklahoma	No	No	No
Oregon	No	Yes	Yes
Pennsylvania	No	Yes	No
Rhode Island	No	Yes	No
South Carolina	No	No	No
South Dakota	South Dakota does not impose a corporate income tax		
Tennessee	No	Yes	No
Texas	No	No	No
Utah	No	No	No
Vermont	No	Yes	No
Virginia	No	No	No
Washington	Washington does not impose a corporate income tax		
West Virginia	No	NR	NR
Wisconsin	No	No	Yes

Legend:
NA Not applicable
NR Not reported

Treatment of Foreign Income Tax Payments

	May Corporations Claim a Credit for Foreign Income Tax	*If Deduction for Foreign Income Tax Is Taken for Federal Purposes, Does State Allow a Deduction for State Purposes?*	*If Credit for Foreign Income Tax Is Taken for Federal Purposes, Does State Allow a Deduction for State Purposes?*
Wyoming	Wyoming does not impose a corporate income tax		

Part 8. CREDITS AND INCENTIVES

Investment, Jobs, and Research Credits

Federal and state lawmakers use business tax credits to implement a wide range of tax policy objectives, including attracting new business investment, increasing employment, and encouraging research and development activities.

Federal Tax Treatment

General Business Credit. For federal tax purposes, a corporation may claim a Code Section 38 general business credit, which is a nonrefundable credit equal to the sum of the current year business credit plus any business credit carryforwards or carryback to such tax year. The current year business credit is the sum of the following credits:

- Investment credit [IRC § 46]
- Work opportunity credit [IRC § 51]
- Alcohol fuels credit [IRC § 40]
- Research credit [IRC § 41]
- Low-income housing credit [IRC § 42]
- Enhanced oil recovery credit [IRC § 43]
- Disabled access credit [IRC § 44]
- Renewable electricity production credit [IRC § 45]
- Empowerment zone employment credit [IRC § 1396]
- Indian employment credit [IRC § 45A]
- Employer social security credit [IRC § 45B]
- Orphan drug credit [IRC § 45C]
- New markets tax credit [IRC § 45D]
- Small employer pension plan startup cost credit [IRC § 45E]
- Employer-provided child care credit [IRC § 45F]
- Railroad track maintenance credit [IRC § 45G]
- Biodiesel fuels credit [IRC § 40A]
- Low sulfur diesel fuel production credit [IRC § 45H]
- Marginal oil and gas well production credit [IRC § 45I]
- Distilled spirits credit [IRC § 5011]
- Advanced nuclear power facility production credit [IRC § 45J]
- Nonconventional source production credit [IRC § 45K]
- New energy efficient home credit [IRC § 45L]
- Energy efficient appliance credit [IRC § 45M]
- Alternative motor vehicle credit [IRC § 30B]
- Alternative fuel vehicle refueling property credit [IRC § 30C]
- Hurricane Katrina housing credit [IRC § 1400P]
- Hurricane Katrina, Rita, or Wilma employee retention credit [IRC § 1400R]
- Mine rescue team training credit [IRC § 45N]
- Agricultural chemicals security credit [IRC § 45O]
- Differential wage payment credit [IRC § 45P]
- Carbon dioxide sequestration credit [IRC § 45Q]
- New qualified plug-in electric drive motor vehicle credit [IRC § 30D]
- Small employer health insurance credit [IRC § 45R]

Investment Credit. The Code Section 46 investment credit is one of the components of the general business credit under Code Section 38. The investment credit equals the sum of the following credits:

- Rehabilitation credit [IRC § 47]
- Energy credit [IRC § 48]
- Qualifying advanced coal project credit [IRC § 48A]
- Qualifying gasification project credit [IRC § 48B]
- Qualifying advanced energy project credit [IRC § 48C]
- Qualifying therapeutic discovery project credit [IRC § 48D]

The Code Section 47 rehabilitation credit equals a specified percentage of the qualified rehabilitation expenditures with respect to a certified historic structure or other qualified rehabilitated building.

Energy Credits. As noted above in the discussion of the general business credit and investment credit, there are numerous provisions designed to promote domestic energy efficiency or domestic energy production. Examples include:

- Section 45 renewable electricity production credit for producing electricity from qualified energy resources, such as wind, biomass, geothermal and solar.
- Section 48 energy credit, which equals a specified percentage of the basis of qualified solar property, geothermal property, qualified fuel cell property, and stationary microturbine property.
- Section 48A qualifying advanced coal project credit and Section 48B qualifying (coal) gasification project credit are both designed to encourage the burning of coal in a more efficient and environmentally friendly manner.
- Section 48C qualifying advanced energy project is a project that reequips, expands, or establishes a manufacturing facility for the production of certain types of property, such as property used to produce energy from the sun, wind, or geothermal deposits.

Research Credit. Congress enacted the Code Section 41 research credit in 1981 in response to concerns that U.S. companies were not spending enough on research and development activities to maintain their competitiveness in an increasingly global economy. The credit is available for incremental research expenses paid or incurred in a trade or business and is claimed as one of the components of the general business credit under Code Section 38.

Employment Credits. The Code Section 51 work opportunity credit equals a specified percentage of the qualified wages paid during an employee's first year of employment. The credit is designed to provide employers with an incentive to hire persons from certain targeted groups, including qualified recipients under the Temporary Assistance for Needy Families (TANF) program, food stamp and Supplemental Security Income (SSI) recipients, veterans, ex-felons, high-risk youth, vocational rehabilitation referrals, and summer youth employees.

The Code Section 1396 enpowerment zone employment credit equals a specified percentage of the qualified wages paid to employees who are residents of the empowerment zones and who perform substantially all their employment services within the zone in the employer's trade or business.

Both employment-based credits are components of the Code Section 38 general business credit.

Bond Credits. Code Section 54 provides a credit to holders of clean renewable energy bonds. Code Section 54A provides a credit to holders of qualified tax credit bonds, which include qualified forestry conservation bonds [IRC § 54B], new clean renewable energy bonds [IRC § 54C], qualified energy conservation bonds [IRC § 54D], qualified zone academy bonds [IRC § 54E], and qualified school construction bonds [IRC § 54F]. Finally, Code Section 54AA provides a credit for holders of build America bonds.

Transferability of Credits. Federal and state lawmakers use business tax credits to achieve a wide range of tax policy objectives, including stimulating new business investment, increasing employment, and encouraging research and development activities. However, a tax credit benefits a business only to the extent it has a pre-credit tax liability that the credit can offset. Thus, even if a business engages in the activity targeted for a credit, it may not benefit from the credit if it has little or no taxable income. Lawmakers can address this issue in a number of ways, including making the tax credit refundable, permitting unused credits to be carried over to another tax year, or permitting the taxpayer who earns the credit to sell, transfer or assign the credit to a third party whose tax liability is sufficient to fully utilize the credit.

State Tax Treatment

State competition for investment in new manufacturing plants and other business facilities is intense because of the economic growth it may foster. As a consequence, most states offer various investment, research, or employment-based tax credits to companies that invest in facilities and create jobs in the state.

State tax credits are generally limited to activities performed or property located within the state's borders. This has led some commentators to suggest that such credits unconstitutionally discriminate against interstate commerce in violation of the Commerce Clause. In *Westinghouse Electric Corp. v. Tully* [466 U.S. 388 (1984)], the Supreme Court ruled that a New York corporate franchise tax credit for the accumulated income of a domestic international sales corporation unconstitutionally discriminated against interstate commerce because the credit created an advantage for domestic international sales corporations that operated within New York.

In *Cuno v. DaimlerChrysler, Inc.* [547 U.S. 332, 2006], an automobile manufacturer agreed to construct a new assembly plant in Toledo, Ohio in exchange for various tax incentives, including a tax credit against the Ohio corporate franchise tax equal to 13.5% of the cost of investments in machinery and equipment. A group of Toledo taxpayers sued, asserting that their state taxes were increased by the tax breaks given to DaimlerChrysler, and that the tax breaks discriminated against interstate commerce in violation of the Commerce Clause. The U.S. Court of Appeals for the Sixth Circuit agreed, ruling that the Ohio investment tax credit unconstitutionally imposed a discriminatory burden on economic activity outside Ohio by providing preferential tax treatment to companies that invested in Ohio rather than elsewhere [No. 01-3960 (U.S. Ct. of App., 6th Cir., Sept. 2, 2004)]. Subsequently, however, the U.S. Supreme Court vacated the Sixth Circuit's decision on the grounds the plaintiffs had no standing in federal court to challenge the State of Ohio's fiscal decisions simply by virtue of their status as Ohio taxpayers, because the alleged injury was too indirect and conjectural. The Court did not address the merits of the underlying discrimination claim, however.

It is important for taxpayers to carefully scrutinize the eligibility requirements for claiming a credit. This point is illustrated by the ruling in *Appeal of Save Mart Supermarkets* [2002-SBE-002 (Calif. State Bd. of Equal., Feb. 6, 2002)], in which a taxpayer that operated supermarkets which contained full-service bakery and meat departments was a qualified taxpayer for purposes of claiming an investment credit for manufacturers. See also *Appeal of Costco* [No. 266592 (Calif. State Bd. of Equal., Oct. 26, 2005)].

The importance of complying with the administrative requirements for claiming a credit is illustrated by the ruling in *Cosmo World of Hawaii, Inc. v Kamikawa* [36 P.3d 814 (Haw. Ct. of App. Oct. 9, 2001], in which the Hawaii Intermediate Court of Appeals held that a taxpayer waived its right to claim a capital goods excise tax credit because it failed to file a claim prior to the statutory deadline.

State-by-State Summary

The following chart, presented in two parts, indicates which states provide investment, jobs, research, or energy credits. The chart also summarizes which states provide a mechanism whereby one taxpayer may sell, transfer or assign unused credits or incentives to another taxpayer.

Investment, Jobs, and Research Credits (Part 1)

Legend:
R&D Research and development
NA Not applicable
NR Not reported

	Does State Allow an Investment Tax Credit?	*Does State Allow a Jobs Credit?*	*Does State Allow a Research Credit?*
Alabama	Yes, various incentive programs; qualifying property includes manufacturing equipment and buildings and fixtures.	No	No
Alaska	Yes, 18% of the federal investment credit to the extent attributable to Alaska property. Special Industrial Inventive Investment Tax Credits: May apply the following percentage of the federal investment credit allowed on only the first $250,000,000 of qualified investment in the state: 100% on first $50,000,000, 80% on investment over $50,000,000, 70% on investment over $100,000,000, 60% on investment over $150,000,000, and 40% on $200,000,000. Gas Exploration and Development Credit: 10% of investment and costs for qualified services for years 2003-2009, 25% of investment and costs for qualified services for years after 2009. Exploration Incentive Credit: Gas Storage Facility Tax Credit: $1.50 for each 1,000 cubic feet of working gas storage capacity.	Yes	Yes

Investment, Jobs, and Research Credits (Part 1)

Legend:

R&D	Research and development
NA	Not applicable
NR	Not reported

	Does State Allow an Investment Tax Credit?	*Does State Allow a Jobs Credit?*	*Does State Allow a Research Credit?*
Arizona	No	Yes, also credit for net increases in qualified employment in healthy forest management zones, for employment of temporary assistance for needy family recipients, and for employment in military reuse zones; employer credit for expenses incurred for providing qualified technology skills training; and credit for expenses incurred for providing dependent day care services for employees.	Yes, similar to federal on Arizona research only
Arkansas	Yes, 10% of investment approved by the Arkansas Department of Economic Development Commission	Yes, several different programs with various methods based on Arkansas Code.	Investment approved by the Arkansas Department of Economic Development Commission

Investment, Jobs, and Research Credits (Part 1)

Legend:

R&D	Research and development
NA	Not applicable
NR	Not reported

	Does State Allow an Investment Tax Credit?	*Does State Allow a Jobs Credit?*	*Does State Allow a Research Credit?*
California	No	Yes, different calculations are required depending on the particular credit. See R&TC § § 23621 (Jobs Tax Credit), 23622.7 (Enterprise Zone Wage Credit), 23622.8 (Manufacturing Enhancement Area Wage Credit), 23623 (New Jobs Credit), 23624 (Prison Inmate Labor Credit), 23634 (Targeted Area Wage Credit), & 23646 (Local Area Military Base Recovery Area Wage Credit)..	Yes, conforms generally to federal credit computation, with modifications to allow a credit at the rate of 15% for qualified research and 24% for basic research expenses. Additionally the definition of gross receipts is modified to include only receipts, minus returns and allowances, from the sale of real, tangible, or intangible property held for sale to customers in the ordinary course of the taxpayer's trade or business that is delivered or shipped to a purchaser in California. As such, receipts for the sale of services are excluded from the definition of gross receipts. A taxpayer without gross receipts as defined will not be eligible to claim the California research credit. For further information, please see http://www.ftb.ca.gov/law/Guidance/2011/20110601.pdf,
Colorado	Yes; 1% of § 38 property as existed in 1986	Yes	Yes
Connecticut	Yes, 5% rate for manufacturing equipment, buildings and fixtures. Conn. Gen. Stat. § 12.217w, fixed capital investment credit; Conn. Gen. Stat § 12-1270, machinery equipment tax credit.	Yes, new jobs creation tax credit; Conn. Gen. Stat § 12-217; displaced electric worker and displaced worker tax credit; Conn. Gen. Stat. § 12-217bb, 12-217hh	Yes, See Conn. Gen. Stat. § § 12-217j; and 12-217n

Investment, Jobs, and Research Credits (Part 1)

Legend:

R&D	Research and development
NA	Not applicable
NR	Not reported

	Does State Allow an Investment Tax Credit?	*Does State Allow a Jobs Credit?*	*Does State Allow a Research Credit?*
Delaware	Yes, 50% of tax; based on investment and employment. Qualifying property includes all fixed assets, manufacturing and pollution control equipment, buildings and fixtures, and 8 times rental of property. Must file Form 700, Tax Credit Schedule.	Yes, $250,000/$100,000 investment and $250 per new employee	NR
District of Columbia	No	No	No
Florida	No, see § 220.191 F.S.	Yes	No
Georgia	Yes, rates from 1% to 10%, computed as a percentage of qualified investment property. Qualifying property includes manufacturing and pollution control equipment, buildings, telecommunications, recycling, defense conversion, and certain water conversion equipment.	Yes, see OCGA § 48-7-40 and DOR Website	Yes, see OCGA § 48-7-40.12 and DOR Website
Hawaii	Yes, see §§ 235-110.3, .4, .7, .8, and .9, HRS.	Yes, see § 235-55.91, HRS.	Yes, see § 235-110.91, HRS.
Idaho	3% of qualified investment of property located in Idaho that would have qualified for federal ITC prior to its general repeal, except for lightweight vehicles and property not used in Idaho. Limitations apply, see § 63-3029B, Idaho Code. Qualifying property includes manufacturing and pollution control equipment.	Yes, the credit is $500 per qualified new employee, or $1,000 per qualified new employee, who in the calendar year ending during the taxable year for which the credit is claimed, received annual earnings at an average rate of $15.50 or more per hour. The credit may not exceed 3.25% of the net income from the business.	Yes, for activities conducted in Idaho. The credit is the sum of (i) 5% of the excess of qualified research payments over the base amount; and (ii) 5% of basic research payments allowable under IRC § 41(e). The credit together with any other credits shall not exceed the amount of tax due. See Idaho Code § 63-3029G.

Investment, Jobs, and Research Credits (Part 1)

Legend:
R&D — Research and development
NA — Not applicable
NR — Not reported

	Does State Allow an Investment Tax Credit?	*Does State Allow a Jobs Credit?*	*Does State Allow a Research Credit?*
Illinois	Yes. See IITA § § 201(e) and 201(f). Qualifying property includes manufacturing and pollution control equipment, buildings and fixtures, tangible property used by a retailer, manufacturer, or a miner of coal or fluorite. A credit is also allowed for tangible, depreciable property used in enterprise zones and by certain high-impact businesses.	Yes, increased employment can affect the ITC rate. See IITA § 201(e).	Yes, reinstated for taxable years ending on and after 12/31/04. 6.5% of the increase in Illinois R&D expenditures over the average expenditures over a 3-year base period
Indiana	No	No	Yes, computed by using Form IT 20 Rec
Iowa	10% rate; qualifying property includes manufacturing equipment, pollution control equipment, buildings and fixtures, and land and improvements to land.	Yes, one-time credit of 6% of unemployment wage base if there is training agreement with community college.	Yes, Iowa allows either the regular method or the alternative simplified method (SAF) in computing the Iowa research credit. The alternative simplified method can be used starting for tax years beginning on or after 1/1/10.
Kansas	Yes, 10% of net investment over base period. Manufacturing equipment, buildings and fixtures, and pollution control equipment.	No new credit for jobs after 12/31/11. Unused jobs credits earned prior to 2012 may be carried forward provided qualifying criteria are met.	Yes, Excess of current year research and development expenditures over average expenditures of last three years multiplied by 6.5%. Maximum of 25% of credit allowed in any one tax year.
Kentucky	No	No	No

Investment, Jobs, and Research Credits (Part 1)

Legend:

R&D	Research and development
NA	Not applicable
NR	Not reported

	Does State Allow an Investment Tax Credit?	*Does State Allow a Jobs Credit?*	*Does State Allow a Research Credit?*
Louisiana	Yes, effective 07/10/2007, Acts 2007, No 400 amends RS 51: 1787 to allow taxpayers in an Enterprise Zone a choice between the current sales tax rebate and an investment income tax credit.	Yes, New Jobs Credit (LSA R.S. 47:287.749); Credit for Hiring Eligible Re-Entrants (LSA R.S. 47:287.748); Credit for Employment of the Previously Unemployed (LSA R.S. 47:6004); Credit for the Employment of Certain First-Time Drug Offenders (LSA R.S. 47:287.752)	Yes, per LSA R.S. 47:6015, for income tax years beginning on or after 1/1/2005, and franchise tax years beginning on or after 1/1/2006, the Department of Economic Development may approve a credit to qualifying taxpayers in an amount equal to 8% of the state's apportioned share of the taxpayer's expenditures for increasing research activities, 20% of the state's apportioned share of the taxpayer's expenditures for increasing research activities, if the taxpayer is an entity that employs 500 or more Louisiana residents, or 25% of the state's apportioned share of eligible expenditures if the taxpayer claims the alternative incremental tax credit pursuant to 26 U.S.C. § 41.

Investment, Jobs, and Research Credits (Part 1)

Legend:

R&D	Research and development
NA	Not applicable
NR	Not reported

	Does State Allow an Investment Tax Credit?	*Does State Allow a Jobs Credit?*	*Does State Allow a Research Credit?*
Maine	Yes, Investment Tax Credit. The credit is based on the federal credit amount, according to the Internal Revenue Code in effect as of 12/31/85, which is based on investment in qualified property. Limitations: the taxpayer must create at least 100 new jobs within 2 years from the date the qualified property was placed in service and invest at least $5,000,000 in one year. The credit is limited to tax liability or $500,000, whichever is less, and cannot be carried back, but can be carried forward up to 7 years. 36 M.R.S.A. § 5215. High Technology Investment Tax Credit. The credit is based on the adjusted basis of eligible equipment. Limitations: the credit is limited to high-tech equipment purchased (or leased) by businesses engaged primarily in high-tech activities. The credit cannot reduce tax below zero or to an amount below the previous year's tax after credits and cannot exceed $100,000 in any one year. The credit cannot be carried back, but can be carried forward for up to 5 years. 36 M.R.S.A. § 5219-M.	Yes, Jobs and Investment Tax Credit. The credit is based on the federal credit amount, according to the Internal Revenue Code in effect as of 12/31/85, which is based on investment in qualified property. Limitations: the taxpayer must create at least 100 new jobs within 2 years from the date the qualified property was placed in service and invest at least $5,000,000 in one year. The credit is limited to tax liability or $500,000, whichever is less, and cannot be carried back, but can be carried forward up to 7 years. 36 M.R.S.A. § 5215.	Research Expense Tax Credit. The credit is based on a percentage of the federal credit for increasing research activities. Limitations: the credit is limited to 5% of the excess qualified research expenses over the previous 3-year average, plus 7.5% of the basic research payments under IRC § 41(e)(1)(A). The credit is limited to the tax liability of the taxpayer. For corporate taxpayers, the credit is further limited to 100% of the first $25,000 in tax liability plus 75% of the tax liability in excess of $25,000. The credit cannot be carried back, but can be carried forward for up to 15 years. 36 M.R.S.A. § 5219-K. Super Research and Development Credit. Taxpayers that qualify for the research expense credit may also qualify for the super research credit. The credit is based on qualified research payments exceeding 150% of the average 3 taxable years immediately preceding 6/12/97. Limitations: the credit is limited to 50% of the tax otherwise due after all other credits. Further, the credit cannot reduce tax liability below the amount due the previous year after credits. The credit cannot be carried back, but can be carried forward for up to 5 years. 36 M.R.S.A. § 5219.
Maryland	No		NR

Investment, Jobs, and Research Credits (Part 1)

Legend:

R&D	Research and development
NA	Not applicable
NR	Not reported

	Does State Allow an Investment Tax Credit?	*Does State Allow a Jobs Credit?*	*Does State Allow a Research Credit?*
Massachusetts	Yes, varies based on year, 90% of qualified purchases. Tangible property, including realty and personal property	Yes, $100 per month per eligible employee	Yes, similar to federal R&D credit
Michigan (Business Tax)	Yes, 2008-2.32% of qualified investment expenses, 2009 and later, 2.9% of qualified investment expenses.		Yes, 2008-1.52% of qualified R&D expenses, 2009 and later, 1.9% of qualified R&D expenses.

Note. The CIT takes effect 01/01/12, and replaces the Michigan Business Tax (MBT) for most taxpayers. However, businesses that have been approved to receive, have received, or have been assigned certain certified credits may elect to file a return and pay the tax imposed by the MBT in lieu of the CIT until the certified credits are exhausted or extinguished.

Minnesota	No	No	Yes, similar to federal
Mississippi	No	Yes, depends on type of business and county classification	$1,000 per employee for each job requiring R&D skills
Missouri	No	Yes, computed by Dept of Economic Development	Yes, computed by Dept of Economic Development
Montana	No	Yes, credit of 1% of new wages for new and expanding corporations	Yes, 5% of qualified expenses for research conducted in Montana

Investment, Jobs, and Research Credits (Part 1)

Legend:

R&D	Research and development
NA	Not applicable
NR	Not reported

	Does State Allow an Investment Tax Credit?	*Does State Allow a Jobs Credit?*	*Does State Allow a Research Credit?*
Nebraska	No	No	Yes, the credit is 15% of federal credit allowed under § 41 of the IRC. For business firms that make expenditures in research and experimental activities defined in § 174 of the IRC on the campus of college or university in Nebraska or at a facility owned by a college or university in this state, the credit is equal to 30% of the federal credit allowed under § 41of the IRC. Multistate businesses must apportion the credit based on the actual amount expended in research and experimental activities or the average property and payroll factors.
Nevada	Nevada does not impose a corporate income tax		
New Hampshire	Yes, see RSA 77-A:5, XI	Yes, see RSA 77-A:5, VII and RSA 77-RSA-A:5, XIV	Yes, see RSA 77-A:5, XIII
New Jersey	Yes, per the terms of the New Jobs Investment Tax Credit Act, N.J.S.A. 54:10A-5.4 to 5.15; Manufacturing Equipment and Employment Investment Tax Credit Act N.J.S.A. 54:10-5.21. Small NJ Based High Technology Business Investment Tax Credit Act N.J.S.A. 54:10A-5.28 to 30. Enterprise Zone Investment Tax Credit	Yes, per the terms of the New Jobs Investment Tax Credit Act, N.J.S.A. 54:10A-5.4 to 5.15; Manufacturing Equipment and Employment Investment Tax Credit Act N.J.S.A. 54:10-5.21. Small NJ Based High Technology Business Investment Tax Credit Act N.J.S.A. 54:10A-5.28 to 30	Yes, similar to federal. N.J. Stat. Ann. 54:10A-5.24, see also N.J.S.A. 54:10A-24b (15 year carry-forward)

Investment, Jobs, and Research Credits (Part 1)

Legend:

R&D	Research and development
NA	Not applicable
NR	Not reported

	Does State Allow an Investment Tax Credit?	*Does State Allow a Jobs Credit?*	*Does State Allow a Research Credit?*
New Mexico	Yes, see New Mexico Publication FYI-106.	Yes, Federal Welfare to Work credit for 50% of amount claimed under 26 U.S.C. § 51A. Job mentorship credit for 50% of wages paid to full time students in accredited New Mexico secondary schools.	Yes, see New Mexico Publication FYI-106.
New York	Yes, credits for investments include: the investment tax credit (ITC) (including an ITC in Empire Zones and the financial services ITC); R&D ITC; a historic properties credit; biofuel production credit; film and commercial production credits; Empire Zone capital credit; brownfields redevelopment credit; qualified emerging technology company (QETC) facilities, operations, and training credit, and a capital credit	Yes, credits rewarding job creation include: credit for employment of persons with disabilities; employment incentive credit calculated on the base of the ITC/ EZ-ITC; Empire Zone wage credit; security officer training tax credit; QETC employment credit	Yes, rate same as ITC, except optional 9% rate if no Employment Incentive Credit taken. Also, QETC credits are research focused.
North Carolina	Yes, manufacturing equipment, building and fixtures and pollution abatement equipment. See Article 3J (G.S. 105-129.80 through G.S. 105-129.89)	Yes, G.S. 105-129.87	Yes, G.S. 105-129.87
North Dakota	No	Yes, only for certain "new industries," percentage of wages for the first 5 years	Yes, 25% of the first $100,000 of qualified expenses, plus a percentage ranging from 8% to 20% for qualified expenses over $100,000. The percentage of expenses over $100,000 I dependent on when the ND research began.
Ohio	Ohio does not impose a corporate income tax		

Investment, Jobs, and Research Credits (Part 1)

Legend:

R&D	Research and development
NA	Not applicable
NR	Not reported

	Does State Allow an Investment Tax Credit?	*Does State Allow a Jobs Credit?*	*Does State Allow a Research Credit?*
Note. Effective 1/1/2010, the Ohio Franchise Tax was fully phased out and business will be taxed on gross receipts through the Commercial Activity Tax. Details about that tax can be found at: http//tax.ohio.gov/divisions/commercial_activities/index.stm			
Oklahoma	1% of qualified property. 2% under certain conditions and if located in an enterprise zone computed on Oklahoma Form 506, Qualifying property includes manufacturing and pollution control equipment and buildings and fixtures but only if related to manufacturing.	Yes, $500 per new job (doubles in enterprise zones)	No
Oregon	Yes, manufacturing equipment, buildings and fixtures	Yes, up to $2,500 of first year wages in youth apprentice program, employer must have participated in program before 11/4/93. Credit 50% of wages up to a maximum of $1,000 per youth for up to two years. Effective for tax years beginning on or after 1/1/98.	Yes, 5% of increase in qualified research expenses and basic research payments or 5% of qualified research expenses that exceed 10% of Oregon sales. Maximum credit of $500,000. Limited to activities in Oregon.
Pennsylvania	No	Yes, based on percentage of qualifying wages	Yes
Rhode Island	Yes, based on cost of property; 4% buildings (manufacturing only), 10% qualified property purchases. Property that qualifies: manufacturing equipment, buildings and fixtures, and certain qualified leases.	Yes	Yes, 22.5% up to $111,111 of expenses, 16% in excess of $111,111.
South Carolina	Yes, manufacturing equipment 1/2% for 3 years,; 1%, 7 years; 2%, 10 year; 2.5%, 15 years S.C. Code § 12-4-60(B)	Yes, $8,000 for Tier IV; $4,250 Tier III, $2,750, Tier II; $1,500, Tier 1 § 12-6-3360	Yes
South Dakota	South Dakota does not impose a corporate income tax		

Investment, Jobs, and Research Credits (Part 1)

Legend:

R&D	Research and development
NA	Not applicable
NR	Not reported

	Does State Allow an Investment Tax Credit?	*Does State Allow a Jobs Credit?*	*Does State Allow a Research Credit?*
Tennessee	Industrial machinery excise tax credit of 1% of purchase price; qualifying property includes manufacturing and pollution control equipment and industrial machinery.	Yes	No
Texas	No	No	No
Utah	As part of Utah's Enterprise Zone Credit for designated areas there is an investment tax credit.	No	6% of qualified research expenses exceeding base amount and 6% of payments to qualified organizations for basic research that exceeds the base amount
Vermont	Yes, 5% to 10% of investment computed by application to the Vermont Economic Progress Council	Yes, by application to Vermont Economic Progress Council, 5% to 10% of increase with prior approval	Yes, by application to Vermont Economic Progress Council 10% with prior approval

Investment, Jobs, and Research Credits (Part 1)

Legend:

R&D	Research and development
NA	Not applicable
NR	Not reported

	Does State Allow an Investment Tax Credit?	*Does State Allow a Jobs Credit?*	*Does State Allow a Research Credit?*
Virginia	Yes, An amount equal to 50% of a taxpayer's qualified investments. No credit shall be allowed to any taxpayer that has committed capital under management in excess of $10 million and engages in the business of making debt or equity investments in private businesses, or to any taxpayer that is allocated a credit as a partner, shareholder, member or owner of an entity that engages in such business. The Qualified Equity and Subordinated Debt Investment Tax Credit is limited to individuals or corporations making investments in businesses related to advanced computing, advanced materials, advanced manufacturing, agricultural technologies, biotechnology, electronic device technology, energy environmental technology, medical device technology, nanotechnology, or any similar technology, medical device technology, nanotechnology, or any similar technology-related field.	Yes, (1) the nonrefundable credit is equal to $1,000 for each qualifying new job in excess of the applicable job threshold. The applicable thresholds are 25 qualifying new jobs in an enterprise zone or economically distressed area, and 50 qualifying new jobs elsewhere in Virginia. (2) Virginia allows a corporate and individual income tax credit for each new "green job" that is created in Virginia. The amount of the credit is $500 for each job that is created and that has an annual salary of $50,000 or more. The tax credit is allowed in the first taxable year in which the job had been filled for at least one year, and for the four succeeding taxable years in which the job is continuously filled. The tax credit is allowed for up to 350 green jobs per taxpayer. (3) Effective for taxable years beginning on and after 01/01/11 but before 01/01/15, Virginia allows an international trade facility tax credit for either capital investment in an international trade facility or increasing jobs related to an international trade facility. The amount of the credit is equal to either $3,000 per new qualified full-time employee that results from increased qualified trade activities by the taxpayer or two percent of the amount of capital	Yes, The credit amount is equal to (1) 15 percent of the first $167,000 in Virginia qualified research and development expenses; or (2) 20 percent of the first $175,000 in Virginia qualified research and development expenses if the research was conducted in conjunction with a Virginia public college or university, to the extent the expenses exceed the Virginia base amount for the taxpayer. The Virginia base amount has the same meaning as ''base amount'' that is defined in § 41(c) of the IRC, but pertains to research and development conducted in Virginia only. The amount of the Virginia tax credit is determined by using the incremental expenses for research and development conducted in Virginia that exceeds the expenses for research and development that constitute the Virginia base amount. Virginia's credit is subject to a $5 million cap. If the total amount of approved tax credits is less that $5 million, the remaining amount will be allocated to taxpayers in an amount equal to 15 percent of the second $167,000 in Virginia qualified research expenses or 20 percent of the second $175,000 in Virginia qualified research expenses if the research was conducted in conjunction with a

Legend:
R&D Research and development
NA Not applicable
NR Not reported

Investment, Jobs, and Research Credits (Part 1)

	Does State Allow an Investment Tax Credit?	*Does State Allow a Jobs Credit?*	*Does State Allow a Research Credit?*
		investment made by the taxpayer to facilitate increased trade activities.	Virginia public college or university, to the extent the expenses exceed the Virginia base amount, on a pro rata basic.
Washington	Washington does not impose a corporate income tax		
West Virginia	Various state credits available	Yes	Yes

Investment, Jobs, and Research Credits (Part 1)

Legend:

R&D Research and development
NA Not applicable
NR Not reported

	Does State Allow an Investment Tax Credit?	*Does State Allow a Jobs Credit?*	*Does State Allow a Research Credit?*
Wisconsin	Yes, various rates depending on the credit claimed. See Wisconsin Publication 123. Qualifying property includes manufacturing equipment, buildings and fixtures.	Yes, (This is not the Enterprise Zone Jobs Credit). For taxable years beginning on or after 1/1/10, the credit is equal to any of the following: (1) The amount of wages that the claimant paid to an eligible employee in the taxable year, not to exceed 10% of such wages, as determined b the Dept. of Commerce (2) The amount of costs incurred by the claimant in the taxable year, as determined by the Dept. of Commerce to undertake training activities.	Yes, research expense credit: 5% of increase in qualified research expenses (as defined in IRC) incurred in Wisconsin over a base period. Increases to 10% for certain qualified research activities (related to internal combustion engines and certain energy efficient products). Alternative incremental research credit computation available, but changes made by P.L 109-432 do not apply. Research facilities credit: 5% of amount paid or incurred to construct and equip new facilities or expand existing facilities used in Wisconsin for qualified research (as defined by IRC). Increase to 10% for certain qualified research activities (related to internal combustion engines and certain energy efficient products. Super research and development credits: For taxable years beginning on or after 1/1/11, an amount equal to the amount of qualified research expenses paid or incurred by the corporation in the taxable year that exceeds the amount calculated as follows: (1) Determine the avg. amount of the qualified research expenses paid or incurred by the corporation in the 3 taxable years immediately preceding the taxable year for which a credit is claimed and (2) multiply the amount determined by 1.25.

Investment, Jobs, and Research Credits (Part 1)

Legend:

R&D	Research and development
NA	Not applicable
NR	Not reported

	Does State Allow an Investment Tax Credit?	*Does State Allow a Jobs Credit?*	*Does State Allow a Research Credit?*
Wyoming	Wyoming does not impose a corporate income tax		

Investments, Jobs, Research Credits (Part 2)

Legend:
R&D Research and Development
NA Not Applicable
NR Not Reported

	Does State Allow an Energy Credit for Businesses?	*If Yes, How is it Computed?*	*Does State Provide a Mechanism for Taxpayers to Sell, Transfer or Assign Unused Credits or Incentives to Another Taxpayer?*	*If Yes, How does the Mechanism Work?*
Alabama	No		No	
Alaska	Yes	18% of federal energy credit	Yes	The only transferable credit available is for the film production tax credit. The taxpayer must complete Form 0405-707 to request approval of transfer of the credit.
Arizona	Yes	See A.R.S. § 43-1164.02 starting 2011	No, generally. Depends on specific credit.	
Arkansas	No		Yes	Varies based on Arkansas code.
California	No		Yes	Permissable assignments, which are made via an irrevocable election on an original return, may only be made to affiliates that are in a unitary relationship both at the time the credit is first earned and also at the time the credit is assigned. See R&TC § 23663.
Colorado	No		Yes	Gross Conservation Easement Credit is transferrable. See Colo. Rev. Stat. § 39-22-522.

Legend:
R&D Research and Development
NA Not Applicable
NR Not Reported

Investments, Jobs, Research Credits (Part 2)

	Does State Allow an Energy Credit for Businesses?	*If Yes, How is it Computed?*	*Does State Provide a Mechanism for Taxpayers to Sell, Transfer or Assign Unused Credits or Incentives to Another Taxpayer?*	*If Yes, How does the Mechanism Work?*
Connecticut	No		Yes	Many of Connecticut's tax credits may be transferred to another taxpayer. For additional information see Informational Publication 2010(13), A Guide to Connecticut's Business Tax Credits
Delaware	No		Yes	Must complete Form 1811CC 0701
District of Columbia	No		No	
Florida	Yes, §§220.192 & 220.193 F.S.	Fla. Stat. §§ 220.192 & 220.193. (expired 06/30/10)	Yes	Applies to certain credits
Georgia	Yes	See GA. Code § 48-7-29.14 and DOR's website.	Yes	Credits may be assigned to affiliated entities as provided by GA. Code § 48-7-42 and the Film Tax Credit may be sold as provided in GA. Code § 48-7-40.26.
Hawaii	Yes	As a percentage of the actual cost, up to a cap per system. The percentage depends on the type of system and whether the credit is refundable. (See Haw. Rev. Stat. § 235-12.5.)	No	

Legend:

R&D Research and Development
NA Not Applicable
NR Not Reported

	Does State Allow an Energy Credit for Businesses?	*If Yes, How is it Computed?*	*Does State Provide a Mechanism for Taxpayers to Sell, Transfer or Assign Unused Credits or Incentives to Another Taxpayer?*	*If Yes, How does the Mechanism Work?*
Idaho	Yes	Idaho offers an income tax credit for: qualified equipment utilizing post-consumer waste or post-industrial waste (Idaho Code § 53-3029D); capital investment in biofuel infrastructure (Idaho Code § 63-3029M).	Yes	Idaho law allows for the "transfer" of the income tax credit for investment in broadband equipment (Idaho Code § 53-3029J). Idaho Income Tax Administrative Rules 719-793 provide information regarding the transfer of these credits. Rule 791.01 states: A taxpayer who intends to transfer qualified credit shall notify the Tax Commission in writing of its intent to transfer the credit at least 60 days prior to the date of transfer. A transfer may not take place prior to the Tax Commission providing its response as to the amount of credit available and the years the credit may be carried forward. Additionally, Idaho law does allow Idaho corporate taxpayers that are part of a unitary group filing a combined report to "use" income tax credits earned by another Idaho corporate taxpayer filing as part of the same unitary group. For

Legend:

R&D	Research and Development
NA	Not Applicable
NR	Not Reported

	Does State Allow an Energy Credit for Businesses?	*If Yes, How is it Computed?*	*Does State Provide a Mechanism for Taxpayers to Sell, Transfer or Assign Unused Credits or Incentives to Another Taxpayer?*	*If Yes, How does the Mechanism Work?*
				example the two credits mentioned above; the Idaho investment tax credit (Idaho Code § 63-3029B); the credit for research activities (Idaho Code § 63-3029G); and the credit for capital investments in biofuel infrastructure (Idaho Code § 63-3029M). Prior permission is not required for the "use" of the credit between members of the same unitary group.
Illinois	No		Yes	Only the film credit (35 ILCS 5/213) and the credit for affordable housing donations (35 ILCS 5/214) may be transferred. Transfers of the film credit are administered by the Department of Commerce and Economic Opportunity. Transfers of the affordable housing donations credit are administered by the Illinois Housing Development Authority.

Investments, Jobs, Research Credits (Part 2)

Legend:
R&D Research and Development
NA Not Applicable
NR Not Reported

	Does State Allow an Energy Credit for Businesses?	*If Yes, How is it Computed?*	*Does State Provide a Mechanism for Taxpayers to Sell, Transfer or Assign Unused Credits or Incentives to Another Taxpayer?*	*If Yes, How does the Mechanism Work?*
Indiana	No		In general no, however one credit, the Coal Gasification Technology Investment Credit, can be assigned by contract, subject to restrictions.	
Iowa	Yes	Companies engaged in the production of wind energy and renewable energy which are approved by the Iowa Utilities Board are eligible for production tax credits. Most of the credits involve wind projects. The credit is $0.01 per kilowatt hour for large wind projects and $0.015 cents per kilowatt hour for small wind projects.	Yes	Tax credit certificates are issued by the Department of Revenue or another state agency. When the credit is transferred, the original certificate is surrendered to the Department of Revenue, and a replacement certificate is issued by the Department of Revenue to the purchaser of the credit.
Kansas	Yes	The credit is 10% of the taxpayer's qualified investment for the first $50,000,000 and 5% of the amount of the taxpayer's qualified investment that exceeds $50,000,000. Such credit shall be taken in 10 equal, annual installments, beginning with the year in which the taxpayer places into service the new renewable electric cogeneration facility.	No	
Kentucky	No		No	

Legend:

R&D — Research and Development
NA — Not Applicable
NR — Not Reported

Investments, Jobs, Research Credits (Part 2)

	Does State Allow an Energy Credit for Businesses?	*If Yes, How is it Computed?*	*Does State Provide a Mechanism for Taxpayers to Sell, Transfer or Assign Unused Credits or Incentives to Another Taxpayer?*	*If Yes, How does the Mechanism Work?*
Louisiana	Yes	50% of the first $25,000 in cost of each residential wind or solar energy system, including installation.	Yes	Unclaimed credits may be transferred or sold to another Louisiana taxpayer, subject to conditions specifically provided for each credit or incentive.
Maine	No		No	
Maryland	Yes	Maryland Clean Energy Incentive Tax Credit, MD. Code Ann., Tax-General § 10-720, allows a credit against the state income tax for electricity produced by certain qualified Maryland facilities from certain qualified energy resources. The tax credit, which must be certified by the Maryland Energy Administration, is generally computed at $0.0085 cents per kilowatt hour of electricity. The tax credit is available to certified electricity that has been produced and put in service on or after 01/01/2006, but before 01/01/2016.	No	
Massachusetts	Yes		Yes	Depends on credit.

Investments, Jobs, Research Credits (Part 2)

Legend:

R&D Research and Development

NA Not Applicable

NR Not Reported

	Does State Allow an Energy Credit for Businesses?	*If Yes, How is it Computed?*	*Does State Provide a Mechanism for Taxpayers to Sell, Transfer or Assign Unused Credits or Incentives to Another Taxpayer?*	*If Yes, How does the Mechanism Work?*
Michigan	Yes	Various targeted credits are allowed under the Michigan Business Tax. See Michigan Compiled Laws 208.1429, 208.1430, 208.1432 and 208.1434 for examples.	Yes	Various Michigan Business Tax credits allow for assignment of all or a portion of the credit, generally within the tax year that the credit is earned. See Michigan Compiled Laws 208.1430, 208.1437, 208.1455 and 208.1457 for more details.
Note. The CIT takes effect 01/01/12, and replaces the Michigan Business Tax (MBT) for most taxpayers. However, businesses that have been approved to receive, have received, or have been assigned certain certified credits may elect to file a return and pay the tax imposed by the MBT in lieu of the CIT until the certified credits are exhausted or extinguished.				
Minnesota	No		No	
Mississippi	Yes	An investment tax credit equal to 5% of investments made in the initial establishment of an eligible facility. It can offset up to 50% of total state income tax liability and has a five year carryforward. (MS Code Ann. § 27-7-22.35)	No	
Missouri	No		Yes	Each credit has its own statutory requirements.
Montana	Yes		No	
Nebraska	Yes		No	
Nevada	Nevada does not impose a corporate income tax			
New Hampshire	No		No	

Investments, Jobs, Research Credits (Part 2)

Legend:

R&D	Research and Development
NA	Not Applicable
NR	Not Reported

	Does State Allow an Energy Credit for Businesses?	*If Yes, How is it Computed?*	*Does State Provide a Mechanism for Taxpayers to Sell, Transfer or Assign Unused Credits or Incentives to Another Taxpayer?*	*If Yes, How does the Mechanism Work?*
New Jersey	No		Yes	Business Retention and Relocation Credit—For fiscal years beginning 07/01/2004, a credit against the corporation business tax (or insurance premiums tax) is provided for retention of jobs in New Jersey. Businesses with unused amounts of credits that cannot be applied by the business prior to the expiration of the credits may transfer the credits for use by other nonaffiliated taxpayers on the Corporation Business Tax and Insurance Premiums Tax returns in exchange for private financial assistance to be provided by the recipient of the Corporation Business Tax Credit Certificate or Insurance Premiums Tax Credit Certificate to assist in the funding of costs incurred by the relocating business. N.J.S.A. 24:1-B-120.2. Corporation Business Tax Benefit Certificate Transfer Program—High-tech companies are allowed to

Investments, Jobs, Research Credits (Part 2)

Legend:
R&D Research and Development
NA Not Applicable
NR Not Reported

Does State Allow an Energy Credit for Businesses?	*If Yes, How is it Computed?*	*Does State Provide a Mechanism for Taxpayers to Sell, Transfer or Assign Unused Credits or Incentives to Another Taxpayer?*	*If Yes, How does the Mechanism Work?*
			trade their unused research and development credits and net operating losses to another corporate entity through a certificate program in exchange for private financial assistance from the entity acquiring the surrendered tax benefits. N.J.S.A.34:1B-7.42a. Film Production Credit—A taxpayer may apply to the Director for a Tax Credit Transfer Certificate in lieu of the taxpayer being allowed any amount of the credit against the taxpayer's tax liability. If allowed, the tax credit transfer certificate may be sold or assigned, in full or in part, to any other taxpayer that may have a tax liability under the Gross Income tax or the Corporation Business tax in exchange for private financial assistance to be provided by the purchaser or assignee to the taxpayer that has applied for and been granted the credit. N.J.A.C. 18:7-3B.6(a) through

Legend:

R&D Research and Development

NA Not Applicable

NR Not Reported

	Does State Allow an Energy Credit for Businesses?	*If Yes, How is it Computed?*	*Does State Provide a Mechanism for Taxpayers to Sell, Transfer or Assign Unused Credits or Incentives to Another Taxpayer?*	*If Yes, How does the Mechanism Work?*
				18:7-3B.6(c).
New Mexico	Yes	See New Mexico Publication FYI-106.	Yes	See NM Publication FYI-106.
New York	Yes	New York allows several energy credits for businesses. These include the Power for Jobs Credit, the Clean Fuel Heating Credit, and the Biofuel Production Credit. For more details, see New York's annual Tax Expenditure Report.	No	
North Carolina	Yes	The tax credit for investing in renewable energy property is equal to 35% of the cost of renewable energy property constructed, purchased, or leased by a taxpayer and placed into service in North Carolina during the taxable year. For business and other non-residential property, the credit is taken in five equal installments beginning with the year the property is placed in service. However, the credit is subject to various ceiling amounts.	No	

Investments, Jobs, Research Credits (Part 2)

Legend:
R&D — Research and Development
NA — Not Applicable
NR — Not Reported

	Does State Allow an Energy Credit for Businesses?	*If Yes, How is it Computed?*	*Does State Provide a Mechanism for Taxpayers to Sell, Transfer or Assign Unused Credits or Incentives to Another Taxpayer?*	*If Yes, How does the Mechanism Work?*
North Dakota	Yes	The credit is allowed for the installation of biomass, geothermal, solar or wind energy devices in a building owned or leased in North Dakota. The credit is equal to 3% of the cost of acquisition and installation in each of the first five years (a total of 15%). The credit is allowed in the year the installation is completed.	Yes	This mechanism applies only to the Research and Experimental Expenditures Credit. For taxpayer's filing a consolidated North Dakota return with more than one North Dakota nexus company, an unused credit may offset another affiliate's liability. For other situations, certain conditions must be met and the taxpayer wishing to sell/transfer the credit must first be certified by the Department of Commerce. The maximum amount of credit that a taxpayer may sell is limited to $100,000 per lifetime. Seller and purchaser must report terms of the sale to the Tax Department.
Ohio	Ohio does not impose a corporate income tax			
Oklahoma	No		Yes	Certain credits are transferrable by statute. Must execute transfer agreement (Form 572) and submit to Oklahoma Tax Commission.

Investments, Jobs, Research Credits (Part 2)

Legend:

R&D Research and Development
NA Not Applicable
NR Not Reported

	Does State Allow an Energy Credit for Businesses?	*If Yes, How is it Computed?*	*Does State Provide a Mechanism for Taxpayers to Sell, Transfer or Assign Unused Credits or Incentives to Another Taxpayer?*	*If Yes, How does the Mechanism Work?*
Oregon	Yes	See ORS 315.354 Energy Conservation Facilities. Generally, the credit is 35% of the certified cost of the facility, spread over 5 years (10% yrs 1-2 and 5% years 3-5), with exceptions, limitations, and carryover provisions.	Yes	Depends on the credit. Generally, Oregon Revised Statute (ORS) § 315.052 allows an income tax credit for corporations "that is transferable may be transferred or sold only once, unless expressly provided otherwise by statute."
Pennsylvania	No		Yes	Taxpayer must complete an application. Not all credits are authorized to be transferred.
Rhode Island	No		Yes	Only for Historic Preservation Tax Credits and Motion Picture Production Tax Credits. Application must be made to the Rhode Island Division of Taxation for written approval and a certificate which must be attached to the return claiming the credits.
South Carolina	Yes	§ 12-6-3587 solar, § 12-6-3588 systems manufacturers, § 12-6-3600 ethanol & biodiesel, § 12-6-3610 facility, § 12-6-3620 biomass and § 12-6-3631 R&D	Yes	Conservation carryovers are approved by the Department of Revenue
South Dakota	South Dakota does not impose a corporate income tax			

Investments, Jobs, Research Credits (Part 2)

Legend:
R&D Research and Development
NA Not Applicable
NR Not Reported

	Does State Allow an Energy Credit for Businesses?	*If Yes, How is it Computed?*	*Does State Provide a Mechanism for Taxpayers to Sell, Transfer or Assign Unused Credits or Incentives to Another Taxpayer?*	*If Yes, How does the Mechanism Work?*
Tennessee	No		No	
Texas	No		No	
Utah	Yes	Utah Code Ann. § 59-7-614 provides for a Renewable Energy Systems tax credit. A business entity is allowed a credit of 10% of the costs of a Commercial Energy System and 25% of the costs of each residential unit it owns or uses under the foregoing statute.	No, however a business enterprise that earns a residential energy credit may assign its right to the credit to an individual taxpayer that purchases the residential unit. Also, a business entity that leases a commercial energy system installed on a commercial unit may essentially assign the credit to the lessee if the lessor irrevocably elects not to claim the credit.	

Investments, Jobs, Research Credits (Part 2)

Legend:

R&D	Research and Development
NA	Not Applicable
NR	Not Reported

	Does State Allow an Energy Credit for Businesses?	*If Yes, How is it Computed?*	*Does State Provide a Mechanism for Taxpayers to Sell, Transfer or Assign Unused Credits or Incentives to Another Taxpayer?*	*If Yes, How does the Mechanism Work?*
Vermont	Yes	Corporations may qualify for a credit of 100% of the Vermont-property portion of the Business Solar Energy Investment Tax Credit component of the Federal Investment Tax Credit allowed under IRC § 48. The credit must be approved by the Vermont Clean Energy Development Board. There is a cap on the total expenditure for this credit.	Yes	The only credit that may be transferred is the Downtown and Village Center Program Tax Credit (32 V.S.A. §§ 5930dd(f), 5930(ff), which may be transferred to a bank or insurance company to be taken against the bank franchise tax or insurance premiums tax respectively. The mechanism is for the applicant to request the credit in the form of a bank credit certificate that a bank may accept in return for cash or adjusting the rate or term of the applicants' mortgage or loan related to the qualified building.

Investments, Jobs, Research Credits (Part 2)

Legend:
R&D Research and Development
NA Not Applicable
NR Not Reported

	Does State Allow an Energy Credit for Businesses?	*If Yes, How is it Computed?*	*Does State Provide a Mechanism for Taxpayers to Sell, Transfer or Assign Unused Credits or Incentives to Another Taxpayer?*	*If Yes, How does the Mechanism Work?*
Virginia	No		Yes	The Virginia Land Preservation Tax Credit and the Biodiesel and Green Diesel Fuels Producers Tax Credit - transferred via forms provided by the Department of Taxation. The Coal Employment and Production Incentive Tax Credit - May be allocated between the electricity generator and person with an economic interest in coal through the contract for the sale of the coal.
Washington	Washington does not impose a corporate income tax			
West Virginia	No		No	

Investments, Jobs, Research Credits (Part 2)

Legend:
R&D — Research and Development
NA — Not Applicable
NR — Not Reported

	Does State Allow an Energy Credit for Businesses?	*If Yes, How is it Computed?*	*Does State Provide a Mechanism for Taxpayers to Sell, Transfer or Assign Unused Credits or Incentives to Another Taxpayer?*	*If Yes, How does the Mechanism Work?*
Wisconsin	No		Yes	A person who is eligible to claim the early stage Seed Investment Credit may sell or otherwise transfer the credit to another person who is subject to tax if the person receives prior authorization from the investment fund manager and the manager then notifies the Department of Commerce and the Department of Revenue of the transfer and submits with the notification a copy of the transfer documents. No person may sell or otherwise transfer a credit more than once in a 12-month period. The Department of Commerce may charge any person selling or otherwise transferring a credit a fee equal to 1% of the credit amount sold or transferred.
Wyoming	Wyoming does not impose a corporate income tax			

Enterprise Zones

States attempt to stimulate economic growth and development in numerous ways. Tax incentives have proven to be a strong marketing tool. Consequently, nearly every state offers some type of corporate tax credit or incentive to attract new businesses, encourage particular activities, or expand economic opportunity in targeted geographic areas.

To encourage development of economically distressed areas, many states have embraced the concept of enterprise zones or similar development programs. An enterprise zone typically is a defined geographic area with certain economic and social characteristics. The size of the enterprise zone varies according to the demographics and economics of the state. Some states establish enterprise zones that are limited to a few city blocks; others designate an entire county for economic expansion.

Enterprise zones and similar development programs are typically available through the state's department of economic development, commerce, or community affairs, or some similar agency, and are designed to enhance opportunities for private investment in certain areas. These incentives are intended to encourage investment in the area and to reduce or remove regulatory barriers to economic development.

Granting tax incentives to businesses is not without its critics, who often object to such programs on public policy and constitutional grounds. In addition, states have begun to realize that tax incentives alone generally will not bring an economic renaissance to a depressed area. As a consequence, some states use "claw back" provisions, which require the taxpayer to reimburse the government for prior benefits if certain conditions established in exchange for those benefits are not satisfied.

Eligibility

Generally, the states are responsible for the designation of enterprise zones. Restrictions may apply to the number of zones that may be authorized or the criteria that may be used to designate them. Many states designate specific industries as eligible for participation; however, a state may make the program available to all businesses. The usual intent of states that designate specific industries is to target businesses that are likely to provide greater social benefits at a lower incentive cost. Many times, a state will base eligibility on a business's standard industrial classification (SIC) code. Generally, states do not narrow their eligibility requirements to a specific type of business entity. The programs are normally available to C corporations, S corporations, partnerships, and individuals. States with enterprise zone programs have promulgated regulations governing the process under which a local business may be certified to receive the various benefits available through the program.

For the most part, local municipalities (or local agencies) are responsible for administering and managing enterprise zones, which nevertheless must meet the designation criteria established by state statute. Normally, an application must be submitted and approved before a company may avail itself of the tax credits or incentives; however, not all tax credits or incentives require certification. Taxpayers usually may participate in the program and qualify for the credits or incentives at any time during the life of an enterprise zone.

Income/Franchise Tax Incentives

Two common types of income/franchise tax incentives are investment tax credits and jobs credits. A state investment credit is usually administered as a percentage of the investments in qualified property and is applied against the state income tax. The definition of qualified property often follows that found in Code Section 179, which applies to new and used tangible personal business property. Most states require that the qualified property not have been previously used in the enterprise zone or the state. Generally, to qualify for the credit, the property must be placed in service on or after the date the zone is designated and on or before the last day of the company's tax year. Unused credits can usually be carried forward to offset the tax liability in subsequent years.

The purpose of a jobs credit usually is to encourage businesses to hire residents of enterprise zones. In most instances, a qualified zone employee means an employee who performs substantially all of his or her services for the employer within the enterprise zone and whose principal place of abode while performing services is within an enterprise zone. The employer receives a tax credit that is typically a percentage of the sum of qualified zone wages paid or incurred in hiring a qualified employee during the tax year or a per diem amount (e.g., $500 per employee). Many times, a cap is imposed or a threshold is required. Unused credits can usually be carried forward.

Sales and Use Tax Incentives

The purchase of certain tangible personal property and services may be exempt from sales and use taxes. Many times, the exemption will apply to property that is used or consumed in a manufacturing or assembly process or in the operation of a pollution control facility within an enterprise zone. If the state already offers such an exemption to taxpayers in general, the definition of the manufacturing process or the types of items that are exempt may be expanded. Sales and use tax exemptions for tangible personal property may require certification that the minimum investment or job creation requirements have been met.

Building materials used in remodeling, rehabilitation, or new construction within an enterprise zone may also be exempt from sales and use taxes. The building materials typically must be used in the zone, and the materials must be permanently affixed to the real property and purchased locally. *Locally* could mean within the zone or within the municipality or unincorporated area of the county that authorized the zone. Sales and use tax exemptions for building materials may not require certification and are generally available to all taxpayers within the zone; however, an affidavit is normally required from the local authority to give to sellers of building materials.

Property Tax Incentives

States generally administer two types of property tax incentives: tax abatement and assessment reduction. Generally, neither incentive requires certification of any minimum investment or job creation requirements.

Tax abatements for all, or a portion, of the taxes on real property generally require improvements to have been constructed or existing improvements to have been renovated or rehabilitated. The abatement typically applies to the taxes on the increase in assessed value attributable to the new construction, renovation, or rehabilitation. Taxes based on the assessed value of the land and the existing improvements continue to be extended and collected. Tax abatements marginally affect the calculation of tax rates. The tax rate for a district is normally calculated by dividing the district's tax levy by its tax base. The lower the tax base, the higher the rate needed to generate the amount of the levy. Eligibility criteria and tax abatement formulas are usually established by local ordinance and may vary within a zone.

Eligible businesses may be able to receive a reduced assessment ratio on all personal and real property for a limited period of time. The tax rate remains the same, but the taxing authority may classify improvements under a special category. Some states do not classify improvements within an enterprise zone at different assessment rates and therefore may offer the tax abatement program. The qualifying business usually needs to report annually to the department of commerce (or similar agency), and tax abatement does not begin until certification is obtained.

Other Tax Incentives

A credit may be available for the utility taxes on gas or electricity consumed within an enterprise zone. It may be an income tax credit, a sales tax credit, or another kind of tax credit. Sometimes, the credit includes an abatement of a portion, or all, of the administrative or miscellaneous charges. A state may also offer lower, "incentive" utility rates as a benefit to large commercial and industrial energy users located within an enterprise zone.

State-by-State Summary

The chart that follows identifies the states that have adopted enterprise zone programs, the types of tax incentives they offer, the manner in which the incentive is recognized, and the areas currently designated as enterprise or development zones.

Enterprise Zones

Legend:

X — State will offer a tax incentive for this type of tax
NA — Not applicable
NR — Not reported

	Does State Offer Tax Incentives for Enterprise Zones?	*If Yes, Types of Tax Incentives?*						*If Yes, Form of Incentives?*	*What Areas Constitute Your Enterprise Zones?*
		Income Taxes	*Franchise Taxes*	*Sales Taxes*	*Property Taxes*	*Unemployment Taxes*	*Other*		
Alabama	Yes	X	X					Credit	As determined by the Alabama Department of Community Affairs
Alaska	No	NA	NA	NA	NA	NA	NA	NA	NA
Arizona	Yes	X			X		X, Premium	As a credit Tax	Contact State Department of Revenue for locations
Arkansas	No						Based on controlling Arkansas Code section	NA	
California	Yes	X	X	X				Credit and/or deduction	42 geographic zones throughout California; see The California Housing and Community Agency Enterprise Zone Map

Enterprise Zones

Legend:

X	State will offer a tax incentive for this type of tax
NA	Not applicable
NR	Not reported

	Does State Offer Tax Incentives for Enterprise Zones?	*If Yes, Types of Tax Incentives?* Income Taxes	Franchise Taxes	Sales Taxes	Property Taxes	Unemployment Taxes	Other	*If Yes, Form of Incentives?*	*What Areas Constitute Your Enterprise Zones?*
Colorado	Yes	X		X	X		Sales tax exemptions	As a credit, sales tax exemptions	See website
Connecticut	Yes	X			X			As a credit	Designated by Department of Economic and Community Development
Delaware	Yes	X					Gross receipts tax	As a credit	Targeted census tracks; contact Department of Revenue.
District of Columbia	Yes	X	X	X	X		X, withholding	Credit, deduction and exemption	Areas marked by the Deputy Mayor for Planning and Economic Development.
Florida	Yes	X		X	X			As a credit	Designated by Legislature
Georgia	Yes	X					As a credit	NR	
Hawaii	Yes	X			X	X	General excise tax	Deduction or credit	NR

Enterprise Zones

Legend:
X State will offer a tax incentive for this type of tax
NA Not applicable
NR Not reported

	Does State Offer Tax Incentives for Enterprise Zones?	*If Yes, Types of Tax Incentives?*						If Yes, Form of Incentives?	What Areas Constitute Your Enterprise Zones?
		Income Taxes	Franchise Taxes	Sales Taxes	Property Taxes	Unemployment Taxes	Other		
Idaho	Yes, similar to Idaho's Urban Renewal areas				X			As a credit	NR
Illinois	Yes	X		X				NR	A list can be obtained from Illinois Department of Commerce and Community Affairs, 620 E. Adams, Springfield, Ill. 62701.
Indiana	Yes	X			X			NR	Enterprise Zone Board designates zones in addition to any zone that the federal government may designate.

Legend:

X	State will offer a tax incentive for this type of tax
NA	Not applicable
NR	Not reported

Enterprise Zones

	Does State Offer Tax Incentives for Enterprise Zones?	*If Yes, Types of Tax Incentives?*						*If Yes, Form of Incentives?*	*What Areas Constitute Your Enterprise Zones?*
		Income Taxes	*Franchise Taxes*	*Sales Taxes*	*Property Taxes*	*Unemployment Taxes*	*Other*		
Iowa	Yes	X		X	X			As a credit	Cannot comprise more than 1% of the area of a county.
Kansas	No							A	
Kentucky	No								
Louisiana	Yes	X	X	X				As a credit	Various; La. Rev. Stat. 51:1781

Enterprise Zones

Legend:

X	State will offer a tax incentive for this type of tax
NA	Not applicable
NR	Not reported

	Does State Offer Tax Incentives for Enterprise Zones?	*If Yes, Types of Tax Incentives?*						*If Yes, Form of Incentives?*	*What Areas Constitute Your Enterprise Zones?*
		Income Taxes	*Franchise Taxes*	*Sales Taxes*	*Property Taxes*	*Unemployment Taxes*	*Other*		
Maine	Yes	X	X				Insurance Premiums Tax	As a credit, and reimbursement	Pine Tree Development Zones are designated as either Tier 1 locations (municipalities in all Maine counties except Cumberland and York, plus municipalities in Cumberland and York that have a high unemployment rate) or Tier 2 locations, (municipalities that do not qualify for Tier 1 designation). Tax benefits for Tier 1 locations are available for 10 years and,

Enterprise Zones

Legend:

X	State will offer a tax incentive for this type of tax
NA	Not applicable
NR	Not reported

	Does State Offer Tax Incentives for Enterprise Zones?	*If Yes, Types of Tax Incentives?* Income Taxes	Franchise Taxes	Sales Taxes	Property Taxes	Unemployment Taxes	Other	*If Yes, Form of Incentives?*	*What Areas Constitute Your Enterprise Zones?*
									for Tier 2 locations, 5 years. The income tax benefit is a credit equal to 100 % of the Maine tax liability for each of the first 5 years of eligibility and 50% of the tax liability in each of the second 5 years of eligibility. There is also an employment tax increment financing reimbursement of 80% of required income tax withholding from qualified

Legend:

X	State will offer a tax incentive for this type of tax
NA	Not applicable
NR	Not reported

Enterprise Zones

	Does State Offer Tax Incentives for Enterprise Zones?	*If Yes, Types of Tax Incentives?*						*If Yes, Form of Incentives?*	*What Areas Constitute Your Enterprise Zones?*
		Income Taxes	*Franchise Taxes*	*Sales Taxes*	*Property Taxes*	*Unemployment Taxes*	*Other*		
									employees.
Maryland	Yes	X			X			As a credit	Areas established by the Secretary of Economic and Community Development.
Massachusetts	Yes	X	X		X			As a credit	NR
Michigan (Business Tax)	No								
Note. The CIT takes effect 01/01/12, and replaces the Michigan Business Tax (MBT) for most taxpayers. However, businesses that have been approved to receive, have received, or have been assigned certain certified credits may elect to file a return and pay the tax imposed by the MBT in lieu of the CIT until the certified credits are exhausted or extinguished.									
Minnesota	Yes	X	X	X	X			As a credit and deduction	Designated by the Department of Employment and Economic Development

Enterprise Zones

Legend:

X	State will offer a tax incentive for this type of tax
NA	Not applicable
NR	Not reported

	Does State Offer Tax Incentives for Enterprise Zones?	*If Yes, Types of Tax Incentives?* Income Taxes	Franchise Taxes	Sales Taxes	Property Taxes	Unemployment Taxes	Other	*If Yes, Form of Incentives?*	*What Areas Constitute Your Enterprise Zones?*
Mississippi	Yes	Offer several other income tax credits and outright exemptions for income and franchise tax							
Missouri	Yes	X						As a credit	This program is administered by Department of Economic Development.
Montana	Yes	X						As a credit	NA
Nebraska	No	X		X				As a credit	NR
Nevada	Nevada does not impose a corporate income tax								
New Hampshire	Yes						Business Enterprise Tax	See RSA 77-A:5, XII and RSA 162-N:6	Designated by the Department of Resources and Economic Development under RSA 162-N.

Enterprise Zones

Legend:

X	State will offer a tax incentive for this type of tax
NA	Not applicable
NR	Not reported

	Does State Offer Tax Incentives for Enterprise Zones?	*If Yes, Types of Tax Incentives?*						*If Yes, Form of Incentives?*	*What Areas Constitute Your Enterprise Zones?*
		Income Taxes	*Franchise Taxes*	*Sales Taxes*	*Property Taxes*	*Unemployment Taxes*	*Other*		
New Jersey	Yes		X	X				As a credit	Designated by the legislature in certain cities.
New Mexico	Yes	X						As a credit	NR
New York	Yes	X	X	X	X			As a credit	Empire Zones have been designated at 84 locations throughout the state. Also certain "regionally significant projects" can be eligible for Empire Zone benefits regardless of location

Note. The Empire Zones Program expired on 6/30/10. Taxpayers certified in the program as of 6/30/10 may continue to receive credits for the duration of their tax benefit period.

Enterprise Zones

Legend:

X State will offer a tax incentive for this type of tax

NA Not applicable

NR Not reported

	Does State Offer Tax Incentives for Enterprise Zones?	*If Yes, Types of Tax Incentives?* Income Taxes	Franchise Taxes	Sales Taxes	Property Taxes	Unemployment Taxes	Other	*If Yes, Form of Incentives?*	*What Areas Constitute Your Enterprise Zones?*
North Carolina	Yes	X	X				Insurance Gross Premiums Tax	As a credit	Enterprise Tiers as determined by the Commerce Department
North Dakota	No	NA	NA	NA	NA	NA	NA	NA	NA
Ohio	Ohio does not impose a corporate income tax								
Note. Effective 1/1/2010, the Ohio Franchise Tax was fully phased out and business will be taxed on gross receipts through the Commercial Activity Tax. Details about that tax can be found at: http//tax.ohio.gov/divisions/commercial_activities/index.stm									
Oklahoma	Yes	X		X				As a credit, enhances (doubles) investment credit	Statutory definition
Oregon	Yes	X			X			As a credit	Scattered throughout state
Pennsylvania	Yes	X	X					As a credit	NR
Rhode Island	Yes	X						As a credit	Specially designated areas, see 42-64.3 R.I.G.L.

Enterprise Zones

Legend:

X	State will offer a tax incentive for this type of tax
NA	Not applicable
NR	Not reported

	Does State Offer Tax Incentives for Enterprise Zones?	If Yes, Types of Tax Incentives?						If Yes, Form of Incentives?	What Areas Constitute Your Enterprise Zones?
		Income Taxes	Franchise Taxes	Sales Taxes	Property Taxes	Unemployment Taxes	Other		
South Carolina	No								
South Dakota	South Dakota does not impose a corporate income tax								
Tennessee	Yes	X	X					As a credit	Economically distressed counties
Texas	Yes			X				As a credit	See Government Code, Chapter 2303
Utah	Yes	X	X					As a credit	Specific areas of counties and cities that have qualified as disadvantaged and applied for designation; for more information contact Utah Department of Economic Development.

Enterprise Zones

Legend:

X	State will offer a tax incentive for this type of tax
NA	Not applicable
NR	Not reported

	Does State Offer Tax Incentives for Enterprise Zones?	*If Yes, Types of Tax Incentives?*						*If Yes, Form of Incentives?*	*What Areas Constitute Your Enterprise Zones?*
		Income Taxes	*Franchise Taxes*	*Sales Taxes*	*Property Taxes*	*Unemployment Taxes*	*Other*		
Vermont	No	NA	NA	NA	NA	NA	NA	NA	NA
Virginia	Yes	X	X			X	Virginia allows an Enterprise Zone business Tax Credit and an Enterprise Zone Real Property Investment Tax Credit for those businesses that already receive the credits. Beginning on and after 7/1/05, the credit was switched to the Enterprise Zone Grant Program, and was capped at $7.5 million per year.	Grants	They are determined by the Governor (See Va. Code §59.1-539)
Washington	Washington does not impose a corporate income tax								

Enterprise Zones

Legend:

X	State will offer a tax incentive for this type of tax
NA	Not applicable
NR	Not reported

		If Yes, Types of Tax Incentives?							
	Does State Offer Tax Incentives for Enterprise Zones?	*Income Taxes*	*Franchise Taxes*	*Sales Taxes*	*Property Taxes*	*Unemployment Taxes*	*Other*	*If Yes, Form of Incentives?*	*What Areas Constitute Your Enterprise Zones?*
West Virginia	No	NA	NA	NA	NA	NA	NA	NA	NA
Wisconsin	Yes	X	X					As a credit	Various areas determined by the Wisconsin Economic Development Corporation
Wyoming	Wyoming does not impose a corporate income tax								

Business Tax Incentives Outside Enterprise Zones

Background

A state's economic future depends, in part, on the degree to which businesses are encouraged to locate, expand, or retain their operations in the state. Businesses consider a number of factors when deciding where to locate their operations, including the availability and cost of labor, proximity to suppliers and markets, transportation costs, the cost of utilities, real estate costs, the regulatory environment, and quality of life issues such as local schools, public services, and recreational opportunities. To a large extent, this is a cost-minimization decision, and therefore differential tax burdens can play a role in determining where a business chooses to locate or expand.

All states, as well as many local governments, have incentive programs in place to attract new business investment. Examples include low-cost financing (e.g., tax-incremental financing, and industrial development or revenue bonds), assistance with construction (e.g., site clearing, grading, road construction, and water, sewer, and utility installation), zoning adjustments, and employee educational and training assistance. Tax incentives have also proven to be a strong marketing tool. Consequently, every state offers tax incentives to attract new businesses, encourage particular activities, or expand economic development in targeted geographic areas.

To obtain the maximum benefit from state incentive programs, it is important for a company to contact the appropriate state and local economic development offices at the early stages of the project. This allows time to identify potential tax and nontax incentives, develop relationships with incentive-granting agencies, and establish procedures to comply with the requirements for receiving the incentives. In addition, certain incentives, such as property tax abatements, may be subject to negotiation. Because many small or mid-sized companies may not have the personnel or resources to identify and take advantage of all the available incentives, it may be beneficial for them to seek assistance from outside consultants.

To help ensure that the state realizes the anticipated economic benefits from providing a corporation with special tax incentives, many states have enacted recapture, or "claw back" provisions, which require the taxpayer to reimburse the government for prior benefits if certain conditions established in exchange for those benefits are not satisfied.

Enterprise Zones

To encourage development of economically distressed areas, many states have embraced the concept of enterprise zones or similar development programs. An enterprise zone typically is a defined geographic area with certain economic and social characteristics. The size of the enterprise zone varies according to the demographics and economics of the state. Some states establish enterprise zones that are limited to a few city blocks; other states designate entire counties for economic expansion. For a more detailed discussion of this topic, see the section in this part entitled Enterprise Zones.

Types of Business Tax Incentives Offered Outside Enterprise Zones

Most states do not limit their business tax incentives to companies that locate facilities in designated enterprise zones, but instead offer an array of business tax incentives that taxpayers can benefit from on a statewide basis. The specific tax incentives offered vary significantly from one state to another, and generally include income tax incentives as well as incentives related to franchise, sales, and property taxes. (Property tax incentives must often be negotiated with local taxing jurisdictions.) Common examples include the following:

- Income tax incentives
  - — Investment credits
  - — Jobs credits
  - — Research and development credits

  - — Energy credits
  - — General income tax incentives (e.g., apportionment formulas that emphasize the sales factor and the lack of a sales throwback rule)
- Property tax incentives
  - — Abatements
  - — Reduced assessment rates
  - — Deferral of tax payments
- Sales and use tax incentives
  - — Exemptions for machinery and equipment used in manufacturing
  - — Exemptions for items consumed in manufacturing

State-by-State Summary

The following chart, presented in two parts, provides information regarding which states offer business tax incentives outside of enterprise zones, the types of business incentives offered, whether the incentives take the form of a credit or a deduction, and the types of requirements that must be met to qualify for the tax incentives.

Business Tax Incentives Outside Enterprise Zones (Part 1)

Legend:

X	Indicates available tax incentives
NA	Not applicable
NR	Not reported

	Does State Offer Tax Incentives for Businesses Other Than Those in Enterprise Zones?	*If Yes, What Types of Tax Incentives Are Available?*					
		Income Taxes	*Franchise Taxes*	*Sales Taxes*	*Property Taxes*	*Unemployment Taxes*	*Other*
Alabama	Yes	X			X		
Alaska	No	NA	NA	NA	NA	NA	NA
Arizona	Yes	X		X	X		
Arkansas	Yes	X		X			
California	Yes	X	X	X			
Colorado	No						
Connecticut	Yes	X	X		X		See 2011 Conn. Pub. Acts 86-Commissioner of Department of Economic and Community Development (DECD) may grant substantial financial assistance including loans. Contact DECD for information.

Note. During the 2011 legislative session, the following incentives were passed: (1) 2011 Conn. Pub. Acts 86, An Act Creating the First Five Program. Available to the first five companies creating investment and job expansion in each income year commencing on or after 1/1/11 and prior to 1/1/13; (2) 2011 Conn. Pub. Acts 6, §78, which allows corporations and insurance companies to increase the cap on the use of tax credits for adding new employees; and (3) 2011 Conn. Pub. Acts 140, §§4-5, which allows taxpayers to establish a "manufacturers reinvestment account" (MRA) that may be used to purchase machinery, equipment, manufacturing facilities or for workforce training, development, or expansion. The funds put into the account are deducted from a corporation's taxable income and are taxed at a different rate.

Legend:

X	Indicates available tax incentives
NA	Not applicable
NR	Not reported

Business Tax Incentives Outside Enterprise Zones (Part 1)

	Does State Offer Tax Incentives for Businesses Other Than Those in Enterprise Zones?	*If Yes, What Types of Tax Incentives Are Available?*					
		Income Taxes	*Franchise Taxes*	*Sales Taxes*	*Property Taxes*	*Unemployment Taxes*	*Other*
Delaware	Yes	X					X, gross receipts tax
District of Columbia	Yes		X	X	X		X, withholding
Florida	Yes	X		X	X		Credit and others
Georgia	Yes	X		X			
Hawaii	NR	NR	NR	NR	NR	NR	NR
Idaho	Yes	X					Credit for qualifying new employees, broadband investment credit. See §§ 63-3029B, E, F, and I.
Illinois	Yes	X		X			
Indiana	Yes	X			X		Various requirements, see IR6-3.1.
Iowa	Yes	X		X	X		

Business Tax Incentives Outside Enterprise Zones (Part 1)

Legend:

X — Indicates available tax incentives
NA — Not applicable
NR — Not reported

	Does State Offer Tax Incentives for Businesses Other Than Those in Enterprise Zones?	*If Yes, What Types of Tax Incentives Are Available?*					
		Income Taxes	*Franchise Taxes*	*Sales Taxes*	*Property Taxes*	*Unemployment Taxes*	*Other*
Kansas	Yes	X		X	X		In addition to depreciation and expensing claimed for federal purposes, an expense deduction from Kansas taxable income is available to businesses that invest in machinery & equipment depreciable under MACRS in IRC § 168 or canned software as defined in IRC § 197 that is located in Kansas (effective for tax year 2012). Specifics are contained in House Substitute for Senate Bill 196. Investment credits may not be claimed if the expensing option is used.
Kentucky	Yes	X					Limited liability entity tax as provided by KRS 141.0401

Business Tax Incentives Outside Enterprise Zones (Part 1)

Legend:

X	Indicates available tax incentives
NA	Not applicable
NR	Not reported

	Does State Offer Tax Incentives for Businesses Other Than Those in Enterprise Zones?	*If Yes, What Types of Tax Incentives Are Available?*					
		Income Taxes	*Franchise Taxes*	*Sales Taxes*	*Property Taxes*	*Unemployment Taxes*	*Other*
Louisiana	Yes	X	X	X			
Maine	Yes	X			X, on equipment		
Maryland	Yes	X			X		
Massachusetts	Yes	X	X		X		
Michigan (Business Tax)	Yes	X			X		
Note. The CIT takes effect 01/01/12, and replaces the Michigan Business Tax (MBT) for most taxpayers. However, businesses that have been approved to receive, have received, or have been assigned certain certified credits may elect to file a return and pay the tax imposed by the MBT in lieu of the CIT until the certified credits are exhausted or extinguished.							
Minnesota	No						
Mississippi	Yes	X	X	X	X		
Missouri	Yes	X					
Montana	Yes	X					
Nebraska	Yes	X	X	X	X		
Nevada	Nevada does not impose a corporate income tax						
New Hampshire	No						

Legend:

X	Indicates available tax incentives
NA	Not applicable
NR	Not reported

Business Tax Incentives Outside Enterprise Zones (Part 1)

	Does State Offer Tax Incentives for Businesses Other Than Those in Enterprise Zones?	*If Yes, What Types of Tax Incentives Are Available?*					
		Income Taxes	*Franchise Taxes*	*Sales Taxes*	*Property Taxes*	*Unemployment Taxes*	*Other*
New Jersey	Yes	X	X		X		Media Content Production Credit: PL 2007 c 257. Business Relocation Tax Credit PL 2007 c 310. Urban Transit Hub Tax Credit: PL 2007 c 346. Sports and Entertainment District: PL 2007 c 30
Note. Offshore Wind Economic Development Credit - P.L. 2010, c. 57. Credit awarded to businesses for offshore wind energy facilities approved by the Economic Development Authority taken over the course of 10 years at a rate of one-tenth of the value of the total credit for each accounting or privilege period starting with the period the business was approved by the EDA.							
New Mexico	Yes	X, See Note		X		X, withholding taxes, compensating taxes	
Note. Effective for personal income taxes for tax years beginning 1/1/04, taxpayers who make payments to a licensed nursing home, licensed intermediate care facility for the mentally retarded, or a licensed residential treatment center may take a refundable credit on personal income tax of up to $10 per day that the expenses are the taxpayer's responsibility. Expenses incurred before 7/1/04 and after 6/30/07, are excluded.							
New York	Yes	X	X	X	X		See New York's annual Tax Expenditure Report.
North Carolina	Yes	X	X				Insurance Gross Premiums Tax

Legend:

X	Indicates available tax incentives
NA	Not applicable
NR	Not reported

Business Tax Incentives Outside Enterprise Zones (Part 1)

	Does State Offer Tax Incentives for Businesses Other Than Those in Enterprise Zones?	*If Yes, What Types of Tax Incentives Are Available?*					
		Income Taxes	*Franchise Taxes*	*Sales Taxes*	*Property Taxes*	*Unemployment Taxes*	*Other*
North Dakota	Yes	X		X	X		
Ohio	Ohio does not impose a corporate income tax						
Note. Effective 1/1/2010, the Ohio Franchise Tax was fully phased out and business will be taxed on gross receipts through the Commercial Activity Tax. Details about that tax can be found at: http//tax.ohio.gov/divisions/commercial_activities/index.stm							
Oklahoma	Yes	X		X	X, local only; not state	Oklahoma Quality Jobs Incentive Program	
Oregon	Yes	X			X		
Pennsylvania	Yes	X	X	X	X		
Rhode Island	No						
South Carolina	Yes	X			X		
South Dakota	South Dakota does not impose a corporate income tax						
Tennessee	Yes	X	X				
Texas	No						
Utah	Yes						See Note.
Note. Partial rebates given to firms engaging in qualifying aerospace and aviation industry projects that bring new, incremental jobs Into the state. In addition, Contingent tax credits may be issued to investors in the Utah fund of funds in connection with the Venture Capital Enhancement Act.							
Vermont	Yes	X		X	X		

Business Tax Incentives Outside Enterprise Zones (Part 1)

Legend:

X	Indicates available tax incentives
NA	Not applicable
NR	Not reported

	Does State Offer Tax Incentives for Businesses Other Than Those in Enterprise Zones?	*If Yes, What Types of Tax Incentives Are Available?*					
		Income Taxes	*Franchise Taxes*	*Sales Taxes*	*Property Taxes*	*Unemployment Taxes*	*Other*
Virginia	Yes	X					X, to qualify for Virginia's major business facility job tax credit, the taxpayer must increase employment by creating more than 25-50 new full-time jobs, depending on location. Virginia has adopted two additional credits that provide incentives for businesses to expand Virginia facilities. Effective for taxable years beginning on and after 01/01/11 but before 01/01/15, Virginia allows an international trade facility tax credit for either capital investment in an international trade facility or increasing jobs related to an

Business Tax Incentives Outside Enterprise Zones (Part 1)

Legend:

X	Indicates available tax incentives
NA	Not applicable
NR	Not reported

	Does State Offer Tax Incentives for Businesses Other Than Those in Enterprise Zones?	*If Yes, What Types of Tax Incentives Are Available?*					
		Income Taxes	*Franchise Taxes*	*Sales Taxes*	*Property Taxes*	*Unemployment Taxes*	*Other*
							international trade facility. The amount of the credit is equal to either $3,000 per new qualified full-time employee that results from increased qualified trade activities by the taxpayer or two percent of the amount of capital investment of the amount of capital investment made by the taxpayer to facilitate increased eligible trade activities. Effective for taxable years beginning on and after 01/01/11, Virginia also offers a wineries and vineyards tax credit, which is equal to 25 percent of the cost of all qualified capital expenditures

Business Tax Incentives Outside Enterprise Zones (Part 1)

Legend:
X — Indicates available tax incentives
NA — Not applicable
NR — Not reported

		If Yes, What Types of Tax Incentives Are Available?					
	Does State Offer Tax Incentives for Businesses Other Than Those in Enterprise Zones?	*Income Taxes*	*Franchise Taxes*	*Sales Taxes*	*Property Taxes*	*Unemployment Taxes*	*Other*
							made in connection with the establishment of new Virginia farm wineries and vineyards and capital improvements made to existing Virginia farm wineries and vineyards.
Washington	Washington does not impose a corporate income tax						
West Virginia	Yes	NR	NR	NR	NR	NR	NR
Wisconsin	Yes, Research Facilities Credit	X	X				
Wyoming	Wyoming does not impose a corporate income tax						

Business Tax Incentives Outside Enterprise Zones (Part 2)

Legend:

X	Condition applies
NA	Not applicable
NR	Not reported

	If Tax Incentives Are Available, What is The Form of The Incentives?		
	Credit	*Deduction/Exemption*	*What Requirements Must Be Met to Qualify for Tax Incentives?*
Alabama	X		Various, must qualify project before undertaking expansion/relocation, increase productive output, and increase employment.
Alaska			
Arizona	X		NR
Arkansas	X	Deduction/Exemption	Based on controlling Arkansas code section. Must qualify project before undertaking expansion or relocation, increase employment.
California	X	X	Increase employment. There is also a credit for television and film production in California, see R&TC § 23685, and a production relocated to California qualifies for this credit.
Colorado			
Connecticut	X	X, (MRA)	Must qualify project before undertaking expansion/relocation and increase employment (for First Five and MRA)

Note. 2011 Conn. Pub. Acts 86 - Commissioner of Department of Economic and Community Development (DECD) may grant substantial financial assistance including loans.

Business Tax Incentives Outside Enterprise Zones (Part 2)

Legend:

X	Condition applies
NA	Not applicable
NR	Not reported

	If Tax Incentives Are Available, What is The Form of The Incentives?		
	Credit	*Deduction/Exemption*	*What Requirements Must Be Met to Qualify for Tax Incentives?*
Delaware	X		Must employ 5 new employees and invest $200,000. Facility must be examined by the Division of Revenue.
District of Columbia	X	X	Requirements specified for qualified high tech Co (QHTC), super market, tax incremental financing.
Florida	X		Must increase employment by a certain percentage and qualify project before undertaking expansion/ relocation.
Georgia	X	Exemption, sales tax	Provide retraining, provide childcare, water conservation, shift from ground water usage, increase port traffic, increase cigarette exports, new manufacturing jobs and property credit, film production credit. Must increase employment by x number of employees, depending on location. Must qualify project before undertaking for investment tax credit. See DOR's website @ www.dor.ga.gov
Hawaii	NR	NR	NR
Idaho	X		Certain assets acquired and additional jobs in businesses engaged in certain activities

Business Tax Incentives Outside Enterprise Zones (Part 2)

Legend:

X	Condition applies
NA	Not applicable
NR	Not reported

	If Tax Incentives Are Available, What is The Form of The Incentives?		
	Credit	*Deduction/Exemption*	*What Requirements Must Be Met to Qualify for Tax Incentives?*
Illinois	X		Must increase employment by 1% to obtain additional benefits. There is a research and development credit and environmental remediation.
Indiana	X		Various requirements, see IC6-3.1.
Iowa			Iowa new jobs and income program. A new provision started in 2003, called the "New Capital Investment Program," which is similar to the new jobs and income program but is available to smaller businesses.
Kansas	X	X	Must qualify project before undertaking expansion/relocation
Kentucky	X		Must qualify project before undertaking expansion/relocation.
Louisiana	X	X	Must increase employment by a certain percentage and qualify project before undertaking expansion/relocation.
Maine	X		Must create at least 100 new jobs ($1,200,000) within 2 years and $5,000,000 in qualified investment in 1st year. (Jobs and Investment Tax Credit, Title 36, § 5215).

Legend:

X Condition applies
NA Not applicable
NR Not reported

Business Tax Incentives Outside Enterprise Zones (Part 2)

	If Tax Incentives Are Available, What is The Form of The Incentives?		
	Credit	*Deduction/Exemption*	*What Requirements Must Be Met to Qualify for Tax Incentives?*
Maryland	X		Numerous incentives available, each having different requirements
Massachusetts	X		Other
Michigan (Business Tax)	X		Business must be located in renaissance zone.
Note. The CIT takes effect 01/01/12, and replaces the Michigan Business Tax (MBT) for most taxpayers. However, businesses that have been approved to receive, have received, or have been assigned certain certified credits may elect to file a return and pay the tax imposed by the MBT in lieu of the CIT until the certified credits are exhausted or extinguished.			
Minnesota			employment
Mississippi	X		An increase in employment
Missouri	X		Per statutory requirement of the credit.
Montana	X		Must increase employment by 30%
Nebraska	X		Must qualify project before undertaking expansion/relocation and employment and investment increases depending upon program, benefits sought, and location.
Nevada			
New Hampshire			
New Jersey	Grants from New Jersey Commerce and Economic Growth Commission	Yes	

Business Tax Incentives Outside Enterprise Zones (Part 2)

Legend:

X — Condition applies
NA — Not applicable
NR — Not reported

	If Tax Incentives Are Available, What is The Form of The Incentives?		
	Credit	*Deduction/Exemption*	*What Requirements Must Be Met to Qualify for Tax Incentives?*
New Mexico	X		Increase in employment. See New Mexico Publication FYI-106.
New York	X	X	See New York's annual Tax Expenditure Report.
North Carolina	X		NR
North Dakota	X	X	Some must be approved by the State Board of Equalization or the Division of Community Services and others must be representative of economic expansion.
Ohio	Ohio does not impose a corporate income tax		
Note. Effective 1/1/2010, the Ohio Franchise Tax was fully phased out and business will be taxed on gross receipts through the Commercial Activity Tax. Details about that tax can be found at: http//tax.ohio.gov/divisions/commercial_activities/index.stm			
Oklahoma	X		NR
Oregon	Exemption on major portion of large capital investments		
Pennsylvania	X		Must increase employment by 20% and have capital expenditures equal 10% of prior year revenues
Rhode Island	X	X	Must increase employment by at least 5%

Business Tax Incentives Outside Enterprise Zones (Part 2)

Legend:

X	Condition applies
NA	Not applicable
NR	Not reported

	If Tax Incentives Are Available, What is The Form of The Incentives?		
	Credit	*Deduction/Exemption*	*What Requirements Must Be Met to Qualify for Tax Incentives?*
South Carolina	X		Must increase employment; increase investment; qualify project before undertaking expansion or relocation in some cases
South Dakota			
Tennessee	X		Must have a $500,000 capital investment, increase employment by creating 25 new jobs and must qualify project before undertaking expansion/relocation
Texas	X		Varies; see Texas Tax Code § § 171.701 through 171.836.
Utah			Must qualify project before undertaking expansion/relocation
Vermont	X		Approval by Vermont Economic Progress Council and compliance with any performance expectations set by the Council
Virginia	X		Must increase employment by creating more than 25-100 new full-time jobs, depending on location
Washington			
West Virginia	NR	NR	NR

Business Tax Incentives Outside Enterprise Zones (Part 2)

Legend:
X Condition applies
NA Not applicable
NR Not reported

	If Tax Incentives Are Available, What is The Form of The Incentives?		
	Credit	*Deduction/Exemption*	*What Requirements Must Be Met to Qualify for Tax Incentives?*
Wisconsin	X		Qualifying project before undertaking expansion or relocation
Wyoming			

Gulf Opportunity Zone

In 2005, the Gulf Coast was substantially damaged by Hurricanes Katrina, Wilma, and Rita. To provide tax relief to help businesses recover from the devastation, Congress enacted Code Section 1400N (Gulf Opportunity Zone Act of 2005, Pub. L. No. 109-135, or "Gulf Zone Act"). The Gulf Zone Act creates a Gulf Opportunity Zone (GO Zone) for the areas within Alabama, Louisiana, and Mississippi affected by Hurricane Katrina, as well as a Rita GO Zone and a Wilma GO Zone for the areas within Florida, Louisiana, and Texas affected by Hurricanes Rita and Wilma [for listings of the applicable parishes and counties, see IRS Pub. 4492 (Jan. 2006)]. The Gulf Zone Act provides numerous tax breaks which affect the computation of federal taxable income, as well as enhanced business tax credits for certain expenditures in the GO Zone.

The Heartland, Habitat, Harvest, and Horticulture Act of 2008 (Pub. L. No. 110-246) extends some of these tax relief provisions to the victims of the tornadoes and storms that hit the Greensboro, Kansas area in May 2007.

Five-Year Net Operating Loss Carryback for GO Zone Losses

Generally, a net operating loss (NOL) can be carried back 2 years and forward up to 20 years. [IRC § 172] The Gulf Zone Act provides a five-year carryback, however, for GO Zone losses arising in any tax year ending on or after August 28, 2005. [IRC § 1400N(k)] Moreover, a GO Zone NOL is not subject to the 90-percent limitation that generally applies to an NOL for alternative minimum tax purposes. A GO Zone loss in a tax year is the lesser of (1) NOL for such tax year, reduced by any specified liability loss for such tax year to which a 10-year carryback applies under Code Section 172(b)(1)(C); or (2) sum of the following expenses for the tax year, including qualified GO Zone casualty losses, moving expenses, temporary employee housing expenses, depreciation of GO Zone property, and repair expenses.

First-Year Bonus Depreciation for GO Zone Property

The Gulf Zone Act permits taxpayers to claim a 50-percent first-year bonus depreciation allowance with respect to qualifying business property acquired on or after August 28, 2005, and placed in service in the GO Zone on or before December 31, 2007 [IRC § 1400N(d)]. In the case of residential rental and nonresidential real property, the placed in service expiration date is December 31, 2009, and December 31, 2010 for property in specified counties or parishes. Substantially all use of the property must be in the active conduct of a trade or business by the taxpayer within the GO Zone. Eligible property includes MACRS property with a recovery period of 20 years or less, MACRS 25-year water utility property, qualified leasehold improvement property, off-the-shelf computer software amortized over 3 years, residential rental property, or nonresidential real property. Bonus depreciation may not be claimed, however, on property used in connection with a private or commercial golf course, a country club, a massage parlor, a hot tub facility, a suntan facility, a liquor store, or a gambling or animal racing property.

Expanded Section 179 Asset Expensing for GO Zone Property

The maximum allowable Code Section 179 expense ($125,000 in 2007 and $250,000 in 2008) is increased by the lesser of $100,000 or the amount of qualified Section 179 GO Zone property placed in service during the tax year. Thus, the annual dollar limitation is $225,000 in 2007, and $350,000 in 2008. The Gulf Zone Act also increases the phase-out threshold ($500,000 in 2007 and $800,000 in 2008) by the lesser of $600,000 or the amount of qualified Section 179 GO Zone property placed in service in the tax year. These increases apply to qualified Section 179 GO Zone property acquired on or after August 28, 2005, and placed in service before January 1, 2008. [IRC § 1400N(e)] The Small Business and Work Opportunity Tax Act of 2007 [Pub. L. No. 110-28] extended the placed in service expiration date through 2008, but only for property in specified counties or parishes [see IRS Notice 2007-36, 2007-17 I.R.B. 1000].

For the increased limits to apply, the property (1) must be qualified GO Zone property, which has the same definition as for purposes of the 50 percent first-year bonus depreciation; and (2) must qualify as Section 179 property, which means it must be tangible personal property that is depreciable under MACRS (or off-the-shelf software amortized over three years) and is acquired by purchase for use in the active conduct of a trade or business. The additional Section 179 allowance may not be claimed, however, on property used in connection with a private or commercial golf course, a country club, a massage parlor, a hot tub facility, a suntan facility, a liquor store, or a gambling or animal racing property.

Demolition and Cleanup Costs in GO Zone

Under Code Section 280B, if a building or other structure is demolished, the demolition costs and debris removal costs are generally added to the basis of the replacement property, rather than deducted currently. However, a Section 165 casualty loss deduction may still be available with respect to the adjusted basis of the structure. To provide some relief, the Gulf Zone Act permits taxpayers to deduct 50 percent of the costs paid on or after August 28, 2005, and before January 1, 2008, to remove debris from, or to demolish structures on, real property that is in the GO Zone, but only if the real property is either (1) held by the taxpayer for use in a trade or business or (2) inventory in the hands of a taxpayer. [IRC § 1400N(f)]The provision applies only to the cost of demolishing structures and removing debris that would otherwise be capitalized. Amounts that could be deducted without regard to this provision continue to be currently deductible.

Environmental Remediation Costs in GO Zone

Under Code Section 198, a taxpayer may elect to deduct, rather than capitalize, environmental remediation expenditures paid in connection with the abatement or control of hazardous substances located on property used in a trade or business. This provision was scheduled to expire with respect to expenditures made after December 31, 2005, but the Gulf Zone Act extended the expiration date to December 31, 2007, for environmental remediation expenditures (including expenditures for the clean-up of petroleum products) paid in connection with a qualified contaminated site located in the GO Zone. [IRC § 1400N(g)]

Replacement Period Extension for Involuntary Conversions of Property in the Hurricane Katrina Disaster Area

Under Code Section 1033, if property is involuntarily converted into money as a result of its complete or partial destruction, any gain that arises from an insurance award need not be recognized to the extent the taxpayer reinvests the amount realized from the conversion into qualifying replacement property within two years after the close of the tax year in which the gain from the conversion is realized. The Katrina Emergency Tax Relief Act of 2005 (Pub. L. No. 109-73) extends the replacement period from two years to five years for property in the Hurricane Katrina disaster area that is involuntarily converted on or after August 25, 2005, due to the hurricane. This extension applies, however, only if substantially all of the use of the replacement property is in the Hurricane Katrina disaster area, which includes Alabama, Florida, Louisiana, and Mississippi.

State-by-State Summary

The following chart, presented in two parts, summarizes which states conform to the following Gulf Zone Act provisions:

- Five-year net operating loss carryback for GO Zone losses;
- First-year bonus depreciation for GO Zone property;
- Expanded Section 179 asset expensing for GO Zone property;
- Demolition and clean-up costs in GO Zone;
- Environmental remediation costs in GO Zone; and

- Replacement period extension for involuntary conversions of property in the Hurricane Katrina disaster area

Gulf Opportunity Zone (Part 1)

Legend:
NA Not applicable
NR Not reported

	Does Your State Conform to the Following Provisions of the Gulf Opportunity Zone Act of 2005?		
	5 Year Net Operating Loss Carryback for Gulf Opportunity Zone Recovery Losses	*50% Additional First-Year Depreciation Deduction on Qualified Gulf Opportunity Zone Property*	*Increase in the Maximum IRC § 179 Expense Amount by an Additional $100,000 for Qualified Gulf Opportunity Zone*
Alabama	No	Yes	Yes
Alaska	Yes	Yes	Yes
Arizona	Yes, information about the AZ NOL CF calculation can be found at A.R.S. § 43-1123, Arizona Administrative Code rule R15-2D-302, and AZ Corporate Income Tax Rulings CTR 91-2, CTR 94-11 and CTR 99-3.	No, A.R.S. § 43-1121(1) requires an addback of the depreciation deducted on the federal return and a subtraction under A.R.S. § 43-1122(1) for depreciation allowable under the Internal Revenue Code computed as if the tax payer had not elected bonus depreciation.	No, Arizona requires an adjustment to addback the federal section 179 expense taken at the federal level in excess of $25,000 and provides for a subtraction of the excess of $25,000 section 179 deduction to be subtracted ratably over a five-year period.
Arkansas	No	No	No
California	No, California does not conform to the provisions in the Katrina Emergency Tax Relief Act of 2005 ("KETRA"). However, under existing authority California allowed victims affected by the hurricanes described in KETRA an extension of time for filing and submitting tax payments.	No	No
Colorado	Yes	Yes	Yes
Connecticut	No written guidance	No written guidance	No written guidance
Delaware	Yes	Yes	Yes
District of Columbia	No	No	No
Florida	No	Yes	Yes

Gulf Opportunity Zone (Part 1)

Legend:
NA Not applicable
NR Not reported

	Does Your State Conform to the Following Provisions of the Gulf Opportunity Zone Act of 2005?		
	5 Year Net Operating Loss Carryback for Gulf Opportunity Zone Recovery Losses	*50% Additional First-Year Depreciation Deduction on Qualified Gulf Opportunity Zone Property*	*Increase in the Maximum IRC § 179 Expense Amount by an Additional $100,000 for Qualified Gulf Opportunity Zone*
Georgia	No	No	Yes
Hawaii	Yes	No	No
Idaho	No, Idaho Code § 63-3022	No, Idaho Code § 63-30220, IRC § 168(k)	Yes
Illinois	No	Yes	Yes
Indiana	No	No	No
Iowa	No	Yes	Yes
Kansas	No	Yes	Yes
Kentucky	No	No	No
Louisiana	No	Yes	Yes
Maine	Yes	Yes	Yes
Maryland	Yes	Yes	Yes
Massachusetts	No	No	Yes
Michigan (Business Tax)	No	Yes	Yes

Note. The CIT takes effect 01/01/12, and replaces the Michigan Business Tax (MBT) for most taxpayers. However, businesses that have been approved to receive, have received, or have been assigned certain certified credits may elect to file a return and pay the tax imposed by the MBT in lieu of the CIT until the certified credits are exhausted or extinguished.

Minnesota	No	Yes	No
Mississippi	No	No	Yes

Gulf Opportunity Zone (Part 1)

Legend:
NA Not applicable
NR Not reported

	Does Your State Conform to the Following Provisions of the Gulf Opportunity Zone Act of 2005?		
	5 Year Net Operating Loss Carryback for Gulf Opportunity Zone Recovery Losses	*50% Additional First-Year Depreciation Deduction on Qualified Gulf Opportunity Zone Property*	*Increase in the Maximum IRC § 179 Expense Amount by an Additional $100,000 for Qualified Gulf Opportunity Zone*
Missouri	Yes	Yes	Yes
Montana	No	Yes	Yes
Nebraska	No	Yes	Yes
Nevada	Nevada does not impose a corporate income tax		
New Hampshire	No	No	No
New Jersey	No	No	No
New Mexico	No	Yes	Yes
New York	Yes	Yes	Yes
North Carolina	No	Yes	Yes
North Dakota	No	Yes	Yes
Ohio	Ohio does not impose a corporate income tax		
Note. Effective 1/1/2010, the Ohio Franchise Tax was fully phased out and business will be taxed on gross receipts through the Commercial Activity Tax. Details about that tax can be found at: http//tax.ohio.gov/divisions/commercial_activities/index.stm			
Oklahoma	Yes	Yes	Yes
Oregon	No	Yes	Yes
Pennsylvania	No	Yes	Yes
Rhode Island	No	No	No
South Carolina	No	No	No
South Dakota	South Dakota does not impose a corporate income tax		

Gulf Opportunity Zone (Part 1)

Legend:
NA Not applicable
NR Not reported

	Does Your State Conform to the Following Provisions of the Gulf Opportunity Zone Act of 2005?		
	5 Year Net Operating Loss Carryback for Gulf Opportunity Zone Recovery Losses	*50% Additional First-Year Depreciation Deduction on Qualified Gulf Opportunity Zone Property*	*Increase in the Maximum IRC § 179 Expense Amount by an Additional $100,000 for Qualified Gulf Opportunity Zone*
Tennessee	No	No	Yes
Texas	No	No	No
Utah	No	Yes	Yes
Vermont	NR	NR	NR
Virginia	Yes	Virginia no longer conforms to this provision. See 2009 Acts of Assembly, Chapter 2	Yes
Washington	Washington does not impose a corporate income tax		
West Virginia	Yes	Yes	Yes
Wisconsin	No	No	No
Wyoming	Wyoming does not impose a corporate income tax		

Gulf Opportunity Zone (Part 2)

Legend:
NA Not applicable
NR Not reported

	Does Your State Conform to the Following Provisions of the Gulf Opportunity Zone Act of 2005?		
	Deduction for 50% of Costs to Remove Debris or to Demolish Structures in the Gulf Opportunity Zone	*Deduction for Qualified Environmental Remediation in Connection with a Contaminated Site*	*5 Year Replacement Period for Nonrecognition of Gain on Involuntary Conversions*
Alabama	Yes	Yes	Yes
Alaska	Yes	Yes	Yes
Arizona	Yes	Yes	Yes
Arkansas	No	Yes	Yes
California	No	No	No
Colorado	Yes	Yes	Yes
Connecticut	No written guidance	No written guidance	No written guidance
Delaware	Yes	Yes	Yes
District of Columbia	No	No	No
Florida	Yes	Yes	Yes
Georgia	No	Yes	Yes
Hawaii	Yes	Yes	Yes
Idaho	Yes	Yes	Yes
Illinois	Yes	Yes	Yes
Indiana	No	No	No
Iowa	Yes	Yes	Yes
Kansas	Yes	Yes	Yes
Kentucky	No	No	No
Louisiana	Yes	Yes	Yes

Gulf Opportunity Zone (Part 2)

Legend:

NA Not applicable

NR Not reported

	Does Your State Conform to the Following Provisions of the Gulf Opportunity Zone Act of 2005?		
	Deduction for 50% of Costs to Remove Debris or to Demolish Structures in the Gulf Opportunity Zone	*Deduction for Qualified Environmental Remediation in Connection with a Contaminated Site*	*5 Year Replacement Period for Nonrecognition of Gain on Involuntary Conversions*
Maine	Yes	Yes	Yes
Maryland	Yes	Yes	Yes
Massachusetts	No	No	No
Michigan (Business Tax)	Yes	Yes	Yes
Note. The CIT takes effect 01/01/12, and replaces the Michigan Business Tax (MBT) for most taxpayers. However, businesses that have been approved to receive, have received, or have been assigned certain certified credits may elect to file a return and pay the tax imposed by the MBT in lieu of the CIT until the certified credits are exhausted or extinguished.			
Minnesota	Yes	Yes	Yes
Mississippi	Yes	No	No
Missouri	Yes	Yes	Yes
Montana	Yes	Yes	Yes
Nebraska	Yes	Yes	Yes
Nevada	Nevada does not impose a corporate income tax		
New Hampshire	No	No	No
New Jersey	Yes	Yes	Yes
New Mexico	Yes	Yes	Yes
New York	Yes	Yes	Yes
North Carolina	Yes	Yes	Yes
North Dakota	Yes	Yes	Yes

Gulf Opportunity Zone (Part 2)

Legend:
NA Not applicable
NR Not reported

	Does Your State Conform to the Following Provisions of the Gulf Opportunity Zone Act of 2005?		
	Deduction for 50% of Costs to Remove Debris or to Demolish Structures in the Gulf Opportunity Zone	*Deduction for Qualified Environmental Remediation in Connection with a Contaminated Site*	*5 Year Replacement Period for Nonrecognition of Gain on Involuntary Conversions*
Ohio	Ohio does not impose a corporate income tax		
Note. Effective 1/1/2010, the Ohio Franchise Tax was fully phased out and business will be taxed on gross receipts through the Commercial Activity Tax. Details about that tax can be found at: http//tax.ohio.gov/divisions/commercial_activities/index.stm			
Oklahoma	Yes	Yes	Yes
Oregon	Yes	Yes	Yes
Pennsylvania	Yes	Yes	Yes
Rhode Island	No	No	No
South Carolina	No	No	No
South Dakota	South Dakota does not impose a corporate income tax		
Tennessee	Yes	Yes	Yes
Texas	No	No	No
Utah	Yes	Yes	Yes
Vermont	NR	NR	NR
Virginia	Yes	Yes	Yes
Washington	Washington does not impose a corporate income tax		
West Virginia	Yes	Yes	Yes
Wisconsin	No	No	No
Wyoming	Wyoming does not impose a corporate income tax		

Part 9. TAX PERIODS AND METHODS

Conformity to Federal Accounting Methods

Virtually all states that tax corporate income piggyback on the federal system by adopting federal taxable income (federal Form 1120, line 28 or line 30) as the starting point for computing state taxable income. This conformity to the federal tax base greatly simplifies the tax compliance process. Despite broad conformity, however, each state deviates from the federal tax base in some respects. This section considers federal and state use of selected accounting methods.

Federal Tax Treatment

Installment Sales. Gains from the sale of property are generally reported in the year in which the property is sold. Consequently, if a seller makes a credit sale with payments spread over a number of years, the taxpayer may find it difficult to pay the tax on the entire gain in the year of the sale. The installment method mitigates this problem by allowing such taxpayers to spread recognition of the gain over the period during which payments are received. Under Section 453 of the Internal Revenue Code (Code), taxpayers can use the installment method for installment sales, except for sales by dealers, sales of inventory, sales of publicly-traded stock or securities, and sales of property regularly traded on an established market.

Long-Term Contracts. Long-term contracts include building, installation, construction, or manufacturing contracts that are not completed in the tax year in which the contract was entered into. Income from long-term contracts is reported upon completion of the contract under the completed-contract method, and as the work progresses under the percentage-of-completion method. Taxpayers generally must use the percentage-of-completion method for federal income tax purposes. The completed-contract method may be used only by smaller companies that have entered into short-term construction contracts, and for home construction contracts. [IRC § 460]

Bad Debts. Generally accepted accounting principles (GAAP) require that a bad debt expense be recorded in the year in which it appears probable that a debt will be uncollectible and the amount of the loss can be reasonably estimated. This is known as the allowance, or reserve, method of accounting for bad debts. For federal income tax purposes, the use of the reserve method generally is not permitted. Instead, most taxpayers must use the specific charge-off method [IRC § 166], under which a bad debt expense is reported in the year in which a specific debt is determined to be either wholly or partially worthless. An exception applies to banks other than a "large bank," which are allowed to use the reserve method. [IRC § 585]

LIFO Inventory. A manufacturer or distributor may determine its inventory costs based on a last-in, first-out (LIFO) cost flow assumption. Because the recordkeeping required by the LIFO assumption can be cumbersome, taxpayers are also allowed to use dollar-value pools and government price indexes, rather than detailed records of actual costs, to compute ending inventory. [IRC § 472]

UNICAP Rules. Certain purchasing, warehousing, and other overhead-type costs must be capitalized as part of ending inventory. Code Section 263A, which contains the uniform capitalization (UNICAP) rules, enumerates the specific costs that must be capitalized. Some of these indirect costs do not have to be capitalized for financial reporting purposes.

Organizational Expenditures. Organizational expenditures are expenses that are directly related to the creation of the corporation, such as legal, accounting, and state incorporation fees. Under Code Section 248, a corporation may elect to deduct in its first tax year up to $5,000 of organizational expenditures. The $5,000 ceiling is reduced by the amount of organizational expenditures in excess of $50,000. Organizational expenditures that cannot be deducted in the first year are amortized over 180 months.

Start-up Expenditures. Start-up expenditures include investigatory, business start-up, and pre-opening costs related to the creation or acquisition of an active trade or business. Examples include employee training, advertising, and the costs of lining up suppliers. Under Code Section 195, a corporation may elect to deduct in its first tax year up to $5,000 of start-up expenditures ($10,000 for tax years beginning in 2010). The $5,000 ceiling is reduced by the amount of start-up expenditures in excess of $50,000 ($60,000 for tax years beginning in 2010). Start-up expenditures that cannot be deducted in the first year are amortized over 180 months.

R&E Costs. Research and experimental (R&E) expenditures include experimental and laboratory costs incidental to the development of a product. Taxpayers may immediately deduct research and experimental expenditures, or capitalize and amortize the expenditures over 60 months. [IRC § 174] Taxpayers also may claim a credit for the incremental research expenses paid or incurred in a trade or business. [IRC § 41]

State-by-State Summary

The following chart, presented in two parts, indicates that, with very minor exceptions, the states conform to the federal accounting methods summarized above. Keep in mind, however, that this chart does not address the issue of conformity (or lack thereof) with respect to every possible federal tax accounting method.

Conformity to Federal Accounting Methods (Part 1)

Legend:
SAF Same as applicable federal rules
NR Not reported

	Installment Method	*Completed Contract Method*	*Percentage-of-Completion Method*	*Reserve Method for Small Banks (Bad Debts)*	*LIFO Inventory Method*	*Simplified Dollar Value LIFO*
Alabama	SAF	SAF	SAF	SAF	SAF	SAF
Alaska	SAF	SAF	SAF	SAF	SAF	SAF
Arizona	SAF	SAF	SAF	SAF	SAF	SAF
Arkansas	SAF	SAF	SAF	SAF	SAF	SAF
California	SAF	SAF	SAF	SAF	SAF	SAF
Colorado	SAF	SAF	SAF	SAF	SAF	SAF
Connecticut	SAF	SAF	SAF	SAF	SAF	SAF
Delaware	SAF	SAF	SAF	SAF	SAF	SAF
District of Columbia	SAF	SAF	SAF	SAF	SAF	SAF
Florida	SAF	SAF	SAF	SAF	SAF	SAF
Georgia	SAF	SAF	SAF	SAF	SAF	SAF
Hawaii	SAF	SAF	SAF	SAF	SAF	SAF
Idaho	SAF	SAF	SAF	SAF	SAF	SAF
Illinois	SAF	SAF	SAF	SAF	SAF	SAF
Indiana	SAF	SAF	SAF	SAF	SAF	SAF
Iowa	SAF	SAF	SAF	SAF	SAF	SAF
Kansas	SAF	SAF	SAF	SAF	SAF	SAF
Kentucky	SAF	SAF	SAF	SAF	SAF	SAF
Louisiana	SAF	SAF	SAF	SAF	SAF	SAF

Conformity to Federal Accounting Methods (Part 1)

Legend:
SAF Same as applicable federal rules
NR Not reported

	Installment Method	*Completed Contract Method*	*Percentage-of-Completion Method*	*Reserve Method for Small Banks (Bad Debts)*	*LIFO Inventory Method*	*Simplified Dollar Value LIFO*
Maine	SAF	SAF	SAF	SAF	SAF	SAF
Maryland	SAF	SAF	SAF	SAF	SAF	SAF
Massachusetts	SAF	SAF		SAF	SAF	SAF
Michigan (Business Tax)	SAF	SAF	SAF	SAF	SAF	SAF
Note. The CIT takes effect 01/01/12, and replaces the Michigan Business Tax (MBT) for most taxpayers. However, businesses that have been approved to receive, have received, or have been assigned certain certified credits may elect to file a return and pay the tax imposed by the MBT in lieu of the CIT until the certified credits are exhausted or extinguished.						
Minnesota	SAF	SAF	SAF	SAF	SAF	SAF
Mississippi	Allow other method	SAF	SAF	SAF	SAF	SAF
Missouri	SAF	SAF	SAF	SAF	SAF	SAF
Montana	SAF	SAF	SAF	SAF	SAF	SAF
Nebraska	SAF	SAF	SAF	SAF	SAF	SAF
Nevada	Nevada does not impose a corporate income tax					
New Hampshire	SAF	SAF	SAF	SAF	SAF	SAF
New Jersey	SAF	SAF	SAF	SAF	SAF	SAF
New Mexico	SAF	SAF	SAF	SAF	SAF	SAF
New York	SAF	SAF	SAF	SAF	SAF	SAF
North Carolina	SAF	SAF	SAF	SAF	SAF	SAF
North Dakota	SAF	SAF	SAF	SAF	SAF	SAF

Conformity to Federal Accounting Methods (Part 1)

Legend:
SAF Same as applicable federal rules
NR Not reported

	Installment Method	*Completed Contract Method*	*Percentage-of-Completion Method*	*Reserve Method for Small Banks (Bad Debts)*	*LIFO Inventory Method*	*Simplified Dollar Value LIFO*
Ohio	Ohio does not impose a corporate income tax					
Note. Effective 1/1/2010, the Ohio Franchise Tax was fully phased out and business will be taxed on gross receipts through the Commercial Activity Tax. Details about that tax can be found at: http//tax.ohio.gov/divisions/commercial_activities/index.stm						
Oklahoma	SAF	SAF	SAF	SAF	SAF	SAF
Oregon	SAF	SAF	SAF	SAF	SAF	SAF
Pennsylvania	SAF	SAF	SAF	SAF	SAF	SAF
Rhode Island	SAF	SAF	SAF	SAF	SAF	SAF
South Carolina	SAF	SAF	SAF	Banks taxed on entire net income.	SAF	SAF
South Dakota	South Dakota does not impose a corporate income tax					
Tennessee	SAF	SAF	SAF	SAF	SAF	SAF
Texas	SAF	SAF	SAF	SAF	SAF	SAF
Utah	SAF	SAF	SAF	SAF	SAF	SAF
Vermont	SAF	SAF	SAF	SAF	SAF	SAF
Virginia	SAF	SAF	SAF	SAF	SAF	SAF
Washington	Washington does not impose a corporate income tax					
West Virginia	SAF	SAF	SAF	SAF	SAF	SAF
Wisconsin	NO	SAF	SAF	SAF	SAF	SAF

Conformity to Federal Accounting Methods (Part 1)

Legend:
SAF Same as applicable federal rules
NR Not reported

	Installment Method	*Completed Contract Method*	*Percentage-of-Completion Method*	*Reserve Method for Small Banks (Bad Debts)*	*LIFO Inventory Method*	*Simplified Dollar Value LIFO*
Wyoming	Wyoming does not impose a corporate income tax					

Legend:
SAF — Same as applicable federal rules
NR — Not reported

Conformity to Federal Accounting Methods (Part 2)

	IRC § 174 Amortization of R&D Costs	*IRC § 195 Amortization of Start-up Costs*	*IRC § 263A Uniform Capitalization*	*IRC § 248 Amortization of Organizational Costs*
Alabama	SAF	SAF	SAF	SAF
Alaska	SAF	SAF	SAF	SAF
Arizona	SAF	SAF	SAF	SAF
Arkansas	SAF	SAF	SAF	SAF
California	SAF	SAF	SAF	SAF
Colorado	SAF	SAF	SAF	NO
Connecticut	SAF	SAF	SAF	SAF
Delaware	SAF	SAF	SAF	SAF
District of Columbia	SAF	SAF	SAF	SAF
Florida	SAF	SAF	SAF	SAF
Georgia	SAF	SAF	SAF	SAF
Hawaii	SAF	SAF	SAF	SAF
Idaho	SAF	SAF	SAF	SAF
Illinois	SAF	SAF	SAF	SAF
Indiana	SAF	SAF	SAF	SAF
Iowa	SAF	SAF	SAF	SAF
Kansas	SAF	SAF	SAF	SAF
Kentucky	SAF	SAF	SAF	SAF
Louisiana	SAF	SAF	SAF	SAF

Conformity to Federal Accounting Methods (Part 2)

Legend:
SAF Same as applicable federal rules
NR Not reported

	IRC § 174 Amortization of R&D Costs	*IRC § 195 Amortization of Start-up Costs*	*IRC § 263A Uniform Capitalization*	*IRC § 248 Amortization of Organizational Costs*
Maine	SAF	SAF	SAF	SAF
Maryland	SAF	SAF	SAF	SAF
Massachusetts	SAF	SAF	SAF	SAF
Michigan (Business Tax)	SAF	SAF	SAF	SAF
Note. The CIT takes effect 01/01/12, and replaces the Michigan Business Tax (MBT) for most taxpayers. However, businesses that have been approved to receive, have received, or have been assigned certain certified credits may elect to file a return and pay the tax imposed by the MBT in lieu of the CIT until the certified credits are exhausted or extinguished.				
Minnesota	SAF	SAF	SAF	SAF
Mississippi	SAF	SAF	SAF	SAF
Missouri	SAF	SAF	SAF	SAF
Montana	SAF	SAF	SAF	SAF
Nebraska	SAF	SAF	SAF	SAF
Nevada	Nevada does not impose a corporate income tax			
New Hampshire	SAF	SAF	SAF	SAF
New Jersey	SAF	SAF	SAF	SAF
New Mexico	SAF	SAF	SAF	SAF
New York	SAF	SAF	SAF	SAF
North Carolina	SAF	SAF	SAF	SAF
North Dakota	SAF	SAF	SAF	SAF

Conformity to Federal Accounting Methods (Part 2)

Legend:
SAF — Same as applicable federal rules
NR — Not reported

	IRC § 174 Amortization of R&D Costs	*IRC § 195 Amortization of Start-up Costs*	*IRC § 263A Uniform Capitalization*	*IRC § 248 Amortization of Organizational Costs*
Ohio	Ohio does not impose a corporate income tax . .			
Note. Effective 1/1/2010, the Ohio Franchise Tax was fully phased out and business will be taxed on gross receipts through the Commercial Activity Tax. Details about that tax can be found at: http//tax.ohio.gov/divisions/commercial_activities/index.stm				
Oklahoma	SAF	SAF	SAF	SAF
Oregon	SAF	SAF	SAF	SAF
Pennsylvania	SAF	SAF	SAF	SAF
Rhode Island	SAF	SAF	SAF	NR
South Carolina	SAF	SAF	SAF	SAF
South Dakota	South Dakota does not impose a corporate income tax			
Tennessee	SAF	SAF	SAF	SAF
Texas	SAF	SAF	SAF	SAF
Utah	SAF	SAF	SAF	SAF
Vermont	SAF	SAF	SAF	SAF
Virginia	SAF	SAF	SAF	SAF
Washington		Washington does not impose a corporate income tax		
West Virginia	SAF	SAF	SAF	SAF
Wisconsin	No	No	SAF	No

Note. Installment method (Wisconsin did not adopt P.L. 106-573, which restored the installment method for accrual basis taxpayers). Regarding amortization and depreciation methods and limitations, Wisconsin generally did not adopt any amortization or depreciation provisions enacted after 12/31/2000.

Conformity to Federal Accounting Methods (Part 2)

Legend:
SAF Same as applicable federal rules
NR Not reported

	IRC § 174 Amortization of R&D Costs	*IRC § 195 Amortization of Start-up Costs*	*IRC § 263A Uniform Capitalization*	*IRC § 248 Amortization of Organizational Costs*
Wyoming	Wyoming does not impose a corporate income tax			

Changing Accounting Methods or Year-End

Federal Tax Treatment

Change in Accounting Method. The term *method of accounting* includes not only the taxpayer's overall method of accounting (cash, accrual, or hybrid) but also the accounting treatment of specific items of income or deduction. [Treas. Reg. § 1.446-1] A taxpayer's overall accounting method determines the year in which income is reported and expenses are deducted. A corporation generally must use the accrual method of accounting, unless it is an S corporation, a personal service corporation (PSC) other than a qualified PSC, a farming business, or has average gross receipts of less than $5 million. [IRC § 448] Examples of accounting methods for specific items include the accounting for research and experimental expenditures [IRC § 174], long-term contracts [IRC § 451], and installment sales. [IRC § 453]A taxpayer elects an accounting method by applying that method when filing an initial tax return. [Treas. Reg. § 1.446-1]

Once an accounting method has been chosen, it generally cannot be changed without IRS consent. Taxpayers wishing to change an accounting method must file Form 3115 with the IRS during the first half of the tax year in which the change is to be made. [Treas. Reg. § 1.446-1 and Rev. Proc. 97-27, 1997-1 C.B. 680] A change in accounting methods usually results in duplications or omissions of items of income or expense. The amount of this net adjustment must be included in income either all at once in the year of the change or by spreading the net adjustment over a number of years. [IRC § 481] Rev. Proc. 2008-52 [2008-36 I.R.B. 587] provides procedures for taxpayers to use to obtain automatic consent for certain types of accounting method changes.

Change in Accounting Period. A newly formed corporation may elect to use a calendar year, fiscal year, or 52-53 week year as its accounting period. The election is made by filing the corporation's initial tax return on the basis of the accounting period selected. S corporations and PSCs generally must adopt a calendar year, unless the corporation has a business purpose for electing a different year, for example, to conform to the corporation's natural business year. [IRC §§ 1378 and 441] A PSC is a regular corporation whose principal activity is the performance of certain personal services that are substantially performed by shareholder-employees.

Once adopted, a taxpayer ordinarily cannot change its accounting period without IRS permission. [IRC § 442] A change in accounting period usually creates a short tax year starting with the end of the old accounting period and ending with the beginning of the new accounting period. A taxpayer wishing to change its accounting period generally must file Form 1128 on or before the fifteenth day of the second calendar month following the close of the short tax year. The IRS will usually approve a change if the taxpayer can establish that there is a substantial business purpose for adopting a different tax year [Treas. Reg. § 1.441-1(c)(2)]. The primary method for establishing a substantial business purpose is to satisfy a mechanical "natural business year" test. A natural business year is one in which at least 25 percent of the taxpayer's gross receipts are received in the last 2 months of the 12-month period. The IRS requires a 47-month history of gross receipts in order to have a 36-month history on which to base calculations required to establish a natural business year, plus an additional 11-month period for comparing the requested tax year with other potential tax years [Rev. Proc 2006-46, 2006-2 C.B. 859].

Section 444 Elections. Many S corporations, partnerships, and PSCs are unable to meet the Internal Revenue Service's strict business purpose test. This led Congress to create the IRC Section 444 election, which allows partnerships, S corporations, and PSCs to elect a tax year that results in a tax deferral of three months or less. The deferral period signifies the number of months from the beginning of the entity's fiscal year to December 31. Therefore, an S corporation or PSC with calendar-year shareholders may elect a September 30, October 31 or November 30 year-end. A Section 444 election is made on federal Form 8716, *Election To Have a Tax Year Other Than a Required Tax Year.*

A partnership or S corporation making a Section 444 election must reimburse the IRS for the benefit of the tax deferral obtained when a fiscal year is used. Under Code Section 7519, the required payment is the product of the maximum tax rate for individuals plus 1 percent times the previous year's taxable income times a deferral ratio. The deferral ratio equals the number of months in the deferral period divided by the number of months in the tax year.

PSCs that elect a fiscal year are not required to reimburse the IRS for the benefit of the tax deferral, but instead must make minimum distributions to shareholders during the deferral period. [IRC § 280H] These minimum distributions are designed to prevent a distribution pattern that achieves a deferral of income at the shareholder level. Roughly speaking, these rules require that deductible payments made to shareholder-employees during the deferral period be made at a rate that is no lower than the rate at which they were made during the previous fiscal year.

State-by-State Summary

Since virtually all states use federal taxable income as the starting point for computing state taxable income, it is not surprising that all but a few states automatically conform to accounting method changes for which IRS permission is obtained, and also permit taxpayers to spread the net adjustment over the same time period used for federal tax purposes (see chart below).

Changing Accounting Methods or Year-End

Legend:

SAF	Same as applicable
NA	Not applicable
NR	Not reported

	Changing Accounting Methods				
	How Does Taxpayer Obtain Permission?	*Can Effect of Change Be Spread Over Future Years?*	*Does Federal Change Require State Change?*	*Must State Year-End Match Federal Year End?*	*Is State Permission Required to Change a Corporation's Tax Year-End?*
Alabama	Automatic with federal permission	SAF	Yes	Yes	No, automatic with federal permission
Alaska	Automatic with federal permission	SAF	Yes	Yes	No, automatic with federal permission
Arizona	Automatic with federal permission	SAF	Yes	Yes	No, automatic with federal permission
Arkansas	Automatic with federal permission	SAF	Yes	Yes	No, automatic with federal permission
California	State permission required, federal Form 3115	SAF	Yes	Yes	No, automatic with federal permission
Colorado	Automatic with federal permission	SAF	Yes	NR	No, automatic with federal permission
Connecticut	Automatic with federal permission	No written guidance	Yes	Yes	No, automatic with federal permission
Delaware	Automatic with federal permission, but also requires a written letter	Yes	Yes	Yes	Yes, with a written letter
District of Columbia	Automatic with federal permission	No	Yes	Yes	Yes, automatic with federal permission

Changing Accounting Methods or Year-End

Legend:
SAF Same as applicable
NA Not applicable
NR Not reported

	Changing Accounting Methods				
	How Does Taxpayer Obtain Permission?	*Can Effect of Change Be Spread Over Future Years?*	*Does Federal Change Require State Change?*	*Must State Year-End Match Federal Year End?*	*Is State Permission Required to Change a Corporation's Tax Year-End?*
Florida	Automatic with federal permission	SAF	Yes	Yes	Automatic with federal permission
Georgia	Automatic with federal permission	When the change is reported in federal taxable income	Yes	Yes	No, automatic with federal permission
Hawaii	Automatic with federal permission	SAF	Yes	Yes	Yes, federal Form 1128; due date SAF
Idaho	Automatic with federal permission	SAF	Yes	Yes	No, automatic with federal permission
Illinois	Automatic with federal permission	SAF	Yes	Yes	No, automatic with federal permission
Indiana	Automatic with federal permission	SAF	Yes	Yes	No, automatic with federal permission
Iowa	Automatic with federal permission	SAF	Yes	Yes	No, automatic with federal permission
Kansas	Automatic with federal permission	SAF	Yes	Yes	No, automatic with federal permission
Kentucky	Automatic with federal permission	SAF	Yes	Yes	No, automatic with federal permission
Louisiana	Automatic with federal permission	SAF	Yes	Yes	No, automatic with federal permission

Changing Accounting Methods or Year-End

Legend:

SAF	Same as applicable
NA	Not applicable
NR	Not reported

	Changing Accounting Methods				
	How Does Taxpayer Obtain Permission?	*Can Effect of Change Be Spread Over Future Years?*	*Does Federal Change Require State Change?*	*Must State Year-End Match Federal Year End?*	*Is State Permission Required to Change a Corporation's Tax Year-End?*
Maine	Automatic with federal permission	SAF	Yes	NR	No, automatic with federal permission
Maryland	Automatic with federal permission	SAF	Yes		No, automatic with federal permission
Massachusetts	Automatic with federal permission, State permission is required	NR	Yes	Yes	No, automatic with federal permission
Michigan (Business Tax)	Automatic with federal permission	SAF	Yes	Yes, the former Single Business Tax (SBT) was repealed 12/31/07 and the new Michigan Business Tax (MBT) became effective 1/1/08. The MBT return of a fiscal year taxpayer whose tax year ends before 12/31/08 will not conform to its federal tax year.	No, automatic with federal permission

Note. The CIT takes effect 01/01/12, and replaces the Michigan Business Tax (MBT) for most taxpayers. However, businesses that have been approved to receive, have received, or have been assigned certain certified credits may elect to file a return and pay the tax imposed by the MBT in lieu of the CIT until the certified credits are exhausted or extinguished.

Legend:
SAF Same as applicable
NA Not applicable
NR Not reported

Changing Accounting Methods or Year-End

	Changing Accounting Methods				
	How Does Taxpayer Obtain Permission?	*Can Effect of Change Be Spread Over Future Years?*	*Does Federal Change Require State Change?*	*Must State Year-End Match Federal Year End?*	*Is State Permission Required to Change a Corporation's Tax Year-End?*
Minnesota	Automatic with federal permission	SAF	Yes	Yes	No, automatic with federal permission
Mississippi	Automatic with federal permission	No	Yes	Yes	No, automatic with federal permission
Missouri	Automatic with federal permission	SAF	Yes	Yes	No, automatic with federal permission
Montana	Automatic with federal permission	SAF	Yes	Yes	No, automatic with federal permission
Nebraska	Automatic with federal permission	SAF	Yes	Yes	No, automatic with federal permission
Nevada	Nevada does not impose a corporate income tax				
New Hampshire	Automatic with federal permission	SAF	Yes	Yes	No, automatic with federal permission
New Jersey	Automatic with federal permission	SAF	Yes		Yes
New Mexico	Automatic with federal permission	SAF	Yes	Yes	No, automatic with federal permission
New York	Automatic with federal permission	SAF	Yes	Yes	No, automatic with federal permission
North Carolina	Automatic with federal permission	NR	Yes	Yes	No, automatic with federal permission

Changing Accounting Methods or Year-End

Legend:
SAF Same as applicable
NA Not applicable
NR Not reported

	Changing Accounting Methods				
	How Does Taxpayer Obtain Permission?	*Can Effect of Change Be Spread Over Future Years?*	*Does Federal Change Require State Change?*	*Must State Year-End Match Federal Year End?*	*Is State Permission Required to Change a Corporation's Tax Year-End?*
North Dakota	Automatic with federal permission	SAF	No	Yes	No, automatic with federal permission
Ohio	Ohio does not impose a corporate income tax				
Note. Effective 1/1/2010, the Ohio Franchise Tax was fully phased out and business will be taxed on gross receipts through the Commercial Activity Tax. Details about that tax can be found at: http//tax.ohio.gov/divisions/commercial_activities/index.stm					
Oklahoma	Automatic with federal permission	SAF	Yes	Yes	No, automatic with federal permission
Oregon	Automatic with federal permission	SAF	Yes	Yes	No, automatic with federal permission
Pennsylvania	Automatic with federal permission	SAF	Yes	Yes	No, automatic with federal permission
Rhode Island	Automatic with federal permission	SAF	Yes	Yes	No, automatic with federal permission
South Carolina	Automatic with federal permission	SAF	Yes		Yes
South Dakota	South Dakota does not impose a corporate income tax				
Tennessee	Automatic with federal permission	SAF	Yes	Yes	No, automatic with federal permission
Texas	Automatic with federal permission	SAF	Yes	Yes	No, automatic with federal permission

Changing Accounting Methods or Year-End

Legend:
SAF Same as applicable
NA Not applicable
NR Not reported

	Changing Accounting Methods				
	How Does Taxpayer Obtain Permission?	*Can Effect of Change Be Spread Over Future Years?*	*Does Federal Change Require State Change?*	*Must State Year-End Match Federal Year End?*	*Is State Permission Required to Change a Corporation's Tax Year-End?*
		No	Yes, except where method is expressly prohibited		No, automatic with federal permission
Utah	Automatic with federal permission	Other method of accounting for change	Yes	Yes	No, automatic with federal permission
Vermont	Automatic with federal permission	SAF	Yes	Yes	No, automatic with federal permission
Virginia	Automatic with federal permission	SAF	Yes	Yes	No, automatic with federal permission
Washington	Washington does not impose a corporate income tax				
West Virginia	Automatic with federal permission	SAF	Yes	Yes	No, automatic with federal permission
Wisconsin	Automatic with federal permission	SAF, however, all remaining adjustments must be taken into account in the last year that a crop is subject to WI taxation.	Yes	Yes	No, automatic with federal permission
Wyoming	Wyoming does not impose a corporate income tax				

Short Tax Year Due to Acquisition of Subsidiary

Federal Tax Treatment

Short Tax Years. For federal income tax purposes, the consolidated return regulations govern the tax treatment of the acquisition of a subsidiary that will file as part of the federal consolidated return group. Those regulations provide that a newly acquired subsidiary must adopt the common parent's annual accounting period in the first year in which the subsidiary's income is includible in the consolidated return; in most cases, that will occur immediately after the acquisition [Treas. Reg. § 1.1502-76].

Depending on the date of acquisition and the new parent's and the acquired corporation's tax years, the acquired corporation generally will have two short tax periods in the year of its acquisition. The first short tax period begins on the first day of the entity's pre-acquisition tax year and ends on the date of acquisition. The second short tax period begins after the date of acquisition and ends on the last day of the new parent's tax year. When an acquired subsidiary was a member of a consolidated return group before the acquisition, the first short-period federal return is due on the due date of the old parent's consolidated return. When a newly acquired subsidiary was not included in a federal consolidated return before its acquisition, the due date of the first short-period return depends on whether the return is due before or after the new parent files its consolidated return.

Net Operating Losses (NOLs). Treasury Regulation Section 1.1502-21 imposes limitations on the carryover of a newly acquired subsidiary's pre-acquisition losses and the carryback of a newly acquired subsidiary's post-acquisition losses within the context of a federal consolidated return. A newly acquired subsidiary generally can use only separate return limitation year (SRLY) or pre-acquisition NOLs to reduce the portion of consolidated taxable income attributable to that entity. Similarly, a newly acquired affiliate can carry back only its share of a consolidated NOL to offset taxable income in a SRLY. The amount of an acquired loss company's NOLs available for use may also be limited under Code Section 382 if there has been a substantial change in the stock ownership of the loss corporation.

State Tax Treatment

Short Tax Years. States generally require a corporation to maintain the same tax year for both federal and state tax purposes. Therefore, most states require a corporation to file a state income tax return for each tax year for which the entity is required to file a federal income tax return. As a result, a newly acquired subsidiary generally is required to file two short-period state income tax returns in the year of its acquisition. For example, in *W.H. Newbold Son & Co. v. Commonwealth* [727 A.2d 640 (Pa. Commw. Ct. 1999)], the court held that a subsidiary that was a member of a federal consolidated group had to file two short-period Pennsylvania corporate tax returns in the year of disposition because the corporation had two federal tax years. In construing the statutory definitions of taxable income and tax year, the court concluded that the Pennsylvania filing requirements applicable to a corporation that was a member of a federal consolidated group were tied to the federal filing requirements applicable to that corporation.

When a newly acquired subsidiary is required to file two short-period returns, the due date of the first short-period return varies among the states. As a general rule, the due date for filing the state tax return covering the pre-acquisition period starts running from the last day of the month in which the acquisition occurred. When the newly acquired subsidiary was a member of a consolidated group, however, several states take the position that the due date for filing the return begins on the last day of the month in which the old parent's tax year ended. The due date of the second return would start to run on the last day of the month in which the entity's new tax year ended.

The states also differ on whether a newly acquired subsidiary can be included in the combined report of selling or acquiring groups in the year of disposition or acquisition. Most combined reporting states provide that a subsidiary can be included in the combined report of both the selling and acquiring groups in the year of disposition or acquisition, as long as the entity is engaged in a unitary business. State tax authorities may argue, however, that the acquiring corporation and the target corporation cannot be engaged in a unitary business in the year of acquisition (instant unity issue).

In nexus combined or consolidated reporting states, the acquisition or disposition of a subsidiary may result in a change in filing status. Depending on the circumstances, that change could be mandatory or optional.

Net Operating Losses (NOLs). In states that permit NOL carrybacks, carryovers, or both, there is a lack of uniformity regarding the treatment of the newly acquired subsidiary's pre-acquisition and post-acquisition NOLs. For separate company reporting states that either start the computation of state taxable income with Line 30 of the federal return (i.e., taxable income after NOL deductions and special deductions) and do not have separate NOL provisions or adopt the federal rules for computing NOLs, the Section 382 limitations may restrict the use of NOLs when there has been a substantial change in the stock ownership of the loss corporation.

In combined or consolidated reporting states, the Section 382 limitations, the SRLY rules, or a requirement that the corporation must have incurred the underlying loss giving rise to a net operating loss deduction in a year in which the entity was subject to tax in that state may limit the use of a newly acquired subsidiary's NOLs, but some states that begin the computation of state taxable income with Line 28 of the federal return (i.e., taxable income before NOL deductions and special deductions) have not adopted the Section 382 provisions.

State-by-State Summary

The chart that follows indicates whether, in the context of the acquisition of a subsidiary, two short-year returns are required, and if so, the due date of the first short-period return and whether the state imposes any limitations on the use of the acquired subsidiary's NOLs. The states were asked to assume that an existing calendar-year federal consolidated group (E) acquires and consolidates with a non-calendar-year corporation (T), forming a new consolidated group (N). Because of the inherent differences between unitary and non-unitary states, the states' responses may vary depending on whether the target corporation (T) and the acquiring corporation (E) are members of a unitary group. In an effort to capture the diversity of potential responses, the questions regarding the acquisition of a subsidiary were asked for each of the following three fact patterns:

1. N files using a calendar year, and T is not part of a unitary group with E or N;
2. N files using a calendar year, and T is part of a unitary group with either E or N; and
3. E and N use different tax years.

Short Tax Year Due to Acquisition of Subsidiary

Assumptions:
(E) Calendar-year consolidated group
(T) Acquisition and consolidation with noncalendar year corporation
(N) Formation of a new consolidated group (E&T)

Legend:

NA	Not applicable
NR	Not reported
SAF	Same as applicable federal rules
SRLY	Separate return limitation year

	N Files Calendar Year; T Not Unitary with E, N			*N Files Calendar Year; T Is Unitary with E or N*			*E and N Use Different Tax Years*		
	Two Short Year Returns Required for T?	*If Yes, Due Date of First Return*	*Limits on Use of T's NOLs*	*Two Short Year Returns Required for T?*	*If Yes, Due Date of First Return*	*Limits on Use of T's NOLs*	*Two Short Year Returns Required for T?*	*If Yes, Due Date of First Return*	*Limits on Use of T's NOLs*
Alabama	Yes	15th day of 3rd month following close of short year	NA	Yes	15th day of 3rd month following close of short year	SAF	Yes	15th day of 3rd month following close of short year	SAF
Alaska	SAF	One month after federal	SAF, except only Alaska NOLs allowed	SAF	1 month after federal	SAF, except only Alaska NOLs allowed	SAF	One month after federal	SAF, except only Alaska NOLs allowed
Arizona	No	NA	NA	Yes	15th day of 4th month after short period	T's share of combined income	Yes	15th day of 4th month after short period	T's share of combined income
Arkansas	Yes	SAF	Yes, Reg 2.26-51-805(f)	Yes	SAF	Yes, Reg 2.26-51-805(f)	Yes	SAF	Yes, Reg 2.26-51-805(f)
California	Yes	SAF	See note	Yes	SAF	See note	Yes	SAF	See note
Note. In a loss year, each entity must separately compute its share of the NOL using intrastate apportionment rules. Likewise, each member of the combined report will have its own NOL carryover that may only be applied against the income intrastate-apportioned to that member in subsequent years. See RTC § 25108									
Colorado	Yes	15th day of 4th month after short period	§ 382; SRLY	Yes	15th day of 4th month after short period	§ 382; SRLY	Yes	15th day of 4th month after short period	§ 382; SRLY

Short Tax Year Due to Acquisition of Subsidiary

Assumptions:
(E) Calendar-year consolidated group
(T) Acquisition and consolidation with noncalendar year corporation
(N) Formation of a new consolidated group (E&T)

Legend:
NA Not applicable
NR Not reported
SAF Same as applicable federal rules
SRLY Separate return limitation year

	N Files Calendar Year; T Not Unitary with E, N			*N Files Calendar Year; T Is Unitary with E or N*			*E and N Use Different Tax Years*		
	Two Short Year Returns Required for T?	*If Yes, Due Date of First Return*	*Limits on Use of T's NOLs*	*Two Short Year Returns Required for T?*	*If Yes, Due Date of First Return*	*Limits on Use of T's NOLs*	*Two Short Year Returns Required for T?*	*If Yes, Due Date of First Return*	*Limits on Use of T's NOLs*
Connecticut									
Delaware	Yes	1st of 4th month after close of taxable year	NA	Yes	1st of 4th month after close of taxable year	NA	Yes	1st of 4th month after close of taxable year	NA
District of Columbia	Yes	SAF	SAF	Yes	SAF	SAF	Yes	SAF	SAF
Florida	Yes	SAF plus 15 days	SAF, Florida SRLY rules	Yes	SAF plus 15 days	SAF, Florida SRLY rules	Yes	SAF plus 15 days	SAF, Florida SRLY rules
Georgia	NR	NR	NR	NR	NR	NR	NR	NR	NR
Hawaii	Yes	3 months and 20 days after close of short year	NA	Yes	3 months and 20 days after close of the taxable year	Up to T's apportioned income	Yes	3 months and 20 days after close of the taxable year	Up to T's apportioned income

Short Tax Year Due to Acquisition of Subsidiary

Assumptions:
(E) Calendar-year consolidated group
(T) Acquisition and consolidation with noncalendar year corporation
(N) Formation of a new consolidated group (E&T)

Legend:

NA	Not applicable
NR	Not reported
SAF	Same as applicable federal rules
SRLY	Separate return limitation year

	N Files Calendar Year; T Not Unitary with E, N			*N Files Calendar Year; T Is Unitary with E or N*			*E and N Use Different Tax Years*		
	Two Short Year Returns Required for T?	*If Yes, Due Date of First Return*	*Limits on Use of T's NOLs*	*Two Short Year Returns Required for T?*	*If Yes, Due Date of First Return*	*Limits on Use of T's NOLs*	*Two Short Year Returns Required for T?*	*If Yes, Due Date of First Return*	*Limits on Use of T's NOLs*
Idaho	SAF	Later of 15th day of 4th month following close of short period or federal due date	IRC § § 381, 382	SAF	Later of 15th day of 4th month following close of short period or federal due date	IRC § § 381, 382	SAF	Later of 15th day of 4th month following close of short period or federal due date	IRC § § 381, 382
Illinois	No, as long as T is nonunitary both before and after the acquisition	NA	NA	No	NA	NA	No	NA	NA
Indiana	No		SAF	No		SAF	No		SAF
Iowa	Yes	45 days after the federal date	SAF	Yes	45 days after the federal date	SAF	Yes	45 days after the federal date	SAF

Short Tax Year Due to Acquisition of Subsidiary

Assumptions:
(E) Calendar-year consolidated group
(T) Acquisition and consolidation with noncalendar year corporation
(N) Formation of a new consolidated group (E&T)

Legend:

NA	Not applicable
NR	Not reported
SAF	Same as applicable federal rules
SRLY	Separate return limitation year

	N Files Calendar Year; T Not Unitary with E, N			*N Files Calendar Year; T Is Unitary with E or N*			*E and N Use Different Tax Years*		
	Two Short Year Returns Required for T?	*If Yes, Due Date of First Return*	*Limits on Use of T's NOLs*	*Two Short Year Returns Required for T?*	*If Yes, Due Date of First Return*	*Limits on Use of T's NOLs*	*Two Short Year Returns Required for T?*	*If Yes, Due Date of First Return*	*Limits on Use of T's NOLs*
Kansas	Yes	SAF plus 1 month	NOL's limited to T's Kansas taxable income	SAF plus 1	15th day of 4th month following close of short period tax year	NOL's limited to T's Kansas taxable income	SAF plus 1	15th day of 4th month following close of short period tax year	NOL's limited to T's Kansas taxable income
Kentucky	Yes	1 month after federal due date	No	Yes	1 month after federal due date	NR	Yes	1 month after federal due date	NR
Louisiana	Yes	15th day 4th month after short period close	No	Yes	15th day 4th month after short period close	No	Yes	15th day 4th month after short period close	No
Maine	SAF	SAF	SAF	SAF	SAF	SAF	SAF	SAF	SAF

Short Tax Year Due to Acquisition of Subsidiary

Assumptions:

(E) Calendar-year consolidated group

(T) Acquisition and consolidation with noncalendar year corporation

(N) Formation of a new consolidated group (E&T)

Legend:

NA	Not applicable
NR	Not reported
SAF	Same as applicable federal rules
SRLY	Separate return limitation year

	N Files Calendar Year; T Not Unitary with E, N			*N Files Calendar Year; T Is Unitary with E or N*			*E and N Use Different Tax Years*		
	Two Short Year Returns Required for T?	*If Yes, Due Date of First Return*	*Limits on Use of T's NOLs*	*Two Short Year Returns Required for T?*	*If Yes, Due Date of First Return*	*Limits on Use of T's NOLs*	*Two Short Year Returns Required for T?*	*If Yes, Due Date of First Return*	*Limits on Use of T's NOLs*
Maryland	Maryland does not accept consolidated federal filings. Each separate corporation must file a separate return each time its income is included in a federal filing.	SAF	SAF	Maryland does not accept consolidated federal filings. Each separate corporation must file a separate return each time its income is included in a federal filing.	SAF	SAF	Maryland does not accept consolidated federal filings. Each separate corporation must file a separate return each time its income is included in a federal filing.	SAF	SAF
Massachusetts	Yes	SAF	See Mass. Regs. Code tit. 830 § 63.32B.1.	No, See DD 93-6	1st day of 3rd month following end of tax year	See CMR 62B.1	See DD 93-6.	NR	See 830 CMR 62.B1
Michigan (Business Tax)	Yes	Last day of 4th month after end of tax period	NA	Yes	Last day of 4th month after end of tax period	NA	Yes	Last day of 4th month after end of tax period	NA

Short Tax Year Due to Acquisition of Subsidiary

Assumptions:
(E) Calendar-year consolidated group
(T) Acquisition and consolidation with noncalendar year corporation
(N) Formation of a new consolidated group (E&T)

Legend:

NA	Not applicable
NR	Not reported
SAF	Same as applicable federal rules
SRLY	Separate return limitation year

	N Files Calendar Year; T Not Unitary with E, N			*N Files Calendar Year; T Is Unitary with E or N*			*E and N Use Different Tax Years*		
	Two Short Year Returns Required for T?	*If Yes, Due Date of First Return*	*Limits on Use of T's NOLs*	*Two Short Year Returns Required for T?*	*If Yes, Due Date of First Return*	*Limits on Use of T's NOLs*	*Two Short Year Returns Required for T?*	*If Yes, Due Date of First Return*	*Limits on Use of T's NOLs*
Note. The CIT takes effect 01/01/12, and replaces the Michigan Business Tax (MBT) for most taxpayers. However, businesses that have been approved to receive, have received, or have been assigned certain certified credits may elect to file a return and pay the tax imposed by the MBT in lieu of the CIT until the certified credits are exhausted or extinguished.									
Minnesota	Yes	SAF	SAF	Yes	SAF	SAF	Yes	SAF	SAF
Mississippi	No	NA	NA	Yes	21/2 months after the date of acquisition	T's NOLs can only offser T's income.	Yes	21/2 months after the date of acquisition	T's NOLs can only offset T's income.
Missouri	Yes	105 days after year-end	SAF	Yes	105 days after year-end	SAF	Yes	105 days after year-end	SAF

Short Tax Year Due to Acquisition of Subsidiary

Assumptions:
(E) Calendar-year consolidated group
(T) Acquisition and consolidation with noncalendar year corporation
(N) Formation of a new consolidated group (E&T)

Legend:

NA	Not applicable
NR	Not reported
SAF	Same as applicable federal rules
SRLY	Separate return limitation year

	N Files Calendar Year; T Not Unitary with E, N			*N Files Calendar Year; T Is Unitary with E or N*			*E and N Use Different Tax Years*		
	Two Short Year Returns Required for T?	*If Yes, Due Date of First Return*	*Limits on Use of T's NOLs*	*Two Short Year Returns Required for T?*	*If Yes, Due Date of First Return*	*Limits on Use of T's NOLs*	*Two Short Year Returns Required for T?*	*If Yes, Due Date of First Return*	*Limits on Use of T's NOLs*
Montana	Yes	15th day of 5th month following close of taxable period	In the case of a consolidation of corporations, the new corporate entity is not allowed a deduction for net operating losses sustained by the consolidated corporations prior to the date of consolidation.	Yes	15th day of 5th month following close of taxable period	In the case of a consolidation of corporations, the new corporate entity is not allowed a deduction for net operating losses sustained by the consolidated corporations prior to the date of consolidation.	Yes	15th day of 5th month following close of taxable period	In the case of a consolidation of corporations, the new corporate entity is not allowed a deduction for net operating losses sustained by the consolidated corporations prior to the date of consolidation.

Short Tax Year Due to Acquisition of Subsidiary

Assumptions:

(E) Calendar-year consolidated group

(T) Acquisition and consolidation with noncalendar year corporation

(N) Formation of a new consolidated group (E&T)

Legend:

NA	Not applicable
NR	Not reported
SAF	Same as applicable federal rules
SRLY	Separate return limitation year

	N Files Calendar Year; T Not Unitary with E, N			*N Files Calendar Year; T Is Unitary with E or N*			*E and N Use Different Tax Years*		
	Two Short Year Returns Required for T?	*If Yes, Due Date of First Return*	*Limits on Use of T's NOLs*	*Two Short Year Returns Required for T?*	*If Yes, Due Date of First Return*	*Limits on Use of T's NOLs*	*Two Short Year Returns Required for T?*	*If Yes, Due Date of First Return*	*Limits on Use of T's NOLs*
Nebraska	Yes, if required to file two federal short period returns	SAF	SAF	Yes, if required to file two federal short period returns	SAF	SAF; also limited to Nebraska income apportioned to T	Yes, if required to file two federal short period returns	SAF	SAF
Nevada	Nevada does not impose a corporate income tax								
New Hampshire	Yes	15th day of the 3rd month following expiration of tax period	NR	NR	NR	NR	NR	NR	NR
New Jersey	Yes	15th day of 4th month following close of year	T keeps NOL	Yes	15th day of 4th month following close of year	T keeps NOL	Yes	15th day of 4th month following close of year	T keeps NOL
New Mexico	Yes	SAF	SAF	Yes	SAF	SAF	Yes	SAF	SAF

Short Tax Year Due to Acquisition of Subsidiary

Assumptions:
(E) Calendar-year consolidated group
(T) Acquisition and consolidation with noncalendar year corporation
(N) Formation of a new consolidated group (E&T)

Legend:
NA Not applicable
NR Not reported
SAF Same as applicable federal rules
SRLY Separate return limitation year

	N Files Calendar Year; T Not Unitary with E, N			*N Files Calendar Year; T Is Unitary with E or N*			*E and N Use Different Tax Years*		
	Two Short Year Returns Required for T?	*If Yes, Due Date of First Return*	*Limits on Use of T's NOLs*	*Two Short Year Returns Required for T?*	*If Yes, Due Date of First Return*	*Limits on Use of T's NOLs*	*Two Short Year Returns Required for T?*	*If Yes, Due Date of First Return*	*Limits on Use of T's NOLs*
New York	Yes	21/2 months after date of T's acquisition	SAF subject to NY modifications	Yes	21/2 months after date of T's acquisition	SAF; subject to NY modifications and limitations	Yes	21/2 months after date of T's acquisition	SAF subject to NY modifications
North Carolina	Yes	Acquisition date	No effect	Yes	Acquisition date	No effect	Yes	Acquisition date	No effect
North Dakota	Yes	15th day of 4th month following close of short period	None	Yes	15th day of 4th month following close of short period	None	Yes	15th day of 4th month following close of short period	None
Ohio	Ohio does not impose a corporate income tax								
Note. Effective 1/1/2010, the Ohio Franchise Tax was fully phased out and business will be taxed on gross receipts through the Commercial Activity Tax. Details about that tax can be found at: http//tax.ohio.gov/divisions/commercial_activities/index.stm									
Oklahoma	SAF	SAF	SAF	SAF	SAF	SAF	SAF	SAF	SAF

Short Tax Year Due to Acquisition of Subsidiary

Assumptions:
(E) Calendar-year consolidated group
(T) Acquisition and consolidation with noncalendar year corporation
(N) Formation of a new consolidated group (E&T)

Legend:

NA	Not applicable
NR	Not reported
SAF	Same as applicable federal rules
SRLY	Separate return limitation year

	N Files Calendar Year; T Not Unitary with E, N			*N Files Calendar Year; T Is Unitary with E or N*			*E and N Use Different Tax Years*		
	Two Short Year Returns Required for T?	*If Yes, Due Date of First Return*	*Limits on Use of T's NOLs*	*Two Short Year Returns Required for T?*	*If Yes, Due Date of First Return*	*Limits on Use of T's NOLs*	*Two Short Year Returns Required for T?*	*If Yes, Due Date of First Return*	*Limits on Use of T's NOLs*
Oregon	SAF	15th day of the month following the federal due date	T cannot be included in Oregon consolidated return. T's losses can only offset T's future income.	SAF	15th day of the month following the federal due date	T's loss can only offset T's income after consolidation with unitary members, subject to federal SRLY limitations applied under state law.	SAF	15th day of the month following the federal due date	T's loss can only offset T's income after consolidation with unitary members, subject to federal SRLY limitations applied under state law and federal provisions for different tax year.
Pennsylvania	SAF	30 days after federal due date	None	SAF	30 days after federal due date	None	SAF	30 days after federal due date	None
Rhode Island	SAF	SAF	SAF	SAF	SAF	SAF	SAF	SAF	SAF
South Carolina	Yes	SAF	SAF	Yes	SAF	SAF	Yes	SAF	SAF

Short Tax Year Due to Acquisition of Subsidiary

Assumptions:
(E) Calendar-year consolidated group
(T) Acquisition and consolidation with noncalendar year corporation
(N) Formation of a new consolidated group (E&T)

Legend:

NA	Not applicable
NR	Not reported
SAF	Same as applicable federal rules
SRLY	Separate return limitation year

	N Files Calendar Year; T Not Unitary with E, N			*N Files Calendar Year; T Is Unitary with E or N*			*E and N Use Different Tax Years*		
	Two Short Year Returns Required for T?	*If Yes, Due Date of First Return*	*Limits on Use of T's NOLs*	*Two Short Year Returns Required for T?*	*If Yes, Due Date of First Return*	*Limits on Use of T's NOLs*	*Two Short Year Returns Required for T?*	*If Yes, Due Date of First Return*	*Limits on Use of T's NOLs*
South Dakota	South Dakota does not impose a corporate income tax								
Tennessee	SAF	15th day of 4th month of second return	NOLs do not go to successor	SAF	15th day of 4th month of second return	NOLs do not go to successor	SAF	15th day of 4th month of second return	NOLs do not go to successor
Texas	No	NA	NA	No	NA	NA	No	NA	NA
Utah	Yes	15th day of 4th month following end of short year	Losses limited to T's separate company income calculated in same manner as losses	Yes	15th day of 4th month following end of short year	Losses limited to T's separate company income calculated in same manner as losses	Yes	15th day of 4th month following end of short year	Losses limited to T's separate company income calculated in same manner as losses
Vermont	SAF	SAF	SAF	SAF	SAF	SAF	SAF	SAF	SAF
Virginia	SAF	SAF	SAF	SAF	SAF	SAF	SAF	SAF	SAF
Washington	Washington does not impose a corporate income tax								
West Virginia	Yes	15th day of 4th month	300K carry back limit	Yes	15th day of 4th month	300K carry back limit	Yes	15th day of 4th month	300K carry back limit

Short Tax Year Due to Acquisition of Subsidiary

Assumptions:
(E) Calendar-year consolidated group
(T) Acquisition and consolidation with noncalendar year corporation
(N) Formation of a new consolidated group (E&T)

Legend:
NA Not applicable
NR Not reported
SAF Same as applicable federal rules
SRLY Separate return limitation year

	N Files Calendar Year; T Not Unitary with E, N			*N Files Calendar Year; T Is Unitary with E or N*			*E and N Use Different Tax Years*		
	Two Short Year Returns Required for T?	*If Yes, Due Date of First Return*	*Limits on Use of T's NOLs*	*Two Short Year Returns Required for T?*	*If Yes, Due Date of First Return*	*Limits on Use of T's NOLs*	*Two Short Year Returns Required for T?*	*If Yes, Due Date of First Return*	*Limits on Use of T's NOLs*
Wisconsin	Yes	SAF	No consolidations for Wisconsin	Yes	SAF	No consolidations for Wisconsin	Yes	SAF	No consolidations for Wisconsin
Wyoming	Wyoming does not impose a corporate income tax								

Part 10. PAYMENT OF TAX

Estimated Tax Payment Requirements (Calendar-Year Corporations)

Federal Tax Treatment

To avoid an underpayment penalty, a corporation that expects to owe more than $500 in federal income tax for the current year is required to pay four installments of estimated tax, each equal to 25 percent of the required annual payment. [IRC § 6655] The required annual payment equals the excess of the sum of the regular income tax and the alternative minimum tax over the allowable tax credits. The amount of the required installments differs for large and small corporations. For a more detailed discussion, see the next section in this part entitled Underpayment Penalty Exceptions.

Federal estimated tax payments for calendar-year taxpayers are due April 15, June 15, September 15, and December 15. For fiscal-year taxpayers, estimated tax payments are due on the fifteenth day of the fourth, sixth, ninth, and twelfth months of their tax year. If those dates fall on a holiday or on a Saturday or Sunday, federal rules provide that the payment is due on the next business day.

Many corporations choose to extend the time for filing a return; however, an extension of time to file does not extend the time for paying the required tax. Therefore, if the total estimated tax payments do not equal or exceed the final tax liability for the year, an additional tax payment is normally due by the original due date of the return, which is the fifteenth day of the third month following the close of the tax year. Generally, any amount of final tax liability not paid by the original due date is subject to interest until the tax is paid with the final return.

State Tax Treatment

States generally require estimated tax payments, but each state has its own dollar threshold, procedures, and due dates for estimated tax payments. For example, not all states require the payment of four equal installments of 25 percent of the estimated annual tax. For example, Massachusetts requires four installment payments of 40 percent, 25 percent, 25 percent, and 10 percent, respectively; whereas New Jersey requires corporations with annual gross receipts of $50 million or more to make three installment payments of 25 percent, 50 percent, and 25 percent, respectively. Some states require a minimum payment to be made in the first installment.

Most states conform to the federal due dates, that is, the fifteenth day of the fourth, sixth, ninth, and twelfth months of the tax year. An example of a state that does not conform to the federal due dates is Florida, which requires estimated tax payments to be made by the first day of the fifth, seventh, and tenth months of the tax year, as well as the first day of the first month of the following tax year. Another example is Kentucky, which requires only three installment payments, due on the fifteenth day of the sixth, ninth and twelfth months of the tax year.

Electronic Funds Transfer

All but the smallest corporations are required to make their federal tax deposits using electronic funds transfer (EFT) from their own accounts to the Treasury Department's account. The requirement to make federal tax deposits using EFT applies to all federal depository taxes, including FICA taxes, FUTA taxes, withheld income taxes, corporate income and estimated tax payments, and excise taxes. An amount deposited by electronic funds transfer is deemed paid on the last day prescribed for filing the applicable return for the return period (without regard to extensions) or, if later, when withdrawn from the payee's account. [IRC § 6302(h), and Treas. Reg. § 31.6302-1(h)] Taxpayers that are required to use EFT must make their federal tax deposits through the Electronic Federal Tax Payment System, whose website is found at www.eftps.gov. [Rev. Proc. 97-33, 1997-2 C.B. 371]

The requirements for using EFT to make estimated tax payments vary from state to state. In addition, a taxpayer that fails to comply with a requirement to remit payment by EFT may be subject to a penalty. For example, California requires a corporation to remit its corporate franchise tax by EFT if any estimated tax installment payment exceeds $20,000 or the total annual tax liability exceeds $80,000. If a corporation that is required to pay its California tax by EFT makes the payment through other means (e.g., a check), it is subject to a penalty of 10 percent of the amount paid, unless the taxpayer can substantiate that the failure to make the payment by EFT was for reasonable cause and not the result of willful neglect. [Cal. Rev. & Tax. Code § 19011]

Recent Developments

Alabama. Effective for tax years beginning on or after January 1, 2010, the Alabama quarterly estimated tax payment threshold for corporations is lowered from $5,000 to $500, which conforms to the federal threshold. [H.B. 504, Apr. 22, 2010]

California. Effective for installments due for tax years beginning on or after January 1, 2009, the first and second quarterly estimated payments are increased from 25 percent to 30 percent, and the third and fourth quarterly installments are decreased to 20 percent of the estimated amount due for the tax year. [A.B. 1452, Sept. 30, 2008]

Effective for installments due for tax years beginning on or after January 1, 2010, the second quarterly estimated payment is increased from 30 percent to 40 percent, the third quarterly installment is eliminated, and the fourth quarterly installment is increased from 20 percent to 30 percent. [A.B. 17, July 28, 2009]

Florida. Effective January 1, 2009, the due dates for Florida corporate estimated income tax payments will be one day earlier than previously required. Specifically, payments of estimated tax will have to be made on or before the last day of the fourth month, the last day of the sixth month, the last day of the ninth month, and the last day of the tax year. For example, a calendar year taxpayer's estimated payments will be due April 30, 2009, June 30, 2009, September 30, 2009, and December 31, 2009. [Tax Information Publication, No. 08C01-08, Fla. Dept. of Rev., Dec. 1, 2008]

New Mexico. For tax years beginning on or after January 1, 2009, taxpayers that will owe at least $5,000 in New Mexico corporate income tax must make a quarterly income tax payment on the fifteenth day of the fourth month of the tax year (April 15 for calendar year taxpayers) equal to 25 percent of the annual estimated tax due. For estimated payments due on or before April 15, 2009, corporations must remit at least 12.5 percent of their annual estimated taxes for the tax year in lieu of the 25 percent that otherwise would be required. The remainder of the estimated taxes due in the first quarter must be remitted with the taxpayer's second-quarter payment by June 15, 2009. [S.B. 80, Feb. 6, 2009] The law regarding estimated payments was inadvertently changed in 2003 to eliminate the first estimated payment and adopt a three-payment schedule. This legislation rectifies this error.

State-by-State Summary

The following chart is presented in two parts. Part 1 indicates, by state, whether estimated tax payments are required, whether estimated tax payments must include the applicable minimum tax, the minimum amount of payment required, and whether estimated tax payments must be made by electronic funds transfer. Part 2 indicates, by state, the due date and percentage of the payment required for each installment, what constitutes timely payment, the interest rate applicable to underpayments, and the penalty imposed on underpayments.

Estimated Tax Payment Requirements (Part 1)
(Calendar-Year Corporations)

Legend:

X	Indicates estimated tax has been timely paid
SAF	Same as applicable federal rules
NA	Not applicable
NR	Not reported

	Does State Require Estimated Payments?	*Must Estimated Payments Include Applicable (Alternative) Minimum Tax?*	*De Minimis Amount Below Which Estimates Not Required*	*Is Electronic Funds Transfer Required for Certain Taxpayers?*
Alabama	Yes	No	$5,000	Yes, mandatory if tax liability ≥ $25,000
Alaska	Yes	Yes	$1,000	Yes, all payments > $100,000
Arizona	Yes	No	$1,000	Yes, mandatory if tax liability ≥ $20,000
Arkansas	Yes	No	$1,000	Yes, required if prior year tax liability $20,000 or more
California	Yes	Yes	No	Yes, see R&TC § 19011-$20,000 payment or $80,000 total. Once threshold is reached, then all payments must be made by EFT.
Colorado	Yes	NA	No	No
Connecticut	Yes	NA	$1,000	Yes, mandatory if tax liability > $10,000
Delaware	Yes	No	NR	Yes
District of Columbia	Yes	Yes	$1,000	Yes, tax liability $25,000 and above
Florida	Yes	Yes	$2,500	Yes, for tax liability ≥ $20,000
Georgia	Yes	NR	$1,500 estimated tax	Yes, taxpayers with estimated payments of $10,000 or more per quarter

Estimated Tax Payment Requirements (Part 1)
(Calendar-Year Corporations)

Legend:

X	Indicates estimated tax has been timely paid
SAF	Same as applicable federal rules
NA	Not applicable
NR	Not reported

	Does State Require Estimated Payments?	*Must Estimated Payments Include Applicable (Alternative) Minimum Tax?*	*De Minimis Amount Below Which Estimates Not Required*	*Is Electronic Funds Transfer Required for Certain Taxpayers?*
Hawaii	Yes	NA	NR	Yes, required for annual tax liability > $100,000
Idaho	Yes	No	$500	Yes, taxpayer request before first payment; required for annual tax liability ≥ $100,000
Illinois	Yes	NA	$400 for corporations	Yes, see 86 III. Admin. Code § 750.300.
Indiana	Yes	NR	$1,000	Yes, if amount due > $10,000
Iowa	Yes	Yes	NR	Yes, must be used if prior year's tax at least $80,000
Kansas	Yes	No	$500	No
Kentucky	Yes	Yes	$5,000	No
Louisiana	Yes	No	$1,000	Yes, for taxpayers who remit tax payments of $5,000 or more per taxable period LA Rev. Stat. 47:1519(A)(3)
Maine	Yes	Yes	$1,000 prior year	Yes, all payroll processors and all corporations with total aggregate liability of $25,000 or more for 2010 and $18,000 or more effective 1/1/2011.
Maryland	Yes	NA	NR	Yes, minimum amount is $20,000

Estimated Tax Payment Requirements (Part 1)
(Calendar-Year Corporations)

Legend:

X	Indicates estimated tax has been timely paid
SAF	Same as applicable federal rules
NA	Not applicable
NR	Not reported

	Does State Require Estimated Payments?	*Must Estimated Payments Include Applicable (Alternative) Minimum Tax?*	*De Minimis Amount Below Which Estimates Not Required*	*Is Electronic Funds Transfer Required for Certain Taxpayers?*
Massachusetts	Yes, See TIR 05-22, 04-12, 03-11 DD 03-15	NA	$1,000	Yes, all
Michigan (Business Tax)	Yes	No	$800 or less	NR
Note. The CIT takes effect 01/01/12, and replaces the Michigan Business Tax (MBT) for most taxpayers. However, businesses that have been approved to receive, have received, or have been assigned certain certified credits may elect to file a return and pay the tax imposed by the MBT in lieu of the CIT until the certified credits are exhausted or extinguished.				
Minnesota	Yes	Yes	$500	Yes, those meeting payment thresholds
Mississippi	Yes	NA	$200	No
Missouri	Yes	No	Yes, $250	No
Montana	Yes	No	Yes	Yes
Nebraska	Yes	NA	Yes, $400	Yes, EFT payments may be required from any corporation that made payments in any prior year exceeding $5,000. The corporation will be notified three months prior to the date the first EFT payment is required to be made. This requirement is being phased in. The minimum threshold beginning 1/1/12 is $13,000.
Nevada	Nevada does not impose a corporate income tax			

Estimated Tax Payment Requirements (Part 1)
(Calendar-Year Corporations)

Legend:

X	Indicates estimated tax has been timely paid
SAF	Same as applicable federal rules
NA	Not applicable
NR	Not reported

	Does State Require Estimated Payments?	*Must Estimated Payments Include Applicable (Alternative) Minimum Tax?*	*De Minimis Amount Below Which Estimates Not Required*	*Is Electronic Funds Transfer Required for Certain Taxpayers?*
New Hampshire	Yes	NA	Yes, $200	Yes, all business organizations with a total tax liability of $100,00 or greater
New Jersey	Yes	Yes	25% of estimated tax liability	Yes, if liability > $20,000
New Mexico	Yes	No	Yes, $5,000	No
New York	Yes, if prior year's tax was in excess of $1,000.	Yes	$250	Yes
North Carolina	Yes, SAF, if tax liability is greater than $500.	NA	NR	NR
North Dakota	Yes	NR	NR	No
Ohio	Ohio does not impose a corporate income tax			
Note. Effective 1/1/2010, the Ohio Franchise Tax was fully phased out and business will be taxed on gross receipts through the Commercial Activity Tax. Details about that tax can be found at: http//tax.ohio.gov/divisions/commercial_activities/index.stm				
Oklahoma	Yes	NA	NR	Yes, for motor fuel tax payments, large sales, and withholding
Oregon	Yes	Yes	$500	Yes, SAF
Pennsylvania	Yes	NA	NR	Yes, if tax payment ≥ $20,000
Rhode Island	Yes, if tax liability is over $500.	NR	Greater than $500	Yes
South Carolina	Yes	NA	Yes	Yes
South Dakota	South Dakota does not impose a corporate income tax			

Estimated Tax Payment Requirements (Part 1)
(Calendar-Year Corporations)

Legend:

X	Indicates estimated tax has been timely paid
SAF	Same as applicable federal rules
NA	Not applicable
NR	Not reported

	Does State Require Estimated Payments?	*Must Estimated Payments Include Applicable (Alternative) Minimum Tax?*	*De Minimis Amount Below Which Estimates Not Required*	*Is Electronic Funds Transfer Required for Certain Taxpayers?*
Tennessee	Yes	NR	$5,000	Yes, if liability > $10,000
Texas	No	NA	NA	Yes, see General Rule 3.9.
Utah	Yes	Yes	$3,000	No
Vermont	Yes	NR	$500	No
Virginia	Yes	No	Yes, $1,000. See Va. Code § 58.1-500 and 23 VAC 10-240-420.	Yes, if average monthly liability > $20,000
Washington	Washington does not impose a corporate income tax			
West Virginia	Yes	No	NR	Yes, if making individual payment of $100,000 or more.
Wisconsin	Yes	No	$500	Yes, if prior year net tax is $40,000 or more.
Wyoming	Wyoming does not impose a corporate income tax			

Estimated Tax Payment Requirements (Part 2)
(Calendar-Year Corporations)

Legend:

X	Indicates estimated tax has been timely paid
SAF	Same as applicable federal rules
NA	Not applicable
NR	Not reported

	Payment Due Date/Percent Payment Required					
	1st	*2nd*	*3rd*	*4th*	*Interest Rate Applicable to Underpayments*	*Penalty Imposed on Underpayments*
Alabama	4/15 25%	6/15 25%	9/15 25%	12/15 25%	SAF	Based on federal interest rate
Alaska	4/15 25%	6/15 25%	9/15 25%	12/15 25%	11%	11%
Arizona	4/15 25%	6/15 25%	9/15 25%	12/15 25%	SAF	See Ariz. Rev. Stat. Ann. § 42-1125.
Arkansas	4/15 25%	6/15 25%	9/15 25%	12/15 25%	NA	10%
California	SAF 4/15 30%	SAF 6/15 40%	SAF 9/15 0%	SAF 1/15 30%	4%, variable	4%, variable
Colorado	4/15 25%	6/15 25%	9/15 25%	12/15 25%	Varies by year	Interest rate
Connecticut	3/15; 30% of prior-year tax or 27% of current-year tax	6/15; 70% of prior-year tax or 63% of current-year tax	9/15; 80% of prior-year tax or 72% of current-year tax	12/15; 100% of prior-year tax or 90% of current-year tax	1% per month	None
Delaware	4/1 50%	6/15 20%	9/15 20%	12/15 10%	1%	1.5% a month
District of Columbia	4/15 25%	6/15 25%	9/15 25%	12/15 25%	10%/yr compounded daily.	20%
Florida	4/30 25%	6/30 25%	9/30 25%	12/31 25%	Floating rate tied to prime	12%
Georgia	4/15 25%	6/15 25%	9/15 25%	12/15 25%	9%	5% a year of total tax
Hawaii	4/20 25%	6/20 25%	9/20 25%	1/20 25%	NA	2/3 of 1% per month upon the amount of underpayment for the period of underpayment

Estimated Tax Payment Requirements (Part 2)
(Calendar-Year Corporations)

Legend:

X	Indicates estimated tax has been timely paid
SAF	Same as applicable federal rules
NA	Not applicable
NR	Not reported

	Payment Due Date/Percent Payment Required					
	1st	*2nd*	*3rd*	*4th*	*Interest Rate Applicable to Underpayments*	*Penalty Imposed on Underpayments*
Idaho	4/15 25%	6/15 25%	9/15 25%	12/15 25%	6% effective 1/1/04 to 12/31/04	Underpayment interest only
Illinois	4/15 22.5%	6/15 45%	9/15 67.5%	12/15 90%	2% of underpayment within 30 days of due date, 5% between 30 and 90 days of due date, 10% between 90 and 100 days of due date, and 15% of any amount paid later than 180 days after the due date.	
Indiana	4/20 25%	6/20 25%	9/20 25%	12/20 25%	NA	10%
Iowa	4/30 25%	6/30 25%	9/30 25%	12/31 25%	.4% per month	NR
Kansas	4/15 25%	6/15 25%	9/15 25%	12/15 25%	NA	2011/2012 is a 5% annual rate, varies with federal rate each year
Kentucky	6/15 50%	9/15 25%	12/15 25%	NA	5%	10% of underpayment
Louisiana	4/15 25%	6/15 25%	9/15 25%	1/15 25%	NA	12% per year
Maine	4/15 25%	6/15 25%	9/15 25%	12/15 25%	NR	Applicable interest rate
Maryland	4/15 25%	6/15 25%	9/15 25%	12/15 25%	13%	25%
Massachusetts	3/15 40%	6/15 25%	9/15 25%	12/15 10%	See TIR 92-6, calculated quarterly	TIR 04-12

Estimated Tax Payment Requirements (Part 2)
(Calendar-Year Corporations)

Legend:

X	Indicates estimated tax has been timely paid
SAF	Same as applicable federal rules
NA	Not applicable
NR	Not reported

	Payment Due Date/Percent Payment Required					
	1st	*2nd*	*3rd*	*4th*	*Interest Rate Applicable to Underpayments*	*Penalty Imposed on Underpayments*
Michigan (Business Tax)	4/30 25%	7/31 25%	10/31 25%	1/31 25%	1% over prime	10% negligence 25% intentional disregard
Note. The CIT takes effect 01/01/12, and replaces the Michigan Business Tax (MBT) for most taxpayers. However, businesses that have been approved to receive, have received, or have been assigned certain certified credits may elect to file a return and pay the tax imposed by the MBT in lieu of the CIT until the certified credits are exhausted or extinguished.						
	Per 85% of prior year's tax liability					
Minnesota	3/15 25%	6/15 25%	9/15 25%	12/15 25%	3%	3%
Mississippi	4/15 25%	6/15 25%	9/15 25%	12/15 25%	1% a month	10% a year
Missouri	4/15 25%	6/15 25%	9/15 25%	12/15 25%	Keyed to prime rate	NA
Montana	4/15 25%	6/15 25%	9/15 25%	12/15 25%	None	12%
Nebraska	4/15 25%	6/15 25%	9/15 25%	12/15 25%	5%	NR
Nevada	Nevada does not impose a corporate income tax					
New Hampshire	4/15 25%	6/15 25%	9/15 25%	12/15 25%	6%	6%
New Jersey	4/15 25%	6/15 25%	9/15 25%	12/15 25%	3% above quarterly prime rate	5% of balance due paid after due date
	For privilege periods beginning on and after 1/1/03, a taxpayer having gross receipts of $50 million or more for the prior privilege period pays:					
	4/15 50%	6/15 50%		12/15 50%		
New Mexico	4/15 25%	6/15 25%	9/15 25%	12/15 25%	IRC quarterly annual rate	2% per month; 20% maximum

Estimated Tax Payment Requirements (Part 2)
(Calendar-Year Corporations)

Legend:

X	Indicates estimated tax has been timely paid
SAF	Same as applicable federal rules
NA	Not applicable
NR	Not reported

	Payment Due Date/Percent Payment Required					
	1st	*2nd*	*3rd*	*4th*	*Interest Rate Applicable to Underpayments*	*Penalty Imposed on Underpayments*
New York	3/15 25%, 40% for taxpayers with a prior year liability of over $100,000.	6/15 25%	9/15 25%	12/15 25%	Prevailing interest rate	10% of any underpayment of tax when the understatement exceeds the greater of 10% of tax required to be shown or $5,000
	Effective 1/1/03 through 12/31/05, the first payment of estimated tax is increased to 30% for taxpayers whose preceding year's tax exceeded $100,000. The remaining quarterly payments will each be reduced from 25% to 23.33%.					
North Carolina	4/15 25%	6/15 25%	9/15 25%	12/15 25%	NA	5%
North Dakota	4/15 25%	6/15 25%	9/15 25%	11/15 25%		None
Ohio	Ohio does not impose a corporate income tax					
Note. Effective 1/1/2010, the Ohio Franchise Tax was fully phased out and business will be taxed on gross receipts through the Commercial Activity Tax. Details about that tax can be found at: http//tax.ohio.gov/divisions/commercial_activities/index.stm						
Oklahoma	4/15 25%	6/15 25%	9/15 25%	1/15 25%	15%	5%
Oregon	4/15 25%	6/15 25%	9/15 25%	12/15 25%	5%	None
Pennsylvania	3/15 25%	6/15 25%	9/15 25%	12/15 25%	8% to 9%	None
Rhode Island	3/15 40%	6/15 60%			12%	5%
South Carolina	4/15 25%	6/15 25%	9/15 25%	1/15 25%	SAF	SAF
South Dakota	South Dakota does not impose a corporate income tax					

Estimated Tax Payment Requirements (Part 2)
(Calendar-Year Corporations)

Legend:

X	Indicates estimated tax has been timely paid
SAF	Same as applicable federal rules
NA	Not applicable
NR	Not reported

	Payment Due Date/Percent Payment Required					
	1st	*2nd*	*3rd*	*4th*	*Interest Rate Applicable to Underpayments*	*Penalty Imposed on Underpayments*
Tennessee	4/15 25%	6/15 25%	9/15 25%	1/15 25%	12.25%	5% a month, up to 25%
Texas	NA	NA	NA	NA	NA	NA
Utah	4/15 22.5%	6/15 45%	9/15 67.5%	12/15 90%	None	9% for 2009
Vermont	4/15 25%	6/15 25%	9/15 25%	12/15 25%		NR
Virginia	4/15 25%	6/15 25%	9/15 25%	12/15 25%	Federal underpayment rate plus 2%; this rate is reduced to the federal short-rate for contested assessments starting nine months after the date of assessment until 30 days after the Department of Taxation issues a determination.	0.5% of tax due per month from original due date to payment date.
Washington	Washington does not impose a corporate income tax					
West Virginia	4/15 25%	6/15 25%	9/15 25%	12/15 25%	NA	9.50%
Wisconsin	3/15 25%	6/15 25%	9/15 25%	12/15 25%	12%	No penalty; however, interest is assessed from unextended due date to date paid at 18%.
Wyoming	Wyoming does not impose a corporate income tax					

Underpayment Penalty Exceptions

Federal Tax Treatment

To avoid an underpayment penalty, a corporation that expects to owe more than $500 in federal income tax for the current year is required to pay four installments of estimated tax, each equal to 25 percent of the required annual payment. [IRC § 6655] The required annual payment equals the excess of the sum of the regular income tax and the alternative minimum tax over the allowable tax credits. Generally, estimated tax payments are due on or before the fifteenth day of the fourth, sixth, ninth, and twelfth months of the corporate tax year. For example, estimated tax payments for calendar-year taxpayers are due April 15, June 15, September 15, and December 15.

Failure to make a required estimated tax payment results in the imposition of a nondeductible penalty. The penalty rate is applied to the amount of the underpayment, and is applied for the period of underpayment. The penalty rate generally equals the federal short-term interest rate (which is adjusted quarterly), plus three percentage points. [IRC § 6621] A corporation computes its estimated tax underpayment penalty on federal Form 2220.

The amount of the required installments differs for large and small corporations. The required installments for a "large corporation" are based on the applicable percentage of the current year's tax. A large corporation must make estimated tax payments equal to 100 percent of the expected tax for the current year to avoid an underpayment penalty. However, the first installment payment for a large corporation may be based on 100 percent of the tax shown on the preceding year's return. For estimated tax purposes, a large corporation is a corporation that had taxable income of $1 million or more for any of the three tax years immediately preceding the tax year involved. For purposes of determining whether a corporation has taxable income of $1 million or more, taxable income is modified to exclude net operating loss or capital loss carrybacks and carryovers. In addition, the $1 million limit is apportioned among members of a controlled group of corporations.

The required installments for a corporation that is not a large corporation are based on the lesser of 1) 100 percent of the current year's tax or 2) 100 percent of the tax shown on the return for the preceding year. The 100 percent of the prior year's tax provision, however, is available only when the corporation filed an income tax return showing a tax liability for the preceding year and the return covered a full 12-month period.

For many companies, the most beneficial method of computing their federal estimated tax payments is the annualized income method. This method allows taxpayers to remit tax based on their annualized taxable income recognized for various monthly periods, as reflected in the table below. Some taxpayers can also take advantage of the adjusted seasonal installment method if it yields lower installment payments. The adjusted seasonal installment method may be used only when the taxable income of the taxpayer for the same six-month period in each of the last three preceding tax years averaged 70 percent or more of its total annual taxable income.

For this purpose, each year a corporation may choose the monthly periods that are used in computing its federal taxable income. Corporations may use the standard monthly periods without any other action on their part. If a corporation elects to use Option 1 or Option 2, it is required to file Form 8842, Election to Use Different Annualization Period for Corporate Estimated Tax, on or before the due date of its first required installment payment.

Annualized Income Alternatives

Installment	*Standard Monthly Periods*	*Option 1 Monthly Periods*	*Option 2 Monthly Periods*
1st	3 months	2 months	3 months
2nd	3 months	4 months	5 months
3rd	6 months	7 months	8 months
4th	9 months	10 months	11 months

Under each method, the required payment is limited to the amount that would be due if total payments for the year up through the required payment equaled 100 percent of the tax that would be due if the income already received during the current year were placed on an annual basis.

State Tax Treatment

States also generally require corporations to make estimated tax payments, and impose a penalty if the payments are not made in timely installments, but the percentage of a corporation's estimated tax that must be paid to avoid the underpayment penalty varies among states.

Most states have adopted exceptions to the underpayment penalty similar to those allowed for federal purposes. In applying the prior year's tax exception, some states depart from the federal rule by not requiring that the corporation file an income tax return reporting a tax liability for the preceding year or that the return cover a full 12-month period. Moreover, some states provide an exception to the penalty for paying an amount greater than or equal to the tax on the prior year's income based on the prior year's facts but using the current year's rates. Consistent with the federal approach, many states impose more burdensome estimated tax requirements on large corporations. Most states conform to the federal definition of a large corporation, but a few states have created their own definition. These states generally prohibit large corporations from using the prior year's tax exception.

Some states have enacted other exceptions to the normal underpayment penalty. For example, Pennsylvania has a "safe harbor" law, under which the state will not impose interest on an underpayment of estimated tax if the taxpayer makes a payment that equals or exceeds the amount that would have been required if the tax were computed using the current year's tax rate and the facts shown on the tax return for and the law applicable to, the "safe harbor' base year. The safe harbor base year is the second preceding tax year or, if the taxpayer had filed its initial return in the previous year, the first preceding tax year [72 P.S. § 10003.3].

States generally do not provide a reasonable cause or extenuating circumstances exception that exempts taxpayers from penalties for underpayments of estimated tax when business or accounting problems make it difficult to estimate the amount of tax due. For example, in *Appeal of Howard Hughes Medical Institute* [No. 246269 (Cal. State Bd. of Equal., Aug. 24, 2004)], the California State Board of Equalization ruled that an unexpected sale in the fourth quarter of the tax year did not relieve the corporation from liability for an underpayment penalty. Likewise, in *Appeal of Stryker* [No. 301164 (Cal. State Bd. of Equal., Dec. 13, 2005)], the imposition of an underpayment penalty was upheld, even though the underpayment was not due to any fault of the taxpayer, but instead resulted from the failure of the taxpayer's bank to process an electronic funds transfer. In *Hollinger International, Inc. v. Bower* [No. 1-04-0392 (Ill. App. Ct., Dec. 12, 2005)], the Illinois Appellate Court ruled that the taxpayer's reliance on its outside CPA firm, which incorrectly computed the taxpayer's estimated tax payments, was insufficient reasonable cause to waive an underpayment penalty.

In P.D. 04-212 [Dec. 3, 2004], the Virginia Department of Taxation ruled that a penalty for underpayment of estimated taxes was properly computed based on the tax shown on the original return, and was not adjusted after the taxpayer filed an amended return that reflected a reduction in Virginia taxable income.

Recent Developments

District of Columbia. For tax years beginning on or after January 1, 2012, a corporation must pay the lesser of 110 percent (under prior law, 100 percent) of the preceding year's tax liability or 90 percent of the current year's tax liability to avoid an underpayment penalty. [D.C.B 19-203, July 22, 2011]

Illinois. For installments of estimated tax due before February 1, 2011, a corporation must pay the lesser of 100 percent of the preceding year's tax liability or 90 percent of the current year's tax liability to avoid an underpayment penalty. For installments due on or after February 1, 2011, and before February 1, 2012, a corporation must pay the lesser of 150 percent of the preceding year's tax liability or 90 percent of the current year's tax liability to avoid an underpayment penalty. [S.B. 2505, Jan. 13, 2011]

Michigan. For tax years beginning on or after January 1, 2008, taxpayers that make federal quarterly estimated income tax payments based on the annualized income installment or the adjusted seasonal installment methods found in Code Section 6655(e) may use the same methodology to calculate estimated tax payments for the Michigan business tax. In addition, the penalty for the underpayment of estimated tax will not be assessed for a tax year that ends before December 1, 2009 if the taxpayer paid 75 percent of the Michigan business tax due for the tax year. [H.B. 4496 and S.B. 98, Apr. 9, 2009]

State-by-State Summary

The chart that follows summarizes the state exceptions to penalties for estimated tax underpayments.

Underpayment Penalty Exceptions

Legend:

X	Indicates that the exception to the underpayment penalty is followed
SAF	Same as applicable federal rules
NA	Not applicable
NR	Not reported

		Exceptions That Are Followed					*Large Corporation Rules*	
	Does State Provide Exceptions to Underpayment Penalties?	*Estimated Taxes Equal the Tax Liability Shown on the Preceding Year's (12-Month) Return*	*Payment of a Percentage of Current Year's Taxes*	*Annualized Income Method*	*Adjusted Seasonal Installment Method*	*Other Exceptions*	*Do Special Large Corporation Rules Apply?*	*Special Estimated Tax Rule*
Alabama	Yes	X	100%	X	X		Yes	Prior year's tax exception not available
Alaska	Yes	SAF	SAF	SAF	SAF		NR	NR
Arizona	Yes	SAF	SAF	SAF	SAF		SAF	SAF
Arkansas	Yes	X	NR	X			No	NA
California	Yes	SAF	SAF	NR	NR		Yes	SAF
Colorado	Yes	X	NR	SAF	SAF		SAF	No exceptions for prior year amount.
Connecticut	Yes		90%	X	X		NR	NR
Delaware	Yes	X, exception if Delaware taxable income is over $200,000 in any of 3 preceding years	80%	X			Yes, large corporation has Delaware taxable income of $200,000 or more in any 3 preceding tax years.	Cannot use exception rule

Underpayment Penalty Exceptions

Legend:

X	Indicates that the exception to the underpayment penalty is followed
SAF	Same as applicable federal rules
NA	Not applicable
NR	Not reported

		Exceptions That Are Followed					*Large Corporation Rules*	
	Does State Provide Exceptions to Underpayment Penalties?	*Estimated Taxes Equal the Tax Liability Shown on the Preceding Year's (12-Month) Return*	*Payment of a Percentage of Current Year's Taxes*	*Annualized Income Method*	*Adjusted Seasonal Installment Method*	*Other Exceptions*	*Do Special Large Corporation Rules Apply?*	*Special Estimated Tax Rule*
District of Columbia	Yes	X	90%	X	X		No	NA
Florida	Yes	X	90%			X, prior years income using current years rates.	No	NA
Georgia	Yes	X	70%	X			No	NA
Hawaii	Yes	X	60%	X	X		SAF	SAF
Idaho	Yes	X	90%	SAF			No	NA
Illinois	Yes	X	90%, provided remaining 10% is paid by extended due date.	X			No	NA
Indiana	Yes	X	80%				No	NA
Iowa	Yes	X	90%	X			No	NA
Kansas	Yes	X	90%	X	X		No	NA

Underpayment Penalty Exceptions

Legend:

X	Indicates that the exception to the underpayment penalty is followed
SAF	Same as applicable federal rules
NA	Not applicable
NR	Not reported

		Exceptions That Are Followed					*Large Corporation Rules*	
	Does State Provide Exceptions to Underpayment Penalties?	*Estimated Taxes Equal the Tax Liability Shown on the Preceding Year's (12-Month) Return*	*Payment of a Percentage of Current Year's Taxes*	*Annualized Income Method*	*Adjusted Seasonal Installment Method*	*Other Exceptions*	*Do Special Large Corporation Rules Apply?*	*Special Estimated Tax Rule*
Kentucky	Yes					X, no penalty, if estimated taxes paid equal the tax liability shown on preceding year's 12 month return provided preceding year's tax was $25,000 or less.	No	NA
Louisiana	Yes	SAF	SAF	SAF	SAF	SAF	NR	NR
Maine	Yes	X	90%	X		No estimates are required if tax liability is less than $1,000.	Yes	Cannot base estimated payments on prior year tax liability, no estimated payments required if tax liability is less than $1,000.

Legend:

X	Indicates that the exception to the underpayment penalty is followed
SAF	Same as applicable federal rules
NA	Not applicable
NR	Not reported

Underpayment Penalty Exceptions

		Exceptions That Are Followed					*Large Corporation Rules*	
	Does State Provide Exceptions to Underpayment Penalties?	*Estimated Taxes Equal the Tax Liability Shown on the Preceding Year's (12-Month) Return*	*Payment of a Percentage of Current Year's Taxes*	*Annualized Income Method*	*Adjusted Seasonal Installment Method*	*Other Exceptions*	*Do Special Large Corporation Rules Apply?*	*Special Estimated Tax Rule*
Maryland	Yes	X	90%				NR	NR
Massachusetts	Yes, see G.h.c.63B.	X	X				Yes, large corporation is defined in IRC § 6655(g).	Cannot rely on previous year liability for estimates
Michigan (Business Tax)	Yes	If prior year tax in Michigan is less than $20,000.	85%	X			No	NA

Note. The CIT takes effect 01/01/12, and replaces the Michigan Business Tax (MBT) for most taxpayers. However, businesses that have been approved to receive, have received, or have been assigned certain certified credits may elect to file a return and pay the tax imposed by the MBT in lieu of the CIT until the certified credits are exhausted or extinguished.

Minnesota	Yes	X	90% year during the 3 taxable years immediately preceding the taxable year involved.	X	X		Yes	SAF

Underpayment Penalty Exceptions

Legend:

X	Indicates that the exception to the underpayment penalty is followed
SAF	Same as applicable federal rules
NA	Not applicable
NR	Not reported

		Exceptions That Are Followed					*Large Corporation Rules*	
	Does State Provide Exceptions to Underpayment Penalties?	*Estimated Taxes Equal the Tax Liability Shown on the Preceding Year's (12-Month) Return*	*Payment of a Percentage of Current Year's Taxes*	*Annualized Income Method*	*Adjusted Seasonal Installment Method*	*Other Exceptions*	*Do Special Large Corporation Rules Apply?*	*Special Estimated Tax Rule*
Mississippi	Yes		90%	X	X		Yes, large corporation is one with taxable income of at least $1 million in any 1 of the 3 immediately preceding tax years.	MS Reg. § 1121
Missouri	Yes	X	90%	X			Yes	See § 143.761 RSMo
Montana	Yes	X	80%	X	X	X	No	NA
Nebraska	Yes	SAF	SAF	SAF	SAF	SAF	Yes	SAF
Nevada	Nevada does not impose a corporate income tax							
New Hampshire	Yes	X	90%	X		First tax period which taxpayer is required to file.	No	NR
New Jersey	Yes	Not necessarily	90%		X		No	NA

Underpayment Penalty Exceptions

Legend:

X	Indicates that the exception to the underpayment penalty is followed
SAF	Same as applicable federal rules
NA	Not applicable
NR	Not reported

		Exceptions That Are Followed					*Large Corporation Rules*	
	Does State Provide Exceptions to Underpayment Penalties?	*Estimated Taxes Equal the Tax Liability Shown on the Preceding Year's (12-Month) Return*	*Payment of a Percentage of Current Year's Taxes*	*Annualized Income Method*	*Adjusted Seasonal Installment Method*	*Other Exceptions*	*Do Special Large Corporation Rules Apply?*	*Special Estimated Tax Rule*
New Mexico	Yes	X	80%	X	X	Equal to 110% year prior tax year	No	NA
New York	Yes	X	91%	X	X	X, payment is misappropriated through no fault of taxpayer.	Yes, allocated ENI over $1 million	Cannot rely on exceptions based on prior year's tax or prior year's facts.
North Carolina	Yes		SAF				SAF	Prior year's tax exception not available
North Dakota	Yes	SAF	SAF, 90%	X	X	SAF	No	NA
Ohio	Ohio does not impose a corporate income tax							

Note. Effective 1/1/2010, the Ohio Franchise Tax was fully phased out and business will be taxed on gross receipts through the Commercial Activity Tax. Details about that tax can be found at: http//tax.ohio.gov/divisions/commercial_activities/index.stm

Underpayment Penalty Exceptions

Legend:

X	Indicates that the exception to the underpayment penalty is followed
SAF	Same as applicable federal rules
NA	Not applicable
NR	Not reported

		Exceptions That Are Followed					*Large Corporation Rules*	
	Does State Provide Exceptions to Underpayment Penalties?	*Estimated Taxes Equal the Tax Liability Shown on the Preceding Year's (12-Month) Return*	*Payment of a Percentage of Current Year's Taxes*	*Annualized Income Method*	*Adjusted Seasonal Installment Method*	*Other Exceptions*	*Do Special Large Corporation Rules Apply?*	*Special Estimated Tax Rule*
Oklahoma	Yes	X	70%	X			Yes, Oklahoma tax if greater than $5 million income for 1 of 3 preceding years	NA
Oregon	Yes	X	100%	X	X		If interest on underpayment for first quarter not imposed due to payment of 1/2 of prior year's tax, the difference between the next lowest	Prior year's tax exception not available, except for first quarter "exception" amount and 1/2 of prior year's tax is added to second installment period required payment.
Pennsylvania	Yes		90%				No	NA
Rhode Island	Yes	X	80%				No	NA
South Carolina	SAF	SAF	SAF	SAF			No	

Underpayment Penalty Exceptions

Legend:

X	Indicates that the exception to the underpayment penalty is followed
SAF	Same as applicable federal rules
NA	Not applicable
NR	Not reported

		Exceptions That Are Followed					*Large Corporation Rules*	
	Does State Provide Exceptions to Underpayment Penalties?	*Estimated Taxes Equal the Tax Liability Shown on the Preceding Year's (12-Month) Return*	*Payment of a Percentage of Current Year's Taxes*	*Annualized Income Method*	*Adjusted Seasonal Installment Method*	*Other Exceptions*	*Do Special Large Corporation Rules Apply?*	*Special Estimated Tax Rule*
South Dakota	South Dakota does not impose a corporate income tax							
Tennessee	Yes	X	100%				No	NA
Texas	NA, estimated franchise tax payments are not required							
Utah	Yes	X	90%	X	X		No	NA
Vermont	Yes	SAF	SAF	SAF	SAF	SAF	NR	NR

Underpayment Penalty Exceptions

Legend:

- X — Indicates that the exception to the underpayment penalty is followed
- SAF — Same as applicable federal rules
- NA — Not applicable
- NR — Not reported

		Exceptions That Are Followed					*Large Corporation Rules*	
	Does State Provide Exceptions to Underpayment Penalties?	*Estimated Taxes Equal the Tax Liability Shown on the Preceding Year's (12-Month) Return*	*Payment of a Percentage of Current Year's Taxes*	*Annualized Income Method*	*Adjusted Seasonal Installment Method*	*Other Exceptions*	*Do Special Large Corporation Rules Apply?*	*Special Estimated Tax Rule*
Virginia	Yes	Taxpayer must have filed an income tax return showing a tax liability for the preceding taxable year and that year must have consisted of 12 months. See Va. Code § 58.1-504(D)(1).	90%	X		No penalty if estimated taxes paid equal the tax computed at the rate applicable to the taxable year but otherwise on the basis of the facts shown on the return of the corporation form, and the law applicable to, the preceding taxable year. See Va. Code § 58.1-504(D)(2).	No	NA
Washington	Washington does not impose a corporate income tax							
West Virginia	Yes	X	90%	X			No	NA

Underpayment Penalty Exceptions

Legend:

X	Indicates that the exception to the underpayment penalty is followed
SAF	Same as applicable federal rules
NA	Not applicable
NR	Not reported

		Exceptions That Are Followed					*Large Corporation Rules*	
	Does State Provide Exceptions to Underpayment Penalties?	*Estimated Taxes Equal the Tax Liability Shown on the Preceding Year's (12-Month) Return*	*Payment of a Percentage of Current Year's Taxes*	*Annualized Income Method*	*Adjusted Seasonal Installment Method*	*Other Exceptions*	*Do Special Large Corporation Rules Apply?*	*Special Estimated Tax Rule*
Wisconsin	Yes, SAF	X, if a small corporation, net income of less than $250,000	90%	X			Yes, if Wisconsin net income greater than $250,000	Cannot rely on prior year's tax for an alternative computation.
Wyoming	Wyoming does not impose a corporate income tax							

Timely Filing of Returns and Payment of Estimated Tax

Federal Tax Treatment

The date on which a tax return is considered to have been filed with or received by the IRS is important for two reasons. First, taxpayers are subject to penalties and interest if they do not comply with the tax return filing requirement. Second, the date a return is filed begins the running of the statute of limitations on the assessment of additional tax or the refund of an overpayment. The timely payment of estimated tax is required to avoid underpayment penalties.

A corporation must file its federal income tax return or an application for extension of time to file by the fifteenth day of the third month following the close of its tax year. [IRC § 6072(b)] In addition, a corporation is required to pay federal estimated taxes if its tax liability for the year can reasonably be expected to be $500 or more. [IRC § 6655] Generally, federal estimated tax payments must be made in four equal installments, due on or before the fifteenth day of the fourth, sixth, ninth, and twelfth months of the corporation's tax year. (For details regarding estimated tax payments, see the section entitled Estimated Tax Payment Requirements.)

In general, when a return is filed or a tax payment is made before the due date, the return or payment is considered to have been filed or made on the due date. A return that is delivered by the U.S. Postal Service is considered to have been delivered on the date of the postmark, not on the date of actual receipt by the IRS. [IRC § 7502]The federal "timely mailed–timely filed" rule provides that any return required to be filed before a specified date that is delivered after that date by the U.S. Postal Service to the office where the return is required to be filed is deemed to have been timely filed if the U.S. postmark stamped on the cover is dated on or before the date prescribed for filing. The same rule applies with respect to determining whether a tax payment has been made by the due date. Accordingly, a return, an extension request, or a tax payment is considered timely filed or made if its mailing envelope bears a U.S. postmark dated on or before the filing or payment due date. In addition to the U.S. Postal Service, the IRS has designated three private delivery services that can be relied upon for purposes of the timely mailed-timely filed rule. They include DHL Express, Federal Express, and United Parcel Service. [IRS Notice 2004-83]

The timely mailed-timely filed rule has been extended to cover returns filed electronically. [Treas. Reg. § 301.7502-1] The date of an electronic postmark given by an authorized electronic return transmitter is deemed to be the filing date if the date of the electronic postmark is on or before the filing due date. A federal tax deposit by electronic funds transfer is deemed paid on the last day prescribed for filing the applicable return for the return period (without regard to extensions) or, if later, when withdrawn from the payee's account. [Treas. Reg. § 31.6302-1(h)]

Finally, when the tax return or tax payment due date falls on a Saturday, Sunday, or legal holiday, the return or payment is treated as having been timely filed or made if it is filed or made on the next business day after the Saturday, Sunday, or legal holiday.

State Tax Treatment

Most states have adopted the federal provision under which an income tax return or estimated income tax payment is deemed to have been filed or made on the date of the U.S. postmark on the envelope in which the return or tax payment is delivered, and under which the certificate of mailing is considered proof that the income tax return or payment was timely mailed.

Different rules may apply to state taxes other than income taxes. In *Washington Department of Licensing v. Exxon Mobil Corporation* [No. 29334-0-II (Wash. Ct. of App., Sept. 9, 2003)], the Washington Court of Appeals ruled that the taxpayer did not make a timely payment of a fuels tax that had a statutory due date which happened to fall on a Sunday. The taxpayer paid the tax by electronic funds transfer on the Monday following the statutory due date. The applicable fuels tax statute provided that the tax was due on or before the statutory due date but did not define "on or before." However, a fuels tax regulation stated that if the due date fell on a weekend, the tax was due on the last business day before the weekend.

While most states have adopted the federal timely mailed–timely filed provisions for purposes of filing tax returns and making tax payments, they have not been adopted for purposes of filing protests and appeals. For instance, the North Carolina Court of Appeals ruled that timely mailing cannot be proved by evidence of the date imprinted on a notice by a private postal meter, even when the appeal is received within the normal period of time allowed for receipt following postmarking by the U.S. Postal Service. For the appeal to be considered timely filed, it had to be received within the appeal period or it had to bear a U.S. Postal Service postmark date that fell before the end of the appeal period. [*In re Bass Income Fund,* No. 92-PTC-179 (N.C. Ct. App. Aug. 2, 1994)] In *Nash v. Department of Revenue* [No. P.98-513 (Ala. ALJ May 5, 1999)], an Alabama administrative law judge ruled that a notice of appeal must be mailed or hand-delivered—not faxed—within the time prescribed. In *W.A. Foote Memorial Hospital v. City of Jackson* [Nos. 244670, 244671, 244672, 246122, and 246124 (Mich. Ct. of App., June 8, 2004)], the Michigan Court of Appeals ruled that for purposes of timely filing a Michigan property tax appeal, the term "certified mail," as used in the state statute, refers to mail sent only by the U.S. Postal Service, and does not include delivery by Federal Express.

State-by-State Summary

The following chart summarizes the state rules governing the timely filing of returns and payment of estimated tax.

Legend:

NR Not reported
SAF Same as applicable federal rules
A Postmark date controls
B Date of receipt controls

Timely Filing of Returns and Payment of Estimated Tax

	A Return Is Considered Timely Filed				*Estimated Tax Is Considered Timely Paid*			
	Delivery by U.S. Mail		*Delivery by Express Mail Carrier*		*Delivery by U.S. Mail*		*Delivery by Express Mail Carrier*	
	Indicator	*Proof of Date with Certificate of Mailing?*	*Date Given to Carrier*	*Date Received by Revenue Department*	*Indicator*	*Proof of Date with Certificate of Mailing?*	*Date Given to Carrier*	*Date Received by Revenue Department*
Alabama	A	Yes	Yes	No	A	Yes	Yes	No
Alaska	A	Yes	Yes	Yes	A	Yes	Yes	Yes
Arizona	A	Yes	No	Yes	A	Yes	No	Yes
Arkansas	A	Yes	No	Yes	A	Yes	No	Yes
California	A	Yes	Yes	Yes	A	Yes	Yes	Yes
Colorado	B	No	No	Yes	B	No	No	Yes
Connecticut	A	Yes	See Policy Stmt 2005(4)		A	Yes	See Policy Stmt 2005(4)	
Delaware	A	Yes	No	Yes	A	Yes	No	Yes
District of Columbia	A	No	Yes	Yes	A	No	Yes	Yes
Florida	A	No	Yes, date carrier identifies as shipping date.	No	A	No	Yes date carrier identifies as shipping date.	Yes
Georgia	A		Yes		A			
Hawaii	A, B	Yes	Yes, for IRS designated private delivery service	NR	A, B	Yes	Yes, for IRS designated private delivery service	NR

Timely Filing of Returns and Payment of Estimated Tax

Legend:

NR	Not reported
SAF	Same as applicable federal rules
A	Postmark date controls
B	Date of receipt controls

	A Return Is Considered Timely Filed				*Estimated Tax Is Considered Timely Paid*			
	Delivery by U.S. Mail		*Delivery by Express Mail Carrier*		*Delivery by U.S. Mail*		*Delivery by Express Mail Carrier*	
	Indicator	*Proof of Date with Certificate of Mailing?*	*Date Given to Carrier*	*Date Received by Revenue Department*	*Indicator*	*Proof of Date with Certificate of Mailing?*	*Date Given to Carrier*	*Date Received by Revenue Department*
Idaho	A, if U.S. mail per IRC § 7502, B if hand delivered	Yes, if U.S. mail per IRC § 7502	Yes, if U.S. mail per IRC § 7502	No, unless hand delivered	A, if U.S. mail per IRC § 7502, B if hand delivered	Yes, if U.S. mail per IRC § 7502	Yes, if U.S. mail per IRC § 7502	No, unless hand delivered
Illinois	A	SAF	If competent evidence shows mailing, filing, and payment on date of mailing for U.S. Postal Service Express Mail.	If other than U.S. Postal Service Express Mail used, date of receipt by revenue department is date used.	A	SAF	If competent evidence shows mailing, filing, and payment on date of mailing for U.S. Postal Service Express Mail.	If other than U.S. Postal Service Express Mail used, date of receipt by revenue department is date used.
Indiana	A	Yes	Yes	No	A	Yes	Yes	No
Iowa	A	Yes	NR	Yes	A	Yes	NR	Yes
Kansas	A	Yes	Yes	No	A	Yes	Yes	No
Kentucky	A	NR	No	Yes	A	NR	No	Yes
Louisiana	A	Yes	The date of registration with the express service		A	Yes	The date of registration with the express service	
Maine	A	Yes	No	Yes	A	Yes	No	Yes
Maryland	A	Yes	No	Yes	A	Yes	No	Yes

Legend:

NR	Not reported
SAF	Same as applicable federal rules
A	Postmark date controls
B	Date of receipt controls

Timely Filing of Returns and Payment of Estimated Tax

	A Return Is Considered Timely Filed				*Estimated Tax Is Considered Timely Paid*			
	Delivery by U.S. Mail		*Delivery by Express Mail Carrier*		*Delivery by U.S. Mail*		*Delivery by Express Mail Carrier*	
	Indicator	*Proof of Date with Certificate of Mailing?*	*Date Given to Carrier*	*Date Received by Revenue Department*	*Indicator*	*Proof of Date with Certificate of Mailing?*	*Date Given to Carrier*	*Date Received by Revenue Department*
Massachusetts	A	Yes	Depends on facts	Depends on facts	A	Yes		
Michigan	A	NR	No	Yes	A	NR	No	Yes

Note. The CIT takes effect 01/01/12, and replaces the Michigan Business Tax (MBT) for most taxpayers. However, businesses that have been approved to receive, have received, or have been assigned certain certified credits may elect to file a return and pay the tax imposed by the MBT in lieu of the CIT until the certified credits are exhausted or extinguished.

Minnesota	A		Yes	No	A		Yes	No
Mississippi	A, B	No	No	No	A, B	No	No	Yes
Missouri	A	Yes	Yes	No	A	Yes	Yes	No
Montana	A	Yes	Yes	No	A	Yes	Yes	No
Nebraska	A	Yes	No	Yes	A	Yes	No	Yes
Nevada	Nevada does not impose a corporate income tax							
New Hampshire	A	Yes	Yes	No	A	Yes	Yes	No
New Jersey	A	Facts and circumstances govern	One day prior to delivery to Revenue Department, see N.J.A.C. 18:2-4.B.		A	Facts and circumstances govern	One day prior to delivery to Revenue Department, see N.J.A.C. 18:2-4.B.	
New Mexico	A	Yes	Yes		A	Yes	Yes	

Timely Filing of Returns and Payment of Estimated Tax

Legend:

NR	Not reported
SAF	Same as applicable federal rules
A	Postmark date controls
B	Date of receipt controls

	A Return Is Considered Timely Filed				*Estimated Tax Is Considered Timely Paid*			
	Delivery by U.S. Mail		*Delivery by Express Mail Carrier*		*Delivery by U.S. Mail*		*Delivery by Express Mail Carrier*	
	Indicator	*Proof of Date with Certificate of Mailing?*	*Date Given to Carrier*	*Date Received by Revenue Department*	*Indicator*	*Proof of Date with Certificate of Mailing?*	*Date Given to Carrier*	*Date Received by Revenue Department*
New York	A	Yes	Will be considered timely filed based on date received by approved carrier.	No	A	Yes	Will be considered timely filed based on date received by approved carrier.	No
North Carolina	A				A		Yes	
North Dakota	A	Yes	Yes	No	A	Yes	Yes	No
Ohio	Ohio does not impose a corporate income tax							
Note. Effective 1/1/2010, the Ohio Franchise Tax was fully phased out and business will be taxed on gross receipts through the Commercial Activity Tax. Details about that tax can be found at: http//tax.ohio.gov/divisions/commercial_activities/index.stm								
Oklahoma	A, B	No	No	Yes	A, B	No	No	Yes
Oregon	A	Yes	No	Yes	A	Yes	No	Yes
Pennsylvania	A; B if hand delivered	Yes	No	Yes	A; B if hand delivered	Yes	No	Yes
Rhode Island	A, B	NR	Yes	Yes	A, B	NR	Yes	Yes
South Carolina	A		SAF		A		SAF	
South Dakota	South Dakota does not impose a corporate income tax							

Legend:

NR	Not reported
SAF	Same as applicable federal rules
A	Postmark date controls
B	Date of receipt controls

Timely Filing of Returns and Payment of Estimated Tax

	A Return Is Considered Timely Filed				*Estimated Tax Is Considered Timely Paid*			
	Delivery by U.S. Mail		*Delivery by Express Mail Carrier*		*Delivery by U.S. Mail*		*Delivery by Express Mail Carrier*	
	Indicator	*Proof of Date with Certificate of Mailing?*	*Date Given to Carrier*	*Date Received by Revenue Department*	*Indicator*	*Proof of Date with Certificate of Mailing?*	*Date Given to Carrier*	*Date Received by Revenue Department*
Tennessee	A	Yes	Yes	No	A	Yes	Yes	No
Texas	A	Yes	Yes		NA	NA	Yes	
Utah	A	Yes, if issued by U.S. Postal Service	Yes	No	A	Yes, if issued by U.S. Postal Service	Yes	No
Vermont	A	Yes	NR	Yes	A	Yes	NR	Yes
Virginia	A, B	Yes		Yes	A, B	Yes		Yes
Washington	Washington does not impose a corporate income tax							
West Virginia	A	Yes	No	Yes	A	Yes	No	Yes
Wisconsin	A	Yes	No	Yes	A	Yes	No	Yes
Wyoming	Wyoming does not impose a corporate income tax							

Use of Credit Cards to Pay Taxes

The IRS may accept as payment for federal tax bills any commercially accepted means authorized by the Treasury Department, including electronic funds transfer, credit cards, and debit cards. [IRC § 6311]Under Treas. Reg. § 301.6311-2, a payment of tax by credit card or debit card generally is deemed to be made when the issuer of the credit or debit card properly authorizes the transaction, provided that the payment is actually received by the IRS in the ordinary course of business. Furthermore, the IRS may not impose any fee or charge on persons paying taxes by credit card or debit card. A fee or charge may, however, be imposed by the issuer of the credit or debit card or by any other financial institution or person participating in the credit or debit card transaction.

Taxpayers can make credit card payments whether they file electronically or file a paper return. Taxpayers can charge taxes on their American Express, MasterCard, Visa or Discover cards. The IRS uses two service providers to accept credit card payments: Official Payments Corporation (www.officialpayments.com) and Link2Gov Corporation (www.PAY1040.com). [IRS Fact Sheet FS-2008-6, Jan. 2, 2008]

Like the federal government, a number of states permit the payment of tax bills by credit card and/or debit card. Some states permit the use of the cards for both current and delinquent taxes. The type of credit cards that may be used (e.g., VISA, MasterCard) and the type of taxes eligible for payment by a credit or debit card (e.g., individual income taxes, corporate income taxes, payroll taxes) vary from state to state.

State-by-State Summary

The following chart, presented in two parts, identifies the states that permit use of credit cards to pay tax bills. For the states that permit credit card use, the chart indicates whether they may be used to pay for current and/or delinquent taxes, which cards may be used, and the type of taxes eligible for payment by credit card.

Use of Credit Cards to Pay Taxes (Part 1)

Legend:

X	Condition applies
NA	Not applicable
NR	No reply

		If Yes, Are Current and Delinquent Taxes Eligible for Payment Via Credit Card?		
	Does State Allow Payment of Tax Via Credit Card?	*Only Current Tax*	*Only Delinquent Tax*	*Both Current and Delinquent Tax*
Alabama	Yes			X
Alaska	No			
Arizona	No			
Arkansas	Yes	X		
California	Yes			X
Colorado	Yes			X
Connecticut	Yes	X		
Delaware	Yes	X		
District of Columbia	Yes			X
Florida	Yes			X
Georgia	Yes			X
Hawaii	Yes, only if payment made in person or via Internet.			X
Idaho	Yes			X
Illinois	Yes	X		
Indiana	Yes			X
Iowa	Yes		X, for sales/use tax and withholding tax	X, for individual income tax
Kansas	Yes			X

Use of Credit Cards to Pay Taxes (Part 1)

Legend:

X	Condition applies
NA	Not applicable
NR	No reply

	Does State Allow Payment of Tax Via Credit Card?	*If Yes, Are Current and Delinquent Taxes Eligible for Payment Via Credit Card?* *Only Current Tax*	*Only Delinquent Tax*	*Both Current and Delinquent Tax*
Kentucky	Yes	X		
Louisiana	Yes			X
Maine	Yes		X	
Maryland	No			
Massachusetts	Yes			X
Michigan (Business Tax)	No			
Note. The CIT takes effect 01/01/12, and replaces the Michigan Business Tax (MBT) for most taxpayers. However, businesses that have been approved to receive, have received, or have been assigned certain certified credits may elect to file a return and pay the tax imposed by the MBT in lieu of the CIT until the certified credits are exhausted or extinguished.				
Minnesota	No			
Mississippi	No			
Missouri	Yes	NR	NR	X
Montana	Yes			X
Nebraska	Yes	X, individual income		X, corporate income/franchise, sales/use, payroll, motor fuels tax
Nevada	Nevada does not impose a corporate income tax			
New Hampshire	No, however recently passed legislation will soon allow credit card payment.			

Use of Credit Cards to Pay Taxes (Part 1)

Legend:

X	Condition applies
NA	Not applicable
NR	No reply

	Does State Allow Payment of Tax Via Credit Card?	*If Yes, Are Current and Delinquent Taxes Eligible for Payment Via Credit Card?* Only Current Tax	*Only Delinquent Tax*	*Both Current and Delinquent Tax*
New Jersey	Individual income tax, 1-888-2PAYTAX			
New Mexico	Yes	X		
New York	Yes	X		
North Carolina	No			
North Dakota	Yes			X
Ohio	Ohio does not impose a corporate income tax			
Note. Effective 1/1/2010, the Ohio Franchise Tax was fully phased out and business will be taxed on gross receipts through the Commercial Activity Tax. Details about that tax can be found at: http//tax.ohio.gov/divisions/commercial_activities/index.stm				
Oklahoma	Yes			X
Oregon	Yes		X	
Pennsylvania	Yes	NR	NR	NR
Rhode Island	Yes			X
South Carolina	Yes			X
South Dakota	South Dakota does not impose a corporate income tax			
Tennessee	Yes	X		
Texas	Yes			X
Utah	Yes, there is a convenience fee added.			X

Use of Credit Cards to Pay Taxes (Part 1)

Legend:

X	Condition applies
NA	Not applicable
NR	No reply

		If Yes, Are Current and Delinquent Taxes Eligible for Payment Via Credit Card?		
	Does State Allow Payment of Tax Via Credit Card?	*Only Current Tax*	*Only Delinquent Tax*	*Both Current and Delinquent Tax*
Vermont	NR	NR	NR	NR
Virginia	Yes, Visa, MasterCard, American Express, Discover.			X
Washington	Washington does not impose a corporate income tax			
West Virginia	No			
Wisconsin	Yes			X
Wyoming	Wyoming does not impose a corporate income tax			

Use of Credit Cards to Pay State Taxes (Part 2)

Legend:

X	Condition applies
NA	Not applicable
NR	No reply

	If Yes, Which Cards Are Eligible for Use in Payment?					*If Yes, Which Taxes Are Eligible for Payment Via Credit Card?*				
	VISA	*Mastercard*	*American Express*	*Discover*	*Other*	*Corporate Income or Franchise*	*Sales/Use*	*Payroll*	*Individual Income*	*Other*
Alabama	X	X	X	X		X			X	
Alaska	NA	NA	NA	NA	NA	NA	NA	NA	NA	NA
Arizona	NA	NA	NA	NA	NA	NA	NA	NA	NA	NA
Arkansas	X	X	X	X			X		X	
California	X	X	X	X		X			X	Fee is 2.5% of the tax amount charged, minimum fee $1.
Colorado	X	X	NA	X	NA	NA	NA	NA	X	NA
Connecticut	X	X							X	
Delaware			X		X			X		
District of Columbia		X	X		ACS Debit or Credit	X	X	X	X	X, gross receipts and ball park fee
Florida	X	X		X			X			
Georgia	X	X	X	X		X	X	X	X	
Hawaii	X	X	X	X, only if paying in person			X	X	X	

Legend:

X Condition applies
NA Not applicable
NR No reply

Use of Credit Cards to Pay State Taxes (Part 2)

	If Yes, Which Cards Are Eligible for Use in Payment?					*If Yes, Which Taxes Are Eligible for Payment Via Credit Card?*				
	VISA	*Mastercard*	*American Express*	*Discover*	*Other*	*Corporate Income or Franchise*	*Sales/Use*	*Payroll*	*Individual Income*	*Other*
Idaho	X	X				X	X	X	X	X
Illinois		X	X	X					X	
Indiana				X		X		X	X	
Iowa	X	X	X	X			X	X	X	
Kansas	X	X	X	X		X	X	X	X	X, privilege tax
Kentucky	X	X		X		X	X	X	X	
Louisiana	X	X	X	X	LDR provides for secured payments of returns through use of 3rd party credit card vendors.	X	X		X	
Maine	X	X							X	
Maryland	NA	NA	NA	NA	NA	NA	NA	NA	NA	NA
Massachusetts	NR	NR	NR	NR	NR				X	
Michigan	NA	NA	NA	NA	NA	NA	NA	NA	NA	NA

Use of Credit Cards to Pay State Taxes (Part 2)

Legend:
X Condition applies
NA Not applicable
NR No reply

	If Yes, Which Cards Are Eligible for Use in Payment?					*If Yes, Which Taxes Are Eligible for Payment Via Credit Card?*				
	VISA	*Mastercard*	*American Express*	*Discover*	*Other*	*Corporate Income or Franchise*	*Sales/Use*	*Payroll*	*Individual Income*	*Other*
Note. The CIT takes effect 01/01/12, and replaces the Michigan Business Tax (MBT) for most taxpayers. However, businesses that have been approved to receive, have received, or have been assigned certain certified credits may elect to file a return and pay the tax imposed by the MBT in lieu of the CIT until the certified credits are exhausted or extinguished.										
Minnesota										
Mississippi	NA	NA	NA	NA	NA	NA	NA	NA	NA	NA
Missouri	X	X	X	X		X	X	X	X	Motor Fuel/ Tobacco, Tire Fee
Montana	X	X				X		X	X	X
Nebraska	X	X	X	X	NA	X	X	X	X	X, Motor Fuels Tax
Nevada	Nevada does not impose a corporate income tax									
New Hampshire	NA	NA	NA	NA	NA	NA	NA	NA	NA	NA
New Jersey	NR	NR	NR	NR	NR				X	
New Mexico	X	X	X				X		X	
New York	X	X	X	X		X, assessments only and only Mastercard and Discover			X	

Use of Credit Cards to Pay State Taxes (Part 2)

Legend:
X Condition applies
NA Not applicable
NR No reply

	If Yes, Which Cards Are Eligible for Use in Payment?					*If Yes, Which Taxes Are Eligible for Payment Via Credit Card?*				
	VISA	*Mastercard*	*American Express*	*Discover*	*Other*	*Corporate Income or Franchise*	*Sales/Use*	*Payroll*	*Individual Income*	*Other*
North Carolina	NA	NA	NA	NA	NA	NA	NA	NA	NA	NA
North Dakota	X	X	X	X			X		X	
Ohio	Ohio does not impose a corporate income tax									
Note. Effective 1/1/2010, the Ohio Franchise Tax was fully phased out and business will be taxed on gross receipts through the Commercial Activity Tax. Details about that tax can be found at: http//tax.ohio.gov/divisions/commercial_activities/index.stm										
Oklahoma	NR	NR	NR	NR	NR	NR	NR	NR	NR	NR
Oregon	X	X				X		X	X	X, local transit taxes
Pennsylvania	X	X	X	X					X	
Rhode Island	X			X		X	X	X	X	
South Carolina	X	X				X	X	X	X	
South Dakota	South Dakota does not impose a corporate income tax									
Tennessee		X	X	X						X, Professional Privilege Tax

Use of Credit Cards to Pay State Taxes (Part 2)

Legend:
X — Condition applies
NA — Not applicable
NR — No reply

	If Yes, Which Cards Are Eligible for Use in Payment?					*If Yes, Which Taxes Are Eligible for Payment Via Credit Card?*				
	VISA	*Mastercard*	*American Express*	*Discover*	*Other*	*Corporate Income or Franchise*	*Sales/Use*	*Payroll*	*Individual Income*	*Other*
Texas		X	X	X			X			Franchise taxes filed via the Web-file option may be paid with a credit card.
Utah		X	X	X		X	X	X	X	Most tax types
Vermont	NR	NR	NR	NR	NR	NR	NR	NR	NR	NR
Virginia	NA	NA	NA	NA	NA	NA	NA	NA	NA	NA
Washington	Washington does not impose a corporate income tax									
West Virginia	NA	NA	NA	NA	NA	NA	NA	NA	NA	NA
Wisconsin	X	X	X	X		X	X	X	X	
Wyoming	Wyoming does not impose a corporate income tax									

Penalties and Interest Rates on Late Payments and Refunds

Penalties

Federal Treatment. Under IRC Section 6651, a corporation that fails to file its federal income tax return by the due date (including extensions) is subject to a penalty, unless the failure to file is the result of reasonable cause and not the taxpayer's willful neglect. The penalty is 5 percent per month of the amount of the tax liability shown on the return (less any prior payments and credits), up to a maximum of 25 percent. The minimum penalty for a return that is more than 60 days late is the lesser of the tax required to be shown on the return or $100 ($135 for returns required to be filed after December 31, 2008). The penalty for a fraudulent failure to file is 15 percent per month, up to a maximum of 75 percent. The failure-to-file penalty is reduced by the failure-to-pay penalty (discussed below) for any month in which both penalties apply unless the failure relates to an assessed deficiency, in which case the IRS may assess both penalties.

If a corporation fails to pay the tax shown on its return, a penalty of 0.5 percent per month of the unpaid tax will be assessed, up to a maximum of 25 percent of the unpaid tax. [IRC § 6651]A penalty will also be imposed if a corporation fails to pay an assessed deficiency of tax within ten days of notice and demand for payment. The penalty will be increased to 1 percent per month beginning either 1) ten days after a notice and demand of an intent to levy has been filed by the IRS or 2) on the day on which a notice and demand for immediate payment is given preceding a jeopardy levy. The penalty will not apply if the failure to pay is attributable to reasonable cause or attributable to failure to pay estimated taxes (for which a different set of penalties applies). If a corporation is granted an automatic filing extension, reasonable cause is presumed to exist, provided that at least 90 percent of the total tax liability was paid by the unextended due date.

State Treatment. As a general rule, states also impose penalties if a tax return or tax payment is not timely filed or paid. Like the maximum federal penalty, the maximum penalty imposed by most states (in cases other than fraud) is 25 percent; however, some states impose maximum penalties that exceed 25 percent. For instance, Delaware's maximum penalty for the late filing of a return is 50 percent. Generally, a state's penalty for late payment of tax is imposed at the same rate as its penalty for late filing.

Interest

Federal Treatment. The Code provides for interest on underpayments and overpayments of tax at adjustable rates. [IRC § 6621] Such interest must be compounded on a daily basis. Interest on underpayments is payable at a federally specified rate from the last day that is prescribed by law for the payment of the tax to the date on which the tax is actually paid. Typically, the last date that is prescribed by law for the payment of tax is the unextended due date of the return to which the tax relates. Thus, interest is generally charged on taxes not paid by the unextended due date even if an extension of time to file is granted.

Interest will also accrue on penalties that have not been paid within ten days after a notice and demand for payment has been made for such penalties.

Interest is payable by the IRS on any overpayment of taxes. It accrues from the date of the overpayment—the date of payment of the first amount that, when added to previous payments, is in excess of the tax liability—to the date that the overpayment is credited or a date that is not more than 30 days before the date of the refund check. If any subsequent payments are made, the date of overpayment of each such payment is the date of the payment.

The interest rate imposed on an underpayment (deficiency) equals the federal short-term rate plus 3 percentage points, except in the case of a large corporate underpayment, where the interest rate equals the federal short-term rate plus 5 percentage points. A large corporate underpayment is any underpayment (including tax, interest, and penalties) by a corporation that exceeds $100,000 for any tax year. The increased rate generally is applicable on the 30th day after the IRS sends the corporation a 30- or 90-day letter, whichever is earlier. The interest rate paid to a corporation on an overpayment (refund) equals the federal short-term rate plus 2 percentage points, except the rate for the portion of a corporate overpayment exceeding $10,000 is the federal short-term rate plus one-half of 1 percentage point. In the case of a noncorporate taxpayer, the overpayment rate equals the federal short-term rate plus 3 percentage points.

IRC Section 6603 permits a taxpayer to make a cash deposit with the IRS for future application against an underpayment of tax that has not been assessed at the time of the deposit. To the extent that the deposit is used to pay a tax liability, the tax is treated as paid when the deposit is made and no interest underpayment is imposed. If the dispute is resolved in favor of the taxpayer, interest is payable on the deposit at the federal short-term rate. [Rev. Proc.2005-18, 2005-13 I.R.B. 798]

State Treatment. States, like the federal government, want to encourage the prompt filing of returns and payment of taxes. Consequently, most states charge interest when the taxpayer is delinquent in its responsibilities. The rate of interest charged, however, varies among the states, and several states impose different rates of interest on different types of taxes. Some states tie their interest rates on underpayments and overpayments of income tax directly to the federal rates, whereas other states tie their rates of interest to the prime interest rate. Still other states have a legislatively set rate of interest. The legislatively set rates of interest generally change infrequently, whereas the rates tied to the prime rate or to the federal rate change quarterly, semiannually, or annually. In some states, the interest rate paid on overpayments of tax is the same rate as the state charges on underpayments of tax.

Like the federal government, the states usually assess interest from the due date of the return; however, unlike the federal government, the states typically calculate such interest as simple interest. The states vary as to whether interest is imposed on state income tax resulting from a federal audit assessment that has been timely reported and remitted to the state.

In a Florida case, *Barnett Banks, Inc. v. Department of Revenue* [No. 98-4101 (Fla. Dist. Ct. App. Aug. 10, 1999)], the court ruled that interest assessed by the Florida Department of Revenue was inappropriate after a federal audit adjustment when a timely filed Florida amended return was filed. The taxpayer had timely filed an amended Florida income tax return after certain IRS audit adjustments were made. The Florida Department of Revenue assessed the taxpayer interest from the time the tax returns were originally due. The court held that a return is considered timely filed if it is filed within 60 days of the IRS adjustment that was agreed to and finally determined for federal income tax purposes. Since the returns were timely filed (within 60 days), no interest was owed by the taxpayer.

In many states, interest on requests for refunds of overpaid tax begins 90 days after the claim is made. A few states calculate interest on overpayments after a longer period of time (e.g., 120 days or 180 days). Other states have adopted a time frame of only 45 or 60 days.

Recent Developments

California. Corporations that underpay their corporation franchise tax liability by more than $1 million for any tax year are subject to a new 20 percent underpayment penalty, in addition to any other penalty that may be imposed. For taxpayers included in a combined report, the underpayments of all the group members are aggregated for purposes of determining whether the $1 million threshold has been reached. The penalty applies retroactively to each taxable year beginning after 2002, for which the statute of limitations has not expired. However, taxpayers will have until May 31, 2009, to report and pay outstanding taxes in order to avoid this penalty. [A.B. 1452, Sept. 30, 2008]

Colorado. To prevent corporations from taking advantage of the state's generous interest rate on overpayments of prime plus 3 percent, interest is no longer payable on overpayments of Colorado corporate income tax if the payments are not made to satisfy a bona fide estimate of tax liability. If a taxpayer's total payments are less than or equal to twice the amount of the actual tax liability, the Department of Revenue bears the burden of proving that such payments were not made to satisfy a bona fide estimate of tax liability. The taxpayer bears the burden of proof if the taxpayer's total payments are more than twice the amount of the actual tax liability. [H.B. 1219, Mar. 24, 2009]

Hawaii. Hawaii reduced the interest rate on refunds of tax overpayments to one-third of 1 percent per month, applicable to claims for refund made on or after January 1, 2009. The previous interest rate was two-thirds of 1 percent per month. [S.B. 1327, May 5, 2009]

State-by-State Summary

The following chart indicates each state's penalty for late filing of a return and late payment of tax, interest rates on late payments and refunds, the date interest begins to accrue, and how the rates change (e.g., with a change in the prime rate or legislatively).

Penalties and Interest Rates on Late Payments and Refunds

Legend:
SAF Same as applicable federal rule
NA Not applicable
NR Not reported

	Penalty for Late Filing of Corporate Income Tax Return	*Penalty for Late Payment of Corporate Income Tax*	*Interest Rate Applicable to Late Payments*	*Interest Rate on Refunds*	*Beginning Interest Accrual Date*	*How Are Interest Rates Determined?*
Alabama	10% or $50., whichever is greater	1% per month, up to 25%	SAF, not compounded	SAF, not compounded	90 days after claim for refund; due date of return for underpayments	SAF
Alaska	5% per month, up to 25%	5% per month, up to 25%	11%, compounded quarterly	11%, compounded quarterly	Due date of return for underpayments, 60 days after claim for refund	Statute
Arizona	4.5% per month, up to 25%	1/2% per month	SAF, compounded annually	SAF, compounded annually	As of due date for underpayments; 60-days after claim for refund	Based on federal rates
Arkansas	5% per month up to 35%	5% per month up to 35%	10% a year, not compounded	10%, not compounded	90 days after claim for refund; as of due date of return for underpayments	Legislative action
California	SAF	SAF	4%, compounded daily	0%, compounded daily	Due date of return for underpayments	Federal change, see RTC § 19521.
Colorado	5% plus 0.5% per month, up to 12%	5% plus 0.5% per month, up to 12%	Varies by year, not compounded	Varies by year, not compounded	From due date of return for underpayments; 45 days after claim for refund	Other

Legend:

SAF	Same as applicable federal rule
NA	Not applicable
NR	Not reported

Penalties and Interest Rates on Late Payments and Refunds

	Penalty for Late Filing of Corporate Income Tax Return	*Penalty for Late Payment of Corporate Income Tax*	*Interest Rate Applicable to Late Payments*	*Interest Rate on Refunds*	*Beginning Interest Accrual Date*	*How Are Interest Rates Determined?*
Connecticut	Greater of 10% of tax due or $50, whichever is greater	Greater of 10% of tax due or $50, whichever is greater	1% per month, not compounded	2/3% per month, not compounded	Due date of return	By statute, Conn. Gen. Stat. §§ 12-226 and 12-227
Delaware	5% per month, up to 50%	5% per month, up to 25%	1% a month, not compounded	1%, not compounded	Begins on 91st day for refunds; as of due date for underpayments	Legislative action
District of Columbia	5% per month, up to 25%	5% per month, up to 25%	10% compounded daily.	6% a year, not compounded	As of due date of return for underpayments	DC Code
Florida	10% per month, 50% maximum, $50 per month not to exceed $300 if no tax liability	10% per month, 50% maximum, $50 per month not to exceed $300 if no tax liability	Tied to prime, not compounded	Tied to the prime rate, not compounded	As of due date of return for underpayments; after 90-day grace period for refunds	Tied to prime rate, updated every six months; see § 220.807
Georgia	5% per month, up to 25%. Total of both cannot exceed 25%	0.5% per month, up to 25%.	12% per year, not compounded	12% per year, not compounded	Due date of return for refunds; 90 days after claim for refund	By statute
Hawaii	5% per month, up to 25%	20% if paid later than 60 days after timely filing	2/3 of 1% per month, not compounded	2/3 of 1% per month	Due date of return for underpayments; 90 days after claim for refund	NR

Penalties and Interest Rates on Late Payments and Refunds

Legend:
SAF Same as applicable federal rule
NA Not applicable
NR Not reported

	Penalty for Late Filing of Corporate Income Tax Return	*Penalty for Late Payment of Corporate Income Tax*	*Interest Rate Applicable to Late Payments*	*Interest Rate on Refunds*	*Beginning Interest Accrual Date*	*How Are Interest Rates Determined?*
Idaho	5% per month, up to 25%; 2% per month penalties may apply from original due date to extended due date if required extension payments were not paid.	5% per month, up to 25%; 2% per month penalties may apply from original due date to extended due date if required extension payments were not paid.	6% for 2004, not compounded	6% for 2004, not compounded	As of due date of return for underpayments and later of due date or date paid for refunds.	Idaho Code § 63-3045; 2% over rate determined under IRC § 1274(d) rate of 10/15 of prior year, round to the nearest whole number.
Illinois	Lesser of 2% of required tax to be shown or $250	20% of tax shown or required to be shown on return.	Rate adjusted semiannually; simple interest calculated on a daily basis	Rate adjusted semiannually; simple interest calculated on a daily basis	Due date of return	Rate adjusted semiannually based on federal underpayment rule under IRC § 621
Indiana	10%	10%	4%	4%	As of due date of return for underpayments; 90 days after claim for refund	2% over what the state earns
Iowa	.4 % per month for 2010	.4% per month for 2010	.7% per month, for 2009 not compounded	.7% per month for 2009, not compounded	Day claim is received for loss carryback; all other refunds, first day of 2nd month after due date or date paid (whichever is later); as of due date of return for underpayments	2% above the average prime rate for 12 months ended 9/30

Penalties and Interest Rates on Late Payments and Refunds

Legend:

SAF	Same as applicable federal rule
NA	Not applicable
NR	Not reported

	Penalty for Late Filing of Corporate Income Tax Return	*Penalty for Late Payment of Corporate Income Tax*	*Interest Rate Applicable to Late Payments*	*Interest Rate on Refunds*	*Beginning Interest Accrual Date*	*How Are Interest Rates Determined?*
Kansas	None if tax is paid with return	1% of unpaid balance of tax due for each month or fraction thereof during which such failure continues, not exceeding 24% in the aggregate, plus interest.	.4167 % per month for 2011/ 2012	.4167% per month for 2011/2012,	Refund interest not paid if refunded within 60 days of refund claim. Interest paid from end date of loss year in the case of capital loss carrybacks.	Legislative action, tied to the federal underpayment rate plus 1% as in effect on July 1 of the year immediately preceding the calendar year for which the rate is being fixed.
Kentucky	2% of tax due for each 30 days or fraction	2% of tax due for each 30 days or fraction	5%	1%	As of due date of re-return for underpayments, 60 days after claim for refund, and 90 days for refunds from NOL/capital loss carrybacks	Each year the rate is based on the prime rate charged by banks. The rate for an underpayment is the prime rate plus 2% and the rate for a refund is the prime rate les 2%.
Louisiana	5% per month, up to 25%	5% per month, up to 25%	15%, not compounded	Louisiana Judicial interest rate, not compounded	From due date of return for underpayments; 90 days after claim for refund	By statute
Maine	The greater of 10% of the tax liability or $25	1% of the unpaid tax up to 25%	Compounded monthly	Compounded monthly	As of due date of return for underpayments; 90 days after claim for refund.	NR

Penalties and Interest Rates on Late Payments and Refunds

Legend:
SAF Same as applicable federal rule
NA Not applicable
NR Not reported

	Penalty for Late Filing of Corporate Income Tax Return	*Penalty for Late Payment of Corporate Income Tax*	*Interest Rate Applicable to Late Payments*	*Interest Rate on Refunds*	*Beginning Interest Accrual Date*	*How Are Interest Rates Determined?*
Maryland	NR	25%	13% a year, not compounded	8%	45 days after claim for refund; as of due date of return for overpayments	3 percentage points above prime; floor is 13%.
Massachusetts	1% per month		See TIR 92-6, 830 CMR 62C.33.1	NR	As of due date of return for underpayments; 90 days after claim for refund	NR
Michigan (Business Tax)	5% for first 2 months; maximum of 25% and 5% per month	5% for first 2 months; maximum of 25% and 5% per month	1% above prime, not compounded	1% above prime, not compounded (9.5% 7/1/00 to 12/31/00)	45 days after claim for refund; as of due date of return for underpayments	1% above prime rate

Note. The CIT takes effect 01/01/12, and replaces the Michigan Business Tax (MBT) for most taxpayers. However, businesses that have been approved to receive, have received, or have been assigned certain certified credits may elect to file a return and pay the tax imposed by the MBT in lieu of the CIT until the certified credits are exhausted or extinguished.

Minnesota	Progressive	Progressive	3%, not compounded	3%, not compounded	As of due date of return for underpayments; 90 days after claim for refund	Bank prime interest rate
Mississippi	5% per month, up to 25%	0.5% per month, up to 25%	1% per month, not compounded	1% per month, not compounded	90 days after claim for refund; as of due date of return for underpayments	Statute

Penalties and Interest Rates on Late Payments and Refunds

Legend:

SAF	Same as applicable federal rule
NA	Not applicable
NR	Not reported

	Penalty for Late Filing of Corporate Income Tax Return	*Penalty for Late Payment of Corporate Income Tax*	*Interest Rate Applicable to Late Payments*	*Interest Rate on Refunds*	*Beginning Interest Accrual Date*	*How Are Interest Rates Determined?*
Missouri	5% per month of tax due, up to 25%	5%	Keyed to prime	Not compounded	120 days after claim for refund; as of due date for underpayments	Prime annually for underpayments, quarterly for overpayments.
Montana	$50 or amount of tax due with return	1.5% per month, up to 18%	12%, compounded daily	12%, compounded daily	As of due date	Legislation
Nebraska	5% per month of tax due	5% per month up to 25%	5%, not compounded	5%, not compounded	As of due date of return for refunds and underpayments	Tied to federal rates, set each 2 years
Nevada	Nevada does not impose a corporate income tax					
New Hampshire	5% per month, up to 25%	10% of underpayment amount	6% a year, not compounded	3%, see RSA 21-J:28	As of due date of return	SAF
New Jersey	5% per month, up to 25%	5% of late tax due	3% above prime a year, compounded annually	Prime, compounded annually	As of due date of return for underpayments; 180 days after claim for refund	Quarterly, based on prime
New Mexico	2% per month, beginning maximum, 01/01/08	2% per month, beginning maximum, 01/01/08	New Mexico statute, not compounded	New Mexico statute, not compounded	120 days after claim for refund; as of due date of return for underpayments	Statute
New York	5% per month (5 months)	0.5%, up to 25%	Varies, depends on the nature of the refund claim.	Varies, depends on the nature of the refund claim.	Depends on the nature of the refund claim; as of due date of return for underpayments	Set by Department, reviewed quarterly

Penalties and Interest Rates on Late Payments and Refunds

Legend:
SAF Same as applicable federal rule
NA Not applicable
NR Not reported

	Penalty for Late Filing of Corporate Income Tax Return	*Penalty for Late Payment of Corporate Income Tax*	*Interest Rate Applicable to Late Payments*	*Interest Rate on Refunds*	*Beginning Interest Accrual Date*	*How Are Interest Rates Determined?*
North Carolina	5% per month, up to 25%	10%	5%, not compounded	5%, not compounded	45 days after due date of refund; due date of returns for underpayments	G.S. § 105-241.1(i)
North Dakota	Greater of 5% or $5	Greater of 5% or $5	12%, not compounded	1% per month, not compounded	Depends on the nature of the claim for refunds; due date of returns for underpayments	Statute
Ohio	Ohio does not impose a corporate income tax					
Note. Effective 1/1/2010, the Ohio Franchise Tax was fully phased out and business will be taxed on gross receipts through the Commercial Activity Tax. Details about that tax can be found at: http//tax.ohio.gov/divisions/commercial_activities/index.stm						
Oklahoma	None	5%	15% a year, not compounded	15% a year, not compounded	90 days after claim for refund; as of due date of return for underpayments	Statute 68 O.S. § 217

Penalties and Interest Rates on Late Payments and Refunds

Legend:

SAF	Same as applicable federal rule
NA	Not applicable
NR	Not reported

	Penalty for Late Filing of Corporate Income Tax Return	*Penalty for Late Payment of Corporate Income Tax*	*Interest Rate Applicable to Late Payments*	*Interest Rate on Refunds*	*Beginning Interest Accrual Date*	*How Are Interest Rates Determined?*
Oregon	5% first 90 days, additional 20% after 90 days and 100% if three consecutive years not filed by due date of the third year's return.	5%	9%	5%	For refunds, 45 days after filing; for underpayment, as of due date of return; for refunds on amended returns, interest accrues 45 days after the due date of the original return or the date the original return is filed, whichever is later.	Annually. Tied to IRS rate; within 1% of IRS. If tax is not paid within 60 days after an assessment, the interest rate is increased by 1/3 of 1% per month (4% annually).
Pennsylvania	10% of first $1,000; 5% of next $4,000; 10% of amount over $5,000	None	NR	NR	As of due date of return for underpayment. As of 75 days after claim for refunds	Treasury bond rate in October of any given year is used for entire subsequent year
Rhode Island	5% per month, up to 25%	1/2% per month, up to 25%	12%, not compounded	12%, not compounded	As of due date of return for underpayments	By law
South Carolina	5% per month, up to 25%	0.5% per month, maximum 25%	SAF, compounded daily	SAF, compounded daily	As of due date of return for underpayments; after 75 days for refund	SAF
South Dakota	South Dakota does not impose a corporate income tax					

Penalties and Interest Rates on Late Payments and Refunds

Legend:
SAF Same as applicable federal rule
NA Not applicable
NR Not reported

	Penalty for Late Filing of Corporate Income Tax Return	*Penalty for Late Payment of Corporate Income Tax*	*Interest Rate Applicable to Late Payments*	*Interest Rate on Refunds*	*Beginning Interest Accrual Date*	*How Are Interest Rates Determined?*
Tennessee	$15 minimum	5% per month, up to 25%	12.25%	12.25%	45 days after claim for refund; as of due date of return for underpayments	Each July 1, see 67-1-801 TCA
Texas	5% up to 30 days late, 10% if later	Prime plus 1% up to 30 days late, 10% if later	4.25%, not compounded	Treasury Pool Rate or Prime plus 1%, whichever is less, not compounded.	Interest begins 60th day after payment due for refund; for underpayments, 60 days after payment date or original due date, whichever is later	See Texas Tax Code § 111.060.
Utah	1 thru 5 days late: Greater of $20 or 2% of unpaid tax; 6 thru 15 days: Greater of $20 or 5% of unpaid tax; 16 or more days late: Greater of $20 or 10% of unpaid tax.	1 thru 5 days late: Greater of $20 or 2% of unpaid tax; 6 thru 15 days: Greater of $20 or 5% of unpaid tax; 16 or more days late: Greater of $20 or 10% of unpaid tax	3% a year, not compounded	3% a year, not compounded	90 days from later of return regular due date or filing date for refunds and 45 days if electronically filed; as of due date of return for underpayments	UCA 59-1-402 provides the rate at 2% above the federal short term rate in effect for the 4th quarter of the preceding year.
Vermont	5% per month, 25% maximum	5% per month, 25% maximum	5%, not compounded	5%, not compounded	As of due date of return for underpayments; 45 days after due date for refunds	NR

Legend:

SAF Same as applicable federal rule
NA Not applicable
NR Not reported

Penalties and Interest Rates on Late Payments and Refunds

	Penalty for Late Filing of Corporate Income Tax Return	*Penalty for Late Payment of Corporate Income Tax*	*Interest Rate Applicable to Late Payments*	*Interest Rate on Refunds*	*Beginning Interest Accrual Date*	*How Are Interest Rates Determined?*
Virginia	6% per month, up to 30%, minimum $100	6% per month, up to 30%, minimum $100	SAF plus 2 points, but not compounded	SAF plus 2 points, but not compounded	60 days after claim for refund; as of due date of return for underpayments	Federal rate plus 2%
Washington	Washington does not impose a corporate income tax					
West Virginia	5% per month, up to 25%	0.5% per month, up to 25%	9.5%, not compounded	8%, not compounded	As of due date of return	Every 6 months based on adjusted prime rates (never below 8%)
Wisconsin	$150 late filing fee	5% of net tax due for each month or fraction thereof that return is late, but not more than 25%; 18% annual interest on balance due.	18%	9%	As of due date of return for refunds and underpayments; however, refunds issued within 90 days of either the filing of the return or the deadline for filing (whichever is later) bear no interest.	By statute
Wyoming	Wyoming does not impose a corporate income tax					

Part 11. FILING REQUIREMENTS

Due Dates and Extensions for Filing Returns

Federal Tax Treatment

A corporation must file its federal income tax return by the fifteenth day of the third month following the close of its tax year. [IRC § 6072(b)] This due date applies to both C corporations and S corporations.

If a corporation is unable to file its federal income tax return by the due date, it may obtain an automatic six-month extension of time to file its return by filing Form 7004, Application for Automatic Extension of Time to File Corporation Income Tax Return, and paying any remaining tax due for the year. The IRS will not notify the taxpayer that the extension has been accepted, but will notify the taxpayer if the extension is not accepted. Beginning in 2005, taxpayers may file Form 7004 electronically.

An automatic extension of time to file a federal income tax return does not extend the time to pay the tax due on the return, and interest is charged if the actual tax due with the return exceeds the tentative tax reported on Form 7004. Moreover, if the tax due with the completed federal return exceeds 10 percent of the total tax paid on or before the original due date for the return, a late-payment penalty is imposed from the original due date of the return until the date the tax is paid.

For a more detailed discussion of what constitutes the timely filing of a return, see the section in Part 10 entitled Timely Filing of Returns and Payment of Estimated Tax.

State Tax Treatment

The due date for state corporate income tax returns varies. The most popular dues dates are the federal return due date and one month after the federal return due date. Some states use different due dates. A few states require all corporate taxpayers, including both fiscal-year and calendar-year taxpayers, to file their returns by the same date. For example, Texas requires all corporations to file their franchise tax return by May 15 after the beginning of the regular annual period. [Tex. Tax Code § 171.152]

Although the procedures for obtaining an extension of time to file a state corporate income tax return vary, all the states permit a corporation to obtain an extension of time to file. A number of states require a corporation to file a separate state extension request, regardless of whether a similar federal extension request has been filed or whether a portion of the corporation's tentative tax is due. Some of these states will provide notification of acceptance, and most states will notify the taxpayer if the extension has been rejected.

Many states provide that any extension of time to file a federal return automatically extends the time to file the corresponding state return. Most of these states require that a copy of the federal request for extension (Form 7004) be filed along with the state return. To facilitate the timely collection of state income tax revenues, however, a number of states apply the automatic extension provision only when the corporation's tentative state tax liability has been paid before the filing of its extension request. Therefore, even though a federal extension normally constitutes an automatic state extension, a separate state extension request or payment voucher form may be required to accompany the payment of the corporation's tax liability that must be paid by the original due date of its return.

Some states no longer require a corporation to file an extension form, regardless of whether the corporation has filed a federal extension request. These states require a payment of any tentative tax due on the original due date of the return, accompanied by a payment voucher form. No penalty for the late filing of the return is assessed if the return is filed within the permitted extension period (generally, within six months of the original due date) and the required percentage of tax is paid by the original due date of the return.

As with the federal return, an extension of time to file a state return generally does not extend the time to pay any tentative tax due on the original due date. Accordingly, to avoid penalties, interest charges, or both, a corporation is required to pay all or a specified percentage of its tentative tax liability before the original due date of its state tax return.

Electronic Filing of Income Tax Returns

For federal tax purposes, corporations with assets of $10 million or more and that file 250 or more tax returns during a tax year (including income tax returns, employment tax returns, excise tax returns, and information returns) are required to file federal Form 1120 or 1120S electronically. A corporation that is required to file electronically but fails to do so may be subject to a failure to file return penalty under Code Section 6651.

Many states also provide corporations with the option to file their state income tax returns electronically, and some states require electronic filing. Most of these states have joined the Federal-State 1120 electronic filing program. To participate in the e-file program, a taxpayer must register and be accepted in both the IRS and state e-file programs. The program allows taxpayers to transmit their federal and state tax returns to the IRS, which validates the federal employer identification numbers and forwards the returns to the appropriate state.

State-by-State Summary

The first chart, presented in two parts, summarizes the due dates and the rules for extending the due date for filing a state tax return. The second chart summarizes which types of corporations are required to file their income tax returns electronically, and which states participate in the Federal-State 1120 electronic filing program.

Legend:

X	Indicates state-allowed extensions for filing returns
NA	Not applicable
NR	Not reported

Note: In all cases, tax return due date is extended for weekends and holidays.

Due Dates and Extensions for Filing Returns (Part 1)

			Circumstances Under Which an Extension Is Allowed						
	Tax Return Due Date for Calendar-Year Corporation	*Same Due Date for S Corporation?*	*Automatic with Federal Extension*	*Automatic State Extension*	*Only if Valid Business Reason*	*Other*	*Maximum Period of Extension (Months)*	*Must Federal Extension Form Be Filed with State Extension Form?*	*If a State Extension Is Not Required (Because the Extension Is Automatic with Federal), Must a State Extension Be Filed if Tax Is Due?*
Alabama	3/15, extended for weekends and holidays	Yes		X			6	No	Yes
Alaska	Same as federal plus 30 days, extended for weekends and holidays	Yes	X				6	Yes	No, full payment required
Arizona	4/15, extended for weekends and holidays	Due by the 15th day of the 3rd month following the close of the taxable year	X	X			6	No	Yes
Arkansas	3/15, extended for weekends and holidays	Yes	X	X			6 months if no federal extension, or 2 months beyond federal extension	No	Yes
California	3/15, extended for weekends and holidays; automatic paperless extension to October 15	Same as C Corporation		X	X	Automatic 7 month paperless	7	No, there is no form. The extension is automatic unless taxpayer owes tax. If the taxpayer owes tax for the year, and is unable to file a return by the 3/15 due date, use FTB Form 3539 (Payment Voucher and Automatic Extension).	
Colorado	4/15, extended for weekends and holidays	NR	X				6	No	No
Connecticut	4/1, extended for weekends and holidays	X, informational return CT-1065/CT-1120SI	X				6	No	NR

Due Dates and Extensions for Filing Returns (Part 1)

Legend:
X — Indicates state-allowed extensions for filing returns
NA — Not applicable
NR — Not reported
Note: In all cases, tax return due date is extended for weekends and holidays.

	Tax Return Due Date for Calendar-Year Corporation	*Same Due Date for S Corporation?*	*Circumstances Under Which an Extension Is Allowed*				*Maximum Period of Extension (Months)*	*Must Federal Extension Form Be Filed with State Extension Form?*	*If a State Extension Is Not Required (Because the Extension Is Automatic with Federal), Must a State Extension Be Filed if Tax Is Due?*
			Automatic with Federal Extension	*Automatic State Extension*	*Only if Valid Business Reason*	*Other*			
Delaware	4/1, extended for weekends and holidays	Yes	X	X			6	Yes	No
District of Columbia	3/15, extended for weekends and holidays	Yes	X	X	X		6	No	NA
Florida	4/1, extended for weekends and holidays	Generally not required to file in Florida unless the corporation is taxed at the federal level.			X	X, normally granted if taxpayer is in compliance with tax due.	6	No, however federal extension would support the request for state extension.	NA
Georgia	3/15, extended if due date falls on weekend or holiday	Yes	X		X, state extension	X	6	No	No, File Form 560-C with payment by regular due date.
Hawaii	4/20, extended for weekends and holidays	Yes				X	6	No	NR
Idaho	4/15, extended for weekends and holidays	Yes			X		6	No	No
Illinois	Same as applicable federal rule	Yes			X		7	Yes, if extension request is based on federal extension longer than the automatic extension.	Yes
Indiana	4/15, extended for weekends and holidays	Yes	X				6	Yes	
Iowa	4/30, extended for weekends and holidays	Yes				Automatic extension if 90% of tax is paid by due date.	6	No	No

Legend:

X Indicates state-allowed extensions for filing returns
NA Not applicable
NR Not reported
Note: In all cases, tax return due date is extended for weekends and holidays.

Due Dates and Extensions for Filing Returns (Part 1)

			Circumstances Under Which an Extension Is Allowed						
	Tax Return Due Date for Calendar-Year Corporation	*Same Due Date for S Corporation?*	*Automatic with Federal Extension*	*Automatic State Extension*	*Only if Valid Business Reason*	*Other*	*Maximum Period of Extension (Months)*	*Must Federal Extension Form Be Filed with State Extension Form?*	*If a State Extension Is Not Required (Because the Extension Is Automatic with Federal), Must a State Extension Be Filed if Tax Is Due?*
Kansas	4/15, extended for weekends and holidays	Yes	X				6	'Yes	No
Kentucky	4/15, extended for weekends and holidays	Yes	X	X		Kentucky extension request form	6	No	Yes
Louisiana	4/15, extended for weekends and holidays	Yes	X	X			7	Yes	No
Maine	3/15, extended for weekends and holidays	Yes	X	X, 7 months		May request additional 30 days	8	No	No
Maryland	3/15, extended for weekends and holidays	Yes		X			6	NR	
Massachusetts	3/15, extended for weekends and holidays	NR		X			6	NR	Yes
Michigan (Single Business Tax—VAT)	4/30, extended for weekends and holidays	Yes		X		Michigan extension form with payments or estimates made	8, with approved federal extension	No	NA
Note. The CIT takes effect 01/01/12, and replaces the Michigan Business Tax (MBT) for most taxpayers. However, businesses that have been approved to receive, have received, or have been assigned certain certified credits may elect to file a return and pay the tax imposed by the MBT in lieu of the CIT until the certified credits are exhausted or extinguished.									
Minnesota	3/15, extended for weekends and holidays	Yes		X			7	No	Yes
Mississippi	3/15, extended for weekends and holidays	Yes		X			6	No	Yes

Legend:

X — Indicates state-allowed extensions for filing returns
NA — Not applicable
NR — Not reported

Note: In all cases, tax return due date is extended for weekends and holidays.

Due Dates and Extensions for Filing Returns (Part 1)

			Circumstances Under Which an Extension Is Allowed						
	Tax Return Due Date for Calendar-Year Corporation	*Same Due Date for S Corporation?*	*Automatic with Federal Extension*	*Automatic State Extension*	*Only if Valid Business Reason*	*Other*	*Maximum Period of Extension (Months)*	*Must Federal Extension Form Be Filed with State Extension Form?*	*If a State Extension Is Not Required (Because the Extension Is Automatic with Federal), Must a State Extension Be Filed if Tax Is Due?*
Missouri	4/15, extended for weekends and holidays	Yes	X	X			6	Yes	Yes
Montana	5/15, extended for weekends and holidays	The return is due on the 15th day of the 3rd month following the close of the taxable period.		X			6	No	NA
Nebraska	3/15, extended for weekends and holidays	Yes	X				7	Yes	No
Nevada	Nevada does not impose a corporate income tax								
New Hampshire	3/15, extended for weekends and holidays	Yes	X				7 months	No	Yes
New Jersey	4/15, extended for weekends and holidays	Yes		X		Tentative return and payment must be filed by original due date, Form CBT-200T.	6	NR	NA
New Mexico	3/15, extended for weekends and holidays	Yes	X				12 months total with good cause	No	No
New York	3/15, extended for weekends and holidays			X (Form CT-5)			Automatic 6 months with up to 2 additional 3-month extensions (maximum 12 months)	No	
North Carolina	4/15, extended for weekends and holidays	Yes				Must file NC Form CD-419, Extension Request Form	7	No	NA

Legend:

X — Indicates state-allowed extensions for filing returns

NA — Not applicable

NR — Not reported

Note: In all cases, tax return due date is extended for weekends and holidays.

Due Dates and Extensions for Filing Returns (Part 1)

			Circumstances Under Which an Extension Is Allowed						
	Tax Return Due Date for Calendar-Year Corporation	*Same Due Date for S Corporation?*	*Automatic with Federal Extension*	*Automatic State Extension*	*Only if Valid Business Reason*	*Other*	*Maximum Period of Extension (Months)*	*Must Federal Extension Form Be Filed with State Extension Form?*	*If a State Extension Is Not Required (Because the Extension Is Automatic with Federal), Must a State Extension Be Filed if Tax Is Due?*
North Dakota	4/15, extended for weekends and holidays.	Yes				If no federal extension, must request state extension	6	Yes	No
Ohio	Ohio does not impose a corporate income tax								
Note. Effective 1/1/2010, the Ohio Franchise Tax was fully phased out and business will be taxed on gross receipts through the Commercial Activity Tax. Details about that tax can be found at: http//tax.ohio.gov/divisions/commercial_activities/index.stm									
Oklahoma	3/15, extended for weekends and holidays	Yes	X	X			Federal plus 1 month	Yes	Yes
Oregon	4/15, extended for weekends and holidays	Yes	X				6	No	No
Pennsylvania	4/15, extended for weekends and holidays	Yes				Must have a federal extension, separate state extension must be filed.	6	Yes	NA
Rhode Island	3/15, extended for weekends and holidays	April 15th		X			6	No	Yes
South Carolina	3/15, extended for weekends and holidays	X	X	X		File Form SC 1120T by original due date.	5 months for S Corporations	No	Yes
South Dakota	South Dakota does not impose a corporate income tax								

Legend:
X — Indicates state-allowed extensions for filing returns
NA — Not applicable
NR — Not reported
Note: In all cases, tax return due date is extended for weekends and holidays.

Due Dates and Extensions for Filing Returns (Part 1)

	Tax Return Due Date for Calendar-Year Corporation	*Same Due Date for S Corporation?*	*Circumstances Under Which an Extension Is Allowed: Automatic with Federal Extension*	*Automatic State Extension*	*Only if Valid Business Reason*	*Other*	*Maximum Period of Extension (Months)*	*Must Federal Extension Form Be Filed with State Extension Form?*	*If a State Extension Is Not Required (Because the Extension Is Automatic with Federal), Must a State Extension Be Filed if Tax Is Due?*
Tennessee	4/15, extended for weekends and holidays	Yes				State extension required provided prepayment equals 90% of current year's liability, if prepayment not needed, federal extension is acceptable.	6	No	NR
Texas	5/15, extended for weekends and holidays	Yes					6 month extension to 11/15 if request made before 5/16 and 90% of current taxes paid or 100% of prior year's tax	No	NR
Utah	4/15, extended for weekends and holidays	Yes		X			6	No	NA
Vermont	3/15, extended for weekends and holidays	Yes	X				6	Yes	No
Virginia	4/15, however, the due date of tax exempt organizations with unrelated business taxable income is 6/15, extended for weekends and holidays	Yes		X			6	No	No
Washington	Washington does not impose a corporate income tax								
West Virginia	3/15, extended for weekends and holidays	Yes	X				6 months, plus reasonable time period	Yes	No

Due Dates and Extensions for Filing Returns (Part 1)

Legend:

X — Indicates state-allowed extensions for filing returns

NA — Not applicable

NR — Not reported

Note: In all cases, tax return due date is extended for weekends and holidays.

			Circumstances Under Which an Extension Is Allowed						
	Tax Return Due Date for Calendar-Year Corporation	*Same Due Date for S Corporation?*	*Automatic with Federal Extension*	*Automatic State Extension*	*Only if Valid Business Reason*	*Other*	*Maximum Period of Extension (Months)*	*Must Federal Extension Form Be Filed with State Extension Form?*	*If a State Extension Is Not Required (Because the Extension Is Automatic with Federal), Must a State Extension Be Filed if Tax Is Due?*
Wisconsin	3/15, extended for weekends and holidays	Yes	X			Automatic 7 month extension or until the original due date of the corporation's corresponding federal return, whichever is later.	Any extension allowed by IRS for filing the federal return automatically extends the Wisconsin due date 30 days after federal extended due date.	N/A, there is no extension form. However, a copy of the federal extension form must be attached to the Wisconsin return.	No
Wyoming	Wyoming does not impose a corporate income tax								

Due Dates and Extensions for Filing Returns (Part 2)

Legend:

X	Indicates state-allowed extensions for filing returns
NA	Not applicable
NR	Not reported
SAF	Same as federal

	State Form Number	*Does State Allow Extension without Federal Extension?*	*If No Tax Is Due and a Federal Extension Is Not Filed, Must a State Extension Form Be Filed?*	*Must Payment of Tax Accompany the Extension?*
Alabama	N/A	Yes	No	No
Alaska	Use federal form; mark Alaska on top.	No	NR	Yes, pay 100% tax due
Arizona	120 EXT	Yes	Yes	Yes, 90% of tax due
Arkansas	AR-1155	Yes	NR	Yes, 100%
California	None required unless payment of tax due, then use FTB 3539	Yes	No	Yes, 100% with voucher. Use FTB Form 3539.
Colorado	NA	Yes	NR	Yes, 90% of tax due
Connecticut	CT-1120EXT	Yes		Yes, 100% of tax due
Delaware	1100 EXT or 1100T-5	Yes	NR	Yes, entire tax due
District of Columbia	FR-128	Yes	Yes	Yes, entire tax due
Florida	F-7004	Yes	NR	Yes, pay 100% tax due
Georgia	IT-303	Yes	Yes	Yes, entire tax due. Use Form 560-C.
Hawaii	N-301 or federal form	Yes	Yes	Yes, entire tax due
Idaho	No form, automatic extension; penalties if required payments are not made by due date	Yes	No	Yes, lesser of 80% of current tax or 100% of previous year. Payments can be made on Form 41EXT, Extension of Time Payment Business Income Tax Returns.

Due Dates and Extensions for Filing Returns (Part 2)

Legend:

X	Indicates state-allowed extensions for filing returns
NA	Not applicable
NR	Not reported
SAF	Same as federal

	State Form Number	*Does State Allow Extension without Federal Extension?*	*If No Tax Is Due and a Federal Extension Is Not Filed, Must a State Extension Form Be Filed?*	*Must Payment of Tax Accompany the Extension?*
Illinois	IL-505-B, only required if tentative tax is due	Yes	No	Yes, entire tax due
Indiana	No form; letter requests are accepted.	Yes		No
Iowa	NA	Yes	No	Yes, 90% of tax by due date, voucher form available for payment
Kansas	E-2	Yes	Yes	Yes, 90% of tax
Kentucky	41A720SL	Yes	Yes	No, tax is paid through estimated payments
Louisiana	CIFT-620EXT	Yes	Yes	Yes, entire tax due
Maine	Extension is automatic	Yes	No	Yes, 90% of tax
Maryland	500E	Yes		Yes, entire tax due
Massachusetts	Form 355-7004	Yes	NR	Yes, entire tax due
Michigan (Business Tax)	Form 4	Yes	NA	Yes, 90% of tax due
Note. The CIT takes effect 01/01/12, and replaces the Michigan Business Tax (MBT) for most taxpayers. However, businesses that have been approved to receive, have received, or have been assigned certain certified credits may elect to file a return and pay the tax imposed by the MBT in lieu of the CIT until the certified credits are exhausted or extinguished.				
Minnesota	PY 81	Yes	No	Yes, 90% tax due

Due Dates and Extensions for Filing Returns (Part 2)

Legend:

X	Indicates state-allowed extensions for filing returns
NA	Not applicable
NR	Not reported
SAF	Same as federal

	State Form Number	*Does State Allow Extension without Federal Extension?*	*If No Tax Is Due and a Federal Extension Is Not Filed, Must a State Extension Form Be Filed?*	*Must Payment of Tax Accompany the Extension?*
Mississippi	83-180	Yes	Yes	Yes, 100% of both income and franchise tax liability from return
Missouri	MO 7004	Yes	Yes	Yes, 90%
Montana	NA	Yes		No
Nebraska	7004N	Yes	Yes	Yes, 100% tax due
Nevada	Nevada does not impose a corporate income tax			
New Hampshire	BT-Ext	Yes	No	Yes, 100%
New Jersey	CBT-200T	Yes	Yes	Yes, entire tax due
New Mexico	RPD-41096	Yes	Yes	No
New York	CT-5	Yes; state extension must be filed if additional tax is due.		Yes; to avoid penalties and invalid extensions, taxpayers must pay amounts sufficient to bring their estimated tax payments up to at least 90% of current year's tax (or 100% of prior year's tax), plus 25% of current year's tax as the first installment for the next year.
North Carolina	CD 419	Yes	Yes	Yes, entire franchise tax and income tax due
North Dakota	F-101	Yes	Yes	No

Legend:

X	Indicates state-allowed extensions for filing returns
NA	Not applicable
NR	Not reported
SAF	Same as federal

Due Dates and Extensions for Filing Returns (Part 2)

	State Form Number	*Does State Allow Extension without Federal Extension?*	*If No Tax Is Due and a Federal Extension Is Not Filed, Must a State Extension Form Be Filed?*	*Must Payment of Tax Accompany the Extension?*
Ohio	Ohio does not impose a corporate income tax			
Note. Effective 1/1/2010, the Ohio Franchise Tax was fully phased out and business will be taxed on gross receipts through the Commercial Activity Tax. Details about that tax can be found at: http//tax.ohio.gov/divisions/commercial_activities/index.stm				
Oklahoma	504	Yes	Yes	Yes, 90% of current year liability
Oregon	20-EXT	Yes	Yes	Yes, entire tax due to avoid late payment penalty
Pennsylvania	Rev. 853	Yes, 60 days	Yes	No
Rhode Island	RI7004	NR	Yes	Yes, 100%
South Carolina	SC1120-T	Yes	No	Yes, 100% of anticipated tax
South Dakota	South Dakota does not impose a corporate income tax			
Tennessee	FAE 173	Yes	Yes	Yes, 90% of tax
Texas	05-164 and 05-165	Yes	Yes	Yes; must pay 90% of current tax due or 100% of previous year tax
Utah	NA, no state form required	Yes	No	Yes, 90%; estimated tax payments are also required. However, penalties and interest apply if payment has not been made to cover the tax later shown to be due on the return.

Due Dates and Extensions for Filing Returns (Part 2)

Legend:

X	Indicates state-allowed extensions for filing returns
NA	Not applicable
NR	Not reported
SAF	Same as federal

	State Form Number	*Does State Allow Extension without Federal Extension?*	*If No Tax Is Due and a Federal Extension Is Not Filed, Must a State Extension Form Be Filed?*	*Must Payment of Tax Accompany the Extension?*
Vermont	BA 403	Yes	Yes	Yes, 100% of tax
Virginia	No form required	Yes	No	Yes, 90% of tax
Washington	Washington does not impose a corporate income tax			
West Virginia	Letter of request	Yes	Yes	Yes, entire tax due
Wisconsin	Copy of federal extension	Yes; state extension need not be filed even if additional tax is due.	No	No
Wyoming	Wyoming does not impose a corporate income tax			

Due Dates and Extensions for Filing Returns (Part 3)

Legend:
NA Not applicable
NR Not reported

	Are Any Corporations Required to File Their Income Tax Returns Electronically?	*Does Your State Participate in the Federal-State 1120 Electronic Filing Program?*
Alabama	No	Yes
Alaska	No	No
Arizona	No	Yes
Arkansas	No	No
California	No	No
Colorado	No	Yes
Connecticut	No	Yes
Delaware	No	Yes
District of Columbia	No	No
Florida	Yes	Yes
Georgia	Yes, C corporations and S corporations, if paying estimated taxes electronically and C corporations that file electronically with the IRS.	Yes
Hawaii	No	No
Idaho	No	Yes
Illinois	No	No
Indiana	No	No
Iowa	No	Yes
Kansas	No	Yes
Kentucky	No	No

Due Dates and Extensions for Filing Returns (Part 3)

Legend:
NA Not applicable
NR Not reported

	Are Any Corporations Required to File Their Income Tax Returns Electronically?	*Does Your State Participate in the Federal-State 1120 Electronic Filing Program?*
Louisiana	No	No
Maine	No	No
Maryland	No	No
Massachusetts	Yes, all	NR
Michigan	Yes, effective 1/1/2010, for the 2009 tax year, software developers producing MBT tax preparation software must support electronic filing (e-file) for all eligible MBT forms that are included in their tax preparation software. All eligible MBT returns prepared using software must be e-filed.	Yes

Note. The CIT takes effect 01/01/12, and replaces the Michigan Business Tax (MBT) for most taxpayers. However, businesses that have been approved to receive, have received, or have been assigned certain certified credits may elect to file a return and pay the tax imposed by the MBT in lieu of the CIT until the certified credits are exhausted or extinguished.

Minnesota	No	No
Mississippi	No	NR
Missouri	No	Yes
Montana	No	Yes
Nebraska	No	No
Nevada	Nevada does not impose a corporate income tax	
New Hampshire	No	No
New Jersey	No	No
New Mexico	No	No
New York	NR	NR

Due Dates and Extensions for Filing Returns (Part 3)

Legend:
NA Not applicable
NR Not reported

	Are Any Corporations Required to File Their Income Tax Returns Electronically?	*Does Your State Participate in the Federal-State 1120 Electronic Filing Program?*
North Carolina	No	No
North Dakota	No	No
Ohio	Ohio does not impose a corporate income tax	
Note. Effective 1/1/2010, the Ohio Franchise Tax was fully phased out and business will be taxed on gross receipts through the Commercial Activity Tax. Details about that tax can be found at: http//tax.ohio.gov/divisions/commercial_activities/index.stm		
Oklahoma	NR	NR
Oregon	No	Yes
Pennsylvania	No	Yes
Rhode Island	No	No
South Carolina	No, preparer e-file mandate	Yes
South Dakota	South Dakota does not impose a corporate income tax	
Tennessee	No	No
Texas	No	No
Utah	No	Yes
Vermont	No	No
Virginia	No	No
Washington	Washington does not impose a corporate income tax	
West Virginia	No	No
Wisconsin	All corporate returns are required to be filed electronically.	Yes
Wyoming	Wyoming does not impose a corporate income tax	

Corporate Amended Return Forms

Federal Tax Treatment

To correct an error in a previously filed federal income tax return, a corporation must file an amended return, using federal Form 1120X, Amended U.S. Corporation Income Tax Return.

Generally, Form 1120X must be filed within three years after the date the original return was due or three years after the date the corporation filed it, whichever is later. In the case of a refund claim, the federal statute of limitations for claiming a refund is generally three years from the date the original return was filed, or two years from the date the tax was paid, whichever is later.

The IRS has not developed a separate form for amending an S corporation's federal income tax return. Instead, to correct a previously filed Form 1120S, U.S. Income Tax Return for an S Corporation, an S corporation must complete the usual Form 1120S and indicate, by checking a box on the front of the return, that the return is an amended one.

State Tax Treatment

If a corporation files an amended federal return, it is generally required to file an amended state tax return. Most states have special statute of limitation rules related to the filing of an amended federal return. These rules generally provide that when a federal return is amended, an amended state return must be filed within 30 to 90 days. If an amended state return is not filed within the designated period, the state statute of limitations on the assessment of tax remains open indefinitely, to the extent of the unreported changes. Although the statutes remain open for assessments, however, most states will not allow a refund of tax if the amended state return resulting from a federal audit adjustment is not filed within the statutory time frame. Many states limit assessments and refunds related to changes in federal taxable income to only those changes that were a result of the IRS adjustments. (For further details regarding the states' statutes of limitations, see the section in Part 12 entitled Statute of Limitations for Assessing Income Taxes.)

An amended state return may be required as a result of a federal income tax audit. An amended state return is usually required to be filed if the correction changes the corporation's state taxable income, apportionment data, or state tax liability, even if the correction does not affect the taxpayer's federal taxable income and does not require the filing of an amended federal return. (For details, see the section in Part 12 entitled Time Limits for Reporting Federal Adjustments and Responding to Notices of Deficiency.)

In general, the states have adopted one of the following three ways to indicate that a state tax return is an amended return:

1. Filing a freestanding amended return form;
2. Checking an "Amended Return" box on the face of the usual corporate return; or
3. Marking "Amended" across the top of the usual corporate return.

A number of states have developed a separate form, similar to federal Form 1120X, on which a corporation is to report any amendments to its previously filed tax return.

In many of the states that have not developed a separate form, the standard corporate forms are similar to the federal S corporation return in that, on the face of the return, a number of boxes or other notations are provided that are to be checked to indicate whether the return is an original return or an amended return. In those states, a corporation must complete the normal corporate return that includes the corrections and then check the "Amended Return" box on the face of the return.

Other states provide that if a previously filed return must be amended for any reason, the taxpayer must complete a new return using the corrected figures and write "Amended" across the top of the return. In some of those states, it may not be necessary to complete the new return in its entirety and all of the schedules that accompany the original tax return.

When the state provides a separate form for amending a return, the form generally includes a section in which the taxpayer explains the reasons for the amendments and enters any necessary computations. When the state does not provide a separate form for amending a return, as a rule the taxpayer is required to attach a statement indicating the reasons for the amendments and reflecting, in detail, any computations necessary to verify the adjustments it is making. If the change involves an item of income, a deduction, or a credit that the original return requires the corporation to support with a schedule or form, the corrected schedule or form must be attached to the amended return. When an amended state tax return is filed, a number of states require that a copy of the amended federal return (if one was filed) be attached to the state return.

In *Appeal of Oceanic Bank* [No. 286855 (Cal. State Bd. of Equal., Feb. 1, 2006)] the taxpayer's amended California corporation franchise tax return did not satisfy the requirements for an informal claim for refund because it did not indicate the specific grounds for a refund claim. Although the amended return included an attachment stating that it was being filed as a protective refund claim for the 1998 tax year, it did not provide the Franchise Tax Board with information regarding the nature or basis of the refund claim.

In *Great Source Education Group, Inc. v. Alabama Department of Revenue* [Ala. Dept. of Revenue, Admin. Law Div., INC. 04-802, Apr. 26, 2005], the court ruled that a taxpayer's letter notifying the Alabama Department of Revenue that an IRS audit was completed and the federal adjustments would result in a refund of Alabama corporate income tax constituted a valid petition for refund because the letter was received within three years of filing the original return. The corporation subsequently filed an amended Alabama return within the one year period required for reporting IRS audit adjustments.

State-by-State Summary

The following chart indicates how a C corporation and an S corporation amend a previously filed state corporate income tax return.

Corporate Amended Return Forms

Legend:

NA	Not applicable
NR	Not reported

	C Corporations	*S Corporations*
Alabama	Taxpayer files usual corporate return and checks a box indicating "Amended Return"	Taxpayer files usual corporate return and checks a box indicating Amended Return
Alaska	Taxpayer files freestanding Form 04-611X.	Taxpayer files freestanding Form 04-611X.
Arizona	Taxpayer files freestanding Form 120X.	Taxpayer files the usual corporate return but checks a box indicating "Amended Return."
Arkansas	Taxpayer files freestanding form AR1100CTX for tax years 2009 and earlier. Taxpayer files same as original return, but checks "Amended" box (for tax years beginning in 2010 and later).	Taxpayer files same as original return, but checks "Amended" box.
California	Taxpayer files freestanding Form FTB 100X.	Taxpayer files freestanding Form FTB 100X.
Colorado	Taxpayer files freestanding Form 1120X.	Taxpayer files a form similar to the original return, but writes "Amended" at the top, Form 106.
Connecticut	Taxpayer files freestanding Form CT-1120X. Year specific if amending CT-1120. Same as original return but check "Amended" box. If amending Connecticut combined return use form CT-1120CR	Same as original return, but check "Amended" box.
Delaware	Taxpayer files freestanding Form 1100X; a form similar to the original return but writes "Amended" at the top; or a letter with schedule of changes	Exempt from CIT, but files a reconciliation informational return, Form 1100S.
District of Columbia	Taxpayer files original return, but write "Amended" on top	Taxpayer files original return, but write "Amended" on top.
Florida	Taxpayer files freestanding Form F-1120X.	Taxpayer files freestanding Form F-1120X.
Georgia	Taxpayer files the usual corporate return, but checks a box indicating "Amended Return," Form 600.	Taxpayer files the usual corporate return, but checks a box indicating "Amended Return," Form 600S.
Hawaii	Taxpayer files freestanding Form N-30X or taxpayer files a form similar to the original return but writes "Amended" at the top.	Taxpayer files a form similar to the original return but writes "Amended" at the top.

Corporate Amended Return Forms

Legend:
NA Not applicable
NR Not reported

	C Corporations	*S Corporations*
Idaho	For 2001 returns and later, taxpayer files the usual corporate return but checks a box indicating Amended Return; for returns prior to 2001, taxpayer files a form similar to the original return but writes "Amended" at the top.	For 2001 returns and later, taxpayer files the usual corporate return but checks a box indicating Amended Return; for returns prior to 2001, taxpayer files a form similar to the original return but writes "Amended" at the top.
Illinois	Taxpayer files freestanding Form IL-1120X.	Taxpayer files freestanding Form IL-843.
Indiana	Taxpayer files the usual corporate return, but checks a box indicating "Amended Return."	NR
Iowa	Taxpayer files freestanding amended return, Form IA 1120X, or files a Form IA 1120, a form similar to the original return, and writes "Amended" at the top.	Taxpayer files a form similar to the original return and writes "Amended" at the top of the form, Form IA 1120S
Kansas	Taxpayer files the usual corporate return, but checks a box indicating "Amended Return," Form K-120.	Taxpayer files the usual corporate return, but checks a box indicating "Amended Return," Form K-120S.
Kentucky	Same as original return, but check "Amended" box	Taxpayer files form similar to original Form 720S and writes "Amended" at the top of the form.
Louisiana	Taxpayer files a form similar to the original return and writes "Amended" at the top of the form.	Taxpayer files a form similar to the original return and writes "Amended" at the top of the form.
Maine	Taxpayer files free-standing form 1120X ME.	Same as original return, but check "Amended Return."
Maryland	Taxpayer files freestanding Form 500X.	Taxpayer files freestanding Form 500X.
Massachusetts	Taxpayer files freestanding Form 355X, or the usual corporate return, but checks box indicating "Amended Return," or files a form similar to the original return and writes "Amended" at the top of the form.	Taxpayer files freestanding Form 355X, or the usual corporate return, but checks box indicating "Amended Return," or files a form similar to the original return and writes "Amended" at the top of the form.
Michigan (Business Tax)	Taxpayer files freestanding Form C-8000X or C-8044 or files original form C8000 or C8044 and writes "Amended" at top of form.	Taxpayer files freestanding Form C-8000X or C-8044 or files original form C8000 or C8044 and writes "Amended" at top of form.

Legend:
NA Not applicable
NR Not reported

Corporate Amended Return Forms

	C Corporations	*S Corporations*
Note. The CIT takes effect 01/01/12, and replaces the Michigan Business Tax (MBT) for most taxpayers. However, businesses that have been approved to receive, have received, or have been assigned certain certified credits may elect to file a return and pay the tax imposed by the MBT in lieu of the CIT until the certified credits are exhausted or extinguished.		
Minnesota	Taxpayer files freestanding Form M-4X.	Taxpayer files freestanding Form M-8X.
Mississippi	Taxpayer files a free-standing amended return, Form 83-170.	Taxpayer files a free-standing amended return, Form 83-170.
Missouri	Taxpayer files Form MO-1120 ,but checks "Amended" box.	Taxpayer files the usual corporate tax return, Form MO 1120S, but checks a box indicating Amended Return.
Montana	Taxpayer files the usual corporate return with a box checked indicating "Amended Return," for years prior to 2004, taxpayer files a form similar to the original return but writes "Amended" at the top.	Taxpayer files freestanding Form CLT-4X. A form similar to the original return with "Amended" at the top and the usual corporate return with a box checked indicating "Amended Return" are also accepted.
Nebraska	Taxpayer files freestanding Form 1120XN.	Taxpayer files a form similar to the original return and writes "Amended" at the top of the form.
Nevada	Nevada does not impose a corporate income tax	. . . .
New Hampshire	Taxpayer files original return, but checks "Amended" box.	Taxpayer files original return, but checks "Amended" box.
New Jersey	Taxpayer files a form similar to the original return, but writes "Amended" at the top, Form CBT-100.	Taxpayer files a form similar to the original return, but writes "Amended" at the top, Form CBT-100S.
New Mexico	Taxpayer files the usual corporate return, but checks a box indicating "Amended Return," Form CIT-1.	Taxpayer files the usual corporate return, but checks a box indicating "Amended Return," Form PTE-1.
New York	Taxpayer files the usual corporate return, but checks a box indicating "Amended Return."	Taxpayer files the usual corporate original return, but checks a box indicating "Amended Return."
North Carolina	Taxpayer files freestanding Form CD-444 or Form CD-405 and marks it "Amended."	Taxpayer files freestanding Form CD-444 or Form CD-405 and marks it "Amended."
North Dakota	Taxpayer files freestanding amended return Form 40X.	Taxpayer files the usual corporate return, but checks a box indicating "Amended Return."

Corporate Amended Return Forms

Legend:
NA Not applicable
NR Not reported

	C Corporations	S Corporations
Ohio	Ohio does not impose a corporate income tax	
Note. Effective 1/1/2010, the Ohio Franchise Tax was fully phased out and business will be taxed on gross receipts through the Commercial Activity Tax. Details about that tax can be found at: http//tax.ohio.gov/divisions/commercial_activities/index.stm		
Oklahoma	Taxpayer files freestanding amended return Form 512X.	Taxpayer files a form similar to the original return, but writes "Amended" at the top of Form 512S.
Oregon	Taxpayer files the usual corporate return, but checks a box indicating "Amended Return."	Taxpayer files the usual corporate return, but checks a box indicating "Amended Return."
Pennsylvania	Taxpayer files freestanding Form RCT-101X.	Taxpayer files freestanding Form RCT-101X.
Rhode Island	Taxpayer files a free-standing amended return, Form RI1120X	Taxpayer files a free-standing amended return, Form RI1120X
South Carolina	Taxpayer files same as original return, but checks "Amended" box	Taxpayer files same as original return, but checks "Amended" box
South Dakota	South Dakota does not impose a corporate income tax	
Tennessee	Taxpayer files the usual corporate return but checks a box indicating amended return, Form FAE 170	Taxpayer files the usual corporate return but checks a box indicating amended return, Form FAE 170
Texas	Taxpayer files a form similar to the original return and writes "Amended" at the top of the form.	Taxpayer files a form similar to the original return and writes "Amended" at the top of the form.
Utah	Taxpayer files the usual corporate return but checks a box indicating amended return.	Taxpayer files the usual corporate return but checks a box indicating amended return.
Vermont	Taxpayer files the usual corporate return, but checks a box indicating amended return.	Taxpayer files the usual corporate return, but checks a box indicating amended return.
Virginia	Taxpayer files same as original return, but checks "Amended" box.	Taxpayer files same as original return, but checks "Amended" box.
Washington	Washington does not impose a corporate income tax	

Legend:
NA Not applicable
NR Not reported

Corporate Amended Return Forms

	C Corporations	*S Corporations*
West Virginia	Taxpayer files freestanding Form WV/CNT-112X and files the usual corporate return but checks a box indicating "Amended Return."	Taxpayer files a form similar to the original return, but writes "Amended" at the top.
Wisconsin	Taxpayer files the usual corporate return but checks a box indicating "Amended Return," or writes "Amended" at the top; Form 4 or 5.	Taxpayer files the usual corporate return but checks a box indicating "Amended Return," or writes "Amended" at the top; Form 5S.
Wyoming	Wyoming does not impose a corporate income tax	

Requirements for Attaching Federal Forms

The vast majority of states that impose a corporate income tax use a corporation's taxable income as reported on Form 1120, U.S. Corporation Income Tax Return, as the starting point for computing state taxable income. The specific starting point is either taxable income before net operating loss and special deductions (Line 28) or taxable income itself (Line 30) from the federal return. The selected federal figure is then adjusted for various state-defined modifications to determine the corporation's state taxable income.

Because a figure reported on the federal return is used as the basis for computing state taxable income, the majority of states require that a complete copy of Form 1120 be attached to the state return. A number of states require that only pages 1 through 4 of the federal return be attached to the state return; several require that all or selected supporting schedules also be attached. A few states require that only selected forms such as Schedule D, Capital Gains and Losses; Form 4797, Sales of Business Property; or Form 4562, Depreciation and Amortization, be attached to the state return. Some states require that taxpayers attach a copy of federal Form 7004 to their state return when an extension of time to file the state return was granted based on the taxpayer filing a Form 7004 to obtain a federal extension.

Some states provide that unless a complete copy of the federal return as filed with the IRS is attached to the state return, the state return is incomplete. In those states, failure to attach the federal return could result in the state imposing penalties for failure to file a complete return or sending the return back to the taxpayer for completion. On the other hand, a few states will accept a federal return attached to the state return in lieu of one or more schedules or pages of the state return, which generally duplicate page 1 or page 4, or both pages 1 and 4, of the federal return.

When a corporation is a member of an affiliated group that files a federal consolidated return, but files *either* a separate state return or a state consolidated or combined return that does not include all of the affiliated members included in the federal return, the attachment requirements of the states vary. Several states require that the federal consolidated income tax return as filed with the IRS, including a breakdown by individual company, be attached to the state return. Other states require that a copy of a pro forma federal return, along with the breakdown for only the corporations included in the state return, be attached to the state return. A pro forma federal return is the federal return that would have been filed if the corporation did not file a federal consolidated return or if the corporation's consolidated affiliated group included only the members included in the state consolidated or combined return. A few states provide that the corporation may attach to the state return *either* the federal consolidated return as filed with the IRS *or* a pro forma federal return along with the breakdown for the corporations included in the state return.

State-by-State Summary

The following chart provides a state-by-state listing of the federal forms that are required to be attached to the state return.

Requirements for Attaching Federal Forms

Legend:

X	Federal forms that must be attached to state return
SAF	Same as applicable federal rules
NA	Not applicable
NR	Not reported

	What Federal Forms Must Be Attached to State Returns?						
	Complete 1120	*Only pages 1-4 of Form 1120*	*Schedule D*	*Form 4797*	*Form 4562*	*Other Forms*	*How Does State Treat a Federal Consolidated Return, Where the Composition of the Consolidated Group Differs for State Purposes?*
Alabama	X						Attach the return filed with the IRS (complete federal consolidated return). Attach a pro-forma return, including federal data for only the state group.
Alaska	X						Attach the return filed with the IRS (complete federal consolidated return).
Arizona	X						Attach a proforma return, including federal data for only the state group.
Arkansas	X						Attach the return filed with the IRS (complete federal consolidated return).
California	X						Attach the "complete" federal consolidated return filed with the IRS
Colorado		X					Attach a proforma return, including federal data for only the state group.

Requirements for Attaching Federal Forms

Legend:

X	Federal forms that must be attached to state return
SAF	Same as applicable federal rules
NA	Not applicable
NR	Not reported

	What Federal Forms Must Be Attached to State Returns?						
	Complete 1120	*Only pages 1-4 of Form 1120*	*Schedule D*	*Form 4797*	*Form 4562*	*Other Forms*	*How Does State Treat a Federal Consolidated Return, Where the Composition of the Consolidated Group Differs for State Purposes?*
Connecticut	X						Attach the "complete" federal consolidated return filed with the IRS.
Delaware	X						State does not permit a consolidated return. Attach a proforma return, including federal data for only the state group.
District of Columbia		X	X	X	X		Attach a proforma return, including federal data for only the state group.
Florida		X				Forms 4626, 1122, 851; supporting details for schedules M-1 and M-2; consolidating schedules	State does not permit a consolidated return unless grandfather election made in 1984.

Requirements for Attaching Federal Forms

Legend:

X	Federal forms that must be attached to state return
SAF	Same as applicable federal rules
NA	Not applicable
NR	Not reported

	What Federal Forms Must Be Attached to State Returns?						
	Complete 1120	*Only pages 1-4 of Form 1120*	*Schedule D*	*Form 4797*	*Form 4562*	*Other Forms*	*How Does State Treat a Federal Consolidated Return, Where the Composition of the Consolidated Group Differs for State Purposes?*
Georgia	X					Proforma return, consolidated schedules upon request.	Permission is required for a state consolidated return. Affiliated members must have nexus to be included in state consolidated return. Attach page 1 and 5 and supporting schedules of federal consolidated return.
Hawaii						Forms 966, 970, 1128, 3115, 6198, 8283, 8582	Attach a proforma return, including federal data for only the state group.
Idaho	X					Complete 1120	Attach the return filed with the IRS (complete federal consolidated return). Attach a copy of the complete federal return for those companies that are less than 80% owned and included in the combined return.
Illinois						Must attach copy of 1120, page 1, and schedules L, M-1, and M-2, or 1120-A, pages 1 and 2.	State does not permit a consolidated return

Requirements for Attaching Federal Forms

Legend:

X — Federal forms that must be attached to state return
SAF — Same as applicable federal rules
NA — Not applicable
NR — Not reported

	What Federal Forms Must Be Attached to State Returns?						
	Complete 1120	*Only pages 1-4 of Form 1120*	*Schedule D*	*Form 4797*	*Form 4562*	*Other Forms*	*How Does State Treat a Federal Consolidated Return, Where the Composition of the Consolidated Group Differs for State Purposes?*
Indiana						Forms 7004, 6765	Attach a proforma return, including federal data for only the state group.
Iowa	X						Attach the return filed with the IRS (complete federal consolidated return).
Kansas	X						Attach the return filed with the IRS (complete federal consolidated return).
Kentucky	X						Attach a proforma return, including federal data for only the state group.
Louisiana						Only those specifically requested by someone conducting a review of the state return	State does not permit a consolidated return.
Maine		X				Forms 4626, 8844, and 5884, as applicable	Attach the return filed with the IRS (complete federal consolidated return).
Maryland	X						

Requirements for Attaching Federal Forms

Legend:

X	Federal forms that must be attached to state return
SAF	Same as applicable federal rules
NA	Not applicable
NR	Not reported

	What Federal Forms Must Be Attached to State Returns?						
	Complete 1120	*Only pages 1-4 of Form 1120*	*Schedule D*	*Form 4797*	*Form 4562*	*Other Forms*	*How Does State Treat a Federal Consolidated Return, Where the Composition of the Consolidated Group Differs for State Purposes?*
Massachusetts	Yes, copies of all schedules and supplemental statements	Attach the return filed with the IRS (complete federal consolidated return).				Maintain records if e-file	See TIR 04-30
Michigan (Business Tax)		X	X	X	X		Federal consolidated return plus a worksheet showing the removal of data for members not included on the combined state return.
Note. The CIT takes effect 01/01/12, and replaces the Michigan Business Tax (MBT) for most taxpayers. However, businesses that have been approved to receive, have received, or have been assigned certain certified credits may elect to file a return and pay the tax imposed by the MBT in lieu of the CIT until the certified credits are exhausted or extinguished.							
Minnesota	X						Attach the return filed with the IRS (complete federal consolidated return).
Mississippi	X						State does not permit a consolidated return.
Missouri	X						Attach a proforma return, including federal data for only the state group.

Requirements for Attaching Federal Forms

Legend:

X	Federal forms that must be attached to state return
SAF	Same as applicable federal rules
NA	Not applicable
NR	Not reported

	What Federal Forms Must Be Attached to State Returns?						
	Complete 1120	*Only pages 1-4 of Form 1120*	*Schedule D*	*Form 4797*	*Form 4562*	*Other Forms*	*How Does State Treat a Federal Consolidated Return, Where the Composition of the Consolidated Group Differs for State Purposes?*
Montana	X					1120 FSC, Schedule N, Form 8873, Form 5471, Schedule M-3	Attach the return filed with the IRS (complete federal consolidated return); also attach complete federal returns for those unconsolidated companies included in the unitary group.
Nebraska	X	X	X	X	X	Schedules supporting totals on any specific line	Attach the return filed with the IRS (complete federal consolidated return).
Nevada	Nevada does not impose a corporate income tax						
New Hampshire		X					State does not permit a consolidated return.
New Jersey					X	Federal and other state forms may be requested as needed for audit.	NA
New Mexico		X					Attach a proforma return, including federal data for only the state group.

Requirements for Attaching Federal Forms

Legend:

X	Federal forms that must be attached to state return
SAF	Same as applicable federal rules
NA	Not applicable
NR	Not reported

What Federal Forms Must Be Attached to State Returns?

	Complete 1120	*Only pages 1-4 of Form 1120*	*Schedule D*	*Form 4797*	*Form 4562*	*Other Forms*	*How Does State Treat a Federal Consolidated Return, Where the Composition of the Consolidated Group Differs for State Purposes?*
New York	X, proforma separate company Form 1120	X, short form CT-4 filers only					Federal consolidated return is ignored.
North Carolina	X						Attach a proforma return, including federal data for only the state group.
North Dakota		X				A schedule of income and deductions by company, supporting consolidated federal taxable income schedule.	Attach the return filed with the IRS (complete federal consolidated return).
Ohio	Ohio does not impose a corporate income tax						
Note. Effective 1/1/2010, the Ohio Franchise Tax was fully phased out and business will be taxed on gross receipts through the Commercial Activity Tax. Details about that tax can be found at: http//tax.ohio.gov/divisions/commercial_activities/index.stm							
Oklahoma	X						Attach the return filed with the IRS (complete federal consolidated return).
Oregon	X						Attach the return filed with the IRS (complete federal consolidated return).

Requirements for Attaching Federal Forms

Legend:

X	Federal forms that must be attached to state return
SAF	Same as applicable federal rules
NA	Not applicable
NR	Not reported

	What Federal Forms Must Be Attached to State Returns?						
	Complete 1120	*Only pages 1-4 of Form 1120*	*Schedule D*	*Form 4797*	*Form 4562*	*Other Forms*	*How Does State Treat a Federal Consolidated Return, Where the Composition of the Consolidated Group Differs for State Purposes?*
Pennsylvania	X						State does not permit a consolidated return.
Rhode Island	X						Attach proforma return, including federal data for only the state group.
South Carolina							Attach a proforma return, including federal data for only the state group.
South Dakota	South Dakota does not impose a corporate income tax						
Tennessee		X				Computation of bonus depreciation adjustment	Attach a proforma return, including federal data for only the state group.
Texas						None	State does not permit a consolidated return.
Utah		X					Attach a proforma return, including federal data for only the state group.
Vermont	X						Attach a pro forma return, including federal data for only the state group.

Requirements for Attaching Federal Forms

Legend:

X	Federal forms that must be attached to state return
SAF	Same as applicable federal rules
NA	Not applicable
NR	Not reported

	What Federal Forms Must Be Attached to State Returns?						
	Complete 1120	*Only pages 1-4 of Form 1120*	*Schedule D*	*Form 4797*	*Form 4562*	*Other Forms*	*How Does State Treat a Federal Consolidated Return, Where the Composition of the Consolidated Group Differs for State Purposes?*
Virginia	X						Proforma accepted with return, complete federal return available to auditor.
Washington	Washington does not impose a corporate income tax						
West Virginia		X				7004, 851, income and expense spreadsheets and beginning and ending balance sheet spreadsheets	Attach a proforma return, including federal data for only the state group or attach the return filed with the IRS (complete federal consolidated return).

Requirements for Attaching Federal Forms

Legend:

X	Federal forms that must be attached to state return
SAF	Same as applicable federal rules
NA	Not applicable
NR	Not reported

	What Federal Forms Must Be Attached to State Returns?						
	Complete 1120	*Only pages 1-4 of Form 1120*	*Schedule D*	*Form 4797*	*Form 4562*	*Other Forms*	*How Does State Treat a Federal Consolidated Return, Where the Composition of the Consolidated Group Differs for State Purposes?*
Wisconsin	X					All schedules attached to federal return	A combined return includes a Form 4R, which reconciles federal taxable income per the federal consolidated return with the starting line (Form 4, line 1) for determining Wisconsin income. Each member of a combined group submits a "complete" copy of the federal return. For members that also file in a federal consolidated return, they may submit a copy of the federal consolidated return, pro-forma federal returns prepared separately for each combined group member, or a spreadsheet showing the line-by-line computation of taxable income of each combined group member included in the federal consolidated returns.
Wyoming	Wyoming does not impose a corporate income tax						

Form 1099 Filing Requirements

Federal Tax Treatment

For federal purposes, taxpayers making certain payments to individuals are required to report those payments at varying thresholds, generally on federal Forms 1099, which are filed annually. The payer provides the payee with the form in January for payments made in the preceding calendar year and reports that information to the IRS in February. There are many different Forms 1099 that are required to be submitted in different situations:

- 1099-A, Acquisition or Abandonment of Secured Property
- 1099-B, Proceeds from Broker and Barter Exchange Transactions
- 1099-C, Cancellation of Debt
- 1099-CAP, Changes in Corporate Control and Capital Structure
- 1099-DIV, Dividends and Distributions
- 1099-G, Certain Government Payments
- 1099-H, Health Insurance Advance Payments
- 1099-INT, Interest Income
- 1099-K, Merchant Card and Third Party Network Payments
- 1099-LTC, Long-term Care and Accelerated Death Benefits
- 1099-MISC, Miscellaneous Income
- 1099-OID, Original Issue Discount
- 1099-PATR, Taxable Distributions Received from Cooperatives
- 1099-Q, Payments from Qualified Education Programs
- 1099-R, Distributions from Pensions, Annuities, Retirement or Profit-Sharing Plans, IRAs, Insurance Contracts, etc.
- 1099-S, Proceeds from Real Estate Transactions
- 1099-SA, Payments from an HSA, Archer MSA, or Medicare+Choice MSA

State Tax Treatment

Only a few states require that a separate Form 1099 be filed at the state level, and a handful of other states require state-level reporting, but only under defined circumstances.

State-by-State Summary

The accompanying chart indicates the state-level filing requirements for Form 1099, the due date if a separate Form 1099 is required to be filed, where the state version of the form can be obtained, and what dollar thresholds exist for filing at the state level.

Form 1099 Filing Requirements

Legend:
NA — Not applicable
NR — Not reported
SAF — Same as applicable federal rules

	Must a Separate "State" Form 1099 Be Filed for Payments to Individuals?	*If a Separate "State" Form 1099 Must Be Filed, What Is the Due Date for the State Version of Form 1099?*	*If a Separate "State" Form 1099 Must Be Filed, What Form Is Required?*	*If a Separate "State" Form 1099 Must Be Filed, What Dollar Threshold Triggers a Filing Requirement?*
Alabama	Yes	SAF	Department's website	NR
Alaska	Alaska does not impose an individual income tax			
Arizona	Only if Arizona withholding is required	28-Feb	Use federal copy.	
Arkansas	No	NA	NA	NA
California	No			
Colorado	No	SAF	NR	
Connecticut	No	NA	NA	NA
Delaware	No	NA	NA	NA
District of Columbia	No	NA	Copy of federal Form 1099	SAF
Florida	Florida does not impose an individual income tax			
Georgia	Yes, only if tax is withheld, the federal Form 1099 should be filed along with Transmittal Form G-1003.	NR	Department's website	NR
Hawaii	No	NA	NA	NA
Idaho	Some federal 1099 forms are required to be filed.	NA	NA	NR

Form 1099 Filing Requirements

Legend:
NA — Not applicable
NR — Not reported
SAF — Same as applicable federal rules

	Must a Separate "State" Form 1099 Be Filed for Payments to Individuals?	*If a Separate "State" Form 1099 Must Be Filed, What Is the Due Date for the State Version of Form 1099?*	*If a Separate "State" Form 1099 Must Be Filed, What Form Is Required?*	*If a Separate "State" Form 1099 Must Be Filed, What Dollar Threshold Triggers a Filing Requirement?*
Illinois	No, but see IITA § 1405.1(a). Also see IITA § 1405.2-.3 and Department of Revenue Regulations § 100.7300(b)(3).	NA	NA	NA
Indiana	No	NA	NA	NA
Iowa	No	NA	NA	NA
Kansas	No	NR	NR	NR
Kentucky	No	NA	NA	NA
Louisiana	No	NA	NA	NA
Maine	No	NA	NA	NA
Maryland	No	NA	NA	NA
Massachusetts	Yes	SAF	Depends on facts, see DD 92-5, 93-5, 94-10	SAF
Michigan (Business Tax)	No	NA	NA	NA
Note. The CIT takes effect 01/01/12, and replaces the Michigan Business Tax (MBT) for most taxpayers. However, businesses that have been approved to receive, have received, or have been assigned certain certified credits may elect to file a return and pay the tax imposed by the MBT in lieu of the CIT until the certified credits are exhausted or extinguished.				
Minnesota	Yes	1/31	Copy of federal Form 1099	SAF
Mississippi	No	NA	NA	NA
Missouri	No	NA	NA	NA

Form 1099 Filing Requirements

Legend:

NA	Not applicable
NR	Not reported
SAF	Same as applicable federal rules

	Must a Separate "State" Form 1099 Be Filed for Payments to Individuals?	*If a Separate "State" Form 1099 Must Be Filed, What Is the Due Date for the State Version of Form 1099?*	*If a Separate "State" Form 1099 Must Be Filed, What Form Is Required?*	*If a Separate "State" Form 1099 Must Be Filed, What Dollar Threshold Triggers a Filing Requirement?*
Montana	No	NA	NA	NA
Nebraska	No	NA	NA	NA
Nevada	Nevada does not impose an individual income tax			
New Hampshire	No	NA	NA	NA
New Jersey	Copies of federal Form 1099 are acceptable. See N.J. Admin. Code § 18:35-8.1.	February 15 following close of tax year	NA	$1,000 or greater
New Mexico	No	NA	NA	NA
New York	No	NA	NA	NA
North Carolina	No	NA	NA	NA
North Dakota	No	NA	NA	NA
Ohio				
Oklahoma	Optional	SAF	Department's Web site	Generally SAF, with exceptions for oil and gas royalties
Oregon	No, except for broker's information returns	NA	Copy of federal Form 1099	SAF
Pennsylvania	Yes	28-Feb	May use federal form	$10
Rhode Island	Yes	NR	Department's website	
South Carolina	No			

Form 1099 Filing Requirements

Legend:

NA	Not applicable
NR	Not reported
SAF	Same as applicable federal rules

	Must a Separate "State" Form 1099 Be Filed for Payments to Individuals?	*If a Separate "State" Form 1099 Must Be Filed, What Is the Due Date for the State Version of Form 1099?*	*If a Separate "State" Form 1099 Must Be Filed, What Form Is Required?*	*If a Separate "State" Form 1099 Must Be Filed, What Dollar Threshold Triggers a Filing Requirement?*
South Dakota	South Dakota does not impose an individual income tax			
Tennessee	No	NA	NA	NA
Texas	Texas does not impose an individual income tax			
Utah	No	NA	NA	NA
Vermont	Yes, for nonresidents	SAF	Copy of federal Form 1099	SAF
Virginia	No	NA	NA	NA
Washington	Washington does not impose an individual income tax			
West Virginia	No	NA	NA	NA
Wisconsin	Yes	2/28 for remuneration excluded from definition of wages; 3/15 for rents and royalties	Copy of federal Form 1099, WI Form 9b may be used instead.	Royalties of $600 or more
Wyoming	Wyoming does not impose an individual income tax			

Taxation of Nonresident Employees

Background

Forty-three states impose personal income taxes. The exceptions are Alaska, Florida, Nevada, South Dakota, Texas, Washington and Wyoming. New Hampshire and Tennessee tax only selected types of income, not including wages. Whether an individual must file returns and pay income tax in a particular state is determined primarily by whether the individual is a resident of the state. An individual is a resident of the state in which his or her "domicile" (i.e., fixed or permanent home) is located.

In contrast to residents, states tax nonresidents only on selected types of income derived from sources within the state's borders. The types of income derived by a nonresident that a source state may tax primarily include: (1) salaries, wages, and other types of income derived from personal services performed within the state, (2) income derived from business activities conducted in the state, and (3) income from real and tangible personal property located in the state. Income from intangibles, such as dividends, interest and capital gains on sales of securities, generally is taxable only by the state of residence.

If a resident of one state derives income from a source within another state, double taxation can result. To mitigate double taxation, states usually allow residents to claim a credit for income taxes paid to other states.

Employee Filing Requirements and Employer Withholding Requirements

Employee business travel can result in a state personal income tax filing requirement for the employee, as well as a state personal income tax withholding requirement for the employer. Because the states have not reached a consensus regarding the threshold level of in-state activity that triggers a tax obligation, the administrative burden can be significant for both parties.

The primary issue for a nonresident employee is whether the employee must file an income tax return and pay tax in the state in which the personal services were performed. A filing requirement generally exists if the employee's income earned within the state exceeds a specified dollar threshold, or if the time spent working in the state exceeds a specified number of days. The portion of an employee's salary or wages attributable to the work done in a state is generally determined by multiplying the employee's annual compensation by a fraction, the numerator of which is the number of working days within the state, and the denominator of which is the total number of working days during the year.

The primary issue for the employer is whether it is required to withhold state personal income taxes on the salary or wages paid to a nonresident employee. As with an employee's filing requirement, a withholding requirement generally exists if the income earned by the employee within the state exceeds a specified dollar threshold or if the time spent by the employee working in the state exceeds a specified number of days. Within a given state, it is possible that the threshold which creates a withholding requirement for the employer may differ from the threshold which creates a filing obligation for the employee. Thus, even if the employer is not required to withhold tax from an employee's wages, that employee may still be required to file a tax return.

Reciprocity Agreements

To ease the compliance burden and prevent double taxation of cross-border commuters, some states have entered into reciprocity agreements. These agreements generally apply only to income from employment, and are aimed at residents who work for an employer that is located across the border in another state. Under a reciprocity agreement, each state agrees not to tax a resident of the other state on salaries and wages that the nonresident receives for working in the state. Instead, such compensation is taxable only by the state in which the employee resides. For example, if States X and Y enter into a reciprocity agreement, State X does not tax the salary that a State Y resident receives for working in State

X. This allows State Y to collect the full tax on the income. Likewise, State Y does not tax the salary that a State X resident receives for working in State Y, which allows State X collects the full tax on the income.

Professional Athletes and Entertainers

In recognition of their high levels of compensation, many states have enacted special tax filing and withholding requirements for professional athletes and entertainers. For example, many states use the duty day method to determine the in-state income earned by nonresident members of a professional athletic team. Duty days generally include all working days from the beginning of pre-season training through the last game in which the team competes. The amount of income earned within a state is determined by multiplying the athlete's annual compensation by a fraction, the numerator of which is the number of duty days within the state, and the denominator of which is the total number of duty days during the year. An alternative approach is to determine a nonresident athlete's in-state income based on the number of games played in the state to the total number of games played everywhere.

Recent Developments

Connecticut. Effective December 2, 2009, employers are not required to withhold tax from compensation paid to a nonresident employee for services performed in Connecticut if the employee is assigned to a primary work location outside of Connecticut and works in Connecticut for 14 or fewer days during the calendar year. This 14-day rule does not exclude the compensation earned by nonresident employees from Connecticut tax; instead, it merely relieves the employer from a withholding obligation. The 14-day rule does not apply to payments made to nonresident athletes and entertainers. [Announcement 2009(9), Ct. Dep't of Rev. Serv., Dec. 2, 2009]

Maine. For tax years beginning on or after January 1, 2011, compensation for personal services performed in Maine as an employee is Maine-source income subject to taxation if the nonresident taxpayer is present in the state performing personal services for more than 12 days during that tax year and earns more than $3,000 in gross income during the year in Maine from all sources. Personal services are not counted toward the 12-day threshold if performed in connection with: (1) presenting or receiving employment-related training or education; (2) a site inspection, review, analysis of management or any other supervision of a facility, affiliate or subsidiary based in Maine by a representative from a company, not headquartered in Maine, that owns that facility or is the parent company of the affiliate or subsidiary; (3) research and development at a facility based in Maine or in connection with the installation of new or upgraded equipment or systems at that facility; or (4) a project team working on the attraction or implementation of new investment in a facility based in Maine.

In addition, a nonresident who is present for business in Maine on other than a systematic or regular basis, either directly or through agents or employees, has Maine-source income derived from or effectively connected with a trade or business in Maine and is subject to taxation by Maine only if the nonresident was present in the state for business more than 12 days during the taxable year and earns or derives more than $3,000 of gross income during the tax year from contractual or sales-related activities. [L.D. 1043, June 20, 2011]

Multistate Tax Commission. In July 2011, the Multistate Tax Commission adopted a Model Mobile Workforce Statute. Under the model statute, an employer would not have to withhold personal income tax on a nonresident employee's compensation if the employee spends less than 20 work days in a state, nor would the traveling employee be required to pay tax to the source state as long as the employee has no other income attributable to the state. Exceptions to the 20-day rule would apply to professional athletes and entertainers, construction workers, and certain key employees.

State-by-State Summary

The following chart summarizes which states have adopted a de minimis rule which exempts the wages of nonresident employees (other than athletes and entertainers) who are temporarily working in your state.

Legend:
NA Not applicable
NR Not reported

Taxation of Nonresident Employees

	Does Your State Impose a Personal Income Tax?	*If Yes, Does Your State Have a De Minimis Rule, Based on the Number of Days Worked or the Amount of Income Earned, Which Exempts the Wages of a Nonresident Employee Who Is Temporarily Working in Your State (Assuming the Employee Is Not an Athlete or Entertainer, and That No Reciprocity Agreement Applies)*	*If Yes, Describe the Exemption*
Alabama	Yes	No	
Alaska	No		
Arizona	Yes	No. See ARS § 43-401.	
Arkansas	Yes	No	
California	Yes	No	
Colorado	Yes	No	
Connecticut	Yes	No	
Delaware	Yes	No	
District of Columbia	No		
Florida	No		
Georgia	Yes	Yes	If wages do not exceed the lesser of 5% of income received for services or $5,000.
Hawaii	Yes	No	
Idaho	Yes	Yes	Nonresidents with $2500 or less of Gross Income from Idaho Sources are not Required to File an Idaho Tax Return, ID Code § 63-3030(2).

Taxation of Nonresident Employees

Legend:
NA Not applicable
NR Not reported

	Does Your State Impose a Personal Income Tax?	*If Yes, Does Your State Have a De Minimis Rule, Based on the Number of Days Worked or the Amount of Income Earned, Which Exempts the Wages of a Nonresident Employee Who Is Temporarily Working in Your State (Assuming the Employee Is Not an Athlete or Entertainer, and That No Reciprocity Agreement Applies)*	*If Yes, Describe the Exemption*
Illinois	Yes	No	There is no *de minimis* rule based on the number of days or amount of income earned, but Illinois does not tax wages of a nonresident even if the services are performed in Illinois, if the services performed in Illinois are merely incidental to the services performed outside of Illinois or the nonresident's base of operations is outside Illinois.
Indiana	Yes	No	
Iowa	Yes	Yes	
Kansas	Yes	No	
Kentucky	Yes	No	
Louisiana	Yes	No	

Taxation of Nonresident Employees

Legend:
NA Not applicable
NR Not reported

	Does Your State Impose a Personal Income Tax?	*If Yes, Does Your State Have a De Minimis Rule, Based on the Number of Days Worked or the Amount of Income Earned, Which Exempts the Wages of a Nonresident Employee Who Is Temporarily Working in Your State (Assuming the Employee Is Not an Athlete or Entertainer, and That No Reciprocity Agreement Applies)*	*If Yes, Describe the Exemption*
Maine	Yes	Yes	A nonresident whose only Maine-source income is from performing personal service as an employee in Maine for no more than 12 days is generally not required to file a Maine return. Nonresident individuals performing certain personal services in Maine for no more than 36 days are generally not required to file a Maine return.
Maryland	Yes	No	
Massachusetts	Yes	Yes	See 830 CMR 62.5A1
Michigan	NR	NR	NR
Note. The CIT takes effect 01/01/12, and replaces the Michigan Business Tax (MBT) for most taxpayers. However, businesses that have been approved to receive, have received, or have been assigned certain certified credits may elect to file a return and pay the tax imposed by the MBT in lieu of the CIT until the certified credits are exhausted or extinguished.			
Minnesota	Yes	Yes	Under $8,000 of total income
Mississippi	Yes	No	
Missouri	Yes	No	
Montana	Yes	No	
Nebraska	Yes	No	

Taxation of Nonresident Employees

Legend:
NA Not applicable
NR Not reported

	Does Your State Impose a Personal Income Tax?	*If Yes, Does Your State Have a De Minimis Rule, Based on the Number of Days Worked or the Amount of Income Earned, Which Exempts the Wages of a Nonresident Employee Who Is Temporarily Working in Your State (Assuming the Employee Is Not an Athlete or Entertainer, and That No Reciprocity Agreement Applies)*	*If Yes, Describe the Exemption*
Nevada	NR	NR	NR
New Hampshire	No		
New Jersey	Yes	No	
New Mexico	Yes	Yes	14 non-current days within the state
New York	NR	NR	NR
North Carolina	Yes	No	
North Dakota	Yes	Yes	Adopted a statute based on the MTC Model Mobile Workforce Statute. This statute will not be effective until tax years beginning after 12/31/12. See note below.

Note. Compensation received by a nonresident for employment duties in North Dakota will be excluded from state source income if all of the following are true:

(1) The employee does not have any other North Dakota source income; (2) The employee does not spend more than 20 "working days" in North Dakota; and (3) The employee's home state provides a substantially similar exemption or does not impose an individual income tax.

Compensation received by a nonresident for employment duties in North Dakota will be excluded from income tax withholding if all of the following are true: (1) the employee does not spend more than 20 "working days" in North Dakota; and (2) the employee's home state provides a substantially similar exemption or does not impose an individual income tax.

The statute provides for exceptions in which the income from employment duties in North Dakota will be taxed and subject to withholding regardless of how much time is spent there: (1) a professional athlete or member or a professional athletic team; (2) a professional entertainer performing services in the performing arts; (3) a person of prominence performing services for compensation on a per event basis; (4) a person performing construction services to improve real property; (5) a "Key Employee" under IRC § 416(i) - generally has a salary of at least $160,000 and is one of the 50 highest paid officers; (6) an employee of a non-corporate employer who is not an officer but otherwise meets the "Key Employee" requirements.

Taxation of Nonresident Employees

Legend:
NA Not applicable
NR Not reported

	Does Your State Impose a Personal Income Tax?	*If Yes, Does Your State Have a De Minimis Rule, Based on the Number of Days Worked or the Amount of Income Earned, Which Exempts the Wages of a Nonresident Employee Who Is Temporarily Working in Your State (Assuming the Employee Is Not an Athlete or Entertainer, and That No Reciprocity Agreement Applies)*	*If Yes, Describe the Exemption*
Ohio	NR	NR	NR
Oklahoma	NR	NR	NR
Oregon	Yes	No	
Pennsylvania	NR	NR	
Rhode Island	No	No	
South Carolina	Yes	Yes	South Carolina gross income ≤ federal personal exemption
South Dakota	NR	NR	NR
Tennessee	No		
Texas	No		
Utah	NR	NR	NR
Vermont	Yes	No	
Virginia	Yes	Yes	Virginia has a filing threshold for all taxpayers. In 2011, the filing threshold is $11,650 for single filers and $23,300 for married taxpayers filing jointly.
Washington	NR	NR	NR
West Virginia	Yes	No	

Taxation of Nonresident Employees

Legend:
NA Not applicable
NR Not reported

	Does Your State Impose a Personal Income Tax?	*If Yes, Does Your State Have a De Minimis Rule, Based on the Number of Days Worked or the Amount of Income Earned, Which Exempts the Wages of a Nonresident Employee Who Is Temporarily Working in Your State (Assuming the Employee Is Not an Athlete or Entertainer, and That No Reciprocity Agreement Applies)*	*If Yes, Describe the Exemption*
Wisconsin	Yes	Yes	If employer can reasonably expect the annual Wisconsin earnings to be less than $2,000
Wyoming	NR	NR	NR

Part 12. OTHER ADMINISTRATIVE ISSUES

Statute of Limitations for Assessing Income Taxes

Federal Tax Treatment

Statutes of limitations set time limits within which an action must be started. Such statutes promote fairness and efficient administration of law by requiring prompt attention to the matter in question. Statutes of limitations typically fix a deadline for assessing additional taxes or claiming a refund. It is often prudent tax planning to file a return in order to start the running of the statute of limitations.

The federal statute of limitations on the ability of the IRS to assess or collect taxes is generally three years from the date that the tax return is filed. [IRC § 6501] For this purpose, a return that is filed before its due date is considered to have been filed on the due date. If no return is filed or a false or fraudulent return is filed, the federal statute of limitations period does not begin to run. In addition, when a taxpayer omits a substantial amount of gross income from a federal return, defined as more than 25 percent of the gross income reported on the return, the federal statute of limitations period is increased to six years. Although the federal statute of limitations period is extended for a substantial omission of income, it is not extended when a taxpayer has overstated the amount of deductions, regardless of the amount of the overstatement.

The federal statute of limitations on the ability of taxpayers to claim a refund or credit with respect to an overpayment of taxes is generally the later of (1) three years from the time the return was filed, or (2) two years from the time the tax was paid. [IRC § 6511] However, if the taxpayer did not file a return for the year of overpayment, the claim for a refund or credit must be filed within two years after the date on which the overpayment occurred.

State Tax Treatment

Most states conform to the three-year federal statute of limitations, as well as to the federal approach of extending the basic limitations period for substantial understatements of income, and providing an unlimited period in which to assess tax when there has been a failure to file a return or when a fraudulent return has been filed. One exception is Texas, which employs a four-year statute of limitations. [Texas Tax Code § 111.201]

Care must be used when dealing with a taxpayer with multistate filings. An audit in one state may require filing amended returns in other states. Failure to do so may result in assessments, including interest and penalties, from the other states or a missed opportunity for a refund. For example, with respect to extended-due-date tax returns, some states grant extensions of time to file for a period that is measured in days. If the period is 180 days instead of six months, the extended due date may not fall as expected on the fifteenth day of the sixth month following the original due date of the return. That may affect the expiration of the statute of limitations.

If a taxpayer fails to report a federal audit adjustment to a state, an unlimited or substantially lengthened period for assessing additional state taxes may exist. For example, in *Gibson v. Levin*[No. 2008-Ohio-4828 (Ohio Sup. Ct., Sept. 30, 2008)], the Ohio Supreme Court ruled that the four-year statute of limitation did not bar an assessment of Ohio personal income tax, because, after the IRS had made an adjustment, the taxpayers failed to file an amended Ohio return before the Tax Commissioner issued the assessment. The four-year statute of limitation never commenced to run in this case, because, to activate the statute, the taxpayers would have had to have (1) filed an amended return, and (2) demonstrated that the four-year limitation period had lapsed between the actual filing of the amended return and the issuance of the assessment. (For details regarding the time limits for reporting federal adjustments, see the section entitled Time Limits for Reporting Federal Adjustments and Responding to Notices of Deficiency in this part.)

Timely Filing of Refund Claims

Courts in Texas and West Virginia have addressed the proper determination of the limitation period when a taxpayer has filed an extension of time to file its original return. Both courts essentially held that an amended return requesting a refund of overpaid tax was timely filed if it was filed within four years (Texas) or three years (West Virginia) of the actual filing of the original return. In other words, like the federal provisions, these state statutes of limitations ran from the date the return was filed pursuant to an automatic extension of time to file, rather than from the original date the return was due. [*Sharp v. IBM*, No. 03-95-00673-CV (Tex. App. Ct., Aug. 14, 1996); *In re Doran & Assocs., Inc.*, No. 22852 (W. Va. Sup. Ct., Oct. 27, 1995)]

In *Utelcom, Inc. v. Egr* [653 N.W.2d 846 (Neb. Sup. Ct. Dec. 6, 2002)], the Nebraska Supreme Court ruled that, in the case of a taxpayer that filed its return after the original due date for the return but prior to the expiration of an automatic seven-month extension, the state's three-year limitation period for claiming a tax refund starts to run on the automatic extended due date for filing a tax return rather than on the date the taxpayer actually filed the return.

In *Graham v. McKesson Information Solutions* [Nos. A06A033 and A06A0334 (Ga. Ct. of App., May 12, 2006)], a corporation whose refund claim was initially denied because it was not timely filed was also denied a refund when it filed a second claim after receiving a federal refund check. The Georgia Court of Appeals ruled that a taxpayer is only allowed to file an amended state return within the 180 day window after a final federal determination if the change to the taxpayer's net income was made by the IRS. The adjustment to the taxpayer's federal net income was not pursuant a final federal determination, which would have necessitated the filing of an amended Georgia return within 180 days of the final determination. Instead the adjustment was made because the taxpayer filed an amended federal return after deciding it had overstated its income for the tax year at issue.

Caution also must be exercised when navigating through procedural statutes to ensure that all deadlines and actions occur timely. The Michigan Tax Tribunal dismissed an appeal because it was not filed properly within the 30-day period from the Department of Treasury's final decision. The taxpayer argued unsuccessfully that the statute of limitations should be tolled, because it was not notified of its right to appeal and it was negotiating a settlement with the tax administrator. [*Curtis Big Boy, Inc. v. Department of Treasury*, No. 146213 (Mich. Ct. App. July 5, 1994)]

Extending the Limitation Period

The Oregon Supreme Court ruled that the Department of Revenue could not redetermine a taxpayer's state income tax liability by using corrected information from an IRS audit report, because the IRS correction was made more than three years after the taxpayer filed the state tax return, and the time limitation for sending a state notice of deficiency could be extended only if a federal correction was initiated within the original three-year period. [*Swarens v. Department of Revenue*, 320 Or. 326, 883 P.2d 853 (1994)] In the case of credit carryovers, however, the Oregon Tax Court in *Smurfit Newsprint Corp. v. Department of Revenue* [Or. T.C. Dec. 23, 1998] ruled that the Department of Revenue may recalculate the amount of tax due in a closed year and consequently change the amount of a carryover deduction or credit for a subsequent year.

In *Louisiana-Pacific Corp. v. Department of Revenue* [No. S-9198 (Ark. Sup. Ct., May 4, 2001)], the Alaska Supreme Court ruled that although an IRS waiver of the federal statute of limitations also extended the statute of limitations for filing an Alaska refund claim, that waiver only applied to the tax issues specified in the federal waiver and did not extend the statute of limitations to unrelated Alaska tax issues.

In *Bridges v. X Communications, Inc.* [No. 03-CA-441 (La. Ct. of App., Nov. 12, 2003)], the Louisiana Court of Appeals ruled that a document waiving the statute of limitations with respect to a tax audit was not valid because it was signed by an employee of the taxpayer who did not have the authority to bind the corporation to such an agreement.

Recent Developments

Utah. In 2008, Utah enacted legislation establishing that a claim for refund must be filed within the later of three years from the due date of the return, including any extensions, or two years from the date the tax was paid. [S.B. 108, Mar. 24, 2009]

State-by-State Summary

The following chart indicates the states' statutes of limitations for assessing tax on corporate taxpayers and the exceptions that extend the general period of limitations. The chart divides the states' statutes of limitations into three categories: (1) basic limitation, (2) limitation when a specified percentage of income is not reported, and (3) failure to file/fraudulent return limitation. The chart also indicates whether a jeopardy assessment can be made for income taxes.

Statute of Limitations for Assessing Income Taxes

Legend:
NA Not applicable
NR Not reported

		Limitations Where Income Is Underreported		Other Limitations		
	Basic Limitation (Years)	*No. of Years*	*Applicable Percentage*	*Failure to File a Return*	*Filing a Fraudulent Return*	*Can Jeopardy Assessment Be Made for Income Taxes?*
Alabama	3 from due date or filing date, whichever is later	6	25%	No limit	No limit	Yes
Alaska	3 from date filed or due date, whichever is later	SAF	SAF	No limit	No limit	Yes
Arizona	4 from date filed or due date, whichever is later	6	25%	No limit	No limit	Yes
Arkansas	3 from date filed or due date, whichever is later	6	25%	No limit	No limit	Yes
California	4 from date filed or due date or 4 years from date return actually filed after due date	6	SAF	No limit	No limit	Yes
Colorado	4-federal statute plus one year; plus federal extensions	SAF	SAF	No limit	No limit	Yes
Connecticut	3 from filing date or extended due date, whichever is later	6	25%	No limit	No limit	Yes
Delaware	3 from date filed or due date, whichever is later	Gross underreporting eliminates statute	Gross underreporting eliminates statute	No limit	No limit	Yes
District of Columbia	3 from date filed or due date, whichever is later	6	25%	No limit	No limit	Yes

Legend:

NA Not applicable

NR Not reported

Statute of Limitations for Assessing Income Taxes

		Limitations Where Income Is Underreported		*Other Limitations*		
	Basic Limitation (Years)	*No. of Years*	*Applicable Percentage*	*Failure to File a Return*	*Filing a Fraudulent Return*	*Can Jeopardy Assessment Be Made for Income Taxes?*
Florida	3 from date return was due or filed, whichever is later	NA	NA	No limit	No limit	Yes
Georgia	3 from filing date or due date of return, including extensions, whichever is later	6	25%	No limit	No limit	Yes
Hawaii	3 from filing date or due date, whichever is later	No difference	NA	No limit	No limit	Yes
Idaho	3 from the due date of the return without regard to extensions or the date the return was filed, whichever is later	No difference	NA	No limit	No limit	Yes
Illinois	3 from filing date	6	25%	No limit	No limit	Yes
Indiana	3 from due date	6	25%	No limit	No limit	Yes
Iowa	3 from filing or due date, whichever is later	6	25%	No limit	No limit	Yes
Kansas	3 from filing date	6	3 years from due date of return or date return is filed, whichever is later	No limit	No limit	Yes
Kentucky	4 from date filed or due date, whichever is later	6	25%	No limit	No limit	Yes

Statute of Limitations for Assessing Income Taxes

Legend:
NA Not applicable
NR Not reported

		Limitations Where Income Is Underreported		*Other Limitations*		
	Basic Limitation (Years)	*No. of Years*	*Applicable Percentage*	*Failure to File a Return*	*Filing a Fraudulent Return*	*Can Jeopardy Assessment Be Made for Income Taxes?*
Louisiana	3 from 12/31 of the year in which the tax is due	NR	NR	See LSA-R.S. 47:1580(c)	See LSA-R.S. 47:1580(A)(4)	Yes
Maine	3 from date filed or due date, whichever is later	6	25%, or if tax liability is less than 1/2 of the tax liability determined by the state tax assessor.	No limit	No limit	Yes
Maryland	3	No difference	NA	No limit	No limit	Yes
Massachusetts	3 from date filed or due date, whichever is later	6	25%	No limit	No limit	Yes
Michigan (Business Tax)	4 from date filed or due date, whichever is later	No difference	NA	No limit	2 years after discovery of fraud	Yes
Note. The CIT takes effect 01/01/12, and replaces the Michigan Business Tax (MBT) for most taxpayers. However, businesses that have been approved to receive, have received, or have been assigned certain certified credits may elect to file a return and pay the tax imposed by the MBT in lieu of the CIT until the certified credits are exhausted or extinguished.						
Minnesota	3.5 years	6.5%	25%	No limit	No limit	Yes
Mississippi	3 from due date including extension, or the date the return was filed, whichever is later	NR	NR	No limit	No limit	Yes
Missouri	3 from date return filed or due date, whichever is later	6	25%	No limit	No limit	Yes
Montana	3 from date filed	No difference	NA	No limit	No limit	Yes

Legend:
NA Not applicable
NR Not reported

Statute of Limitations for Assessing Income Taxes

		Limitations Where Income Is Underreported		*Other Limitations*		
	Basic Limitation (Years)	*No. of Years*	*Applicable Percentage*	*Failure to File a Return*	*Filing a Fraudulent Return*	*Can Jeopardy Assessment Be Made for Income Taxes?*
Nebraska	3 after due date of return	6	25%	No limit	No limit	Yes
Nevada	Nevada does not impose a corporate income tax					
New Hampshire	See RSA 21-J:29, I(a)	6	25%	No limit	No limit	Yes
New Jersey	4 from payment date or filing date, whichever is later	No difference	NA	No limit	No limit	Yes
New Mexico	3 from year end of the calendar year in which the return is originally due	6	25%	7 years	10 Years	Yes
New York	3 from date return filed or due date, whichever is later	6	25%	No limit	6 years; no limit if intent to evade	Yes
North Carolina	3 years from due date of the return or the date the return was filed, whichever is later	NR	NR	NR	NR	Yes
North Dakota	3 from date filed, or due date, whichever is later	6	25%	10 years	No limit	Yes
Ohio	Ohio does not impose a corporate income tax					

Note. Effective 1/1/2010, the Ohio Franchise Tax was fully phased out and business will be taxed on gross receipts through the Commercial Activity Tax. Details about that tax can be found at: http://tax.ohio.gov/divisions/commercial_activities/cat_general_information.stm

Statute of Limitations for Assessing Income Taxes

Legend:
NA Not applicable
NR Not reported

		Limitations Where Income Is Underreported		*Other Limitations*		
	Basic Limitation (Years)	*No. of Years*	*Applicable Percentage*	*Failure to File a Return*	*Filing a Fraudulent Return*	*Can Jeopardy Assessment Be Made for Income Taxes?*
Oklahoma	3 from date paid unless given consent to extend IRS audit	NR	NR	No limit	No limit	Yes
Oregon	3 from date filed or return date, whichever is later; or within 2 years of notification of federal audit adjustment	5	25%	No limit	No limit	Yes
Pennsylvania	18 months from receiving date of tax return No difference	No difference	NA	No limit	No limit	Yes
Rhode Island	3 from date filed	6	25%	No limit	No limit	No
South Carolina	Generally 3 from due date or date filed, whichever is later.	6	20%, understatement of total tax	No limit	No limit	Yes
South Dakota	South Dakota does not impose a corporate income tax					
Tennessee	3 years from end of the year filed	No difference	NA	No limit	No limit	Yes
Texas	4 years from the date the tax is due and payable; exceptions exist.	None	25%	None, per Texas Tax Code § 111.205	None, per Texas Tax Code § 111.205	Yes

Legend:
NA Not applicable
NR Not reported

Statute of Limitations for Assessing Income Taxes

		Limitations Where Income Is Underreported		*Other Limitations*		
	Basic Limitation (Years)	*No. of Years*	*Applicable Percentage*	*Failure to File a Return*	*Filing a Fraudulent Return*	*Can Jeopardy Assessment Be Made for Income Taxes?*
Utah	Generally 3 from filing date; however, if federal waiver is signed the federal waiver extended period plus six months applies.	NA	NA	No limit	No limit	No
Vermont	3 from due date of return or date filed, whichever is later	No difference	NA	No limit	No limit	Yes
Virginia	3 from later of due date or filing date of return, 6 years for listed as abusive tax avoidance transactions.	No difference unless fraud	NR	No limit	No limit	Yes
Washington	Washington does not impose a corporate income tax					
West Virginia	3 from date filed	No difference	NA	No limit	No limit	Yes
Wisconsin	4 from unextended due date of return or when filed, whichever is later	6	25%	No limit	No limit	Yes
Wyoming	Wyoming does not impose a corporate income tax					

Time Limits for Reporting Federal Adjustments and Responding to Notices of Deficiency

Reporting Federal Adjustments

Virtually all states that tax corporate income piggyback on the federal system by adopting federal taxable income as the starting point for computing state taxable income. This practice is known as "piggybacking" and is the reason changes to federal taxable income have a direct and immediate impact on the tax base of those states. Taxpayers, therefore, are required to report all "federal changes" in a timely manner.

Federal changes arise most often from audits of the related federal returns or from filing amended federal returns. States generally require taxpayers to notify the state of any federal change once the federal adjustment is either "final" or a "final determination" has been made. Federal changes are generally reported by filing an amended state corporate income tax return and attaching to it a copy of the final federal revenue agent's report (RAR). Some states require only a copy of the RAR.

The time periods within which taxpayers must report federal changes to states vary. Most states require that federal changes be reported within between 30 and 90 days of the date on which the federal changes become final. Many states treat the time periods for reporting federal changes that increase state tax differently from the time periods for reporting federal changes that result in state refunds. Late notification of federal changes that increase state tax can result in additional penalties and interest. Late notification of federal changes that reduce state tax can bar refunds. In addition, many states keep the statute of limitations for assessment of tax (but not for refunds) open indefinitely for items included in an RAR until the state is notified of the RAR. Therefore, from a planning perspective, a taxpayer should notify each state that is affected by a federal change, since state corporate income tax may have been paid to (and refunds may be due from) numerous states.

Federal changes must be reported to states regardless of whether state statutes of limitations on assessments or refunds otherwise bar assessment or refund. When the assessment period is otherwise closed, however, the majority of states can recover additional state tax due resulting only from federal changes. Similarly, taxpayers are generally limited to refunds of state tax resulting only from the federal changes when the time period under the state statute of limitations on refunds has passed. Finally, federal changes must be reported even if they were in error but no action was taken to contest them and they became final.

Methods for notifying state tax authorities that a federal adjustment has been made also vary. Although virtually all the states responded that they require an amended state return to be filed with a copy of the federal RAR attached, many states do not statutorily require that an amended return be filed. Instead, the law provides only that the state be notified of the change. Some states have a specific form or require that the RAR details be reported on the next annual tax return. A few states permit the taxpayer to file either a copy of the RAR or an amended return with a copy of the RAR attached.

In 2003, the Multistate Tax Commission adopted a Model Uniform Statute for Reporting Federal Tax Adjustments with Accompanying Model Regulation. [Available at http://www.mtc.gov/.].

State Determination Letters, Notices of Deficiency, Proposed Assessments, and the Like

The state corporate income tax base can also be increased by action taken by state revenue departments. The U.S. Constitution, however, requires the states to provide due process of law before taxpayers' money (or property) can be taken to satisfy an alleged tax debt. That constitutional guarantee is why determination letters, which provide a time limit within which taxpayers can contest a proposed increase of tax, are sent to taxpayers.

At the conclusion of an unsettled state tax audit, the state revenue department issues a determination letter granting the taxpayer a limited number of days (often, just 30 days) within which to pay or protest the audit findings to a higher administrative level. Informal appeals, however, are not available in every state and some states restrict them to "audit issues" as opposed to "legal issues." Generally taxpayers can be represented at these appeals by CPAs acting under duly executed powers of attorney. (See the section entitled Notification Procedure to Represent Corporate Clients in this part for further details on eligibility and procedures for representing taxpayers.)

After a taxpayer's unsuccessful attempt at audit appeals or after the 30-day limit has passed without protest, the state revenue department generally issues a formal letter called a "Notice of Deficiency," "Notice of Tax Liability," "Notice of Proposed Assessment," or the like. Formal notices generally grant taxpayers 90 days within which to file formal protests. Taxpayers must exercise extreme care and pay attention to detail in responding to assessment notices. Some states use the date of receipt, not the postmark date, when determining whether correspondence is timely. Accordingly, allowance must be made for the mailing time. Registered or certified mail with a return receipt requested is advisable for all responses to assessment notice mailings.

Formal protests are generally filed with revenue departments' offices of administrative review or with state tax courts. The benefit granted to taxpayers is that the tax, interest, and penalties generally do not have to be paid before they have their "day in court." Administrative law judges or tax court judges preside at formal hearings. Both the government and the taxpayer are represented. In some states taxpayers can be represented by CPAs acting under duly executed powers of attorney. If the time limit passes without contest, the alleged tax debts become "final" and states may lawfully lien, levy, and seize taxpayers' property in satisfaction of those final liabilities. Every formal protest should include the following:

- A concise statement of the issues in dispute
- A complete recital of all relevant facts
- Application of favorable statutes, regulations, cases, and administrative rulings
- Reasons, if any, why adverse authority does not apply or can be distinguished in the case

As an alternative to allowing taxpayers to file formal protests in state tax court or within the office of administrative hearings, many states provide statutory procedures allowing taxpayers to file refund suits directly in state courts. These state courts also hear appeals from state offices of administrative review and state tax courts. One consideration in taking tax cases directly to state courts or appealing to state courts is that taxpayers generally must either post bond in the amount in dispute or pay the amount in dispute "under protest" in order to have access to state courts. In addition, the statutory procedures in these states can be complex and taxpayers must be represented by attorneys licensed to practice law in that state or out-of-state attorneys granted permission by the court to represent taxpayers in those disputes.

From a planning perspective, a taxpayer should not wait for the conclusion of a state audit, pay additional tax, and then find that the period of limitations for refunds in other states has expired. Double taxation can be avoided by filing "protective" claims for refunds with other states in which tax has already been paid on the same item.

Recent Developments

Connecticut. A taxpayer must file an amended Connecticut corporate income tax return within 90 days of the date of the final determination on an amended federal return. [H.B. 5494, June 7, 2010]

Maine. A taxpayer must file an amended Maine corporate income tax return within 180 days (previously, 90 days) of the date of the final determination on an amended federal return. In addition, a taxpayer may request a credit or refund of Maine tax within 3 years from the date the return was filed or 3 years from the date the tax was paid, whichever period expires later. [L.D. 100, Feb. 8, 2011]

Nebraska. Effective January 1, 2009, Nebraska taxpayers have 60 days (previously, 90 days) to file a petition for redetermination in order to contest a notice of deficiency. If the petition is not filed or postmarked within the 60-day limitation period, the notice of deficiency becomes final. [Rev. Rul. 99-09-1, Neb. Dept. of Rev., Jan. 7, 2009]

Ohio. In *Gibson v. Levin*[No. 2008-Ohio-4828 (Ohio Sup. Ct., Sept. 30, 2008)], the Ohio Supreme Court ruled that the four-year statute of limitation did not bar an assessment of Ohio personal income tax, because, after the IRS had made an adjustment, the taxpayers failed to file an amended Ohio return before the Tax Commissioner issued the assessment. The four-year statute of limitation never commenced to run in this case, because, to activate the statute, the taxpayers would have had to have (1) filed an amended return, and (2) demonstrated that the four-year limitation period had lapsed between the actual filing of the amended return and the issuance of the assessment.

State-by-State Summary

The following chart is presented in two parts. Part 1 outlines how finalized federal audit adjustments are to be reported to a state and specifies the state-imposed time limits for reporting federal adjustments and the time limit for responding to state-issued determination letters. Part 2 addresses whether an amended return that is required by an RAR adjustment is limited to federal RAR adjustments, clarifies whether a refund can be received by filing a state return after the final RAR is issued, and identifies the statute of limitations period for filing a refund claim.

Time Limits for Reporting Federal Adjustments and Responding to Notices of Deficiency (Part 1)

Legend:

RAR	Revenue agent report
NA	Not applicable
NR	Not reported

	How Are Finalized Federal Audit Adjustments Reported to the State?	*Deadline for Reporting a Federal Revenue Agent's Final Adjustment*	*Deadline for Filing a Response to a Determination Letter*
Alabama	Amended return and copy of RAR	1 year	Addressed in Letter
Alaska	Amended return and copy of RAR	60 days after final determination	60 days
Arizona	Amended return and copy of RAR, or copy of RAR only, at taxpayer's option	90 days after final determination	45 days
Arkansas	Amended return and copy of RAR	90 days after final determination	60 days
California	Copy of RAR only with letter and/or schedules as necessary; can provide a schedule if it is sufficient to allow for a California computation of tax	6 months, see RTC Sec 18622	90 days for appeal from claim determination and 30 days for appeal from determination on unpaid amounts
Colorado	Amended return and copy of RAR	30 days after final determination	30 days
Connecticut	Amended return and copy of RAR report	90 days after final determination	60 days
Delaware	Amended return and copy of RAR, or copy of RAR only, at taxpayer's option	90 days after final determination	90 days after date on determination letter
District of Columbia	Amended return and copy of RAR	90 days after final determination	30 days
Florida	Amended return and copy of RAR	60 days after final determination	60 days
Georgia	Amended return and copy of RAR, or copy of RAR only, at taxpayer's option	180 days after final determination	30 days
Hawaii	Amended return and copy of RAR	90 days after final determination	NA
Idaho	Amended return and copy of RAR, or copy of RAR only, at taxpayer's option. Amended return required for refund.	60 days after final determination	63 days after notice is mailed

Time Limits for Reporting Federal Adjustments and Responding to Notices of Deficiency (Part 1)

Legend:

RAR	Revenue agent report
NA	Not applicable
NR	Not reported

	How Are Finalized Federal Audit Adjustments Reported to the State?	*Deadline for Reporting a Federal Revenue Agent's Final Adjustment*	*Deadline for Filing a Response to a Determination Letter*
Illinois	Amended return and copy of RAR	120 days after final determination	60 days from notice of deficiency
Indiana	Amended return and copy of RAR	120 days after final determination	60 days from date of notice
Iowa	Amended return and copy of RAR, or copy of RAR only, at taxpayer's option	None. Statute of limitations for assessment remains open until 6 months after receipt of federal audit from the taxpayer.	60 days
Kansas	Amended return and copy of RAR	180 days from closed agreement	60 days from date of notice
Kentucky	Amended return and copy of RAR	Within 30 days of its conclusion	45 days from date of ruling
Louisiana	Amended return and copy of RAR	60 days after taxpayer's receipt of such adjustments from the IRS (LSA-R.S. 47:287.614(c))	60 days
Maine	Amended return and copy of RAR	90 days	30 days
Maryland	Amended return and copy of RAR, or copy of RAR only, at taxpayer's option	90 days after final determination	30 days to appeal an assessment
Massachusetts	Amended return and copy of RAR, see TIR 04-13	3 months from notice of determination, see TIR 04-13	30 days
Michigan (Business Tax)	Amended return and copy of RAR	120 days after final determination	4 years from return due date or 120 days after final adjustments, whichever is later

Note. The CIT takes effect 01/01/12, and replaces the Michigan Business Tax (MBT) for most taxpayers. However, businesses that have been approved to receive, have received, or have been assigned certain certified credits may elect to file a return and pay the tax imposed by the MBT in lieu of the CIT until the certified credits are exhausted or extinguished.

Minnesota	Amended return and copy of RAR	180 days after final determination	60 days

Time Limits for Reporting Federal Adjustments and Responding to Notices of Deficiency (Part 1)

Legend:
RAR — Revenue agent report
NA — Not applicable
NR — Not reported

	How Are Finalized Federal Audit Adjustments Reported to the State?	*Deadline for Reporting a Federal Revenue Agent's Final Adjustment*	*Deadline for Filing a Response to a Determination Letter*
Mississippi	Amended return and copy of RAR	30 days after final determination	NR
Missouri	Amended return and copy of RAR	90 days after final determination	90 days
Montana	Amended return and copy of RAR	90 days after final determination	30 days
Nebraska	Amended return and copy of RAR	60 days after final adjustment	60 days from the date the deficiency notice was mailed
Nevada	Nevada does not impose a corporate income tax		
New Hampshire	Amended return and a copy of RAR	6 months	60 days
New Jersey	IRA-100 or copy of amended return CBT-100	90 days after final determination	90 days
New Mexico	Amended return and copy of RAR	30 days after RAR	Have 30 days to file written protest.
New York	Form CT-3360 and copy of RAR	90 days after final determination, 120 days for combined filers	90 days
North Carolina	Amended return and copy of RAR	2 years	30 days
North Dakota	Amended return and copy of RAR, or schedule with copy of RAR only for tax due	90 days after final determination	30 days
Ohio	Ohio does not impose a corporate income tax		
Note. Effective 1/1/2010, the Ohio Franchise Tax was fully phased out and business will be taxed on gross receipts through the Commercial Activity Tax. Details about that tax can be found at: http://tax.ohio.gov/divisions/commercial_activities/cat_general_information.stm			
Oklahoma	Amended return and copy of RAR	1 year	30 days

Time Limits for Reporting Federal Adjustments and Responding to Notices of Deficiency (Part 1)

Legend:
RAR Revenue agent report
NA Not applicable
NR Not reported

	How Are Finalized Federal Audit Adjustments Reported to the State?	*Deadline for Reporting a Federal Revenue Agent's Final Adjustment*	*Deadline for Filing a Response to a Determination Letter*
Oregon	Amended return and copy of RAR, or copy of RAR only, at taxpayer's option, or a schedule showing the adjustments and the recomputation of the tax, with a copy of the RAR, or other information sufficient to inform the department of each item on the income tax return that has been changed or corrected.	2 years after state is notified	90 days
Pennsylvania	RCT-128c and copy of RAR	30 days	NR
Rhode Island	Amended return and copy of RAR	60 days	30 days
South Carolina	Copy of RAR only	180 days	90 days
South Dakota	South Dakota does not impose a corporate income tax		
Tennessee	Amended return and copy of RAR, or copy of RAR only, at taxpayer's option	2 years from state notice	NR
Texas	An amended report is required within 120 days after RAR finalized.	120 days	30 days
Utah	Amended return and copy of RAR, or copy of RAR only, at taxpayer's option	90 days after final determination	30 days from notice date
Vermont	Amended return and copy of RAR	30 days	60 days
Virginia	Amended return and copy of RAR	90 days after final determination	3 years from due date, or 1 year from final determination
Washington	Washington does not impose a corporate income tax		

Time Limits for Reporting Federal Adjustments and Responding to Notices of Deficiency (Part 1)

Legend:
RAR Revenue agent report
NA Not applicable
NR Not reported

	How Are Finalized Federal Audit Adjustments Reported to the State?	*Deadline for Reporting a Federal Revenue Agent's Final Adjustment*	*Deadline for Filing a Response to a Determination Letter*
West Virginia	Amended return and copy of RAR, or copy of RAR only, at taxpayer's option	90 days after final determination	90 days after final determination
Wisconsin	Amended return and copy of RAR, or copy of RAR only, at taxpayer's option	90 days after final determination	60 days after receipt of notice
Wyoming	Wyoming does not impose a corporate income tax		

Time Limits for Reporting Federal Adjustments and Responding to Notices of Deficiency (Part 2)

Legend:

RAR Revenue agent report
SAF Same as applicable federal rules
NA Not applicable
NR Not reported

	Is Amended Return That Is Required by RAR Adjustment (Otherwise Closed by Statute) Limited to Federal RAR Adjustments?	*If Tax Year Is Otherwise Closed by Statute, Can a Refund Be Received on Filing a State Return After the Final Federal RAR Is Issued?*	*Deadline for Filing a Valid Claim for Refund?*
Alabama	Yes	Yes	3 years from date return was filed
Alaska	Yes	Yes	3 years from date filed or 2 years from date paid
Arizona	Yes	Yes	4 years from due date or date filed, whichever is later
Arkansas	Yes	Yes	3 years from date return was filed
California	Yes	Yes, RTC § 19311 if within 2 years of final federal determination	4 years from the due date of return or 1 year of overpayment
Colorado	No	Yes	1 year longer than the federal statute of limitations
Connecticut	No written guidance	Yes	3 years from due date or extended due date
Delaware	Yes	Yes	2 years after the RAR has been finalized, within 3 years of return due date, or within 2 years of time tax was paid
District of Columbia	Yes	Yes	3 years from date return was filed
Florida	Yes	Yes	2 years
Georgia	Yes	Yes	3 years from the later of date tax is paid or return was due. For RAR, one year of filing RAR with GA

Time Limits for Reporting Federal Adjustments and Responding to Notices of Deficiency (Part 2)

Legend:

RAR	Revenue agent report
SAF	Same as applicable federal rules
NA	Not applicable
NR	Not reported

	Is Amended Return That Is Required by RAR Adjustment (Otherwise Closed by Statute) Limited to Federal RAR Adjustments?	*If Tax Year Is Otherwise Closed by Statute, Can a Refund Be Received on Filing a State Return After the Final Federal RAR Is Issued?*	*Deadline for Filing a Valid Claim for Refund?*
Hawaii	Yes	Yes	3 years from due date or filing date or 2 years from payment date
Idaho	Yes	Yes	1 year if 3-year statute has expired
Illinois	Yes	Yes	3 years from date return filed (including extension); or 1 year after tax payment date, whichever is later
Indiana	Yes	Yes	3 years from latter of due date of return or payment of tax
Iowa	Yes	Yes	6 months from finalization of the federal audit
Kansas	Yes	Yes	180 days
Kentucky	No	No	4 years from date return was filed
Louisiana	Yes	Yes	Within prescriptive period
Maine	Yes	Yes	3 years from date filed and date tax was paid
Maryland	Yes	Yes	Within 1 year after federal adjustment
Massachusetts	No		3 years from date return was filed
Michigan (Business Tax)	Yes	Yes	4 years from original due date

Note. The CIT takes effect 01/01/12, and replaces the Michigan Business Tax (MBT) for most taxpayers. However, businesses that have been approved to receive, have received, or have been assigned certain certified credits may elect to file a return and pay the tax imposed by the MBT in lieu of the CIT until the certified credits are exhausted or extinguished.

Time Limits for Reporting Federal Adjustments and Responding to Notices of Deficiency (Part 2)

Legend:

RAR	Revenue agent report
SAF	Same as applicable federal rules
NA	Not applicable
NR	Not reported

	Is Amended Return That Is Required by RAR Adjustment (Otherwise Closed by Statute) Limited to Federal RAR Adjustments?	*If Tax Year Is Otherwise Closed by Statute, Can a Refund Be Received on Filing a State Return After the Final Federal RAR Is Issued?*	*Deadline for Filing a Valid Claim for Refund?*
Minnesota	No	Yes	$3^1/2$ years from due date or filing date
Mississippi	Yes	Yes	3 years
Missouri	Yes	Yes	1 year and 90 days
Montana	No	Yes	3 years from original due date of return or 1 year from the date of overpayment
Nebraska	Yes	Yes	2 years and 60 days after final adjustment
Nevada	Nevada does not impose a corporate income tax		
New Hampshire	Yes	Yes	Within 3 years from due date of tax or within 2 years from date tax was paid whichever is later
New Jersey	Yes	Yes	4 years from payment or filing, whichever is later
New Mexico	Yes	Yes	1 year from final determination letter date
New York	Yes	Yes	2 years + 90 days after final federal determination
North Carolina	No	Yes	3 years
North Dakota	Yes	Yes, if there is a federal waiver	3 years
Ohio	Ohio does not impose a corporate income tax		

Time Limits for Reporting Federal Adjustments and Responding to Notices of Deficiency (Part 2)

Legend:
RAR Revenue agent report
SAF Same as applicable federal rules
NA Not applicable
NR Not reported

	Is Amended Return That Is Required by RAR Adjustment (Otherwise Closed by Statute) Limited to Federal RAR Adjustments?	*If Tax Year Is Otherwise Closed by Statute, Can a Refund Be Received on Filing a State Return After the Final Federal RAR Is Issued?*	*Deadline for Filing a Valid Claim for Refund?*
Note. Effective 1/1/2010, the Ohio Franchise Tax was fully phased out and business will be taxed on gross receipts through the Commercial Activity Tax. Details about that tax can be found at: http://tax.ohio.gov/divisions/commercial_activities/cat_general_information.stm			
Oklahoma	No	Yes	1 year
Oregon	No	Yes	Within 3 years from date return is filed; 2 years from RAR; or 2 years after payment of assessed tax
Pennsylvania	Yes	Yes	NR
Rhode Island	Yes	Yes	3 years for years 12/97 and after
South Carolina	Yes	Yes, claim must be filed within 90 days of IRS changes.	Later of 3 years from original due date, 3 years from date of timely filed return was filed or 2 years from the date of payment.
South Dakota	South Dakota does not impose a corporate income tax		
Tennessee	Yes	Yes	2 years from date of RAR
Texas	Yes	Yes	4 years
Utah	Not if federal waivers are in effect	Only if federal waivers are in effect for the years being amended	Generally 3 years after return is filed
Vermont	Yes	Yes	3 years from due date or 6 months after notice of federal adjustment
Virginia	Yes, if filed after 3 years from due date.	Yes	1 year from federal or state final determination or 3 years from due date

Time Limits for Reporting Federal Adjustments and Responding to Notices of Deficiency (Part 2)

Legend:

RAR	Revenue agent report
SAF	Same as applicable federal rules
NA	Not applicable
NR	Not reported

	Is Amended Return That Is Required by RAR Adjustment (Otherwise Closed by Statute) Limited to Federal RAR Adjustments?	*If Tax Year Is Otherwise Closed by Statute, Can a Refund Be Received on Filing a State Return After the Final Federal RAR Is Issued?*	*Deadline for Filing a Valid Claim for Refund?*
Washington	Washington does not impose a corporate income tax		
West Virginia	Yes	Yes	6 months after final determination
Wisconsin	Yes	Yes	4 years from unextended due date of the original return. 4 years from the notice date of an assessment for adjustments made as the result of an audit if the tax has been paid and an appeal was not previously filed.
Wyoming	Wyoming does not impose a corporate income tax		

Tax Audit Procedures

The concept of sampling hinges on the premise that sample items within a large population can be evaluated for particular characteristics in order to estimate the distribution of those characteristics in the population. State auditors use sampling techniques to evaluate the accuracy of taxpayer records and to estimate tax liabilities associated with inaccuracies. Most states that apply such techniques do not employ true statistical sampling methodologies, which require the taking of a truly "random" sample of transactions from which to make inferences about the likely errors to be found in the entire population of those transactions. Although sampling is frequently used in sales and use tax audits, its application in corporate income and franchise tax audits has been limited.

If the taxpayer is engaged in a large number of transactions that incur transaction tax such as sales and use taxes, the use of statistical sampling by the tax authority in auditing the taxpayer's books and records may save considerable time and expense without materially sacrificing accuracy. For a more in-depth discussion of statistical sampling issues, see the section entitled Sampling in Auditing Sales and Use Taxes in Volume 2.

In 2008, the MTC approved a model statute and accompanying regulation, Model Uniform Statistical Sampling Statute and Accompanying Regulation, which read as follows:

> Statute. Audit Procedures—For purposes of administering this act, the Department may, when examining returns or records and making assessments or refunds, use statistical sampling techniques or other sampling techniques.
>
> Regulation. Audit Procedures—
>
> 1. For purposes of administering this act, the Department is authorized to use judgmental, probability and statistical sampling techniques.
>   a. Judgmental sampling means any approach to sampling where the sample is selected based on convenience and judgment, showing characteristics where some elements of the population are subjectively favored over others, or where the chance of selection is unknown.
>   b. Probability sampling means any approach to sampling where the sample units are selected into the sample based on known probabilities, and includes any sample using a method in which every element of a finite population has a known but not necessarily equal chance of being selected.
>   c. Statistical sampling means any approach to sampling that has the following characteristics:
>   i. Use of probability sampling techniques to select the sample; and
>   ii. Use of probability theory to evaluate

State-by-State Summary

The chart that follows examines whether a state uses statistical sampling in conducting corporate income tax audits, whether the state conducts income and sales and use tax audits simultaneously, and whether the state assesses a taxpayer for out-of-pocket costs incurred in conducting an out-of-state audit.

Tax Audit Procedures

Legend:
NA Not applicable
NR Not reported

	Does State Allow Use of Statistical Sampling in Corporate Income Tax Audits?	*Are Income Taxes and Sales & Use Taxes Audited at the Same Time?*	*Does State Assess Taxpayer for Costs Incurred in Conducting Out-of-State Audit?*
Alabama	No	No	No
Alaska	No	No	No
Arizona	No	No	No
Arkansas	No	Yes	No
California	No	No	No
Colorado	No	No	No
Connecticut	No written guidance	No	No
Delaware	Yes	Yes (gross receipts tax)	No
District of Columbia	No	Yes	No
Florida	No	Sometimes	No
Georgia	No	NR	No
Hawaii	Yes	Yes	No
Idaho	No	No	No
Illinois	Yes	Yes	No
Indiana	Yes	Yes	No
Iowa	No	Yes	No
Kansas	No	No	No
Kentucky	No	Yes	No
Louisiana	No	No	No
Maine	No	No	No

Tax Audit Procedures

Legend:
NA Not applicable
NR Not reported

	Does State Allow Use of Statistical Sampling in Corporate Income Tax Audits?	*Are Income Taxes and Sales & Use Taxes Audited at the Same Time?*	*Does State Assess Taxpayer for Costs Incurred in Conducting Out-of-State Audit?*
Maryland	No	No	No
Massachusetts	No, not generally	Yes	No
Michigan (Business Tax)	No	Yes	No
Note. The CIT takes effect 01/01/12, and replaces the Michigan Business Tax (MBT) for most taxpayers. However, businesses that have been approved to receive, have received, or have been assigned certain certified credits may elect to file a return and pay the tax imposed by the MBT in lieu of the CIT until the certified credits are exhausted or extinguished.			
Minnesota	No	No	No
Mississippi	No	Yes	NR
Missouri	Yes	Yes	No
Montana	No	No state sales tax	No
Nebraska	No	Yes	No
Nevada	Nevada does not impose a corporate income tax		
New Hampshire	No	No	No
New Jersey	No	Yes	No
New Mexico	No	No	No
New York	No	No	No
North Carolina	No	Yes	No
North Dakota	No	No	No
Ohio	Ohio does not impose a corporate income tax		
Note. Effective 1/1/2010, the Ohio Franchise Tax was fully phased out and business will be taxed on gross receipts through the Commercial Activity Tax. Details about that tax can be found at: http://tax.ohio.gov/divisions/commercial_activities/cat_general_information.stm			

Tax Audit Procedures

Legend:
NA Not applicable
NR Not reported

	Does State Allow Use of Statistical Sampling in Corporate Income Tax Audits?	*Are Income Taxes and Sales & Use Taxes Audited at the Same Time?*	*Does State Assess Taxpayer for Costs Incurred in Conducting Out-of-State Audit?*
Oklahoma	No	No	No
Oregon	No	No state sales tax	No
Pennsylvania	No	Yes	No
Rhode Island	Yes	Yes	No
South Carolina	No	Yes	No
South Dakota	South Dakota does not impose a corporate income tax		
Tennessee	No, but possible for sales factor	Yes	No
Texas	Yes	No	No
Utah	No	No	No
Vermont	NR	Yes	No
Virginia	No	Yes	No
Washington	Washington does not impose a corporate income tax		
West Virginia	No	Yes	No
Wisconsin	Yes	Yes	No
Wyoming	Wyoming does not impose a corporate income tax		

Membership and Participation in the Multistate Tax Commission

The Multistate Tax Commission (MTC) was created in 1967, and its main offices are located in Washington, D.C. The MTC is an intergovernmental agency whose purpose is to make state tax laws governing multistate business enterprises more equitable and effective. A state becomes a member of the MTC by enacting the Multistate Tax Compact (Compact) into legislation. The Compact is a model statute, the primary objective of which is to promote uniformity in state tax administration. The most important feature of the Compact is the adoption of the Uniform Division of Income for Tax Purposes Act (UDITPA), which is found in Article IV of the Compact. UDITPA was drafted in 1957 by the National Conference of Commissioners on Uniform State Laws and is a model law for allocating and apportioning the income of a multistate business enterprise.

Under Article I of the Compact, the specific purposes of the Compact are to:

(1) Facilitate proper determination of state and local tax liability of multistate taxpayers, including the equitable apportionment of tax bases and settlement of apportionment disputes.

(2) Promote uniformity or compatibility in significant components of state tax systems.

(3) Facilitate taxpayer convenience and compliance in the filing of tax returns and in other phases of tax administration.

(4) Avoid duplicative taxation.

The MTC provides a vehicle through which the participating states can achieve these objectives.

The MTC engages in a wide variety of activities to promote equitable and efficient state tax systems. In particular, the MTC promulgates model statutes, regulations, and other guidelines for taxing multistate business enterprises. Other MTC activities include its Taxpayer-Initiated Joint Audit Program, Alternative Dispute Resolution Program (arbitration and mediation procedures to resolve tax controversies involving two or more states), Multistate Voluntary Disclosure Program, and Multistate Tax Shelter Voluntary Compliance Program.

MTC Membership

There are several ways in which a state can participate in the MTC, including as a Compact member, sovereignty member, or associate member.

Compact members are states that have enacted the Multistate Tax Compact into their state laws. These states govern the MTC and participate in a wide range of projects and programs. There are roughly 20 Compact member states, including Alabama, Alaska, Arkansas, California, Colorado, District of Columbia, Hawaii, Idaho, Kansas, Michigan, Minnesota, Missouri, Montana, New Mexico, North Dakota, Oregon, South Dakota, Texas, Utah, and Washington.

Sovereignty members are states that support the purposes of the Compact through participation in, and financial support for, the general activities of the MTC. The sovereignty member states include Georgia, Kentucky, Louisiana, New Jersey, South Carolina, and West Virginia.

Associate members are states that participate in MTC meetings and consult and cooperate with the MTC and its other member states or, as project members, participate in MTC programs or projects. There are roughly 20 associate or project member states, including Arizona, Connecticut, Florida, Illinois, Indiana, Iowa, Maine, Maryland, Massachusetts, Mississippi, Nebraska, New Hampshire, New York, North Carolina, Ohio, Oklahoma, Pennsylvania, Rhode Island, Tennessee, Vermont, Wisconsin, and Wyoming.

Delaware, Nevada, and Virginia are not members of the MTC.

Model Income Tax Statutes and Regulations

One of the principal ways in which the MTC promotes uniformity in state tax systems is to promulgate model regulations, statutes, and other guidelines regarding the taxation of multistate business enterprises. Over the years, the MTC has adopted the following model apportionment regulations (year adopted):

- Allocation and Apportionment Regulations (1973, revised through 2010), which set forth rules concerning the application of UDITPA
- Special Rule: Construction Contractors (1980)
- Special Rule: Railroad (1981)
- Special Rule: Airlines (1983)
- Special Rule: Trucking companies (1986, revised 1989)
- Special Rule: Television and radio broadcasting (1990, revised 1996)
- Special Rule: Publishing (1993)
- Recommended Formula for the Apportionment and Allocation of Net Income of Financial Institutions (1994)

The MTC has also adopted the following model statutes governing corporate income taxes (year adopted):

- Factor Presence Nexus Standard for Business Activity Taxes (2002)
- Model Statute Requiring the Add-back of Certain Intangible and Interest Expenses (2006)
- Model Statute for Combined Reporting (2006)
- Model Statute on Compilation of State Tax Return Data (2006)
- Model Statute on Disclosure of Reportable Transactions (2006)
- Tax Avoidance Transaction Voluntary Compliance (2006)

Guidelines adopted by the MTC include, among other things, the Statement of Information Concerning Practices of Multistate Tax Commission and Signatory States Under Public Law 86-272 (1986, revised 1993, 1994, and 2001).

Recent Developments

At its annual meeting in July 2011, the MTC voted to adopt the following three proposals as uniformity recommendations to the states:

- Model Mobile Workforce Statute,
- Model Statute for Disallowance of Deductions for Certain Payments to Captive Real Estate Investment Trusts, and
- Amendment to Model Statute for Combined Reporting Section 1.I. – Definition of "Tax Haven" for Purposes of Water's Edge Election.

State-by-State Summary

The following chart identifies which states are members of the MTC, participate in the MTC joint audit programs, or have adopted the various MTC model apportionment regulations and statutes. For ease of presentation, the chart is divided into three parts, as follows:

- Part 1: MTC Membership, Joint Audit Programs, Pub. L. No. 86-272
- Part 2: Adoption of Model Apportionment Regulations
- Part 3: Adoption of Model Apportionment Statutes.

Membership and Participation in the Multistate Tax Commission (Part 1)

MTC Membership, Joint Audit Programs, PL 86-272

Legend:

NA Not applicable

NR Not reported

State	*What Type of Membership Does Your State Have in the MTC?*	*Does Your State Participate in the MTC Joint Income Tax Audit Program?*	*Does Your State Participate in the MTC Joint Sales Tax Audit Program?*	*Has Your State Adopted the Statement of Information Concerning Practices of MTC and Signatory States under Public Law 86-272 (1986)?*
Alabama	Compact	Yes	Yes	Yes
Alaska	Compact	Yes	No	Yes
Arizona	Associate	No	No	No
Arkansas	Compact	Yes	Yes	No
California	NR	No	No	Partly, as of 1/1/11, California applies the *Finnegan* throwback rule
Colorado	Compact		Yes	Yes
Connecticut	Associate	No	No	No
Delaware	Non-Member	No	No	No
District of Columbia	Compact	Yes	Yes	Yes
Florida	NR	No	No	To some extent
Georgia	Sovereignty	No	Yes	No
Hawaii	Compact	Yes	Yes	Yes
Idaho	Compact	Yes	Yes	Yes
Illinois	Associate	No	No	To some extent
Indiana	Associate	No	No	No
Iowa	Non-Member	No	No	To some extent

Membership and Participation in the Multistate Tax Commission (Part 1)

MTC Membership, Joint Audit Programs, PL 86-272

Legend:
NA Not applicable
NR Not reported

State	*What Type of Membership Does Your State Have in the MTC?*	*Does Your State Participate in the MTC Joint Income Tax Audit Program?*	*Does Your State Participate in the MTC Joint Sales Tax Audit Program?*	*Has Your State Adopted the Statement of Information Concerning Practices of MTC and Signatory States under Public Law 86-272 (1986)?*
Kansas	Compact	Yes	Yes	No
Kentucky	Sovereignty	Yes	Yes	No
Louisiana	Sovereignty	No	No	Yes
Maine	NR	No	No	Yes
Maryland	Sovereignty	No	NR	No
Massachusetts	Associate	NR	NR	No
Michigan (Business Tax)	Compact	Yes	Yes	No
Note. The CIT takes effect 01/01/12, and replaces the Michigan Business Tax (MBT) for most taxpayers. However, businesses that have been approved to receive, have received, or have been assigned certain certified credits may elect to file a return and pay the tax imposed by the MBT in lieu of the CIT until the certified credits are exhausted or extinguished.				
Minnesota	Associate	Yes	No	No
Mississippi	Sovereignty	No	No	No
Missouri	Compact	Yes	Yes	No
Montana	Compact	Yes	No	Yes
Nebraska	Non-Member	Yes	Yes	
Nevada	Nevada does not impose a corporate income tax			
New Hampshire	Associate	No	No	To Some extent
New Jersey	Sovereignty	Yes	Yes	Yes

Membership and Participation in the Multistate Tax Commission (Part 1)
MTC Membership, Joint Audit Programs, PL 86-272

Legend:
NA Not applicable
NR Not reported

State	*What Type of Membership Does Your State Have in the MTC?*	*Does Your State Participate in the MTC Joint Income Tax Audit Program?*	*Does Your State Participate in the MTC Joint Sales Tax Audit Program?*	*Has Your State Adopted the Statement of Information Concerning Practices of MTC and Signatory States under Public Law 86-272 (1986)?*
New Mexico	Compact	Yes	No	No
New York	Associate	No	No	No
North Carolina	Associate	No	No	No
North Dakota	Compact	Yes	Yes	Yes
Ohio	Ohio does not impose a corporate income tax			
Note. Effective 1/1/2010, the Ohio Franchise Tax was fully phased out and business will be taxed on gross receipts through the Commercial Activity Tax. Details about that tax can be found at: http://tax.ohio.gov/divisions/commercial_activities/cat_general_information.stm				
Oklahoma	Associate	No	No	No
Oregon				
Pennsylvania	Associate	No	No	No
Rhode Island	Non-Member	No	No	To some extent
South Carolina	Sovereignty			No
South Dakota	NA	NA	NA	NA
Tennessee	Associate	No	No	No
Texas	Compact			P.L 86-272 does not apply
Utah	Compact	Yes	Yes	Yes
Vermont	Associate	No	No	No
Virginia	Non-Member	No	No	No

Membership and Participation in the Multistate Tax Commission (Part 1)

MTC Membership, Joint Audit Programs, PL 86-272

Legend:
NA Not applicable
NR Not reported

State	*What Type of Membership Does Your State Have in the MTC?*	*Does Your State Participate in the MTC Joint Income Tax Audit Program?*	*Does Your State Participate in the MTC Joint Sales Tax Audit Program?*	*Has Your State Adopted the Statement of Information Concerning Practices of MTC and Signatory States under Public Law 86-272 (1986)?*
Washington	Washington does not impose a corporate income tax			
West Virginia	Sovereignty	Yes	Yes	To some extent
Wisconsin	Associate	Yes	Yes	No
Wyoming	Wyoming does not impose a corporate income tax			

Membership and Participation in the Multistate Tax Commission (Part 2)

Adoption of Model Apportionment Regulations

Legend:
NA Not applicable
NR Not reported

	Has Your State Adopted the Following MTC Model Apportionment Regulations? (Year MTC Adopted)							
State	*General Apportionment (1973)*	*Construction Contractors (1980)*	*Railroads (1981)*	*Airlines (1983)*	*Trucking Companies (1986)*	*TV and Radio Broadcasting (1990)*	*Publishing (1993)*	*Financial Institutions (1994)*
Alabama	Yes	Yes	Yes	Yes	Yes	Yes	Yes	Yes
Alaska	Yes	Yes	No	Yes	Yes	No	No	To some extent
Arizona	Yes	No	No	No	No	No	No	No
Arkansas	No	Yes	No	No	No	To some extent	To some extent	Yes
California	Partly	Partly, see CCR tit. 18, § 25137-2	Partly, see CCR tit. 18, § 25137-9	No, see CCR tit. 18, § 25137-7	Partly see CCR tit. 18, § 25137-11	No, see CCR tit. 18, § 25137-8	No, see CCR tit. 18, § 25137-12	Partly see CCR tit. 18, § 25137-4.1 & § 25137-4.2
Colorado	Partly	Partly	Partly	Partly	Partly	Partly	Partly	Partly
Connecticut	No	No	No	No	No	No	No	No
Delaware	Yes	No	No	No	No	No	No	No
District of Columbia	Yes	Yes	No	No	No	No	No	No
Florida	To some extent	No	To some extent	No	To some extent	No	No	No
Georgia	No	No	No	No	No	No	No	No
Hawaii	To some extent	Yes	No	No	No	Yes	Yes	No
Idaho	Modified slightly	Yes	Yes	Yes	Yes	Yes	Yes	Yes
Illinois	To some extent	No	No	No	No	No	No	No
Indiana	To some extent	To some extent	To some extent	To some extent	To some extent	To some extent	To some extent	To some extent

Membership and Participation in the Multistate Tax Commission (Part 2)

Adoption of Model Apportionment Regulations

Legend:
NA Not applicable
NR Not reported

State	*Has Your State Adopted the Following MTC Model Apportionment Regulations? (Year MTC Adopted)*							
	General Apportionment (1973)	*Construction Contractors (1980)*	*Railroads (1981)*	*Airlines (1983)*	*Trucking Companies (1986)*	*TV and Radio Broadcasting (1990)*	*Publishing (1993)*	*Financial Institutions (1994)*
Iowa	To some extent	To some extent	To some extent	To some extent	To some extent	To some extent	To some extent	To some extent
Kansas	Yes	No	No	Yes	No	No	No	To some extent
Kentucky	No	No	No	No	No	No	No	No
Louisiana	No	No	No	No	No	To some extent	No	No
Maine	To some extent	To some extent	To some extent	To some extent	To some extent	To some extent	To some extent	To some extent
Maryland	No	No	No	No	No	No	No	No
Massachusetts	No	No	No	To some extent	To some extent	No	No	To some extent
Michigan (Business Tax)	No	No	No	No	No	No	No	No
Note. The CIT takes effect 01/01/12, and replaces the Michigan Business Tax (MBT) for most taxpayers. However, businesses that have been approved to receive, have received, or have been assigned certain certified credits may elect to file a return and pay the tax imposed by the MBT in lieu of the CIT until the certified credits are exhausted or extinguished.								
Minnesota	No	No	No	No	No	No	No	No
Mississippi	To some extent	No	To some extent	To some extent	To some extent	No	No	To some extent
Missouri	Yes	Yes	Yes	Yes	Yes	No	No	No
Montana	Yes	Yes	Yes	Yes	Yes	Yes	Yes	No
Nebraska								
Nevada	Nevada does not impose a corporate income tax							

Membership and Participation in the Multistate Tax Commission (Part 2)

Adoption of Model Apportionment Regulations

Legend:

NA	Not applicable
NR	Not reported

State	*Has Your State Adopted the Following MTC Model Apportionment Regulations? (Year MTC Adopted)*							
	General Apportionment (1973)	*Construction Contractors (1980)*	*Railroads (1981)*	*Airlines (1983)*	*Trucking Companies (1986)*	*TV and Radio Broadcasting (1990)*	*Publishing (1993)*	*Financial Institutions (1994)*
New Hampshire	To some extent			To some extent	To some extent	To some extent	To some extent	To some extent
New Jersey	No	No	No	No	No		No	No
New Mexico	Yes	Yes	Yes	Yes	Yes	Yes	Yes	Yes
New York	To some extent	To some extent	To some extent	To some extent	To some extent	To some extent	To some extent	To some extent
North Carolina	To some extent	To some extent	To some extent	To some extent	To some extent	No	No	No
North Dakota	Yes	No	Yes	Yes	Yes	Yes	Yes	Yes
Ohio	Ohio does not impose a corporate income tax							
Note. Effective 1/1/2010, the Ohio Franchise Tax was fully phased out and business will be taxed on gross receipts through the Commercial Activity Tax. Details about that tax can be found at: http://tax.ohio.gov/divisions/commercial_activities/cat_general_information.stm								
Oklahoma	To some extent	To some extent	To some extent	To some extent	To some extent	To some extent	To some extent	To some extent
Oregon								
Pennsylvania	To some extent	No	No	No	No	No	No	No
Rhode Island	No	No	No	To some extent	No	No	No	No
South Carolina	No	No	No	No	No	No	No	No
South Dakota	South Dakota does not impose a corporate income tax							
Tennessee	To some extent	No	No	No	No	No	No	No
Texas	No	No	No	No	No	No	No	No

Membership and Participation in the Multistate Tax Commission (Part 2)

Adoption of Model Apportionment Regulations

Legend:
NA Not applicable
NR Not reported

	Has Your State Adopted the Following MTC Model Apportionment Regulations? (Year MTC Adopted)							
State	*General Apportionment (1973)*	*Construction Contractors (1980)*	*Railroads (1981)*	*Airlines (1983)*	*Trucking Companies (1986)*	*TV and Radio Broadcasting (1990)*	*Publishing (1993)*	*Financial Institutions (1994)*
Utah	Yes	Yes	Yes	No	Yes	No	Yes	Yes
Vermont	No	No	No	No	No	No	No	No
Virginia	No	No	No	No	No	No	No	No
Washington	Washington does not impose a corporate income tax							
West Virginia	To some extent							
Wisconsin	No	No	No	No	No	No	No	No
Wyoming	Wyoming does not impose a corporate income tax							

Membership and Participation in the Multistate Tax Commission (Part 3)

Adoption of Model Apportionment Statutes

Legend:
NA Not applicable
NR No reply

State	*Has Your State Adopted the Following MTC Model Statutes? (Year MTC Adopted)*					
	BAT Factor Presence Nexus Standard (2002)	*Intangible and Interest Expense Add-Back (2006)*	*Combined Reporting (2006)*	*Compilation of State Tax Return Data (2006)*	*Disclosure of Reportable Transactions (2006)*	*Tax Avoidance Transaction Voluntary Compliance (2006)*
Alabama	No	Partly	No	No	No	Yes
Alaska	No	No	Yes	No	No	No
Arizona	No	No	No	No	No	No
Arkansas	No	No	No	No	No	No
California	No	No, not applicable to state	No, see CCR, tit. 18, § 25106.5-0 through -11	No, see CCR, tit. 18, § 25106.5-0 through -11	No, see RTC § 18407	No
Colorado	Partly	No	No	No	Partly	No
Connecticut	No	No	No	No	No	No
Delaware	No	No	No	No	No	No
District of Columbia		Yes	No		Yes	Yes
Florida	No	No	No	No	No	No
Georgia	No	No	No	No	No	No
Hawaii	No	No	No	No	No	No
Idaho	No	No	No	No	No	No
Illinois	No	No	No	No	No	No
Indiana	No	To some extent	No	No	No	No
Iowa	No	No	No	No	No	No

Membership and Participation in the Multistate Tax Commission (Part 3)

Adoption of Model Apportionment Statutes

Legend:
NA Not applicable
NR No reply

State	*Has Your State Adopted the Following MTC Model Statutes? (Year MTC Adopted)*					
	BAT Factor Presence Nexus Standard (2002)	*Intangible and Interest Expense Add-Back (2006)*	*Combined Reporting (2006)*	*Compilation of State Tax Return Data (2006)*	*Disclosure of Reportable Transactions (2006)*	*Tax Avoidance Transaction Voluntary Compliance (2006)*
Kansas	No	No	Yes	No	No	No
Kentucky	To some extent	To some extent	To some extent	To some extent	To some extent	To some extent
Louisiana	No	No	No	No	No	No
Maine	No	No	To some extent	No	No	To some extent
Maryland	No	No	No	No	No	No
Massachusetts	No	Yes	No	No	No	No
Michigan (Business Tax)	No	No	No	No	No	No
Note. The CIT takes effect 01/01/12, and replaces the Michigan Business Tax (MBT) for most taxpayers. However, businesses that have been approved to receive, have received, or have been assigned certain certified credits may elect to file a return and pay the tax imposed by the MBT in lieu of the CIT until the certified credits are exhausted or extinguished.						
Minnesota	No	No	No	No	No	No
Mississippi	No	To some extent	No	No	No	No
Missouri	No	No	No	No	No	No
Montana	No	No	No	No	No	No
Nebraska						
Nevada	Nevada does not impose a corporate income tax					
New Hampshire	No	No	No	No	No	No
New Jersey	No	No	No	No	No	Yes

Membership and Participation in the Multistate Tax Commission (Part 3)
Adoption of Model Apportionment Statutes

Legend:
NA — Not applicable
NR — No reply

State	BAT Factor Presence Nexus Standard (2002)	Intangible and Interest Expense Add-Back (2006)	Combined Reporting (2006)	Compilation of State Tax Return Data (2006)	Disclosure of Reportable Transactions (2006)	Tax Avoidance Transaction Voluntary Compliance (2006)
	Has Your State Adopted the Following MTC Model Statutes? (Year MTC Adopted)					
New Mexico	No	No	No	No	No	No
New York	To some extent	To some extent	To some extent	To some extent	To some extent	To some extent
North Carolina	No	No	No	No	No	To some extent
North Dakota	No	No	No	No	No	
Ohio	Ohio does not impose a corporate income tax					
Note. Effective 1/1/2010, the Ohio Franchise Tax was fully phased out and business will be taxed on gross receipts through the Commercial Activity Tax. Details about that tax can be found at: http://tax.ohio.gov/divisions/commercial_activities/cat_general_information.stm						
Oklahoma	No	To some extent	No	No	No	No
Oregon						
Pennsylvania	No	No	No	No	No	No
Rhode Island	No	No	No	No	No	No
South Carolina	No	No	No	No	No	No
South Dakota	South Dakota does not impose a corporate income tax					
Tennessee	No	No	No	No	No	No
Texas	No	No	No	No	No	No
Utah	No	No	No	No	No	No
Vermont	No	No	No	No	No	No
Virginia	No	No	No	No	No	No

Membership and Participation in the Multistate Tax Commission (Part 3)
Adoption of Model Apportionment Statutes

Legend:
NA Not applicable
NR No reply

State	*Has Your State Adopted the Following MTC Model Statutes? (Year MTC Adopted)*					
	BAT Factor Presence Nexus Standard (2002)	*Intangible and Interest Expense Add-Back (2006)*	*Combined Reporting (2006)*	*Compilation of State Tax Return Data (2006)*	*Disclosure of Reportable Transactions (2006)*	*Tax Avoidance Transaction Voluntary Compliance (2006)*
Washington	Washington does not impose a corporate income tax					
West Virginia	No	No	Yes	No	Yes	Yes
Wisconsin	No	No	To some extent	No	To some extent	To some extent
Wyoming	Wyoming does not impose a corporate income tax					

Partial Payments of Income Tax Assessments

Assessments

When a taxing jurisdiction determines that a taxpayer has not filed a complete and accurate return on or before the due date, or did not remit the requisite tax, the jurisdiction has the authority to assess the taxpayer for the tax due. Such assessments usually include interest on the unpaid amount of tax, and may also include penalties. Generally speaking, an assessment will be issued if a taxpayer fails to timely file a prescribed return, files an inaccurate return, fails to remit the full amount of tax due with the return, files a return with a material omission or misstatement, or files a fraudulent return.

Assessment methods and procedures vary by state, but generally upon discovery of a tax delinquency a state will issue a "tentative" or "proposed" assessment to the taxpayer in the form of a deficiency notice. This proposed assessment usually serves as notice to the taxpayer that the tax commissioner or director has discovered a tax deficiency and has computed adjustments giving rise to the proposed assessment for the tax period at issue. Administrative procedures provide taxpayers that have been served with notice of a tax deficiency a specified period of time in which to respond to the state. Generally, during this period, which usually ranges from 30 to 60 days, the taxpayer may pay the assessment, petition for administrative relief, or file suit in the court of claims for the jurisdiction at issue.

If the taxpayer petitions for administrative relief or protests the assessment, the taxpayer is normally required to remit the portion of the assessment that is not contested. Some states require payment of all or a portion of the assessment, depending on the component of the assessment being protested, at the time the petition for reassessment is submitted in order for the taxpayer to contest the proposed assessment. In most states, the petition is considered in an informal administrative hearing. Some states have information and reconsideration hearings at both the audit level and the appeals level. Other states have specific tax administrative hearing courts. These courts have the power and duty to review final determinations by the state's department of revenue of any assessments, reassessments, determinations, findings, or orders. Special administrative hearing courts may or may not require the taxpayer to be represented by an attorney.

If the taxpayer fails to respond to the notice within the time required, the administering agency will issue the assessment as a final determination, and the taxpayer is usually deemed to have waived the right to protest the assessment. In many states, the taxpayer's only remedy at this point is to pay the assessment, including all penalties and interest, and then file a claim for refund or file suit in the appropriate court of claims.

Tax may be paid under protest, although many states may treat payment of the assessment made prior to, or at the time of filing of, the protest as a claim for refund. Some states require that all liabilities resulting from an assessment—including penalties and interest—be paid prior to protesting such assessment.

Interest

The rate of interest charged to taxpayers for underpayment of tax is usually set by statute and is often the same as the rate paid to taxpayers in refunds. The rate varies by state, and may also vary by type of tax. The interest rate often fluctuates between years and may be a function of the rate in effect under IRC Section 6621, may be tied to another index, or may be specified by statute. For example, some states base interest on the prime rate in effect at the beginning of the tax year.

In the case of tax delinquencies, interest usually accrues from the initial due date of the tax or return until the date of payment or receipt by the jurisdiction. Most states impose interest on both the tax due and any penalties that are imposed, although some states impose interest on only the outstanding tax due. Interest is usually simple interest, calculated on a daily or monthly basis, but a few states impose compound interest.

States take different positions with respect to the ability of a taxpayer to protest and/or have interest abated. For example, Massachusetts does not permit abatement of assessed or accrued interest on unpaid taxes or penalties unless the underlying tax or penalty on which the interest is computed is also abated. [Mass. Regs. Code tit. 830, § 62C.33.1(4)(c), (6)(c)] Missouri permits corporations to protest interest, as long as a protest is filed within 30 days from the date the notice of assessment was mailed. [Mo. Code Regs. Ann. tit. 15, § 30-150.210] In Colorado, the executive director is given statutory authority to waive any penalty or interest. [Colo. Rev. Stat. § 39-21-112(8)]

Penalties

Penalties may be assessed either at a flat amount for each instance of noncompliance, or as a percentage of the tax outstanding. Some penalties are imposed on a monthly or daily basis during the period of noncompliance. Most states assess penalties for late filing or nonfiling of returns, late payment, failure to file correct information returns, failure to remit tax due, negligence, willful neglect, and fraud. The amounts and rates of penalties will often vary depending on the reason for noncompliance and the egregiousness of the infraction.

Some states may also assess penalties and interest on erroneous tax refunds. For example, if a Massachusetts taxpayer accepts a refund as a result of an error made by the Department of Revenue, the taxpayer has 30 days to return the refund. If the refund is not returned within 30 days, then the amount demanded may be collected like a tax which may result in the imposition of interest and penalties. [Tech. Info. Release No. 06-011, (Mass. Dept. of Rev., July 2006)]

Many states provide a waiver of penalties if the taxpayer shows that a failure to file a return or pay tax at the required time was due to reasonable cause. The definition of reasonable cause may vary by state and often revolves around the application of the statutory criteria demonstrating reasonable cause to the facts at hand.

For example, Kentucky defines reasonable cause to include the destruction or unavailability of the taxpayer's records by a catastrophic event, death or serious illness of the taxpayer or tax return preparer, erroneous advice from the Department of Revenue, inability to obtain records in the custody of a third party, undue hardship, human error, erroneous advice by a tax adviser, reliance on substantial legal authority, and tax modernization. [Ky. Emergency Reg. 103 KAR 1:040E, adopted Feb. 6, 2006].

Most states consider whether the taxpayer made a good faith effort to determine the proper tax liability and to file and pay the liability in a timely fashion. A good faith effort is usually demonstrated when the taxpayer exercised ordinary business care and prudence. The taxpayer's filing history is also considered when making a good faith determination. Isolated computational or transcriptional errors may not indicate a lack of good faith.

In *Strathmore Finance Company, Inc. v. Dept. of Treasury* [No. 311682 (Mich. Tax Trib. May 10, 2006)], the Michigan Tax Tribunal upheld a penalty assessment because the taxpayer did not prove that the failure to timely file or pay a tax was due to reasonable cause and not to willful neglect. For this purpose, willful neglect means something more than negligence but less than fraud. The taxpayer had received a penalty waiver for earlier tax years, but did not correct the decade-long problem of high turnover in the accounting department and changes in outside CPA firms. The Tribunal concluded that the taxpayer did not exercise ordinary business care and prudence, and failed to mitigate the risk of future penalties.

Some states provide other standards by which penalties may be abated. Missouri permits abatement on a showing that the failure to make a timely payment was devoid of any intent to evade the tax, including when a taxpayer is in its first year of doing business in the state. [Mo. Code Regs. Ann. tit. 15, § 30-150.200(2)(D)] In Florida, reasonable cause may exist even though the circumstances indicate that slight negligence resulted in noncompliance. [Fla. Admin. Code Ann. r. 12-13.007(2)]

In limited circumstances, a taxpayer's reliance on a paid advisor or paid preparer may constitute reasonable cause when the taxpayer relied in good faith on written advice of an advisor and the advisor acted with full knowledge of all of the essential facts. Informal advice, advice based on insufficient facts, advice received when facts were deliberately concealed, or obviously erroneous advice is not grounds for a finding of reasonable cause. States that include provisions for waiver of penalties for reliance on a paid advisor or preparer generally provide explicit guidelines for when such reliance will constitute reasonable cause.

In *Tiger Steak, Inc. v. Dept. of Revenue* [No. INC. 05-722 (Ala. Dept. of Rev., Admin. Law Div. Dec. 28, 2005)], an Alabama S corporation's penalty for the late filing of a composite return for nonresident shareholders was waived for reasonable cause because the S corporation relied on the advice of a competent tax adviser that the due date to file the return had been extended. The tax adviser had timely filed an extension request for the S corporation's return, but mistakenly believed that this extension would also extend the filing deadline for the nonresident shareholders' composite return.

In *Hollinger International, Inc. v. Bower* [No. 1-04-0392 (Ill. App. Ct., Dec. 12, 2005)], the Illinois Appellate Court ruled that the taxpayer's reliance on its outside CPA firm, which incorrectly computed the taxpayer's estimated tax payments, was insufficient reasonable cause to waive an underpayment penalty. The court determined that the taxpayer did not exercise ordinary business care and prudence in relying on its accountant, even though it had done so for many years without ever having made an underpayment of estimated taxes.

Although most states will permit a taxpayer to protest assessed penalties, payment of all or part of the assessment may be required prior to consideration of penalty relief.

Application of Partial Payments

Most states have a statutory ordering for the application of partial payments. Statutory ordering is fairly evenly split between application first to penalties, then to interest, and finally to tax; and application first to tax, then to penalties, and finally to interest.

Many states allow taxpayers to specify how a partial payment is to be applied, although the ability to direct payment may depend on whether payment is voluntary. As a general rule, a taxpayer may not direct involuntary payments. In most instances, prior payments generally may not be applied to penalties or interest assessed after the date of those payments.

When available, the taxpayer's ability to direct the ordering of the application of assessment payments is an important consideration. Interest may be a substantial component of the overall assessment. Accordingly, the ordering of the application of payments among the components of tax, interest, and penalty may have the effect of increasing the interest amount initially assessed. In states that impose interest on outstanding tax and penalties, the application of payments is very important to the amount of interest that a taxpayer ultimately pays on the assessment of underpaid tax. When payment is applied first to tax, then to penalties, and finally to interest, paying down interest-bearing tax and penalty amounts first prevents the further accrual of interest, whereas assessments in states that apply payments to penalties or interest first result in further accrual of interest amounts on the unpaid portion of the assessed tax.

State-by-State Summary

The chart that follows indicates the order in which the states apply a partial payment to assessed tax, interest, and penalties; whether taxpayers may direct the application of partial payments to those components; and whether the application of partial payments is negotiable.

Legend:
X — The payment can be applied in this manner
NA — Not applicable
NR — Not reported

Partial Payments of Income Tax Assessments

	How Is That Payment Applied?				
	Tax First, Then Penalty, Then Interest	*Penalty First, Then Interest, Then Tax*	*Some Other Ordering Required*	*As Indicated by Taxpayer*	*Subject to Negotiation Between the Parties*
Alabama			Interest, tax, penalty		
Alaska	X			X	
Arizona	X			X	
Arkansas			Tax, interest, penalty		
California	X			X	
Colorado		X			
Connecticut		X			
Delaware	X				
District of Columbia		X			
Florida			If not indicated by taxpayer; interest, penalty, tax		
Georgia			Tax, interest, penalty	X	
Hawaii			Interest, penalty, tax		
Idaho			Returned check charges, interest, tax, penalty		
Illinois					
Indiana		X			
Iowa		X			

Legend:

X	The payment can be applied in this manner
NA	Not applicable
NR	Not reported

Partial Payments of Income Tax Assessments

	How Is That Payment Applied?				
	Tax First, Then Penalty, Then Interest	*Penalty First, Then Interest, Then Tax*	*Some Other Ordering Required*	*As Indicated by Taxpayer*	*Subject to Negotiation Between the Parties*
Kansas			Tax, interest, penalty		
Kentucky	X			X	
Louisiana			Tax, penalty, interest		
Maine	X				
Maryland		X			
Massachusetts	X			X	
Michigan (Business Tax)			Interest, penalty, tax	X	
Note. The CIT takes effect 01/01/12, and replaces the Michigan Business Tax (MBT) for most taxpayers. However, businesses that have been approved to receive, have received, or have been assigned certain certified credits may elect to file a return and pay the tax imposed by the MBT in lieu of the CIT until the certified credits are exhausted or extinguished.					
Minnesota		X			
Mississippi		X			
Missouri		X			
Montana	X				
Nebraska	X			X	
Nevada	Nevada does not impose a corporate income tax				
New Hampshire		X			
New Jersey	X				
New Mexico	X				

Partial Payments of Income Tax Assessments

Legend:
X — The payment can be applied in this manner
NA — Not applicable
NR — Not reported

	How Is That Payment Applied?				
	Tax First, Then Penalty, Then Interest	*Penalty First, Then Interest, Then Tax*	*Some Other Ordering Required*	*As Indicated by Taxpayer*	*Subject to Negotiation Between the Parties*
New York	X			X	X
North Carolina		X			
North Dakota	X				
Ohio	Ohio does not impose a corporate income tax				
Note. Effective 1/1/2010, the Ohio Franchise Tax was fully phased out and business will be taxed on gross receipts through the Commercial Activity Tax. Details about that tax can be found at: http://tax.ohio.gov/divisions/commercial_activities/cat_general_information.stm					
Oklahoma	X				
Oregon		X			
Pennsylvania	X			X	
Rhode Island			Tax, interest, penalty		
South Carolina	X				
South Dakota	South Dakota does not impose a corporate income tax				
Tennessee	X				
Texas	X				
Utah		X			
Vermont		X			
Virginia	X				
Washington	Washington does not impose a corporate income tax				

Partial Payments of Income Tax Assessments

Legend:

X	The payment can be applied in this manner
NA	Not applicable
NR	Not reported

	How Is That Payment Applied?				
	Tax First, Then Penalty, Then Interest	*Penalty First, Then Interest, Then Tax*	*Some Other Ordering Required*	*As Indicated by Taxpayer*	*Subject to Negotiation Between the Parties*
West Virginia			Tax, interest, penalty		
Wisconsin		X			
Wyoming	Wyoming does not impose a corporate income tax				

Notification Procedure to Represent Corporate Clients

Federal Tax Treatment

Corporations often require assistance when dealing with the IRS. A taxpayer can grant a "qualified representative" permission or authority to represent it and perform any or all acts the taxpayer would perform. Because such acts constitute practice before the IRS, they can be performed only by a qualified person and only when evidence of authorization to perform the acts has been furnished to the IRS. Accordingly, representatives must have evidence of recognition and authorization from the corporations they are representing to assure the IRS that it is not disclosing confidential information to unauthorized persons.

To designate a qualified representative for federal tax purposes, corporations and other taxpayers must complete and file Form 2848, Power of Attorney and Declaration of Representative. The execution of this form gives the designated representative the authority to do the following:

1. Receive and inspect confidential tax information;
2. Receive (but not endorse or collect) refund checks;
3. Execute a waiver of the restrictions on assessment or collection of a deficiency in tax or execute a waiver or notice of disallowance of a claim for credit or refund;
4. Execute a consent to extend the statute of limitations for assessment or collection; and
5. Execute a closing agreement.

The taxpayer can deny the representative any of those powers by providing an exclusionary statement on Form 2848.

For the power of attorney to be considered valid, the corporation must indicate that it pertains only to specific types of taxes and to specified tax years. A general reference to types of taxes and tax years is unacceptable.

If the taxpayer wants to limit the activity of its representative solely to the inspection and receipt of confidential tax information, the taxpayer should file Form 8821, Tax Information Authorization. That form authorizes *any* designated person to receive or inspect tax information of a confidential nature.

For corporations, Form 2848 or Form 8821 is not required in the following situations:

1. The representative attends a conference with the IRS and the taxpayer is present; or
2. The representative serves only as a witness for the taxpayer.

State Tax Treatment

Most states follow the federal guidelines regarding authorized representation, requiring execution of a power of attorney form or a written authorization to represent the corporate taxpayer. Although power of attorney forms vary from state to state, they are generally similar to federal Form 2848. The list of powers granted to the representative may be amended by the taxpayer; accordingly, additional powers may be granted or listed powers may be struck. Although some states have developed their own power of attorney forms, a number of states require a corporate taxpayer to complete federal Form 2848 authorizing a representative to act on its behalf.

Some states grant tax return preparers limited authority of representation without requiring the filing of a power of attorney or other special authorization form. Typically, as part of the tax return, those states incorporate authorization for the state's tax authority to discuss directly with the return preparer items contained on the return. When questions relating to the return arise, such limited authority provides administrative ease for the taxpayer, the state's tax authority, and the tax return preparer.

State-by-State Summary

The following chart summarizes each state's requirements for appointing representatives in audit and nonaudit situations.

Notification Procedure to Represent Corporate Clients

Legend:

X	These procedures must be followed when representing corporate clients
SAF	Same as applicable federal rules
NA	Not applicable
NR	Not reported

	Must Notify State That a Person Will Represent Corporate Clients in:		*Applicable State Form*	
	Audit Situations	*Nonaudit Situations*	*Name*	*Number*
Alabama	X	X	Power of attorney	2848A
Alaska	X	X	Power of attorney	04-775
Arizona	X	X	NR	Audit Situations 285A; Nonaudit Situations 285
Arkansas	X	X	Power of attorney; for nonaudit situations may also check box on return	AR 1100CT or AR 1100CTX
California	X	X	Power of attorney	FTB 3520
Colorado	X	X	Power of attorney	DR 0145
Connecticut	X	X	Power of attorney	LGL-001
Delaware			NA	NA
District of Columbia	X	X	Federal form	DC POA
Florida	X	X	Power of attorney	DR-835
Georgia	X	X	Power of attorney is required unless officer or employee.	RD-1061
Hawaii	X	X	Power of attorney	N-848
Idaho	X	X	Power of attorney	
Illinois	X	X	Power of attorney	IL-2848
Indiana	X	X	Power of attorney	POA1
Iowa	X	X	Power of attorney	IA 2848

Notification Procedure to Represent Corporate Clients

Legend:

X	These procedures must be followed when representing corporate clients
SAF	Same as applicable federal rules
NA	Not applicable
NR	Not reported

	Must Notify State That a Person Will Represent Corporate Clients in:		*Applicable State Form*	
	Audit Situations	*Nonaudit Situations*	*Name*	*Number*
Kansas	X	X	Power of attorney	DO-10
Kentucky	X	X	Power of attorney or letter of authorization	NA
Louisiana	X	X	Power of attorney	R-7006
Maine		X	Power of attorney	2848-ME
Maryland	X	X	NA	NA
Massachusetts	X	X	Power of attorney	Form M-2848
Michigan (Business Tax)	X	X	Power of attorney	Form 151
Note. The CIT takes effect 01/01/12, and replaces the Michigan Business Tax (MBT) for most taxpayers. However, businesses that have been approved to receive, have received, or have been assigned certain certified credits may elect to file a return and pay the tax imposed by the MBT in lieu of the CIT until the certified credits are exhausted or extinguished.				
Minnesota	X	X	Power of attorney	REV-184
Mississippi	X	X	Power of attorney	NR
Missouri	X	X	Power of attorney	MO-2827
Montana	Yes	Yes	Power of Attorney	NR
Nebraska	X	X	Power of attorney	Form 33
Nevada	Nevada does not impose a corporate income tax			
New Hampshire	X	X	Power of attorney	DP 2848

Notification Procedure to Represent Corporate Clients

Legend:

X	These procedures must be followed when representing corporate clients
SAF	Same as applicable federal rules
NA	Not applicable
NR	Not reported

	Must Notify State That a Person Will Represent Corporate Clients in:		*Applicable State Form*	
	Audit Situations	*Nonaudit Situations*	*Name*	*Number*
New Jersey	X	X	Appointment of Taxpayer Representative	M-5008-R
New Mexico	X	X	Power of attorney or NM DI-6	Power of attorney or NM DI-6
New York	X	X	Power of attorney	POA1
North Carolina	X	X	Power of attorney	Power of attorney
North Dakota	X	X	Authorization to Disclose Tax Information and Designation of Representative	Form 500
Ohio	Ohio does not impose a corporate income tax			
Note. Effective 1/1/2010, the Ohio Franchise Tax was fully phased out and business will be taxed on gross receipts through the Commercial Activity Tax. Details about that tax can be found at: http://tax.ohio.gov/divisions/commercial_activities/cat_general_information.stm				
Oklahoma	X	X	Power of attorney	NA
Oregon	X	X	Power of attorney and declaration of representative	150-800-005
Pennsylvania	No	No	NA	NA
Rhode Island	X	X	NR	RI 2F48
South Carolina	X	X	Power of attorney	SC2848
South Dakota	South Dakota does not impose a corporate income tax			
Tennessee	Yes	Yes	Power of attorney	RV-F0103801 or FAE 170/174
Texas	X	If claim for refund	Power of attorney	01-137 for refunds

Notification Procedure to Represent Corporate Clients

Legend:

X	These procedures must be followed when representing corporate clients
SAF	Same as applicable federal rules
NA	Not applicable
NR	Not reported

	Must Notify State That a Person Will Represent Corporate Clients in:		*Applicable State Form*	
	Audit Situations	*Nonaudit Situations*	*Name*	*Number*
Utah	X	X	Power of attorney	2848
Vermont	No, if officer	No, if officer	NA	NA
Virginia	X, if person other than an officer is authorized to sign returns	X	X, notification is not required to represent a taxpayer, but is required if an agent desires copies of future correspondence.	Par 101
Washington	Washington does not impose a corporate income tax			
West Virginia	X	X	NR	WV-2848 and WV ARI-001
Wisconsin	X	X	Power of attorney	A-222
Wyoming	Wyoming does not impose a corporate income tax			

Use of Private Contractors

In General

In an effort to enhance tax compliance in the face of limited state resources, some states have entered into contracts with independent third parties to identify nonfilers and/or to assist in performing audits. In many situations, those third parties are compensated based on a percentage of the taxes collected from the newly identified taxpayers. Many states use private contract auditors for unclaimed property and property tax audits.

As to whether the use of private contract auditors is good public policy, the decisions of the highest-level state courts that have addressed the issue are split. In *Sears, Roebuck & Co. v. Parsons* [260 Ga. 824, 401 S.E.2d 4 (1991)], the Georgia Supreme Court held that a contract authorizing a private company to conduct personal property tax audits on behalf of a county where the audit firm would be compensated on a contingent fee basis "offend[ed] public policy" and was void. In contrast, in *Philip Morris U.S.A. v. Cabarrus County Board of Equalization* [335 N.C. 227, 436 S.E.2d 828 (1993)], the North Carolina Supreme Court held that a personal property audit contract between a county and a private firm in which the private firm was compensated on a contingent fee basis did not violate North Carolina public policy. In *Lonky v. Municipal Tax Collection Bureau* [N.J. Super. Ct. App. Div. Oct. 16, 1998], the Superior Court of New Jersey, Appellate Division, upheld the Division of Taxation's contingent fee contract with a commercial tax collector. The court was convinced that statutory authority exists for what the Municipal Tax Collection Bureau does and found that the statute does not prohibit contingent fee arrangements with private tax collecting agents hired by the Division of Taxation.

State-by-State Summary

The following chart, presented in two parts, identifies the states that employ private contractors to assist in the administration of tax laws. For the states that contract with private companies, the chart indicates how such entities are compensated and in what activities the entities can be engaged (e.g., nexus reviews, audits, collection of tax).

Use of Private Contractors (Part 1)

Legend:
NA Not applicable
NR No reply
X Applicable fee arrangement

	Does State Employ Private Contractors to Assist in Administration of Tax Law?	*If Yes, How Are These Contractors Compensated?* Hourly Fee	Fixed Fee	Contingent Fee	Other
Alabama	No				
Alaska	No				
Arizona	No				
Arkansas	No				
California	Yes		X	X	
Colorado	Yes		X		
Connecticut	Yes				
Delaware	Yes	X			
District of Columbia	Yes				Sliding scale
Florida	Yes				Negotiated contract
Georgia	Yes	X	X	X	
Hawaii	Yes	X	X		
Idaho	No				
Illinois	Yes			X	
Indiana	Yes			X	
Iowa	Yes			X	
Kansas	Yes			X	
Kentucky	Yes			X	

Use of Private Contractors (Part 1)

Legend:
NA Not applicable
NR No reply
X Applicable fee arrangement

	Does State Employ Private Contractors to Assist in Administration of Tax Law?	*If Yes, How Are These Contractors Compensated?* Hourly Fee	Fixed Fee	Contingent Fee	Other
Louisiana	Yes			X	
Maine	Yes	X			
Maryland	No				
Massachusetts	Yes, collection agencies only				Depends on contract
Michigan (Business Tax)	Yes			X	
Note. The CIT takes effect 01/01/12, and replaces the Michigan Business Tax (MBT) for most taxpayers. However, businesses that have been approved to receive, have received, or have been assigned certain certified credits may elect to file a return and pay the tax imposed by the MBT in lieu of the CIT until the certified credits are exhausted or extinguished.					
Minnesota	Yes			X	
Mississippi	Yes			X	
Missouri	Yes			X	
Montana	No				
Nebraska	Yes			X	
Nevada	No				
New Hampshire	NR				
New Jersey	Yes	X	X	X	
New Mexico	Yes			X	

Use of Private Contractors (Part 1)

Legend:
NA Not applicable
NR No reply
X Applicable fee arrangement

	Does State Employ Private Contractors to Assist in Administration of Tax Law?	*If Yes, How Are These Contractors Compensated?* Hourly Fee	Fixed Fee	Contingent Fee	Other
New York	No				
North Carolina	Yes			X	
North Dakota	No				
Ohio	Ohio does not impose a corporate income tax				
Note. Effective 1/1/2010, the Ohio Franchise Tax was fully phased out and business will be taxed on gross receipts through the Commercial Activity Tax. Details about that tax can be found at: http://tax.ohio.gov/divisions/commercial_activities/cat_general_information.stm					
Oklahoma	Yes		X		
Oregon	Yes	X, for auditors		X, for collection agencies 15% to over 30% for out-of-state accounts	
Pennsylvania	Yes			X	
Rhode Island	No				
South Carolina	Yes			X	
South Dakota	South Dakota does not impose a corporate income tax				
Tennessee	No				
Texas	Yes		X		
Utah	Yes			X	
Vermont	No				
Virginia	Yes				

Use of Private Contractors (Part 1)

Legend:
NA Not applicable
NR No reply
X Applicable fee arrangement

	Does State Employ Private Contractors to Assist in Administration of Tax Law?	*If Yes, How Are These Contractors Compensated?* Hourly Fee	Fixed Fee	Contingent Fee	Other
Washington	Washington does not impose a corporate income tax				
West Virginia	Yes		X	X	
Wisconsin	Yes		X		
Wyoming	Wyoming does not impose a corporate income tax				

Use of Private Contractors (Part 2)

Legend:
NA Not applicable
NR No reply
X Condition applies

	In What Activities Do Private Contractors Engage?				
	Nexus Reviews	*Assessment of Tax Via Audit*	*Collection of Outstanding Delinquent Tax Receivable*	*Other*	*If Hired Under a Contingent Fee Arrangement, What Range of Fee Is Authorized?*
Alabama	NA	NA	NA	NA	NA
Alaska	NA	NA	NA	NA	NA
Arizona	NA	NA	NA	NA	NA
Arkansas	NA	NA	X, out of state only	NA	NA
California			X		
Colorado			X		NA
Connecticut			X		
Delaware		X	X		NA
District of Columbia	NA	NA	X	NA	NA
Florida		X	X		NA
Georgia			X		NR
Hawaii			X	X, general excise and income tax audits of mainland corporations	NR
Idaho	NA	NA	NA	NA	NA
Illinois			X		From 14% to 25%
Indiana			X		From 10% to 15%
Iowa			X		Varies by contract

Use of Private Contractors (Part 2)

Legend:

NA	Not applicable
NR	No reply
X	Condition applies

	In What Activities Do Private Contractors Engage?				
	Nexus Reviews	*Assessment of Tax Via Audit*	*Collection of Outstanding Delinquent Tax Receivable*	*Other*	*If Hired Under a Contingent Fee Arrangement, What Range of Fee Is Authorized?*
Kansas	NA	NA	X	NA	NA
Kentucky	Yes		X		Negotiated
Louisiana			X		NA
Maine			X		
Maryland	NA	NA	NA	NA	NA
Massachusetts			X		Depends on contract
Michigan (Business Tax)	X	X	X		From 1% to 30%
Note. The CIT takes effect 01/01/12, and replaces the Michigan Business Tax (MBT) for most taxpayers. However, businesses that have been approved to receive, have received, or have been assigned certain certified credits may elect to file a return and pay the tax imposed by the MBT in lieu of the CIT until the certified credits are exhausted or extinguished.					
Minnesota			X		
Mississippi			X		33% over and above the tax due
Missouri			X		
Montana	NA	NA	NA	NA	NA
Nebraska				Collection of outstanding delinquent tax receivable outside Nebraska	Rates vary depending on the agreement with private contractors.
Nevada	NA	NA	NA	NA	NA
New Hampshire	NA	NA	NA	NA	NA

Use of Private Contractors (Part 2)

Legend:
NA — Not applicable
NR — No reply
X — Condition applies

	In What Activities Do Private Contractors Engage?				
	Nexus Reviews	*Assessment of Tax Via Audit*	*Collection of Outstanding Delinquent Tax Receivable*	*Other*	*If Hired Under a Contingent Fee Arrangement, What Range of Fee Is Authorized?*
New Jersey			X, known deficiencies and delinquencies		NA
New Mexico	NA	NA	X	NA	NA
New York	NA	NA	NA	NA	NA
North Carolina			X		Up to 20%
North Dakota	NA	NA	NA	NA	NA
Ohio	Ohio does not impose a corporate income tax				
Note. Effective 1/1/2010, the Ohio Franchise Tax was fully phased out and business will be taxed on gross receipts through the Commercial Activity Tax. Details about that tax can be found at: http://tax.ohio.gov/divisions/commercial_activities/cat_general_information.stm					
Oklahoma	X		X		NA
Oregon		X	X		From 15% to over 30% for out-of-state
Pennsylvania			X		NR
Rhode Island	NA	NA	NA	NA	NA
South Carolina			X		NR
South Dakota	South Dakota does not impose a corporate income tax				
Tennessee	NA	NA	NA	NA	NA
Texas		X	X		NA

Legend:
NA Not applicable
NR No reply
X Condition applies

Use of Private Contractors (Part 2)

	In What Activities Do Private Contractors Engage?				
	Nexus Reviews	*Assessment of Tax Via Audit*	*Collection of Outstanding Delinquent Tax Receivable*	*Other*	*If Hired Under a Contingent Fee Arrangement, What Range of Fee Is Authorized?*
Utah			X		Approximately 11% of amounts collected on assigned cases
Vermont	NA	NA	NA	NA	NA
Virginia	NA	NA	X	NA	NA
Washington	Washington does not impose a corporate income tax				
West Virginia	X		X		NA
Wisconsin	X	X	X		
Wyoming	Wyoming does not impose a corporate income tax				

Voluntary Disclosure

In General

Most states offer taxpayers some type of voluntary disclosure procedure, whereby a taxpayer can voluntarily disclose previously unpaid tax liabilities to state tax authorities. In exchange for bringing these unpaid taxes to a state's attention, the state usually waives the penalties that would otherwise be imposed on the unpaid taxes, and places a limit on the number of prior years for which taxes must be paid. Depending on the state and the facts of the case, interest may or may not be charged on the delinquent tax payments.

The purpose of a voluntary disclosure program is to promote tax compliance and generate additional tax revenues by providing nonfilers with an incentive to voluntarily pay taxes due for prior years. One of the justifications for enacting a voluntary disclosure program is that it allows the state to collect unpaid taxes that would not otherwise be detected through traditional audits. A taxpayer generally is not eligible to enter into a voluntary disclosure agreement if state tax authorities have already identified the taxpayer as an audit target (e.g., through an audit notice or nexus questionnaire).

The essential features of a voluntary disclosure agreement are the period covered by the agreement ("look-back period"), the method of computing taxes due for prior years, and the amount of any interest and penalty charges. In many states, taxpayers have the option of seeking a voluntary disclosure agreement through a third party. This allows the taxpayer to remain anonymous until an agreement can be reached with state tax authorities regarding the amount of taxes, interest, and penalties due. The amount of assessment for prior years' taxes generally is subject to negotiation.

At its website, the Texas Comptroller of Public Accounts describes the policy underlying its voluntary disclosure agreements (dated March 2007), as follows:

> The Texas Comptroller of Public Accounts is committed to promoting taxpayer compliance. In an effort to accomplish this objective, a Voluntary Disclosure Agreement is available to taxpayers who want to comply with our tax laws. Standard written agreements will be made available for all taxes administered by our agency to which we can enter into such agreements.
>
> In our commitment to fairness in the administration of our taxes, we adhere to the following general guidelines:
>
> - Liabilities due to failure to collect taxes and/or file the applicable reports will be limited to reports due four years from the initial taxpayer contact date.
> - All taxes that were actually collected by the seller need to be remitted (i.e., there is no four-year limitation on tax collected not remitted).
> - Statutory penalties will be waived.
> - Interest will be waived on taxes voluntarily disclosed and paid that were not collected.
> - Agreements will be offered to taxpayers who have not been contacted regarding an audit or investigation, either verbally or in writing.

In 2009, the Ohio Department of Taxation announced a voluntary disclosure program for the commercial activity tax (CAT). To be eligible, a taxpayer must enter into a voluntary disclosure agreement prior to any contact from the department through any audit, compliance, or criminal investigation programs. To participate, a taxpayer must submit certain information in writing and then the department will prepare a voluntary disclosure agreement and send it to the taxpayer. The taxpayer must sign and return the agreement, after which the taxpayer must register for the tax and file all applicable returns and pay all corresponding liabilities and interest from the agreed start date through the present date. [CAT Information Release 2008-01, Ohio Department of Taxation, May 2009]

Amnesty Programs

Another method of inducing taxpayers to come forward and pay any outstanding tax liabilities is an amnesty program. Amnesty programs typically waive part or all of the penalties or interest that would otherwise be due on the unpaid taxes if the taxes are paid during the amnesty period. In response to shortfalls in tax revenues caused by the economic recession, numerous states enacted amnesty programs from 2008 to 2011. The Federation of Tax Administrators (FTA) provides a listing of state tax amnesty programs offered since 1982 at its website [www.taxadmin.org, last updated May 5, 2011]. According to the FTA, seven states and the District of Columbia offered amnesty programs in 2010. These programs generally lasted one or three months.

State-by-State Summary

The following chart summarizes which states offer voluntary disclosure programs, the number of years for which unpaid taxes are collected (look-back period), and whether penalties are abated.

Voluntary Disclosure

Legend:
X Condition applies
SAF Same as federal
NR Not reported

	Does State Offer a Voluntary Disclosure Program for Non-Filer Registration?	*If Yes, Which Viewpoint Is Taken Regarding Filing by Taxpayers?*		*If a Look-Back Perspective Is Employed, How Many Years Are Typically Required to Be Filed?*	*Are Penalties Abated When a Taxpayer Comes Forward with Prior Liabilities?*	*If No Voluntary Disclosure Program, Are Penalties Required If Non-Filer Comes Forward?*
		Look-Back?	*Prospective Filing?*			
Alabama	Yes	X		3	Yes	Yes
Alaska	Yes	X		5	Yes	
Arizona	Yes	X	Yes	6	Yes	
Arkansas	Yes	X		3	Yes	
California	Yes	X		6	Yes, only specified penalties are waived under RTC § 19191. Interest and statutory fees may not be waived.	
Colorado	Yes	X		3 years for sales and use tax, 4 years for income tax	Yes	Yes
Connecticut	Yes	Yes		Depends, usually 3 years	Yes	NR
Delaware	No, individual basis					
District of Columbia	Yes	X		3-5	Yes	
Florida	Yes	X		3	Yes	Yes, unless tax was collected but not remitted
Georgia	Yes	X		3	Yes	

Voluntary Disclosure

Legend:
X — Condition applies
SAF — Same as federal
NR — Not reported

	Does State Offer a Voluntary Disclosure Program for Non-Filer Registration?	*If Yes, Which Viewpoint Is Taken Regarding Filing by Taxpayers?*		*If a Look-Back Perspective Is Employed, How Many Years Are Typically Required to Be Filed?*	*Are Penalties Abated When a Taxpayer Comes Forward with Prior Liabilities?*	*If No Voluntary Disclosure Program, Are Penalties Required If Non-Filer Comes Forward?*
		Look-Back?	*Prospective Filing?*			
Hawaii	Yes	X		All open years	Yes	Occasionally
Idaho	Yes	X		Depends upon circumstances	Penalties are set by statute; taxpayer may request a waiver.	Yes
Illinois	Yes, 86 Ill. Admin. Code 210.126	X		4	Yes	No, irrespective of voluntary disclosure, a taxpayer may petition for abatement of penalty or interest in accordance with 86 Ill. Admin. Code 210.126.
Indiana	Yes	X		Varies	Yes	Occasionally
Iowa	Yes	X		3 to 5	Yes	Yes
Kansas	Yes	X		3	Yes	NA
Kentucky	Yes	X		4	Yes	Yes
Louisiana	Yes	X	X, depends on whether nexus has been established for prior periods	All open periods	Yes	Yes
Maine	Yes	X		3 or case by case	Yes	

Legend:

X	Condition applies
SAF	Same as federal
NR	Not reported

Voluntary Disclosure

	Does State Offer a Voluntary Disclosure Program for Non-Filer Registration?	*If Yes, Which Viewpoint Is Taken Regarding Filing by Taxpayers?*		*If a Look-Back Perspective Is Employed, How Many Years Are Typically Required to Be Filed?*	*Are Penalties Abated When a Taxpayer Comes Forward with Prior Liabilities?*	*If No Voluntary Disclosure Program, Are Penalties Required If Non-Filer Comes Forward?*
		Look-Back?	*Prospective Filing?*			
Maryland	Yes	X		3	Yes, code requires assessment of interest and penalties.	Occasionally
Massachusetts No, see TIR 02-13 and 01-8	Yes, TIR 03-17 & 11-1	X			Depends on facts	
Michigan (Business Tax)	Yes	X		4	Yes	Yes
Note. The CIT takes effect 01/01/12, and replaces the Michigan Business Tax (MBT) for most taxpayers. However, businesses that have been approved to receive, have received, or have been assigned certain certified credits may elect to file a return and pay the tax imposed by the MBT in lieu of the CIT until the certified credits are exhausted or extinguished.						
Minnesota	Yes	X		3	Occasionally	
Mississippi	Yes	X		3 to 5	No	Yes, but not interest
Missouri	Yes	X		4	Yes	
Montana	Yes				Yes	
Nebraska	Yes	X		3	Yes	NR
Nevada	Nevada does not impose a corporate income tax					
New Hampshire	Yes	X		3	NR	Occasionally
New Jersey	Yes	X		4	No	Yes

Voluntary Disclosure

Legend:
X — Condition applies
SAF — Same as federal
NR — Not reported

	Does State Offer a Voluntary Disclosure Program for Non-Filer Registration?	*If Yes, Which Viewpoint Is Taken Regarding Filing by Taxpayers?* Look-Back?	*Prospective Filing?*	*If a Look-Back Perspective Is Employed, How Many Years Are Typically Required to Be Filed?*	*Are Penalties Abated When a Taxpayer Comes Forward with Prior Liabilities?*	*If No Voluntary Disclosure Program, Are Penalties Required If Non-Filer Comes Forward?*
New Mexico	No, instead a managed audit program with 7-year look-back and no penalty or interest.					
New York	Yes	X		As far back as necessary to fully disclose a tax liability.	Yes, if they qualify for the voluntary disclosure program	NA
North Carolina	Yes	X		3	NR	Yes
North Dakota	Yes	X		3	Yes	Yes
Ohio	Ohio does not impose a corporate income tax					

Note. Effective 1/1/2010, the Ohio Franchise Tax was fully phased out and business will be taxed on gross receipts through the Commercial Activity Tax. Details about that tax can be found at: http://tax.ohio.gov/divisions/commercial_activities/cat_general_information.stm

Oklahoma	Yes	X, case by case basis X, case by case basis	NR	NR	Occasionally	
Oregon	Yes	X		Varies depending upon circumstances	Yes	Yes
Pennsylvania	Yes	X		5	No	Yes
Rhode Island	Yes	X		Reasonable amount of time	NR	Occasionally

Voluntary Disclosure

Legend:
X Condition applies
SAF Same as federal
NR Not reported

	Does State Offer a Voluntary Disclosure Program for Non-Filer Registration?	*If Yes, Which Viewpoint Is Taken Regarding Filing by Taxpayers?*		*If a Look-Back Perspective Is Employed, How Many Years Are Typically Required to Be Filed?*	*Are Penalties Abated When a Taxpayer Comes Forward with Prior Liabilities?*	*If No Voluntary Disclosure Program, Are Penalties Required If Non-Filer Comes Forward?*
		Look-Back?	*Prospective Filing?*			
South Carolina	No	NA	NA	NA	NA	Yes
South Dakota	South Dakota does not impose a corporate income tax					
Tennessee	Yes	X	X	6	No	Yes
Texas	Yes	X		4	Yes	Yes
Utah	Yes	X		3	No	Yes
Vermont	Yes	X		3	No	Penalties are not required.
Virginia	Yes	X		3	Yes	Occasionally
Washington	Washington does not impose a corporate income tax					
West Virginia	Yes	X		3	Yes	Yes
Wisconsin	Yes, the Wisconsin Tax Shelters Voluntary Compliance Program under Wis. Stat. § 71.805 ran from 1/1/08 to 5/31/08	X		4	Occasionally	Yes
Wyoming	Wyoming does not impose a corporate income tax					

Offers in Compromise

An offer in compromise is an agreement between a taxpayer and the IRS that resolves the taxpayer's tax liability. [IRC § 7122; Treas. Reg. § 301.7122-1] It is a type of settlement, usually made at the collection stage, whereby the IRS agrees to accept less than full payment of the tax assessed. The IRS is empowered to settle, or compromise, for one of the following reasons:

1. Doubt as to liability—there is doubt as to whether the assessed tax is correct.
2. Doubt as to collectibility—there is doubt that the taxpayer could ever pay the full amount of tax, penalty, and interest assessed.
3. Promotion of effective tax administration—there is no doubt that the assessed tax is correct and no doubt that the amount owed could be collected, but there is some type of exceptional circumstance; specifically, the collection of the tax would create an economic hardship or be unfair or inequitable.

An offer in compromise generally is used for taxpayers experiencing financial difficulties. From the taxpayer's perspective, the benefits of a compromise are that it closes the taxpayer's entire liability, including taxes, interest, and penalties, for the tax years covered by the agreement. It also often allows a taxpayer to pay the IRS less in taxes than would otherwise be due. The IRS's reasons for accepting an offer in compromise include a desire to 1) resolve accounts receivable that cannot be collected in full or on which there is a legitimate dispute as to what is owed, 2) collect what could reasonably be collected at the earliest time possible and at the least cost to the government, 3) give taxpayers a fresh start to enable them to comply with the tax laws voluntarily, and 4) collect funds that may not be collectible through any other means. [Internal Revenue Manual ch. 5.8.1]

A taxpayer generally is eligible to request an offer in compromise if, in the taxpayer's judgment, it either does not owe an assessed tax (doubt as to liability) or cannot pay the tax liability in full (doubt as to collectibility), or there is an exceptional circumstance that the taxpayer would like the IRS to consider (promotion of effective tax administration). A taxpayer is not eligible for consideration of an offer in compromise on the basis of doubt as to collectibility or an exceptional circumstance if the taxpayer has not filed all of the required federal tax returns or is involved in an open bankruptcy proceeding. In addition, a taxpayer that wants to submit an offer based on either doubt as to collectibility or an exceptional circumstance must provide the IRS with information regarding its current financial situation. [Internal Revenue Manual ch. 5.8.3]

There are three payment plans that the taxpayer and the IRS may agree to: 1) cash paid within 90 days or less, 2) a short-term deferred payment of more than 90 days and up to 24 months, and 3) deferred payment terms over the remaining statutory period for collecting the tax.

As part of the Tax Increase Prevention and Reconciliation Act of 2005 [P.L. 109-222], Congress amended Section 7122 to require taxpayers to make nonrefundable partial payments with any offer in compromise submitted after July 15, 2006. This requirement reflects Congressional concerns that some taxpayers were abusing the offer in compromise process by concealing information and making frivolous offers, and that the IRS's lengthy review process may lead to a substantial delay in the government's collection of the compromised liability.

Federal Form 656, Offer in Compromise, is the official compromise agreement, and the instructions provide a detailed description of the settlement procedure.

State-by-State Summary

The following chart, presented in three parts, indicates whether a state department of revenue is authorized to accept offers in compromise, the form used to start the offer in compromise process, the types of taxes for which an offer in compromise can be made, and the conditions under which an offer in compromise can be made.

Offers in Compromise (Part 1)

Legend:
NA Not applicable
NR Not reported

	Is the Department of Revenue/Taxation Authorized to Accept Offers in Compromise?	*Is There a Special Form That Must Be Filed to Start the Offer in Compromise Process?*	*If the Department of Revenue/Taxation Is Not Authorized to Accept Offers in Compromise, Is There Another Way to Obtain an Offer in Compromise?*
Alabama	No	NA	NR
Alaska	Yes	No	NA
Arizona	Yes	No	NA
Arkansas	Yes	Yes, Form REG 2000-4	NA
California	Yes	Yes, Form 4905	NA
Colorado	Yes	No	NA
Connecticut	Yes	No	
Delaware	Yes	No	NA
District of Columbia	Yes	Yes	NA
Florida	Yes	No	NA
Georgia	Yes	Yes, Form OIC-1	NA
Hawaii	Yes	Yes, Form CM-1	NA
Idaho	Yes	No	NA
Illinois	No. Ill. Admin. Code tit. 86, § 210.126.	NA	Yes. See Ill. Comp. Stat. 2505/39b20.1.
Indiana	Yes	No	NA
Iowa	Yes	No	NA
Kansas	Yes	Yes, written petition	NA
Kentucky	Yes	Yes, Form 12AO18-KY	NA
Louisiana	Yes	R-20211 and R-20212	NA

Offers in Compromise (Part 1)

Legend:
NA Not applicable
NR Not reported

	Is the Department of Revenue/Taxation Authorized to Accept Offers in Compromise?	*Is There a Special Form That Must Be Filed to Start the Offer in Compromise Process?*	*If the Department of Revenue/Taxation Is Not Authorized to Accept Offers in Compromise, Is There Another Way to Obtain an Offer in Compromise?*
Maine	Yes	Yes, Debtor Financial Statement	NA
Maryland	NR	NR	NR
Massachusetts	Yes	NR	NA
Michigan (Business Tax)	No	NA	NR
Note. The CIT takes effect 01/01/12, and replaces the Michigan Business Tax (MBT) for most taxpayers. However, businesses that have been approved to receive, have received, or have been assigned certain certified credits may elect to file a return and pay the tax imposed by the MBT in lieu of the CIT until the certified credits are exhausted or extinguished.			
Minnesota	Yes	No	NA
Mississippi	No	NA	NR
Missouri	Yes	Form MO-656	NA
Montana	Yes	Yes, Form MDOR 01C002L	NA
Nebraska	Yes	No	NA
Nevada	No	NA	Yes, request for penalty and/or interest relief after full payment of tax
New Hampshire	NR	NR	NA
New Jersey	Yes, N.J. Stat. Ann. §. 54:53-7 et seq.	No	NA
New Mexico	No	No	
New York	Yes	Forms DTF4, DTF4.1, DTF5	NA
North Carolina	Yes	NR	NA
North Dakota	Yes	No	NA

Offers in Compromise (Part 1)

Legend:
NA Not applicable
NR Not reported

	Is the Department of Revenue/Taxation Authorized to Accept Offers in Compromise?	*Is There a Special Form That Must Be Filed to Start the Offer in Compromise Process?*	*If the Department of Revenue/Taxation Is Not Authorized to Accept Offers in Compromise, Is There Another Way to Obtain an Offer in Compromise?*
Ohio	Ohio does not impose a corporate income tax		
Note. Effective 1/1/2010, the Ohio Franchise Tax was fully phased out and business will be taxed on gross receipts through the Commercial Activity Tax. Details about that tax can be found at: http://tax.ohio.gov/divisions/commercial_activities/cat_general_information.stm			
Oklahoma	No	NA	No
Oregon	Yes	Yes, Application for Settlement Offer, Form 150-101-157	NA
Pennsylvania	No	NA	NR
Rhode Island	Yes	Yes	NA
South Carolina	Yes	Yes, SC 656	
South Dakota	South Dakota does not impose a corporate income tax		
Tennessee	No	NA	Yes. A taxpayer can submit a settlement to the Commissioner in relation to an assessment after the informal hearing process. This is done by correspondence and at the Commissioner's discretion as to how the settlement will be handled.
Texas	Yes	No	NA
Utah	Yes	No	NA
Vermont	Yes	No	NA
Virginia	Yes	No	NA
Washington	Washington does not impose a corporate income tax		

Offers in Compromise (Part 1)

Legend:

NA	Not applicable
NR	Not reported

	Is the Department of Revenue/Taxation Authorized to Accept Offers in Compromise?	*Is There a Special Form That Must Be Filed to Start the Offer in Compromise Process?*	*If the Department of Revenue/Taxation Is Not Authorized to Accept Offers in Compromise, Is There Another Way to Obtain an Offer in Compromise?*
West Virginia	Yes	Yes	NA
Wisconsin	Yes	Yes, Forms A212 and A213	NA
Wyoming	Wyoming does not impose a corporate income tax		

Offers in Compromise (Part 2)

Legend:

X — Indicates taxes for which an offer in compromise can be made

NR — Not reported

If the Department of Revenue/Taxation Is Authorized to Accept Offers in Compromise, Identify the Taxes for Which an Offer in Compromise Can Be Made

	Income Tax	*Franchise Tax*	*Uncollected Sales/Use Tax*	*Collected, but Unremitted Sales/Use Tax*	*Employment Taxes*	*Income Tax Withheld from Payroll*	*Other*
Alabama	Offers in Compromise cannot be accepted						
Alaska	X						
Arizona	X		X	X		X	
Arkansas	X		X	X		X	X, all types administered by DFA
California	X						
Colorado	X		X	X		X	
Connecticut	X	X	X				
Delaware							X, gross receipts
District of Columbia	X	X	X	X		X	X, gross receipts
Florida	X		X				X, other taxes administered by the Department
Georgia	X		X	X		X	X, Net Worth
Hawaii	X	X	X	X		X	X, any tax administered by the Department of Taxation

Offers in Compromise (Part 2)

Legend:
X Indicates taxes for which an offer in compromise can be made
NR Not reported

	If the Department of Revenue/Taxation Is Authorized to Accept Offers in Compromise, Identify the Taxes for Which an Offer in Compromise Can Be Made						
	Income Tax	*Franchise Tax*	*Uncollected Sales/Use Tax*	*Collected, but Unremitted Sales/Use Tax*	*Employment Taxes*	*Income Tax Withheld from Payroll*	*Other*
Idaho	X	X	X	X		X	X, all taxes administered by the Tax Commission
Illinois	Offers in Compromise cannot be accepted						
Indiana	X	X	X	X		X	
Iowa	X	X	X	X		X	
Kansas	X	X	X	X			X, Excise Tax
Kentucky	X		X	X		X	X, Coal Severance Tax
Louisiana	X	X	X	X	X	X	Excise and severance tax
Maine	X	X	X	X		X	X, Excise Tax
Maryland	NR	NR	NR	NR	NR	NR	NR
Massachusetts	X		X	X		X	
Michigan	Offers in Compromise cannot be accepted						
Note. The CIT takes effect 01/01/12, and replaces the Michigan Business Tax (MBT) for most taxpayers. However, businesses that have been approved to receive, have received, or have been assigned certain certified credits may elect to file a return and pay the tax imposed by the MBT in lieu of the CIT until the certified credits are exhausted or extinguished.							
Minnesota	X	X	X	X		X	
Mississippi	Offers in Compromise cannot be accepted						

Offers in Compromise (Part 2)

Legend:

X — Indicates taxes for which an offer in compromise can be made

NR — Not reported

	If the Department of Revenue/Taxation Is Authorized to Accept Offers in Compromise, Identify the Taxes for Which an Offer in Compromise Can Be Made						
	Income Tax	*Franchise Tax*	*Uncollected Sales/Use Tax*	*Collected, but Unremitted Sales/Use Tax*	*Employment Taxes*	*Income Tax Withheld from Payroll*	*Other*
Missouri	X	X	X	X		X	
Montana	X	NA	NA	NA	X	X	Any tax administered by the department
Nebraska	X	X	X	X		X	
Nevada	Offers in Compromise cannot be accepted						
New Hampshire							
New Jersey	X	X	X	X		X	X, Director's authority is with respect to "the tax laws of the state." N.J.S.A. § 54:53-7
New Mexico							X, depends upon circumstances
New York	X	X	X	X	X	X	X, local taxes administered by the Department
North Carolina	X	X	X				
North Dakota	X						
Ohio	Ohio does not impose a corporate income tax						

Note. Effective 1/1/2010, the Ohio Franchise Tax was fully phased out and business will be taxed on gross receipts through the Commercial Activity Tax. Details about that tax can be found at: http://tax.ohio.gov/divisions/commercial_activities/cat_general_information.stm

Offers in Compromise (Part 2)

Legend:
X — Indicates taxes for which an offer in compromise can be made
NR — Not reported

	If the Department of Revenue/Taxation Is Authorized to Accept Offers in Compromise, Identify the Taxes for Which an Offer in Compromise Can Be Made						
	Income Tax	*Franchise Tax*	*Uncollected Sales/Use Tax*	*Collected, but Unremitted Sales/Use Tax*	*Employment Taxes*	*Income Tax Withheld from Payroll*	*Other*
Oklahoma	Offers in Compromise cannot be accepted						
Oregon	X				X	X	Excise tax and all tax programs administered by the department
Pennsylvania	Offers in Compromise cannot be accepted						
Rhode Island	See Regulation OC 98-1						
South Carolina	X	X	X	X		X	
South Dakota	South Dakota does not impose a corporate income tax						
Tennessee	Offers in Compromise cannot be accepted						
Texas		X	X	X			X, gross receipts, business permit, severance, and inheritance taxes
Utah	X	X	X	X		X	
Vermont	X	X	X	X		X	
Virginia	X	X	X			X	Any tax administered by the Virginia Department of Taxation
Washington	Washington does not impose a corporate income tax						

Offers in Compromise (Part 2)

Legend:
X — Indicates taxes for which an offer in compromise can be made
NR — Not reported

	If the Department of Revenue/Taxation Is Authorized to Accept Offers in Compromise, Identify the Taxes for Which an Offer in Compromise Can Be Made						
	Income Tax	*Franchise Tax*	*Uncollected Sales/Use Tax*	*Collected, but Unremitted Sales/Use Tax*	*Employment Taxes*	*Income Tax Withheld from Payroll*	*Other*
West Virginia	X	X	X	X		X	X, all taxes administered under W.Va. Code § 11-10-1 et seq.
Wisconsin	X	X	X	X		X	
Wyoming	Wyoming does not impose a corporate income tax						

Offers in Compromise (Part 3)

Legend:
X — Indicates conditions required in order for an offer in compromise to be made
NR — Not reported

	If the Department of Revenue/Taxation Is Authorized to Accept Offers in Compromise, Identify the Conditions Required in Order for an Offer in Compromise to Be Made				
	Tax Liability Has Finally Been Fixed	*Taxpayer Has Exhausted Its Protest Rights*	*Taxpayer Has Been Discharged in Bankruptcy*	*Taxpayer Has Shown by Proof to Be Insolvent*	*Other*
Alabama	Offers in Compromise cannot be accepted				
Alaska	X				
Arizona	X				
Arkansas	X	X	X	X	
California	X				
Colorado					Case by case basis
Connecticut	X			X	X, doubt as to amount of liability
Delaware	NR	NR	NR	NR	NR
District of Columbia	X			X	
Florida	X, bill issued			X, inability to pay	X, taxpayer has shown doubt as to liability or collectability
Georgia					X, has to be either doubt as to liability or doubt as to collectability. A $100 fee must be submitted.
Hawaii	X		X	X	

Offers in Compromise (Part 3)

Legend:
X — Indicates conditions required in order for an offer in compromise to be made
NR — Not reported

	If the Department of Revenue/Taxation Is Authorized to Accept Offers in Compromise, Identify the Conditions Required in Order for an Offer in Compromise to Be Made				
	Tax Liability Has Finally Been Fixed	*Taxpayer Has Exhausted Its Protest Rights*	*Taxpayer Has Been Discharged in Bankruptcy*	*Taxpayer Has Shown by Proof to Be Insolvent*	*Other*
Idaho					The taxpayer must make the offer in writing. However, the Tax Commission may compromise the tax liability, penalties, or both, only if one or more circumstances exist: doubt as to liability, doubt as to collectability, or extreme hardship of taxpayer; IDAPA 35.02.01.500.
Illinois	Offers in Compromise cannot be accepted				
Indiana					See IC 6-8.1-3-17.
Iowa	X	X	X		
Kansas			X	X	Doubt as to liability, doubt as to collectability
Kentucky				X	

Legend:

X — Indicates conditions required in order for an offer in compromise to be made

NR — Not reported

Offers in Compromise (Part 3)

	If the Department of Revenue/Taxation Is Authorized to Accept Offers in Compromise, Identify the Conditions Required in Order for an Offer in Compromise to Be Made				
	Tax Liability Has Finally Been Fixed	*Taxpayer Has Exhausted Its Protest Rights*	*Taxpayer Has Been Discharged in Bankruptcy*	*Taxpayer Has Shown by Proof to Be Insolvent*	*Other*
Louisiana					(A) There is serious doubt as to the collectability of the outstanding judgment; (B) there is serious doubt as to the taxpayer's liability for the outstanding judgment; or (C) the administration and collection costs involved would exceed the amount of the outstanding liability (see LSA R.S. 47:295 and 1578(4))
Maine	X	X	X		X, doubt of liability or collectability
Maryland	NR	NR	NR	NR	NR
Massachusetts	X	X	X	X	See 830 CMR 62C.37A.1
Michigan (Business Tax)	Offers in Compromise cannot be accepted				
Note. The CIT takes effect 01/01/12, and replaces the Michigan Business Tax (MBT) for most taxpayers. However, businesses that have been approved to receive, have received, or have been assigned certain certified credits may elect to file a return and pay the tax imposed by the MBT in lieu of the CIT until the certified credits are exhausted or extinguished.					
Minnesota					Based on the issues of the specific case
Mississippi	Offers in Compromise cannot be accepted				

Offers in Compromise (Part 3)

Legend:
X — Indicates conditions required in order for an offer in compromise to be made
NR — Not reported

If the Department of Revenue/Taxation Is Authorized to Accept Offers in Compromise, Identify the Conditions Required in Order for an Offer in Compromise to Be Made

	Tax Liability Has Finally Been Fixed	*Taxpayer Has Exhausted Its Protest Rights*	*Taxpayer Has Been Discharged in Bankruptcy*	*Taxpayer Has Shown by Proof to Be Insolvent*	*Other*
Missouri	X				
Montana	X	X	X		Generally, must demonstrate present and future inability to pay (temporary inability to pay not sufficient), or the offer is in the best interest of the department or the most cost effective resolution.
Nebraska	X	X			
Nevada	Offers in Compromise cannot be accepted				
New Hampshire	NR	NR	NR	NR	NR
New Jersey					X, doubt as to liability or doubt as to collectability
New Mexico					X, depends upon circumstances
New York	X, only for offers issued on doubt as to collectability	X	X, or insolvent	X, or recent discharge in bankruptcy	X, doubt as to liability
		Answered as if condition is taken separately, not *all* necessary conditions			
North Carolina	NR	NR	NR	NR	NR

Offers in Compromise (Part 3)

Legend:
X — Indicates conditions required in order for an offer in compromise to be made
NR — Not reported

	If the Department of Revenue/Taxation Is Authorized to Accept Offers in Compromise, Identify the Conditions Required in Order for an Offer in Compromise to Be Made				
	Tax Liability Has Finally Been Fixed	*Taxpayer Has Exhausted Its Protest Rights*	*Taxpayer Has Been Discharged in Bankruptcy*	*Taxpayer Has Shown by Proof to Be Insolvent*	*Other*
North Dakota					X, taxpayer can make a settlement offer at any point.
Ohio	Ohio does not impose a corporate income tax				
Note. Effective 1/1/2010, the Ohio Franchise Tax was fully phased out and business will be taxed on gross receipts through the Commercial Activity Tax. Details about that tax can be found at: http://tax.ohio.gov/divisions/commercial_activities/cat_general_information.stm					
Oklahoma	Offers in Compromise cannot be accepted				
Oregon	X	X			Taxpayer must be in compliance with all Oregon tax return filing requirements for all years and tax programs administered by the department and must demonstrate an inability to pay the amounts due in full.
Pennsylvania	Offers in Compromise cannot be accepted				
Rhode Island					See OC 98-1 Regulation

Offers in Compromise (Part 3)

Legend:

X Indicates conditions required in order for an offer in compromise to be made

NR Not reported

	If the Department of Revenue/Taxation Is Authorized to Accept Offers in Compromise, Identify the Conditions Required in Order for an Offer in Compromise to Be Made				
	Tax Liability Has Finally Been Fixed	*Taxpayer Has Exhausted Its Protest Rights*	*Taxpayer Has Been Discharged in Bankruptcy*	*Taxpayer Has Shown by Proof to Be Insolvent*	*Other*
South Carolina					Amount cannot be collected through liquidation of assets or monthly installment plan; and DOR cannot collect more than the taxpayer is offering.
South Dakota	South Dakota does not impose a corporate income tax				
Tennessee	Offers in Compromise cannot be accepted				
Texas	All factors taken into consideration.	All factors taken into consideration.	All factors taken into consideration.	All factors taken into consideration.	All factors taken into consideration.
Utah	X		X	X	
Vermont	NR	NR	NR	NR	NR
Virginia					X, doubtful liability or doubtful collectability; reasonable cause for penalties
Washington	Washington does not impose a corporate income tax				
West Virginia	X	X	X	X	
Wisconsin	X	X	X	X	
Wyoming	Wyoming does not impose a corporate income tax				

ASC 740 and Uncertain Income Tax Positions

Background

In June 2006, the Financial Accounting Standards Board (FASB) issued "Interpretation No. 48, Accounting for Uncertainty in Income Taxes-an Interpretation of FASB Statement No. 109." The FASB issued FIN 48 to make financial reporting of income taxes more relevant and comparable by clarifying how companies should account for uncertainty in income taxes. In 1992, the FASB issued Statement No. 109, Accounting for Income Taxes, but did not provide specific guidance on how to deal with uncertain income tax positions. As of September 2009, FAS 109 was re-codified and is now referred to as FASB ASC Topic 740 – Income Taxes.

In terms of applying ASC 740-10 (formerly FIN 48) to state and local taxes, it is important to highlight that it applies only to "income taxes." It does not apply to sales and use taxes. For purposes of ASC 740-10 (formerly FIN 48), a "tax position" means a position in a previously filed tax return or a position expected to be taken in a future tax return. A tax position can result in either a permanent reduction of income taxes or a deferral of income taxes to future years. Examples of a tax position include, but are not limited to, a decision not to file a tax return in a jurisdiction, an allocation of income between jurisdictions, the characterization of income, or a decision to exclude income.

The financial reporting effect of a tax position is determined through a two-step process called recognition and measurement. The first step in the process is recognition. The tax benefit of a tax position is recognized only if, based solely on the technical merits of the position, the corporation determines that it is more likely than not that the tax position will be sustained upon examination, appeal, or litigation. In making this determination, it is presumed that the examining taxing authority has full knowledge of all relevant information.

In the second step of the process, a tax position that meets the more-likely-than-not recognition threshold is measured to determine the amount of tax benefit to recognize in the financial statements. The measurement is based on the largest tax benefit that has a more than 50 percent likelihood of being realized upon ultimate settlement with the taxing authority.

A tax position that previously failed to meet the more-likely-than-not recognition threshold is recognized in the first subsequent financial reporting period in which that threshold is met. Likewise, a previously recognized tax position that no longer meets the more-likely-than-not recognition threshold is derecognized in the first subsequent financial reporting period in which that threshold is no longer met.

Difficulties Posed by State Nonfiling Positions

To comply with ASC 740-10 (formerly FIN 48), a corporation must catalog all of its state and local income tax issues by jurisdiction and analyze each position in each jurisdiction under the standards for recognizing and measuring the benefits of a tax position. In this regard, the position that a corporation is not required to file an income tax return in a particular state poses unique challenges. As discussed in Part 2, Activities Creating Franchise or Income Tax Nexus, nexus is a grey area of the law. In particular, there is a substantial controversy over whether a corporation must file returns and pay income tax in a state in which it derives a significant amount of income but has no physical presence.

In *Quill Corp. v. North Dakota* [504 U.S. 298 (1992)], the Supreme Court ruled that, at least for purposes of sales and use tax nexus, an in-state physical presence is required to satisfy the "substantial nexus" test under the Commerce Clause. The Court did not, however, address the issue of whether the physical presence test also applied to income tax nexus. Just one year later in *Geoffrey, Inc. v. South Carolina Tax Commissioner* [437 S.E.2d 13 (S.C. July 6, 1993), *cert. denied*, 114 S. Ct. 550 (1993)], the South Carolina Supreme Court ruled that an in-state physical presence is not an absolute requirement for establishing constitutional nexus for income tax purposes. The most recent high profile economic nexus cases are *Lanco, Inc. v. Division of Taxation* [908 A.2d 176 (N.J. 2006); *cert. denied*, U.S. Sup. Ct., 06-1236, June 18, 2007] and *Tax Commissioner v. MBNA America Bank, N.A.* [640 S.E.2d 226 (W. Va. 2006); *cert. denied*, U.S. Sup. Ct.,

06-1228, June 18, 2007]. In *Lanco*, the New Jersey Supreme Court concluded that "the better interpretation of *Quill* is the one adopted by those states that limit the Supreme Court's holding to sales and use taxes." In *MBNA America Bank, N.A.* [640 S.E.2d 226 (W. Va. 2006); *cert. denied*, U.S. Sup. Ct., 06-1228, June 18, 2007], the West Virginia Supreme Court of Appeals concluded that the *Bellas Hess* physical presence test "applies only to state sales and use taxes and not to state business franchise and corporation net income taxes," and that MBNA had "a significant economic presence sufficient to meet the substantial nexus" test under the Commerce Clause. In both the *Lanco* and *MBNA America Bank* cases, the taxpayers' petitions for a writ of certiorari were denied by the Supreme Court.

Because nexus is a grey area of the law, a corporation may find it difficult to determine that the more-likely-than-not recognition threshold has been met with respect to a nonfiling position. In such cases, the corporation may have to reserve the full potential income tax liability for a state, even though the corporation believes it does not have nexus in that state and therefore does not file a return. Recording this contingent liability on the corporation's financial statements is problematic, because if the corporation never files a return, the statute of limitations never closes.

In a letter to the FASB dated January 8, 2007 (FASB File Reference 1215-U01), the Council On State Taxation observed that "the problem with FIN 48 and nexus is so great that at least one accounting firm has publicly suggested that businesses should consider filing and paying taxes in jurisdictions where they may not have nexus because the alternative under FIN 48 (indefinite reserves, interest, and penalties) is too large a dollar figure for the financial statement to bear."